W9-ASR-603

CRITICAL COMPANION TO

William Faulkner

A Literary Reference to His Life and Work

A. NICHOLAS FARGNOLI

MICHAEL GOLAY

ROBERT W. HAMBLIN

Facts On File

An imprint of Infobase Publishing

Critical Companion to William Faulkner: A Literary Reference to His Life and Work

Facts On File, Inc.
An imprint of Infobase Publishing
132 West 31st Street
New York NY 10001

Library of Congress Cataloging-in-Publication Data

Fargnoli, A. Nicholas.
Critical companion to William Faulkner : a literary reference to his life and
work / A. Nicholas Fargnoli, Michael Golay, Robert W. Hamblin.
    p. cm.
Rev. ed. of: William Faulkner A to Z. c2002.
Includes bibliographical references and index.
ISBN 978-0-8160-6432-8 (acid-free paper) 1. Faulkner, William, 1897–1962
—Encyclopedias. 2. Novelists, American—20th century—Biography—Encyclopedias.
3. Yoknapatawpha County (Imaginary place)—Encyclopedias. 4. Mississippi—In literature
—Encyclopedias. I. Golay, Michael, 1951– II. Hamblin, Robert W. III. Fargnoli,
A. Nicholas. William Faulkner A to Z. IV. Title.
PS3511.A86Z459 2008
813'.52—dc22
[B]
2007032361

Facts On File books are available at special discounts when purchased in bulk
quantities for businesses, associations, institutions, or sales promotions.
Please call our Special Sales Department in New York at (212) 967-8800 or
(800) 322-8755.

You can find Facts On File on the World Wide Web at http://www.factsonfile.com

Text design by Erika K. Arroyo

Printed in the United States of America

VB Hermitage 10 9 8 7 6 5 4 3 2 1

This book is printed on acid-free paper and contains
30 percent postconsumer recycled content.

CONTENTS

ACKNOWLEDGMENTS

With sincere gratitude, we acknowledge our friends and colleagues who have graciously helped us in preparing *Critical Companion to William Faulkner*. Because of their assistance, our task was all the easier. We add their names here along with the names of those who aided us in the writing of *William Faulkner A to Z*, this book's predecessor: Don Bowden, Matthew J. Bruccoli, J. D. Chapman, Wenhui Chen, Cynthia Cox, Joan Crane, Christina Deane, Larry Donato, Kathleen Duffy, Alessandro Fargnoli, Gioia Fargnoli, Giuliana Fargnoli, Harriett Fargnoli, Sister Elizabeth Gill, O.P., Joel Greenberg, Gregory A. Johnson, Robert Kinpoitner, Mark Lerner, Robert Martin, Trisha O'Neill, Brian Quinn, Regina Rush, Norman Weil, and the Reference Department at the Great Neck Library.

Special recognition and gratitude must be given to Jeff Soloway, executive editor at Facts On File, whose insights and professionalism are equaled only to his patience. Gratitude is also owed to Anne Savarese, our previous editor, who facilitated the publication of *William Faulkner A to Z*; to the Committee for Faculty Scholarship and Academic Advancement at Molloy College for funds to help with photo-reproduction costs; and to Southeast Missouri State University for its support for this project.

When writing *William Faulkner A to Z*, we acknowledged Eva Weber of Northampton, Mass., for having contributed to the entries on 39 Faulkner short works from the *Collected Stories* and *Uncollected Stories*; a debt of gratitude is again mentioned.

INTRODUCTION AND GUIDE TO USE

Critical Companion to William Faulkner is an expanded and updated version of William Faulkner A to Z. More than 80,000 words have been added to the text. Character entries throughout the book and Critical Commentary sections on Faulkner's major works have been significantly expanded, and entirely new sections providing excerpts from contemporary reviews have been added. Other new features include further-reading lists for Faulkner's major novels and short stories and an appendix providing a detailed chronology of one of Faulkner's greatest and most complicated works, As I Lay Dying. In addition, the text throughout has been revised and augmented in the light of the latest scholarship. Joining the authors of the previous edition is Robert W. Hamblin of the Center for Faulkner Studies at Southeast Missouri State University.

The organization of the text also differs in this new volume. In keeping with Facts On File's Critical Companion series, the entries in this book are categorically arranged to assist the reader, especially the student reader, in finding information quickly and easily. Part I contains a short biography of Faulkner. Part II consists of entries on Faulkner's works; most entries contain composition and publication information, a synopsis and critical analysis, and descriptions of important characters and some related items. Entries on major works also contain excerpts from selected contemporary

reviews. Part III contains entries, in alphabetical order, on people, places, events, and topics related to Faulkner. Fictional places that appear in several of Faulkner's works, such as Yoknapatawpha County, appear here; a few fictional places that are specific to an individual work appear as subentries to the main work entry in Part II. Part IV contains the appendixes including, among other things, primary and secondary bibliographies, library holdings, Faulkner's appendix to The Sound and the Fury and his Nobel Prize acceptance speech, and a dateline.

References to works covered in entries in Part II or to related items covered in entries in Part III are given in SMALL CAPITAL LETTERS the first time they appear in any entry.

Like its predecessor, Critical Companion to William Faulkner offers the general reader and nonspecialist a clear and organized supplement to the reading of William Faulkner's works. Faulkner is one of the most important literary figures in American literature and is recognized worldwide as a stylistic innovator, but his work can also be bewildering at times because of his complex, sometimes convoluted, prose style and narrative techniques. Understanding his plots, themes, and characters can be difficult for any reader. The primary goal of this volume is to assist students and general readers in their quest to understand, enjoy, and situate in a larger literary and historical context the works and

In 1987, the United States Postal Service issued a commemorative first-class stamp bearing Faulkner's likeness. (*Stamp Design © 1987 U.S. Postal Service. Reproduced with permission. All rights reserved.*)

life of this great American writer and Nobel laureate. It is also our intention to provide those already familiar with Faulkner's works a convenient one-volume reference source.

Faulkner's published writings span a period of more than 40 years and include poems, short stories, novels, essays, speeches, screenplays, and letters. His literary works contain well in excess of a thousand named characters, some of whom appear in several different works. Unfortunately for the reader and scholar, there are times when Faulkner is inconsistent with either the names of his characters or with their spellings. For instance, the surname McCallum first appeared as MacCallum, and the character V. K. Ratliff was first called V. K. Suratt. The reader might bear in mind that Faulkner himself seemed unconcerned about such discrepancies. "What I am trying to say is, the essential truth of these people and their doings is the thing," he once told an editor. We have attempted to minimize the confusion that may surround a character's identity by placing and describing that character after each work in which he or she appears. We also provide a cross-reference to any other work in which that character appears.

Faulkner's works have endured for several reasons but—to adapt a concept from Aristotle—primarily because the highest achievement of art is an expression of the human spirit and of the universal element of life. Faulkner catches the imagination *and* the emotions of his readers, and he can be at once serious and comic as he portrays the struggles of the human heart in conflict with itself.

We are indebted to the many scholars and critics who, through the insights and ideas in their writings, have provided us with valuable historical and critical information. Like all major writers whose works are characterized by complexity and depth of purpose and meaning, William Faulkner is an author one must read in communion with others. Faulkner's mythic Yoknapatawpha County—his "little postage stamp of native soil," as he referred to it—occupies a permanent place in the world's literary geography and conjures up a world with boundless interpretative possibilities. If Faulkner drew much of his inspiration from his native Mississippi, he also wrote of what he knew best, and he was not indifferent to trying new narrative techniques that he thought best expressed his characters and themes. His works are peopled with vivid and memorable characters—too numerous to list in this brief introduction—who often face the harshest of conflicts and struggles. Many of Faulkner's major works, such as *The Sound and the Fury, As I Lay Dying, Light in August, Go Down, Moses,* and *Absalom, Absalom!*, are viewed as exemplary modernist texts and precursors to postmodernism. Faulkner's "little postage stamp" has grown to planetary size. He is translated and read in many languages throughout the world, and his literary influence on later writers endures.

Critical Companion to William Faulkner provides readers easy access to information on a wide range of topics directly related to the study of Faulkner's life and works. However, this reference book, like all reference guides, is not a substitute for the enjoyment of reading Faulkner; it is meant to aid and enrich the reading experience.

With the exception of *Soldiers' Pay* (New York: Liveright Publishing Corporation, 1997), *Mosquitoes* (New York: Boni & Liveright, 1927), *Knight's Gambit* (New York: Random House, 1949), and *Sartoris* (Random House, 1956), citations from Faulkner's writings are from the Vintage editions of his works.

PART I

Biography

William Faulkner

(1897–1962)

Novelist, author of *The SOUND AND THE FURY, LIGHT IN AUGUST, ABSALOM, ABSALOM!, GO DOWN, MOSES, The HAMLET,* and other works, winner of the 1949 NOBEL PRIZE IN LITERATURE (awarded 1950), and by critical consensus a leading literary artist of the 20th century.

Born William Cuthbert Falkner in NEW ALBANY, MISSISSIPPI, on September 25, 1897, he was the first child of MURRY CUTHBERT and MAUD BUTLER FALKNER and the great-grandson of the soldier, author, banker, and railroad builder WILLIAM CLARK FALKNER, known as the Old Colonel, a near-legendary figure and the prototype of Colonel John Sartoris of Faulkner's fictional JEFFERSON, MISSISSIPPI, and YOKNAPATAWPHA COUNTY.

The novelist's mythic Yoknapatawpha has become a permanent feature of the world's literary geography, a suffering, defeated place, a haunt of grotesque and villainous Snopeses and Sutpens, with a troubled heritage of slavery and war. But it is an enduring and timeless place too, peopled with ordinary men and women such as Dilsey Gibson, V. K. Ratliff, and Isaac (Ike) McCaslin who rise to heroic stature and in whom hope has not died.

Faulkner's ancestry was mostly Scots or Scots-Irish. He evidently regarded the violent, impulsive, grasping, creative Old Colonel as his spiritual father. W. C. Falkner, born in 1825, migrated from North Carolina via Missouri to northern Mississippi, settling in RIPLEY, MISSISSIPPI, in the early 1840s. He read law, served in the Mississippi militia during the Mexican War, and established himself during the 1850s as a prosperous, slaveholding lawyer, businessman, and farmer.

With the coming of the Civil War, a calamity that would live in his great-grandson's imagination, Falkner raised a volunteer company, the MAGNOLIA RIFLES, and in May 1861 won election as colonel of the 2nd Mississippi Infantry. In July 1861 he fought at the battle of First Manassas (*see* BULL RUN), where his rather ostentatious bravery (he had two horses shot from under him) caught the attention of his superior officers.

Colonel William Clark Falkner's monument, Ripley, Mississippi *(Harriett and Gioia Fargnoli)*

Denied reelection to the regimental command in the spring of 1862, probably on account of his martinet approach to discipline, he returned to Mississippi, raised a regiment of irregular cavalry, and carried out intermittent raids on federal communications lines before leaving the army for good in October 1863. His early retirement did not, however, deter federal troops from burning his Ripley home in 1864.

After the war, the Old Colonel rebuilt his law practice and, like the fictional John Sartoris, gained influence, power, and prosperity as a banker and railroad developer. He also found time to write; his melodramatic novel *The White Rose of Memphis,* published in 1881, remained in print for 30 years and reportedly sold 160,000 copies. He followed up this publishing success with *The Little Brick Church,* another novel, in 1882, and *Rapid Ramblings in Europe,* an account of his travels, in 1884.

Ripley sent Falkner to the Mississippi legislature on November 5, 1889, but he did not live to take his seat. Late on the afternoon of election day, his business and political rival RICHARD J. THURMOND shot and fatally wounded him on the Courthouse Square, an assassination Faulkner would fictionalize in the novels SARTORIS (1929) and The UNVANQUISHED (1938).

The Old Colonel's son, JOHN WESLEY THOMPSON FALKNER (1848–1922), expanded the family's banking and railroad enterprises and made successful forays into Mississippi politics. He married SALLIE MCALPINE MURRY (FALKNER) in 1869; she delivered their first child, Murry Cuthbert FALKNER, the following year. The Young Colonel moved his family from Ripley 40 miles southwest to the LAFAYETTE COUNTY town of OXFORD, MISSISSIPPI, in late 1885 and established a law practice there. His legal, business, and political affairs flourished into the early years of the new century, in spite of the near-legendary drinking bouts that sent him from time to time to the KEELEY INSTITUTE of Memphis for "the cure." The Young Colonel's alcoholism would pass from him through his son Murry to his novelist grandson. (See ALCOHOLISM, FAULKNER AND.)

A good deal less is known of the background of Faulkner's mother's family. The Butlers were among the earliest settlers of Lafayette County. Maud Falkner, born in 1871, the daughter of Charles Edward and Lelia Swift BUTLER, claimed Texas patriot Sam Houston and the Confederate general Felix Zollicoffer as kinsmen and boasted of several forebears who had fought in the Civil War. Charles Butler served for a dozen years as the Oxford town marshal. He abandoned his wife and two children in 1887, vanishing with as much as $3,000 in town funds and, so the gossip ran, with a beautiful young octoroon mistress. Faulkner never knew his maternal grandfather, and he remained always reticent about his Butler antecedents.

The infant Willie, as his parents called him at first, was a colicky newborn, and his mother recalled rocking him in a stiff-backed chair for many hours a night during the first year of his life. He survived early frailties to grow up tough and durable, if small in size. The Falkners moved from New Albany to Ripley, where Murry worked for the family-owned GULF & CHICAGO RAILROAD, in November 1898. Two more sons—Billy's brothers Murry Charles (known as Jack) and John Wesley Thompson III (known as Johncy)—were born there before the family removed permanently to Oxford, the Young Colonel's seat, on September 24, 1902, a day before Billy Falkner reached his fifth birthday.

Murry Falkner's decline began in this period. His father's abrupt and unexpected sale of the Gulf & Chicago, for $75,000 in May 1902, robbed him of his vocation, and he mourned the loss. Though the Young Colonel backed Murry financially in a succession of small businesses, nothing could replace his beloved railroad. His wife vetoed his dream of resettling in Texas and raising cattle, and he slipped ever deeper into the shadow of his powerful and successful father.

Strains in the Falkners' marriage were only too evident. They were temperamentally incompatible. Maud Falkner was steely and determined, her husband feckless and alcoholic. Her interests lay in books and pictures; his in guns, dogs, and horses. Billy Falkner grew up in a tense, emotionally edgy household in which his mother held dominion. She ran the place on Second South Street with the assistance of a capable, ever-present lieutenant, CAROLINE (Callie) BARR, who had been born into slavery and who was known as Mammy. Murry seemed to fail at everything he attempted. Weak or absent fathers modeled on Murry Falkner would recur in Faulkner's fiction; the theme of family decline would run through much of his work.

The elder Falkner ran a livery stable and a cottonseed oil mill, sold coal oil, and operated a hardware store on Confederate Square in Oxford. The coming of factory-made automobiles doomed the livery stable. Murry sold the South Street house and moved the family into a more modest place on North Street to raise money to buy himself into the hardware business. But he chafed at the sedentary life of a merchant and showed no aptitude for the work.

Yet aspects of Billy Falkner's boyhood were idyllic. Woods stretched out behind the Falkners' first Oxford home, a large one-story frame house with a barn and paddock; six blocks up the street lay the Oxford Square. With a population of 1,800, three times Ripley's, Oxford in the first decade of the 20th century had a four-faced clock in the courthouse tower, dry goods, confectioners and other stores on the square, a new 140-foot-high water tower, and the UNIVERSITY OF MISSISSIPPI.

There were the immemorial pastimes of small-town boyhood: pickup games of football and baseball, explorations of the nearby woods and fields with Mammy Callie, hit-and-run raids on enemy neighborhoods. Billy absorbed Civil War lore from cronies of his grandfather, a leader of the SONS OF CONFEDERATE VETERANS fraternal organization, and entertained his brothers with scraps of speeches picked up at soldier reunions. "Now what air more noble," he used to mimic one old orator, "than to lie on the field of battle with your car-case full of canyon balls." Their father took the boys for

Sunday afternoon rides in the trap, and on summer and autumn weekends they would journey farther afield, to the Club House, the family's hunting and fishing lodge in the TALLAHATCHIE RIVER bottoms 15 miles north of Oxford. In time, he would play football for Oxford High School.

The Big Place, the Old Colonel's home, served as the center of Falkner social life. It had wide porches and a finished attic, venues where the young Falkners gathered with the neighborhood children, among them Lida Estelle Oldham, who in due course became Billy's particular friend.

Billy's three brothers (DEAN SWIFT [FAULKNER], the fourth Faulkner son, arrived in August 1907) looked up to him as the great organizer and improviser. One summer, he directed the boys and his cousin Sally Murry in assembling a virtually full-

Faulkner (middle row, second from left) and his schoolmates at Oxford Graded School in 1908 *(Brodsky Collection, Center for Faulkner Studies, Southeast Missouri State University)*

scale airplane from plans in *American Boy* magazine, using his mother's bean poles for a frame and newspapers applied with flour paste as the skin. The boys and their cousin launched Billy from the edge of a 10-foot-deep ditch at the back of the Falkner's lot. The frail craft broke apart on takeoff.

Billy Falkner, age 8, entered the first grade in Oxford's all-white elementary school in September 1905. He did well in Miss Annie Chandler's class—well enough to be allowed to skip second grade. Maud Falkner was literate, conversant with books and the arts. She taught the Falkner boys to read and introduced them to James Fenimore Cooper, Charles Dickens, Mark Twain, Robert Louis Stevenson, and the Grimm brothers and later to Shakespeare, Balzac, Poe, Kipling, and Conrad. For some reason, though, Billy turned against formal education. "I never did like school," he would recall, "and stopped going to school as soon as I got big enough to play hooky and not get caught." By the autumn of 1909, when he was in the sixth grade, he found himself in more or less constant trouble for skipping class, failing to turn in his homework, and general inattention to matters at hand. A 1911 report card, otherwise positive, noted a "lack of progress in grammar and language."

But he was learning in other ways, observing, experiencing, storing up material that his imagination would one day transform. Oxford taught him early the nuances of the South's rigid system of racial subordination. The majority of Oxford's African Americans lived in Freedmantown, the black quarter north of the railroad tracks. Many, domestic servants for the most part, inhabited cabins in the yards behind the big houses of the white folks. The Falkners employed Callie Barr and other blacks as servants, and the boys always had black playmates. There may have been black Falkner cousins too, for circumstantial evidence suggests that the Old Colonel had fathered a "shadow family" with one of his former slaves, though these Falkners were never acknowledged.

Black-white relations were easy, often affectionate, so long as blacks made no bid to breach the racial barrier. Whites reacted fiercely to any attempt to cross the line. Race and racial identity would become major themes of Faulkner's mature fiction, most pervasively in the novels *Light in August, Absalom, Absalom!,* and *Go Down, Moses.* (*See* RACE, FAULKNER AND.)

So he picked up his novelist's education outside the schoolroom. Helping out at his father's livery stable, he absorbed the lore of horses and horsetrading that would infuse the SNOPES TRILOGY, *The REIVERS,* and other works. Relations with his father grew steadily more difficult as Billy reached adolescence. Murry called him "Snake Lips," a dig at his Butler features; Billy had the Butler physical form, short and slight. Murry only too plainly favored the second son Jack, a Falkner in build: tall, bulky, florid.

Between them, Estelle Oldham and Billy's friend PHILIP AVERY STONE, the son of a prominent lawyer and banker, taught him more than any Oxford school. To impress Estelle, a popular girl, Billy affected the dress and manners of a dandy. He learned to recognize the Beethoven sonatas she played on the piano in the Oldham parlor, and he tried to dance. There were many rivals for Estelle's attention, but even so, she and Billy seemed to have an understanding.

Falkner dropped out of high school after the 10th grade and went to work in his grandfather's bank. He had met Phil Stone in the summer of 1914 and had tentatively shown him his adolescent verse. Four years Falkner's senior, Stone was educated at the UNIVERSITY OF MISSISSIPPI and Yale. Cultured, cosmopolitan, and fluent, he talked literature with Billy, loaned him books, and introduced him to classic and modern writers; in effect, he shaped the young artist's viewpoint and style, or so he afterward claimed.

Stone's teaching encompassed the Lafayette County hill people and the MEMPHIS underworld as readily as the literary moderns. Falkner explored the MISSISSIPPI DELTA wilderness with Stone; his father's Delta hunting camp would form the model for the camp in the novella "The Bear" (in *Go Down, Moses*). The novelist would also exploit the entrée Stone provided into the world of gamblers and prostitutes in a number of stories and novels, from SANCTUARY (1931) to *The Reivers* (1962).

War in Europe filled Billy Falkner's thoughts and imagination in 1915 and 1916. He had actually seen an airplane by then, and he devoured newspaper and magazine accounts of the flying aces of the western front; he would salt his war allegory *A FABLE* with the names of the British, French, and Canadian air aces. (*See* FLYING, FAULKNER AND.) The United States entered World War I in the spring of 1917, but by then Falkner's motives for action had become more personal than patriotic. LEMUEL OLDHAM refused to accept Billy Falkner as a suitor for his daughter. Estelle's mother maneuvered her into an engagement with a young lawyer named CORNELL FRANKLIN, and they were married in April 1918. Billy sought escape at a U.S. Army Air Corps recruiting office.

The air service turned him down, citing his short stature (he stood five feet, five inches tall), according to the biographer JOSEPH BLOTNER. He fled Oxford all the same, traveling to New Haven, Connecticut, where Phil Stone was studying law at Yale. Faulkner briefly worked as a clerk in an office of the Winchester Repeating Arms Company there before managing to pass himself off as an expatriate Englishman named William Faulkner (he had added the *u* to the family name on his application for the Winchester job) and enlisting as a cadet in the ROYAL AIR FORCE. Around the same time, Jack Falkner enlisted as a private soldier in the U.S. Marine Corps.

Faulkner—he would retain the *u*, part of the fictional biography he created for the RAF—reported to ground school in Toronto, Canada, in July 1918. Jack landed in France in August. For all his later elaboration of himself as a wounded flying hero, Faulkner proved an indifferent cadet. As it happened, he never came near the cockpit of an airplane, let alone flew solo, crashed, or shot down German fighters over France, as he later suggested he had done. (He would, however, obtain a pilot's license in 1933.) Jack was badly wounded in the Argonne Forest in early November, shot in the head and leg during the Saint-Mihiel offensive. He would need months in hospital to recover. After the armistice of November 11, 1918, the RAF moved swiftly to cut its trainees loose. Faulkner arrived home in Oxford in December with $42.58 in severance pay, a promise of an eventual honorary second lieutenant's commission, and an added 18 pounds to his slender frame.

William Faulkner in 1914 *(Brodsky Collection, Center for Faulkner Studies, Southeast Missouri State University)*

For weeks afterward, Faulkner roamed about Oxford in his British officer's uniform, playing the returned war hero and accepting the salutes of authentic veterans. He even walked with a manufactured limp. This was the second of the many roles he would play, following that of Oxford dandy. The biographer Frederick Karl regards the RAF experience as crucial in Faulkner's artistic development. "The war turned Billy into a storyteller, a fictionalist, which may have been the decisive turnabout of his life," he wrote. The returned flyer retained the clipped, formal, buttoned-down pose of the English officer through the autumn of 1919, when he enrolled as a special student at Ole Miss and reprised the role of dandy.

He studied French, Spanish, and English, taking only the classes that interested him, indifferent to much of the college life around him. Faulkner's earliest published works date from this time: two drawings in the Ole Miss yearbook and an adaptation of Mallarmé's "L'Après-Midi d'un Faune," in

The New Republic of August 6, 1919. In November, the student newspaper, *The* MISSISSIPPIAN, accepted the short story "Landing in Luck," his first published prose work. Nine Faulkner poems appeared in *The Mississippian* during the spring semester of 1920.

His social life was hit or miss. He joined the Sigma Alpha Epsilon fraternity and a drama club known as the Marionettes but ran afoul of many of the Ole Miss hearties, his mannerisms and airs earning him the unflattering sobriquet of "Count No-'Count." His "decadent" poems inspired a set of parodies, including "Une Ballade d'une Vache Perdu," about the lost and wandering heifer Betsey. Bored, feeling out of place, he withdrew from Ole Miss in mid-November 1919.

Murry Falkner had been business manager at Ole Miss, a patronage appointment, since 1918. The job came with a house on campus, and Billy would keep a room at his parents' home for a full decade. This secure base gave him the freedom to wander and to perfect the latest of his poses, that of the hard-drinking bohemian poet.

He journeyed to New York in the fall of 1921 at the invitation of the author STARK YOUNG, an Oxford native. Faulkner worked briefly in the Doubleday Bookstore at a Lord & Taylor department store for ELIZABETH PRALL, a future wife of SHERWOOD ANDERSON. Phil Stone worried that his friend would lose his artistic bearings in the great city and recalled him to Oxford after a few weeks. In the interval, Stone and others had arranged the job of University of Mississippi postmaster for him, a sinecure with a salary of $1,500 a year.

Faulkner converted the post office into a private club. He and his cronies read, played cards, drank, and sometimes shut down the office altogether to play the university's "golfing pasture." He mishandled the mail. He tossed magazines and journals into the trash. He set aside periodicals that caught his fancy to read himself before passing them on. He ignored the requests of patrons. "It was amazing," Jack Falkner recalled, "that under his trusteeship any mail ever actually got delivered." Astonishingly, he held onto the job for three years. A postal inspector finally turned up to investigate the scandalous opera-

tion. Whether he was fired or arranged for his own removal, Faulkner took the loss of the job—and the salary—with equanimity.

"I reckon I'll be at the beck and call of folks with money all my life," he said afterwards, "but thank God I won't ever again have to be at the beck and call of every son-of-a-bitch who's got two cents to buy a stamp."

Meantime, Phil Stone arranged and subsidized the publication of Faulkner's first book, *The* MARBLE FAUN, a collection of poems. The FOUR SEAS COMPANY of Boston released an edition of 1,000 copies on December 15, 1924. Stone wrote the preface; Faulkner dedicated the book to his mother. ("Phil Stone and Mother were the first ones to believe in Bill," Johncy Falkner would write.) He presented a signed copy to Estelle Oldham Franklin, by now the mother of two young children: a girl, MELVINA VICTORIA FRANKLIN, and a boy, MALCOLM ARGYLE FRANKLIN. She and Franklin had settled first in Hawaii and then in Shanghai, but by the mid-1920s their marriage was in trouble and she was spending long furloughs at home in Oxford. When not attending to the Oxford boy-scout troop he headed or going off to immerse himself in the bohemian world of NEW ORLEANS's Vieux Carré, eight hours from Oxford by train, Billy was as attentive to her as ever.

Through Elizabeth Prall, he met Sherwood Anderson in New Orleans, and he found an outlet for verse, essays of criticism, and prose sketches in the new little magazine, *The* DOUBLE DEALER, published there. He also placed a series of vignettes of local life in the NEW ORLEANS TIMES-PICAYUNE newspaper—and was even paid for the privilege. "I have turned in 5 of my stories and collected $20 for them," he wrote home proudly. "I write one in about 3 hours. At that rate I can make $25 a week in my spare time." He was writing constantly, drinking heavily, and playing the part of wounded war hero to the hilt. He persisted in walking with a limp and let it be known that he had suffered a serious head wound.

All the while, Faulkner worked on his first novel, originally titled MAYDAY, eventually published as SOLDIERS' PAY. He followed a disciplined writing routine. He was up early, his portable typewriter clacking away. Sometimes he kept a glass of whiskey and water at hand. He did not permit interruptions. "His concentration was a formidable engine," recalled his Vieux Carré flatmate, the painter WILLIAM SPRATLING, "and one could not get in its way. Bill would not even see you or hear you if you tried to get his attention." Faulkner regarded 3,000 words as a good day's work. He would allow himself afternoons off for long walks around the city. At night, he drank heavily.

Anderson agreed to recommend the book, completed in May 1925, to his publisher, HORACE LIVERIGHT. Liveright accepted it on behalf of the firm of BONI & LIVERIGHT. With publication assured and a $200 advance in hand, Faulkner sailed for Europe with Spratling in July.

He traveled in Italy, Switzerland, France, and England, working fitfully on short stories and a manuscript titled ELMER, which would grow to novel length but never be published during his lifetime. He spent time in Paris but shied from making an approach to JAMES JOYCE or lesser expatriate literary figures settled there. "I knew of Joyce," he said many years later, "and I would go to some effort to go to the café that he inhabited to look at him. But that was the only literary man that I remember seeing in Europe in those days." With money running short, he sailed for home from Cherbourg, France, on December 9.

Boni & Liveright published *Soldiers' Pay* on February 25, 1926. Reviews were mixed, but the novel did anticipate themes and even scenes of more powerful work to come. Faulkner spent part of the spring in New Orleans and the summer at the Stones' beachfront house in PASCAGOULA, MISSISSIPPI, where he worked on his second novel, *MOSQUITOES*, and ineffectually courted a Tennessee-born artist and sculptor named HELEN BAIRD. He completed the manuscript on September 1, with a dedication "To Helen." Liveright published it on April 30, 1927. Helen Baird married the New Orleans lawyer Guy Lyman on May 4.

By then, Faulkner had put aside a manuscript he called *FATHER ABRAHAM*, in which the fateful Flem Snopes made his first appearance, and turned to work on a novel originally titled *FLAGS IN THE DUST*, launching the Sartoris saga. The

two works were the origin of Faulkner's legendary Yoknapatawpha County. A recent biographer suggests that Faulkner envisioned a Yoknapatawpha cycle from the start. "He had been reading Dickens and Balzac," Jay Parini writes, "and wished to create a shelf of books that had some unity and purpose." Faulkner completed *Flags* in late September and sent it on to Liveright, whose letter of rejection reached him late in November. The publisher judged the novel hopeless, and advised the author to withdraw it altogether. "It is diffuse and non-integral with neither very much plot development nor character development," Liveright wrote. "We think it lacks plot, dimension and projection." Faulkner sank into depression and gloom, but he recovered quickly from this episode and set about scheming to free himself from Boni & Liveright and to find a publisher for the Sartoris novel. (HARCOURT, BRACE AND COMPANY would publish it as *Sartoris* in January 1929.)

He turned to two stories, "That Evening Sun Go Down" and "A Justice," that introduced a family called the Compsons. Early in 1928, he began a story called "Twilight" about a little girl named Candace (Caddy) Compson and her brothers Quentin, Jason, and Benjy, the genesis of *The Sound and the Fury*.

Faulkner claimed long afterward that Liveright's rejection (a new firm, CAPE & SMITH, would publish the tale of the Compsons) had freed him to approach what would become arguably his finest work, and the one nearest his heart—"the book I feel tenderest towards," he told an interviewer many years later. He forgot, he said, about commercial publishing, about making money, about recognition.

"Twilight" touched off an astonishing creative explosion. Faulkner would produce much of his best work between 1928 and 1936: *The Sound and the Fury*, published in October 1929; *AS I LAY DYING*, written in a short burst—47 days—during his night-shift supervisory job at the Ole Miss power plant and published in October 1930; *Sanctuary*, published in February 1931; *Light in August*, published in October 1932; and *Absalom, Absalom!*, published in October 1936.

He achieved both money and literary fame against a backdrop of private agonies: alcoholism, financial troubles, and an impending marriage to Estelle Franklin, a mésalliance that would prove destructive for each partner. The impressionistic and technically difficult *The Sound and the Fury* was an immediate critical success. "A great book," Faulkner's friend Lyle Saxon called it in a *New York Herald Tribune* review, a judgment that has stood the test of time, and *Sanctuary,* when it appeared in 1931, eased his financial burden, at least for a time.

Work provided Faulkner an escape from his torments. With pen in hand, he could forget his miseries—or at least transform them into fictions. Estelle's divorce had come through finally in late April 1929. A single woman with two children, she had been intensely uncomfortable in conservative Oxford, and her family, working through her sister DOT OLDHAM, brought pressure to bear on her longest-running beau, William Faulkner. They were married in the parsonage of the College Hill Presbyterian Church in Oxford on June 20, 1929.

The newlyweds went off to Pascagoula for their honeymoon. Faulkner corrected the galley proofs of *The Sound and the Fury* there, a project that left him

The historical marker outside of College Church. *(Harriett and Gioia Fargnoli)*

nervy and out of sorts. He became withdrawn and silent, and he drank heavily. Estelle's nerves were raddled, and she executed what may have been an attempt to drown herself by walking far out into the bay one evening. Faulkner's shouts alerted a neighbor, who pulled her to safety on the shore.

He and Estelle returned to Oxford in the autumn of 1929, taking a two-bedroom apartment on University Avenue, handy to Faulkner's new job as night supervisor at the Ole Miss power plant. Faulkner set out deliberately to create a "masterpiece" during the long overnights in the boiler room; the result, in six weeks, was *As I Lay Dying.*

In the spring of 1930, Faulkner, on the strength of several short-story sales, bought the "old Shegog place," a dilapidated antebellum house on the outskirts of Oxford, for $6,000, payable in monthly installments of $75 each. The Faulkners took possession in June. Rather grandly, Faulkner renamed it ROWAN OAK, after a tree that represents good fortune, safety, and security in Scottish folklore.

At first, Rowan Oak represented anything but security. Estelle did not like the house: It lacked running water and electricity; the windows would not open; there were rumors that it was haunted. Faulkner went further into debt fixing the place up. Estelle became pregnant that summer; Faulkner corrected proofs of *As I Lay Dying* and saw the book into print in October. The Faulkners' first child, Alabama, named for a favorite Faulkner great-aunt, was born prematurely on January 11, 1931, and lived only nine days.

But Faulkner loved Rowan Oak. The house and the grounds represented shelter from a hostile world. Even Oxford was changing. The Square had been paved over, the horse troughs removed, the elm trees felled. Faulkner's grandfather, the Young Colonel, had died in 1922, and the Big Place, once a proud landmark, afterward knew indignity and abuse, a metaphor for Falkner family decline: The mansion was cut up into apartments, and the corner lot sold off for a gasoline station.

To a degree, Rowan Oak enabled Faulkner to shut out these changes. He could *work* there, allow his imagination to shape his surroundings as he wanted them to be. *Sanctuary,* anyway, brought a

Faulkner's bedroom at Rowan Oak. *(Harriett and Gioia Fargnoli)*

temporary financial reprieve. Faulkner set out to write an attention-grabber with this book, set in the Memphis underworld and peopled with gangsters and an ambiguous heroine, a blonde Ole Miss student named Temple Drake. He succeeded.

Like some of his critics, Faulkner himself always seemed slightly queasy about *Sanctuary,* which includes a lurid scene involving a rape with a corncob. Jay Parini, for one, regards his portrayal of Temple Drake as "hardly less than a form of misogyny." Faulkner's first view of the galleys in December 1930 sent him into a panic, and he began furiously to rewrite it. Cape & Smith published the revised manuscript on February 19, 1931. By early March, it was selling 1,500 copies a week. For better or worse, it remained the book most closely associated with Faulkner's name during his lifetime.

He began there in August 1931 what would become *Light in August,* the novel some critics judge his most satisfying work artistically; the novel's genesis was in a short story whose central character, GAIL HIGHTOWER, is obsessed with his grandfather, a Civil War soldier. He set the novel aside briefly in the autumn of 1931 for trips to a writers' conference in Charlottesville, Virginia, and to New York City, where he found he had become the latest lion of the literary set. "I have learned with astonishment that I am now the most important figure in American letters," he wrote Estelle. He finished

Light in August at Rowan Oak in February 1932, sending the manuscript off to his publisher, Cape & Smith, in mid-March. But the house, Estelle's extravagances, and his own profligacy (he would lay out several thousand dollars for a powerful airplane in 1933) left him in low water financially. Then Cape & Smith went into bankruptcy, another victim of America's Great Depression. The firm failed, owing Faulkner $4,000 in royalties.

Relief came in the spring of 1932 in the form of Faulkner's first offer from Hollywood, a $500-a-week screenwriting contract with METRO-GOLD-WYN-MAYER. The novelist set off for the first of what would be a series of involvements, some of them unredeemably miserable, with "the industry." Faulkner had scant aptitude for the job and still less liking for California.

Word of his father's death on August 7, 1932, reached him in Hollywood. Murry had lost his university job in a political shuffle in the late 1920s and afterward had failed rapidly. Heavy drinking accelerated the decline; he died of a heart attack a few days short of his 62nd birthday, leaving Faulkner head of the family. "It was a natural role for him, and he assumed it at once, without fanfare but with dignity and purpose," Jack Falkner recalled. Murry Falkner's passing meant added financial burdens for the novelist. So did an increase to his own immediate family, which already included Estelle's children, various Oldhams, Callie Barr and other

A partial view of Faulkner's study at Rowan Oak. *(Harriett and Gioia Fargnoli)*

servants, and his youngest brother Dean. His and Estelle's only surviving child, JILL FAULKNER, was born on June 24, 1933. Jill would succeed Caddy Compson as his "heart's darling," but life at Rowan Oak with a drunken, emotionally unstable mother and a drunken, often absent father would be the reverse of idyllic for her.

Faulkner's money troubles mounted, and by the summer of 1935 he was approaching the edge of bankruptcy. Meantime, he was furiously at work on a new novel, with a title he would borrow from the biblical story of a son of King David who rose against his father. *Absalom, Absalom!* evolved from the 1931 short story "EVANGELINE." In the story, a young man named Henry Sutpen kills his sister's suitor, Charles Bon, after he discovers that Bon has a trace of black blood. Faulkner took up the Sutpen saga again with the short story "WASH" of 1933. He began to convert the stories and characters into a novel, called "Dark House" at first, early in 1934, using Quentin Compson as the narrator. Faulkner worked on the novel through much of 1934 and then set it aside for a time as "not quite ripe." During the fallow period, he turned out the novel *PYLON*, a minor work in which he indulged his fascination with barnstorming flyers of the early years of aviation.

Returning to *Absalom*, Faulkner worked on the last stages in an abyss of debt and grief. The director HOWARD HAWKS came to his financial rescue late in 1935 with a screenwriting offer of $1,000 a week. But nothing could assuage the pain of the death of his youngest brother, Dean Swift Faulkner, who at age 28 was killed in an airplane crash during an airshow near PONTOTOC, MISSISSIPPI, on November 10, 1935. Faulkner had introduced Dean to aviation; he blamed himself for his brother's death and said long afterward that he still saw Dean's shattered form in nightmares.

He completed *Absalom, Absalom!* on the last day of January 1936. Faulkner had been drinking heavily for some weeks, and he finally suffered a total collapse. The bout ended with his first visit to the sanitarium at BYHALIA, MISSISSIPPI, where, for a few days, Dr. Leonard Wright enforced a regimen of vitamins, drugs, and rest.

Faulkner's recuperative powers were astonishing. He was in Hollywood by the end of February 1936, coauthoring the script for *The Road to Glory*, working on another movie called *Banjo on My Knee*, and single-mindedly pursuing Hawks's Memphis-born aide and "script girl," META CARPENTER. She was wary: Faulkner was married, older, and pretty obviously a hard drinker. He persisted; she finally consented to go out to dinner with him, the beginning of a tortured, on-again, off-again 15-year affair.

The Hollywood tour inaugurated a bleak decade for Faulkner. It began with the promise of his first real love, Meta. He had just completed one of his masterworks, and he had settled in with his fifth—and last—major publisher, RANDOM HOUSE, which brought out *Absalom* in October 1936.

But the coming years would bring debt, heartache, despair. One by one, his books would go out of print, and he would lapse into obscurity. Using some of his Hollywood earnings, he bought GREENFIELD FARM, a run-down Lafayette County hill farm, in 1938; in playing the role of farmer, yet another Faulkner persona, he would know stretches of something like peace. "He had been a lot of things in his life," his brother Johncy observed, "but he always liked farmers and farming." This was the backdrop to the last of Faulkner's greatest works—*The Hamlet* (1940) and "The Bear," part of *Go Down, Moses* (1942). There were other works, too: short stories, the linked Civil War stories collectively titled *The Unvanquished* (1938) and the novel *The WILD PALMS* (1939), which sold well for a time, as many as 1,000 copies a week. But he also spent long stretches buried in Hollywood film studios.

Estelle refused to agree to a divorce—or rather, threatened to ruin him in exchange for one. So the Faulkners remained together, locked in conflict. Meta Carpenter married an Austrian émigré pianist later in 1936, but she and Faulkner would rekindle their affair during the novelist's Hollywood periods.

There came, too, a brief burst of critical appreciation that would have to last Faulkner through much of the 1940s. In "William Faulkner: The Novel and Form," the poet and critic CONRAD

AIKEN, writing in *The* ATLANTIC MONTHLY, magazine in November 1939, acknowledged the difficulty of reading Faulkner but asserted that he more than repaid the effort. Aiken likened Faulkner's sometimes clotted prose style to "the exuberant and tropical luxuriance" of a great jazz band.

Less gratifying, doubtless, was the cover story in TIME magazine at the beginning of the year. For the cover portrait, Faulkner wore a tan shirt open at the collar, suspenders (or galluses, in the language of a Faulkner character); his dark hair and moustache were neatly trimmed. Below the portrait ran Faulkner's statement of his literary purpose: "To make men stand on their hind legs and cast a shadow."

In a longish essay, part profile and part review of *The Wild Palms*, *Time* presented Faulkner to a mass audience as the author of "a series of bitter, imaginative, extraordinarily powerful but extremely uneven books." This and the Aiken piece were virtually the last word on Faulkner for a half-decade. He had appeared on the cover of *Time* in January 1939; by January 1941 he could not raise $15 to pay the Rowan Oak light bill, and he owed $600 to an Oxford grocer.

The Hamlet, the first novel in what would become the Snopes trilogy, appeared to mixed reviews in March 1940. Faulkner counted on *The Hamlet* to sell; he would be disappointed in this. He then wrote reams of what he called "trash" in an effort to remain solvent. He revised "The Bear" from memory for the high-paying SATURDAY EVENING POST so that he could make a quick sale.

Faulkner was disappointed, too, at failing to find a niche in the war effort. He had begun to cast around for a role after the fall of France in 1940. When the United States entered World War II after the Japanese attack on Pearl Harbor in December 1941, he tried to join the navy and then the army air corps. None of the services had need of an alcoholic middle-aged novelist. *The Post* published "Shingles for the Lord" in the summer of 1942, the last Faulkner story in a major national magazine for seven years. Desperate, he agreed that summer to a contract at $300 a week—far

less than he had commanded in the mid-1930s—with the WARNER BROTHERS studio. He neglected to read the fine print. The agreement contained seven years of options, essentially an indenture to Jack Warner.

As it happened, despite his misgivings about Hollywood, Faulkner actually developed into a competent screenwriter. While at Warner Bros. he received screen credit for co-scripting a couple of good films that both starred HUMPHREY BOGART: *To Have and Have Not* (1944), loosely adapted from an Ernest Hemingway novel, and *The Big Sleep* (1946), based on the detective novel of the same title by Ramond Chandler. He also authored or coauthored a number of partial and full-length scripts that never found their way to the screen but have been posthumously published: *The De Gaulle Story, Battle Cry, Country Lawyer, Stallion Road,* and *Mildred Pierce*. While Faulkner's royalties from Random House for 1942 did not exceed $300, his $300–500 monthly salary from Warner Bros. at least paid the bills. In return, Faulkner did heavy duty at the studio from 9:30 to 5 weekdays, Saturdays until 1.

Faulkner fled Hollywood for the last time in September 1945, determined to free himself from Warner Brothers no matter what the cost. About this time too, the critic MALCOLM COWLEY undertook the literary reclamation project that would vault the novelist into his rightful place in the front rank of literary artists.

"In publishing circles your name is mud," Cowley wrote him in 1944. "They are all convinced your books won't sell. Now when you talk to writers, it's quite a different story; there you hear almost nothing but admiration, and the better the writer the greater the admiration is likely to be" (*The Faulkner-Cowley File*, 9–10).

Of his 17 books, only the equivocal *Sanctuary* remained in print in 1945. On the other hand, Faulkner's reputation stood high in France. The translator MAURICE COINDREAU had been interested in his work since the early 1930s and recommended it to the Paris publisher Gaston Gallimard (*see* GALLIMARD EDITIONS) in 1931 after reading *The Sound and the Fury* and *As I Lay*

Dying. Gallimard had taken to Faulkner, and the French had responded.

"For the young people of France, Faulkner is a god," the philosopher and novelist Jean-Paul Sartre told Cowley (Williamson, 268), and the American critic launched the Faulkner boom with an appreciative essay, "William Faulkner's Human Comedy," in the *New York Times Book Review* of October 29, 1944. He followed up in *The Saturday Review* in April 1945 with "William Faulkner Revisited," in which he advised reading Faulkner's novels a second time. "You form an utterly new judgment of his aims, his shortcomings and his achievements as a novelist," Cowley wrote. "He deserves a much more important place in American literature than almost any of his critics have been willing to grant."

To further "redress the balance between his worth and his reputation," Cowley proposed an anthology of Faulkner's work to the Viking Press. *The PORTABLE FAULKNER* (1946) contained selections from the novelist's major works. Cowley wrote the introduction and prefaces to the book's seven sections. Faulkner himself supplied character genealogies and an updated map of Yoknapatawpha County that he had originally used as an appendix to *Absalom, Absalom!.* The only point of contention was Cowley's biographical sketch. Here Faulkner's fantasies about his RAF experience returned to haunt him. "You're going to bugger up a fine dignified distinguished book with that war business," he wrote Cowley (*The Faulkner-Cowley File,* 82). In the event, Cowley simply noted that the novelist had been in the RAF. For his part, Faulkner pronounced himself thoroughly satisfied with the "spoonrivering" (i.e., anthologizing) of his major works.

"The job is splendid," the novelist wrote the anthologist in April 1946. "Damn you to hell anyway. . . . By God, I didn't know myself what I had tried to do, and how much I had succeeded" (*The Faulkner-Cowley File,* 91).

Cowley's lobbying helped persuade Random House to bring out a joint Modern Library edition of *The Sound and the Fury* and *As I Lay Dying.* But it was a lesser work, *INTRUDER IN THE DUST* (1948), a thinly plotted murder mystery with an underly-

Faulkner at home in Mississippi in 1950, shortly before he won the Nobel Prize in literature *(AP/Wide World Photos)*

ing racial theme, that saved Faulkner financially. MGM paid $50,000 for the film's rights and shot much of the movie in Oxford in early 1949. The film had its premiere in Oxford's Lyric Theater in October.

Reprints of *Light in August, The Wild Palms, Go Down, Moses,* and *The Hamlet* were issued in 1949. In November, Random House published *KNIGHT'S GAMBIT,* a series of detective stories featuring the lawyer Gavin Stevens, recycled from *Intruder.* Faulkner also arranged the 60-story scheme of the *Collected Stories,* the third (and last) anthology of his short fiction, which Random House would release in 1950. The Swedish Academy considered Faulkner for the NOBEL PRIZE IN LITERATURE.

Three members of the Nobel committee dissented, however, and the academy withheld the award for 1949. In November 1950, Faulkner learned that he would be given the prize after all "for his powerful and independent artistic contribution in America's new literature of the novel." It carried a cash gift of $30,000.

Faulkner declined at first to travel to Sweden to claim the prize. Pressures were brought to bear, and in December, he and Jill flew to Stockholm. There he met Else Jonsson, the widow of the Swedish translator of his works, with whom he would have an intermittent affair, begun in Sweden and continued in Paris. The Nobel presentation speech judged him "the unrivaled master of all living British and American novelists as a deep psychologist" and "the greatest experimentalist among twentieth-century novelists."

Pale, nervous, quaking with stage fright, Faulkner raced through his acceptance speech. No one sitting more than a few feet from the dais could interpret his rapid murmurings. But the printed version remains indelible, one of the best known of all Nobel acceptances.

"I believe that man will not merely endure: he will prevail," Faulkner said. "He is immortal, not because he alone among creatures has an inexhaustible voice, but because he has a soul, a spirit capable of compassion and sacrifice and endurance."

Faulkner's literary reputation was secure. True, there had been quibbles in the United States with the Nobel decision. A fair number of critics and reviewers in his own country had always been ambivalent about his work (see CRITICISM, FAULKNER AND). Leslie Fiedler categorized Faulkner as a sentimentalist—"not a writer with the occasional vice of sentimentality, but one whose basic mode of experience is sentimental, in an age when the serious 'alienated' writer emblazons anti-sentimentality on his coat of arms" (Quoted in Parini, *One Matchless Time*, 324). The *New York Herald* drew back from an "open quarrel" about the prize, "even though one would have preferred the choice of a laureate more smiling in a world which is gradually getting darker." Faulkner could afford to ignore this sort of dissent now.

But as his fame approached its peak, his private life remained a shambles. JOAN WILLIAMS came into his life in the summer of 1949. A star-struck 19-year-old Bard College student from Memphis

with an ambition to write, she ignored the "PRIVATE—KEEP OUT" sign Faulkner had painted himself and posted at the entrance of the Rowan Oak drive and knocked on his door, commencing a strange and pathetic love affair. For the next few years, he pursued her relentlessly. She tried to fend him off. Estelle learned of the entanglement and intervened; there were drunken scenes, talk of divorce, almost unbearable tension.

Faulkner sailed on Sardis Reservoir, played at being a farmer, and worked on the manuscript of what would become *A FABLE*, an allegorical fiction set in France during World War I—the only one of his novels not sited in the South.

This book caused Faulkner a lot of trouble. At times, he seemed to look for excuses—even film work—to lay the manuscript aside. He had begun the allegory, which revolved around a Christlike

Having shunned publicity for most of his career, in his later years Faulkner began to use his fame to influence causes in which he believed. *(Library of Congress, Prints and Photographs Division, Carl Van Vechten Collection, [LC-USZ62-424851])*

Faulkner at the University of Virginia, site of an important Faulkner archive *(William Faulkner Collection, Special Collections Department, Manuscripts Division, University of Virginia Library. Photo by Ralph Thompson.)*

figure and a mutiny in a French army regiment, as early as 1943. He found it slow going, perhaps because he had come to regard it, wrongly, as his masterwork. He finished it finally in November 1953, working out the final details during a visit to SAXE COMMINS's home in Princeton, New Jersey.

With the Nobel award, the Howells Medal from the American Academy of Arts and Letters, and National Book Awards for the *Collected Stories* and *A Fable*, Faulkner became a public figure. He continued, though, to resist publicity. ROBERT COUGHLAN's 1954 profile for *Life*, filled with details about his private life, enraged and mortified him.

"What a commentary," he complained in a letter to Phil Mullen, the editor of the hometown OXFORD EAGLE. "Sweden gave me the Nobel Prize. France gave me the Legion d'Honneur. All my native land did for me was to invade my privacy over my protest and my plea" (*Selected Letters*, 354).

Yet Faulkner was prepared to use his fame and influence to further causes in which he felt an interest. A conservative Democrat, skeptical of the New Deal and a conventional Cold Warrior, he undertook cultural goodwill trips for the U.S. State Department to South America in 1954 and to Japan, the Philippines, and Europe in 1955. In 1956, he chaired the writers' group of President Eisenhower's "People to People" program, which aimed to transmit American culture into Communist Eastern Europe, and he became notorious for his brief, unhappy involvement in the Civil Rights movement in the South, in which he pulled off the difficult feat of alienating partisans on all sides of the issue (*see* RACE, FAULKNER AND).

His cautious endorsement of integration infuriated the Oxford Falkners and brought him hate mail, threatening phone calls, and the sobriquet "Weeping Willie." The writer and educator W. E. B. DuBois, a founder of the National Association for the Advancement of Colored People (NAACP), challenged him to a debate on the steps of a Mississippi courthouse on his gradualist approach to desegregation, a challenge he wisely declined.

Faulkner dropped out of the great racial controversy and turned back to his work. He took up the Snopes saga again, finishing *The* TOWN, the second book in the trilogy, following *The Hamlet*, in August 1956. At home, he and Estelle negotiated an armistice in their long and bitter war. Estelle entered Alcoholics Anonymous in 1955. She took his latest (and last) affair with a younger woman gently, worrying mainly that Jill, who had married in 1954, would learn of his involvement with JEAN STEIN. Jean herself brought things to an abrupt close in February 1957, touching off a drinking binge that landed Faulkner in the hospital yet again.

But his last years brought a measure of stability, if not serenity. In 1957 and 1958, Faulkner was writer-in-residence at the UNIVERSITY OF VIRGINIA, where a group of English Department admirers that included his future biographer Joseph Blotner attended him faithfully. Jill and her husband, PAUL D. SUMMERS, had settled in Charlottesville, and the Faulkners decided to move there permanently to be near Jill and the grandchildren; Jill delivered the second of three sons, named William Cuthbert Faulkner Summers, in December 1958. Faulkner attended University of Virginia football games (the play-by-play announcer, in a halftime interview, introduced the famous fan to his radio audience as the winner of the "Mobile Prize for Literature") and took up fox hunting in the rolling hills of Albemarle County, proudly wearing the pink coat of the FARMINGTON HUNT CLUB.

Faulkner closed out the Snopes chronicle with *The* MANSION, published in November 1959. Maud Falkner, 88 years old, died in Oxford in October 1960. Faulkner finished his last novel, *The Reivers*, comic but elegiac too in its casting back to his Oxford boyhood, in August 1961. Dedicated to his grandchildren, it was chosen by the Book-of-the-Month Club as its main selection.

He took two hard falls from horses in Virginia early in 1962, aggravating old back injuries. In June, his horse threw him violently as he rode along the Old Taylor Road near Rowan Oak. He reached for his usual remedy: prescription painkillers and whiskey. Soon he was deep into another alcoholic episode, incoherent, undernourished, virtually comatose.

On July 4, Estelle and his nephew JAMES (Jimmy) FAULKNER resolved to take him to Wright's Sanitarium in Byhalia. To their surprise, he offered no protest. Dr. Wright himself admitted him at 6 P.M. on July 5. At 1:30 in the morning of July 6, 1962,

Faulkner's grave. *(Harriett and Gioia Fargnoli)*

William Faulkner sat up in bed and then collapsed, dead of a heart attack. He is buried in Oxford's St. Peter's Cemetery, at the foot of a hill and underneath a large oak tree, in a setting suggestive of the natural world that he loved so well.

PART II

Works A to Z

Absalom, Absalom!

Considered a masterpiece of 20th-century American literature, this novel, published in October 1936, brought to a close a seven-year burst of creativity in which Faulkner produced *The SOUND AND THE FURY* (1929), *As I LAY DYING* (1930), *LIGHT IN AUGUST* (1932), and other works. Some critics rate *Absalom, Absalom!* as Faulkner's finest work.

The novel chronicles the rise and fall of the YOKNAPATAWPHA COUNTY planter Thomas Sutpen, a western Virginian of obscure origins who comes into frontier northern Mississippi in the 1830s to fulfill a grand design to achieve wealth, position, and power. He buys 100 square miles of virgin land from a CHICKASAW INDIAN chief, builds a mansion and plantation with the enforced labor of Haitian slaves and a captive French architect, marries into a respectable JEFFERSON, MISSISSIPPI, family, and attempts to complete his design by establishing a Sutpen dynasty.

Absalom, Absalom! had its beginnings in the short story "WASH" (1933). The story introduces Wash Jones, a feckless poor white man who looks after Sutpen's estate while he is away with Lee's army during the Civil War. Sutpen returns to find his wife dead, one son dead and the other a fugitive, and his plantation in ruins. He seduces Wash's 15-year-old granddaughter, Milly Jones, in hopes of producing an heir. When she bears him a daughter, he repudiates her. Wash then cuts him down with a rusted scythe, kills Milly and the baby, and burns down the fishing shanty that had been their home.

Harper's magazine bought "Wash" in November 1933, paying $350 for it. On a sheet of manuscript dated February 11, 1934, Faulkner began the novel that would become *Absalom, Absalom!* At first, he titled it *Dark House*, which he earlier had

Sanctuary of College Church where Faulkner was married. Faulkner may have had this church in mind as the scene of Thomas Sutpen's marriage to Ellen Coldfield. *(Harriett and Gioia Fargnoli)*

used provisionally and then discarded for *Light in August*. Faulkner promised his publisher, HARRISON SMITH, the manuscript for the autumn of 1934. With money difficulties and other worries to distract him, he would miss the target by 18 months. He did, at least, find a title he liked: "*Absalom, Absalom!*; the story is of a man who wanted a son through pride, and got too many of them and they destroyed him" (*Selected Letters*, 84). The biblical Absalom, the third of King David's 17 sons, avenges the rape of his sister by her half brother Amnon and later rises against his father and attempts to seize his throne.

Money troubles forced Faulkner to interrupt work on *Absalom* to return to Hollywood to write film scripts, and he set aside the big book altogether late in 1934 to turn out the minor novel PYLON, published in 1935. By March 1935, he had returned to *Absalom*. On March 30, he wrote the title at the top of a sheet of paper, underlining it twice, and after a couple of false starts, he opened with Quentin Compson and Miss Rosa Coldfield in her dark room on a "long still hot weary dead September afternoon" in 1909, just before Quentin heads north to begin his freshman year at Harvard.

Again beset with money troubles, Faulkner suspended work on *Absalom* in the summer of 1935, returning to California for another eight-week term writing for the movies. By mid-October, he was back in Oxford, launched into the middle chapters of the novel. Faulkner wrote the final chapters in a state of deep grieving for his younger brother Dean (*see* FAULKNER, DEAN SWIFT), who died in an airplane crash on November 10, 1935. He worked away at the manuscript at his mother's house where he had moved temporarily to care for her and Dean's pregnant widow; by December, he could see ahead to the tale's conclusion. By mid-month, however, he was in Hollywood again, where he finished the draft early in January 1936. Then he began to drink heavily, even though he told friends and acquaintances that he felt confident about the book. He returned to Oxford before the end of the month and continued to tinker with the manuscript. Finally, he appended a date to the last page: "31 Jany 1936."

SYNOPSIS

The basic story is simple. Thomas Sutpen arrives in Jefferson from parts unknown on a Sunday in June 1833. He acquires land from the Chickasaws through questionable means and with his half-wild slaves hacks out a plantation he calls SUTPEN'S HUNDRED. In 1838, he marries Ellen Coldfield, the daughter of a Jefferson merchant of tender conscience and strict principles. She bears him two children, Judith and Henry Sutpen. During Christmas 1860, Judith falls in love with her brother's UNIVERSITY OF MISSISSIPPI friend, Charles Bon. Sutpen forbids the marriage. Henry and Charles go off together to fight in the Civil War; Sutpen separately goes to war at the head of a Mississippi volunteer infantry regiment. Ellen dies in January 1863. In May 1865, at the war's end, Henry kills Bon at the gates of Sutpen's Hundred and disappears. In 1869, Sutpen's factotum, the squatter Wash Jones, kills Sutpen for seducing and then abandoning his granddaughter Milly.

Faulkner tells the story through Quentin Compson, the doomed Harvard undergraduate of *The Sound and the Fury*. It opens with Quentin preparing to call on Miss Rosa Coldfield, an embittered old spinster who has chosen to pass on to him the story of her monstrous brother-in-law, Sutpen. "Maybe you will enter the literary profession," Miss Rosa tells him, ". . . and maybe some day you will remember this and write about it" (5). Quentin's father, Jason Richmond Compson, has heard some of the Sutpen story through his own father, General Jason Lycurgus Compson II, Sutpen's only friend in Yoknapatawpha County; Mr. Compson passes along what he knows to Quentin. As the novel runs its course, Quentin and his Harvard roommate Shrevlin McCannon together reconstruct the Sutpen story.

Miss Rosa, Mr. Compson, Quentin, and Shreve painstakingly assemble the story of the parvenu Sutpen and the working out of his design. Long flashbacks recount Sutpen's childhood; his first marriage, in Haiti, to Eulalia Bon, a planter's daughter with a taint of black blood, and the birth of their son Charles; and his arrival in Yoknapatawpha County. Faulkner sketches vivid and dramatic scenes, as toward the end of chapter 1 when Rosa tells of Sutpen's "raree show," the master stripped to the waist to fight one of his Haitians with his little son Henry and his daughters Judith and Clytemnestra (Clytie, whose mother was a slave) Sutpen looking on.

In chapters 2 and 3, Mr. Compson fills in details of the history of the house of Sutpen as he and Quentin sit on the front gallery in the cigar smoke- and wisteria-scented twilight: the arrival of Charles Bon, the coming of the war and Sutpen's role in it, Sutpen's father-in-law Goodhue Coldfield's withdrawal and slow suicide, Henry's and Bon's early war service, and Ellen's deathbed request of Rosa to look after Judith. At the end of chapter 3, Wash rides to Jefferson, 12 miles distant, to summon Miss Rosa to Sutpen's Hundred: "Hello. Hello. . . . Air you Rosie Coldfield?" (63).

Faulkner withholds the reason for Wash's errand to develop more of the history of Henry, Charles, and Judith. Mr. Compson speculates that Sutpen had found evidence of Bon's involvement with a New Orleans octoroon woman and used it as a pretext for forbidding the marriage of Bon and Judith. Henry refuses to accept the explanation and breaks with his father out of love for Bon. But Mr. Compson seems to find his theory inadequate to explain events. What he does not know is that Bon is Sutpen's son by the racially mixed Haitian wife whom he had renounced. At the close of the chapter, Faulkner returns to Wash's journey into Jefferson: "Air you Rosie Coldfield? Then you better come on out yon. Henry has done shot that durn French feller. Kilt him dead as a beef" (106).

Miss Rosa again takes up the story in chapter 5, with Quentin as her listener. Judith directs the building of Bon's coffin; after his burial, she, Rosa, and Clytie begin the hard labor of restoring the plantation after four years of wartime neglect. The section, mostly flashbacks, ends with Rosa's eerie and mysterious revelation to Quentin that something is alive in the house: "Something living in it. Hidden in it. It has been out there for four years living hidden in that house" (140).

In chapter 6, Quentin, now at Harvard, takes over the story. In a letter dated January 10, 1910, Mr. Compson informs his son of Miss Rosa's death and burial. Faulkner here introduces a new charac-

ter, the Canadian Shreve, who provides an outsider's detachment as the last of the tale unfolds. The action advances beyond the time of the short story "Wash" and the 1869 killing of Thomas Sutpen. Judith and Clytie raise Charles Bon's son by his octoroon mistress, Charles Etienne St. Valery Bon. Part black himself, the younger Charles marries a full-blood African American; their child is the feeble-minded Jim Bond, Sutpen's last heir. Judith nurses Charles Etienne through a yellow fever outbreak in 1884; they both die of the disease at Sutpen's Hundred. The chapter ends with Quentin preparing to drive to the mansion with Miss Rosa to flush out whoever is in hiding there.

Quentin continues the story in chapter 7, with occasional interjections, queries, and summarizations from Shreve. It is early material: Sutpen's origins in western Virginia, his drunken father's move to the Tidewater, a liveried slave's dismissal of the boy from the front door of a Virginia plantation— the initial motivation for Sutpen's design. Quentin reconstructs Sutpen's arrival in Haiti, his marriage to Eulalia Bon, and his abandonment of her when he learns of her taint. (Their son Charles's courtship of Judith will be her revenge.) Sutpen explains his flight from Eulalia to General Compson, his only friend: with her black blood, she could not be part of his plan, so he left her behind.

The chapter concludes with Wash's killing of Sutpen, much of it lifted from the short story, and with Quentin's disclosure to Shreve, withheld almost until the end, that Milly's child had not been the heir Sutpen wanted, but a girl.

So it ends for Sutpen. He never understands where he has gone wrong. He never learns where he failed, though he believes it is not through moral retribution, not even through bad luck, but because he had made a miscalculation somewhere along the way. General Compson diagnosed Sutpen's trouble as a sort of innocence of the nature of reality, an inability to fully reckon the consequences of his actions.

Chapter 8 concerns Quentin's relentless exploration of the Henry-Bon-Judith triangle. Bon still wants to marry Judith; even more, he wants Sutpen to acknowledge him as his son. In the end, Henry is prepared to accept incest but not miscegenation.

Quentin and Shreve recreate Henry's last interview with his father in an army bivouac in North Carolina in the late winter of 1865. Chapter 8 closes with Shreve's imagined account of the shooting at the gates of Sutpen's Hundred.

In chapter 9, the novel's last and shortest, Quentin relates his night journey with Miss Rosa to the gaunt mansion at Sutpen's Hundred. Quentin follows her upstairs and catches a glimpse of the "something" living there—the spectral Henry, who has come home to die. In the final sequence, he again takes up his father's letter and reads of the death of Rosa, and of Henry and Clytie, and of the destruction of the great house by fire.

CRITICAL ANALYSIS

A work of structural and technical complexity, *Absalom* is an inquiry into the elusive nature of truth. "The whole novel is 'about' the inextricable confusion of fact and fiction, of observation and interpretation, involved in any account of human experience," the critic MICHAEL MILLGATE wrote in his study *William Faulkner.* Closer to the bone, it is an intense, demanding, difficult and often painful exploration of the themes of guilt, shame, and racial injustice. Above all, racism and slavery corrupt individuals and their society; they lead ultimately to Sutpen's destruction and to the deserved destruction of the Old South.

Structurally, the novel is organized around a series of "moments of recognition, truth and disillusion," according to Millgate, among them the encounter of Sutpen and Henry in the library at Sutpen's Hundred; Henry's shooting of Bon; Sutpen's conditional proposal of marriage to Rosa Coldfield; and Wash Jones's recognition that Sutpen has betrayed him and his subsequent killing of Sutpen. Faulkner presents each moment, wrote Millgate, "in a kind of tableau arrested at a particular point in time and held in suspension while it is looked at, approached from all sides, inspected as if it were an artifact."

Most of the "facts" of the story are established in chapter 1, and the facts are incontrovertible. "What is always in doubt, however, and always open to interpretation or conjecture, is the inner meaning of these observable events and the whole

intricate sequence of cause and effect which links them to one another," Millgate wrote. It is left to the reader to sort out the story's significance.

Faulkner presents three (four, counting Shreve, who synthesizes other accounts and adds his own gloss) different, sometimes conflicting interpretations of Sutpen. Miss Rosa, the only one of the narrators to have known Sutpen personally, regards him as a demon, an ogre. Mr. Compson's version, which derives mostly from his father, General Compson, is balanced and judicious; that said, it fails to account for the power of Sutpen's obsession. In their frigid dormitory room in Cambridge, Massachusetts, Quentin and Shreve collate information from both informants to move closer to what Millgate calls a "poetic truth." Quentin finally pieces together his own version of the tale in a long collaboration with Shreve. Quentin's view of the Sutpen saga is tragic and romantic; Shreve's is that of a fascinated, often baffled outsider.

With multiple narrators offering multiple individual versions, "The novel becomes, in effect, a grammar of narrative," asserts Faulkner's most recent biographer, Jay Parini, "one of those rare novels that opens up the hood of fiction to show what's inside."

As Faulkner confidant and biographer JOSEPH BLOTNER has observed, the introduction of Quentin, the passionate and bewildered central figure in *The Sound and the Fury,* turned out to be a master stroke. "I use Quentin because of his sister, and I use his bitterness which he has projected on the South in the form of hatred of it and its people to get more out of the story than a historical novel would be," Faulkner explained to his editor Hal Smith (*Selected Letters,* 79). Quentin's own complex feelings for his sister Caddy (Compson) in the earlier novel make him imaginatively alert to the incestuous triangle of Henry, Judith, and their half brother Bon. Quentin listens quietly as Miss Rosa relates the Sutpen story, though his nerves are jangling. Rosa's tone is frenzied. The language of the opening chapter is complex and confused, the atmosphere violent.

The liveried slave's rejection of young Sutpen is the key to the narrative. The scene and all that flows from it led Parini to invoke the Hindu concept of Karma; "evil acts engender evil acts." Sutpen marries into a slaveholding family to further his ambitions. He discards his wife; the act comes back to haunt him through their son Bon. Sutpen's son Henry destroys Bon and thus is lost to Sutpen. In an effort to beget another heir, Sutpen corrupts Milly, whose grandfather destroys Sutpen (Milly and her baby too) in retribution. Virtually everyone who comes into close contact with Sutpen suffers from it.

From the start, critics remarked on Faulkner's taste for melodrama. In an early review, Bernard De Voto observed that Faulkner had borrowed melodramatic devices and scenes from earlier works: Wash's hammering together Bon's coffin, as in *As I Lay Dying;* the incest theme from *The Sound and the Fury;* the intolerable agonies that beset a mixed-race character, as when Charles Etienne Bon endures "cruelties almost as unceasing as those that made Joe Christmas [of *Light in August*] the most persecuted child since Dickens." Michael Millgate emphasizes gothic elements in *Absalom,* especially the manic exaggeration of Miss Rosa's narrative. He detects affinities between *Absalom* and Charlotte Brontë's *Jane Eyre,* specifically in the similarities of Sutpen and the domineering St. John Rivers and of Rosa Coldfield and Jane Eyre, two innocents wounded by equivocal offers of marriage.

Some critics have identified strains of Christian symbolism and of homoeroticism in *Absalom.* Surely, Jay Parini asserts, the name Charles Bon is significant. "Charles the Good" dies at age 33; he can be regarded as having taken on not only his father's sins but the sins of the South as well. The textual scholar NOEL POLK sees homoerotic undertones in the relationship between Henry and Bon and perhaps between Quentin and Shreve. Indeed, Mr. Compson speculates than Bon "loved Henry the better of the two," and regarded Judith as the shadow of his actual love (86).

Hyatt Waggoner sums up a larger meaning of the novel, perhaps the ultimate meaning, in a commentary on Henry's killing of Charles Bon: "When the Old South was faced with a choice it could not avoid, it chose to destroy itself rather than admit brotherhood across racial lines." Adopting his father's fatally corrosive racial notions, Henry destroys Bon in order to prevent Bon's interracial union with his half-sister Judith.

This, surely, is the immemorial curse of the South that outrages Quentin Compson and gives rise to the despairing denial that brings the novel to a close:

"Why do you hate the South?" Shreve asks him.

"'I dont hate it,' Quentin said quickly, at once, immediately; 'I dont hate it,' he said. *I dont hate it* he thought, panting in the cold air, the iron New England dark: *I dont. I dont! I dont hate it! I don't hate it!*" (303).

CRITICAL RECEPTION

With many revisions, Faulkner sent the typescript of *Absalom, Absalom!* along to his new publisher, RANDOM HOUSE, which had absorbed SMITH & HAAS at the beginning of 1936. Hal Smith, now at Random House, received the concluding pages in June. Faulkner continued revising up to the last minute. He added, too, a chronology of events, a genealogy of characters, and a hand-drawn map of Yoknapatawpha County with identifications of 27 places that had figured in his novels and short stories up to then.

He read and corrected the galleys in August. The official publication date, with 6,000 copies printed, was October 26. Random House soon followed with a second printing of 2,500 copies and a third, in mid-November, of another 1,400. The early reviews, as ever with Faulkner, were mixed. In *The New Yorker,* CLIFTON FADIMAN famously called *Absalom* "the most consistently boring novel by a reputable writer to come my way during the last decade." *Time,* in an unsigned review, called it "the strangest, longest, least readable, most infuriating and yet in some respects the most impressive novel that William Faulkner has written." Bernard De Voto, in the *Saturday Review,* treated the new work with grudging respect tinged with sarcasm.

"It is now possible to say confidently that the greatest suffering of which American fiction has any record occurred in the summer of 1909 and was inflicted on Quentin Compson," De Voto wrote. That is when, in *The Sound and the Fury,* "he made harrowing discoveries about his sister Candace," while only a month or so later in the new work he "had to watch the last act of doom's pitiless engulfing of the Sutpens, another family handicapped by a curse."

Reviewers complained of the novel's technical complexity, of the improbabilities of the characters' actions ("Just why," De Voto wondered, "did not Thomas Sutpen, recognizing Charles Bon as his mulatto son, order him off the plantation, or bribe or kill him, or tell Judith either half the truth, or Henry all of it?") and of long patches of apoplectic prose.

"In the first paragraph of the novel," Graham Greene observed pedantically in the *London Mercury*, "there are forty-one adjectives in twenty-seven lines qualifying only fifteen nouns."

The novelist probably saw only a few of the notices, and he doubtless shrugged off the ones he did read. "Faulkner is probably the one man in the world who doesn't give a damn what the rest of its inhabitants might think, so long as he has a place to sleep, eat and write, with an occasional jug of corn thrown in for recreational hours," Laurence Bell remarked in *Literary America*. In any case, later critics, taking a longer view, would right the balance.

The critic CLEANTH BROOKS called *Absalom* the greatest and least well understood of Faulkner's works. The difficulty of the writing, he argued, "is the price that has to be paid for the novel's power and significance." Millgate viewed *Absalom*'s structural complexity as fundamental to its meaning. Irving Howe agreed and found *Absalom* the most nearly structurally perfect of all Faulkner's novels.

"Faulkner's greatest risk, *Absalom, Absalom!* is never likely to be read widely; it is for aficionados willing to satisfy the large and sometimes excessive demands it makes upon attention," Howe concluded. "Wild, twisted and occasionally absurd, the novel has, nonetheless, the fearful impressiveness which comes when a writer has driven his vision to an extreme."

Frederick Karl, a Faulkner biographer, judges *Absalom* the "Everest" of Faulkner's achievement, one of the great novels of modernism, and the only American work of fiction that can stand with those of Proust, Mann, Kafka, Conrad, Woolf, and Joyce.

For more on *Absalom, Absalom!*, see *Faulkner in the University*, 34–35, 36, 46–47, 71, 73, 74– 77, 79–81, 93–94, 97–98, 119, 273–275, and 281; *Selected Letters*, 92, 94, 96, and 280; and *Faulkner at Nagano*, 42–43.

EXCERPTS FROM CONTEMPORARY REVIEWS OF *ABSALOM, ABSALOM!*

Excerpt From George Marion O'Donnell's review, "Mr. Faulkner Flirts with Failure," published in the Nashville Banner, *October 25, 1936, Magazine Section, 8:*

. . . Returning for his setting to the Mississippi country of *Sartoris* and *As I Lay Dying* and *The Sound and the Fury*, Mr. Faulkner has built his new novel, *Absalom, Absalom!* around [Thomas Sutpen], who stands out as a new sort of figure in Southern fiction, in all his demoniac fierceness and strength. And with him in the book live also the people who lived around him and wondered at him during his lifetime. For in this novel, Mr. Faulkner has presented at once one man's life, the way of life in which he existed, a whole section of the country, and a whole passage of time.

But the story and the characters are not revealed in any conventional fashion. Mr. Faulkner is still experimenting with form; and this is probably a healthy sign, indicating that he is not yet finished as a novelist and is not likely to be finished for some time, despite the major artistic defects of his two previous books, *Light in August* (the formal structure of which does not stand the test of rereading), and *Pylon* (which is probably the worst of Mr. Faulkner's novels). For this new book, Mr. Faulkner has adopted a strange device: the story is revealed only as it takes form in the understanding of Quentin Compson (one of the Compson family who appeared in *The Sound and the Fury*) and becomes so much a part of him that he can say of himself: "I am older at 20 than a lot of people who have died"—and say this without speaking falsely, without speaking with the world-weariness of youth. This taking form of the story in Quentin's understanding occurs in the summer before he leaves for Harvard in 1910, and in the winter of his first year at Harvard, long after most of the events in the narrative have taken place.

Quentin functions as an actor, insofar as he is present at the startling denouement of the story.

But primarily, Quentin might be called a Special Listener; his part is to hear people talk about Sutpen and about the doings surrounding him and his family. Those whom Quentin hears are his father, who tells what his own father knew and told him, and Miss Rosa Coldfield, Sutpen's sister-in-law whom he insulted.

Sometimes Mr. Faulkner reports their actual speech to Quentin. Sometimes he follows Quentin's mind as he thinks of the story. Sometimes he reports Quentin's speech as he tells the story to his roommate at Harvard. Sometimes the roommate, who has evidently heard parts of the story before this particular telling, interrupts Quentin to recount these parts of it. And in the last three sections of the book, all of these methods are combined, sometimes in such a manner that reading is difficult, the story is obscured, and it becomes necessary to refer to the beginning of a passage to determine just what character is acting as narrator. This is undoubtedly a stylistic fault. Difficulty is probably legitimate in fiction; but it has a very tenuous legitimacy, being always dangerous because it may perform the decidedly illegitimate function of standing between the reader and his final understanding of the characters and of the story, instead of helping him toward that understanding.

Moreover, when Quentin's roommate tells Quentin all over again parts of the story which Quentin himself must have told to the roommate, then the process seems a little ridiculous. It cannot fail to call to mind the device by which inexperienced dramatists make their exposition of antecedent action—those tense moments in which a husband reminds his wife that they have been married for five years and now have two children!

However, these are not major faults. Though the method of construction in this book is a dangerous one, it appears to succeed. The book seems narrowly to evade formlessness; yet it does manage the evasion, because of Mr. Faulkner's device of using Quentin as his Special Listener, even if it does not achieve perfect formal coherence.

One might question at times the realism of the narrator's speech, because they speak often in a kind of prose-poetry familiar to readers of *The Sound and the Fury*. But this is defensible in *Absalom, Absalom!* on the grounds that Mr. Faulkner is dealing with characters who speak and think in the elaborate, Latinesque, sometimes oratorical style characteristic of the antebellum South. And it is defensible on the different ground that Mr. Faulkner is not writing just what can be said in narrative speech; he is writing all that cannot be said (trying thereby to project the very experience itself) along with what can be narrated. And experiences actually are projected in *Absalom, Absalom!* by means of this style. Here, too, Mr. Faulkner is daring; here, once more, he is flirting with failure. A novel can not be so complex and artistic a presentation of experience as a poem, since a novel necessarily excludes more of the minutiae of an experience, giving only the essentials where a poem may give much more of rich detail. And the ignoring of this limitation is a dangerous thing. Mr. Faulkner, however, is a conscientious and profound artist. And it is more likely that he deliberately accepts the danger than that he accidentally stumbles into it. That he does accept the danger, and still manages to defy it successfully, is once more evidence of Mr. Faulkner's artistry. For by this acceptance Mr. Faulkner manages to recreate the story of Sutpen whole, as it would be revealed in life, yet richer than life itself because of the strong, controlled power of his art.

With all of its minor stylistic and formal defects, *Absalom, Absalom!* is fiction of a high order of excellence, strong from its roots in the life of a people and in a land and in a time, rich from the experience of that people, and beautiful from its sincere telling by one of that very race, who has mastered his art as have few of his contemporaries.

Excerpt from Peter Monro Jack's review, "Nightmares of Evil," published in the New York Sun, October 30, 1936, 30:

For his new book William Faulkner has done a map of Jefferson, Yoknapatawpha county, Mississippi, with the simple legend: Area, 2,400 square miles; population, whites, 6,298; Negroes, 9,313. William Faulkner, sole owner and proprietor. A queer sort of country to own, hag-ridden and haunted with the ghosts of grotesquely gallant confederate colonels, incestuous and miscegenating younger sons, neurotic old maids of proud and prodigious memories, the violent and erratic passions of girls, and slavery in all its clownish or driveling or threatening aspects; and all of it living luridly in the loving, brooding desperate brain of Faulkner, to whom this lost country is a symbol of the world.

His work has gained in force, complexity and popularity, but as to quality I am not so sure. "The Sound and the Fury" still remains for me his best book. It had an almost poetic pliancy, an enticing and exciting secretiveness, even a furtiveness that went with its theme, a dance of hidden meanings that always receded and always attracted. Mr. Faulkner coarsened his material in "Sanctuary." He reduced it to catch words and claptrap in many of his popular short stories. He made it too explicit in "Light in August," which put gentleness against violence, innocence against evil, Lena, Byron and Hightower against Christmas and Miss Burden, explanations against enigmas, almost as in a morality play.

Now he has done a novel impossible to overlook in any responsible discussion of contemporary literature, but as to its ultimate value I can only hazard a guess. It has not the style of "The Sound and the Fury." It has no character as appealing as Lena in "Light in August." It has not the sensational savagery of "Sanctuary." It will lie near to all of them, and also near to the evocative nostalgia of "Sartoris." But I think it is underplayed and overwritten. When Arnold Bennett said Faulkner wrote like an angel, he started things. Now Faulkner wants to write like a barrel of angels. . . .

The texture of the story, for all its retellings and all its superabundance of words, is amazingly interesting. It is a story of suspense, not of drama, of expectation rather than surprise, a prolonged nightmare of the re-enactment of an inevitable evil and it belongs strongly and assertively to the important literature of our time.

Excerpt from Bernard DeVoto's review, "Witchcraft in Mississippi," published in the Saturday Review of Literature, *15 (Oct. 31, 1936), 3–4, 14:*

. . . Although the story is told in approximations which display a magnificent technical dexterity—more expert than Mr. Dos Passos's, and therefore the most expert in contemporary American fiction—and although the various segments are shredded and displaced, it is not a difficult story to follow. It is not, for instance, so darkly refracted through distorting lenses as *The Sound and the Fury.* Though plenty of devices are employed to postpone the ultimate clarification, none are introduced for the sole purpose of misleading the reader, and in an access of helpfulness, Mr. Faulkner has included not only an appendix of short biographies which make clear all the relationships, but also a chronological chart which summarizes the story. If you study both of them before beginning the book, you will have no trouble. . . .

The drama of *Absalom, Absalom!* is clearly diabolism, a "miasmal distillant" of horror, with clouds of sulphur smoke billowing from the pit and flashes of hellish lightning flickering across the steady phosphorous-glow of the graveyard and the medium's cabinet. And it is embodied in the familiar hypochondria of Mr. Faulkner's prose, a supersaturated solution of pity and despair. In book after book now he has dropped tears like the famed Arabian tree, in a rapture of sensibility amounting to continuous orgasm. The medium in which his novels exist is lachrymal, and in *Absalom, Absalom!* that disconsolate fog reaches its greatest concentration to date. And its most tortured prose. Mr. Faulkner has always had many styles at his command, has been able to write expertly in many manners, but he has always been best at the phrase, and it is as a phrase-maker only that he writes well here. Many times he says the incidental thing perfectly, as "that quiet aptitude of a child for accepting the inexplicable." But, beyond the phrase, he now—deliberately—mires himself in such a quicksand of invertebrate sentences as has not been seen since *Euphues.* There have been contentions between Mr. Faulkner and Mr. Hemingway before this; it may be that he is matching himself against the Gertrude-Steinish explosions of syntax that spattered *Green Hills of Africa* with bad prose. If so, he comes home under wraps: the longest Hemingway sentence ran only forty-three lines, whereas the longest Faulkner sentence runs eighty lines and there are more than anyone will bother to count which exceed the thirty-three line measure of his page. They have the steady purpose of expressing the inexpressible that accounts for so much of

Mr. Faulkner, but they show a style in process of disintegration. When a narrative sentence has to have as many as three parentheses identifying the reference of pronouns, it signifies mere bad writing and can be justified by no psychological or esthetic principle whatever. . . .

Excerpt from Mary-Carter Roberts's review, "Faulkner's Style Dwarfs Material in New Novel," published in the Washington Evening Star, October 31, 1936, 2–B:
Fighting with his own prose like a man slashing his way through a forest of falling velvet curtains armed only with a dull knife, William Faulkner here writes another novel of human disintegration in terms of the far South. It is on the whole a fine performance, though its excellence rests on Mr. Faulkner's formidable prowess as a consistent stylist rather than on any significance in his material. . . .

Through the sheer pounding music of his prose he has invested his conventional stuff with conviction and significance. He writes here as he has in past novels—that is, as if he were the only writer in the world, and as if no one were expected to read his book except himself. To him, obviously, the story of the Sutpen plantation has been immensely tragic. Is conventionality simply has not occurred to him. He writes with newness about it, with a profound personal sense of the horror of its decay and degeneration, not as if he were telling the tale to some other persons, but as if, from that cycle of human regression he had drawn such a dark and dreadful beauty that for his own sake alone he must needs reproduce and preserve it. And so we have a novel that stands high among its contemporaries simply as a prose structure, a signal triumph of style over content and an example of artistic conviction as a force to give old tales new life and significance.

Beyond that there is not much to say about the work.

Excerpt from Harold Strauss's review, "Mr. Faulkner Is Ambushed in Words," published in The New York Times Book Review, November 1, 1936, 7:
. . . Nor is [*Absalom, Absalom!*] strange for its time-stopping intensity and for its detailed and hyper-

sensitive examination of the flow of mental images during moments of violent physical action—matters in which Faulkner is a recognized master. No, it is strange chiefly because of the amazing indirectness with which Faulkner has managed to tell a basically simple story. In fact, he does not tell the story of Thomas Sutpen—of his descent upon Jefferson in 1833 with his twenty wild Negroes and his eventual fate—at all; rather, he gets inside the mind of a young man by the name of Quentin Compson, who went to Harvard in 1910 and who by accident was impelled slowly to piece the old story together and who was permitted to witness its epilogue. . . .

That, and the style. Faulkner has always written in an involved style, but his earlier writing shines with the clear light of eloquence against the obscurity of the intricate page-long sentences in "Absalom, Absalom!"—sentences that occasionally deal simultaneously with the doings of young Quentin in 1910 and of the Sutpens in 1860. The truth seems to be that Faulkner fears banality. . . . He has been complex before, but never uncommunicative.

Occasionally there are passages of great power and beauty in this book, passages which remind us that Faulkner is still a writer with a unique gift of illuminating dark corners of the human soul. There are other passages which, while hardly communicative, drop into a pure blank verse and are estimable for their sheer verbal music. For the rest, "Absalom, Absalom!" must be left to those hardy souls who care for puzzles.

Excerpt from Mary Colum's review, "Faulkner's Struggle with Technique," published in Forum and Century, January 1937, 35–36:
. . . [Faulkner] is making a struggle with form and with language; but his form in this novel seems to me to be too incoherent, and his long, trailing sentences are often difficult, if not exasperating, reading. He is too dazzled by wondrously involved sentences and wondrously involved sounds. Yet there are powerful scenes in the book, all done in the narrative manner in which there is no action and hardly any dialogue, all related by different people. . . .

Yet, while this book of Faulkner's shows a powerful talent, it is an unsuccessful novel. We regret that this should be the net result of all that power for creating situation and atmosphere and producing sentences of deep import and beauty. His people all have the same kind of tension; they all feel the same terror; all the narrators in the story relate their tales in the same manner, with the same kind of words. Yet it is giving great praise to *Absalom, Absalom!* to say that it actually brings *Wuthering Heights* to our minds.

William Faulkner is struggling with a difficult technique, and one cannot help believing that, if he had the opportunity (as writers in other countries naturally have) of threshing out his technical ideas around a café table, his accomplishment would not be so incoherent as it is. Obviously he has studied Joyce and Proust, as well as *Wuthering Heights* and *The Fall of the House of Usher;* but Joyce knew George Moore, and George Moore knew [Edouard] Dujardin—who invented the interior monologue—and he knew Zola and Turgenev; and, as for the artists Proust talked with and studied, the list is too long to write down. . . .

Excerpt from William Plomer's review, "Fiction," published in The Spectator, February 26, 1937, 376:

I understand that in America Mr. Faulkner's latest book has had what is called a mixed reception, some regarding it as another triumph of his peculiar talent and some as a reduction almost to absurdity of his peculiar mannerisms. You may find it fascinating or exasperating, or both. Here is the old original Faulknerian bag of tricks—"the deep South dead since 1865 and peopled with garrulous outraged baffled ghosts." Readers somewhat baffled, if not actually outraged, by Mr. Faulkner's syntax and his tremendous manoeuvrings in search of a meaning will at any rate recognise his vigour and may easily find themselves caught up into the world of romantic horror which he has created. . . .

Now this book has a perfectly logical plot and various merits and beauties, but reading it tends at times to be little easier than it would be to knit with barbed wire. The legend of Colonel Sutpen, who arrived on the banks of the Mississippi early in the last century to build a mansion and found a family, is not presented; it has to be found out. But luckily Mr. Faulkner is always ready to construct a mountain from which we may catch a glimpse of

some significant molehill, and as clues to his purpose he provides on this occasion a map, a who's who, and a chronological table. . . .

Excerpt from Oswell Blakeston's review, published in Life and Letters To-day 16 (Summer 1937): 155–156:

Certainly Mr. Faulkner merits the best rejection slip of the month. He has laboured with such very long sentences in this very long novel. As his inspiration has thinned, so his writing has thickened. Attempting to recapture the strange atmosphere, caught so effortlessly in *Sanctuary* he has worked one or two tricks which deserve critical underlining. A less obvious example (muddling of time sequence has become hack convention) is the elaborate description of the beginning of an incident (when Sutpen is arrested by the Vigilance Committee) followed by but a hint as to its conclusion (how did he really get out of that mess?). The result is that the reader is left with an expansion of imaginative possibilities—or isn't! And one wonders if it is not because the corncob fitted so startlingly into *Sanctuary* that Mr. Faulkner believes it necessary to sprinkle horrors into succeeding volumes—Sutpen amusing himself by setting two naked negroes to fight one another in the bloody manner of mad dogs.

Still he must not be denied his spell. If you have the patience to tackle this over-written (therefore lacking in dramatic emphasis) tale, you do get a queer feeling of listening at old closed gates in the corridors of Mississippi–American-Civil War history. Characters are never seen face to face; they blur into the shade of Sutpen, who descends on a small community, builds a house with his own hands, and doom for his house with his coloured mistresses. It is all rather like running your head into a cobweb in a dark barn; and there is a certain rich magic about this overspun labour.

Excerpt from Frederick Laws's review published in The New Statesman and Nation, March 6, 1937, 380:

Life is short, and *Absalom, Absalom!* is very long. Even Mr. Faulkner's sentences are longer than anyone else's. He includes everything that Racine left out. Without using the technique of James Joyce he attempts the same all-inclusiveness. If he wrote as well as Joyce or gave evidence of a similar quality of mind the difficulty experienced in reading him might be forgivable. Unfortunately he heaps up images interminably only to produce a slag tip.

CHARACTERS IN *ABSALOM, ABSALOM!*

Akers A coon hunter, he treads accidentally on one of Thomas Sutpen's "wild negroes" buried in swamp mud. Some years later, witnessing Sutpen's return from NEW ORLEANS with four wagonloads of fancy furnishings for the mansion at SUTPEN'S HUNDRED, Akers rushes into the HOLSTON HOUSE bar to report: "Boys, this time he stole the whole durn steamboat" (34).

Benbow, Judge As the executor of Goodhue Coldfield's estate, Benbow sells the remains of the family store for Coldfield's daughter, Miss Rosa Coldfield. She refuses to accept money for the sale, so the judge leaves baskets of provisions on her front porch at night and pays down the debts she contracts in local stores.

Judge Benbow continues to support Miss Rosa long after she had exhausted the proceeds from the sale of the store, drawing from a fund that he established with his winnings on MEMPHIS horse races. He also pays for the $200 headstone Rosa ordered for the grave of her niece, JUDITH SUTPEN.

Judge Benbow also appears in *THE UNVANQUISHED* and *THE HAMLET*.

Benbow, Percy The son of Judge Benbow, he discovers after his father's death that the judge had kept an accounting of his bets on Memphis horse races and credited the winnings to Miss Rosa COLDFIELD's mythical account.

Bon, Charles A wealthy and sophisticated New Orleansian, Bon's background is shadowy. Ignorant of his father's identity, he leaves New Orleans at age 28 at the encouragement of his revenge-seeking mother, Eulalia Sutpen, to study law at the UNIVERSITY OF MISSISSIPPI in OXFORD, MISSISSIPPI. There he makes friends with Thomas Sutpen's son Henry Sutpen. As Eulalia Bon had hoped and planned, Charles goes to SUTPEN'S HUNDRED with Henry, meets Henry's sister (and his own half sister) Judith Sutpen, and causes her to fall in love with him. So far as the younger Sutpens are aware, Bon has no parents, only a legal guardian; Henry knows nothing of Bon's octoroon wife and son.

When Bon discovers that Thomas Sutpen is his father, he tells himself that he will give up Judith in return for Sutpen's acknowledgment that Bon is his son. Sutpen refuses. Bon insists that he will marry Judith; in response, Sutpen tells Henry that Bon is married and, eventually, that he is his half brother, hoping that Henry will somehow resolve the matter. Instead, Henry repudiates his father and his birthright but agonizingly decides to accept the relationship between Bon and Judith.

At the outbreak of the Civil War, Henry and Bon enlist together in the Confederate UNIVERSITY GREYS. Now an officer, Bon carries the wounded Henry off the battlefield at Pittsburg Landing (SHILOH) in 1862. Nearly four years of war do not soften Bon's resolve, and Judith waits for him patiently. As the conflict approaches its end, Sutpen, now a colonel in a Mississippi infantry regiment, raises the stakes again. He sends an orderly with a summons for Henry in his camp in a North Carolina pine grove. He tells Henry that Bon must not marry Judith because Bon's mother is "part negro," not of Spanish descent as he had once believed.

Henry cannot countenance miscegenation. After the Confederate surrender, he and Bon return to Mississippi. Bon refuses to give up Judith, and Henry kills him at the gates of Sutpen's Hundred on May 3, 1865.

QUENTIN COMPSON's father speculates that Bon "loved Henry the better of the two"—that he regarded Judith as the shadow of his actual love (86).

Bon, Charles Etienne St. Valery The son of Charles Bon and his octoroon mistress, he comes to SUTPEN'S HUNDRED as an orphan in December 1871 when he is 12 years old. Although Judith Sutpen and the servant Clytemnestra (*see* Sutpen, Clytemnestra) try to shield him from knowledge of his black blood, he figures it out on his own. Embittered, he flees Sutpen's Hundred, eventually returning with a mentally retarded black woman, "coal black and ape-like" (166), as his wife. They

live hermitlike with their son, Jim Bond, in a dilapidated slave cabin on the Sutpen estate. He dies of
yellow fever in 1884 and is buried near his father in
a cedar grove at Sutpen's Hundred.

Bond, Jim   The "hulking, slack-mouthed" (173)
son of Charles Etienne St. Valery Bon and his feeble-minded wife, he lives in solitude in a cabin
behind the haunted mansion at SUTPEN'S HUN-
DRED. Bond is, like his mother, mentally deficient.
He leads Miss Rosa Coldfield and Quentin Compson to their buggy after they had seen Henry Sutpen lying ill in an upstairs room in the mansion on
a September night in 1909. Bond disappears when
the old house burns down later that night.

Coldfield, Aunt   The "strong, vindictive" (49)
spinster aunt of Ellen Coldfield Sutpen and Miss
Rosa Coldfield, she goes furiously door to door in
JEFFERSON in 1838 to build a crowd for Ellen's wedding. She acts as a stern surrogate mother for Miss
Rosa, whose natural mother dies giving birth to her
in 1845.

Perhaps tiring of her position in the Coldfield
household, she climbed out a window and vanished
one night, eloping (as it turned out) with a horse
and mule trader.

Coldfield, Goodhue   A Tennessee-born storekeeper in JEFFERSON, MISSISSIPPI, he breaks up a
business partnership with his son-in-law, Thomas
Sutpen, over a question of mercantile ethics.
Deeply religious and a Methodist steward, he is, by
report, "a man with a name for absolute and unde-
viating and even puritan uprightness" (32).

Goodhue argues against secession in 1860.
When war comes in 1861, he closes the store and
withdraws from affairs in protest of war's waste.
After Confederate troops ransack his store, he dons
the heavy black coat he wore 52 times a year, climbs
up to the attic, and nails the door shut behind him.

For three years, Coldfield subsists on food his
daughter Rosa hoists up to his attic cell. He starves
himself to death in 1864.

Coldfield, Rosa   A key figure in the Sutpen saga,
"one of the ghosts which had refused to lie still"

(4), she is the younger daughter of the JEFFERSON,
MISSISSIPPI, storekeeper Goodhue Coldfield and
sister of Ellen Coldfield Sutpen. Rosa blames her
father, as the agent of the pregnancy, for her mother's death in childbirth with her but dutifully takes
over the management of the household when the
spinster aunt who reared her elopes with a mule
trader. Rosa supplies her father with food after he
nails himself in his attic to hide from the Confederate provost marshals.

After the deaths of her father and of Ellen, who
is 27 years her senior, Miss Rosa goes to live at
SUTPEN'S HUNDRED to look after her niece, Judith
Sutpen. She had long regarded her brother-in-
law Thomas Sutpen as an ogre, but she believes
the Civil War has changed him, and she allows
herself to consider what appears to be his offer of
marriage.

The offer, it turns out, is conditional. Sutpen
insults Rosa by proposing that they marry only if
they first produce a son to replace Henry Sutpen,
who has disappeared after killing Judith's suitor,
Charles Bon. Furious, Rosa returns to her father's
home, surviving on unacknowledged handouts
from Judge Benbow. For 43 years from the day of
Sutpen's proposal, she dresses in "eternal black"
(3) to remind herself—and perhaps the world—of
the insult.

One evening in September 1909, Miss Rosa
sends for young Quentin Compson and narrates
her version of Sutpen's history. She has kept her
hatred for Sutpen alive over the years, and she
wants Quentin to tell the story of the family's
destruction.

Miss Rosa persuades Quentin to escort her to
Sutpen's Hundred, which she has not seen since
the spring of 1866. She knows that "there is something living in that house," and when they discover
the invalid Henry in an upstairs room, she sends for
an ambulance. Thinking Rosa has called the police,
the servant Clytemnestra sets fire to the old, rotted
mansion. Clytie and Henry perish in the flames.
Rosa dies in January 1910; Quentin asserts that in
fact "she died young of outrage in 1866" (142).

Compson, Jason Lycurgus II (General)   The
closest thing to a friend and confidant Thomas

Sutpen ever had, he is the grandfather of Quentin Compson, who narrates the Sutpen story in *Absalom*. General Compson knew Sutpen as a poor young man and loaned him seed cotton to help him make a start in YOKNAPATAWPHA COUNTY as a planter.

During the 30 years of their acquaintance, Compson manages to extract much of Sutpen's story from him. After the Civil War, the general transmits a version of the Sutpen saga to his son Jason Richmond Compson, who in turn passes it on to Quentin, who balances Rosa Coldfield's embittered narrative with his grandfather's more judicious account. General Compson died in 1900.

He also appears in *The UNVANQUISHED*, GO DOWN, MOSES, INTRUDER IN THE DUST, *The REIVERS*, and in the short stories "BEAR HUNT" and "MY GRANDMOTHER MILLARD AND GENERAL BEDFORD FORREST AND THE BATTLE OF HARRYKIN CREEK." He is referred to in *REQUIEM FOR A NUN* and *The TOWN*.

Compson, Jason Richmond (Mr. Compson; Jason III) The son of General Jason Lycurgus Compson II and the father of Quentin Compson, he is an attorney of faded Southern gentility, disillusioned and cynical. Fond of whiskey and windy speeches, he nevertheless is attentive to Quentin and, in the twilight on the veranda of the family home, helps him piece together the saga of Thomas Sutpen.

He also appears in *The SOUND AND THE FURY* and in the novel's appendix (*see* Appendix), the short stories "THAT EVENING SUN" and "A JUSTICE," and is referred to in GO DOWN, MOSES ("The BEAR").

Compson, Mrs. She is General Jason Lycurgus Compson's wife and the grandmother of Quentin Compson. Mrs. Compson is discomfited when Aunt Coldfield bursts into her parlor one day in 1838 to make certain that she and her husband were planning to attend the wedding of her niece Ellen Coldfield (Sutpen) and Thomas Sutpen.

Mrs. Compson also appears in *The UNVANQUISHED* and in the short story "MY GRANDMOTHER MILLARD AND GENERAL BEDFORD FORREST AND THE BATTLE OF HARRYKIN CREEK"; she is referred to in *The TOWN*.

Compson, Quentin The son and oldest child of Jason Richmond Compson, he is 20 years old in September 1909 when Miss Rosa Coldfield chooses to transmit the Sutpen saga to him and to include him in the doomed dynasty's fiery final chapter.

Quentin is about to leave for his freshman year at Harvard when Miss Rosa summons him. Though he is young and seemingly has his life before him, he broods on the past, his person "an empty hall echoing with sonorous defeated names" (7). The themes of sexuality, the brother-sister relationship, and death are major concerns seen through Quentin's eyes. When retelling the story of the Sutpens to his Harvard roommate Shrevlin MacKenzie, Quentin reflects especially on Henry Sutpen's killing of his sister Judith's fiancé, Charles Bon, who unbeknown to her is her half brother. Quentin is aware that Henry is compelled to commit this act to defend the Southern notion of womanly honor and uphold Southern notions of racial propriety, for Charles also has a trace of black blood through his mother. However, it is not incest that forces Henry's hand but miscegenation. Even though Charles passes as a white man, he cannot be one. These themes resonate in Quentin's mind.

Quentin drives Miss Rosa the 12 miles to SUTPEN'S HUNDRED that hot, airless September night and they break into the rotting mansion. Miss Rosa strikes down the servant Clyemnestra Sutpen, who attempts to bar their way, and they climb the stairs to the second floor where both glimpse the long-vanished Henry lying ill in bed. Believing the police are coming for Henry, Clytie sets fire to the house; both she and Henry perish in the flames.

Quentin ends his narration of the Sutpen saga (and the novel) with a tortured denial when MacKenzie asks him: "Why do you hate the South?" (303).

Quentin Compson is a central figure in *THE SOUND AND THE FURY*. He also appears in Faulkner's appendix to the novel (*see* Appendix) and narrates the short stories "THAT EVENING SUN," "A JUSTICE," and "LION." Quentin is referred to in *The MANSION*.

de Spain, Major (Cassius) As sheriff of YOKNAPA-TAWPHA COUNTY, de Spain leads a posse to Wash Jones's shack, the site of Thomas Sutpen's murder, and in self-defense shoots and kills Wash when he lunges toward de Spain with a scythe.

De Spain also appears or is mentioned in GO DOWN, MOSES, INTRUDER IN THE DUST, The HAM-LET, The TOWN, The MANSION, and The REIVERS and in the short stories "BARN BURNING," "WASH," "A BEAR HUNT," and "SHALL NOT PERISH."

French Architect, the Character in ABSALOM, ABSALOM! A good architect, an artist, he designs the mansion at SUTPEN'S HUNDRED in two years of more or less enforced servitude to Thomas Sutpen. The architect's escape and Sutpen's pursuit supply the occasion for Sutpen's narration of the details of his early life to General Compson.

Hamblett, Jim A magistrate, he tries Charles Etienne Bon for fighting at a "negro ball" in 1879. (164) When Hamblett begins to lecture Bon about his duties as a white man, General (Jason Lycurgus II) Compson, aware of Bon's mixed racial background, intervenes, quashes the indictment, pays Bon's fine, and gives him money to leave town.

Ikkemotubbe A CHICKASAW INDIAN chief, he sells Thomas Sutpen 100 square miles of Yoknapa-tawpha bottomland, the future SUTPEN'S HUNDRED.

Ikkemotubbe also appears in GO DOWN, MOSES, INTRUDER IN THE DUST, The REIVERS, and the short story "A JUSTICE" and is mentioned in REQUIEM FOR A NUN, The TOWN, and the short stories "RED LEAVES" and "A COURTSHIP."

Jones, Melicent The daughter of Wash Jones and the mother of Milly Jones, she is rumored to have died in a MEMPHIS brothel. She is mentioned by name in the novel's appendix.

Jones, Milly The 15-year-old granddaughter of Thomas Sutpen's factotum, Wash Jones, Milly accepts candy, beads, and ribbon from Sutpen, then 60, the opening phase of a seduction that results in her bearing his child, a girl. Disappointed because he wants a son, Sutpen insults her and appears to cast her aside.

Wash avenges the insult by slaying Sutpen with a scythe. Thinking he is protecting Milly from a future of pain and degradation, Wash cuts her throat with a butcher's knife and then meets his own death at the hand of Sheriff de Spain.

Jones, Wash A squatter in an abandoned fishing shack at SUTPEN'S HUNDRED, he is the admirer, man-of-all-work, and sometime scuppernong-arbor drinking companion of Thomas Sutpen. When Miss Rosa Coldfield first sees him in 1865, he is "a gaunt gangling man" of indeterminate age, pale-eyed and malarial (69). It is Wash who bears the first report that Henry Sutpen has killed his sister's suitor, Charles Bon, outside the gates of the estate.

Jones builds the coffin in which Bon is buried, and he later reluctantly turns to and helps his hero Sutpen restore the ruined plantation. He offers consolation to Sutpen, who after two or three drinks and reflections on the Civil War would lather himself into a mood of furious undefeat, call for his horse and pistols, and threaten to ride to Washington and shoot Lincoln and Sherman.

Wash abets Sutpen's seduction of his grand-daughter Milly Jones, carrying ribbons and beads and candy from Sutpen to the girl. He has misgivings, but in the end he persuades himself that Sutpen is an honorable man and will look after her.

Sutpen repudiates Milly when she delivers a daughter instead of the son he wanted to replace the vanished Henry and carry out his grand design. Thus betrayed, Wash attacks and kills Sutpen with a rusted scythe. A little later, he slits Milly's throat, thinking he is sparing her from suffering. When the scythe-wielding Wash rushes at Sheriff de Spain, the sheriff shoots and kills him.

Wash also appears in the eponymous short story, published in 1934. Faulkner reworked "WASH" for a key episode of *Absalom*.

Luster One of the Compsons' black servants. Luster leads the horses over a flooded ditch the day Quentin Compson and his father, hunting quail, approach Thomas Sutpen's grave in the cedar grove of the SUTPEN'S HUNDRED estate.

McCaslin, Theophilus (Filus, Uncle Buck) Twin brother of Amodeus (Uncle Buddy) McCaslin and father of Issac McCaslin, he and his brother are the inheritors of old Lucius Quintus Carothers McCaslin's vast YOKNAPATAWPHA COUNTY plantation holdings.

Uncle Buck assists at Charles Bon's funeral, helping to carry the coffin from the house to the gravesite. He gives the rebel yell (the Confederate battle cry) in lieu of the Catholic ceremonial, the words of which none of the funeral party know.

McCaslin is an important figure in GO DOWN, MOSES. He also appears in *The* UNVANQUISHED, *The* TOWN, and *The* HAMLET.

Negress, the A "bright, gigantic" servant, she attends Charles Bon's Octoroon Mistress when she and her son visit Bon's grave at SUTPEN'S HUNDRED. She gives the distraught mistress occasional whiffs from a smelling-bottle.

Pettibone A wealthy Tidewater Virginia planter, he inspires both awe and ambition in young Thomas Sutpen. Sutpen's father works off his resentment of Pettibone by thrashing one of his slaves. When one of Pettibone's servants turns the ragged boy away from the front hall of the mansion, he vows to acquire wealth and power equivalent to the planter's someday.

Octoroon Mistress, the (Charles Bon's) The unnamed "morganatic" wife of Charles BON, she is a New Orleans courtesan, one-eighth black. She brings their son to visit SUTPEN'S HUNDRED in 1870, where she weeps over Bon's gravesite.

Sartoris, Colonel John Patriarch of the founding family of Faulkner's YOKNAPATAWPHA COUNTY cycle, Sartoris with Thomas Sutpen raised a volunteer infantry regiment in JEFFERSON after Mississippi seceded from the Union in 1861. The Sartoris womenfolk sewed the regimental colors out of silk dresses.

After the CIVIL WAR, Sartoris violently opposes the new order that the victorious Yankees are try-

ing to impose. Sutpen rebuffs him in his night-riding efforts to mobilize Yoknapatawpha County planters against Reconstruction.

Faulkner modeled the character of the hard, violent, and imaginative John Sartoris on his great-grandfather, the soldier and railroad builder WILLIAM CLARK FALKNER. Sartoris appears in SARTORIS, *and* THE UNVANQUISHED, GO DOWN MOSES, REQUIEM FOR A NUN, *The* HAMLET, *The* TOWN, *The* MANSION, and *The* REIVERS, and in the short stories "BARN BURNING," "SHALL NOT PERISH," "MY GRANDMOTHER MILLARD AND GENERAL BEDFORD FORREST AND THE BATTLE OF HARRYKIN CREEK," and "THERE WAS A QUEEN."

Shreve (Shrevlin McCannon) Quentin Compson's HARVARD UNIVERSITY roommate from Alberta, Canada, he urges Quentin to "Tell about the South" (142). Bespectacled and matter-of-fact, Shreve intently absorbs the saga of the Sutpens, taking in Quentin's tale with "cherubic and erudite amazement" (206). With an inquisitive mind probing the nuances of Southern history and a lively imagination, he actively contributes to the reconstruction of the story and at times—especially in the novel's last chapter—becomes as much a part of it as Quentin does.

He is referred to only as Shreve in *Absalom*; his name appears as Shrevlin McCannon in the novel's genealogy. As Shreve MacKenzie, he is Quentin's Harvard roommate in *The* SOUND AND THE FURY.

Sutpen, Clytemnestra (Clytie) The daughter of Thomas Sutpen and one of his slaves, she is the mainstay of the doomed household at SUTPEN'S HUNDRED. Born with a "sphinx face" (109), she is tough, strong, and capable; Clytie could "cut a cord of wood or run a furrow better" than Sutpen's white handyman Wash Jones (124).

While Thomas Sutpen is at war, Clytie and Sutpen's white daughter Judith Sutpen take a subsistence from the land and keep the place intact. Clytie helps Judith fashion a wedding dress and veil out of rags and scraps that should have been used to make bandages for the Confederate wounded. She takes responsibility for the orphaned Charles Etienne Bon when his mother dies in New Orleans in 1871 and teaches him to farm. She risks her own life to nurse her half sister Judith and Charles Etienne during a yellow fever outbreak in 1884. Finally, she raises Charles Etienne's feebleminded son, Jim Bond.

In the end, Clytie guards the last of the Sutpen secrets: Henry Sutpen, who vanished after killing his sister Judith's suitor Charles Bon (Charles Etienne's father) in 1865 and returned 40 years later to live as an invalid in his old home. Rosa Coldfield discovers him there in September 1909, despite Clytie's frantic efforts to prevent Rosa from mounting the stairs to Henry's room.

Later, Miss Rosa sends for an ambulance to fetch Henry. Clytie panics, mistaking the ambulance for a police wagon. Believing the authorities are about to arrest and hang Henry for shooting Charles Bon, she sets the house afire; she and Henry perish in the flames.

According to Miss Rosa, Clytie "in the very pigmentation of her flesh represented the debacle" that brought down the Sutpen family (126).

Sutpen, Ellen Coldfield The older daughter of Goodhue Coldfield, she marries Thomas Sutpen in 1838 and moves into the great house at SUTPEN'S HUNDRED even though she knows little or nothing about him and actually fears him. Quentin Compson thinks of her as a "Niobe without tears"; to her spinster sister Rosa Coldfield, she is a "blind romantic fool" (8, 10).

Ellen bears two children conceived of the "demon," Henry (born 1839) and Judith (born 1841), and settles uneasily into the role of grand lady of the plantation. She watches helplessly as they grow up beyond her reach.

Over time, Sutpen corrupts her. She stops going into town altogether, instead bidding the merchants and her social inferiors to wait upon her at Sutpen's Hundred, over which she presides with an air "a little regal" (54). She becomes obsessed with the furnishings of the plantation house, with menus, even with how the elegant meals are prepared. She also welcomes Charles Bon, the suave young man from New Orleans, as her daughter's suitor, as a model of comportment for her son, and as an ornament to her household.

Ellen's dreams are shattered on Christmas Eve, 1860, when her husband and son quarrel and Charles Bon abruptly leaves for New Orleans. She withdraws and sickens; only the bafflement in her coal-black eyes suggests anything of life. She summons Miss Rosa, then 17, to her deathbed and asks her to look after Judith, who is four years younger than her aunt. Ellen dies in January 1863.

Sutpen, Eulalia Bon The daughter of a wealthy Haitian sugar planter, said to be part Spanish; she marries Thomas Sutpen in 1827 and bears him a son. When Sutpen discovers that she is part black, he repudiates and divorces her.

A "somber vengeful" (263) Eulalia Bon resettles in New Orleans, where her son, Charles Bon, matures into a suave and elegant young man. Plotting retribution, she arranges for him to attend the UNIVERSITY OF MISSISSIPPI, even though at age 28 he is a bit old for college. There he meets Sutpen's son (Henry Sutpen) by his second wife, Ellen Coldfield Sutpen.

Henry and Charles Bon become friends, as Eulalia had hoped, and Bon is taken to SUTPEN'S HUNDRED. There, according to her plan, Henry's sister, Judith Sutpen, falls in love with him. When Sutpen learns his son with "a little spot of negro blood" hopes to marry his daughter, Eulalia has her revenge, although it is not clear whether she lives to savor it. She dies in New Orleans on a date unknown, possibly by the hand of her lawyer.

Sutpen, Henry The son of Thomas and Ellen Coldfield Sutpen, he is a proud and sensitive rustic—"a grim humorless yokel out of a granite heritage" (86)—who falls under the sway of the cosmopolitan Charles Bon at the university and takes him home to SUTPEN'S HUNDRED at the first opportunity.

There Bon meets Henry's sister, Judith Sutpen, and they become engaged. On Christmas Eve 1860, Thomas Sutpen tells Henry that Bon is his half brother and that the marriage must be prevented. Henry refuses to accept this. He surrenders his home and birthright, even though he leaves Sutpen's Hundred knowing that he has been told the truth.

As the Compsons note, Henry never thinks; he acts. When war breaks out, he and Bon enlist together in a Mississippi infantry regiment. Henry is wounded at SHILOH; Charles carries him off the battlefield, and he recovers. He gradually comes to accept the notion of incest, perhaps in concert with his own unconscious desires. Dukes and kings had married their sisters, Henry tells himself.

Toward war's end, with Johnston's army in North Carolina, Henry and his father cross paths. Colonel Sutpen summons Henry and informs him that Charles is part black. Henry will not accept miscegenation. After the war, he and Charles return to JEFFERSON, MISSISSIPPI. When Charles refuses to give up Judith, Henry shoots and kills him at the gates of Sutpen's Hundred on May 3, 1865, and disappears.

In about 1905, ailing and elderly, Henry returns home to die. In 1909, fearing that he will be exposed, arrested, and hanged, the servant Clytemnestra Sutpen (old Thomas Sutpen's daughter by one of his slaves) sets fire to the rotten, decrepit house. Henry and Clytie perish in the flames.

Sutpen, Judith The daughter of Thomas and Ellen Coldfield Sutpen, she is her father's daughter: strong-willed, tough, and determined to get what she wants. She whips the horses into a race-course frenzy on the long ride to church; she slips out of the house to watch her father fight in the ring with one of his slaves.

Judith falls in love with her brother Henry Sutpen's friend Charles Bon and waits patiently for him through the Civil War, even though there is no courtship, no engagement; they were together three times in two years, a total of 12 days. She scratches a living out of the family place, SUTPEN'S HUNDRED, with the help of her servant half sister, Clytemnestra Sutpen, and her father's white handyman Wash Jones. She seems barely aware of the havoc her choice has caused, for Bon, evidently unknown to her, is Sutpen's son (and thus her half brother) by his first wife, who has black blood. In any case, there is no evidence that she knows why her father and brother fall out on Christmas Eve 1860 or that she ever quarreled with her father over Bon.

Judith loses Bon when Henry shoots and kills him at the gate of Sutpen's Hundred on their return from North Carolina in 1865. In 1884, she helps Clytie nurse Bon's son (by a mistress or wife in New Orleans) through an attack of yellow fever, catches the disease herself, and dies. Her gravestone identifies her only as the daughter of Ellen Coldfield; there is no mention of her father.

The critic CLEANTH BROOKS found Judith a sympathetic figure: "Judith is doomed by misfortunes not of her making, but she is not warped and twisted by them," Brooks observes. "Her humanity survives them."

Sutpen, Thomas The son of a poor white western Virginia farmer, he is the flawed, corrupt, doomed creator and master of SUTPEN'S HUNDRED, the plantation he hacks out of the YOKNAPATAWPHA COUNTY wilderness in the 1830s. In early youth, with his debased family now living a hardscrabble existence in the wealthy Virginia Tidewater, a snub from a servant of the planter Pettibone ignites his ambition. To avenge the slight, he decides he must have what Pettibone has—land and slaves—so conceiving a design to build a dynasty, he applies all his furious energies to the task

Sutpen leaves home at age 14 and ventures to a Haiti sugar plantation, where he eventually marries the wealthy planter's daughter; he casts her and their son aside when he learns that she is part black. Big and gaunt, with a short reddish beard and pale eyes "at once visionary and alert" (24), he reaches JEFFERSON, MISSISSIPPI, on a Sunday morning in June 1833 with only a horse, a saddlebag, and two pistols to his name, "seeking some place to hide himself" (9). Sutpen inveigles a hundred square miles of virgin bottomland out of a Chickasaw chief, forces a captive French architect to design a mansion the size of a courthouse for him, and marries into a respectable Jefferson family. He and his wife, Ellen Coldfield Sutpen, produce a son and dynastic heir, Henry Sutpen, and a daughter, Judith Sutpen.

In due course, the town of Jefferson accepts Sutpen. He grows richer and richer; by 1860 he is the largest landowner and cotton planter in Yoknapatawpha County. Sutpen corrupts his wife; Ellen fills the mansion with fine things and takes on the airs of a great lady. Then Charles Bon, Sutpen's son by his revenge-driven Haitian wife, arrives to threaten the design. Henry and Bon have become friends at the university; Henry brings him to Sutpen's Hundred during the holidays, and Judith falls in love with him almost at first sight. Sutpen then makes a grave miscalculation. Rather than acknowledge Bon openly as his son, he calls Henry into the library on Christmas Eve 1860 and reveals the relationship, with the expectation that Henry will resolve the matter for him.

War comes; Henry and Bon enlist together in a Mississippi regiment; Henry gradually learns to accept the notion of incest in the courtship of Charles and his sister. Sutpen too goes off to fight for the Confederacy. He is an excellent soldier, efficient and brave, and he has a citation for valor from the hand of General Lee himself to prove it. Toward war's end his path crosses Henry's in North Carolina, and he finally tells Henry that Bon has black blood. This Henry will never accept. When Bon refuses to repudiate Judith, Henry shoots and kills him at the gates of Sutpen's Hundred and vanishes.

So Sutpen's design is in shambles. Nearing 60, a widower since 1863, he is forced to start over. The plantation is a ruin, but he takes this in hand with his usual fierce efficiency. His effort to establish a new dynasty leads, however, to fresh disaster. Sutpen offers to marry his deceased wife's sister, Miss Rosa Coldfield, on the condition that she will first deliver him a son; outraged, she refuses and returns to her father's house in Jefferson. He then gets the adolescent granddaughter of his lackey Wash Jones with child, but when she delivers a girl, he rejects and insults her. The betrayal enrages Jones and on August 12, 1869, he attacks Sutpen with a rusted scythe and kills him. He is buried in a cedar grove near his son Bon; his daughter Judith reads the service.

Sutpen never knows where he failed. He turns to his only friend and confidant, General Jason Lycurgus Compson II, in an effort to discover the flaw in his design. Compson speculates that his trouble was innocence, an inability to comprehend that actions have consequences. Sutpen believes he failed, not through moral retribution, not even through bad luck, but because he had made a miscalculation somewhere along the way.

Sutpen also appears in *The* UNVANQUISHED, GO DOWN, MOSES, REQUIEM FOR A NUN, and *The* REIVERS.

Willow, Colonel   A Confederate officer, he tells Thomas Sutpen of his son Henry's wounding at the battle of SHILOH in 1862. Charles Bon carries Henry, who is hit in the shoulder, safely off the battlefield.

FURTHER READING

Backman, Melvin. *"Absalom, Absalom!"* In *Faulkner: The Major Years,* 88–112. Bloomington: Indiana University Press, 1966.

Bloom, Harold, ed. *Modern Critical Interpretations of William Faulkner's* Absalom, Absalom! New York: Chelsea House, 1987.

Brooks, Cleanth. *"Absalom, Absalom!"* In *William Faulkner: First Encounters,* 192–224. New Haven: Yale University Press, 1983.

———. "History and the Sense of the Tragic (*Absalom, Absalom!*)." In *William Faulkner: The Yoknapatawpha Country,* 295–324. Baton Rouge: Louisiana State University Press, 1990.

———. "The Narrative Structure of *Absalom, Absalom!*" In *William Faulkner: Toward Yoknapatawpha and Beyond,* 301–328. Baton Rouge: Louisiana State University Press, 1990.

———. "Thomas Sutpen: A Representative Southern Planter?" In *William Faulkner: Toward Yoknapatawpha and Beyond,* 283–300. Baton Rouge: Louisiana State University Press, 1990.

Clarke, Deborah L. "Familiar and Fantastic: Women in *Absalom, Absalom!*" *Faulkner Journal* 2.1 (Fall 1986): 62–72.

Cowley, Malcolm. "*Absalom, Absalom!* as a Legend of the Deep South." In *Readings on William Faulkner,* edited by Clarice Swisher, 142–148. San Diego: Greenhaven, 1998.

Goldman, Arnold, ed. *Twentieth Century Interpretations of* Absalom, Absalom!. Englewood Cliffs, N.J.: Prentice Hall, 1971.

Hamblin, Robert W. "'Longer Than Anything': Faulkner's 'Grand Design' in *Absalom, Absalom!*" In *Faulkner and the Artist,* edited by Donald M. Kartiganer and Ann J. Abadie, 269–293. Jackson: University Press of Mississippi, 1996.

Howe, Irving. *"Absalom, Absalom!"* In *William Faulkner: A Critical Study,* 221–232. Chicago: University of Chicago Press, 1957.

Kinney, Arthur F. *Critical Essays on William Faulkner: The Sutpen Family.* Boston: G. K. Hall, 1996.

Kuyk, Dirk, Jr. *Sutpen's Design: Interpreting Faulkner's Absalom, Absalom!.* Charlottesville: University Press of Virginia, 1990.

Lind, Ilse Dusoir. "The Design and Meaning of *Absalom, Absalom!*." In *William Faulkner: Three Decades of Criticism,* edited by Frederick J. Hoffman and Olga W. Vickery, 278–304. New York: Harbinger, 1963.

Matthews, John T. "Marriages of Speaking and Hearing in *Absalom, Absalom!*" In *The Play of Faulkner's Language,* 115–161. Ithaca: Cornell University Press, 1982.

Millgate, Michael. *"Absalom, Absalom!"* In *The Achievement of William Faulkner,* 150–164. Lincoln: University of Nebraska Press, 1978.

Porter, Carolyn. "*Absalom, Absalom!*: (Un)Making the Father." In *The Cambridge Companion to William Faulkner,* edited by Philip M. Weinstein, 168–196. New York: Cambridge University Press, 1997.

Ragan, David Paul. *Annotations to William Faulkner's Absalom, Absalom!.* New York: Garland, 1991.

Sundquist, Eric J. "*Absalom, Absalom!* and the House Divided." In *Faulkner: The House Divided,* 96–130. Baltimore: Johns Hopkins University Press, 1985.

Waggoner, Hyatt. "Past and Present: *Absalom, Absalom!*" In *Faulkner: A Collection of Critical Essays,* edited by Robert Penn Warren, 175–185. Englewood Cliffs, N.J.: Prentice Hall, 1966.

"Adolescence" (Uncollected Stories)

Written sometime around 1922, this short story was first published posthumously in 1979 by RANDOM HOUSE in *Uncollected Stories of William Faulkner.* With somewhat of a fairy tale-like plot and with many poetic passages, "Adolescence" is about a young girl, Juliet BUNDEN, who, after the death of her mother and subsequent remarriage of her father, moves in with her grandmother. With the tumult of her four brothers, indifferent father, and hateful stepmother ended, the young heroine finds her new home peaceful and satisfying. The pastoral happiness of her life is intensified when she and Lee HOLLOWELL, a boy about her own age of 13, befriend one another. Seeing Juliet swimming nude in a brook or river, Lee strips off his clothes to join her, and they swim together in all innocence, an innocence that lasts throughout the duration of their relationship. The bucolic setting of their encounters is highly suggestive of an untainted Garden of Eden, and for nearly four years, Juliet and Lee remain in an idyllic friendship that comes to an end when her grandmother discovers them lying together in a blanket. Assuming that she has come upon a scene of lust and uncleanliness, GRAMMAW Bunden chases Lee away and castigates Juliet for having ruined herself and for having lost her virtue to a no-good, lazy Hollowell. Ordering Juliet home, the grandmother threatens her. Juliet, however, seems oblivious. Finally, the grandmother admits that she has told Juliet's father, Joe Bunden, about her wrongdoing and that he is arranging a marriage for her.

Angered and upset, Juliet swears not to marry any man chosen by her hated father. That night after a heated confrontation with her grandmother, Juliet makes a mysterious trip to town. A few days later Juliet learns that her father and Lee's, Lafe Hollowell, both moonshiners, have been killed by federal Revenue agents. When she takes a lonely walk to the creek where she first met Lee several years before, she sees a figure walking toward her and mistakenly thinks that it is he; instead, it is Bud, her now fatherless little brother. After comforting him and after giving him a parcel of food and all her savings—just a few dollars—she watches him leave for good. A melancholy wistfulness comes over Juliet as she finally realizes that life must go on and that her childhood innocence is ending.

Faulkner used some of the scenes and ideas from this short piece in novels such as SOLDIERS' PAY, MOSQUITOES, and *The* WILD PALMS. Not unlike the short stories "MISS ZILPHIA GANT" and "FRANKIE AND JOHNNY," "Adolescence" deals with the conflict between a parent figure and her daughter, a theme that Faulkner employed in a few of his early short pieces. In "Adolescence," this conflict—handled through the device of an adversarial, possessive, and destructive mother figure—is seen first between Juliet and her stepmother, then between Juliet and her grandmother. In the case of "Adolescence" and "Miss Zilphia Gant," the parent figure comes on the daughter with a boy in compromising circumstances and the interference disturbs the tranquil relationship that the young ones have worked out between themselves. One of Faulkner's recurring themes throughout his fiction is the end of innocence. (For further information regarding "Adolescence," *see Uncollected Stories of William Faulkner,* 704).

CHARACTERS

Bunden, Bud   Juliet Bunden's younger brother. After his father is killed by Revenue agents, Bud seeks out Juliet's help before he starts out on his own.

Bunden, Joe   Juliet Bunden's stern and unreasonable father. Joe's first wife, Juliet's mother, dies, leaving Joe with four sons and a daughter. When he remarries, his daughter and new wife quickly come to despise each other, forcing him to send Juliet to live with her grandmother. Joe and his partner Lafe Hollowell are killed at their moonshine still by Revenue agents apparently tipped off by Juliet herself.

Bunden, Juliet   The oldest child and only daughter of Joe Bunden, Juliet is the heroine of "Adolescence." After Juliet's mother dies, her father remarries a woman whom Juliet comes to hate, and she is sent to live with her grandmother. Juliet spends her summers swimming and fraternizing with Lee Hollowell, a neighbor, until she is falsely accused by the grandmother of immoral sexual behavior with Lee. Afraid that her father is about to force her to marry a man of his choosing, Juliet makes a mysterious trip to town. The following night, her father and his partner, Lafe Hollowell (Lee's father), are both killed by Revenue agents, who raid their secret moonshine still. The text clearly hints at Juliet's involvement in alerting the agents.

Grammaw (Bunden)   Juliet Bunden's uncompromising grandmother with whom Juliet lives after her father, a widower, marries a woman Juliet hates.

When discovering Juliet and Lee Hollowell innocently lying naked together in a horse blanket, the grandmother becomes enraged, calls Juliet a slut, and prohibits her from ever seeing Lee again. She also informs Juliet's father of the apparent wrongdoing so he can arrange to get her married.

Hollowell, Lafe   Lee Hollowell's father and Joe Bunden's moonshine partner. Lafe and Joe are killed by Revenue agents who raid their moonshine whiskey still. (The story seems to indicate that Joe's daughter Juliet, in an act of vengeance, tipped the Revenue agents off.)

Hollowell, Lee   Juliet Bunden's friend and confidant. In Edenic childhood innocence, Lee and Juliet spend their time together swimming, hunting, and fishing.

"Afternoon of a Cow" (Uncollected Stories)

First published in a French translation, "L'Après-midi d'une Vache," by MAURICE EDGAR COINDREAU in the June/July 1943 issue of *Fontaine* (27–28), "Afternoon of a Cow" was intended by Faulkner to be taken as a light-hearted spoof. Faulkner himself thought it was particularly funny (*see Selected Letters of William Faulkner,* 246). When Coindreau was visiting Faulkner in Hollywood in late June 1937 to discuss the French translation of *The SOUND AND THE FURY,* Faulkner read the story to him. The original English version was first published in 1947 in *Furioso* II, 5–17, and reprinted in *Parodies: An Anthology from Chaucer to Beerbohm—and After,* edited by Dwight Macdonald (New York: Random House, 1960) and in *Uncollected Stories of William Faulkner* (1979). Faulkner borrowed from "Afternoon of a Cow" when he was writing *The HAMLET.* For further information, *see Selected Letters of William Faulkner,* 224, 245, 246; *Uncollected Stories of William Faulkner,* 702–703; and the entry on *The MISSISSIPPIAN.*

"Afternoon of a Cow" is a tongue-in-cheek short story that Faulkner passed off as the work of Ernest V. Trueblood. The story generates interest because it uses Faulkner himself as a character, much in the manner of a postmodernist writer such as Paul Auster. The story reports on a frightened cow that has fallen into a ditch during a fire. The character Faulkner, along with OLIVER, a black butler, and Ernest Trueblood, the first-person narrator of the tale, rush to its rescue. At first they are unsuccessful. In its fear and distress, the cow empties its bladder and bowels on Faulkner, shattering the dignity of the scene. The story ends with Faulkner stripping in the door of the stable and washing. Later, wrapped in a horse blanket, he and his friends drink to the cow.

CHARACTERS

Faulkner   Main character and hero who rescues a cow that has fallen into a ditch. A writer and Southern gentleman (but supposedly not William Faulkner himself), he is also referred to as Mr. Bill. (*Also see* the character Faulkner in MOSQUITOES.)

Oliver   A minor character who helps Faulkner rescue a cow during a fire.

Trueblood, Ernest V.   Trueblood is the narrator of "Afternoon of a Cow." He is the pseudonym Faulkner used when he published MAURICE EDGAR COINDREAU's French translation of the short story in *Fontaine* 27–28 (June/July 1943), 66–81.

"Al Jackson" (Uncollected Stories)

A short piece in the form of two letters written in 1925 by Faulkner to SHERWOOD ANDERSON. First published posthumously in 1979 in *Uncollected Stories of William* Faulkner.

SYNOPSIS

In New Orleans together, Faulkner and Anderson vied to outdo each other in creating a series of tall tales about the imaginary Al Jackson, a "fish-herd" and surviving descendant of President Andrew Jackson. Here Faulkner relates what was told to him of Al Jackson's remarkable family members by a riverboat pilot. His father, old man Jackson, tried to raise sheep on swampy pastureland, but the sheep were transformed into aquatic creatures. In trying to catch the sheep, Al's brother Claude Jackson gradually turned into a shark that chased women swimmers. In the second letter, Faulkner tells what he has learned of Al's sister Elenor, who eloped with a tin peddler, and of his brother Herman, who died of brain convulsions after reading all of Walter Scott's works. Al felt responsible for this because he had helped Herman invent a system of making pearl buttons from fish scales, the profits from which enabled Herman to obtain an education.

CRITICAL COMMENTARY

Similar Al Jackson anecdotes also appear in *Mosquitoes*, related by the character Dawson Fairchild, who is based, at least in part, on Anderson. Faulkner wrote this material at the time of the early prose later assembled in *New Orleans Sketches*. Although exceedingly slight and trivial in comparison with Faulkner's principal canon, the Al Jackson stories show Faulkner's delight in the oral tall-tale tradition, and his and Anderson's collaboration in storytelling anticipates Faulkner's later partnership with PHIL STONE, the Oxford lawyer, in swapping stories about the Snopes clan. These actual collaborations with Anderson and Stone parallel the manner in which Gavin Stevens and V. K. Ratliff serve as complementary narrators in *The* TOWN and *The* MANSION.

CHARACTERS

Jackson, Al   The central character in the short story. He is a web-footed descendant of Andrew Jackson who with his father runs the largest fish ranch in the world. *Also see* MOSQUITOES.

Jackson, Claude   The brother of fish rancher Al Jackson. He turns into a shark while herding amphibious sheep and becomes notorious for chasing blonde women swimmers off Gulf Coast beaches. *Also see* MOSQUITOES.

Jackson, Elenor ("Perchie")   The sister of Al Jackson, she elopes with a tin peddler.

Jackson, Herman   He earned a university education with the help of his brother Al and then died of brain convulsions brought on by his reading of Sir Walter Scott's novels.

Jackson, Old Man A descendant of Andrew Jackson and the father of Al, Claude, Elenor, and Herman Jackson. A one-time bookkeeper, he becomes a fish rancher when the sheep on his swampy Louisiana estate turn gradually into fish. *Also see* MOSQUITOES.

Wife of Old Man Jackson She won her Sunday School tatting championship at age seven and captured a husband at age 12 with her great talent in playing the melodeon.

"All the Dead Pilots" (Collected Stories)

This short story was first published in *These 13* (1931) and again slightly revised in *Collected Stories* (1950).

SYNOPSIS

"All the Dead Pilots" is set in France in the last years of World War I. Framing the story is a melancholy elegy for all the dead aviators, including those who survived the war to grow older in a kind of living death. The nameless narrator is a British officer who now works as a censor; he tells the tragicomic tale of Johnny Sartoris, an American flyer in the British ROYAL AIR FORCE. Sartoris obsessively seeks revenge on his morally bankrupt British squadron leader, Spoomer, who stole first Sartoris's London sweetheart and then his Amiens girlfriend. As Amiens comes under German fire, Sartoris tracks Spoomer to a tryst and steals his uniform. He dresses a drunken ambulance driver in the uniform and puts the man into Spoomer's bed at the airbase. Spoomer is caught when he sneaks back the next morning disguised in women's clothing; he is demoted and sent back to England. Sartoris himself is demoted for dereliction of duty and courageously dies in combat over German lines on July 4, 1918. The censor learns this when he opens the flyer's

final letter to his aunt, the official letter announcing his death, and a parcel of his pathetic personal effects. The narrator reflects that a life of such reckless intensity could not, by its nature, last long.

CRITICAL COMMENTARY

Though "All the Dead Pilots"—a story Faulkner was particularly fond of—has not been as extensively discussed as other Faulkner short stories such as "A ROSE FOR EMILY" or "BARN BURNING," readers who do comment on the story often stress its humor and the narrator's tone or attitude in telling a story that occurred more than a decade before. In his assessment of the "All the Dead Pilots," Hans H. Skei mentions that the attitudes of the unnamed narrator "are crucial to an understanding of the story's significance. The lack of personal involvement on the part of the narrator and the distance in time makes this a more romantic story, in the sense that it gives another distorted impression of what the pilots were like, seen in retrospect thirteen years later" (*William Faulkner: The Novelist as Short Story Writer*, 133).

HELPFUL RESOURCES

Theresa M. Towner and James B. Carothers, *Reading Faulkner: Collected Stories*, pp. 275–289.

CHARACTERS

Elnora An offstage character mentioned in Sartoris's letter to his great-aunt Jenny. A black servant in the Sartoris household, Elnora knitted socks for Sartoris, but he gave them away. (For other details concerning this character, *see* SARTORIS.)

Ffollansby One of Sartoris's fellow corps members.

Isom An offstage character mentioned in Sartoris's letter to his great-aunt Jenny. He is a black servant in Aunt Jenny's houshold. (*See* SARTORIS for other details.)

Kaye, Major C. The British officer who notifies Mrs. Virginia Sartoris of her nephew's, Johnny Sartoris's, death.

Kitchener (Kit) Sartoris's London girlfriend. She is nicknamed Kit because, as Ffollansbye explains, she is involved with many soldiers—including Spoomer, Sartoris's superior officer.

Kyerling, R. A British flyer who witnesses Johnny Sartoris's death in action over France on July 4, 1918.

Sartoris, Johnny An American aviator flying with the Royal Air Force. Sartoris is killed on July 4, 1918, while in combat over France during World War I. He is drawn as rash, reckless, and vengeful in the short story where he and his superior officer, Spoomer, are rivals for the affections of two women. (*Also see* SARTORIS and "WITH CAUTION AND DISPATCH"; he is referred to in *The* TOWN, *The* MANSION, and the short story "THERE WAS A QUEEN."

Sartoris, Mrs. Virginia (Aunt Jenny) Sartoris's great-aunt, an offstage character. (*Also see* Virginia (Jenny) Du Pre in SARTORIS, and Jenny Du Pre in SANCTUARY, *The* UNVANQUISHED, and "THERE WAS A QUEEN"; she is mentioned in *The Town* and *The Mansion*. In *Requiem for a Nun*, she is referred to as Mrs. Virginia Depre.)

Spoomer The nephew of a British army corps commander and thus a man of influence. The American Johnny Sartoris, Spoomer's rival for the affections of the French girl 'Toinette, manages to outwit Spoomer, who is recalled to England and assigned to a ground school.

'Toinette A French girl, she is the object of affection of the rival ROYAL AIR FORCE flyers Spoomer and Sartoris.

"Ambuscade" (Uncollected Stories)

Humorous short story, first published in the September 29, 1934, issue of the SATURDAY EVENING POST.

SYNOPSIS

The focal characters are Bayard Sartoris, the narrator, and his black playmate Marengo ("Ringo"),

both 12 years old. The setting is the Sartoris plantation near Jefferson, just after the fall of the strategic fortress of Vicksburg in July 1863. Colonel John Sartoris's mother-in-law, Rosa Millard, manages the place while Sartoris is off in Tennessee fighting in the war. The action involves the boys' firing at a Yankee officer (killing his horse) and then hiding under the flowing skirts of Granny Millard when the enemy comes to investigate. The gallant officer accepts Granny's explanation that there are no children on the premises, even though he clearly knows she is lying. After the Yankee soldiers have moved on, Granny prays for forgiveness for her lie and then makes Bayard and Ringo wash their mouths with soap for calling the Yankee officer a "bastard."

CRITICAL COMMENTARY

The first-person narration by a youthful, innocent protagonist, the war games the children play, and the comic, mannerly interplay of Granny and the Yankee colonel mask the harsh reality of the war being waged in places like Vicksburg, Corinth, and Chickamauga. Faulkner significantly revised the story for use as the opening chapter of *The* UNVANQUISHED (1938), adding more detailed descriptions of hardships on the home front and filling out the portrait of Colonel Sartoris to build him into a more imposing figure.

CHARACTERS

For the list of characters in this story, *see* the entry on *The* UNVANQUISHED.

As I Lay Dying

The title of Faulkner's fifth novel. Dedicated to HAL SMITH, *As I Lay Dying* was first published on October 6, 1930, by Jonathan Cape and Harrison Smith of New York (*see* CAPE & SMITH). In this novel, Faulkner for the first time identifies by name his fictional YOKNAPATAWPHA COUNTY (*As I Lay Dying*, 203). In the misleading introduction to the 1932 Modern Library edition of SANCTUARY, an introduction which he suppressed in later editions of that novel but which was reprinted in the "Editor's Notes" of the 1993 Vintage edition, Faulkner included a comment about his writing *As I Lay Dying*. In the summer of 1929—the summer he married Estelle Oldham Franklin—Faulkner began to work the night shift in the power plant at the University of Mississippi: "I shoveled coal from the bunker into a wheelbarrow and wheeled it in and dumped it where the fireman could put it into the boiler. About 11 o'clock the people would be going to bed, and so it did not take so much steam. . . . I had invented a table out of a wheelbarrow in the coal bunker, just beyond a wall from where a dynamo ran. . . . There was no more work to do until about 4 A.M., when we would have to clean the fires and get up steam again. On these nights, between 12 and 4, I wrote *As I Lay Dying* in six weeks, without changing a word. I sent it to [Harrison (Hal)] Smith and wrote him that by it I would stand or fall" (*Sanctuary*, 323). Although Faulkner did in fact change and augment passages, he wrote the novel very quickly, between October 25 and December 11, 1929, during a period from around 1926 through 1933 that was marked by an extraordinary burst of creative energy. In addition to his writing such exceptional novels as *The Sound and the Fury* and *Light in August* and such enduring short stories as "A Rose for Emily," "Dry September," and "That Evening Sun," Faulkner was also writing screenplays. (For further comments by Faulkner relating to *As I Lay Dying*, see *Selected Letters of William Faulkner*, *Faulkner in the University*, and *Lion in the Garden*.)

SYNOPSIS

Note: For a day-by-day chronology of events and a diagrammatic outline of the plot of this novel, *see* appendix (page 521).

As the novel opens, Addie awaits death from some unspecified cause. Although she is probably only in her early fifties, Addie appears to welcome her approaching death as the realization of her father's prophecy: "the reason for living was to get ready to stay dead a long time" (*As I Lay Dying*, 169). At last, she believes, she will have rest, something her husband Anse has not afforded her in the years of their marriage. Incompetent,

lazy, manipulative, and shrewd in getting others to do for him, Anse seemingly never has given a thought to Addie's feelings. Even now with her impending death, he seems more preoccupied with being inconvenienced rather than grieved by it and intent on getting to Jefferson to buy a set of teeth.

Addie's children each react differently to her imminent death and burial. As the novel opens, Cash, the oldest son and a carpenter by trade, is stoically fashioning Addie's coffin in the yard outside the room where she lies dying, and before nailing the boards together, he takes each one up to the window for her approval (*As I Lay Dying*, 43). Characteristic of his personality, Cash does what needs to be done, in a workmanlike, unemotional, and almost mechanical manner. Darl, the next son, is driven by a painful, apparently unreturned, love for his mother and a deep jealousy of Jewel, Addie's favorite. Darl seems to be the smartest of the Bundrens, the most imaginative but the most psychologically troubled. (By the end of the novel, he is taken off to the state mental institution in Jackson.) He is also the most intuitive. Dewey Dell, for instance, is very well aware that Darl, without having been told and without having voiced the fact, knows that she is pregnant (*As I Lay Dying*, 27). Of the 59 monologues in the novel, Darl narrates 19, far more than anyone else. Driven by a hatred of his brother, Darl manipulates Jewel into going with him to deliver a load of lumber, thus preventing Jewel from being with Addie when she dies. In vivid detail, Darl imagines the scene of their mother's death as Jewel, ankle-deep in mud, is working on the broken wheel of their wagon filled with lumber. (The problems with transporting the lumber prefigure the problems the Bundrens will have in transporting Addie's body to the grave.) Like his brother Cash, Jewel is instrumental in getting his mother's corpse to Jefferson for burial and together these two brothers are heroic in their efforts; their heroic acts, as Cleanth Brooks suggests in *William Faulkner: The Yoknapatawpha Country* (142–143), are a major theme of the novel. The pregnant 17-year-old Dewey Dell uses the trip as a chance to purchase an abortifacient with the 10 dollars her lover Lafe gave her, but her naïve attempts fail. Rebuffed by the druggist in Mottson, she is advised to marry Lafe and have the child. Vardaman, like his older half-brother Jewel, has difficulty in accepting the death of his mother. Upset and acting like the young child that he is, he assumes that she will suffocate in the coffin and consequently drills holes in it that bore into her face. In the shortest chapter of the novel—five words only—Vardaman states, "My mother is a fish" (*As I Lay Dying*, 84), a line that associates in his mind a link between his dead mother and the fish that he caught on the day of her death.

The rains that delayed Darl and Jewel in transporting the lumber have flooded the Yoknapatawpha River. One bridge is submerged, another too damaged for a wagon to cross, and when the Bundrens foolishly attempt to ford the river, their wagon overturns, the mules drown, and Cash fractures the same leg he had fractured once before. Courageously Jewel saves the coffin and Cash's tools. Shortly afterwards, Anse trades Jewel's beloved horse for a new team of mules and the journey continues. Traveling five days with a body that has been dead for just over a week, the Bundrens cause consternation and alarm among the townspeople of Mottson, whose marshal forces Anse to move on, for by this time the odor from Addie's decomposing corpse is repugnant to the passersby. Anse, however, will not leave until after he buys a small amount of cement to set Cash's leg. Meanwhile, Dewey Dell visits the druggist. After they continue their journey, they stop for the night at the farm of a man named Gillespie where they store the coffin in the barn. During the night, the barn unexpectedly catches fire. Jewel, Darl, Gillespie, and his son rush into the flames to save the livestock. Jewel returns and single-handedly fetches his mother's coffin, becoming badly burned in the process. The fire, however, unlike the flooded river, is not an act of God. It was purposely set by Darl in an attempt to end the farce of his father's burial march. But the journey goes on.

As the Bundrens approach Jefferson, Jewel angrily responds to a comment made by one of three Negroes walking by the wagon, but by the time Jewel—who is suffering from burns—turns to curse them, a white man walking 10 feet behind gets the brunt of Jewel's anger and draws a knife. Dewey Dell and Anse help Darl defuse the situ-

ation. The Bundrens arrive at the cemetery and Addie is finally laid to rest. After leaving the gravesite, Dewey Dell, who learns from Vardaman that Darl set fire to Gillespie's barn, frantically attacks Darl before Jewel has the chance to subdue him. Two men have been summoned to take Darl to the state institution in Jackson, and one of them pulls Dewey Dell away while the other, along with Anse and Jewel, pins Darl to the ground. It is either the state institution for Darl or a lawsuit that Gillespie will bring against the Bundrens. Gillespie "knowed some way," Cash narrates in his penultimate monologue, "that Darl set fire to [the barn]" (*As I Lay Dying*, 232). Shortly after, Dewey Dell, still intent on obtaining a drug to produce an abortion, goes to a drug store in Jefferson. She is told by the soda jerk Skeet MacGowan, who pretends to be a medical doctor, to come back at night. She returns only to be swindled and sexually taken advantage of. Meanwhile, Cash's leg is reset by doctor Peabody, and Anse returns the shovels he used to dig Addie's grave. When Anse finds out that Dewey Dell has $10—money which she has not yet spent on an abortion drug—he takes it from her to buy false teeth. Before the Bundrens leave Jefferson the next morning, Anse not only has a new set of teeth but a new wife. In the last line of the novel, he introduces his children to a duck-shaped woman whom he calls "Mrs. Bundren."

CRITICAL COMMENTARY

As I Lay Dying is one of Faulkner's shortest novels, but it is also one of his most innovative and acclaimed. In it, he presents the story of the death and burial journey of Addie Bundren, as told from multiple perspectives and in the individual voices of Addie's husband, children, neighbors, and strangers. In one of the more moving and important passages of the novel, Addie herself speaks. Her monologue appears to occur five days after her own death, if the reader adheres to a strict and literal chronological time line of the chapters. However, it takes place on the day she dies (or perhaps a day or two before). The critic IRVING HOWE rightly sees Addie's single monologue as reflecting her dying thoughts. "This soliloquy," he writes, "is one of Faulkner's most brilliant rhetorical set-pieces, placed about two-thirds of the way through the novel and establishing an intense moment of stillness which overpowers, so to speak, the noise of the Bundren journey" (*William Faulkner: A Critical Study*, 176). By positioning Addie's monologue at this late point in the novel *and* immediately between Cora's and Whitfield's, two narratologically relevant and informative chapters, Faulkner intensifies the dramatic irony of the novel's title and skillfully etches the depth of Addie's character and subtlety of her motives.

In *As I Lay Dying*, horror is piled on horror and absurdity on absurdity. In this respect, the novel may be more mock-heroic than heroic. The love and devotion Anse ostensibly shows for his wife may be, from his point of view, partly genuine, but his motives are also self-serving. Ironically, Addie had despised him for years, calling him dead (*As I Lay Dying*, 173), and the promise she asked of him, that she be buried with her ancestors, had no meaning for her, except as a cruel and capricious trick. Even Anse's performance in carrying out the promise is logically flawed or at best short-sighted. He brings no shovel with which to dig Addie's grave. When doctor Peabody is resetting Cash's leg, he gets wind of this fact and sarcastically remarks: "'Of course he'd have to borrow a spade to bury his wife with. Unless he could borrow a hole in the ground. Too bad you all didn't put him in it too'" (*As I Lay Dying*, 240).

Faulkner described the work on several occasions as a "tour de force." *As I Lay Dying* is told in 59 monologues of varying lengths. Most of them represent the thoughts of the Bundrens themselves (Anse, husband and father, narrates 3 chapters; Addie, wife and mother, 1; Cash, the eldest son, 5; Darl, the second son, 19; Jewel, the third son, 1; Dewey Dell, the fourth child, a pregnant teenage girl, 4; and Vardaman, the youngest son, 10). Sixteen chapters are narrated by eight nonfamily members (Cora 3, Tull 6, Peabody 2, Armstid 1, Samson 1, Whitfield 1, MacGowan 1, and Moseley 1); these 16 sections of the novel punctuate and comment upon the story told by the Bundrens, giving the outsiders' perspectives on what seems like a foolish odyssey—foolish because it takes six days in the July heat of Mississippi to accomplish, and the Bundrens do not start on the journey until three days after Addie dies. During the burial odyssey, Addie's body is decomposing, repelling townsfolk and attracting vultures.

Some readers may judge the journey heroic, some absurd. Addie's husband, a selfish man who routinely relies on others, has hidden motives—as do other family members—to make the 40-mile trip from rural FRENCHMAN'S BEND to JEFFERSON. Intent on fulfilling his promise to bury his wife with her family, Anse subjects himself and his children to many hardships, including crossing a flooded river and rescuing Addie's coffin from a burning barn. "I took this family," Faulkner said in response to a question, "and subjected them to the two greatest catastrophes which man can suffer—flood and fire" (*Faulkner in the University*, 87). In combining the ludicrous with the honorable, Faulkner achieves great literary and technical success. In this respect, the critic CLEANTH BROOKS has commented, "Faulkner has daringly mingled the grotesque and the heroic, the comic and the pathetic, pity and terror, creating a complexity of tone that has proved difficult for some readers to cope with" (*William Faulkner: The Yoknapatawpha Country*, 141). One of the major themes of the novel, Brooks contends, is "the nature of the heroic deed" (142–143), and closely related to this theme is that of self-determination. Each of the Bundrens is resolute in pursuing his or her own intentions, whether they are fully realized or not. Critics have also discussed the themes of death and burial and of the nature of consciousness and being. In his study of *As I Lay Dying*, André Bleikasten sees the novel as dealing "with an almost endless agony, a prolonged suspension between life and death" (*Faulkner's As I Lay Dying*, 115).

Readers of both *As I Lay Dying* and *The Sound of the Fury* almost immediately recognize a similar narrative strategy in the two novels. With the exception of the last chapter of *The Sound and the Fury*, told by an omniscient narrator, both novels employ the INTERIOR MONOLOGUE, a narrative technique that may at first cause confusion for some readers. But this device also provides direct insight into the personality of a character and permits readers to probe into the intimate thoughts and sensations unique to a particular character. The interior monologue affords readers a direct channel into a character's inner self and perception of the world.

Unlike *The Sound and the Fury*, however, *As I Lay Dying* can also be read as a comic novel. Though there are humorous passages in the former work, the latter contains classic elements of Bergsonian comedy. In his essay on the elements of laughter, first published in 1900, Henri Bergson identifies a central constituent of the comic character as one who "always errs through obstinacy of mind or of disposition. . . . At the root of the comic there is a sort of rigidity which compels its victims to keep strictly to one path, to follow it straight along, to shut their ears and refuse to listen" ("Laughter," 179–180). Bergson's description especially typifies Anse Bundren with his uncompromising determination against all odds—and literally against flood and fire—to bury Addie in Jefferson. Each Bundren in his or her own way—Anse, Cash, Darl, Jewel, Dewey Dell, Vardaman, and even Addie herself—appears to have a single-mindedness of purpose that borders on the relentless or the absurd. "Every comic effect," Bergson notes, "implies contradiction in some of its aspects. What makes us laugh is alleged to be the absurd realised in concrete shape, a 'palpable absurdity'. . ." (177). Although the ultimate goal of burying Addie with her family is achieved, Anse involves his children in an adventure that on more than one occasion poses serious threats to their well-being, and yet each child—with the exception of Darl—manages to endure the struggles of the journey from rural Frenchman's Bend to Jefferson and back again. In Bergson's terms, the comic element "consists of a certain *mechanical inelasticity*, just where one would expect to find the wideawake adaptability and the living pliableness of a human being" (67). An inelasticity of character—"the sign of an eccentricity," according to Bergson (73)—and a rigid momentum or obstinacy define much of the comic element in the novel.

The comic is not automatically eliminated or even diminished if a reader were to judge the Bundrens' resolve in fulfilling Addie's wish an heroic accomplishment. The comic is the privilege of the observer not the observed unless the latter momentarily step outside themselves. The comic is also something that can be at once incongruous and unexpected. Anse's introduction of the new Mrs. Bundren to his unsuspecting and incredulous children at the end of the novel is a fitting humorous conclusion to a work structured throughout with comic elements.

EXCERPTS FROM CONTEMPORARY REVIEWS OF *AS I LAY DYING*

From Margaret Cheney Dawson's review, "Beside Addie's Coffin," published in the New York Herald Tribune Books, *October 5, 1930, 6:*

. . . This meaty tale comes to us through the consciousness of first one and then another of the characters. The method Mr. Faulkner used in his last novel, *The Sound and the Fury*, is here greatly modified, so that though something of that extraordinary madness hangs like a red mist over it, the lines of demarcation are mercifully clear. This is a great concession and a boon to people who are ready to weep with exhaustion from the effort to interpret and absorb what might be called a sort of photographic mysticism. But even so it cannot be said that for such readers *As I Lay Dying* will prove much of a picnic. Parts of it are written with that tense, defiant obscureness, the self-sufficient dislocation of thought which withdraws itself from facile understanding; and other passages, clear in themselves, are absolutely unhinged from the point of view of the character whose mind they expose and whose impressionistic portrait they seem to contradict. . . .

The fecundity of an imagination like this is amazing, and the ingenuity, too, with which it skips from one sphere of action to another. One wonders what would happen if it were compressed into an even sterner form if Mr. Faulkner were to experiment with tradition? Something in the way his strength mounts when he externalizes his subject matter suggests that it would be very exciting. But surely, whatever the next move is, he will not lack for audience any one who had followed his work thus far.

From Ted Robinson's review, "Faulkner's New Book Engrossing," published in the Cleveland Plain Dealer, *October 12, 1930, Amusement Section, 17:*

. . . I don't know much about this man Faulkner; but now that I know that *The Sound and the Fury* was not a mere tour de force, I am certain that he is one of the two or three original geniuses of our generation.

From Julia K. W. Baker's "Literature and Less," New Orleans Times-Picayune, *October 26, 1930, 33*

Most of the men and women of promise who have contributed to the brilliance of recent American literature have shown an unfortunate tendency, after a splendid beginning, to go backwards or to stand still. Their promissory notes have not matured. . . . William Faulkner is a noteworthy exception. . . .

Mr. Faulkner's new novel, *As I Lay Dying*, is a worthy companion piece to *The Sound and the Fury*. It lacks the intensity and driving power that make the latter one of the most remarkable of American novels, but it has an integrity of conception and firmness of handling that make it a distinctive and noteworthy work. It fulfills the promise of *Soldiers' Pay*. It represents, in construction and technique, an advance beyond *The Sound and the Fury*. Mr. Faulkner continues to develop toward simplicity and power. . . .

As I Lay Dying is a horrible book. It will scandalize the squeamish. But it is an admirable book, one to delight those who respect life well interpreted in fine fiction without attempting to dictate what subjects an author shall choose. . . .

The style, save in the passages of conversation, which are excellent, is not strictly in dialect. Mr. Faulkner repeatedly uses rhetorical devices of his own, and a vocabulary such as a Bundren never dreamed of, to render the thought in the mind. He does this particularly when the thought is so vague that a Bundren would be inarticulate, merely sensible of his feelings. . . .

Mr. Faulkner has in a few instances exaggerated to attain the horror he desired, but the story as a whole is convincing. *As I Lay Dying* is a distinguished novel. With *The Sound and the Fury* it entitles William Faulkner to rank with any living writer of fiction in America. All but a scant half dozen—Dreiser, Anderson, Hemingway among them—he far surpasses.

From Clifton P. Fadiman's "Morbidity in Fiction," 131 The Nation, *November 5, 1930, 500–501:*

In his fourth novel Mr. Faulkner has to an extent departed from the irritating obscurity which marked *The Sound and the Fury*. It still seems that his is a far more involved technique than his material actually required: impudent analysis might reduce this story to the dimensions of simple melodrama. But as people are always triumphantly reminding us, the same thing can be done with *Hamlet*.

Mr. Faulkner has a set of romantic obsessions which he treats in a highly intellectual manner. He is fascinated by characters who border on idiocy; by brother-and-sister incest; by lurid religious mania; by physical and mental decay; by peasants with weird streaks of poetry; by bodily suffering; by the more horrifying aspects of sex. Though his approach is always objective, he specializes in emotional extremes—is a sort of prose Robinson Jeffers. . . .

Despite the enthusiasm which has greeted Mr. Faulkner's work, it is difficult to believe him an important writer. . . .

But no one can doubt that the author of *As I Lay Dying* has a really interesting mind, apparently untouched by the major intellectual platitudes of our day. His cosmos is awry; but it is his own, self-created. Genuine idiosyncrasy is rare among our younger novelists. For the most part they explain themselves too easily; they are conveniently ticketed. Mr. Faulkner cannot be so ticketed; that is one reason why he deserves attentive consideration.

Kenneth White's review of As I Lay Dying, *published in* The New Republic, *November 19, 1930, 27:*

Fiction dealing with Southern poor whites tends, whether it need to or not, to confine itself within a small circle of events beyond which few authors seem capable of carrying it. Mr. Faulkner has enlarged this circle but little and added practically not at all to the temper or range of activity peculiar, in literature at least, to these people, but he has increased the intensity and explicitness of their emotional states and experiences. Working within the frame of an extremely simplified external plot he has attempted to reconstruct the complete affective and factual experience of a poor and ignorant family. The method used, telling the same events as seen through the minds of the different characters, offers many pitfalls of unintelligibility and obscurity of reference, which Mr. Faulkner has largely avoided. As the family's grim history unrolls in all its repellent details, one is forced to admire the ingenuity Mr. Faulkner displays in keeping his various strands tightly knit and in contriving the steadily increasing horror. The style, save for occasional passages of meaningless word juggling, is well adapted to the material; and the colloquial idiom these farmers speak is excellently handled. *As I Lay Dying* does not offer a pleasant or inspiring view of humanity, but it is an uncommonly forceful book.

From Basil Davenport's "In the Mire," Saturday Review of Literature, *November 22, 1930, 362:*

. . . There is a disadvantage in this experimental method for a writer of Mr. Faulkner's remarkable imaginative power, which is that many of his characters would in fact be quite unable to find words for their deep and complex feelings; for Mr. Faulkner knows, as few poets do, that thoughts which lie too deep for tears are not the peculiar possession of who can express them. In this difficulty, he cuts the knot; at times his people think in bad grammar and in dialect, as they would actually speak; at other times they think in sentences most skillfully constructed from a rich vocabulary to give as nearly as possible an impression of their incommunicable thoughts. The compromise cannot be called entirely successful, but the facing of the problem is another evidence of Mr. Faulkner's self-reliant experimentalism.

In all other respects, the method entirely justifies itself. As the characters speak, they disclose all the violent forces that have made their stagnant lives; the dying woman recalls the love-affair that led to the birth of one of the children; the daughter is continually gnawed with anxiety over her concealed pregnancy; the others show the secret antipathies and alliances that have been formed in the family. One boy shows flashes of what may be genius, but by the end of the story he has gone mad.

Mr. Faulkner's power is especially in his presentation of mental abnormality. To his studies of it may be given the very high praise that they convince without demonstrating. That is, in the earlier classics of insanity, Maupassant's "Le Horla" and Mrs. Gilman's "The Yellow Wall Paper," the disease may be seen developing step by step, one might almost say logically; they stop one's heart by the terrible necessity with which each stage follows upon the other. But Mr. Faulkner's equally breathtaking madmen are like Lear or Ophelia, in this respect at least, that one believes in them at once; they convince the feelings, which are harder to reach than the reason.

. . . Some readers will prefer *The Sound of the Fury*, finding its effect heightened by the interludes in the past, and its brief passages of humor and tenderness; others will prefer the crushing, almost deadening effect of *As I Lay Dying*. But whichever one puts first, these two novels establish Mr. Faulkner as one of the most original and powerful of our newer novelists.

From John Brophy's review, "New Fiction," published in British journal Time and Tide, *October 19, 1935, 1,490–1,491:*

. . . Mr. William Faulkner is deliquescent jelly, he is a cloud of smoke with a suspicion of flame at the centre, he is the raging volcano which at long last produces a very small mouse. *As I Lay Dying* appears to be one of his earlier novels, and one of his worst. Addie Bundren, the farmer's wife dies, and the coffin is carried a long journey to its burial place. The minor incidents of this journey afford Mr. Faulkner an opportunity for disclosing the private lives, the amours and hatreds and miseries, of a "poor white" family. Each chapter is headed with the name of a character, who then speaks his piece. The technique is unconvincing, for these soliloquies mingle illiterate idioms with poetic eloquence and psychological jargon. . . .

Excerpted from Sean O'Faolian's review of British edition of As I Lay Dying, "Selected Fiction," published in The Fortnightly Library, *138 (December 1935), 637–638:*

. . . [W]ith Faulkner one does not need to understand—the impact is like a storm, and one does not question storms. *As I Lay Dying* has all his primitive, earthy, dark forcefulness, and his personality is so intense that it works freely on us; even if it is a little daft and does tie Mr. Faulkner up in knots of technical reticences. . . . It is not a charming book: it denigrates humanity like most modern American work; but even a reading of one incident, such as that called *Moseley*, or *Samson*, will suffice to affirm Faulkner's inimitable power.

ADAPTATIONS

Adaptations of *As I Lay Dying* include a dramatized version of the novel by Jean-Louis Barrault in 1935; Valerie Bettis's ballet with music by Bernardo Segall and costumes by Kim Swados, first performed by Choreographers' Workshop at Hunter College in New York City on December 19, 1948; a CBS *Camera Three* television version on October 7, 1956; and Robert Flynn's play first performed in 1960 at Baylor University in Waco, Texas. Faulkner recorded a selection from the novel on Caedmon Records (TC-1035) in 1954.

CHARACTERS

Albert The fountain clerk in Moseley's drugstore in Mottson (MOTTSTOWN). He tells Moseley about the townspeople's reaction to the stench of Addie Bundren's decaying body coming from the Bundrens' wagon, which is stopped in front of Grummet's hardware store, and how the marshal insisted that the Bundrens move on because no one can stand the smell. (By this time, Addie Bundren had been dead for eight days.)

Alford (Dr.) A JEFFERSON, MISSISSIPPI, physician. In *As I Lay Dying,* he is referred to by Skeet Mac-Gowan as having an office upstairs from the drugstore that Dewey Dell goes to for medication that will produce an abortion. (*Also see SARTORIS.*)

Armstid A poor farmer who lives in the vicinity of FRENCHMAN'S BEND. He narrates chapter 43— "Armstid"—of *As I Lay Dying.* In this novel (as well as in *LIGHT IN AUGUST*), he is portrayed as a kind and considerate person who helps both neighbor and stranger. He attends Addie's funeral and gives overnight shelter to the Bundrens, whose mishap while crossing the flooded river causes them to lose their mules. (*Also see Light in August; The HAMLET,* where his first name, Henry, is given, and where he is portrayed as a greedy fool and in a much different light; *The TOWN* and *The MANSION,* where in both he is an off-stage character living in the Jackson

asylum; and the short stories "SPOTTED HORSES" and "SHINGLES FOR THE LORD."

Armstid, Lula (Mrs. Armstid) Armstid's wife. She attends to Cash, whose leg is broken, and prepares supper for the Bundrens after their mishap crossing the flooded river. (She also appears in "SHINGLES FOR THE LORD," *The HAMLET,* and *LIGHT IN AUGUST*; in the latter novel, her first name is Martha. For further information, *see Faulkner in the University*, 30–31).

Bud *See* Bundren, Vardaman.

Bundren, Addie The central character of *As I Lay Dying.* Addie is the wife of Anse Bundren and the mother of Cash, Darl, Jewel, Dewey Dell, and Vardaman. (Jewel, however, is not Anse's son, but the product of an adulterous affair with the preacher WHITFIELD.) Addie's death at the beginning of the novel precipitates her family's burial odyssey to JEFFERSON, MISSISSIPPI, where her putrefying corpse is laid to rest. Out of spite, Addie made Anse agree to burying her in Jefferson with "her people," and Anse treats this request as a solemn vow. In the one chapter that she narrates, Addie recalls her father saying "that the reason for living was to get ready to stay dead a long time" (169). She also reflects on her life and family. A former schoolteacher, she hated her students and looked forward to the times when they did something wrong so she could whip them. A memory from this period in her life reveals the sadomasochistic pleasure she derived from thrashing her students:

> When the switch fell I could feel it on my flesh; when it welted and ridged it was my blood that ran, and I would think with each blow of the switch: Now you are aware of me! Now I am something in your secret and selfish life, who have marked your blood with my own for ever and ever. (170)

In her monologue, Addie expresses a pessimistic philosophy of life and a deep skepticism of words; "living is terrible," she pronounces, and "words are no good; . . . [they] dont ever fit even what they are trying to say at" (171). Throughout her life, Addie, who adheres to her own beliefs, is not swayed by the opinions of other.

(*Also see* the short story "SPOTTED HORSES," where a Mrs. Bundren is referred to as a potential customer by the narrator. For further information, *see Faulkner in the University*, 109, 110–111, 112, 113, 114–115, 263.)

Bundren, Anse He is a farmer near FRENCHMAN'S BEND, Addie's husband, and the father of four of Addie's five children: Cash, Darl, Dewey Dell, and Vardaman. (Her son Jewel is not his; he is the offspring of an illicit affair with Whitfield, the local preacher.) When Addie dies, Anse fulfills his promise to bury her with her people in JEFFERSON. (The burial journey forms the central motif and plot of the novel.) Characterized as a lazy and selfish person, Anse's work is often done by others, for he claims that if he sweats he will die, a belief that dates back to a case of apparent sunstroke when he was 22, and one of his motivations for going to Jefferson is to buy a new set of teeth. Perhaps another is to get a wife. The day after he buries Addie (the day the Bundrens start for home), Anse appears with a new Mrs Bundren, and the novel ends with his introducing her to his spellbound children. Anse narrates chapters 9, 26, and 28. (For further information, *see Faulkner in the University*, 109, 110 111, 112, 114, and 265.)

Bundren, Cash Anse and Addie's eldest son, and brother of Darl, Jewel, Dewey Dell, and Vardaman. Cash is a carpenter by trade who constructs his mother's coffin while she is dying. As he puts the coffin together outside his mother's window, he shows her each piece of lumber before he sets it in place. He once suffered a broken leg from a fall from a church roof. The same leg is broken again when the Bundrens attempt to ford the flooded river on their journey to bury Addie in JEFFERSON. Cash, like other members of his family, has a secondary motive in wanting to go to Jefferson; he wants to obtain a "graphophone" (235), that is a phonograph. Cash narrates chapters 18, 22, 38, 53, and 59. (For further information, *see Faulkner in the University*, 114–115 and 121.)

Bundren, Darl Anse and Addie's second son. Darl is intelligent, imaginative and jealous. He is also mentally unstable. Darl maneuvers his brother Jewel away from their mother's bedside when she is near death because he knows that Jewel is Addie's favorite. Darl is the Bundren most affected by the horror and growing absurdity of the journey to bury Addie 40 miles away in JEFFERSON. On the fifth day of the journey (the eighth day after Addie's death), he sets fire to Gillespie's barn to cremate his mother's putrefying remains and to end a senseless journey. His brother Vardaman witnesses Darl's act of arson and tells their sister, Dewey Dell. By the end of the novel, Darl is taken by two officials to the state mental institution in Jackson, and Gillespie drops his threat of a lawsuit against the Bundrens.

In a lecture he gave on American literature at the University of Virginia in 1957, Faulkner was asked whether Darl was out of his mind from the beginning or whether his insanity was the result of the journey to bury his mother's remains. Faulkner answered, "Darl was mad from the first. He got progressively madder because he didn't have the capacity—not so much of sanity but of inertness to resist all the catastrophes that happened to the family" (*Faulkner in the University*, 110). Darl narrates 19 chapters in the novel, more than any other character: 1, 3, 5, 10, 12, 17, 21, 23, 25, 27, 32, 34, 37, 42, 46, 48, 50, 52, and 57. (For further information, *see Faulkner in the University*, 112–13, 115, 121, 263–64.)

Bundren, Dewey Dell Anse and Addie Bundren's only daughter; her four brothers are Cash, Darl, Jewel, and Vardaman. A 17-year old, Dewey Dell is pregnant and seeking a remedy to cause an abortion before anyone discovers her condition, though she is not exactly sure what she needs. Her boyfriend, Lafe, has given her $10 and told her to ask for help at drugstores. When the Bundrens stop in Mottstown on their way to Jefferson to bury Addie, Dewey Dell requests assistance from the druggist Moseley, who sternly rebuffs her. On the day Addie is buried, she seeks help from Skeet MacGowan, a clerk in a pharmacy in Jefferson. Thinking that he is a doctor, she accepts a dose of phony medicine that smells like turpentine and plans to return at 10 P.M. for the rest of the medicine and for the operation. "It wont hurt you," MacGowan promises to encourage her to come back later that night. "You've had the same operation before. Ever hear about the hair of the dog?" (247). (The phrase refers to the belief that like cures like.) When she returns that evening, her brother Vardaman is with her; as he is waiting outside, MacGowan takes Dewey Dell to the basement of the drugstore and has sex with her, convincing her that this is part of the treatment. Earlier that same day, Anse takes her $10 to buy himself a new set of teeth. Dewey Dell narrates chapters 7, 14, 30, and 58 of the novel. (For further information, *see Faulkner in the University*, 112–113.)

Bundren, Jewel   Addie Bundren's son, the product of her adulterous affair with the preacher Whitfield. This fact is unknown to Jewel and his putative father Anse. Only his half brother Darl suspects Jewel's otherness, and he taunts him with it. By working nights, Jewel buys one of Flem Snopes's half-tamed spotted horses. Jewel is his mother's favorite, although she appears to be harder on him than on her other children. At first, Jewel denies the imminence of his mother's death and accompanies his brother Darl on a misadventure to deliver a wagonload of lumber. Addie dies while they are off with the wagon. On the burial journey to JEFFERSON, Jewel insists on fording the swollen river rather than detouring to another bridge, and this impetuosity (one of his character traits) leads to the drowning of the mules, to Cash's broken leg, and to a near fight with a stranger as the Bundrens enter Jefferson. To obtain a replacement span of mules, Anse trades Jewel's beloved horse. Jewel rushes into the Gillespies' burning barn to save the animals and his mother's corpse from the flames and later helps turn in Darl for starting the fire. Jewel, like his mother, narrates only one chapter of *As I Lay Dying*, namely, the fourth. (For further information, *see Faulkner in the University*, 109, 110, 113, 125, and 126.)

Bundren, Mrs.   A JEFFERSON, MISSISSIPPI, woman in *As I Lay Dying* who lends Anse BUNDREN two shovels so that he can bury his deceased wife, Addie. Anse chooses her house to ask for the loan because he hears a gramophone playing there. She

is described as "duck-shaped." In the last line of the novel, Anse introduces her to his incredulous children as "Mrs Bundren"; she is his new wife. (For further information, *see Faulkner in the University*, 111.)

Bundren, Vardaman   He is Anse and Addie's youngest son. (Once in the novel Vardaman is referred to as Bud by Dr. Peabody, 60.) Vardaman cannot accept his mother's death and blames Dr. Peabody's arrival for causing it. In a wild rage, Vardaman chases the doctor's horses off. He is also afraid that his mother will suffocate when she is laid in her coffin; consequently, the night after her death, he drills holes in the top of the coffin, inadvertently ripping into her face. At one point in Vardaman's confused thoughts, he identifies his mother with a fish (84), an apparent connection in his mind between his mother and the fish he caught on the day she died. The traumatized and frightened Vardaman reiterates this connection on the journey to bury her. In a particularly poignant passage in one of the chapter's that he narrates, Vardaman reveals his innermost thoughts:

> Cash is my brother. *But Jewel's mother is a horse. My mother is a fish. Darl says that when we come to the water again I might see her and Dewey Dell said, She's in the box; how could she have got out? She got out through the holes I bored, into the water I said, and when we come to the water again I am going to see her. My mother is not in the box. My mother does not smell like that. My mother is a fish.* (196)

Unwittingly, Vardaman identifies his mother with a horse and perceptively, though unconsciously, observes that his half brother Jewel's affection toward a spotted pony is the life-giving and nourishing force of Jewel's existence. Vardaman is an observant child. He is the one who sees his brother Darl set fire to Gillespie's barn. On his mind throughout the journey to bury his mother is a toy train he once saw in a JEFFERSON store; he is disappointed when it is no longer there.

Vardaman narrates chapters 13, 15, 19, 24, 35, 44, 47, 49, and 56. (For further information, *see Faulkner in the University*, 110–11, 115, 139.)

Gillespie A farmer in *As I Lay Dying*. Gillespie shows compassion to Anse Bundren and his family by allowing them to stay overnight and store the coffin containing Addie's remains in his barn. During the night, the barn catches fire. Gillespie and his son rush into the flames to rescue their horses and cow. Darl and Jewel Bundren also help with the rescue of the livestock, and Jewel single-handedly returns when the fire is even more intense to save his mother's coffin and remains. Later it is discovered that Darl set the fire. Gillespie insists that Darl be held accountable, but by the end of the novel, Darl is escorted to the asylum in Jackson, and the Bundrens avoid a lawsuit.

Gillespie, Mack Gillespie's son in *As I Lay Dying*. Mack's father welcomes the Bundrens to his farm and lets them stay the night on their journey to bury Addie in JEFFERSON. When a fire breaks out in the barn, Mack helps his father, Darl, and Jewel save the livestock.

Grimm, Eustace A minor character in *As I Lay Dying*. A young tenant farmer living about 10 or 12 miles from FRENCHMAN'S BEND, Eustace works a farm belonging to one of his cousins, a Snopes. After the Bundrens lose their mules when they foolishly attempt to ford the flooded river, Eustace goes to Armstid's place with the pair of mules that Anse Bundren acquired for Jewel's horse. Despite his family's fears that he would ride off to Texas rather than give up his beloved horse, Jewel, as Eustace informs Anse, did in fact hand it over. (Eustace also appears in other works; *see The* HAMLET and the short story, "LIZARDS IN JAMSHYD'S COURTYARD," which Faulkner revised for the novel.)

Grummet The owner of the hardware store in Mottson (MOTTSTOWN) where Anse Bundren buys 10 cents' worth of cement to fashion a makeshift cast for Cash's broken leg.

Houston A neighbor who attends Addie Bundren's funeral.

Jody The name of the boy who works in the drugstore in JEFFERSON. Jody acts as a lookout for Skeet MacGowan, who takes advantage of Dewey Dell once he finds out that she is seeking a drug to terminate her pregnancy. Jody is a voice of conscience, which MacGowan ignores.

Lafe The farmhand who impregnates Dewey Dell. Lafe never actually appears in *As I Lay Dying*, but Dewey Dell relates the story of their lovemaking in the woods by the Bundrens' field. He gives Dewey Dell $10 to buy a drug to abort her pregnancy.

Lawington, Miss An offstage character in *As I Lay Dying*. According to Cora Tull, Miss Lawington gave her advice to buy a good breed of chickens and told her of a woman in JEFFERSON who needs special cakes for a party. (Cora bakes the cakes but is disappointed to find out that the unnamed buyer has changed her mind.)

Littlejohn One of the Bundrens' neighbors present at Addie's funeral; he is gathered on the porch with other men. Littlejohn is a family name of early farmers in YOKNAPATAWPHA COUNTY. The name appears in *The* HAMLET, INTRUDER IN THE DUST, and *The* MANSION.

MacCallum Minor character in *As I Lay Dying*; he is Rafe's twin brother. MacCallum does not recognize the Bundrens when they pass by on their way to JEFFERSON to bury Addie. When Quick identifies them, MacCallum, unaware of the Bundrens' burial journey, wonders why they are so far from home. On and off for 12 years, MacCallum has been trading with Samson, who, in the single chapter that he narrates, cannot remember his first name. (In SARTORIS, Rafe's twin is Stuart. Faulkner is not always consistent with the names of his characters or with the spelling of their names. MacCallum was Faulkner's early spelling of McCallum, a fictional family name in YOKNAPATAWPHA COUNTY. The name appears as MacCallum in Faulkner's third novel, *Sartoris* (1929), and in *As I Lay Dying* (1930), but the spelling later changed.)

MacCallum, Rafe MacCallum's twin brother, referred to in *As I Lay Dying*. *Also see* SARTORIS, "Knight's Gambit" in KNIGHT'S GAMBIT, and the short story "The TALL MEN"; in the latter two works the name is spelled McCallum (*see* the Mac-Callum entry above). Rafe is also referred to in *The MANSION*.

McGowan, Skeet Minor character in *As I Lay Dying*; he narrates one chapter. He is a clerk and soda jerker in Uncle Willy Christian's drugstore in JEFFERSON. McGowan takes sexual advantage of Dewey Dell when she comes into the drugstore to buy an abortifacient by convincing her that it is the treatment that will cure her problem. (He also appears in *INTRUDER IN THE DUST*, *The TOWN*, and *The MANSION*.)

Moseley A pharmacist in Mottson (MOTTSTOWN). He refuses to help Dewey Dell when she asks him for a drug to abort her pregnancy, but he tells her instead to marry Lafe, the father of the child, and raise babies. What she wants to do, he explains, is illegal. Moseley narrates chapter 45 of the novel.

Peabody, Doctor Lucius Quintus He attends Addie on her deathbed and saves Cash's broken and festering leg. Dr. Peabody is a 70-year-old man and weighs 225 pounds. He is quick-witted with a mordant sense of humor. When he arrives at the Bundrens', he has to be hauled up the hill leading to the house by a rope. (Peabody narrates chapters 11 and 54 of the novel. He also appears in *SARTORIS*, *The SOUND AND THE FURY*, *The HAMLET*, *The TOWN*, *The REIVERS*, and in the short story "BEYOND.")

Quick, Lon (père; big Lon) An offstage character in *As I Lay Dying*. He is referred to as old man Lon (113) and old Lon Quick (134). In exchange for clearing his field, Quick trades Jewel Bundren a spotted horse, a descendant of one of the wild ponies Flem Snopes brought from Texas to auction off in FRENCHMAN'S BEND. (Jewel's father later trades the horse for a new team of mules when his are drowned fording the flooded river.) Quick also appears in *The HAMLET*, the short story "SPOTTED HORSES" (revised for *The Hamlet*), and "Tomorrow" (in *KNIGHT'S GAMBIT*).

Quick, Lon (fils; little Lon) The son of old Lon Quick in *As I Lay Dying*. Quick finds Doc Peabody's team of horses after Vardaman, thinking that Peabody caused his mother's death, chased them off. Quick attends Addie's funeral, where he reports that the river is rising rapidly. Later, as the Bundrens pass by Samson's farm on their way to bury Addie in JEFFERSON, Quick tells them the bridge is out.

Samson A minor character in *As I Lay Dying* and narrator of chapter 29, "Samson." A kindly neighbor of the Bundrens, Samson puts them up overnight at his farm when they are on their way to JEFFERSON to bury Addie. Confused by Anse's insistence on taking his wife's body to Jefferson even though two bridges have been washed away, Samson suggests that they bury her at New Hope, or, if they must go to Jefferson, that they go up by Mount Vernon, where a bridge is still standing. (Samson also appears in *SARTORIS*.)

Samson, Rachel Samson's wife. She insists that the Bundrens, who are on their way to bury Addie in JEFFERSON, stay the night at the Samson farm. She prepares the Bundrens dinner and the next morning reprimands her husband for not insisting that they stay for breakfast before leaving. Rachel says that it is "a outrage" for the family to drag the dead body of Addie "up and down the country," and she blames "all the men in the world" for what women must go through (117).

Snopes An offstage character in *As I Lay Dying* who trades a team of mules to Anse Bundren in exchange for Jewel's horse. Eustace Grimm delivers the mules to Anse at Armstid's farm. Snopes is a "nephew" of Flem Snopes living in the region of FRENCHMAN'S BEND, but it is questionable whether he is Flem's actual nephew, since Flem's only brother, Colonel Sartoris Snopes, according to the short story "BARN BURNING," ran away as a child and was never heard from again. In "SHINGLES FOR THE LORD" and "HOG PAWN," a Snopes without a first name also appears. (Snopes is the family name that Faulkner gives to a group of people who live in and around the rural area of

Frenchman's Bend and JEFFERSON; *see* SNOPES and SNOPESISM in Part III.)

Snopes, Flem An offstage character in *As I Lay Dying*. The most cunning, greedy, and successful of the Snopes family, Flem appears as a major character in other works by Faulkner. Jewel Bundren's spotted horse that he got from Lon Quick in exchange for clearing Quick's field is a descendant of one of the wild ponies that Flem auctioned off. *Also see* SARTORIS, *The* HAMLET, *The* TOWN, *The* MANSION, and other works Faulkner revised for these novels: FATHER ABRAHAM (fragment of a novel revised and incorporated into *The Hamlet*), "SPOTTED HORSES" (revised from *Father Abraham* and recast in *The Hamlet*), "CENTAUR IN BRASS" (revised for *The Town*), "LIZARDS IN JAMSHYD'S COURTYARD" (revised for *The Hamlet*), and "By the People" (revised for *The Mansion*); Flem is referred to in *The* REIVERS.

Suratt An itinerant salesman in *As I Lay Dying*. He offers Cash Bundren a gramophone for eight dollars. Suratt also appears in SARTORIS, where his initials V. K. are given, and in the short story "LIZARDS IN JAMSHYD'S COURTYARD"; he is referred to in the short story "CENTAUR IN BRASS" and, though not identified, is the narrator of the short story "SPOTTED HORSES." Faulkner later changed his name to V. K. Ratliff; *see The Snopes Trilogy* (*The* HAMLET, *The* TOWN, *The* MANSION) and *Big Woods* ("A BEAR HUNT"). For more information, *see Selected Letters of William Faulkner*, 197.

Tull, Cora One of Addie Bundren's neighbors. A pious woman who speaks her mind on religious matters, Cora is Vernon Tull's domineering wife and the overbearing mother to her daughters. She has been friendly with Addie for many years, although there is latent hostility between them. In the past, Cora had tried to get Addie to be repentant and religious. With her daughters Eula and Kate, Cora attends Addie on her deathbed. She narrates chapters 2, 6, and 39 of the novel. (*Also see The* HAMLET, *The* MANSION, and the short story "SPOTTED HORSES," which Faulkner revised for *The Hamlet*. She is referred to in *The* TOWN.)

Tull, Eula Cora and Vernon Tull's daughter. Eula attends Addie Bundren in the last week of her life, and it is implied that she would like Darl to marry her.

Tull, Kate Cora and Vernon Tull's daughter. As with her sister Eula, Kate helps care for the dying Addie Bundren. Kate looks on Jewel Bundren as a potential mate.

Tull, Vernon A farmer in the vicinity of FRENCHMAN'S BEND, Tull is a kind, amiable and mild-mannered man dominated by his wife. He is a compassionate neighbor to the Bundrens and others. Tull aids the Bundrens in crossing the swollen river, but he is too shrewd to let them use his mules to ford it. He helps save Cash from drowning and helps find his tools when the Bundren wagon overturns trying to ford the flooded Yoknapatawpha River. Tull narrates chapters 8, 16, 20, 31, 33, and 36 of *As I Lay Dying*. (*Also see The* HAMLET, *The* TOWN, "SPOTTED HORSES," "THE HOUND," "LIZARDS IN JAMSHYD'S COURTYARD"—all three stories were revised for *The Hamlet*—and "SHINGLES FOR THE LORD." Tull is referred to in *The* MANSION.)

Varner, Jody An offstage character in *As I Lay Dying*. Jody is Will Varner's (Uncle Billy's) ninth of 16 children, born in 1888, the same year the bridge that is washed away was first built. Jody helps in his father's business matters and is the only one of Varner's children to live at home as an adult. (*Also see* LIGHT IN AUGUST, *The* HAMLET, *The* TOWN, *The* MANSION, and the short stories "FOOL ABOUT A HORSE" and "SPOTTED HORSES"; both were revised for *The Hamlet*.

Varner, Will (Uncle Billy) One of Anse Bundren's neighbors. Uncle Billy attends Addie's funeral and, when talking with Peabody, Armstid, and others, gives the date when the bridge that is washed away was built, 1888. Among other things, Varner is a veterinarian and the proprietor of the general store in FRENCHMAN'S BEND. He sets Cash's broken leg after the Bundrens' wagon overturns crossing the swollen Yoknapatawpha River. *Also* *see* LIGHT IN AUGUST, The HAMLET, INTRUDER IN THE DUST, The TOWN, The MANSION, and the stories "SPOTTED HORSES," "LIZARDS IN JAMSHYD'S COURTYARD," "Tomorrow" (in KNIGHT'S GAMBIT), "SHINGLES FOR THE LORD" and "BY THE PEOPLE" (revised for *The Mansion*).

Whitfield (Rev.)   The preacher who was once Addie Bundren's lover; their affair produced Jewel, Addie's favorite child. Whitfield narrates chapter 41. As Addie lies dying, the remorseful Whitfield plans a visit to confess his transgression to Anse. When he arrives at the Bundrens and finds out that Addie is already dead, he quickly changes his mind and no longer sees the need to ask for forgiveness. Whitfield interprets Addie's death as a clear sign from God that the affair is to be kept secret. Because the bridge is washed away, Whitfield had to ride his horse through the swelling Yoknapatawpha River. Soaked from the waist down, he performs the funeral service. Whitfield also appears in *The* HAMLET, "Tomorrow" (KNIGHT'S GAMBIT), and "SHINGLES FOR THE LORD."

RELATED INFORMATION

Mount Vernon   Fictional place. Described as 18 miles from JEFFERSON, Mount Vernon is possibly Faulkner's name for Abbeville, a village north of OXFORD, MISSISSIPPI. The road to Mount Vernon is offered as an alternate route for the flood-harassed Bundrens in *As I Lay Dying*.

New Hope   Fictional place not far from FRENCHMAN'S BEND in *As I Lay Dying*. New Hope, as Vernon Tull points out in the novel, is not quite three miles away from the Bundren farm and is the place where Anse's folks are buried (29–30).

Samson's Bridge   Fictional place, spanning the Yoknapatawpha River in *As I Lay Dying*. The Bundrens had planned to cross this bridge on their way to Jefferson to bury Addie, but it is washed away by flooding. (*See* SARTORIS, where the bridge seems to span the Tallahatchie River; it is also referred to *LIGHT IN AUGUST* and in the short story "SPOTTED HORSES.")

FURTHER READING

Blotner, Joseph. "How *As I Lay Dying* Came to Be." In *Readings on William Faulkner*, edited by Clarice Swisher, 113–119. San Diego: Greenhaven, 1998.

Bleikasten, André. *Faulkner's As I Lay Dying.* Bloomington: Indiana University Press, 1973.

Brooks, Cleanth. "*As I Lay Dying.*" In *William Faulkner: First Encounters*, 78–95. New Haven: Yale University Press, 1983.

———. "Odyssey of the Bundrens (*As I Lay Dying*)." In *William Faulkner: The Yoknapatawpha Country*, 141–166. Baton Rouge: Louisiana State University Press, 1990.

Cox, Dianne L. *William Faulkner's As I Lay Dying: A Critical Casebook.* New York: Garland, 1985.

Howe, Irving. "*As I Lay Dying.*" In *William Faulkner: A Critical Study*, 175–191. Chicago: University of Chicago Press, 1957.

Luce, Dianne C. *Annotations to William Faulkner's As I Lay Dying.* New York: Garland, 1990.

Millgate, Michael. "*As I Lay Dying.*" In *The Achievement of William Faulkner*, 104–112. Lincoln: University of Nebraska Press, 1978.

Morris, Wesley with Barbara Alverson Morris. "A Writing Lesson: *As I Lay Dying* as tour de force." In *Reading Faulkner*, 150–175. Madison: University of Wisconsin Press, 1989.

Sundquist, Eric J. "Death, Grief, Analogous Form: *As I Lay Dying.*" In *Faulkner: The House Divided*, 28–43. Baltimore: Johns Hopkins University Press, 1985.

Vickery, Olga W. "The Dimensions of Consciousness: *As I Lay Dying.*" In *William Faulkner: Three Decades of Criticism*, edited by Frederick J. Hoffman and Olga W. Vickery, 232–247. New York: Harbinger, 1963.

Wadlington, Warwick. As I Lay Dying: *Stories Out of Stories.* New York: Twayne, 1992.

"Barn Burning"
(Collected Stories)

This is one of Faulkner's most anthologized short stories and considered by many as one of his best. After several rejections, the story was first published in *Harper's Magazine* 179 (June 1939), 86–96, and a year later won the O. Henry Memorial Award. Faulkner had originally planned to use "Barn Burning" as the opening chapter of *The HAMLET*, where a different and shortened version of the story appears. In the novel, Faulkner eliminates Ab Snopes's son, Sarty, effecting less sympathy toward the Snopeses. In *William Faulkner: A Critical Study*, Irving Howe rightly points out that Sarty "is one of the very few Snopeses treated sympathetically by Faulkner" (266; see SNOPESISM).

The 1980 film version of "Barn Burning" (part of an educational series on American short stories produced by Learning in Focus, Inc.) used Rowan Oak, Faulkner's home, as the home of Major de Spain (played by Faulkner's nephew Jimmy Faulkner). Sarty (Shawn Wittington) and his father, Al Snopes (Tommy Lee Jones), walk up the path to the house. *(Harriett and Gioia Fargnoli)*

SYNOPSIS

"Barn Burning" concerns the emotional plight of the 10- or 11-year-old son of a sharecropper, Sarty, whose full name is Colonel Sartoris Snopes after the legendary Civil War hero Colonel John Sartoris (*see* "Characters" under *SARTORIS* and *The UNVANQUISHED*). As the narrative progresses, Sarty finds himself pitted against his own emerging sense of honesty and manhood and the arsonous tendencies of his poor, embittered father, Ab, who settles disputes with his landlords by burning down their barns. The story opens with Ab being accused of arson by Mr. Harris. Though the justice of the peace, for lack of evidence, does not convict Ab, he does advise him to leave the area and never to return. Ab and his family move on to a two-room tenant farmhouse owned by Major de Spain. But even before he starts farming the land, Ab causes a problem for himself and his family by intentionally soiling an expensive new rug when he enters de Spain's house. He then makes matters worse by further damaging the rug after de Spain orders him to clean it. De Spain brings him to court and this time a judge rules against him. Later that night, Ab takes revenge by burning down de Spain's barn. Though Sarty runs to warn de Spain, he is too late; the barn is set ablaze. As he is fleeing from de Spain's mansion, he hears shots being fired. He also realizes that he cannot return to his family. After spending the night outdoors, he leaves for good and never looks back.

CRITICAL COMMENTARY

Some readers may speculate that the shots Sarty hears after de Spain rides past him in pursuit of

Ab Snopes have actually killed his father, as Sarty may have unconsciously hoped for but kept suppressed. This interpretation that Snopes was shot, however, has no conclusive textual basis, and since he appears later in *The Hamlet*, evidence shows that he was not killed or, as the 1985 film adaptation depicts, even wounded by de Spain.

The critic CLEANTH BROOKS considers "Barn Burning" one of the finest examples of Faulkner's great theme of the human heart in conflict with itself (*William Faulkner: First Encounters*, 19). Old enough to understand and sympathize with his father's anger and lot in life, Sarty's conflict, as Brooks points out, is one of being "caught between loyalty to his father . . . and his own sense of honor and decency" (17). Variations on the theme of loyalty and conflict are found in many of Faulkner's works.

"Barn Burning" is told from a narrative perspective sympathetic toward Sarty, whose feelings and thoughts are woven in and out of the narrative line. Many readers view "Barn Burning" as the story of a child's coming of age, of a child's initiation into the conflicts and struggles of an adult world that he must eventually face and resolve for himself. At the beginning of the story, Sarty experiences "frantic grief and despair" when he is called on to testify at his father's trial. Although Sarty knows the truth, he also knows that his father expects him to lie and that he *"will have to do hit"* (*Collected Stories of William Faulkner*, 4). The judge is reluctant to question the boy and finally the plaintiff, Mr. Harris, demands that the boy be dismissed. That evening when the Snopeses are camping, Ab, who suspects that his son would have told the truth (or, if the reader takes Sarty's thoughts at face value, would have wanted to tell the truth even though he was willing to lie), confronts Sarty, who, when ordered to answer, says yes (8). The apparent contradiction between what Sarty thought he had to do to help his father and the answer to his father's question seems to reveal the emerging conflict that he has yet to resolve. The answer that he gives his father expresses not so much what he was expected to do but what he would have wanted to do, an inclination that does not materialize until the end of the story when he runs off to warn Major de Spain. At first Sarty is naively hopeful that his father will change but soon realizes that he will not alter his ways. Sarty feels compelled to break from his family and the blood kinship impressed upon him by his father.

Some readers may view the story from a very different angle and see Ab Snopes as a victim of an unjust economic system that exploits tenant farmers and one that creates conditions that force families to live in poverty. Denied the sufficient means to support his family, Ab is denied basic human decency contributing to his embitterment and anger. Ab's actions, though not justified, can be understood in this light. Like any successful work of art, "Barn Burning" lends itself to multiple interpretations.

REPUBLICATION AND ADAPTATIONS

"Barn Burning" was reprinted in *A Rose for Emily and Other Stories*, in *Collected Stories of William Faulkner*, in *The Faulkner Reader*, and in *Selected Stories of William Faulkner*. On August 17, 1954, a television adaptation of the story by Gore Vidal, starring E. G. Marshall, James Reese, Beatrice Straight, Charles Taylor, and Peter Cookson, aired on the CBS dramatic series *Suspense*. In 1985, a film version of the story, starring Tommy Lee Jones, Diane Kagan, Shawn Wittington, and Faulkner's nephew, JAMES

MURRY (Jimmy) FAULKNER, was produced by Learning in Focus, Inc., an educational series on American short stories hosted by Henry Fonda.

For more information, *see Selected Letters of William Faulkner*, 108, 116, 197, 202, 274, 275, 278, and Diane Brown Jones, *A Reader's Guide to the Short Stories of William Faulkner*, 3–32.

CHARACTERS

de Spain, Major (Cassius) He is the owner of the land that Ab Snopes farms. Major de Spain charges Ab Snopes 20 bushels of corn for having ruined his wife's expensive French rug. A judge reduces the charge to half that amount when Ab sues, but that does not stop Ab from taking revenge by burning down de Spain's barn. Major de Spain also appears in ABSALOM, ABSALOM!, The TOWN, "LION," "The OLD PEOPLE," "The BEAR," and "WASH." He is referred to in The MANSION, INTRUDER IN THE DUST, The REIVERS, "DELTA AUTUMN," "A BEAR HUNT," and "SHALL NOT PERISH."

Harris (Mr.) He is the farmer in Grenier County who brings Ab Snopes to trial and accuses him of burning down his barn. The short story opens with the trial. Although Snopes is obviously guilty, he cannot be convicted because of the lack of hard evidence, but the Justice demands that Snopes leave the country before dark. (This incident is referred to in the first chapter of The HAMLET.)

Lizzie She is Sarty's aunt. Lizzie urges Sarty's mother to let him leave the house and try to prevent his father from setting Major de Spain's barn on fire.

Sarty *See* Snopes, Colonel Sartoris.

Snopes, Ab(ner) He is Sarty's mean-spirited father, known for burning down barns. A "wiry figure," Snopes walks "a little stiffly" from having been shot in the heel by a Confederate provost, when trying to steal a horse ("Barn Burning," 5). Accused by Mr. Harris of burning down his barn, Ab is not convicted for the arson because of lack of evidence. When renting from Major de Spain, Snopes ruins an expensive rug belonging to the de Spains. On top of Snopes's payment as a tenant farmer, Major de Spain takes him to court to charge him an extra 20 bushels of corn to pay for the damaged rug. Even though the judge reduces the charge to 10 bushels, Snopes is not satisfied and he takes revenge by burning down de Spain's barn. (A different version of the story is found in The HAMLET.) Ab Snopes, one of the first Snopeses in YOKNAPATAWPHA COUNTY, also appears in several other works: The UNVANQUISHED, The Hamlet, The TOWN, and The MANSION, and the short story "MY GRANDMOTHER MILLARD AND GENERAL BEDFORD FORREST AND THE BATTLE OF HARRYKIN CREEK." Throughout these works, as in "Barn Burning," Ab is an unscrupulous scavenger.

In response to a question while at the University of Virginia, Faulkner explained that Ab Snopes was "a hanger-on" and "sort of a jackal" that stayed "around the outskirts of the kill to get what scraps might be left," and "nobody would have depended" on him because he "probably . . . wouldn't have held together when the pinch came" (*Faulkner in the University*, 250). Snopes appears to have been married twice. His first wife was a woman from JEFFERSON named Vynie (*see The Hamlet*); his second is named, Lennie, and with her he has four children: Flem (*see The Hamlet*), Sarty, and twin girls, one of whom is named Net (in "Barn Burning").

Snopes, Colonel Sartoris (Sarty) He is the 10- or 11-year-old son of the sharecropper Ab Snopes. Confronted and disturbed by his embittered father's barn-burning, Sarty faces the choice between his father's unjustifiable actions and a moral sense of honesty. He chooses the latter and runs away from home for good. "Barn Burning" is narrated from Sarty's perspective.

Snopes, Lennie She is Ab Snopes's wife and Sarty's mother. When he is leaving to burn down de Spain's barn, Ab tells her to hold on to Sarty, but she is unable to do so; the boy bolts loose and runs to warn de Spain. (*Also see The HAMLET.*)

Snopes, Net She is one of Ab Snopes's twin daughters described by the narrator as big and bovine. Net tries to stop Sarty from running off to warn Major de Spain of his father's intent to burn down the landowner's barn.

HELPFUL RESOURCES

Brooks, Cleanth. "Short Stories." In *William Faulkner: First Encounters*, 7–42. New Haven: Yale University Press, 1983.

Towner, Theresa M., and James B. Carothers, *Reading Faulkner: Collected Stories.* Jackson: University Press of Mississippi, 2006, 3–20.

Jones, Diane Brown. *A Reader's Guide to the Short Stories of William Faulkner*, New York: G.K. Hall, 1994, 3–32.

Yunis, Susan S. "The Narrator of Faulkner's 'Barn Burning.'" *Faulkner Journal* 6 (1991): 23–31.

Zender, Karl F. "Character and Symbol in 'Barn Burning.'" *College Literature* 16 (1989): 48–59.

"Bear, The" (Uncollected Stories)

Short story extracted and shaped from a longer work in progress (the version that became a chapter in GO DOWN, MOSES) and first published in the May 9, 1942, issue of the *Saturday Evening Post*. This version of "The Bear" became the basis of the film treatment of Faulkner's story.

SYNOPSIS

An unnamed young boy is now old enough to accompany the hunters on their November hunting trip into the big woods. Even before he has become old enough to join the hunt, however, he has heard stories of Old Ben, the huge, legendary bear that has escaped hunters and dogs for so long that he now seems immortal. The boy dreams of seeing the great bear, and in the hope of achieving this goal, he subjects himself to the tutelage of Sam Fathers, a man of mixed-race ancestry who is the most admired and skillful of all the hunters. From Sam, the boy learns to love and respect the wilderness and the creatures that inhabit it. He learns how to handle a rifle, track game, use a compass, and read the seasonal changes in the woods.

On his first hunt, when he is only 10, the boy listens excitedly with the other hunters as the dogs chase Old Ben in the distance, but though he discovers a huge footprint left by the giant bear, he does not see the animal; when the wounded and cowering dogs return to the camp, Sam explains that they do not yet have the dog that can hold the great bear. The following June, while the older hunters sit in camp eating and drinking and swapping stories, the boy roams the woods, hoping to see Old Ben. Sam tells the boy that if he will leave his gun behind, the bear might show himself, so the boy goes unarmed into the woods. When he still does not see the bear, he thinks his watch, compass, and protective stick might be hindrances as well, so he lays those aside. Shortly thereafter he views the bear moving across an open glade. The bear stops momentarily to look at the boy and then disappears again into the big woods.

The narrative jumps ahead to the time when the boy is 14. By now, under Sam's guidance, the boy, having already killed both a deer and a bear, has become a better woodsman than most of the older hunters in the camp. This year the boy sees Old Ben twice and, though he has his rifle with him each time, he declines to fire at the bear. On the second occasion, the boy's little fyce dog charges Old Ben, and the boy races to rescue the dog, pulling it back to safety as the bear looms directly over them. Holding the dog tightly, the boy watches the bear retreat into the woods.

Later the boy discusses with his father why he did not shoot at the bear when he had a chance. The father walks to a bookcase, takes out a book, and reads a passage to the boy: "She cannot fade, though thou hast not thy bliss, for ever wilt thou love, and she be fair." When the boy objects that the poet is writing about a girl, the father counters that he is writing about "truth" and "all things that touch the heart—honor and pride and pity and justice and courage and love." The boy thinks to himself that it is perhaps such qualities that he has seen demonstrated in the encounter of the bear, dog, and himself in the woods. And now he understands why he did not fire his rifle at the bear.

CRITICAL COMMENTARY

One of the finest hunting narratives in the English language, "The Bear" is both a story of initiation and a lyrical paean to nature, specifically the wilderness and the old bear that rules over that domain. The education of the boy is twofold: the lessons of experience learned from the old hunter Sam Fathers and the lessons of reflection and introspection learned from the dialogue with his father. From his novitiate with Fathers the boy learns to love and respect the big woods and all its creatures, as well as the skill, courage, and patience required for the hunt. Old Ben, who seems modeled partly on Thomas Bangs Thorpe's "The Big Bear of Arkansas" and partly on Sir James George Frazer's sacred bear of anthropology in *The Golden Bough*, is a mythic, almost divine creature. Significantly, his first appearance to the boy is presented in language that suggests a mystical vision. The boy yearns for the discipline and insight that will make him worthy of such a vision.

Faulkner's poetic treatment of the boy's immersion in the wilderness places "The Bear" within the genre of nature writing. William H. Rueckert writes: "'The Bear' is one of our most profound ecological fictions and belongs with Thoreau's *Walden*. Such texts require deep meditation and mediation because they are about the relation of the self to nature—the non-human universe—and relate the formation of the self to the forms of nature in ways that should concern us all in this age of possession, manipulation, exploitation and destruction of nature for purely human ends" (*Faulkner from Within*, 199).

The passage of poetry that the father reads to the boy is from Keats's "Ode on a Grecian Urn," one of Faulkner's favorite poems. The theme of the passage is the relationship of the real and the ideal, more precisely, the challenge of finding the ideal within the real. The definition of "truth" that the father offers the boy not only references the end of Keats's ode ("Beauty is truth, truth beauty,"— that is all / "Ye know on earth, and all ye need to know") but also anticipates the list of virtues that Faulkner will enumerate in his Nobel Prize acceptance speech. The point of the discussion seems to be that it is not enough to possess lived experience: One needs also to derive understanding and wisdom from that experience.

The link between the idealization of Old Ben and Keats's famous poem about the universality and permanence of great art suggests that "The

Bear" belongs with other Faulkner works, such as The MARBLE FAUN and the "Foreword" to The FAULKNER READER, that examine the interrelationship of life and art.

The version of "The Bear" that appears in Go Down, Moses is significantly different from the magazine version. In the novel, the "boy" is Ike McCaslin, the boy's father becomes Ike's cousin McCaslin ("Cass") Edmonds, and the role of Sam Fathers is considerably expanded. In addition, a long section that does not appear in the magazine version parallels Ike's experience in the woods with his reading of an old family ledger that reveals the miscegenation and incest of his grandfather, Lucius Quintus Carothers McCaslin.

CHARACTERS

For the list of characters in this story, *see* the entry on GO DOWN, MOSES.

"Bear Hunt, A" (Collected Stories)

Short story, a comic tale of revenge in the oral storytelling tradition. "A Bear Hunt" appeared in three versions; the version in Collected Stories was the second. In the earliest, published in the SATURDAY EVENING POST (February 10, 1934), Ratliff is named V. K. Suratt and Old Man Ash is Old Man Bush. In the last version, for Big Woods (1955), Provine becomes Lucius Hogganbeck, a part Indian, and the first narrator is identified as Quentin Compson.

SYNOPSIS

The nameless narrator introduces the events, which occurred at Major de Spain's hunting camp during the annual bear hunt. Nearby is the sinister and ancient Indian mound where de Spain camped as a boy. The narration then is taken over by V. K. Ratliff, the itinerant sewing-machine salesman (a central figure in the SNOPES TRILOGY) who participates in the tricking of the shiftless Lucius "Luke" Provine.

Ratliff stops in at the hunting camp to find that Provine, suffering from a horrendous case of hiccups, is keeping his companions awake and scaring away the game. The hiccups have resulted from Provine's gluttony, and all the usual remedies have failed. Ratliff suggests that Provine seek a cure from the Indian healer John Basket, who lives near the mound. De Spain's black servant, Old Man Ash, overhears this advice and precedes Provine to the site. He warns Basket that a revenue man is on the way and needs a good scare. When Provine arrives, the Indians tie him to a pyre as if to burn him alive and then let him escape. The terrified Provine indeed does lose his hiccups, but thrashes Ratliff for his role in the prank. Ratliff elicits the rest of the tale from Old Man Ash: Decades earlier, Provine had burned off his exceptionally fine celluloid collar. Ash at last has exacted his revenge and regained his dignity.

CRITICAL COMMENTARY

With its use of Southwestern yarn-spinning humor, colloquial style, shifting narrations, movement backward and forward in time, and dramatization of the influence of the past upon the present, "A Bear Hunt" exhibits a number of Faulkner's favorite narrative devices. The inclusion of the story in "The County" section of Collected Stories demonstrates that Faulkner viewed the story and characters as representative of his fictional YOKNAPATAWPHA COUNTY.

CHARACTERS

Ash, Old Man Major de Spain's camp cook, he arranges for John Basket and his Indian associates to frighten Lucius ("Luke") Provine. Ash seeks revenge for Provine's having burned a fine celluloid collar of Ash's some 20 years before.

Basket, John He is the leader of the Indians who cures Lucius Provine of the hiccups by scaring him.

Bonds, Jack Now deceased, he was a member, along with Lucius Provine and his brother, of the gang of youths that terrorized the town by racing their horses through the streets and firing their pistols into the air.

de Spain, Major   One of the hunters and owner of the hunting camp.

McCaslin, Uncle Ike   A member of the hunting party.

Provine, Lucius   The victim of a practical joke unwittingly instigated by V. K. Ratliff and executed by Old Man Ash and John Baskett. Ash's role in the plot is in revenge for an earlier grievance against Provine.

Provine, Mrs.   The wife of the improvident Lucius Provine, she takes in sewing to support the family.

Ratliff, V. K.   An itinerant sewing machine salesman who is a principal character in a number of Faulkner's stories and novels. Here, he suggests that Provine seek a cure for his hiccups from Indian healer John Basket.

"Big Shot, The"
(Uncollected Stories)

This short story was written around 1929 and first published posthumously in *Uncollected Stories of William Faulkner*. (For more information, *see Uncollected Stories of William Faulkner*, 707; *also see* "DULL TALE," a reworking of the material in "The Big Shot.")

SYNOPSIS

"The Big Shot" is written as a retelling of a story by an unnamed narrator who reports the words of his friend Don Reeves about Dal Martin, a Memphis political boss and contractor. Martin is an uneducated yet shrewd and successful multimillionaire. The story also concerns Popeye, the bootlegger and murderer in the novel SANCTUARY. "The Big Shot" centers on Popeye's arrest for running a stop sign and nearly killing a pedestrian while transporting a carload of bootleg whiskey to Martin's house. Reeves recaps Martin's history, delving back into his childhood as a sharecropper's illiterate son who pulled himself into financial and political prominence

through sheer will and desire. But Martin's money and connections cannot push his daughter, Wrennie (Miss Laverne), onto a higher social plane, which is his deepest desire. Martin attempts to bribe Dr. Blount, one of the city's distinguished citizens, into including his daughter in the next Chickasaw Guards debutante ball. At first Dr. Blount turns Martin out for offering him a cash bribe. But he relents when Martin returns several weeks later with the offer to build an art gallery in honor of Dr. Blount's grandfather. Blount comes to regret his action, however, and tries to renege; when Martin does not allow him out of the bargain, Blount commits suicide. Martin's social triumph is tragically (and ironically) obliterated at the end of the story when his daughter is run over and killed by Popeye, who, freed from jail, is rushing to deliver liquor to Martin's house.

CRITICAL COMMENTARY

In "The Big Shot" (and its revision, "Dull Tale"), Faulkner touches on themes that resonate in his later fiction: the unscrupulous quest for power, rapacity, and the pursuit of social respectability and approbation. The character traits of Popeye and Wrennie Martin, respectively, anticipate Popeye and Temple Drake in *Sanctuary*; Dal Martin foreshadows Thomas Sutpen in ABSALOM, ABSALOM! and Flem Snopes in the Snopes trilogy.

CHARACTERS

Blount, Dr. Gavin   He is a member of the old aristocracy in MEMPHIS. Dr. Blount's grandfather was killed in the Civil War riding with NATHAN BEDFORD FORREST, the Confederate cavalry general. Dr. Blount invites young women to make their debuts into Memphis society at the annual Chickasaw Guards Ball. He is bribed by Dal Martin, the nouveau riche contractor and political boss, to add Wrennie (Miss Laverne)—Martin's daughter—to the exclusive list in exchange for the building of an art gallery dedicated to Dr. Blount's grandfather. At first Dr. Blount agrees, but when he reconsiders and asks to be let out of the bargain, Martin refuses. With his honor gone, Dr. Blount commits suicide. (*See* "DULL TALE" where Dr. Blount's character is essentially the same and "A RETURN" where he is the grandnephew of a senior officer killed in the Civil War. Dr. Blount prefigures Gail Hightower in *LIGHT IN AUGUST* and Horace Benbow in *SARTORIS* and *SANCTUARY*.)

Govelli   He is a bootlegger who supplies whiskey to Dal Martin. In "The Big Shot," the infamous Popeye of *SANCTUARY* works for Govelli.

Martin, Dal   He is the main character in the story (and a major character in the story's revision, "DULL TALE"). Illiterate and uneducated, Martin rises from poverty as a sharecropper's son to a wealthy political boss and crooked contractor in Memphis. His rise in status has its origins in the disdainful treatment he received as a child from a wealthy landowner. In his dealings, Martin employs and protects the bootleggers Popeye and Govelli. One of his obsessions is to seek a better, more sophisticated and respectable life than his own for his daughter Wrennie. (Martin's character foreshadows that of Thomas Sutpen in *ABSALOM, ABSALOM!* and of Flem Snopes in the *SNOPES TRILOGY*.)

Miss Wrennie   She is the spoiled daughter of Dal Martin. (As a character, she foreshadows Temple Drake in *SANCTUARY* and *REQUIEM FOR A NUN*. Like Temple, she has a reckless personality.) Dal Martin bribes Dr. Blount to include his daughter on the invitation list to the Chickasaw Guards Ball, but before this major social event, she is run over and killed by Popeye. (She also appears in Faulkner's retelling of the story in "DULL TALE.")

Popeye   A bootlegger who works for Govelli. Popeye accidentally runs over and kills Wrennie Martin, the only child of the powerful political boss, Dal Martin. *Also see SANCTUARY* (where he is a major character) and *A REQUIEM FOR A NUN* (where he is referred to).

Big Woods

Random House brought out this collection of four of Faulkner's previously published hunting pieces in 1955. Faulkner wrote four brief prose narratives

linking the stories, together with a coda. Edward Shenton, who had done the drawings for *The UNVANQUISHED*, supplied the illustrations.

The four stories, all of which are discussed at length elsewhere in this volume, are, in order, "The BEAR," "The OLD PEOPLE" (*see GO DOWN, MOSES*), "A BEAR HUNT," and "RACE AT MORNING." The revised versions of the two stories from *Go Down, Moses* are shorn of the themes of racial injustice and retribution, miscegenation and incest, leaving what some critics regard as the minor theme of the destruction of the wilderness.

Faulkner omitted part 4 of "The Bear," which reveals the guilty heritage of the twins Theophilus (Buck) and Amodeus (Buddy) McCaslin. As the biographer Frederick Karl notes, the excision converts the story into "an adventure piece—a commercialization of the inner tale." There were only minor changes to the other pieces. Lucius Provine becomes Lucius Hogganbeck, Boon Hogganbeck's 40-year-old son, in "A Bear Hunt." Faulkner added a dozen or so lines to "Race at Morning."

The introductory narratives for *Big Woods* are drawn from previous work, including *REQUIEM FOR A NUN*, the essay "MISSISSIPPI," and several short stories. They are elegiac, the 58-year-old Faulkner's mournful tribute and farewell to the vanished wilderness. The epilogue ends on a bitter note: "No wonder the ruined woods I used to know don't cry out for retribution. The very people who destroyed them will accomplish their revenge" (*Big Woods*, 224).

The publication date was October 14, 1955. The reviews were mostly favorable, although as the critic MALCOLM COWLEY observed, "the virtues of *Big Woods* have been achieved too much at the cost of other books from which the material was taken by right of eminent domain."

Most critics agree the excisions from "The Bear" and "The Old People" lessen the stories' power and literary merit. Barbara L. Pittman, writing in the *Mississippi Quarterly* (1996), however, argues for a different kind of symbolic power in the revised stories, which appeared in a changed, and changing, historical context. "Faulkner creates an elaborate narrative system, supported by the accompanying illustrations, that instructs the formation of myth to replace the loss of the actual wilderness," she writes. "In this process, *Big Woods* exhibits the dual apocalyptic movement of doom and revelation as it writes itself from history to myth."

For Pittman, the loss of the wilderness accompanies the loss of white dominance in America and, particularly, the South, in the wake of the Supreme Court's challenge to racial segregation in *Brown v. Board of Education* (1954): "For Faulkner to refigure his earlier text about racial injustice into the 'nice book' [Faulkner's phrase] that laments the loss of [white domination] not only reveals some of the frustration and tension that moderate Southern whites were feeling as their society was daily dissected by the national media, but also speaks the unspeakable desire to dominate."

"Black Music"
(*Collected Stories*)

Short story that first appeared in DOCTOR MARTINO AND OTHER STORIES (1934).

SYNOPSIS

This comic story concerns a mythical metamorphosis in a 20th-century Virginian arcadia. The tale is revealed through a dialogue between the protagonist and the nameless, at times sarcastic, narrator, who has traveled to the Latin American port town of Rincón. There he hears of a mysterious old American expatriate, Wilfred Midgleston, who is poor and, above all, happy. Other disreputable American exiles, including one who apparently had to flee his homeland because of thievery, attribute a similar past to Midgleston. The narrator treats the old man to a hearty breakfast and learns the truth.

Midgleston is content with his simple life, sleeping under a roll of tar paper in a rat-infested attic over a cantina. He tells of the event that altered his life. Once a Brooklyn draftsman, he was sent to Virginia to deliver architectural blueprints to a wealthy Park Avenue matron, Mrs. Carleton (Mathilda) Van Dyming, who was building a vacation compound with classical-style structures and an outdoor Greek theater in a vineyard run wild. On the journey, he saw a faun's head with goat's

horns and beard suspended outside the window of the train. He collapsed, and was revived by alcohol. When he arrived at the station, he bought a tin flute, continued to imbibe on the wagon ride to the construction site, and was transformed into a faun. In a modern reenactment of a Dionysian orgy, he played the flute while chasing Mrs. Van Dyming through the old vineyard, together with the prize bull he had released.

The Van Dymings consequently abandoned their plans for the property and Midgleston disappeared. To prove that the event, which he believes was ordained by the pagan gods, actually happened, Midgleston produces several yellowed newspaper clippings, including one headlined "Maniac at Large in Virginia Mountains." Since he later was presumed dead, his generous life insurance policy went to his wife, who then moved to Park Avenue and married a more socially acceptable fellow. For Midgleston, his temporary transformation radically changed his life to one he has found more spiritually amenable.

CRITICAL COMMENTARY

No critic to date has argued that this story belongs with Faulkner's best, yet Faulkner thought enough of the story to allow it to be included in the "Beyond" section of *Collected Stories*. The story focuses on a character who has "been something outside the lot and plan for mortal human man to be" (*Collected Stories*, 805). Michael Millgate groups the story with "Beyond" and "The Leg" in its "preoccupation with the world of the supernatural" (*Achievement*, 274). Hyatt H. Waggoner finds in the opening lines of the story, a description of an ordinary man granted a brief "apotheosis . . . above his lost earth like that of Elijah of old" (*Collected Stories*, 799), a tension running throughout Faulkner's work and finding ultimate expression in *A FABLE* (*William Faulkner: From Jefferson to the World*, 227).

Because the story is set in Rincón and Mrs. Widrington, the wife of an office manager, allows the character the use of the attic above the cantina, readers tend to identify Midgleston with the unnamed protagonist of "CARCASSONNE." However, the ages and temperaments of the two characters seem greatly different.

CHARACTERS

Carter He is the architect for whom Wilfred Midgleston works when he has the strange experience that causes him to believe he is a faun. Under this delusion, Midgleston chases Mrs. Van Dyming through the woods of her Virginia estate.

Harris, Elmer He is the police chief who heads up the Van Dyming investigation of the strange case of the faun chasing Mrs. (Matilda) Van Dyming through the woods of her Virginia estate.

Midgleston, Martha She is the wife of an architectural draftsman who fancies himself a faun. When her husband is presumed dead, she collects his insurance money, remarries, and moves to Park Avenue in New York City.

Midgleston, Wilfred A middle-aged architectural draftsman assigned to help design a group of buildings in the Grecian style for a wealthy financier named Carleton Van Dyming, he has a strange experience in which he imagines himself a faun. Naked and carrying a tin whistle, he chases Van Dyming's wife through the woods of their Virginia estate. Midgleston disappears and is presumed dead. In fact, he turns up alive and in dire poverty in Latin America, living in an attic above a cantina with a roll of tar paper for a bed.

Unnamed narrator The individual to whom Midgleston tells his strange story.

Van Dyming, Carleton A wealthy financier, he buys an estate in Virginia and indulges his wife Mattie's ambition to put up classical-style buildings modeled on the Acropolis and the Coliseum on the property.

Van Dyming, Matilda (Mattie) The former Matilda Lumpkin of Poughkeepsie, New York, she marries the rich New York financier Carleton Van Dyming and talks him into putting up classical-style buildings on their newly acquired Virginia estate.

Wilfred Midgleston, a draftsman working for Van Dyming's architect, has a strange experience in which he imagines himself a faun. Naked and carrying a tin whistle that Mrs. Van Dyming mistakes for a knife, he chases her into the Virginia woods. She flees in terror, with the faun and her husband's prize bull in pursuit, and finally faints. The "madman" vanishes without a trace.

Widrington He manages a company that does business in a port town in a small Latin American country. His firm owns the cantina building in whose attic Wilfred Midgleston finds shelter.

Widrington, Mrs. The wife of a company manager in the Latin American town where Wilfred Midgleston turns up, she gives the fugitive Midgleston permission to sleep in the attic above the company-owned cantina.

Mrs. Widrington also appears in the short story "CARCASSONNE," where her husband is identified as the manager of a Standard Oil Company office.

"By the People"

Short story first published in the October 1955 issue of *Mademoiselle*. Faulkner revised it to be included in chapter 13 of *The MANSION*. The story was also published in *Prize Stories 1957: The O. Henry Awards*, selected and edited by Paul Engle and Constance Urdang (Garden City, N.Y.: Doubleday, 1957), and in *40 Best Stories from Mademoiselle, 1935–1960*, edited by Cyrilly Abels and Margarita G. Smith (New York: Harper, 1960).

SYNOPSIS

Told from the point of view of Charles Mallison, Gavin Stevens's nephew, this amusing and comical story concerns V. K. Ratliff's scheme to defeat Clarence Eggleston Snopes, a bigoted and self-serving Mississippi legislator, in his bid to win a congressional election against a wounded Korean War veteran, Colonel Devries. A Medal of Honor winner, Devries was in charge of a unit of African-American troops. In his plot to assure that Uncle Billy (Will Varner), the biggest landowner in FRENCHMAN'S BEND and Snopes's sponsor, will become angry enough to withdraw his support and force Snopes to step down, Ratliff arranges for two boys to artfully scent Snopes's trouser legs with damp switches from a dog thicket that cause dogs to trail, sniff, and urinate on him, thus making him look foolish. To Uncle Billy, Snopes becomes too much of an inept embarrassment to represent the citizens of Frenchman's Bend and BEAT FOUR.

CRITICAL COMMENTARY

As JOSEPH BLOTNER points out, when writing the story Faulkner drew ideas from the commencement speech he gave at his daughter Jill's high school graduation on May 28, 1951 (*see Faulkner: A Biography*, 592). In his analysis of the story, Robert W. Hamblin comments that in addition to being a tall tale "in the southwestern yarn-spinning tradition," "By the People" "pits a concern for a democratic ideal of government . . . against the political machinations and ethical abuses of a demagogue like Senator Snopes" and has roots in the American tradition of political satire that "reaches back to such early works as Hugh Henry Breckenridge's *Modern Chivalry* (1792–1815)" (*A William Faulkner Encyclopedia*, edited by Robert W. Hamblin and Charles A. Peek, 57). For further information, *see Selected Letters of William Faulkner*, 373.

"Carcassonne" (Collected Stories)

Short narrative piece, almost a prose poem, first published in *These 13* (1931).

SYNOPSIS

Here Faulkner employs the dreams and fantasies of an unnamed protagonist in what appears to be a meditation on the creation of art and on the divided psyche of the artist. The focal character lives in a rat-infested attic of a cantina in the port city of Rincón. His benefactress, Mrs. Widrington, wife of the Standard Oil Company office manager, allows him to sleep over the cantina, which is owned by her husband's company, and encourages him to become a poet. Sleeping under a roll of tar paper, amid the scurrying rats, the protagonist "nightly peruse[s] the fabric of dreams" (*Collected Stories*, 896), envision-

ing the heroic actions of medieval crusaders, images of crucifixion and resurrection, and himself "on a buckskin pony *with eyes like blue electricity and a mane like tangled fire, galloping up the hill and right off into the high heaven of the world*" (895). All such images of escape and transcendence are countered by objections from the character's "skeleton," which prefers quietness and peace: "I know that the end of life is lying still," the skeleton tells the poet. "You haven't learned that yet" (899). The poet rejects the skeleton's counsel, however, and the story ends with another flight of the poet's imagination.

CRITICAL COMMENTARY

The visionary content, with its allusions to religion, history, and literature, sharply contrasts with the dreamer's physical existence. His body lies beneath tar paper in the rat-infested attic, yet his imagination soars free and far. Just as the viewpoint shifts between the real and the imaginary, the tone shifts between despair and hopefulness. The story has much in common with popular medieval dramatizations of the debate between the body and the soul, with the religious elements of the medieval narrative being replaced in Faulkner's version by the conflict between fact and fancy, the real and the ideal, the restricted and the transcendent.

Although many readers and critics dismiss this story as negligible in the Faulkner canon, Faulkner himself described the story as "a piece that I've always liked," further noting that the story is about "a young man in conflict with his environment." In the same observation Faulkner went on to link the content of the narrative to his own initial interest in poetry and to explain that "fantasy" seemed better suited to the story's purpose than "simple realism" would have been (*Faulkner in the University*, 22). MICHAEL MILLGATE views the story's buckskin pony as "an American-bred Pegasus" (*Achievement*, 261), the winged horse provided by the Muses to serve poets. Robert W. Hamblin links the imagery of the story to Faulkner's stated artistic credo of "saying No to death" (*see* "'Carcassonne': Faulkner's Allegory of Art and the Artist," *Southern Review* 15.2 [1979]: 355–365). Noel Polk, stressing the placement of the story as the culminating chapter of *These 13*, views the protagonist as a failed Prufrock-type inhabiting a modern waste land ("William Faulkner's 'Carcassonne,'" *Studies in American Fiction* 12 (1984): 29–43).

The real Carcassonne is a city in southwestern France, the site of one of the finest remains of medieval fortifications in all of Europe. Although Faulkner apparently never visited Carcassonne (he may have first learned about it in the French classes he took with Professor Calvin Brown at the University of Mississippi in 1919–20), the city came to represent for him, much like Xanadu did for Keats, a symbol of the creative imagination. Once asked to comment on the source of Southern literature, Faulkner said, "I myself am inclined to think it was because of the bareness of the Southerner's life, that he had to resort to his own imagination, to create his own Carcassonne" (*Faulkner in the University*, 136). In ABSALOM, ABSALOM! Thomas Sutpen's effort to realize his dynastic dream is compared to "a madman who creates within his very coffin walls his fabulous immeasurable Camelots and Carcassonnes" (160). In "Carcassonne in Mississippi: Faulkner's Geography of the Imagination" (*Faulkner and the Craft of Fiction*, ed. Doreen Fowler and Ann J. Abadie, 148–171), Robert W. Hamblin argues that Faulkner's Yoknapatawpha is best understood as a fusion of the real (Oxford and Lafayette County) and the imaginary (Carcassonne).

CHARACTERS

Luis He operates the cantina and allows the pauper-poet to sleep in the garret.

unnamed protagonist The "tramp" or "poet" (or both) whose dreams and fantasies provide the principal content of the story. Though trapped in poverty and living in a "rat-infested" room, he dreams of heroic actions and romantic transcendence: "*I want to perform something bold and tragical and austere.*" In another story, "BLACK MUSIC," also set in Rincón, a character named Wilfred Midgleston is given permission by Mrs. Widrington to sleep in the attic above the cantina, leading some readers to assume the protagonist of "Carcassonne" is also Midgleston.

Widrington, Mrs. Her husband is identified as the manager of a Standard Oil Company office, and the company owns the building in which the cantina is located. A benefactress of sorts to the protagonist, she encourages him to be a poet. She also appears in the story "BLACK MUSIC."

"Centaur in Brass" (Collected Stories)

First published in *American Mercury* 25 (February 1932), 200–210, "Centaur in Brass" was revised for publication in *Collected Stories of William Faulkner;* Faulkner revised it further and used it as the first chapter of *The TOWN*, the second novel in the SNOPES TRILOGY. For more information, *see Selected Letters of William Faulkner*, 197, 274, and 278, and Diane Brown Jones, *A Reader's Guide to the Short Stories of William Faulkner*, 154–169.

SYNOPSIS

"Centaur in Brass" concerns Flem Snopes's prolonged but unsuccessful attempt at stealing brass safety valves from the power plant in JEFFERSON. The story opens with a brief summary of Flem's immediate past and his arrival in Jefferson with his wife and her infant daughter, but soon turns to Flem's appointment as plant superintendent and his unscrupulous greed. To accomplish his ends, Flem exploits his wife's erotic appeal to Major Hoxey, the town's rich bachelor mayor, and plays Tom-Tom, the day fireman at the power plant, against Turl, the night fireman. But Flem's scheme backfires when he orders Turl to recover the brass that Tom-Tom is in fact hiding on his property for Flem. Instead of finding brass on the day Turl goes hunting for it, he discovers Tom-Tom's much younger wife alone. Once Flem suspects why Turl is not delivering the wares, he alerts Tom-Tom to what Turl is doing. Just before sundown one evening, Tom-Tom puts on one of his wife's nightgowns and lies in wait on a cot in the back porch for the unsuspecting Turl. When Turl arrives, Tom-Tom chases him with a butcher knife until the two men fall exhausted into a ditch and realize what Flem has done. To get even with Flem, the two men decide to dump the brass in the water tank.

COMMENTARY

The themes of sexual and economic opportunism vividly play off each other in "Centaur in Brass," a story which, according to John T. Matthews, "suggests that the age-old economic foundation of erotic desire takes on particular clarification in capitalism's transition to mass market practices" ("Shortened Stories: Faulkner and the Market" in *Faulkner and the Short Story*, 29). The story is also a foreshadowing of Flem's unscrupulous greed that dominates the SNOPES TRILOGY.

CHARACTERS

Conner, Buck   He is the city marshal of JEFFERSON who investigates the missing brass fittings at Jefferson's power plant. (*Also see* LIGHT IN AUGUST.)

Harker, Mr.   A veteran sawmill engineer, Mr. Harker runs the power plant in JEFFERSON. (*Also see* The TOWN.)

Hoxey, Major   He is the mayor of Jefferson when Flem Snopes arrives from FRENCHMAN'S BEND. A Yale graduate and wealthy bachelor, Major Hoxey appoints Flem superintendent of the municipal power plant after starting an adulterous affair with Flem's beautiful wife, Eula, an affair that Flem exploits. The mayor is also referred to as Colonel Hoxey. (A similar character with a similar function is Manfred de Spain in The TOWN.)

Snopes, Flem   After marrying Eula Varner in FRENCHMAN'S BEND, Flem moves with his wife and her infant daughter to JEFFERSON. His arrival was "preceded by a reputation for shrewd and secret dealings" ("Centaur in Brass," 149). Knowing that the mayor, Major Hoxey, and his wife are having an affair, Flem exploits their adultery in furthering his plans to achieve his goals. He devises a scheme to get possession of the solid brass fittings at the power plant but it backfires. Once the two unwitting accomplices, Turl and Tom-Tom, become aware of what Flem has in mind, they dump the brass fittings into the water tank, leaving Flem with the responsibility to pay for them. (Flem is an important character and appears in several of Faulkner's works; *see* SARTORIS, The HAMLET, The TOWN, The MANSION and in previously written works Faulkner revised for these novels: FATHER ABRAHAM (fragment of a novel revised and incorporated into *The Hamlet*), "SPOTTED HORSES" (revised from *Father Abraham* and recast in *The Hamlet*), and "LIZARDS IN JAMSHYD'S COURTYARD" (revised for *The Hamlet*); Flem is also referred to in AS I LAY DYING and The REIVERS.

Suratt   He is an itinerant sewing machine agent, who lost his half-interest in a small restaurant in JEFFERSON to Flem Snopes. Suratt is an offstage character referred to at the beginning of the story. (*Also see* SARTORIS, AS I LAY DYING, and the short story "LIZARDS IN JAMSHYD'S COURTYARD"; in the first of these three works his initials, V. K., are used. (Faulkner later changed his name to V. K. Ratliff; *see* The HAMLET, The TOWN, The MANSION, and *Selected Letters of William Faulkner*, 197.)

Tom-Tom   He is the African-American fireman who reads the gauges on the day shift at the power plant in Jefferson. A 60-year-old who looks about 40, Tom-Tom is a big man weighing 200 lbs. and married to a young woman, his third wife, whom he keeps in seclusion. When he catches his night-shift counterpart, Turl, sneaking up to his house one night to be with his wife, Tom-Tom chases him with a butcher knife until they fall into a ditch. Once they realize their unwitting role in Flem Snopes's scheme to steal the solid brass fittings at the power plant, Tom-Tom and Turl put the fittings into the town's water tank. (In the revised version of the story in *The TOWN*, Tom-Tom is a minor character whose full name is Tom Tom Bird, with no hyphen; in the novel, he is married for a fourth time.)

Turl   He is one of two African-American firemen at the power plant in JEFFERSON in 1910. Turl works at night under Mr. Harker; his counterpart, Tom-Tom, works during the day. When Flem Snopes becomes superintendent of the plant, he exploits both men in his attempt to steal the solid brass safety valves. Flem orders Turl to retrieve the brass Tom-Tom is hiding on his property, but the 30-year-old Turl begins an affair with Tom-Tom's much younger wife and one night is caught. After a struggle between Turl and Tom-Tom, both men realize what Flem is up to and decide to throw the brass into the water tank. (In the revised version of the story in *The TOWN*, Turl is a minor character whose full name is Tomey's Turl Beauchamp.)

Collected Stories of William Faulkner

Published in 1950, this volume brought together 42 short stories written over a period of two decades. (*See* entries for individual stories.)

ALBERT ERSKINE, an editor at RANDOM HOUSE, began preparations for the collection in early 1948, making up a list of stories to be included and passing it along to Faulkner's longtime editor, ROBERT K. HAAS. By November, Haas, the editor SAXE COMMINS, and Faulkner himself had chosen the 42 pieces to be arranged in six sections: "The Country," "The Village," "The Wilderness," "The Wasteland," "The Middle Ground," and "Beyond." Faulkner arranged the order of the stories but he did not write a foreword, as MALCOLM COWLEY had suggested, to illustrate the volume's themes and connections.

Collected Stories contains much of Faulkner's best short fiction, including "A ROSE FOR EMILY," "BARN BURNING," "DRY SEPTEMBER," "RED LEAVES," "THAT EVENING SUN," and "UNCLE WILLY." Notably absent from the omnibus are the seven stories of *The* UNVANQUISHED, the seven stories of GO DOWN, MOSES, and four stories, including "SPOTTED HORSES," that Faulkner wove into *The* HAMLET.

Random House published the *Collected Stories* on August 21, 1950. The early reviews were mostly enthusiastic, always respectful. Harry Sylvester, writing in the *New York Times Book Review*, did not like the "Beyond" section, in which four of the six stories contained supernatural elements, but praised the volume overall and classified Faulkner as a great writer.

"One thing remains to distinguish him above all American writers since James and perhaps since Melville—he simply knows so much more than they," Sylvester wrote.

The poet and critic Horace Gregory, in an essay in the *New York Herald Tribune Weekly Book Review*, ranked Faulkner with James, Kafka, Dostoyevsky, Joyce, and D. H. Lawrence. Writers of such stature are not bound by the ordinary rules, he suggested, and even their failures have value.

"The first impression that the book conveys is one of an Elizabethan richness: here is the variety of life itself, its humors, its ironies, its ancient tempers, its latest fashions, its masks of horror, its violence, its comedy, its pathos," Gregory wrote. "It is gratuitous to say that the stories are uneven in depth, quality and interest."

In March 1951, Faulkner won a National Book Award for *Collected Stories*.

"Dangerous Man, A" (Uncollected Stories)

Written about 1929, "A Dangerous Man" was published posthumously in *Uncollected Stories of William Faulkner*.

SYNOPSIS

This short story tells of a slightly deaf but extremely aggressive man, Mr. Bowman, who unquestioningly defends himself and Southern womanhood. The story is told by an unnamed male observer who claims that women know more than men. This narrator-observer seems attuned to the gossip of the village and to Mr. Bowman's hypervolatility. The title of the story itself is taken directly from the narrator's first description of Mr. Bowman, who, at the beginning of the story, unhesitatingly accompanies Zack Stowers on his way to defend Mrs. Stowers's honor against two drummers (traveling salesmen). The drummers claim to be unjustly accused. Mr. Bowman, with a reputation for fierceness—he once disarmed and killed a robber in the railway express office he managed—is willing to fight both men at once, but Stowers keeps him from doing so. There is much irony and humor behind this scene, for Mr. Bowman's wife, a large, shrewish woman, secretly is carrying on an affair with Wall, an insurance salesman. For all the narrator's protestations of deference to women, he seems unaware that his tale mocks not only the highly strung Mr. Bowman but, by extension, the honor of Southern womanhood.

CRITICAL COMMENTARY

In his brief discussion of the theme of solipsism in Faulkner, James Ferguson points out that this theme, though "almost never explicitly stated in Faulkner's best and most mature short fiction," is clearly present in "A Dangerous Man" and in "Frankie and Johnny," another early Faulkner story Ferguson discusses in reference to solipsism (*Faulkner's Short Fiction*, 51). Mr. Bowman perceives or interprets a world that he more or less creates for himself.

CHARACTERS

Bowman, Mr.   The appositive title character in the short story. Willing to defend the honor of southern womanhood and the rights of southern husbands at the smallest provocation, Mr. Bowman is volatile, vain, impetuous, brave, and thoughtless. He works as the agent in an express office, a sinecure he received as the result of having disarmed and killed a robber when he was stationed in an office in a small town. Blinded by his own dangerousness and pride, Mr. Bowman is unaware that his wife, who actually runs the office where they work, is carrying on an affair while he is attending to the business of delivering packages. Faulkner depicts Mr. Bowman as partially deaf, perhaps symbolic of his never hearing about the affair.

Bowman, Mrs.   Mr. Bowman's stout, ill-tempered wife. She takes care of the inner workings of the express office that she and her husband manage, while he delivers packages throughout the town and the surrounding region. Mr. and Mrs. Bowman argue and bicker frequently. She uses his absences as the opportunity to carry on an affair with Wall, a traveling insurance salesman.

Joe, Mr.   *See* Bowman, Mr. who is referred to as Mr. Joe by the Bowmans's cook.

Minnie Maude   The 22-year-old ticket seller at the Rex Theater across the street from the express office where the Bowmans work. In her conversation with the unnamed narrator of the story, she divulges that Mrs. Bowman is having an illicit affair with a traveling insurance salesman named Wall.

Stowers, Zack   After his wife is supposedly insulted by a traveling salesman, Stowers seeks Mr. Bowman's help. Stowers beats the alleged offender with his fists while Mr. Bowman fights a second salesman, who is unfortunate enough to be with the first.

Wall   An insurance salesman. Minnie Maude tells the narrator of the story that Wall is having an affair with the wife of the story's main character, Mr. Bowman. Wall is described as a dapper-Dan type with a handsome but effeminate face.

Wiggins, Mrs.   The owner of the boardinghouse where Minnie Maude lives.

"Death Drag"
(*Collected Stories*)

This short story was first published in the January 1932 issue of *Scribner's Magazine* 91, 34–42; it was reprinted with minor revisions as "Death-Drag" in *Doctor Martino and Other Stories*, The PORTABLE FAULKNER, and *Collected Stories of William Faulkner*. For more information, *see Selected Letters of William Faulkner*, 205, 207, 278; FAULKNER IN THE UNIVERSITY, 48, 68.

SYNOPSIS

This short story concerns three barnstormers who come to a small Southern town to put on their aeronautical show of death-defying acts. Jock, the pilot, is a former World War I aviator. His two cohorts are Ginsfarb, the wing walker, and Jake, the driver. In the act, Ginsfarb hangs onto a rope ladder and leaps from the airplane into a moving car that Jake drives on the runway. As the airplane circles close to the ground, Ginsfarb grabs the ladder and pulls himself back into the aircraft in a maneuver called the "death drag."

There is an undercurrent of distrust among the three men, who are tied together by their act. Ginsfarb, who takes most of the physical risks, feels he deserves more money. The other two are more interested in making whatever they can and then leaving town before the local authorities discover that the plane is not properly licensed.

Although "Death Drag" is told from the first person point of view, from the perspective of one of the townspeople witnessing the events, the story incorporates much from Captain Warren, who knew

Jock at flight school in World War I. During the performance described in the story, the act ends in what appears to be tragedy, but which turns out to be almost slapstick humor. As Ginsfarb hangs from the ladder, he demands to know how much money he will get, but Jake refuses to tell him. The plane circles again, and again the argument between the hanging acrobat and the driver takes place. As the plane climbs to circle around once more, Ginsfarb lets go of the ladder and falls to the ground. The onlookers are horrified, but, miraculously, Ginsfarb hits the rotted roof of an old barn, falls into a hayloft, and emerges with only a deep cut on his face and a ripped coat. The pilot lands and punches Ginsfarb. Captain Warren gives them money and sends them on their way, still arguing.

CRITICAL COMMENTARY

In response to a question at the University of Virginia, Faulkner explained that "Death Drag" is a story about "a human being in conflict with his environment and his time. This man who hated flying, but that was what he had to do, simply because he wanted to make a little money" (*Faulkner in the University*, 68). Faulkner's characterization in the short story, particularly that of Ginsfarb, has drawn critical attention. IRVING HOWE, who judges the story "a small masterpiece," comments that the focus of "Death Drag" is on one figure, "a Jewish merchant whom bankruptcy has driven to the extreme resort of stunt jumping." Willing to risk his life again and again, Ginsfarb, according to Howe, appears as "a large aching figure of modern loneliness, Jew and stunt jumper, alien by birth and need" (*William Faulkner: A Critical Study*, 220). Faulkner's artistic exploitation of anti-Semitic stereotypes has also attracted critical attention.

HELPFUL RESOURCES

Theresa M. Towner, and James B. Carothers, *Reading Faulkner: Collected Stories*, 107–112; and Diane Brown Jones, *A Reader's Guide to the Short Stories of William Faulkner*, 204–220.

CHARACTERS

Black   He is the driver of the car that brings the aviators into JEFFERSON from the rudimentary airfield on the edge of town.

Ginsfarb   He is the wing walker in the story. Ginsfarb is called Demon Duncan in the printed advertisements for the air show that he, Jock, and Jake put on in small Southern towns. As explained by Jock to his former Royal Flying Corps mate, Captain Warren, Ginsfarb throws himself from the wing of the aircraft (a trick called the death drop), hangs from beneath the aircraft at the end of a rope ladder, jumps to the roof of a car, and then once more grabs the rope ladder and pulls himself back up to the airplane (called the death drag). Ginsfarb feels that he is underpaid for the risks he takes, and the story revolves around his insistence on being paid more money. At the end of the story he goes on strike, more or less, and jumps from the airplane. Miraculously, Ginsfarb crashes through the rotted roof of an old barn and lands safely in a hayloft; he sustains only a cut on the face and a ripped coat.

Harris   He rents his car to the touring aviators for the "death drag" stunt.

Jake   He is the third member of the barnstorming troupe in the story. Jake is the man who drives the car that Ginsfarb leaps onto from a rope ladder suspended beneath the airplane.

Jock   A veteran World War I aviator with shaky nerves, Jock is the pilot of Ginsfarb's stunt plane. He is a ne'er-do-well barnstormer, badly dressed in dirty overalls, traveling the small towns of the South, staging air shows with his friends Ginsfarb and Jake. At one of the towns where Jock lands, he is greeted by Captain Warren, another World War I veteran, whom Jock had known in flight training school.

Jones   He is the secretary of the Fair Association in JEFFERSON. One of the stuntmen seeks him out to arrange details of the air show.

Vernon   He is a waiter in the restaurant where Jock tells Captain Warren about the ups and downs of his work as a stunt pilot.

Warren, Captain   He is a former member of the Royal Flying Corps who had trained as a pilot in

Canada, where he met Jock. He and Jock meet again in the small southern town when Jock and two friends, Ginsfarb and Jake, come to put on an air show; he is very hospitable to Jock. Captain Warren significantly adds to the narrative line of the story. (He also appears in KNIGHT'S GAMBIT.)

"Delta Autumn" (Uncollected Stories)

Short story, first published in the May–June 1942 issue of *Story* and significantly revised to appear as the sixth of the seven chapters in Go DOWN, MOSES (1942).

SYNOPSIS

This hunting story is set in *circa* 1940 in what little remains of the big woods—it is now a 200-mile car ride from JEFFERSON to reach the hunting grounds. Isaac McCaslin, an old man who is known throughout YOKNAPATAWPHA COUNTY as "Uncle Ike," accompanies a group of younger men on the hunt. One of the men, Don Boyd, typically uses these trips to rendezvous with a woman with whom he is having an affair: Thus the hunters joke about hunting "does." On this trip, however, Boyd is determined to end what has become a troublesome relationship with the woman. However, instead of courageously facing her with his decision, he leaves some money along with a one-word message—"No"—for Uncle Ike to deliver to her when she shows up at the camp. When Uncle Ike meets and talks with the young woman, he is shocked to learn not only that she is pregnant with Boyd's child but also that she is part black. Now it is Ike's turn to say no: He advises her to return north and marry into her own race. The woman rebukes Ike for his attitude: "Old man," she asks him, "have you lived so long that you have forgotten all you ever knew or felt or even heard about love?" After the woman has left, the hunting party returns to camp with word that Boyd has shot a deer. Ike knows without being told that it is a doe.

CRITICAL COMMENTARY

While the issue of race becomes the principal focus of "Delta Autumn" as revised for Go Down, Moses, race is only a subtext of the original story. The main subject of the first version, as the title symbolizes, is the diminishment of the big woods and the changed nature of the hunters who frequent them. Uncle Ike recalls the old days when the wilderness had been only 30 miles from Jefferson, the hunters traveled in wagons instead of cars, and the woods were filled with bear, deer, and wild turkey. But now the woods are disappearing and, just as disappointing to Ike, the hunters seem to be lesser men than those with whom he hunted in his youth. These hunters are not as committed to the woods and the hunting; they had just as soon use a shotgun as a rifle, and they have no regrets about shooting does. In this connection, Faulkner's story invites comparison with John Steinbeck's "The Leader of the People," in which another aging character laments the decline from the heroism and adventure of the past.

Much of the critical discussion of "Delta Autumn" focuses on Uncle Ike's treatment of the young woman. Some critics have seen in Ike's attitude a compromise with segregation. Certainly, by today's standards, Ike's advice to the woman appears racist, but the setting of the story is the South of the early 1940s, and in that context Ike no doubt thought his advice to be not only practical but also in the best interest of the woman and her child. Significantly, Uncle Ike's harshest criticism is not directed to the woman but to Boyd's irresponsibility and cowardice. Faulkner himself regarded Ike both as a man of his time and a passive figure. Passivity, according to the novelist, explains Ike's bleak comment that racial harmony and justice may be a thousand years in the future (*see also Faulkner in the University*, 246).

When Faulkner reworked "Delta Autumn" for inclusion in Go Down, Moses, he made a number of major changes, most notably converting the character of Don Boyd into Carothers ("Roth") Edmonds and making the mulatto mistress into a descendant, like Ike and Roth, of old Lucius Quintus Carothers McCaslin. Thus the twin actions of miscegenation and incest committed decades earlier by Ike's grandfather have now been repeated by

Ike's cousin Roth. Through a significant addition, Faulkner somewhat softened Ike's rejection of the young woman by having the old hunter make a gift to the woman of a prized hunting horn. These and other changes to the original version of the story were designed to make the story conform to the overall theme of GO DOWN, MOSES: the problematic and tragic legacy of race in American history.

CHARACTERS

Boyd, Don A member of the hunting party who is having an affair with a mulatto woman. Wanting to break off the affair, Boyd leaves money and a message for Uncle Ike McCaslin to deliver to the woman when she shows up at the hunting camp.

For a list of the other characters in this story, *see* the entry on GO DOWN, MOSES.

Doctor Martino and Other Stories

A collection of 14 short stories published by SMITH & HAAS in April 1934. With the exception of "Black Music" and "The LEG," all of the stories had been previously published: "HONOR" (July 1930), "FOX HUNT" (September 1931), "Doctor Martino" (November 1931), "DEATH DRAG" (January 1932), "TURN ABOUT" (*See* "TURNABOUT") (March 5, 1932), "Smoke" (April 1932), "Mountain Victory" (December 1932), "THERE WAS A QUEEN" (January 1933), "BEYOND" (September 1933), "Elly" (February 1934), "Pennsylvania Station" (February 1934), and "WASH" (February 1934). (For further publication details, *see* Appendix.)

Doctor Martino and Other Stories was Faulkner's second collection of stories to be published; the first was *These 13*. In his study of Faulkner's works, MICHAEL MILLGATE comments that with the exception of "Wash" and "The Hound," the stories in this second collection do not show "Faulkner at his best" (*The Achievement of William Faulkner*, 265). As JOSEPH BLOTNER points out, "The reviews . . . tended to go to either extreme" (*Faulkner: A Biography*, 330–331); in general, however, they were unfavorable. A few of the stories were incorporated into larger works.

"Don Giovanni" (Uncollected Stories)

Written sometime about 1925, this short story was posthumously published in *Uncollected Stories of William Faulkner*. Faulkner often recycled elements from earlier works into later ones. In "Don Giovanni," Morrison and Herb respectively are obvious prototypes for Dawson Fairchild and Ernest Talliaferro in MOSQUITOES. For further information, *see Uncollected Stories of William Faulkner*, 705.

SYNOPSIS

"Don Giovanni" is a humorous short story about the self-deceptions of Herb, a vain middle-aged widower who, tired of celibacy and worried about his thinning hair, decides to go a-courting. He prides himself on what he thinks is his thorough understanding of the psychology of women, mostly gained from years working as a buyer of women's clothing for a large department store. When visiting his friend Morrison (who unsuccessfully tries to avoid him), Herb discusses his tactical plan for an evening out with Miss Steinbauer. He tells Morrison that the ingredients of romantic success are boldness and indifference. Enamored of his own schemes, Herb is oblivious to Morrison's observations and cynicism. His bold plan to win over Miss Steinbauer by making her jealous fails miserably; he returns to Morrison's apartment to recount his moves and ask where he went wrong. Finally, at home, he decides that he has not been bold and cruel enough. He telephones Morrison to share this insight with him, and as he is explaining that he has to be cruel and brutal, a woman on Morrison's line sarcastically retorts: "'You tell 'em, big boy; treat 'em rough'" (*Uncollected Stories of William Faulkner*, 488). The story ends with Herb holding a dead phone in his hand and the round receiver staring him in the mouth.

CRITICAL COMMENTARY

Throughout the story, Faulkner incorporates obvious Freudian allusions to sexuality and suppressed emotions; he also subtly alludes to T. S. Eliot's poem "The Love Song of J. Alfred Prufrock" (references to Herb's thinning hair, for instance, echo Prufrock's self-descriptions). The last line of the story—"A click: [Herb] held dead gutta percha in his hand and dead gutta percha was a round Ó, staring at his mouth" (488)—resonates with poetic justice. Faulkner's poignant use of the term gutta percha, a plant whose sap (a latex also called gutta percha) is used to insulate marine telegraph cables and other wires, ironically underscores the title of the short story and Herb's utter failure in his understanding of women. The term also ironically underscores Herb's lack of communication—he is holding a "dead gutta percha" (a metonymy for telephone)—and positions him, like Prufrock at the end of his love song, lingering "in the chambers of the sea" until "human voices wake us, and we drown" ("The Love Song of J. Alfred Prufrock," in T. S. Eliot, *The Waste Land and Other Poems* [New York: Harvest, 1962], 9).

CHARACTERS

Herb (Herbie)   He is the main character in the short story, a wholesale women's-clothing buyer for a large department store and a lonely widower. Vain, worried about his thinning hair, and tired of celibacy, Herb decides to practice his psychology of women on the unsuspecting Miss Steinbauer. He ignorantly assumes that a woman falls for a bold and indifferent man. Instead of feeling humiliated when his plans fail, he thinks he has learned from the fiasco and decides, as he incredulously explains on the phone to the disinterested Morrison, to try harder next time by adding cruelty to his boldness. The short story ends with Herb holding a dead phone line and displaying a remarkable insensitivity to women. Although confronted with his own folly, Herb is unaware of his misunderstanding of women. (In depicting the character of Ernest Talliaferro in MOSQUITOES, Faulkner draws on his treatment of Herb.)

Morrison   He is Herb's disinterested friend and sounding board in the short story. Although he tries to give advice to Herb, Morrison reluctantly tolerates his friend's fantasies about how to seduce women.

Steinbauer, Miss   She is the woman who goes out on a date with Herb, the story's main character, and pushes him over for another man. (Faulkner based the character Jenny Steinbauer in MOSQUITOES on Miss Steinbauer; *also see Uncollected Stories of William Faulkner, 705.*)

"Dry September" (Collected Stories)

Short story that first appeared in *Scribner's Magazine* (January 1931) and was included in *These 13* (1931).

SYNOPSIS

On a stifling evening that follows 62 days of drought, the barber Hawkshaw tries to calm an agitated group by insisting that Will Mayes, the reported attacker, is a good man. This attempt proves futile and the mob, led by the war veteran John McLendon, rushes off to take action; Hawkshaw follows them, hoping to discourage mob violence. The viewpoint shifts to the white spinster Minnie Cooper, the apparent rape victim. Her life, empty and idle, has been one of romantic disappointments. The story implies that she has possibly made up the story of the assault to gain attention for herself. The racists seize Mayes, and when the black man attempts to fight off his attackers, Hawkshaw joins the others in striking him. As the kidnappers drive Mayes to an isolated spot, Hawkshaw leaps from the car and walks back toward town. On the way he is passed by the returning car, this time without Mayes. That same evening, Miss Cooper walks with friends to the cinema. During the film she becomes hysterical and is taken home. McLendon also returns home, where he treats his wife with brutality.

CRITICAL COMMENTARY

Widely acknowledged as one of Faulkner's best stories, "Dry September" employs a technique that forces the characters, and the readers, to try to construct what actually occurred from fragments of gossip, ambiguous hearsay, and things left unsaid.

Was Miss Minnie actually raped, and, if so, was Will Mayes the culprit? Why does Hawkshaw strike Mayes, when he seems to have accompanied the mob to seek to protect the black man? What happens to Mayes? What accounts for McLendon's violent attitude and behavior? What role, if any, does the weather play in the characters' actions? What accounts for Miss Minnie's nervous breakdown? All such questions demonstrate the ambiguity and irresolution that characterize the narrative.

"Dry September" is one of Faulkner's most frequently anthologized stories, and many critics list it among his finest short stories. Hans Skei calls it "classical in its tragic intensity." Joseph Reed commends the way "atmosphere, metaphor, theme, character, structure, merge in frustration, compulsion, entrapment, and isolation." John Vickery and others have linked it to an archetypal scapegoat ritual, as described by James Frazer in *The Golden Bough.*

CHARACTERS

Butch He tries to inflame the men in a barbershop against Will Mayes, a black man who is accused of attacking a middle-aged white woman, Miss Minnie Cooper.

Cooper, Miss Minnie A spinster of about 40, she is said to have been "attacked, insulted, frightened" by a black man named Will Mayes, and a lynch mob forms to avenge her.

Hawkshaw The barber who tries to talk the leader of the lynch mob out of murdering Will Mayes, who is accused of attacking a white spinster. Hawkshaw also appears in the short story "HAIR," in which his name is given as Henry Stribling.

McLendon, Captain (Jackson) He leads a lynch party. In *The TOWN* and *The MANSION*, he is a cotton buyer who organizes a JEFFERSON, MISSISSIPPI, company of soldiers known as Sartoris Rifles during World War I.

Mayes, Will A mob abducts and apparently lynches him over Hawkshaw's protest when Mayes, who is black, is accused of assaulting a white spinster, Minnie Cooper.

"Dull Tale" (Uncollected Stories)

This short story essentially reworks the plot of "The BIG SHOT." "Dull Tale," however, is told from the third-person omniscient point of view, concentrating on Dr. Gavin Blount, a relatively minor character in "The Big Shot." "Dull Tale" was written sometime near 1929 or 1930 but published posthumously in *Uncollected Stories of William Faulkner.*

SYNOPSIS

As in the earlier story, the crux of "Dull Tale" is wangling an invitation to the annual debutante coming-out party for Miss Laverne Martin (referred to as Miss Wrennie in "The Big Shot"). Miss Martin's father, Dal Martin, is a wealthy self-made contractor and political boss. He first attempts to get his daughter invited to the Nonconnah Guards ball (called the Chickasaw Guards ball in "The Big Shot") by offering a cash bribe to Dr. Blount, head of the Nonconnah Guards. After this ploy fails, Martin offers to build a new armory; this too is spurned. Finally Martin offers to build an art gallery for the city of MEMPHIS and to name it in memory of Dr. Blount's grandfather, a hero of the Confederate army who was killed riding with NATHAN BEDFORD FORREST. This enticement garners the coveted invitation. Unlike in "The Big Shot," in "Dull Tale" Miss Laverne Martin attends the ball but is snubbed and treated shabbily. (In "The Big Shot," she never gets to the ball because she is accidently killed by the bootlegger Popeye who runs her over while driving a carful of whiskey to Mr. Martin's house.) Dr. Blount, who had predicted that Miss Martin would not fit in and would not have a good time, is filled with shame at the self-knowledge of "selling out." As in "The Big Shot," Dr. Blount cannot live with his guilt and kills himself. Self-conscious and upset, Miss Martin leaves the ball before it ends and goes home where she cries on her father's lap. Reflecting more his own ambitions than sympathy for his daughter, Martin, in the story's last lines, says to her: "'There now. The fool. The durn fool. We could have done something with this town, me and him'" (546).

CRITICAL COMMENTARY

Faulkner's reworking of the material in "Dull Tale" is a definite improvement on "The Big Shot." By using a third-person point of view and the central consciousness of Dr. Blount, Faulkner, as James Ferguson points out, "turned the work into a very characteristic study of an obsessed, solipsistic consciousness in the process of discovering some unpleasant truths about himself" (*Faulkner's Short Fiction*, 101). In "Dull Tale," as in "The Big Shot," Faulkner introduces themes that are found in his later fiction: greed, corruption, the quest for power, and the desire for social acceptance or respectability. The character traits of Popeye and Miss Laverne Martin anticipate those of Popeye and Temple Drake in SANCTUARY; and Dal Martin foreshadows Thomas Sutpen in ABSALOM, ABSALOM! and Flem Snopes in the SNOPES TRILOGY.

CHARACTERS

Blount, Dr. Gavin   He is responsible for inviting the young women of Memphis to make their debuts at the annual Nonconnah Guards Ball. Bribed by Dal Martin, a socially inferior self-made millionaire and political boss, to put his daughter on the very exclusive list of debutantes, Dr. Blount comes to regret his decision and ends up killing himself.

Dr. Blount's family heritage can be traced back to a grandfather who was killed riding in the Confederate cavalry with general Nathan Bedford Forrest during the Civil War. (*Also see* "The BIG SHOT" and "A RETURN"; Dr. Blount anticipates the characters of Gail Hightower in LIGHT IN AUGUST and Horace Benbow in SARTORIS and *Sanctuary*.)

Martin, Dal   A major character in the short story, Martin is a newly made millionaire and political boss who, like other Faulkner characters, desperately seeks social respectability. He bribes Dr. Blount to put his daughter Laverne's name on the prestigious debutante list of Memphis socialites. A sharecropper's son, Martin was born into poverty, and the treatment he received as a child from a landowner spurred him

on to become wealthy. His purpose, as he explains to Dr. Blount, is to give his daughter a better start in life than he had so she in turn can do the same for her children. (Martin foreshadows Thomas Sutpen in ABSALOM, ABSALOM! and of Flem Snopes in the Snopes trilogy; *also see* "The BIG SHOT.")

Martin, Miss Laverne   She is Dal Martin's spoiled and self-centered daughter. Her father bribes Dr. Blount to place her name on the invitation list for Memphis debutantes, but when she attends the Nonconnah Guards Ball, she does not enjoy the evening—as Dr. Blount had anticipated—and leaves before it is over, an indication that she is not welcome into Memphis society. She arrives home in tears. (*Also see* "The BIG SHOT" where she is referred to as Miss Wrennie. Laverne foreshadows Temple Drake in SANCTUARY and REQUIEM FOR A NUN and, like Temple, tends toward recklessness.)

"Elly" (Collected Stories)

Short story, the first version of which, titled "Selvage" or "Salvage," was a revision of a story originally written by Faulkner's wife, (Lida) ESTELLE OLDHAM FAULKNER. "Elly" first appeared in *Story* (February 1934) and was included in DOCTOR MARTINO AND OTHER STORIES (1934).

SYNOPSIS

The daughter of a respectable family in JEFFERSON, MISSISSIPPI, Elly fluctuates between boredom with the monotony of her small-town existence, despair over her future, and rebellion against the Southern way of life personified by her apparently malevolent grandmother. After flirting with numerous beaus, Elly fixates on and pursues Paul de Montigny, a young man of black ancestry who insists he will never marry her. She uses Paul to taunt her grandmother. Eventually Elly becomes engaged to Philip, a suitable young man with a future in banking. When her mother asks Elly to go with Philip to bring back her grandmother for the wedding, Elly instead decides to make the trip with Paul, and Philip agrees to the substitution. Stopping on the drive to Mills City, Elly and Paul sexually consummate their relationship, but Paul still refuses to marry her. Over her grandmother's strong opposition, Paul spends the night in Elly's uncle's house before their return to Jefferson the next day. On the drive back, Elly grabs the steering wheel and sends the car over a precipice. She is thrown free, while Paul and her grandmother are killed.

CRITICAL COMMENTARY

Faulkner biographer Frederick Karl believes "Elly" is loosely based on the triangle between Faulkner, Estelle, and her first husband Cornell Franklin. Many scholars compare Elly's frustrated and willful character to such other Faulkner women as Emily Grierson, Candace (Caddy) Compson, Temple Drake Stevens, and Minnie Cooper. Edmond Volpe considers the story a "brilliantly wrought" study of a woman "torn by irreconcilable forces unravelling into madness."

CHARACTERS

Ailanthia Elly's grandmother. Aware that Elly's lover Paul has black blood, Ailanthia is deeply disturbed by the connection. Elly hates her grandmother and urges Paul to kill her. In the end, Elly causes the car crash that takes the old woman's life.

de Montigny, Paul A young man, part African American, he becomes the lover of the bored, restless JEFFERSON, MISSISSIPPI, girl Elly but refuses to marry her. She retaliates by causing the crash of de Montigny's car, which kills him and a second passenger, Elly's grandmother. Elly herself survives the crash.

Elly (Ailanthia) Bored and restless, she drops her fiancé, an assistant bank cashier in JEFFERSON, MISSISSIPPI, for Paul de Montigny. When de Montigny refuses to marry her, she causes the car crash that kills him and her disapproving grandmother, whom she detests.

Philip He is an assistant bank cashier in JEFFERSON, MISSISSIPPI, engaged to Elly. She is in love with Paul de Montigny, who refuses to marry her.

Elmer

The title of an unfinished novel Faulkner began to write while in Paris in 1925. A typescript was published posthumously in *Mississippi Quarterly* 36 (summer 1983): 343–447, and later, in a limited edition, edited by Dianne L. Cox with a foreword by James B. Meriwether, by Seajay Press of Northport, Alabama, in 1983. Faulkner mentioned putting the novel aside in a September 1925 letter to his mother. Although Faulkner abandoned the work, he appropriated ideas from it in MOSQUITOES, *If I Forget Thee, Jerusalem* (*The WILD PALMS*), and *The HAMLET*; in 1935, this unfinished work provided the basis of the short story "A Portrait of Elmer" (posthumously published in *Uncollected Stories of William Faulkner*, 610–641).

For more information, *see Selected Letters of William Faulkner*, 13, 16, 17, 20, 31, 32, and 63; Thomas L. McHaney, "The Elmer Papers: Faulkner's Comic Portraits of the Artist" in *Mississippi Quarterly* 26 (summer 1973): 281–311, or in *A Faulkner Miscellany*, edited by James B. Meriwether (Jackson: University Press of Mississippi, 1974), 37–69; Cleanth Brooks, *William Faulkner: Toward Yoknapatawpha and Beyond* (Baton Rouge: Louisiana State University Press, 1990), 100–128; and *Uncollected Stories of William Faulkner*, 710.

Essays, Speeches, and Public Lectures by William Faulkner

Collection of Faulkner's articles, speeches, forewords, book reviews, and public lectures, edited by JAMES B. MERIWETHER. The collection was published by RANDOM HOUSE in 1966. In addition to several public letters on various topics, a few book reviews (including one of ERNEST HEMINGWAY's *The Old Man and the Sea*), two forewords, and an introduction (including the introduction to the Modern Library edition of SANCTUARY and the foreword to *The FAULKNER READER*), the collection contains essays on various writers such as SHER-WOOD ANDERSON and ALBERT CAMUS, on Faulkner's impressions of Japan (also published in FAULKNER AT NAGANO) and of New England, and on social issues such as race relations. The speeches include his eulogy for CAROLINE BARR and his NOBEL PRIZE acceptance speech. Not included in the collection are a few unpublished public letters, early reviews, and essays Faulkner wrote when he was a student at the UNIVERSITY OF MISSISSIPPI and when he was a fledgling poet.

"Evangeline" (Uncollected Stories)

This short story was written in 1931. It introduces the doomed Sutpen family of YOKNAPATAWPHA COUNTY and forms the basis for Faulkner's novel ABSALOM, ABSALOM! (1936). Rejected by two magazines, "Evangeline" remained unpublished until 1979, when the editor and biographer JOSEPH BLOTNER included it in Uncollected Stories of William Faulkner. Faulkner wrote "Evangeline" during the intense burst of creativity that produced The SOUND AND THE FURY (1929) and AS I LAY DYING (1930). He finished the story in late June or early July, just six weeks or so before he began work on another of his major novels, LIGHT IN AUGUST (1932). In quick succession, the SATURDAY EVENING POST and Women's Home Companion turned it down.

SYNOPSIS

The story is told from the perspective of an unnamed narrator. Charles Bon is a close friend of Henry Sutpen, Judith's brother. When Henry accompanies Bon to his home in NEW ORLEANS just before the outbreak of the Civil War, he discovers secrets about his friend that make it impossible, in his view, for Bon to marry his sister. Henry returns home alone and orders Judith to break off the engagement, although he will not explain the reasons for his demand. Bon and Judith, however, marry over his objection. When the war begins, Henry and Bon join the Confederate army and are away for four years. With the South's surrender, Henry returns home with Bon's corpse—he has been killed, Henry announces, by the "last shot of the war."

Old Colonel Sutpen, Henry and Judith's father, dies in 1870. Judith dies about 1885, and her ghost is said to haunt the old house. The narrator goes out to the Sutpen place to try to unravel the mystery, and an old servant named Raby, part Indian, fathered by Colonel Sutpen, takes him upstairs to a dark, sealed room. Raby lights a candle and the narrator sees the dying Henry lying in a soiled bed. When they return downstairs, Raby tells the narrator that Bon had been married to another woman in New Orleans; she also announces that Henry is her brother. But she refuses to reveal the rest of the story.

The inquisitive narrator discovers that Henry had killed Bon, "the last shot of the war." He learns this final detail, however, only after Raby burns down the house with herself and Henry inside. A photo of Bon's New Orleans wife survives inside a fire-blackened metal case. Inspecting it, the narrator sees "all the ineradicable and tragic stamp of negro blood"—to Henry Sutpen, something worse than bigamy or divorce, and so intolerable that he saw no choice but to kill Bon for marrying his sister.

CRITICAL COMMENTARY

"Evangeline," which Faulkner extensively reworked for Absalom, Absalom!, has obvious gothic elements and, as James Ferguson points out, characteristics of the mystery or detective story, an interest that stayed with Faulkner (see Faulkner's Short Fiction, 77.) Absalom, Absalom! replaces the flip, slangy tone of the nameless narrator and his friend Don with a more objective and even sympathetic tone of Quentin Compson and his roommate Shreve (Shrevlin McCannon). The give and take between Don and the narrator and the reconstruction of details, however, anticipate Quentin and Shreve's involvement in the narration. Faulkner also adds the element of incest to the novel where Charles Bon is Thomas Sutpen's son, and thus half brother to Judith and Henry.

As Faulkner's biographer Frederick Karl notes, the title alludes to Henry Wadsworth Longfellow's poem about two lovers separated by events beyond their control. In Faulkner's telling, miscegenation, bigamy, and murder keep Judith Sutpen and her suitor Charles Bon apart.

CHARACTERS

Bon, Charles Henry Sutpen's roommate at the University of Mississippi. When accompanying Bon on a visit home to NEW ORLEANS, Henry finds out that Bon is married and that his wife is partly black; he leaves for home, cutting his stay short. Meanwhile, Bon had met Henry's sister Judith, and against Henry's objections, marries her before the two go to war. When the South surrenders, Henry kills Bon—"the last shot of the war"—and carts his body home to Judith to bury. (*Also see* Charles Bon in the Character entries following *ABSALOM, ABSALOM!*)

(Bon, Mrs. Charles) Although not given a name in the story, she is Charles Bon's NEW ORLEANS wife with whom he has a son. An ostentatious and vainglorious woman, she travels with her nine-year-old son to Judith's home in rural Mississippi to visit Bon's grave. She does not know that Judith was also married to her husband. Once she arrives, Judith immediately recognizes that she is partly black, a suspicion that she certainly had when she saw the photo Bon kept of her in the metal case that Judith found.

Don An amateur artist by avocation, an architect by vocation, Don is the narrator's friend. While on vacation and sketching in the Mississippi countryside, Don becomes intrigued with the story surrounding the Sutpen plantation and wires the narrator to come and investigate.

Raby The old servant the unnamed narrator meets at the ruined Sutpen plantation. She is half Indian and a half sister to Henry and Judith Sutpen. Although she informs the unnamed narrator of the events that transpired (she needed to unburden her mind), he is left to figure out on his own the

reason why Henry killed Charles Bon, his sister's husband. After Raby burns down the Sutpen home with Henry, an old man now, dying in his bedroom, the narrator comes to understand Henry's motive when he sees the features in the picture of Bon's NEW ORLEANS wife in a metal case that Judith had hammered shut.

Sutpen, Colonel Henry and Judith's father. After fighting for the Confederacy, he returns home in defeat and dies five years later in 1870. He was never fully aware of Henry's opposition to Judith's marriage to Charles Bon. (*Also see* Thomas Sutpen in the Character entries following *ABSALOM, ABSALOM!*)

Sutpen, Henry Colonel Sutpen's son and Judith's brother. Henry is Charles Bon's roommate at the University of Mississippi and his close friend, until he finds out that Bon, who is engaged to marry Judith, is not only already married but married to a woman who is partly black. When the Civil War breaks out, the two young men, however, ride off together to fight for the Confederacy. Henry fires "the last shot of the war"; he kills Bon and transports his body back to Judith to bury. He leaves the night of his arrival, but returns years later when Judith is dying. The "ghost" in the story refers to Henry's 40-year furtive presence in the Sutpen house. Although by the end of the story he is dying an old man, his half sister, Raby, an old servant, sets the house ablaze, and both, of course, die. (*Also see* Henry Sutpen in the Character entries following *ABSALOM, ABSALOM!*)

Sutpen, Judith Colonel Sutpen's daughter and Henry's sister. Through her brother, she meets Charles Bon and later, against her brother's objections, marries him the very day he leaves with Henry to fight for the Confederacy in the Civil War. During the years Bon is away, Judith receives letters from him and keeps a room ready, anticipating his return. But when he arrives, he is dead, killed by Henry, who leaves the very same night that he arrives. When preparing for his burial, Judith comes across a small metal case with a picture of

Bon's NEW ORLEANS wife, a woman with black features. Realizing that she had been betrayed, Judith hammers the case shut, but, nonetheless, writes the woman to inform her of the death. Although very poor, Judith, sometime after the death of her father in 1870, begins to send this woman money. A year after Bon's New Orleans wife visits with their nine-year-old son, Judith dies, but not before she writes to her brother, who returns home for good. (*Also see* Judith Sutpen, in the Character entries following ABSALOM, ABSALOM!)

unnamed narrator A newspaper writer by profession. While on vacation in Mississippi, his friend Don wires him to come and inquire about the "ghost" haunting the antebellum home once owned by Colonel Sutpen. The narrator investigates and with Raby's help learns about the Sutpen family and discovers the purported ghost, the dying Henry Sutpen.

Fable, A

This is Faulkner's 16th novel, published on August 2, 1954, by RANDOM HOUSE; it is dedicated to his daughter, Jill. Faulkner spent about nine years writing *A Fable* and considered it to be his most significant work. The novel incorporates a revision of NOTES ON A HORSETHIEF, published in 1951. During the time of writing *A Fable*, Faulkner also wrote and published other works including INTRUDER IN THE DUST and REQUIEM FOR A NUN. In 1955, *A Fable* received both the Pulitzer Prize for fiction and the National Book Award.

SYNOPSIS

The plot of the novel is fairly simple. Sometime in late May 1918, in the fourth year of trench warfare in France during World War I, a French regiment, for reasons that are never made particularly clear, is ordered to attack a small hill held by the Germans. The commanding officer is certain the attack will fail. Instead, it never takes place. The regiment mutinies and simply, completely, adamantly refuses to leave its trenches to make any

attack whatsoever. Major General Charles Gragnon, the division commander who passed along the order to attack despite knowing it would be disastrous, orders the arrest of the entire regiment and demands that every man in it be shot for cowardice or disobedience to orders. He knows that his career is also over, and he is fearful that the war will be lost as well. For an anxious hour, while the mutinous regiment is placed under arrest, disarmed, and withdrawn, General Gragnon expects a massive German counterattack in this sector. But the Germans do not take advantage of the weakness in the French line. Indeed, peace, or rather peacefulness, breaks out along the whole front, and within hours of the troops' refusal to attack, all the French troops are disengaged. They do not pull back from their trenches anywhere, but they stop firing, stop probing, stop trying

William Faulkner's draft of the "Tuesday" outline of the novel *A Fable*, c. 1952. Faulkner wrote these notes and others on his study wall in his home at Rowan Oak. *(Brodsky Collection, Center for Faulkner Studies, Southeast Missouri State University)*

to kill the Germans. The British and American troops flanking the French line also stand down, and the Germans, mysteriously, do not attack. They too become inactive, and an unintended armistice occurs.

An investigation of the incident reveals that the mutiny was incited or inspired by 13 soldiers in the French army, although four of them, including their leader, Corporal Stefan, whose last name is never given, are not French nationals. (Throughout the novel, Stefan is mostly referred to simply as "the Corporal.") For four years up and down the lines, these soldiers have advocated peace or a kind of military civil disobedience and have traveled as a unit to visit with the Americans and British troops as well as the French and even, it would seem, with the Germans. The Corporal's message is simple: "Thou shalt not kill."

The French higher command imprisons the regiment and segregates the ringleaders. The Corporal is brought before the French commander-in-chief (called the Old General) in a scene that CLEANTH BROOKS compares to the meeting of the Grand Inquisitor and Christ in Dostoyevsky's novel *The Brothers Karamazov* (*see William Faulkner: Toward Yoknapatawpha and Beyond,* 231–232). The old marshal recognizes the Corporal as his own son, but he is unable to tempt him or steer him away from his mission of peace. In the end, the old marshal is compelled to order the execution of the Corporal and of Major General Gragnon; for the latter's sake, his death is made to appear the result of an enemy bullet on the field of battle, an honorable way to die.

CRITICAL COMMENTARY

As Faulkner mentions in his acknowledgments to the novel, the basic idea for *A Fable* goes back to the scriptwriter and producer William Bacher and the director Henry Hathaway. *Also see Faulkner at the University,* 27, where, in response to a question at the University of Virginia, he more or less says the same thing but makes an unmistakable allusion to the allegory or parable found in "The Grand Inquisitor" section of Dostoyevsky's *The Brothers Karamazov,* one of Faulkner's favorite novels, according to his biographer JOSEPH BLOTNER

(*Faulkner,* 588). In Dostoyevsky's tale of the Grand Inquisitor, Christ returns during the Inquisition only to be rejected.

The title of *A Fable* itself offers the key to its understanding and lends perspective to the reader. Although it contains many passages of powerful, and even horrifying, realism, the novel is an intended fable or parable with obvious tall-tale elements. But the blending of the fabulous and realistic, according to Cleanth Brooks, is unsuccessful because it is not always "clear where the fabulous leaves off and the realistic begins" (*William Faulkner: Toward Yoknapatawpha and Beyond,* Baton Rouge, 230–231).

A Fable is complex and to some critics a masterpiece. In a review of the novel published in *Perspectives U.S.A.* (No. 10, 1955), the literary critic and writer Delmore Schwartz called it "a unique fulfilment of Faulkner's genius" (127). Other reviews, however, were negative, and many critics thought that Faulkner's ambitions were too lofty. The novel uses techniques of religious allegory and employs numerous religious symbols. There are obvious parallels between the figure of the Corporal and Christ. Readers, for example, readily note that the Corporal has 12 disciples and is also followed by three women, one named Marthe (also called Magda), one Marya, and one unnamed prostitute from Marseilles—like the Martha, Mary, and Mary Magdalene of the Gospels. When the Corporal is brought before the old marshal, he is tempted, as Jesus was during his 40 days in the desert. Further, evidence is presented that the Corporal has died and been buried at least three times during the war. Polchek, one of the Corporal's disciples, a Judas figure, betrays him; another called Pierre Bouc, like Peter, denies knowing him at all. In Corporal Stefan's death scene, Faulkner continues other Christ parallels. The Corporal is 33 when he is executed. He is shot to death, standing tied to a fence post between two thieves, Lapin and Casse-Tête ("Horse"). When he falls dead into a shallow trench, a coil of barbed wire forms a crown of metal thorns about his head; his body is given to his fiancée (the prostitute from Marseilles) and sisters, who bury it in a cavelike sepulcher on the family farm, and it mysteriously disappears from the grave during an artillery barrage. All of this action takes place within a week. The order to attack is given on Monday; by 3 in the afternoon on Tuesday, the fighting has ceased; by Wednesday, Corporal Stefan is caught (after Polchek betrays him) and put in prison; and by Friday, the corporal is executed. Like an epic, the novel opens *in medias res,* on the Wednesday after the mutiny.

Faulkner, also, much like Mark Twain, uses elements of the American tall tale in *A Fable*. A subplot of the novel concerns a British soldier to whom all the other men of his regiment are indebted. Before the war, this soldier had been a groom for a trainer of a race horse. Through various outrageously unbelievable events, the soldier and a black stable worker (*see* Rev. Toby Sutterfield) contrive to steal an injured race horse and run it at small tracks throughout America. The thoroughbred is supposedly a miracle horse, capable of winning races while running on only three good legs, but it can also be seen as a metaphor, which, according to Schwartz, Faulkner adeptly incorporates into his overall concerns of the novel: "The horse is . . . the cause of belief and nobility in other human beings just as the illiterate corporal is, an identification which does not become explicit until, after much mystery, the corporal's true nature is made clear" ("Faulkner's 'A Fable,'" *Perspectives U.S.A.*, 130).

Another character whose story is rife with hyperbole is the runner, a British soldier who had risen from the ranks to become an officer. Then after about seven months, he tried unsuccessfully to resign his commission, so while on leave the runner makes such a public spectacle of himself that he is broken back into the ranks. It is the runner who discovers a scheme that resembles another tall tale. In order to arrange a secret parley between the Allies and a German general, the Allies provide blank ammunition for hundreds of antiaircraft guns and for a flight of three SE5 fighter planes. The German general flies to the meeting through this fabricated "safe" corridor to discuss with his enemy counterparts how to get the fighting to begin again—how, in short, to undo the Corporal's work.

In a final scene entitled "Tomorrow" (a title with an apocalyptic overtone), one last tall tale or fable is retold. After the end of the war, a squad of 12 soldiers, commanded by Landry, a fussy sergeant, is sent to a battered fortress in the lines around Verdun. Their orders are to find and bring back to Paris a body of a French soldier unidentified and unidentifiable by name, regiment, or rank to be buried with honor in the Tomb of the Unknown Soldier with a perpetual flame. The soldiers complete the first part of their mission, but the body they find they sell to a woman who claims that the soldier is her son. Needing another body to fill the coffin they carry, the soldiers, led by Picklock, use the watch they stole from a dead German officer to buy a replacement body found by a farmer in the nearby village of Vienne-la-pucelle. This replacement is the Corporal, unwittingly or miraculously disinterred to become the honored Unknown Soldier, underscoring the anonymity of war. This scene demonstrates Faulkner's use of irony in *A Fable*, sometimes heavy-handed irony.

Faulkner began to write the novel in December 1944, during the last winter of World War II, and completed it in November 1953, just after the end of the Korean conflict. In 1950 Faulkner was awarded the NOBEL PRIZE IN LITERATURE, and in his acceptance speech expressed some of his beliefs about humanity and the role of the novelist. *A Fable* reflects these beliefs and concerns, as MICHAEL MILLGATE explains in his study of Faulkner: "the whole novel is in the nature of a gloss upon this most famous of Faulkner's public statements. It is thus a 'committed' novel, a book with a message. . . ." (*William Faulkner*, 99). The novel shows the deep disgust Faulkner felt toward war as a solution to human struggles and as act of statecraft. It also shows his mistrust of political and military leaders and displays a type of pacifism reminiscent of Leo Tolstoy's.

In his review of *A Fable*, MALCOLM COWLEY observed that the novel "is based on a contradiction between feeling and logic. The feeling of the novel is deeply pacifist. . . . Faulkner's logic, on the other hand, says that some wars are right, or at least necessary, and that the men who refuse to have any part in them are fools. If the corporal is a fool, he cannot be truly Christlike" ("Faulkner's Powerful New Novel: Biblical Overtones, Daring Symbols," *New York Herald Tribune Books*, August 1, 1954, 8).

For more information, *see Faulkner at Nagano*, 7, 9, 23, 46–47, 50–51, 129–30, 159–60; *Faulkner in the University*, 25–26, 27, 51–52, 62–63, 85–86; and *Selected Letters of William Faulkner*. Faulkner recorded a portion of the novel for Caedmon (TC-1035).

CHARACTERS

Angelique She is a blind woman who leads a crippled man and takes a child from Marthe. She accuses Marthe's half brother Stefan (the Corporal) of murdering Frenchmen. Although it is not entirely clear from the text, it appears that the child is related to Angelique, and not to Marthe or her sister Marya.

Ball, Albert (1896–1917) He is a British World War I flying ace referred to in *A Fable*. Ball, Barker, Bishop, McCudden, Mannock, and Rhys Davids, were real persons mentioned in the novel, but neither he nor they appear as characters. The French aviators Fonck and Guynemer, and the German flyers Boelcke, Immelmann (it appears in the novel as *Immelman*), Richthofen, and Voss are also cited (*see* 73–74). Shot down in northern Frannce on May 7, 1917, Ball was killed before the Royal Flying Corps (RFC) of the British Army was renamed the Royal Air Force (RAF) in 1918. *See also* FLYING, FAULKNER AND.

Barker, William (1894–1930) He is an historical aviator referred to in *A Fable*. (*See* Ball, Albert.)

Beale, Colonel He is the British army officer who identifies the French army corporal Stefan as a British soldier called Boggan, whom Beale had seen killed at the Battle of Mons in 1914, four years before the setting of the novel. Beale is one of three men who confuse Stefan with other soldiers who had been already killed and buried during World War I. In this, Faulkner seems not to suggest that Stefan is immortal; instead, he seems to imply that Stefan is an Everyman, a soldier who is like all other soldiers in the ranks, even to the extent of exactly resembling three others.

Beauchamp, Philip Manigault An African-American private from Mississippi who has ambitions to become an undertaker, he is the third of three soldiers who volunteer for an unknown mission in exchange for which they will be issued a three-day pass to Paris. A proud man, he reacts quickly to Buchwald's use of the derisive "Sambo" for him, telling Buchwald that his name is pronounced "Mannygo" but spelled *Manigault*. The mission they are sent on is the execution of Major General Gragnon. Manigault is described as strong and graceful. It is he who holds Gragnon while Buchwald pulls the trigger.

Bidet, General He is the group commander of the portion of the French army that contains the regiment that mutinies. Bidet (as his name seems to imply) is described as being overly preoccupied with the excretory functions of the soldiers in his command, but he is nonetheless a good soldier. He ranks just below the old general. Bidet denies Major General Gragnon's demand to have all the 3,000 men of the regiment executed for mutiny.

Bishop, William ("Billy") (1894–1956) He is an historical aviator referred to in *A Fable*. Flying for Britain's ROYAL AIR FORCE, Bishop was Canada's top ace fighter pilot in World War I. *See also* Ball, Albert.

Bledsoe, Sergeant A British soldier, he attempts to prevent the runner from reaching the front lines and seeking to further the cause of Corporal Stefan. The runner uses the flat of a pistol to dispose of Bledsoe without having to kill him. The runner also uses the pistol on Horn and Lieutenant Smith.

Blum, Major He identifies Corporal Stefan as the man who took the winnings from a group of gambling American soldiers and gave it to a pair of newlyweds. This is the third time that Blum has seen the corporal perform a generous deed (Stefan also found the money to save the sight of a young girl, and raised money to send an old and grief-stricken man home to his relatives).

Boelcke, Oswald (1891–1916)   He is an historical German aviator referred to in the novel. *See* Ball, Albert.

Boggan   He is a person referred to in the novel. Colonel Beale of the British army saw a soldier named Boggan brutally killed during the 1914 Battle of Mons, yet he identifies Corporal Stefan as being the same man. Stefan is one of three avatars of the "ubiquitous corporal" (236) who has supposedly died. Another is Brzewski, who was buried at sea in 1917. These references underscore the theme of humanity's resurrection from its own brutality and centers on the main character of *A Fable* through which Faulkner enunciates his vision of the futility of conflict and war and announces his belief in the spirit's constant urging for peace and brotherhood.

Bouc, Pierre (Piotr)   Pierre Bouc is the false identity assumed by one of the 12 followers of Corporal Stefan. Three times, he pointedly denies knowing the corporal and begs to be removed from the cell where the group is held. The corporal produces a regimental order that identifies Piotr as "Pierre Bouc," and asserts that the man was included by mistake. After Stefan is questioned by the old general, however, Piotr demands to be reincluded with the 12 and admits his true identity. He is one of the four Zsettlani in the group.

Bridesman, Major   He is a British fighter pilot commanding the group to which Levine belongs; he is one of three flyers who are issued blank machine-gun ammunition and who escort the German general to the conference with Allied generals. Bridesman knows that the incident was fixed to allow the German to arrive safely, but he is too cautious to investigate why.

Brzewski   He is one of the three avatars of Corporal Stefan. Captain Middleton identifies the living Stefan as Brzewski, an American soldier who died of flu on a transport ship and was buried at sea in late 1917. *See also* Boggan and Brzonyi.

Brzonyi   Brzonyi is the surname that Captain Middleton at first mistakenly uses to identify Corporal Stefan when he tells of burying the American soldier Brzewski at sea in 1917. Middleton's use of the surname Brzonyi could indicate Corporal Stefan's last name as it was known in the French army.

Buchwald   He is one of the three American soldiers (along with Philip Manigault Beauchamp and Sergeant Wilson) in World War I who execute Major General Gragnon. Buchwald is described as a hard-faced man who is at least somewhat aware that the duty he and the others volunteered for (with the offer of a three-day pass in Paris as an inducement) will be a shameful act. Buchwald actually fires the German pistol that kills Gragnon. (He uses a German pistol to make it look like the enemy killed Gragnon.) After the war, Buchwald becomes a bootlegger and crime lord in America.

Burk   An aviator, Burk is one of Gerald David Levine's tent mates.

Casse-tête   He is one of the two thieves who are executed on either side of Corporal Stefan. Also called Horse, he is apparently brain-damaged or possibly retarded. Able to speak only the word *Paris*, he is executed without even knowing what is about to happen to him. Casse-tête is a companion of Lapin, who is honorably loyal to him. Just before he and Lapin are killed, Corporal Stefan tells the anxious Casse-tête, "It's all right. . . . We won't go without you" (325). This comment is an allusion to Christ's remark on the cross to the repentant thief (*see* Luke 23:39–43). In French, *casse-tête* can mean several things, a truncheon or a brain teaser (a puzzler).

Collyer   He is a British Royal Air Force officer, adjutant to Gerald Levine's squadron. Collyer orders the hangars and airfield shut down in preparation for the arrival of the German general.

Conventicle   He is a Welsh flight sergeant in Levine's squadron. Conventicle apparently has taken Levine under his wing, and Levine feels a kind of kinship for him.

Corporal   In the novel, this appellation is used most often for Stefan, the mystical leader of the 13 French soldiers whose pacifist beliefs incite the mutiny in the novel. In these entries, he is called Corporal Stefan for clarity, but this combined form is never used in *A Fable*. (See Stefan, Corporal.)

Cowrie, Captain   He is the British RAF (Royal Air Force) officer. Captain Cowrie shares a hut with Major Bridesman.

De Marchi   A British Royal Air Force officer, he shares a hut with Burk and Levine.

Demont   He is Marthe Demont's husband. A Frenchman by birth, Demont had been in the garrison in Beirut when he and Marthe met and married. He acted as father to the young Stefan (then approximately nine years old). He meets Marthe and her sister Marya with a cart when they bring Stefan's body back to be buried on the family farm. His concern is for his wife, but even more for the farm, which he describes as ruined. He dies not long after Stefan is buried, after yet another artillery barrage destroys the land once again and causes Stefan's body to disappear.

Demont, Marthe (Magda)   She is Corporal Stefan's half sister. After she marries Demont, a Frenchman, she brings her brother to France. Marthe informs the old general that Stefan is his son, conceived out of wedlock in some unnamed Middle Eastern country. The result of that pregnancy, she tells the old general, was to destroy her family. Her mother left their village, taking the two girls with her, and they traveled until Christmas Eve, when Stefan was born. The mother died in childbirth, but before dying she revealed to Marthe (then called Magda) the name of Stefan's father. It was Marthe's desire to force some recognition out of the old general that induced her to go to France. Marthe buries Stefan on the farm.

De Montigny, Captain   A minor character in the novel, De Montigny interviews the relatives of Corporal Stefan before the old general sees them.

Fonck, Rene (1894–1953)   He is an historical aviator referred to in the novel. *See Ball, Albert.*

Gargne, Monsieur   He is the French *patronne* (landlord) of the apartment house where the runner lived while studying architecture in Paris.

General (the German General)   One of the generals in the novel, he arrives in a two-seater plane at the British airfield in France to meet with his enemy counterparts so together they can resume World War I. The fighting has temporarily halted on both sides because of the mutiny caused by Corporal Stefan and his disciples.

Gragnon, Charles (Major General)   He is the commander of the division of the French army chosen to make an attack. The regiment he designates to make the doomed attack mutinies and refuses to leave the trenches. When Gragnon realizes what has happened, he orders the arrest of the entire 3,000-man unit and demands that they be shot for cowardice. Gragnon himself is executed by a trio of American soldiers who are instructed to shoot him with a German pistol to imply that he was killed while leading his troops in the attack, thereby enabling the French high command to cover up the mutiny. Gragnon's own pride demands that the world know what happened to him, and he refuses to face his killers. Even while Philip Manigault Beauchamp is holding Gragnon and Buchwald is aiming the gun, Gragnon manages to twist his head so that he is shot in the back. Buchwald tells Beauchamp, a would-be undertaker, to fill in the bullet hole with wax; they shoot Gragnon again, this time in front.

Guynemer, Georges (1894–1917)   He is an historical aviator referred to in the novel. (See Ball, Albert.)

Hanley   He is a Royal Air Force (RAF) aviator and Levine's hut mate.

Harry, Mr.   This is the name used by Toby Sutterfield to refer to the English groom. Sutterfield pronounces Mr. Harry as "Mistairy." In the novel,

Harry is more commonly called "the sentry." He is a private in the British army and renowned among the troops for a sort of "bank" he runs. He lends each man enrolled in his informal financial organization 30 shillings. They, in turn, repay him at usurious rates, but the sentry is in essence betting the men that they will live until next payday. An angry and unpleasant man, he had been a groom employed at an English racing stable until he bonded with a spectacularly gifted race horse. When the horse is sold to an Argentine millionaire, he accompanies it. The horse is resold to an American, and the sentry goes to America, too. The train carrying the sentry, the horse, and Sutterfield (a groom at the American's horse farm) is derailed in a Mississippi swamp and the horse is badly hurt. The sentry and Sutterfield doctor the horse and steal it, racing it at small racetracks all across America. In a small valley in eastern Tennessee, the sentry becomes a Mason. The runner convinces the sentry to lead his regiment into no-man's-land where they meet a like-minded unarmed German battalion. While the two units mingle in peace, a combined German and Allied barrage kills nearly all of them.

Henri   A minor character, he is a French army commander whose troops include the mutinous regiment under Major General Gragnon.

Horn   He is the British soldier who is knocked out by the runner when he frees Mr. Harry, the sentry.

Immelmann, Max (1890–1916)   World War I aviator referred to in the novel. Germany's first "ace," he developed an aerial combat maneuver known as the Immelmann Turn. A British pilot shot him down in June 1916. (The name appears in *A Fable* with only one *n*, Immelman.) (*Also see* Ball, Albert.)

Irey   He is the jailer in the American horse racing section of the novel. Irey holds the Reverend Toby Sutterfield and Sutterfield's grandson for the theft of the horse. An ineffectual man, he is unable to stop a mob from entering the courthouse, but he is able to help the two prisoners escape. (Irey also appears in the novella *NOTES ON A HORSETHIEF*, the earliest version of which was published in a limited edition in 1950. This story was later revised and used in *A Fable*; this section of the novel appeared as a short story in *Vogue* in 1954.)

James, Lieutenant Colonel   He is the commander of the battalion that the runner joins after having been demoted from officer to common soldier.

Jean   One of the 12 disciples of Corporal Stefan, Jean sits on the corporal's left when the prisoners eat on Thursday night (a parallel to Christ's Last Supper, also on a Thursday evening). Jean comments on Polchek's lack of appetite.

Lallemont   He is the commander of the French army corps that includes Major General Gragnon's division. He orders Gragnon to make the attack that results in the mutiny led by Corporal Stefan. A friend of Gragnon's, Lallemont had been a fellow subaltern in the same division at the start of their careers.

Landry, Sergeant   He commands a squad of 12 French soldiers who are sent to a fortress in the Verdun region with orders to bring back an unidentified and unidentifiable body of a French soldier to be buried in the Tomb of the Unknown Soldier. A fussy man who neither smokes nor drinks, Landry has served far behind the actual fighting line during World War I.

Lapin   He is the thief and murderer executed next to Corporal Stefan. Lapin is the friend and protector of Casse-tête.

Levine, Gerald David   He is an 18-year-old inexperienced fighter pilot in the novel, who, nonetheless, notices that the bullets he is firing at the German general's aircraft are blanks. He asks Major Bridesman, his commander, for the truth about this, but is rebuffed. Although he has dreamed of glory flying and fighting for England, Levine, a Jew, feels estranged from his fellows. He considers himself and his honor betrayed by the subterfuge and commits suicide.

Luluque   He is one of Corporal Stefan's followers. A Midian, Luluque asks for grace to be said at their meal in prison.

McCudden, James (1895–1918)   He is an historical aviator referred to in the novel. McCudden received the Victoria Cross for bravery three months before dying in a flying accident. (*See* Ball, Albert.)

Mannock, Edward (1887–1918)   British World War I fighter pilot referred to in the novel. Ground fire brought down Mannock's aircraft in July 1918 and he died in the wreckage. (*See* Ball, Albert.)

Martel, General   A former commander of the old general, Martel does not appear in the novel in person, but is referred to in a conversation as one whose signature was required on a citation for the old general when he was a younger officer. Seemingly supernatural occurrences twice prevent this action.

Marya   She is the older sister of Marthe (Demont) and half sister of Corporal Stefan. Marya is described as looking younger than her sister because she is to a degree mentally deficient, but she has good instincts about the actions of others and is a true support to her family.

Middleton, Captain   He is an American officer, who is confronted with Corporal Stefan. He states that a man identical to Stefan was in his command but died and was buried at sea in 1917.

Milhaud, Madame   She is the proprietor of a bistro where the British aviators used to eat and drink near the aerodrome.

Monaghan, Captain   He is an American aviator flying in the Royal Air Force (RAF). Monaghan witnesses the murder of the German pilot by the German general and attacks the killer. He is dragged away by Bridesman and Thorpe. (*Also see* Monaghan under Characters in *SARTORIS*, "Ad Astra," and "Honor" (where he is given the first name Buck.)

Morache   He is one of a detail of 12 soldiers sent to collect a body to be buried in the Tomb of the Unknown Soldier, but because they needed money to buy liquor, the soldiers sold this body to a peasant woman. To obtain a second body, Picklock uses a watch Morache stole from a dead German officer to buy a substitute body, which is that of Corporal Stefan.

the old general (the Generalissimo, the marshal, the old marshal)   He is the unnamed supreme commander of the allied American, British, and French forces in World War I. Through an illicit affair in a Middle Eastern country, he is the father of Corporal Stefan, who leads the mutiny at the center of the novel. He meets with Stefan on two occasions and offers him not only his freedom but great wealth and worldly power if he will renounce his 12 disciples and embrace the war. The old general is said to be from an ancient French family. Throughout his life, he is seen by many as the "hope of France." But the old general has consistently gone his own way, volunteering for harsh outposts and unglamorous assignments. He refuses to use his family connections to make his way to the pinnacle of the French military. Nevertheless, his brilliance and talent bring him the highest rank and honors. Like Satan in the New Testament, the old general tempts Stefan to renounce his way of life. When the corporal refuses to follow in his father's bloody footsteps, the old general orders his execution, along with the execution of Major General Gragnon, who commanded the division that included the mutinous regiment (although Gragnon's death is made to appear as if it occurred during battle). The old general is committed to carrying on the war until the very last soldier has died. He arranges for the mutiny to be covered up as a failed attack. In the final scene of the novel the old general is buried with great pomp while the mauled and maimed runner attempts to disrupt the funeral.

Osgood, Captain   He is a pilot in Lieutenant Levine's Royal Air Force (RAF) squadron.

Paul He is one of Corporal Stefan's disciples. Considered second in command, Paul is designated to be in charge in Stefan's absence.

Picklock A French private whose name comes from his civilian profession, Picklock leads a 12-man detail assigned to the task of getting a body to bury in the Tomb of the Unknown Soldier. After the detail obtains a body from a fortress in Verdun, Picklock steals brandy from Sergeant Landry's briefcase. In a drunken stupor, the men sell the body to a bereaved old woman, who is convinced that it is her dead son. Still in need of a body, Picklock and Morache trade a stolen German officer's watch with a farmer for a replacement. This second body is that of Corporal Stefan, who is thus resurrected and buried with honor as the Unknown Soldier.

Piotr *See* Bouc, Pierre.

Polchek He is one of the 12 followers of Corporal Stefan. Polchek corresponds to Judas in Christ's passion story. He betrays the corporal, telling the old general about the planned mutiny. In return, he is freed from the prison during the last meal they share. He later repents his action, and after the war's end he seeks out Marthe and Marya at their farm. He offers them 29 coins, and adds the symbolic 30th from his pocket. When they refuse his money and his expiation, Polchek leaves in despair. On his way through their doorway he appears "as if he actually were hanging on a cord against the vacant shape of the spring darkness" (366).

Rhys Davids, Arthur (1897–1917) British World War I aviator referred to as Rhys Davies. After a short but highly effective career as a fighter pilot on the Western Front, he vanished in flight near Roulers, France, in October 1917. (*See* Ball, Albert.)

Rhys Davies *See* Rhys Davids, Arthur.

Richthofen Referred to in *A Fable* and known as the "Red Baron," Richthofen appears in SARTORIS as a German military aviator and flight instructor; *see* Characters under *Sartoris*. (*See* Ball, Albert.)

the runner He is a British soldier, who is promoted from a common enlisted man to officer's rank. After five months as an officer, he requests that he be made a common soldier again. His request is denied and he is forced to act in so outrageous manner while on leave that the British authorities have no recourse but to strip him of his rank. He becomes a regimental messenger. In this capacity, he travels the front lines and the rear areas extensively and is able to learn much about the Allied armies. An intelligent, sensitive man, the runner had been an architect before the war. He was among the first of the men of London to enlist in the army, but by 1918 he has become convinced of the stupidity and evil of war. When he learns of the mutiny led by Corporal Stefan, he attempts to prolong the temporary cease-fire into an actual armistice. He convinces Mr. Harry, the sentry, to use his influence to get another battalion to cross into no-man's-land and make peace with the enemy. This action leads both armies to lay down a powerful barrage upon the peaceful mingled British and German soldiers, killing all but the runner, who is horribly maimed. The runner later interrupts the funeral of the old general after the war. An outraged crowd beats him in spite of his injuries and leaves him bleeding in the gutter. One individual, also a veteran of World War I, comes to his aid. The runner says he is not going to die. The old soldier tells the runner that he is not laughing at him. "What you see," says the good samaritan in the final five words of the book, "are tears" (370).

Sibleigh Mentioned in *A Fable*, he appears in SARTORIS as a ROYAL AIR FORCE aviator in France. *See* Characters under *Sartoris*; *also see* "WITH CAUTION AND DISPATCH," where he is also mentioned.

Smith, Lieutenant He is the officer subdued by the runner when the latter frees Mr. Harry (the sentry) from the guardhouse.

Stefan, Corporal He is the leader of the mutiny central to the plot in *A Fable*. The mutiny involves a French regiment's refusal to make a foolhardy attack against the Germans. Corporal Stefan and his 12 followers attempt to bring about peace through a kind of civil disobedience in the army. The group—reminiscent of Jesus and his 12 disciples—has visited widely on both the Allied and the German sides of the lines and has a following among common soldiers. The effect Stefan has had on both adversaries is evident in the Germans' puzzling refusal to take advantage of the French regiment's mutiny. This, too, is ascribed to Stefan and his effect on young soldiers of both sides. Stefan is betrayed by one of his own followers, arrested, and brought before the French supreme commander, who is, in fact, his father. The supreme commander offers Stefan wealth and power if he will renounce his mission of peace. Stefan refuses to turn on his followers, and the supreme commander orders his execution. Stefan thus becomes a martyr to peace, as is foretold, in a way, by his name. (St. Stephen was the first Christian martyr.)

Faulkner uses a multitude of allusions and parallels to Christ and other ironic plot twists in creating Corporal Stefan. When Stefan is executed, for example, he is tied to a post between two thieves who are being shot for crimes committed against civilians. Stefan's body is flung backward into a ditch where a rusty, discarded coil of barbed wire forms a crown of thorns on his head. Later, his half sisters Marya and Marthe (Demont) claim the body. He is buried in a makeshift sepulcher, but an artillery barrage causes the grave and the body to disappear. Later, Picklock trades a dead German officer's watch for a body, presumably Stefan's, found by Marya and Marthe's neighbor. The body is transported to Paris, where it is given a full military burial as France's famous Unknown Soldier.

Sutterfield, Rev. Toby   He is an African-American stable hand, who, with the British groom Mr. Harry (which Sutterfield pronounces "Mistairy"), is traveling with a marvelously swift racehorse via railway through a Mississippi swamp when the train is derailed and one of the horse's legs is badly injured. Because both Sutterfield and Mr. Harry believe the horse should continue doing what it does best—racing and winning—rather than be destroyed or put out to stud, they steal the horse and doctor it as best they can. The horse then races at small tracks across the southeastern United States against competition which, for the most part, it can outrun on its three good legs. During this nomadic existence, Sutterfield,

a self-ordained country minister, baptizes Mr. Harry, who in turn makes Sutterfield a Mason. This connection is important later in the novel when Mr. Harry returns to England to become a soldier known as the sentry. As a soldier, Mr. Harry has a kind of hypnotic hold over the men in his regiment who are willing to invest their pay with him. Sutterfield gains the confidence of a wealthy American woman whose son had been killed in the air war above France. He convinces her to support an organization, *Les Amis Myriades et Anonymes à la France de Tout le Monde* (The Many and Anonymous Friends of France throughout the World), that he creates to promote peace. While traveling in France, and now called Monsieur Tooleyman (a corruption of *Tout le Monde*), Sutterfield finds the sentry but is rebuffed by his former comrade. Another soldier, the runner, discovers the connection between Sutterfield and the sentry and uses it to get the sentry's assistance in his campaign to turn the impromptu cease-fire, brought about by the French regiment's mutiny, into a permanent peace. Sutterfield, the sentry, and the runner lead a battalion of British troops into no-man's-land, where they lay down their weapons and are greeted by similarly disarmed German soldiers. The high commands on both sides, however, crush this peace movement by ordering a barrage on the unarmed men in no-man's-land, and both Sutterfield and the sentry are among those killed.

Theodule   He is a French soldier, who was killed in 1916 somewhere near Fort Valaumont. His mother goes seeking his body in 1919 after the end of the war and encounters Sergeant Landry and his detail. They have been given orders to bring back to Paris the body of an unidentifiable Frenchman for burial in the Tomb of the Unknown Soldier. When she sees Landry's men carrying a body, Theodule's mother is certain it is her son, and she bribes the men with 100 francs to allow her to take the body for burial.

Thorpe   A minor character, he is a British aviator under Major Bridesman's command.

Tooleyman (Monsieur Tooleyman)   Tooleyman is an English mispronunciation of the French expression *Tout le Monde* used by Rev. Toby Sutterfield as a pseudonym while in France. It is derived from *Les Amis Myriades et Anonymes à la France de Tout le Monde* (The Many and Anonymous Friends of France throughout the World), an organization he heads.

Voss, Werner   He is a World War I German aviator referred to in the novel. (*See* Ball, Albert.)

Wilson, Sergeant   He is an American sergeant referred to by an Iowan as the best in the army. (*See* Buchwald.)

Witt   He is a British flight commander in the novel.

Zsettlani   This is the name that is used to identify the four foreign members of the group of 13 soldiers in the French army who are led by Corporal Stefan in a failed attempt to end World War I. The four include Stefan himself, Polchek, Piotr (also called Pierre Bouc), and one other. Although its precise meaning is unclear, the word "Zsettlani" is apparently a collective noun referring to the common provenance of these men, perhaps connected to a Middle Eastern ethnic group or nationality or perhaps a dialect shared by these four (see *A Fable*, 292, 301, and 361).

FURTHER READING

Brooks, Cleanth. "Man's Fate and Man's Hope (*A Fable*)." In *William Faulkner: Toward Yoknapatawpha and Beyond*, 230–250. Baton Rouge: Louisiana State University Press, 1990.

Butterworth, Nancy, and Keen Butterworth. *Annotations to Faulkner's* A Fable. New York: Garland, 1989.

Howe, Irving. "A Fable." In *William Faulkner: A Critical Study*, 268–281. Chicago: University of Chicago Press, 1957.

King, Richard H. "A Fable: Faulkner's Political Novel?" *Southern Literary Journal* 17 (1985): 3–17.

Millgate, Michael. "A Fable." In *The Achievement of William Faulkner*, 227–234. Lincoln: University of Nebraska Press, 1978.

Polk, Noel. "Woman and the Feminine in *A Fable*." In *Faulkner and Women*, edited by Doreen Fowler and Ann J. Abadie, 180–204. Jackson: University of Mississippi Press, 1986.

———, and Kenneth L. Privratsky, eds. "*A Fable*": *A Concordance to the Novel*. 2 vols. Ann Arbor, Mich.: UMI Research Press, 1981.

Pritchett, V. S. "Time Frozen: *A Fable*." In *Faulkner: A Collection of Critical Essays*, edited by Robert Penn Warren, 238–242. Englewood Cliffs, N.J.: Prentice Hall, 1966.

Rice, Philip Blair. "Faulkner's Crucifixion." In *William Faulkner: Three Decades of Criticism*, edited by Frederick J. Hoffman and Olga W. Vickery, 373–381. New York: Harbinger, 1963.

Straumann, Heinrich. "An American Interpretation of Existence: Faulkner's *A Fable*." In *William Faulkner: Three Decades of Criticism*, edited by Frederick J. Hoffman and Olga W. Vickery, 349–372. New York: Harbinger, 1963.

Urgo, Joseph R. "Conceiving the Enemy: The Rituals of War in Faulkner's 'A Fable.'" *Faulkner Studies* 1.2 (1992): 1–19.

Father Abraham

An unfinished novel Faulkner started writing about 1926. A limited edition with an introduction and textual notes by JAMES B. MERIWETHER was published posthumously by Red Ozier Press, New York, in 1983. In 1984 a facsimile edited by Meriwether, with wood engravings by John DePol, was published by RANDOM HOUSE.

This unfinished work forms the basis of *The* HAMLET; a portion of it was written as "SPOTTED HORSES," a short story that Faulkner again revised and enlarged for chapter 1 of book 4 of *The Hamlet*.

Faulkner at Nagano

This is the title of a book that contains a collection of interviews, colloquies, short written statements, and the Nobel Prize address. Edited with a preface by Robert A. Jelliffe, *Faulkner at Nagano* was published by Kenyusha, Ltd., Tokyo, in July 1956. On an invitation of the Exchange of Persons Branch of the United States Department of State as part of a round-the-world trip, Faulkner went to Japan in August 1955 to participate in the Summer Seminars in American Literature at Nagano. Over a period of 10 days, Faulkner met and spoke with seminar members—about 50 Japanese teachers of American literature—and freely answered their many questions and inquiries recorded in the book. Like any collection of interviews and statements by Faulkner, this volume contains valuable bits of information regarding Faulkner's own writings and brief comments he voiced on other authors and their works. Some of the writers Faulkner touches on are ERNEST HEMINGWAY, SHERWOOD ANDERSON, André Gide, Theodore Dreiser, John Steinbeck, Edgar Allan Poe, Oscar Wilde, and T. S. Eliot. Many of the interviews were reedited and rearranged for publication in *Esquire* 50 (December 1958): 139, 141–42.

Faulkner in the University

This is the title of a comprehensive collection of the conferences Faulkner held at the University of Virginia when he was writer in residence there for the

Faulkner on the campus of the University of Virginia *(William Faulkner Collection, Special Collections Department, Manuscripts Division, University of Virginia Library. Photo by Ralph Thompson.)*

spring terms (February to June) of 1957 and 1958. First published by the University Press of Virginia in 1959, these transcripts of 36 recorded sessions were edited by Frederick L. Gwynn and JOSEPH L. BLOTNER; a new edition with an introduction by Douglas Day was published in 1995. During these sessions, Faulkner freely responded to hundreds of questions on a variety of topics relating to his writings and his views on literature and art, race and society, and other writers. Faulkner's responses provide readers with an invaluable, although not always trustworthy, resource for scholarship. (For further information, *see* UNIVERSITY OF VIRGINIA.)

Faulkner Reader, The

Published by RANDOM HOUSE in 1954, *The Faulkner Reader* is a selection from Faulkner's works. With a foreword by Faulkner, the selection contains his Nobel Prize address; one complete novel, *The* SOUND AND THE FURY; several important short stories, including "A ROSE FOR EMILY," "BARN BURNING," "THAT EVENING SUN," and "DRY SEPTEMBER"; and selections from GO DOWN, MOSES ("The BEAR"), *The* WILD PALMS ("Old Man"), *The* HAMLET ("SPOTTED HORSES"), and other works. Faulkner's editor at Random House, SAXE COMMINS, was responsible for the edition. In the foreword, Faulkner reflects on the notion of the artist as uplifting the human heart, an idea that he said came from the foreword of a book written by the Polish Nobel laureate Henryk Sienkiewicz (1846–1916) that was in his grandfather's library. This was the first foreword, Faulkner wrote, that he "ever took time to read" (vii). The notion of uplifting the human heart and that of the role of the writer Faulkner had incorporated in his 1950 Nobel Prize acceptance speech.

Flags in the Dust

An early Faulkner novel, substantially condensed and released in 1929 as SARTORIS. In 1973 RAN-

DOM HOUSE issued, under Faulkner's original choice of title, Douglas Day's reconstruction of Faulkner's text, based on a composite typescript archived in the Faulkner collection at the UNIVERSITY OF VIRGINIA.

SYNOPSIS

Set in JEFFERSON, MISSISSIPPI, just after World War I, this slow-paced and discursive novel treats members of four different families: the upper-class Sartorises and Benbows, the poor white Snopeses, and the black Strothers.

As the novel opens, the elderly Bayard Sartoris, president of the bank, and his friend, old man Will Falls, reminisce about the past, particularly the exploits of Bayard's father, John Sartoris, a brave Confederate colonel during the Civil War and a railroad builder after the war. Falls has brought a pipe that belonged to the colonel to present to old Bayard. Falls and the pipe are among several characters and objects in the novel that provide a tangible link between the past and the present.

When Simon Strother, old Bayard's black servant, comes with the carriage to drive his employer home at the end of the day, he informs the old man that his grandson, young Bayard Sartoris, has been seen in town earlier in the day, having just returned home from the war. Both young Bayard and his twin brother John have been pilots during the war, and John was killed in a dogfight with German flyers. Bayard had sought to prevent John's engagement in a foolish dogfight and lives with the traumatic memory of having seen his brother's plane shot down by the Germans. Bayard has also recently lost his young wife and baby, who both died in childbirth.

Three other characters have also returned home from the war: Horace Benbow, who has served in a noncombatant role as an officer with the YMCA and who has brought home from Europe a glass-blowing machine; Montgomery Ward Snopes, who accompanied Benbow as an assistant; and Caspey, Simon's lazy and insolent grandson, who brings home a belligerent and confrontational attitude toward whites.

Young Bayard, who seems bent on self-destruction, scandalizes his family and the community by purchasing a racing automobile and driving it dangerously around town and on the narrow roads of the county. He also rides an untamed stallion through the streets and engages in drinking sprees with both white and black companions. His great-great-aunt, Virginia du Pre, the widow of the first Bayard Sartoris (Carolina Bayard), who was killed in a foolhardy raid of a Yankee supply camp at Manassas, thinks young Bayard's recklessness is typical of the entire Sartoris clan: "Sartoris. It's in the blood. Savages, every one of 'em. No earthly use to anyone."

When Bayard wrecks his new automobile and is confined to bed with injuries, Narcissa Benbow, Horace's sister and Aunt Jenny's young friend, visits him, frequently reading him books while he convalesces. Narcissa is a troubled young woman who shares a near-incestuous love with her brother and is terribly upset that Horace is having an affair with the married Belle Mitchell. Narcissa is also receiving suggestive love letters from an anonymous source, subsequently revealed to be Byron Snopes, a bookkeeper in old Bayard's bank.

Horace, a lawyer who had been a Rhodes scholar at Oxford during his student days, is a dreamer and sybarite who is having difficulty settling into a responsible life and career. He spends much of his time strolling and talking with his sister, reading books, and producing beautiful objects with his glass-blowing apparatus. While waiting for Belle to secure a divorce from her husband Harry, Horace has a brief, tempestuous affair with Belle's sister Joan.

Against her best judgment and will power, Narcissa falls in love with Bayard and secures from him a promise that he will quit driving so fast. As soon as the automobile has been repaired, however, Bayard resumes his dangerous ways. His grandfather now accompanies him as a passenger on some of the drives through the countryside.

Byron Snopes, who bribes a young boy, Virgil Beard, to serve as his copyist, continues to send unsigned love letters to Narcissa, who hides them in her dresser drawer. She tells Aunt Jenny about the letters, but no one else. One day, fearing that Virgil is going to expose his actions, Snopes plots to rob the bank, leaving the vault open at closing time so he can reenter the bank and take the money during the night. Before he returns to the bank, he slips into Narcissa's house, steals one of her undergarments, and takes the packet of letters, substituting a new one in their place. He then robs the bank and leaves town.

Young Bayard and Narcissa are married. But Bayard has another automobile wreck; and his grandfather, a passenger in the car, dies from a heart attack caused by the accident. Following the accident, Bayard disappears, riding his horse into the countryside to the McCallums's farm, where he goes hunting with his longtime friends. Several days later he heads back home, loses his way, and spends Christmas day with a Negro family.

Horace and Belle marry and move to another town, but Horace is unhappy and writes sad, longing epistles to his sister Narcissa. He associates his unhappiness with the detestable smell of the shrimp he regularly carries home to Belle. She is unhappy too, missing the new car and the luxurious life style she had with Harry.

Still unable to find peace with himself and his life, Bayard leaves Narcissa, who is now pregnant, and Jefferson. After wandering for several months from Mexico to San Francisco to Chicago, he dies in Dayton, Ohio, in the crash of an experimental plane he is test piloting. On that same day his son is born, and Narcissa names the child Benbow Sartoris. "Do you think," Aunt Jenny asks her, "that because his name is Benbow, he'll be any less a Sartoris and a scoundrel and a fool?"

Interspersed into the narrative summarized above are comic episodes involving the Strother family: Simon, the patriarch, who carries on with young women and who persuades old Bayard to repay money he has stolen from his black church; Isom, who helps Aunt Jenny in her flower beds—when he can be found; and Caspey, who impresses younger blacks with his fabricated stories of war exploits, and who shows signs of becoming an "uppity" black until old Bayard hits him over the head with a stick of stove wood. However, this story, too, turns tragic, as Simon is found dead from a blow with a blunt instrument in the house of one of his young lovers.

CRITICAL COMMENTARY

Together with the posthumously published *Father Abraham*, which dates from roughly the same period, *Flags in the Dust* is Faulkner's first important excursion into his fictional YOKNAPATAWPHA

COUNTY. Looking back over his career years later, Faulkner said this novel contains "the germ of [his] apocrypha" (*Faulkner in the University*, 285).

Begun in the autumn of 1926, *Flags in the Dust* is the story of generations of the Sartoris clan, loosely based on the Falkners of north Mississippi, with a diverse collection of secondary characters and events that reappear in later novels and stories. Faulkner here calls his fictional county Yocona and the county town Jefferson. With *Father Abraham*, which introduces the hill-country Snopes clan, and *Flags*, which involves the planter-class Sartorises, Faulkner established the fictional opposites of his mythical Yoknapatawpha.

While the setting of the novel is distinctly southern, *Flags in the Dust* exhibits many features in common with the post–World War I Lost Generation novels and poems produced by several American and European authors of the 1920s, including ERNEST HEMINGWAY, F. Scott Fitzgerald, T. S. Eliot, and Eric Maria Remarque. As CLEANTH BROOKS, who titles his discussion of *Sartoris* as "The Waste Land: Southern Exposure," has noted, "*Flags in the Dust* powerfully conveys the difference between the older members of a traditionalist society, still sure of itself and possessing a clearly defined code of manners and conduct, and its younger members who have been jarred loose by the new ideas, events and experiences."

Some critics find Faulkner's treatment of African Americans in this novel to be condescending and even racist. Certainly the portrayals here are less positive than the later characterizations of blacks in such works as *The Sound and the Fury* and *Go Down, Moses*. Nevertheless, the descriptions of Bayard and Ratliff's fellowship with blacks and Bayard's spending Christmas day in a black community show considerable sympathy for black behavior and culture.

EXCERPTS FROM CONTEMPORARY REVIEWS OF *FLAGS IN THE DUST*

Richard Adams's review, "At Long Last, Flags in the Dust," published in The Southern Review 10 (1974); 878–888:

. . . It has been fairly generally known that *Sartoris* was a heavily cut version of the book that Faulkner wrote in 1926 and 1927 and tried unsuccessfully to publish under the title *Flags in the Dust.* . . . Now, at last, some forty-six years after Faulkner finished writing it, a book entitled *Flags in the Dust* has been printed and put on the market. The blessing, however, turns out to be somewhat mixed, and mixed in a way that makes the degree of it more than somewhat hard to assess. . . .

. . . These doubts and problems [regarding the text] notwithstanding, *Flags in the Dust* is an important increment. Its value lies partly in the simple fact that it makes, by my rough count, a net addition of something like twenty thousand words to what had been previously printed in *Sartoris*.

The mere quantitative gain is not so important as the qualitative differences, which lie mainly in the fact that Yoknapatawpha County is more fully present in the book Faulkner wrote than in the one Harcourt, Brace published. Even on the basis of a dubiously reliable text, we can arrive more confidently at certain conclusions about Faulkner's literary career than we could with no available text. These conclusions will help us, I believe, in a continuing effort to account for Faulkner's sudden, surprising, and spectacular development as a writer between 1926 and 1928. . . .

CHARACTERS

For a list of characters in this novel, *see* the entry on SARTORIS.

FURTHER READING

Andrews, Karen M. "Toward a 'Culturalist' Approach to Faulkner Studies: Making Connections in *Flags in Dust*." *Faulkner Journal* 7.1–2 (fall 1991–spring 1992): 13–26.

Berg, Allison. "The Great War and the War at Home: Gender Battles in *Flags in the Dust* and *The Unvanquished*." *Women's Studies—An Interdisciplinary Journal* 22.4 (1993): 441–453.

Cohen, Philip. "*Flags in the Dust*, *Sartoris*, and the Unforseen Consequences of Editorial Surgery." *Faulkner Journal* 5.1 (1989): 25–43.

Gray, Richard. "Ancestor Worship, Patricide and the Epic Past: *Flags in the Dust* and *Sartoris*." In *The Life of William Faulkner*, 127–136. Oxford: Blackwell, 1994.

McDaniel, Linda Elkins. *Annotations to William Faulkner's* Flags in the Dust. New York: Garland, 1991.

"Fool About a Horse" (Uncollected Stories)

A short story first published in August 1936 in SCRIBNER'S MAGAZINE 100, 80–86. A revision was included in book 1 of *The* HAMLET; the original version was reprinted in *Uncollected Stories of William Faulkner*. For more information, *see Selected Letters of William Faulkner*, 90, 92, 115, and *Uncollected Stories of William Faulkner*, 684–685.

SYNOPSIS

"Fool About a Horse" is a humorous short story concerning the harmless trickery involved in horse trading. Told from the perspective of a 12-year-old boy, the story recounts a day in the life of Pap, the boy's father, who is intent on vindicating the honor of YOKNAPATAWPHA COUNTY by outwitting the horse-and-mule trader Pat Stamper, thus beating him at his own game. However, Pap loses and even ends up trading his wife Vynie's cream separator for the very same horse he had traded Pat earlier that same day. Vynie does get the separator back, but at the cost of Pap's horse and mule.

CRITICAL COMMENTARY

The critic James Ferguson rightly points out that "Fool About a Horse" is an example of the "exuberant delight in oral storytelling that is so basic an aspect of Faulkner's art" and that the pleasure this work and others such as "SPOTTED HORSES" and "SHINGLES FOR THE LORD" give the reader "surely derives as much from the telling as from what is told, from the sense they convey of not just the fun in but the joy of storytelling" (*Faulkner's Short Fiction*, 116). Oral tradition was very much a part of Faulkner's youth, and it significantly contributed to his skillful use of comic language and the tall tale. "Fool About a Horse" owes much of its success to Faulkner's manipulation of point of view, comic dialect, and tone.

CHARACTERS

Jim   He is the horsetrader Pat Stamper's black assistant and an artist at disguising mules and horses that Stamper trades. (*Also see The* HAMLET.)

Kemp, Beasley   A minor character in the short story, Beasley trades a horse with Pap. (*Also see The* HAMLET.)

Pap   The main character in this humorous tale, Pap tries to outwit the horse-and-mule trader Pat Stamper but always loses. When Pap trades his wife Vynie's cream separator for a horse, he unwittingly gets the same horse he had earlier that day traded with Pat. To get her separator back, Vynie has to trade a mule and a horse with Stamper.

Short, Herman   A minor character in the short story, Herman swaps Pat Stamper a mule and buggy for a horse which he then sells to Beasley Kemp for eight dollars.

Stamper, Pat   A master horsetrader, Stamper easily fools Pap when the latter trades his wife's cream separator for a horse. (*Also see The* HAMLET *and* The MANSION.)

Varner, Jody   A minor character in the short story, Jody is Will Varner's son, who hears from Pap that Beasley's horse came from Kentucky. (*Also see As I Lay Dying, Light in August, The* HAMLET, *The* TOWN, *The* MANSION, *and* "SPOTTED HORSES.")

Varner (Will)   He is the owner of the country store in FRENCHMAN'S BEND that Pap and his son, the unnamed narrator of the short story, pass by after the foolish Pap gets Beasley's broken-down horse in a trade. (Varner appears in several of Faulkner's works; *see* LIGHT IN AUGUST, *The* HAMLET, INTRUDER IN THE DUST, *The* TOWN, *The* MANSION, SARTORIS, and the short stories "SPOTTED HORSES," "LIZARDS IN JAMSHYD'S COURTYARD" (these stories along with "THE HOUND" and "Fool About a Horse" Faulkner revised for *The Hamlet*), "Tomorrow" (in KNIGHT'S GAMBIT), "SHINGLES FOR THE LORD" and "BY THE

PEOPLE" (revised for *The Mansion*); Varner is also referred to in As I LAY DYING.

Vynie   She is Pap's wife, also referred to as Mammy by her son, the 12-year-old narrator of the story. Determined to get the separator back that her husband lost in a deal with Pat Stamper, Vynie trades Stamper a mule and a horse.

"Frankie and Johnny" (Uncollected Stories)

Written sometime around 1925, this short story was first published in the *Mississippi Quarterly* 31 (summer 1978): 454–464; it is included in the *Uncollected Stories of William Faulkner*, edited by Joseph Blotner, 338–347. For more information, *see Uncollected Stories*, 698.

SYNOPSIS

The short story traces the brief love affair of a small-time gangster, Johnny, and Frankie, a poor young woman he picks up on the street, the protagonist of the story. Frankie is usually adept at giving men like Johnny the brush-off, but he catches her at a moment of particular vulnerability and they become sweethearts. Frankie's mother, a widow (and an apparent prostitute), warns Frankie away from Johnny. When Frankie becomes pregnant with Johnny's child, Johnny leaves, but this predicament seems to liberate rather than entrap Frankie. Through her pregnancy, she comes into her own. When her mother frets about Frankie's condition, Frankie calls her a fool and bluntly retorts by saying that she was not trying to force Johnny to marry her by getting pregnant. In a moment of insight, Frankie affirms that she does not need a man to keep her and challenges her mother to do the same.

CRITICAL COMMENTARY

The Faulkner critic James Ferguson sees "Frankie and Johnny" as one of several examples—in this case an early example—showing Faulkner's "compassionate characterizations of women in difficult or impossible situations" (*Faulkner's Short Fiction*, 74).

CHARACTERS

Frankie's father (unnamed) A small-time boxer who expected a son when Frankie was born. He eventually took a great deal of pride in having a daughter, who was very much like him, and his last thoughts were of her when he drowned attempting to save a woman bather at Ocean Grove Park.

Frankie's mother (unnamed) Indulging in self-pity, she vainly instructs Frankie in the way of the world and the difficulties women face.

Frankie The protagonist in the short story. She falls in love with Johnny, a minor gangster-type character. At the conclusion of the story, Frankie is carrying Johnny's child but swears she needs no man to keep her.

Johnny The young gangster-type character in the short story. He is able to penetrate through Frankie's hard, defensive shell but abandons her when he finds out that she is pregnant with his child.

"Go Down, Moses" (Uncollected Stories)

Short story first published in the January 25, 1941 issue of *Collier's* and only slightly revised as the last chapter of GO DOWN, MOSES (1942).

SYNOPSIS

The story opens with a census taker's interview of a 26-year-old black man, Samuel Worsham ("Butch") Beauchamp, the grandson of Mollie Beauchamp, as he awaits execution in an Illinois prison for the killing of a policeman in Chicago. The scene then shifts to Gavin Stevens's law office in JEFFERSON, MISSISSIPPI, where the elderly Mollie is seeking the lawyer's help in locating her grandson, whom she insists Carothers Edmonds, the owner of the farm on which the Beauchamps live, had "sold into Egypt," like "Benjamin." "Pharaoh got him," she says.

Stevens recalls Beauchamp as a young troublemaker who, five or six years earlier, had been chased off the Beauchamp farm for breaking into the commissary store. His troubles continued in town, as he was in and out of jail for gambling and fighting and then was arrested for attempted robbery. But somehow he managed to escape from his cell and disappeared.

When Stevens begins to make inquiries, Wilmoth, the editor of the local newspaper, shows him the story about Beauchamp's pending execution. Miss Belle Worsham, a respected member of the white community, comes to Stevens's office, expressing concern for Mollie. Stevens learns that Mollie's parents had been slaves owned by Miss Worsham's grandfather, and she and Mollie had grown up together. Stevens and Miss Worsham agree to try to keep Mollie from knowing the details of Butch's disgraceful end.

After Miss Worsham tells Stevens that Mollie will want the body brought back home, Stevens, Wilmoth, and a number of Jefferson merchants take up a collection to bring Beauchamp's body to Jefferson for burial. Now Stevens realizes that he must inform Mollie about the circumstances of her grandson's death. However, when he tries to talk with her, she just sits swaying back and forth in her chair and repeating that Edmonds had sold her Benjamin to Pharaoh, "and now he dead."

The next day a sizeable group of townsmen, black and white, watch as the casket is removed from the train and placed in a hearse arranged for by Stevens. As the body is transported through town on the way to the farm for burial, Mollie and Miss Worsham follow in Stevens's car, driven by a man Stevens has hired, and Stevens and Wilmoth follow in Wilmoth's car. At the edge of town, however, the two white men drop out of the procession; on the way back to town, Wilmoth informs Stevens that Mollie has asked that the notice of Butch's death be printed in the paper. At the end of the story Stevens finally understands that Mollie does not care how her grandson died: She merely wanted him to be buried at home in a proper, dignified manner, with casket, flowers, hearse, and a funeral procession through the town square.

CRITICAL COMMENTARY

The title of this story (borrowed from the title of a well-known Negro spiritual) and its allusions to the Old Testament narrative of the Hebrews' bondage in Egypt signal the story as a treatment of the legacy of slavery in America. The story is generally recognized as one of Faulkner's most astute handlings of the complex issue of race relations in the South during the 1940s. While the races are clearly segregated, the story shows that there can also be crossings of the barriers, as represented by the lifelong relationship between Mollie Beauchamp and Belle Worsham ("It's our grief," the white woman says) and by the white community's charitable act of paying for Butch's funeral. Still, such interrelationships stop far short of equality: For example, to Stevens, Mollie is "an old nigger woman" while the white woman is Miss Worsham; and the collection to pay for the funeral may represent an unstated confession that the white community has somehow been complicit in Butch's death. Stevens, while presented as a gentle and sympathetic individual, exhibits a condescending attitude toward blacks and, as a result, constantly misreads the grandmother's feelings and intentions. He is clearly uncomfortable listening to the ritualistic expressions of mourning by the black family. Stevens and Wilmoth's turning aside from the funeral procession may be taken to symbolize the division that remains between whites and blacks.

CLEANTH BROOKS finds the main theme of this story, as in so much of Faulkner's work, to be the importance of community, particularly the role that women play in representing and defending its claims (278). Richard Gray sees the story as more paradoxical, offering "a contrast between 'nature' and 'culture', the primal simplicity of black people and the mired complexity of whites" (286). Glenn Meeter, who thinks the story has been undervalued, stresses the heroic role of Mollie Beauchamp: "If Old Carothers McCaslin was a founding Abraham, Mollie here makes good her claim as a matriarchal Rachel, claiming the McCaslin property as the land

of promise for its black as well as its white inhabitants" (*A William Faulkner Encyclopedia*, 148).

CHARACTERS

For the list of characters in this story *see* the entry on GO DOWN, MOSES.

Go Down, Moses

A Faulkner masterwork, this novel, published in 1942, began life as a series of short stories, some of which had appeared previously in print. Desperate for money, Faulkner in the spring of 1941 conceived the notion of welding the stories into a larger work. He shaped the novella "The Fire and the Hearth" and the short stories "Was," "PANTALOON IN BLACK," "The OLD PEOPLE," "The BEAR," "DELTA AUTUMN" and "GO DOWN, MOSES" into a novel that related the story of the McCaslin family, white and black. Critics have remarked on the novel's thematic kinship with ABSALOM, ABSALOM!, particularly in its emphasis on race, inheritance and identity. As it evolved, the improvisational *Go Down, Moses*, spanning nearly a century, became Faulkner's most important exploration of black-white relations, and by critical consensus the last of his truly great achievements.

SYNOPSIS

As it happened, Faulkner found the task of building the novel rather more difficult than the cut-and-paste job that produced The UNVANQUISHED out of a set of previously published short stories in 1938. "There is more meat to it than I thought," he wrote his editor at RANDOM HOUSE, ROBERT K. HAAS, in early December 1941. "I am at it steadily, and have been." For one thing, this project involved substantial rewriting. "The Fire and the Hearth," which Faulkner had originally intended to lead off *Go Down, Moses*, required the extensive reworking of source material in four existing short stories.

The short story "A POINT OF LAW," published in *Collier's* in June 1940, formed the basis for the first section of chapter 1 of "The Fire and the Hearth." The story turned on the comic circumstance of the black tenant farmer Lucas Beauchamp's daughter Nathalie Beauchamp Wilkins and her husband George Wilkins establishing a still on Lucas's place. Faulkner opened with a new introductory passage detailing Lucas's troubles with Wilkins and the relationship between the entwined white and black families of the McCaslin plantation. The plantation owner, the elder Carothers (Roth) Edmonds, is a collateral descendant of Lucius Quintus Carothers McCaslin, the founder of the estate and of the two family lines. Faulkner added most of the second section, a long flashback that develops Lucas's troubled relationship with Zachary Edmonds, Carothers's father.

Chapter 2 of the novella is a revised version of the short story "GOLD IS NOT ALWAYS," published in The ATLANTIC MONTHLY in November 1940, which details Lucas Beauchamp's growing obsession with finding treasure allegedly buried on the McCaslin plantation. Faulkner based the concluding chapter 3 on an unsold story called "An Absolution," later retitled "Apotheosis." The narrative relates Lucas's wife Molly's bid to divorce him because of his treasure-hunting mania. The novelist added significant new material, including a brief history of the black family line of old Lucas Quintus Carothers McCaslin.

Faulkner reworked the short story "Almost," written in 1940 but unsold, into "Was," the piece that he eventually would select to lead off the novel. In "Almost," the boy narrator Bayard relates the story of Theophilus (Uncle Buck) McCaslin's chase of the slave Tomey's Turl Beauchamp to a neighboring plantation where his lover lives. In the revised version, the narrator is nine-year-old McCaslin (Cass) Edmonds, the older cousin of Isaac (Ike) McCaslin, who will become the novel's central figure. Ike has not yet been born in 1859, the year the story takes place; he will hear about events secondhand. Jason Prim of "Almost" becomes Hubert Beauchamp, the owner of the plantation to which Tomey's Turl continually runs.

Faulkner made few alterations to the manuscript of "Pantaloon in Black," published in HARPER'S MAGAZINE in October 1940. Substantial changes were required for "The Old People," written in 1939 and originally published in Harper's in September 1940. The young narrator of the story is given a name, Ike McCaslin, the orphaned son of Buck McCaslin.

In the revision of the hunting story "Delta Autumn," written in December 1940 and published in Story magazine in May 1942, a character named Don Boyd becomes the younger Roth Edmonds, a tormented figure who repudiates his black mistress. Here Faulkner changed his original plan, deciding he needed a hunting piece to precede "Delta Autumn," which he set near the end of Ike McCaslin's long life. The result was the incomparable novella "The Bear." It opens with Ike at 16 and flashes back to a younger Ike. Section 2 of "The Bear" incorporates material from the short story "LION," published in Harper's in December 1935. Section 3 details the killing of the larger-than-life bear, Old Ben. In section 4, Ike repudiates the land and his heritage in expiation of his family's guilt: his grandfather's incest and miscegenation. In the novella's conclusion, Ike returns to the vanishing woods for the last time and muses upon his patrimony.

The short story "Go Down, Moses" narrates Molly Beauchamp's quest to bring her grandson, executed for a murder in Illinois, back to JEFFERSON, MISSISSIPPI, for burial. The title story brings the novel to a close. Faulkner wrote that he conceived the idea for it in July 1940 when he saw a coffin unloaded from a train. Faulkner initially called the young man Henry Coldfield Sutpen and identified him as the grandson of one of Thomas Sutpen's slaves. He eventually settled on the name Samuel Worsham Beauchamp. The Post rejected the story. Collier's accepted it for publication on January 25, 1941.

CRITICAL COMMENTARY

With the final lineup of "Was," "The Fire and the Hearth," "Pantaloon in Black," "The Old People," "The Bear," "Delta Autumn" and "Go, Down, Moses," Faulkner had conjured up a powerful work of art. With revisions and additions, he transformed the separate elements into a searching exploration of YOKNAPATAWPHA COUNTY blacks and whites together and apart, comic and tragic by turns.

Looking ahead to "The Bear," "Was" opens with old Ike McCaslin, "a widower now and uncle to half a county and father to no one" (3). The story proper begins in section 2, with Uncle Buck and his twin Uncle Buddy, sons of old Carothers McCaslin; the slave Tomey's Turl; his girlfriend Tennie Beauchamp; the spinster Miss Sophonsiba Beauchamp; and a poker game. After the cards are dealt, Tennie returns to the McCaslin place and Buck marries Sophonsiba. Ike hears the story of his parents' courtship and marriage from his cousin and surrogate father, Cass Edmonds, born in 1850 and 16 years Ike's senior.

The plot is comic, with Buck McCaslin summoning all his poker-playing skills in an attempt to get his brother out of trouble with Sophonsiba, although Buddy does marry her in the end. But there is an underlying seriousness in the story. After all, when Tomey's Turl runs away, he is hunted down like an animal, with dogs. Then too, Buck and Buddy McCaslin are inarticulate abolitionists. They refuse to live in their father's mansion and they prod their slaves into working their way toward emancipation.

"The Fire and the Hearth," the second-longest story in the novel, set in 1940, is a comic exploration of Lucas Beauchamp's money obsession, with a long dramatic flashback detailing Lucas's confrontation with his white landlord, Zack Edmonds. Lucas's wife Molly, called to Edmonds's home when his wife dies in childbirth, nurses the Edmonds son and stays on at the big house for six months. A jealous and resentful Lucas breaks into Edmonds's bedchamber and, in a violent confrontation at daybreak, demands Molly's return. He imagines himself the first McCaslin's rightful heir, and feels it is his duty to reclaim his wife.

In the concluding section of the story, Molly, exasperated by Lucas's continuing search for buried treasure on the Edmonds place, files for a divorce. With the intervention of Roth Edmonds (the son of Zack), Lucas agrees to drop his quest and Molly withdraws her suit.

Faulkner develops Lucas Beauchamp and Isaac McCaslin, black and white descendants of the original McCaslin, as the central figures of *Go Down, Moses*. The character of Lucas is more than a racial contrast and far more than a comic figure. Lucas regards Ike as weak. In his view, Ike allowed his cousin Cass Edmonds (Zack's father) to seize the McCaslin lands from him. By novel's end, Lucas has emerged as a powerful figure, with the pride, strength, and independence of old Lucius Quintus Carothers McCaslin himself.

Yet the burden of a slaveholding and racist past oppresses all the characters, black and white, a reality Faulkner powerfully expresses in a scene involving Lucas and Molly's seven-year-old son Henry and his inseparable white playmate, Roth Edmonds. Henry first confronts the South's rigid racial code when Roth suddenly refuses to share a pallet on the floor with him; he later eats alone at the Beauchamp table, served by Henry's mother. "He entered into his heritage," the narrator says of Roth. "He ate its bitter fruit." In an early review, the critic Lionel Trilling identifies this as one of the best passages in the novel, and one of the most crucial.

In "Pantaloon in Black," which the critic CLEANTH BROOKS likened to a story by ERNEST HEMINGWAY, the tough, inarticulate hero, Rider, suffers deeply over the death of his young wife, Mannie. As Brooks notes, he expresses his grief in violence: shoving others aside and filling in his wife's grave himself, manhandling logs at the sawmill where he works, drinking himself into a stupor, and finally slashing the throat of the white night watchman who has long been cheating the black millhands at craps.

"Pantaloon" has only a passing connection with the other six stories in *Go Down, Moses;* Trilling and others have suggested it diminishes the novel's coherence. Rider, as it happens, is another of Roth Edmonds's tenants. Just as Lucas Beauchamp had done, he builds a permanent fire in the hearth on the night of his wedding. Brooks speculates that Faulkner decided to include the story in *Go Down, Moses* "simply because it reveals one more aspect of the world in which 'The Bear' takes place."

That said, it does share with the others the broad theme of black-white relations. Whether ill-placed or not, the story itself is intense and moving—not, as Trilling once suggested, "like every other lynching story we have ever read." "Pantaloon" means fool; presumably Faulkner suggests Rider is a fool, and a doomed one at that, for challenging the South's racial code. And Faulkner achieves a sustained lyrical mastery in his evocations of Rider's physicality. "The story is keyed to Rider's body," the critic Philip Weinstein has written, "the sentences moving in mimickry of his powerful motion."

"The Old People," the fourth story in the novel, forms the essential introduction to "The Bear." The boy in the story is Ike McCaslin. The piece is essentially a character sketch of the woodland genius Sam Fathers, part black, part CHICKASAW INDIAN. In an act of self-emancipation, Fathers quits the plantation, where he is a skilled and highly independent blacksmith, for a life in the big woods. When Ike kills his first buck, Fathers cuts the animal's throat, dips his hands in the warm blood, and wipes them on the boy's face. Priestlike, he officiates at this initiatory rite as Ike's mentor and spiritual father. He teaches the boy pride, humility, and reverence for the land.

In a discussion with UNIVERSITY OF VIRGINIA students in the 1950s, Faulkner addressed the question of Ike's education in the school of Fathers, Boon Hogganbeck, and the other hunters: "They didn't give him success but they . . . gave him what would pass for wisdom—I mean wisdom as contradistinct from the schoolman's wisdom. . . . They gave him that," he said (*Faulkner in the University*, 54). In the end, Ike passes on what he learns from Fathers to following generations. Some critics have seen this notion of mentorship as a new theme of Faulkner's, what Karl F. Zender calls "scenes of instruction."

"The Bear" contains some of Faulkner's best writing. He worked on it through the summer of 1941, completing section 1 in July. The opening introduces the annual ritual, the quest for the near-mythical bear, Old Ben (194), in Trilling's phrase "a kind of forest cousin to Moby-Dick." In the short story "Lion," the genesis of section 2, the narrator, Quentin Compson, is a boy of 16, and Ike McCaslin an old man. In the recast version, told by an omniscient narrator, Ike is the 13-year-old student-in-woodcraft of Sam Fathers. Section 3 opens with a comic interlude in which Ike, now 16, accompanies Boon Hogganbeck on a mission to Memphis to restock the hunting camp's whiskey supply. On their return, they join in the climactic last hunt for Old Ben, Ike observing

from muleback. Old Ben is brought to bay; the dog Lion springs on the bear; Boon Hogganbeck throws himself onto the creature's back and drives his knife into its heart. With the destruction of the bear—the symbolic destruction of the wilderness—Sam Fathers collapses. Boon carries the dog, nearly disemboweled in his encounter with Old Ben, back to camp. The section ends with the deaths of Sam and Lion.

In need of cash, Faulkner in November recast the first three sections of "The Bear," simplified the story line for a mass audience, and offered it to the *Saturday Evening Post*. The magazine responded with a request for Faulkner to alter the ending. The novelist proved accommodating. The *Post* bought the revision, with symbolic elements removed in favor of an uncomplicated story of a boy's rite of initiation, for $1,000 for publication in May 1942.

With the cash infusion, Faulkner returned to the larger work. He had promised the final manuscript for December 1, 1941, but needed extra time to work on section 4, the philosophical center of the novella. Here Ike at 21 discovers painful aspects of his and his clan's past, a documentary record in the yellowing pages of McCaslin plantation ledgers. Quoted selectively, they reveal his grandfather's crimes—rape, incest, miscegenation. They may raise other issues, too, though Ike may not see them. Critics Richard Godden and NOEL POLK offer an alternative reading of the ledgers, arguing they hint at a homosexual relationship between Uncle Buck and Uncle Buddy, or possibly that Buck purchased the hapless slave Percival Brownlee—he can not do a clerk's job, he has no artisan skills and he is not strong enough to work in the fields—for his own sexual use.

He decides to renounce the land and heritage of his fathers, turning over his inheritance to his second cousin (and surrogate father) Cass Edmonds. "Freed" by the mystic woodsman Sam Fathers, Ike can no longer accept the sins of the family's founder nor carry the burden of the larger guilt of slavery. Entries in the old plantation ledgers bring the full extent of old Carothers's outrageous behavior home to Ike: the old man's seduction—in effect, the rape—of his own daughter, whom he had fathered by his slave Eunice.

Ike argues—as Abraham Lincoln had done in his second inaugural address—that God brought on the Civil War to destroy slavery and expiate the sin of it. Ike thus regards the Confederacy's defeat as providential. In long discussions with Cass, he speaks of basing his hopes for the future of the descendants of slaves on their capacity to endure. Ike and Cass argue over the "curse" of the South. Cass believes the land is cursed; Ike responds that the curse lies on "us."

In section 5, the renunciation of the land wrecks Ike's marriage and leaves him a sort of recluse, cut off from the life of the town. Ike revisits the scene of the hunt and finds lumbermen slashing away at the woods. An epoch has ended with the killing of Old Ben. The novella closes on a comic and ironic note. Passing Sam Fathers's grave and the place where Lion is buried, Ike encounters Boon Hogganbeck. The forest canopy is alive with the scurrying of squirrels, a suggestion of the vanishing woods' old abundance. Frustrated and clumsy as ever, Boon fumbles with his jammed gun while the squirrels caper mockingly overhead. Boon tells Ike not to touch the squirrels: "They're mine!"

The relationship of the first three sections of the novella to the fourth "philosophical" section has long engaged Faulkner critics. In his study *William Faulkner*, IRVING HOWE argues that the story would be more satisfying in some ways with section 4 omitted. "The narrative would flow more evenly toward its climax; there would be a more pleasing unity of tone; and the meaning, never reduced to the brittle terms of Isaac's political and moral speculations, would be allowed to rest in a fine implication," he suggests. Nonetheless, Howe concedes that the fourth section makes the story richer and more challenging for the reader.

In "Delta Autumn," the sixth of the seven stories in *Go Down, Moses*, Faulkner emphasizes the historical wrong done to blacks and the parallel wrong of man's destruction of his natural heritage. The story is set in 1940 in what remains of the big woods—it is a 200-mile car ride now to reach the hunting grounds. Ike, here an old man, witnesses the younger Roth (Carothers) Edmonds repeat the sin of Carothers McCaslin: miscegenation and a form, perhaps, of incest. Edmonds has repudiated

his mistress, a young black woman who, unknown to him, is a granddaughter of James Beauchamp (Tennie's Jim), Lucas's brother, who had migrated north in the 1890s.

Ike meets the young woman and advises her to return north and marry into her own race. Some critics have seen in Ike's attitude a compromise with segregation. Faulkner himself regarded Ike both as a man of his time and a passive figure. Passivity, according to the novelist, explains Ike's bleak comment that racial harmony and justice may be a thousand years in the future (*Faulkner in the University*, 246).

The story "Go Down, Moses" brings the novel to a close. Samuel Worsham Beauchamp, the grandson of Lucas and Molly Beauchamp, flees Yoknapatawpha for a life of petty crime in Chicago. He kills a policeman, is convicted and executed. Molly blames Roth Edmonds for his death, because Roth ran him off the plantation for breaking into the commissary.

Members of the white community recognize their complicity in young Beauchamp's end. As Trilling has observed, the novel in general and "Delta Autumn" in particular deal less with the fate of blacks than with "the spiritual condition of white men who have that fate at their disposal." Gavin Stevens, the editor of the local newspaper, and a number of Jefferson merchants take up a collection to bring his body home to Jefferson for burial. Though Stevens and his well-meaning friends miss the larger implications of the Beauchamps' loss, they recognize the symbolic importance of the journey for Molly.

CRITICAL RECEPTION

Faulkner sent off the last of *Go Down, Moses* to New York to his editors at Random House in mid-December. On January 21, 1942, Faulkner dedicated *Go Down, Moses* to the long-time family retainer CAROLINE BARR, whom Faulkner knew as Mammy. A traditional figure, Callie Barr is in sharp contrast to the independent Lucas Beauchamp of the novel—a contrast that suggests Faulkner's own ambiguous response to race and caste.

The book was published on May 11, 1942. In typical fashion, the early reviewers expressed annoyance at the hard labor to which Faulkner's difficult prose sentenced them. The anonymous reviewer of the *Times Literary Supplement* found Faulkner "an exasperating writer" with his "prodigious, mountainous, dizzily soaring wordiness."

Writing in *The Nation* in May 1942, Trilling agreed: "Mr. Faulkner's new book is worth effort but not, I think, the kind of effort which I found necessary: I had to read it twice to get clear not only the finer shades of meaning but simple primary intentions, and I had to construct an elaborate genealogical table to understand the family connections," he wrote. Trilling wondered, too, why Faulkner had included "Pantaloon in Black," which he regarded as misplaced and inferior in conception and execution. That said, he nonetheless judged the novel important and enduring: "The six McCaslin stories are temperate and passionate, and they suggest more convincingly than anything I have read the complex tragedy of the South's racial dilemma."

Even Faulkner's champion MALCOLM COWLEY, delivering a glowing assessment of Faulkner's career in *The Saturday Review* in April 1945, found himself exasperated in trying to negotiate a 1,600-word sentence in the fourth section of "The Bear." He wrote, "It is probably the longest sentence in American fiction, and longer than any in English or Irish fiction, except for Molly Bloom," the soliloquy that concludes Joyce's *Ulysses*. In showing off his technical dexterity, Cowley suggests, Faulkner may have weakened the impact of the story of Uncle Buddy and Uncle Buck freeing their slaves.

Writing in the Book Review of *The New York Times* not long after *Go Down, Moses* appeared, Horace Gregory offered a generally positive assessment, inviting a comparison of Faulkner with Melville and Hawthorne. "He is one of the few writers of our day who deserves increasing respect and admiration."

Random House initially published the book as *Go Down, Moses and Other Stories*. Faulkner objected, insisting on the work's unity as a novel. In subsequent editions beginning in 1949, the title became simply *Go Down, Moses*. Later critics generally do not quibble over the form of *Go Down, Moses*, and most rank its most powerful component, "The Bear," with *The SOUND AND THE FURY*,

LIGHT IN AUGUST and *ABSALOM, ABSALOM!* as one of the peaks of Faulkner's achievement.

EXCERPTS FROM CONTEMPORARY REVIEWS OF *GO DOWN, MOSES*

Excerpt from Lionel Trilling's review, "The McCaslins of Mississippi," published in The Nation, May 30, 1942, 632–633:
. . . Mr. Faulkner's literary mannerisms are somewhat less obtrusive than they have been, but they are still dominant in his writing, and to me they are faults. . . . Mr. Faulkner's new book is worth effort but not, I think, the kind of effort which I found necessary: I had to read it twice to get clear not only the finer shades of meaning but the simple primary intentions, and I had to construct an elaborate genealogical table to understand the family connections.

These considerations aside, Mr. Faulkner's book is in many ways admirable. The six McCaslin stories are temperate and passionate, and they suggest more convincingly than anything I have read the complex tragedy of the South's racial dilemma. The first of the stories is set in 1856; it is the humorous tale of the chase after the runaway Tomey's Turl—it takes a certain effort to make sure that this is a slave, not a dog—of how old Buck McCaslin is trapped into marriage by Miss Sophonisba Beauchamp and her brother Hubert (rightly the Earl of Warwick), and of the poker game that is played for Tomey's Turl; the humor is abated when we learn that Turl is half-brother to one of the poker players. The last story is set in 1940; its central figure is the Negro murderer Samuel Worsham Beauchamp, descendant of Tomey's Turl and related to the McCaslins through more lines than one.

The best of the book does not deal directly with the Negro fate but with the spiritual condition of the white men who have that fate at their disposal. . . .

Excerpt from Robert Littell's review, published in The Yale Review, 31 (Summer 1942), 8:
. . . Here is a collection of William Faulkner's latest short stories, *Go Down, Moses*, full of crazy, incomprehensible, and sometimes rather wonderful people. Too often, a Faulkner story gives one the feeling of having come into a theatre at the end

of the second act—with this difference, that it's usually possible to catch up on a play and find out what it's all about, while if Mr. Faulkner doesn't want you to find out what it's all about, you won't.

Excerpt from Malcolm Cowley's review, "Go Down to Faulkner's Land," published in **The New Republic,** *June 29, 1942, 900:*
. . . Perhaps the best way to judge the book is neither as a novel nor as a series of novellas; neither as magazine nor as personal writing; but simply as another instalment of the Mississippi legend on which Faulkner has now been working for more than fifteen years. It is, as everyone knows by this time, the story of an imaginary county called Yoknapatawpha—area, 2,400 square miles; population, 15,611 by Faulkner's last census, which was printed at the end of "Absalom, Absalom!" At least a fifth of its people, Negro and white, have by now appeared in one or more of his stories. And these stories, although they differ in quality, and although the seven in "Go Down, Moses" are only his second-best, have each the effect of making the legend as a whole seem more impressive. There is no other American writer, and not many novelists anywhere, who have succeeded in presenting the life of a whole neighborhood, with all its social strata, all its personal conflicts, humor and much more that its share of violent crimes.

And there is no other American writer who has been consistently misrepresented by his critics, including myself. . . .

Excerpt from Margharita Widdows's review, published in **The Annual Register,** *1942, 324:*
In Go Down, Moses, and Other Stories . . . Mr. William Faulkner was more Faulkneresque than ever—more tortuous in style, more torrential in his rain of epithets, more frenzied: but at the same time not to be disregarded as one spokesman from America.

Kate O'Brien's review, published in **The Spectator,** *"Fiction," October 30, 1942, 418:*
Blame the times or blame me, but I find myself hopelessly out of sympathy with the thickening self-consciousness and sentimentality in which Mr. Faulkner continues to bury and further bury his original great talent. *Go Down, Moses* is a mighty wedge of ponderous writing, of Mississippi, of negroes and half-Indians, and great dogs and bears and all kinds of odd "Deep South"-ers. Atmospherically it is sometimes magnificent; but the characters are immense exaggerations—and that would be fine if they were not so curiously tedious, so literary. The seven stories are linked together in place and in theme; they deal, poetically, sentimentally and heavily, with the passing of the master-slave days, with the approach of modern decadence to the wild, and with the dreams of great hunters. But they are written in a manner too bogus and pretentious to support their intention of tragedy.

Excerpt from Phillip Toynbee's review, published in **The New Statesman and Nation,** *October 31, 1942, 293:*
There is nothing lucid about Faulkner, and his lack of lucidity is evidently deliberate. . . . The sentences roll on, inversions after qualification often a full paragraph in length. To understand one must re-read, and understanding brings nothing but irritation that so simple a statement shouldn't have been simply stated. With all the qualifications of subjectivity, this is a wonderfully dull book. It is dull because the reward nowhere near justifies the intellectual effort. . . . Faulkner's book has the faults of exhaustion.

CHARACTERS

Acey ("Pantaloon in Black") A black hand at the JEFFERSON, MISSISSIPPI, sawmill where Rider works, he tries to console Rider over his wife Mannie's death. Acey advises Rider against returning home after Mannie's funeral. "She be wawkin yit," Acey tells him.

Alec, Uncle ("Pantaloon in Black") A tall, lean and frail old man, he is the husband of Rider's aunt, who looked after him when he was a boy. When Rider's wife dies, Alec and his wife try to persuade him to come back to his childhood home.

Beauchamp, Amodeus McCaslin ("The Bear") The son of the slaves Tomey's Turl and Tennie Beauchamp, he dies on the day of his birth.

Beauchamp, Henry ("The Fire and the Hearth")
The son of Lucas and Molly Beauchamp, he and
Carothers (Roth) Edmonds, the scion of an old
planter family, are childhood friends.

Henry first confronts the South's rigid racial
code at about age seven, when Roth suddenly
refuses to share a pallet on the floor with him, and
later eats alone at the Beauchamp table, served by
Henry's mother. "He entered into his heritage," the
narrator says of Roth. "He ate its bitter fruit."

**Beauchamp, Hubert ("Was," "The Bear," and
"Delta Autumn")**   A "bluff burly roaring child-
like man," he is the bachelor owner of an estate
just over the edge of the next county from the
McCaslins. His leading ambition is to marry off his
sister Sophonsiba. When Theophilus McCaslin—
Uncle Buck—blunders into her bed by mistake,
Mr. Hubert sees his chance.

A poker game seals the engagement. Uncle
Buck's low hand means he will marry Sophonsiba
and buy the slave Tennie Beauchamp, whose lover,
the McCaslin slave Tomey's Turl, chronically steals
away to the Beauchamp place to see her.

Buck's twin Amodeus—Uncle Buddy—arrives
and persuades Hubert to play another hand of stud
poker. More skilled at cards than his brother, he
wins Uncle Buck's release for the engagement and
gets Tennie for free into the bargain.

Beauchamp appears in two other stories in *Go
Down, Moses,* "The Bear" and "Delta Autumn."
In "The Bear," he deposits 50 gold pieces into a
silver cup as a gift for his nephew and godson Isaac
McCaslin on his 21st birthday. When Ike reaches
his majority and opens the gift, he finds copper
coins and IOUs for the gold pieces and a tin cof-
feepot in place of the cup.

In "Delta Autumn," the part African-American woman with whom the McCaslin descendant
Carothers Edmonds is involved mentions Hubert
Beauchamp as the man who lost Tennie in a card
game.

**Beauchamp, James Thucydus (Tennie's Jim)
("The Fire and the Hearth," "The Old People,"
and "The Bear")**   Born into slavery in 1864. He
is the eldest son and first surviving child of the

slaves Tomey's Turl and Tennie Beauchamp and
the brother of Lucas Beauchamp. In "The Fire and
the Hearth," he leaves home, heads north, and
doesn't stop until he has crossed the Ohio River.
He vanishes on his 21st birthday, leaving his $1,000
legacy unclaimed.

In "The Old People," Tennie's Jim is a servant in the hunting camp of Major DE SPAIN. He
reprises that role in "The Bear," with the special
duty of looking after the camp dogs. He goes to
Hoke's Station to fetch Dr. Crawford to attend
Sam Fathers and the dog Lion, both injured in the
climactic battle with the bear. In "Delta Autumn,"
he is the grandfather of Roth Edmonds's mistress.

Tennie's Jim also appears in *The* REIVERS.

**Beauchamp, Lucas Quintus Carothers McCaslin
("Fire and the Hearth" and "The Bear")**   An
important figure in the YOKNAPATAWPHA COUNTY
cycle, he is the grandson of old Lucius Quintus
Carothers McCaslin, a planter and slaveholder,
and a slave woman and is fiercely proud of his
mixed racial heritage. In his view, his descent from
old Cass sets him above his Edmonds landlords, to
whom Isaac McCaslin has passed the estate, for
they are "woman-made," connected to the founder
only through the female line.

Born in 1874, he is the youngest of the children
of Tomey's Turl and Tennie Beauchamp, who
is old Cass's daughter by a slave. Lucas is presented as the oldest living McCaslin descendant
on the hereditary land—"not only the oldest man
but the oldest living person" there, a man with "a
face composed, inscrutable, even a little haughty,
shaped in the pattern of his great-grandfather
McCaslin's face."

In "The Fire and the Hearth," Lucas confronts
Zack Edmonds over his wife Molly's long stay as
a nurse in the Edmonds home, and he bests the
white man in a violent confrontation at dawn.
Later in the story, he defies Roth Edmonds, Zack's
son and heir, by distilling illegal whiskey on the
plantation. His overarching pride nearly leads to
tragedy; his greed—he is obsessed with the notion
of buried treasure—nearly costs him his marriage.
In the end, Molly and Edmonds persuade him to
give up his hopeless search for wealth.

In "The Bear," Lucas, the only one of the Beauchamp children to remain on the McCaslin plantation, appears in Isaac McCaslin's doorway on his 21st birthday and demands his share of a $1,000 legacy from old Cass. He may have stayed behind on the old place, but he is nonetheless independent for that.

He also appears as a key character in INTRUDER IN THE DUST, and in *The* REIVERS.

Beauchamp, Molly (Aunt Molly; Mollie) ("The Fire and the Hearth," "Delta Autumn," and "Go Down, Moses")   The wife of Lucas Beauchamp, she is a longtime loyal servant of the Edmonds family.

In "The Fire and the Hearth," a young Molly, born a "town woman" and new to country life when she marries Lucas, nurses her son Henry Beauchamp and the motherless Carothers Edmonds (Roth) as though they were brothers, and stays on at Zack Edmonds's place long after the death of Edmonds's wife—too long, in her husband's judgment. Lucas finally confronts Edmonds, and Molly returns to their cabin on the Edmonds plantation.

Later in the same story, the elderly Molly moves, with Roth Edmonds's help, to obtain a "voce" (divorce) from her husband, who has become obsessed with a search for buried treasure. Lucas agrees to abandon his quest, and the suit is withdrawn.

In "Go Down, Moses," the novel's title story, Mollie (Faulkner has varied the spelling of her name) has a premonition that disaster has visited her petty criminal grandson, Samuel Worsham Beauchamp (Butch), and she wants him back in JEFFERSON, MISSISSIPPI. Gavin Stevens, the county attorney, learns that Butch has been convicted and executed for killing a Chicago policeman. With the help of Stevens and Miss Belle Worsham, Mollie recovers his body and insists on a proper burial at home, with flowers, a hearse, and a notice in the Jefferson newspaper.

Molly also appears in retrospective scenes in INTRUDER IN THE DUST.

Beauchamp, Samuel Worsham (Butch) ("Go Down, Moses")   The grandson of Mollie (Molly) Beauchamp, who raised him, he is a small-time criminal who is finally tried, convicted, and executed at age 26 for killing a policeman—shooting him in the back—in Chicago.

With the assistance of the Yoknapatawpha County attorney, Gavin Stevens, his grandmother brings his body home to Jefferson, Mississippi, for burial.

Beauchamp, Sophonsiba (1) (Sibbey) ("Was")   A spinster, pretentious and silly, she fancies herself the mistress of "Warwick," her name for her bachelor brother Hubert Beauchamp's plantation. Mr. Hubert's great ambition is to see Miss Sophonsiba married; her choice settles on Theophilus McCaslin, familiarly known as Uncle Buck.

Sibbey is overdone and over-dressed, all "earrings and beads clashing and jangling like little trace chains on a toy mule." She indulges in a lot of perfume, and roaches her hair under a lace cap. Her most vivid characteristic, though, is a roan tooth that flicks and glints fascinatingly between her lips.

Through a misadventure, Uncle Buck becomes engaged to Miss Sophonsiba. His twin brother, Amodeus McCaslin—Uncle Buddy—wins back Buck's freedom in a hand of stud poker with Hubert, but he eventually marries her anyway and they become the parents of a central figure in "The Bear," Isaac (Ike) McCaslin.

Beauchamp, Sophonsiba (2) (Fonsiba) ("The Fire and the Hearth" and "The Bear")   Born in 1869, she is the daughter of the slaves Tomey's Turl and Tennie Beauchamp and is Lucas Beauchamp's sister. In "The Fire and the Hearth," she goes away to live in Arkansas.

In "The Bear," Isaac McCaslin tracks Fonsiba down in Arkansas to deliver her a $1,000 legacy. He finds her married to a black small farmer and living in near-destitution. Ike arranges for the money to be paid out to her in monthly installments of three dollars so that she will always have a subsistence.

Beauchamp, Tennie ("Was," "The Fire and the Hearth," "The Bear," and "Delta Autumn")   The slave of Hubert Beauchamp, she moves to the McCaslin place, home of her lover, Tomey's Turl, when Amodeus McCaslin acquires her in a card game in 1859.

In "The Fire and the Hearth," Tennie has married Tomey's Turl; their children are James, Sophonsiba, and Lucas Beauchamp. Tennie also appears in "The Bear" and "Delta Autumn."

Birdsong ("Pantaloon in Black")   The white night watchman at the sawmill in JEFFERSON, MISSISSIPPI, where Rider works, he runs a rigged craps game and has been cheating the hands out of their wages for 15 years.

The grieving Rider, who has been steadily drinking whiskey, confronts Birdsong about his crooked dice. When Birdsong reaches for his pistol, Rider cuts his throat with a razor. Birdsong's kin avenge him by lynching Rider.

Brownlee, Percival (Spintrius) ("The Bear")   When Theophilus McCaslin acquires Brownlee from the slave trader Nathan Bedford Forrest, he finds that Brownlee can do neither office nor plantation work and tries to set him free; for a long time, Brownlee refuses to leave. He turns up in the mid-1880s as "the well-to-do proprietor of a select New Orleans brothel."

Compson, Jason Lycurgus II (General) ("The Old People")   He is a senior member of the hunting party that goes deep into the BIG BOTTOM country of the Tallahatchie River each November.

General Compson is the grandfather of Quentin Compson, who narrates the Sutpen story in ABSALOM, ABSALOM! He also appears in The UNVANQUISHED, INTRUDER IN THE DUST, The REIVERS, and in the short stories "A BEAR HUNT" and "MY GRANDMOTHER MILLARD AND GENERAL BEDFORD FORREST AND THE BATTLE OF HARRYKIN CREEK." He is referred to in REQUIEM FOR A NUN and The TOWN.

Crawford, Dr. ("The Bear")   The camp physician at the HOKE'S STATION sawmill, he treats the dog Lion, Sam Fathers, and Boon Hogganbeck after the climactic battle with the bear, Old Ben. Dr. Crawford treats Fathers for shock and exhaus-

tion, and after Fathers dies determines that he "just quit."

Daisy ("The Bear")   The wife of Uncle Ash Wiley, she is the black cook at Major de Spain's hunting camp in the Big Bottom.

Dan ("The Fire and the Hearth")   One of the African-American lotmen on the Edmonds plantation, he turns the draft animals out to pasture in the morning and brings them in each evening. Dan helps Carothers Edmonds search for the missing mule Alice Ben Bolt.

de Spain, Major (Cassius) ("The Old People," "The Bear," and "Delta Autumn")   A Confederate cavalry commander in the Civil War, he is a landowner and sheriff of Yoknapatawpha County. After the hunters kill the bear, de Spain sells the Big Woods timber rights to a Memphis logging company.

de Vitry, Soeur-Blonde ("The Old People")   the New Orleans friend of the Chickasaw chief Ikkemotubbe, he gives the chief his sobriquet of *du homme*—Doom. The name is doubly apt because Doom attains power by using poison to frighten off the incumbent chief, Moketubbe.

De Vitry also appears in the short stories "RED LEAVES" and "A COURTSHIP."

Edmonds, Alice ("The Bear")   She is the wife of McCaslin (Cass) Edmonds, who succeeds to ownership of the McCaslin plantation. She teaches Sophonsiba Beauchamp (2), the daughter of the slaves Tomey's Turl and Tennie Beauchamp, to read and to write a little.

Edmonds, Carothers (Roth) ("The Fire in the Hearth," "Pantaloon in Black," "Delta Autumn," and "Go Down, Moses")   The grandson of McCaslin Edmonds and the son of Zack, he inherits the old McCaslin plantation and supports his cousin Isaac McCaslin, the true heir who long ago relinquished his claim to the place.

The midwife Molly Beauchamp delivered the newborn Roth when the country was in flood and the doctor unable to reach the Edmonds place. He grows up to serve in the U.S. forces in World War I. A bachelor, he is a man of "choleric shortness of temper"; he reminds Isaac (Uncle Ike) McCaslin of old Lucius Quintus Carothers McCaslin, the founder of the clan.

In "The Fire and the Hearth," Edmonds is the often exasperated landlord of Lucas Beauchamp, Molly's husband, and George Wilkins. In "Delta Autumn," he fathers a child with his mistress, a young Northern schoolteacher, then leaves her. Unknown to him, she is part black and is the great-great-great granddaughter of old Carothers.

The harsh, cynical Edmonds's private code prohibits marriage, and his mistress understands this. All the same, she goes with their infant son to the hunting camp in the Delta in search of him. Expecting her, he leaves the camp and asks his elderly kinsman Uncle Ike to offer her a thick sheaf of banknotes and invite her to leave.

In "Go Down, Moses," he evicts Lucas and Molly (Mollie) Beauchamp's grandson Samuel Beauchamp for robbing the plantation commissary.

Edmonds also appears in INTRUDER IN THE DUST and is an offstage character in *The* TOWN.

Edmonds, McCaslin (Cass) ("Was") As the nine-year-old narrator of "Was," the first story in *Go Down, Moses*, set in the years before the Civil War, he accompanies his great-uncle Theophilus McCaslin (Uncle Buck) to the Beauchamp place, a half-day's ride distant, and is fascinated by Miss Sophonsiba Beauchamp's roan tooth.

In "The Old People," Cass is presented as the cousin of Uncle Buck's son Isaac (Ike) McCaslin, 16 years Ike's senior and "more his brother than his cousin and more his father than either." Cass traces Sam Fathers's complicated racial heritage for Ike, allows Sam to go off and live permanently in Major de Spain's hunting camp, and takes Ike on his first hunting trip into the big woods.

In "The Fire and the Hearth," Cass, a descendant of the McCaslins in the female line, takes control of the McCaslin estate, seizing it from the true heir (Ike). Faulkner significantly revises this arrangement in "The Bear." In that story, Ike rejects his patrimony on his 21st birthday and forces the reluctant Cass to accept it. Ike struggles

to explain his complex, sophisticated, and even mystical notions of responsibility to the land and his belief that it carries a curse.

Cass Edmonds also appears in *The* TOWN, *The* REIVERS, and the short story "A BEAR HUNT."

Edmonds, Roth *See* Edmonds, Carothers.

Edmonds, Zachary (Zack; Cousin Zack) ("The Fire and the Hearth") He is the son of McCaslin (Cass) Edmonds and the landlord of Lucas Beauchamp. After Zack's wife dies in childbed, Lucas's wife Molly nurses Edmonds's infant son along with her own boy, Henry Beauchamp.

Molly stays on at the Edmonds place for nearly six months. Her husband becomes jealous, perhaps suspecting a sexual involvement with Zack. Lucas fetches Molly home, then confronts Zack in his bedroom at dawn, first with a knife, then with Zack's pistol. The pistol misfires.

He also appears in *The* REIVERS.

Ewell, Walter ("The Old People," "The Bear," "Delta Autumn," and other works) A member of the annual hunting party that gathers at Major de Spain's camp by the TALLAHATCHIE RIVER valley, he is a crack shot—his rifle never misses. Ewell is present for young Isaac McCaslin's first kill on the hunt.

He also appears in *The* MANSION, *The* REIVERS, and the short stories "A BEAR HUNT" and "RACE AT MORNING."

Fathers, Sam (Had-Two-Fathers) ("The Old People," "The Bear," and "Delta Autumn") The son of the Chickasaw chief Ikkemotubbe ("Doom") and a quadroon slave, he is for many years the blacksmith on the McCaslin plantation where, doing "white man's work" such as carpentry and blacksmithing, he is treated with the deference due a skilled craftsman.

Also a skilled hunter, Fathers teaches woodcraft to Isaac McCaslin, showing him "when to shoot and when not to shoot, when to kill and when not to kill." When Ike is nine years old, Sam leaves the plantation to live alone in the woods. In "The Old People," after 12-year-old Ike kills his first buck,

Fathers smears the animal's hot blood on the boy's face as a coming-of-age ritual.

He teaches Ike humility, patience, and reverence and respect for the land. In "The Bear," Fathers has left the plantation and is living in a hut deep in the woods not far from Major de Spain's hunting camp. For years he is the chief woodsman during the annual hunt for the wily, seemingly indestructible bear the hunters call Old Ben.

Finally Old Ben is brought down, slain by Boon Hogganbeck with the assistance of Lion, the dog Fathers has trained for the purpose. Some of the party find Fathers lying facedown in the trampled mud. Dr. Crawford, summoned from the sawmill at HOKE'S STATION, sews up the mortally wounded Lion and examines Sam.

The hunters break camp, and only Boon and Ike stay behind. With Old Ben dead, Fathers realizes that the wilderness that has been his life is no more. Following Fathers's instructions, Boon builds a Chickasaw grave platform of freshly cut saplings bound between four posts, kills Fathers, and lifts his blanket-wrapped body onto the platform. In the end, McCaslin Edmonds and Major de Spain return to the woods, drive Boon away, and bury Fathers.

Sam Fathers also appears in INTRUDER IN THE DUST, The REIVERS, the short story "RED LEAVES" (as Had-Two-Fathers), and the short story "A JUSTICE."

Gowan, Judge ("The Fire and the Hearth") Lucas Beauchamp and his son-in-law George Wilkins are tried in Gowan's court for making illegal whiskey. He lets them off when they promise to pour out their supply of liquor and destroy the stills.

Henry ("The Fire and the Hearth") He is the toothpick-chewing old deputy marshal in the court of Judge Gowan, who tries Lucas Beauchamp and George Wilkins for making illegal whiskey. Henry also appears in "A POINT OF LAW," a short story that Faulkner revised for the novel.

Hogganbeck, Boon ("The Old People," "The Bear," and "Delta Autumn") The grandson of a Chickasaw woman, he is the large, rough, uneducated, hard-drinking, good-hearted handyman at

Major de Spain's hunting camp. Faulkner notes carefully that Boon is a white man and that his Indian blood is not chief's blood. Isaac McCaslin remarks the difference every time he sees Boon with Sam Fathers.

A violent, insensitive man "with the mind of a child," he is also hardy, generous and faithful. In "The Bear," he is as devoted to the old dog Lion as he is to his patron de Spain.

In the climactic scene, the bear Old Ben swipes at Lion, mortally wounding him. A notoriously bad shot, Boon leaps on the bear and stabs him to death. When Fathers, equating the slain bear to the vanishing wilderness, loses the will to live, he instructs Boon to kill him and place his blanket-wrapped body on a Chickasaw grave platform.

Boon Hogganbeck is a principal character in THE REIVERS and is referred to in INTRUDER IN THE DUST, The TOWN, and the short story "A BEAR HUNT."

Hulett ("The Fire and the Hearth") The court clerk in the interrupted divorce proceeding between Lucas and Molly Beauchamp, he accuses Lucas of being "uppity" for keeping his hat on inside the building.

Ikkemotubbe ("The Old People") Known as "Doom," *du homme*, the man, he threatens the reigning Chickasaw chief, his cousin Moketubbe, with poison, frightens him into abdicating, and assumes the tribal leadership himself. He performs a marriage ceremony joining a quadroon woman pregnant with his child to one of his slaves. She delivers a boy named Had-Two-Fathers, who will become the hunter Sam Fathers of Go Down, Moses and other works. Later, he sold Fathers, his mother and his step-father to Lucius Quintus Carothers McCaslin.

Isham ("Delta Autumn") An elderly African-American servant at the MISSISSIPPI DELTA hunting camp, he prepares a 4 A.M. breakfast for the hunters.

Issetibbeha ("The Old People," "The Bear") A CHICKASAW INDIAN chief, he is the uncle of the ambitious Ikkemotubbe (called Doom). After his death, his son Moketubbe succeeds him, but Ikke-motubbe forces him to abdicate.

Jobaker (Joe Baker) ("The Old People," "The Bear") A CHICKASAW INDIAN, he is a market hunter and fisherman who lives as a hermit in a "foul little shack" on the Edmonds place miles from any other dwelling. The only man to dare to approach his hut is Sam Fathers. When he dies, Fathers buries him in a secret place and sets fire to the shack.

Jonas ("Was") An ostler, he is one of the slaves on the plantation of the McCaslin twins, Amodeus and Theophilus.

Ketcham ("Pantaloon in Black") He is the jailer to whom Rider is delivered after Rider slashes Bird-song's throat in a dispute over a crooked dice game.

Legate, Will ("Delta Autumn") A member of the MISSISSIPPI DELTA hunting party, he is the grandson of Bob Legate, one of the hunters who used to gather each autumn at Major de Spain's camp in the BIG BOTTOM 60 years back. He teases Roth (Carothers) Edmonds about his interest in "does," an allusion to the young woman who seeks him out at the camp.

McAndrews ("Pantaloon in Black") He is the foreman of the JEFFERSON, MISSISSIPPI, sawmill where Rider works. McAndrews expects Rider to take the day off for his wife's burial, but he shows up for work anyway.

McCaslin, Eunice ("The Bear") A slave on the McCaslin plantation, Lucius Quintus Carothers McCaslin purchased her for $650 in New Orleans in 1807. Eunice married Thucydus McCaslin in 1809. She drowns herself in a creek on Christmas Day 1832 after she learns that her daughter Toma-sina (Aunt Tomey) is pregnant with the child of her own father, the white master.

McCaslin, Isaac (Cousin Ike, Uncle Ike) ("Was," "Fire and the Hearth," "The Old People," "The Bear," and "Delta Autumn") The son of Theophilus (Buck) McCaslin, born in 1866 the only child of an old man, he is a complex figure who repudiates his patrimony, the family plantation, because he believes that no man can claim title to the land and that, in any case, slavery has laid a curse upon the YOKNAPATAWPHA COUNTY holdings. He owns nothing, and desires to own nothing.

Ike appears in "The Fire and the Hearth" as an old man, "a widower now and uncle to half a county and father to no one," living in a jerry-built bungalow in JEFFERSON, MISSISSIPPI, surviving on whatever his kinsman Roth (Carothers) Edmonds, now owner of the McCaslin place, chooses to give him. He is the boy narrator of "The Old People." At age 12, he slays his first buck, has its warm blood smeared on his face, and thus completes the rite of passage into manhood.

In "The Bear," Ike at age 10 is permitted to join Major de Spain's hunting camp for the first time. From his part-Chickasaw mentor Sam Fathers he learns woodcraft and gains a deep understanding of the relationship between man and the natural world. The years-long quest for Old Ben, the bear, is the symbol of that relationship. Ike finally catches a glimpse of the bear when he lays aside his gun, watch and compass, the instruments of civilization, and strikes deep into the woods.

The hunters abandon the camp after the killing of Old Ben and the death of Sam Fathers, and Major de Spain sells the timber rights to his holdings to a Memphis lumber company. When Ike returns after a long interval he finds the wilderness transformed: a large planing mill at HOKE'S STATION, long stacks of steel rails, piles of crossties, and a logging line into the woods.

Ike discovers the interrelationships of master and slave and the painful details of the "curse and taint" of slavery when he studies the plantation ledgers his father and uncle had kept: his grandfather's incest; the old man's slave daughter's suicide when she learns her daughter is pregnant with her father's child; his father's fumbling efforts to free his slaves. He finds in the ledgers an account of his grandfather's legacy to his black son Terrel (Tomey's Turl Beauchamp) and his three children, and attempts to find them and deliver it.

Ike relinquishes the McCaslin estate, all but forcing it on his older cousin (and father figure) McCaslin Edmonds, and supports himself by working as a carpenter. Though he marries, he remains childless, and never attempts to reclaim his patrimony.

In "Delta Autumn," Ike, now an old man, draws the unpleasant task of sending away Roth Edmonds's mistress, who is part black—the granddaughter, it turns out, of Jim Beauchamp (Tennie's Jim), the son of Tomey's Turl and once a servant at the hunting camp. The encounter deeply disturbs him.

Faulkner presents Ike as a passive figure, a man overwhelmed, a pessimist. He is powerless to protect his beloved wilderness; he is helpless in the face of injustice. In "Delta Autumn," he tells Roth's bereft mistress that maybe in a thousand years whites and blacks will get along, but not now.

Ike stands for a sort of static decency that he hoped to pass on to future generations, an attitude the conservative in Faulkner understood and admired. "He was trying to teach what he knew of respect for whatever your lot in life is," the novelist remarked, "that if your lot is to be a hunter, you slay the animals with the nearest approach you can to dignity and decency" (*Faulkner in the University*, 54).

Isaac McCaslin is mentioned in *The* HAMLET, INTRUDER IN THE DUST, *The* TOWN, *The* MANSION, *The* REIVERS, and the short stories "A BEAR HUNT" and "RACE AT MORNING."

McCaslin, Lucius Quintus Carothers ("The Fire and the Hearth," "The Old People" and "The Bear")   Born in North Carolina in 1779 and the first McCaslin in YOKNAPATAWPHA COUNTY, he obtains the large grant of CHICKASAW INDIAN land that became the McCaslin plantation. Old Carothers is responsible for the tangled McCaslin racial history. He fathers Tomey's Turl (Beauchamp) by a slave girl who is his own daughter, and so is Lucas Beauchamp's grandfather. He dies in 1837.

He is mentioned in INTRUDER IN THE DUST and *The* REIVERS.

McCaslin, Theophilus (Filus, Uncle Buck) ("Was," "The Fire and the Hearth," and "The Bear")   The twin brother of Amodeus (Uncle Buddy) McCaslin and father of Issac McCaslin, he and his brother are the inheritors of old Lucius Quintus Carothers McCaslin's vast YOKNAPATAWPHA COUNTY plantation holdings.

In "Was," Uncle Buck finds himself engaged to Miss Sophonsiba Beauchamp after he accidentally creeps into her bed one night. Though his brother frees him from the unwanted commitment by winning a hand at poker, he marries her anyway.

At age 60 Uncle Buck is "lean and active as a cat," a vivid figure with white hair, a growth of white stubble, and hard gray eyes. He is a comic character, but he and his brother also represent Faulkner's notion of good men. In "The Fire and the Hearth," for instance, in the 1850s he and Uncle Buddy begin to carry out their scheme to free their father's slaves.

Uncle Buck also appears in *The* HAMLET.

McCaslin, Thucydus Roskus ("The Bear")   A McCaslin slave, the husband of Eunice McCaslin, he refused old L. Q. C. McCaslin's legacy of 10 acres and a $200 cash gift from McCaslin's sons in favor of a work arrangement to gain his freedom. He sets up as a blacksmith in JEFFERSON, MISSISSIPPI, in 1841 and lives until 1854.

Mannie ("Pantaloon in Black")   Rider's wife, she dies only six months after their wedding. The couple had just settled into an emotionally satisfying life together on the Edmonds place, and Rider's grief knows no bounds.

Maydew ("Pantaloon in Black")   The Jefferson sheriff, he investigates Rider's killing of the sawmill night watchman Birdsong, mindful of the fact that Birdsong clan votes helped him win election to the sheriff's office.

Moketubbe ("The Old People")   He is the fat, indolent son of the CHICKASAW INDIAN chief Issetibbeha. He succeeds as chieftain when his father dies, but soon abdicates in favor of his cousin Ikkemotubbe after Ikkemotubbe poisons his eight-year-old son.

Moketubbe is also mentioned in *The* REIVERS and in the short stories "RED LEAVES" and "A COURTSHIP."

Oscar ("The Fire and the Hearth") A lot man on the Edmonds place, he helps Dan look after the mules.

Phoebe (Fibby) ("The Bear") A slave Lucius Quintus Carothers McCaslin brought with him from North Carolina, she is the wife of Roscius (Roskus). Old McCaslin frees her on his death; she remained on the place until her death in 1849.

Rideout, Dr. ("The Fire and the Hearth") Roth Edmonds summons him to attend Molly Beauchamp after she is found semiconscious in the creek bottom where her husband Lucas has been treasure-hunting. She collapses there after running away with the handle of the divining machine Lucas uses in his search for buried wealth.

Rider ("Pantaloon in Black") An African-American sawmill hand, he lives quietly and industriously with his newlywed wife, Mannie, in a cabin he rebuilds on Carothers Edmonds's place. When Mannie dies only six months after the wedding, he is inconsolable and refuses offers of succor from his friends and the old aunt who raised him.

Grieving and desperate, he becomes drunk on moonshine and joins a crooked dice game at the mill. When he accuses Birdsong of cheating (the night watchman has rigged the game and has been fleecing the hands for 15 years), Birdsong reaches for his pistol. Rider, a lithe and powerful six-footer, slashes his throat with a razor.

Rider is arrested and jailed for the murder. Birdsong's kinsmen take him from his cell and hang him from a bell rope in the black schoolhouse two miles from the sawmill.

Roscius (Roskus) ("The Bear") One of the original McCaslin slaves, he is the husband of Phoebe. L. Q. C. McCaslin frees both Roskus and Phoebe on his death in 1837; both refuse to leave the plantation. Roskus dies in 1841.

Rouncewell ("Go Down, Moses") He owns the store in JEFFERSON, MISSISSIPPI, that Butch (Samuel Worsham) Beauchamp breaks into, his first serious trouble with the law.

Sartoris, Bayard (old) ("The Bear") The son of Colonel John Sartoris, founder of the prominent JEFFERSON, MISSISSIPPI, family, he is the inheritor of his father's banking and related business interests. Along with four other Jefferson men, he is an overnight visitor to Major de Spain's hunting camp in the Big Bottom.

Semmes, Mr. ("The Bear") He is a MEMPHIS distiller. Major de Spain sends Isaac McCaslin and Boon Hogganbeck to Semmes to replenish the supply of whiskey for the hunting camp in the Big Bottom.

Sickymo ("The Bear") A former slave, he becomes a U.S. marshal in JEFFERSON, MISSISSIPPI, after the Civil War. His half-white sister was the mistress of a Federal officer. Sickymo used to steal his master's grain alcohol, dilute it with water, and sell it from a cache in the roots of a big sycamore behind the drug store, an enterprise that gave him his name.

Stevens, Gavin ("Go Down, Moses") Modeled partly on Faulkner's longtime friend Philip Avery Stone, Stevens is an attorney from a prominent family in JEFFERSON, MISSISSIPPI, and as the Jefferson city attorney arranges to bring the body of the executed killer Samuel Worsham Beauchamp home from Chicago.

Thisbe, Aunt ("The Fire and the Hearth") She fixes a "sugar tit" (pacifier) for the infant Roth Edmonds after Molly Beauchamp, who had been nursing the boy, returns home at her husband Lucas's command.

Tom ("The Fire and the Hearth") A county commissioner in JEFFERSON, MISSISSIPPI, he books Lucas Beauchamp and George Wilkins after their arrest for distilling illegal whiskey.

Tomey, Aunt (Tomasina) ("The Fire and the Hearth" and "The Bear") A slave, she is the daughter of the old planter Lucius Quintus Carothers McCaslin, the mother of McCaslin's slave son, Tomey's Turl (Beauchamp), and the grandmother of Lucas Beauchamp. Tomey dies giving birth to Turl (Terrel) in June 1833.

Tomey's Turl (Terrel) ("Was") Born in June 1833, a son of the old master Lucius Quintus Carothers McCaslin and a slave girl, Tomey, who also was McCaslin's daughter, he is the lover (and later the husband) of Tennie (Beauchamp). He used to clothe himself in a white Sunday shirt when he fled the McCaslin plantation to visit Tennie at Hubert Beauchamp's place. In "Delta Autumn," Faulkner notes he has no last name.

Wilkins, George ("The Fire and the Hearth") The husband of Lucas Beauchamp's daughter Nathalie Beauchamp Wilkins, he is a "jimber-jawed clown" in Lucas's estimation, a swaggerer who manages to look "foppish even in faded overalls." George secretly follows his father-in-law's example and sets up a still on Roth Edmonds's plantation. When Lucas reports him for making what he derides as "hog swill," both are caught and charged with distilling illegal whiskey.

Wilkins, Nathalie Beauchamp ("The Fire and the Hearth") The youngest child of Lucas and Molly Beauchamp, at 17 she marries the flashy but rather simple George Wilkins in secret and takes his side when her father turns him in for making illegal whiskey.

Beauchamp has long been distilling whiskey discreetly himself, and both men end up being hauled into court. As the case is presented, Beauchamp learns that George and his daughter have been husband and wife for several months. Though small and thin, Nathalie is tough; she negotiates with her father for a stove, a new back porch, and a well for George's place.

Wilmoth ("Go Down, Moses") The editor of the JEFFERSON, MISSISSIPPI, newspaper, he helps Gavin Stevens raise money to bring the body of the killer Samuel Worsham Beauchamp, executed in Illinois, home for burial.

Worsham, Belle ("Go Down, Moses") A JEFFERSON, MISSISSIPPI, spinster, she is the granddaughter of the planter who owned the slave parents of Mollie (Molly) Beauchamp and her brother Hamp.

Though she is poor, Miss Belle feels an obligation to help bring Samuel Beauchamp's body home from Chicago for a decent burial, whatever the cost.

Worsham, Hamp ("Go Down, Moses") The brother of Mollie (Molly) Beauchamp, an old man with blurred eyes and the head of a Roman general, he and his wife live with Miss Belle Worsham, a penniless JEFFERSON, MISSISSIPPI, spinster, and help support her through the sale of chickens and vegetables.

Worsham, Samuel ("Go Down, Moses") He is the father of the Jefferson spinster Miss Belle Worsham. Mollie (Molly) Beauchamp names her grandson for him.

Wyatt, Henry ("Delta Autumn") A member of the MISSISSIPPI DELTA hunting party, he recalls a time before the arrival of the logging companies when the Big Woods were far richer in game.

Wylie, Uncle Ash ("The Old People," "The Bear") The black cook in the Big Woods hunting camp, he is "as deft in the house as a woman." He accurately forecasts the weather, too, predicting a warm-up and rain that would allow the hunters to go after their quarry, the bear Old Ben.

FURTHER READING

Brooks, Cleanth. *"Go Down, Moses."* In *William Faulkner: First Encounters*, 129–159. New Haven: Yale University Press, 1983.

———. "The Story of the McCaslins (*Go Down, Moses*)." In *William Faulkner: The Yoknapatawpha Country*, 244–278. Baton Rouge: Louisiana State University Press, 1990.

Kinney, Arthur F. Go Down, Moses: *The Miscegenation of Time.* New York: Twayne, 1996.

Kuyk, Dirk, Jr. *Threads Cable-Strong: William Faulkner's* Go Down, Moses. Lewisburg, Pa.: Bucknell University Press, 1983.

Litz, Walton. "Genealogy as Symbol in *Go Down, Moses.*" *Faulkner Studies* 1.4 (1952): 49–53.

Matthews, John T. "The Ritual of Mourning in *Go Down, Moses.*" In *The Play of Faulkner's Language,* 212–273. Ithaca: Cornell University Press, 1982.

Millgate, Michael. *"Go Down, Moses."* In *The Achievement of William Faulkner,* 201–214. Lincoln: University of Nebraska Press, 1978.

Sundquist, Eric J. "Half Slave, Half Free: *Go Down, Moses.*" In *Faulkner: The House Divided,* 131–159. Baltimore: Johns Hopkins University Press, 1985.

Taylor, Nancy Dew. *Annotations to William Faulkner's* Go Down, Moses. New York: Garland, 1994.

Thornton, Weldon. "Structure and Theme in Faulkner's *Go Down, Moses.*" *Costerus* 3 (1975): 73–112.

Tick, Stanley. "The Unity of *Go Down, Moses.*" In *William Faulkner: Four Decades of Criticism,* edited by Linda W. Wagner. East Lansing: Michigan State University Press, 1973.

Wagner-Martin, Linda, ed. *New Essays on* Go Down, Moses. New York: Cambridge University Press, 1996.

"Gold Is Not Always" (Uncollected Stories)

Humorous short story published in *American Mercury* in November 1940; revised and incorporated into "The Fire and the Hearth," the second chapter of GO DOWN, MOSES (1942).

SYNOPSIS

"Gold Is Not Always" details Lucas Beauchamp's growing obsession with finding treasure allegedly buried on the McCaslin plantation. When a young salesman calls on Lucas to collect payment for the divining machine that Lucas has ordered from a St. Louis company, Lucas goes to his landlord, Carothers (Roth) Edmonds, hoping to borrow $300 to cover the purchase price. Edmonds rebuffs the request, scoffing at the idea of a buried treasure and reminding Lucas that he has $3,000 of his own in the local bank. Lucas, however, refuses to spend his own money; instead, he persuades the salesman to trade him the machine for a mule, with the understanding that Lucas will buy the mule back for $300 once the treasure has been found.

Later that same day, Edmonds discovers that one of his best mules is missing from the barn. When Edmonds and two helpers track the footprints of the mule through briars and heavy undergrowth deep into a creek bottom, they find Lucas, his son-in-law George Wilkins, and the salesman using the divining machine. While Edmonds and the salesman, who has a signed bill of sale from Lucas, argue over the ownership of the mule, Lucas continues his search for the buried treasure. Edmonds, after ordering Lucas to return the mule to the barn by the next morning, departs in frustration and anger.

Now more desperate than ever to find the treasure, Lucas searches all night long. The next morning, after a night of futility, he arranges with the salesman to keep the machine for another night, agreeing to pay an extra $25 for the use. Lucas sends George to the bank with a check for $50, telling him to get the money in silver dollars. When George returns, Lucas buries the money in an old rusted can in the orchard near his house. That night, when the search resumes, Lucas makes sure the salesman is the one using the machine when the money is discovered.

Now it is the salesman who is obsessed with finding the remainder of the treasure. For the use of the machine for the rest of the night he returns the bill of sale for the mule to Lucas, signs over the ownership of the divining machine to Lucas, and agrees to pay Lucas the rental fee of $25 per night. He also agrees to pay Lucas half of any treasure he finds, including that share of the $50 he has already uncovered. Lucas sends George to return the mule to Edmonds.

Three days later Lucas goes to see Edmonds. Lucas describes his dealings with the salesman, who has apparently left the area, and explains that, now that he owns the machine outright, he and George will continue to look for the buried treasure. Exasperated, Edmonds orders Lucas to leave: "Go home. And don't come back. Don't ever come back. When you need supplies, send your wife after them."

CRITICAL COMMENTARY

This surface text of this story, which turns on a version of the ancient salted-mine trick (which Faulkner had previously used in *The* HAMLET), deals with human greed. With Lucas's obsession for the missing treasure, Faulkner dramatizes the almost-universal human desire for easy wealth, for getting something for nothing. But the more powerful subtext of the narrative—indeed, the real story—concerns the relationship of Lucas, a black sharecropper, with his white landlord and the white salesman. A popular story line in Southern literature from slave days onward treats the actions of a black character who, unequal in status and judged inferior by whites, must exercise craftiness and guile in his dealings with his white "betters." Faulkner had previously created such a character in his portrayal of Simon Strother in *SARTORIS / FLAGS IN THE DUST*, but Lucas Beauchamp is by far Faulkner's most successful characterization of the type. As readers know from other stories in which he appears, Lucas Beauchamp is part white, a descendant of the McCaslin patriarch, Lucius Quintus Carothers McCaslin; and, partly for that reason, Lucas refuses the role of the subservient black that the white society seeks to impose on him. In *INTRUDER IN THE DUST* (1948) this refusal takes the form of stubborn, militant resistance; in "Gold Is Not Always" Lucas bests the whites by using his intelligence and wit.

CHARACTERS

For the character list for this story *see* the entry on
GO DOWN, MOSES.

"Golden Land"
(Collected Stories)

First published in *American Mercury* in May 1935, this piece is Faulkner's only short story explicitly

reflecting his impression of Hollywood; it was later republished in *Collected Stories of William Faulkner* in 1950.

SYNOPSIS

"Golden Land" portrays southern California as a pseudoparadise undermined by moral decay. The uneventful action follows the real estate entrepreneur Ira Ewing, Jr., through one day: He awakens with his usual hangover, fights with his wife and son over breakfast, visits his mother, stops for a business errand, and goes with his mistress to the beach.

Ewing may live in luxury, but he is an alcoholic, his marriage is in tatters, and his children are an embarrassing disappointment. His son is effeminate, with transvestite tendencies; his daughter, a movie extra, is embroiled in a lurid scandal. His widowed mother, for whom he provides a house and everything else she needs, still yearns for the one thing he will not allow her—to return to her Nebraska home. Nebraska's bleak prairies and its staunch pioneer values contrast with the sunny gardens and ephemeral culture of expediency in Los Angeles. Ewing does not hesitate to exploit his daughter's notoriety for his own commercial gain, and even his mother exploits her grandchildren for money after their relationship breaks down. She finally accepts that California is to be her home until the end of her days.

CRITICAL COMMENTARY

In his biography of Faulkner, JOSEPH BLOTNER mentions that "Golden Land" is "a story from Faulkner's last sojourn in California" and is "imbued with the distaste and unhappiness he had felt. The terrain, the climate, the architecture, the people, their behavior, their dress—all displeased him" (*Faulkner* 342). James Ferguson arrives at a similar conclusion when he writes, "Whatever coherence the largely unsuccessful 'Golden Land' has is thematic: at the most obvious level, Faulkner's contempt for Hollywood as a false and meretricious Eden; at a deeper level, the idea that we define ourselves as human beings only through our willingness to acknowledge and confront the harsher realities of life" (*Faulkner's Short Fiction*, 137). Other autobiographical elements appear to be present in the story as some readers who know of Faulkner's drinking (*see* ALCOHOLISM, FAULKNER AND) unhesitatingly make a connection between Faulkner and the story's main character, the alcoholic Ira Ewing, Jr. However readers may judge the merits of this story, its setting remains unique to Faulkner's short fiction.

HELPFUL RESOURCES

Theresa M. Towner and James B. Carothers, *Reading Faulkner: Collected Stories,* 371–384 Diane Brown Jones, *A Reader's Guide to the Short Stories of William Faulkner,* 476–486.

CHARACTERS

Ewing, Ira, Jr. He runs away from his family's bleak Nebraska farm at 14, jumps a freight train that carries him to California, and becomes a successful real estate dealer in Beverly Hills. But he and his wife are at daggers drawn, his children are awful, and he drinks to escape the wreckage of his life. Ewing has a mistress who seems to love him. He visits his widowed mother every day but fails to keep the tragedy of his family life from her.

Ewing, Ira, Sr. A Nebraska pioneer, a wheat farmer, and a part-time preacher, he tries to teach his son Ira Ewing, Jr., "something about fortitude." Ewing's widow comes to live with Ira Jr. in Beverly Hills.

Ewing, Samantha (1) The widowed mother of Ira Ewing, Jr., the Beverly Hills real-estate tycoon, she is alone and homesick for Nebraska, although she lives without material want in Glendale, California, in the former home of her son and his family. Because Ira handles all her finances, Mrs. Ewing cannot put aside money for train fare back to Nebraska and realizes she is trapped in California, doomed to live there to the end of her days. Ira tries to keep his children's troubles from her, but she learns the sorry details from her gardener, Kazimura.

Ewing, Samantha (2) Ira Ewing, Jr.'s, daughter. She is a promiscuous would-be starlet who lands extra parts under the name of April Lalear. Samantha turns up in the newspapers as one of three people charged in a case involving sex orgies.

Ewing, Voyd The effeminate son of Ira Ewing Jr., he favors women's underwear. Voyd and his father detest each other. Ira discovers the underwear when he puts the youth to bed drunk, and he beats him even though he is unconscious.

Kazimura Samantha Ewing's gardener, he shows her a newspaper that recounts the equivocal doings of her granddaughter, a would-be starlet who seeks to advance her Hollywood career by taking part in sex orgies.

Green Bough, A

A collection of poems with illustrations by Lynd Ward, published in April 1933 by HARRISON SMITH and ROBERT K. HAAS. Of the 44 poems, 13 were previously published (*see* Appendix for specific titles and dates), and most were composed during the first half of the 1920s; earlier versions of a few of the poems are found elsewhere in Faulkner, for example, in MISSISSIPPI POEMS and in his novels MOSQUITOES and SOLDIERS' PAY. Several of the poems in *A Green Bough* were reprinted in *Mississippi Verse,* a collection edited by Alice James and published in 1934 by the University of North Carolina Press, Chapel Hill. *A Green Bough* was reproduced photographically from its original edition (along with *The MARBLE FAUN*) and published in 1965 by RANDOM HOUSE.

The poems in *A Green Bough,* like most of Faulkner's poetry, reflect the influence of such writers as T. S. Eliot, A. E. HOUSMAN (in particular, the poems of *A Shropshire Lad*), Algernon Charles Swinburne, John Keats, and others. Although in general the poems in this collection are more convincing as poems than the poetry in *The Marble Faun,* they, like the earlier volume, tend to be overly "literary," an observation made by CLEANTH BROOKS in his discussion of Faulkner's poetry (*William Faulkner: Toward Yoknapatawpha and Beyond,* 17). However, *A Green Bough,* as Michel Gresset discusses in *Fascination: Faulkner's Fiction, 1919–1936,* is an important step in Faulkner's apprenticeship and in his artistic development as a prose writer. *Also see* Judith Sensibar, *Faulkner's Poetry: A Bibliographic Guide to Texts and Criticism.* (For more information, see *Selected Letters of William Faulkner*, 37, 55, 59–60, 67, and 138; and *Faulkner in the University*, 4.)

"Hair" (Collected Stories)

Short story first was published in *American Mercury* (May 1931) and included in *These 13* (1931).

SYNOPSIS

The private life of Henry Stribling, known as Hawkshaw, is vastly different from how he is perceived by the public, most of whom regard him as pathetic or perhaps even perverted. Set in JEFFERSON, MISSISSIPPI, the story is narrated by an unnamed traveling salesman who also hears of and witnesses Hawkshaw's activities elsewhere.

After Hawkshaw arrives to work as a barber, the townspeople gossip about his attentions to the orphan girl Susan Reed, even after she matures into an apparently promiscuous young woman. Speculation about the two continues while the narrator learns and conceals the truth. In fact a man of exceptional integrity and devotion, Hawkshaw once was engaged to a young woman who died. He paid for her burial and later the funerals of her parents, paid off her father's mortgage debt, and now takes his annual April vacation on the anniversary of her death in order to tend to the house and yard. In the end everybody, including the narrator, is astounded to hear that Hawkshaw has married Susan, whose yellow-brown hair is the same color as that of his dead fiancée.

CRITICAL COMMENTARY

This story mirrors the familiar theme of appearance versus reality, as the narrator learns that Hawkshaw is a quite different person from the one the townspeople have long assumed. Technically, "Hair" demonstrates Faulkner's habit of treating his subject indirectly, linking viewpoint and truth to subjectivity and perspective.

CHARACTERS

Bidwell A storekeeper in Division, the town on the Mississippi–Alabama line where the Starnes family lives.

Burchett The name of the couple with whom Susan Reed lives. The exact relationship between Susan and the Burchetts is uncertain, causing some people to question its character. Mr. Burchett also appears in the short story "MOONLIGHT," where he is identified as the uncle and guardian of Susan, who in this story has no last name. Mr. Burchett catches Susan and her young beau fumbling and kissing in the hammock and drives the boy off with kicks and blows.

Burchett, Mrs. She and her husband take Susan Reed into their home. Mrs. Burchett treats Susan harshly and even beats her for wearing makeup. Mrs. Burchett also appears in the short story "MOONLIGHT," in which Susan refers to her as Aunt Etta. Susan tells her aunt that she is going to a show with her friend Skeet when she actually plans to meet her boyfriend, whom she has been told not to see again.

Cowan, Mrs. Owner of the boarding house in Jefferson where Hawkshaw lives.

Ewing, Mitch The freight agent at the depot in Jefferson.

Fox, Matt A coarse, fat, gossiping barber, he works in Maxey's shop in Jefferson.

Maxey A barber who owns the shop in which Hawkshaw works.

Reed, Susan An orphan, she lives with Burchett and his wife and is regarded as something of a loose woman by JEFFERSON, MISSISSIPPI, standards. She marries the barber Henry Stribling (Hawkshaw). With no last name, Susan also appears in the short story "MOONLIGHT," where she is the 16-year-old girlfriend of the unnamed protagonist. Told by her uncle and guardian, Mr. Burchett, not to see her boyfriend, Susan disobeys, writes a provocative note to her beau, and meets with him at an empty house one night. She rejects her boyfriend's amorous advances, however, and tells him she would rather go to a show.

Starnes, Mrs. Sophie Starnes's mother. Regarding her background as superior to that of her daughter's fiancé, the barber Henry Stribling, she allows Stribling to do her yardwork when he comes to visit each April on his vacation.

Starnes, Sophie   She is engaged to the barber Henry Stribling (Hawkshaw), but dies before they can be married.

Starnes, Will   The lazy, debt-ridden father of Sophie Starnes, Henry Stribling's fiancée. When he dies, Stribling pays off the mortgage on his house.

Stevens, Gavin   The district attorney in Jefferson. He is the only one to whom the narrator tells the story of Hawkshaw's background in Alabama.

Stribling, Henry (Hawkshaw)   The son of a tenant farmer, Hawkshaw learns barbering at a school in Birmingham, Alabama, saves money, rents a little place, and prepares to send for his fiancée, Sophie Starnes. She dies before they can be married. Moving to JEFFERSON, MISSISSIPPI, where he finds work in Maxey's barbershop, he falls in love with the orphan girl Susan Reed and eventually marries her. In "DRY SEPTEMBER," Hawkshaw tries to talk the leader of the lynch mob out of the killing of Will Mayes, who is accused of attacking a white spinster.

Hamlet, The

This is the first novel of the Snopes trilogy (*The HAMLET, The TOWN,* and *The MANSION*) and one of Faulkner's most humorous works; all three are dedicated to Faulkner's close friend PHIL STONE. In Faulkner's original plan for the trilogy, *The Hamlet* was tentatively called *The Peasants,* the title he later gave to book 4 of the novel (*see Selected Letters of William Faulkner,* 107).

Although published on April 1, 1940, *The Hamlet,* as Faulkner remarked, began as short stories written in the late 1920s (*see Faulkner in the University,* 14). The novel, therefore, contains versions of several previously published and one unpublished story: "SPOTTED HORSES" (*Scribner's,* June 1931 [in chapter 1, book 4]), "The HOUND" (*Harper's,* August 1931 [in chapter 2, book 3]), "FOOL ABOUT

A HORSE" (*Scribner's,* August 1936 [in chapter 2, book 1]), "LIZARDS IN JAMSHYD'S COURTYARD" (The *Saturday Evening Post,* February 27, 1932 [in chapter 3, book 1, and chapter 2, book 4]), a portion of "BARN BURNING" (*Harper's,* June 1939 [in chapter 1, book 1]), and "AFTERNOON OF A COW" (written in 1937 but not published until after *The Hamlet* in a French translation in 1943 [in the second section of chapter 1, book 3]). Faulkner explains the compositional history of the work in an August 1945 letter to MALCOLM COWLEY, in which he notes that he conceived *The Hamlet* as a novel from the outset (*see Selected Letters of William Faulkner,* 197). Several short stories Faulkner produced when writing the novel found their way into it as well. Another source for *The Hamlet* is the fragment of the novel FATHER ABRAHAM, which Faulkner abandoned sometime around 1927 when he began FLAGS IN THE DUST (published under the title *Sartoris*).

SYNOPSIS

The novel takes place about 1907 and begins the Snopes saga with the arrival of the sharecropper Ab Snopes and his ambitious and unscrupulous son Flem in YOKNAPATAWPHA COUNTY's rural village of FRENCHMAN'S BEND. *The Hamlet* describes how this unsuspecting town, accustomed to the autocratic dealings of Will Varner, Frenchman's Bend's principal landowner, is forced to adapt to the rise to power of the Snopes clan, whose varied activities dominate most of the action of the novel and some of which produce grotesquely humorous episodes, such as Isaac Snopes's romantic obsession with a cow and Mink Snopes's ludicrous attempt to remove the murdered body he stuffed into the empty hollow of a tree trunk. The Snopeses alter the social and economic conditions of a village whose denizens, ironically, become inadvertent participants in their own exploitation and demise.

The novel opens with the image of the decayed ruins of the OLD FRENCHMAN PLACE, a pre–Civil War plantation with overgrown gardens and neglected fields. The rumor of buried money on the premises reinforces an image of unrealistic hopefulness on the part of anyone foolish enough to dig for it. By the end of the novel Flem, the most successful Snopes, dupes even the shrewdest of observers, V. K. Ratliff. Snopes sells Ratliff and two others the worthless plantation, and with prospects for even greater success—the subject matter of the second and third novels in the trilogy—departs from Frenchman's Bend for JEFFERSON, MISSISSIPPI. "'Couldn't no other man have done it,'" an unidentified character says at the close of the novel. "'Anybody might have fooled Henry Armstid. But couldn't nobody but Flem Snopes have fooled Ratliff'" (The Hamlet, 405).

The Hamlet is a comic novel that mingles irony and satire with deep human pathos. The effectiveness of the ironic and humorous tone that Faulkner achieves is partly the consequence of having Ratliff narrate much of the novel. An astute and detached observer of events, Ratliff is at times also an active participant in them, reinforcing the novel's ironic and satiric elements. The novel consists of four major divisions, each contributing to the delineation of the Snopes takeover and Flem's ultimate successes: book 1, "Flem"; book 2, "Eula"; book 3, "The Long Summer"; and book 4, "The Peasants."

Book 1 opens with a brief account of the history of Frenchman's Bend and an amusing description of Will Varner pictured leisurely sitting on a chair his blacksmith made from an empty flour barrel, a substitute (and mock) throne from which he surveys his holdings. Against this tranquility and the security of a landowner contemplating his next foreclosure, Jody, Varner's son, rents a farm to Ab Snopes, a tenant farmer and reputed barn burner, a fact Jody discovers only after the deal. To protect his property (a form of fire insurance, as Ratliff wryly remarks to Will Varner [25]), Jody hires Flem as a clerk in his store. Flem uses this opportunity to advance his interests and business schemes. Among his successful ventures, he builds and furnishes a new blacksmith shop that forces Varner's to close. In addition to introducing the Snopes family and detailing Flem's entrepreneurial maneuvers, this first book also includes the memorable account of Ab Snopes's horse dealings, a story Faulkner first used in "Fool About a Horse." It contains an episode that captivates readers: the air-bloated horse Ab Snopes unwittingly gets as a trade from Pat Stamper.

In book 2, "Eula," the title character (Eula Varner Snopes) is portrayed in heightened language evocative of Greek mythology and her presence associated with the revelry and ripeness of a Dionysic era. At the age of eight when she starts school at her brother Jody's insistence, Eula, as seen through the eyes of her schoolteacher Labove, is likened to an earth goddess of fecundity. When Labove one morning turns from the blackboard, he beholds before him "a face eight years old and a body of fourteen with the female shape of twenty, which on the instant of crossing the threshold brought into the bleak, ill-lighted, poorly-heated room . . . a moist blast of spring's liquorish corruption, a pagan triumphal prostration before the supreme primal uterus" (126). In juxtaposition to the mock heroic description of this modern-day Helen is Jody's satiric and coarse comment: "'She's like a dog! Soon as she passes anything in long pants she begins to give off something. You can smell it! You can smell it ten feet away!'" (99).

Of the four books, book 2 is the shortest but also the most concentrated in its account of a single character (Eula) and the most dramatic in its delineation of the *immediate* (and at times *frenzied*) effect she has on others. Although serene and inert in herself, Eula causes strong emotions and strange behavior in those around her. Labove's mad passion for her is likened to "a man with a gangrened hand or foot [who] thirsts after the axe-stroke which will leave him comparatively whole again" (131). Eula discovers his after-school ritual of kneeling and placing his face on the still-warm bench where she sat during the day, and wards off Labove's bungled attempt to ravish her with a blow to the face that knocks him and the bench over. That night Labove leaves Frenchman's Bend for good, but others faithfully take his place. By the time Eula is 15, a half dozen young men engage in a savage Sunday night rite of beating up on one another. A year after that, Hoake McCarron, an outsider living 12 miles from Frenchman's Bend, begins to court Eula. Three months later when he learns that she is pregnant with his child, he vanishes. Jody wants revenge and Varner a practical solution, which the latter finds in his clerk Flem Snopes. Flem marries Eula out of greed and, on their wedding day, gets money and the deed to the Old Frenchman Place from Varner. Eula and Flem honeymoon in Texas until after her baby, Linda, is born. Book 2 ends with Ratliff's imagined and imaginative description of Flem outwitting the Prince of Evil and ultimately possessing hell itself.

The passions and obsessions of love and greed dominate book 2. In book 3, variations on these passions ironically play off one another through the characters of Ike Snopes, Jack Houston, and Mink Snopes. Though the language in some passages of book 3 is as heightened as that in the previous book, there is a marked change in the narrative tone, particularly in the section relating Ike Snopes's infatuation for Houston's cow. However the reader may judge (and react to) Ike's sexual behavior, a tone of tenderness and compassion nonetheless comes through the episode.

Book 3, "The Long Summer," opens with Ratliff meeting Will Varner on his way to preside over the trial that will take place in the makeshift courtroom of VARNER'S STORE. As justice of the peace, Varner hears the suit Mink brings against Houston for taking possession of the scrub-yearling Mink claims is his. When Ratliff, the normally impartial observer, hears that the ruling favors Mink, he provides a commentary in mock imitation of the proverb-prone I. O. Snopes: "'Snopes can come and Snopes can go, but Will Varner looks like he is fixing to snopes forever. Or Varner will Snopes forever—take your pick'" (179).

In the next section, the lyrical description of Ike's devotion to Houston's cow elevates his passions to the level of unselfish love, which Ike is able to mimic but is incapable of ever knowing. The sentiments and emotions as well as the sexual overtones and pastoral imagery in this episode are a powerful and ironic evocation of the Song of Solomon with its themes of the tenderness of love and of the union, separation, and reunion of lovers. If Ike's ingenuous love provides a sharp contrast to the love stories of Houston and Mink that immediately follow as flashbacks in the narrative, it also provides a contrast to the scheming devices others in the novel employ in their daily dealings. Houston and Mink, however, may be as much the victims of fate as the simpleminded Ike is. Houston

has failed in his attempt to flee "not from his past, but to escape his future" and learned that one "cannot escape either of them" (234). He abruptly ends a seven-year common-law marriage to a woman he had taken from a brothel and returns to Frenchman's Bend to marry his former schoolmate, Lucy Pate (Houston). Within six months, she is killed by the stallion he bought as a wedding present. Houston "grieved for her for four years in black, savage, indomitable fidelity" (227). Later, he becomes the victim of Mink Snopes's revenge for having taken possession of his scrub-yearling. Houston is murdered by a man whose own life reflects the forces of a fate that make escape improbable.

In trying as a young man to escape a sharecropper's life of poverty and degradation, Mink plans to run off to sea but ends up instead in a logging camp in southern Mississippi. When it goes out of business, he marries the owner's nymphomaniac daughter and returns to "his native country" to become a sharecropper. His murder of Jack Houston is as much an act of defiance and reclamation of honor as it is revenge. After shooting him, Mink has to repress the desire to leave a signed note on the body: "*This is what happens to the men who impound Mink Snopes's cattle . . .* But he could not, and here again, for the third time since he had pulled the trigger, was that conspiracy to frustrate and outrage his rights as a man and his feelings as a sentient creature" (242). When Mink arrives home at dusk, his wife knows what has happened, confronts him, and leaves after he strikes her several times.

When he hears the baying of Houston's hound during the night, Mink returns to the dead body, drags it through slime, and hides it in the hollow shell of a pin oak, in which he himself almost gets stuck. He later meets with his wife and, although he has no money with which to run away, refuses to accept the $10 she has for him because he realizes she got it by selling herself either to Will or to Jody Varner. His cousin Lump tries several times to con Mink into taking him to the body in order to steal the money he believes is still in Houston's purse. Mink, however, refuses. At two different times, he knocks Lump unconscious so he will not interfere with his plans to retrieve the body from the hollow of a tree. (Mink had seen buzzards circling over the tree during the day, revealing the location of Houston's corpse.) As Mink hurls the decaying body from the river bank, he notices that one of its limbs is missing, and while searching for the missing arm, he is arrested. Book 3 ends with Mink in jail in Jefferson and his wife and two children boarding at Ratliff's house. Eck Snopes informs Ratliff that he paid the full amount ($20) for Ike's cow so it could be destroyed and replaced it with a wooden effigy worth two bits. A folk remedy for the cure of beastiality suggested by the village minister, Whitfield, required slaughtering the animal and having Ike eat of it.

In book 4, "The Peasants," Flem returns from Texas with Buck Hipps, who auctions off the wild ponies the two brought with them. Hipps opens the auction by giving Eck a horse, which by the end of the day runs through Mrs. Littlejohn's yard, up the steps of her hotel, through the front door, and into Ratliff's room. Taking his wife's hard-earned money, Henry Armstid bids five dollars on one of the wild ponies, and when he tries to capture it, he is injured. The wild horses run through Mrs. Littlejohn's lot toward an open gate and scatter throughout Frenchman's Bend. Armstid, with a broken leg, is carried into Mrs. Littlejohn's hotel. Eck's horse gallops into Vernon Tull's wagon as he and his family are crossing a bridge on their way home. Tull is knocked unconscious when his "frantic mules" (336) pull him from the wagon. Hipps assures Mrs. Armstid that Flem will return the five dollars. Flem, of course, pockets the money. The Armstids file suit against Flem and the Tulls against Eckrum Snopes, but both plaintiffs lose. Although the episode recounts financial losses and physical injuries and is set against the backdrop of another of Flem's schemes to exploit those around him, the description of the auction, of the bidding, and of the breaking loose of the wild ponies is one of the most humorous passages in Faulkner.

The last part of the novel reintroduces the legend of the buried pre–Civil War money at the Old Frenchman place. Armstid, Ratliff, and Bookwright watch Flem digging at night and assume he is looking for the treasure; in fact he is salting the worthless property to lure them into buying it. The next night the three arrive with Uncle Dick Bolivar, a

diviner, to help them search for the money. They find the three bags of coins Flem buried to trick them and buy the place a few days later. When Ratliff and Bookwright examine the dates of their coins (dates all much later than 1861), they realize that they have been duped. Armstid, however, mulishly continues to dig. On his way to Jefferson, where he is moving with his family and where he now possesses Ratliff's share of a restaurant, Flem goes three miles out of his way to pass by the Old Frenchman Place to have one more look at the foolish Armstid. The second novel of the Snopes trilogy, *The Town*, continues the story of Flem's pursuit of money.

For more on *The Hamlet*, see the books *Faulkner in the University* and *Selected Letters of William Faulkner*.

CRITICAL RECEPTION AND COMMENTARY

Most reviews of the novel were favorable. One reviewer, the critic MALCOLM COWLEY, observed that "*The Hamlet* is a new sort of novel for William Faulkner, less somber, more easygoing and discursive. Except for a few short stories, it makes better reading than anything else he has written since *Sanctuary*. . . . The new quality I find in this book," Cowley continued "—new to Faulkner at least—is friendliness. Pity he has often shown in the past, but never before the amused liking that he extends to almost all the people of Frenchman's Bend" ("Faulkner by Daylight," published in *The New Republic* 102 [April 15, 1940]: 510). IRVING HOWE points out that "The strength of *The Hamlet*, a strength typical of Faulkner, lies in its characterization" (*William Faulkner: A Critical Study*, 248). Faulkner's characters are convincingly sketched and their stories—even those that touch upon pathos and violence—account for the humor in *The Hamlet* and provide a source of unity. The novel is a vivid portrait of the residents in and around the rural hamlet of Frenchman's Bend.

The unity of the novel has been a concern to many readers. Some judge *The Hamlet* episodic because it incorporates versions of several short stories. Malcolm Cowley, for instance, in his introduction to "Spotted Horses" published in *The Portable*

Faulkner, comments that *The Hamlet* "is halfway between a novel and a cycle of stories" (366). But other critics find unity through the novel's themes; one theme in particular is that of emerging SNOPE-SISM. Howe cautions readers against condemning *The Hamlet* as having been "loosely strung together," a "pointless" criticism because, according to Howe, the novel is meant to be that way. He argues that unity is achieved through the major theme of "the demoralization of Frenchman's Bend by the Snopes clan" and that the novel focuses attention on this theme "with reasonable frequency" (*William Faulkner: A Critical Study*, 244). Other readers find unity in the work's central character, Flem Snopes. In his assessment of the problem, Edmond L. Volpe writes: "Episodic the novel certainly is, presenting as it does the stories of many characters, some of whom (like Labove and Houston) have no contact with Flem; but the book as a whole is unquestionably unified, each episode revealing directly or indirectly the character of the central figure" (*A Reader's Guide to William Faulkner*, 307). Just how some episodes "indirectly" reveal the character of Flem *is* questionable, however. In his assessment of three major critical attitudes toward the question of the novel's unity (namely, that it is episodic, that it is unified through the theme of encroaching Snopesism, and that the novel's unity is achieved through the recurring stories of barter and love), Melvin Backman argues that:

> . . . one must concede that Flem plays little or no part in the stories of Labove's obsessional passion for Eula Varner, the development and seduction of Eula, the romance of the idiot and the cow, the feud between Jack Houston and Lucy Pate, and Mink Snopes's murder of Jack Houston. These stories, which constitute Books Two and Three, occupy literally the center of the novel; they are generally uninfluenced by the Snopes theme and are at variance with the humor that prevails in the tales of barter. They emit another tone—intense, tortured and strange—and suggest that a darkness underlies the novel's comic mood. Intermittently, however, comedy breaks through the somber drama to fuse distress with laughter,

pathos with violence, and despair with hilarity. The result is a unique counterpoint that combines diverse elements into a kind of whole. (*Faulkner: The Major Years*, 141)

This "unique counterpoint" combining apparently diverse elements into artistic unity is not atypical of Faulkner's narrative strategies, which often disrupt a reader's expectation of a straightforward go-ahead plot or storyline and redirect the reader's attention onto the text itself. Displacing the primacy of plot and engaging the reader's imagination in the dynamic of the text are modernist tendencies. (*See* MODERNISM.)

After reviewing the compositional history of *The Hamlet*, Michael Millgate concludes that even though the writing of the novel was sporadic and stretched over a decade it was "conceived as a single whole," and the period of composition afforded Faulkner time to revise, expand—it is one of his longer works—and integrate the novel. The final product, according to Millgate, "far from being a series of loosely connected incidents, demands consideration as a carefully organised and wholly organic structure" (*The Achievement of William Faulkner*, 185–186). As an example of Faulkner's adeptness and artistry in integrating into *The Hamlet* two previously published short stories, "Spotted Horses" and "Fool About a Horse," Millgate explains that these straightforward and humorous stories of the trickery of horse-trading, stories clearly within the tall tale tradition, perform a different function in the novel by presenting readers with "characters who in the short stories are little more than conventional counters" but in the novel these characters "become fully known to us as individuals, as human beings capable of suffering" (186). Millgate judges the reworking of "Spotted Horse" into *The Hamlet* "a brilliant variation on the traditional horse-trade theme, but it also tells us a great deal about the economic and social relationship operating within the world of Frenchman's Bend and brings out with painful clarity the suffering implicit for the losers in a horse-trade and for their wives and families—something which lies wholly beyond the limits of the tall tale" (186). The episode, as Millgate notes, also underscores the unbridled rapacity and utter heartlessness of Flem Snopes, who is on his way to realizing his ambitions. The novel closes with Flem and his wife Eula and her daughter leaving Frenchman's Bend for Jefferson where Flem will eventually become president of a bank and owner of a mansion.

FILM ADAPTATION

In 1958, *The Long, Hot Summer,* a film version of *The Hamlet,* directed by Martin Ritt and starring Paul Newman, Joanne Woodward, Anthony Franciosa, Orson Welles, Lee Remick, Angela Lansbury, and Richard Anderson, was released by Twentieth Century–Fox. The screenplay was written by Irving Ravetch and Harriet Frank, Jr., and based on book 3 ("The Long Summer") of the novel and on the short stories "BARN BURNING" and "SPOTTED HORSES."

CHARACTERS

Armstid, Henry   A poor farmer who lives in the rural area of FRENCHMAN'S BEND. In book 4 of *The Hamlet,* Armstid is presented as a selfish, greedy, foolish, and impetuous person who ends up making a spectacle of himself. At the auction of the wild ponies that Flem Snopes and Buck Hipps drove up from Texas, Armstid takes his wife's hard-earned money to buy a horse he cannot afford and breaks his leg trying to catch it. By the end of the novel, he mortgages all he owns and, with V. K. Ratliff and Odum Bookwright, purchases the OLD FRENCHMAN PLACE, a worthless piece of property that Flem tricks the three into buying. Armstid goes mad in his futile attempt at digging up the treasure rumored to be buried there, and eventually he is put away in an insane asylum in Jackson.

Armstid appears in *As I LAY DYING* and *LIGHT IN AUGUST,* where only his surname is used and where he is portrayed as a kind and considerate person who helps both neighbor and stranger; *also see* the short story "SHINGLES FOR THE LORD." In *The TOWN* and *The MANSION,* he is an offstage character living in the Jackson asylum.

Armstid, Mrs.   Henry Armstid's wife. In addition to long hours and heavy manual work (there are times when she pulls a plow with her husband), she earns money by weaving at night. In book 4 of

The Hamlet, she unsuccessfully tries to prevent her inconsiderate husband from using her hard-earned money ($5.00) to bid on one of the wild ponies Flem Snopes and Buck Hipps are auctioning off. Though Buck is willing to give the money back to her, Flem pockets it, and when she brings suit against him, she loses. *Also see LIGHT IN AUGUST* (where her first name is Martha), *As I LAY DYING* (where she is called Lula, and "SHINGLES FOR THE LORD" (where, like in *The Hamlet,* no first name is given). (For further information, *see Faulkner in the University,* 30–31).

Benbow, Judge   An offstage character referred to in the opening pages of the novel. In the narrative description of Will Varner, Judge Benbow is mentioned as having said of Varner that a milder-mannered man never bled a mule or stuffed a ballot box. *See ABSALOM, ABSALOM!* and *The UNVANQUISHED* ("An Odor of Verbena").

Bolivar, Uncle Dick   An old diviner in *The Hamlet* who helps V. K. Ratliff, Odum Bookright, and Henry Armstid search for the treasure rumored to be buried at OLD FRENCHMAN PLACE. Employing a forked peach branch as a divining rod, Uncle Dick finds only the three sacks of coins that Flem Snopes used to salt the worthless property. For his service, Ratliff pays him a dollar. Uncle Dick is said to eat frogs, snakes, and bugs. He also appears in the short story "LIZARDS IN JAMSHYD'S COURTYARD," which Faulkner incorporated into this section of *The Hamlet.*

Bookwright, Odum   A bachelor farmer in the area of FRENCHMAN'S BEND. With V. K. Ratliff and Henry Armstid, he is tricked by Flem Snopes into buying OLD FRENCHMAN PLACE, a worthless piece of property believed to contain buried treasure. This episode is also referred to in *The MANSION.* (Although presented as a bachelor, at one point Bookwright refers to his wife in a remark he makes to Ratliff; *see The Hamlet,* 76.)

Cain   A storekeeper in Jefferson. In *The Hamlet,* Cain sells Ab Snopes a milk separator for Snopes's wife, Vynie.

De Spain, Major (Cassius) A retired major of the Confederate cavalry and, after the Civil War, a landowner and sheriff of YOKNAPATAWPHA COUNTY. In the short story "Barn Burning" and as retold in book 1 of *The Hamlet* (where details of the burning barn episode slightly differ from those in the short story), De Spain charges his tenant farmer Ab Snopes 20 bushels of corn for having ruined his wife's expensive French rug. A judge reduces the charge to 10 bushels when Ab sues, but that does not stop Ab from taking revenge by burning down De Spain's barn. *Also see* ABSALOM, ABSALOM!, *The* TOWN, *The* MANSION, INTRUDER IN THE DUST, *The* REIVERS, and the short stories "BARN BURNING," "LION," "THE OLD PEOPLE," "THE BEAR," and "WASH"; he is referred to in "DELTA AUTUMN," "A BEAR HUNT," and "SHALL NOT PERISH." His last name also appears as de Spain.

De Spain, Mrs. (Lula) Wife of Major De Spain. As would be expected, she is very upset when the tenant farmer Ab Snopes soils her expensive rug imported from France. The spiteful and embittered Ab Snopes intentionally walks across it in his manure-covered boots. This episode from book 1 of *The Hamlet* is a retelling of the same incident in the short story "BARN BURNING."

Doshey An old family name in the area of FRENCHMAN'S BEND. In *The Hamlet*, Doshey is the family name of Eustace Grimm's first wife. She is one of the Calhoun County Dosheys.

Freeman In book 4 of *The Hamlet*, Freeman is one of the men lounging about on the gallery of VARNER'S STORE and the first to recognize Flem Snopes as he returns from Texas with the wild ponies. Freeman later buys one of them at the auction. When the horses break loose, he suggests that the men catch one wild horse at a time. Freeman also appears in "SPOTTED HORSES," the short story Faulkner revised for this section of *The Hamlet*.

Freeman, Mrs. Freeman's wife. Mrs. Freeman sees Eck Snopes's wild pony break its neck when it runs into the rope Eck and his son tie across the end of a lane on her property.

George One of Sheriff Hub Hampton's deputies. Mink Snopes is handcuffed to him when being taken to jail for murdering Jack Houston.

Grenier, Louis A Huguenot, Grenier is one of the early settlers of YOKNAPATAWPHA COUNTY and owner of a vast plantation which becomes FRENCHMAN'S BEND. He is the first settler to bring slaves to the county and the county's first cotton planter. The ruined mansion on the original property is the OLD FRENCHMAN PLACE eventually acquired by the landowner Will Varner. Flem Snopes gets possession of this worthless property when he marries Varner's daughter Eula and later tricks V. K. Ratliff, Odum Bookwright, and Henry Armstid into buying it. (*See* SANCTUARY, where the bootlegger Lee Goodwin uses Old Frenchman Place as a hideout.) *Also see* REQUIEM FOR A NUN. Grenier is referred to in KNIGHT'S GAMBIT ("Hand Upon the Waters"), *The* TOWN, *The* REIVERS, and as a Paris-trained architect and something of a dilettante in INTRUDER IN THE DUST. *The Hamlet* mentions a county named Grenier (*see* Related Places on page 132). Grenier's last descendant is the dull-witted squatter Lonnie Grinnup.

Grimm, Eustace A young tenant farmer living about 10 or 12 miles from FRENCHMAN'S BEND. Eustace helps his cousin Flem Snopes trick V. K. Ratliff, Odum Bookwright, and Henry Armstid into buying OLD FRENCHMAN PLACE, a worthless piece of property said to contain buried treasure. Worried that Eustace might buy the property before they have the chance, the three partners quickly purchase the land after they dig up the three bags of coins Flem buried as bait. Only after the sale does Ratliff realize the role Eustace played in Flem's scheme. Eustace appears in "LIZARDS IN JAMSHYD'S COURTYARD," the short story Faulkner revised for this section of *The Hamlet*. *Also see* As I LAY DYING.

Grumby, Major A roughneck referred to by V. K. Ratliff when the latter recounts Ab Snopes's horse dealings during the Civil War. For specifics, *see* "Riposte in Tertio" and "VENDÉE" in *The* UNVANQUISHED.

Hampton The steady, capable sheriff of YOKNAPA-TAWPHA COUNTY. In *The Hamlet*, he arrests Mink Snopes for having killed Jack Houston and takes him to the JEFFERSON, MISSISSIPPI, jail. *Also see* INTRUDER IN THE DUST (where his first name is Hope), *The* TOWN, and *The* REIVERS. (Faulkner was not consistent in giving Hampton a first name; he has no first name in *The Hamlet* or in *The Reivers*, but in *The Town* and *The* MANSION his first name is Hub.)

Hipps, Buck He is the Texan who auctions off the wild ponies he and Flem Snopes herd up to FRENCHMAN'S BEND (*see* book 4, "The Peasants," part 1 of chapter 1). Although in partnership with the unscrupulous Flem, Hipps shows a genuine sensitivity toward Mrs. ARMSTID, whose foolish and impetuous husband, Henry, takes her hard-earned money to buy a horse. Hipps refuses to sell him one and returns the five dollars to his wife. When Henry forces the money from her to give to Flem, Hipps tells her she can get it back the next day, but the greedy Flem keeps it. (An earlier version of this episode appears in FATHER ABRA-HAM, where Hipps is identified by his first name. He asks people to call him Buck in *The Ham-let*, but the narrator refers to him exclusively as the Texan. In the short story "SPOTTED HORSES," another version of the episode, Buck is referred to as "the Texas man" by the narrator and by his first name by Flem.)

Hoake A well-to-do landowner, he is the father of Alison Hoake McCarron; he leaves his prop-erty to his grandson, Hoake McCarron. When his only daughter elopes with McCarron, he sits with a loaded shotgun across his knees and waits 10 days for their return.

Holland, Anse Referred to Old Man Anse Holland in *The Hamlet*, he rents farms to V. K. Ratliff's father and Ab Snopes. Without Anse's knowledge, Snopes trades Anse's worn-out sor-ghum mill and straight plow stock to Beasley Kemp for a horse. (In the short story "A FOOL ABOUT A HORSE," an earlier version of the epi-sode than the one found in the novel, Holland's

bob-wire and busted tools are traded.) *Also see* "Smoke" in KNIGHT'S GAMBIT.

Houston, Jack He is a childless widower and farmer in the vicinity of FRENCHMAN'S BEND. At 16, Houston leaves home to avoid a romantic involve-ment with his country schoolgirl friend Lucy Pate, whom he marries 13 years later when he returns to home. While away, he works at different jobs, one of which is a locomotive fireman, and lives with a woman for seven years after taking her from a brothel in Galveston. Before leaving for Mississippi, he shares his money with his common-law wife. Six months after he is married to Lucy she is killed by the stallion he gave her as a wedding present. At this time, he becomes embittered and isolated.

The idiot Ike Snopes is in love with Houston's cow and steals it; after tracking him down, Hous-ton in disgust gives Ike the cow. At 33, Houston, arrogant and forceful, is killed by Mink Snopes, the result of a dispute over Mink's stray yearling that Houston penned up. References to Houston appear in *The* TOWN—in one place his first name appears as Zack (36) and in another Jack (78); in *The* MAN-SION; and in an earlier published short story, "The HOUND," where he is referred to as a "prosperous and overbearing man" (*Uncollected Stories of Wil-liam Faulkner*, 157).

Houston, Lucy Pate She is Jack Houston's schoolgirl friend and later his wife. Six months after marrying Houston, she is fatally kicked by the stal-lion he gave her as a wedding present. (In editions prior to the 1961 Vintage paperback edition of *The* TOWN, the second novel of the SNOPES TRIL-OGY, her name is Letty Bookwright, and she is the youngest daughter of Cal Bookwright.)

Jim (1) He is one of Sheriff Hampton's deputies. When Mink Snopes is arrested for having killed Jack Houston, Jim drives the wagon that takes Snopes to jail.

Jim (2) In *The Hamlet* (and in "FOOL ABOUT A HORSE"), he is the horsetrader Pat Stamper's black assistant. Jim is an artist at disguising mules and horses that Stamper trades.

Kemp, Beasley A minor character, Beasley trades a horse with Ab Snopes. (*Also see* the short story, "FOOL ABOUT A HORSE.")

Labove (1) He is the father of the schoolteacher by the same name. On a business trip in an adjacent county, Will Varner happens to meet Labove at dusk and is invited to spend the night in his cabin. Varner also happens to be on the lookout for a schoolteacher, and when he finds out that Labove's son is a university student who at one time wanted to be a teacher, Varner suggests to Labove that his son come over to FRENCHMAN'S BEND to see him about the job.

Labove (2) He is a student at the university who takes a teaching job in FRENCHMAN'S BEND before graduating. Although he does not care for football, he plays to pay for his education, and during the summer he works in sawmills. Labove sends football cleats to his family so they will have shoes to wear outdoors. Will Varner provides him with a horse to ride the 40 miles from the university in OXFORD, MISSISSIPPI, to Frenchman's Bend so Labove can keep up with his schooling and continue to play football.

Stricken by the sensuous beauty of Varner's 13-year-old daughter, Eula, Labove decides to stay on as a teacher after he graduates and is admitted to the bar. He is so enamored of Eula that he kneels at her bench to feel her body warmth after his students leave for the day. When Eula discovers him one afternoon, he attempts to ravage her but fails. Eula knocks him down. Labove abruptly leaves town for good, knowing that Eula was so unimpressed that she would not even bother to tell her brother of the attempted rape.

Littlejohn, Mrs. She is the owner and sole manager of Littlejohn's Hotel in FRENCHMAN'S BEND. A hard-working and kindhearted woman, she provides a place in her barn for the idiot Ike Snopes, who does various chores for her, and she helps Henry Armstid when he breaks his leg trying to catch the wild pony he thinks he bought from the Texan Buck Hipps. When one of the wild horses that escape comes running toward her, she daunt-

lessly breaks a washboard over its face. This episode is found in the earlier works FATHER ABRAHAM and "SPOTTED HORSES," which Faulkner incorporated into *The Hamlet*, and is again referred to in *The TOWN*. Mrs. Littlejohn also appears in "LIZARDS IN JAMSHYD'S COURTYARD" (revised for *The Hamlet*). (For more information, *see Faulkner in the University*, 66.)

In *The Hamlet* and INTRUDER IN THE DUST, Littlejohn is a family name of early farmers in YOKNAPATAWPHA COUNTY. *Also see* AS I LAY DYING and *The MANSION*.

McCallum, Anse (old) He is a self-reliant yeoman farmer in northeast YOKNAPATAWPHA COUNTY. Old Anse trades 14 rifle cartridges for two wild horses, which he brings back home from Texas and turns into a good team. *Also see* "The TALL MEN" and SARTORIS (where his name appears as Virginius MacCallum).

McCallum, Old Man Hundred-and-One This is a name that V. K. Ratliff uses when talking about Flem Snopes and his wife, Eula, who have been married for 29 days. Although the exact identity of the person is not certain, it appears that Ratliff is speaking metaphorically. McCallum is a family name in YOKNAPATAWPHA COUNTY, dating back to the Civil War.

McCarron He is the father of Hoake McCarron. Before eloping with Alison Hoake (McCarron), he made his living by playing poker, but after his marriage he became a decent husband, who successfully ran his father-in-law's farm. He apparently died in a gambling house 10 years after he was married.

McCarron, Alison Hoake She is Hoake McCarron's mother. A determined and independent woman, she climbed out of a second-story window to elope with her husband. She is also referred to in *The TOWN*.

McCarron, Hoake He is one of Eula Varner's suitors. At 23, he looks older. Following a scandal involving the wife of an instructor at the agricultural college he was attending, Hoake withdrew.

By chance one day he happens to ride through FRENCHMAN'S BEND and sees Eula, whom he begins to visit to the ire of her other admirers. When he is abused by his rivals, he fights them off with Eula's help but suffers a broken arm, which Will Varner sets. After Varner goes to bed, Hoake—with his splinted arm supported by Eula—takes her virginity. When he finds out three months later that she is pregnant, he leaves for Texas, as do the other suitors. *Also see* The TOWN *and* The MANSION.

McCaslin, Isaac (Cousin Ike, Uncle Ike) Although mentioned in *The Hamlet*, where he allowed Ab Snopes and his family to live in his storehouse when Ab worked for him, he appears in other works, principally in GO DOWN, MOSES. He is also referred to in INTRUDER IN THE DUST, *The Town*, *The MANSION, The REIVERS*, and the short stories "A BEAR HUNT" and "RACE AT MORNING."

McCaslin, Theophilus (Filus, Uncle Buck) He is referred to by V. K. Ratliff in connection with the horse thief Ab Snopes, whose crippled leg, according to Uncle Buck, was a result of a gunshot wound Colonel John Sartoris gave him for trying to steal the colonel's horse. *Also see* ABSALOM, ABSALOM! and GO DOWN, MOSES.

Mitchell, Hugh A minor character in the novel, he is one of the men lounging on the gallery of Whiteleaf's store when Ab Snopes comes by with a horse he says came from Kentucky. Knowing that is not true, Mitchell identifies the horse as once belonging to Herman Short, Pat Stamper, and Beasley Kemp, and mockingly asks whether Snopes gave Beasley 50 cents for it.

Odum, Cliff He is a minor character in *The Hamlet*, a farmer in FRENCHMAN'S BEND who helps Ab Snopes's wife get her milk separator back from Pat Stamper in exchange for a cow.

Pate, Lucy *See* Houston, Lucy Pate.

Peabody, Doctor Lucius Quintus He sells V. K. Ratliff a bottle of whiskey to give to Ab Snopes when Pat Stamper outwits Snopes on a horse trade.

Doc Peabody appears in several other works; *see* SARTORIS, *The* SOUND AND THE FURY, AS I LAY DYING, *The* TOWN, *The* REIVERS, and the short story "Beyond."

Quick, Lon Uncle Ben Quick's son, Lon operates the sawmill in FRENCHMAN'S BEND. He is the first to bid on one of the wild ponies Buck Hipps auctions off. When the horses escape, Quick fails to capture his. *Also see* the short story "SPOTTED HORSES" (revised for *The Hamlet*), KNIGHT'S GAMBIT ("Tomorrow," where his first name is Isham), and AS I LAY DYING.

Quick, Uncle Ben In *The Hamlet*, he is an old man who raises goats. He is Lon Quick's father. *Also see* KNIGHT'S GAMBIT ("Tomorrow").

Ratliff, V. K. (Vladimir Kyrilytch) One of the main characters and narrators in the Snopes Trilogy (*The Hamlet, The* TOWN, and *The* MANSION) and *Big Woods* ("A BEAR HUNT"). Ratliff is an itinerant salesman with a "bland affable . . . face" and "a pleasant, lazy, equable voice" (*The Hamlet*, 14). Much of the action in the trilogy is recounted through his narrative voice, which is often dispassionate, ironic, and humorous. Ratliff is a shrewd observer of events and the major source of news throughout the counties in which he sells sewing machines and, later on, other items such as radios and televisions. In *The Hamlet*, the first novel of the trilogy, Ratliff discerns early on and before others the danger Flem Snopes poses to the community. By the end of the novel he is nevertheless duped by Flem into buying the OLD FRENCHMAN PLACE, where he and his co-owners, Henry Armstid and Odum Bookwright, foolishly expect to find treasure rumored to be buried on the property. To pay for his third of the Old Frenchman Place, Ratliff sells his share of a sidestreet restaurant he owned in partnership with his cousin Aaron Rideout. (In *The Town* and *The Mansion*, Aaron Rideout's name is changed to Grover Cleveland Winbush.)

Ratliff lives in Jefferson with his widowed sister, who keeps house for him as he travels through several counties selling his sewing machines more often on promissory notes than for hard cash. On several occasions, Ratliff proves himself a humane and compassionate person. In *The Hamlet,* he opens his home to the displaced Mrs. Mink Snopes and her children, for whom he buys new overcoats. He also leaves money with Mrs. Littlejohn for the dimwitted boy Ike Snopes and puts an end to the spectacle of watching Ike's bestiality with a cow in Mrs. Littlejohn's barn. *Also see The Town and The Mansion.*

In addition to the Snopes trilogy, Ratliff appears in the short story "A Bear Hunt" and under the name V. K. Suratt in "LIZARDS IN JAMSHYD'S COURTYARD," "CENTAUR IN BRASS," SARTORIS, and AS I LAY DYING. In responding to a question on the characters in his novels who best adjust to progress, Faulkner exclusively identifies Ratliff as one who is able to accept without "anguish" or "grief" the inevitability of change in culture and environment. In Faulkner's words, Ratliff "possesses what you might call a moral, spiritual eupepsia" (*Faulkner in the University*, 253). In an August 1945 letter to MALCOLM COWLEY, Faulkner mentioned that the short story "Spotted Horses" produced a character he "fell in love with: the itinerant sewing-machine agent named Suratt," whose name Faulkner changed to Ratliff because "[l]ater a man with that name turned up at home" (*Selected Letters of William Faulkner*, 197).

Rideout A minor character in the novel, he is Aaron Rideout's brother and V. K. Ratliff's cousin.

Rideout, Aaron A minor character in *The Hamlet,* Rideout is V. K. Ratliff's cousin and with him a half-owner of a sidestreet restaurant in Jefferson. (Faulkner changes his name to Grover Cleveland Winbush in *The TOWN* and *The MANSION*.)

Sam A minor character in *The Hamlet,* he is Will Varner's African-American manservant who carries around Varner's daughter Eula when she is a child. When Flem Snopes leaves FRENCHMAN'S BEND for JEFFERSON, MISSISSIPPI, Sam helps Lump and Eck Snopes load his wagon.

Sartoris, Bayard (old) Modeled on Faulkner's paternal grandfather, JOHN WESLEY THOMPSON

FALKNER, Bayard Sartoris is the son of Colonel John Sartoris, founder of the prominent Jefferson family, and inheritor of his father's banking and related business interests. In *The Hamlet,* the story of his giving Ab Snopes a beating for his role in the death of his grandmother is told. *Also see SARTORIS, The UNVANQUISHED, The TOWN, GO DOWN, MOSES,* ("The Bear"), *REQUIEM FOR A NUN, The MANSION, The REIVERS,* and the short stories "A ROSE FOR EMILY" and "There was a Queen."

Sartoris, Colonel John Modeled on Faulkner's great-grandfather, WILLIAM CLARK FALKNER, Colonel John Sartoris is an important figure in the history of Yoknapatawpha County. He is referred to in *The Hamlet* when V. K. Ratliff mentions Uncle Buck McCaslin's story of how Ab Snopes got his club foot. Colonel John Sartoris shot the horsethief Snopes when he attempted to steal the Colonel's horse during the Civil War. *See* especially SARTORIS, where he is referred to, ABSALOM, ABSALOM!, *The UNVANQUISHED,* and *REQUIEM FOR A NUN;* he is referred to also in *LIGHT IN AUGUST, The SOUND AND THE FURY, GO DOWN, MOSES* ("The Bear"), *The TOWN, The MANSION, The REIVERS,* and in the short stories "BARN BURNING," "SHALL NOT PERISH," "MY GRANDMOTHER MILLARD AND GENERAL BEDFORD FORREST AND THE BATTLE OF HARRYKIN CREEK," and "THERE WAS A QUEEN."

Short, Herman A minor character in *The Hamlet.* Herman swaps Pat Stamper a mule and buggy for a horse which he then sells to Beasley Kemp for eight dollars. He also appears in the short story "FOOL ABOUT A HORSE," which was revised and used in *The Hamlet.*

Snopes, Ab An unscrupulous scavenger, Ab Snopes is one of the first Snopeses in YOKNAPATAWPHA COUNTY. In response to a question Faulkner was asked while at the University of Virginia, the author said that this Snopes was "a hanger-on" and "sort of a jackal" that stayed "around the outskirts of the kill to get what scraps might be left," and "nobody would have depended" on him because he "probably . . . wouldn't have held together when the pinch came" (*Faulkner in the University*, 250).

Ab Snopes was married twice. One wife, named Vynie, is a woman from Jefferson. In *The Hamlet,* he trades Vynie's milk separator to Pat Stamper for a team of horses Snopes had lost to him. To get the separator back, Vynie gives Stamper the Snopeses' cow. (*See* the short story "BARN BURNING," where his second wife is named Lennie.) Ab has four children: Flem, Colonel Sartoris (in "Barn Burning"), and twin girls, one of whom is named Net (in "Barn Burning"). Snopes does not join the Confederate army during the Civil War but stays on at Colonel John Sartoris's plantation. In collaboration with Sartoris's mother-in-law, Miss Rosa (Granny) Millard, he sells back to the federal troops the horses and mules Granny Millard steals from them. According to Uncle Buck McCaslin, Snopes was shot in the foot by Colonel John Sartoris for attempting to steal the Colonel's "clay-bank riding stallion during the War" (*The Hamlet*, 18; *see* the short story "Barn Burning," where Snopes was shot by a Confederate provost). Because of his connection with the death of Granny Millard, as Ratliff narrates in *The Hamlet,* he was severely beaten by Colonel Sartoris's son Bayard and others (32). But Snopes is especially known as a barn-burner, and his reputation is known throughout FRENCHMAN'S BEND; *see* "Barn Burning" and *also see* THE UNVANQUISHED, THE TOWN, and THE MANSION, and the short story "MY GRANDMOTHER MILLARD AND GENERAL BEDFORD FORREST AND THE BATTLE OF HARRYKIN CREEK."

Snopes, Eckrum (Eck) He is one of Flem Snopes's cousins. Although Eck has no blacksmithing experience, he works for his cousin (or uncle), I. O. Snopes, in the blacksmith shop in FRENCHMAN'S BEND. (The narrative is not clear as to the relation of I. O. Snopes and Eck; *see The Hamlet*, 225.) When the cow that the idiot Ike Snopes sexually possesses is to be destroyed, the ingenuous and gullible Eck is persuaded by I. O. to pay for most of the cost of the animal. Eck later buys the boy a 25-cent toy cow substitute. At the auction of the wild ponies, Buck Hipps starts the bidding off by giving Eck a horse. When after the auction his horse escapes along with the others and upsets the wagon carrying Vernon Tull and his family across

the bridge, Eck offers to pay damages, but the judge rules that Eck holds no liability because he never legally owned the horse.

Within a year of his marriage, at 16, his wife had a son, whom Eck named Wallstreet Panic 10 years after the child was born. *Also see* FATHER ABRAHAM, "SPOTTED HORSES," and *The Town*; Eck is referred to in *The MANSION*.

Snopes, Eula Varner *See* Varner, Eula.

Snopes, Flem The shrewdest and most successful of the Snopes, Flem is at the center of the SNOPES TRILOGY. Avaricious and unscrupulous in his efforts for economic gain, Flem outwits and manipulates those around him to achieve his ends. In *The Hamlet,* he is aptly described as having "eyes the color of stagnant water, and projecting from among the other features in startling and sudden paradox, a tiny predatory nose like the beak of a small hawk (57). This description evinces the predatory nature of a rapacious, insensitive, and acquisitive man.

Flem is Ab Snopes's son by Ab's second wife. Soon after Ab moves to the FRENCHMAN'S BEND area and becomes Will Varner's tenant farmer, Varner's son Jody hires Flem as a clerk in VARNER'S STORE. Jody sees Flem as fire insurance against Ab's tendencies to burn the barns of his employers. During his clerkship, Flem stops giving credit to the customers and even charges Will Varner for his tobacco. The quiet but scheming Flem quickly rises from store clerk to Varner's assistant, helping him settle his business accounts and going along with him on Jody's roan to appraise cotton crops. In the meantime, Flem takes over Jody's role as superviser of the cotton gin, forcing Jody to return to clerking in the store. Flem lends money at high interest rates to the townsfolk, deals in cattle, builds a new blacksmith shop that puts I. O. Snopes out of business, sells the blacksmith shop to Varner for a profit; and, to advance his ambitions even further, marries Varner's daughter Eula, who is pregnant with another man's child. As part of the dowry he gets the OLD FRENCHMAN PLACE that he tricks V. K. Ratliff, Henry Armstid, and Odum Bookwright into buying. To avoid Mink Snopes's trial for having killed Jack Houston, Flem does not return with his wife and daughter to Frenchman's Bend after his honeymoon in Texas. When he does return, he is accompanied by Buck Hipps, the Texan who auctions off the wild ponies. Flem, however, never admits that he is in partnership with Hipps. Flem's unscrupulous greed is especially apparent when he refuses to refund Mrs. Armstid the five dollars her husband took from her to buy a horse, and he even lies to her by saying that Hipps took the money with him. *The Hamlet* ends with Flem, Eula, and her baby moving to Jefferson. As they are departing in their wagon, he takes one last look at the mad Henry Armstid furiously and foolishly digging for the treasure he relentlessly believes is buried at the Old Frenchman Place.

Flem appears in several of Faulkner's works; *see* SARTORIS, *The* TOWN, *The* MANSION, and in previously written works Faulkner revised for these novels: FATHER ABRAHAM (fragment of a novel revised and incorporated into *The Hamlet*), "SPOTTED HORSES" (revised from *Father Abraham* and recast in *The Hamlet*), "CENTAUR IN BRASS" (revised for *The Town*), "LIZARDS IN JAMSHYD'S COURTYARD" (revised for *The Hamlet*), and "BY THE PEOPLE" (revised for *The Mansion*); Flem is also referred to in *As I* LAY DYING and *The* REIVERS.

Snopes, I. O. He is a minor character in the novel. This proverb-prone Snopes leases Will Varner's blacksmith shop, even though he has no blacksmithing expertise, and later takes the teaching position that Labove vacates in FRENCHMAN'S BEND. He counsels Mink Snopes, who is accused of Jack Houston's murder, and cons his kinsman Eck Snopes into paying most of the cost to destroy the cow to which Ike Snopes is amorously attached. Although thought to be single, I. O. has two wives. The first shows up one day in Frenchman's Bend with a baby (Montgomery Ward Snopes), causing I. O. to leave for Jefferson where he replaces Flem Snopes in the restaurant.

I. O. also appears in *The* SOUND AND THE FURY, *The* TOWN, FATHER ABRAHAM (fragment of a novel incorporated into *The Hamlet*), and the short stories "SPOTTED HORSES" (revised for *The Hamlet*) and "MULE IN THE YARD" (revised for *The Town*). He is also referred to in *The* MANSION.

Snopes, Isaac (Ike) He is Flem Snopes's dim-witted cousin, who is sexually attracted to Jack Houston's cow. After Ike runs away with it, Houston in disgust gives him the animal, which Ike keeps in Mrs. Littlejohn's barn. Unaware that he is being watched, Ike has sex with the cow in view of the men lounging at VARNER'S STORE until V. K. Ratliff puts a stop to it and has the cow destroyed. To replace the lost animal, the kindhearted Eck Snopes buys the boy a toy cow. (For further information, *see Faulkner in the University*, 131–132.)

Snopes, Launcelot (Lump) A minor character in *The Hamlet* and referred to in *The* MANSION, Lump replaces his cousin Flem Snopes as the clerk at VARNER'S STORE. A man without moral scruples, Lump takes a plank off Mrs. Littlejohn's barn so he and others can spy on Ike Snopes having sex with a cow. He also lies to protect his cousin Mink Snopes, who is accused of Jack Houston's murder. Prior to Mink's arrest, Lump tried to persuade his cousin to steal and share with him the money that the dead Houston still had in his pocket. Lump also perjures himself at the Armstid v. Snopes trial when he says that he saw Flem give Armstid his money back. In fact, Flem did not.

Snopes, Linda She is the daughter of Eula Varner and Hoake McCarron, conceived out of wedlock and born after Eula marries Flem Snopes. In *The Hamlet*, she is an infant when Flem and Eula leave FRENCHMAN'S BEND for JEFFERSON. *Also see The* TOWN and *The* MANSION.

Snopes, Mink (M. C.) Single-minded, determined, and vindictive, Mink retaliates against Jack Houston by killing him. In *The Hamlet* (and as retold in *The* MANSION), Houston charged him a poundage fee for his yearling that strayed into Houston's pasture. It was the fee, an insult to his pride, that incensed Mink to commit the murder. A few days after having stuffed Houston's body into a hollow tree trunk, Mink, fearing that the odor of Houston's body will be detected, retrieves the body and throws it into a nearby river. An arm, however, is missing from the decayed corpse, and when Mink goes back to find it, he fights off Houston's dog, is arrested and taken to jail in JEFFERSON where he spends more than two months before being sent to the state penitentiary at PARCHMAN; the year is 1908. Mink expects his cousin Flem to rescue him, but Flem intentionally avoids his kinsman.

Also see the short story "The Hound," which Faulkner revised for book 3 of *The Hamlet*. In the short story, the main character is a bachelor named Ernest Cotton, who winters Houston's hog, but in the novel Faulkner changed Cotton's name to Mink Snopes and has Houston winter Snopes's scrub yearling. (For Faulkner's remarks on Mink, *see Faulkner in the University*, 262).

Snopes, Mrs. (1)   A minor character in the novel (and in the short story "BARN BURNING"), she is Ab Snopes's second wife and mother of his children. She accompanies Ab, when as a sharecropper he attends to one of Will Varner's farms. See "BARN BURNING" where her first name appears as Lennie.

Snopes, Mrs. (2)   Mink Snopes's wife, she unwittingly indicts her husband by telling everyone that Mink did not kill Houston. *Also see The MANSION* where she is referred to as Yettie.

Snopes, Saint Elmo   Referred to in the novel, he is I. O. Snopes's son; he takes candy from VARNER'S STORE.

Snopes, Vynie   She is Ab Snopes's first wife. With Cliff Odum's help, she gets her milk separator back from Pat Stamper in exchange for a cow. She also appears in the short story "FOOL ABOUT A HORSE."

Snopes, Wallstreet Panic (Wall)   Eck Snopes's son. Wall was not given a first name until he was about 10 years old. Eck chose the name with the hope that his son would become as rich as those who ran the Wall Street panic. Like his father, Wall is not a typical Snopes. He helps his father in his futile attempt to catch the two wild ponies bought at the auction. He also appears in *The TOWN* and *The MANSION*.

Stamper, Pat   He is a master horsetrader who outwits his rivals. When Ab Snopes realizes he has been duped in a trade, Stamper agrees to take back the worthless mules that Ab got in exchange for a horse. Finally, Stamper ends up with the mules and Mrs. Snopes's milk separator, while Ab unknowingly gets the same horse back, disguised. *Also see The MANSION* and the short story "FOOL ABOUT A HORSE," which Faulkner revised for *The Hamlet*.

Trumbull   He is the blacksmith in FRENCHMAN'S BEND, who ran Will Varner's blacksmith shop until it was taken over by I. O. Snopes and his cousin Eck Snopes. (This episode is also referred to in *The TOWN*.)

Tull, Cora (Mrs. Vernon)   A minor character in *The Hamlet*, where she unsuccessfully sues Eck Snopes for the injuries her husband suffered from one of Eck's wild horses. The judge, however, dismisses the case because Eck was never given a bill of sale for the horse. *Also see AS I LAY DYING, The MANSION*, and the short story "SPOTTED HORSES," which Faulkner revised for *The Hamlet*; she is referred to in *The TOWN*.

Tull, Vernon   A farmer in the vicinity of FRENCHMAN'S BEND, Tull, a minor character in the novel, is injured by one of Eck Snopes's wild ponies, severely enough to be out of work for a few days. *Also see AS I LAY DYING, The TOWN*, and the short stories "SPOTTED HORSES," "The HOUND," "LIZARDS IN JAMSHYD'S COURTYARD" (all three revised by Faulkner for *The Hamlet*), "TWO SOLDIERS," and "SHINGLES FOR THE LORD." He also is referred to in *The MANSION*. (When Faulkner revised "Lizards in Jamshyd's Courtyard" for *The Hamlet*, he substituted Tull with Odum Bookwright in reference to the men who foolishly dig for buried treasure at the OLD FRENCHMAN PLACE.)

Varner, Jody   He is Will Varner's son, who rents a farm to the tenant farmer (and reputed barn-burner) Ab Snopes and hires Ab's son Flem as a clerk in the Varner store. The only one of Varner's adult children to live at home, Jody helps in his father's business matters. He is also responsible for making sure that his sister Eula, unlike their mother, gets at least some formal education. In one of the funnier passages in *The Hamlet,* when Eula is found to be pregnant, Jody becomes so irate about defending the honor of the Varner name that he has to be subdued by his father and his gun taken away. Jody also appears in As I Lay Dying, Light in August, *The Town, The Mansion,* and the short stories "Fool About a Horse" and "Spotted Horses" (both of which were revised for *The Hamlet*).

Varner, Eula The 16th and youngest child of Will and Maggie Varner. Eula is Flem Snopes's wife and the mother of an infant daughter. In "Eula," book 2 of *The Hamlet,* she is caricatured in vivid mythic terms redolent of the chaotic revelry of Dionysian times. Like an earth goddess stirring the sexual appetite in men, she is enticing, aloof, and unattainable, but like her father, she is lazy. At age eight, Eula starts school at the insistence of her brother Jody, who is compelled to transport her on his horse because of her reluctance to walk any distance. By 10, she is taller than her mother. At 14, she is the indifferent and oblivious target of the amorous obsessions of her teacher, Labove, whose attempt to ravish her in the schoolhouse fails when she resists him with a blow to his face that knocks him over. By 15, rivals for her affection fight over her on Sunday nights, and by 16, fully aware of her sexuality and seductiveness, Eula successfully helps Hoake McCarron fight off his attackers. When, three months later, Hoake realizes that Eula is pregnant with his child, he leaves Frenchman's Bend. To save face and to protect his daughter, Will Varner arranges Eula's marriage to Flem. While on an extended honeymoon in Texas, Eula's daughter and only child, Linda, is born. After their return, they move to Jefferson. For other details regarding Eula, *see* especially *The Town* and *also see* Father Abraham and "Spotted Horses," which Faulkner revised for *The Hamlet.*

Varner, Mrs. (Maggie) A minor character in *The Hamlet,* she is Will Varner's wife and mother of 16 children (including Jody and Eula). One of the finest housewives in the area, she wins prizes at the annual county fair for preserving fruits and vegetables. In *The Hamlet,* V. K. Ratliff refers to her as Miss Maggie (86). *Also see* As I Lay Dying, *The*

Town, The Mansion, and Father Abraham (fragment of a novel Faulkner incorporated into *The Hamlet*).

Varner, Will (Uncle Will) A robust, Rabelaisian man, Varner is the father of 16 children, fountainhead of advice, and a practical-minded individual with diverse business interests. Of his 16 children, only Jody and his sister Eula (until her wedding midway through *The Hamlet*) remain at home. Although lazy by natural temperament but, nonetheless, active in the life of the community at Frenchman's Bend, the 60-year-old Varner is identified as a veterinarian, usurer, holder of mortgages, supervisor and largest landholder in one county, justice of the peace in another county, and election commissioner in both. In addition to owning the store in Frenchman's Bend, the cotton gin, and the combined grist mill and blacksmith shop, he held title to the Old Frenchman Place before signing it over to Flem Snopes and his daughter Eula on the day of their wedding. Will Varner appears in many of Faulkner's works: Light in August, Intruder in the Dust, *The Town, The Mansion,* and in the short stories "Spotted Horses," "Lizards in Jamshyd's Courtyard," "Fool About a Horse" (all three revised by Faulkner for *The Hamlet*), "Tomorrow" (in Knight's Gambit), "Shingles for the Lord," and "By the People" (revised for *The Mansion*). Varner is also referred to in As I Lay Dying.

Whitfield He is the minister of the local church. Although he never attended seminary and holds no degrees, Whitfield, "a harsh, stupid, honest, superstitious and upright man" (223), was ordained by Will Varner. Whitfield suggests to I. O. Snopes and V. K. Ratliff that the only way to cure Ike Snopes of his sexual attraction to Houston's cow is to kill the animal and make him consume some of the meat. He is referred to as Brother Whitfield by I. O. Snopes. Whitfield also appears in As I Lay Dying, "Tomorrow" (Knight's Gambit), and "Shingles for the Lord."

Winterbottom He runs a boardinghouse in Frenchman's Bend where Launcelot Snopes lives. Winterbottom also appears in Light in August and the short story "SPOTTED HORSES," revised by Faulkner for *The Hamlet*.

RELATED PLACES

Grenier County   Fictional place, sharing a southern border with YOKNAPATAWPHA COUNTY. In *The Hamlet*, Ab Snopes burns the barn of a Grenier County farmer named Harris.

Littlejohn's Hotel   The boardinghouse in FRENCHMAN'S BEND owned and run by Mrs. Littlejohn. It is one of only two multistory houses (Will Varner's being the other) in this rural hamlet. The sewing machine salesman V. K. Ratliff stays here when he is travelling in the area, and in the lot next to the hotel the Texan Buck Hipps auctions off the wild ponies. The hotel is also is mentioned in *The TOWN*. During Faulkner's time, there was an actual Littlejohn's Store on the New Albany Road (now Mississippi Route 30) northeast of OXFORD, MISSISSIPPI.

Whiteleaf Bridge   Fictional place in southeastern YOKNAPATAWPHA COUNTY. It carries the road to FRENCHMAN'S BEND across fictional Whiteleaf Creek. The bridge figures in *The Hamlet* and *INTRUDER IN THE DUST*.

EXCERPTS FROM CONTEMPORARY REVIEWS OF *THE HAMLET*

From Stephen Vincent Benet's review, "Flem Snopes and His Kin," published in **The Saturday Review of Literature** *(April 6, 1940), 7:*
In the Snopes family, Mr. Faulkner has created what is probably the finest sub-human species in contemporary American literature. Compared to the Snopes, the Joads are the country-club set and Jeeter and his brood folks of high social consciousness, well adjusted to their environment. To create a set of characters with the acquisitiveness of the gypsy-moth and the morality of the swamp-moccasin, and to watch them writhing and squirming in their environment with blind ferocity of maggots, is in itself an achievement. It is as even greater achievement that the dark magic of Mr. Faulkner's style makes these creatures continuously interesting. Mr. Faulkner may be a great many things—he is seldom, if ever, dull. He can be clotted and con-fused, but his writing, at its best, has an hallucinative power which keeps one reading, like a man in the toils of nightmare, till the last page is turned. In "The Hamlet," his peculiar power is at its best. There are fewer of the long, winding sentences that strangle themselves to death in their own subordinate clauses—there is all of the earthy force that Mr. Faulkner can summon, like a spirit out of the ground, when he chooses to do so. Reading "The Hamlet" is like listening to the gossip of a country store, with its cruelty, its extravagance, its tall stories, and its deadly comment upon human nature—but a gossip translated, heightened, and made into art. It is, I suppose, an unpleasant book; it may well be a repellent book to many readers. It is also, not always but frequently, superbly written. Nor is "unpleasant," the first adjective this particular reviewer would think of Mr. Faulkner is too good for that. . . .

Excerpt from Malcolm Cowley's review, "Faulkner by Daylight," published in **The New Republic**, *102 (April 15, 1940), 510:*
The Hamlet is a new sort of novel for William Faulkner, less somber, more easygoing and discursive. Except for a few short stories, it makes better reading than anything else he has written since *Sanctuary*. . . .

The Hamlet is different from any of the novels in the Sartoris cycle. Reading it one feels that Faulkner has suddenly emerged from his Gothic midnight into the light of day. . . .

The principal theme of the novel is the rise of Flem Snopes, by consistent meanness, from clerking in the village store to lording over the whole community. Very soon he has peopled Frenchman's Bend with a whole swarm of his relatives, little men gnawing at money like rats at cheese. One of them, Mink Snopes, commits murder for pure spite. Another, Ike Snopes, is an idiot boy who falls in love with a cow (and this passage is the least effective in the novel because it seems deliberately intended to be shocking). Flem Snopes himself cheats the shrewdest man in the county by making him dig for an imaginary treasure. The book is composed of separate episodes like these, tragic, sensational or hilarious. Some of them have little to do with the Snopes family; and they are bound together chiefly by dealing with a community where Faulkner seems to have known every single inhabitant from birth to deathbed.

The new quality I find in this book—new to Faulkner at least—is friendliness. Pity he has often shown in the past, but never before the amused liking that he extends to almost all the people of Frenchman's Bend. He likes their back-country humor, he likes the clean look of their patched and faded shirts, he likes the lies they tell when swapping horses. In a curious way, he even likes the invading tribe of Snopeses; at least he likes to write about them. . . .

Excerpt from Richard Church's review, published in John O' London's Weekly *(September 20, 1940), 663:*

. . . There is a calmness of spirit, evincing itself in outbreaks of humour and grotesquerie that play like summer lightning round the cloudy fabric of Mr. William Faulkner's new novel, *The Hamlet*. . . . That cloudy fabric is the style of the man, the very essence of his creative force. . . . In *The Hamlet*, however, his fancy, rather than his imagination, takes charge, and the result is a most ingenious tale of rural life in the Southern States, showing the queer social parasitism resulting from the decay of the aristocratic estates after the Civil War. . . .

FURTHER READING

Beck, Warren. *Man in Motion: Faulkner's Trilogy.* Madison: University of Wisconsin Press, 1961.

Backman, Melvin. "The Hamlet." In *Faulkner: The Major Years,* 139–159. Bloomington: Indiana University Press, 1966.

Brooks, Cleanth. "Faulkner's Savage Arcadia: Frenchman's Bend (*The Hamlet*)." In *William Faulkner: The Yoknapatawpha Country,* 167–191. Baton Rouge: Louisiana State University Press, 1990.

———. "The Hamlet." In *William Faulkner: First Encounters,* 96–128. New Haven: Yale University Press, 1983.

Holmes, Catherine D. *Annotations to William Faulkner's* The Hamlet. New York: Garland, 1996.

Howe, Irving. "The Hamlet." In *William Faulkner: A Critical Study,* 243–252. Chicago: University of Chicago Press, 1957.

Matthews, John T. "*The Hamlet*: Rites of Play." In *The Play of Faulkner's Language,* 162–211. Ithaca: Cornell University Press, 1982.

Millgate, Michael. "The Hamlet." In *The Achievement of William Faulkner,* 180–200. Lincoln: University of Nebraska Press, 1978.

Helen: A Courtship

Cycle consisting of an introductory poem and 15 sonnets, written between June and September 1925. In part, it is Faulkner's declaration of love to the sculptor HELEN BAIRD. Critics see echoes of the English poet A. E. HOUSMAN. Faulkner presented the hand-lettered, hand-bound poem cycle to Baird, dated Oxford, Mississippi, June 1926. She rejected him as a suitor, however, and married the New Orleans lawyer Guy Lyman. Together with MISSISSIPPI POEMS, *Helen: A Courtship* was published posthumously in 1981 by Tulane University and Yoknapatawpha Press.

"Hog Pawn" (Uncollected Stories)

This short story was written in about October 1954 and published posthumously in *The Uncollected Stories of William Faulkner.* A revised version was included in chapter 14 of book 3, "Flem," of *The* MANSION. For more information, *see Uncollected Stories of William Faulkner,* 697.

SYNOPSIS

"Hog Pawn" is short story about the eccentric behavior of a cantankerous, vindictive, and penny-pinching old man, Otis Meadowfill, who, among other threatening things, shoots at his neighbor's hog as it strays onto Meadowfill's property. When an oil company approaches Meadowfill to buy a portion of his land, he refuses to sell. Since the legal ownership of the land is in dispute—it either belongs to Meadowfill's neighbor Snopes or to Meadowfill's daughter, Essie Meadowfill (Smith), to whom Meadowfill transferred the property when he applied for relief under the Roosevelt administration—the oil company needs both parties to agree to sell. Eventually the town attorney (and sometime private eye) Gavin Stevens becomes involved. After finding the booby trap that Snopes attached to the window Meadowfill shoots from, Stevens settles the dispute between the two neighbors. Confronted with the evidence, the usurious Snopes must sell his lot to Essie. The story ends on a happy note: Essie will marry the World War II veteran McKinley Smith, sell the land to the oil company and, together with her husband, buy a farm.

CRITICAL COMMENTARY

Several disparate themes—a father's opposition to the marriage of his daughter, a defiant older man in conflict with his neighbor, and perennial struggles with SNOPESISM and its defeat—merge in "Hog Pawn," but, as James Ferguson comments, "the triumph of 'good guys' and the defeat of the Snopeses through various machinations in 'By the People' and 'Hog Pawn' seem unconvincing because the stories are turgid, listless, dull—and unfunny" (*Faulkner's Short Fiction*, 76).

"Hog Pawn" is narrated by Gavin Stevens's nephew Chick Mallison.

CHARACTERS

Mallison, Charles Jr. (Chick) Gavin Stevens's nephew and narrator of the short story. At Stevens's request, Chick accompanies his uncle when the latter confronts Snopes about the booby-trap and the deed to the strip of land an oil company wants to buy. *Also see* INTRUDER IN THE DUST, KNIGHT'S GAMBIT, *The* TOWN, *and The* MANSION.

Meadowfill, Essie Otis Meadowfill's daughter. When she graduates as valedictorian from high school, she makes the highest grades ever and is offered a $500 scholarship and a job from the president of a bank. But she declines both, having already found a job with the telephone company. However, she wants to borrow the money as a loan, to be paid back from her salary, to have a bathroom built in her house. (*See The* MANSION where Faulkner changed some minor details when

he incorporated the story into "Flem," the third book of the novel, chapter 14. For example, the name of the bank president, Mr. Holland, is given, and Essie has a job in the bank for life.) By the end of the shorty story, she marries McKinley Smith, an ex-marine sergeant in World War I (a corporal in *The Mansion*). With the help of Gavin Stevens, she gets Orestes Snopes's deed to a strip of land that she sells to an oil company to buy a farm.

Meadowfill, Mrs. Otis's wife, a "gray dredge" of a woman.

Meadowfill, Otis Mean-spirited father of Essie Meadowfill who sits in a second-hand wheelchair to guard his property against any intruders including his neighbor's hog that strays onto his land. Taking a warped sense of delight in using his old single-shot .22 to sting the hog, Meadowfill sits in ambush until the animal appears after breakfast. By the end of the story—and after Meadowfill is the outraged victim of the booby trap his neighbor Snopes, the owner of the hog, sets up—the disputed about a strip of land between Meadowfill and Snopes is resolved by Uncle Gavin.

Smith, McKinley An ex-marine sergeant, who marries Essie Meadowfill. Son of an Arkansas tenant farmer, Smith buys a small lot that Essie picked and builds a home. (*See The* MANSION, where he is identified as an ex-marine corporal and the son of a tenant farmer from east Texas and where he buys a small lot in Eula Acres to build his home.)

Snopes In the short story, Snopes, a bachelor without a first name, feuds with his neighbor, Otis Meadowfill. This Snopes, who buys and sells and who lends "small sums, secured by usurious notes, to Negroes and small farmers" (*Uncollected Stories*, 315), has a deed that covers part of Meadowfill's vacant lot, which an oil company wants to buy. On several occasions, Snopes's hog strays into Meadowfill's rundown orchard and roots "among the worthless peaches on the ground beneath his worthless and untended trees" (316). When Meadowfill takes revenge by routinely shooting at the hog with an old, ineffective, single-shot .22, only to sting and goad the animal back home, Snopes seeks legal advice from Gavin Stevens (referred to as Uncle Gavin in the story) but ends up hatching his own plan of retaliation, ironically triggered by Stevens's suggestion to give the hog away. As a ploy, Snopes presents it as a gift to Meadowfill's future son-in-law, McKinley Smith, and then rigs a booby-trap aimed at Meadowfill. After Stevens uncovers the scheme, he confronts Snopes, gets the deed to the strip of land the oil company wants to purchase, and hands it over to Meadowfill's daughter, Essie.

When Faulkner revised "Hog Pawn" for *The Mansion*, the third novel of the SNOPES TRILOGY, he gave this Snopes the first name Orestes (Res). In *As I Lay Dying* and "SHINGLES FOR THE LORD," there is a Snopes without a first name.

Uncle Gavin (Stevens, Gavin) The narrator Chick Mallison's uncle, an attorney who gets involved in the feud between Snopes and the cantankerous Otis Meadowfill. (Stevens is a significant character in several of Faulkner's works; *see* LIGHT IN AUGUST, *The Town, The Mansion,* INTRUDER IN THE DUST, KNIGHT'S GAMBIT, and REQUIEM FOR A NUN; *also see* GO DOWN, MOSES, "HAIR," "THE TALL MEN," and "BY THE PEOPLE." He is referred to in "A Name for the City" (revised for the prologue to act 1 of *Requiem for a Nun*).

"Hound, The" (Uncollected Stories)

SYNOPSIS

The story recounts Ernest Cotton's murder of Jack Houston and Cotton's ludicrous and pathetic attempt at getting rid of the body. Not content with the meager one dollar fee that the court awards him for wintering Houston's stray hog, Cotton shoots Houston in revenge for what he believes is an unpardonable injustice. Cotton first forces Houston's corpse into the rotten shell of a cypress tree. A few days later, he notices vultures flying above it, so he returns during the night to disentangle the decaying body from the tree trunk and

toss it into a river. When he realizes that one of the body's limbs is missing, he goes back to search for it and gets caught by the sheriff and his deputies.

CRITICAL COMMENTARY

"The Hound" is a story of the internal psychological processes of a man obsessed with his own code of honor and self-worth in conflict with the norms of societal justice. The critic James Ferguson comments that "the anguish and terror the protagonist has gone through have been so intense that our reactions at the end of the story are not those of relief or triumph but of exhaustion—and of compassion for Cotton" (*Faulkner's Short Fiction,* 76).

This short story was first published in August 1931 in HARPER'S MAGAZINE 163, 266–274, and reprinted in *Doctor Martino and Other Stories* (1934) and in *A Rose for Emily and Other Stories by William Faulkner* (1945). Faulkner revised the story for book 3 of *The HAMLET*. The original version is reprinted in *Uncollected Stories of William Faulkner*. In the revision, Faulkner changed the name of the main character from Ernest Cotton to Mink Snopes. Unlike Cotton, a bachelor, Snopes is a married man with two children. Faulkner also changed the conflict that occurs between Houston and Mink. In the short story, Cotton winters Houston's hog, but in the revision found in *The Hamlet* Houston winters Snopes's scrub yearling and the court awards Houston three dollars for pasturage. The revised story is referred to in *The TOWN* and *The MANSION*.

For more information, *see Selected Letters of William Faulkner,* 115, 197, 202, and 430, and UNCOLLECTED STORIES OF WILLIAM FAULKNER, 688–689.

CHARACTERS

Cotton, Ernest The central character in "The Hound," Cotton is not fully satisfied with the reward he receives for housing Jack Houston's stray hog over the winter. A resentful and proud man who feels taken advantage of, Cotton later settles the matter by killing Houston. When after the murder he is talking with other men (including the sheriff) at VARNER'S STORE, his attitude is bluntly divulged in a comment that he makes about Houston's dog and at the same time it appears (though the reader cannot be certain) that he stops himself from revealing that he killed Houston (*Uncollected Stories*, 157). The story ends with his arrest.

In Faulkner's revision of "The Hound" for book 3 of *The HAMLET*, Cotton's name is changed to Mink Snopes and he is no longer a bachelor but married with two children.

Houston, Jack The owner of the stray hog that Ernest Cotton winters. In the story, Houston is described as a "prosperous and overbearing man" (*Uncollected Stories of William Faulkner*, 157). When the court awards Cotton only a one-dollar fee for wintering the stray hog, the indignant Cotton shoots and kills Houston. (For a further discussion of Houston's character, *see The HAMLET*.)

Snopes A minor character in the story. The clerk at VARNER'S STORE, Snopes ends up with the shotgun that Ernest Cotton used to kill Jack Houston and threw into a swamp. When Cotton comes to the store one afternoon, Snopes shows the gun to him but Cotton denies that it is his.

Tull, Vernon A farmer in the rural area of FRENCHMAN'S BEND. He recognizes the shotgun that a black squirrel hunter found in a swamp as belonging to Ernest Cotton. When showing the mud-caked gun to Cotton, Snopes, the clerk at VARNER'S STORE, refers to Tull as having said that it belongs to him. Cotton lies to Snopes and says that he has one like it and it is at home. (Tull also appears in *As I LAY DYING*, *The HAMLET*, *The TOWN*, "SPOTTED HORSES," "LIZARDS IN JAMSHYD'S COURTYARD," "TWO SOLDIERS," and "SHINGLES FOR THE LORD"; he is referred to *The MANSION*.)

"Idyll in the Desert" (Uncollected Stories)

Short story first issued as a limited signed edition of 400 copies on December 31, 1931, by RANDOM HOUSE.

SYNOPSIS

The nameless narrator engages in conversation with a mail rider, Lucas Crump, who relates a rambling tale laced with sardonic wit. Ten years earlier, Crump took Darrel Howes (or House), a tuberculosis patient, by wagon to the isolated Arizona cabin where Howes hoped to recover his health. On his weekly route Crump delivered food and mail to him and, when his condition worsened, prepared meals and cut firewood for him. A telegram to New York brought his lover, who abandoned her two children and husband in order to care for Howes. Howes recovered and left; the woman, who had become infected herself, stayed on. Over the next eight years Crump faithfully watched over her, with the financial assistance of her husband. The two men let her believe that the envelopes of cash paying for her stay came from Howes. Near the end, Crump took her by stretcher to the train. Coincidentally getting off the train were Howes and his new bride; Howes did not recognize his former lover. When she arrived dead at her destination, her husband did not recognize her either, as she had aged so much from her ordeal.

CRITICAL COMMENTARY

A story of devotion and self-sacrifice in the face of ingratitude, "Idyll in the Desert" is characterized by irony and a pessimism bordering on despair. It is an "idyll" only because it has a pastoral setting and narrates a simple tale; the tone and content are altogether nonidyllic. James B. Carothers views the story as a treatment of "the perfidy of men and the thankless devotion of their women" (*William Faulkner's Short Stories*, 104).

CHARACTERS

Crump, Lucas A mail rider with a route in the Arizona desert, he befriends the tubercular Darrel Howes and, later, Howes's lover, who arrives to care for him and then becomes infected herself.

Howes (or House), Darrel A tuberculosis patient, he comes to the Arizona desert to recover and is looked after by the mail rider Lucas Crump and, later, by his lover who abandons her family in New York to come to him. Howes eventually recovers and leaves. His lover, however, has become infected and must stay behind. When Howes, traveling with his new wife, accidentally encounters the woman years later, he fails to recognize her.

Hughes, Manny The postmaster in Blizzard, Arizona, he helps Lucas Crump deceive Darrel Howes's consumptive ex-lover about the source of the support payments she receives in the mail.

Lewis, Matt A livery stable owner, he helps Lucas Crump look after the tuberculosis patients at Sivgut in the Arizona desert.

Painter A grocer, he extends credit to Lucas Crump so Crump can supply groceries to the consumptive Darrel Howes.

If I Forget Thee, Jerusalem

See WILD PALMS, *The*

Intruder in the Dust

A novel, published in 1948, it explores the South's racial predicament delivered through the medium of a murder mystery. *Intruder in the Dust* attracted considerable attention when it first appeared. The subject was timely—an antilynching measure was then before Congress, and the 1948 Democratic Party platform called for civil rights for blacks, which led to the Dixiecrat revolt of southern Democrats—so *Intruder* found an eager if somewhat divided audience. Thus it became Faulkner's best-selling book since SANCTUARY (1931). Few critics today rank it with his best work, though some say it grades among the strongest of the later novels.

Faulkner suggested he came up with the idea for the novel as a means of taking advantage of a current fashion for detective stories. "My children were always buying them and bringing them home," he told an audience at the UNIVERSITY OF VIRGINIA in the 1950s. In fact, the plot outline for *Intruder* dated at least as far back as the spring of 1940 when, short of money and looking for a quick cash infusion, he wrote ROBERT HAAS at RANDOM HOUSE that he had an idea for a "blood-and-thunder mystery novel which should sell." Faulkner had seen far enough into the story in 1940 to know that it would entail a "negro, himself in jail for the murder and about to be lynched," solving the crime in self-defense.

As the idea developed, it took on a deeper significance for Faulkner. Though a "mystery-murder," he wrote his agent, HAROLD OBER, "the theme is more relationship between Negro and white . . . the premise being that the white people in the south . . . owe and must pay a responsibility to the Negro. But it's a story. Nobody preaches in it."

SYNOPSIS

According to the biographer JOSEPH BLOTNER, Faulkner based the plot on an actual event in OXFORD, MISSISSIPPI, in the late 1930s in which the authorities accused a black man of killing a white. While the jury deliberated, a mob of 75 whites broke into the Oxford jail, seized the prisoner, carried him away, and hanged him along a country road.

For the central character, he reclaimed Lucas Beauchamp from GO DOWN, MOSES (1942). Now in his late 60s, a descendant of the YOKNAPATAWPHA COUNTY planter and slaveholder Lucius Quintus Carothers McCaslin, Beauchamp is fiercely independent and stubbornly proud of his mixed racial heritage and "syriac" features. Contemptuous, too, of Mississippi's strict racial conventions, he refuses to adopt an attitude of submissiveness. His defiant bearing, coupled with some sketchy circumstantial evidence, makes him an automatic suspect when Vinson Gowrie, a member of a large clan of hill country white farmers, is found murdered.

Faulkner turned to the story in early 1948 when he found himself in trouble with the intractable manuscript, a work of many years, that would become A FABLE (1954). He wrote to Ober that he envisioned the new project as a short novel, perhaps 120 pages in length. As he thought it through, however, the manuscript would grow to more than twice the originally projected size, and carry a heavy freight of social implication.

David Brian as John Stevens, Juan Hernandez as Beauchamp, and Claude Jarman, Jr., as Chick Mallison in the film version of Faulkner's *Intruder in the Dust. (Museum of Modern Art/Film Stills Archive)*

Faulkner uses a familiar device to develop the story, one he had turned to before. Lucas Beauchamp attempts to unravel the mystery of Vinson Gowrie's killing with the assistance of two juvenile inseparables, 16-year-old Charles (Chick) Mallison, the nephew of attorney Gavin Stevens, and Chick's black friend Aleck Sander, the son of the Mallisons' cook, Paralee. The novelist enlists the elderly spinster Eunice Habersham to provide timely assistance to Chick and Aleck. The two boys' partnership recalls that of Bayard Sartoris (3) and Ringo Strother, who with Granny Rosa Millard foil the Yankee invaders and homegrown bushwhackers in Civil War-era northern Mississippi in *The* Unvanquished (1938).

The time is the recent past—*Intruder* "happened about 1935 or '40," according to Faulkner. The novel opens with a favorite Faulkner device, an extended flashback. Out hunting near the Beauchamp place, Chick falls into an icy creek; Lucas Beauchamp pulls him out of the water, dries him off, takes him home and feeds him. Chick offers money for the hospitality. Lucas angrily rejects it, flinging the coins to the floor. Chick broods on his solecism for a long time afterward, wondering how he could make up for it. He gives the Beauchamps a Christmas present: cigars for Lucas, snuff for his wife, Molly Beauchamp. Later, he sends Molly a dress. Lucas responds with a gift of a gallon of sorghum molasses.

"They were right back where they had started," the narrator observes; "it was all to do over again."

Chick's opportunity for repayment comes when Lucas is accused of the Gowrie killing. Lucas had tumbled onto Crawford Gowrie's steady theft of lumber from his brother Vinson and his business partner, Sudley Workitt. Anticipating exposure, Crawford kills Vinson and manages to make it appear that Lucas, who is seen standing over the corpse with a recently discharged pistol in his pocket, is the culprit.

Lucas is arrested and jailed. Gowrie friends and kin talk of forming a lynch mob. Attorney Stevens visits Lucas in his cell and advises him to plead guilty when he goes before the judge the next day and be sent to the penitentiary for his own protection.

When Chick visits him in jail, Lucas asks him to dig up the Gowrie grave at CALEDONIA CHAPEL out in BEAT FOUR, a lonely country district peopled by clannish and violent white hill farmers. He enlists Aleck's assistance, and Miss Habersham agrees to help out. The body, it turns out, is not Vinson's but that of a shady CROSSMAN COUNTY timber buyer named Jake Montgomery. They return later with the sheriff and the Gowries to exhume the body; this time the casket is empty. The boys eventually find Montgomery's body in a shallow grave and Vinson's in quicksand under the highway bridge. Crawford Gowrie is exposed as the killer, and Lucas goes free.

CRITICAL COMMENTARY

Faulkner wrote a draft of the novel in six weeks in early 1948, finishing in late February with a promise to RANDOM HOUSE of the final manuscript by June 1. For the first time in his writing career, he struggled with a title, and even asked agents and editors for help with it. He considered several words suggesting sleight of hand to pair with "in the dust"—shenanigan, skullduggery, and jugglery. He finally settled on intruder as "the best yet."

Historian James T. Campbell has remarked that Faulkner was perhaps "the last writer of significant talent, white or black, to address the Negro presence in the United States without going through the conduit of protest or pity or role-model boost-

erism." To the novelist, blacks were an organic part of the southern world; they belonged. He described his black characters without self-consciousness, dealing with them no differently than the whites who people his stories and novels.

The story is told from the point of view of Chick Mallison. As he becomes a man in the course of the novel, he shows a growing comprehension of the white community's attitudes on race. Whites resented Lucas Beauchamp because he acted more like his white McCaslin ancestors than a descendant of slaves. Gradually Chick comes to understand the brutal, dehumanizing reality of white-black relations in Yoknapatawpha County.

Faulkner has Gavin Stevens ponder the larger problem. Biographer Jay Parini suggests Stevens occupies a "limbo position" between Jefferson's blacks and racist whites. Stevens takes a gradualist view not unlike Faulkner's own: Justice must prevail, blacks must be permitted the advantages of full citizenship someday soon, but the problem is the South's to solve, free of northern interference. In a series of long, murky passages, Stevens articulates his views on the South and on southern resistance to the federal government's halting but increasingly forceful support of the Civil Rights movement.

Random House published the novel on September 27, 1948. With its timely content, it drew an immediate response from reviewers. "*Intruder in the Dust* does not come to us merely as a novel: it also involves a tract," the critic Edmund Wilson wrote in *The New Yorker*. "The book contains a kind of counterblast to the anti-lynching bill and to the civil rights plank in the Democratic platform." Wilson reads Gavin Stevens's speeches "as something in the nature of a public message delivered by the author himself," one that reserves the racial question to the white South itself, free of outside intervention. That said, Wilson found the novel impressive, particularly in its delineation of the character of Lucas Beauchamp, certainly one of Faulkner's stronger creations, white or black.

Wilson and others have noted that Faulkner's lack of attention to workmanlike detail mars *Intruder*. "One of the more snarled-up of Faulkner's books," in Wilson's words, it contains some of the longest sentences in literature in English, major syntactical failures, convoluted parenthetical asides and slipshod punctuation.

That said, "Even when the prose goes to pieces, the man and his milieu live," Wilson concluded.

Writing in the *Hudson Review*, the novelist Eudora Welty called *Intruder* "a double and delightful feat, because the mystery of the detective-story plot is being raveled out while the mystery of Faulkner's prose is being spun and woven before our eyes."

Like Wilson, the critic MALCOLM COWLEY focused on the novel's political message. "The tragedy of intelligent Southerners like Faulkner is that their two fundamental beliefs, in human equality and in Southern independence, are now in violent conflict," Cowley wrote in the *New Republic*.

From an African-American perpective, southern white confusions were beside the point. Writing in *The Chicago Defender*, a black newspaper, Gertrude Martin found *Intruder in the Dust* "bigoted," the two main black characters, Beauchamp and Aleck Sander, scarcely more than symbols. "His latest work adds nothing to Faulkner's stature as a writer," Martin wrote, "and definitely stamps him as one of those Southerners who, like Lot's wife, keep their faces turned backwards."

The book sold well, some 15,000 hardcover copies in the first year, and Random House attracted a lucrative screen rights offer from Hollywood: METRO-GOLDWYN-MAYER paid $50,000 for a movie version of *Intruder*. Filmed on location in Oxford in the spring of 1949, the movie generated much local controversy; residents objected to the making of a movie in their town that portrayed the South negatively. There were also difficulties with housing the biracial cast in segregated Oxford. Juan Hernandez, a Puerto Rican actor who played Lucas Beauchamp, ended up staying in the home of G. W. Bankhead, Oxford's black undertaker.

Faulkner read the script and approved most of the scenes. He liked the film, which he saw in preview in MEMPHIS in September. A crowd of 800—tickets cost $2.60—filled Oxford's Lyric Theatre

for the formal opening of *Intruder in the Dust* on October 11, 1949.

CHARACTERS

Beauchamp, Lucas Quintus Carothers McCaslin

An important figure in the YOKNAPATAWPHA COUNTY cycle, he is the grandson of old Lucius Quintus Carothers McCaslin, a planter and slaveholder, and a slave woman and is fiercely proud of his mixed racial heritage. In his view, his descent from old Cass sets him above his Edmonds landlords, to whom Isaac McCaslin has passed the estate, for they are "woman-made," connected to the founder only on the female side.

Born in 1874, he is the youngest of the children of Tomey's Turl and Tennie Beauchamp, who is old Cass's daughter by a slave. Lucas is presented as the oldest living McCaslin descendant on the hereditary land.

Lucas Beauchamp dominates *Intruder in the Dust*, leaving the other characters, particularly the windy, speechifying Gavin Stevens, in the shade. He is an old man in the novel, still farming on the Edmonds estate, proud as ever of his descent from Carothers McCaslin, sturdy, dignified and unintimidated by—even contemptuous of—Yoknapatawpha's rigid racial conventions. Faulkner gives him a white man's accoutrements—a heavy gold watch chain, a gold toothpick, an old hand-made beaver hat. And Beauchamp says "ma'am" and "sir" to whites he encounters, just as other whites do.

When he is wrongly charged with murder, he learns "what every white man in that whole section of the country" had been thinking about him for a long time:

"We got to make him be a nigger first. He's got to admit he's a nigger. Then maybe we will accept him as he seems to intend to be accepted" (*Intruder*, 18).

The victim is a white man, Vinson Gowrie, a member of a large hill country clan. Beauchamp discovers that Crawford Gowrie has been stealing timber from brother Vinson and his partner, Sudley Workitt. To protect himself, Crawford kills Vinson and makes it seem as if Lucas is the murderer. The authorities jump to that conclusion, and Beauchamp is arrested and jailed.

Innumerable Gowries mobilize and threaten to lynch Beauchamp. From the Jefferson jail, he gains the help of young Chick (Charles, Jr.) Mallison, Chick's black friend Aleck Sander, and the elderly spinster Eunice Habersham (a childhood friend of his wife, Molly) in opening Vinson's grave as a means of proving his innocence: he claims his gun was not the one that killed the victim.

The Jefferson sheriff keeps the lynch mob at bay, Vinson's body is exhumed, the real murderer is revealed at last, and Lucas goes free.

Lucas Beauchamp is Faulkner's personification of the South's tortured racial history, with its patterns of intimacy, for better and mostly for worse, of blacks and whites. He is a rarity in mainstream American fiction of the time, a fully developed African-American male character who is proud, haughty, and courageous.

He also appears in GO DOWN, MOSES and *The REIVERS*.

Beauchamp, Molly (Aunt Molly; Mollie) The wife of Lucas Beauchamp, she is a longtime loyal servant of the Edmonds family.

Molly has died before Lucas's arrest for murder, and she appears only in retrospective scenes in *Intruder in the Dust*. Faulkner describes her as "a tiny old almost doll-sized woman" characteristically dressed in a spotless white headcloth and an ornamented straw hat.

She is a more fully developed character in GO DOWN, MOSES.

Bookwright A family name in the FRENCHMAN'S BEND section of YOKNAPATAWPHA COUNTY. In the novel, Bookwright's name is included with the early settlers of the area Frenchman's Bend.

Dandridge, Maggie Miss Maggie is Chick (Charles, Jr.) Mallison's grandmother. Lucas Beauchamp confuses her with Chick's mother, Margaret Stevens Mallison.

Downs, Mrs. Something of a sorceress, she is an old white woman who tells fortunes, cures hexes, and finds missing objects. Mrs. Downs lived on the edge of town in a house "that smelled like a fox den."

Edmonds, Carothers (Roth) The grandson of McCaslin Edmonds and the son of Zack, he inherits the 2,000-acre McCaslin plantation 17 miles from Jefferson, and is Lucas Beauchamp's landlord. At the time of Lucas's arrest for murder, he is in NEW ORLEANS being operated on for gallstones.

Edmonds also appears in GO DOWN, MOSES and is an offstage character in *The TOWN*, where he signs a note to help Lucius Hogganbeck buy a Model-T Ford.

Ephraim The father of Paralee, the Mallisons' cook, he dozes all day in a rocking chair, and walks the roads around Jefferson at night. Ephraim uses his extrasensory powers to find a ring belonging to Maggie Mallison. Something of a homespun philosopher, he tells Charles (Chick) Mallison, Maggie's son, not to bother with men when he needs something done "outside the common run," but to apply to women and children instead.

Fraser, Doyle He is the son of storekeeper Squire Adam Fraser. Vinson Gowrie is murdered near the Fraser store and Lucas Beauchamp is falsely accused of the crime. Fraser once restrained a drunken white sawmill hand from attacking Lucas; he protected Lucas from a potential lynch mob when whites idling at his store found him standing over Gowrie's body.

Fraser, Squire Adam He owns the store near where Vinson Gowrie is shot to death. Lucas Beauchamp is falsely accused of the murder; after his arrest, Fraser checks in with the sheriff to make sure he's safe from the white mob.

Gowrie An old family name in YOKNAPATAWPHA COUNTY, it is prominent in *Intruder in the Dust* and *The TOWN*.

Gowrie, Amanda Workitt The late wife of N. B. Forrest Gowrie, the eldest of old Nub Gowrie's six sons, she is buried in the Gowrie family plot in the pinewoods.

Gowrie, Bilbo   He and his twin brother Vardaman Gowrie are the fourth and fifth of the six sons of the old widower Nub Gowrie. The boys are named for powerful populist Mississippi politicians Theodore G. Bilbo and James K. Vardaman. The Gowrie twins help their father open the grave of the murdered Vinson Gowrie.

Gowrie, Bryan   The third son of Nub Gowrie, he runs the Gowrie family farm, and manages it so efficiently that it feeds them all.

Gowrie, Crawford   The second of Nub Gowrie's six sons, he is drafted into the U.S. Army in early November 1918 and, with "bad luck guessing," deserts the night of November 10—just hours before the Armistice ends the war. In consequence, he serves a one-year prison sentence in Fort Leavenworth.

Crawford deals in lumber in partnership with his brother Vinson Gowrie and Uncle Sudley Workitt. Lucas Beauchamp witnesses him stealing lumber from his partners and threatens him with exposure. Crawford kills Vinson, and tries to frame Lucas for the crime.

When Crawford observes a third man, the blackmailer Jake Montgomery, removing Vinson's body from its grave, he kills Montgomery too, buries him in Vinson's grave, and dumps Vinson's body into a bed of quicksand.

Through the investigations of Chick Mallison (Charles Mallison Jr.), Aleck Sander, and Eunice Habersham, Crawford's crimes are ultimately discovered. He kills himself in the Jefferson jail with a single shot from a Luger pistol.

Gowrie, N. B. Forrest   Nub Gowrie's oldest son, he manages a cotton plantation in the MISSISSIPPI DELTA above Vicksburg.

Gowrie, Nub   A fierce, ill-tempered widower, a short, lean, weathered old man with one arm and "a nose like the hooked beak of an eagle," he is a YOKNAPATAWPHA COUNTY hill farmer and the father of six grown sons.

Nub refuses at first to allow the authorities to open the grave of his murdered son Vinson Gowrie. He only relents when he is told that Vinson's body has been removed.

Chick (Charles Mallison Jr.) imagines old Nub at the head of a lynch mob out to avenge his son's killing.

Nub Gowrie is mentioned in *The* MANSION.

Gowrie, Vardaman   One of six sons of old Nub Gowrie, he is the twin of Bilbo Gowrie. With the sheriff looking on, Vardaman and Bilbo open their brother Vinson (Gowrie)'s grave and find Jake Montgomery's body there.

Gowrie, Vinson   The youngest son of Nub Gowrie, 28 years old, he is involved in a number of business enterprises, among them a lumber partnership with his brother Crawford (Gowrie), who has been stealing from him. When Lucas Beauchamp discovers the theft and threatens to reveal it, Crawford kills Vinson and tries to pin the crime on Beauchamp.

Good with money, Vinson was "the first Gowrie who could sign his name to a check and have any bank honor it."

Greenleaf   The Greenleafs were early settlers in YOKNAPATAWPHA COUNTY.

Grenier, Louis   One of the first settlers of YOKNAPATAWPHA COUNTY, he is of Huguenot ancestry and is characterized as a Paris-trained architect and something of a dilettante. He appears in REQUIEM FOR A NUN and is referred to in KNIGHT'S GAMBIT, *The* TOWN, and *The* REIVERS.

Grinnup, Lonnie   He is the last descendant of Louis Grenier, architect, lawyer, and one of the founders and the first great landowner of YOKNAPATAWPHA COUNTY. Cheerful and dim, Grinnup squats in a riverside shack on the last scrap of land still owned by his family.

He also appears in KNIGHT'S GAMBIT.

Habersham, Doctor   He is Eunice Habersham's grandfather. In antebellum YOKNAPATAWPHA COUNTY, Molly Beauchamp had been one of his slaves; Molly and Miss Habersham were girls together. With Louis Grenier and Alexander Holston, Habersham is one of the founders of JEF-FERSON, MISSISSIPPI. Doctor Samuel Habersham appears in REQUIEM FOR A NUN and is mentioned in *The* TOWN.

Habersham, Eunice A 70-year-old spinster who lives in an unpainted columned house on the edge of JEFFERSON, MISSISSIPPI, and the descendant of one of the three "first families" of YOKNAPATAW-PHA COUNTY, she earns a subsistence by selling chickens and vegetables from the back of an old pickup truck.

Miss Eunice takes an interest in the Lucas Beauchamp murder case because her grandfather once owned Molly Beauchamp's parents as slaves. Eunice accompanies Charles (Chick) Mallison, Jr., and Aleck Sander to the Gowrie burial plot and helps the boys persuade the sheriff to reopen his investigation into Vinson Gowrie's murder.

She also appears in *The* TOWN.

Halladay, Jim He is the district attorney, with an office in Harrisburg 60 miles distant from Jefferson. Halladay needs to originate the petition to exhume Vincent Gowrie's body.

Hampton (Hope or Hubert [Hub]) For a dozen years he is the efficient, capable sheriff of YOKNAPA-TAWPHA COUNTY. A countryman in his 50s, "a farmer and the son of farmers," he owns the house he had been born in and lives in a rented place in Jefferson during his terms in office.

Hampton takes Lucas Beauchamp into custody for the murder of Vinson Gowrie and protects him from a Gowrie-led lynch mob. When Chick Malli-son and Aleck Sander, with help from Miss Eunice Habersham, present Hampton with evidence that Lucas is not the killer, he agrees to reopen the case. In the end, Crawford Gowrie is revealed as his brother's murderer and Lucas goes free.

He also appears in *The* HAMLET, *The* REIVERS, *The* TOWN, and *The* MANSION.

Hampton, Mrs. (Hope) She is the wife of the YOKNAPATAWPHA COUNTY sheriff, Hope Hampton.

Hogganbeck, Boon An important comic char-acter in GO DOWN, MOSES and *The* REIVERS, he is mentioned in passing in *Intruder*.

Holston, Alexander With Doctor Habersham and Louis Grenier, he is one of the three original settlers of YOKNAPATAWPHA COUNTY. He is men-tioned as a tavern-keeper in *Intruder in the Dust*, and his name lives on in the Holston House, a hotel on the square in Jefferson.

Holston is fleshed out in the prose prologue to act 1 of REQUIEM FOR A NUN.

Ingraham The name of one of the early YOKNAPATAWPHA COUNTY farm clans, it has passed into common usage as Ingrum, just as Urquhart has evolved into Workitt.

Ingrum, Willy He is the talkative JEFFERSON, MISSISSIPPI, town marshal. When the sheriff, Hope Hampton, wants to move Lucas Beauchamp from the jail to a safer place, he gives Willy a false route and destination so that he will pass it along and throw the Gowrie lynch mob off the scent.

Joe A young African-American tenant of Caroth-ers Edmonds, he accompanies Chick Mallison and Aleck Sander on a rabbit hunt.

Legate, Will An excellent shot and by reputation the best deer hunter in YOKNAPATAWPHA COUNTY, he stands guard outside the JEFFERSON, MISSISSIPPI, jail to protect Lucas Beauchamp from a lynch mob. He later escorts Beauchamp from the besieged jail to the sheriff's house.

Legate also appears in GO DOWN, MOSES and in the short story "RACE AT MORNING."

Lilley He owns a small store with business chiefly from the JEFFERSON, MISSISSIPPI, black community. All the same, he offers to join the mob that forms to lynch Lucas Beauchamp, the supposed killer of Vinson Gowrie. As Gavin Stevens notes, there are no hard feelings on Lilley's part; he is simply acting like a white man, "implicitly observing the rules" of the racial relationship.

Littlejohn This is the family name of farmers in early YOKNAPATAWPHA COUNTY. Littlejohns are mentioned in *The HAMLET, AS I LAY DYING* and *The MANSION*.

McCallum, Buddy   The father of young Anse and Lucius McCallum and a World War I veteran, he trades a "war trophy," a German Luger automatic pistol, to Crawford Gowrie for a pair of foxhounds in the summer of 1919. Gowrie used the weapon to murder his brother, Vinson.

Buddy McCallum also appears in *SARTORIS* (where his name is spelled MacCallum), *The TOWN*, and the short story "THE TALL MEN."

McGowan, Skeets   He is the clerk in a Jefferson drug store from whom Chick Mallison hopes to buy tobacco for the jailed Lucas Beauchamp. McGowan also appears in *AS I LAY DYING, The TOWN*, and *The MANSION*.

Mallison, Charles, Jr. (Chick)   The 16-year-old nephew of Gavin Stevens, he is the precocious investigator of Vinson Gowrie's murder. The novel is told from Chick's point of view.

His relationship with Lucas Beauchamp has a rocky start. Beauchamp, who is black, pulls Chick out of an icy creek and takes him home to his cabin to recuperate. Supposing he is following the rules of Mississippi racial relationships, Chick offers him a 70-cent tip for drying him off and feeding him. Beauchamp brusquely refuses payment. When Chick sends Christmas presents (cigars, snuff, a dress for Beauchamp's wife) in a further attempt to pay off the debt, Beauchamp responds with a gift of sorghum molasses, leaving the two "right back where they started."

With his young black friend Aleck Sander, Chick finally settles accounts by undertaking to prove Beauchamp's innocence of the Gowrie murder. Along the way, he gains an awareness of the perversities of Mississippi's law-flouting racial code.

Chick Mallison also appears in *KNIGHT'S GAMBIT, The TOWN, The MANSION*, and the short story "HOG PAWN."

Mallison, Charles, Sr.   He is the querulous, ineffectual father of Charles (Chick) Mallison, Jr., one of the boy heroes of *Intruder*. Mallison's brother-in-law Gavin Stevens seems to run his household.

He also appears in *The TOWN* and *The MANSION*.

Mallison, Margaret Stevens (Maggie)   She is Charles Mallison, Sr.'s wife, the mother of Chick Mallison, and the twin sister of Gavin Stevens. An overprotective mother, she is said to have never forgiven her son for learning to button his pants.

Maggie Mallison also appears in *KNIGHT'S GAMBIT, The TOWN*, and *The MANSION* and is mentioned in *REQUIEM FOR A NUN*.

Maycox, Judge   He is the judge to whom Gavin Stevens applies for an order to exhume murder victim Vinson Gowrie. The judge issues the order.

Montgomery, Jake   A "shoestring" timber dealer with other business interests, including a speakeasy/brothel across the Tennessee line, he buys lumber that he knows Crawford Gowrie has stolen from his brother Vinson Gowrie and Vinson's partner, Sudley Workitt.

Jake also knows that Crawford killed Vinson and framed Lucas Beauchamp for the crime. He digs up Vinson's body, evidently with the idea of showing the sheriff that Crawford is the murderer. Crawford discovers Jake in the act and kills him, dumping his body into Vinson's grave.

When Chick Mallison and company find the corpse and rebury it, Crawford exhumes it and deposits it in a shallow grave. Sheriff Hampton finds Montgomery's body there. "By getting himself murdered and into Vinson's grave," says Gavin Stevens, "Jake probably saved Lucas' life."

Mosby, Uncle Hogeye   He is an epileptic inmate of the YOKNAPATAWPHA COUNTY poorhouse. The town boys used to achieve a thrill watching him fall into a foaming fit.

Paralee   The Mallisons' cook, she is the mother of Chick Mallison's friend and fellow detective, Aleck Sander.

Sander, Aleck   He is Chick Mallison's 12-year-old friend and his collaborator, with Miss Eunice

Habersham, in the exhumation of Vinson Gowrie, an attempt to prove Lucas Beauchamp innocent of a murder charge. Because Aleck is black, his involvement in Gowrie business is riskier than that of his white fellow detectives.

Aleck's motives for helping Beauchamp are pure, and he makes it clear he's not interested in a reward. "I ain't rich," he says. "I don't need money."

He reappears in *The Town* as the son of Big Top and Guster Sander and the friend and sidekick of Chick Mallison.

Skipworth The BEAT FOUR constable, he arrests Lucas Beauchamp for the murder of Vinson Gowrie, takes him to his home, and holds him overnight, standing guard with a shotgun and protecting him from the mob until Sheriff Hampton can arrive to take him to the county jail.

Stevens, Gavin A prominent Jefferson attorney, Stevens defends Lucas Beauchamp against a charge of murdering Vinson Gowrie. Stevens, a 50-year-old bachelor, is Jefferson's intellectual, a Phi Beta Kappa with a master's degree from HARVARD UNIVERSITY. Something of a windbag, he delivers long, rambling soliloquies on race relations in the South.

Stevens initially doubts Beauchamp's innocence, and he decides to try to persuade him to plead guilty to a manslaughter charge in return for a lesser sentence. When evidence produced by his nephew Chick Mallison and his allies exonerates Beauchamp, Stevens refuses to bill him for his services, accepting only $2 for expenses.

Stevens is a major character in KNIGHT'S GAMBIT, REQUIEM FOR A NUN, *The Town* and *The MANSION*. He also appears in LIGHT IN AUGUST, GO DOWN, MOSES, and several short stories. Some readers see Stevens as Faulkner's mouthpiece, particularly in *Light in August* and *Intruder in the Dust.*

Tubbs, Euphus The potbellied, timid jailer in Jefferson, Mississippi, he complains that, at $75 a month, he is not paid enough to stand up to a lynch mob. But he reluctantly agrees to do his duty and protect his prisoner, Lucas Beauchamp, a black man accused of killing Vinson Gowrie, a white man.

Tubbs also appears in REQUIEM FOR A NUN and *The MANSION.*

Tubbs, Mrs. She is the wife of Euphus Tubbs, the JEFFERSON, MISSISSIPPI, jailer. Mrs. Tubbs also appears in REQUIEM FOR A NUN and *The MANSION.*

Workitt, Uncle Sudley A distant kinsman of the Gowries with the honorary title of "uncle," he is murder victim Vinson Gowrie's partner in a lumber business. Vinson's brother Crawford Gowrie stole lumber from the partners, and ended up committing double murder trying to cover his crime.

FURTHER READING

Basset, John E. "Gradual Progress and *Intruder in the Dust.*" *College Literature* 13 (1986): 207–216.

Brooks, Cleanth. "The Community in Action (*Intruder in the Dust*)." In *William Faulkner: The Yoknapatawpha Country,* 279–294. Baton Rouge: Louisiana State University Press, 1990.

Brylowski, Walter. "The Theme of Maturation in *Intruder in the Dust.*" In *Readings on William Faulkner,* edited by Clarice Swisher, 172–176. San Diego: Greenhaven, 1998.

Hamblin, Robert W. "Teaching *Intruder in the Dust* Through Its Political and Historical Context." In *Teaching Faulkner: Approaches and Methods,* edited by Stephen Hahn and Robert W. Hamblin, 151–162. Westport, Conn.: Greenwood Press, 2000. Reprinted in *A Gathering of Evidence: Essays on William Faulkner's* Intruder in the Dust, edited by Michel Gresset and Patrick Samway, S.J., 57–73. Philadelphia: Saint Joseph's University Press, 2004.

Millgate, Michael. "*Intruder in the Dust.*" In *The Achievement of William Faulkner,* 215–220. Lincoln: University of Nebraska Press, 1978.

Rigsby, Carol R. "Chick Mallison's Expectations and *Intruder in the Dust.*" *Mississippi Quarterly* 29 (1976): 386–399.

"Justice, A" (*Collected Stories*)

Short story that first appeared in *These 13* (1931). The steamboat episode was revised for *Big Woods* (1955). Events in "A Courtship" precede this story.

SYNOPSIS

This story recounts the return home of Ikkemotubbe, now named Doom and corrupted by the white man's ways, and his rise to power through murder, intimidation, and ruthless exploitation of even his closest friends. The tale is framed by an adult Quentin Compson looking back to his boyhood, when he heard the story from his grandfather's carpenter Sam Fathers.

Using a laconic, comic tone, Sam tells how, long ago, Doom gave him the name Had-Two-Fathers. With what may be an Indian storytelling strategy of deception, he relates an elliptic and ambiguous tale that implies rather than spells out key events. After Doom gains power, probably by poisoning the old Chickasaw Indian chief and his son, he forces his men and his slaves to transport, by means of heroic exertions, a stranded steamboat through the wilderness. At the same time he renders justice to a black slave whose wife is pursued obsessively by Craw-ford, Sam's "pappy." Doom gives the man his best fighting cock in order to defeat Craw-ford's bird. When the black man's wife bears a light-skinned baby, Doom names him Had-Two-Fathers. According to this story, Craw-ford appears to be the biological father, but Faulkner has stated elsewhere that Doom actually is the father (*Selected Letters*, 208). Doom forces Craw-ford and Herman Basket to erect a palisade fence around the black man's cabin. Once it is complete, the man shows them a new baby, this time seemingly completely black. Quentin Compson, innocent at age 12, does not quite grasp the role of violence and sex in this saga; its meaning only becomes clearer to him when he is older.

CRITICAL COMMENTARY

Diane B. Jones, in her detailed survey of the criticism devoted to this story, identifies the critics' principal concerns as "race, power, patriarchy, and the narrative technique used in this framed story" (353).

CHARACTERS

Basket, Herman A Chickasaw Indian, he is a friend of Crawfishford, the father of Sam Fathers.

Callicoat, David Captain of the steamboat that makes four trips a year up the river along which Doom's Chickasaw people live.

Compson, Caddy Quentin's sister. When she visits her grandfather's farm, a Negro boy takes her and Jason fishing.

Compson, Grandfather The owner of the Compson farm four miles outside of JEFFERSON, MISSISSIPPI, he takes his grandchildren with him for a visit to the farm.

Compson, Jason Quentin's younger brother. He accompanies Caddy on the fishing trip.

Compson, Quentin The narrator of the frame of the story. On a visit to the farm, Caddy and Jason go fishing, but Quentin prefers to go to the blacksmith shop to talk with Sam Fathers, who tells him the story of how he came to be named "Had-Two-Fathers."

Crawfishford (Craw-ford) A boyhood friend of Doom and Herman Basket, he is the Chickasaw Indian father of Sam Fathers by a slave woman.

Fathers, Sam (Had-Two-Fathers) The son of a quadroon woman and the Chickasaw Indian, Crawfishford. He becomes the carpenter and blacksmith on the Compson farm and tells young Quentin Compson how he got his Indian name.

Ikkemotubbe A Chickasaw chief, he performs a marriage ceremony joining a quadroon woman to one of his slaves. She delivers a boy named Had-Two-Fathers, and Ikkemotubbe later sells the bride, groom, and child to the white planter Carothers McCaslin.

Sometimes-Wakeup The brother of the poisoned Chickasaw chief, he prudently concludes he does not want to succeed as head of the tribe. The post goes instead to the poisoner, Doom (Ikkemotubbe).

Roskus Black servant of the Compsons. The adult Quentin recalls that Roskus would drive the surrey carrying the 12-year-old Quentin, his grandfather, his sister Caddy, and his brother Jason from their home in town to the farm.

Stokes, Mr.   Manager of the Compson farm. Sam Fathers works there as a blacksmith and carpenter.

Knight's Gambit

Collection of five previously published short stories and an eponymous novella, published by Random House on November 27, 1949.

SYNOPSIS

In "Smoke," crabbed, violent Anselm Holland Sr. (Old Anse) is found dead with his foot in his horse's stirrup—an obvious attempt to make the killing look like an accident. Suspicion immediately falls upon one of his twin sons, Anselm Holland Jr. (Young Anse). The real murderer, who kills because he covets the Holland farm, is a cousin of the twins, Granby Dodge. Under suspicion by Judge Dukenfield, Dodge hires a Memphis gangster to kill the judge. Gavin Stevens, a lawyer, ultimately unravels the mystery by tracing the "city cigarette" the hitman smokes.

The plot of "Monk," the second story in the collection, turns on a false murder accusation that sends the feeble-minded Stonewall Jackson Odlethrop, known as Monk, to prison for life. There he kills the prison warden at the instigation of another convict. In sorting out the details of Monk's starcrossed career, Stevens shows compassion for Monk, doubly a victim, and a reformer's contempt for Mississippi's corrupt prison system.

In "Hand Upon the Waters," Stevens, now county attorney, identifies the murderer of Lonnie Grinnup, a degraded descendant of one of the first of the Yoknapatawpha County settlers. A fisherman, he is found drowned on his own trotline. As Stevens discovers, Boyd Ballenbaugh has killed the cheerful, childlike Lonnie to collect on his insurance policy.

"Tomorrow" turns on the murder of a young bravo called Buck Thorpe. A Frenchman's Bend farmer named Bookwright is accused of killing him for running off with Bookwright's 17-year-old daughter. The jury is prepared to find the homicide justifiable, for Thorpe seems born for the hangman. But one juror holds out. As Stevens discovers, juryman Stonewall Jackson Fentry had taken the orphan Thorpe into his home as a boy.

In "An Error in Chemistry," a man named Joel Flint murders his wife and father-in-law; he is arrested, but escapes from jail and vanishes. Flint hid the old man's body, which was never found; this allows him to impersonate his wife's grieving father, sell the man's farm, and go off with the proceeds. Stevens discovers the ruse and brings Flint, a conjuror by trade, to justice.

In "Knight's Gambit," the boy narrator Chick Mallison watches his Uncle Gavin play a potentially deadly chess game involving the vicious young Max Harris, Captain Gualdres, and the two unwitting women, mother and daughter. In the end, Stevens prevents the murder; Gualdres marries the girl, and the middle-aged sleuth wins the hand of his middle-aged sweetheart.

CRITICAL COMMENTARY

Knight's Gambit is typically considered one of Faulkner's slighter works. The stories are "whodunits" (Faulkner's label), detective pieces with the lawyer and sometime county attorney Gavin Stevens as chief investigator and central character. Along with the Yoknapatawpha County setting and a gallery of the plain people of Mississippi, Stevens, who appears at the end of GO DOWN, MOSES (1942) and as a major player in INTRUDER IN THE DUST (1948), The TOWN (1957), and The MANSION (1959), gives the collection of six pieces written from 1931 to 1948 such unity as it possesses.

Early reviewers of *Knight's Gambit* were not greatly impressed. *Commonweal* called the book a "rather miserable and mawkish performance." In a left-handed compliment, the *Saturday Review of Literature* judged *Knight's Gambit* just the thing for readers put off by the novelist's more difficult works. Writing in *The New Yorker*, the critic Edmund Wilson could hear faint echoes of Faulkner at his best: "In spite of all one can say against the book, certainly very inferior Faulkner, none of these stories, however farfetched, fails to awaken that anxious suspense as to what is going to be revealed, to summon that troubled emotion in the presence of human anomaly, which make the strength of his finer fiction." Significantly, Irving Howe totally ignored both the volume and its individual stories in his critical study of Faulkner's works. Most recent scholars, as typified by the following remark of Jay Parini, have not elevated their opinion of the book: "The collection as a whole, though periodically engaging, lacks the febrile intensity of major Faulkner."

Nevertheless, *Knight's Gambit* has not been without its defenders. MICHAEL MILLGATE finds an overall unity in the book by identifying Gavin Stevens as the title character: "a knight of many gambits, as embodiment of justice, a fearless, skillful and yet compassionate campaigner for the right." Similarly, Richard Gray views Stevens as "a magisterial figure" whose ideal goal is to be "a solid citizen in a solid community." Robert Hamblin extends this view by identifying Stevens as "a traditionalist in a corrupt modern world" and pointing out how he seeks, at least somewhat successfully, to protect Yoknapatawpha County from its invasion by underworld murderers, thugs, and bootleggers from Memphis and New Orleans.

CHARACTERS

Ballenbaugh, Boyd ("Hand Upon the Waters") Knowing that his older brother Tyler Ballenbaugh is the beneficiary of Lonnie Grinnup's insurance policy, he kills Grinnup in order to collect the insurance. Boyd is killed at the hands of Joe, a deaf and mute orphan whom Grinnup had adopted.

Ballenbaugh, Tyler ("Hand Upon the Waters") The older brother of Boyd Ballenbaugh and a farmer with a reputation for self-sufficiency and violence, he insures Lonnie Grinnup's life on a $5,000 policy with a double indemnity for accidental death. The Ballenbaughs are thus suspects in Grinnup's murder. When Tyler confronts Boyd about it, Boyd shoots him; a moment later, the deaf and mute orphan Joe shoots and kills Boyd, avenging his foster father, Grinnup.

Berry, Ben ("An Error in Chemistry") He is the deputy sheriff of doubtful competence who searches the house of murder suspect Joel Flint.

Blake, Jim ("Hand Upon the Waters") He helps carry Lonnie Grinnup's body away from the coroner's office for burial.

Bookwright ("Tomorrow") A well-off farmer, husband, and parent who turns himself in at four in the morning to Will Varner and admits to having killed the brawling, swaggering Buck Thorpe for eloping with Bookwright's 17-year-old daughter. The jury is deadlocked and the case put down for retrial.

Canova, Signor (Joel Flint) ("An Error in Chemistry") An illusionist (his advertising slogan is "He Disappears While You Watch Him"), he is in fact Joel Flint, the Yankee murder suspect.

Cayley, Miss ("Knight's Gambit") A country girl, she is the daughter of Hence Cayley. Max Harriss gives her an engagement ring, but her father disapproves of him and she refuses to wear it.

Cayley, Hence ("Knight's Gambit") The father of Miss Cayley, he disapproves of Max Harriss, a well-off young man from NEW ORLEANS who courts her.

Dodge, Granby ("Smoke") A cousin of the Holland twins, he is the beneficiary of one of them, Virginius Holland. In his quest to inherit the Holland property, Dodge murders old Anselm Holland, the father of the twins, and hires a MEMPHIS gangster to kill Judge Dukenfield. Gavin Stevens eventually foils him.

Dukinfield, Judge ("Smoke") The executor of old Anselm Holland's will. Granby Dodge has him killed to further his scheme of inheriting the Holland property. *See also The TOWN and The MANSION.*

Ewell, Bryan ("An Error in Chemistry") One of Sheriff Hub Hampton's deputies, he is sent to watch Wesley Pritchel, Joel Flint's father-in-law.

Fentry, G. A. ("Tomorrow") A YOKNAPATAW-PHA COUNTY hill farmer, he is the father of the stubborn juryman Stonewall Jackson Fentry.

Fentry, Jackson Longstreet ("Tomorrow") A waif, he is taken in and raised by Stonewall Jackson Fentry. His Thorpe uncles eventually claim him.

Fentry, Stonewall Jackson ("Tomorrow") A "little, worn, dried-out hill man," he refuses as a juror to acquit Bookwright for the killing of Buck Thorpe. Fentry had raised the orphaned Thorpe.

Flint, Ellie Pritchel ("An Error in Chemistry") The "half wit" spinster daughter of the misanthropic Wesley Pritchel, she marries Joel Flint in order to escape her father. Flint later murders Ellie and her father and tries to collect the proceeds from the sale of Pritchel's farm.

Flint, Joel ("An Error in Chemistry") A Yankee, an outlander who operates a "pitch" in a street carnival and sometimes goes by the name of Signor Canova, master of illusion, he marries the spinster daughter of the irascible old hill farmer Wesley Pritchel. Flint later murders his wife and father-in-law, then impersonates the old man in a bid to collect on the illegal sale of his farm.

Fraser ("Monk") He is a childless widower, an old moonshiner whose whiskey is highly regarded. Stonewall Jackson (Monk) Odlethrop lives with him after the death of his grandmother, Mrs. Odlethrop.

Frazier, Judge ("Tomorrow") The judge who presides over the trial of Bookwright for the murder of Buck Thorpe. The trial ends in a hung jury.

Gambrell, C. L. ("Monk") He is warden of the prison in which the wrongly convicted Stonewall Jackson (Monk) Odlethrop is an inmate. At fellow prisoner Bill Terrel's instigation, Monk kills the warden.

Grenier, Louis ("Hand Upon the Waters") Mentioned as one of the first settlers of YOKNAPA-TAWPHA COUNTY. Grenier's last descendant is the dull-witted squatter Lonnie Grinnup.

Grinnup, Lonnie ("Hand Upon the Waters") Grinnup squats in a riverside shack on the last scrap of land still owned by his family. A murder victim, he is killed for his insurance.

Gualdres, Captain ("Knight's Gambit") An Argentine army officer, he is a house guest of the Harrisses and the fiancé of Miss Harriss, whose brother, Max Harriss, suspects he really wants to marry their mother for her money. Gualdres eventually marries Miss Harriss and volunteers for a U.S. Army cavalry regiment.

Harriss ("Knight's Gambit") A wealthy NEW ORLEANS bootlegger, he ostentatiously rebuilds his wife's deteriorated, once noble Jefferson, Mississippi, house. Harriss eventually is the victim of a gangland-style killing. *See also The* MANSION.

Harriss, Max ("Knight's Gambit") The son of the bootlegger Harriss, he resents the fact that Captain Gualdres can outride him on his own horses and once outfenced him with a hearth-broom. He tries to arrange for a wild horse to kill Gualdres.

Harriss, Melisandre Backus ("Knight's Gambit") The childhood sweetheart of Gavin Stevens, she marries a wealthy NEW ORLEANS bootlegger, with whom she has two children. After her husband's death she and her two children live in Jefferson. Stevens prevents her son Max from murdering his sister's suitor, Captain Gualdres. Max enlists in the army, and Stevens marries Mrs. Harriss.

Harriss, Miss ("Knight's Gambit") The daughter of a wealthy bootlegger (Harriss) and Melisandre Backus Harriss (Stevens), she marries the Argentine fortune hunter Captain Gualdres.

Hogganbeck, Melissa ("Knight's Gambit"). She is Chick Mallison's history teacher. Miss Hogganbeck changes the name of the course to "World Affairs." She also appears as a history teacher in *The* TOWN.

Holland, Anselm, Jr. (Young Anse) ("Smoke")
The son of Anselm (Old Anse) Holland, Sr., with whom he constantly feuds, and the twin of Virginius Holland, he runs away from home in his teens and returns a decade later to demand his share of the family property. Old Anse and Virginius refuse him.

Holland, Anselm, Sr. (Old Anse) ("Smoke")
The "crazed, hate-ridden" father of the twins Anselm (Young Anse) and Virginius Holland. Granby Dodge murders him in a bid to get possession of the Holland property. Old Anse also appears in *The* HAMLET and other works.

Holland, Cornelia Mardis ("Smoke") She is the deceased wife of Anselm (Old Anse) Holland and the mother of the twins, Young Anse and Virginius Holland.

Holland, Mr. ("Tomorrow") The jury foreman in the murder trial of Bookwright, accused of killing Buck Thorpe.

Holland, Virginius (Virge) ("Smoke") The son of Anselm (Old Anse) Holland and the twin of Anselm Holland, Jr. (Young Anse). A good farmer, he longs to take over the mistreated land from his father and restore it to productivity. But the old man eventually drives him away and he sets to farming his cousin Granby Dodge's land.

Ike ("Hand Upon the Waters") The head of the party that carries Lonnie Grinnup away for burial.

Job, Uncle ("Smoke") Judge Dukinfield's black doorkeeper, he sees and hears nothing when the judge is murdered. *See also The* TOWN.

Joe ("Hand Upon the Waters") A deaf and mute orphan, a ward of Lonnie Grinnup. Joe kills Lonnie's murderer, Boyd Ballenbaugh.

Killegrew, Hampton ("Knight's Gambit") The night marshal in JEFFERSON, MISSISSIPPI, he passes the time in the pool hall or the Allnite Inn.

McCallum, Rafe ("Knight's Gambit") A farmer and expert horse breeder and trader, he sells Max Harriss the wild stallion that Harriss means to use to kill Captain Gualdres. McCallum, Gavin Stevens, and Chick Mallison arrive just in time to save Gualdres.

McWilliams ("Knight's Gambit") The conductor of the railroad that serves Jefferson.

Mallison, Charles, Jr. (Chick) The young nephew of Gavin Stevens, he serves as Stevens's aide and the narrator of several tales in *Knight's Gambit* (namely, "Monk," "Tomorrow," "An Error in Chemistry"; although not narrated by him, the tale "Knight's Gambit" is told from Mallison's point of view). He is also a principal character in INTRUDER IN THE DUST, *The* TOWN, and *The* MANSION.

Mallison, Margaret Stevens (Maggie) ("Knight's Gambit") The mother of Chick Mallison and the twin sister of Gavin Stevens. Maggie is the childhood friend of Gavin's future fiancée, Melisandre Backus Harriss. *See also* INTRUDER IN THE DUST.

Markey, Robert ("Knight's Gambit") A MEMPHIS lawyer and politician, he studied at Heidelberg with Gavin Stevens. At Stevens's request, Markey has Max Harriss shadowed while Harriss is in Memphis.

Matthew ("Hand Upon the Waters") With Ike, Pose, and Jim Blake, he helps carry away Lonnie Grinnup's body for burial.

Mitchell ("Hand Upon the Waters") A storekeeper, he is the banker to which Lonnie Grinnup entrusted his burial money.

Nate ("Hand Upon the Waters") A black neighbor of Lonnie Grinnup. Gavin Stevens stops at Nate's cabin in the night and asks Nate to report him missing if he has not returned from Grinnup's camp by daylight.

Odlethrop, Mrs. ("Monk") Stonewall Jackson (Monk) Odlethrop's presumed grandmother, she dies when Monk is six or seven years old.

Odlethrop, Stonewall Jackson (Monk) ("Monk") Mentally deficient, he is falsely accused of murder and sentenced to life in prison. When the real killer confesses five years later, Monk is pardoned; however, he refuses to leave the prison. At another convict's instigation, he murders the prison warden, Gambrell, and is executed for the crime.

Paoli ("Knight's Gambit") Max Harriss's fencing master.

Pose ("Hand Upon the Waters") With Ike, Jim Blake, and Matthew, he helps carry Lonnie Grinnup's body from the coroner's office to the burial ground.

Pritchel, Wesley ("An Error in Chemistry") The foul-tempered father-in-law of Joel Flint and the owner of a back country farm with valuable deposits of clay. Flint murders him in a bid to obtain possession of the farm.

Pruitt, Mrs. ("Tomorrow") A white-haired old lady in a clean gingham sunbonnet and dress, she helps her son Rufus Pruitt narrate the story of the Fentrys to Gavin Stevens, breaking in frequently to correct him or to add details.

Pruitt, Rufus ("Tomorrow") A hill country neighbor of G. A. Fentry, he tells Gavin Stevens the story of Fentry and his infant son. Pruitt's loquacious mother interrupts to correct him or supply details.

Quick, Isham ("Tomorrow") He finds the half-drawn pistol in the hand of Buck Thorpe, whom the farmer Bookwright has just killed for attempting to elope with his daughter. Later, after the Bookwright murder trial ends in a hung jury, Quick recalls the Fentry-Thorpe connection (Stonewall Jackson Fentry raised the orphaned Thorpe) and explains it to Gavin Stevens.

Quick, (Uncle) Ben ("Tomorrow") Owner of the sawmill where Stonewall Jackson Fentry works, he is the father of Isham Quick.

Rouncewell, Mrs. ("Tomorrow") She owns the JEFFERSON, MISSISSIPPI, boardinghouse where the Bookwright jury deliberates. She also appears as a minor character in *The TOWN*, *The MANSION*, and *The REIVERS*.

Smith, Miss ("Tomorrow") Stonewall Jackson Fentry marries the pregnant Miss Smith, a "downstate" girl whose name actually is Thorpe, and rears her son after she dies in childbirth.

Stevens, Gavin The chief investigator in all of the crime stories in *Knight's Gambit*. Stevens is a major character in several of Faulkner's important works: *Knight's Gambit*, *INTRUDER IN THE DUST*, *REQUIEM FOR A NUN*, *The TOWN* (in which he narrates chapters 2, 5, 8, 13, 15, 17, 20 and 22), and *The MANSION* (in which he narrates chapter 10). He also appears in *LIGHT IN AUGUST*, "HAIR," *GO DOWN, MOSES*, "THE TALL MEN," "HOG PAWN" (revised for chapter 14 of *The Mansion*), and "BY THE PEOPLE" (revised for chapter 13 of *The Mansion*); he also is referred to in "A Name for the City" (revised for the prologue to act 1 of *Requiem for a Nun*).

Modeled partly on Faulkner's longtime friend PHILIP AVERY STONE, Gavin Stevens is an attorney from a prominent family in JEFFERSON, MISSISSIPPI, Faulkner's fictional counterpart of OXFORD, MISSISSIPPI. He is the son of Judge Lemuel Stevens and twin of Margaret Stevens Mallison; in *The Mansion*, he marries the widow Melisandre Backus Harriss (Stevens), a childhood sweetheart and one of his sister's childhood friends. Gavin is a Don Quixote figure whose romantic idealism can appear as foolishness to others around him, in particular to his sister. When, for example, he defends the honor of the married Eula Varner Snopes, whose dancing with Manfred de Spain shocks onlookers, he gets his face bloodied by Manfred. What Gavin seems to be doing here, according to his nephew, Chick Mallison, on whom Gavin has a considerable influence, is defending the ideal of women's chastity and virtue. Throughout *The Town* and *The Mansion*, Gavin is preoccupied with preventing the spread of SNOPSEISM. As part of this mission he takes an active interest in the education of Eula's teenage daughter Linda Snopes (Kohl) by discussing poetry with her and giving her catalogues of colleges she might like to attend. Although Gavin's interest in Linda may be an unconscious sublimation of his romantic feelings for her mother, he shows such genuine and singular kindness toward the daughter that, after Eula's suicide, his friend and ally against Snopesism, V. K. Ratliff, half-jokingly suggests that he marry Linda. Gavin, of course, declines (*The Town*, 351).

Gavin is Jefferson's "intellectual," a Phi Beta Kappa with a master's degree from HARVARD UNIVERSITY, a doctorate from Heidelberg University in Germany, and a law degree from the UNIVERSITY OF MISSISSIPPI. During World War I, he served in the American Field Service and YMCA in France from 1915 through 1918. His professional positions include county attorney, acting city attorney, and district attorney. In *Light in August*, Stevens, described as a tall and disheveled man, is the young district attorney who tells the sheriff that Joe Christmas will plead guilty to the murder of Joanna Burden. Stevens also reflects on the factors that lead up to Christmas's death and offers an interpretation that focuses on Christmas's inner struggles caused by the mixture of white and black blood flowing in his veins (*see especially* 448–449). Always thoughtful and humane, Stevens assures the elderly Mrs. Hines that her grandson Joe Christmas's body will be on the train to MOTTSTOWN in the morning to be buried there.

In *Intruder in the Dust*, after initial skepticism, Stevens becomes persuaded of Lucas Beauchamp's innocence and defends him aggressively against a murder charge. He also delivers long, rambling soliloquies on race relations in the South. In *Requiem for a Nun*, Gavin takes his nephew's wife, Temple Drake Stevens, to the governor's office in the middle of the night so the governor can hear Temple's plea for Nancy Mannigoe, who is to be executed for having killed Temple's six-month-old baby.

Some readers see Gavin Stevens as Faulkner's mouthpiece, particularly in *Light in August* and

Intruder in the Dust, but such an assumption cannot be justified. Faulkner was too skilled as an artist to identify with any of his characters, even though some of these characters may echo some of his sentiments. Faulkner does not intrude into his fictional works to present his opinions. (For more information, *see Faulkner in the University*, 25, 72, 118, 140–141 and 201; and James Farnham's "Faulkner's Unsung Hero: Gavin Stevens" in *Arizona Quarterly* [summer 1965], 115–132, where Farnham discusses Stevens's significance in the Snopes trilogy and how, by the end of *The Mansion*, he becomes a realist in his view of humanity). Horace Benbow, a precursor of Gavin Stevens, shares a similar educational background and other personal characteristics.

Stevens, Captain ("Tomorrow") An influential citizen of Jefferson, he is the father of Gavin Stevens. *See also* The TOWN and *The* MANSION.

Terrel, Bill ("Monk") A convict serving a 20-year term for manslaughter, he incites the slow-witted Stonewall Jackson (Monk) Odlethrop to murder Warden C. L. Gambrell in revenge for Gambrell's twice denying him parole.

Thorpe, Buck ("Tomorrow") A brawler, gambler, and moonshiner known to his friends as Bucksnorter, he comes to a violent end when he runs off with the 17-year-old daughter of a FRENCHMAN'S BEND farmer named Bookwright. The outraged father shoots Thorpe, who is found with a half-drawn pistol in his hand.

Varner, Will (Uncle Billy) ("Tomorrow") The justice of the peace and chief officer of the district to whom Bookwright surrenders himself for having killed Buck Thorpe. Varner appears in several of Faulkner's novels and stories and is a principal character in *The* HAMLET, *The* TOWN, and *The* MANSION.

Warren, Captain ("Knight's Gambit") Chick (Charles) Mallison asks him how a 16-year-old can enlist to fight in World War II. Warren advises him to wait.

West, Doctor ("Smoke") Owner of the drugstore in which Judge Dukinfield's murderer buys a pack of rare cigarettes. The identification of the cigarettes helps Gavin Stevens solve the Dukinfield murder.

Workman, Mr. ("An Error in Chemistry") An adjuster for the insurance company that underwrote a $500 policy for Ellie Pritchel Flint.

Light in August

One of Faulkner's masterpieces, published in 1932, the novel narrates the contrasting stories, one broadly comic, the other tragic, of Lena Grove and Joe Christmas. *Light in August* is peopled with a gallery of compelling secondary characters who move about in a succession of richly imagined YOKNAPATAWPHA COUNTY scenes.

"Few American novels are so lavish in dramatic incident, so infused with images of sensation, so precisely fixed in place and weather," the critic IRVING HOWE wrote in *Willam Faulkner; A Critical Study*. Most commentators rank it among Faulkner's greater works, along with *The SOUND AND THE FURY* (1929), *As I LAY DYING* (1930), *ABSALOM, ABSALOM!* (1936), *The HAMLET* (1940) and "THE BEAR" (1942).

SYNOPSIS

More conventional in structure than its great experimental predecessors, *The Sound and the Fury* and *As I Lay Dying*, *Light in August* is told chronologically over eleven days of present time, with long flashbacks. Lena Grove frames the story. The novel opens with Lena along the road heading westward to JEFFERSON, MISSISSIPPI, in search of the father of her unborn child. As she approaches the town near midday of Saturday, smoke is visible on the horizon: she arrives some hours after Joanna Burden's murder and the burning of her house. The core of the book is the story of Miss Burden's killer, Joe Christmas, in a flashback that takes up seven central chapters. The book returns to the present with the aftermath of the Burden murder and the

destruction of Christmas, and closes with Lena on the move once again, heading north from Jefferson on a futile search for the newborn's father.

The external events of the story are succinctly told. Lena Grove, a simple, trusting country girl from Alabama, comes to Jefferson in search of her lover, Lucas Burch, who abandons her after he learns of her pregnancy. Through a similarity of surnames she meets Byron Bunch, a meek and withdrawn bachelor who works as a sawmill hand and is also a choirmaster in a country church. Byron falls in love with Lena at once and looks after her until her child is born.

A counterpoint to Lena is Joanna Burden, a descendant of New England abolitionists and long a resident of Jefferson, though she is an outcast there. Her killer is also her illicit lover, the bootlegger Joe Christmas. Joe has long passed as white; after the killing, Burch (alias Joe Brown), his junior partner in the whiskey-running enterprise, denounces him to the sheriff as black, a claim that instantly persuades the sheriff of his guilt. Christmas is caught and jailed; he escapes and flees to the house of the Reverend Gail Hightower, like Miss Burden a Jefferson pariah. A self-appointed guardian of the community, the aptly named Percy Grimm, pursues Christmas into Hightower's kitchen, fires five shots into him, and castrates him with a butcher's knife as he dies.

Meantime, the reclusive Hightower, drawn back into the life of the town through his involvement with Byron Bunch, Lena Grove, and Christmas, is midwife to the birth of Lena's child. After he delivers a beating to the overmatched Bunch, the unspeakable Lucas Burch vanishes again. The novel closes with Lena and her baby moving placidly off in search of him, with the faithful Bunch trailing along as escort and protector.

The extended flashback develops the story of Joe Christmas. Faulkner introduces him as a foundling left on the steps of a MEMPHIS orphanage on Christmas night; hence his name. His mad grandfather, Eupheus (Doc) Hines, believing Joe's father is black, has placed him there. In a memorable scene, a young girl named Alice, who has befriended the child Joe, wakes him up to say goodbye when she is released from the orphanage. Joe is introduced to sex in another vivid scene. He innocently eavesdrops on the dietician Miss Atkins's lovemaking with an intern. Dreading exposure, she tells the matron that Joe is black, figuring he will then be sent away to the "nigger orphanage."

The matron instead arranges for Joe to live with a YOKNAPATAWPHA COUNTY poor white farmer, Simon McEachern, and his wife. A strict and fanatic Calvinist, McEachern literally tries to beat his religion into the boy. Joe hates McEachern, but he stoically accepts the thrashings. He despises his foster mother and rejects her efforts to make life easier for him. Joe acknowledges a bleak justice in Calvinistic patterns of crime and punishment, and resents Mrs. McEachern for trying to alter the pattern through pity or sentimentality. Lying rigid in his bed, reflecting on punishment and injustice, he thinks, "'She was trying to make me cry. Then she thinks that they would have had me'" (169).

Joe runs from home at age 17, a flight touched off when McEachern follows him to a dance hall and confronts him there with the prostitute Bobbie Allen. Joe breaks a chair over his foster father's head and leaves him unconscious, perhaps dying, on the dance floor. But Bobbie turns on him when he tells her he is part black, abandoning him abruptly to return to Memphis with Max and Mame Confrey, proprietors of the brothel where she works. Joe wanders for the next 15 years. Recurrent, usually deliberate, acts of violence mark his progress. Eventually he turns up in Jefferson, finds work in a sawmill, and becomes the lover of the spinster outcast Joanna Burden.

Their lovemaking, if that is what it should be called, is savage. Joanna's frigidity dissolves into nymphomania and finally into religious mania. With her sudden religious conversion, or perhaps relapse, Joanna comes to believe that because Joe is part black she has sinned against the stern Calvinist God of her forebears in her sexual encounters with him. A fatalistic calm settles on Joe as he makes his way to the Burden house for the final scene. "So now it's all done, all finished," he thinks, enters the house through the kitchen, and mounts the stairs. Joanna demands that Joe kneel with her and pray for forgiveness. When he refuses, she threatens him with an old Civil War pistol. The weapon misfires.

Insensate with rage, he slashes at her throat with a razor, nearly taking her head off.

Joe sets the house afire and takes flight. After a week on the run he approaches Mottstown, only 20 miles from Jefferson, and prepares to give himself up, marching up and down the main street until someone recognizes him. Joe surrenders and is taken to the Mottstown jail. His lunatic grandfather, full of racial hatred and religious fervor, tries to whip up the townspeople into a lynch mob. Joe is escorted to Jefferson, where he briefly breaks free of his captors. The avenger Percy Grimm tracks him down for the final chilling scene in Hightower's kitchen.

Christmas having accepted his terrible fate, *Light in August* ends as it began, with the serene Lena Grove on the track of Lucas Burch. "My, my," she says in the novel's last lines. "A body does get around. Here we aint been coming from Alabama but two months, and now it's already Tennessee" (507).

CRITICAL COMMENTARY

Faulkner began the novel in OXFORD, MISSISSIPPI, on August 17, 1931. He originally called it "Dark House," a title he would later briefly consider for *Absalom, Absalom!* According to the biographer JOSEPH BLOTNER, the novelist's wife suggested the change when she observed the unique qualities of light on an uncharacteristically cool and clear August evening. Another story persists that Faulkner borrowed the title from a Mississippi folk idiom for giving birth: a pregnant woman would be "light in August," or in whatever month her child appeared. Faulkner himself said it had to do with "a peculiar quality to light" in northern Mississippi on a couple of days each August.

Faulkner, not always reliable on such matters, claimed he launched the novel without a plan, only the image of a young pregnant woman walking along a road. By January 1932, the orphan Joe Christmas had taken over the novel. Faulkner found himself absorbed in his story of a boy doomed and alone, caught up in a violent, intensely painful, and self-defeating search for a sense of his identity and a place in society.

Christmas "deliberately evicted himself from the human race," Faulkner once said, because he did not know where he belonged. "That was his tragedy, that to me was the tragic, central idea" of the novel, that ". . . he didn't know what he was, and there was no way possible in life for him to find out" (*Faulkner in the University*, 72).

The recurrent pattern is for Joe to seek out trouble wherever he finds himself, flaunting what he suspects is his black blood, telling whites he is black, telling blacks he is white. Faulkner deliberately leaves the question vague. Doc Hines rejects his daughter Milly Hines's claim that the father is Mexican, but has no proof that he is black; when Joanna Burden quizzes Joe about his parents, he admits he doesn't really know.

Christmas's torment about his background causes most of his adult troubles. As the critic MICHAEL MILLGATE observes, "He is perpetually made aware of society's inflexible requirement that a man be *either* black *or* white and act accordingly."

While many critics have remarked on the comparative straightforwardness of narrative technique in *Light in August*, Millgate emphasizes the demands on the reader of Faulkner's extensive use of flashbacks. He withholds or delays the introduction of characters; he withholds or delays an explanation of events. In Millgate's view, Faulkner is attempting "to incorporate within the structure of a conventional novel the technique of multiple reflection" that gave *As I Lay Dying* its peculiar power.

In a succession of vividly narrated episodes, then, Faulkner introduces the themes of man in tension with nature, alienation from the community, and man's inability to fulfill himself outside the community. Present, too, is the American South's peculiar obsession with race and with the region's tortured past—Faulkner's first direct, extended confrontation with southern racial prejudice.

Some critics have questioned whether the episodes that make up *Light in August*, powerful as they are individually, reveal a coherent pattern of meaning. Not long after the novel appeared, CONRAD AIKEN anticipated later criticism in arraigning it for a lack of unity. Generally admiring of Faulkner's work, Aiken judged *Light in August* a failure on this ground.

Critic CLEANTH BROOKS asked, "What possible relation is there between the two main characters,

Lena and Joe Christmas, who go their separate ways, the one placidly, the other violently?" Answering his own question, Brooks suggested that the concept of community unifies the novel. Most of the characters in *Light in August* bear a special relationship to the community. They are strangers or outcasts. The community protects Lena, as when the initially disapproving Mrs. Armstid relents and gives her a few coins out of her small hoard. It persecutes Gail Hightower and destroys Christmas.

Faulkner biographer Joseph Blotner observed that the novelist integrates Lena into the Christmas plot through her relationship with Lucas Burch, the father of her child; under the alias Joe Brown, he joins Christmas in the bootlegger trade. She is, as virtually every commentator has noted, the life-bearing counterpoint to the doomed Christmas. So the link between Lena and Christmas is plain enough, even though they never actually meet. They have much in common: both are in flight, both have been deceived and abandoned, both end up in Jefferson. But their fates are painfully different.

More recent critics see unity in the thematic links among the major characters: cold, Calvinistic Joanna Burden is offered in contrast to the pagan Lena Grove; the past-obsessed Gail Hightower is antithetical (Faulkner's word) to Joe Christmas, a man without a past; the placid outcast Lena is paired with the furious outcast Joe; the saintly Byron Bunch in in contrast to the itinerant good-for-nothing Lucas Burch, who lives "on the country, like a locust" (6).

Faulkner's most recent biographer, Jay Parini, argues that Faulkner's use of symbols unifies *Light in August*. The novel is "beautifully integrated in symbolic terms," Parini writes; this gives coherence to the parallel stories of the major characters. One such linking device is the smoke that rises above the Burden place on the morning after Joanna's murder; this is what Lena sees first as she approaches Jefferson at the end of her two-month journey from DOANE'S MILL.

There is symbolism, too, in the names of characters, Lena Grove recalling Greek and Roman myth; Hightower the man out of the common run, noble and misunderstood; Joanna bearing the burden of the South's racial history; and above all Joe Christmas who, at the end, Christlike, is the picture of patient, accepting suffering at the hand of Percy Grimm.

Faulkner plainly is sympathetic to Christmas, subject as he is to the oppressions of Miss Atkins, mad Doc Hines, Simon McEachern, and others. Race and heredity are not really his problem, Faulkner seems to be saying; he is a victim of his upbringing and of society at large.

"The pressures that mold him into an Ishmael have," as Faulkner knows, nothing to do with biology as such," Brooks observes. "The decisive factor is the attitude that the world takes toward Joe and the attitude that he takes—toward other men and toward himself."

Faulkner plays the novel's final scene for humor, with Lena wandering northward into Tennessee with Byron Bunch in tow; Brooks and other critics argue that in spite of everything the closing sequence makes the predominant mode of the novel comedy. But Faulkner's humor has a deeper purpose than occasional relief from the pressures of the story. "Its function," asserts Brooks, "is to maintain sanity and human perspective in a scene of brutality and horror."

CRITICAL RECEPTION

Faulkner finished *Light in August* in Oxford on February 19, 1932. Extensive revisions occupied him until mid-March, when he sent off the 165,000-word, 507-page manuscript to his publishers, HARRISON SMITH and ROBERT K. HAAS. He reportedly experienced a kind of revulsion when the first copies reached him at ROWAN OAK in the early autumn, not at all how he felt at his first sight of *The Sound and the Fury* printed and bound. He also had no interest in reading the reviews, the first of which appeared in the *Saturday Review*, the *New York Times*, the *New York Tribune* and the *Nation*. Most reviewers treated Faulkner as a major novelist, but most also had reservations about his latest work.

Writing in the *New York Sun* in October 1932, the novelist James T. Farrell remarked that Faulkner draws readers in with his sensationalism, his obsession with psychopathology; this becomes

troubling only on reflection. "When one strives to reconstruct or to tell a Faulkner plot in retrospect one sees this melodrama clearly, but when one is reading, one is swept along by the man's driving pen," Farrell wrote. He predicted that Faulkner would limit himself as a novelist through his preoccupation with insanity and violence.

A British reviewer, the poet Richard Aldington, discerned a deeper purpose in Faulkner's choice of material, in his stern Calvinist characters with their obsessions about the past and about race. "In spite of the hard-boiled style in which Mr. Faulkner writes, there cannot be the slightest doubt of his meaning and sympathies," Aldington wrote in the London *Evening Standard* in February 1933. "He is engaged in the not very popular task of criticising the fundamental assumptions of his own people." F. R. Leavis, in the June 1933 number of the journal *Scrutiny*, faulted Faulkner for falling short of "an intimate and subtle rendering" of Joe Christmas's consciousness. Because Christmas is seen from the outside, the furies that drive him, and the necessity of his killing Joanna Burden, are not entirely clear.

As noted, critics early and late struggled to find coherence in *Light in August*. In the last analysis, the critic Irving Howe regarded the issue of unity as a phantom. In novels, he wrote, "the actual relation between form and content is almost always unfinished and improvisatory, rarely as neat as critics like to suppose." Howe argued that Faulkner's moral vision, his power, overcome the book's structural flaws: "In *Light in August* a new voice is heard, partly Faulkner's own and partly, as it were, an over-voice speaking for the memories and conscience of a people. . . . [T]his voice records the entire Yoknapatawpha story."

EXCERPTS FROM CONTEMPORARY REVIEWS OF *LIGHT IN AUGUST*

Excerpt from James T. Farrell's review, "The Faulkner Mixture," published in the New York Sun, October 7, 1932, 29:
William Faulkner's most apparent literary virtues are an impressive stylistic competence and a considerable virtuosity in construction and organization. It is his sheer ability to write powerfully that

carries many readers through the consistently melodramatic and sensational parts that occur regularly in his writings.

For instance, when one strives to reconstruct or to tell a Faulkner plot in retrospect one sees this melodrama clearly, but when one is reading, one is swept along by the man's driving pen. Technically, he is the master of almost all American writers who fit under such a loose and general category as "realists." He has probably forgotten more about literary tricks than such writers as Ernest Hemingway or Sherwood Anderson will ever learn. . . .

In *Light in August,* Faulkner adopts many of the tricks and mannerisms that have been termed "modernistic," and this without any great profit. Particularly, in some of the early pages, he is very free with metaphors, and they grow monotonous. He adopts the habit of using two verbs where one would often do. . . .

Excerpt from Floyd Van Vuren's review, "William Faulkner Attains New Maturity in Light in August," *published in the* Milwaukee Journal, *October 8, 1932, 4:*
A compelling power urges the reader through the 400 closely printed pages of this new novel by William Faulkner, the much acclaimed author of *Sanctuary, The Sound and the Fury* and *These Thirteen.* It is a power which transcends that of his earlier books, as if the power apparent in them was only a promise of the vital force that pervades *Light in August.*

The new book introduces a sounder and a more mature William Faulkner, a William Faulkner, it is true, who has not yet entirely conquered the art of the novelist, but who has now mastered the style and literary mannerisms to which in the past he was willing sometimes to sacrifice clarity and vitality. If Mr. Faulkner finds, after *Light in August* attains, as it will inevitably, to best sellerhood, that he is less a cult than he has been heretofore it will be because he has removed the taint of obscurity from his writing and has put more of his inherent strength and force as a novelist into his story than he has into its writing.

Which is not to say, however, that Mr. Faulkner is not still indebted, in *Light in August,* to James Joyce and the earlier followers of Joyce. His Joycean

heritage is still apparent, but now it does not get in the way of the story Faulkner has to tell and his style and mannerisms seem more an integral part of his novel. The tendency toward style for style's sake has disappeared and his mannerisms have attained purpose. . . .

It is not without contemplation that one discovers that the actual events in the story all take place within the limits of a few days. In reading *Light in August* it is as though the reader has lived through many lifetimes, so completely has he felt and realized to the full the significance or the futility of the lives of Mr. Faulkner's characters.

Excerpt from Henry Canby's review, "The Grain of Life," published in the Saturday Review of Literature, *October 8, 1932, 153–156:*
Those interested in the career of William Faulkner, and they are many, have waited with some concern for the appearance of his next book. They have felt that his earlier stories had shown a powerful grasp upon character and scene, a poetic vision that set him apart from the prosaic realists of the day, but a hurt mind tending with an alarming descent toward morbidity and the macabre. Was he to be another Southerner racked to pieces by his own talents, or a power in American literature?

"Light in August" may not be the final answer, but it is an answer. It is a novel of extraordinary force and insight, incredibly rich in character studies, intensely vivid, rising sometimes to poetry, and filled with that spirit of compassion which saves those who look at life too closely from hardness and despair. If the writing is sometimes as slovenly as at other times it is pointed and brilliant, if there are scenes too macabre, characters in whom fantasy transcends its just limits, and an obscurity, or rather, a turgidity in symbolism which is often annoying, this is merely to say that it is not a perfect work of art. Men of Faulkner's experience and training seldom make of their work one perfect chrysoprase; but there is no reason to suppose with this writer that he will be congenitally unable to shape his imagination into its own best form. He needs self-discipline, and the discipline of study and reading, but he can be trusted to find his own way.

The more so, since Faulkner possesses what so many powerful writers of modern fiction lack, a strong and constant sense for narrative. This novel through all its complexities, and its quiet periods of analysis, drives on like the current of a Spring river, gathering in tributaries as it goes, sweeping through backward curves, but always moving at flood intensity. There is not one plot, there are several; there is, one might almost say, no plot to the novel (was there a plot in "Vanity Fair"?) but a theme, the opposition of those whom life accepts and those whom it rejects, which gathers up all plots, all characters, as it goes. . . .

"Light in August" is by any standard a remarkable book. It will puzzle many readers, it will shock many readers, it will terrify many readers if they are honest in their reading. But I think that no one can deny it the praise of life caught in its intensities both good and bad, and, without cheap sentiment or melodrama, made to seem rich, humorous, distressing, thrilling, violent, lovable, disgusting, everything that life is and can be except the imagination of great minds highly touched which does not enter this book.

I think that Faulkner, like the revivalist preachers, overdoes his fantasy. I think that his analysis of destiny crushing the unfortunate and yet not letting the sparrow fall is adulterated by the romanticism of the Fundamentalist preachers he listened to in his youth. This is in a curious fashion a Methodist book. I think that, like all the American writers who deal with the vitalities of American experience, he lacks restraint in both style and incident, probably because he has no precedent for narrative such as his and must make one. But that he is one of the most powerful, vigorous, and interesting writers now practising English prose admits of no doubt. Let the skeptic, alarmed by his violence, or doubtful of his symbolism, compare "Light in August" with the post-Hardy novels of a roughly equivalent English life. There is no comparison in originality, force, and intrinsic imagination, only contrast. This man can go far.

Excerpt from J. Donald Adams's review, "Mr. Faulkner's Astonishing Novel," published in The New York Times Book Review, October 9, 1932, 6, 24:

With this new novel, Mr. Faulkner has taken a tremendous stride forward. To say that *Light in August* is an astonishing performance is not to use the word

lightly. That somewhat crude and altogether brutal power which thrust itself through his previous work is in this book disciplined to a greater effectiveness than one would have believed possible in so short a time. There are still moments when Mr. Faulkner seems to write of what is horrible purely from a desire to shock his readers or else because it holds for him a fascination from which he cannot altogether escape. There are still moments when his furious contempt for the human species seems a little callow.

But no reader who has followed his work can fail to be enormously impressed by the transformation which has been worked upon it. . . . In a word, Faulkner has admitted justice and compassion to his scheme of things. . . .

Light in August is a powerful novel, a book which secures Mr. Faulkner's place in the very front rank of American writers of fiction. He definitely has removed the objection made against him that he cannot lift his eyes above the dunghill. There are times when Mr. Faulkner is not unaware of the stars. One hesitates to make conjectures as to the inner lives of those who write about the lives of others, but Mr. Faulkner's work has seemed to be that of a man who has, at some time, been desperately hurt; a man whom life has at some point badly cheated. There are indications in the book that he has regained his balance.

Excerpt from George Marion O'Donnell's review, "A Mellower Light," published in the Memphis Commercial Appeal, October 9, 1932, Section IV, 4:

. . . For though *Light in August* is more human and less mordant than *Sanctuary*, it is decidedly tragic and decidedly unconventional in tone.

Mr. Faulkner utilizes almost 500 pages in the telling of his story. The plot is luxuriant, teeming with a thousand suggestions and implications and complications, but clearcut and lucid at last. As in his other books, Faulkner sheds lights gradually upon the events that make up his narrative. There are long flash-backs in which one learns the life history of each of his major characters in turn; and these flash-backs, with their abrupt transitions from the present to the past, from one set of characters to another, give to the narrative a slight looseness that stands in the way of perfection, though it does not impair the cumulative effect of the whole.

The method which Mr. Faulkner has utilized in *Light in August* is interesting. It is simpler than any other he has used in his writing, yet it is a synthesis of all these methods. The author has employed third person, past tense, and present tense narration, the stream of consciousness, first person narration and conversation, blending the various methods that he has used separately in previous books into a whole that is admirably effective if not always smooth. The synchronization gives the impression that Faulkner is striving for a novel-form in which all modes will be blended into a perfect narrative. This perfection is not attained in *Light in August,* but it is approached.

In every respect *Light in August* is quieter than the author's earlier works. It is more restrained, less brutal, more leisurely and dignified in its movement. The author still possesses his power for dramatic, gripping writing about tragic events, and his descriptive epithets are usually so apt as to be startling; but the prose is less staccato than that of *Sanctuary,* being more like the prose of *Sartoris* and of portions of *The Sound and the Fury.* Even the characters are more human and less pathological than one expects Faulkner's characters to be.

On the whole *Light in August* is a greater work than any other book William Faulkner has written. It is more mature, broader in outlook, nearer to the final, truthful revelation of human potentialities for which the author is striving. It is a novel that no one who is interested in the growth of American literature can afford to neglect. And that William Faulkner is one of the major writers of our generation is proved here anew.

Excerpt from Evan Shipman's untitled review of **Light in August**, *published in the* **New Republic 72 (October 26, 1932), 300–301:**
At the present time, most of the interesting writers are cautiously feeling their way with a realism that reduces the scope of their work in an effort toward absolute honesty. William Faulkner is in strong contrast to this tendency; his risk is considerable. He fills that realistic scene with drama; his characters are moved by exceptional and perverse impulses; their lives proceed toward violent ends. His powerfully individual books are written in a prose that at its best is poetic, at its worst confused and tedious. He has been highly praised; the strange, fervent quality of his work compared to the great Russians. But one feels that what is with them an evangelical force is with Faulkner a savage weariness with the puppets he means to destroy.

Light in August, his sixth or seventh novel, combines all the faults and some of the interesting qualities of his previous books. For instance the lack of unity in the handling of diverse themes is so marked as to seem a willful misleading of the reader. The extravagant style becomes ridiculous when, as often in four hundred pages, it is applied to the commonplace. It is hardly a supple medium. Much of the violence appears to be as formal a matter as in an Elizabethan "tragedy of blood." On the other hand, when describing a situation which justifies his elaborate prose, Faulkner controls the rhetoric so that it becomes an ideal expression of his nervous intensity. And he has a rare feeling for the poetry of rural speech; he indicates, contrasts, the difference in tempo of neighboring ways of life in the South with a perception that identifies him seriously with his country. . . .

Excerpt from Herbert Agar's review, published in the British journal, **The English Review 56 (February 1933), 226:**
Mr. William Faulkner is one of the best known of the young American writers. His new book, "Light in August". . . , has all the repulsive qualitites that his public has learned to love. It is what is known as "powerful" and "courageous."

Excerpt from Helen Fletcher's review of **Light in August**, *published in* **Time and Tide (February 4, 1933), 120–122:**
Light in August is as brave as it is compassionate. A grand and unforgettable book.

CHARACTERS

Alice A 12-year-old girl with motherly instincts, she takes care of Joe Christmas in the orphanage. Alice wakes him up to say a tearful good-bye when she wins her release.

Allen, Bobbie   She is a waitress at a cheap restaurant who doubles as a prostitute. Small, "slight, almost childlike" with overlarge hands, Bobbie has a "musing, demure" appearance in the eyes of Joe Christmas.

At 17, Joe, unaware that she is a prostitute, has a love affair with Bobbie Allen. The stern Simon McEachern, Joe's foster father, confronts them at a dance; Joe attacks him with a chair when he calls Bobbie a harlot. But she rejects Joe and leaves town with her MEMPHIS employers, Max and Mame Confrey.

Armstid, Henry   A poor farmer, he is a kind and considerate person who helps both neighbor and stranger. Courting his wife's displeasure, he provides overnight shelter for the stranger Lena Grove, and the next day takes her in his wagon to VARNER'S STORE, where she can catch a lift to JEFFERSON, MISSISSIPPI.

Thinking of his wife's grudging reaction to the plainly pregnant and unmarried Lena, he observes that "women folks are likely to be good without being very kind" (12).

Armstid also appears in AS I LAY DYING, THE HAMLET, *The* TOWN and *The* MANSION and in the short story "SHINGLES FOR THE LORD."

Armstid, Mrs. (Martha)   The wife of the poor farmer Henry Armstid, "a gray woman with a cold, hard, irascible face" (15), she taps her small store of egg money to see the travel-weary Lena Grove on her way to JEFFERSON, MISSISSIPPI. Although indignant about Lena's pregnancy and contemptuous of her naiveté, Mrs. Armstid is sympathetic too.

Mrs. Armsid also appears in AS I LAY DYING, where she is called Lula, in *The* HAMLET, and in the short story "SHINGLES FOR THE LORD." (For more on her, *see Faulkner in the University*, 30–31).

Atkins, Miss   A dietician in the orphanage where Joe Christmas lives, she is a "fullbodied, smooth, pink and white" 27-year-old who panics when she suspects that Joe has overheard her making love with an intern named Charley. She fears Joe will betray her to the matron.

As it happens, Joe had been too sick from eating the dietician's pink toothpaste to notice anything. But Miss Atkins does not know this, and she decides to tell the matron that Joe is an African American, in the hope that the authorities will deliver him to the "nigger" orphanage. The matron arranges for Joe's adoption by Simon McEachern and his wife.

Beard, Mrs.   "A comfortable woman, with red arms and untidy grayish hair" (84), Mrs. Beard operates the Jefferson boardinghouse where Byron Bunch has a room. Lena Grove boards with her when she first arrives in Jefferson.

Bedenberry, Brother   He is the pastor of a black country church. After Joanna Burden's murder, Joe Christmas tries to "snatch him outen the pulpit" as he preaches during a night-time revival meeting (323). When Brother Bedenberry's grandson tries to avenge him, Joe fractures his skull with a bench leg.

Buford   He is a deputy sheriff assigned to the Joanna Burden murder case. Buford handles the dogs in the Joe Christmas manhunt. Christmas briefly escapes from Buford's custody before Percy Grimm tracks him down and kills him.

Bunch, Byron   Hardworking, upright, and devout, "a small man who won't see thirty again" (47), Bunch befriends the outcasts Lena Grove, Joe Christmas, and Gail Hightower. For seven years, six days out of the seven, he has worked at the planing mill in JEFFERSON, MISSISSIPPI, and on Sundays he rides 30 miles out of town to lead the choir of a country church.

Bunch is the disgraced and solitary Hightower's sole link with the world; they meet and talk only at night. He encounters Lena by the accident of his name, which is close to that of her seducer, Lucas Burch. Falling in love with her virtually at first sight, Bunch finds her a home, talks Hightower into delivering her baby, and finally tracks down Burch for her.

Lena seems not so much indifferent to as unaware of Bunch's attentions, and he prepares to leave Jefferson. In a final encounter, Burch (Joe Brown) pummels him and then jumps a freight train to make a final escape from his responsibilities. Byron Bunch stays on after all, resuming his role as Lena's protector. He is with her, traveling slowly north into Tennessee, as the novel closes.

Burch, Lucas (Joe Brown)   A drifter, a man who is "just living on the country, like a locust" (6), Burch is Lena Grove's seducer. After he learns she is pregnant, he leaves Doane's Mill, Alabama, for Mississippi, saying he will send for her later. When six months pass with no word from Burch, Lena strikes out on foot for the west, asking after him along the way; he is identifiable by a narrow white scar below his lower lip "as white as a thread of spittle" (273).

Burch finds work in a JEFFERSON, MISSISSIPPI, planing mill under the name Joe Brown, but soon leaves the job to go into the bootlegging trade with Joe Christmas. He is later found lying drunk in Joanna Burden's burning house and is taken into custody as a suspect in her murder. He persuades the authorities that Christmas, whom he exposes as black, is the real killer and claims the $1,000 reward.

Before Burch can collect, Byron Bunch brings him to Lena. Desperate to escape this complication, he gives up his claim to the reward money and hops a freight train for parts unknown.

Burden, Beck   She is one of three daughters of the elder Calvin and Evangeline Burden.

Burden, Calvin (the elder)   The youngest of 10 children of Nathaniel Burrington (1), a New Hampshire minister, he ran away to California at age 12, calling himself Burden because he couldn't spell his real name. He grows into a "tall, gaunt, nordic" young man, passionate and prone to violence.

In his early 20s, Burden migrates eastward to Missouri, where he met and married his wife, Evangeline (Burden). In Missouri he learns to hate slavery, and he kills a man in a dispute over the question. He teaches his children, three daughters and a son, to hate it too. A skirmish with Kansas pro-slavery guerrillas costs him an arm in 1861.

After the Civil War he moves to JEFFERSON, MISSISSIPPI, to promote black suffrage. Colonel John Sartoris shoots him dead in an election dispute there.

The shooting is detailed in SARTORIS, *The UNVANQUISHED*, and other works.

Burden, Calvin (the younger)   The son of Nathaniel and Juana Burden and grandson of the Missouri abolitionist Calvin Burden (the elder), he served as ringbearer at his parents' wedding as a 12-year-old.

Colonel John Sartoris kills Calvin, age 20, and his, Calvin's, grandfather in a JEFFERSON, MISSISSIPPI, boardinghouse in a Reconstruction-era dispute "over a question of Negro voting" (248). The younger Calvin's father buries both men on a cedar knoll in a pasture a couple of miles from the Burden house. His half sister Joanna Burden is born 14 years after his death.

Burden, Evangeline   She is the wife of the elder Calvin Burden and the mother of Nathaniel Burden.

Burden, Joanna   She is the daughter of Nathaniel Burden and his second wife, and the granddaughter of the murdered abolitionist Calvin Burden (the elder). Although she is a native of JEFFERSON, MISSISSIPPI, the white community treats her as an outcast for her support of schools and colleges for African Americans throughout the South, damning her doubly as "a Yankee, a lover of Negroes" (46). She allows Joe Christmas to live in one of the tumbledown cabins on the old Burden place.

Though she dresses plainly in an "apparently endless succession of clean calico house dresses" (233), Joanna is comely; she looks 30 by candlelight when she and Joe Christmas become lovers, but she is actually 41. (This would place the present-time action of the novel in 1921.) They barely talk, and Joe feels he hardly knows her, but their nighttime lovemaking is savage, sometimes hard and brutal on Joe's part, frantic and furious on hers.

Something shifts in Joanna, and she abruptly turns to the fierce and uncompromising religion of her Calvinist ancestors. She furiously attempts to convert Christmas, whom she now envisions as a missionary to African Americans. When he resists and refuses to pray with her, she aims an ancient pistol at him. It misfires; Christmas attacks her with a razor, slashing her throat. He sets the house afire, but Hamp Waller, passing by, saves her body from the flames.

Joanna Burden is a powerful, disturbing figure, endowed "with pathos and tragic dignity," wrote the critic CLEANTH BROOKS.

She (or, rather, her mailbox) is referred to in *The* MANSION.

Burden, Juana The Spanish (or rather Mexican) wife of Nathaniel Burden, she bears so close a resemblance to the elder Calvin Burden's late wife that he calls out "Evangeline!" when he first meets her.

Burden, Nathaniel The son of the elder Calvin Burden, he runs away from home at 14 and stays away for 16 years, though his family hears of him twice by word of mouth: once from Colorado, later from Mexico. Nathaniel finally returns home in 1866 to find a minister to marry him to Juana, the mother of his son, 12-year-old Calvin Burden (the younger).

Nathaniel Burden comes to JEFFERSON, MISSISSIPPI, to bury his father and son, victims of Colonel John Sartoris's determination to prevent Reconstruction-era blacks from voting. On Juana's death, he sends to New Hampshire for the wife who becomes Joanna Burden's mother. Nathaniel is buried near the two Calvins on a cedar knoll in a pasture not far from the Burden house.

Burden, Sarah She is one of three daughters of Calvin and Evangeline Burden.

Burden, Vangie She is one of three daughters of Calvin and Evangeline Burden.

Burrington, Nathaniel (1) A New England minister, he is the father of the elder Calvin Burden, who runs away from home at age 12.

Burrington, Nathaniel (2) Joanna Burden's nephew, he lives in Exeter, New Hampshire. He offers a reward of $1,000 for the capture of Joanna's killer.

Bush, Lem A neighbor of the Hineses, he takes Milly Hines to the circus in his wagon. He returns alone, however, when Milly elopes with a member of the troupe. Milly later gives birth to the boy who will become the orphan Joe Christmas.

Carruthers, Miss The organist in the Rev. Gail Hightower (2)'s JEFFERSON, MISSISSIPPI, church, she has been dead for 20 years when Hightower imagines her at her usual place in the organ loft for Sunday and Wednesday services.

Charley A medical intern, Charley found Joe Christmas on the orphanage doorstep on Christmas night. He makes love to the dietician Miss Atkins while Joe is hiding in her clothes closet. She worries that Joe will expose them, but he has become too ill from eating her pink toothpaste to notice anything.

Christmas, Joe The illegitimate son of Milly Hines and a dark-skinned man rumored to be part African American, he passes his first five years in the orphanage where his grandfather left him on Christmas night (hence his name). He then goes to live with adoptive parents, the harsh and puritanical Simon McEachern and his wife, on their hardscrabble Mississippi farm.

He endures the strict discipline of McEachern with stoicism. The old man whips him for not polishing his boots to his satisfaction and for failing to memorize his catechism. Joe accepts this, and coldly resists his foster mother's attempts at tenderness.

Joe rebels finally, going his own way at age 17 in pursuit of the waitress and prostitute Bobbie Allen. He assaults McEachern with a chair when McEachern confronts the couple at a dance hall. Afraid Joe has killed McEachern and will bring her trouble with the police, Bobbie drops him later that night. One of Max Confrey's thugs beats and robs Joe before the Confreys and their entourage leave Mississippi for MEMPHIS.

The episode leads to a 15-year period of wandering for Joe Christmas. He migrates aimlessly, west to Missouri and Oklahoma, south to Mexico, north to Chicago and Detroit, then back to Mississippi. "He looked like a tramp, yet not like a tramp either . . . there was definitely something rootless about him, as though no town or city was his, no street, no walls, no square of earth his home" (31). He is bitter, defiant, proud, and in conflict about his identity. He moves back and forth between black and white worlds, courting trouble, brawling, insulting and abusing women, seeming to live only to inflict pain and to be hurt in his turn.

Christmas drifts to JEFFERSON, MISSISSIPPI, and becomes the lover of Joanna Burden, the white spinster outcast whose abolitionist half brother and grandfather paid for their support of black suffrage with their lives. He lives in a "tumbledown negro cabin" on the Burden place, and works for a time in a planing mill, then quits the job to become a full-time bootlegger.

In time, Joe begins to resent Joanna. She tells him she is pregnant; then they quarrel over Joanna's sudden religious mania. He believes she is trying to domesticate him, "to make of him something between a hermit and a missionary to negroes" (271). In a climactic scene in Joanna's bedroom, she attempts to shoot him; he slashes her throat with a razor, sets her house on fire, and flees.

In the end, Joe's ambiguities outrage the community, which hates and fears him as much for who he is as for what he has done. A lynch mob headed by the aptly named Percy Grimm finds Christmas in sanctuary in the house of Gail Hightower, the failed minister. Hightower attempts to shield Joe, but Grimm finds his quarry in the kitchen and empties his automatic weapon into him. Just before Christmas dies, Grimm castrates him with a butcher's knife.

Christmas dominates *Light in August*. His story is a tragedy, set against Lena Grove's comedy. He shows Faulkner's concern with race and identity. Like a lost child, Christmas wanders aimlessly, drawn to life but unable to connect with it, and fated to die.

A student once asked Faulkner if he intended any Christ symbolism in Joe Christmas. He said no, and he also refused to characterize Joe as a bad man, in spite of his horrific crime.

"I don't think he was bad, I think he was tragic," Faulkner said. "And his tragedy was that he didn't know what he was and would never know, and that to me is the most tragic condition that an individual can have—to not know who he was." (*Faulkner in the University*, 117–118)

Cinthy A former slave who returns home in 1866 to become the cook for the first Gail Hightower, she retails his Civil War exploits to his grandson and namesake. The older Hightower is a Civil War casualty, shot dead with a fowling piece in a raid on a JEFFERSON, MISSISSIPPI, henhouse. The story haunts the younger Gail's imagination.

Confrey, Mame She is the amply constructed blonde wife of Max Confrey, proprietor of the restaurant and brothel where Bobbie Allen works. Decent at bottom, she leaves money in the fob pocket of Joe Christmas's trousers after her husband and another man beat him unconscious.

Confrey, Max He and his wife Mame Confrey run a combination restaurant and brothel. Bobbie Allen works for the Confreys as a waitress and prostitute; the Confreys disapprove when she and Joe Christmas become lovers.

Conner, Buck The city marshal of JEFFERSON, MISSISSIPPI, Conner is involved in the Joanna Burden murder investigation and escorts Lucas Burch to jail as the hunt for Joe Christmas, Joanna's killer, proceeds. He threatens to gag Burch if he doesn't keep quiet and let the other prisoners sleep.

He also appears in the short story "CENTAUR IN BRASS" and as Buck Connors in the novel *The Town*.

Dollar He is a storekeeper in MOTTSTOWN. Eupheus (Doc) Hines sits in front of Dollar's store while his wife tries to see Joe Christmas in his jail cell. Dollar later tells the townsfolk that the Hineses are intent on following Christmas in the police car to the jail in Jefferson.

Gillman He owns the Arkansas sawmill in which Eupheus (Doc) Hines once worked as foreman.

Grimm, Percy A 25-year-old captain in the Mississippi National Guard, the son of a hardware merchant, he compensates for having been too young to fight in World War I by carrying out his duties as a part-time soldier with fanaticism. Grimm's articles of faith are physical courage, blind obedience and an unshakeable belief in the superiority of the white race.

He tracks down and captures Joe Christmas after Joanna Burden's murder, shoots him, then castrates him with a butcher's knife. Faulkner once said that in Grimm he had created a Nazi before he ever knew Nazis existed.

Grove, Lena A country girl from the Alabama hamlet of DOANE'S MILL, an orphan since the summer of her 12th year, she sets out from her brother's place on foot for Mississippi in search of her lover, Lucas Burch, by whom she is pregnant, because he has not yet carried out his promise to send for her.

Grove frames the tragic story of Joe Christmas, supplying the novel's beginning and end. Critics see her as one of Faulkner's several embodiments of the female: some portray her as an earth goddess, others as a near saint. She is a carrier of life, a symbol of hope and endurance requiring—and deserving of—protection. Lena is serene, simple, trusting, and not overly intelligent.

When Lena decides to seek out Burch after months of waiting, she reaches JEFFERSON, MISSISSIPPI, and, through a similarity in names, comes under the watchful eye of the sawmill hand Byron Bunch.

Though he falls in love with her, Byron eventually brings Lena and Burch (who is living in Jefferson under the alias of Joe Brown) together. When Burch flees, Byron takes Lena and the newborn on the road again in what he thinks is a renewed search for the child's father.

As always, Lena advances confidently into the unknown, taking what comes. "My, my. A body does get around," she says at the novel's close. "Here we aint been coming from Alabama but two months, and now it's already Tennessee" (507).

Lena's last odyssey is comic in effect, making *Light in August*, in the words of the critic IRVING HOWE, "a comedy that underscores the tragic

incommensurability between the fates of Joe Christmas and herself."

Grove, McKinley The brother of Lena Grove, 20 years her senior, he takes her into his DOANE'S MILL, ALABAMA, home after their father dies. A hard man, he has no sympathy for her when she becomes pregnant—"swolebellied," as he puts it—and calls her a whore.

Halliday He recognizes the fugitive Joe Christmas on the street in MOTTSTOWN and figures this qualifies him for the $1,000 reward for his capture.

Hightower, Gail (1) A self-taught lawyer and a Civil War cavalryman, a "hale, bluff, rednosed man with the moustache of a brigand chief" (471), he is the grandfather of Gail Hightower (2), the solitary and introspective failed minister who tries to save Joe Christmas. The younger Gail is obsessed with his grandfather's wartime exploits; he was shot dead in a raid on a Jefferson henhouse during Van Dorn's attack on the Yankee supply lines.

Hightower, Gail (2) The only child of an intimidating 50-year-old father and an invalid mother, he grows up regarding his parents as phantoms. As an adult he decides that he has "skipped a generation" and is the figurative son of his Civil War cavalryman grandfather, the first Gail Hightower.

Obsessed with his grandfather's legend, which he learns in vivid detail from the house servant Cinthy, he decides at seminary that he must follow his pastor's vocation in JEFFERSON, MISSISSIPPI, the town where the first Gail was shot dead in a henhouse in an absurd ending to a wartime raid on a federal supply depot. His young wife helps him arrange the appointment. He takes up the post, and for several years he preaches hysterical sermons that weirdly blend Presbyterianism with his grandfather's soldierly exploits. The congregation is baffled at first. Eventually it comes to see the pastor as "a figure antic as a showman, a little wild: a charlatan preaching worse than heresy" (488).

His Presbyterians never accept him, and the rumors that swirl around his marriage prove his undoing. He is thought to be an "unnatural" husband and to lapse into homosexual practices. His wife makes several unexplained trips out of town—to meet a lover in MEMPHIS, it turns out. When she is killed in a fall from a window of the Memphis hotel room where she and her lover had registered as husband and wife, the terrible truth comes out: "His wife went bad on him" (59). The church turns against Hightower and forces him to resign.

Hightower stays on in Jefferson in a small, unpainted, obscure house. In the novel's present time, he is 50 years old, flaccid in "soft and sedentary obesity" (89), living in what the townspeople call his disgrace. He fails at his second vocation, that of an art teacher and photographer, and withdraws, hermitlike, into his bungalow. The town persecutes him, but he refuses to leave.

Byron Bunch, his only friend, rekindles his interest in life. Other people's troubles seem to restore his link to the world. He befriends Lena Grove and delivers her baby. He hears out the story of Mrs. Hines and her mad husband. In the end, he does his best to save Joe Christmas from the lynch mob, swearing that he and Christmas had been together on the night of Joanna Burden's murder. But in this, as in so much else, he fails.

Faulkner, according to the critic IRVING HOWE, developed Hightower as a "reflective consciousness" to register the conduct of Christmas, Bunch, Lena Grove, and other characters. But Howe and others find him inadequate in some ways.

Hightower is "too vague, too drooping, too formless, in a word too much a creature of defeat and obsession, to compel our interest or our belief," wrote the critic ALFRED KAZIN.

Hines, Eupheus (Doc) A deranged religious fanatic, a dirty, goat-bearded little old man, he lives in idleness in the black section of MOTTSTOWN; his neighbors see to his sustenance even though his vocation is delivering harangues on white supremacy in African-American churches.

Hines is the killer of his daughter Milly Hines's lover, alleged to be part black, and the de facto killer of Milly herself, for whom he refuses to call a doctor when she goes into labor; she eventually dies in childbirth. Hines places the surviving child

on the steps of the white orphanage where he finds work as a janitor.

After his grandson, called Joe Christmas, is given up for adoption at age five, old Hines does not see him again until he is taken captive in Mottstown and accused of murder. The old man urges the townspeople to lynch him.

Hines, Milly The daughter of Eupheus Hines, she runs off with a circus employee said to be a Mexican but rumored to be part black. Her father shoots and kills the Mexican; Milly dies in childbirth. Their child, dubbed Joe Christmas, spends the first five years of his life in an orphanage.

Hines, Mrs. A fat, dumpy woman "with a face like that of a drowned corpse" (348), she is the wife of Eupheus Hines and the mother of Milly Hines. For 30 years she does not know whether Milly's child is dead or alive. When she learns her grandson is the murderer Joe Christmas, she begs Gail Hightower (2) to save him from the lynch mob.

Jupe He is one of a party of black men and women Joe Christmas accosts along a road outside Jefferson. He calls Christmas "whitefolks" and asks him what he wants.

Kennedy, Watt "A tub of a man" (292), he is the sheriff who investigates the fire at the Burden place and leads the hunt for Joe Christmas.

McEachern, Joe *See* Christmas, Joe.

McEachern, Mrs. The wife of Simon McEachern, she is a "small woman . . . , a little hunched, with a beaten face" (147) who looks 15 years older than her vigorous husband. She tries to protect her foster son, Joe Christmas, from the hard, brutal Simon McEachern, but Joe rejects her kindnesses and steals from her little store of carefully hoarded money. Joe finds her soft attentions far more objectionable than the "hard and ruthless justice of men" (169).

McEachern, Simon The rugged, vigorous, and fanatically Calvinistic foster father of Joe Christmas, he tries to beat his version of morality into the boy, without success. He is older than 40, with cold, light-colored eyes, a "thickish man with a close brown beard and hair cut close" (141).

Joe fails to learn his catechism. He sells a heifer without permission. He becomes interested in girls and otherwise violates Simon's stern code. One night Simon observes Joe slipping out of the house and follows him on horseback to a dance hall. There he confronts Joe and the waitress Bobbie Allen. When Simon calls Bobbie a harlot, Joe strikes him with a chair, leaving him unconscious on the dance floor.

McLendon, Captain In a barbershop, he over-hears the boasts of the drunken Joe Brown (Lucas Burch) and discusses Joe Christmas's bootlegging activities with a man named Maxey.

McLendon appears in *The* TOWN (where he is styled Jackson McLendon), *The* MANSION, and the short story "DRY SEPTEMBER."

Maxey In the barbershop, Captain McLendon and Maxey overhear Joe Brown's (Lucas Burch) drunken boasts about his hijacking of a liquor truck with bootlegger Joe Christmas.

He also appears in the short story "HAIR."

Metcalf He is the jailer in MOTTSTOWN. Mrs. Hines appeals to him to allow her to see Joe Christmas, who is being held there.

Mooney He is a foreman in the JEFFERSON, MISSISSIPPI, planing mill where Byron Bunch, Joe Brown (Lucas Burch), and Joe Christmas all work.

Peebles, E. E. A black attorney with an office on Beale Street in MEMPHIS, he handles Joanna Burden's legal affairs. Peebles is notified of Miss Burden's death.

Pomp He is the husband of Cinthy and the ser-vant of the Civil War cavalryman Gail Hightower (1). Refusing to believe his master has been killed, he goes off in search of him and is killed in his turn when he crosses the Federal lines and attacks a Yankee officer with a shovel.

Russell He is a sheriff's deputy in MOTTSTOWN, where the murderer Joe Christmas is briefly held in jail. From his place behind the desk, Mrs. Hines, who had come to ask permission to see Christ-mas, appeared to him as "a toy balloon with a face painted on it" (353).

Salmon A garage-keeper in MOTTSTOWN, he offers to take Eupheus Hines and his wife to JEFFER-SON, MISSISSIPPI, in his "rent car" for the steep fare of three dollars. Mrs. Hines decides that Salmon is too expensive.

Simms The manager, or perhaps owner, of the JEFFERSON, MISSISSIPPI, planing mill, he hires Joe Christmas and Joe Brown (Lucas Burch).

Stevens, Gavin A "tall, loose-jointed man with a constant corncob pipe, with an untidy mop of iron gray hair" (444), Stevens is the Harvard-educated district attorney for YOKNAPATAWPHA COUNTY. A member of an old Jefferson family, he has a way with the country people; Stevens puts Eupheus Hines and his wife on the train after their grandson Joe Christmas is lynched and promises to send Christmas's body after them in the morning.

Stevens is an important figure in a number of Faulkner works. He appears in KNIGHT'S GAMBIT, INTRUDER IN THE DUST, REQUIEM FOR A NUN, *The* TOWN, *The* MANSION and GO DOWN, MOSES and in the short stories "THE TALL MEN," "HOG PAWN," "BY THE PEOPLE," and "A Name for the City."

Thompson, Pappy Joe Christmas assaults this 70-year-old worshipper at a night revival service after Christmas murders Joanna Burden.

Thompson, Roz The six-foot-tall grandson of Pappy Thompson, he goes after Pappy's assailant, Joe Christmas, with a razor. But Christmas strikes first, fracturing Roz's skull with a bench leg as he enters the darkened church.

Varner, Jody A clerk at his father's store, Jody tells Lena Grove that the fellow working at the planing mill is named Bunch, not Burch; he then sells her crackers, cheese, and a 15-cent box of "sour-deans" (sardines). He also appears in *As I Lay Dying*, *The Hamlet*, *The Town*, *The Mansion*, and the short stories "Fool about a Horse" and "Spotted Horses"

Varner, Will (Uncle Billy)   The father of Jody Varner, he is the owner of the crossroads country store where Lena Grove inquires about Lucas Burch, the father of the child she is carrying, and buys cheese, crackers and sardines. He also appears in *As I Lay Dying*, *The Hamlet*, *Intruder in the Dust*, *The Town*, *The Mansion*, and in the stories "Spotted Horses," "The Hound," "Lizards in Jamshyd's Courtyard," "Fool about a Horse," "Tomorrow" (in *Knight's Gambit*), "Shingles for the Lord" and "By the People."

Vines, Deacon   A deacon in a black country church, he sends someone off on a mule to alert the sheriff when Joe Christmas begins to smash up the sanctuary.

Waller, Hamp   A countryman driving to Jefferson in a mule-drawn wagon, he discovers the fire at the Burden place. Waller recovers Joanna Burden's nearly decapitated body from the burning house; his wife phones the sheriff to report the fire.

Waller, Mrs.   The wife of Hamp Waller, she telephones the sheriff at around 11 o'clock in the morning to report the Burden house is on fire.

Winterbottom   He and Armstid take a break from negotiating the sale of a cultivator to gossip about the pregnant Lena Grove as she passes on her way to Jefferson, Mississippi, in search of Lucas Burch, the father of her unborn child. He also appears in *The Hamlet* and the short story "Spotted Horses."

FURTHER READING

Backman, Melvin. *"Light in August."* In *Faulkner: The Major Years*, 67–87. Bloomington: Indiana University Press, 1966.

Berland, Alwyn. Light in August: *A Study in Black and White*. New York: Twayne, 1992.

Bloom, Harold, ed. *Modern Critical Interpretations of William Faulkner's* Light in August. New York: Chelsea, 1988.

Brooks, Cleanth. "The Community and the Pariah (*Light in August*)." In *William Faulkner: The Yoknapatawpha Country*, 47–74. Baton Rouge: Louisiana State University Press, 1990.

———. "Faulkner's Women: *Light in August* and *The Hamlet*." In *On the Prejudices, Predilections, and Firm Beliefs of William Faulkner: Essays by Cleanth Brooks*, 80–91. Baton Rouge: Louisiana State University Press, 1987.

———. "*Light in August.*" In *William Faulkner: First Encounters*, 160–191. New Haven, Conn.: Yale University Press, 1983.

Howe, Irving. *"Light in August."* In *William Faulkner: A Critical Study*, 200–214. Chicago: University of Chicago Press, 1957.

Kazin, Alfred. "The Stillness of *Light in August*." In *Faulkner: A Collection of Critical Essays*, edited by Robert Penn Warren, 147–162. Englewood Cliffs, N.J.: Prentice Hall, 1966.

Longly, John L. "Joe Christmas: The Hero in the Modern World." In *Faulkner: A Collection of Critical Essays*, edited by Robert Penn Warren, 163–174. Englewood Cliffs, N.J.: Prentice Hall, 1966.

Millgate, Michael. *"Light in August."* In *The Achievement of William Faulkner*, 124–137. Lincoln: University of Nebraska Press, 1978.

———, ed. *New Essays on* Light in August. New York: Cambridge University Press, 1987.

Minter, David L., ed. *Twentieth Century Interpretations of* Light in August. Englewood Cliffs, N.J.: Prentice Hall, 1969.

Moseley, Edwin M. "Christ as Social Scapegoat: Faulkner's *Light in August*." In *Pseudonyms of Christ in the Modern Novel: Motifs and Methods*, 135–151. Pittsburgh: University of Pittsburgh Press, 1962.

Pitavy, François L., ed. *William Faulkner's* Light in August: *A Critical Casebook*. New York: Garland, 1982.

Sundquist, Eric J. "The Strange Career of Joe Christmas." In *Faulkner: The House Divided*, 63–95. Baltimore: Johns Hopkins University Press, 1985.

Ruppersburg, Hugh M. *Reading Faulkner*: Light in August. Jackson: University Press of Mississippi, 1994.

Vickery, John B., and Olga W. Vickery, eds. *Light in August and the Critical Spectrum.* Belmont, Calif.: Wadsworth, 1971.

Wittenberg, Judith Bryant. "Race in *Light in August*: Wordsymbols and Obverse Reflections." In *The Cambridge Companion to William Faulkner,* edited by Philip M. Weinstein, 146–167. New York: Cambridge University Press, 1997.

"Lion" (Uncollected Stories)

Short story first published in the December 1935 issue of *Harper's* and incorporated into sections 3 and 5 of "The BEAR" in GO DOWN, MOSES (1942).

SYNOPSIS

The narrator, Quentin Compson, recalls the time when, as a 16-year-old boy, he accompanied Major de Spain, Boon Hogganbeck, Uncle Ike McCaslin, and others on the annual December hunt in the big woods. When the men run out of whiskey, de Spain sends Hogganbeck, a dim-witted giant who is part-Indian, into MEMPHIS to buy some more—and sends Quentin along to make sure Boon returns. Boon is concerned that the hunt not be resumed until he returns: He loves Lion, the best of Major de Spain's hunting dogs, and wants to be with him on the hunt. Boon and Ad, the Negro cook, compete for the mastiff's affection, even allowing the dog to sleep with them. Quentin is eager to return to camp because he knows that the next day the men will engage in their yearly pursuit of Old Ben, the legendary bear that has eluded the hunters for years. As soon as the whiskey purchase is made, Boon starts drinking, but Quentin is able to nurse him onto the train and get him and the suitcase full of liquor back to camp. The next morning the hunters and dogs go in pursuit of Old Ben, and Uncle Ike leads Quentin to a stand in the woods where the bear might be seen. Quentin does not see the bear but hears the dogs giving chase in the distance. Back in camp Quentin learns from de Spain that Old Ben has killed one of the dogs, Kate, and escaped across the river. De Spain also tells him that the dogs, led by Lion and followed by Boon and Ad, have continued the pursuit on the other side of the river. After dark, long after the other hunters have returned to camp, Boon enters the lodge, bleeding heavily from a multitude of wounds and holding a gravely-wounded Lion in his arms. Later Uncle Ike explains to the others what Ad said had happened: Lion bravely charged the bear—the only dog in the pack with the courage to do so—and Boon rushed to the aid of Lion. In the epic struggle Boon killed the bear with his knife, but not before Old Ben had severely mangled the dog. Now, ignoring his own hurts, Boon demands a mule so he can ride to a nearby village to fetch a doctor to treat Lion's wounds. The next day people gather from all over the region to gaze at the corpse of Old Ben and to see the gallant dog that had finally brought the giant bear to bay. Lion survives throughout the day, almost as if he is waiting to hear all of the stories of his mighty exploits and take one final look at the woods, but then dies that night. Boon mourns his death by getting drunk. In a coda to the main narrative Quentin explains that Major de Spain never again returns to the hunting camp after the deaths of Old Ben and Lion. The following summer Quentin requests and receives permission to hunt squirrels on the property, and he arranges to meet Boon there. Entering the woods once more, Quentin realizes that, with Old Ben and Lion gone, the hunt and the woods will never be the same. As he approaches the spot where he will meet Boon—a large clearing marked by a huge gum tree—he hears a strange clanking noise. Walking closer, he sees Boon seated on the ground beside the tree, hammering on his rifle as a colony of squirrels scamper from limb to limb above his head. "Get out of here!" Boon screams. "Don't touch them! They're mine!"

CRITICAL COMMENTARY

Like "The Bear," "The OLD PEOPLE," and "DELTA AUTUMN," this story is a poignant elegy to the lost wilderness. The double deaths of Old Ben and Lion signal the end of an era. The ironic ending, with Boon frantically repairing his rifle so he can shoot the squirrels (significantly, not a deer or bear) before someone else can, dramatizes the enormity of the change from the days when the great hunters exhibited a shared camaraderie and a mutual respect in their pursuit of the big game. Quentin recognizes the loss, and he understands why de Spain chooses not to return to the hunting camp. At the same time, Quentin's narration of the story celebrates the legendary past and serves to keep the characters and events alive in memory. When Faulkner incorporated "Lion" into section 3 of "The Bear" in *Go Down, Moses*, he altered the text considerably. The novel's version employs an omniscient narrator, and the youthful Quentin Compson becomes Ike McCaslin. In addition, for obvious symbolic purposes, Faulkner makes the death of Sam Fathers coincident with those of Old Ben and Lion; and he uses the incident with Boon and the squirrels as the culminating scene of section 5 of the story. James B. Carothers has analyzed these changes, noting how the "self-contained, simple, and direct" short story becomes "interdependent, complex, and oblique" in the novel (*William Faulkner's Short Stories*, 89).

CHARACTERS

Compson, Quentin The 16-year-old narrator who participates in the annual hunt with the older men. He narrates the story retrospectively, thereby demonstrating how real and significant the characters and events remain in his memory.

For a list of the other characters in this story *see* the entry on GO DOWN, MOSES.

"Lizards in Jamshyd's Courtyard" (*Uncollected Stories*)

This short story was first published on February 27, 1932, in the SATURDAY EVENING POST 204, 12–13, 52, 57; it was revised and included in book 4 of *The* HAMLET. The original version is reprinted in UNCOLLECTED STORIES OF WILLIAM FAULKNER. For more information, *see* UNCOLLECTED STORIES OF WILLIAM FAULKNER, 686–688.

SYNOPSIS

"Lizards in Jamshyd's Courtyard" is a humorously told short story about the craftiness of Flem Snopes and his unscrupulous business practices. The setting is the bucolic hamlet of FRENCHMAN'S BEND, where the sewing machine agent and itinerant salesman, Suratt, stays about every six weeks when travelling through the countryside. On one of his stopovers, Flem overhears Suratt's plans to buy and sell goats and intervenes by purchasing them before Suratt has the chance. Although he buys from Suratt the contract to sell the goats, Flem makes a much greater profit than the one dollar Suratt gains from the deal. Three years later, Flem pulls off yet another scheme that involves Suratt and two residents of Frenchman's Bend, Henry Armstid and Vernon Tull. Taking full advantage of the rumor that there is buried treasure on OLD FRENCHMAN PLACE, a worthless piece of property, Flem purchases it from Will Varner and salts it with a few small canvas sacks of silver dollars. He knows that Suratt and the others will spy on him, so he pretends that he is digging for the money that was buried during the Civil War. The night after Suratt, Armstid, and Tull watch Flem, they arrive with the diviner Uncle Dick to help them locate the coins, which they eventually do. Convinced that there is a trove of coins to be dug up, they unhesitatingly buy the property from Flem, but once Suratt and Bookwright examine the dates on their coins, they realize that they have been duped. Armstid, however, the one who has the most to lose, refuses to stop digging and becomes obsessed with finding what is not there. Every evening his wife brings him cold food in a pail as onlookers from all around gaze in rapt attention at his folly.

CRITICAL COMMENT

In discussing Faulkner's sense of the literary marketplace, John T. Matthews argues that "Lizards in Jamshyd's Courtyard" reflects "on its own status as a work of art in the age of commodification." Armstid's "spectators themselves become a part of the spectacle" the readers of the story perceive ("Shortened Stories: Faulkner and the Market," in *Faulkner and the Short Story*, edited by Evans Harrington and Ann J. Abadie, 21). But Faulkner's aesthetic goals are not compromised by his awareness of mass literary consumption.

CHARACTERS

Armstid, Henry A struggling farmer in the area of FRENCHMAN'S BEND who goes heavily into debt to buy a third of the worthless OLD FRENCHMAN PLACE. Along with Suratt and Vernon Tull, Henry is duped by Flem Snopes and makes a spectacle of himself by tenaciously digging for coins rumored to be buried at the property. Henry continues longer after Suratt and Tull give up the very first night after they buy the property.

Armstid, Mrs. Henry Armstid's wife. She prepares food for him which she puts in a tin pail and drops off at OLD FRENCHMAN PLACE where her foolish husband is relentlessly digging for treasure that is not there.

Dick, Uncle An old diviner, a frail man with a long white beard, who lives alone in a mud-daubed hut and eats bugs, frogs, and snakes. Suratt, Vernon Tull, and Henry Armstid get him to help them find coins rumored to have been buried at OLD FRENCHMAN PLACE during the Civil War. Using a divining rod, Uncle Dick locates a few bags of coins, which Flem Snopes planted as a ruse to sell the property. *Also see* Uncle Dick Bolivar in *The* HAMLET; Faulkner revised "Lizards in Jamshyd's Courtyard" for this novel.

Grimm, Eustace One of Flem Snopes's relatives from the adjoining county. The narration implies that Eustace at Flem's request travelled the ten or twelve miles from his home to FRENCHMAN'S BEND to help con Suratt, Henry Armstid, Vernon Tull into buying the OLD FRENCHMAN PLACE, a worthless piece of property rumored to contain coins that were buried there during the Civil War. Posing as an interested party in purchasing the property, Eustace heartens the three men to buy it before he does. *Also see The* HAMLET *and* AS I LAY DYING.

Littlejohn, Mrs. An offstage character referred to in the short story. She owns a boarding house. *Also see The* HAMLET *and* The TOWN.

Snopes, Flem Runs Varner's Store in FRENCHMAN'S BEND. Flem is an unscrupulously shrewd businessman, who tricks Suratt, Vernon Tull, and Henry Armstid into buying the worthless OLD FRENCHMAN PLACE at a considerable price. He is an important figure throughout the Snopes trilogy; *see The* HAMLET, *The* TOWN, *and The* MANSION. *Also see* SARTORIS, FATHER ABRAHAM, "SPOTTED HORSES," *and* "CENTAUR IN BRASS"; Flem is also referred to in *As I LAY DYING and The* REIVERS.

Suratt A convivial itinerant sewing machine salesman. With the aid of a relative, Flem Snopes dupes Suratt, Vernon Tull, and Henry Armstid into buying the valueless OLD FRENCHMAN PLACE. Earlier in the short story, Suratt finds out that Flem buys the very goats that he (Suratt) was planning to buy and sell to a breeder. *Also see As I LAY DYING and* V. K. Suratt in SATORIS; he is referred to in "CENTAUR IN BRASS" and though not identified is the narrator of "SPOTTED HORSES." Faulkner changed Suratt's name to V. K. Ratliff, a character who plays an important role in the SNOPES TRILOGY; *see The* HAMLET, *The* TOWN, *and The* MANSION. *Also see* Big Woods ("A BEAR HUNT").

Tull, Vernon A well-off bachelor, who, along with Suratt and Henry Armstid, is fooled into buying the worthless OLD FRENCHMAN PLACE. *Also see As I LAY DYING, The* HAMLET, *The* TOWN, "SPOTTED HORSES," "THE HOUND," "TWO SOLDIERS" *and* "SHINGLES FOR THE LORD"; he is referred to in *The* MANSION.

Varner, Will Owner of Varner's Store where Flem Snopes works. An offstage character in the short story, (Will) Varner (sometimes referred to as Uncle Billy) is the major landowner in the area of FRENCHMAN'S BEND and an important character who either appears or is referred to in several of Faulkner's works; *see the following: The* HAMLET, *The* TOWN, *The* MANSION, LIGHT IN AUGUST, INTRUDER IN THE DUST, *and* KNIGHT'S GAMBIT ("Tomorrow"), AS I LAY DYING, "SPOTTED HORSES," "THE HOUND," "SHINGLES FOR THE LORD," "FOOL ABOUT A HORSE," *and* "BY THE PEOPLE."

Mansion, The

The third novel of the SNOPES TRILOGY, published by Random House on November 13, 1959, two and a half years after the second volume, *The* TOWN (May 1957), and 19 years after the first volume, *The* HAMLET (April 1940). Like the first two volumes of the trilogy, *The Mansion* is dedicated to Phil Stone, Faulkner's close friend. Chapter 13 of *The Mansion* is a revision of "BY THE PEOPLE," a short story first published in Mademoiselle 41 (October 1955). When writing The Mansion, Faulkner refashioned "HOG PAWN," a short story posthumously published in UNCOLLECTED STORIES OF WILLIAM FAULKNER, and included it in chapter 14 of the novel.

To this third volume, Faulkner added a prefatory note in which he informs the reader that discrepancies and contradictions in the novel are the result of the author's growth over three decades. He explains that he now knows his characters better and knows "more about the human heart and its dilemma" than he did when he first began the trilogy. Several months before its publication, ALBERT ERSKINE of Random House and the Faulkner textual critic JAMES B. MERIWETHER went through *The Mansion* to reconcile discrepancies between this volume and the first two novels of the trilogy. In a February 10, 1959, letter to Erskine, Faulkner expresses his gratitude to him and offers a few general guidelines governing the correction of inconsistencies (*see Selected Letters of William Faulkner*, 423–424).

SYNOPSIS

The Mansion is divided into three major parts, with 18 chapters. The first part, "Mink" (chapters 1–5), covers the period in the life of Mink Snopes from 1907, the year of his troubles with Jack Houston, until his release from prison in September 1946. In 1908, Mink was convicted of killing Houston and sent to the Mississippi State Penitentiary at PARCHMAN. There are three narrators in this first section: omniscient (chapters 1, 2, and 5); V. K. Ratliff, the sewing machine salesman (chapter 3); and Montgomery Ward Snopes, Mink's cousin (chapter 4).

The second part of the novel, "Linda" (chapters 6–11), focuses on Linda Snopes Kohl and her life in

JEFFERSON, MISSISSIPPI, after her return from Spain, where her husband, Barton Kohl, fighting for the Loyalists in the Spanish civil war, died when his aircraft was shot down. In 1927, the year her mother, Eula Varner Snopes, committed suicide, Linda left Jefferson for New York City, where she met and lived with Kohl for several years before marrying him. In August 1937, she returned to Jefferson from Spain as a widow whose eardrums were shattered by the sound of a shell that exploded while she was driving an ambulance; the accident left her deaf. This second part of the novel also touches upon the complex relationship between Linda and Gavin Stevens, and upon her life with Flem. There are three narrators in this second section of the novel (incidently, the same three as in *The Town*): Ratliff (chapters 6, 7); Charles (Chick) Mallison, Jr., Gavin Stevens's nephew and a former prisoner of war during World War II (chapters 8, 9, 11); and Gavin Stevens, the county attorney (chapter 10).

The third part, "Flem" (chapters 12–18), returns to Mink and covers the days immediately following his pardon from prison on September 26, 1946. During this time Mink purchases a $10 pistol in MEMPHIS and returns to Jefferson to kill his cousin Flem Snopes.

The basic story line of *The Mansion* revolves around Mink and his resolve to kill Flem for not having come to his assistance when on trial for the murder of Houston. The single thought of avenging Flem's betrayal of blood kinship and clan loyalty sustains Mink throughout his 38 years at the state penitentiary; nothing will deter him from accomplishing that end, even the prospect of being hanged for the crime.

Whether Flem could have intervened or not does not matter to Mink, who simply sees Flem's failure to help as disloyalty. While serving time at Parchman for bootlegging, Montgomery Ward Snopes, bribed by Flem, persuades Mink to escape in a woman's dress and sunbonnet and tries to convince him that Flem is looking out for his welfare. The abortive attempt is a ludicrous failure, and Flem in fact intended it to add time to Mink's sentence. Holding no bitterness against Montgomery Ward, Mink drily remarks in the warden's office that Flem "hadn't ought to used that dress" (86).

Mink is certain that the day will come to avenge the wrong committed against him. It is a matter of patience and waiting, and in stoical anticipation of that day, he views the present moment as an extraneous reality that no longer matters; it is something to be endured. In his response to the warden's remark that he has been in prison for three years—"'Have I? . . . I aint kept count'" (51)—Mink reveals an attitude of extreme indifference. When, 35 years later, the day nears, Mink is absolutely convinced as though by divine decree that the rusted and virtually dysfunctional pistol he buys to shoot his cousin Flem will fire: "*It's got to shoot* he thought. *It's jest got to. There aint nothing else for hit to do. Old Moster jest punishes; He dont play jokes*" (398). When the moment finally does come, the gun does not fire at first, but the determined Mink is undeterred. His second attempt is successful.

Responsible for getting Mink pardoned, Linda Snopes plays a major role in Flem's death. She knows very well that once Mink leaves the prison at Parchman he will return to Jefferson to avenge the wrong Flem committed against him and at the same time avenge the wrong Flem has done Linda, her mother, and the many others whom he exploited throughout his rapacious life. Immediately after shooting Flem, Mink attempts to escape through a locked door. As he is scrabbling at the doorknob, he is startled by the voice behind him and when he whirls around he sees Linda standing in the hallway door. In a panic, he throws the pistol at her, which she catches and gives back to him. Linda helps him escape.

It is not until the last chapter (chapter 18) that Gavin Stevens, the romantic idealist and county prosecutor whose duty it is to protect even a citizen as despicable as Flem, realizes what Linda has done. Stevens is forced to confront and accept his own moral vulnerability and weakness when he and V. K. Ratliff find Mink—not to arrest him, but to give him the money that Linda wants him to have.

CRITICAL COMMENTARY

In *The Mansion*, Faulkner portrays Mink as a man of honor and pride and as a character who elicits the reader's sympathies. The narrator in the opening pages of the novel explains that Mink is a victim of bad luck. In the last chapter of the first part of the novel, chapter 5, the narration ends with Mink's reaffirming thought: "*Not justice; I never asked that; jest fairness, that's all*" (106). Even though Mink is first seen as a convicted murderer who contemplates a second murder, Faulkner presents him as the novel's hero (or, more accurately, the novel's anti-hero). Mink kills Houston and later Flem not for personal profit or gain, but for honor and from a deep sense of wounded pride. What causes Mink's anger is not having to pay Houston for feeding the cow through the winter but the one-dollar fee that the court added to the cost of what Mink was ordered to pay. It is the insult that sparks Mink's deed.

In the confrontation between Mink and Houston, some critics see Faulkner touching upon the universal conditions of human life, upon the forces that cause struggle, and upon the need for endurance. If Mink evokes sympathy in the reader, he does so because he is willing to defend his integrity and to stand against the forces of life that give one an accidental advantage over another. Mink, in his own way, clearly and powerfully understands the insult against the dignity of his person. But in presenting him as a man of honor, Faulkner does not attempt to hide serious flaws in his character. Mink is mean to his family, and while in prison he completely dismisses them from his life. His lawyer sees him as a snake. But the more the reader understands Mink's attitude and his deep sense of pride, the more the reader can sympathize with him and understand the motive behind his killing Flem, a man who represents nothing but greed.

In a review of *The Mansion* titled "The Last of the Snopeses," in the November 14, 1959, issue of the *Saturday Review*, the critic Granville Hicks remarked, "one feels [in Faulkner's novels after 1948] strength of will and mastery of technique rather than the irresistible creative power that surged forth so miraculously in the earlier work" (21). Some critics and readers may share this view and some may find the novel thematically diffuse or lacking in structural unity. Others, however, find the novel a fitting culmination to a well-conceived trilogy. In his review, "End of the Snopeses," published in the *Washington Post* on November 15, 1959, Paul H. Stacy concludes:

Technically there are puzzles. *The Mansion* is a large cubist painting put together in enormous chunks.

Points of view change, minor themes and characters push to the foreground, transitions are startling, repetitions and variations confuse, and digressions and broken continuity often halt the pace completely. This means that the book (particularly the last third) is often tough going.

But one hesitates before assuming that toughness is a defect, for clearly *The Mansion* is not merely a suitable climax to a trilogy that is monumental in scope and technique; it is, even by itself, as impressive as very few books are—very few indeed (7-E).

For further information, *see Selected Letters of William Faulkner*, 107, 115, 406, 411, 416, 418, 419, 423–424, 425–426, 427, 429–430, 431, 432, 433, 438, 439, 455.

EXCERPTS FROM CONTEMPORARY REVIEWS OF *THE MANSION*

Excerpt from R. E. L. Masters's review, "Faulkner Concluding Novel of Snopes Family Is Unwieldy, Irritating and Dull," published in the **Shreveport Times,** *November 1, 1959, 4-G:*
All in all, *The Mansion* is a tedious tale, made more irritating in places by the here false-ringing language of rural Mississippi, crammed with superfluous material, and unduly complicated by the presence of characters who add nothing and detract considerably.

Mr. Faulkner, as it has become painfully evident in recent years, is not the writer he once was. Despite occasional flashes of brilliance, something has gone out of his work—or he is trying to do too much. One waits in vain for another novel as lean and taut and true as *Sanctuary*, or some of the other, earlier works.

Excerpt from Elizabeth Jennings's review, published in **The Listener,** *January 19, 1961, 151:*
In the course of a recently published interview, William Faulkner declared, 'I like to think of the world I created as being a kind of keystone in the Universe. . . . My last book will be the Doomsday Book, the Golden Book, of Yoknapatawpha County.' Whether or not *The Mansion*, the final volume in the trilogy about the Snopes clan, turns out to be the last of Mr. Faulkner's novels, it is undoubtedly one of his finest. Though part of a series, this book can nevertheless be read on its own; the beautifully controlled inevitability of the plot fits into the shape and design of a single novel. The world of Yoknapatawpha County—the cotton fields, the gas stations, the small townships, the huge, sprawling cities—are recreated along with the lives of the characters. With Mr. Faulkner, the setting and the lives are one and the same thing and both depend finally on 'the old patient biding unhurried ground' of the American Deep South. Dogged by destiny yet defiant and self-assertive even in the face of it, men can, in this world, be mean or heroic, worthless or noble. What Hemingway said in *The Old Man and the Sea* applies exactly to Mr. Faulkner's conception of humanity—'a man can be destroyed but not defeated.'. . .

In an illuminating article recently published in *Encounter*, Miss Iris Murdoch has suggested that the modern novel tends to divide itself into two categories, 'the crystalline' and 'the journalistic', and that 'fantasy' has replaced 'imagination' in the minds and works of most contemporary novelists. William Faulkner is obviously the great exception to this theory. . . .

Excerpt from Irving Howe's review, "Faulkner: End of a Road," published in the **New Republic,** *December 7, 1959, 17–18, 20–21:*
The Snopeses have always been there. No sooner did Faulkner come upon his central subject—how the corruption of the homeland, staining its best sons, left them without standards or defense—than Snopesism followed inexorably. Almost anyone can detect the Snopeses, but describing them is very hard. The usual reference to "amorality," while accurate, is not sufficiently distinctive and by itself does not allow us to place them, as they should be placed, in a historical moment. Perhaps the most important things about the Snopeses is that they are what comes afterward: the creatures that emerge from the devastation, with the slime still upon their lips. . . .

. . . If the Snopes trilogy, bringing together nearly the best and nearly the worst in Faulkner's career, is both imposing and seriously marred, *The Mansion*, taken more modestly, as a novel in its own right, has some superb sections. Perhaps the reader who is not so steeped in Faulkner's work and cares nothing about its relation to his previous books is in the best position to accept it with pleasure. For whenever Mink Snopes appears, the prose becomes hard, grave, vibrant, and Faulkner's capacity, as Malcolm Cowley has well put it, for "telling stories about men or beasts who fulfilled their destiny," comes into full play. Like the convict in *The Wild Palms*, Mink drives steadily toward his end, without fear or hope, unblinking and serene.

Excerpt from David L. Stevenson's review, "Faulkner's Subliminal World," published in **New Leader,** *February 1, 1960, 26–27:*

Faulkner is the only living, functioning American novelist who, during the past quarter century, has produced a sustained body of work of a very high order, with an identifiable tone and style that is itself a special creation. And yet, we are apparently too close to him to feel wholly comfortable in exploring in public our sense of his very great stature as a writer. Indeed, it has recently seemed much more tempting to critics to indulge their carping faculties at his expense and to let themselves go in chiding his failure to be 100 percent genius. . . .

Hence my final praise of *The Mansion* is that in it Faulkner reasserts those elements of perception which have always been his greatest strength. This new novel, once again, gives us the uncommon, exhausting and deeply rewarding pleasure of letting go our surface identity. For the length of time it takes to read the novel, we are plunged, if only momentarily, into the almost inscrutable pool of feeling that lurks below all our superficial and incessant questing for satisfaction and happiness.

CHARACTERS

Albert   A minor character in *The Mansion*. A member of Brother Joe C. Goodyhay's religious community, Albert drives the truck containing the lumber to build a chapel, but the owner of the property has changed his mind.

Allanovna, Myra   Owner of a men's tie store in New York City. When V. K. Ratliff is in New York for Linda Snopes's wedding, Allanovna, who also designs the ties, gives one to Ratliff.

Allison, Miss   A relative of Manfred de Spain, Miss Allison is a retired, old-maid school teacher from California. She returns to JEFFERSON, MISSISSIPPI, with her mother to live in the de Spain mansion that Flem Snopes had bought from Manfred. After Flem's death, Linda Snopes Kohl gives the house back to the de Spain family as a partial vindication of the past.

Armstid, Henry   An off-stage character living in the Jackson asylum. Armstid, a poor farmer eking out a living in the rural area of FRENCHMAN'S BEND, was one of Flem Snopes's gullible victims in buying the worthless OLD FRENCHMAN PLACE. His maniacal determination to keep digging for a treasure when there was none on the property eventually led to his being institutionalized; see The HAMLET and the opening pages of The TOWN.

Armstid also appears in AS I LAY DYING, LIGHT IN AUGUST, and in the short stories "SPOTTED HORSES" (revised for *The Hamlet*) and "SHINGLES FOR THE LORD."

Backus, Melisandre   See Stevens, Melisandre Backus Harriss.

Backus, Mr.   The father of Melisandre Backus in *The MANSION*. A widower, he spends his time drinking whiskey in the summer and reading Horace in the winter. Rumor has it that Backus died of a broken heart when Melisandre, his only child, married a wealthy NEW ORLEANS bootlegger by the name of Harriss.

Baddrington, Harold (Plex, Plexiglass)   A World War II pilot whose plane is shot down over Germany. Charles Mallison is one of the crew members. Although Plex manages a one-engine landing, the crew are rounded up by the Germans and taken to the prisoner-of-war camp at Limbourg. Because Baddrington is obsessed with cellophane (which he calls plexiglass), he is nicknamed Plex or Plexiglass.

Barron, Jake A convict with Mink Snopes at PARCHMAN, the state penitentiary in Mississippi, he is killed by a guard when he tries to escape in 1943. A fellow prisoner who does escape, Shuford H. Stillwell, holds Mink responsible for Barron's death because Mink did not go along with the plan.

Benbow The son of (young) Bayard and Narcissa Benbow Sartoris, born on the day his father was killed flying an experimental airplane at the Dayton testing field. Referred to in *The Mansion*, Benbow at 17 years old is deemed one of the best bird shots in YOKNAPATAWPHA COUNTY. He appears at various ages in *SARTORIS*, *SANCTUARY*, and the short story "THERE WAS A QUEEN"; he is referred to in *KNIGHT'S GAMBIT* ("Knight's Gambit") and *The TOWN*.

Benbow, Narcissa *See* Sartoris, Narcissa Benbow.

Benjy (Compson, Benjamin) The idiot son of Jason Richmond Compson (*see* Characters under *The SOUND AND THE FURY*). In *The Mansion*, Benjy is referred to as having died when he sets his house on fire. Benjy is committed to the state asylum in Jackson in 1933, but his mother insists that her son Jason have Benjy brought home. According to Jason, "his mother whined and wept" (322) until he gave in.

Biglin, Luther Jailor in Jefferson. During the day, Luther takes care of the jail and its prisoners; at night he sits outside Flem Snopes's window to protect his life from any threat that the newly released convict Mink Snopes might pose. Ironically, Luther is not at his post when Mink enters the house to kill Flem.

Biglin, Mrs. Luther (Miz Biglin) Luther Biglin's wife. When coming home from the movies (sometime between 7 and 10 P.M.), she wakes her husband, who protects Flem Snopes by sitting outside his window.

Binford, Lucius An offstage character referred to in *The Mansion* and in *SANCTUARY*. He is the front man for the brothel that his lover Miss Reba Rivers runs in MEMPHIS (*see* Characters under *The REIVERS*).

Binford, Mr. One of Reba Rivers's dogs, named after her late lover and landlord, Lucius Binford. The other, Miss Reba, she named after herself. In the chapter he narrates in *The Mansion*, Montgomery Ward Snopes characterizes them as "two damn nasty little soiled white dogs" (72).

Bishop, Ephriam (Eef) He is Jefferson's sheriff when Flem Snopes is killed. Eef alternates his term as sheriff with old Hub Hampton and then later with Hub's son, Hub, Jr.

Bookwright A family name common in the FRENCHMAN'S BEND region. Several Bookwrights appear in the novel. The name appears in the short story "BY THE PEOPLE," which Faulkner revised for *The Mansion*. *Also see* "Tomorrow" (the fourth section of *KNIGHT'S GAMBIT*), *INTRUDER IN THE DUST*, and *The TOWN*.

Bookwright, Calvin (Cal) A bootleg whiskeymaker in *The Mansion* and *The REIVERS*. In *The Mansion*, Bookwright is an old man who sells only to a select few people, of whom V. K. Ratliff is one. *Also see The Reivers* and *The TOWN*.

Bookwright, Herman One of Eula Varner's suitors referred to by V. K. Ratliff. Herman Bookwright and Theron Quick leave town one night once they find out that Eula is pregnant.

Bookwright, Homer A minor character who believes that Mrs. Tubbs, like everybody else, wants to know about Montgomery Ward Snopes's pornographic pictures. He also appears in the short stories "SHINGLES FOR THE LORD" and "SHALL NOT PERISH."

Bookwright, Odum An offstage character. The episode of his having been duped along with V. K. Ratliff and Henry Armstid into buying the worthless OLD FRENCHMAN PLACE is referred to in *The Mansion*; *see The HAMLET*.

Brummage, Judge The presiding judge at Mink Snopes's murder trial. He gives Mink a life sentence.

Buffaloe, Mr.   Referred to in *The Mansion*, Buffaloe keeps the steam-driven electric plant running in Jefferson. (*Also see* The TOWN and *The* REIVERS.)

Candace (Compson)   An offstage character referred to in the novel. Candace is the second child and only daughter of Jason Richmond Compson and his wife, Caroline Bascomb Compson (*see* Characters under *The* SOUND AND THE FURY where she is usually referred to as Caddy). After her failed marriage, she makes arrangements with her parents to rear her infant daughter, Quentin. She appears in the short stories "THAT EVENING SUN" and in "A JUSTICE."

Christian, Uncle Willy   An old Jefferson drugstore proprietor. Two thieves rob the drug cabinet in his store when the night watchman is up the alley enjoying Montgomery Ward Snopes's peep show. (*Also see* the short story "UNCLE WILLY" and the novels, *The* TOWN and *The* REIVERS.)

Compson, Mrs. Caroline Bascomb   Referred to not by name but as Jason Compson's mother. Jason gave in to her insistence—to her whining and crying—that Benjy, her retarded son, be brought home from the Jackson asylum. (*See* Characters under *The* SOUND AND THE FURY.) She appears in the short story "THAT EVENING SUN."

Compson, Jason   The third child of Jason Richmond Compson and his wife, Caroline Bascomb Compson; he is their second son. His brother Quentin committed suicide; his sister Candace's short-lived marriage ended in divorce, and her infant daughter, also named Quentin, was reared by his mother; and his idiot brother Benjy was institutionalized in Jackson. (*See* Characters under *The* SOUND AND THE FURY). In *The Mansion*, Jason brings Benjy home to assuage his whining mother, but within two years after his return, Benjy burns the house down with himself in it. Jason then buys a new home in town with his mother and later buys back the property his father had sold years before. This property Jason sells to Flem Snopes, tricking him into buying land that was rumored to be, but not suitable for, a government airfield.

When he realizes that Flem will make a hefty profit because the land will be used to build new housing for JEFFERSON's growing population, Jason unsuccessfully tries to find a flaw in the original deed to the property. *Also see* "THAT EVENING SUN" and "A JUSTICE"; he is also referred to in *The* TOWN.

Compson, Quentin (1)   One of the founders of JEFFERSON; he is referred to in the novel. In 1821, Quentin Compson was granted land from the Chickasaw matriarch Mohataha. *Also see* REQUIEM FOR A NUN and Faulkner's appendix to *The* SOUND AND THE FURY reprinted in Appendix.

Compson, Quentin (2)   The oldest child and son of Jason Richmond Compson and his wife, Caroline Bascomb Comspon, he is referred to in the novel. At the end of his freshman year at Harvard, he committed suicide by drowning. (For further details, *see The* SOUND AND THE FURY). Quentin also appears in ABSALOM, ABSALOM! and in the short stories "THAT EVENING SUN," "A JUSTICE," and "LION."

Compson, Quentin (3)   Candace's daughter. Quentin was reared by her grandmother, Mrs. Compson. She is referred to in the novel as having climbed down the rainpipe (outside her bedroom window) and as having run off with a carnival worker. (For further details, *see The* SOUND AND THE FURY).

Crack   Referred to in *The Mansion*, Crack is First Sergeant in the Sartoris Rifles, a JEFFERSON, MISSISSIPPI, U.S. Army company organized in 1917 by Captain McLendon in honor of Colonel John Sartoris.

Dad   The man who works for Brother J. C. Goodyhay. Dad robs Mink Snopes of all the money he has, $10.

de Spain, Major   Manfred de Spain's father, a retired major of the Confederate cavalry and landowner. Major de Spain is referred to in the novel. *Also see* ABSALOM, ABSALOM!, *The* HAMLET, *The* TOWN, INTRUDER IN THE DUST, *The* REIVERS, "BARN BURNING," "LION," "The OLD PEOPLE," "The BEAR," and "WASH"; he is referred to in "DELTA AUTUMN,"

"A BEAR HUNT," and "SHALL NOT PERISH." (Sometimes the last name appears as De Spain.)

de Spain, Manfred   Former mayor of Jefferson. In *The TOWN*, Manfred carried on a long love affair with Eula Varner Snopes, Flem's wife. He is referred to throughout *The Mansion*. For further information, *see The Town*. (Sometimes the last name appears as De Spain.)

Devries, Colonel   A decorated veteran of World War II. He is elected to Congress after his opponent, Clarence Eggleston Snopes, withdraws from the race. Devries has had one leg amputated because of a war injury. He also appears in the short story "BY THE PEOPLE," which Faulkner revised for the novel.

Dilazuck   The owner of a livery stable.

Dukinfield, Judge   An offstage character referred to in *The Mansion*. See "Smoke" (*KNIGHT'S GAMBIT*) and *The TOWN*.

Du Pre, Mrs.   Bayard Sartoris's aunt. She is referred to in the novel as having engineered Bayard's marriage to Narcissa Benbow. She appears in *SARTORIS*, *The UNVANQUISHED*, *SANCTUARY*, and in the short story "THERE WAS A QUEEN." She is also referred to in *The TOWN*, as Aunt Jenny Sartoris in "All the Dead Pilots," and as Mrs. Virginia Depre in *REQUIEM FOR A NUN*. (On some occasions, her name appears as Genevieve Du Pre and Virginia Sartoris.)

Ewell, Walter   One of the members of the hunting parties that meet annually at Major de Spain's camp by the TALLAHATCHIE RIVER. For more information, *see GO DOWN MOSES* ("The Old People," "The Bear," "Delta Autumn"), *The REIVERS*, and the short stories "A BEAR HUNT" and "RACE AT MORNING."

Gavin, Uncle   *See* Stevens, Gavin.

Gihon   A federal agent. He meets with Gavin Stevens and informs him that Linda Snopes Kohl carries a Communist Party card. He expects Stevens, who is Linda's friend, to convince her to give up her party membership and to give Gihon the names of other members in exchange for immunity.

Goodyhay, Brother J. C.   A former Marine sergeant turned preacher. During World War II, he saved a soldier from dying during an enemy attack in the Pacific. When Mink Snopes (who worked on Goodyhay's chapel for a few days after his release from prison) was robbed of $10, Goodyhay started a collection for him to make up the loss.

Gowrie, Nub   A hill farmer and father of six sons. An ill-tempered widower, Nub is mentioned in reference to Mink Snopes (Mink alleges that he sold his cow to Gowrie) and then as the Beat Nine farmer from whom Flem Snopes might have bought the whiskey which Flem used to frame his cousin Montgomery Ward Snopes. *Also see INTRUDER IN THE DUST.*

Grier, Res (Pap)   An offstage character in *The Mansion*. He is the father of a young soldier killed in World War II and one of the volunteers who helped put the roof on Reverend Whitfield's church. See "SHINGLES FOR THE LORD," "TWO SOLDIERS," and "SHALL NOT PERISH" (in *Collected Stories*).

Hait, Lonzo   An offstage character referred to in *The Mansion* and *The TOWN*. (He is also referred to in the short story "MULE IN THE YARD," which Faulkner extensively revised for *The Town*.) With I. O. Snopes, Hait participates in a scheme to have mules killed on train tracks in order to collect damages from the railroad companies.

Hampton, Hub (Old Hub)   The YOKNAPATAWPHA COUNTY sheriff referred to in *The Mansion* and described as "a meat-eating Hard-Shell-Baptist deacon whose purest notion of pleasure was counting off the folks he personally knowed was already bound for hell" (53). The story of his arresting Montgomery Ward Snopes is recounted in the novel by V. K. Ratliff. *Also see The HAMLET* and *The REIVERS* (where in both novels Hampton's first name is not given), *The TOWN*, and *INTRUDER IN THE DUST* (where his first name is Hope).

Hampton, Hubert, Jr. (Little Hub) In *The Mansion*, Sheriff Hub Hampton's son, who, like his father, alternates a four-year term as sheriff with Ephriam Bishop.

Harriss A wealthy New Orleans underworld figure and bootlegger married to Melisandre Backus. After his father-in-law's death, he transforms his wife's deteriorated house in JEFFERSON, "a simple familiar red-ink north Mississippi cotton plantation . . . [,] into a Virginia or Long Island horse farm" (196). *Also see* KNIGHT'S GAMBIT ("Knight's Gambit"), where he is killed, gangland style.

Harriss, Mrs. *See* Stevens, Melisandre Backus.

Henry A black man who works on Jack Houston's farm. He is present when Mink Snopes tries unsuccessfully to get his cow back from Houston.

Hogganbeck, Lucius An offstage character in the novel. The son of Boon Hogganbeck (*see* "The OLD PEOPLE," "The BEAR," and *The REIVERS*), Lucius runs a car service, an "automobile jitney" (35), in Jefferson. *Also see The* TOWN *and* "A BEAR HUNT." His full name is Lucius Priest Hogganbeck. In "A Bear Hunt" (*Collected Stories*), he is called Lucius Provine, "the Butch" Provine, or Luke. When "A Bear Hunt" was revised for *Big Woods*, Faulkner changed his name to Lucius (Luke) Hogganbeck and he was a member of the Provine gang.

Holcomb, (Sister) Beth A member of Brother J. C. Goodyhay's religious congregation. Right after his release from prison, Mink Snopes does yard work for her because he needs money to travel to MEMPHIS and JEFFERSON. After she feeds Mink dinner, she sends him on to Brother Goodyhay's, four miles down the road.

Holland, Mr. The president of the Bank of Jefferson. As a gesture of kindness, Holland has a needed bathroom installed in Otis Meadowfill's home despite Meadowfill's outrage and gives Meadowfill's daughter, Essie Meadowfill (Smith), a job for life in the bank.

Holston, Alexander One of the three original settlers of YOKNAPATAWPHA COUNTY (*see* REQUIEM FOR A NUN) and the late owner of a public house known as the Holston House, which "still clung to the old ways, not desperately nor even gallantly: just with a cold and inflexible indomitability, owned and run by two maiden sisters . . . who were the last descendants of the Alexander Holston" (383). *Also see* ABSALOM, ABSALOM! He is mentioned in INTRUDER IN THE DUST, KNIGHT'S GAMBIT ("Hand Upon the Waters"), and *The* TOWN.

Houston, Jack An offstage character in *The Mansion*. He was a childless widower and farmer in the rural area of FRENCHMAN'S BEND, murdered at 33 years old by Mink Snopes over a dispute regarding Mink's stray yearling that Houston penned up. (For further details, *see The* HAMLET and the Character entries on Jack Houston and Mink Snopes.) Houston is also referred to in *The* TOWN; in the Vintage paperback edition his first name in one place appears as Zack (36) and in another as Jack (78). This discrepancy is corrected in The Library of America edition, *Faulkner Novels: 1957–1962*, where the first name Zack appears in both cases (33 and 69). *Also see* the short story "The HOUND."

Jabbo, Captain A prison guard at the Mississippi state penitentiary at PARCHMAN, where Mink Snopes serves time for the murder of Jack Houston. Captain Jabbo kills Jake Barron when Barron tries to escape.

Killegrew, Hunter The deputy who escorts Montgomery Ward Snopes to PARCHMAN (Mississippi's state penitentiary).

Kohl, Barton Linda Snopes's husband. Kohl is a sculptor, a communist, and a Jew. Before getting married, Barton and Linda live together for several years in Greenwich Village. In 1936, right after they marry, they leave for Spain and fight for the Loyalists during the Spanish civil war. He is killed when his airplane is shot down by the Germans.

Kohl, Linda Snopes Daughter of Eula Varner Snopes and Hoake McCarron. Linda was conceived out of wedlock and born after Eula married Flem Snopes. She grows up in Jefferson and, until her late teens, she assumes that Flem is her father. (For other details, *see* The HAMLET and The TOWN.) After her mother commits suicide in 1927 (*see* The *Town*), Linda moves to Greenwich Village, where she meets and lives with Barton Kohl, an avowed communist. They marry and together go to Spain to fight with the Loyalists in the Spanish civil war. Her husband is killed when his airplane is shot down, and she is wounded when a shell explodes near the ambulance she is driving, leaving her completely deaf. She returns to Jefferson in August 1937 and lives with Flem, although she has virtually nothing to do with him. She clearly sees Flem for what he is, an enemy, a rapacious and exploitative person largely responsible for her mother's suicide.

For a time during World War II, she works for the war effort in PASCAGOULA. When Linda returns to Jefferson, she spends her time drinking boot-legged whiskey and walking around aimlessly until she finds another cause to live for: to have Mink Snopes pardoned of the crime of killing Jack Houston. She plays a key role in his release from prison in 1946, knowing all along that he will avenge his treatment by Flem. Linda is in the house when Mink sneaks in to kill Flem, and she helps him find his way out. Later, through Gavin Stevens, she gives him money with which to run away and plans regularly to send him money to live on. Before leaving Jefferson for good, as a final act of justice Linda gives the mansion, which once belonged to Manfred de Spain's family, back to Manfred's only living relatives.

Ledbetter, Mrs. A minor offstage character in *The Mansion* (and *The* TOWN). She lives in Rocky-ford and buys a sewing machine from V. K. Ratliff.

Littlejohn A minor character in the novel, owner of a half-Airedale terrier. *Also see* The HAMLET and INTRUDER IN THE DUST, where Littlejohn is a family name of early farmers in YOKNAPATAWPHA COUNTY, and AS I LAY DYING.

Long, Judge A minor character in *The Mansion* (and in *The* TOWN). Judge Long is the federal judge of the district that includes JEFFERSON, MISSISSIPPI. In *The Mansion*, Judge Long sentences Montgom-ery Ward Snopes to two years in the state peniten-tiary for possessing a gallon of moonshine whiskey, which was planted in his photography store by Montgomery's kinsman, Flem Snopes.

Ludus The jailed husband of Miss Reba Rivers's black maid, Minnie. After he quit his job, Ludus loafed around, ate from Miss Reba's kitchen, and stole money from his wife which he gave to other women. When Minnie confronted him, Ludus hit her with a flatiron.

Maggie *See* Mallison, Maggie.

McCallum, Rafe An offstage character referred to in the novel. Melisandre Harriss Backus's maniac son either "bought or tricked or anyway got" (*The Mansion*, 255) Rafe's wild stallion. Believing that his sister's fiancé, an Argentine steeplechaser and cavalry officer, was marrying for money, the maniac brother intent on killing the fiancé put the horse into a stall knowing the Argentine would go to it. The plot, however, was foiled by Uncle Gavin (Gavin Stevens), who reached Rafe in time to get to the stall first. Rafe is referred to in AS I LAY DYING; *also see* SARTORIS where his full name appears as Raphael Semmes MacCallum, "Knight's Gambit" (KNIGHT'S GAMBIT), and the short story "The TALL MEN." (The surname MacCallum is a variant and earlier spelling of McCallum; the former spelling occurs in *Sartoris* and *As I Lay Dying*.)

McCarron, Hoake Linda Snopes's biological father. With the encouragement of Gavin Stevens, he attends Linda's wedding in New York City. Although he introduces himself to her as an old friend of the family, Linda knows who he really is. *See* The HAMLET for further details. In *The* TOWN, he is an offstage character.

McCaslin, Ike (Isaac, Uncle Ike) An offstage character in *The Mansion*, who owns a hardware store in Jefferson (the McCaslin Hardware Com-pany that Jason Compson runs in the novel). An octogenarian in *The Mansion*, Ike and Walter Ewell are regarded as the best hunters in YOKNAPATAW-PHA COUNTY. At the time of the novel, Ike's days are mostly spent hunting and fishing. The narrator explains that Ike refused to sell Mink Snopes buckshot shells that Mink would have used to kill Jack Houston. Ike is also referred to in *The* HAMLET, *The* TOWN, INTRUDER IN THE DUST, *The* REIVERS, and the short stories "A BEAR HUNT" and "RACE AT MORNING." For further details, *see* the following works in which he appears: GO DOWN, MOSES ("Was," "Fire and the Hearth," "The Old People," "The Bear," and "Delta Autumn").

McGowan, Skeets   A minor character in *The Mansion*. He is a clerk and soda jerker in Uncle Willy Christian's drugstore in Jefferson. Skeets's bantering with Tug Nightingale so angers Tug that he gives Skeets a beating. By the time Tug is subdued, Skeets is in an ambulance on his way to the hospital. He is also a minor character in AS I LAY DYING (where his name appears as Skeet MacGowan), INTRUDER IN THE DUST, and *The* TOWN.

McLendon, Captain (Mack)   An offstage character in the novel. A cotton buyer, McLendon during World War I organized a Jefferson company of soldiers known as the Sartoris Rifles in honor of the legendary Civil War hero Colonel John Sartoris. Mack took Tug Nightingale in as a house guest when the latter's father, a dyed-in-the-wool confederate resentful of the North, disowned Tug for joining the Yankee army. In *The* TOWN, he is referred to as Jackson McLendon and in "DRY SEPTEMBER" simply as McLendon. *Also see* Captain McLendon under Characters in LIGHT IN AUGUST.

Mallison, Charles, Jr. (Chick)   The nephew and companion of Gavin Stevens. In *The Mansion*, Chick studies law for two years at HARVARD UNIVERSITY before taking one more year at the UNIVERSITY OF MISSISSIPPI. He tours Europe at his Uncle Gavin's insistence, and considers becoming the lover of the radical Linda Snopes Kohl, who has just returned home to Jefferson from fighting with the Loyalists in the Spanish civil war, the war in which her husband was killed. After World War II breaks out, Chick joins the Air Force and is

shot down over Germany. When returning home in September of 1945 from a World War II prisoner of war camp, Chick resumed the struggle against the Snopes clan, and he arrives in Jefferson in time to witness the shrewd V. K. Ratliff engineer the election defeat of the rabble-rousing, race-baiting Senator Clarence Eggleston Snopes. Chapters 8, 9, and 11 of *The Mansion* are narrated by him. *Also see* INTRUDER IN THE DUST, KNIGHT'S GAMBIT, *The* TOWN, REQUIEM FOR A NUN, and the short story "HOG PAWN."

Mallison, Charles, Sr.   Chick Mallison's father; he plays no role in the novel. *See* INTRUDER IN THE DUST and *The* TOWN.

Mallison, Maggie (Margaret Stevens)   Chick Mallison's mother, Gavin Stevens's twin, and the wife of Charles Mallison, Sr. Maggie is referred to in the novel. *See* INTRUDER IN THE DUST, KNIGHT'S GAMBIT, and *The* TOWN. She is also mentioned in REQUIEM FOR A NUN.

Meadowfill, Essie   *See* Smith, Essie Meadowfill.

Meadowfill, Mrs.   Otis Meadowfill's wife and mother of Essie Meadowfill Smith. She is described as a "gray drudge of a wife" (328).

Meadowfill, Otis   An unfriendly, cantankerous, and nasty man in Jefferson. Until his one child, Essie (*see* Essie Meadowfill Smith), helps support the household, Meadowfill does his own grocery shopping at side-street stores where he looks for leftovers at bargain prices. When his neighbor—a paralytic old lady—dies, he immediately buys her wheelchair to sit in, from which he guards his property against intruders, including the hog belonging to his neighbor Orestes Snopes. The animal trespasses onto his property daily and is met not with a solid bullet but with the sting of tiny shot cartridges fired from a single-shot .22 rifle. (Killing the hog would probably have been too definitive for the contentious Meadowfill, who seems to savor the sadistic pleasure of routinely annoying the animal.) When an oil company wants to buy his plot of land and the adjacent lot legally belonging to Flem

Snopes, Meadowfill refuses to sell, thus preventing the company from building a gas station. Eventually the town's attorney, Gavin Stevens, intervenes, settling the dispute in favor of the Meadowfills. *Also see* the short story "HOG PAWN," which Faulkner revised for the novel.

Meeks, Doc   A minor character; he is a salesman of patent medicine.

Minnie   Miss Reba Rivers's black maid. Minnie's lazy husband, Ludus, steals money from her, and when he is confronted he injures her ear with a flatiron. Minnie also appears in *SANCTUARY* and *The REIVERS*.

Mohataha   An offstage character in *The Mansion; also see REQUIEM FOR A NUN.* She is the CHICKASAW INDIAN matriarch who, in 1821, grants Quentin (MacLachan) Compson land that becomes very valuable in Jefferson. (*Also see* Faulkner's Appendix to *The SOUND AND THE FURY*, reprinted in Appendix, where Jason Lycurgus Compson (II) fits the time period when the land was granted by Mohataha.)

Nightingale, Mr.   Father of Tug Nightingale. A widower, he is a staunch, inflexible Baptist, who believes that the earth is flat and that General Lee's surrender at Appomattox was a betrayal of the South. When, in 1917, Tug, his only surviving child, joins the Sartoris Rifles organized by Captain McLendon, Nightingale disinherits him because he believes that his son has become a traitor by joining the Yankee army.

Nightingale, Tug   A member of the Jefferson military company known as the Sartoris Rifles, organized by Captain McLendon in 1917. When his widowed father (an unrelenting Confederate) finds out that his only surviving child joined the Yankee army, Tug is disinherited. After the company trained in Texas, it was sent overseas, where Tug became a cook. In 1919, Tug returns to Jefferson and once again becomes a barn and fence painter.

Quick, Solon   The constable in FRENCHMAN'S BEND during the time Jack Houston is having a

problem with Mink Snopes's cow. *Also see* the short stories "SHINGLES FOR THE LORD" and "SHALL NOT PERISH."

Quick, Theron   A minor offstage character referred to in *The Mansion*. He was one of Eula Varner Snopes's suitors who attacked Hoake McCarron when he was riding with Eula in a wagon. Struck by Eula with the handle of a buggy whip, Theron is knocked unconscious. He and Herman Bookwright leave FRENCHMAN'S BEND quickly when they find out that Eula is pregnant. (This episode occurred during the time period of *The HAMLET*, although it is not recounted in that novel.)

Ratcliffe, Nelly   An offstage character referred to in the novel. She is V. K. Ratliff's great grandmother. Nelly, a farmer's daughter in Virginia, married Vladimir Kyrilytch, whom she found hiding out in a hayloft. Left to fend for himself after the defeat at Saratoga, this first V. K. had been a mercenary in General Burgoyne's army. He took Nelly's last name, which later became Ratliff.

Ratliff, V. K. (Vladimir Kyrilytch)   A main character in the SNOPES TRILOGY (*The HAMLET, The TOWN,* and *The Mansion*) and one of the major narrators of these novels. An itinerant salesman, Ratliff is an ideal person (or narrator) for spreading news and recounting events. Ratliff narrates chapters 3, 6, and 7 of *The Mansion*. In chapter 7 of this novel, the reader learns that he is a descendent of a Russian mercenary, Vladimir Kyrilytch, who fought on the side of the British during the Revolutionary War and escaped when General Burgoyne surrendered at Saratoga. "[W]e didn't know his last name," Ratliff says to Gavin Stevens, "or maybe he didn't even have none until Nelly Ratliff, spelled Ratcliffe then, found him" hiding in a hayloft (*The Mansion*, 165). When Nelly became pregnant with his child, the first Vladimir married her, and a son in each succeeding generation was given his first two names; one moved to Tennessee, and the next one to Mississippi. For other details regarding Ratliff, *see The Hamlet, The Town,* and *Big Woods* ("A BEAR HUNT"). He also appears under the name V. K. Suratt in "LIZARDS

IN JAMSHYD'S COURTYARD," "CENTAUR IN BRASS," *SARTORIS*, and *AS I LAY DYING*.

Reba, Miss   The name of one of Reba Rivers's two dogs. Reba Rivers named one after herself and the other, Mr. Binford, after Lucius Binford, her late landlord for 11 years and her lover.

Rivers, Reba (Miss Reba)   Madam of a MEMPHIS brothel and well-known throughout town. Some of the most important men in Memphis (bankers, medical doctors, lawyers, and even police captains) frequent her tightly run establishment to drink and be with women. Miss Reba owns two small, soiled white dogs that she names Miss Reba and Mr. Binford, one after herself and the other after Lucius Binford, her late landlord and lover. The naive Fonzo Winbush and Virgil Snopes stay at her brothel, mistakenly thinking that it is a boarding-house. *Also see SANCTUARY and The REIVERS.*

Rouncewell, Mrs.   A minor character in the novel. For a time, she operates the Commercial Hotel. *Also see KNIGHT'S GAMBIT ("Tomorrow"), The TOWN and The REIVERS.*

Rouncewell   Referred to in the novel as "that Rouncewell boy" (59). While climbing down a drain pipe to go to a late movie, he saw two fellows robbing Uncle Willy Christian's drugstore. (*Also see The TOWN;* he is probably Mrs. Rouncewell's son, Whit.)

Sartoris, Bayard (young)   An offstage character referred to in the novel. Bayard served in the ROYAL AIR FORCE during World War I, and after his return in the spring of 1919 he "bought the fastest car he could find and spent his time ripping around the county or back and forth to Memphis" (*The Mansion*, 188–89). Thinking that she can put a stop to his reckless behavior, Mrs. Du Pre (young Bayard's aunt) gets him to marry Narcissa Benbow. After a serious car crash in which his grandfather, Colonel Sartoris, dies of a heart attack, Bayard, who walked away unharmed from the accident, abandons his pregnant wife to seek even riskier adventure by becoming a test pilot of a plane that

costs him his life. For further details *see SARTORIS* and the short story "Ad Astra"; Bayard is also referred to in *The TOWN, REQUIEM FOR A NUN,* and "THERE WAS A QUEEN."

Sartoris, Benbow   *See* Benbow.

Sartoris, Colonel   An offstage character in the novel. Although his first name is Bayard, in *The Mansion* he is exclusively referred to as Colonel Sartoris. He is the son of the legendary Colonel John Sartoris, the first Sartoris in YOKNAPATAWPHA COUNTY and founder of the prominent Sartoris family (*see* Characters under *SARTORIS* and *The UNVANQUISHED*). He died of a heart attack when the car driven by his grandson (also named Bayard) crashed. For other details, *see* Bayard Sartoris (old) under Characters in *Sartoris, The Unvanquished,* and "MY GRANDMOTHER MILLARD AND GENERAL BEDFORD FORREST AND THE BATTLE OF HARRYKIN CREEK"; he is also referred to in *The HAMLET, REQUIEM FOR A NUN, The TOWN,* and *The REIVERS, GO DOWN, MOSES* ("The BEAR") and the short stories "A ROSE FOR EMILY" and "THERE WAS A QUEEN."

Sartoris, Colonel   An offstage character in *The Mansion*. The first Sartoris in YOKNAPATAWPHA COUNTY, he is the legendary Colonel John Sartoris, railroad builder and successful business man. (In *The Mansion* his first name is not used). In 1917, McLendon organized a Jefferson company of soldiers known as the Sartoris Rifles in honor of Colonel Sartoris.

For further information regarding this character, *see The UNVANQUISHED* and *REQUIEM FOR A NUN.* Colonel Sartoris is referred to in *SARTORIS, The SOUND AND THE FURY, ABSALOM, ABSALOM!, LIGHT IN AUGUST, GO DOWN, MOSES* ("The BEAR"), *The HAMLET, The TOWN, The REIVERS,* and in the short stories "BARN BURNING," "SHALL NOT PERISH," "MY GRANDMOTHER MILLARD AND GENERAL BEDFORD FORREST AND THE BATTLE OF HARRYKIN CREEK," and "THERE WAS A QUEEN."

Sartoris, John   Referred to in the novel, he is the deceased twin brother of (young) Bayard Sartoris. During World War I, in July of 1918, John—a pilot in the ROYAL AIR FORCE—was shot down on a mission over France. *See* Characters under "ALL THE DEAD PILOTS" and "WITH CAUTION AND DISPATCH"; he is also mentioned in *SARTORIS*, *The TOWN*, and "THERE WAS A QUEEN."

Sartoris, Narcissa Benbow An offstage character in the novel referred to by her maiden name, Narcissa Benbow. Her marriage to Bayard Sartoris was orchestrated by Bayard's aunt, Mrs. Du Pre. Narcissa was pregnant when her husband abandoned her and became a widow the day their son Benbow was born. For other details, *see* Characters under *SARTORIS*, *SANCTUARY*, and "THERE WAS A QUEEN." She is also referred to by her maiden name in *The TOWN*.

Smith, Essie Meadowfill Otis Meadowfill's daughter. When she graduates as valedictorian from high school in 1942, she makes the highest grades ever and is offered a $500 scholarship from Mr. Holland, the president of the Bank of Jefferson. She turns down the scholarship, however, and instead borrows the same sum of money from the bank president to have a bathroom installed in her home. Mr. Holland gives Essie a job for life, and soon after World War II she marries McKinley Smith, an ex-marine corporal. With the help of Gavin Stevens, she gets Orestes Snopes's deed to a strip of land that she sells to an oil company to buy a farm. She also appears in the short story "HOG PAWN," which Faulkner revised for *The Mansion*. (A few minor details were changed when Faulkner revised the piece for the novel. In the short story the bank president's name is not given and Essie declines not only the money that he offers her but the job as well; she chooses to work for the telephone company instead. Her husband in the short story is an ex-marine sergeant and not a corporal.)

Smith, McKinley The son of a tenant farmer from east Texas and an ex-marine corporal who marries Essie Meadowfill. He buys a small lot in Eula Acres where he builds a home. He also appears in the short story "HOG PAWN," which Faulkner

revised for *The Mansion*. (In the short story, he is identified as an ex-marine sergeant.)

Snopes, Ab According to the first novel of the SNOPES TRILOGY, *The HAMLET*, Ab Snopes is clearly Flem's father, the reputed barn burner, but in *The Mansion* that relationship is not stated. In the latter novel, Ab is an offstage character referred to as being old and as having been evicted from a house owned by Will Varner for not having paid rent in two years. For other details relating to Ab Snopes, *see The UNVANQUISHED*, *The Hamlet*, *The TOWN*, "BARN BURNING," and "MY GRANDMOTHER MILLARD AND GENERAL BEDFORD FORREST AND THE BATTLE OF HARRYKIN CREEK."

Snopes, Admiral Dewey A minor offstage character, Admiral Dewey is Eck Snopes's younger son and brother of Wallstreet Panic Snopes. Because these three are atypical in that they are not rapacious and dishonest Snopeses, their kinsman Montgomery Ward Snopes says that "they dont belong to us: they are only our shame" (*The Mansion*, 83). *Also see The TOWN.*

Snopes, Bilbo A minor offstage character referred to by Montgomery Ward Snopes as one of the true (i.e., greedy and dishonest) Snopeses. *Also see The TOWN.*

Snopes, Byron An offstage character; he and his four wild children are briefly referred to in *The Mansion*. Byron stole money from Colonel Sartoris's bank and took off to Texas, and in the late 1920s, he sent his unruly children to his relative Flem Snopes (*see The TOWN* for further details). Byron also appears in *SARTORIS* and the theft (but not his name) is referred to in the short story "THERE WAS A QUEEN" (*Collected Stories*, 739).

Snopes, Clarence Eggleston The Mississippi State Senator from YOKNAPATAWPHA COUNTY. He previously was Constable of FRENCHMAN'S BEND until Uncle Billy Varner, annoyed by Clarence's tough-guy tactic of pistol-whipping someone in the name of the law, engineered his election to the state legislature. Though later Clarence is a formidable candidate for the U.S. Congress, V. K. Ratliff singlehandedly eliminates him from the race by getting two boys to sneak up behind Clarence and without his knowledge rub the back of his trouser legs with damp switches from a dog thicket, causing dogs to sniff and urinate on the unsuspecting Clarence. This spectacle forces Varner to withdraw his support and Clarence to withdraw from the congressional race. *Also see* The TOWN, SANCTUARY, and "BY THE PEOPLE" (which Faulkner revised for *The Mansion*).

Snopes, Doris   An offstage character referred to in *The Mansion*. Doris is Clarence Eggleston Snopes's youngest brother, a 17-year old living in FRENCHMAN'S BEND; he resembles his brother Clarence in size, shape, and mentality. When Byron Snopes's four wild children are in Frenchman's Bend, Doris becomes a victim of their sinister machinations. Caught hold of alone, Doris is taken by them to the woods and tied to a stake, and would have been burned alive had his screams not been heard. (Referred to here in *The Mansion*, this episode is slightly different in *The TOWN*.)

Snopes, Eck (Eckrum)   An offstage character, father of Wallstreet Panic and Admiral Dewey Snopes. Because Eck, a cousin of Flem Snopes, is honest and kindhearted, and so too his sons, Wallstreet Panic and Admiral Dewey, Montgomery Ward Snopes does not consider them true Snopeses. Such human qualities make Montgomery Ward comment that "they dont belong to us: they are only our shame" (*The Mansion*, 83). *Also see* FATHER ABRAHAM, The HAMLET, The TOWN, and "SPOTTED HORSES."

Snopes, Eula Varner   One of the major characters in the SNOPES TRILOGY, although during the time period of *The Mansion*, the last of the three novels, Eula does not appear. References to her, however, abound in the novel and her death by suicide is retold. The daughter of Will Varner (Uncle Billy), Eula is Linda Snopes's mother and Flem Snopes's wife. Before her death, Eula had a long-term affair with the banker Manfred de Spain, JEFFERSON's mayor. For other details, *see* especially

The HAMLET and *The* TOWN; Eula also appears in the fragment FATHER ABRAHAM and the short story "SPOTTED HORSES," which Faulkner revised for *The Hamlet*.

Snopes, Flem   The son of the sharecropper Ab Snopes and a central character in the SNOPES TRILOGY. Although often in the background, Flem is in the forefront of much of the action of the three novels and frequently the focus of the narrative. His presence is pervasive throughout the trilogy. The greediest and most successful Snopes, the insensitive Flem manipulates others to satisfy his own ends, and throughout the trilogy he has no qualms about his treatment toward anyone who stands in his way, whether relative or neighbor. By the time of *The Mansion*, Flem has achieved financial success and lives in Manfred de Spain's ancestral home, which he redecorates to look like Mount Vernon. Portrayed as a man without family or friends, Flem lives alone until Linda, deaf from a war injury, returns in August 1937 from the Spanish civil war.

Concerned with maintaining respectability, Flem devises a plan to have his relative, Montgomery Ward Snopes, arrested when he becomes an embarrassment to Flem for running a photography shop as a front for peep shows, and sent to the state prison at PARCHMAN where Mink Snopes is also serving time. Fearing that Mink will seek revenge for his failure to show up at Mink's murder trial, Flem bribes Montgomery to entice Mink to escape, thus protecting himself against any threat Mink might pose to him. As expected, Mink is caught, and his prison term extended another 20 years. But when the 63-year-old Mink is finally pardoned in 1946, he travels to Jefferson with the sole intend of killing Flem, who at the moment right before his death at Mink's hands seems indifferent and almost resigned to its inevitability. *Also see* SARTORIS, *The* HAMLET, *The* TOWN, FATHER ABRAHAM, and the short stories "SPOTTED HORSES," "CENTAUR IN BRASS," and "LIZARDS IN JAMSHYD'S COURTYARD"; Flem is also referred to in *As I* LAY DYING and *The* REIVERS.

Snopes, I. O.   A minor offstage character in the novel. A bigamist, I. O. with one wife is the father of Montgomery Ward (and Saint Elmo, who is not mentioned in *The Mansion* but appears in *The HAMLET*) and with another wife the father of Clarence, Doris, and the twins Vardaman and Bilbo. (For a Snopes Family Tree, *see* Appendix.) I. O. also appears in *The SOUND AND THE FURY*, *The HAMLET*, *The TOWN*, *FATHER ABRAHAM* (fragment of a novel incorporated into *The Hamlet*), and the short stories "SPOTTED HORSES" (revised for *The Hamlet*) and "MULE IN THE YARD" (revised for *The Town*).

Snopes, Lump (Launcelot)   A minor character referred to in the novel, Lump replaced his cousin Flem Snopes as the clerk at VARNER'S STORE; *see The HAMLET*. He also appears in "The HOUND," which Faulkner revised for *The Hamlet*.

Snopes, Linda   *See* Kohl, Linda Snopes.

Snopes, Mink (M. C.)   A poor farmer in the rural area of FRENCHMAN'S BEND currently serving time at PARCHMAN for murdering Jack Houston. (*See The HAMLET*; Houston had charged Mink a poundage fee to cover the cost of pasturing his yearling, and Mink, interpreting that penalty as an injustice and an indignity, killed Houston.) While in prison, Mink was persuaded by his cousin Montgomery Ward Snopes (also serving time on charges of bootlegging) to escape, but the attempt backfired and more time was added to Mink's term; in all, he served 38 years. Linda Snopes Kohl orchestrates his pardon, but when he is offered money from Gavin Stevens to stay away from JEFFERSON forever, he refuses to accept it. The 63-year-old Mink is resolute in his determination to kill the indifferent Flem Snopes for not having come to his assistance during his murder trial. (Whether Flem could have actually done anything or not was not the question for Mink. He expected Flem to do something to intervene in his behalf, to rescue him, because, he believed, blood relatives do whatever is necessary to help. But Flem never even showed up, forcing Mink to take revenge.) Before getting to Jefferson, Mink goes to MEMPHIS where he buys a pistol and three rounds of ammunition for $10. (At one point while in Memphis, Mink unknowingly is near the brothel that his younger daughter runs and that he himself had visited 47 years before.) Five days after his release from Parchman, Mink kills Flem in his home, and on the following night, Stevens and V. K. Ratliff find Mink hiding in the cellar of his abandoned cabin. Stevens has the money Linda set aside for Mink, and this time he takes it. Before departing, Stevens asks him where he will be in three months to receive the next payment. *Also see The Hamlet* and *The TOWN*.

Snopes, Montgomery Ward   I. O. Snopes's eldest child by his first wife, whom I. O. did not divorce before marrying a second woman. (For the names of his siblings, *see* the entry on I. O. Snopes above.) Montgomery Ward narrates chapter 4 of *The Mansion*. With Gavin Stevens, Montgomery Ward goes to France during World War I and runs a canteen for the YMCA. He turns part of it into a club and hires a young French girl for the entertainment of any soldier who wants more than chocolate bars. After he returns to JEFFERSON, he opens an arty photography shop where he shows pornographic postcards from France. Flem Snopes has Montgomery Ward arrested, but not for pornography. Instead, he has him arrested for having moonshine liquor on his premises, which Flem himself planted there. Because of Flem's scheme, Montgomery Ward is sent to the penitentiary in PARCHMAN for the crime, a lesser offense than had he been convicted of pornography, which would have landed him time in a federal prison in Atlanta. With Montgomery Ward at Parchman (where Mink Snopes is also serving time), Flem, knowing that Mink would certainly get caught, uses Montgomery Ward to convince Mink to escape dressed in women's clothes. (Flem suspects that Mink, who is in prison for the murder of Jack Houston, is determined to take revenge on him for not having come to Mink's aid during the murder trial.) After Montgomery Ward is released from prison, he travels to Los Angeles where he gets a lucrative job working in the motion picture industry. *Also see The TOWN* and *SARTORIS*.

Snopes, Orestes (Res)   Otis Meadowfill's neighbor who lives in the converted Compson carriage house owned by Flem Snopes. Res, a bachelor, buys and sells scrubby cattle and hogs and uses Meadowfill's worthless and untended orchard as a boundary hog-lot fence. When, out of revenge, Meadowfill declines to sell his property to an oil company after he learns that a 13-foot strip of land that he thought he owned is actually deeded to Flem Snopes, Res (who works for his relative Flem) hatches a plan to force Meadowfill to sell. (The condition the oil company stipulates is that both property owners must sell or the deal is off.) Meanwhile, one of Res's loose hogs starts trespassing onto Meadowfill's property and rooting among his rotting peaches, causing Meadowfill to shoot at it. Res visits the attorney Gavin Stevens for legal advice at which time he makes it known to Stevens that he will give the errant hog away. After presenting it as a gift to McKinley Smith, Meadowfill's future son-in-law, Res sets a booby trap so that the next time Meadowfill lifts the windowscreen to shoot at the hog Meadowfill himself would also get shot. Res's plan, however, backfires by Stevens's intervention, and the deed to the strip of land ends up in the hands of Meadowfill's daughter.

Res also appears, but without a first name, in the short story "HOG PAWN," which Faulkner revised for *The Mansion*.

Snopes, Vardaman   A minor character in *The Mansion*. Bilbo Snopes's twin, Vardaman is I. O. Snopes's son by his second wife. (I. O. is still married to his first wife at the time.) Vardaman is included in Montgomery Ward Snopes's family list of "just another Snopes son of a bitch" (*The Mansion*, 87).

Snopes, Virgil   A minor (and humorous) character in *The Mansion*; he is Wesley Snopes's youngest son. With Fonzo Winbush, Virgil goes to barbers' college in MEMPHIS. While there, the two rent a room from Reba Rivers but do not know that her house is a brothel. They think that the women "were all Reba's nieces or wards or something just in town maybe attending female equivalent of barbers' colleges themselves" (*The Mansion*, 73). When Virgil's kinsman Clarence Snopes happens upon Virgil one night at a different brothel, Clarence learns of Vir-

gil's "really exceptional talent" (73) of sexually satisfying two girls in succession. He brags about Virgil's powers to lure others into betting against him, but Clarence would usually win. Virgil also appears in SANCTUARY and is referred to in *The TOWN*.

Snopes, Wallstreet Panic   A minor character in the novel. Wallstreet is Eck Snopes's son and Admiral Dewey's brother. Because of their un-Snopesian disposition of decency, kindness, and fairness, Eck and his two sons are not counted as real Snopeses by Montgomery Ward (see *The Mansion*, 83). Wallstreet not only does not look like a Snopes; he does not act like one. "[A]ll Wallstreet evidently wanted to do," V. K. Ratliff observes, "was run a wholesale grocery business by the outrageous un-Snopesish method of jest selling ever body exactly what they thought they was buying, for exactly what they thought they was going to pay for it" (*The Mansion*, 153). Starting off as a delivery boy in a side-street grocery store, Wallstreet put himself and his brother through school, created a wholesale grocery supply company in JEFFERSON, and then after moving to MEMPHIS established a wholesale grocery business in Mississippi, Tennessee, and Arkansas. When Flem Snopes dies, Wallstreet attends his funeral. For other details, *see The HAMLET* and *The TOWN*.

Snopes, Wat (Watkins Products)   A minor character in *The Mansion*. He is the carpenter Flem Snopes hires to renovate his house and to convert the Compson carriage house into a two-storey residence.

Snopes, Wesley   A minor offstage character in *The Mansion*, referred to as Uncle Wesley or Uncle Wes by his nephew, Montgomery Ward, and portrayed as fumbling with the skirt of a young girl while directing the singing of a hymn. Wes is Byron and Virgil's father. For other details regarding his character, *see The TOWN*; his first name is not given in that novel.

Snopes, Yettie   A minor offstage character, she is Mink Snopes's wife. Illiterate, she has a letter written (probably by Mrs. Tull) and sent to her husband in the state penitentiary at PARCHMAN asking him when he wants her to visit and whether she should bring their daughters. When the warden reads the letter to Mink and asks him for a reply, he says to tell her not to come because he will be out soon. *See The* HAMLET where she also appears, but her name is not used.

Spoade A minor offstage character from Charleston, South Carolina, who went to HARVARD UNIVERSITY with Chick Mallison. His father, also called Spoade, went to Harvard with Chick's uncle Gavin Stevens in 1909 and also with Quentin Compson in 1910 (*see The* SOUND AND THE FURY). Spoade invites Chick to Charleston during a Christmas break.

Stamper, Pat A minor character in the novel known for his horse trading throughout north Mississippi, Tennessee, Alabama, and Arkansas. He is the Fritz Kreisler of horse and mule traders, the person others aspire to be like; no one outwits Pat Stamper when trading horses or mules. *Also see The* HAMLET and the short story "FOOL ABOUT A HORSE," which Faulkner revised for *The Hamlet*.

Stevens, Gavin A major character in *The Mansion* and in several other works. Gavin is partly modeled on PHILIP AVERY STONE, Faulkner's lifelong friend. Judge Lemuel Stevens's son, Margaret Stevens Mallison's twin, and Chick Mallison's uncle, Gavin is an attorney from a prominent family in JEFFERSON, an intellectual, a romantic idealist, an active county attorney, and a staunch opponent of SNOPESISM. Gavin is a Phi Beta Kappa with a master's degree from HARVARD UNIVERSITY, a doctorate from Heidelberg University in Germany, and a law degree from the UNIVERSITY OF MISSISSIPPI. During World War I, he served in the American Field Service and YMCA in France from 1915 to 1918. Before marrying the widow Melisandre Backus Harriss, a childhood sweetheart and one of his sister's childhood friends, Gavin spends a considerable amount of time with Linda Snopes Kohl. *Also see The* TOWN, KNIGHT'S GAMBIT, INTRUDER IN THE DUST, REQUIEM FOR A NUN, LIGHT IN AUGUST, GO DOWN, MOSES, "HAIR," "The TALL MEN,"

"HOG PAWN" (revised for chapter 14 of *The Mansion*), and "BY THE PEOPLE" (revised for chapter 13 of *The Mansion*); he also is referred to in "A Name for the City" (revised for the prologue to act 1 of *Requiem for a Nun*). Gavin narrates chapter 10 of *The Mansion*.

Some readers see Gavin Stevens as Faulkner's mouthpiece, particularly in *Light in August* and *Intruder in the Dust*, but such an assumption cannot be justified. Faulkner was too skilled as an artist to identify with any of his characters, even though a few of these characters may echo some of his sentiments. Faulkner does not intrude into his fictional works to present his opinions. (For more information, *see* FAULKNER IN THE UNIVERSITY, 25, 72, 118, 140–41 and 201; and James Farnham's "Faulkner's Unsung Hero: Gavin Stevens" in *Arizona Quarterly* [summer 1965], 115–32, where Farnham discusses Stevens's significance in the SNOPES TRILOGY and how, by the end of *The Mansion*, he becomes a realist in his view of humanity). Horace Benbow, a precursor of Gavin Stevens, shares a similar educational background and other personal characteristics (*see* SANCTUARY).

Stevens, Melisandre Backus Harriss Gavin Stevens's wife. After the death of her husband, a wealthy New Orleans bootlegger, Melisandre, in 1942, marries Gavin, her childhood friend. She has two children by her first marriage. Gavin's sister, Margaret Mallison, had all along suggested to her brother that he marry her. *Also see The* TOWN, where she is identified by her maiden name, Melisandre Backus, and KNIGHT'S GAMBIT ("Knight's Gambit"), where she appears as Mrs. Harriss.

Stillwell, Shuford H. Mink Snopes's fellow inmate at the Mississippi state penitentiary at PARCHMAN. A gambler, he is in prison for having cut the throat of a Vicksburg prostitute. In 1943, Stillwell escapes and in the attempt another inmate, Jake Barron, is killed by a guard. Because Mink did not go along with the plan, Stillwell blames him for Barron's death and threatens his life, forcing the warden not to consider parole for Mink. A few years later, however, Stillwell dies in a deconsecrated church when it collapses on him in the Mexican quarter of San Diego. Soon afterward, Mink is pardoned and goes free. As revealed in a conversation with the warden, Stillwell's death seems to be an expected consequence of Mink's absolute confidence in the judgment of God.

Strutterbuck, Captain   A patron at Miss Reba Rivers's brothel in MEMPHIS, where he meets Montgomery Ward Snopes. According to Reba, Strutterbuck is a veteran of two wars, the Spanish-American War and World War I. After his time with Thelma, one of the girls, Strutterbuck tries to skip out without paying but is stopped by Minnie and Reba. He hands Reba a two-dollar money order, but before she lets him out she tells him to button himself up.

Strutterbuck, Q'Milla   The name on the two-dollar money order that Captain Strutterbuck gives to Miss Reba Rivers. Wondering whether the money order is from his sister or daughter, Miss Reba asks her black maid Minnie to guess; she deems his wife.

Thelma   The new girl at Miss Reba Rivers's brothel in MEMPHIS. One of her first customers is Captain Strutterbuck, who almost cheats her out of her fee.

Triplett, Earl   He ran Uncle Ike McCaslin's hardware store until Jason Compson takes over. Earl took over the business from McCaslin as Jason, who started working there while in high school, would later take it over from Earl. *Also see The SOUND AND THE FURY.*

Tubbs, Euphus   The jailer in JEFFERSON. He tells Montgomery Ward Snopes, who has been jailed for having had five gallons of moonshine whiskey in his photography shop, that he is better off going to PARCHMAN (in Mississippi) instead of Atlanta because Parchman is closer and because "a native Missippi jailor can get the money" for his keep and not strangers in another state (*The Mansion*, 60). Tubbs takes advantage of Montgomery Ward's jail time by having him help out his wife in the kitchen

and the garden, and, trying to capitalize even more, Tubbs wants to release him before his bond is posted so he (Tubbs) can pocket the meal money. *Also see INTRUDER IN THE DUST and REQUIEM FOR A NUN.*

Tubbs, Miz (Mrs.)   Wife of Euphus Tubbs, JEFFERSON's jailor. To keep the early morning sun from waking Montgomery Ward Snopes, she hangs an old shade over his cell window. Tubbs has Montgomery Ward, who is waiting to be sentenced, help his wife in her kitchen and garden. *Also see INTRUDER IN THE DUST and REQUIEM FOR A NUN.*

Tull, Miz (Mrs.)   The person Mink Snopes assumes wrote the letter his wife sent to him in prison. *Also see AS I LAY DYING* (where her first name appears as Cora), *The HAMLET,* and the short story "SPOTTED HORSES," which Faulkner revised for *The Hamlet;* she is referred to in *The TOWN.*

Tull, Vernon   A minor offstage character in the novel. A genuinely kind and good-natured person, Tull is a farmer in the area of FRENCHMAN'S BEND. He (or Solon Quick or someone else) may have been the person who saw the last bear in the area scuttle across Will Varner's mill dam and into bushes and trees. *Also see AS I LAY DYING, The HAMLET, The TOWN,* and the short stories "SPOTTED HORSES," "THE HOUND," "LIZARDS IN JAMSHYD'S COURTYARD," "TWO SOLDIERS," and "SHINGLES FOR THE LORD."

Turpin   A young man in FRENCHMAN'S BEND. When he was trying to avoid the draft, Gavin Stevens and V. K. Ratliff looked for him at Mink Snopes's abandoned and run-down house. On their way to find Mink hiding there years later, Stevens and Ratliff recall the Turpin episode.

Varner, Jody (Uncle Jody)   A minor character in the novel, Jody is Will Varner's son, Eula Varner Snopes's older brother, and Linda Snopes Kohl's uncle. Still living at home, Jody is visited one afternoon by his niece and explains to her Flem Snopes's scheme to have Montgomery Ward Snopes sent to the state penitentiary at PARCHMAN and Flem's role in Mink Snopes's doomed attempt at escaping from prison dressed in what Jody characterized as MOTHER HUBBARD in a sunbonnet (*The Mansion*, 367). *Also see* AS I LAY DYING, LIGHT IN AUGUST, *The* HAMLET, *The* TOWN, and the short stories "FOOL ABOUT A HORSE" and "SPOTTED HORSES."

Varner, Miz (Mrs.) Will Varner's wife, mother of Jody and Eula Varner Snopes. Referred to in the novel as having given her husband the papers Linda signed so Flem can get the inheritance she would receive from her grandfather, Will Varner.

Varner, Will (Uncle Billy) A principal land-owner and businessman in FRENCHMAN'S BEND, sometimes referred to as Uncle Billy. He is the father of Jody and Eula Varner Snopes and the grandfather of Linda Snopes Kohl. The gallery of VARNER'S STORE is a hub for men in and around Frenchman's Bend to relax and talk. Among other things, Varner is the justice of the peace and actively involved in the politics of the county. He privately appoints Clarence Snopes as constable and then supervisor of Beat Two; later, through a talent for blackmail, Clarence becomes the county representative in Jackson, but loses Varner's support for U.S. Congress when V. K. Ratliff engineers an embarrassing prank against him; (*see* the entry on Clarence Eggleston Snopes above). For other details regarding Will Varner, *see* especially the first two novels of the SNOPES TRILOGY, *The* HAMLET *and The* TOWN; *also see* LIGHT IN AUGUST, INTRUDER IN THE DUST, and the short stories "SPOTTED HORSES," "LIZARDS IN JAMSHYD'S COURTYARD," "Tomorrow" (in KNIGHT'S GAMBIT), "SHINGLES FOR THE LORD" and "BY THE PEOPLE" (revised for *The Mansion*). Varner is referred to in AS I LAY DYING.

Vladimir Kyrilytch Referred to in *The Mansion*, he is V. K. Ratliff's patronymic ancestor who fought in General Burgoyne's army during the Revolutionary War battle at Saratoga in October 1777. Though he does not know his ancestor's last name, Ratliff explains to Gavin Stevens that after the British defeat at Saratoga the army was abandoned in Virginia without money or food. The first V. K., a Russian emigré, faced an additional difficulty because he did not know the language. He was hiding in a hayloft when Nelly Ratcliffe first saw him and started feeding him. After she became pregnant, they married, and he took her last name, which eventually became Ratliff. The oldest son of each successive generation is named Vladimir Kyrilytch and "spends half his life trying to keep anybody from finding it out" (*The Mansion*, 166).

Wesley (Wes), Uncle *See* Snopes, Wesley.

Wattman, Jakeleg A bootlegger who lives at Wyott's Crossing. To show her the route so she will know how to get there on her own, Gavin Stevens and V. K. Ratliff drive Linda Snopes Kohl to Jakeleg's so-called fishing camp for liquor.

Winbush, Fonzo A minor character in the novel. Fonzo is Grover Cleveland Winbush's nephew. With Virgil Snopes, he attends barber school in MEMPHIS. Upon their arrival in Memphis, the two country youths get a room at Miss Reba Rivers's brothel thinking it a boardinghouse. Montgomery Ward Snopes explains that Fonzo and Virgil heeded the advice of a Mrs. Winbush, who suggested that they stay at a house run by a Christian motherly type.

Winbush, Grover Cleveland With Flem Snopes, Grover is part owner of a sidestreet restaurant in JEFFERSON. After Flem forces him out of the restaurant business, Grover becomes Jefferson's night marshal, but when the town's drugstore is robbed he is fired for having been at one of Montgomery Ward Snopes's peep shows instead of patrolling the streets. *Also see The* TOWN *and The* HAMLET; in *The Hamlet*, this character's name appears as Aaron Rideout.

Winbush, Mrs. A woman who gives advice to Virgil Snopes and Fonzo Winbush. According to Montgomery Ward Snopes, she told Virgil and Fonzo before they left for barber school in MEMPHIS to rent a room from a mature, Christian, motherly woman. Unwittingly, the two naive youths ended up at Miss Reba Rivers's brothel.

FURTHER READING

Beck, Warren. *Man in Motion: Faulkner's Trilogy.* Madison: University of Wisconsin Press, 1961.

Brooks, Cleanth. "Faulkner's Revenger's Tragedy (*The Mansion*)." In *William Faulkner: The Yoknapatawpha Country,* 219–243. Baton Rouge: Louisiana State University Press, 1990.

Creighton, Joanne V. "The Dilemma of the Human Heart in *The Mansion.*" *Renascence: Essays on Value in Literature* 25 (1972): 35–45.

Kang, Hee. "A New Configuration of Faulkner's Feminine: Linda Snopes Kohl in *The Mansion.*" *Faulkner Journal* 8.1 (1992): 21–41.

Millgate, Michael. "*The Mansion.*" In *The Achievement of William Faulkner,* 245–252. Lincoln: University of Nebraska Press, 1978.

Polk, Noel. "Idealism in *The Mansion.*" In *Faulkner and Idealism: Perspectives from Paris,* edited by Michel Gresset and Patrick Samway, 112–126. Jackson: University Press of Mississippi, 1987.

Marble Faun, The

Faulkner's first published book, a pastoral poem of 19 eclogues, with a prologue and epilogue. The book's preface is by Faulkner's lifelong friend and onetime mentor, PHIL STONE. *The Marble Faun* was published by the FOUR SEAS COMPANY, Boston, in December 1924. One early reviewer, John McClure, writing in the *New Orleans Times-Picayune Magazine* (January 25, 1925, 16), commented that the best a young poet can achieve is failure with honor. In his opinion, this is the case with Faulkner, but the book is "rich in promise" and "successful in part." He is "a born poet, with remarkable ability," McClure observes, and, although the poem is not a complete success, it "contains scores of excellent passages." Years later, the critic CLEANTH BROOKS, although a bit harsher in his assessment, commented that the poem in several ways is "awkward and stumbling" but "there are occasional few passages of authentic poetry." The major shortcoming of *The Marble Faun,* Brooks argues, is that "the young poet is hag-ridden by the necessity of finding rhymes, and sometimes is forced into quasi-nonsense in his effort to come up with a rhyme. The meter fares not much better: often a line is metrically broken-backed" (*William Faulkner: Toward Yoknapatawpha and Beyond,* 6). Faulkner even judged himself a "failed poet." At the University of Virginia in 1957, for instance, he remarked: "I've often thought that I wrote the novels because I found I couldn't write the poetry, that maybe I wanted to be a poet, maybe I think of myself as a poet, and I failed at that, I couldn't write poetry, so I did the next best thing" (*Faulkner in the University,* 4; *also see Lion in the Garden,* edited by JAMES B. MERIWETHER and MICHAEL MILLGATE, 217). In a technical sense, Faulkner may have been a failed poet—that is, not a craftsman of verse—but he more than compensated in his prose for any failure, a prose extraordinarily poetic and suffused with a commanding cadence and rhythm.

Though Faulkner wrote most of the verses in *The Marble Faun* in 1919, a few years before they were published, he arranged them into a seasonal pattern and cycle of days and nights for their publication. The plaintive voice in the poems is that of the marble faun, mourning his imprisonment to dreams and sighs for things he knows, "yet cannot know" (prologue, line 32). The faun's reflections on beauty, art, nature, and youth within a pastoral setting unmistakably reveal Faulkner's indebtedness especially to romantic and symbolist poets of the late 19th century. Indebtedness to Keats's "Ode on a Grecian Urn" is also apparent, but unlike that ode, which elevates art above nature, *The Marble Faun,* as Brooks has pointed out, places life above art: "it is the inferiority of art to life that is stressed—'wild ecstasy' that has become frozen into a 'cold pastoral,' the unaging faun who has been turned into inanimate marble" (5). *The Marble Faun* has been reexamined by various critics and particularly by Judith L. Sensibar in *The Origins of Faulkner's Art.*

Marionettes, The

A play Faulkner wrote in the fall of 1920 for a UNIVERSITY OF MISSISSIPPI drama group called the

Marionettes. A one-act verse drama showing the influence of the symbolist movement of the late 19th century, it draws on elements of commedia dell'arte, or masked comedy, to relate a story of seduction and abandonment.

Faulkner produced six or eight hand-lettered copies of the play and illustrated it with 10 drawings by his own hand. Four copies survive. The biographer Frederick Karl judges *The Marionettes* not playable, and regards it as "a stillborn poem with strong visual effects." Faulkner withdrew from the university not long after completing the play.

Edited with an introduction by NOEL POLK, *The Marionettes: A Play in One Act* was published by the University Press of Virginia in 1977. (For more information, *see Selected Letters of William Faulkner*, 89, and Lothar Hönnighausen's essay "Faulkner's Graphic Work in Historical Context" in *Faulkner: International Perspectives*, 139–73.)

Mayday

A hand-lettered book that Faulkner wrote, illustrated, bound, and dedicated to HELEN BAIRD, with whom Faulkner was in love, and whom he wanted to marry, although she did not have the same feelings toward him. Faulkner dated the book "27 January, 1926." Edited with an introduction by CARVEL COLLINS, *Mayday* was published in 1976. Collins comments that Faulkner gave Baird "the only known copy" (3).

A fable of a young knight, Sir Galwyn of Arthgyl, *Mayday* is a story about a young man's search for the woman he is to love. After dismissing the three princesses he meets on his journey—Yseult, Elys, Aelia—the disillusioned Sir Galwyn finally encounters the woman he desires: Death. In his perceptive introduction, Collins discusses the historical and literary context behind the composition of *Mayday* and its place within Faulkner's writings. Collins also convincingly shows parallels between Sir Galwyn in this work and Quentin Compson in *The SOUND AND THE FURY*. One obvious parallel is their suicides by drowning.

"Mississippi"

Essay presenting a fictionalized memoir of the Falkner family's native place, published in *Holiday* magazine in 1954. The editors of the glossy travel-and-leisure magazine approached Faulkner about writing the essay in 1952, offering $2,000 for a 7,500-word piece.

As critics have noted, Faulkner used the dramatic method of *REQUIEM FOR A NUN* (1951) in the essay, opening with a prologue that recounts the history of Mississippi up to the time of the author's childhood. From there, "Mississippi" becomes autobiographical, with Faulkner appearing as "the boy." His African-American servants NED BARNETT and CAROLINE BARR (Mammy Callie) assume important roles in the narrative. Faulkner freely conceded that he introduced fictional details when he thought they would improve the story.

The concluding sections of "Mississippi" deal with Mammy Callie's decline and death and foreshadow Faulkner's own passing—nine years remained to him when he finished the essay in March 1953. Although he emphasized that he hated the racial intolerance, injustice, and inequality that mar so much of Mississippi's history, he ended with an expression of love for his home country. In a passage that recalls Quentin Compson in *The SOUND AND THE FURY* (1929), Faulkner wrote that he loved Mississippi not for its virtues but in spite of its faults.

Ned Barnett's tombstone, Ripley, Mississippi. *(Harriett and Gioia Fargnoli)*

Holiday published "Mississippi," which came in 3,000 words longer than the contract had stipulated, in April 1954.

Mississippi Poems

A minor collection of poems Faulkner presented in typescript to his friend Myrtle Ramey in December 1924. Faulkner revised eight of the 12 poems to include in A GREEN BOUGH, published in 1933. With an introduction by JOSEPH BLOTNER and an afterword by LOUIS DANIEL BRODSKY, *Mississippi Poems* was published posthumously in 1979 by Yoknapatawpha Press, Oxford, Mississippi, and was reissued in 1981 by Tulane University, New Orleans.

"Miss Zilphia Gant" (Uncollected Stories)

A short story first published separately as *Miss Zilphia Gant* in June 1932 by the Book Club of Texas (Dallas), with a preface by Henry Nash Smith, and later reprinted in UNCOLLECTED STORIES OF WILLIAM FAULKNER. For more information, *see Uncollected Stories of William Faulkner*, 700.

SYNOPSIS

The short story centers on the development of the title character, Miss Zilphia Gant, whose mother (Mrs. Gant) rears her as a virtual prisoner. In one respect, the main character is Zilphia's mother who passes on to her daughter her growing hatred of men and distrust of almost everyone. The genesis of Mrs. Gant's misanthropy is her husband Jim, a horse-trader who leaves her for another woman when Zilphia is a baby. Jim sends his hulking half-wit assistant to tell his wife that he is never coming back. When Mrs. Gant tracks down her unfaithful husband and his mistress in MEMPHIS, she kills them both with a borrowed pistol.

Three months later, Mrs. Gant sells her house and moves to JEFFERSON where she purchases a dressmaking shop. She lives with her daughter in a small room behind the shop and never lets her out until it is time for the girl to attend school. Even then she is reluctant to allow Zilphia any freedom. When Mrs. Gant finds Zilphia, now a teenager, lying with a boy in the woods, she takes her out of school and confines her once more to the dress shop. Zilphia becomes a seemingly docile young woman, while her mother grows less and less womanlike each passing day. When the dress shop is painted, Zilphia falls in love with the painter. They elope and are married before a justice of the peace. The itinerant painter urges Zilphia to go away with him and never see her overbearing mother again, but Zilphia cannot. Hand in hand, the newlyweds go back to the house where Mrs. Gant asserts her fierce power once again, driving off her son-in-law and imprisoning her daughter. When Mrs. Gant dies two days later, Zilphia starts running her mother's business. Expecting to hear from her husband, Zilphia waits six months, but receives no word. She then hires a detective to find him and discovers that he remarried. She also learns that her husband and his new wife had a baby, that the wife died in childbirth, and that the husband was hit and killed by a car. Zilphia goes away for three years and returns with a wedding band and a three-year-old child, whom she calls Zilphia. She rears the girl in the same room, with barred windows, in the back of the dressmaking shop that once belonged to her mother.

CRITICAL COMMENTARY

Although first published in 1932, "Miss Zilphia Gant" was written in 1928, and many critics see a connection between this early story and two later ones, "A ROSE FOR EMILY" and "DRY SEPTEMBER"; among other things, all three concern repressed sexuality, revenge, violence, and isolation. In "Miss Zilphia Gant," Faulkner introduces themes that recur in his other works.

CHARACTERS

Gant, Jim A horse and livestock trader who leaves his wife and baby daughter, Zilphia, to run off with the woman at the tavern, Mrs. Vinson; he intends never to return. His vindictive wife tracks Gant and his paramour down in MEMPHIS and kills them both.

Gant, Miss Zilphia (Zilphy)   The title character, Zilphia is the daughter of Jim Gant and his wife, who is referred to as Mrs. Gant throughout the short story. Mrs. Gant murders Zilphia's father for infidelity and displays a lifelong hatred and distrust of men. Unsuccessfully, Zilphia attempts to break away from her domineering mother. Even after Zilphia, without permission, marries a painter, her own neuroses force her to return to her mother, who drives off the husband and imprisons Zilphia once more. After her mother dies (two days after Zilphia's return), Zilphia waits for her husband to reappear, but he does not. She eventually hires a detective and discovers that her husband has gone to MEMPHIS and has remarried. When Zilphia finds out that her husband's wife died during childbirth and that the husband was killed by a car, she leaves town and returns three years later with a three-year-old daughter.

Gant, Mrs.   The domineering and vengeful mother in the short story, whose rage at having been left by her husband, Jim, leads her to find him and his mistress, Mrs. Vinson, in MEMPHIS, where she murders them both. She rears her daughter almost as a prisoner, attempting to keep her away from the opposite sex.

Vinson, Mrs.   A bartender in a tavern where stock traders gather. Mrs. Vinson induces the married Jim Gant to run off with her to MEMPHIS. Jim's wife, however, tracks the errant pair down and murders them.

"Mistral" (Collected Stories)

This short story first appeared in *These 13* (1931).

SYNOPSIS

"Mistral" concerns two young American hikers as they attempt to solve the mystery of what has taken place in a northern Italian village. In an atmosphere rife with gothic gloom, tolling bells, and the piercing cold wind (*mistral*), the two catch glimpses of the drama's protagonists: a beautiful girl, her soldier sweetheart, and her dead fiancé in his coffin. They meet only briefly with the main figure,

the girl's guardian and village priest, who is in a state of agony. The revelation of the ambiguous events through fragments of gossip and the hikers' own questionable conjectures is hindered by the prejudices and dissimulations of their informants, a shifting language barrier, and probably by their own ever-increasing inebriation.

What emerges is the possibility that the priest attempted to sever the attachment between the girl and her sweetheart by arranging to have the young man drafted into the army. He then manipulated a rich man into becoming engaged to the girl, although she was able to delay the wedding for three years. When the soldier finally was due to return, the priest forced the marriage to take place, but on its eve the fiancé died, perhaps of poison. The perpetrator of this deed may have been the soldier's aunt, who left the church when her nephew was drafted. Some villagers attribute the priest's spiritual torment to his lustful passion for his ward, but it may be due instead to his recognition that his unethical machinations have led to a man's death, have cost him the respect and loyalty of his parishioners, and have compromised his mission as a man of God. In the end, the truth remains obscure as the two travelers move on, fortified by yet another swig of brandy.

CRITICAL COMMENTARY

According to James Ferguson, "the basic narrative strategy" of this short story is similar to Faulkner's story, "Snow": Both concentrate on "the attempts by two young men to piece together elaborate and ominous mysteries." The focus on resolving a mystery appears in other works, and, as Ferguson rightly observes, "clearly fascinated Faulkner and was to receive its most elaborate embodiment in his masterpiece, *Absalom, Absalom!*" (*Faulkner's Short Fiction*, 31).

CHARACTERS

Cavalcanti   Family name in the short story. Giulio Farinzale's aunt, who keeps a wineshop on the edge of town, is a Cavalcanti.

Don   He appears in both this short story and its companion piece, "Snow." A young American, he and the American friend who narrates the story become mixed up in a complicated situation involving a priest, a girl, and her lover in an Italian village during the season of the mistral.

Farinzale, Giulio Returning from a tour in the army, Giulio intends to reclaim his girlfriend, a wild young woman and a ward of the village priest. The priest had arranged for her betrothal to a rich young man of the parish.

"Moonlight" (Uncollected Stories)

A posthumously published short story about the relationship between two teenagers, and the failure of one to seduce the other.

SYNOPSIS

Displaying a carefree and humorous depiction of youthful uncertainty, "Moonlight" concerns an attempted seduction of a 16-year-old girl, Susan, by the unnamed protagonist, also 16. The protagonist, smarting from the humiliation of being literally kicked off Susan's premises by her uncle and guardian, Mr. Burchett, wants both to seduce Susan—although he does not seem too sure what seduction actually entails—and to take revenge against her uncle. Susan sends the protagonist a note saying that she will meet him surreptitiously and be his for the night. He sends his best friend Skeet to fetch Susan. After the two meet and after some kissing, the protagonist realizes that all Susan wants to do is go to a show. She drinks none of the moonshine whiskey that he brought and resists his clumsy seduction attempt. "Moonlight" ends with the protagonist quieting the frightened Susan. As she is clinging to him saying that he scared her he feels nothing, "no despair, no regret, not even surprise" (*Uncollected Stories*, 503), and even his thoughts are elsewhere.

CRITICAL COMMENTARY

"Moonlight" is a moody, but poetic, and in many ways amusing, short story about young love. Unlike other unfinished sketches published after Faulkner

died, this piece is a fully realized story. According to Faulkner, the first and earlier version of "Moonlight" (a 16-page typescript) was written sometime between 1919 and 1921 and is perhaps the first short story Faulkner ever wrote (*see* JAMES B. MERIWETHER, *The Literary Career of William Faulkner*, 87). JOSEPH BLOTNER points out that the version published in *Uncollected Stories*, a 14-page typescript, is "much closer to the mature style of Faulkner than the 16-page version which may represent its earliest form after the manuscript" (*Uncollected Stories of William Faulkner*, 706). For more information, *see* UNCOLLECTED STORIES OF WILLIAM FAULKNER, 706, and Diane Brown Jones, *A Reader's Guide to the Short Stories of William Faulkner*, 142–43, 144, 178.

CHARACTERS

Burchett, Mr. Susan's uncle and guardian. Mr. Burchett catches Susan and her young beau fumbling and kissing in the hammock and drives the boy off with kicks and blows. (*Also see* the short story "HAIR.")

Burchett Mrs. (Aunt Etta) Susan's aunt. Susan tells her aunt that she is going to a show with her friend Skeet when she actually plans to meet her boyfriend (the unnamed protagonist), whom she has been told not to see again. (*Also see* the short story "HAIR.")

Susan The 16-year-old girlfriend of the unnamed protagonist. Told by her uncle and guardian, Mr. Burchett, not to see her boyfriend, Susan disobeys, writes a provocative note to her beau saying that she will clandestinely meet him and be his for the night. But all she really wants to do is have him take her to a show in town. When they meet at an empty house, she fights off his amorous advances and becomes hysterical. (*Also see* the short story "HAIR," where an orphan by the name of Susan Reed lives with Burchett and his wife.)

Skeet The 16-year-old friend of the unnamed protagonist in the short story. The unnamed protagonist offers Skeet moonshine whiskey to help arrange a clandestine meeting with his girlfriend Susan.

unnamed protagonist Susan's 16-year old friend who is set on seducing her. When one night the two rendezvous, his clumsy attempt fails and actually frightens Susan to the point of hysterics. He is finally able to calm her.

Mosquitoes

Faulkner's second novel, published in April 1927, is a work of apprenticeship, derivative, uneven, and tedious in places, though critics agree that it foreshadows the powerfully original fiction that followed.

"*Mosquitoes* is Faulkner's least respected novel and it is very easy to see why," wrote the critic CLEANTH BROOKS. "There is almost no story line; nothing of real consequence happens to any of its characters." Brooks adds, however, that the novel does show Faulkner's "zest for language and his power to handle it."

Faulkner wrote most of the book in the summer of 1926 in the Gulf Coast resort of PASCAGOULA, MISSISSIPPI. Living and working conditions were pleasant. His room in the spacious seafront cottage of PHILIP STONE's family came equipped with a daybed, a chair, and a table for his portable typewriter. But he often worked outdoors, on one of the wooden benches that curved around the big live oaks in front of the place. Faulkner wrote a first draft on plain white paper, in a tiny script, striking off a fair copy on the typewriter when he reached the end of a section. He worked for several hours early in the morning, took a long break in the heat of the day, and went back to the manuscript for a stretch in the afternoon.

SYNOPSIS

In *Mosquitoes*, Faulkner assembles a gallery of ill-matched characters for a sailing party aboard the yacht *Nausikaa* in Lake Ponchartrain outside NEW ORLEANS. The protagonist, Ernest Talliaferro, a wholesale buyer of women's clothing, is a widower approaching middle age whose clumsy attempts at ingratiating himself with women invariably fail. Faulkner biographer JOSEPH BLOTNER and others see echoes of Eliot's ineffectual Prufrock from

the poem "The Love Song of J. Alfred Prufrock"; Brooks calls him "a kind of cultural flunky and go-between" for the dilettantish Patricia Maurier, a wealthy New Orleans matron with artistic interests. Dawson Fairchild, an Indiana novelist, is patently modeled on SHERWOOD ANDERSON. Gordon (no surname given) is a sculptor with little to say; his is the only work for which there is any evidence of serious artistic ability. Gordon might be a fictionalized version of Faulkner's New Orleans friend WILLIAM SPRATLING. Mark Frost is a poet who talks a lot and produces very little. Critic MICHAEL MILLGATE has suggested Frost might be a satirical Faulkner self-portrait. Patricia Robyn, Mrs. Maurier's epicene niece, is an early Faulkner type, suggesting Faulkner's love interest of about this time, HELEN BAIRD, to whom *Mosquitoes* is dedicated. Patricia boards *Nausikaa* with her twin brother, Theodore Robyn, known as Josh and sometimes Gus, and with a working-class couple she has picked up in the French Quarter, the lush and disturbing Jenny Steinbauer and her boyfriend Pete Ginotta, whose brother is a bootlegger. Dorothy Jameson, a painter, prefers still lifes to portraits and is rather desperate for a man. Eva Wiseman is a poet; Faulkner takes her work seriously. Her brother Julius, whose last name is hinted at as Kauffman, is called "the Semitic man" more often than not, and is an articulate if obsessive literary theorist. Major Ayers, a stage Englishman, promotes a remedy for constipation. David West is somewhat miscast as the yacht's steward.

Mosquitoes opens on an evening in August with Talliaferro delivering an invitation to join the yachting party to the studio of the sculptor Gordon. The characters gather. *Nausikaa* floats gently out into Lake Ponchartrain in a cloud of mosquitoes whose constant buzzing suggests the conversation on board. The yacht runs aground. Patricia and the steward West slip away in a small boat and wander about for hours in a swamp, but thirst, heat, and mosquitoes drive them back to the *Nausikaa*. Brooks speculates on the significance of the title insect (incidentally, never mentioned by name in the text) in his study of Faulkner's early work, *Toward Yoknapatawpha and Beyond* (1978): "My guess is that they stand for the unpredictable and annoying aspects of reality that human beings have to reckon with." At any rate, one character or another is usually slapping at one.

The characters divide into groups: the older men, who do a lot of drinking among themselves; the older women, who play cards listlessly; and the younger members of the party, who inhabit a self-centered world of their own. Patricia Maurier ineffectually tries to organize dancing to the Victrola. There is lots of windy chatter. There is action of a sort too: Talliaferro's clumsy efforts to attract Jenny; Dorothy Jameson's attempted seduction of Pete Ginotta; Patricia Robyn's elopement with David West; an equivocal scene in a bunk involving Patricia and Jenny, portions of which the publisher cut from the original manuscript.

After four days, the *Nausikaa* returns to New Orleans. The party disperses, and Gordon, Fairchild, and Kauffman wander the city's red light district, a scene strongly suggestive of the Circe episode in JAMES JOYCE's *Ulysses* (1922). *Mosquitoes* ends as it began, with Talliaferro alone, though Faulkner suggests Mrs. Maurier somehow has entrapped him into a promise of marriage.

CRITICAL COMMENTARY

Many critics characterize *Mosquitoes* as a *roman à clef*; Faulkner draws scenes and characters more or less directly from his life in the artistic community in the Vieux Carré of New Orleans in the early 1920s. It is self-consciously a novel of ideas, according to Joseph Blotner. *Mosquitoes* is full of talk, most of it circling around two inexhaustible topics, literature and sex. One of the characters even complains of the incessant drone. Eva Wiseman, tiring of Fairchild's interminable tall tale about fish farmers with webbed feet, says finally: "Dawson, shut up. We simply cannot stand any more" (88). Blotner, Brooks, and others identify T. S. Eliot, James Joyce, Aldous Huxley (*Chrome Yellow*, 1921) and D. H. Lawrence (*Women in Love*, 1920) as Faulkner's chief literary influences. Some of the content is daring for its time. Faulkner mentions masturbation, conception, constipation, evacuation, lesbianism, syphilis, and perversion in the course of the novel's 349 pages. He also indulges in artistic name-dropping: Byron, Shelley, Swinburne, Ibsen, Chopin, Grieg, Sibelius.

Faulkner uses a commonplace device, of the sort familiar to readers of English country house murder mysteries, to gather his characters: he brings a mixed group together for a cruise on *Nausikaa* under the aegis of Mrs. Maurier. The characters are thus conveniently captive in one place for as long as the novelist requires them. The structure of *Mosquitoes* is simple. A prologue introduces the characters. Sections titled "The First Day" through "The Fourth Day" follow. The time of day captions the subsections. An epilogue in which the characters scatter closes the novel.

Faulkner develops a theme of the aridity of talk; his characters divide, too, into those who act and those who reflect. For all her passivity, Jenny exerts a powerful attraction over the men and women of the yachting party, a form of action. By land, her boyfriend Pete delivers contraband liquor in a powerful car. The sculptor Gordon has little to say; he spanks the bratty Patricia Robyn rather than lectures her, and allows his work in marble to speak for him. The talkers—Talliaferro, Fairchild, Kauffman—do little but create constellations of words. As narrator, Faulkner makes clear where he stands:

"Talk, talk, talk: the utter and heartbreaking stupidity of words. It seemed endless, as though it might go on forever. Ideas, thoughts, became mere sounds to be bandied about until they were dead" (186).

Faulkner's execution of the talk is a weakness of *Mosquitoes*. He has not yet fully developed his remarkable ear for patterns, nuances and idioms of speech; the dialogue sounds forced, clumsy in places. The humor often is strained, adolescent—for example, Fairchild's irritating running gag about the serving of grapefruit with every meal. That said, Faulkner provides relief from the talk with occasional fine lyrical passages that hint at the glories to come.

What will become a Faulknerian habit of borrowing and recycling from his earlier works, published and unpublished, is much in evidence here. He lifts an image of New Orleans as "an aging and yet still beautiful courtesan" from one of the NEW ORLEANS SKETCHES in *The DOUBLE DEALER*. He shanghais the characters of Talliaferro, Fairchild, and Jenny Steinbauer from the unpublished short story "DON GIOVANNI."

Most significantly, Faulkner begins to develop the means by which he will telescope the universal into the local in the greater works of YOKNAPATAWPHA COUNTY, his "little postage stamp of native soil." Julius Kauffman states the aesthetic briefly by remarking that life essentially is the same everywhere.

CRITICAL RECEPTION

Faulkner finished *Mosquitoes* in Pascagoula on September 1, 1926, except for revisions. In OXFORD, MISSISSIPPI, Phil Stone's law office provided typing services, and Faulkner mailed the completed manuscript to publisher HORACE LIVERIGHT in New York before the end of the month. Editors there deleted four substantial passages, including a two-page stretch of Fairchild conversation that equated writing with perversion, and the cabin-bunk scene hinting at lesbianism involving Patricia Robyn and Jenny Steinbauer. They corrected his punctuation, too.

The publication date was April 30, 1927. The first reviews appeared in mid-June. CONRAD AIKEN wrote the first major one, for the *New York Evening Post*, which praised the characters and dialogue. In the *New York World*, Ruth Suckow reported that the writing was occasionally good, "when it isn't Joyce," but the "all too recognizable mixture of suavity, brilliance, cynicism, tragedy, philosophy, obscenity, pure nature and thoughts on art" did not greatly impress her.

MAUD BUTLER FALKNER once said *Mosquitoes* earned her novelist son about $400. It was true that the book did not sell especially well. By the end of 1930, combined sales of *Mosquitoes* and Faulkner's first novel, SOLDIERS' PAY, were a little short of 4,000 copies.

Faulkner himself turned against the novel not long after its publication, calling it "trashily smart." MALCOLM COWLEY would judge *Mosquitoes* a very bad early novel. Faulkner took a more generous view toward the end of his long literary career. "If I could write that over," he told students at the University of Virginia, "I probably wouldn't write it at all. I'm not ashamed of it, because that was the chips, the badly sawn planks that the carpenter produces while he's learning to be a first-rate carpenter" (*Faulkner in the University*, 257).

CHARACTERS

Ayers, Major A florid Briton with ill-fitting false teeth, he is one of Dawson Fairchild's drinking companions on Mrs. Patricia Maurier's yacht *Nausikaa*. For "certain private reasons" (304), possibly a criminal matter, Ayers seems unable to return to Britain.

Ayers is continually alert to merchandising possibilities. In the novel's epilogue, Major Ayers consults with the businessman Mr. Reichman about selling salts (a laxative) to Americans, for he thinks "all Americans are constipated" (304).

Broussard He owns the New Orleans restaurant that the novelist Dawson Fairchild patronizes.

Ed The captain of Patricia Maurier's yacht, *Nausikaa*, he grudgingly gives the Robyn twins a tour of the yacht's engine room and explains the workings of the engine to the mechanically minded Theodore Robyn.

Fairchild, Dawson A novelist with a taste for mischief, Fairchild is the malicious guiding spirit of the yachting party aboard the *Nausikaa*. Burly, "forty-odd" years old and a native of Indiana, he resembles a "deceptively sedate walrus of middle age" (80).

Fairchild is fond of his own voice and has a habit of riding a joke too hard, as with his running commentary on Mrs. Maurier's insistence on serving grapefruit with every meal. His friend Julius Kauffman regards him as an "emotional eunuch" (137). All the same, Ernest Talliaferro considers him as an authority on love. Fairchild prankishly urges the inexperienced Talliaferro to be forceful with women. Talliaferro tries out the new attitude, but women are not impressed.

Faulkner A sunburned, shabbily dressed, self-confessed professional liar, he tells the voluptuous Genevieve (Jenny) Steinbauer that if the straps of her dress were to break she'd "devastate the country" (145).

Frost, Mark Frost is a "ghostly young man, a poet who produced an occasional cerebral and obscure poem in four or seven lines" (54). He spends most of his time abstractedly smoking cigarettes. Frost calls on Miss Dorothy Jameson after the yacht trip and misses an amorous opportunity when, not long after she has retired to her bedroom to change into something more comfortable, he dashes out of her house to catch a streetcar.

Ginotta   The father of Joe and Pete Ginotta, he regrets his sons' Americanization of his modest New Orleans Italian restaurant; they convert it into a speakeasy.

Ginotta, Joe   The 25-year-old son of an Italian restaurateur, Ginotta, he refurbishes the family restaurant in New Orleans and converts it into a nightclub. Shrewd and taciturn, Joe also runs a profitable bootlegging business on the side.

Ginotta, Mrs.   The deaf and silent wife of Ginotta, she is reduced after his death to pottering about the modernized kitchen of the family restaurant, preparing Italian dishes for her Americanized sons. She refuses to enter the brassy speakeasy her son Joe has developed.

Ginotta, Pete   A flashy young man with "queer golden eyes" (300), he delivers liquor for his bootlegger brother, Joe Ginotta. With his girlfriend, Jenny Steinbauer, he goes aboard the *Nausikaa* at Patricia Robyn's invitation. Pete seems a misfit on the yachting party; when he first boards, Mrs. Maurier mistakes him for the steward.

Gordon   An artist and sculptor with a red beard, icy blue eyes and "face like that of a heavy hawk" (12), he joins the *Nausikaa* yachting party out of an interest in Patricia Robyn. After the yachting trip, Gordon makes a bust of Patricia Maurier that so effectively captures her essence that his friends regard it with astonishment.

Hooper   A businessman and Rotarian with the face of a "thwarted Sunday school superintendent" (34), he arranges to have lunch with the novelist Dawson Fairchild to satisfy his curiosity about NEW ORLEANS bohemian life.

Helmsman, the   The unnamed steersman of Mrs. Maurier's yacht *Nausikaa*, he predicts rough weather for the next day on the first night out in the lake.

Jackson, Al   He is a character in one of Dawson Fairchild's fabulous tales, a web-footed descendant of Andrew Jackson who with his father runs the largest fish ranch in the world. He wears congress boots to hide his unusual feet.

Jackson, Claude   He is the brother of fish rancher Al Jackson in Dawson Fairchild's fantasy story. Claude turns into a shark while herding amphibious sheep and becomes notorious for chasing blonde women swimmers off Gulf Coast beaches.

Jackson, Old Man   A character in a Dawson Fairchild tale, he is a descendant of Andrew Jackson and is the father of Al and Claude Jackson. A one-time bookkeeper, he becomes a fish rancher when the sheep on his swampy Louisiana estate turn gradually into fish.

Jameson, Dorothy   A member of the *Nausikaa* yachting party, she is a portrait painter who works in a "bold humorless style" (101), a reckless driver, and a virgin who is desperate for success with men.

Dorothy tries to arrange a date with the bootlegger Pete Ginotta but drives him off with her abrupt intensity. Then, when the yacht returns to NEW ORLEANS, she attempts to seduce the poet Mark Frost, who flees in alarm at her approach.

Kauffman, Julius (1)   He is the "Semitic man," the worldly, sophisticated brother of the poet Eva Wiseman. Kauffman and the novelist Dawson Fairchild are close friends and drinking companions; Kauffman pokes fun of Fairchild's circle of self-conscious artists.

It is unclear why Faulkner refers to him only as the Semitic man, withholding his name till late in the novel.

Kauffman, Julius (2)   The grandfather of Julius Kauffman (1), he helped old Maurier, the defunct husband of the owner of the yacht *Nausikaa*, make a series of lucrative "but rather raw" land deals under the Yankee occupation of NEW ORLEANS during the Civil War.

Maurier   A one-time plantation overseer, he makes or steals a fortune during the Civil War, enabling him to acquire the estate on which he had been the prewar "head servant" and eventually to win the hand of Patricia Maurier. She dutifully gives up the boy she loves to marry him for his ill-gotten fortune.

Maurier, Patricia   The wealthy, Northern-born widow of the Civil War profiteer Maurier, she recklessly gathers together a party of artists for a cruise aboard her yacht, the *Nausikaa*. Mrs. Maurier seeks out the company of artists without really understanding what they are about; in consequence, the party is a social disaster.

Julius Kauffman (1) narrates the tragedy of her life to Dawson Fairchild and the sculptor Gordon: She gave up the penniless boy she loved to marry Maurier's fortune. Once a beauty, Mrs. Maurier has an aging double-chinned face that characteristically wears an "expression of infantile astonishment." (17) But Gordon captures her essence in a sculpture that shows "something thwarted back of it all." (326)

Reichman   Major Ayers approaches Reichman for financial backing for the laxative he hopes to launch in the American market. The narrative does not indicate whether Reichman invested in the product.

Robyn, Henry   He is the father of Patricia Robyn and Theodore Robyn and the brother of Patricia Maurier. His daughter calls him Hank.

Robyn, Patricia   The thin, boyish, slangy and absent-mindedly provocative niece of Patricia Maurier, she slips off to Mandeville with David West, the *Nausikaa*'s steward who has fallen in love with her, when the yacht runs aground. They are lost in a swamp for a time and made miserable by swarms of mosquitoes, and their adventure goes nowhere. "It's a mess, David," she tells him. "I didn't know it was going to be like this" (212). When they return

to the *Nauskikaa*, the lovelorn West quits his steward's job and disappears.

Robyn, Theodore (Gus; Josh)   He is Patricia Robyn's mechanically minded twin brother. Robyn detaches a piece of the *Nausikaa*'s machinery to make a tobacco pipe, an inadvertent sabotage of the steering gear that causes the yacht to run aground.

His sister's attentions annoy him; he erupts when she insists she is going north to Yale with him in September.

Roy   He is a boyfriend of Jenny Steinbauer's friend Thelma.

Steinbauer, Genevieve (Jenny)   She and her boyfriend, Pete Ginotta, are members of the *Nausikaa* yachting party, present by the invitation of the impulsive Patricia Robyn, who met Jenny while buying a bathing suit. She and Pete hardly fit in with the others. Pete is associated with bootleggers, and Jenny is neither artistic nor intelligent, though her sexual allure—her sleepy manner and "vague ripe prettiness" (56)—is disturbing to the men aboard the yacht and to Patricia and Dorothy Jameson, too.

Talliaferro, Ernest   A northern Alabama native whose real name is Tarver, he is a 38-year-old widower with thinning hair, a former clerk in the women's clothing section of a department store. Forty-one days in Europe have given Talliaferro a "worldly air and a smattering of esthetics and a precious accent" (33). With this veneer, he rises to the position of factotum to the wealthy Mrs. Maurier.

Talliaferro admits to the sex instinct as his "most dominating compulsion" (9), but he is a failure with women. He decides he's too nice to them, and must learn to "dominate them from the start" (348). The novelist Dawson Fairchild advises Talliaferro mischievously about women, with results wounding to his self-esteem.

Thelma   A friend of Jenny Steinbauer, she witnesses a drowning at the swimming and dancing resort of Mandeville. Jenny mentions her to Patricia Robyn.

Walter (1)   He is Patricia Maurier's industrious African-American servant, "a yellow negro in a starched jacket" (46).

Walter (2)   He is a member of the tugboat crew that pulls the grounded yacht *Nausikaa* off the mud.

West, David   A young drifter from Indiana; "just traveling around" (123) he finds work as steward aboard the yacht *Nausikaa*, where he falls in love with Patricia Robyn after she half-consciously encourages him. They flee the yacht together but become lost and discouraged; Patricia makes her feelings—or rather the lack of them—clear to him. When they return, David vanishes.

Wiseman, Eva Kauffman   The elder sister of Julius Kauffman who has discarded an unsatisfactory husband, she is the author of a volume of verse titled *Satyricon in Starlight*, which Major Ayers derides as "the syphilis book" because he regards it as risque.

All the same, Mrs. Wiseman seems a sensible woman, the only grown-up aboard the *Nausikaa* (for instance, she tires easily of Dawson Fairchild's childish humor), and the men of the yachting party are fond of her.

FURTHER READING

Arnold, Edwin T. *Annotations to William Faulkner's Mosquitoes.* New York: Garland, 1989.

Brooks, Cleanth. "A Fine Volley of Words (*Mosquitoes*)." In *William Faulkner: Toward Yoknapatawpha and Beyond*, 129–151. Baton Rouge: Louisiana State University Press, 1990.

Wittenberg, Judith Bryant. "Configurations of the Female and Textual Politic in *Mosquitoes*." *Faulkner Studies* 1.1 (1991): 1–19.

LaLonde, Christopher A. "*Mosquitoes* and the Rites of Passage: Making Space and Time." In *William Faulkner and the Rites of Passage*, 37–64. Macon, Ga.: Mercer University Press, 1995.

Millgate, Michael. "*Mosquitoes*." In *The Achievement of William Faulkner*, 68–75. Lincoln: University of Nebraska Press, 1978.

"Mr. Acarius"

A short story about an idealist, Mr. Acarius, who has the odd notion that to experience humanity or the human condition at its grittiest, he needs to be committed to a hospital ward for alcoholics. He asks his old friend and doctor, Ab Cochrane, for advice in this pursuit, and they arrange for him to be admitted to an expensive private clinic. To get there, he goes on a binge reminiscent of his college days. Though an idealist, Mr. Acarius is also a wealthy collector and a snob. He speaks of his Picassos and drinks only the finest scotch. Once in the ward, however, Mr. Acarius finds himself not in touch with reality or the human condition as he imagined it to be but instead cooped up with self-destructive liars and manipulators who are escaping from life and incapable of dealing with its complications and vicissitudes. Unable to bear the situation he had created for himself, Mr. Acarius escapes from the hospital. Once outside, he is stopped by the police. In the nick of time, his doctor intercedes and helps his patient to his apartment in an upper-class neighborhood, where the first thing Mr. Acarius does is to pour his supply of liquor down the drain.

CRITICAL COMMENTARY

A humorous story that reflects, perhaps, Faulkner's own bouts with alcoholism, "Mr. Acarius" has been described by James Ferguson as having "some psychological and biographical interest, but it is unpleasantly frenetic and uncontrolled, certainly one of the strangest stories he ever wrote" (*Faulkner's Short Fiction*, 46). Originally entitled "Weekend Revisited" (a title evocative of F. Scott Fitzgerald's short story "Babylon Revisited" [1931]), "Mr. Acarius" was written in early 1953 but published posthumously, first in the *Saturday Evening Post* 238 (October 9, 1965), and later in UNCOLLECTED STORIES OF WILLIAM FAULKNER.

CHARACTERS

Acarius, Mr.   Main character in the short story. In order to experience the depths of humanity and to be one with it, which includes its debasement, Mr. Acarius convinces his doctor to admit him to a clinic for alcoholics. While there, he is disillusioned by his fellow drunks and their machinations. He leaves the clinic and vows never to drink again.

Cochrane, Dr. Ab   A medical doctor with a wry sense of humor. Dr. Cochrane admits the title character, Mr. Acarius, into a clinic for alcoholics at his own request to identify with humanity's suffering souls. Upset with what he finds, the idealist Mr. Acarius flees from the hospital, and when he is stopped by the police, Dr. Cochrane intervenes and takes his patient home, where Mr. Acarius admits to his misconception about humanity.

Goldie   The serious-minded nurse in the short story.

Hill, Dr.   The physician in charge of the clinic in the short story.

Lester, Miss Judy   Watkins's girlfriend. She smuggles half-pint bottles of whiskey into the clinic for alcoholics by hiding them in her brassiere.

Miller   Alcoholic patient of Dr. Hill in the short story. He arranges for liquor to be smuggled into the clinic in the brassiere of Miss Judy Lester, a visitor.

Watkins   One of the inmates in the clinic. His girlfriend, Miss Judy Lester, smuggles booze to the patients by hiding half-pint bottles in her brassiere.

"Mule in the Yard" (*Collected Stories*)

A short story first published in SCRIBNER'S MAGA-ZINE, 96 (August 1934), 65–70 and later, in 1950, in COLLECTED STORIES OF WILLIAM FAULKNER. The story was significantly revised and incorporated in chapter 16 of the second volume of the SNOPES TRIL-OGY, THE TOWN. For more information, *see Selected Letters of William Faulkner,* 79, 197, 274, 278, and 304, and Diane Brown Jones, *A Reader's Guide to the Short Stories of William Faulkner,* 248–59.

SYNOPSIS

The short story is about Mrs. Mannie Hait outwitting the scheming mule trader I. O. Snopes, with whom her late husband had worked before losing his life in one of Snopes's scams. When Snopes's mules get loose in Mrs. Hait's yard, one kicks over the bucket of smoldering ashes that Mrs. Hait leaves by the open cellar door to run after the animals. The house catches on fire and burns down. But instead of suing Snopes, Mrs. Hait offers to buy the offending mule for $10, an amount $50 less than what the railroad paid Snopes for each mule that was killed on the tracks 10 years before in a swindle. Mrs. Hait is evening the score, for her husband died tying Snopes's mules to the tracks and Snopes never paid Hait's widow what he owed Hait. When Snopes argues that the mule is worth $150, Mrs. Hait calmly tells him that he can claim the mule up the road a piece where she hid it. After he leaves, Mrs. Hait's friend old Het asks what she did with the mule and learns that she shot it. Het happily remarks, "'Dat's whut I calls justice'" (*Collected Stories,* 264).

CRITICAL COMMENTARY

"Mule in the Yard," according to MICHAEL MILL-GATE, "one of Faulkner's greatest comic *tours de force,* has its furious crescendoes of farcical activity" (*The Achievement of William Faulkner,* 236). The ironic pattern of Mannie Hait's victory over a Snopes significantly adds to the humor, for she uses tactics not unlike those used by Snopes, one of which is deception. This short story can also be seen, as John T. Matthews argues, as an example of the empowerment of woman in the male market (*see* "Shortened Stories: Faulkner and the Market," in Evans Harrington and Ann J. Abadie, editors, *Faulkner and the Short Story,* 29–35).

CHARACTERS

Hait   An offstage character, he is Mrs. Hait's deceased husband who conspired with I. O. Snopes in a scam to have mules killed on train tracks in order to collect damages from the railroad companies. Ironically, Hait himself loses his life when tying mules to the tracks, but his wife receives a substantial payment from the railroad. Hait is also referred to in *The Town* and *The Mansion* where his first name, Lonzo, is given.

Hait, Mrs. (Mannie)   Hait's widow and main character in the short story who gets even with the conniving I. O. Snopes. She received $8,500 from the railroad company when her husband was killed by a train as he was tying Snopes's mules to the tracks; the two (Snopes and Hait) were scheming to be awarded damages. The stingy Snopes never paid Mrs. Hait what he would have given her husband. When Mrs. Hait's house burns down as a result of the scuttle of hot ashes having been knocked over by one of Snopes's loose mules running wild through her yard, she does not sue him. Instead, she offers to buy the mule for $10, $50 less than what the railroad paid him for each mule that was killed on the tracks 10 years earlier. Snopes, of course, rejects the offer, and when he asks where the mule is Mrs. Hait tells him, and he leaves. But she had already settled the score by having shot the animal. *Also see The Town.*

Het (Old Het)   African-American character in the short story. Het is the first to notice that the scuttle of live ashes is not by the open cellar door of Mrs. Hait's house and the first to smell smoke. Knowing that the house is burning, she warns Mrs. Hait to get her money out. *Also see The Town.*

Snopes, I. O.   Mrs. Hait's adversary. One of Snopes's mules that run loose into Mrs. Hait's yard kicks over a bucket of hot ashes setting her house on fire. Snopes takes no responsibility for her loss. Ten years before, he schemed with her husband to tie his (Snopes's) mules to railroad tracks to assure that they would be killed by an on-coming train. Although receiving $60 a mule, Snopes paid Hait only $50 even though several were killed at a time. When Hait himself was killed along with five mules, Snopes never paid Hait's widow the money he would have given her husband. She, however, received $8,500 as compensation, and 10 years later (the time period of "Mules in the Yard"), Snopes still believes that the money, or at least a portion of · it, should have gone to him. By the end of the short story, Snopes is outwitted by Mrs. Hait.

I. O. Snopes appears as a minor character in several other works: *The Sound and the Fury*, *The Hamlet*, *Father Abraham* (fragment of a novel incorporated into *The Hamlet*), *The Town*, and the short story "Spotted Horses"; he is also referred to in *The Mansion*.

Spilmer   A neighbor of Mrs. Hait. The ravine ditch behind Splimer's is where Mrs. Hait takes and shoots Snopes's mule. *Also see The Town.*

"My Grandmother Millard and General Bedford Forrest and the Battle of Harrykin Creek" (Collected Stories)

Comic short story that first appeared in *Story* (March–April 1943). It is closely related to the Sartoris family chronicles in *The Unvanquished*.

SYNOPSIS

Set during the Civil War era, this story recounts a legendary Sartoris family episode. Granny Rosa Millard, an accomplished strategist, saves the family treasures from the Yankees, outwits the wily horse thief Ab Snopes, and manipulates the Confederate General Nathan Bedford Forrest into allowing a besotted young couple to wed. The narrator, Bayard Sartoris, recalls the events he witnessed as a boy, beginning with Granny's repeated rehearsals of burying their silver. This plan is thwarted when the Yankees arrive suddenly; Cousin Melisandre instead is sent to hide with the trunk in the outhouse. The marauders shatter the privy with a battering ram but are chased off single-handedly by a Confederate officer, Philip Backhouse. He is smitten with the young woman, who is unhurt, and comically preens himself for their formal introduction. She finds him attractive, but when she hears his name, a coarse reminder of her recent fright, she renounces any future between them. With the complicity of General Forrest, the recklessly courageous Backhouse is declared dead in the made-up

Harrykin Creek battle and is replaced by one Lieutenant Philip Backus. Thus the marriage can take place.

CRITICAL COMMENTARY

This wildly comic and even slightly bawdy tale demonstrates the influence of the Southwestern yarnspining tradition upon Faulkner. The tale's sole serious note is an ironic consideration of the word *freedom* and of its differing meanings for the family slaves and for the white Southerners who fight for the Confederacy.

CHARACTERS

Backhouse, Philip S. A young Confederate officer, he is so infatuated with Bayard Sartoris's cousin Melisandre that he becomes a hazard in the field. She, however, is put off by his name. General Forrest and Rosa Millard concoct a fiction in which Lieutenant Backhouse is killed in battle and an equally dashing officer, Philip St-Just Backus, emerges in his place. The lieutenant, actually the same man with his last name sanitized, marries Melisandre soon after.

Compson, Mrs. Wife of General Compson, a Confederate officer. When the Yankee scouts come into JEFFERSON, MISSISSIPPI, she sits fully dressed on a wicker basket of silver in the outhouse.

Forrest, General Nathan Bedford Legendary Confederate general who cooperates with Rosa Millard's scheme to arrange the marriage of Lieutenant Backhouse and Melisandre.

Holston, Dr. A JEFFERSON, MISSISSIPPI, physician during the Civil War, he warns the Compsons that Yankee troops are approaching their place in northern Mississippi.

Joby A slave on the Sartoris plantation.

Louvinia A female slave on the Sartoris plantation.

Lucius A slave on Sartoris plantation, he thinks only of his freedom and looks to the Yankees to deliver it.

Melisandre, Cousin (Melisandre Backus) A young girl living on Sartoris plantation during the Civil War, she retires into the privy with the family silver when the Yankees arrive. The Federals knock over the privy, or backhouse, but the dashing Lieutenant Philip S. Backhouse arrives to chase them off. Melisandre cannot see her way clear to marrying him, however, until his name is converted to Backus.

Millard, Grandfather He is the late husband of Granny Rosa Millard.

Millard, Miss Rosa (Granny) The grandmother of young Bayard Sartoris, she manages the Sartoris plantation during the Civil War when the master is away with the Confederate army. She and General Forrest conceive the plan that enables Melisandre to marry Lieutenant Backhouse.

Phildelphia A female slave on the Sartoris plantation.

Ringo A young black slave on the Sartoris plantation, he is a boyhood companion to Bayard Sartoris.

Roxanne, Aunt A black servant of Mrs. Compson.

Sartoris, Bayard The narrator of the story, he is the son of Colonel John Sartoris.

Sartoris, John Back home briefly after his regiment in Virginia had voted him out as colonel, he reorganizes a cavalry unit to serve with General Nathan Bedford Forrest's command.

Snopes, Ab A "horse-captain" in Colonel Sartoris' cavalry, he steals horses from the Yankees.

New Orleans Sketches

Collection of 11 short pieces and 16 prose sketches that Faulkner wrote for the NEW ORLEANS TIMES-

PICAYUNE and the DOUBLE DEALER while he was living in NEW ORLEANS in 1925. Edited with an introduction by CARVEL COLLINS, the collection was published by Rutgers University Press in 1958; an expanded and revised edition was published by RANDOM HOUSE in 1968. Prior to Collins's collection, 11 of the 16 prose sketches, titled "Mirrors of Chartres Street," with an introduction by William Van O'Connor, were published in *Faulkner Studies* in 1953. In 1954, two other sketches appeared in *Faulkner Studies*. In 1955, these 13 sketches, edited by Ichiro Nishizaki, were published as *New Orleans Sketches by William Faulkner*.

As Collins more or less demonstrates in his introduction, these sketches provide readers with an opportunity to view in Faulkner's early writings anticipatory themes, techniques, and character traits found in his later works. Collins also situates Faulkner in his New Orleans setting. In his review of Collins's edition, Joseph V. Ridgely concludes with a comment worth repeating: "Essentially . . . these early Faulkner pieces are amateur, derivative and overblown; and their chief interest may well lie in raising the question as to how their author, only four years later, could produce *The Sound and the Fury*" (*Modern Language Notes* 74 [February 1959], 176). (For information regarding titles, *see* Appendix.)

Notes on a Horsethief

Novella, with decorations by Elizabeth Calvert, published in February 1951 (though dated 1950) by the Levee Press, Greenville, Mississippi; revised and incorporated into *A FABLE* (1954). The revised version was also published in the July 1954 issue of *Vogue* and in *Perspectives U.S.A.* 9 (autumn 1954), 24–59. In August 1947 when Faulkner was working on *A Fable,* he described the novella in a letter to his editor ROBERT K. HAAS as being a tall tale that begins a few years before World War I with one of the British soldiers in the novel, who at the time (1912) is a groom. He goes to the United States with an exceptional race horse and meets a black stable worker. Together they steal the horse after

it breaks its leg to prevent it from being retired as a stud. These men know that the horse is a champion and wants only to race. They run the horse, but not for their own financial gain, at small tracks throughout the South before they are caught by the police. (*See Selected Letters of William Faulkner*, 253–254.)

Although *Notes on a Horsethief* contains obvious elements of the tall tale, Faulkner nonetheless skillfully integrates the story into the larger framework of the novel. For further information, *see Selected Letters of William Faulkner*, 123–124, 256, 257, 258, 260–262, 264, 266.

"Nympholepsy"

A short story about the thoughts and sensations of a young unnamed farm laborer on his way home after a day's work. JAMES B. MERIWETHER dates the composition of the story in early 1925. It was first published in the *Mississippi Quarterly* 26 (Summer 1973), 403–409, and again in *A Faulkner Miscellany*, edited by Meriwether (Jackson: University Press of Mississippi, 1974, 149–155); it is also published in UNCOLLECTED STORIES OF WILLIAM FAULKNER, edited by JOSEPH BLOTNER (New York: Vintage International, 1997, 331–337). For more information, *see Uncollected Stories of William Faulkner*, 698.

SYNOPSIS

In "Nympholepsy," a young farm hand becomes momentarily and dimly aware of greater possibilities than he is living when he sees, in the distance, a woman walking across a field. Enraptured by her presence, he moves to overtake her, but he slips into a stream and imagines that he fleetingly feels a woman's thigh and breast. He drags himself out of the water, his clothes wet and heavy, and sees a woman—or the apparition of a woman, a nymph—running away through a wheat field. Unsure of the feelings welling up inside of him, he becomes confused and frightened of some unknown but "troubling Presence," now gone but still mocking him. Feeling again the exhaustion and emptiness of his long working day, he heads back to his rooming house in town, continuing with the monotonous cycle of his life.

CRITICAL COMMENTARY

The tone of the short story in particular is achieved through Faulkner's use of vivid and sensual imagery, including the religious or sexual. The dream world and reality play off each other in "Nympholepsy," and, as David Minter points out, the story, like Faulkner's early poetry, abounds in echoes of Swinburne, Shelley, Keats, and others; Minter also observes that "though the deficiencies and inadequacies of reality provide the need and occasion of the dream, reality has the first and last word, and it remains unaltered" ("Carcassonne," "Wash," and "Voices of Faulkner's Fiction" in *Faulkner and the Short Story,* edited by Evans Harrington and Ann J. Abadie, 88). In his assessment of the story, James Ferguson comments that "one has no real sense that Faulkner knows where he is going or what he is trying to achieve in 'Nympholepsy'" (*Faulkner's Short Fiction,* 21). "Nympholepsy," like many of Faulkner's early short works published in Uncollected Stories of William Faulkner, is clearly an apprentice piece.

CHARACTER

unnamed protagonist   A young farm hand. At dusk on his way home to a rooming house after work, the young man reminisces on his day. His thoughts are interrupted when he slips off a log bridging a stream. Once ashore, he sees (or imagines) a young woman in the distance, in a wheat field; he pursues her but she vanishes.

"Old People, The" (*Uncollected Stories*)

Short story, first published in the September 1940 issue of *Harper's Magazine,* revised as the fourth chapter in the novel, Go Down, Moses (1942).

SYNOPSIS

Narrated by a young boy who remains unnamed, the piece is essentially a character sketch of the woodland genius Sam Fathers, part black, part Chickasaw Indian. Although he lives for a time in one of the Negro cabins on the boy's father's plantation, he relates to white men "with gravity and dignity and without servility or recourse to that impenetrable wall of ready and easy mirth which Negroes sustain between themselves and white men, bearing himself toward father not only as one man to another but as an older man to a younger one." In an act of self-emancipation, Fathers quits the plantation, where he works as a blacksmith and carpenter, for a life in the big woods, looking after the hunters' camp and guiding the seasonal hunts. When the boy kills his first buck, Fathers cuts the animal's throat, dips his hands in the warm blood, and wipes them on the boy's face—a priest-like, initiatory rite that establishes Fathers as the boy's mentor and spiritual father. On a later hunt, Fathers guides the boy deep into the Big Bottom, away from the other hunters, to a place where he knows the boy will get a view of a huge buck that hunters have occasionally caught sight of but not been able to kill. As the huge deer passes by, slowly and unafraid, the boy stands with his rifle in hand, safety off, but declining to shoot, while Fathers says, in tribute, "Oleh, Chief. . . . Grandfather." Riding in the surrey on the way home from the hunt, the boy tells his father about seeing the big buck; and his father says, "I know you did. So did I. Sam took me in there once after I killed my first deer."

CRITICAL COMMENTARY

This story, like "The Bear" and "Lion," is an elegy to the old times of the big woods and the people and animals who inhabited them. Sam's tribute to the big buck is simultaneously a tribute to his ancestors and the wilderness, which is rapidly disappearing with the encroachment of civilization. Fathers finds his fulfillment and purpose in teaching others not only to hunt but also to love and respect the woods and the creatures that live there. As the boy's father explains at the end of the story, Sam, the big buck, and the natural world teach lessons of humility, joy, beauty, grief, endurance, continuance—"all the blood hot and fierce and strong for living, pleasuring."

CHARACTERS

For a list of the characters in this story, *see* the entry on Go Down, Moses.

"Once Aboard the Lugger" (I and II)

Two short stories set among bootleggers out of NEW ORLEANS sometime during Prohibition in the mid-1920s. "Once Aboard the Lugger" (I) was first published in *Contempo* I, 1, 4, and reprinted in UNCOLLECTED STORIES OF WILLIAM FAULKNER. "Once Aboard the Lugger" (II) was first published posthumously in *Uncollected Stories of William Faulkner*. For more information, *see Selected Letters of William Faulkner*, 41–42, 56, and *Uncollected Stories of William Faulkner*, 699–670.

SYNOPSIS

In "Once Upon the Lugger" (I), a young man serving as the boat's engineer recalls a voyage into the Gulf of Mexico, where the three crew members and the boat's captain uncover a buried cache of alcohol, probably from Cuba, and prepare to smuggle it back into Louisiana. In "Once Aboard the Lugger" (II), the second short story involving the fateful bootlegging run of a crew out of New Orleans, something happens to stop the progress of the smugglers' boat, now loaded with bootleg alcohol. The pumps must be used to bail out the boat, and the engine has been shut down. As the lugger drifts, another boat comes alongside and rival bootleggers hijack the cargo at gunpoint. Pete, Joe's ineffectual younger brother, is taken unawares and unarmed. The hijackers kill Pete and another crew member, pistol-whip the captain, and then make their escape.

CRITICAL COMMENTARY

James Ferguson considers the second of these two stories, in particular, a story of initiation; "the narrator," Ferguson writes, "learns a great deal from the sudden intrusion of irrationality, of raw evil into the world of the mundane" (*Faulkner's Short Fiction*, 61–62).

CHARACTERS

Ed One of two rival bootleggers in "Once Aboard the Lugger" (II). He is apparently a drug user ("hophead") and dangerous.

Joe Pete's older brother in "Once Aboard the Lugger" (I). Joe sends Pete on the bootlegging trip

that ultimately results in Pete's death in "Once Aboard the Lugger" (II).

Pete A 19-year old in "Once Aboard the Lugger" (I) and (II). Apparently, this is his first bootlegging trip out into the Gulf of Mexico, and he becomes violently seasick. His seasickness in essence causes a delay when the crew, short one man because of Pete's incapacity, digs up the buried alcohol on an unnamed island. The delay is significant because in "Once Aboard the Lugger" (II), another bootlegger overtakes Pete's boat and hijacks the alcohol, killing Pete and a black crew member in the process.

"Pantaloon in Black" (Uncollected Stories)

Short story first published in the October 1940 issue of *Harper's Magazine* and, slightly revised, incorporated as the third chapter of GO DOWN, MOSES (1942).

SYNOPSIS

Rider, a large, strong, 24-year-old black man who is head of a timber gang at the local sawmill, joins with other mourners in shoveling dirt into the grave of his young wife Mannie. Following the funeral, he returns to the house that they had shared together. Although they had rented the house from a white landowner, Rider and Mannie had worked weekends to make numerous repairs and improvements. Before he married Mannie, Rider had known nothing but hard work, heavy drinking, crap games, and promiscuity. But Mannie had given him love, order, and purpose. Now Rider is inconsolable. When his aunt and uncle counsel him to accept Mannie's death as God's will, Rider angrily denounces God: "Whut Mannie ever done ter Him? Whut He wanter come messin' wid me and—"

The next day Rider throws himself into near superhuman work at the mill, at one point amazing the other workers by single-handedly unloading a huge log from a truck and tossing it down the skidway. Then he walks off the job and heads to the bootlegger's house in the woods, where he purchases a gallon of whiskey. The bootlegger tries to persuade him to take only a pint instead, but Rider insists on the whole gallon. After consuming the liquor, he goes to see his aunt, who again fails to convince him to turn to the Lord for consolation and strength.

That night, still drunk, Rider returns to the sawmill to participate in the crap game that is regularly held by the mill workers. Shortly an argument ensues, the white night watchman Birdsong pulls a pistol from his pocket, and Rider slits his throat with a razor.

The story concludes with a deputy sheriff's telling his wife what happened to Rider. After being arrested and jailed, Rider goes into a violent rage, ripping the cot from the floor, hurling it against the wall, and then tearing the steel door of the jail from its hinges. He is finally subdued by the other prisoners, but later he is taken from the jail by a lynch mob and hanged. To the deputy all of Rider's actions—from his behavior at his wife's funeral to the violent behavior in the jail—are just further evidence of blacks' animalistic nature and behavior. To the deputy's wife the whole story is a complete bore and nuisance, as she is in a hurry to get to a picture show.

CRITICAL COMMENTARY

Generally recognized as one of Faulkner's most powerful stories dealing with race and race relations, "Pantaloon in Black" is a masterpiece of irony, understatement, and indirection. No other character in the story recognizes the depth of Rider's love for Mannie or his grief over her death. The deputy sheriff views Rider, as he does all blacks, as subhuman: "They look like a man and they walk on their hind legs like a man, and they can talk and you can understand them and you think they understand you, at least now and then. But when it comes to normal human feelings and sentiments of human beings, they might just as well be a damn herd of wild buffaloes." His wife is more interested in a card game and a movie than she is in the lynching of a black man. This gulf of understanding between the two races is established early in the story when the narrator describes the objects that decorate the black cemetery as having "a profound meaning and fatal to touch, which no white man could have read." No other story in all of Faulkner's

work better dramatizes the pathos of race relations in the South during the 1940s.

CLEANTH BROOKS likens "Pantaloon in Black," with its tough, inarticulate protagonist who suffers deeply over the death of his young wife to a story by Ernest Hemingway (*Yoknapatawpha Country*, 255). As Brooks notes, Rider expresses his grief in violence: shoving others aside and filling in his wife's grave himself, manhandling logs at the sawmill where he works, drinking himself into a stupor, and finally slashing the throat of the white night watchman who has long been cheating the black mill hands at craps. William H. Ruecker, who believes "Pantaloon" to be "one of Faulkner's most perfect short fictions," observes that "Rider is one of Faulkner's great sufferers and, like other great sufferers in Faulkner (black or white), suffering dignifies him and increases his moral stature" (*Faulkner from Within*, 189, 190). Terrell L. Tebbetts interprets the love story of Rider and Mannie as a rejection of "the polarization of male and female." Tebbetts notes: "This most masculine man became another man when he found and married his Mannie, his loving relationship with Mannie 'manning' Rider more fully than he could ever 'man' himself" (in *Faulkner and Postmodernism*, ed. Duvall and Abadie, 92).

"Pantaloon" has only a passing connection with the other stories in GO DOWN, MOSES. Rider, as it happens, is another of Roth Edmonds's tenants. Just as Lucas Beauchamp had done, he builds a permanent fire in the hearth on the night of his wedding. Brooks speculates that Faulkner decided to include the story in *Go Down, Moses* "only because it reveals one more aspect of the world in which 'The Bear' takes place" (257).

CHARACTERS

For a list of the characters in this story *see* the entry on GO DOWN, MOSES.

"Peter" (Uncollected Stories)

Short sketch concurrent with the pieces in NEW ORLEANS SKETCHES (1958), probably originally intended for newspaper publication in 1925 but not issued until its inclusion in *Uncollected Stories* (1979).

SYNOPSIS

The nameless narrator (probably Faulkner himself) has accompanied his artist friend Spratling on a sketching expedition into the Negro district. As customers enter and leave, the young mulatto boy Peter, on watch for his mother and the other prostitutes, speaks with the two men about his own life, his mother's affairs, and of his more innocent longing to learn to spin a top. Peter asks the artist to draw him, but is too restless to hold his pose. Their conversation is punctuated by ragtime music from the Victrola and by sexually explicit exclamations from within the rooms. Finally Peter's mother comes down and ends the sketching session, to the boy's dismay.

CRITICAL COMMENTARY

Like the other newspaper and magazine sketches that Faulkner wrote in NEW ORLEANS in 1925, "Peter" adumbrates techniques, character types, and motifs that Faulkner would later employ with considerably more sophistication in his major fiction. For example, here one finds an early use of an observer narrator, an innocent youth, and the ironic counterpointing of contrasting actions or dialogue.

CHARACTERS

Chinaman A customer of Peter's mother, a prostitute.

Eagle Beak A dockworker who cohabits with Peter's mother.

Peter A young mulatto whose mother works in a brothel, he asks the artist Spratling to do a sketch of him as part of Spratling's tour of the black quarter. Peter has trouble holding a pose, though, and finally his mother comes down and puts an end to the sitting.

Peter's mother A prostitute in a NEW ORLEANS brothel.

Spratling An artist, he is sketching the mulatto boy Peter in a black-quarter brothel when the boy's mother objects and puts an end to the session. The character is named for WILLIAM M. SPRATLING, who

was Faulkner's close friend and NEW ORLEANS neighbor who accompanied him on his European trip.

"Point of Law, A" (Uncollected Stories)

Comic short story that was published in *Collier's* in June 1940 and subsequently formed the basis for the first section of chapter 1 of "The Fire and the Hearth" in GO DOWN, MOSES (1942).

SYNOPSIS

The black tenant farmer Lucas Beauchamp is concerned that George Wilkins, whom Lucas opposes as a suitor to his daughter Nat (not knowing the couple are already secretly married), has established a still on Lucas's place. Lucas is not worried about the competition, since George has not yet learned how to make good whiskey; rather, he is concerned that George, whom Lucas considers a fool, will bring the law down on both of them. So Lucas goes to visit his landlord, Carothers Edmonds, and informs him that Wilkins has a still hidden on the farm. Lucas knows that Edmonds, who has forbidden any whiskey on the place, will report the information to the sheriff. Unknown to Lucas, however, his daughter Nat has followed him to Edmonds' house, and she tells her husband what her father has done. Early the next morning Lucas's wife shakes him out of bed and leads him to the back porch, where Lucas sees George's still sitting in the yard and the porch filled with containers of homemade whiskey. Before Lucas can demolish the evidence, the sheriff appears to arrest him. He has already arrested George, who sits in the sheriff's car with Nat.

At the pretrial hearing at which Edmonds posts bond for both accused men, Lucas learns a point of law: that kinfolks cannot testify against each other. He now invites Wilkins to marry Nat, but the daughter refuses until Lucas agrees to pay for a rebuilt porch, a new cookstove, and a well for the couple. Lucas agrees to all of these demands, only to discover during the trial that George and Nat have been married for almost a year. When they produce the wedding certificate for the judge, he orders the whiskey poured out, the stills destroyed, and the case thrown out of court.

Three weeks later Nat complains to her father that George has not yet begun work on the porch or the well; moreover, he has spent the money Lucas gave him on a new still. When Lucas confronts George about the matter, George explains that the new still is much better than either of the first two. Lucas tells George he knows just the place to hide it. He has decided that he can do business with this son-in-law after all.

CRITICAL COMMENTARY

James B. Carothers dismisses this story as "minstrel comedy" (*William Faulkner's Short Stories*, 93), and CLEANTH BROOKS links it, along with the other parts of "The Fire and the Hearth" in GO DOWN, MOSES, to the Uncle Remus stories in which Brer Rabbit outwits Brer Fox and Brer Bear. Yet, as Brooks goes on to acknowledge, the human traits of greed, deception, and irresponsibility seem "thoroughly grounded in human nature, not in some patronizing idea of the Negro character" (*Yoknapatawpha Country*, 249).

CHARACTERS

For the characters in this story *see* the entry on GO DOWN, MOSES.

William Faulkner in Paris in 1925. *(Brodsky Collection, Center for Faulkner Studies, Southeast Missouri State University)*

Portable Faulkner, The

Anthology of Faulkner's works, published in 1946 and revised in 1974. The writer and critic MALCOLM COWLEY assembled the anthology, which includes shorter works—notably, "The BEAR"—and excerpts from the novels *The SOUND AND THE FURY* (1929), *SANCTUARY* (1931), *ABSALOM, ABSALOM!* (1936), *The UNVANQUISHED* (1938), *The WILD PALMS* (1939), and *The HAMLET* (1940).

Cowley conceived the project at a time when Faulkner's 17 books were effectively out of print. Cowley asked, "How could one speak of Faulkner's value on the literary stock exchange? In 1944 his name wasn't even listed there."

An essay on Faulkner in the *New York Times Book Review* represented Cowley's initial effort to "redress the balance between his worth and his reputation." *The Portable Faulkner* followed. Cowley and Faulkner collaborated on the selections and arrangement; Faulkner provided a set of character genealogies titled "The Compsons" and a map of YOKNAPATAWPHA COUNTY.

Cowley recounted their literary relationship, which continued until Faulkner's death, in *The Faulkner-Cowley File: Letters and Memories* (Viking, 1966). (*Also see* CRITICISM, FAULKNER AND.)

"Portrait of Elmer, A" (Uncollected Stories)

Short story derived from *Elmer*, the unfinished experimental novel Faulkner wrote in Paris in

1925. Although the story dates from the 1930s, "A Portrait of Elmer" was first published in 1979 in UNCOLLECTED STORIES OF WILLIAM FAULKNER. See *also* the entry on ELMER.

SYNOPSIS

The story opens with an American, Elmer Hodge, sitting at a Parisian sidewalk café with his Italian friend Angelo. In an interior monologue, Elmer meditates on his present surroundings, his impatience with Angelo, his plans to establish himself as an artist, and his hope of again meeting Myrtle Monson, a Texan to whom he is attracted and who now is in Paris with her mother. He then recalls their first meeting in Houston. In a series of flashbacks of Elmer's earlier life, Elmer first recalls the house fire that occurred when he was five and that introduces his disintegrating family. Only his sister, Jo Hodge, is heroic. She senses his artistic potential, sending him a box of paints after she leaves home. At age 14, Elmer is attracted to a cruel, beautiful boy and is devoted to the middle-aged teacher who encourages his aspirations; he flees when she makes a physical overture. At age 15, his sexual initiation takes place with Velma, a neighbor girl. In another flashback, Elmer returns to Houston wounded from World War I, longing for Myrtle, to find his mother dead and his father cheerful. The point of view shifts briefly to Angelo, who thinks of his own war days, delights in the women passing by and considers Elmer with contempt. Elmer next thinks back to his liaison at age 18 with Ethel, who refused to marry him yet bore his son. This rejection sent him on the road as a menial laborer and hobo. He ended up in a Michigan lumber camp, where the cook encouraged him to join the Canadian army. During training he was injured by a grenade and shipped back from England. While in New York, he thought he saw his sister Jo at a war rally. A second meditation by Angelo gives way to an account of Elmer's parents' marriage and of the discovery of the oil in his father's yard that funded his European trip. Elmer paints a watercolor landscape that is to be his introduction to the Paris art world. In the farcical conclusion, he is forced to use this painting to wipe himself when Myrtle and her mother unexpectedly visit his room.

CRITICAL COMMENTARY

This satirical portrait of the artist as a young man, with its echoes of T. S. Eliot and JAMES JOYCE, is notable for its play with chronology, interior monologue, and point of view—features that would come to characterize Faulkner's later, and much greater, fiction. The content and themes of the story also adumbrate the later works: obsession with sexuality and death, art as substitution for unfulfilled longing, the search for identity and security. Frederick Karl asserts: "In some undefined, shadowy way, the questing, yearning, fear- and anxiety-ridden Elmer, the young man divided between desire and artistic achievement, is a prototypical Faulkner protagonist, no less than Stephen Hero of Joyce's earliest fiction evolves into the protagonists of his mature novels" (*William Faulkner: American Writer,* 261). Michael Zeitlin identifies the main theme of Faulkner's story as an exploration of "the paradoxical relationship between life and art" (*A William Faulkner Encyclopedia,* 298). Richard Gray believes that the material from which the story was shaped is highly autobiographical, so much so that Faulkner was unable to achieve the necessary aesthetic distance from the subject: "Faulkner is not so much using autobiography in *Elmer* as allowing himself to be swamped by it," Gray states (*The Life of William Faulkner,* 106).

CHARACTERS

Angelo   A hard-bitten World War I veteran, he is the Italian friend of the American artist Elmer Hodge.

Ethel   One of Elmer Hodge's Houston girlfriends, she has a baby by the 18-year-old Elmer but refuses to marry him.

Gloria   She is a singer and dancer in a NEW ORLEANS nightclub, a consort of Mr. Monson.

Hodge, Elmer   A would-be artist from Texas, he has lived an adventurous life for one so young. He is a father at 18; a tramp; a wounded convalescent in an army hospital in England; and finally a painter in Paris in love (or so he thinks) with a wealthy young Texas woman. Elmer's courtship of Myrtle

Monson ends in farce in his Paris room when he is forced to use one of his paintings to wipe himself.

Hodge, Jo Elmer Hodge's sister, she sends him a box of paints in recognition of his artistic potential.

Hodge, Mr. He is Elmer Hodge's father. Oil is discovered in the yard of his Houston, Texas, home.

Hodge, Mrs. Elmer Hodge's mother, she dies while Elmer is convalescing from a training camp wound in England. Her husband seems happier after her death.

Merridew, Velma She introduces the aspiring artist Elmer Hodge to sex when he is 15.

Monson, Mr. A Texas oil magnate, he is the father of Myrtle.

Monson, Mrs. She escorts her daughter Myrtle Monson on a post–World War I tour of Europe, where they meet the American would-be artist Elmer Hodge.

Monson, Myrtle A wealthy young woman from Houston, Texas, she is the object of the American artist Elmer Hodge's affection. They meet first in Texas and, later, in Europe where Myrtle is traveling with her mother.

"Priest, The"

A short story written in 1925 and first published posthumously in the *Mississippi Quarterly* 29 (Summer 1976), 445–450, where it was edited with an introduction by JAMES B. MERIWETHER The story is reprinted in UNCOLLECTED STORIES OF WILLIAM FAULKNER.

SYNOPSIS

"The Priest" contains almost no action other than a short walk taken by the protagonist, an unnamed seminarian, on the eve of his ordination. Although

he seems completely sincere in his beliefs and is prepared to make the church his profession, he finds himself racked with guilt over physical desires and sexual curiosities that he has long suppressed. He notices girls everywhere and wonders about their simple daily chores and pleasures. Troubled by his thoughts of youth and women, he momentarily questions his religious commitment and philosophy. Although he believes his ordination will give him enough grace to renounce earthly desires, the unnamed priest-to-be is not completely convinced. The story ends with his promise to purge his soul and a prayer to the Blessed Virgin.

CRITICAL COMMENTARY

This early short narrative portrays the protagonist with an indefinite future and as an outsider in the world around him, a theme that Faulkner skillfully exploited throughout his mature writings.

CHARACTERS

Gianotti, Father An older priest referred to by the unnamed seminarian in the short story.

unnamed seminarian The protagonist of the short story. While he is out for a walk on the night right before his ordination, he seriously questions his vocation. His doubts, however, linger and are not completely eradicated.

Pylon

One of Faulkner's non-YOKNAPATAWPHA COUNTY novels. *Pylon* was first published by HARRISON SMITH and ROBERT K. HAAS in March 1935. A corrected text by NOEL POLK was published in 1985 by the LIBRARY OF AMERICA (volume 1 of Faulkner's collected works: *Novels 1930–1935*), and again with illustrations by David Tamura in 1987 by Vintage. A film adaptation of the novel, titled *The Tarnished Angels*, was released by Universal-International in 1957, directed by Douglas Sirk and starring Rock Hudson as Burke Devlin (the unnamed reporter in the novel), Robert Stack as Roger Shumann, Dorothy Malone as Laverne Shumann, Jack Carson as

Jiggs, and Chris Olsen, as Jack Shumann. (*Also see* FILM, FAULKNER AND; FLYING, FAULKNER AND; OMLIE, VERNON C.)

SYNOPSIS

The setting of the novel is New Valois, Franciana, a thinly disguised NEW ORLEANS, LOUISIANA, during a three-day air show celebrating the opening of Feinman Airport at Mardi Gras time. The title refers to one of the posts marking a designated flight course for aircraft competing in events. The plot concerns a strange ménage à trois arrangement between Jack Holmes (a parachuter), Roger Shumann (a racing pilot), and Laverne Shumann, mother of the young boy Jack Shumann. After the child was born (and not knowing whether Holmes or Shumann was the child's father), Laverne married Shumann when the two men cast dice to determine who would marry her and act as the legal father of the child. She gave the boy the first name of the man she did not marry.

Shumann manages to outfly pilots in more powerful, more modern aircraft to win second place in the first race. In covering the air show, the unnamed reporter becomes intrigued with the relationship between Roger, Laverne, and Jack, and tries to convince the editor, Hagood, to run a piece about them. Hagood tells him to write only about the news of the air show or risk being fired. The reporter does not care, however, about his editor's threat and continues to investigate and enter into their private lives. Knowing that Shumann must wait a couple of days to collect the second-place winnings, the reporter allows this unconventional family and the team's mechanic, Jiggs, to stay in his flat. In the second race, Shumann crashes his plane because Jiggs, who was hung over, failed to maintain its engine properly. The reporter continues to assist Shumann in his pursuit of winning the last race with the largest purse in the competition, $2,000. He helps get a new airplane from the famous but retired pilot, Matt Ord. Knowing that the plane is unsafe because its engine is too powerful for its frame, Ord will not sell the plane and wants it grounded. However, Shumann and the reporter go behind Ord's back and sign a promissory note for the plane, which is accepted by

an authorized agent of Ord's corporation. At first, Schumann flies well in the new airplane, but when he is about to take the lead, his aircraft begins to break up. Courageously maneuvering away from the crowds, Shumann takes his plane over the lake, where he crashes and dies. His body is lost forever.

As the novel closes, Jiggs joins the pilot Art Jackson to become a parachuter and gives gifts to Holmes, Laverne, and little Jack before they travel to Ohio, where Roger's father, Dr. Carl Shumann, lives. Holmes and Laverne (who is now pregnant, she believes, with Holmes's child) leave her son with Dr. Shumann and his wife, Roger's mother, to rear. Although angry over not knowing the true paternity of the child, Dr. Shumann, nonetheless, takes the boy with the condition that Laverne never see him again. She leaves at night while little Jack is asleep. When Dr. Shumann discovers the $175 that the reporter hid as a gift in the boy's toy airplane, he talks about it with his wife, who convinces him that Laverne was hiding the money from Roger. Assuming that Laverne made the money illegally by prostituting herself, Dr. Shumann burns it. Back in New Valois, the reporter writes the story of Roger Shumann's death, after which he goes out to get drunk.

CRITICAL COMMENTARY

In addition to Shakespearean references (for example, Macbeth's "tomorrow and tomorrow and tomorrow"), throughout *Pylon*, Faulkner shows his indebtedness in particular to JAMES JOYCE and T. S. Eliot. For instance, in the second chapter of the novel, "An Evening in New Valois," there are a few journalistic captions characteristic of the Aeolis episode in Joyce's *Ulysses* (chapter 7); portmanteau words also abound in the novel. The penultimate chapter of *Pylon* is entitled "Lovesong of J. Alfred Prufrock," after Eliot's well-known poem "The Love Song of J. Alfred Prufrock." Eliot's long poem, *The Waste Land,* is also evoked through the treatment of the novel's central characters as they face an indefinite future. The very description of the airport itself in the opening chapter of the novel states that it has been "raised up" and "created out" of a wasteland. The novel ends with the reporter's obituary of Shumann and on a literal note of despair that the reporter "savagely" pencils in beneath the obituary for his editor to read.

Pylon may be Faulkner's most self-consciously modernist work. As Daniel J. Singal points out in *William Faulkner: The Making of a Modernist*, "the aviators in *Pylon* are viewed through a Modernist lens that preserves their standing as heroes but strips away virtually all the glamour. Distinctly ordinary men and women from nondescript midwestern backgrounds, they have chosen to risk their lives racing dangerous aircraft in order to escape the humdrum existence to which they would otherwise be consigned" (192–193).

In response to a question at the University of Virginia, Faulkner explained that he wrote *Pylon* to get away from writing ABSALOM, ABSALOM! (*Faulkner in the University*, 36). Because *Pylon* was written very quickly (according to JOSEPH BLOTNER, the last few months of 1934), it "must have given Faulkner a sense of freshness and even release," as CLEANTH BROOKS comments in *William Faulkner: Toward Yoknapatawpha and Beyond* (178).

CHARACTERS

Atkinson Minor character in the novel. He is Matt Ord's business associate. Atkinson and Ord manufacture airplanes.

Bullitt, Mrs. She is the wife of the pilot Bob Bullitt.

Bullitt, Bob (R. Q.) A minor character in the novel. Bullitt is one of the pilots competing in the air shows celebrating the opening of Feinman Airport in New Valois, Franciana.

Burnham, Lieutenant Frank Minor character in *Pylon*. One of the pilots competing in the air shows celebrating the opening of Feinman Airport in New Valois, Franciana, Burnham is the first fatality of the events. He burns to death when his rocket plane crashes.

Chance, Vic A minor character in the novel. Chance wants to build a plane for Roger Shumann, one of the competing pilots in the air meets at Feinman Airport, but neither Shumann nor Chance has the money.

Cooper A minor character, Cooper is sent by his editor Hagood to replace the unnamed reporter covering the air meet celebrating the opening of Feinman Airport in New Valois, Franciana.

Despleins, Jules Minor character in the novel, he is a French pilot who performs aerial acrobatics at the opening of Feinman Airport in New Valois, Franciana.

Feinman, Colonel H. I. The man who builds the airport named after him in New Valois, Franciana. He is an attorney and chairman of the Sewage Board. Wanting to make sure the paying public get their money's worth of air events, Feinman gives permission to Roger Shumann to fly Matt Ord's unsafe plane, which causes Shumann's death.

Grady A minor character, he is one of several reporters present when Roger Shumann's plane comes apart and crashes. Grady tries to put an end to the other reporters' gossip about Shumann's unconventional ménage à trois marriage.

Grant, Joe Minor character in the novel. Grant is one of the pilots in the air meets celebrating the opening of Feinman Airport in New Valois, Franciana.

Hagood The city editor of the newspaper the unnamed reporter writes for. Angered by the reporter's obsession with the private sex lives of the pilot Roger Shumann, his wife Laverne, and the parachuter Jack Holmes, Hagood fires the reporter for not writing about the news of the air show celebrating the opening of Feinman Airport at New Valois, Franciana. In the end, however, Hagood rehires the reporter and even loans him money.

Hank The announcer of the air events and races in *Pylon*. He explains to the pilots that two and a half percent will be taken from the prize money to cover the cost of new programs.

Holmes, Jack The parachuter or jumper who accompanies the pilot Roger Shumann in the novel. In a ménage à trois relationship, Holmes openly lives with Shumann and his wife Laverne. After Laverne's son is born, Holmes and Shumann roll dice to decide who will marry her and be the child's legal guardian. Shumann wins, but the boy is named Jack, after Holmes. When Shumann crashes his plane in the lake and dies, Holmes asks the reporter to send the body to Shumann's father in Ohio, but the body is never found. At the end of the novel, Laverne and Holmes go to Ohio to leave little Jack with Shumann's father, with whom the boy will now live. Laverne is also pregnant at this time with (she believes) Holmes's child.

Hurtz, Mr. An offstage character referred to in *Pylon*. He marries the reporter's mother and honeymoons in Santa Monica.

Jiggs Roger Shumann's drunken airplane mechanic. Hung over the morning of Shumann's second air race, Jiggs does not properly maintain the plane's engine, causing Shumann to crash. Although the plane is destroyed, the pilot survives to race again in what will prove to be his last flight. After Shumann dies, Jiggs becomes a parachute jumper for the stunt pilot Art Jackson. At the end of the novel, Jiggs pawns his new boots to buy gifts for Shumann's widow, Laverne, and son Jack.

Jug A newspaper photographer in *Pylon*.

Leblanc A minor character, Leblanc is a police officer at Feinman Airport during the celebration of its opening. He is persuaded by the reporter not to arrest Roger Shumann's mechanic, Jiggs, who is drunk.

Mac The desk clerk in the Bayou Street police station where the drunken airplane mechanic, Jiggs, is being held for vagrancy. The reporter, who borrowed money from Hagood, his editor, pays Mac a $10 fine to have Jiggs released.

Marchand Minor character in *Pylon*. A Cajun, Marchand works for Matt Ord's aircraft company.

In Ord's absence, Marchand sells Ord's unsafe airplane to Roger Shumann and the reporter.

Monk A minor character in the novel. He is a crew member of one of the pilots. Jiggs puts a bill in Monk's hand to give to Art Jackson for flying the parachute jump.

Myers, Al One of the pilots competing in the air meet celebrating the opening of Feinman Airport in New Valois, Franciana.

Ord, Matt Famous (retired) pilot in *Pylon* and with Atkinson owner of the Ord-Atkinson Aircraft Corporation. Behind Ord's back, Roger Shumann and the reporter buy an unsafe plane from an authorized agent of the Ord-Atkinson corporation to fly in one of the air races celebrating the opening of Feinman Airport in New Valois, Franciana. Although Ord tries his best to ground the plane (its engine is too powerful for its frame), Colonel H. I. Feinman permits Shumann to fly it. The plane breaks apart and Shumann dies in the crash.

Ord, Mrs. Matt Ord's wife.

Ott, Jimmy One of the competing pilots mentioned in *Pylon*.

the reporter He is the tall, emaciated, unnamed cadaverlike reporter sent by the city editor, Hagood, to cover the air shows celebrating the opening of Feinman Airport in New Valois, Franciana. The reporter is a figure resembling T. S. Eliot's J. Alfred Prufrock in his unrealized dreams and sexual desires. He is enamored with the obvious ménage à trois relationship between the racing pilot Roger Shumann, his attractive wife Laverne (with whom the reporter can only imagine a relationship), and Jack Holmes, the parachute jumper. Although told by the city editor not to get involved in the trio's private sexual lives and to report only news of the air show, the reporter does not heed this advice and is fired. During the course of the air meets, the reporter gives over his apartment to the three and their child, little Jack, and also strikes up a drinking relationship with their mechanic, Jiggs.

When Shumann's plane crashes, the reporter helps the uninjured pilot acquire another plane, which proves to be fatal to Shumann. Holmes, Laverne, and little Jack depart for Ohio after Shumann's death, and the reporter, rehired by Hagood, writes Shumann's obituary before going to Amboise Street to get drunk.

In response to a question about the naming of his character, Faulkner commented that they name themselves and the few that do not he left nameless. "There was one in *Pylon*, for instance, he was the central character in the book, he never did tell me who he was" (*Faulkner at Nagano*, 78–79).

Sales, Mac   A minor character in *Pylon*. A federal agent, Sales inspects airplanes.

Shumann, Dr. Carl   The pilot Roger Shumann's father. Although he wanted his son to be a physician, Dr. Shumann bought Roger his first plane. When Roger dies in a crash at an air meet, Roger's wife, Laverne, and their friend Jack Holmes take the little boy Jack to live with Roger's parents in Ohio. Dr. Shumann agrees to take the child on the condition that Laverne never see him again.

Shumann, Jack   Laverne Shumann's six-year-old son. Born in a hangar in California, Jack's paternity is uncertain. His father is either Jack Holmes, the parachute jumper, or Roger Shumann, the pilot. The three adults live openly in a ménage à trois. After the child is born, Laverne marries Shumann when the two men cast dice to determine who will act as the child's legal father; she gives the boy Jack Holmes's first name. When Roger dies in a crash, Laverne and Holmes take little Jack to live with Roger's father in Ohio.

Shumann, Laverne   The young woman openly living in ménage à trois arrangement with Roger Shumann, a pilot, and Jack Holmes, a parachute jumper. After giving birth to her son, whose paternity is uncertain, Laverne marries Roger when the two men roll dice to determine who the child's legal father will be. She gives the boy Holmes's first name. Flashbacks in the novel show Laverne to have been a sexually active and adventurous teen-

ager. Infatuated with her way of life and sexually attracted to her, the reporter explains to Shumann that he would like to have sex with her. But she will have nothing to do with him. When Shumann dies in the last air race at Feinman Airport, Laverne departs with Holmes and her son for Ohio, where she leaves little Jack with Shumann's parents. Pregnant with Holmes's child, Laverne travels on with Holmes, never to see her son again.

Shumann, Roger   One of the racing pilots in *Pylon*. Although his father wanted him to be a physician, Shumann became a pilot instead, and with his father's money bought his first plane. He competes in the air meets that are part of the opening celebrations of Feinman Airport in New Valois, Franciana. Living openly in a ménage à trois, Shumann arrives with his wife, Laverne, Jack Holmes, the parachute jumper, and their son little Jack. In the opening race of the meet, Shumann takes second place, beating out pilots with more powerful and more modern planes. In the second race, he crashes because the plane's engine was not properly maintained by Shumann's hungover mechanic, Jiggs. Desperate for money, Shumann is determined to fly in the last and biggest race of the meet with a purse of $2,000. Assisted by the reporter, Shumann buys a plane that proves to be fatally unsafe because its engine is too powerful for its frame. As he is about to take the lead in the last race, his aircraft breaks up and crashes in the lake. Shumann's body is not to be found.

Shumann epitomizes alienation in the mechanized world of speed and daring, and his life a commodity to be used. When Colonel H. I. Feinman permits the unworthy plane to compete in the last race, he is thinking more of entertaining the paying crowd than safeguarding Shumann's life.

FURTHER READING

Brooks, Cleanth. "People Without a Past (*Pylon*)." In *William Faulkner: Toward Yoknapatawpha and Beyond*, 178–204. Baton Rouge: Louisiana State University Press, 1990.

Howe, Irving. "*Pylon*." In *William Faulkner: A Critical Study*, 215–220. Chicago: University of Chicago Press, 1957.

Johnson, Suzanne Paul. *William Faulkner's* Pylon: *Annotations for the Novel*. New York: Taylor & Francis, 1989.

Matthews, John T. "The Autograph of Violence in Faulkner's *Pylon*." In *Southern Literature and Literary Theory*, edited by Jefferson Humphries, 247–269. Athens: University of Georgia Press, 1990.

Millgate, Michael. *"Pylon."* In *The Achievement of William Faulkner*, 138–149. Lincoln: University of Nebraska Press, 1978.

Torchiana, Donald. "*Pylon* and the Structure of Modernity." *Modern Fiction Studies* 3 (1957–1958): 291–308.

Zeitlin, Michael. "Faulkner's *Pylon*: The City in the Age of Mechanical Reproduction." *Canadian Review of American Studies* 22 (1991): 229–240.

"Race at Morning" (Uncollected Stories)

Short story that first appeared in the *Saturday Evening Post* (March 5, 1955) and was revised for *Big Woods* (1955).

SYNOPSIS

Narrated by a 12-year-old boy, the story describes an annual deer hunt. Abandoned two years earlier by his tenant farmer parents, the boy was adopted informally by the widower, Mister Ernest, who was their landlord and a farmer himself. The story opens on the eve of the hunt, when the boy spots a magnificent 12-point buck swimming in the river. After supper the hunters play poker and tease the boy, who obviously is quite intelligent, about his lack of schooling. Before dawn they begin the chase on horseback, following a pack of dogs through the Mississippi bayou country. With Mister Ernest and the boy in pursuit, the buck evades the other hunters and begins to circle back to its territory. Mister Ernest empties his rifle of ammunition before aiming and snapping his rifle at the buck when it presents a clear target. After the two find their way back to camp in the dark by using a compass, Mister Ernest explains his deliberate refusal to kill the deer, saying that the joy of the hunt rather than the kill is what is important; the privilege of hunting is a reward for the hard work of cultivating the land during the rest of the year. He then dismays the boy by announcing that he now must start school.

CRITICAL COMMENTARY

Another of Faulkner's several initiation stories, "Race at Morning" traces the growth of the narrator, a young boy, under the tutelage of a sensitive, caring adult male. The boy's disappointment at the end of the story that he now has to enroll in school ironically ignores the fact that his education has already begun: From Mister Ernest's example and instruction the boy is learning an ethical attitude toward nature and responsibility toward other people. James B. Carothers writes of the book of which this story becomes a part: "The entire *Big Woods* collection is elegiac in tone, a celebration of the land, a lament for its passing, and for the passing of the men who hunted it" (*William Faulkner's Short Stories*, 102).

CHARACTERS

Dan The mule that Mr. Ernest and the boy ride during the hunt for the big buck.

Eagle A hunting dog.

Edmonds, Roth A member of an old YOKNAPATAWPHA COUNTY family, he joins the November deer hunt. *See also* GO DOWN, MOSES.

Ernest, Mister A farmer, he is the adoptive father of the 12-year-old narrator, whose parents have abandoned him. During the November hunt, Ernest intentionally allows a prize buck to escape unharmed so the hunters can stalk it the next year.

Ewell, Walter One of the hunters. In other stories he is identified as a member of the annual hunting parties that gather at Major de Spain's camp in the Tallahatchie River bottom. He has the reputation of being a crack shot—his rifle never misses. Ewell also appears in *The* MANSION, *The* REIVERS, and "A BEAR HUNT."

Legate, Will(y) Another member of the hunting party. Legate also appears in GO DOWN, MOSES and INTRUDER IN THE DUST.

McCaslin, Isaac (Uncle Ike) The oldest and most highly respected of the hunters. The narrator says of him: "He had been hunting deer in these woods for about a hundred years, I reckon, and if anybody would know where a buck would pass, it would be him." *See also* GO DOWN, MOSES, in which Ike, both as a boy and a man, is a major character.

Simon The African-American cook at the November deer hunting camp.

"Raid" (Uncollected Stories)

Short story first published in the November 3, 1934, issue of the *Saturday Evening Post* and revised as the third chapter of The UNVANQUISHED (1938).

SYNOPSIS

During the Civil War Granny Rosa Millard, the mistress of Sartoris plantation, in the company of her young grandson Bayard Sartoris and his black playmate Ringo, pursues a unit of federal troops into Alabama in search of compensation for two stolen mules, some missing silver, and two runaway slaves, Loosh and Philadelphy. The pursuers stop over briefly at the Hawkhurst plantation, where cousin Drusilla Hawk, whose fiancé has been killed at Shiloh, burns for revenge. Drusilla dresses like a man, rides well, and is willing to learn to shoot and wants to enlist in Colonel Sartoris's cavalry. Miss Rosa tracks down the Union colonel Nathaniel Dick, who agrees to provide compensation. Through a comedy of errors involving a play on the mules' names (Old Hundred and Tinney), he gives Miss Rosa a chit for 110 mules, 110 runaways, and 10 chests of silver.

CRITICAL COMMENTARY

Narrated by the youthful Bayard Sartoris, "Raid" reflects the paradoxical nature of the Southerners'

life during the Civil War. On the one hand, the story dramatizes the courage and fortitude of those, especially the women, left on the home front. On the other hand, in employing deceit and accepting the Yankees' overpayment, Granny strays from the strict code of behavior that has governed her life. All of the events become part of the initiation experience of the young Bayard. In significantly revising the story for inclusion in *The UNVANQUISHED*, Faulkner added a lengthy section in which Drusilla describes the Yankees' futile chase of a Confederate locomotive—a story that has become part of the local lore of ongoing Southern resistance against insurmountable odds and inevitable defeat.

CHARACTERS

For the list of characters in this story *see* the entry for *The* UNVANQUISHED.

"Red Leaves" (Collected Stories)

Short story first published in the *Saturday Evening Post* (October 25, 1930) and revised for *These 13* (1931). Its final sections were reworked as a prelude to "The OLD PEOPLE" in *Big Woods* (1955).

SYNOPSIS

The runaway black slave of the Chickasaw chief Issetibbeha must be recaptured so that, according to tribal custom, the servant can be buried with his master. As they seek him in the slave quarters, two older Indians recall the death of the chief's father, Doom (Ikkemotubbe), and how it took three days to catch his slave. Grumbling about the burden of slavery on the tribe, they go to the new chief to announce the slave's disappearance. Speculation over Issetibbeha's relationship with his son Moketubbe suggests the possibility of patricide.

An account follows of Doom's rise to power. Issetibbeha succeeds him and uses profits from slave breeding to travel to Paris, returning with a useless fancy bed and red-heeled shoes, which fascinate Moketubbe.

The point of view shifts to the hunted servant who, remembering his own journey from Africa, watches from hiding as Issetibbeha dies. He begins to run but keeps circling back, chased by the Indians who drag the obese Moketubbe along on a litter. At night the chief's servant seeks out the other slaves; they give him food but already regard him as dead. A snake bites him, and he submits to capture on the seventh day. Accepting a last meal, he is unable to swallow. The story ends as he is about to be slain.

CRITICAL COMMENTARY

This story, rich in ironies, paradoxes, and ambiguities interwoven with poetic imagery and mythic symbolism, is one that many critics place among Faulkner's best. Jay Parini considers "Red Leaves" one of only a few Faulkner short stories that are "classic examples of the genre, complete in themselves, on a par with the novels as self-sufficient works of art" (323). For most readers the vigorous black man seems superior, morally and culturally, to the corrupt Moketubbe. Historian Don H. Doyle, who views the Indians' laziness and depravity as the result of white and European influence, calls the story "one of the most haunting portrayals of slavery in American fiction" and adds: "it is poignant testimony of the power of fiction to imagine what historians can rarely document, the inner thoughts of a slave" (124). James B. Carothers argues that "the world of 'Red Leaves' is a world of despair, in which the only dignified response is the stoic acceptance of the inevitable" (*William Faulkner's Short Stories*, 76).

CHARACTERS

Berry, Louis A CHICKASAW INDIAN, he helps track down one of the dead chief Issetibbeha's runaway slaves, who by tribal tradition must be caught and put to death before the chief can be buried.

de Vitry, Soeur-Blonde The NEW ORLEANS friend of the Chickasaw chief Ikkemotubbe, he gives the chief his sobriquet of *du homme*—Doom.

Had-Two-Fathers A Chickasaw Indian who assists Three Basket in removing the red-heeled slippers from the dying Moketubbe.

Ikkemotubbe Issetibbeha's father, known as "Doom"—*du homme,* the man, doom. As a young man he spent some time in NEW ORLEANS. As chief he forced his slaves to haul a wrecked steamboat overland for 12 miles so he could use it as his house.

Issetibbeha Son of the CHICKASAW INDIAN chief Ikkemotubbe and successor to his father as tribal chief. After his death, his son Moketubbe succeeds him.

Moketubbe The fat, indolent son of the CHICKASAW INDIAN chief Issetibbeha. He succeeds as chief when his father dies.

The Negro The slave who is Issetibbeha's body servant for 23 years. When Issetibbeha dies, the slave runs away in an attempt to escape being buried with his chief, but he is subsequently captured.

Three Basket A CHICKASAW INDIAN, squat, paunchy, and approaching old age, he wears an enameled snuffbox clamped through one ear. Three Basket complains of having to supervise the chief's slaves at their work. He assists in capturing the runaway slave.

Reivers, The

Faulkner's last novel, published in 1962, is a funny, reminiscent, elegiac and sentimental coming-of-age story with a plot involving an automobile, a stolen racehorse, and fallen women. Some critics have compared the novel favorably to Mark Twain's *Huckleberry Finn. The Reivers* attempts an affectionate recovery of a vanished world, a past seen through a haze of nostalgia—the automobile is both a symbol of change and the agent of corruption—and with much of the violence, misery and evil endemic to Faulkner's work airbrushed out. Unusually for Faulkner, the story has a happy ending.

With *The* MANSION, the third novel in the SNOPES TRILOGY published in 1959, Faulkner had declared his serious writing life at an end. For some reason, though, he revived an old idea, one he had first proposed to ROBERT K. HAAS at RANDOM HOUSE some 20 years before.

"It is a sort of Huck Finn," he wrote Haas in May 1940. "He goes through in miniature all the experiences of youth which mold a man's character. They happen to be the very experiences which in his middle class parents' eyes stand for debauchery and degeneracy and actual criminality; through them he learned courage and honor and generosity and pride and pity."

Faulkner is "in his happiest mood" in *The Reivers,* critic Brooks Atkinson observed in a 1962 appreciation of the novel. "His story of townsfolk on the loose, soberly trying to control a mad situation they have created, is pure comedy."

SYNOPSIS

Set in 1905 in Faulkner's mythical JEFFERSON, MISSISSIPPI, and in the Tenderloin district of MEMPHIS, *The Reivers* opens in present time—1961—with the words "GRANDFATHER SAID." With that announcement, Lucius (Loosh) Priest, 65 years old, relates to his grandson the crowning story of his own childhood. He looks back, sometimes fondly, sometimes censoriously, on himself as an 11-year-old; his partners and corrupters Boon Hogganbeck and Ned William McCaslin; the "borrowed" Winton Flyer automobile in which they all escape to Memphis; Miss Reba Rivers's brothel; and the horse that ultimately wins a fixed race and thus frees them from the direst consequences of their wrongdoing. In the end, the scheming Ned commits a good deed, young Loosh learns the code of the gentleman, and the dim and loveable Boon happily weds his favorite whore, Miss Corrie (Everbe Corinthia Hogganbeck).

The Reivers reintroduces familiar characters and situations. The Priests are the "cadet branch" of the McCaslin-Edmonds clan of GO DOWN, MOSES. Boon Hogganbeck is an antic figure out of the novella "The BEAR." Ned McCaslin is a cousin of Lucas Beauchamp of *Go Down, Moses* and INTRUDER IN THE DUST. Faulkner lifted Miss Reba's brothel from SANCTUARY. There are coming-of-age parallels with Ike McCaslin of "The Bear" and Chick Mallison of *Intruder.*

Boon concocts the scheme; the circumstance that young Loosh's parents are away for the funeral of his maternal grandfather in Bay St. Louis provides the opportunity. Boon dearly loves Loosh's grandfather Lucius (Boss) Priest's Winton Flyer. The car is his "soul's lily maid." He is infatuated, too, with one of Reba's girls, Miss Corrie. So Boon enlists Loosh as collaborator in a mock-heroic automobile odyssey from Jefferson to Memphis, 85 miles distant. Ned stows away in the trunk of the car and is only discovered when he breaks wind a few miles into the journey.

The travelers encounter and surmount two physical obstacles early on: Hurricane Creek and Hell Creek Bottom. They break for the night at Ballenbaugh's, a roadhouse with a violent and romantic past, and arrive at Miss Reba's house on CATALPA STREET the next day. A bit later, Ned turns up at the brothel with a racehorse in tow, which he has acquired in exchange for the car.

Ned plans to take the racehorse—Coppermine, renamed Lightning—to the town of PARSHAM, TENNESSEE, to race against a local favorite, with the Winton Flyer as stakes. Ned's motives are pure: He hopes to free his cousin Bobo Beauchamp from the snares of a $128 debt to a white man. With the assistance of Boon, Lucius, and the girls at Miss Reba's, he arranges for Lightning to be shipped by railroad to Parsham for the race with Colonel Linscomb's champion, Acheron. If Lightning wins, Ned will be able to pay off Bobo's debt *and* recover Boss Priest's car.

Meantime, a 15-year-old minor criminal named Otis advances young Loosh's knowledge of the seamy side of life. He informs Loosh that Miss Corrie is a prostitute and that he, Otis, has made money by allowing men to observe her at work through a peephole. When Loosh attacks Otis with his fists, Otis slashes at him with a knife.

Touched by Loosh's devotion, Miss Corrie decides to reform and live a life of virtue. She even reverts to her given name, Everbe Corinthia, which she had discarded as frumpish. But Lightning loses the first race, and a corrupt, bullying deputy sheriff named Butch Lovemaiden inserts himself into the action. Pursuing Everbe, he provokes a clash with a jealous Boon, who with Ned lands briefly in jail. Everbe gives herself to the deputy as the price for freeing Boon. When Loosh learns of her fall, he is devastated.

There is urgency now, for the Priests are due home soon from Bay St. Louis. Lightning wins the second race as Ned employs an artifice—in the form of a sardine (the horse responds to sardines)—to make the creature run faster. Lightning wins a third heat, but Acheron's backers contest the result. A fourth race, with Acheron's owner Colonel Linscomb and Grandfather Priest now present, is arranged to decide matters. When Ned fails to appear with the sardine, Acheron wins. As it turns out, Ned has bet on the colonel's horse. He wins big and bails out Bobo. And Grandfather Priest recovers his car with out-of-pocket expenses of $496—a figure Ned regards as cheap at the price.

Lucius returns to Jefferson with his grandfather, chastened and miserable. His father's offer to whip him for his misdeeds strikes him as wholly inadequate as a punishment. Grandfather Priest tells him the only way he can atone for his crimes is to simply live with them.

Boon Hoganbeck eventually returns to Jefferson with his bride, Everbe Corinthia. They move into a tiny house that Boon buys from Grandfather Priest. In time, they produce an heir and name him Lucius Priest Hoganbeck.

CRITICAL COMMENTARY

After a slow start, Faulkner "suddenly got hot" and completed *The Reivers* in a rush, finishing the first draft on August 21, 1961. He originally titled the work *The Horse Stealers: A Reminiscence*, then shortened it to *The Stealers*, then hit on *The Reavers*. He did not like the spelling, though, finding it sounded "too peaceful, bucolic: too much like Weavers" (*Selected Letters of William Faulkner*, 456). In the end, he settled on the archaic Scots spelling of the word, *reivers*—robbers or plunderers.

Most of the second-draft revisions were minor, name changes and such: for example, Mr. van Grafe, Coppermine's owner, became Mr. Van Tosch. Faulkner's agent, HAROLD OBER, arranged for excerpts to be published in the SATURDAY EVENING POST and *Esquire*. BENNETT CERF wrote to say that the Book-of-the-Month Club had accepted *The Reivers* as a future selection.

Fittingly, Faulkner dedicated *The Reivers* to the five children of his daughter, JILL FAULKNER, stepdaughter VICTORIA (FRANKLIN) FIELDEN, and stepson MALCOLM FRANKLIN. In the spring of 1962, he read from an advance copy to appreciative audiences at the U.S. Military Academy at West Point and the UNIVERSITY OF VIRGINIA. Random House published the novel on June 4, 1962.

In *Faulkner: Essays* the critic WARREN BECK contends that the book has been too readily dismissed as light and sentimental. "*The Reivers* merits recognition for a true virtuosity that combines exuberance, implicativeness, and commitment, as a narrative wherein humor and wit spring from judicious insight, a nice fusion of value judgments and hearty tolerant interest," he wrote.

Beck judged *The Reivers* "a substantial work, significant in the Faulkner canon." He saw sentimentality as one of its strengths, particularly the comic but also moving love story of Boon Hoganbeck and Miss Corrie. These were Faulkner's people, ones whose courage and strength he understood and admired. "Her reformation and marriage to Boon may be disparaged as facile sentimentality," Beck wrote, "but that implies denial of the way common vital people break through adverse circumstance into idealistic assertion, and thus 'endure.'"

George Plimpton wrote the first major review of Faulkner's last novel for the *New York Herald Tribune*. He listed other "boys' stories" it brought to mind including Stevenson's *Treasure Island* and Twain's *Huckleberry Finn*. Writing in the *New York Times Book Review*, IRVING HOWE classified *The Reivers* as "a deliberately minor work," adding that it was to "The BEAR" what *Tom Sawyer* was to *Huckleberry Finn*. The critic Leslie Fiedler, in a review in the Manchester (England) *Guardian*, found parts of the book unbearably sentimental, "as bad as anything he has ever done." In a rather severe and humorless commentary in the *Christian Science Monitor*, Roderick Nordell called Faulkner's seriousness of purpose into question. "Is this enough?" Nordell asked of *The Reivers*. "No would have to be the answer of those who hoped that he might follow the Snopes trilogy with a probing of the troubled present rather than a diversion into the past."

Howe saw continuity with Faulkner's earlier works, particularly the recurrent theme, present in "'The Bear" and elsewhere, of "the relaxation of the sense of social duty, or to put it more colloquially, the need every once in a while to play hookey, so that men can bear going back to the tedium and trouble of life." *The Reivers* follows the earlier pattern, too, he went on, in that it is a simple fable, "transparent in its significance," then elaborated and "adorned with dark, violent and, at times, obscure complications of plot."

But Howe cautioned against overanalysis of Faulkner's last work.

"We have tended to forget that before all else he is a literary *performer*, a self-made virtuoso aiming to dazzle, incite and give pleasure. We forget, above all, that he can be a brilliant comic writer, blessed with a repertoire of gifts for folk extravaganza, deadpan humor and surrealist hi-jinks."

Faulkner never paid much attention to reviewers or critics. At any rate, in the case of *The Reivers*, he could have seen only the earliest notices before his death on July 6, 1962, only a month after the book was published.

EXCERPTS FROM CONTEMPORARY REVIEWS OF *THE REIVERS*

Excerpt from Granville Hicks's review, "Building Blocks of a Gentleman," published in the Saturday Review, *June 2, 1962, 27:*

Once one accepts the fact that *The Reivers* isn't a major Faulkner novel, nor, I should say, was meant to be, one can settle down to enjoy it, for minor Faulkner may be very good, and this is. It is not comparable, of course, to *Light in August* or *Absalom, Absalom!* but I liked it better than I did either *The Town* or *The Mansion*, the considerably more pretentious novels that preceded it. The novel that it most closely resembles is *Intruder in the Dust*; it is less topical and less grim, but it has the same kind of excitement. . . .

Once the story gets under way, it moves at a splendid pace. Faulkner's characters are always setting out on perilous pilgrimages or undertaking almost or quite impossible tasks: the funereal mission of the Bundren family in *As I Lay Dying*;

Lena Grove's long pursuit of Lucas Burch in *Light in August*; Thomas Sutpen's grand design in *Absalom, Absalom!*; the convict's quest in *The Old Man*. In *The Reivers*, as in *Intruder in the Dust*, a boy finds himself confronted with a task that has to be done over and over again, but Lucius Priest is even younger than Chick Mallison, and perhaps that makes his gallantry all the more admirable. . . .

The style is basically that which Faulkner has cultivated since *Intruder in the Dust*: a voice that starts out, qualifies, interrupts itself, lunges ahead, and sometimes never gets anywhere at all—which is the way voices do behave, as anyone can tell who keeps an ear open at a party. It is a style that is really a good deal like Henry James's, except that James tucked away the qualifications and digressions in neatly grammatical phrases and clauses, as most people don't do in ordinary speech. Faulkner has used the style here with somewhat more restraint than he has sometimes shown—there are fewer breathless, nonstop sentences—and on the whole it is well suited to the kind of story he is telling. . . .

Excerpt from R. A. Jelliffe's review, "Fabulous Tale Has Humor, Wisdom, and Rare Artistry," the Chicago Sunday Tribune, *June 3, 1962, Magazine of Books, 1–2:*

Nothing in Faulkner's previous work, nothing in *Sanctuary*, for instance, or in *A Fable*, to mention only two of his former novels, quite prepares the reader for this latest production. *The Reivers* is in an entirely different vein from its predecessors.

The range of the author's work, that is to say, the variation in theme and tone, is astonishing. He shifts at will, it would seem, from dire sensationalism, from the macabre representation of warped and thwarted human nature, to the symbolic portrayal of religious mysticism, the reproduction, in terms of World War II, of the central legend of our Christian faith. And now, with an equally amazing change of key, he captures our fascinated attention with an absorbing situation, a story steeped in a solution of the plausibly preposterous. . . .

If the author, as he has testified on occasion, liked best of all his novels, *The Sound and the Fury*, because it "caused him the most trouble," he might well, by the same reasoning, it might seem, like this one least; for *The Reivers* sounds as if it had been written effortlessly, as if it were a piece of unpremeditated art.

Excerpt from Clifton Fadiman's review published in the Book-of-the-Month Club News, *July 1962, 1–5:*

... Novel isn't quite the right word to describe *The Reivers*, even though the book is designed to fill its niche in the vast structure of the Yoknapatawpha saga, and mentions characters we have met before. Somehow it doesn't have the feel of fiction. Mr. Faulkner's subtitle "A Reminiscence" has the proper sound, suggesting a long, complicated, true anecdote. Like *Huckleberry Finn*, about a boy very different from the young hero of *The Reivers*, the story may have been drawn from the author's own early experience. But, whether or not autobiographical, here is a tale pervaded by reality. One overhears it being told.

A highly sophisticated folk comedy, with touches of broad humor, *The Reivers* has, playing through it like light, a quality rather rare in Faulkner, a curious tenderness. I intend no left-handed compliment in saying that to enjoy it there is no need to be a Faulkner devotee. I am not one, yet *The Reivers* caught, held and delighted me, despite the impediments of the famous style, the crisscross structure, the acrobatic play with time sequences. Not as ambitious as Mr. Faulkner's major efforts, it is more successful than some of them. Faulkner fans will revel in it; those who have tried to be Faulkner fans but haven't been able to make the grade should give themselves another chance with *The Reivers*; and those who have never read Faulkner now have the opportunity to enjoy a fresh experience....

CHARACTERS

Alice   She is Miss Ballenbaugh's African-American cook. Boon Hogganbeck gives her a ride in the Winton Flyer during the stopover at Ballenbaugh's en route to MEMPHIS.

Avant, Jim   He is mentioned as a "hound man" from Hickory Flat, Mississippi, who attends the annual Grand National trials in PARSHAM, TENNESSEE.

Ballenbaugh (1)   An enormous man with no known antecedents, he becomes the proprietor of Wyott's Ferry on the TALLAHATCHIE RIVER before the Civil War just as mule- and ox-drawn wagons are replacing riverboats as freight and cotton carriers on the Vicksburg-to-Memphis route.

Ballenbaugh (2)   He is the son of the proprietor of the old tavern and ferry at Wyott's Crossing, and succeeds his father in 1865, not long after he returns from the Civil War with a small fortune in U.S. banknotes sewn into his coat lining. When Colonel Sartoris's railroad drives the mule-team freighters out of business, the younger Ballenbaugh sets up a still and converts the place into a resort for drunks, fiddlers, gamblers, girls, and sinful characters of all sorts. It becomes "a byword for miles around for horror and indignation."

For a generation or so, successive sheriffs leave Ballenbaugh's tavern alone. Finally, in the summer of 1886, the crusading Baptist parson Hiram Hightower cleans up Ballenbaugh's by force.

When Lucius Priest, Boon Hogganbeck, and Ned William McCaslin stop there on the way to MEMPHIS in 1905, Ballenbaugh's is a placid inn catering to hunters and fishermen.

Ballenbaugh, Miss   A sober maiden of 50, thin and iron-gray, she succeeds the uproarious younger Ballenbaugh (2) as owner of the inn at Wyott's Crossing on the TALLAHATCHIE RIVER. She farms the place, and also operates a store and boardinghouse that cater to hunters and fishermen.

Lucius Priest, Boon Hogganbeck, and Ned William McCaslin spend a night at Miss Ballenbaugh's on their way to MEMPHIS in May 1905.

Ballott, Mr.   He is the day foreman of Maury Priest's livery stable in JEFFERSON, MISSISSIPPI. When Mr. Ballott leaves for the day, Boon Hogganbeck is in charge.

Beauchamp, Bobo   He is Lucas Beauchamp's cousin, reared in YOKNAPATAWPHA COUNTY by Aunt Tennie. Bobo migrates to MEMPHIS, where he finds work as Mr. Van Tosch's groom and manages to fall $128 in debt, payable on Monday, to a white man.

Bobo confides his troubles to Ned William McCaslin in a Memphis barroom and so unwittingly sets in motion the elaborate scheme in which Ned "borrows" Mr. Van Tosch's horse Coppermine (later Lightning) and leaves the Priest automobile with Bobo's creditor.

Beauchamp, Lucas Quintus Carothers McCaslin An important figure in the YOKNAPATAWPHA COUNTY cycle, the grandson of the planter/slave-holder Lucius Quintus Carothers McCaslin, he is the patriarch of the black McCaslin family line.

Beauchamp is present offstage in *The Reivers*. The narrator's grandmother recalled descriptions of old Carothers McCaslin from her mother; Lucas, she said, "looked (and behaved: just as arrogant, just as iron-headed, just as intolerant) exactly like him except for color" (*Reivers*, 229).

Beauchamp, Tennie's Jim He is the grandfather of Bobo Beauchamp, the feckless young man whose MEMPHIS escapades touch off the series of events that leads to the horse race at PARSHAM, TENNESSEE.

Binford, Mr. (Lucius) The "landlord" or front man for his lover Miss Reba Rivers's MEMPHIS brothel, he handles the money, deals with the tradesmen and distillers, settles the tax bill, bribes the police, and enforces strict house rules.

A small man with a heavy moustache and striking eyes, Mr. Binford is honest, meticulous, and "more faithful than many husbands" but for one flaw, a weakness for betting on horses. He offers to take 15-year-old Otis, the visiting nephew of one of the girls, to the zoo, but they end up at the track instead. When Otis discloses that Mr. Binford has lost $40 on a "horse and buggy," Miss Reba throws him out—and not for the first time.

He is referred to in SANCTUARY and, as Lucius Binford, in *The MANSION*.

Binford, Mrs. The name Miss Reba Rivers uses when she signs in at the hotel in PARSHAM; it is the last name of her business associate and lover.

Bookwright, Calvin (Cal) He is a distiller of fine bootleg whiskey. Boon Hogganbeck gives the stable hand Ludus two dollars for a gallon of Uncle Cal's liquor; Ludus returns with an inferior whiskey instead, touching off a confrontation with Boon.

Briggins, Lycurgus The steady, reliable 19-year-old grandson of Uncle Parsham Hood, he collaborates with Ned McCaslin in preparing the horse Lightning (Coppermine) for the race against Colonel Linscomb's horse. Efficient too, young Briggins tracks Otis with his uncle's hounds and forces him to return the gold tooth that he stole from Mrs. Rivers's maid Minnie.

Briggins, Mary She is Uncle Parsham Hood's daughter and the mother of Lycurgus Briggins.

Buffaloe, Mr. A mechanical genius, "grease-covered and soot-colored," he keeps the JEFFERSON, MISSISSIPPI, steam-driven electric plant running and builds an automobile of his own that spooks Colonel Sartoris's matched carriage horses one afternoon on the square, causing them to bolt. This event is part of the chain of causation that compels "Boss" Priest to acquire an automobile of his own.

Caldwell, Sam A railroad flagman who is kin to a high railroad official, he is a patron and admirer of Everbe Corinthia (Hogganbeck)—Miss Corrie, one of Reba's (*see* Rivers, Reba) girls.

At Corrie's request, Sam arranges for rail transportation of Ned McCaslin and the horse Lightning (Coppermine) from MEMPHIS to PARSHAM. His contributions are essential to the success of Ned's scheme to race Lightning and win money to pay off Bobo Beauchamp's debt. Ned becomes a fervent admirer of the efficient and mannerly Caldwell. As he put it, "When Mr. Sam Caldwell runs a railroad, it's run, mon."

Callie, Aunt An African American and a long-time servant of the Priest family, she nurses each Priest infant in turn, beginning with Maury Priest, Sr., Lucius Priest's father.

Charley A railroad worker in the switch yard at the Union depot in MEMPHIS, he helps Boon Hogganbeck and Sam Caldwell move the boxcar so the horse Lightning (Coppermine) can be loaded for the short train trip from Memphis to PARSHAM, TENNESSEE, for the races.

Christian, Mr. He owns the drugstore on the square in JEFFERSON, MISSISSIPPI.

Clapp, Walter Mr. Van Tosch's horse trainer, he suspects that Ned McCaslin might be trying a ruse—bringing in a ringer—in order to win the PARSHAM horse race.

Compson, General A recurring character in the YOKNAPATAWPHA COUNTY cycle, head of a prominent JEFFERSON family, he is a veteran of the Civil War battle of SHILOH and of General Johnston's Atlanta campaign. In *The Reivers*, General Compson is presented as a shareholder in the "corporation, a holding company" that is Boon Hogganbeck.

De Spain, Major A prominent citizen of JEFFERSON, MISSISSIPPI, he owns the hunting camp in the Delta wilderness 20 miles west of town and, with General Compson and the McCaslins, is a shareholder in the Boon Hogganbeck enterprise, a "mutual protective benefit association," with all benefits to Boon and all the responsibilities of protection to the corporation.

De Spain, Manfred He is a JEFFERSON banker, the son of Major de Spain. By 1940, he has sold off the "lease, land and lumber" of the hunting camp in the Delta wilderness generations of Jefferson men have used for the annual autumn hunt.

Ed The telegraph operator at the PARSHAM railroad depot, he is one of the judges of the horse race between Lightning (Coppermine) and Acheron.

Edmonds, Carothers A descendant of McCaslin (Cass) Edmonds, he is the present (1961) incumbent of the McCaslin plantation 17 miles outside JEFFERSON.

Edmonds, Louisa (Cousin Louisa) She is the wife of Zachary Edmonds, the owner of the old McCaslin plantation in 1905. Lucius Priest (Loosh) is supposed to stay with the Edmondses when his parents travel to Bay St. Louis for the funeral of Grandfather Lessep. Instead, Lucius goes off to MEMPHIS with Boon Hogganbeck and Ned McCaslin.

Edmonds, Zachary (Zack; Cousin Zack) He is the son of the first Carothers Edmonds and is master of the old McCaslin plantation. Lucius Priest (Loosh) is supposed to stay with Cousin Zack and his wife when his parents travel to Bay St. Louis in May 1905 for the funeral of Grandfather Lessep.

Edmonds, McCaslin (Cass) He took over ownership of McCaslin plantation after the Civil War and raised young Isaac McCaslin as his surrogate father.

Ephum A black employee of Miss Ballenbaugh, he accepts Boon Hogganbeck's invitation for a ride in the Priest car. Because the Ballenbaugh inn is segregated, Ned McCaslin spends the night at Ephum's place.

Ewell, Walter He is a long-time patron of Major De Spain's hunting camp, and one of the best shots in YOKNAPATAWPHA COUNTY.

Fathers, Sam (Had-Two-Fathers) The son of a Chickasaw chief and a quadroon slave, he is an expert in woodcraft. Old Lucius Priest mentions Sam in connection with Major De Spain's hunting camp in the Delta wilderness west of JEFFERSON.

Fittie, Aunt An Arkansas brothel operator, she raised Everbe Corinthia (Hogganbeck) after her mother's death and "started her out as soon as she got big enough," according to Miss Corrie's nephew, Otis.

Gabe A short, powerfully built African American with a badly twisted leg from an on-the-job injury, he works as a blacksmith in Maury Priest, Sr.'s livery stable.

Grenier, Louis A Huguenot, he came west to Mississippi in the 1790s and helped found the frontier settlement of JEFFERSON.

Grinnup, Old Dan A drunken hanger-on at the Priest livery stable, he is the debased descendant of Louis Grenier, one of the three original YOKNAPATAWPHA COUNTY settlers. Grinnup's daughter was the wife of the stable foreman Ballott, and Maury Priest, Sr., tolerated him because he had hunted with his father as a boy.

Hampton (Hope or Hubert [Hub]) The steady, capable sheriff of YOKNAPATAWPHA COUNTY, Hampton briefly detains Boon Hogganbeck after a shooting incident in 1905. Faulkner was not consistent in giving Hampton a first name; he has none in *The Reivers*.

Hampton, Hub (Little Hub) Hub Hampton's grandson and in 1961 is "or will be again next year" sheriff of JEFFERSON, MISSISSIPPI.

Hightower, Hiram He is a Baptist parson, a giant of a man and a Civil War veteran of NATHAN BEDFORD FORREST's cavalry, with whom he fought six days a week and served as a company chaplain on the seventh. In 1886, he uses his fists and his Bible to subdue and convert the uproarious riverside settlement of the younger Ballenbaugh (2).

Hogganbeck, Boon He is a comic central figure, the 41-year-old night assistant to Mr. Ballott at the Priest livery stable. "Tough, faithful, brave and completely unreliable," Boon takes loving responsibility for Boss (Lucius) Priest's Winton Flyer, one of JEFFERSON, MISSISSIPPI's, first cars, keeping it gleaming and driving it whenever he can. Along with young Lucius Priest, he develops a plan to "borrow" the Flyer for a trip to MEMPHIS when the senior Priests leave town for Grandfather Lessep's funeral.

The two, with Ned McCaslin as a stowaway in the boot of the Flyer, embark on a series of adventures involving a Memphis brothel, the prostitutes who work there, a racing horse, and an obnoxious deputy sheriff named Butch Lovemaiden. In the end, the travelers return safely to Jefferson. Boon marries one of the prostitutes and names their first-born after Lucius Priest.

Hogganbeck is an important figure in GO DOWN, MOSES and is referred to in INTRUDER IN THE DUST, *The* TOWN, and the short story "A BEAR HUNT."

Hogganbeck, Everbe Corinthia (Miss Corrie) She is one of the girls in Miss Reba Rivers's brothel, and a particular favorite of Boon Hogganbeck.

A small-town Arkansas madam named Aunt Fittie takes in Everbe after her mother dies and introduces her to the business at age 11 or 12. A big girl, "young too, with dark hair and blue eyes," personable appealing and gentle, she advances to work in the better-paying MEMPHIS house of Miss Reba and begins to call herself Miss Corrie, figuring that the name Everbe Corinthia is "too countrified" for her sophisticated patrons. When her adolescent nephew Otis, a budding criminal, comes from Arkansas on a visit, she gives him five cents a day to keep quiet about her full name.

When Boon visits the CATALPA STREET house, jealousy overwhelms him and he demands to have Miss Corrie all to himself, much to Reba's disgust.

Miss Corrie and the innocent young Lucius Priest are drawn to each other from the start. When Otis coarsely details her background to Lucius and explains "pugnuckling," some sort of sexual act, Lucius flies into a rage and attacks him. His action so touches Corrie that she tearfully promises him that she will quit the oldest profession for good. She even refuses Boon.

With Boon and Lucius, Miss Corrie becomes caught up in Ned McCaslin's horseracing scheme. She persuades Sam Caldwell, another of her admirers, to arrange railroad transportation from Memphis to PARSHAM, TENNESSEE, for Ned and the horse Lightning (Coppermine), and she breaks her vow and entertains Deputy Sheriff Butch Lovemaiden so he will release Ned and Lightning from custody. Lucius is devastated by her fall from grace.

After the race, Miss Corrie renews her pledge and declines to go back to Memphis with Miss Reba. She and Boon eventually marry, set up in a little house in JEFFERSON, MISSISSIPPI, and produce a son whom they name for Lucius Priest.

Hogganbeck, Lucius Priest (Luke) He is the son of Boon Hogganbeck and his bride, the quondam prostitute Everbe Corinthia Hogganbeck, named for Lucius Priest, a companion on the MEMPHIS adventure that leads to the Hogganbecks' marriage.

Luke appears in *The* TOWN, *The* MANSION, and in the short story "A BEAR HUNT."

Hood, Uncle Parsham A "lean, dramatic old man" with white hair and a white moustache and imperial, a patrician, the "aristocrat and judge of us all," he involves himself in the doings, sometimes sordid, occasionally dangerous, of the horse racing partnership of Boon Hogganbeck, Lucius Priest, and Ned McCaslin.

Hood's grandson, Lycurgus Briggins, is a key ally of Ned's. Hood himself provides crucial information that allows Lightning (Coppermine) to win a decisive race—he notices that the horse runs well until he sees nothing but empty track ahead, then slows. Ned contrives to lure him on to greater efforts by rewarding him at the finish line with a pungent and aromatic "sourdeen" (sardine).

Eleven-year-old Lucius, homesick and confused, turns to "Uncle Possum" for safety, security, and authority in a hostile adult world. In the face of disapproval from PARSHAM, TENNESSEE's, white community, he insists on staying in Hood's home. He confides in him, seeks comfort from him, and always calls him "sir."

Things all come right in the end, thanks in no small part to Hood, who gains a much-deserved $20 in gambling winnings for his church.

Jackie She is one of the girls in Miss Reba Rivers's CATALPA STREET brothel. Reba leaves Jackie in charge during the excitement over the stolen horse and automobile with instructions to keep the house shut till evening, even "if every horny bastard south of St. Louis comes knocking."

Legate, Bob He is one of the regulars at Major De Spain's annual autumn hunt in the big woods.

Lessep, Alexander He is the great uncle of the narrator, Lucius (Loosh) Priest.

Lessep, Grandfather He is the maternal grandfather of Lucius (Loosh) Priest, a college classmate of Maury ("Boss") Priest, Sr.; they were groomsmen at each other's weddings. Lucius makes the excursion to MEMPHIS with Boon Hogganbeck and Ned McCaslin in "Boss" Priest's Winton Flyer automobile when the adult Priests attend Grandfather Lessep's funeral in Bay St. Louis 300 miles from JEFFERSON, MISSISSIPPI.

Lessep, Grandmother She is Lucius (Loosh) Priest's maternal grandmother.

Linscomb, Colonel A lawyer, he owns Acheron, the horse that races Lightning (Coppermine); the half-mile track on which the races are run; and a considerable plantation near the little town of PARSHAM.

Colonel Linscomb is host to Grandfather Lucius Priest when he comes up to Parsham to recover his automobile, his grandson, and his retainers Boon Hogganbeck and Ned McCaslin. Ned narrates the tangled story of the horseracing scheme in the colonel's fine office, and details of the fourth—and final—race between Acheron and Lightning are worked out there.

A hospitable man, he invites Miss Reba Binford (*see* Rivers, Reba) into his home for supper. She politely declines. "No matter how long your wife stays at Monteagle, she'll come back home some day and you'll have to explain it," Reba tells him.

Lovemaiden, Butch A coarse, bullying, race-baiting deputy from Hardwick, the county seat 13 miles from PARSHAM, he turns up in the little town when he hears of a horse race about to be run there.

Lovemaiden, brandishing his badge and smelling of sweat and whiskey, launches an aggressive pursuit of Miss Corrie (Everbe Hogganbeck) and touches off a violent conflict with Boon Hogganbeck. He uses his authority to goad Boon into attacking him; this lands Boon and Ned McCaslin in jail. He then suggests to Miss Corrie that they will go free if she submits to his gross attentions.

Boon is duly freed, but when he learns the details he assaults Lovemaiden and beats him badly;

Mr. Poleymus, the Parsham constable, asserts his authority and both Boon and Lovemaiden are arrested and taken to the Hardwick jail.

When they are released, Boon attacks him again, this time for calling Corrie a whore.

Ludus   One of Maury Priest's black teamsters, he borrows a company wagon overnight to pay a clandestine visit to a girlfriend in the country, setting off a chain of events that ends when Boon Hogganbeck shoots at him in broad daylight on the JEFFERSON, MISSISSIPPI, square. Boon goes after Ludus because, instead of buying Calvin Bookwright's fine whiskey as he had been instructed to do, he delivered inferior "rot gut" liquor.

"Boss" Priest pretends to fire Ludus for keeping a team out overnight without authorization, but in fact only docks him a week's pay.

Luster   A black employee of the Priest livery stable, he is shoeing a mule when Boon Hogganbeck bursts in looking for John Powell's pistol. Later, Luster helps carry a girl who is slightly wounded in Hogganbeck's shooting spree to the doctor's office.

Lytle, Horace   A specialist in fine bird dogs, he comes to PARSHAM once a year, in February, for the Grand National trials. He once refused an offer of $5,000 for one of his dogs.

McCaslin, Cousin   The uncle of Zachary Edmonds, he owned the mare that Ned McCaslin surreptitiously bred to a farm jack. The offspring, addicted to the sardines Ned offers him as an inducement to run, proves to be the fastest mule in YOKNAPATAWPHA COUNTY. When he dies, unbeaten, at 22, he is buried on the McCaslin plantation.

McCaslin, Delphine   She is Sarah Priest's African-American cook, and one of the four wives (in succession) of Ned McCaslin. Lucius Priest covers his escape to MEMPHIS with Boon Hogganbeck (and with Ned as a stowaway) by telling his relatives he is staying with Ned and Delphine while his parents are away at Grandfather Lessep's funeral.

McCaslin, Isaac (Cousin Ike)   The grandson of old L. Q. C. McCaslin, he is an important figure in the YOKNAPATAWPHA story. In 1905, approaching 40, he keeps the hardware store in JEFFERSON, living alone in a room above it. Ike agrees to take Loosh Priest fishing on Sunday, part of the alibi meant to cover the trip to MEMPHIS in the Winton Flyer.

Ike McCaslin is a central figure in GO DOWN, MOSES.

McCaslin, Lancaster   He is the father of L. Q. C. McCaslin, and thus the founder of the McCaslin clans, black and white.

McCaslin, Lucius Quintus Carothers   The first McCaslin in YOKNAPATAWPHA COUNTY, he obtained the large grant of CHICKASAW INDIAN land that became the McCaslin plantation. Old Carothers is responsible for the tangled McCaslin racial history. He fathers Tomey's Turl (Beauchamp) by a slave girl who is his own daughter, and so is Lucas Beauchamp's grandfather.

McCaslin, Ned William   He is Grandfather Lucius Priest's coachman, a black grandson of old Lucius Quintus Carothers McCaslin, born in the McCaslin backyard in 1860. Proud of his mixed heritage, he is independent, shrewd, and resourceful enough to survive, even prosper, in a white man's world on his own terms. What the narrator calls his "Uncle Remus act" is a mask worn for strange whites, and not at all expressive of Ned's real character.

When he hears of Boon Hogganbeck's and young Lucius Priest's plans for a weekend trip to MEMPHIS in May 1905, he manages to stow himself away in the back of Grandfather Priest's Winton Flyer. He is soon discovered and accepted, grudgingly on Boon's part, into the party. In Memphis, he runs across his cousin Bobo Beauchamp, who tells him he is $128 in debt to a white man, and that the debt comes due on Monday. Ned concocts an elaborate scheme to bail out Bobo that involves the Winton Flyer and a racehorse named Coppermine (later Lightning).

Without Boon's knowledge, Ned trades the car for the horse. He then enlists Boon, Lucius, the girls in Miss Reba's (*see* Rivers, Reba) brothel, and others in his plan. With the help of a railroad flagman admirer of Miss Corrie's (Everbe Corinthia Hoganbeck), he arranges for Coppermine to be transported to the little Tennessee town of PARSHAM, where it will run against the local champion, Colonel Linscomb's Acheron. With the proceeds, Ned expects to pay down Bobo's debt and recover the Winton Flyer.

The intervention of a bullying deputy named Butch Lovemaiden complicates matters. Butch aggressively pursues Everbe, driving Boon to fits of jealous rage. For a time, Ned, Boon, and the horse are held in jail. With the help of Uncle Parsham Hood and his grandson Lycurgus Briggins, and an act of sacrifice on Everbe's part, Butch is confounded and the races finally come off.

Using the secret of the "sourdean" (sardine) to spur on Lightning, Ned wins enough to free Bobo from debt. But the intervention of Colonel Linscomb and Grandfather Priest force major last-minute alterations. A final race is run; Ned does not appear with the sardine; Acheron wins. But Ned has slyly bet on the colonel's horse, and he wins big for himself, with $20 to spare for Uncle Parsham's church. Coppermine/Lightning reverts to Mr. Van Tosch, and Grandfather Priest gets his car back—at a cost of $496.

Ned keeps his winnings for, as he confesses to young Lucius, it is too late for him to give up his ill-gotten gains. But he is proud of Lucius for refusing his share.

Faulkner once described *The Reivers* as "a sort of Huck Finn" (David L. Minter, *Faulkner: His Life and Work*, 246). If that is so, Ned McCaslin would be Faulkner's Jim, the runaway slave in Mark Twain's great novel who teaches Huck imperishable lessons about their common humanity. In a similar way, Ned helps young Lucius to adulthood and to his estate as a good man.

McCaslin, Theophilus ("Uncle Buck") The father of Cousin Isaac McCaslin, twin brother of Amodeus McCaslin ("Uncle Buddy"), he is said to have galloped into MEMPHIS with a Confederate cavalry unit, ridden into the lobby of the GAYOSO HOTEL, and almost captured a Yankee general.

Uncle Buck and his brother figure prominently in GO DOWN, MOSES.

McDiarmid, Mr. He manages the eating room at the railroad depot in PARSHAM and is one of the judges of the race between the horses Coppermine (Lightning) and Acheron. By reputation, McDiarmid "could slice a ham so thin that his entire family had made a summer trip to Chicago on the profits from one of them."

McWillie The 19-year-old son of Colonel Linscomb's chauffeur, he is the overconfident jockey of the horse Acheron in the races against Coppermine (Lightning).

Minnie Miss Reba Rivers's black maid, she has a stunning removable gold tooth, a bauble she saved for three years to acquire. It has a mesmerizing effect on men. Otis, the visiting nephew of Miss Corrie (Everbe Corinthia Hoganbeck), one of Miss Reba's girls, manages to steal the tooth; young Lycurgus Briggins ultimately recovers it for Minnie.

Otis A rising gangster from Kiblett, Arkansas, he is the nephew of Miss Corrie (Everbe Corinthia Hoganbeck), an ill-mannered, perverse, greedy and thieving 15-year-old who passes for 10.

Miss Corrie takes Otis in to save him from his family's hardscrabble farm. All the same, this wizened, worldy-wise and depraved adolescent extorts whatever he can from everyone he meets. He looks through a peephole into Aunt Fittie's Arkansas whorehouse, where Miss Corrie used to work; he charges Miss Corrie five cents a day to keep mum about her real name; he provokes Loosh Priest into a fight and slashes his fingers with a pocket knife; he sells out the MEMPHIS brothel landlord Mr. Binford, whose only weakness is horses, for 85 cents; he steals Minnie's prized removable gold tooth.

Peabody, Dr. He is a JEFFERSON, MISSISSIPPI, physician with an office on the courthouse square. Doc Peabody treats a black passerby after Boon Hogganbeck fires a wild pistol shot that grazes her on the buttocks.

Peyton, George   A famous bird-dog specialist, "his name as magical among bird-dog people as Babe Ruth and Ty Cobb among baseball aficionados," he comes to PARSHAM, TENNESSEE, once a year for the Grand National trials.

Poleymus   He is the honest, capable constable of PARSHAM, TENNESSEE. When Mr. Poleymus learns that the deputy Butch Lovemaiden is abusing his authority in his bid to sleep with the reformed prostitute Everbe Corinthia (Hogganbeck), he strips Butch of his badge and jails him. He "may be little and he may be old," Ned William McCaslin says of him, "but he's a man, mon."

After the races, he hires Everbe as nurse and companion to his invalid wife.

Powell, John   The black head hostler of the Priest livery stable in JEFFERSON, MISSISSIPPI, he is the proud owner of a pistol, "the living symbol of his manhood," that he bought from his father the day he turned 21. Strictly against the rules, Powell brings the weapon to work with him, a fact known to all but never acknowledged, even by Maury Priest, whose gentlemanly code bars him from taking notice.

An enraged Boon Hogganbeck takes the pistol from its resting place in Powell's jumper pocket and fires several times at the stable hand Ludus, who has cheated him out of a jug of fine whiskey.

Priest, Alexander   He is the infant brother of the narrator, Lucius (Loosh) Priest.

Priest, Alison Lessep   She is the wife of Maury Priest, Sr., and the mother of young Lucius Priest and his brothers—Lessep, Maury, Jr., and Alexander Priest. She and her husband are away in Bay St. Louis for her father's funeral when Boon Hogganbeck, Lucius, and Ned McCaslin set out for MEMPHIS. Learning of the extent of her son's crimes on her return, she hovers in the background, near tears, in an agony over the punishment about to be inflicted on him.

Priest, Lessep   He is one of young Lucius Priest's younger brothers.

Priest, Lucius (Boss Priest; Grandfather)   The father of Maury Priest, Sr. and the grandfather of the narrator, young Lucius Priest, he is a leading citizen of JEFFERSON, MISSISSIPPI, a "negotiable paper wizard" whose bank is a rival of Colonel Bayard Sartoris's Merchants and Farmers Bank.

He buys an early automobile, a Winton Flyer, simply to spite his business rival, who has forced through a municipal ordinance banning motor vehicles on Jefferson's streets. Soon, at Boon Hogganbeck's instigation, rides in the Flyer become a family institution.

Boss Priest turns up in PARSHAM, TENNESSEE, to collect the runaways and the car. He treats the escapade as minor, and even bets—ill-advisedly—on Lightning (Coppermine) to win the fourth heat against Colonel Linscomb's Acheron.

When young Lucius practically begs for a punishment for his transgressions, Grandfather tells him that he will have to live with the tangle of lies and deceptions associated with the Memphis trip because "[a] gentleman accepts the responsibility of his actions."

When Boon returns to Jefferson with his bride, Everbe Corinthia (Hogganbeck), Boss Priest sells them a small house for 50 cents a week, payable on Saturdays.

Priest, Lucius (Loosh)   The narrator of *The Reivers*, he is a member of a prominent, privileged JEFFERSON, MISSISSIPPI, family. In 1961, he spins out for his grandson the tale of his four-day adventure in MEMPHIS in May 1905, when he was a boy of 11.

With his parents away attending Grandfather Lessep's funeral in Bay St. Louis, 300 miles distant, Lucius acquiesces in, and even helps advance, Boon Hogganbeck's plan to borrow the family car, a Winton Flyer, for a trip to Memphis and the CATALPA STREET brothel of Reba Rivers.

As the trip unfolds, Lucius gradually loses his innocence. Events force his early entry into grown-up life, and he becomes a willing and faithful servant of "non-virtue." He learns about commercial sex, racing, and gambling, and picks up fresh lessons in duplicity, loyalty, betrayal, and racial bigotry.

Loosh enjoys an early triumph. He is immediately taken with Miss Corrie (Everbe Corinthia

[Hogganbeck]), Boon's particular interest at Miss Reba's, and she with him. When 15-year-old Otis, Everbe's odious nephew, explains his aunt's role at Miss Reba's, Lucius attacks him. When Everbe learns that Lucius has risen to her defense, she is so touched that she vows to give up her work.

Nevertheless, he is drawn deeper into the grown people's schemes. Even though he is guilt-racked and homesick, Loosh does not ask Boon and Ned McCaslin to give up their racing scheme and carry him home. On the contrary, he agrees to replace the unreliable Otis as jockey aboard Lightning (Coppermine).

Lucius is fully engaged now, both as the defender of Everbe's virtue against the assaults of Boon and the corrupt deputy Butch Lovemaiden, and as Lightning's rider. There is no turning back. He has entered the adult world.

At Uncle Parsham Hood's insistence, Ned tells Lucius that Everbe has "entertained" Butch and that Boon has beaten them both. Inconsolable, the boy turns to Hood for solace. The next day, when Lucius wins the decisive third heat, he refuses to accept the money Miss Reba has made for him.

Lucius returns to Jefferson changed forever, innocence and childhood lost beyond recall. But he sees with a shock that home has not changed at all. He seeks, even begs for, punishment for his crimes. His father's display of the razor strop seems inadequate to the moral dimension of the case. Finally, Grandfather Priest intervenes and tells him he must take responsibility for his actions.

Boon eventually returns to Jefferson with Everbe Corinthia as his bride. As the tale closes, Lucius meets their newborn son, his namesake, Lucius Priest Hogganbeck.

Priest, Maury, Jr. He is a younger brother of the narrator, Lucius (Loosh) Priest.

Priest, Maury, Sr. He is the ineffectual father of the narrator, Lucius (Loosh) Priest, and the owner of the Priest livery stable in JEFFERSON, MISSISSIPPI.

After Lucius's MEMPHIS adventure, Maury takes his son to the cellar for a whipping, a wholly inappropriate punishment for his crimes.

Priest, Sarah Edmonds She is the wife of the elder Lucius Priest and grandmother of the narrator, young Lucius Priest. A proud woman, she refuses to allow her daughter-in-law to tidy her after she is spattered with tobacco juice during a breathless ride in the Winton Flyer.

Rainey, Paul A Wall Street financier and hound expert, he acquires a large tract of Mississippi land as a hunting preserve. Rainey once took his pack of bear hounds to Africa "to see what they would do on a lion or vice versa."

Rhodes, Miss She is young Lucius Priest's teacher. When Loosh's mother refuses to write an excuse for him, Miss Rhodes allows him to make up the week's worth of schoolwork he missed during the jaunt to MEMPHIS.

Rivers, Reba (Miss Reba) An imposing woman with a "hard handsome face and hair that was too red," she is the madam of the brothel on CATALPA STREET in MEMPHIS where Boon Hogganbeck takes Lucius Priest. Kindhearted and compassionate, she insists, for example, that her black maid Minnie stay with her in her room at the hotel in PARSHAM, TENNESSEE. When signing into the hotel for the horse races, she uses the name Mrs. Binford; Binford is her lover and the "front man" for the brothel.

Rouncewell A JEFFERSON, MISSISSIPPI, oil company agent, he supplies the fuel for Grandfather Priest's Winton Flyer.

Rouncewell, Mrs. She operates a boardinghouse, the former COMMERCIAL HOTEL, in JEFFERSON, MISSISSIPPI.

Sartoris, Bayard The "young colonel," a familiar figure in the YOKNAPATAWPHA saga, owns a bank in competition with Lucius ("Boss") Priest. His fiat banning motor vehicles from JEFFERSON provoked Priest in to buying an automobile, a Winton Flyer, for the sole purpose of flouting the edict.

Snopes, Flem The founder of the Snopes dynasty, he led "his tribe out of the wilderness behind

Frenchman's Bend" to supplant the Compsons, Sartorises and Priests as JEFFERSON's elite. In 1961, at the time Lucius Priest narrates the story, Flem has been dead for about a dozen years.

Stevens, Judge He inhabits a law office on the courthouse square just down the gallery from Dr. Peabody. Stevens approves issue of two legally dubious "mutual double-action bonds" to keep the peace between Boon Hogganbeck and Ludus. Though he is not given a first name, he certainly is the recurring Gavin Stevens of the YOKNAPATAWPHA cycle.

Sutpen, Thomas He is mentioned as the one-time YOKNAPATAWPHA COUNTY grandee who ends up ruined by his own "kingly dream." Sutpen is a key character in the novel ABSALOM, ABSALOM!.

Thomas, Son The youngest of the drivers at Maury Priest's livery stable, he has the misfortune of being the one to whom Ludus confides his contemptuous opinion of Boon Hogganbeck. Boon shoots at Ludus but misses, and later tells Judge Stevens that had he been in possession of a second pistol, he would have shot at Son too.

Van Tosch A Chicago man who moved to MEMPHIS to breed and train racehorses, he owns Coppermine (Lightning), a horse that refuses to run for him. Van Tosch's employee Bobo Beauchamp steals the animal as part of an elaborate scheme to discharge his $128 debt to a white man.

Later, in PARSHAM, TENNESSEE, Van Tosch agrees to let Coppermine race a fourth heat on his friend Colonel Linscomb's private track in hopes of learning Ned McCaslin's secret for making him run.

Vera She is one of the girls in Miss Reba's brothel. Vera is on a visit to her family in Paducah, Kentucky, in May 1905, when Boon Hogganbeck and his entourage visit Miss Reba's place. Boon and young Loosh Priest use her room for a changing room while she's away.

Virgil He is a desk clerk at the hotel in PARSHAM, TENNESSEE. Virgil lets slip that deputy sheriff Lovemaiden's writ does not run beyond Hardwick, the county seat. "We don't have a law officer right here in Parsham," he says; "we aint quite that big yet."

Watts, Birdie She keeps the brothel on the opposite side of CATALPA STREET from Miss Reba Rivers.

Winbush, Mack He owns a place eight miles out of JEFFERSON, MISSISSIPPI, from which he sells bootlegger Calvin Bookwright's high-quality whiskey.

Wordwin The cashier in Grandfather Priest's Bank of Jefferson, he is entrusted with the task of going to MEMPHIS by train and driving Grandfather's new Winton Flyer to JEFFERSON, MISSISSIPPI. A man-about-town, Wordwin has been a groomsman in 13 weddings in 10 years.

Wyott (1) An early YOKNAPATAWPHA COUNTY settler, he built a store and ran a ferry on the Memphis road at the crossing of the TALLAHATCHIE RIVER. When Ballenbaugh displaced him, he moved eight miles inland from the river and turned to farming.

Wyott (2) He is a family friend of the Priests. Maury Priest took his son Loosh bird-hunting on the Wyott place the previous Christmas. Boon Hogganbeck and Loosh are near the Wyott place eight miles out of JEFFERSON, MISSISSIPPI, on the way to MEMPHIS when they discover the stowaway in the car, Ned McCaslin.

FURTHER READING

Brooks, Cleanth. "The World of William Faulkner (*The Reivers*)." In *William Faulkner: The Yoknapatawpha Country*, 349–368. Baton Rouge: Louisiana State University Press, 1990.

Carothers, James B. "The Road to *The Reivers*." In *A Cosmos of My Own: Faulkner and Yoknapatawpha*, edited by Doreen Fowler and Ann J. Abadie, 95–124. Jackson: University Press of Mississippi, 1981.

Millgate, Michael. "*The Reivers*." In *The Achievement of William Faulkner*, 253–258. Lincoln: University of Nebraska Press, 1978.

Moses, Edwin. "Faulkner's *The Reivers:* The Art of Acceptance." *Mississippi Quarterly* 27 (1974): 307–318.

Urgo, Joseph R. *Faulkner's Apocrypha: "A Fable," Snopes, and the Spirit of Human Rebellion.* Jackson: University Press of Mississippi, 1989, 27–33.

Wittenberg, Judith Bryant. "*The Reivers:* A Conservative Fable?" In *Faulkner: After the Nobel Prize,* edited by Michel Gresset and Kenzaburo Ohashi, 201–228. Kyoto, Japan: Yamaguchi, 1987.

Yoshida, Michiko. "Faulkner's Comedy of Motion: *The Reivers.*" In *Faulkner: After the Nobel Prize,* edited by Michel Gresset and Kenzaburo Ohashi, 197–210. Kyoto, Japan: Yamaguchi, 1987.

Requiem for a Nun

Published in September 1951, *Requiem for a Nun* is one of Faulkner's most experimental novels, told partly in the form of a play in three acts and partly in prose. Faulkner himself in a May 1950 letter to his publisher ROBERT K. HAAS referred to it as "a story told in seven play-scenes, inside a novel" and "an interesting experiment in form" (305). Each act is preceded by a prose passage that tells a portion of the history of YOKNAPATAWPHA COUNTY and the town of JEFFERSON, MISSISSIPPI. In the overall scheme of Faulkner's work, the prose sections of *Requiem* are the author's sole chronological history of his fictional county, and they can be read as a summary or overview of the history of Jefferson, from its founding in the early 1800s up to the time period of the novel (1950) with a glance at the city a decade and a half into the future. Although the history in each preface is not insignificant to Faulkner, the retelling, as NOEL POLK points out, "is essentially just one more of the tools of his trade, which he used in much the same way that he used myth and literary allusion, as a device for the illumination of character. History, the past, is only one of many things that concern him and his people" (Polk, *Faulkner's "Requiem for a Nun": A Critical Study,* 3).

Thematically, each prose section within the novel has a symbolic meaning and its setting is the stage-set for the drama that follows, a drama that is in the here-and-now. These three prose sections add the dimension of time, an overarching view of the meaning of three institutions with great societal significance: the courthouse, the statehouse, and the jailhouse.

In 1994, THE LIBRARY OF AMERICA published the text of *Requiem for a Nun* established by Noel Polk; see JOSEPH BLOTNER and Noel Polk, eds., *William Faulkner: Novels 1942–1954.*

SYNOPSIS

Though the title of *Requiem for a Nun* goes back to 1933 (*see Selected Letters,* 75), Faulkner started in earnest to write the novel in early 1949. (For a discussion of the composition of this work, *see* Noel Polk, *Faulkner's* Requiem for a Nun: *A Critical Study,* 237–245.) *Requiem* is a sequel to Faulkner's 1931 novel SANCTUARY, and as such this 15th Faulkner novel follows up on the subsequent lives of Temple Drake, who by now has become Temple Drake Stevens; her husband, Gowan Stevens; Gowan's uncle, Gavin Stevens; and Nancy Mannigoe, whom Temple hires as a nanny for her two children. (It is Nancy to whom the word *nun* in the title of the novel refers; *see Faulkner in the University,* 196.) Temple and Gowan are central characters in *Sanctuary,* the action of which occurs some eight years prior to the opening of *Requiem.* In that earlier novel, Temple is a 17-year-old first-year college student and Gowan a few years older. Gowan's heavy drinking sets in motion the chain of events leading to the horrifying incidents of *Sanctuary.* Soon after the ending of that novel, Gowan does what he considers to be the honorable thing—he marries Temple.

Requiem for a Nun opens on the final day of Nancy's trial for having killed Temple's six-month-old daughter. Because the experiences of *Sanctuary* leave a mark upon Temple, she employs Nancy, a drug user and sometime prostitute, precisely because Nancy is someone Temple can talk to, someone who understands her. In scene one, Nancy, having already been found guilty of the murder, is sentenced to die by hanging. After the sentence is pronounced, Temple, Gowan, and Gavin Stevens return to Gowan's house, where Gavin, Nancy's defense attorney, is made to feel unwelcome.

He waits until his nephew goes out of the room before confronting Temple, demanding to know what really happened and why Nancy murdered the child. Although Temple refuses to answer, she indicates that there are reasons and that the murder was not the act of a madwoman or that of a vicious psychopath. But Temple cannot squarely face the questions, and flees with her son to California.

Temple, however, cannot stay away forever. She returns to Jefferson the week before Nancy's scheduled execution. Giving her husband a sleeping pill one night so that she can be sure of not being overheard, Temple asks Gavin Stevens to come to see her. She confesses that, in a very real sense, she had a hand in the death of her own daughter and wants to stop the execution, even though there is no doubt that Nancy did the actual killing. Although Stevens thinks that it may be too late, he suggests that they go to Jackson to appeal directly to the governor. At the close of act 1, Temple asks how much she will have to tell, a concern that echoes her experiences in *Sanctuary*, in which she gave perjured testimony against the innocent Lee Goodwin. Wanting to make up for the mistakes of eight years ago and for the consequences of her actions in the immediate past, Temple agrees to speak frankly to the governor. At the very end of the act, the reader learns what Temple does not suspect: Her husband Gowan has overheard the entire conversation.

The second prose section of *Requiem* tells the story of the founding of the state capital, Jackson. In contrast to the almost comical founding of Jefferson, Jackson was carefully selected. Its site on a hill was chosen by three wise men, commissioners sent out by the state government, and it was deliberately named for the hero Andrew Jackson, a planter, a backwoods lawyer, a duelist, a slaveowner, and the architect of the Indian removals which, in essence, gave Mississippi, Alabama, northern Georgia, eastern Tennessee, and Florida to the white man. The power of the statehouse over the citizens of Mississippi crystallizes in this prose introduction.

In the dramatic act that follows, Temple confesses to the governor that she was ready to abandon her husband and son and run off with Pete, the younger brother of Alabama Red, Temple's lover in *Sanctuary*. (In the earlier novel, the bootlegger and gangster Popeye first rapes Temple with a corncob, then virtually imprisons her in a MEMPHIS brothel and watches while Red and Temple are having sex; once he sees that Temple is falling in love with Red, Popeye murders him.) Before Red's murder, Temple had written love letters to him explicit enough to be used by Pete to blackmail her eight years later.

In an attempt to stop Temple from running off with Pete, Nancy smothers Temple's infant daughter, an act that also costs Nancy her own life, which she is willing to sacrifice. Many of Temple's decisions result in someone's death: Tommy's, Goodwin's, and Red's in *Sanctuary*, and in *Requiem*, her baby's and Nancy's. Temple now realizes that it is up to her to stop this cycle of evil, but it is too late: the governor has already refused to grant a stay of execution for Nancy.

In scene 3 of act 2, when the governor is away from his office, Gowan silently takes his place behind the desk. Kneeling and with her face in her arms as she speaks, Temple, assuming that she is speaking to the governor, finishes her confessions, not to the man who has the authority to stop the execution, but to her husband. In a scene of telling power, Temple acts as though her confession were equivalent to a public execution. Gowan tells Temple that he, too, is sorry for all that has happened since their ill-fated trip to a baseball game in northern Mississippi; but the past is done, unchangeable. It is over. Lingering a bit with Gavin, Temple reflects with him on why the governor had refused to grant clemency. She agrees with Gavin and, by extension, with Nancy, when Gavin says: "You came here to affirm the very thing which Nancy is going to die tomorrow morning to postulate: that the little children, so long as they are little children, shall be intact, unanguished, untorn, unterrified" (181). Act 2 ends as Temple and Gavin are leaving the governor's office; her last words as they head home are: "To save my soul—if I have a soul. If there is a God to save it—a God who wants it—" (182).

The third prose section of *Requiem* concerns the history of the Jefferson jail, which, as Faulkner points out, predates both the courthouse and the statehouse, and even the naming of Jefferson itself. Because the original log walls of the first impromptu jail are themselves walled in by the bricks of the current 20th-century jail, the reader can interpret the jail as a symbol not only of justice, law, and order, but also as the first social institution necessary to restrain the primitive rages of humanity before civilization can be built. Faulkner undercuts the jail's meaning, however, in two crucial ways. First, jails can be repositories of blind justice. For example, three persons lawfully convicted are innocent. Lee Goodwin was not the murderer of Tommy; Popeye, executed in Birmingham, Alabama, was the killer of both Tommy and Red, but not of the man for whose death he is hanged; and Nancy Mannigoe is innocent of murder, although not of homicide, because of her motives and the absence of malice aforethought. Second, true murderers, like Wiley Harpe (Big Harpe) simply remove the wall of the jail and walk off. The ominous dread of the jail is also undercut by Faulkner's apparent digression about Cecilia Farmer, the daughter of the Jefferson town jailer in 1861. At that time, as in the time of *Requiem*, the jailer and his family lived in the jail. Described as lazy and weak, Cecilia cuts her name into the glass of a jailhouse window in early April 1861. Legend then has it that during a retreat in 1864 a Confederate soldier sees Cecilia sitting at that same window and returns to marry her the next year. The jail, therefore, becomes a tourist attraction and the setting of sentimental stories instead of an emblem of society's implacable justice.

The events of act 3 are quickly told. With Gavin Stevens, Temple visits Nancy in her cell on the morning before her execution and explains that Nancy is not solely responsible for the death of the baby. Temple confesses that she wanted to go to the governor and to "tell him that it wasn't you who killed my baby, but I did it eight years ago that day when I slipped out the backdoor of that train . . ." (235). Temple learns what Nancy already knows: such an act of confession would not and could not also be an act of expiation. Somebody has to suffer for the death of Temple's infant. Nancy, who actually held the blanket over the struggling baby's nose and mouth, must die for that dreadful act, while Temple, whose actions and plans forced Nancy to commit the crime, must live with its consequences. Stevens and Nancy listen to Temple's reflections on her state of mind. Nancy advises Temple to trust in God, and adds that suffering is a way of staying out of "devilment" (237).

CRITICAL COMMENTARY

Suffering is a major theme of *Requiem for a Nun*. The acceptance of all human suffering as the consequence of living is central to the novel. In *Sanctuary*, Faulkner shows the inevitability of evil, its pervasiveness and its potential presence within us all—even a seemingly innocent 17-year-old college student. In *Requiem*, Faulkner attempts to show that evil can, in fact, be resisted, but that suffering is the price we pay (or the reward we get) for succumbing to it. But through suffering and the recognition of one's guilt, there is spiritual redemption.

In 1951, with the help of Albert Marre, Ruth Ford, and Lemuel Ayers, Faulkner worked on an adaptation of *Requiem for a Nun* for the stage. On November 26, 1957, the play, directed by Tony Richardson, with Ruth Ford as Temple, Beatrice Reading as Nancy, and Zachary Scott as Gavin Stevens, premiered at the Royal Court Theatre in London. On January 28, 1959, the play opened at the John Golden Theatre in New York City. (*Requiem for a Nun: A Play*, adapted to the stage by Ruth Ford, was published by Random House in 1959.) In his note to the play, Faulkner comments: "This play was written not to be a play, but as what seemed to me the best way to tell the story in a novel" (i). The world premiere of the play was in Paris on September 20, 1956. The stage adaptation was by ALBERT CAMUS. *Sanctuary* and *Requiem for a Nun* were adapted to film; *see* FILM, FAULKNER AND.

For further information, *see Selected Letters of William Faulkner* and *Faulkner in the University*, 79, 86, 96, 122, 196, and 266.

EXCERPTS FROM CONTEMPORARY REVIEWS OF *REQUIEM FOR A NUN*

Excerpt from Malcolm Cowley's review, "In Which Mr. Faulkner Translates Past into Present," published in the **New York Herald Tribune Books**, *September 30, 1951, 1, 14:*

Requiem for a Nun is among the most successful of Faulkner's many experiments in narrative form. . . .

Requiem for a Nun—the nun is Nancy, of course—is a drama conceived on a level of moral consciousness that made me describe it as being genuinely tragic. In that respect it is vastly superior to *Sanctuary*, where the only morality was in the dim background of the author's mind. Yet the comparison between the old book and the new isn't as simple as this would make it seem. *Sanctuary* had the compelling power of nightmare images and there were meanings hidden beneath the surface of a headlong and violent story. *Requiem for a Nun* propounds the sort of traditional wisdom that we must respect, because we feel that it has been learned at the cost of suffering. It has a much richer surface than *Sanctuary*, but I would guess that it has less beneath the surface. Faulkner is writing now with more attention to logic and with somewhat less help from his subconscious mind. . . .

Excerpt from Carvel Collins's review, "Mississippi's Nobel Prize Winner Experiments with Play Form in Middle of His Newest Novel," published in The Delta Democrat-Times, *September 30, 1951, 15:*
. . . The book has its excellent aspects and some that are not so good. At times the play moves swiftly and at others it drags. The two most skillful of the three expository preludes give the play magnitude in this book form because they expand our sense of the past, but they are more interesting in themselves and most interesting in relation to all of Faulkner's fiction about Yoknapatawpha County. . . .

Excerpt from Richard Match's review, "The 'New' Faulkner," published in the New Republic, *November 5, 1951, 19–20:*
I have two reasons for believing that *Requiem for a Nun* is not a major addition to the body of William Faulkner's work: (1) it adds no memorable character to the Faulkner gallery, and (2) it is totally implausible. On the other hand, for a couple of equally good reasons, this new book will always rate a nod from future Faulkner commentators. First: in form it is something new for the author, being a play within a novel, or, more exactly, an organic and (potentially) effective fusion of the two forms, a play-novel. Second: whatever it lacks, *Requiem* does contribute a double-barreled footnote to the immortal Yoknapatawpha saga; it is at once a reca-pitulation of Yoknapatawpha County's history, from Chickasaw signal fire to drugstore neon sign, and a sequel to the story of its best-known sinner, Temple Drake. . . .

Excerpt from David Paul's review, "The Faulkner Stammer," published in The Observer, *February 15, 1953, 9:*
Mr. Faulkner's new novel, to echo one of his stylistic foibles, recapitulates, renews, re-exemplifies all the faults and the virtues, the heights of passion and depths of bathos in a writer whose qualities, it seems to me, are more controversial than is generally allowed. The book is written on two levels. Essentially it is a repetition of that tempting experiment, the novel written as a drama, complete with imaginary stage setting and lighting, detailed stage directions and dialogue. Before each act there is a rhapsodic prologue, a solemn invocation, as it were, to the places in which the drama is situated, these being the Courthouse at Jefferson, in Yoknapatawpha County, the State Governor's office in Jackson City, and finally the Jail-house in Jefferson. . . .

CHARACTERS

Coldfield The family name of an early settler in the YOKNAPATAWPHA COUNTY and one of several such family names mentioned in the novel. For specific members of the family, *see* ABSALOM, ABSALOM!

Compson A family name of one of the early settlers in YOKNAPATAWPHA COUNTY and one of several such family names mentioned in the novel. *See* Jason Lycurgus Compson I below and for specific members of the family *see* especially *The* SOUND AND THE FURY and ABSALOM, ABSALOM!

Compson, Jason (Lycurgus I) Referred to in act 1, "The Courthouse" (and in Faulkner's appendix to *The* SOUND AND THE FURY). Jason is the son of Charles Stuart Compson, a British soldier during the Revolutionary War, and the father of General Jason Lycurgus Compson II. (However, according to Faulkner's appendix to *The Sound and the Fury*, Jason I was the grandfather of General Compson.) In 1779, Jason I is taken by his grandfather, Quentin MacLachan, from Carolina to Kentucky. In 1811, he becomes a clerk in the Chickasaw Agency at Okatoba in Mississippi, and later is the agent's partner. He trades his swift mare with Ikkemotubbe for a square mile of land where he builds his home, known as the Compson place. (In *The* MANSION, a different Compson is identified; in 1821 Quentin [MacLachan] Compson [II] was granted land from the Chickasaw matriarch Mohataha.) One of the founders of JEFFERSON, MISSISSIPPI, Jason's square mile "was to be the most valuable land in the future town of Jefferson" (*Requiem*, 12). (For Faulkner's descriptions of the Compsons, *see* Appendix.)

Compson, General (Jason Lycurgus II) The son of Jason (Lycurgus) Compson (I) and a Confederate (brigadier) general during the Civil War. A decade after the war, General Compson, together with Colonel John Sartoris and the carpetbagger Redmond, build a railroad. After a quarrel among the three owners ten years later, Sartoris and Redmond buy out Compson's share. For other details regarding this character, *see* ABSALOM, ABSALOM!, *The* UNVANQUISHED, GO DOWN MOSES ("The OLD PEOPLE," "The BEAR," and "DELTA AUTUMN"), INTRUDER IN THE DUST, *The* TOWN, *The* REIVERS, "My GRANDMOTHER MILLARD AND GENERAL BEDFORD FORREST AND THE BATTLE OF HARRYKIN CREEK," and Faulkner's appendix to *The* SOUND AND THE FURY where General Compson is the grandson of Jason I and the son of the governor Quentin MacLachan Compson II (*see* Appendix).

Du Pre, Mrs. Virginia (Sartoris) An offstage character referred to in the novel. She is Colonel John Sartoris's sister. For further details *see* Virginia Du Pre in SARTORIS and *The* UNVANQUISHED, Miss Jenny in SANCTUARY and "THERE WAS A QUEEN." She is also referred to as Mrs. Du Pre, Mrs. Jennie Du Pre, and Miss Jenny Du Pre in *The* TOWN, as Mrs. Du Pre in *The* MANSION, and as Aunt Jenny and Mrs. Virginia Sartoris in "ALL THE DEAD PILOTS."

Farmer The turnkey (jailer) in JEFFERSON during the Civil War.

Farmer, Cecilia Farmer's daughter. Out of boredom, with a diamond ring she scratches her name and the date on a windowpane of her father's jail. At the end of the war, she meets and marries a former Confederate soldier and moves with him to his farm in Alabama. (*Also see* Celia Cook in *The* UNVANQUISHED.)

Gombault, "Uncle Pete" Referred to in the novel as "a lean clean tobacco-chewing old man, incumbent of a political sinecure under the designation of United States marshal" (*Requiem*, 313). *Also see* Gombault in *The* TOWN and the short story "The TALL MEN."

Grenier, Louis One of the first settlers of YOKNAPATAWPHA COUNTY and owner of a vast plantation which becomes FRENCHMAN'S BEND. The ruined mansion on the original property is the OLD FRENCHMAN PLACE, once owned by Will Varner in *The* HAMLET and later the bootlegger Lee Goodwin's hideout in SANCTUARY. Grenier is the first settler to bring slaves to the county and the county's first cotton planter. Grenier, a Huguenot, is also referred to in INTRUDER IN THE DUST, KNIGHT'S GAMBIT ("Hand Upon the Waters"), *The* TOWN, and *The* REIVERS. *The Hamlet* mentions a Grenier County. *See Intruder in the Dust* where Lonnie Grinnup, the dull-witted squatter, is identified as Grenier's last descendant.

Habersham, Doctor Samuel A pioneer medical doctor and, with Louis Grenier and Alexander Holston, one of the original settlers and founders of JEFFERSON. Until he resigned in protest, Habersham was the first Chickasaw agent of the settlement, which at one time was known by his name: "as Doctor Habersham's, then Habersham's, then simply Habersham" (7). His motherless son married one of Issetibbeha's granddaughters and in the 1830s emigrated to Oklahoma with her "dispossessed people" (7). Doctor Habersham is referred to in INTRUDER IN THE DUST and *The* TOWN.

Hare One of the legendary highway men associated with the early history of YOKNAPATAWPHA COUNTY. Like Mason, another bandit, Hare threw his murder victims into remote wilderness streams.

Harpes Two of the Natchez Trace bandits or highwaymen named in the legendary early history of YOKNAPATAWPHA COUNTY. Legend has the Harpes (Big Harpe in particular) associated with the jailbreak, but by that time they were either dead or gone away. Wiley Harpe, also held in jail, may have been a murderer. They are also referred to as the mad Harpes.

Harpe, Big *See* Harpes.

Harpe, Wiley *See* Harpes.

Henry The governor of Mississippi, whom Temple Drake Stevens and Gavin Stevens visit during the middle of the night to ask for a stay in the execution of Nancy Mannigoe. He denies their pleas.

Holston, Alexander (Alec; Uncle Alec) In *Requiem for a Nun*, he is identified with Doctor Samuel Habersham and Louis Grenier as one of the three original settlers of YOKNAPATAWPHA COUNTY. Holston arrives "as half groom and half bodyguard to Doctor Habersham, and half nurse and half tutor to the doctor's eight-year-old motherless son" (6–7). He is the owner of the lock whose humorous role in the early history of the settlement is narrated in the prose prologue to act 1, "The Courthouse (A Name for the City)," and is also the first publican in the county, proprietor of the tavern known during the time period of *Requiem* as the Holston House. *Also see* ABSALOM, ABSALOM!; Holston is mentioned in INTRUDER IN THE DUST, KNIGHT'S GAMBIT ("Hand Upon the Waters"), The TOWN, and The MANSION.

In *Requiem*, Holston, who dies a generation before the Civil War, is said to be a childless bachelor, but in the later time frame of "SKIRMISH AT SARTORIS" (a short story revised with the same title as chapter 6 of The UNVANQUISHED), there appears a Mrs. Holston, and in *The Mansion*, the Holston House is "owned and run by two maiden sisters ... who were the last descendants of Alexander Holston" (383).

Ikkemotubbe The CHICKASAW INDIAN chief, Mohataha's son and Issetibbeha's successor, with whom Jason Lycurgus Compson I trades his race horse for a square mile of land that was to become the most valuable piece of property in the future town of JEFFERSON. *Also see* ABSALOM, ABSALOM!, GO DOWN, MOSES ("THE OLD PEOPLE"), *The TOWN*, "A JUSTICE," and in the following three works where his name appears as Doom: The REIVERS, "RED LEAVES," and "A COURTSHIP."

Issetibbeha A CHICKASAW INDIAN chief, Mohataha's brother and Ikkemotubbe's immediate predecessor. Faulkner's treatment of this character is not always consistent; *also see* GO DOWN, MOSES ("THE OLD PEOPLE" and "THE BEAR"), The TOWN, The REIVERS, "RED LEAVES," and "A COURTSHIP."

Jailor, The *See* Tubbs, Mr.

Maggie (Aunt Maggie) An offstage character in the novel. Maggie is Margaret Stevens Mallison, Gavin Stevens's twin sister and Chick Mallison's mother. *See* INTRUDER IN THE DUST, KNIGHT'S GAMBIT ("Knight's Gambit"), The TOWN, and The MANSION.

Mannigoe, Nancy Nanny to Temple Drake Stevens's two children. In scene 1 of act 1 of *Requiem*, Nancy, described as a tramp, drunkard, and casual prostitute, is found guilty of the murder of Temple's six-month-old daughter and sentenced to death by hanging. Nancy's crime is the result of her desperate attempt to prevent Temple from leaving her husband and home for Pete, the younger brother of her late lover, Red (*see* SANCTUARY). In choosing a dope fiend as a servant, Temple shows a persistent attraction to evil and sees in Nancy a person with whom she is comfortable conversing. However, in a discussion prior to the murder (in scene 2 of act 2 of the novel), Nancy angers Temple by bluntly confronting her with the possible fate of the child if Temple leaves her husband: ". . . maybe taking her with you will be just as easy, at least until the first time you write Mr. Gowan or your pa for money and they dont send it as quick as your new man thinks they ought to, and he throws you and the baby both out" (161). To Nancy's anguished thinking, Temple's daughter is as good as dead, and by smothering the baby in her cradle, Nancy believes she is merely stopping a cycle of evil that began in *Sanctuary*. Through Nancy, Temple, who is well aware of the consequences of her past deeds, is forced to face her own responsibility and guilt, but Temple's direct appeal to the governor for a stay in Nancy's execution is unsuccessful.

In response to a question at the University of Virginia, Faulkner identified Nancy as the nun in the novel's title (*Faulkner in the University*, 196; for other information, *see Selected Letters*, 298.) *Also see* "THAT EVENING SUN" where she is a central character and where only her first name is used.

Mason   One of the legendary gang leaders referred to as part of the early history of YOKNAPATAWPHA COUNTY. He threw his murder victims into remote wilderness streams; *also see* Hare. By the time of the jailbreak by the Natchez Trace bandits, Mason and his ruffians were either dead or scattered.

McCaslin   The family name of an early settler in YOKNAPATAWPHA COUNTY and one of several such family names mentioned in the novel. Specific members either appear or are referred to in other works; *see* especially GO DOWN, MOSES, *The* UNVANQUISHED, and *The* REIVERS.

Mohataha   The CHICKASAW matriarch referred to in the novel; she is Issetibbeha's sister and Ikkemotubbe's mother. Mohataha leaves Mississippi and leads her people to Oklahoma. *Also see The* MANSION.

Mulberry   The metonymic name given to a black man who sold illegal whiskey that he concealed under a mulberry tree. A U.S. marshal during Reconstruction days, he was still known as Mulberry in 1925. He worked various jobs, such as janitor and furnace-attendant, for several lawyers, medical doctors, and a bank.

Murrel, John   The head of a gang of robbers referred to in the early history of YOKNAPATAWPHA COUNTY. The bandits associated with the jailbreak belonged to his organization. Murrel stood in the tradition of Hare, Mason, and the mad Harpes, and in this respect he was their heir, who turned "his heritage of simple rapacity and bloodlust . . . into a bloody dream of outlaw-empire" (*Requiem for a Nun*, 194). (His last name appears both as Murrel and Murell in the novel.)

Peabody, Doctor   Doctor Samuel Habersham's successor. In the early history of YOKNAPATAWPHA COUNTY, Doctor Peabody is one of the men who agree on naming their new city JEFFERSON. (A Doctor Peabody appears in other works—SARTORIS, AS I LAY DYING, *The* SOUND AND THE FURY, *The* HAMLET, *The* REIVERS, and "BEYOND"—but because of an age discrepancy cannot be the same character who appears in *Requiem for a Nun*.)

Pete   The younger brother of Temple Drake Stevens's deceased lover, Red. Pete has letters Temple wrote to his brother and intends to blackmail her, but a romantic interest develops between them. Their plans to run off with each other are foiled when Temple's six-month-old daughter is murdered by her nanny, Nancy Mannigoe.

Pettigrew, Thomas Jefferson   The small and seemingly insignificant mail rider after whom the town of JEFFERSON is named. Pettigrew shows a remarkable durability riding between the original settlement in northern Mississippi, which settlement later became the town of Jefferson, and Nashville to deliver the mail every three weeks. He rides unarmed through bandit and Indian territories, showing almost casual bravery, using only a hunting horn to mark his coming and going. Pettigrew's physical courage is matched by his moral rectitude, which forces him to object to Jason Lycurgus Compson I's plan to pay Alec Holston $15 for a lost lock out of funds provided by the federal government for the CHICKASAW INDIAN removal. Pettigrew's acquiescence, however, is bought when the settlers offer to name the town Jefferson in his honor.

Ratcliffe   Post trader associated with the Chickasaw agency trading-post and an early settler in the region that becomes JEFFERSON.

Red, Alabama An offstage character referred to in the novel, he was Pete's older brother and Temple Drake Stevens's lover; *see* the Character entry for Temple Drake under SANCTUARY. During the time period of *Requiem*, Alabama Red is deceased; for other information regarding this character, *see* Red under *Sanctuary*.

Redmond A carpetbagger from Missouri described as "a cotton- and quartermaster-supplies speculator, who had followed the Northern army to Memphis in [18]61" (200). After the Civil War, with Colonel Sartoris and General Compson, he built a railroad. Sparked by a quarrel years later, Redmond and Sartoris bought Compson's interest in the business. A year after that, Redmond and Sartoris had a disagreement, and a year later, motivated by physical fear Redmond, killed Sartoris and fled. *Also see The* UNVANQUISHED ("An Odor of Verbena") where his first name, Ben, appears and *SARTORIS* where his name is Redlaw.

Sartoris The family name of an early settler in YOKNAPATAWPHA COUNTY and one of several such family names mentioned in the novel. Specific members either appear or are referred to in other works; for example, *see SARTORIS, The* UNVANQUISHED, the SNOPES TRILOGY (*The* HAMLET, *The* TOWN, and *The* MANSION), *The* REIVERS, "BARN BURNING," "THERE WAS A QUEEN," and "MY GRANDMOTHER MILLARD AND GENERAL BEDFORD FORREST AND THE BATTLE OF HARRYKIN CREEK."

Sartoris, Bayard Colonel John Sartoris's son, a banker. Through his initiative, a law is enacted prohibiting mechanically propelled vehicles from being operated on the streets of JEFFERSON, a result of his having passed a "popping and stinking" one while riding in a horse-drawn carriage (*Requiem*, 208). Ironically, the older Bayard dies of a heart attack in a car that his grandson Bayard is driving recklessly. For more information regarding his character, *see SARTORIS and The* UNVANQUISHED; he is mentioned in *The* HAMLET, *The* TOWN, *The* MANSION, *The* REIVERS and in the short stories "A ROSE FOR EMILY" (where he is referred to with the title Colonel, out of respect for his father) and "THERE WAS A QUEEN."

Sartoris, Colonel John Bayard's father. Considered a newcomer in YOKNAPATAWPHA COUNTY when the county is only about a half dozen years old, John Sartoris arrives with slaves and gear, and, like Louis Grenier and Thomas Sutpen, Sartoris has money. In 1861, Sartoris is the first person in JEFFERSON to be seen in a Confederate uniform. He raises and organizes an infantry regiment and serves as a colonel. After the Battle of Second Manassas (the Second Battle of Bull Run), however, Sartoris is deposed of his position and returns home to his plantation, but not for long. He musters up a small group of irregular cavalry and joins NATHAN BEDFORD FORREST in Tennessee. A decade after the Civil War, Sartoris, together with Redmond and General Compson, builds a railroad. The three men are partners for ten years until Sartoris and Redmond buy Compson's share, and about two years after that Sartoris is assassinated by Redmond, the result of a serious disagreement. For other details regarding Colonel John Sartoris, *see SARTORIS, The* UNVANQUISHED, *LIGHT IN AUGUST, ABSALOM, ABSALOM!, The* HAMLET, *The* TOWN, *The* MANSION, GO DOWN, MOSES ("The BEAR"), *The* REIVERS, and the short stories "BARN BURNING," "SHALL NOT PERISH" "GRANDMOTHER MILLARD AND GENERAL BEDFORD FORREST AND THE BATTLE OF HARRYKIN CREEK," and "THERE WAS A QUEEN." In *The* SOUND AND THE FURY, Quentin Compson, when thinking about death, momentarily calls to mind his grandfather and Colonel Sartoris.

Faulkner modeled Colonel John Sartoris on his great-grandfather; *see* WILLIAM CLARK FALKNER. *Also see Faulkner in the University*, 253–254.

Stevens The family name of an early settler in the YOKNAPATAWPHA COUNTY and one of several such family names mentioned in the novel.

Stevens, Bucky The young son and only surviving child of Gowan and Temple Drake Stevens. While in California with his mother, who is escaping from the circumstances surrounding the death of her infant daughter, Bucky's questions cause Temple to return to JEFFERSON and attempt to save Nancy Mannigoe from being executed for having been found guilty of killing Temple's baby daughter.

Stevens, Gavin   An attorney from a prominent JEFFERSON family, he is Gowan Steven's uncle. Gavin takes his nephew's wife, Temple Drake Stevens, to visit the governor in the middle of the night so the governor can hear her plea for Nancy Mannigoe, who is to be executed for having killed Temple's six-month-old baby. Her attempt to convince the governor to spare Nancy's life is unsuccessful.

Partly modeled on his friend, PHILIP AVERY STONE, Stevens is an important character in several of Faulkner's works; for other details regarding his character, *see* KNIGHT'S GAMBIT, INTRUDER IN THE DUST, *The* TOWN, *The* MANSION, LIGHT IN AUGUST, GO DOWN, MOSES ("Go Down, Moses"), "HAIR," "The TALL MEN," "HOG PAWN," and "BY THE PEOPLE." *Also see Faulkner in the University,* 25, 72, 118, 140–141 and 201.

Stevens, Gowan   Gavin Stevens's nephew and Temple Drake's husband. Gowan and Temple have two children, the younger of whom is killed by their nanny, Nancy Mannigoe. A recovered alcoholic, Gowan married the woman he deserted at OLD FRENCHMAN PLACE; *see* SANCTUARY. *Also see The* TOWN where he is Chick Mallison's first cousin once removed (their grandfathers are brothers) and Gavin's 13-year-old cousin, not his nephew. (Faulkner is not always consistent with some of his characters.)

Stevens, Temple Drake   Gowan Stevens's wife and mother of two small children, the younger of whom is smothered to death by their nanny, Nancy Mannigoe. Now in her mid-20's, Temple, the 17-year-old coed who eight years earlier had been abandoned by the drunken Gowan Stevens at OLD FRENCHMAN PLACE, abducted to MEMPHIS and forced into prostitution, and flirts with the very evil confronting her. (For other details regarding Temple Drake, *see* SANCTUARY.) In *Requiem for a Nun,* Gowan has stopped drinking, but her attempt at a conventional life as wife and mother of two children fails. Letters that she wrote to her lover

Red (referred to as Alabama Red in *Requiem*), letters she does not want her husband to see, are being used by Red's brother, Pete, to blackmail her. Temple's plans to take her infant daughter and run away with Pete—her way of avoiding blackmail—are foiled when her maid Nancy kills the child to prevent Temple from running off. Temple, however, wants Nancy saved from execution. Gowan's uncle, the attorney Gavin Stevens, takes Temple to meet with the governor, to whom she recounts the events of *Sanctuary,* admits her past guilt, and tells of her attraction to evil. But her attempt is futile; Nancy will be hanged. Among other issues, the problem of suffering and moral restitution plague Temple's thoughts and conversations throughout *Requiem.* For further information, *see Faulkner in the University,* 96 and 196.

Sutpen   The family name of an early settler in YOKNAPATAWPHA COUNTY and one of several such family names mentioned in the novel. *See* Thomas Sutpen below.

Sutpen, (Thomas)   An early settler in YOKNAPATAWPHA COUNTY. Sutpen brings with him a Paris architect responsible for designing the Georgian colonial mansion at SUTPEN'S HUNDRED. For other details, *see* ABSALOM, ABSALOM! where Sutpen is a central character.

Tubbs, Mr.   The JEFFERSON jailer who guards Nancy Mannigoe, accused of killing Temple Drake Stevens's baby daughter. *Also see* INTRUDER IN THE DUST and *The* MANSION (where his first name Euphus is given).

Tubbs, Mrs.   The jailer's wife. An offstage character, who, according to her husband, usually has a bottle or two of soda in her icebox. *Also see* INTRUDER IN THE DUST and *The* MANSION.

Vitelli, Popeye   An offstage character in the novel, Popeye is a major figure in SANCTUARY where, among other things, he is a gangster and murderer; his last name, however, is not used in that novel, nor is it used in the short story "The BIG SHOT" where he also appears as a bootlegger.

FURTHER READING

Brooks, Cleanth. "Discovery of Evil (*Sanctuary* and *Requiem for a Nun*)." In *William Faulkner: The Yoknapatawpha Country*, 116–140. Baton Rouge: Louisiana State University Press, 1990.

Fowler, Doreen. "Time and Punishment in Faulkner's *Requiem for a Nun*." *Renascence* 38.4 (1986): 245–255.

Graham, Philip. "Patterns in Faulkner's *Sanctuary* and *Requiem for a Nun*." *Tennessee Studies in Literature* 8 (1963): 39–46.

Millgate, Michael. "*Requiem for a Nun*." In *The Achievement of William Faulkner*, 221–226. Lincoln: University of Nebraska Press, 1978.

Polk, Noel. *Faulkner's* Requiem for a Nun: *A Critical Study*. Bloomington: Indiana University Press, 1981.

"Retreat"
(Uncollected Stories)

Short story first published in the October 13, 1934 issue of the *Saturday Evening Post* and revised when included as the second chapter in The UNVAN-QUISHED (1938).

SYNOPSIS

As the Civil War drags on, the Confederate cause is nearly lost and the Yankees are swarming all around Sartoris plantation; Granny Rosa Millard, the mistress of the plantation, buries the family silver and seeks to make her way, along with her young grandson Bayard Sartoris and his black companion Ringo, to safety in MEMPHIS. However, Bayard and Ringo become separated from Granny, who must then plot her retreat back home. A Union patrol confiscates two Sartoris mules, Old Hundred and Tinny. Bayard and Ringo help Colonel Sartoris's partisans capture a company of Yankees, but Colonel Sartoris intentionally allows the prisoners to escape so he can devote his full attention to finding and safeguarding Granny. Enemy soldiers burn the Sartoris plantation, and the slave Loosh leads them to the treasure and, reluctantly

accompanied by his wife, Philadephia, walks away from Sartoris a free man.

CRITICAL COMMENTARY

Narrated by the youthful Bayard, this story contrasts the boy's heroic, larger-than-life image of his father—made even more heroic by the courageous, though improbable capture of the Yankee soldiers—with the chaos, confusion, and violence that the encroaching war has brought to the very door of Sartoris plantation. The separation of Granny and the boys, albeit temporary, and the acts of betrayal and abandonment by Loosh dramatize the effect of the war upon the Sartoris family and their slaves. The reader understands both Loosh's proclamation of his freedom ("I going. I done been freed. . .") and his wife's anxiety that they may be headed, as Granny insists they are, toward "misery and starvation" (*Uncollected Stories*, 35). For young and old, black and white, the war has brought disruption and paradox—and movement that, even when it appears to be progress, may be better characterized as "retreat."

CHARACTERS

For a list of the characters in this story *see* the entry on The UNVANQUISHED.

"Return, A"
(Uncollected Stories)

Short story, almost a novella, rejected by the *Saturday Evening Post* and first published in *Uncollected Stories* (1979). It is a revision of "ROSE OF LEBANON" (1930).

SYNOPSIS

The story follows the lives of Lewis Randolph and her son Randolph Gordon from the Civil War to a 1930 MEMPHIS dinner party. In 1861, Lewis, a plantation owner's daughter, elopes with the gallant and doomed Charles Gordon as he departs for the front. She returns home to give birth to her son. By then the full catastrophe of the war—starvation, destruction, wasted lives, and senseless slaughter— has befallen the South. Lewis keeps things going by laboring alongside the blacks. Randolph goes to MEMPHIS, where he works his way up to bank president. Obsessed with history, Dr. Gavin Blount, a grandnephew of Charles Gordon's commander, seeks out Randolph. Blount romanticizes the Civil War and idealizes Lewis, whom he imagines as a flower of Southern womanhood. When he finally meets the old woman, she rebuffs his fanciful recreation of the past by flinging a bowl of soup at him. Although Blount shifts his perspective, his future is in doubt. His skewed vision of the mythic South contrasts with Randolph's materialistic new South and with the indomitable Lewis, who survives by substituting for her original future of idleness and needlepoint a life of self-sufficiency and self-determination.

CRITICAL COMMENTARY

This story mirrors the early 20th century literary and cultural debate between the defenders and the detractors of the Old South. Authors such as Thomas Nelson Page and Thomas Dixon romanticized the antebellum South and the Confederate cause and sought to preserve the old ways, while other writers, among them Ellen Glasgow and W. E. B. DuBois, advocated change and accommodation. Faulkner, although he was in some respects a cultural traditionalist, belongs more to the second category than the first. The satirical portrait of Blount seems designed to show the folly of an unthinking, uncritical idealization of the past. James Ferguson believes "A Return" contains "some of the richest prose Faulkner ever wrote" but argues that the climactic scene in which Mrs. Randolph throws the bowl of soup at Blount "is much too slight to bear the weight of the lengthy, leisurely, and detailed exposition" (*Faulkner's Short Fiction*, 121).

CHARACTERS

Awce A slave owned by the Randolphs.

Blount, Dr. Gavin The grandnephew of a senior officer killed in the Civil War, Dr. Blount romanticizes the war and idealizes the war widow Lewis Randolph, but she rejects Blount's rosy view of the

past by throwing soup in his face. He also appears in "The BIG SHOT" and "DULL TALE."

Gordon, Charles A Confederate officer, gallant but doomed, he marries the planter's daughter Lewis Randolph at the outset of the Civil War and leaves her a widowed mother.

Gordon, Randolph The son of the indomitable but unsentimental Civil War widow Lewis Randolph.

Heustace, Mr. and Mrs. Henry Guests at the dinner party that Randolph Gordon arranges for his mother.

Joanna A slave who serves as nurse to Lewis Randolph.

Lissy (Melissandre) Daughter of Joanna and Awce.

Lucius Black servant to Lewis Randolph.

Randolph, Lewis A planter's daughter, she marries a gallant Confederate officer, Charles Gordon, at the outset of the Civil War and carries on with their son in great hardship after Charles is killed and the South is in ruins. Lewis views her long life and achievements in unsentimental terms.

Will A slave owned by the Randolphs.

"Rose for Emily, A" (Collected Stories)

Faulkner's first published short story in a nationally recognized magazine. It appeared in the April 1930 issue of the *Forum* (133, 233–238); a revision of the story was published in *These 13* (1931), *A Rose for Emily and Other Stories* (1945), The PORTABLE FAULKNER (1946), COLLECTED STORIES OF WILLIAM FAULKNER (1950), *The Faulkner Reader* (1954), *A Rose for Emily* (1956), and *Selected Short Stories of William Faulkner* (1962).

SYNOPSIS

"A Rose for Emily" is about Miss Emily Grierson, an elderly woman who lived the last 10 years of her life as a recluse. Told from the first person plural point of view (an indication that the narrator is speaking from the collective perspective of the town), the story opens with Miss Emily's funeral, which the whole town attends: "the men through a sort of respectful affection for a fallen monument, the women mostly out of curiosity to see the inside of her house" (*Collected Stories*, 119), as though by seeing it they would bring to light a hidden secret of her personality. In fact, a secret is exposed at the end of the story when the narrator ties together various clues sprinkled throughout this gothic tale, or ghost story as Faulkner referred to it (*Faulkner in the University*, 26). Between the opening and closing paragraphs, the narrator tells just enough information about Miss Emily's personal life, the mental health of her family, her restrictive father, the stench that came from her house 40 years before, and, in particular, about her romance with the Yankee construction foreman, Homer Barron, who was last seen entering her kitchen door one evening. With the exception of a period of six or seven years, during which time Miss Emily gave lessons in china-painting, her life remained a mystery to the town until her death. Those who went to Miss Emily's house to look through it after the funeral knew that there was one upstairs room that "no one had seen in forty years" (*Collected Stories*, 129) that would have to be broken into. The room was decked like a bridal chamber. In the bed were the skeletal remains of Homer Barron, and on one of the pillows a strand of Miss Emily's gray hair.

CRITICAL COMMENTARY

A highly anthologized work, "A Rose for Emily" has received a considerable amount of criticism, leading Diane Brown Jones, the compiler of a lengthy bibliography on the work, to remark: "The critical canon of 'A Rose for Emily' has become as bloated as the character herself" (*A Reader's Guide to the Short Stories of William Faulkner*, 133). A good deal of that critical attention is directed to the masterly, suspenseful structure featuring Faulkner's typical flashbacks and flash-forwards in time, with numerous related attempts to create an accurate chronology of the narrated events; but most of the discussion of the story centers on theme and characterization. Early critics focused on the gothic elements, noting similarities in setting and tone with Edgar Allan Poe's "The Fall of the House of Usher"; CLEANTH BROOKS and ROBERT PENN WARREN extended this parallel by citing how the respective houses of the two stories mirror the traits of their inhabitants (*Understanding Fiction*, 409–410). In this connection it is tempting to see the story, as some readers do, as a symbolic, tragic representation of the Southern tradition, Emily's refusal to accept change, first in the death of her father and then in the loss of Homer, being viewed as emblematic of the South's historical reluctance to embrace change and progress. Several critics, among them Irving Malin, Norman Holland, and Jack Sherting, analyze Emily's relationship with her father, seeing the tragic conclusion of the relationship with Homer as a logical consequence of the repression and abuse Emily experienced at the hands of Mr. Grierson. Feminist interpretations like Judith Fetterley's expand this application, arguing that the murder of Homer is Emily's revenge against a tyrannical patriarchal system that has made her into a stereotype of the southern "lady." Still other critics interpret the story as a clash between a declining aristocracy and a burgeoning middle class (Old South versus New South); between social expectations and individuality; and between normal and abnormal psychology (with particular attention to the question of necrophilia). A few recent readers argue that Homer Barron is gay (citing the narrator's observation that Homer "liked men" and Homer's own remark that "he was not a marrying man" [*Collected Stories*, 126]) and that it is his homosexuality that triggers Emily's distress and violence. Despite the abundance of criticism devoted to the story, too little attention has been paid to one ironic, though fascinating aspect of the narrative: the close parallels between Emily Grierson and Faulkner's characterization of the artist. Emily, as a teacher of china painting, is something of an artist (she carefully arranges the upstairs bedroom containing Homer's corpse as an artistic tableau); and, like Faulkner's ideal artist types, she is an individualist, fiercely independent of the community, and she embraces death-defying actions that create illusions of immortality. Cleanth Brooks argues against all narrow thematic readings of the story, preferring to view it as "an excellent example of Faulkner's skillful craftsmanship" (*William Faulkner: First Encounters*, 7) and finding in it the expression of a universal concern: "a warning against the sin of pride: heroic isolation pushed too far ends in homicidal madness" (*William Faulkner: First Encounters*, 14).

For more information, *see Selected Letters of William Faulkner*, 47, 63, 278; *Faulkner in the University*, pp. 47–48, 58–59, 87–88, 184–185, 199; and Diane Brown Jones, *A Reader's Guide to the Short Stories of William Faulkner*, 87–141.

CHARACTERS

Barron, Homer A Yankee road construction foreman, who has an affair with Miss Emily Grierson. When he breaks it off, Miss Emily poisons him and keeps his corpse in her bridal chamber.

Grierson, Miss Emily A JEFFERSON spinster, who is romantically taken up with the Yankee construction foreman Homer Barron. Miss Emily poisons him when he attempts to end their relationship and morbidly keeps his body in a locked upstairs room. At the end of the story, the townspeople find a strand of her gray hair on a pillow next to Homer's skeletal remains, an indication of Miss Emily's state of mind. In her way of perceiving and judging things, some readers may argue, she preserves her honor by killing the lover who was about to desert her. Faulkner commented that Miss Emily knew that murdering someone is wrong and that she was expected to marry and never take a lover. According to Faulkner, "she knew she was doing wrong, and that's why her life was wrecked. . . . [S]he was expiating her crime" (*Faulkner in the University*, 58). For more information, *see Faulkner in the University*, 26, 47–48, 87–88, 184–185.

Sartoris, Colonel An offstage character who, when he was mayor of JEFFERSON in 1894, remitted Miss Emily Grierson's taxes to relieve her of the burden of paying what she could not afford. To protect the pride of a woman who would not

accept charity, Colonel Sartoris invented a story that her father had loaned money to the town and the remission of her taxes was repayment. For other details regarding Colonel Sartoris (also referred to as old Bayard Sartoris), *see SARTORIS, The UNVANQUISHED, The HAMLET, The TOWN, The MANSION, GO DOWN, MOSES* ("The BEAR"), *REQUIEM FOR A NUN, The REIVERS*, and "THERE WAS A QUEEN."

Stevens, Judge Eighty-year-old mayor of JEFFERSON, who receives complaints about a smell coming from Miss Emily Grierson's property. Very much the gentleman, he sees to it that the actions taken to eliminate the odor do not publicly embarrass her. Judge Stevens arranges for a few men to spread lime on Miss Emily's property at night. (His relationship to the Stevens family and, in particular, to Judge Lemuel Stevens and Gavin Stevens is not certain; one commentator suggests that this 80-year-old mayor may be Gavin's grandfather.)

Tobe Miss Emily Grierson's black servant.

Wyatt An elderly woman, "crazy" by repute. Miss Emily Grierson's father fell out with his Alabama kin over a question of the old lady's estate.

FURTHER READING

Allen, Dennis W. "Horror and Perverse Delight: Faulkner's 'A Rose for Emily.'" *Modern Fiction Studies* 30 (1984): 685–696.

Brooks, Cleanth. "Short Stories." In *William Faulkner: First Encounters*, 7–42. New Haven: Yale University Press, 1983.

Brown Jones, Diane. *A Reader's Guide to the Short Stories of William Faulkner*. New York: G. K. Hall, 1994, 87–114.

Heller, Terry. "The Telltale Hair: A Critical Study of Faulkner's 'A Rose for Emily.'" *Arizona Quarterly* 28 (1972): 301–318.

Inge, M. Thomas, ed. *William Faulkner: "A Rose for Emily."* Columbus: Charles E. Merrill, 1970.

Powell, Janice A. "Changing Portraits in 'A Rose for Emily.'" *Teaching Faulkner* 11 (1997): 1–4.

Towner, Theresa M., and James B. Carothers. *Reading Faulkner: Collected Stories*. Jackson: University Press of Mississippi, 2006, 63–73.

"Rose of Lebanon"

Short story, posthumously published in 1995. *See* entry for "A RETURN."

Salmagundi

Five reprinted poems and three reprinted prose pieces published in April 1932 by Casanova Press in Milwaukee. The collection is edited with an introduction by Paul Romaine. A poem by ERNEST HEMINGWAY, "Ultimately," appears on the back cover. (*See* Appendix for titles.)

Sanctuary

Faulkner's sixth novel, first published by CAPE & SMITH on February 9, 1931; a corrected text of the novel by JOSEPH BLOTNER and NOEL POLK was published in 1985 in *William Faulkner: Novels 1930–1935*, volume 1 of Faulkner's collected works in the LIBRARY OF AMERICA series. *Sanctuary: The Original Text*, edited, with an afterword and notes, by Noel Polk, was published in 1981 by RANDOM HOUSE; the corrected text with Faulkner's introduction in the editors' note was published by Vintage International, in December 1993.

SYNOPSIS

The novel opens with Popeye in a tight black suit watching Horace Benbow drinking from a spring near the OLD FRENCHMAN PLACE, a gutted plantation house. Horace, who is escaping from his marital problems, is traveling from his home in Kinston to JEFFERSON where he used to live and where his widowed younger sister, Narcissa Benbow Sartoris, still lives with her 10-year-old son, Benbow. Assuming that Horace is a revenue agent, the bootlegger Popeye, an undersized man with a dark pallor, bulging eyes and a chinless face, mistakenly thinks he has a gun in his pocket, but it is only a book. Popeye leads Horace to Old Frenchman Place, where he is given dinner. He meets Lee Goodwin, another bootlegger, and others, including Goodwin's father, Pap, a blind and deaf man. Goodwin's common-law wife, Ruby Lamar, cooks for the men. After dinner, some of them sit on the porch, talking and drinking from a jug that they pass around. Popeye, however, is not one of them, for he has such a weak stomach alcohol would kill him. By the time Benbow gets a lift into Jefferson on Popeye's truck loaded with moonshine for MEMPHIS, he is drunk.

The next afternoon, Horace is in Jefferson at his sister's house. There he meets Gowan Stevens, a student at the University of Virginia, who boasts that he has learned how to drink like a gentleman. While Gowan and Narcissa walk in the garden after dinner, Horace mocks Stevens's claim. Later, Gowan leaves for a date with Temple, who attends the state university in nearby OXFORD. After they go to a dance, he gets very drunk, retches, and passes out. When he wakes up the next morning in front of the railroad station, the special train leaving for a baseball game in Starkville, where he was to drive Temple, has already left, so he speeds on to Taylor, a town the train will pass through. Just as the train starts to pull out of the station, Temple sees his car and jumps off the train to be with him, but his appearance—a wild face, disheveled hair, ruined shirt—disgusts her. Instead of taking her back to Oxford as Temple requests, Stevens hurries on to Starkville to beat the train. On the way, he stops off at Goodwin's for a bottle of bootlegged whiskey, hits a tree lying across the dirt road leading up to Old Frenchman Place and wrecks his car, which turns on its side. Gowan and Temple are led to the house by the feeble-minded Tommy, one of Goodwin's men. In the kitchen Temple meets Ruby, who tells her to wait in the dining room, where the men will be served dinner. Van, one of the bootleggers, attempts to seize Temple but is stopped by Goodwin. Moving slowly at first, Temple backs out of the dining room and once in the hallway runs out of the house and down the road, but then, as Temple is still running, she pivots and heads directly back to the house as Tommy is coming out with some food for her to eat, which she refuses. As she starts looking for Ruby, Gowan and the bootleggers come out onto the porch where Tommy is still holding the plate of ham for Temple.

Van makes a snide remark about Tommy's intent, suggesting that the food is a seduction technique. (Temple's very presence at Old Frenchman Place rouses the sexual appetite of the men, in particular of Van and Goodwin.) After a few contentious words with Gowan, Van goes into the kitchen to sweet-talk Temple into going for a walk with him but is rebuffed by Ruby and told to leave. Meanwhile, Tommy, who follows (and overhears) Van, comes back out with a jug of moonshine that the men pass back and forth to one another and complains to Goodwin that Van is frightening Temple. Dim-witted as he may be, Tommy is able to size up the situation on the porch and knows that a fight is brewing between Van and Gowan. Temple by this time is in a bedroom where she props up a chair against the door to secure it, but Van breaks in when he and Goodwin carry the drunken Gowan (who has been beaten unconscious) into the room. After they throw him onto the bed, Van approaches Temple and roughly rips open the raincoat she has on, but Goodwin beats him down. Later that evening, Ruby, as she is standing in the dark near the door, watches Goodwin come in and take the raincoat off Temple and leave. Ruby becomes aware of Popeye's presence and then Tommy's. Popeye stands over Temple gazing at her lying on the bed and shortly after he leaves followed by Tommy. Cognizant of what could happen to Temple if she is not protected, Ruby takes the 17-year-old coed to the barn after the men leave to transport their whiskey and stays with her until dawn.

By the next morning, Gowan, ashamed and hungover, speaks with Ruby about getting a car. Without breakfast or even coffee, he sets off in search of transportation thinking that he would drive Temple back to the university. However, he realizes that he cannot face her, so he pays the driver and directs him to pick her up and take her back to the university. Gowan then hitchhikes a ride into town. When Temple awakes, she cautiously goes back to the house, enters the bedroom and notices that the bed Gowan slept on is empty. She picks up her dress and hat from the floor, brushes them off before putting them on, and returns to the back porch where she washes her face. As she is using her compact, Temple notices

Ruby watching from the kitchen door. After greeting her, Temple asks for the bathroom and is told to use the barn. Instead she goes down to the bottom of the hill and eventually realizes that someone is watching her, but sees only the outline of a man crouching. (The narrative is not definite as to who this person may be; although it may be Goodwin, it could also be Popeye or Tommy.) Temple goes back to the house and, upset, tells Ruby what had happened. She then runs off to the barn and frightened of Goodwin, who is drunk, sees Tommy and asks him to protect her.

Popeye enters the barn from the rear and pulls himself up into the loft. Temple hears him cross the floor before he descends down the ladder to reach the door of the crib which he orders Tommy to open. Once inside, the sexually impotent Popeye kills Tommy and rapes Temple with a corncob. He later drives her to a Memphis brothel run by Reba Rivers. To telephone the sheriff, Ruby walks two miles to Tull's house (the closest neighbor and the same one Gowan visited to get a car). When the sheriff arrives at Old Frenchman Place, he arrests Goodwin for Tommy's murder and takes him to jail in Jefferson.

Horace Benbow, who had spent two days at his sister's house, is now staying at their family home in Jefferson, a home unoccupied for ten years. By this time Tommy's body has been brought to an undertaker's parlor where a coroner was unsuccessful in finding out the dead man's last name. Horace, an attorney, interviews Goodwin in jail, whom he will defend against the murder charges, and also provides a place for Ruby and her infant child to stay. He first takes them to his family's house, but when his sister and Miss Jenny object he ends up getting them a hotel room, knowing that Ruby has no money; a few days later, he finds a place on the edge of town for Ruby and her child to stay. Although Goodwin is innocent, he is fearful of Popeye, a man too good with a gun.

Ruby, however, tells Horace about Temple and mentions that she saw Popeye drive off with her the day Tommy was murdered. Horace goes to the state university to inquire about the coed and happens to meet the state senator Clarence Snopes on the train back to Jefferson. Snopes explains that a

Jackson paper published a story saying that Temple was sent by her father, Judge Drake, to an aunt in Michigan. At a later date, Benbow meets Snopes again, and for a price, the senator informs him that Temple is at Reba Rivers's house of prostitution in Memphis. When he visits Temple there (where she has been for about three weeks) and hears her story, Horace knows that he needs her to testify at Goodwin's trial.

A few days after Horace leaves Memphis for Jefferson, Popeye brings Red to Temple and watches as they have sexual relations. Several days later, Temple bribes Minnie, Miss Reba's black servant, to let her sneak out to make a phone call. Later that evening, after several drinks during the day, Temple skips out again, but this time Popeye sees her as she is leaving. Refusing to go back to Miss Reba's, she has Popeye drive her to the Grotto, a nightclub on the outskirts of Memphis, to meet Red. On the way, she ridicules Popeye's impotence and voyeurism. Irritated, Popeye reaches over with one hand to cover her mouth and shut her up. The nails of his fingers go into her cheek and the ring he is wearing prevents her from closing her lips, but even after he removes his hand, she continues to ridicule him. At the Grotto, Temple dances with Popeye and drinks heavily. As she is sitting at a table with him, Red, who recently arrived at the nightclub, asks her to dance, but she refuses. Intoxicated and confused, she thinks that she passed out and that by this time Popeye had already killed Red. Her first reaction seems to be one of gratification, but it is immediately followed by a sense of loss and sexual longing. Knowing that Temple is inebriated, Popeye gets her up to dance. As she listens to the music, she becomes aware that Red has not been killed and feels relief and desire. She is then taken to the crap table and, coached by Popeye, she wins. After he takes over, she sneaks off to a room and waits for Red, whom she drunkenly embraces when he arrives, and explains that Popeye is intent on killing him. After the two leave the room together, Red disingenuously tells Temple to wait in the corridor as he goes off to play craps. For a moment, Temple thinks she is dancing again as two men, under Popeye's orders, lead her out of the night club, and as she is being taken out Red

with the gambling cup lifted in his hand gives her "a short, cheery salute" (*Sanctuary*, 240). When she is driven out of the parking lot, she sees Popeye sitting in a parked car. That night Popeye murders Red and leaves Memphis with Temple. Red's funeral is held at the Grotto, with Gene, one of his bootlegger friends, supplying the drinks. When a rowdy party breaks out, the coffin falls from its platform and the corpse slowly tumbles out; in the center of Red's forehead is a bullet hole.

Horace phones Miss Reba the day after the funeral (and the day before Goodwin's trial is to begin, June 20th) and finds out that Temple is no longer there. Goodwin, innocent but also terrified of Popeye, does not want Ruby to testify, but she does. When Temple appears at the trial, she gives false testimony that it was Goodwin who violated her and killed Tommy. The jury takes eight minutes to convict Goodwin of the crime, and later that night, a vengeful mob rushes the jail and drags Goodwin out to burn him to death. Horace himself is almost overcome by the crowd. Stunned, the dejected and defeated Horace leaves Jefferson for Kinston to return to his wife, whom he had planned to leave at the beginning of the novel.

Popeye is arrested in Birmingham on his way to visit his mother in Pensacola and charged for the murder of a policeman in a small Alabama town. This murder occurred the same night that Red was killed. Refusing legal assistance and with no defense, Popeye is convicted, and ironically is hanged for a murder he did not commit. By this time, Temple is in Paris with her father, bored and discontented.

CRITICAL COMMENTARY

Sanctuary is Faulkner's most shocking treatment of the indomitable power of evil, causing one reviewer, Henry Seidel Canby, to comment that with this novel sadism "has reached its American peak" ("The School of Cruelty," *Saturday Review of Literature* 7 [May 21, 1931]: 674). Within weeks of its publication, however, the novel became a best-seller and attracted the attention of Hollywood. Though many readers reacted with outrage or horror and dismay, others saw literary value in the novel and praised its provocative powers. *Sanctuary* is much more than the potboiler Faulkner made it out to be (*see* especially *Faulkner in the University,* 90–91).

The title of the novel has ironic overtones. In addition to meaning holy or consecrated, the word *sanctuary,* derived from the Latin *sanctus,* means inviolable, that which is safe from profanation or violation. A sanctuary can also mean a safe haven. But virtually nothing—as the novel's idealistic attorney, Horace Benbow, voices when speaking with Miss Jenny—is inviolable or safe from the pervasiveness of evil: "'[T]here's a corruption about even looking upon evil, even by accident; you cannot haggle, traffic, with putrefaction'" (129). Horace is ultimately ineffectual against the power of evil, and once defeated by it his ideals of justice and southern womanhood fade into illusions. The same does not happen, however, to the young woman Temple Drake, who significantly contributes to Benbow's defeat and despair and whose first name is a mock evocation of sanctity. Through the gangster Popeye's brutal defilement, she responds to the presence of evil in her own nature. The critic Edmond L. Volpe suggests: "Her horrible corn-cob rape by Popeye does not initiate her moral collapse; it merely releases her from the restrictive convention which society has imposed upon her" (*A Reader's Guide to William Faulkner,* 144). The realization of evil within human nature and the response of human beings to it thematically inform the novel.

Sanctuary is Faulkner's darkest novel, in that, with the discovery of evil, comes disillusionment and defeat. Though the motive (or motives) behind Temple's false statements at Goodwin's trial are not clear, the fact that she perjures herself is in itself a form of corruption. Horace's idealism, especially as it relates to justice and the integrity and inviolability of southern womanhood, is shattered. He knows that Temple *was* brutally raped and violated, but he soon discovers that she perverts justice and violates truth by lying under oath, actions that lead to the violent death of the man who neither raped her nor killed Tommy. (Although the narrative clearly indicates Goodwin's sexual intentions when Temple was at OLD FRENCHMAN PLACE, he was not able to act on them because of the circumstances.) The image and sanctity of southern womanhood are at the center of the prosecutor's argument: "You have just heard the testimony of the chemist and the gynecologist—who is, as you gentlemen know, an authority on the most sacred affairs of the most sacred thing in life: womanhood—who says that this is no longer a matter for the hangman, but for a bonfire of gasoline" (283–284). Though stricken from the record, the provocative statement of his last 18 words foreshadows Goodwin's death. In effect, the innocent Goodwin is being tried not for murder but for sadistically violating a woman, the *idea* of which is so absolutely reprehensible to the town that death is a fitting punishment.

Some early critics charged Faulkner with sensationalism and with exploiting violence and sex, but the novel is rightly seen as an important work in Faulkner's canon with significant moral concerns. It is not merely a potboiler written to make money, for it contains, in spite of lurid passages—which in themselves actually help create part of the powerful effect of the novel—many of the major themes found throughout Faulkner's works: the discovery of the nature of reality and evil, disillusionment, the problem of corruption, and the quest for justice. The struggle of the human spirit in the face of defeat and despair is as much a part of *Sanctuary* as it is of any of Faulkner's major novels, including *The* SOUND AND THE FURY. *Sanctuary* was not the product of "a cheap idea . . . deliberately conceived to make money" as Faulkner in the introduction to the 1932 Modern Library edition misled readers in believing (*see* Appendix).

For further information, *see Faulkner in the University,* 9, 49, 74, 85–86, 90–91, 96; *Selected Letters of William Faulkner,* 18, 53, 54, 58, 61, 65, 68, 92, 106, 423; *Faulkner at Nagano,* 9, 62–64, 76, 80, 125–126, 143, 190.

FILM ADAPTATIONS

In 1933, Paramount released a film, *The Story of Temple Drake,* based on the novel. Directed by Stephen Roberts, it stars Miriam Hopkins as Temple Drake, Jack La Rue as Trigger (Popeye), William Gargan as Stephen Benbow (Horace Benbow), Sir Guy Standing as Judge Drake (Temple's father), Florence Eldridge as Ruby, Irving Pichel as Lee Goodwin, and Elizabeth Patterson as Aunt Jenny

(Miss Jenny). Chapter 25 of the novel was published under the title "Uncle Bud and the Three Madams" in The PORTABLE FAULKNER (1946). In 1954, *Sanctuary* was issued together with REQUIEM FOR A NUN (a sequel to the novel) by the New American Library; a film adaptation based on the two works and titled *Sanctuary* was released in 1961 by Twentieth Century–Fox, directed by Tony Richardson and starring Lee Remick as Temple Drake Stevens, Yves Montand as Candy Man (Popeye), Harry Townes as Ira Stevens (Gavin Stevens), Bradford Dillman as Gowan Stevens, and Odetta as Nancy (Nancy Mannigoe).

EXCERPTS FROM CONTEMPORARY REVIEWS OF *SANCTUARY*

Excerpt from John Chamberlain's review, "Dostoyefsky's Shadow in the Deep South," published in The New York Times Book Review, *February 15, 1931, 9:*

One finishes Mr. Faulkner's "Sanctuary" in that limp state which follows a frightening encounter in the dark or the sudden sickening realization that one has just escaped sudden death. The book has an immediate power that one must go outside of American fiction since the chase in "Moby Dick" to encounter. Dostoyefsky's "The Brothers Karamazoff" is the nearest analogue to "Sanctuary"—and by this we do not mean that Faulkner is a Dostoyefsky or that "Sanctuary" is anything like as big a book as the story of the Karamazoffs. For one thing, the emotion that Mr. Faulkner plays upon to the point of fraying his reader's nerves is that of fear, whereas Dostoyefsky evokes both fear and exaltation. But the power to suggest a hundred horrors behind the immediate horror, the power to tell a complicated story of human evil working out its strange and inevitable destiny without respect of persons that is in "Sanctuary" is undeniable. . . .

Excerpt from Margaret Cheney Dawson's review, "Power and Horror," published in the New York Herald Tribune Books, *February 15, 1931, 3:*

Terrible and hideous and frightening are little limp words that reach weakly for a meaning and fall far short of it. There is no adjective that by itself could describe what Mr. Faulkner has here created,

nor any that could compass the evil that he has drawn out of the world's black and secret pockets. For what he has done is to write not only of horrible things, but to write of them in words that sweat some final distillation, some ultimate essence of horror inseparable from his own sentences. Like mist over a bog at night this emanation hangs over the story. But it does not obscure it. Both technically and, I think, intellectually, he is clearer now than ever before. He is not only comprehensible; he is inescapable. And no one should read "Sanctuary" who is not willing to bear the scars. . . .

Excerpt from Robert Sherwood's review, published in Scribner's Magazine, *April 1931, 13:*

. . . The pace of "Sanctuary" is breathless, frantic. The reader is rushed along stumbling, groping, through the leaping phrases, sentences, paragraphs of exquisite prose, escaping wildly from one unidentifiable horror to find himself colliding suddenly, in the semidarkness, with another. It is a nightmare and yet, in the end, all of it is clear—too clear. Mr. Faulkner does not address himself to the reader's intellect. He chooses to ignore that surface element and speaks, with evangelical fervor, to the senses. In this respect he is comparable to Conrad.

I don't know if "Sanctuary" is Mr. Faulkner's one masterpiece, or if it is just another step in his sure progress. But I do know that it is a great novel.

Excerpt from L. A. G. Strong's review of Sanctuary, *published in* The Observer, *January 3, 1932, 4:*

. . . [I]n Mr. Faulkner's work flame burns very strongly, though it is often coloured green and blue with sulphurous exhalations. His study is the soul, and, though its setting is arbitrary, there is more fury and conflict in his work than in that of any modern author I have read, and I strongly suspect him of genius.

CHARACTERS

Belle   Horace Benbow's wife and mother of Little Belle. At the beginning of *Sanctuary*, Benbow is planning to leave his wife and she herself departs for Kentucky, where her mother lives. By the novel's end, however, she returns when Benbow's sister, Narcissa Benbow Sartoris, informs her that Horace is coming home after his miserable failure in defending the innocent Lee Goodwin. As the narrative makes clear, there are obvious differences between Belle and her husband, particularly in relation to the rearing of Little Belle, her daughter from a previous marriage. *Also see* SARTORIS where she is a minor character as the wife of Harry Mitchell.

Belle, Little   Daughter of Belle Mitchell Benbow and her first husband, Harry Mitchell (*see* SARTORIS). In *Sanctuary*, Little Belle is Horace Benbow's stepdaughter, although there is no indication in *Sanctuary* or *Sartoris* that she has taken his last name. Disingenuous toward Benbow, Little Belle, a teenager very much interested in boys, treats him more as an annoyance than the father figure he would like to be in her life.

Benbow, Belle Mitchell   *See* Belle.

Benbow, Horace   One of the major characters in *Sanctuary*, Horace is an attorney and an idealist. He unsuccessfully defends the bootlegger Lee Goodwin against the false charges of raping Temple Drake and murdering Tommy. At the beginning of the novel, Horace, who is unhappily married, is leaving his wife Belle and stepdaughter Little Belle in Kinston and on his way to a vacant family home in JEFFERSON that he and his sister, Narcissa Benbow Sartoris, still own. (During the action of the novel, Horace stays there.) He first comes across the bootleggers Popeye, Goodwin, and the others at OLD FRENCHMAN PLACE when he stops at a spring for water, and after a few too many drinks and dinner, he is given a lift into town.

Horace Benbow is one of Faulkner's intellectual and idealistic characters who are often in conflict with the immoral world around them. Well educated, philosophical, talkative, and committed to justice as a guiding principle in human affairs, Horace, like his fictional counterpart Gavin Stevens at the end of *The* MANSION, confronts in himself the bitterness of reality and moral compromise or failure. By the end of *Sanctuary*, Horace is a defeated man and painfully discovers the pervasiveness of evil and the powerlessness when fighting against it. He loses the case when defending Goodwin because the principal witness, the rape victim herself, Temple, lies under oath. When Goodwin is pulled from his jail cell the evening of his conviction and burned to death by a mob, Horace is also attacked, but escapes. Two days later, resigned and beaten, Benbow leaves Jefferson to return to his wife. (For other details regarding Horace Benbow, *see* his character entry under SARTORIS.)

Binford, Mr.   An offstage character referred to in the novel. For eleven years, Mr. Binford was the landlord (or front man) for his lover Miss Reba Rivers's brothel in MEMPHIS. During the time frame of *Sanctuary*, he has been dead for two years. According to Minnie, Miss Reba's black maid at the brothel, the day after he died Miss Reba got two dogs that she named Miss Reba and Mr. Binford. *Also see The* REIVERS; in *The* MANSION, he is referred to as Lucius Binford.

Bory   *See* Sartoris, Benbow.

Bud, Uncle   A minor character in the novel, Uncle Bud is a young boy, about five years old, from a farm in Arkansas. He is with Miss Myrtle when she and Miss Lorraine visit Miss Reba (*see* Rivers, Reba) shortly after Red's funeral. As the women drink, cry, and commiserate with one another, Uncle Bud sneaks himself some beer, gets sick, and vomits.

Buddy   *See* Drake, Hubert.

Doc   One of the three young men Gowan Stevens picks up as he is driving into town after taking Temple Drake back to her dorm from the dance. Though it is very late at night, Stevens is able to find bootleg liquor with their help.

Drake, Hubert   The youngest of Temple Drake's four brothers, whom she calls Buddy. The brothers are with their sister and father when Temple testifies at Lee Goodwin's trial in JEFFERSON.

Drake, Judge   Temple Drake's father, a judge in Jackson. After Temple falsely testifies at Lee Goodwin's trial, he takes her to Paris. Temple's failure to speak the truth under oath costs Goodwin his life.

Drake, Temple A major character in *Sanctuary*. The daughter of a judge, Temple is a 17-year-old university student at Ole Miss with the reputation of being a loose young woman. Her plans to go to a college baseball game are thwarted when her date, the hungover Gowan Stevens, wrecks his car at OLD FRENCHMAN PLACE where he had planned to buy bootleg liquor from Lee Goodwin. The following day, Temple is abandoned by Gowan. Frightened and apprehensive, she hides in the corn crib from Goodwin and has the feebleminded Tommy on the lookout. However, the sexually impotent and perverted Popeye gets Tommy to open the crib door and then shoots him in the back of the head before sexually violating Temple with a corncob. Temple is driven to a MEMPHIS brothel where Popeye introduces her to Red, who becomes her john. A month later, she wants to run away with Red, but Popeye murders him.

During her stay at the brothel, Goodwin is charged with Tommy's murder. His attorney, Horace Benbow, tracks Temple down in Memphis to interview and expects her to testify on Goodwin's behalf at the trial, but when she appears, she perjures herself and identifies Goodwin as the murderer and rapist. At the end of *Sanctuary*, Temple, bored and sullen, is with her father at the Luxembourg Gardens in Paris, concluding a gray day and summer and year (*Sanctuary*, 316). Temple is a complex character, and in the discovery evil—as frightening and as painful as that discovery is—she also discovers in her own nature an affinity to it. For further information, *see Faulkner in the University*, 96 and 196.

Ed *See* (Walker), Ed.

Fonzo A minor (and comic) character in the novel, Fonzo attends barber school in MEMPHIS with Virgil Snopes. When these two country youths arrive there from JEFFERSON, they get a room at Miss Reba's brothel thinking it a boardinghouse, and when the two intentionally go to another brothel, Fonzo, worried that Miss Reba might find out, voices his concern to Virgil that she might not allow them to room "'in the house with them ladies no more'" (*Sanctuary*, 196). This episode with Fonzo and Virgil provides a humorous aside to an otherwise violent novel and is a striking example of how Faulkner weaves together both the comic and tragic elements. (The episode is also recounted by Montgomery Ward Snopes in chapter 4 of *The* MANSION where Fonzo's surname, Winbush, is used.)

Frank Ruby Lamar's undaunted, but unwise, lover who was shot to death by her angry father. An offstage character referred to by Ruby when she is talking with Temple Drake in the kitchen at OLD FRENCHMAN PLACE, Frank had ignored Ruby's warning against standing up to her father when he was courting her.

Gene A MEMPHIS bootlegger. At Red's funeral, held at the nightclub called the Grotto, Gene provides the liquor free of charge.

Goodwin, Lee A bootlegger falsely accused of murdering the dimwitted Tommy and of raping Temple Drake with a corncob. Although sexually stirred (as are the other men) by Temple's presence at OLD FRENCHMAN PLACE, Goodwin is innocent of the rape and murder, but he does nothing to defend himself against the charges or to incriminate Popeye, the actual rapist and murderer, because he fears Popeye's revenge. Goodwin is opposed to having his common-law wife, Ruby Lamar, testify at his trial, but his lawyer, Horace Benbow, puts her on the witness stand nonetheless. The night of his conviction, an angry mob pulls Goodwin from his jail cell and burns him to death.

Some readers may question the consistency of Goodwin's character. His cowardice and fear of Popeye (at least while Goodwin is in jail) do not seem to square with his past deeds that occurred prior to the time frame of the novel. An ex-convict, Goodwin, when serving in the Philippines, had killed a fellow soldier over a woman and was sent to Leavenworth prison. He was released to fight in World War I and awarded two medals. After the war he returned to prison, but was later pardoned. In *Sanctuary*, his behavior toward Van at Old Frenchman Place also seems to demonstrate that Goodwin is not one who is easily intimidated.

Graham, Eustace The ambitious, manipulative district attorney with a clubfoot who prosecutes Lee Goodwin for a murder and a rape that he did not commit. During the trial, Graham intentionally incites the jury's anger when he says that the accused should be burned to death. Although that statement is stricken from the record, Goodwin is found guilty and later that night is taken from his jail cell and burned to death. *Also see* SARTORIS.

Harris Owner of a livery stable. In his office Eustace Graham (Lee Goodwin's prosecutor) played poker during his university days. Harris did not trust the way Graham dealt the cards.

Isom A black servant, Isom is Narcissa Benbow Sartoris's driver. *Also see* SARTORIS.

Jenny, Miss The outspoken and determined sister of Colonel John Sartoris, Miss Jenny is Narcissa Benbow Sartoris's great-great-aunt through the latter's marriage to Bayard Sartoris (*see* Virginia Du Pre in SARTORIS). She lives in her large family home with the widowed Narcissa and her son, Bory. Although she does not hesitate to speak her mind or to criticize, Miss Jenny can also be sympathetic and understanding. She is supportive of Narcissa's brother Horace Benbow's defense of the falsely accused Lee Goodwin. For other works in which Miss Jenny appears, *see* "An Odor of Verbena" (*The* UNVANQUISHED) and "THERE WAS A QUEEN" (where she is also called Virginia Du Pre); she is referred to as Mrs. Du Pre (Mrs. Jennie Du Pre and Miss Jenny Du Pre) in *The* TOWN, as Mrs. Du Pre in *The* MANSION, as Aunt Jenny (Mrs. Virginia Sartoris) in "All the Dead Pilots," and as Mrs. Virginia Depre in REQUIEM FOR A NUN.

Joe The proprietor of the Grotto, where Red's funeral is held. He wants the orchestra to play American songs only, but not jazz.

Jones, Herschell A minor offstage character referred to by Miss Jenny in a conversation with Horace Benbow. Herschell had been visiting the widowed Narcissa Benbow Sartoris prior to the time Gowan Stevens started showing up.

Lamar, Ruby The bootlegger Lee Goodwin's common-law wife who cooks for him and the other men at their hideout, the OLD FRENCHMAN PLACE; she is the mother of a sickly baby not yet a year old. With the frightened Temple Drake, Ruby is both protective and scornful. Prior to the time frame of the novel, she paid Goodwin's legal fees by sexually giving herself to the lawyer, who failed in getting him out of Leavenworth prison, and when Horace Benbow decides to defend Goodwin against the false charges of murder and rape, Ruby tells him that she cannot afford to pay and assumes that he will accept sexual favors instead. Although Benbow takes on the case, he does not sexually exploit her. She is also referred to in the novel as Mrs. Goodwin.

Lorraine, Miss With Miss Myrtle, she visits and drinks with Reba Rivers on the day of Red's funeral.

Luke An OXFORD, MISSISSIPPI, bootlegger, from whom Gowan Stevens gets liquor.

Minnie A minor character, Minnie is Reba Rivers's black maid. *Also see The* MANSION and *The* REIVERS.

Mitchell Belle's ex-husband and Little Belle's father; he is referred to in the novel. *See* Harry Mitchell in SARTORIS.

Myrtle, Miss A minor character in the novel. Accompanied by Miss Lorraine and a child named Uncle Bud, Miss Myrtle visits Reba Rivers after Red's funeral. The three women attended his funeral and later console themselves at Miss Reba's brothel by drinking and pouring out their feelings to one another.

Pap A blind and deaf old man at OLD FRENCHMAN PLACE. Lee Goodwin and the others seem to be providing for him.

Popeye Gangster and bootlegger who kills the half-wit Tommy and rapes Temple Drake with a corncob. Popeye is sexually impotent, and although he is a bootlegger he himself cannot consume alcohol, for it would kill him. On the same day Popeye rapes Temple at OLD FRENCHMAN PLACE, he drives her to a MEMPHIS brothel on MANUEL STREET run by Reba Rivers. When Popeye brings Red to her room, he voyeuristically watches him and Temple have sex, but when they become lovers and plan to run away together, Popeye kills him. On his yearly visit to his mother in Pensacola, Popeye is arrested in Birmingham and convicted of a crime he did not commit. Popeye is hanged for the murder of a police officer in a small Alabama town; ironically, the murder occurred on the same night that Popeye killed Red.

In an interview at the University of Virginia, Faulkner said that Popeye was not intended to be a symbol of evil but became one "in modern society only by coincidence" (*Faulkner in the University*, 74). Many readers, however, see in this character not merely a manifestation of moral indifference but of evil itself. The description of Popeye in the opening pages of the novel presages a sinister being: "His face had a queer, bloodless color as though seen by electric light; against the sunny silence, . . . he had that vicious depthless quality of stamped tin" (*Sanctuary*, 4). A reader's interpretation of Popeye may be slightly altered by the last chapter, which Faulkner added when revising the galleys of the novel in late 1930. The physical, psychological, and medical information on Popeye that the narrator provides may add, for some readers, a sympathetic perspective on the character.

Popeye first appeared in the short story "The BIG SHOT," written around 1929 but not published in Faulkner's lifetime. Popeye is also referred to in REQUIEM FOR A NUN where his last name appears as Vitelli.

Quinn, Doctor The physician for Reba Rivers's girls at the brothel. He is the one called to treat the bleeding Temple Drake after Popeye drops her off on the day he rapes her with a corncob. He is an offstage character.

Reba, Miss *See* Rivers, Reba.

Red The tall collegiate-looking young man who is Temple Drake's lover while she is at Reba Rivers's brothel in MEMPHIS. The gangster Popeye first introduces him to Temple, but when he finds out that she intends to run off with Red, Popeye kills him. At his funeral, which takes place at his hangout, the Grotto, a disturbance breaks out and his body falls out of the coffin, revealing the bullet wound to his forehead. He is referred to as Alabama Red in REQUIEM FOR A NUN.

Rivers, Reba (Miss Reba) Madam of the brothel on MANUEL STREET in MEMPHIS where Popeye takes Temple Drake. Known throughout Memphis, Miss Reba runs a tight establishment where some of the biggest men in town—lawyers, bankers, doctors, and police captains—go to drink and be with women. Miss Reba has two small, soiled white dogs that she names Miss Reba and Mr. Binford, one after herself and the other after Lucius Binford, her late landlord and lover. The unsuspecting and naive Fonzo and Virgil Snopes stay at her brothel, mistakenly thinking that it is a boardinghouse. (This episode is retold in The MANSION.) *Also see* Miss Reba in The REIVERS.

Sartoris, Benbow (Bory) Narcissa Benbow Sartoris's young son. His father, Bayard Sartoris (*see* SARTORIS), died flying an poorly constructed experimental airplane on the day Bory was born. *Also see The* TOWN, *The* MANSION, *KNIGHT'S GAMBIT* ("Knight's Gambit"), and the short story "THERE WAS A QUEEN."

Sartoris, Narcissa Benbow Horace Benbow's younger sister, a widow with one son. She thwarts her brother's efforts at defending the falsely accused Lee Goodwin and at helping Goodwin's common-law wife, Ruby Lamar. *Also see* SARTORIS and the short story "THERE WAS A QUEEN"; she is referred to by her maiden name, Miss Narcissa Benbow, in *The* TOWN.

Shack One of the two university students traveling on the same train Horace Benbow takes to OXFORD, MISSISSIPPI, to inquire about Temple Drake. Shack and his unnamed companion ride without paying; they convince the conductor that they have already given him their tickets.

Snopes, Clarence Eggleston The self-aggrandizing and corrupt state senator, who knows the whereabouts of Temple Drake. He readily sells that information to Horace Benbow. As other Snopeses, Clarence appears in several works; *see The* TOWN, *The* MANSION, FATHER ABRAHAM (revised for *The* HAMLET) and the short story "BY THE PEOPLE" (revised for *The Mansion*).

Snopes, Virgil A minor character in the novel who adds a humorous touch to the narrative; he is a relative of Clarence Eggleston Snopes. With Fonzo, Virgil attends barber college in MEMPHIS. In one of the most comic scenes in the novel, these two country boys from JEFFERSON take a room at Reba Rivers's brothel, thinking it a boardinghouse. When they visit other brothels in the city, they worry that Miss Reba will find out and evict them for their behavior. For other details regarding Virgil, *see The* MANSION; he is referred to in *The* TOWN.

Stevens, Gowan A college student at the University of Virginia who drinks heavily under the illusion that he can hold his liquor as a gentleman should. He comes back to JEFFERSON to see Narcissa Benbow Sartoris (who, many years his senior, rejects his offer to marry him), and meets Temple Drake, a student at the state university in OXFORD, MISSISSIPPI. He takes Temple to a dance and plans to drive her to a baseball game in Starkville the next day, but his intentions are thwarted by his drinking. His actions set in motion a major concern of the novel: the materialization and effects of evil. Instead of driving Temple directly to the game, Gowan first takes her to OLD FRENCHMAN PLACE to resupply himself with liquor. As he approaches the property, his car crashes into a tree lying across the road and the two are stranded at the dilapidated plantation until the following afternoon. On the morning of that next day, the hungover Gowan, ashamed of his drunkenness and severely beaten by Van, one of the bootleggers, abandons Temple. Left alone, she witnesses a murder and is raped by Popeye with a corncob. Temple is then driven to a brothel in MEMPHIS.

In *A Reader's Guide to William Faulkner*, Edmond L. Volpe observes that Gowan "represents the corruption of a social class whose moral code is nothing more than an empty concept of the gentleman. . . . His conscience responds only to his failure to live up to [that] code. . . ." (148). Gowan strives to redeem himself by giving up drinking and marrying Temple a year or two later (*see* REQUIEM FOR A NUN). *Also see The* TOWN.

Tommy A feebleminded man who works for the bootlegger Lee Goodwin at OLD FRENCHMAN PLACE. Though he frightens Temple Drake at first when she arrives at the hideout, he brings her food and later tries to protect her against the other men, but Popeye shoots him in the back of the head before raping Temple with a corncob.

Tull A farmer two miles from OLD FRENCHMAN PLACE. Ruby Lamar phones the sheriff from his house when Tommy is murdered. *Also see* Vernon Tull in *As I Lay Dying*, *The* HAMLET, *The* TOWN, *The* MANSION, and the short story "SHINGLES FOR THE LORD"; a Tull who is the father of girls is also referred to in the short story "TWO SOLDIERS."

Van One of the bootleggers at OLD FRENCHMAN PLACE. He badly beats up and knocks out the drunken Gowan Stevens, but when he attempts to take sexual advantage of Temple Drake, Lee Goodwin overpowers him.

(Walker), Ed Lee Goodwin's jailer in JEFFERSON. Although his last name is not used in the novel, his wife is referred to as Mrs. Walker.

Walker, Mrs. The jailer's wife who shelters Ruby Lamar and her infant child at the jail when the hotel in town forces them to leave.

FURTHER READING

Arnold, Edwin T. and Dawn Trouard. *Reading Faulkner: Sanctuary*. Jackson: University Press of Mississippi, 1996.

Backman, Melvin. "*Sanctuary*." In *Faulkner: The Major Years*, 41–49. Bloomington: Indiana University Press, 1966.

Bassett, John E. "*Sanctuary*: Personal Fantasies and Social Fictions." *South Carolina Review* 13.1 (fall 1981): 73–82.

Bloom, Harold, ed. *Modern Critical Interpretations of William Faulkner's* Sanctuary. New York: Chelsea, 1988.

Boon, Kevin A. "Temple Defiled: The Brainwashing of Temple Drake in Faulkner's *Sanctuary*." *Faulkner Journal* 6.2 (1991): 33–50.

Brooks, Cleanth. "Discovery of Evil (*Sanctuary* and *Requiem for a Nun*)." In *William Faulkner: The Yoknapatawpha Country*, 116–140. Baton Rouge: Louisiana State University Press, 1990.

Canfield, J. Douglas, ed. *Twentieth Century Interpretations of* Sanctuary. Englewood Cliffs, N.J.: Prentice-Spectrum, 1982.

Graham, Philip. "Patterns in Faulkner's *Sanctuary* and *Requiem for a Nun*." *Tennessee Studies in Literature* 8 (1963): 39–46.

Matthews, John T. "The Elliptical Nature of *Sanctuary*." *Novel: A Forum on Fiction* 17 (1984): 246–265.

Millgate, Michael. "*Sanctuary*." In *The Achievement of William Faulkner*, 113–123. Lincoln: University of Nebraska Press, 1978.

Howe, Irving. "*Sanctuary*." In *William Faulkner: A Critical Study*, 192–199. Chicago: University of Chicago Press, 1957.

Rousselle, Melinda McLeod. *Annotations to William Faulkner's* Sanctuary. New York: Garland, 1989.

Sundquist, Eric J. "*Sanctuary*: An American Gothic." In *Faulkner: The House Divided*, 44–60. Baltimore: Johns Hopkins University Press, 1985.

Tate, Allen. "Faulkner's *Sanctuary* and the Southern Myth." *Virginia Quarterly Review* 44 (1968): 418–427.

Vickery, Olga. "Crime and Punishment: *Sanctuary*." In *Faulkner: A Collection of Critical Essays*, edited by Robert Penn Warren, 127–136. Englewood Cliffs, N.J.: Prentice Hall, 1966.

Sartoris

Faulkner's third novel, published in 1929. *Sartoris* is the revised and sharply cut FLAGS IN THE DUST, the story of the Sartoris clan of fictional JEFFERSON, MISSISSIPPI. Faulkner scholars regard it as the last work of his artistic apprenticeship.

With *Sartoris*, Faulkner first enters a world of his own invention, the YOKNAPATAWPHA COUNTY of his best work. After a promising but uncertain start with SOLDIERS' PAY (1926) and MOSQUITOES (1927), he had found his themes, his place, his characters, and his voice. "Beginning with *Sartoris*," the novelist told JEAN STEIN in a PARIS REVIEW interview in the 1950s, "I discovered that my own little postage stamp of native soil was worth writing about and that I would never live long enough to exhaust it. . . . so I created a cosmos of my own." Elsewhere, Faulkner advises readers to go to *Sartoris* first, because the novel "has the germ of my apocrypha in it."

SYNOPSIS

Set just after World War I, with flashbacks to the Civil War era, *Sartoris* is the story of two generations of planter class Mississippians set in the broad social context of a changing South. The older generation includes old Bayard Sartoris (3) and Aunt Jenny Du Pre; the younger includes the Sartoris twins, Bayard's grandsons Johnny Sartoris and young Bayard Sartoris (4), and their contemporaries Horace Benbow and his sister Narcissa Benbow (Sartoris). The twins' and the Benbows' parents are absent and barely mentioned, allowing Faulkner to juxtapose the stable, traditional generation of the Civil War with the restless and alienated young men and women of the post–World War I wasteland. Complicating the generational conflicts are new technologies, symbolized by the rise of the automobile, and competition from the long-supressed white and black underclasses.

The book opens in the spring of 1919 with the furtive return from France of young Bayard Sartoris, a World War I aviator racked with guilt over the death in combat of his twin John, who jumped out of his burning airplane without a parachute. There is no meaning to Bayard's life. He finds release in violence and in reckless behavior: riding a wild stallion through the streets of JEFFERSON, driving a powerful car fast over rough country roads, drinking himself insensible.

Bayard joylessly marries Narcissa Benbow but is unable to settle down with her. He kills old Bayard in a car accident and, ashamed to return home, takes refuge with the MacCallums, stolid, self-sufficient yeoman farmers from the hill country northeast of Jefferson. He leaves the MacCallums' farm after a few days, knowing they are bound soon to hear of the manner of his grandfather's death. He spends Christmas Eve in the stable of a black sharecropper family. The next day his host drives him to the nearest railroad station, and he leaves Jefferson for good, moving restlessly from place to place: Mexico, South America, the U.S. West Coast, and finally Chicago. He finally succeeds in killing himself by going aloft in an obviously unsafe experimental airplane that breaks up shortly after takeoff and plummets back to earth. He dies the same day Narcissa gives birth to another male Sartoris to carry on the line.

Horace Benbow, too, is a veteran of France, but as a noncombatant: He had been a YMCA secretary and, as such, an object of derision to the fighting men. A dabbler in the arts, he is dreamy, aesthetic, ineffectual. Faulkner presents Horace and young Bayard as opposed romantics, one a man of reflection, the other a man of action; both are equally out of place in the rapidly changing world of 1920s Jefferson. Horace becomes involved with a married woman, Belle Mitchell (Benbow). She divorces, and much to Narcissa's disgust—she regards Belle as "dirty"—he marries her. Like Bayard, Horace has destroyed himself, even though he lives on.

CRITICAL COMMENTARY

Remarking on the lost generation theme, the critic MICHAEL MILLGATE has observed that Faulkner has placed a "'Twenties' hero, a type who had appeared in the work of other novelists, . . . within the context of an intensely localized Southern setting." In this reading, young Bayard's relations with the land are his efforts to heal his psychic wounds. Indeed, the strengths of *Sartoris* lie in Faulkner's evocation of the spirit of place and in his variegated portrait of the South and its people: the gentry, poor whites and black sharecroppers, independent farmers, the town professional classes. There is a lot of local color: details about Aunt Jenny's garden; the furnishings and atmosphere of the "office," old Bayard's study at SARTORIS, the family seat; the contents of Dr. Peabody's consulting room; Hub's ramshackle

hill farm. Faulkner carefully records the cycle of the seasons, from old Bayard's driving home past tilled fields and budding trees in the spring to his grandson's taking charge of plantation affairs through the long, hot summer to the hunting scenes with the MacCallums in the iron chill of December.

Faulkner is less successful with his characters. Bayard lacks depth and his obsessions are unconvincing. After all, he had little or nothing to do with his brother Johnny's death, beyond failing to talk him out of going aloft in his outgunned Sopwith Camel in the first place. Bayard watches helplessly as Johnny kicks himself free of the airplane and falls to his death. Why does Bayard blame himself?

"Young Bayard's story consists mainly of his repeated attempts to get himself killed," Millgate asserted, "and it is one of the weaknesses of the novel that the pressures driving him are never made entirely clear."

John W. Corrington provided one possible explanation, identifying Bayard's demons as fear and uncertainty of his own courage. These insecurities impelled him to prove through his foolhardy behavior that he can "as easily and gracefully fulfill the demands of the Sartoris myth as did Johnny."

Faulkner himself offers two partial answers. In *Sartoris*, Aunt Jenny explains it by reference to congenital Sartoris recklessness, something in the blood; early in the novel, she tells the story of her brother, the first Bayard Sartoris (1), a Confederate cavalryman who lost his life in an antic raid of a Yankee headquarters in search of anchovies. In an interview many years later, Faulkner suggested the World War I experience as the cause of Bayard's dislocation.

The anxieties of the younger generation contrast with the stability of other characters in *Sartoris*. Old Bayard, the crotchety banker who refuses to own an automobile, and Aunt Jenny, sharp-tongued and shrewd, are survivors of the heroic age of the Civil War and its aftermath. (Faulkner developed their stories in The UNVANQUISHED and other works.) The MacCallums, hill-country farmers, are rooted in the land. Another solid countryman is V. K. Suratt, the sewing machine salesman who will become the incomparable Ratliff of later works. African-American characters, even when they are rather crude stereotypes played for comic effect, as in Simon Strother, the obsequious coachman, seem more animated than young Bayard and Horace Benbow.

CRITICAL RECEPTION

Faulkner wrote *Flags in the Dust* in 1926–27. With rejection slips from several publishing houses, he turned in the late summer of 1928 to his friend and sometime agent BEN WASSON for help in placing the orphaned manuscript. HARCOURT, BRACE & COMPANY agreed to take the book on, with the condition that Faulkner cut it substantially. According to JOSEPH BLOTNER, Faulkner's biographer, the novelist vehemently objected to cutting *Flags* and wanted no part of the job. But he authorized Wasson to rework the book, figuring it would remain unpublished otherwise. The fact is Faulkner had moved on to pressing business with another work. While Wasson worked on *Flags*, Faulkner prepared the final typescript of one of his masterpieces, *The SOUND AND THE FURY*.

"The trouble is that you had about six books in here," Wasson told him. "You were trying to write them all at once."

The contract with Harcourt called for the deletion of about 25,000 words, leaving a novel of about 110,000 words. An editor at Harcourt retitled the book. Wasson's editing substantially reduced the role of the Horace Benbow character, which in *Flags* is a counterpoint to that of young Bayard Sartoris. Passages about Benbow's love affairs and his incestuous feelings for Narcissa were deleted or shortened. Wasson dropped a long account of Narcissa Benbow's reflections on young Bayard's boyhood and cut or deleted several scenes involving Byron Snopes, the author of a series of obscene letters to Narcissa.

The result is a tauter novel, but many Faulknerians were not impressed with Wasson's work. CLEANTH BROOKS found more of Yoknapatawpha in *Flags*, more of Faulkner's "attempts to do justice within the confines of one novel to the landed gentry, the yeomen whites, black people, and even the Snopeses." Frederick Karl argued that Wasson had drained the book of characteristic Faulkner, turning a daring work of fiction into a safe one. According to Millgate, the cuts altered the novel's

"internal balance;" in the end, more was lost than gained.

Faulkner dedicated the revised, shortened and retitled novel to SHERWOOD ANDERSON; Harcourt published it on January 31, 1929, with an initial printing of about 2,000 copies. The first reviews appeared a few weeks later. Like HORACE LIVERIGHT, Faulkner's first publisher, an anonymous critic in the *New York Times* found *Sartoris* seriously deficient, a "work of uneven texture, confused sentiment and loose articulation." Henry Nash Smith, writing in the *Dallas Morning News*, took a more generous view: "He learns his trade and broadens his thought almost vividly from chapter to chapter; and he is young."

Sartoris marks an important stage in Faulkner's development. There are fewer purple patches than in earlier work. As Michael Millgate observes, Faulkner's characteristic "obsession with time, death and the omnipresence of the past" is much in evidence.

The strength of the novel is the Yoknapatawpha world, a source for characters, scenes, and episodes that Faulkner would exploit in later work—after all, the Snopeses make their first appearance here. Faulkner had carried over moods suggesting T. S. Eliot's *The Waste Land* from his earlier, more self-consciously literary work. After *Sartoris*, the influence of Eliot's poem would all but disappear.

"Bayard may be a lost soul, Horace an ineffectual dreamer," Cleanth Brooks wrote. "But the folk society that lies around them goes on in its immemorial ways."

EXCERPTS FROM CONTEMPORARY REVIEWS OF *SARTORIS*

Excerpt from an anonymous annotation of Sartoris, *published in Everyman, 3 March 1932, 181:*
For full beauty of writing there is nothing to surpass to-day what this writer can do; he is gaining for himself an unchallengeable position.

Excerpt from Mary Ellen Chase's review, "Some Intimations of Immortality," published in Commonweal 10 (June 5, 1929), 134–35:
Mr. William Faulkner's *Sartoris* brings to the mind of at least one reader the saying of Mrs. Robert

Louis Stevenson about R. L. S.: "His faults are so much more lovable than other people's virtues." *Sartoris* has faults, but they are the faults of a style and a method crammed with virtues. There is such a wealth of figures, mostly good, that sentences too often seem mannered. Favorite words become intrusive, "sibilant," "myriad." Incidents are so well told that they seem detached, unable through their very individuality and power to take their place in the story. Characters live so completely and fully in themselves that they mingle with difficulty. In short, Mr. Faulkner's ingredients are so dear to him that he hates the stirring of them into a smooth whole.

Nevertheless, perhaps even because of these things, *Sartoris* is a memorable book. It is the name and story of a southern family whose troubled, overwhelming personality was so prodigal that even the dead Sartorises could not stay in heaven, must come back to linger on in their pipes, in the odor of the honeysuckle, in the rooms where they had once lived, and above all in the perturbed and desperate desires of their grandchildren. Thus they obtain their own immortality and ensure, sadly enough, the torturing mortality of succeeding generations of their name. . . .

Excerpt from L. A. G. Strong's review, published in The Spectator, *Feb. 27, 1932, 296, 298:*
If we accept the work of a man of genius—and Mr. Faulkner is one of the few living writers who may safely be accused of genius—we must accept it as it stands. It is useless to deplore his choice of subject; to say, of Lawrence, that he was a great writer but for his obsession, or, of Joyce, that it is a pity he is going so far towards music. Genius demands plain yes or no: and he that is not for it is against it. Very little reflection will show that this must be the case, for any work of high quality is the work of a whole man, and we cannot accept half a man's personality and reject the rest. Nor are we ever in a position to decide how much the quality of a work of art derives from the artist's preoccupation with any particular subject. Mr. Faulkner, therefore, has to be rejected or swallowed whole; and I swallow him whole. His new novel is, on the surface, less sinister than *Sanctuary*, and far easier to read than *The Sound and the Fury*. . . .

Sartoris shows Mr. Faulkner in a new light. His writing has an occasional tendency to take the bit between its teeth and run away with him, but it has gained in simplicity without losing any of its nervous and muscular force. . . .

Excerpt from Helen Fletcher's review, published in Time and Tide, *Feb 27, 1932, 230:*
. . . Not the least of William Faulkner's many virtues is that he permits you to enjoy beauty, comfort and sanitation without loss of Art. . . . I cannot better explain the spell this author has for me than by saying that more than any writer he is capable of transfusing sunlight. It is claimed by Faulkner's enemies that his prose is rendered unreadable by the unfortunate tendency of his sentences to swallow themselves. Let me state at once that in *Sartoris* we have none of this. Kipling himself could not have written anything more straightforward than this narrative. . . .

This is a much easier book to read than its three predecessors, and for that reason it is harder to assess. I think on the whole the auguries are good and that the new simplicity gives proof that the author is rapidly becoming master of his individual and difficult world. . . .

CHARACTERS

Abe   A black employee of the elder Dr. Peabody. Peabody's surgeon son, young Loosh (Lucius Peabody), skillfully repairs the leg of a hunting dog Abe had shot by accident. He is one of the gillies at the fishpond on the Peabody place.

Alford, Dr.   A physician in his thirties, a newcomer to JEFFERSON, he has a "a face like a mask—a comforting face, but cold" (96). He diagnoses old Bayard Sartoris's wen (a cyst), but when he suggests that it be removed immediately, Sartoris testily objects and applies Will Falls's home remedy instead. Later, however, Dr. Alford accompanies Sartoris to a specialist in MEMPHIS. He unaggressively courts Narcissa Benbow (*see* Sartoris, Narcissa) before she marries young Bayard Sartoris.

Dr. Alford is referred to in AS I LAY DYING; his office is on the upstairs from the Jefferson drugstore where Dewey Dell Bundren goes for help.

Beard, Mrs. She is the "lank-haired" wife of the JEFFERSON, MISSISSIPPI, grist mill owner Will C. Beard and the mother of the simple-minded Virgil Beard, who takes down Byron Snopes's obscene letters to Narcissa Sartoris. When Snopes comes to call, she is mopping the hallway floor with "drab fury."

In *LIGHT IN AUGUST*, Mrs. Beard operates the boardinghouse where Byron Bunch has a room. Lena Grove boards with her when she first arrives in Jefferson.

Beard, Virgil He is the son of Will C. Beard, who owns the grist mill in JEFFERSON, MISSISSIPPI. A somewhat simple boy, with straw-colored hair, bland eyes, and a secretive mouth, Virgil takes down Byron Snopes's love letters to Narcissa Sartoris. As payment, Byron promises him an air gun. When Snopes delays delivery of the prize, Virgil threatens him by saying he remembers every word of all the letters. When he finally gets the gun, he kills a mockingbird with it.

Beard, Will C. The father of Virgil Beard, he is the accomplice of Byron Snopes in sending obscene letters to Narcissa Sartoris. He owns W. C. Beard's Mill in a shabby commercial district of JEFFERSON.

His wife owns the boardinghouse where Byron Bunch and Lena Grove stay in *LIGHT IN AUGUST*.

Benbow, Belle Mitchell A plump young woman with "a cleverly rouged face," she is the restless and discontented wife of Harry Mitchell, the inattentive mother of Little Belle Mitchell, and the illicit lover of Horace Benbow. She later divorces Mitchell and marries Benbow. Belle is "cannily stupid," with only a surface understanding; at the piano, she plays "saccharine melodies . . . with a shallow skill" (194).

She appears as Horace Benbow's estranged wife in *SANCTUARY*.

Benbow, Francis The grandfather of Horace Benbow and Narcissa Benbow Sartoris, he brought home a Barbados lantana in a top-hat box in 1871 and planted it in a fence corner of the Benbow lawn.

Benbow, Horace The older brother of Narcissa Benbow Sartoris, he distinguished himself as a student and won a Rhodes Scholarship at Oxford University in England. When he returned to JEFFERSON, MISSISSIPPI, just before his father's death, he took up the profession of the law from "a sense of duty to the family tradition" (175), not because he had any particular interest in or aptitude for it. During World War I, Benbow served a tour in France as a noncombatant with the YMCA, for which he is ridiculed at home.

A sensitive and artistic person "with an air of fine and delicate futility" (161), Benbow is a contrast to his sister's furious and despairing husband, young Bayard Sartoris. He carries on an affair with Belle Mitchell (Benbow) in the face of Narcissa's disapproval. He marries her after her divorce and takes an active but ineffective role in the upbringing of her daughter, Little Belle Mitchell.

Like other intellectual and idealistic Faulkner characters, Benbow is often in conflict with the immoral world around him. Well educated, philosophical, talkative, and committed to justice as a guiding principle in human affairs, Horace ultimately confronts in himself the bitterness of reality and moral compromise.

In *SANCTUARY*, he defends the falsely accused rapist and murderer Lee Goodwin.

Benbow, Julia The wife of Will Benbow and mother of Narcissa Benbow Sartoris and Horace Benbow, she was a "right sweet-natured girl," the usually acerbic Aunt Sally Wyatt said of her. Julia "died genteelly" when Narcissa was seven years old (174–175).

Benbow, Little Belle Mitchell She is the daughter of Harry and Belle Mitchell. Her mother neglects Little Belle and finds her a nuisance as she (the mother) carries on her love affair with Horace Benbow.

She also appears in *SANCTUARY*.

Benbow, Narcissa *See* Sartoris, Narcissa Benbow.

Benbow, Will The father of Narcissa Benbow Sartoris and Horace Benbow. A lawyer, he dies not long after Horace returns home from Oxford, England; Horace inherits the family law practice. Will is buried near his sweet-tempered wife, Julia.

Bird, Uncle He heads the delegation from the Second Baptist Church that calls on Simon Strother, the treasurer, for an accounting of the church funds. As it happens, Strother has given church money to an alluring young mulatto woman named Meloney Harris. Uncle Bird asks old Bayard Sartoris (3) to repay the $67.40 Simon embezzled from the church building fund.

Brandt, Dr. He is the MEMPHIS specialist in blood and glandular diseases to whom Dr. Alford refers old Bayard Sartoris (3), whose wen Alford believes to be cancerous. Bayard goes under protest; he has been using old Will Falls's folk remedy for the wen, and it comes off cleanly at Dr. Brandt's touch. Even so, Brandt sends a bill for $50.

Buck The sober, good-natured, horse-faced town marshal of JEFFERSON, MISSISSIPPI, he obeys a directive from Virginia Du Pre (Aunt Jenny) and takes young Bayard Sartoris into protective custody after Sartoris and two friends, Mitch and Hub, carry out a whiskey-fueled serenade beneath Narcissa Benbow's window (*see* Sartoris, Narcissa Benbow). Buck sends Mitch and Hub home and gives up his bed in the jailkeeper's quarters to Bayard, who had been shaken up in a fall from a wild stallion earlier in the day.

Butler, Joe Byron Snopes uses Joe Butler as the addressee for his obscene letters to Narcissa Benbow Sartoris. This way, Virgil Beard, who writes the letters for Snopes, will not know that they are intended for Narcissa.

Comyn A military aviator known to his friends as "that big Irish devil," he is involved in a wartime brawl in the Cloche-Clos café in Amiens, France. He clears out the place by blowing on a military policeman's whistle.

Comyn also appears in the short story "AD ASTRA."

Deacon *See* ROGERS, DEACON.

Du Pre, Virginia (Genevieve Du Pre; Virginia Sartoris) The strong-minded sister of Colonel John Sartoris, Aunt Jenny is an admired type of traditional Southern woman, slender, with a "sad, resolute face" and a sharp if honest tongue.

Aunt Jenny had been married only two years when her South Carolinian husband was killed in a Civil War battle. She comes to her brother's home seven years a widow in 1869, manages the household after his death in a shooting, and lives to see her twin grandnephews, the younger generation male Sartorises, die violently.

Jenny Du Pre also appears in SANCTUARY, *The UNVANQUISHED* and the short story "THERE WAS A QUEEN" and is mentioned in *The TOWN* and *The MANSION*. She is referred to as Aunt Jenny Sartoris in the short story "ALL THE DEAD PILOTS" and as Mrs. Virginia DEPRE in *REQUIEM FOR A NUN*.

Elnora She is the pleasant, placid African-American daughter of Simon Strother and a servant in the home of old Bayard Sartoris (3). Elnora's son Isom hero-worships her brother Caspey Strother, a returned veteran of World War I with a fund of exaggerated war stories.

She also appears in the short stories "ALL THE DEAD PILOTS" and "THERE WAS A QUEEN." In the latter story, she is identified as the half sister of old Bayard.

Eunice The Benbows' black cook, she makes an irresistible chocolate pie.

Falls, Will A 93-year-old inmate of the county poor farm, Falls is given to retelling the near-legendary exploits of Colonel John Sartoris, with whom he fought in the Civil War. He treks into Jefferson at intervals to reminisce with old Bayard Sartoris (3)—and to report on the doings of Sartoris's rackety grandson. Despite opposition from the local medical establishment, Falls successfully treats Bayard's wen (or cyst) with a home remedy his grandmother obtained from a Choctaw Indian.

Fothergill, Zeb A Confederate soldier, he rode with Colonel John Sartoris's partisan cavalry in north Mississippi during the Civil War. Fothergill rustled a fine horse "outen one of Sherman's cavalry pickets on his last trip into Tennessee," Will Falls recalls (224).

Frankie   A young guest at Belle Mitchell Benbow's, she had "the first bobbed head in town" (186). Frankie plays tennis on the Mitchell court with Horace Benbow.

Graham, Eustace   A lawyer, he tries to introduce a drunken young Bayard Sartoris to Mr. Gratton, a World War I veteran, in Deacon's café. Graham's attempt nearly touches off a brawl when Sartoris insults Gratton. (*Also see* SANCTUARY.)

Gratton, Mr.   He is a veteran of the western front in World War I. Young Bayard Sartoris brushes off Eustace Graham's attempt to introduce him to Gratton in Deacon's café, nearly touching off a fight.

Harris, Meloney   She leaves service with Belle Mitchell to open a beauty parlor. One of her admirers, Simon Strother, an elderly servant of old Bayard Sartoris (3), gives her money he embezzles from the Second Baptist Church. He later is found dead in Meloney's cabin, his head crushed.

Henry, Uncle   A black sharecropper, he supplies one of his dogs for young Bayard Sartoris's possum hunt, which begins behind his house.

Houston   A black waiter in Deacon's café, he serves young Bayard Sartoris (4) and Rafe MacCallum lemons, cracked ice and sugar for a midday toddy made from MacCallum's home-distilled whiskey.

Hub   A country boy with brown forearms and a new straw hat, he, his friend Mitch, and young Bayard Sartoris (4) serenade Narcissa Benbow (Sartoris) at the close of a long night's drinking.

Isom   The 16-year-old black servant of the Sartorises, he is the son of Elnora and the grandson of Simon Strother. Isom is in awe of his returned-soldier uncle, Caspey Strother, and listens wide-eyed to Caspey's highly colored war stories.

He also appears in SANCTUARY.

Joe   One of the tennis players at Belle Mitchell's (*see* Benbow, Belle Mitchell), he makes up a double with Harry Mitchell.

John Henry   With the help of his reluctant father, he pries young Bayard Sartoris (4) from under the wreck of his car where it comes to rest in the creek and drives Sartoris to JEFFERSON, MISSISSIPPI, in a mule-drawn farm wagon, using his straw hat to screen the injured man's face from the sun.

Jones   Known as Doctor, he is the African-American janitor in the Sartoris's bank, elderly and querulous—much like his patron, old Bayard Sartoris (3), who allows him to steal his tobacco and pilfer the bank's coal supply.

MacCallum, Buddy (Virginius MacCallum, Jr.)   The youngest of six sons of Virginius MacCallum, Sr., he is a World War I veteran whose father resents his service with the "Yankee" army. He won a "charm" (or medal) in the fighting in Flanders, but wouldn't say what he had done to earn it. Buddy's bachelor brothers count on him someday "to marry and perpetuate the family name" (334).

In INTRUDER IN THE DUST, *The* TOWN and the short story "The TALL MEN," he appears as Buddy McCallum.

MacCallum, Henry   He is the second of six sons of Virginius MacCallum, Sr., a self-reliant farmer. Squat, tubby, and 50 years old, there is "something domestic, womanish" about Henry (313). He runs the family still—whiskey for home consumption only—and is in charge of the kitchen.

MacCallum, Jackson   He is the eldest of hill farmer Virginius MacCallum, Sr.'s six sons. Like his brothers Lee and Stuart, he is named for a Confederate general. Jackson's ambition is to mate a hound to a tame fox, creating a new breed of hunting dog "with a hound's wind and a fox's smartness and speed" (326).

MacCallum, Lee   One of six sons of the farmer Virginius MacCallum, Sr., he is moody and withdrawn, but with a good tenor voice that makes him much in demand for Sunday services. By report, he keeps company with a woman in MOUNT VERNON six miles distant.

He appears as Lee McCallum in the short story "The TALL MEN."

MacCallum, Raphael Semmes (Rafe)   A son of Virginius MacCallum, Sr. and Stuart's twin, he is "a broad squat man with a keen weathered face and gray temples" (121). Named for a Confederate sea raider, he is known as Rafe. As boys, the Sartoris twins used to hunt foxes and coons with him. Rafe and young Bayard Sartoris (4) get drunk together in Deacon's café the day Bayard is thrown from the wild stallion.

He appears as Rafe McCallum in KNIGHT'S GAMBIT and the short story "The TALL MEN" and is referred to in AS I LAY DYING and The MANSION.

MacCallum, Stuart   A son of Virginius MacCallum, Sr. and Rafe MacCallum's twin, he is a competent farmer and a clever trader with "a respectable bank account of his own" (316).

He appears as Stuart McCallum in the short story "The TALL MEN."

MacCallum, Virginius, Jr.   *See* MacCallum, Buddy.

MacCallum, Virginius, Sr. (Virginius McCallum)   A self-reliant yeoman farmer in the hills of northeast YOKNAPATAWPHA COUNTY and the father of six grown sons, he is host for several days to a grieving and guilt-ridden young Bayard Sartoris, whose reckless driving led to the accident that brought on the heart attack that claimed his grandfather.

Shaggy and silver-haired, 77 years old, a twice-widowed veteran of Robert E. Lee's Army of Northern Virginia, he oversees the running of the family farm in semiretirement. When young Bayard observes that he no longer sees the old man in JEFFERSON, one of the sons remarks that this unreconstructed Confederate has not gotten over his son Buddy's service in the "Yankee" army during World War I, and won't come to town "until the Democratic party denies Woodrow Wilson" (124).

He appears as Old Anse McCallum in The HAMLET and the short story "The TALL MEN."

Mandy   She cooks for Virginius MacCallum, Sr., and his six grown sons. A cheerful woman, she fills the door "with her homely calico expanse" (314).

Marders, Sarah (Mrs. Marders)   She is a friend of Belle Mitchell (Benbow) and a regular visitor to her house. Horace Benbow calls Mrs. Marders an "old cat" because she passes on her suspicions about his intimacy with Belle to his sister.

Mitch   A freight agent in JEFFERSON, MISSISSIPPI, Mitch, his friend Hub, and young Bayard Sartoris (4) serenade Narcissa Benbow (Sartoris) at the close of a riotous evening, drawing the attention of the Jefferson town marshal. Mitch sings "Good Night, Ladies" in a "true, oversweet tenor" (148).

Mitchell, Belle   *See* Benbow, Belle Mitchell.

Mitchell, Harry   The talkative, generous and likeable husband of Belle Mitchell (Benbow), he is a successful cotton speculator. His wife is contemptuous of him, and she eventually leaves him for Horace Benbow. Young Bayard Sartoris (4) catches sight of Mitchell in a Chicago bar after the breakup. The woman he is with is trying to steal his diamond stickpin.

Mitchell is referred to in SANCTUARY.

Mitchell, Little Belle   The daughter of Belle Mitchell Benbow and her first husband, Harry Mitchell, she becomes Horace Benbow's stepdaughter. Her mother is indifferent to her, but Benbow finds her appealing.

Little Belle also appears in SANCTUARY.

Monaghan (Buck, Captain)   He and young Bayard Sartoris (4) were aviators together in France during World War I. They meet again in Chicago, where Monaghan refuses to test-fly an experimental aircraft.

He also appears in the short stories "Ad Astra," and "Honor" and as Captain Monaghan in A FABLE.

Moore, Brother   He is part of the Second Baptist Church delegation that asks Simon Strother for an accounting of church funds for which Strother is responsible, and then requests old Bayard Sartoris (3) to cover the $67.40 shortfall.

Myrtle   She is Dr. Alford's receptionist. Aunt Jenny Du Pre bullies her into allowing old Bayard Sartoris (3) to see the doctor without an appointment.

Peabody, Doctor Lucius Quintus   Eighty-seven years old and at 310 pounds "the fattest man in the whole county" (97), he is a long-standing friend of the Sartoris family and had been Colonel John Sartoris's regimental surgeon during the Civil War. Dr. Peabody has long since stopped keeping accounts and charging fees, and cheerfully accepts a meal of corn pone and coffee or a measure of corn for his services. In Faulkner's words, he filled a room with his "bluff and homely humanity" (98).

Dr. Peabody and Dr. Alford consult about old Bayard Sartoris's wen, disagreeing on the diagnosis. A home remedy eventually causes the wen to fall off.

He also appears in *The Sound and the Fury*, *As I Lay Dying*, *The Hamlet*, *The Town*, and *The Reivers*, and in the short story "Beyond."

Peabody, Lucius   The son of Dr. Lucius Quintus Peabody, with a "big boned and roughly molded face" (376), he is known as young Loosh. A prominent surgeon, he lives in New York and visits his father and other Jefferson, Mississippi, connections once or twice a year.

Ploeckner   A protégé of the German aviator Richtofen, he shot down Johnny Sartoris, the twin brother of young Bayard Sartoris (4), in combat over France during World War I.

Rachel   Belle Mitchell's (Benbow) "mountainous" African-American domestic, she is said to be one of Jefferson's best cooks. Rachel regards Belle as ruthless and self-centered, and takes the husband's part in the Mitchells' marital wars. Harry Mitchell gives Rachel a glass of whiskey from time to time.

Redlaw   A former partner of Colonel John Sartoris in a railroad building enterprise, he shoots and kills the colonel on September 4, 1876, on the square in Jefferson, Mississippi.

In *The Unvanquished*, the character is presented more fully as the lawyer, railroad developer, and Sartoris rival Ben Redmond, and the shooting incident is described in greater detail.

Reno   A clarinet player, one of three black musicians who join young Bayard Sartoris (4) and his friends in the serenade of Narcissa Benbow (Sartoris). Reno bemoans the loss of his hat when Bayard accelerates the car to 55–60 MPH.

Res   He is the cashier in old Bayard Sartoris's bank.

Richard (Dick)   He is one of the MacCallums' black servants, and probably a tenant on the MacCallum farm.

Richthofen   A German military aviator, he is the instructor of Ploeckner, the flyer who shoots down Johnny Sartoris. The actual Baron Manfred von Richthofen (1892–1918), known as the "Red Baron" from the color of his airplane, was Germany's top ace in World War I.

He is referred to in *A Fable*.

Rogers, Deacon   The proprietor of a grocery-café on the courthouse square in Jefferson, Mississippi, he enjoys an illicit midday toddy mixed with the home-distilled whiskey young Bayard Sartoris (3) and Rafe MacCallum bring to his place.

The café is mentioned in *The Sound and the Fury*.

Sartoris, Bayard (1)   The infant son of young Bayard Sartoris (4) and his first wife, Caroline White Sartoris. Mother and child died on October 27, 1918, probably of influenza.

Sartoris, Bayard (2)   He is the younger brother of Colonel John Sartoris. General J. E. B. Stuart's aide-de-camp in 1862, he is killed just before the second battle of Manassas in an antic cavalry raid, a call on the headquarters of the Yankee General Pope in search of anchovies. Aunt Jenny Du Pre delights in retelling the anecdote. Stuart is alleged to have said that Sartoris "was a good cavalry officer and a fine cavalryman, but that he was too reckless" (18).

Sartoris, Bayard (3) (old) The son of Colonel John Sartoris, founder of the prominent JEFFERSON, MISSISSIPPI, family, he is the inheritor of his father's banking and related business interests. The character, according to Faulkner biographer JOSEPH BLOTNER and others, is modeled on Faulkner's paternal grandfather, JOHN WESLEY THOMPSON FALKNER.

Bayard is old, irascible, hard of hearing, and resentful of the changes coming rapidly upon Jefferson. Even as the automobile, a symbol of modernity, becomes dominant, old Bayard insists that his old coachman Simon Strother drive him to and from his bank in the family carriage. Change triumphs over old Bayard, though—perhaps it is speed that seduces him, for he begins to take pleasure in rides in his grandson young Bayard's (Sartoris) recklessly piloted car.

On occasions of death, Bayard ascends to the attic of the family mansion to open his father's trunk, which contains the colonel's cavalry saber and faded gray uniform coat. In an old brass-bound Bible he records the death in 1918 of Johnny Sartoris and the passing a few months later of Johnny's wife and infant son. It is the first time Bayard has opened the trunk since the death of his own son in 1901.

He dies of a heart attack induced when young Bayard crashes the car in which he is a passenger.

Old Bayard also appears in *The UNVANQUISHED, The HAMLET, GO DOWN, MOSES, REQUIEM FOR A NUN, The MANSION* and *The REIVERS* and in the short stories "A ROSE FOR EMILY" and "THERE WAS A QUEEN."

Sartoris, Bayard (4) (young) The grandson of old Bayard SARTORIS (3), a violent, noisy, impulsive, drunken, despairing, guilt-ridden American veteran of the ROYAL AIR FORCE, he mourns the death in aerial combat of his twin brother, Johnny Sartoris.

Young Bayard, 26 years old, illogically holds himself responsible for Johnny's death, but his own destructive behavior leads to the death of old Bayard, whose weak heart gives out when his grandson takes him on a fast car ride through the YOKNAPATAWPHA COUNTY countryside.

With his air of "leashed cold violence," there is something of the bully in young Bayard; he terrifies old Simon Strother by driving the car recklessly, and takes pleasure in roaring too close to mule-drawn wagons, making the animals buck and rear. And as his Aunt Jenny Du Pre says of him, "He never cared a snap of his fingers for anyone except John" (56).

Young Bayard marries Narcissa Benbow (Sartoris), a character scarcely less neurotic that he is himself. He dies violently in the crash of a faulty experimental aircraft on the day their son is born.

He also appears in *The TOWN* and *The HAMLET* and in the short stories "Ad Astra" and "THERE WAS A QUEEN."

Sartoris, Benbow The son of young Bayard Sartoris (4) and Narcissa Benbow Sartoris, he is born on June 11, 1920, the day his father is killed test-flying an experimental airplane. Aunt Jenny Du Pre assumes he will be called John, for young Bayard's twin brother; Narcissa, perhaps hoping to break the Sartoris cycle of violent male death, names him after her family instead.

He appears at various ages in *SANCTUARY, KNIGHT'S GAMBIT, The TOWN,* and *The MANSION,* and in the short story "THERE WAS A QUEEN."

Sartoris, Caroline White The first wife of young Bayard Sartoris (4), she is a slipshod housekeeper, according to the sharp-tongued Aunt Jenny Du Pre, who refers to her as "that fool girl" (93). Caroline and her infant son died on October 27, 1918, probably of influenza, while her husband was in France serving with the ROYAL AIR FORCE.

Sartoris, Colonel John He is the head of the founding family of Faulkner's YOKNAPATAWPHA COUNTY cycle. Faulkner modeled the character of the hard, violent, and imaginative John Sartoris on his great-grandfather, the soldier and railroad builder WILLIAM CLARK FALKNER.

Sartoris serves as an officer in Lee's army in the Civil War and later as the commander of a unit of partisan cavalry in northern Mississippi. After the war, he violently opposes Yankee "carpetbaggers," rebuilds his ruined plantation, develops a railroad, and defeats his bitter business rival to win election to the Mississippi legislature.

He tires of violence at the last, however. He faces his rival Redlaw alone and unarmed and is shot to death on the courthouse square in JEFFERSON on September 4, 1876. His monument is a larger-than-life statue that gazes out from the town cemetery across the valley toward the railroad he built.

The long-dead, by then legendary Sartoris is a hovering spirit in *Sartoris*—"that arrogant shade which dominated the house" (113). The novel opens with a spiritual communion between the colonel, the former soldier Will Falls, and the colonel's son, old Bayard Sartoris (3). Falls leaves, but the old colonel remains a palpable presence.

Later, Bayard climbs to the attic to rummage among his father's preserved things: a blue forage cap of Mexican War vintage, a heavy cavalry saber and a pair of dueling pistols, a gray Confederate coat, his wife's gowns, the family Bible.

In the larger context of the Yoknapatawpha cycle, Colonel Sartoris stands at the head of an aristocratic family of the type that will pass from the scene with the rise of the Snopeses (*see* SNOPESISM). Self-assured, with a firm code to live by, he is a standard by which neurasthenic younger generations of Sartorises are measured and found wanting.

Faulkner saw in his own family history a pattern of slow decline, and acknowledged similarities in character and experience between the founder of the Sartoris clan and his grandfather (*Faulkner in the University*, 254).

Colonel John Sartoris appears in The UNVANQUISHED, The SOUND AND THE FURY, ABSALOM, ABSALOM!, GO DOWN, MOSES, REQUIEM FOR A NUN, The HAMLET, The TOWN, The MANSION, and The REIVERS, and in the short stories "BARN BURNING," "SHALL NOT PERISH," "MY GRANDMOTHER MILLARD AND GENERAL BEDFORD FORREST AND THE BATTLE OF HARRYKIN CREEK," and "THERE WAS A QUEEN."

Sartoris, John (1) (Johnny) The twin brother of young Bayard Sartoris (4), he is killed in combat while flying with the ROYAL AIR FORCE over France in July 1918. His brother's grieving for him and self-reproach for failing to prevent his death is a motif of *Sartoris*.

He is drawn as rash, reckless, but with a *joie de vivre* lacking in his twin. Bayard claims bitterly that he was "drunk, or a fool" on the morning of his last flight (45). Johnny left a wife and infant son; both followed him into the grave a few months later, victims of the influenza epidemic of 1918.

Johnny Sartoris also appears in the short stories "ALL THE DEAD PILOTS" and "WITH CAUTION AND DISPATCH" and is referred to in *The TOWN*, *The MANSION*, and the short story "THERE WAS A QUEEN."

Sartoris, John (2) He is the son of old Bayard Sartoris (3), and the father of the twins young Bayard Sartoris (4) and John (Johnny) Sartoris (1). He dies of "yellow fever and an old Spanish bullet wound" in 1901 (90).

John Sartoris also appears in the short story "THERE WAS A QUEEN."

Sartoris, Lucy Cranston The wife of John Sartoris (2) and mother of the twins Bayard Sartoris (4) and John (Johnny) Sartoris (1), she dies when the boys are young. The censorious Aunt Sally Wyatt says she spoiled the twins.

Sartoris, Narcissa Benbow The sister of Horace Benbow and the second wife of young Bayard Sartoris (4), she is obsessively interested in the emotional life of her ineffectual brother, but in other relationships she is a conventional young southern woman.

Rather joylessly in love with young Bayard from the start, she eventually marries him; she delivers their son on the day her husband is killed in the crash of an experimental airplane. Narcissa does not seem to mourn the loss. She remains what she has been—an unhappy, emotionally inarticulate young woman.

She also appears in SANCTUARY and the short story "THERE WAS A QUEEN." She is referred to by her maiden name, Narcissa Benbow, in *The* TOWN and *The* MANSION.

Sartoris, Virginia *See* Du Pre, Virginia.

Sibleigh He is a ROYAL AIR FORCE aviator in France, a comrade of young Bayard Sartoris (4). Flying an obsolescent aircraft, Sibleigh decoyed a pursuing German fighter so Bayard could shoot it down.

He is mentioned in *A* FABLE and the short story "WITH CAUTION AND DISPATCH."

Smith, Mrs. She operates the switchboard for Dr. Brandt, the MEMPHIS specialist in blood and glandular diseases that old Bayard Sartoris (3) sees for treatment of his wen.

Snopes The name of a "seemingly inexhaustible family" of aggressive instincts, Snopeses had been filtering into JEFFERSON from the hamlet of FRENCHMAN'S BEND since about 1910. The first Snopeses are introduced in the unpublished fragment FATHER ABRAHAM, then issued onto the traditional world of Jefferson in *Sartoris.*

Members of the clan spread into Jefferson's small businesses, "where they multiplied and flourished." In the larger Yoknapatawpha cycle, the Snopeses are avatars of the "New South"—the encroachment of a modern and material world and the erosion of planter-class control in the early years of the 20th century. "The older residents looked on with amusement at first," says Faulkner's narrator. "But this was long since become something like consternation" (173).

Snopes, Byron A bookkeeper in the Sartoris bank, he develops an obsession with Narcissa Benbow (Sartoris) and contracts with Virgil Beard, in whose mother's boarding house he lives, to write anonymous love letters to her. He breaks into Narcissa's bedroom late one night and steals away with one of her undergarments and a packet of the let-

ters he had written her. Injured in the drop from the upper story of the house, he hobbles into the bank, steals all the banknotes he can find in the vault, and vanishes.

He also appears in *The* TOWN and *The* MANSION; Narcissa relates the story of the theft in the short story "THERE WAS A QUEEN."

Snopes, Flem The first "Snopes," he migrated to JEFFERSON to work behind the counter of a small restaurant catering to country folk. With this foothold, he infiltrated his kin into town and, with them, used rapacious methods to grow increasingly rich and powerful. By 1916, "to old Bayard's [Sartoris] profane astonishment and unconcealed annoyance, he became vice president of the Sartoris bank" (172). Three years later, Flem is manager of the Jefferson light and power plant.

This important character also appears in *The* HAMLET, *The* TOWN, and *The* MANSION and in the short stories "SPOTTED HORSES," "CENTAUR IN BRASS" and "LIZARDS IN JAMSHYD'S COURTYARD." Flem Snopes is referred to in AS I LAY DYING and *The* REIVERS.

Snopes, Montgomery Ward Turned down for military service in World War I because of a bad heart, he holds a position in the YMCA with Horace Benbow. As it happens, he faked the heart condition by traveling to MEMPHIS for his induction physical "with a plug of chewing tobacco beneath his left armpit" (15). Benbow regards him as a parasite.

He has a larger role in *The* TOWN and *The* MANSION.

Sol A black porter at the railroad station in JEFFERSON, MISSISSIPPI, he delivers the hand luggage Horace Benbow left on the platform.

Straud, Dr. A medical researcher and colleague of young Loosh Peabody, he is an experimenter with electricity.

Strother, Caspey Son of Simon Strother. An African American, he returns from army service during World War I with ideas about racial equality that are taboo in JEFFERSON, MISSISSIPPI. "I don't take nothin' fum no white folks no mo'," he announces. "War done changed all that" (62). But after verbal and physical battering (old Bayard Sartoris knocks him down the stairs with a piece of stovewood), he comes to accept his subordinate station.

Strother, Euphrony She is Simon Strother's wife.

Strother, Joby The grandfather of Sartoris retainer Simon Strother, he was a slave/servant of Colonel John Sartoris. Joby makes up the fire on the Christmas afternoon long ago when Aunt Jenny Du Pre first tells the story of the death of the reckless Confederate cavalryman Bayard Sartoris (2).

He also appears in The UNVANQUISHED.

Strother, Louvinia The wife of Joby Strother, she equips Colonel John Sartoris with his boots and pistols so he can escape from a Yankee patrol come to search the Sartoris plantation.

She also appears in The UNVANQUISHED and the short story "MY GRANDMOTHER MILLARD AND GENERAL BEDFORD FORREST AND THE BATTLE OF HARRYKIN CREEK."

Strother, Simon The elderly black coachman and butler of old Bayard Sartoris (3), he is the grandson of Joby Strother, a servant of Colonel John Sartoris, and he still talks to the old colonel 40 years after his death. Simon admires Sartorises but he loves horses; he detests young Bayard Sartoris's (4) car as unfit for a gentleman to ride in.

Simon conceives a passion for the attractive young Meloney Harris and gives her money he embezzles from the building fund of the Second Baptist Church. He is later found dead, his head bashed in, in Meloney's cabin.

Sue She is the sister of the young countryman Hub. Sue takes up Hub's milking chores while he goes into JEFFERSON, MISSISSIPPI, with his drinking companions V. K. Suratt and young Bayard Sartoris (4).

Suratt, V. K. An itinerant sewing machine salesman from a sharecropper background, he drives young Bayard Sartoris (4) home in his Ford after Sartoris's wild ride on an untamed stallion. Later, Suratt, Sartoris, and a young rustic named Hub drink moonshine companionably.

Affable and loquacious, with a "shrewd, plausible face" (141), Suratt is said to know nearly everyone in YOKNAPATAWPHA COUNTY.

He also appears in As I LAY DYING and in the short story "LIZARDS IN JAMSHYD'S COURTYARD." Faulkner later changed his name to V. K. Ratliff.

Tobe A hostler, he has a gentle way with a wild stallion no one else can handle. The horse throws young Bayard Sartoris (4) after a wild ride through JEFFERSON, MISSISSIPPI.

Van Dorn (Earl Van Dorn) A Confederate cavalry commander in north Mississippi, General Van Dorn raided Union General ULYSSES S. GRANT's supply lines in 1863. In the novel, Van Dorn rides into Holly Springs and burns Grant's stores while Colonel John Sartoris is home laying by his corn crop. Old Will Falls calls him a "putty good man" (223).

Wagner, Hal An alias Byron Snopes uses to disguise his identity as the author of a letter to Narcissa Benbow Sartoris. He tells Virgil Beard he handles "Wagner's" business because he rarely comes to town.

Watts He owns a hardware store in JEFFERSON, MISSISSIPPI.

Winterbottom, Mrs. She runs the Jefferson boardinghouse in which Colonel John Sartoris kills the two Burdens, carpetbaggers working for black suffrage. He offers to pay for cleaning up the mess.

Wyatt, Aunt Sally A spinster kinswoman of the Benbows, "a potty little woman in a lace cap" (170), something of a busybody and gossip, she stays with Narcissa Benbow (Sartoris) while her brother is in France with the YMCA during World War I.

Wyatt, Miss Sophie She is one of two spinster sisters of Aunt Sally Wyatt. When Sally returns from living with the Benbows after Horace Benbow returns from France, Miss Sophie asks Narcissa Benbow (Sartoris) to take her back.

FURTHER READING

Backman, Melvin. "*Sartoris*." In *Faulkner: The Major Years*, 3–12. Bloomington: Indiana University Press, 1966.

Brooks, Cleanth. "The Waste Land: Southern Exposure (*Sartoris*)." In *William Faulkner: The Yoknapatawpha Country*, 100–115. Baton Rouge: Louisiana State University Press, 1990.

Kinney, Arthur F., ed. *Critical Essays on William Faulkner: The Sartoris Family*. Boston: G. K. Hall, 1985.

Millgate, Michael. "Faulkner's First Trilogy: *Sartoris*, *Sanctuary*, and *Requiem for a Nun*." In *Fifty Years of Yoknapatawpha: Faulkner and Yoknapatawpha, 1979*, edited by Doreen Fowler and Ann J. Abadie, 90–109. Jackson: University Press of Mississippi, 1980.

Millgate, Michael. "*Sartoris*." In *The Achievement of William Faulkner*, 76–85. Lincoln: University of Nebraska Press, 1978.

Pilkington, John. "The Poles of Historical Measurement: *Sartoris*." In *The Heart of Yoknapatawpha*, 3–33. Jackson: University Press of Mississippi, 1981.

Singal, Daniel J. "Discovering Yoknapatawpha." In *William Faulkner: The Making of a Modernist*, 93–112. Chapel Hill: University of North Carolina Press, 1997.

"Sepulture South: Gaslight" (Uncollected Stories)

This short story was first published in December 1954 in *Harper's Bazaar* 84–85, 138, 140–141, and later reprinted in Uncollected Stories of William Faulkner. For more information, *see Selected Letters of William Faulkner*, 373, and *Uncollected Stories of William Faulkner*, 703–704.

SYNOPSIS

"Sepulture South: Gaslight" concerns an unnamed narrator's memories of the death and burial of his grandfather. The story indicates much more than mere sorrow, however. It shows the familial and social effects of death. In the society depicted, ties are dissolved when a death occurs; the black house servants, superstitiously—or through a kind of custom—leave the service of the house after a death. Death, in a sense, frees the servants, but not the family. The central conflict in "Sepulture South: Gaslight" is the narrator's inability to come to terms with death, which the narrator calls an ignominy that God should not allow. The horror of death has a hold on the narrator, who returns three or four times a year to the graveyard to consider death, not only of his own family, but also of all humans.

CRITICAL COMMENTARY

Told from the first person singular point of view, the story is a meditation on death. Though the domestic help are able to view death as a rite of passage, the narrator sees it as a horror and a burden, but also as something that ties humanity together. At the end of the story, he explains that he visits the cemetery several times a year and, while gazing upon the graves and monuments there—some undeniably associated with the Civil War—contemplates how they shield the dead from the inhumanity of the living. The story, as James Ferguson explains, "conveys with warm nostalgia but without sentimentality the atmosphere and tonality of the distant past, of a childhood in the Deep South" (*Faulkner's Short Fiction*, 48). Because it contains both fictional and autobiographical elements, "Sepulture South: Gaslight" may be less of a short story than, as Ferguson remarks, "a personal essay" or "a kind of semifictional autobiographical reminiscence" that is at once lyrical, poetic, and evocative (49).

CHARACTERS

Arthur The black servant of the family in the short story. Along with his wife, Liddy, he feels that he must leave the household upon the death of the narrator's grandfather.

Alice, Aunt The narrator's aunt; she is married to his father's brother, Charles (Uncle Charley).

Although self-determined, she is expected to comfort her husband upstairs in the house when the wake is being held. She orders Uncle Rodney not to drink.

Charley, Uncle The narrator's uncle on his father's side. Upset by his father's death, Uncle Charley is comforted by his wife, Aunt Alice.

Liddy The black cook in the short story. With her husband, Arthur, she leaves the family she is working for shortly after the death of the family's grandfather. Her quitting is seen as a rite of passage or superstition, which she follows regretfully but faithfully. Liddy's predecessor had left seven years before, when the grandmother died.

Maggie The narrator's younger sister, but old enough to mind the young children when Liddy asks her to take them down to the pasture and play.

Rodney, Uncle The youngest brother of the narrator's father. A bachelor and a dandy, Uncle Rodney is his mother's favorite and that of other women also. He is a traveling salesman for a wholesale house in St. Louis. On his brief visits home, he carries with him an air of sophistication, which does not go over well with the townsfolk. At his father's wake, which takes place in the home, he begins to drink until his sister-in-law (Aunt Alice) puts an immediate stop to it; she does not want the smell of alcohol on his breath at a time like this. (*Also see* the short story "THAT WILL BE FINE" where an Uncle Rodney with similar traits appears; his character prefigures that of Maury Bascomb in *The SOUND AND THE FURY*.)

unnamed narrator Although an older man when narrating the story, he was a 14-year-old boy and oldest grandchild at the time of his grandfather's wake. The tone of the short story, especially at the end, betrays a melancholy mood.

Wedlow, Mr. The jeweler in the short story. He beautifully inscribes the formal death notice of the narrator's grandfather.

"Shall Not Perish"
(Collected Stories)

First published in the July–August 1943 issue of *Story* XXIII, 40–47, "Shall Not Perish" is reprinted in *Collected Stories of William Faulkner* (1950) and *A ROSE FOR EMILY* (1956); it is a companion piece to "TWO SOLDIERS," narrated by the same person, Pete Grier's unnamed younger brother.

SYNOPSIS

A story about mourning, "Shall Not Perish" opens with the sad news of the death of Pete Grier, killed by the Japanese during World War II. The news arrives in April, the middle of the planting season, and although Pete's death devastates the family, the endless cycle of sowing and harvesting must continue. Three months later, in July, the unnamed son of Major de Spain, another soldier from YOKNAPATAWPHA COUNTY, dies in the war. Mrs. Grier and her only surviving child, the nine-year-old narrator, take the bus from FRENCHMAN'S BEND to JEFFERSON to make a mourning call on the major. After their visit, Mrs. Grier and her son go to a small local museum that displays paintings of all parts of the United States. The narrator is reminded of his senile grandfather, who sometimes reacted violently to western movies, shouting out the names of long-dead Union and Confederate leaders in a vision of the Civil War. The museum, and its exhibit in particular, reinforces the notion that Frenchman's Bend, as the narrator explicitly indicates, is a microcosm of the United States. By implication, "Shall Not Perish" depicts the United States as omnipotent and a cause worth dying for.

The story centers on a conversation between Mrs. Grier and Major de Spain; the major understandably voices despair and anger over the death of his only son in uncompromising tones. But Mrs. Grier, perhaps as the mouthpiece for Faulkner himself, responds in terms that anticipate the sentiments of love and honor and compassion and sacrifice Faulkner expressed in his Nobel Prize acceptance speech in December 1950. Mrs. Grier's timely visit prevents de Spain from committing suicide.

CRITICAL COMMENTARY

In several respects "Shall Not Perish" is as unrealistic as its companion piece, "TWO SOLDIERS," and both stories are regrettably jingoistic. Virtually nothing in Faulkner's earlier fiction, as James Ferguson writes, prepares us "for the saccharine inanities of 'Two Soldiers' and 'Shall Not Perish'" (*Faulkner's Short Fiction*, 42). Nonetheless, the descriptions of the paintings in the museum, and the boy's response to them, represent one of the finest tributes to art in all of Faulkner. For more information, *see Selected Letters of William Faulkner*, 149, 150, 151, 274.

HELPFUL RESOURCES

Theresa M. Towner and James B. Carothers, *Reading Faulkner: Collected Stories*, 54–60; and Diane Brown Jones, *A Reader's Guide to the Short Stories of William Faulkner*, 73–83.

CHARACTERS

Bookwright, Homer Takes the unnamed narrator's father to town in his cattletruck. When the father returns to the farm at sundown, the young narrator notices that in addition to carrying a sack of flour and a package, his father also has a newspaper, a clear sign to the narrator that another boy, like his brother Pete Grier, must have been killed in the war. (The paper reports the death of Major de Spain's son.) *Also see The MANSION and "SHINGLES FOR THE LORD."*

de Spain, Major The father of a 23-year-old aviator killed while fighting the Japanese during World War II. Distraught and despondent over the untimely death of his son, de Spain contemplates suicide, but Mrs. Grier, who is paying her respects and who had lost a son three months earlier in the same conflict, convinces him otherwise.

Father (Mr. Grier) The unnamed narrator's father, a farmer in FRENCHMAN'S BEND. *Also see* Pap in "TWO SOLDIERS" and Res Grier in "SHINGLES FOR THE LORD"; he is also referred to in *The MANSION*.

Grier, Mrs. The main character, grieving for her son Pete who was killed by the Japanese in World War II. Her younger and only surviving son

is the narrator of the short story. When she learns of the death of Major de Spain's son, also killed by the Japanese three months after her own son's death, she makes a sympathy call on the dejected de Spain. Her courage, sympathy, and directness help the grieving de Spain to draw back from the brink of suicide. (In her speech to Major de Spain, Mrs. Grier appears to be speaking in Faulkner's own voice, prefiguring some of the sentiments in his Nobel Prize speech in 1950. *Also see* "TWO SOLDIERS."

Grier, Pete The young narrator's 18-year-old brother killed by the Japanese in World War II. The short story opens with the news of his death. *Also see* "TWO SOLDIERS."

Killegrew, Old Man An old farmer two miles away from the Griers. In December 1941, Pete Grier and his younger brother (the narrator of the story) would walk to Old Man Killegrew's house to listen to the radio reports about Pearl Harbor and Manila. This news was a motivation behind Pete's decision to enlist. *Also see* "SHINGLES FOR THE LORD" and "TWO SOLDIERS."

Millard, Mrs. Rosa An offstage character. A feisty woman, she held her ground against the Yankees while her son-in-law Colonel (John) Sartoris was away for four years fighting in the Civil War. *Also see The UNVANQUISHED and "MY GRANDMOTHER MILLARD AND GENERAL BEDFORD FORREST AND THE BATTLE OF HARRYKIN CREEK"*; she is referred to in *The HAMLET*.

Mother *See* Grier, Mrs.

Quick, Mrs. Solon Quick's wife.

Quick, Solon The owner and operator of a school-bus truck he built himself, Solon drives Mrs. Grier to JEFFERSON for her visit to the grieving Major de Spain. *Also see* "SHINGLES FOR THE LORD" and *The MANSION*.

Sartoris, Colonel (John) An offstage character referred to in the short story. The legendary Colonel Sartoris, an officer in the Confederate army, is Mrs. Rosa Millard's son-in-law. *Also see* SARTORIS, *The* SOUND AND THE FURY, LIGHT IN AUGUST, ABSALOM, ABSALOM!, *The* UNVANQUISHED, *The* HAMLET, REQUIEM FOR A NUN, *The* TOWN, *The* MANSION, *The* REIVERS, GO DOWN, MOSES ("The BEAR"), and the short stories "BARN BURNING," "MY GRANDMOTHER MILLARD AND GENERAL BEDFORD FORREST AND THE BATTLE OF HARRYKIN CREEK," and "THERE WAS A QUEEN."

unnamed narrator Pete Grier's 9-year-old brother. He had accompanied Pete in December 1941 to listen to the news about Pearl Harbor and Manila being broadcast from Old Man Killegrew's radio. Upon hearing that Pete was killed in the war, the narrator becomes emotional and has to be settled down by his father. Three months later, the young boy—an astute observer—immediately realizes the import of seeing a newspaper in his father's hand: another soldier from YOKNAPATAWPHA COUNTY was killed by the Japanese. He accompanies his mother to JEFFERSON to mourn the death of Major de Spain's son. *Also see* "TWO SOLDIERS."

"Shingles for the Lord" (Collected Stories)

Comic short story first published in the *Saturday Evening Post* (February 13, 1943). The tale was revised for *Collected Stories.*

SYNOPSIS

When Res Grier and his son, who narrates the story, arrive late for their day of voluntary labor in putting a new roof on their church, the minister scolds Grier and the other workers tease him. Solon Quick, a former Works Progress Administration (WPA) employee, jokingly calculates Grier's owed man-hour work units. Finally the men start splitting shingles—the others efficiently, the angry Grier violently and slowly. When Solon offers to complete the rest of Grier's work in return for Grier's half-interest in a hunting dog, Grier figures out a way to outwit Solon. Grier and the boy

secretly come back at night to strip the old shingles from the roof. However, Grier's attempt at trickery backfires. Their lantern falls over and ignites the church, which burns down despite heroic efforts by all. The minister calls Grier an arsonist and bans him from joining the volunteers who will raise a new church. The boy recognizes the essential indestructibility of the church, the powerful faith of the rebuilders, and his father's fallibility. Back at home, a befuddled Grier insists he will join the work crew the next morning.

CRITICAL COMMENTARY

Stephen Hahn finds that the story "engages, in a comic vein, some typically Faulknerian themes, such as the relation of the segmenting and rigidifying power of words compared to the fluidity of life" (*Teaching Faulkner* Web site). Joseph R. Urgo believes the principal concerns of the story to be "the changing understanding of work and its relation to personal profit and community service, as well as the relationship of grace and works" (*A William Faulkner Encyclopedia*, 351).

CHARACTERS

Armstid A neighboring farmer, he helps put out the fire that consumes the old, dried-out church building.

Armstid, Mrs. Armstid's wife, who also assists in fighting the fire.

Bookwright, Homer One of the voluntary workers, he arrives early to help shingle the church. He also appears in "SHALL NOT PERISH" and *The MANSION.*

Grier boy The narrator of the story.

Grier, Mrs. The mother of the young unnamed narrator. She also appears as the main character in "SHALL NOT PERISH."

Grier, Res ("Pap") The father of the narrator and one of the volunteer roofers at Reverend Whitfield's church. Unintentionally he burns the church down.

Killegrew An old farmer, he loans his tools (a froe and maul) to Pap Grier, one of the volunteer roofers of the church. *See also* "Two Soldiers" and "Shall Not Perish."

Quick, Solon One of the volunteers on the roofing job at the Reverend Whitfield's church. Quick draws Res Grier into the deal over a dog—a deal that ends up destroying the church. Quick also appears as a minor character in "Shall Not Perish."

Snopes A member of the rapacious family that plays a significant role in Faulkner's fiction, he assists with the roofing of Reverend Whitfield's church.

Tull Half owner with Pap Grier of a hunting dog. He is one of the church members who help with the rebuilding of Reverend Whitfield's church.

Whitfield, Reverend The pastor of a rural church near Frenchman's Bend, Whitfield asks his congregation to help build a new church after the old one burns down. He also appears in *As I Lay Dying*, in which he is a major character, as well as *The Hamlet* and "Tomorrow" (*Knight's Gambit*).

"Skirmish at Sartoris"

Short story (originally titled "Drusilla"), first published in the April 1935 issue of *Scribner's Magazine* and subsequently revised and incorporated into *The Unvanquished* (1938).

SYNOPSIS

Set during Reconstruction and narrated by a youthful and sometimes naive Bayard Sartoris, the story recounts how, on election day in Jefferson, Bayard's father, Colonel John Sartoris, prevents freed slaves from voting by shooting two carpetbaggers (Calvin Burden and his grandson), confiscating the ballot box, and holding the election on the Sartoris plantation. The story of the double homicide was first related in *Sartoris* (1929) and repeated, with some variations, in *Light in August* (1932).

As a comic counterpoint, the ladies of the community force Drusilla Hawk to marry Colonel Sartoris. Drusilla, who had disguised herself as a man and fought with Colonel Sartoris during the war, is now living in a platonic relationship with Sartoris and helping him restore the plantation. But the ladies, believing Drusilla compromised and scandalized by the situation, insist on the couple's marriage. The ending is conventionally happy: the interfering carpetbaggers have been defeated, and Drusilla and Sartoris are joined.

CRITICAL COMMENTARY

There are two skirmishes in this story: the one between Colonel Sartoris and the carpetbaggers and the one between the women of the town and Drusilla. The humor of the second masks but does not eradicate the violence of the first. Moreover, the story of Drusilla's marriage may not be as humorous as it appears on the surface. John Pilkington suggests that the community's demand that Drusilla conform to "the code of behavior expected from a Southern girl of a good family" may be taken to illustrate "the growing inflexibility of Southern society" (*The Heart of Yoknapatawpha*, 207). In this regard the Jefferson ladies' violence to individual rights and freedom is less bloody but no less arbitrary and dictatorial than the actions of Colonel Sartoris on election day.

Appropriately for a young and naive narrator, Bayard draws no conclusions about the morality or immorality of either his father's or the community's actions. The reader, however, is keenly aware of the contrast between the violent and problematic actions of the story and the innocence and inexperience of the youthful narrator.

CHARACTERS

For a list of the characters in this story *see* the entry on *The Unvanquished*.

"Snow" (Uncollected Stories)

Written sometime around 1942, "Snow" was published posthumously in *Uncollected Stories of*

WILLIAM FAULKNER. (*Also see* this story's companion piece, "MISTRAL.") For more information, *see Selected Letters of William Faulkner*, 149, 151, 161, 272; and *Uncollected Stories of William Faulkner*, 711–712.

SYNOPSIS

Set in Switzerland, a somewhat unusual setting in Faulkner's fiction, "Snow" is closer to the more abrupt style of ERNEST HEMINGWAY than to that normally associated with Faulkner's own more discursive and meandering voice. In the short story, an American man remembers an incident from before World War II, when he and a friend from Alabama were climbing in the Swiss mountains. They witnessed a funeral and learned the details of a strange affair that had its beginnings the previous autumn. Two mountain guides had been asked to take a German amateur climber on what was reputedly an easy climb. One of the guides, Brix, was engaged to be married and had, in fact, postponed his wedding day to take the client up the mountains. The German, von Ploeckner (also referred to as the Big Shot), insisted that the wedding take place; thus the bride accompanied them on the climb. Brix and his bride were married in a mountaintop village, with the Big Shot paying all expenses and signing the marriage contract as a witness. On the way back, however, the four climbers met with an accident, and Brix fell to his death. The Americans, Don and the unnamed narrator, witnessed the retrieval of Brix's body, which had to wait until the spring thaw, and were intrigued by the expensively dressed woman who mourned for him. She was, in fact, his bride, and had gone off with von Ploeckner after Brix's death.

The story is framed by the narrator's seeing a newspaper article that reports the murder of a Nazi general, the same von Ploeckner, by his companion, whom the narrator recognizes as the Mrs. Brix he and Don had seen in the Swiss village years before.

CRITICAL COMMENTARY

Throughout many of Faulkner's works is the presence of a mystery that needs resolution, a strategy that appears to have caught Faulkner's imagination.

James Ferguson points out that "the basic narrative strategy of 'Mistral' and 'Snow'—the attempts by two young men to piece together elaborate and ominous mysteries—clearly fascinated Faulkner and was to receive its most elaborate embodiment in his masterpiece, *Absalom, Absalom!*" (*Faulkner's Short Fiction*, 31).

CHARACTERS

Brix The (last) name of the mountain guide in the short story. With Emil Hiller, he leads the amateur German mountaineer von Ploeckner on a climb during which Brix is killed in an accident.

Brix, Mrs. Brix's new bride; she accompanies her husband, his partner Emil Hiller, and the amateur mountain climber von Ploeckner. On that climb, an accident occurs, causing Brix's death. Mrs. Brix subsequently leaves the village with von Ploeckner. Years later, she stabs him to death.

Don A friend of the unnamed narrator. Through a powerful spyglass, Don is the first to spy Brix's funeral going on in the village and later finds out from a waiter details about Brix's widow and von Ploeckner. (Don also appears in "MISTRAL," the companion piece to this short story.)

Hiller, Emil A mountain guide who works for Brix. Together, the two lead the amateur German mountain climber von Ploeckner on a climb. Hiller survives the accident that kills Brix.

Soldiers' Pay

Faulkner's first novel, originally titled MAYDAY, published by BONI & LIVERIGHT, on February 25, 1926, on the recommendation of the American writer SHERWOOD ANDERSON, whom Faulkner met in NEW ORLEANS in 1924.

SYNOPSIS

Soldiers' Pay is the story of a doomed and severely wounded World War I flier, Donald Mahon; his homecoming to Charlestown, Georgia; and the fiancée, Cecily Saunders, whom he had left behind when going to war. Reviews of the novel were mixed, but *Soldiers' Pay* anticipates many of the themes and even the scenes of the far better novels to come.

Although the setting of the novel is the fictional town of Charlestown, Georgia, *Soldiers' Pay* is not about the South. Instead, it is a story of post–World War I America, and its setting could be any small American town. The town itself can be viewed as a kind of "first draft" of Faulkner's more famous JEFFERSON, MISSISSIPPI; like Jefferson, the YOKNAPATAWPHA COUNTY seat, Charlestown is built around a courthouse square with its obligatory statue of a Confederate soldier. However, the people about whom Faulkner writes in *Soldiers' Pay* are very different from the citizens of Yoknapatawpha County. If the characters in Faulkner's first piece of extended fiction have parents and children, their history and the history of their region go no further than that.

World War I just ended, *Soldiers' Pay* opens with two soldiers, Joe Gilligan and Julian Lowe, drinking on a train. The demobilized Gilligan is returning from the trenches in France, but the 19-year-old Lowe never reached the front lines; a cadet, his flight training was not yet complete when the armistice was signed. On the train, they meet Donald Mahon, a pilot who had been shot down and badly injured; his face is dreadfully scarred. Gilligan's experience tells him that Mahon will not live long, and his pity leads him to take the wounded man under his care. Lowe, however, is both horrified by Mahon's injuries and intensely envious of the heroic status the wounds supposedly confer. He wishes he could have those precious and awful accomplishments for his own. Lowe considers his youth and inexperience as burdens and feels robbed of a chance for glory. In this respect, he is an innocent romantic. Also on the train is Mrs. Margaret Powers, a young woman returning from service with the Red Cross. Unlike Lowe, Mrs. Powers sees no romance or glory in war. Her husband was killed in France, and although she did not love him, she is now a war widow who knows the pain of loss, an experience that may partly explain her motive in helping Mahon reach home.

Lowe falls in love with Mrs. Powers, and although he leaves the action of *Soldiers' Pay* by the end of the first chapter, his love letters to her punctuate the novel with a kind of longing that Mrs. Powers cannot reciprocate because, for her, the war changed everything. Her fate is to be with Mahon, trying to make his last days as comfortable and as meaningful as possible. Mrs. Powers is the only civilian in the novel who is truly aware of the war and its devastating effects. To others, the reality of war was distant, something "over there." Mrs. Powers and Gilligan form a pact to help the dying Mahon, who cannot help himself. His eyesight is failing and his memory fades almost completely. They know where to take Mahon only from letters they find in his pockets.

Through the eyes of Januarius Jones, the novel turns from the soldiers and the war widow to Mahon's family in Charlestown. Jones, one of the stranger characters Faulkner has ever created, is a corpulent, lazy sensualist. He comes with no more history than a brief reference to being "lately a fellow of Latin in a small college" (52), and his nature is that of a Pan or a satyr. When he first meets Donald Mahon's father, the Episcopal rector Joseph Mahon, who thinks his son has been killed in the war, Jones is invited to have lunch with him. At lunch, Jones meets Emmy, the rector's servant, and Cecily, Donald's fiancée. Both women also believe that Donald was killed in the war. Emmy, who had once been intimate with Donald, grieves for him, and Cecily, who had planned to marry him, is seeing George Farr, although out of consideration for Rector Mahon, she does not announce her new affection. In his goatish way, Jones is attracted to both women, but Cecily immediately sees through him. During the lunch, and afterward, he aimlessly and meaninglessly pursues her, leaving the reader with the impression that for him sex is nothing more than a matter of conquest and surrender. As Jones and Cecily duel with words, Mrs. Powers comes to the house and informs the rector that his son has returned.

The remainder of *Soldiers' Pay* concerns the ramifications stemming from Donald's return. Reverend Mahon is overjoyed that his son is home, but Cecily is horrified at the thought of marrying this ruined man and her family is not sure how to take the news. Emmy is crushed that he does not remember her at all. Instead of envying Mahon's heroism as Lowe did, George Farr has only contempt for the wounded soldier and a growing desire for Cecily. Mrs. Powers and Gilligan decide to stay on in Charlestown to take care of Mahon, something no one else in the novel is capable of doing. When Doctor Baird, a specialist, is brought in to see Mahon, he confirms what Gilligan has always maintained—Mahon is doomed. The doctor tells Mrs. Powers that he will surely die and "'should have been dead these three months were it not for the fact that he seems to be waiting for something'" (150). The rector, however, believes that his son will get well. Stoically accepting the fact that Donald will be blind, Reverend Mahon points out that his son is to marry Cecily and suggests that the wedding date be moved up. But knowing that Cecily does not want to keep her promise to Donald, Mrs. Powers disagrees with the rector, who ultimately defers to her. Cecily is moved by both pity and revulsion. At one point, she tearfully tells Donald that she will marry him, but soon regrets her words. When her parents attempt to stop the wedding, Cecily at first resists them. She then loses her virginity to George Farr, making herself feel unworthy of Donald's love, and later elopes with Farr.

Mrs. Powers knows that what Mahon is waiting for is his own wedding. Marrying will complete his journey in life, and, as she rightly suspects, will free him to die. She also knows that Cecily will never marry Mahon and therefore suggests to Emmy that she marry him. Emmy, who is lovingly taking care of Donald and whose passion for him has not subsided, refuses. She will not take Cecily's leavings. Mrs. Powers accepts this news calmly, probably already having made up her mind on what to do next. When Rector Mahon tells Mrs. Powers what she already knows—that Cecily has broken the engagement and that Donald will not be married—she tells him that she intends to marry Donald herself. Soon after the wedding, Mahon dies, reliving for one quick moment the day he was shot down over France. Whatever he was waiting for has passed.

In the final chapter of the novel, Mahon is buried. Jones, who has become obsessed with Emmy, uses the occasion of Donald's funeral to seduce her while she is alone in the house. Afterward, Margaret Powers declines to marry Gilligan, who has loved her from the start.

CRITICAL COMMENTARY

Although *Soldiers' Pay* may not be a great novel, it does contain elements that Faulkner would later employ in his masterpieces. Charlestown, like Jefferson, is a small bucolic southern town with a courthouse in the middle of the square. The novel anticipates Faulkner's propensity to manipulate multiple story lines within an overarching narrative. Faulkner also introduces themes that appear in later novels such as the dependence of men upon their women, the agonizing sense of loss and despair, and the tangled skein of desire and love and of reticence and fear. The characters, too, in *Soldiers' Pay*, prefigure later characters Faulkner will create. The helpless Donald Mahon, for example, anticipates someone like *The SOUND AND THE FURY*'s Benjy Compson, another desperately wounded individual who seeks love.

For more information, *see Selected Letters of William Faulkner*, 20, 27, 28, 31–32, 38, 40, 58, 141; *Faulkner in the University*, 60–61; and *Faulkner at Nagano*, 141–142.

CHARACTERS

Baird, Doctor The medical specialist from Atlanta called in to examine the severely wounded Donald Mahon after the latter comes home to Charlestown, Georgia, at the end of World War I. Doctor Baird tells Mrs. Margaret Powers that there is little hope for Mahon's recovery and mentions that the ex-soldier is hanging on to life only because of some task he had set himself before he was wounded, but since has forgotten. The impetus of that self-appointed goal keeps Mahon going.

Bleyth, Captain A ROYAL AIR FORCE pilot traveling with the cadet Julian Lowe when the novel opens.

Burney, Dewey A boy from the Charlestown, Georgia, area who had been caught stealing sugar. A friend of Donald Mahon, Dewey was permitted to enlist in the American army instead of being sent to jail. While in France in World War I, he panics and kills Lieutenant Richard Powers, the husband of Mrs. Margaret Powers. Later killed in the war, Burney is thought of as a war hero and one of the honored dead in Charlestown.

Burney, Mr. Dewey Burney's morose and quiet father, who takes all his ideas from his wife. His occupation is sawing and nailing boards together.

Burney, Mrs. Dewey Burney's mother. She basks in the reflected glow of her son's "heroic" death in France during World War I, which gives her social standing in Charlestown, Georgia. She speaks cruelly to Mrs. Margaret Powers; ironically, both are unaware that Dewey Burney went berserk while in combat and killed his lieutenant, Richard Powers, Margaret's husband.

Coleman, Mrs. One of the leading women of the village of Charlestown, Georgia, and a friend of Minnie Saunders.

Dough, James Mrs. Wardle's nephew. In World War I, he flew for two years with the French air corps, sustaining wounds that crippled his arm and cost him a leg. He sits and watches the dancing at Mrs. Worthington's.

Ed A police officer. At a train station, Ed tries to arrest the returning ex-soldiers Joe Gilligan and Julian Lowe for being intoxicated and disorderly on the train, but Gilligan and Lowe outwit him and reboard the train to continue their journey.

Emmy The servant at Rector Mahon's house. Emmy had been a childhood companion of the rector's son, Donald. When they were young, Donald and Emmy dammed up the creek to make a swimming hole, where they would innocently swim together on hot afternoons and then nap on an old blanket. When Emmy's drunken father discovers what they are doing, he forbids her from seeing Donald again. One night, however, when she is 16 and Donald 19, Donald comes for her and they spend the night together swimming and making love. Although Donald is engaged to Cecily Saunders at the time, Emmy believes that this night proves that he loves her more than Cecily. Soon after, Emmy leaves her home and lives with a seamstress, Mrs. Miller. Rector Mahon finds her there and takes her into his home while Donald is overseas during World War I. When the wounded Donald returns, he does not recognize Emmy, who is heartbroken by his amnesia. After Donald dies (in the last chapter of the novel), Emmy is seduced by Januarius Jones.

Farr, Cecily Saunders *See* Saunders, Cecily.

Farr, George The young man in Charlestown, Georgia, who takes up with Cecily Saunders after her fiancé, Donald Mahon, is presumed dead in France during World War I. When Mahon returns, Cecily drops Farr. Confused and upset, he persists in his attentions, and Cecily eventually begins to go for rides with him again. Finally, Cecily allows Farr to seduce her so that she can get out of her promise to marry Donald, who is crippled, horribly scarred, and going blind. Farr and Cecily elope, but they return to Charlestown before Donald's death.

Gary, Dr. A physician who examines Donald Mahon. He is insensitive in his manner of telling Donald's father, Rector Mahon, that his son will lose his sight. He is romantically interested in Cecily Saunders.

Gilligan, Joseph A character sometimes called Yaphank (World War I slang for a soldier). At the start of *Soldiers' Pay*, Gilligan is a drunken soldier on the train with Julian Lowe, Captain Bleyth, and Donald Mahon. Gilligan takes on the task of bringing the severely wounded Donald home to Charlestown, Georgia, although he knows that Donald is doomed to die soon. He allies himself with Mrs. Margaret Powers, and together they remain in Charlestown to take care of Donald. A realist, Gilligan tells Mrs. Powers that Donald's fiancée, Cecily Saunders, will abandon him—and she does. Gilligan, the strongest male character in the novel, shows compassion for Donald, Donald's father (Rector Mahon), and even for Cecily Saunders.

He has no illusions about life, yet no lasting bitterness, either. A "downhome" intellectual, Gilligan reads Gibbon and Rousseau to Mahon. He also has a strong moral sense and is protective of Lowe, Mrs. Powers, Emmy, Donald, and others whom he respects. Gilligan disapproves of Januarius Jones and George Farr and is contemptuous of Cecily Saunders. He and Mrs. Powers are Faulkner's moral agents in the novel. At the end of *Soldiers' Pay*, he proposes to Margaret Powers, now twice-married and twice-widowed (she marries Donald Mahon shortly before he dies); but she, also a realist, turns him down. In a moment of unobtainable longing, Gilligan runs after Margaret's train, thinking in vain that she has changed her mind.

Green, Captain   A local community leader who recruited the company of soldiers from the Charlestown, Georgia, area, which included Dewey Burney and Rufus Madden, who are both killed in France.

Henderson, Mrs.   The interfering and disapproving elderly woman on the train; she inquires about Donald Mahon's health.

Henry   An African-American porter on the Buffalo-bound train at the start of the novel.

Jones, Januarius   A highly charged character in the novel. Jones is a literal bastard who views life as a series of contests between men and women; sexual conquest to him means domination. He meets Rector Mahon early on the day that the rector's wounded son, Donald, is brought home by Joe Gilligan and Mrs. Margaret Powers at the end of World War I. The overweight and pompous Jones is described as a goatlike satyr. He has taught Latin at a small college and has some intellectual pretensions. The narrator presents Jones as one of the careless civilians of the era right after World War I. Jones hangs around Cecily Saunders and Emmy, attempting to seduce one or both of them. Seeing through him, Gilligan warns Jones to stay away from Mrs. Powers. At the end of *Soldiers' Pay*, Jones takes advantage of the empty house (and of Emmy's even emptier broken heart) to seduce Emmy during Donald's funeral.

Lowe, (Cadet) Julian   A 19-year-old would-be fighter pilot, who at first assists Joe Gilligan and Mrs. Margaret Powers with the badly wounded Donald Mahon on the train. Lowe, who had been in his final weeks of training when the armistice was signed, feels that the war ended too soon. He falls in love with the widow Mrs. Powers and asks her to marry him. Her reluctance, Lowe believes, has something to do with Mahon's wound, a wound which Lowe interprets as a sign of heroism. When Mrs. Powers realizes that Lowe will be a hindrance, she gently, but firmly, sends him home to San Francisco so that she and Gilligan might bring Mahon home to die in his father's house in Charlestown, Georgia. Lowe continues to write to Mrs. Powers throughout the novel.

Lufbery   A soldier referred to by Cadet Julian Lowe. Lufbery is an offstage character.

Madden, Rufus   One of the soldiers in the company raised in Charlestown, Georgia, by Captain Green. Madden witnesses the killing of Captain Dick Powers by Dewey Burney, but he keeps the information to himself. Madden survives World War I and returns to Georgia, where he meets Mrs. Powers.

Mahon, Donald   The wounded and doomed soldier at the center of *Soldiers' Pay*. Lieutenant Mahon, a fighter pilot, was shot down and very badly wounded toward the end of World War I. He is the son of Rector Mahon of Charlestown, Georgia. In addition to having lost much of his memory, Donald has physical injuries that include a withered right arm, damage to his sight, and horrible scarring. Cadet Julian Lowe, the widowed Mrs. Margaret Powers, and Joe Gilligan meet Mahon on a train, and the latter two bring him home to his father.

A man who had little time for society and the social graces, Donald Mahon is one of Faulkner's "natural men," whose relationship to the physical world, women, sex, and other aspects of the human condition is unforced and unself-conscious. In several places, the narrator even describes him as a faun. Before the war, Mahon and Emmy, a Charlestown girl of lower socioeconomic status than he, had had a longstanding friendship, but Emmy's love for Mahon is unrequited after his engagement to Cecily Saunders. Upon Mahon's return, however, Cecily is unable to bear the thought of marrying him; she marries George Farr instead. When a doctor called in to examine Mahon's eyes tells Mrs. Powers that he will go blind and soon die, Mrs. Powers marries Mahon. She has grown to love him, and instinctively knows that Mahon survived his injuries to come home to marry. Once this task is completed he dies in peace.

Mahon, Margaret Powers *See* Powers, Mrs. Margaret.

Mahon, Rector (Uncle Joe) Donald Mahon's father. An Episcopal minister, Rector Mahon is a big, genial man who refuses to admit to himself that his beloved son will in fact die of his war wounds.

Maurier, Harrison One of Cecily Saunders's beaux referred to in passing in the novel; he is from Atlanta. Mr. Robert Saunders, Cecily's father, wants his daughter to have nothing to do with him, whom he dismisses with the description of having slick hair and smoking cigarettes.

Miller, Mrs. A seamstress in Charlestown, Georgia. Emmy lives with her for a short time after leaving her father's house and before being taken in as a servant by Rector Mahon.

Mitchell, Mrs. One of the townspeople in the novel.

Nelson, Callie (Aunt Callie, ole Cal'line) An elderly black woman who was formerly a nanny for the young Donald Mahon. After the wounded Mahon is brought back to Charlestown, Georgia, Aunt Callie helps to nurse him. (*Also see* BARR, CAROLINE, the person in Faulkner's life who served as a model for this character.)

Nelson, Loosh Aunt Callie Nelson's grandson. He is a veteran of World War I and wears his uniform while visiting the wounded Donald Mahon.

Powers, Mrs. Margaret A wise, compassionate woman, Mrs. Powers inspires confidence and love in those who meet her. A war widow (probably in her early to mid-20s), she meets the drunken Joe Gilligan, Cadet Julian Lowe, and severely wounded lieutenant Donald Mahon on a train. With Gilligan's help, she takes charge of getting Mahon back home to his father in Charlestown, Georgia. Mrs. Powers remains in Charlestown helping Gilligan and Aunt Callie Nelson take care of the dying Mahon. When Mahon's fiancée, Cecily Saunders, refuses to go through with marrying him, Mrs. Powers weds Mahon, who, as she expects, dies soon after. When Joe Gilligan asks Margaret to marry him, she refuses, saying that twice a widow was enough. Throughout the novel, Mrs. Powers receives letters from Cadet Lowe, who at the beginning of the novel had also asked her to marry him.

Powers, Richard (Dick) An officer who is killed by one of his own men, Dewey Burney. Powers was very briefly married to Margaret Powers, with whom he spent three days before going overseas to fight in World War I.

Price A store owner referred to in the novel.

Rivers, Lee A young swain of Charlestown, Georgia, proud of his dancing ability and of his status as a former Princeton student. Lee is disliked by nearly everyone in the novel. He is especially enamored of Cecily Saunders.

Saunders, Cecily (Cecily Saunders Farr) A beautiful but cold young woman, Cecily is engaged to be married to Donald Mahon, but because he has been missing in action during World War I and is presumed dead, Cecily begins to date George Farr, a local young businessman. When the wounded Mahon is brought back to Charlestown, Georgia, by Mrs. Margaret Powers and Joe Gilligan, Cecily is torn between keeping her promise to marry Mahon and being repulsed by the hideous scar on his face. Farr, even while acknowledging that Cecily's suitor has returned from the war, nevertheless continues to pursue her. Cecily eventually allows George to seduce her, hoping that the status of a fallen woman would force Mahon's father, Rector Mahon, to absolve her of her engagement to Donald. She finally elopes with Farr.

Saunders, Minnie   Cecily's mother. After Cecily's badly wounded and scarred fiancé, Donald Mahon, returns to Charlestown, Georgia, from World War I, Mrs. Saunders seeks to end the engagement. In this matter, she is an overbearing wife who dominates her equivocating husband, Robert.

Saunders, Robert, Jr. (Bob)   Cecily's younger brother. Fascinated by the idea of Donald Mahon's horrible war injury, he begs to see it in person and later brings his friends. Seen swimming naked by Mrs. Margaret Powers and Joe Gilligan, he vows to get even by spying on them. After catching them kissing and eavesdropping on their conversation, he tells his sister that Mrs. Powers loves Donald and will take him away from her. Later, moved by Mahon's funeral procession, Bob runs home and cries in the arms of his family's servant, a black cook.

Saunders, Robert, Sr.   Cecily and young Robert's father. At first he feels that Cecily ought to keep her promise to marry Donald Mahon, despite his horrible wounds. For a time, Mr. Saunders is very stern with his daughter in her objections to marrying Mahon, but his domineering wife eventually changes his opinion.

Schluss   A traveling salesman of women's underclothes. Schluss meets the soldiers Joe Gilligan and Cadet Julian Lowe on the train. Asked by the conductor to look after the soldiers, who are inebriated, he himself gets drunk. When he leaves the train at Buffalo, the police arrest him instead of the soldiers for whom they were called.

Tobe   The Saunderses' black servant.

Wardle, Mrs.   One of the townfolks of Charlestown, Georgia.

White, Hank   One of the drunken men on the train with Joe Gilligan and Cadet Julian Lowe.

Willard   Rector Mahon's neighbor, who, according to the rector, has good fruit in his orchard next to his small house.

Worthington, Mrs.   One of the townfolks in Charlestown, Georgia. A widow of some means, she has her driver take the suffering World War I veteran Donald Mahon to the dance she sponsors so he can listen to music, which he likes.

Yaphank   *See* Gilligan, Joseph.

FURTHER READING

Brooks, Cleanth. "A Payment Deferred (*Soldiers' Pay*)." In *William Faulkner: Toward Yoknapatawpha and Beyond*, 67–99. Baton Rouge: Louisiana State University Press, 1990.

Millgate, Michael. "*Soldiers' Pay*." In *The Achievement of William Faulkner*, 61–67. Lincoln: University of Nebraska Press, 1978.

———. "Starting Out in the Twenties: Reflections on *Soldiers' Pay*." *Mosaic* 7 (1973): 1–14.

Yonce, Margaret J. *Annotations to William Faulkner's Soldiers' Pay*. New York: Garland, 1990.

Zeitlin, Michael. "The Passion of Margaret Powers: A Psychoanalytic Reading of *Soldiers' Pay*." *Mississippi Quarterly* 46 (1993): 351–372.

"Sorority, The"

Faulkner wrote this six-paragraph essay in 1933 for a young visitor to Rowan Oak. The visitor, a close friend and junior college classmate of Faulkner's stepdaughter, Victoria Franklin, asked Faulkner to copy in his own hand her sorority pledge as a keepsake for her. Later, when she deciphered Faulkner's miniscule, enigmatic handwriting, she realized that Faulkner had not simply copied her pledge but instead had composed an original, idealized description of a sorority. Jane Isbell Haynes, a Faulkner collector and scholar, acquired the manuscript in 1982; the next year she arranged for Seajay Press to publish it in a limited edition booklet titled *A Sorority Pledge* and containing a facsimile and transcription of the manuscript along with her afterword on the provenance of the document. Haynes donated the manuscript to Southeast Missouri State University's Center for Faulkner Studies in 2007.

SYNOPSIS

Presented in the voice of the sorority, the manuscript employs a highly lyrical style and imaginative figures of speech to describe the positive effects the organization will have upon its members. For example, the speaker says: "I am the musician who directs noble sentiments to play; the chemist who converts ungenerous personalities into individuals of great worth." The various pursuits and activities of the sorority—"education, truth, music, laughter"—are presented as means to produce "common sisterhood" and "queenly women." The essay concludes with the assertion: "I am the University of Friendship, the College of Sisterly Love, the School for the Better Making of the Women. I AM THE SORORITY!"

CRITICAL COMMENTARY

While hardly a serious literary work, "The Sorority" shows a personable, gracious, and playful side to Faulkner's personality. It seems doubtful that Faulkner would have written this manuscript at the request of an adult; but Faulkner liked children and young people, and the gift of this manuscript is typical of his kind, generous treatment of the youth with whom he was acquainted.

Sound and the Fury, The

This is Faulkner's fourth novel. It was first published by CAPE & SMITH on October 7, 1929, and is sometimes considered his greatest work of fiction. Told from four very different and contrasting points of view, the novel concentrates on the breakdown of the Compson family over a period of three decades, from around 1900 to 1928. In response to questions about the novel, Faulkner explained that he started it with the image of a young girl, Caddy Compson, climbing a tree in order to look through the parlor window at her dead grandmother laid out in the

house. The book had its inception, Faulkner said, "with the picture of the little girl's muddy drawers" and her brothers, who "didn't have the courage to climb the tree," waiting to hear "what she saw" (_Faulkner in the University_ 1; cf. _The Sound and the Fury_, 39). Caddy is the central character in the novel, and the relationship that her three brothers—Quentin, Jason, and Benjy—have to her is the novel's integrative theme seen from multiple perspectives. Although Caddy's presence is pervasive throughout _The Sound and the Fury_, she does not actually appear in the novel and, in sharp contrast to her brothers, each of whom narrates a chapter (though one can question whether Benjy has the language to narrate anything), Caddy offers no narration of her own, leaving readers to speculate on what her rendering of events would have been. By around 1912 (a year or so after Caddy had left her family and infant daughter), Dilsey's husband Roskus remarks that Caddy's name is not spoken in the Compson household (_The Sound and the Fury_, 31).

Sometime in early 1928, Faulkner had started the novel as a short story titled "Twilight," but the material was too complex to be confined to that genre. Toward the end of that same year, in a letter to his great-aunt Bama (ALABAMA LEROY FALKNER MCLEAN), Faulkner comments about the book he is writing: "the damndest book I ever read. I dont believe anyone will publish it for 10 years" (_Selected Letters_ 41). The book, however, was published a year later. Faulkner also wrote an appendix to the novel about 20 years after it was published. In an interview at the University of Virginia, Faulkner explained that the appendix was another attempt at trying "to make that book . . . match the dream" (_Faulkner in the University_, 84; for a reprint of Faulkner's appendix to _The Sound and the Fury_, see Appendix of this volume). On several occasions, Faulkner referred to _The Sound and the Fury_ as his "best failure" and the one that he loved "the most" (_Faulkner in the University_ 61, 32, 77; _also see Faulkner at Nagano_, 9). Much of the last chapter of the novel, "April Eighth, 1928," was published under the title "Dilsey" in The PORTABLE FAULKNER (1946); the first appearance of Faulkner's appendix to the novel, "1699–1945 The Compsons," also appeared in this volume. _The Sound and the Fury_ was published together with *As I Lay Dying* by the Modern Library in 1946; in this volume, the appendix appears as a foreword, titled "Compson 1699–1945." The complete novel was also published with the appendix at the end in *The Faulkner Reader* (1954), and in 1984, a corrected text edited by Noel Polk was published by Random House. A film adaptation of *The Sound and the Fury,* with the screenplay by Irving Ravetch and Harriet Frank Jr. was released by Twentieth Century–Fox in March 1959; directed by Martin Ritt, the film starred Yul Brynner as Jason (Jr.), Joanne Woodward as (Miss) Quentin, Margaret Leighton as Caddy, Jack Warden as Benjy, and Ethel Waters as Dilsey. In 1957, Faulkner recorded two excerpts from *The Sound and the Fury* and two from *Light in August*; the recording is titled *William Faulkner Reads from His Works* (M-G-M E3617). In 2008 *The Sound and the Fury (April Seventh, 1928)*, a dramatic adaptation based on the novel's first chapter, was performed by the Elevator Repair Service ensemble in New York City.

SYNOPSIS

Chapter 1: April Seventh, 1928

The novel opens on Saturday, April 7th, 1928, Benjy's 33rd birthday. He and his 14-year-old black caretaker, Luster, are standing by the fence that separates the Compson property from a golf course. The course had once been a pasture belonging to the Compsons and had provided an idyllic space for Benjy and his siblings during their childhood. The pasture was sold to pay for Quentin's education at Harvard University and Caddy's wedding. Benjy's reflections flutter between the present and the past and at times are permeated with unsettling flashbacks as when, for example, he recalls certain incidents relating to Caddy's wedding. Emotionally, Benjy is very much a child whose thoughts and memories often revolve around his absent sister, the one person in his life who he instinctively feels loved him. Especially aware of odors, Benjy is often reminded of her by the smell of trees and leaves. The scenes with Luster take place during the present, while the scenes with T. P., Dilsey's younger son, are set sometime between 1906 or 1907 and 1912 and those with Versh, Dilsey's older son, between 1898 and 1900, when Benjy was a small child. The presence of Benjy's attendants helps the reader discern the approximate time period of the scenes taking place in Benjy's mind; Faulkner also indicates time shifts with the change from Roman type to italic. The scenes reflect Benjy's deepest memories and a thought pattern determined by sensations and associations. In a letter to Ben Wasson, the summer before the novel was published, Faulkner identifies some but not all of the time periods in the chapter: "The ones I recall off-hand," Faulkner writes, "are: Damuddy dies. Benjy is 3. (2) His name is changed. He is 5. (3) Caddy's wedding. He is 14. (4) He tries to rape a young girl and is castrated. 15. (5) Quentin's death. (6) His father's death. (7) A visit to the cemetery at 18. (7) [sic] The day of the anecdote, he is 33" (*Selected Letters,* 44).

Benjy's fragmented narrative begins with Luster searching along the fence for his lost quarter, the money he needs for admission to the traveling carnival show performing for the last night in Jefferson before it moves on the next day to Mottston (Mottstown). As Benjy and Luster go through a broken section of the fence, Benjy gets caught, provoking the first time change in the narrative. Benjy is reminded of when Caddy unsnagged him on their way to delivering Uncle Maury's billet doux to Mrs. Patterson one cold winter day right before Christmas. (This time period is around 1908.) Although not able to articulate the sensation, Benjy is somehow aware of Caddy's absence and begins to moan. Irritated with Benjy, Luster, who does not understand Benjy's inner thoughts, assumes that he is moaning because he no longer can see the golfers. As they pass the carriage house, Benjy is reminded of a trip to the cemetery to visit the graves of his brother Quentin, who committed suicide on June 2nd, 1910, and his father, who died in 1912. (The time period of the visit is around 1913.) Luster and Benjy go through the Compsons' dilapidated barn and Benjy is again reminded of the letter that he and Caddy carried to Mrs. Patterson two days before Christmas. Benjy's thoughts switch to the time when another letter that he alone carried to Mrs. Patterson was intercepted by her husband. (This time period is probably the summer or spring of 1908.)

Luster continues to look for his lost quarter as the two walk to the branch where servants from nearby homes are washing laundry. When Benjy hears a golfer call for his caddie, who is looking for the lost ball that Luster found in the water, he begins to moan again, thinking of his absent sister and the time he was playing in the branch with her and his brothers. (This period is around 1900: Versh is Benjy's caretaker, Benjy's name had not yet been changed from Maury, and his maternal grandmother, Damuddy, is dying; the name change occurred sometime soon after Damuddy's death.) Still intent on finding the quarter, Luster begins to move on, and Benjy's thoughts switch to the scene when T. P. gets him drunk at Caddy's wedding, held at the Compsons' on April 25th, 1910. This scene ends with Benjy being taken "up the bright hill" (*The Sound and the Fury*, 22) triggering yet another association with the branch and Damuddy's death. (The time period is again 1900.)

Other remembrances (and different time periods) are interwoven into Benjy's thoughts at this moment as one memory slides into another. Benjy recalls, for example, Roskus's comment, "'Taint no luck on this place. . . . They aint no luck going be on no place where one of they own chillen's name aint never spoke'" (*The Sound and the Fury*, 29), an indication of a period around 1912, a period sometime after Quentin's suicide, Caddy's short-lived marriage, the birth of Caddy's daughter (also named Quentin), Caddy's subsequent departure from Jefferson, and Mr. Compson's death. Benjy's thoughts return to Caddy's wedding and then again to Damuddy's funeral when he and his brothers caught sight of Caddy's muddy drawers as she was climbing up the tree to peek into the parlor window (*The Sound and the Fury*, 39). Luster momentarily leaves Benjy and goes back to get the golf ball, thinking that he might be able to sell it to one of the golfers. When he returns, he notices that Miss Quentin and her boyfriend with the red tie are in the swing together and feebly attempts to direct Benjy to walk a different way. Benjy, nonetheless, sees the two and his thoughts light on the time he came across his sister in the swing with her boyfriend Charlie. (Caddy is around 16 or 17 years old and the time period is 1908 or 1909.) This remembrance—one of the more moving passages in the novel—reflects a sensitive and genuine concern that Caddy has toward her retarded brother. Charlie, however, is indifferent to Benjy's presence and unappreciative of Caddy's sentiments toward him. He coarsely insists that they continue in their amorous caresses. But Caddy's love is too protective of Benjy to give in to Charlie's insistent entreaties. Just because Benjy does not talk does not mean he cannot see, Caddy remonstrates (*The Sound and the Fury*, 47).

Caddy's daughter, however, is not as tolerant or affectionate toward Benjy as was her mother. Unsympathetic and annoyed with him, she decides to tell Dilsey that Luster lets Benjy follow her wherever she goes. Before Miss Quentin returns, Luster unsuccessfully tries to sell a golf ball to her boyfriend, who works with the carnival, but he is more interested in the metal box that Luster found and gave to Benjy to play with. Labeled Agnes Mabel Becky, the box contained three condoms, a sure sign of Miss Quentin's nightly activities after she climbs down the tree next to her bedroom window (*The Sound and the Fury*, 50).

Benjy and Luster go along the fence where the latter continues to look in the grass for the quarter. Moaning as he waits for the schoolgirls to pass by, Benjy's thoughts turn to the times he waited for Caddy to come home. This time period is after Caddy's wedding and when T. P. was his caretaker. It is also when Benjy escaped through the gate to pursue the Burgess girl on her way home from school and his subsequent castration. Benjy vividly remembers the bright lights and whirling shapes as he falls unconscious before the operation (*The Sound and the Fury*, 53). Luster, who is not very patient with Benjy or even at times polite, has no understanding of Benjy's frustrations. Addressing him as a looney, Luster tells Benjy to stop bellowing and slobbering. When the golf ball Luster found is taken by a golfer, Luster taunts Benjy until Dilsey intervenes. They go into the kitchen where Dilsey places Benjy's birthday cake on the table. Benjy's thoughts float back to the time he was looking at the fire when his mother was telling him his new name. Attracted to fire, Benjy sees the lighted candles on his cake, but Luster is the one who blows them out causing Benjy to cry. After the cake is cut, Benjy's thoughts continue to flash back and forth to the period of his name change that he associates with the sound of the clock and rain and with Caddy's crying. Not being watched by Luster or Dilsey for a moment, Benjy burns his hand on the stove door. Stirred by the commotion, Mrs. Compson comes down from her room. To quiet Benjy, Luster takes him to the family library and builds a fire. Again Benjy returns in thought to the time of his name change, to a time his mother was sick and he was being put to bed, and to the time his brother Jason cut up the paper dolls that he and Caddy made together.

Dilsey prepares supper and calls Miss Quentin. Jason is already present. Benjy's thoughts continue to roam from one episode to another. He thinks of his brother Quentin's fight at school supposedly over someone putting a frog in Caddy's (or someone else's) desk—the identity of the person Quentin refers to is uncertain (68). Mr. Compson, however, sees through Quentin's fabrication. The fight was most likely in retaliation to an attack on Caddy's character; her classmates may have known of her promiscuity. This incident occurred around 1908 or 1909, the same period of time associated with the loss of Caddy's virginity (68–69). Ignorant of specifics, Benjy nonetheless seems to intuit that something was wrong when Caddy came inside in a hurry and was confronted by her parents. Though Caddy put her hands out to Benjy, he started pulling at her dress.

As he is having dinner and overhearing the spat between Jason and Miss Quentin, Benjy thinks back to his early childhood (1900 or a little after), Versh's comment about his name change, and Caddy's willingness to feed him so he would not cry. Miss Quentin gives Luster a quarter for the show, but before he leaves he has to put Benjy to bed. As he undresses, Benjy sees himself naked and begins to cry. Luster, perhaps for the first time all day, understands Benjy's plight and says: "*Looking for them aint going to do no good. They're gone*" (73). Luster takes Benjy to the window where the two watch Miss Quentin climb down the tree and run across the lawn. As he is falling asleep, Benjy's last thoughts are of his sister Caddy holding him.

Chapter 2: June Second, 1910

The second chapter, titled "June Second, 1910," is narrated by Quentin, the oldest Compson child. He is a romantic idealist and a Hamlet-like figure,

pensive and brooding. This is the day of his suicide in Cambridge, Massachusetts, where he is a student at Harvard. Like Benjy, Quentin's reminiscences mainly revolve around Caddy, but unlike Benjy, he punctuates them with literary allusions, musings about time, and thoughts of death. Though Benjy is mentally deficient and Quentin is not, there are, nevertheless, parallels between their thoughts: Both brothers have a deep longing for Caddy.

He begins the last day of his life by skipping classes and with thoughts that linger on his father, time, and death. Before he leaves his dorm room, he breaks the crystal and hands of the watch given to him by his father. This act of destruction—and the cut he gets from the broken glass—are apt precursors of the day to come and his ultimate act of self-destruction. Quentin waits until his roommate, Shreve MacKenzie, rushes off to class before carefully packing his trunk and writing a letter to his father and another to Shreve. Dressed in his best suit, Quentin leaves his room, goes to breakfast at Parker's, buys a cigar, and visits two different shops: a jeweler's, where he shows the jeweler his watch, and a hardware store, where he buys two six-pound flatirons that will be used to weigh him down when he jumps off a bridge into the Charles River. (Although referred to in the novel, Quentin's suicide is not narrated.)

Feeling that he was never successful in protecting Caddy and her honor, Quentin recalls several humiliating incidents, including conversations with his father about having committed incest with her, something which in fact he did not do, and the time he was easily overpowered when trying to beat up Caddy's lover, Dalton Ames, who even put his pistol into Quentin's hands. He thinks too of the library conversation he had with Caddy's fiancé, Sydney Herbert Head, on the day before her wedding and how irritated and annoyed he became with him as he (Head) tried to ingratiate himself. (Time periods in this chapter, like those in Benjy's, can be discerned by the references Quentin makes to people and events.) Quentin recalls, too, his father's words implying that Caddy did not want his protection. He also remembers the time when he suggested to Caddy that they agree to a murder-suicide pact, but when she was willing to go through with it Quentin was unable to act. "In the end," the critic CLEANTH BROOKS observes, "it is not the body of his sister but the river of death to which Quentin gives himself" (*William Faulkner: The Yoknapatawpha Country*, 332).

After leaving the hardware store, Quentin boards a streetcar not knowing its destination and gets off near an open draw bridge that is letting a schooner go through. He crosses to the opposite side of the river and leans over the railing looking at the Harvard boathouses. Noticing various shadows including his own, he remembers the saying: "a drowned man's shadow was watching for him in the water all the time" (90). Here is one of the several references Quentin makes to drowning, indicating to the reader the means by which he will commit suicide. Throughout the day, Quentin is also especially cognizant of shadows, an image that Stephen M. Ross and Noel Polk rightly observe as continuing "a figurative pattern begun in Benjy's narrative" and as alluding "to the passage from *Macbeth* [5.5.23–28] that is the source of the novel's title" (*Reading Faulkner: The Sound and The Fury*, 53). Quentin spots Gerald Bland, a classmate and member of the rowing team, and momentarily reflects on his reputation as a lady's man, but then his thoughts eventually turn to Caddy and his own family. As he is walking on, he sees Deacon, a gregarious black man, and gives him a letter to be delivered to Shreve the next day. Shortly after leaving Deacon, he runs into his roommate Shreve, who asks Quentin why he is dressed up and what he is carrying. Avoiding the truth that he has flat-irons, Quentin—who had purposely purchased the two smaller six-pound flatirons knowing that they would look like a pair of shoes when wrapped (*The Sound and the Fury*, 85)—answers that his package contains shoes that had been resoled.

As Quentin continues on and boards another trolley, his thoughts start wandering to various conversations that occurred in the Compson household, to his mother's defense of her family, the Bascombs, and to her preference for her son Jason. One of many—and often pessimistic—aphorisms of his father that he recalls throughout the day occurs to him at this time: "a man is the sum of his misfortunes" (104). Whenever the streetcar comes to a

stop, Quentin can hear his broken watch ticking. He eventually gets off the car and boards another to go back to the interurban station. His thoughts turn to Gerald Bland and Bland's mother, wondering why she would have sent him a note earlier in the morning, to Caddy's lover Dalton Ames, and to her fiancé Herbert Head. Quentin recalls when before the wedding he imagined shooting Herbert's voice "*through the floor of Caddy's room*" (105). These three male figures—Bland, Head, and Ames—merge together at times in Quentin's consciousness and preoccupy his thoughts, and when linked to Caddy they underscore the threat that sexuality poses to him.

Quentin gets off the streetcar and starts walking into a wooded area toward a stone bridge. Observant of the foliage, he compares it with what he is used to at home. The association of trees and shadows seems to have sparked within him the memory of a conversation he had had with Caddy when she was pregnant. Quentin's rendering of details reflects a dark and spectral moment in Caddy's recognition of her own sexual struggles which she voiced right before her wedding: "*There was something terrible in me at night I could see it grinning at me I could see it through them grinning at me through their faces it's gone now and I'm sick*" (112). As past events and conversations (many relating to his own fears of sexuality) weave in and out of his thoughts of Caddy, Quentin walks to the end of the bridge to hide the flat-irons that he will later use when he drowns himself. He then leans on the bridge railing and looks into the water. Quentin notices a trout swimming and hears a rumor from the three boys who arrive that people have been trying to catch this fish for 25 years and that there is a store in Boston offering a fishing rod as a reward to the person who catches it.

After a brief conversation with the boys, Quentin moves on and sits at the roadside until the same boys come by. As he walks along and chats with them, he remembers bits of conversations with his father and sister, and in particular Caddy's pithy but pragmatic retort when he informed her that Herbert Head was caught cheating at cards and on exams: "*Well what about it I'm not going to play cards with*" (123). It seems virtually impossible for Quentin to come to grips with Caddy's pregnancy and loss of honor; his thoughts just a moment or two before this remembrance indicate his inability to accept Caddy's pregnancy and his unrealistic attitude toward her solution. When he asks why must she marry, Caddy answers: *"Do you want me to say it do you think that if I say it it wont be"* (122). Denial will not make the pregnancy disappear.

After the boys depart, Quentin stops at a bakery where he meets a little Italian girl, whom he affectionately calls "sister," a term that resonates with meaning for him. (At the very beginning of this chapter, he thinks of Saint Francis calling death "little sister" and links the thought to Caddy; throughout the day, Quentin is preoccupied with thoughts of his sister and his own death.) The little girl leaves the bakery with Quentin, who decides to take her for ice cream. When they finish and come out of the drugstore, Quentin sees for a second time a buggy with a white horse and is reminded of Doc Peabody and Caddy, who told Quentin that she would not see a medical doctor until after her wedding. Quentin's thoughts then turn to his father's views and his own—undoubtedly influenced by his father—of women, menstruation, and sexuality (128).

Although he says goodbye to the little girl and starts on his way back to the university, she keeps following him and when asked where she lives she does not answer. Quentin tries to find out from others but to no avail. After taking her to various houses, thinking one might be hers, he gives the girl a quarter and flees, only to once again find her following him. As Quentin was attempting to get away from the little girl, his thoughts mingled different episodes that occurred sometime in his early adolescence and teens; they include, among others, his questioning Caddy about letting a boy kiss her, her reply that she did not let him but made him kiss her (a reply that angered Quentin), and Caddy's poking fun at Quentin when finding him with Natalie (133–135). The little girl continues to follow Quentin as he crosses the river, where some boys are swimming. When the girl's brother Julio and the town marshal Anse catch up to him and the girl, the brother jumps him and has to be pulled away by the marshal. Quentin is arrested on kidnapping charges and taken to court. On the way, he meets Mrs. Bland in her car with her son Gerald, Spoade,

Shreve, and two girls unknown to Quentin, Miss Daingerfield and Miss Holmes. Shreve, Spoade, and Gerald follow Quentin and Anse to the squire. After being questioned by the town judge, Quentin is ordered to pay six dollars in fines and one dollar to Julio, who is not pleased with the decision.

After this ordeal, Quentin and his friends return to Mrs. Bland, who has prepared a picnic for her son. Quentin's thoughts begin to drift further and further away from the conversation and he becomes more and more detached from the others. He thinks of his sister's sexual experiences and the lack of his own, of his real (or imagined) confession to his father of having committed incest with Caddy, and of his unsuccessful attempt at killing her and himself. His reminiscence of the failed attempt to stab Caddy with a knife indicates that she herself seemed to know all along that he would not be able to go through with it. When his thoughts turn to the fiasco of his fighting Caddy's lover Dalton Ames, Quentin reaches an emotional crescendo and momentarily confuses Gerald Bland with Ames. He starts a fight, but Bland, who has been taking boxing lessons, easily wins. Bloodied and beaten, Quentin returns to his dorm room, where he attempts to clean the bloodstains on his clothes with gasoline. The smell of gasoline evokes in him the memory of his brother Jason's aversion to the smell and of his sister having the first car in Jefferson, a gift from Herbert Head before her wedding. Many other memories of his family life flood his mind as he washes and dresses again before departing the room for the last time.

Chapter 3: April Sixth, 1928
The third chapter of *The Sound and the Fury* is narrated by Quentin's younger brother Jason and takes place on Good Friday, April 6th, 1928. Jason, resentful, cynical, deceptive, and hard-hearted, is his mother's favorite, and like her, he is self-absorbed, but where her character plays the role of the suffering victim—hypochondriacal, put-upon, and weak—Jason snarls, bullies, and belittles. Jason does not have to dwell too much on the past to fuel his bitter hatred of his sister, whom he blames for his lost opportunity at a bank job that her fiancé Herbert had once promised him. Caddy's disgrace

and divorce from Herbert meant the end of Jason's hopes, and her daughter, Quentin, who has lived in the Compson household since infancy to be reared by Mrs. Compson, is but a daily reminder of what was denied him. Named after her deceased uncle, Caddy's daughter Quentin is now 17 years old.

Jason's chapter clearly shows his relationship with his family and his attitude toward each member, dead or alive. His niece especially is resented and his brother Benjy seen as an unnecessary burden whom Jason would like nothing better than to send to an asylum. The chapter opens with Jason dwelling on Quentin's absence from school and his mother's child-rearing practices. As the chapter progresses a stark picture of a dysfunctional family emerges. Jason's comments and treatment of others portray an embittered person trapped within his own rancor. As he comes into the kitchen to confront Quentin about school, Quentin is asking for another cup of coffee from Dilsey. Physically removing Quentin to the dining room, he is intent on whipping her with his belt until Dilsey intervenes. Quentin runs off to her room to get ready for school as Mrs. Compson is coming down the stairs. Jason goes to his car to get ready to drive Quentin to school to make sure she attends and notices that Luster had not put the spare tire on the back of the car as he had been told to do; angered, he backs out of the garage without it. When she appears, the two of them continue to argue and on the way to school Jason threatens her once again with a whipping. After he drops her off, he goes to the post office before going to work. He arrives late for work, but Earl, Jason's boss, says nothing except to order him to help Uncle Job uncrate the cultivators that came in. Once the task is done, Jason wastes no time in opening the letter from Caddy, which contains a check intended for Quentin's use. (All along Caddy has been sending her mother monthly checks to support her daughter.) About ten o'clock, Jason goes for a soft drink with a drummer (a salesman) with whom he shares his unsolicited opinions of the hard-working farmer and the stock market. He then goes to the telegraph office where he gets an update on cotton prices and wires Caddy.

When he returns to the store, he reads a letter from his lady friend Lorraine, a MEMPHIS prosti-

tute, and mulls over the value of money; money is Jason's preoccupation and readers are easily struck by the irony in his comments (194). After he tears up and burns her letter, he is called to the front of the store where he impatiently waits on customers. His thoughts, critical of his deceased brother and father and indicative of his embitterment, turn to his father's funeral, conversations with his mother, and to the time his father went to get Caddy's infant daughter to take back home. At the funeral, Jason, although not directly identifying the emotion, "began to feel sort of funny" (202) and decided to leave the grave site and walk around a bit. After the family left, he came back toward the grave and noticed his sister standing there, alone. The Compsons had not informed Caddy of her father's death, but she had read it in the newspaper. At the grave site, Caddy made arrangements with Jason to see her baby daughter, a toddler by now, and agreed to pay him a hundred dollars. When Jason got to the designated spot, he had Mink, the driver of the carriage, slow down and, lifting the child to the window as Caddy came closer, ordered him to whip the horses and speed on. The next day, Caddy confronted Jason at the store. After she left he suspected that she would go to the house and Dilsey would let her see Quentin. When he went home, he found out that Caddy in fact had been there to see her daughter and her brother Benjy. He later threatened Caddy that if she ever does that again Dilsey will be fired, Benjy sent off to the mental institution in Jackson, and Quentin taken away by their mother.

When Earl comes up to the front of the store and goes to lunch, the narrative turns to present time (210). Jason retreats to the back to open Caddy's letter to Quentin and finds to his dismay a $50 money order in it and not a check. He will now need Quentin's signature. As he is hunting for a blank check that he plans to fill out to give his mother, pretending it is the one from Caddy, Quentin comes into the store. (Each month Mrs. Compson burns the $200 check Caddy sends her. Because of her pride, she does not accept "charity" from "a fallen woman"; in her opinion it is "the wages of sin" [220]. Jason, however, tricks his mother into destroying a fake check and deposits most of the money from the real one into her account, having her think that he is generously giving her his monthly earnings; he pockets the rest. Jason is his mother's power of attorney.) On this day, Quentin expects from her mother a letter with money in it, money that she plans to use in leaving Jefferson. She asks whether the letter arrived, but Jason avoids telling her. When he returns from waiting on a customer, he catches her with Caddy's letter and, before she can open it, beats "her knuckles on the desk" (212) to wrest it away. He forces her to sign the money order without seeing the amount and gives her a meager $10. After Quentin leaves, Jason, who no longer has any blank checks to forge, goes out to find some elsewhere. Unsuccessful at the printing shop, he finds old man Simmons, who gives him the key to the old opera house where papers from the defunct Merchants' and Farmers' Bank had been stored. Jason comes across "a pad on a Saint Louis bank" (216) which he uses to write the phony check that he gives his mother.

Before going home for lunch, Jason stops at the telegraph office to get an update on the stock market. It is down twelve points. Once at home, he gives his mother the letter from Caddy which he had resealed. At first, Mrs. Compson is hesitant to burn the check. She also received a letter from her brother Maury asking for money. On his way back to the store, Jason stops at the bank and again at the telegraph office where he finds out that his cotton stock dropped another point; and again he berates the operator for not having kept him informed. Arriving late to work, Jason tells Earl that he went to the dentist, lies about having gone home for lunch, and mentions nothing about going to the bank and the telegraph office. Because of his respect and sympathy for Mrs. Compson, Earl puts up with Jason's rudeness and has never informed her that her son—contrary to what he may have led his mother to believe—did not invest in Earl's business the thousand dollars he got from her; instead he bought a car with it.

When the band for the show starts up, Jason goes out to the back. As he is talking with a black man, he spots his niece walking with a fellow from the show, the fellow wearing the red tie. Not pleased with Quentin's appearance and knowing that she left school early, Jason decides to follow her. Quen-

tin, however, manages to elude him. While standing in the street, Jason is self-conscious and for a moment reflects on how he might be viewed by others because of his family's reputation. Any sympathy he has is strictly for himself and not for the plight of others (233). As Jason is standing there, a boy comes up to him with a telegram from his broker. After signing for it, Jason tears it open and, anticipating what it will say, reads that his account has been closed. He thinks about getting his money back and not playing the market anymore.

About 3:30 P.M. Jason returns to the store and tells Earl that he (Jason) has to go home. On his way up to his room, his mother asks whether he has seen Quentin, who should be home by now. Impatient with her, Jason goes into his room, which he keeps locked whether he is in it or not. He gets his hidden box of money and counts it out before leaving. As he is driving into town, he notices Quentin riding in a car with the fellow wearing the red tie. He gives chase for a while before spotting the car, not far from Ab Russell's barn. At this time, Jason is suffering from a terrible headache. He parks his car and on foot cuts across a plowed field to sneak up on Quentin and her friend, but he gets there too late and hears their car start and drive off fast with the horn blowing. When Jason gets to his car and drives off, he realizes that Quentin and her friend let the air out of one of his tires. He muses over the irony that the spare had not been put on the car and that the air pump was missing. After borrowing a pump from Russell to inflate the tire, Jason returns to town.

Jason stops at the telegraph office and finds out that his stock dropped 40 points by the close of the day. Angered, he takes his frustrations out on the telegraph operator and has him send a message back to the broker collect. He then returns to the hardware store and again argues with Earl. Jason sees that Uncle Job has set up the cultivators and hears singing and the band playing. He momentarily reflects on several different topics ranging from money to child-rearing practices to what he deems are annoying pigeons and sparrows that flock around the courthouse. Earl comes to the back with packages for Job to take out. When Job returns from tending to his own business, Jason accuses him of having sneaked off to the show. After Earl and Jason lock up the store for the day, Jason stops at a drugstore, buys cigars, and talks about baseball before going home.

When Jason walks into his kitchen, he finds out from Luster that Dilsey is upstairs keeping Quentin and Mrs. Compson from quarreling with one another. After coming back down, Dilsey chides Jason for being late and explains that Quentin complained to Mrs. Compson that he was following her around, which Jason denies. When Luster brings up the show, Jason is reminded that he has two tickets and is willing to sell one to Luster for a nickel. Luster, however, has no money (something that Jason probably knows) and, out of spite, Jason burns both tickets. Immediately after, he goes into the living room and reads the paper. Luster and Benjy eventually follow. When Dilsey calls Jason to supper, he does not go into the dining room until after he has her get Mrs. Compson and Quentin to come down to eat. During the dinner conversation, Jason purposely says and does things that he knows will agitate Quentin and lies to his mother when she asks why he was late coming home. Fully aware that Quentin is upset and listening to everything that he is saying, Jason prevaricates a story that he loaned his car to a man from the show, who needed it to follow his brother-in-law riding with a woman from town. Before angrily running up to her room, Quentin complains to her grandmother that Jason mistreats her and blames him for making her do what she does. After she is upstairs, Mrs. Compson says that she inherited "headstrong traits" from both her mother and her uncle Quentin, and then in a morbid self-pitying tone she comments: "Sometimes I think she is the judgment of both of them upon me" (260–261). She continues complaining to Jason that his brother Quentin and sister Caddy took sides with their father against her and Uncle Maury and that Mr. Compson himself favored them over Jason.

Finally, Mrs. Compson goes upstairs, but before going to her own room she says goodnight to Quentin and then locks the girl's bedroom door. Jason finishes a cigar before going upstairs for the night. As he passes Quentin's room, he does not hear a sound and thinks for a moment how quiet she

must study. After saying goodnight to his mother, Jason enters his room and counts his money. Benjy is already asleep in another room. Jason hears "the Great American Gelding," as he refers to him, "snoring away like a planing mill" (263). For a moment, Jason reflects on Benjy's castration as having happened too late and on two unnamed others who he thinks should undergo something similar. Since their identities are not revealed by Jason, the reader can only speculate as to who they might be. The context, however, seems to indicate that one of them may be his own niece Quentin. The chapter ends with Jason thinking of recouping his losses in the stock market and then celebrating over it.

Chapter 4: April Eighth, 1928

The final chapter of the novel is told in the third person and takes place on Easter Sunday, April 8th, 1928. As the opening words of the chapter intimate, the day begins badly for Dilsey in more ways than one. Her grandson Luster has not done his chores, so when she walks into the Compsons' house, she finds it cold and must carry in the firewood on her own before building a fire and making breakfast. Knowing that Dilsey is inside, Mrs. Compson calls from the head of the stairs for a hot water bottle. After taking the bottle from her, Dilsey yells for Luster and tells him to take in more firewood and dress Benjy. When he brings Benjy into the kitchen, Luster says that he has been accused of breaking Jason's bedroom window. At breakfast, Jason complains once again about the broken window and fumes at his bad fortune. He insists that Quentin be awakened and told to join the family for breakfast. While Dilsey is upstairs calling her, Jason, who knows that the window was broken the night before, suddenly becomes aware of what might have happened. He rushes to Quentin's locked room, but not having the key he snatches a set of keys from his mother's pocket in order to open Quentin's door. When Jason realizes that Quentin did not sleep there during the night, he races to his own room and discovers that his strongbox, hidden under a floorboard in his closet, has been pried open and the money taken. Dismayed and angered, he calls the sheriff to tell him he has been robbed and to have a car ready by the time he gets there. Jason runs off without having eaten breakfast and when he arrives at the sheriff's house, he expects him to find and arrest Quentin. Jason again explains what happened, but the sheriff wonders where Jason would have gotten the money and suspects that he was taking it from Quentin all along. Knowing that Jason was partly the cause of Quentin's running away in the first place, the sheriff decides not to go after her. He even questions Jason on what he expects to do with Quentin once he finds her. Although Jason maintains that he will do nothing, the sheriff, who hears the bitterness in his voice, knows better. Jason leaves to chase after Quentin on his own but fails in his attempt to find her and recover the money.

As he is driving to Mottson, Jason imagines a file of soldiers entering the courtroom with him and dragging out the manacled sheriff as just punishment for not helping him and, in Jason's opinion, for not doing his job as a man of the law. These strange fantasies reflect a spiteful mind as Jason attempts to vindicate his failures and missed opportunities. The smell of gasoline causes Jason headaches and he is forced to stop the car to search for a handkerchief with camphor that he might have left in the seat, but there was none. Instead of going back home for the camphor, Jason decides to drive on and think of something that will divert attention away from his headache. First he thinks of Lorraine, then of the money that was taken, and finally of Quentin; he is infuriated that he was outwitted by a girl. He stops at a gas station to ask about the show and is told that the tent is not yet up but that the train cars are in. When he arrives at the train station, Jason scouts around before getting out of his car. Obsessively intent on getting the money that Quentin took, Jason overlooks the possibility that his niece may not even be there. Upon entering one of the cars, Jason interrogates and manhandles an older worker and, after knocking him to the floor, leaves. The man finds a hatchet and follows Jason out. Hearing him, Jason turns as the man jumps from the train car, and as Jason is falling to the ground, he thinks that he is about to die. Jason hits the back of his head on the rail and is helped up by some other men and told to leave. Before going, Jason explains that he was looking for

a girl and a man with a red tie. One of the men tells Jason that they were kicked out because of a stunt they pulled. Jason goes to his car, slowly drives off and finds a drugstore, but it is closed. After waiting awhile, Jason gets a black man to drive him to Jefferson for four dollars.

During the time Jason is trying to hunt down his niece, Dilsey cleans up the kitchen and gets ready to attend Easter services. She takes with her Frony (her daughter), Luster, and Benjy. At church they listen to a sermon by a visiting minister from St. Louis, Reverend Shegog. Although the preacher starts off slowly, he gradually builds to a crescendo that moves Dilsey to tears. On the way home from the service, Dilsey makes a comment with apocalyptic overtones to an uncomprehending Frony: "I seed de beginnin, en now I sees de endin" (297). After the four of them get back, Dilsey tells Luster to play with Benjy in the backyard as she and Frony go to the cabin. Once Dilsey changes her clothes, she walks over to the house, but before making lunch she attends to Mrs. Compson. Believing that her granddaughter has killed herself, Mrs. Compson asks Dilsey whether she has yet found the suicide note and remarks that her son Quentin had enough consideration to leave one; it would be the least that her granddaughter could do.

After lunch, Luster takes Benjy to the cellar and tries again to perform a trick that he saw the night before at the carnival, but Dilsey has them go outside. When Luster takes Benjy to the fence by the golf course, Benjy starts moaning, and Luster provokes him even more by whispering his sister's name, Caddy. Dilsey calls Luster to bring Benjy to her and takes him into the cabin. As Luster is getting the slipper from the house to quiet Benjy, Dilsey holds and rocks him on the bed, "wiping his drooling mouth upon the hem of her skirt" (316). (The slipper, referred to here by Dilsey as a shoe [316], once belonged to Caddy and is used now as a pacifier by Benjy, or, as Stephen M. Ross and Noel Polk infer, "has become a fetish for Benjy" ([Reading Faulkner; "The Sound and the Fury," 35].) Reluctantly, Dilsey decides to let Luster take Benjy for a ride in the carriage to the cemetery and insists that he go the exact same route that T. P. always takes, but once in town by the monument of the Confederate soldier Luster, who wants to show off in front of a group of black people, turns left instead of right, causing Benjy to start bellowing again. Jason, who is now in Jefferson after his futile attempt at finding Quentin and the carnival man with the red tie, hears Benjy's roaring and runs up to the carriage. With the back of his hand, he smacks Luster aside and takes control of the reins so the horse can go to the right of the monument. Jason then hits Luster over the head with his fist and scolds him for going left instead of right; he also strikes Benjy, breaking the flower stalk that Benjy is holding, and tells him to shut up. Jason commands Luster to take Benjy home and threatens him with his life if he ever takes Benjy off the property again. The novel ends with a quiescent Benjy returning to the Compson home, with serene and empty eyes looking upon each passing object "in its ordered place" (321).

CRITICAL COMMENTARY

The Sound and the Fury was published to a number of favorable reviews. Lyle Saxon, for instance, in *New York Herald Tribune Books* on October 13, 1929, rightly observed that Faulkner "achieved a novel of extraordinary effect." The narrative technique of the INTERIOR MONOLOGUE prevalent throughout the novel is a clear influence of JAMES JOYCE's *Ulysses*. The use of this narrative device, as Michael Groden has pointed out in "Criticism in New Composition: *Ulysses* and *The Sound and the Fury*," published in *Twentieth Century Literature* 21 (October 1975), provided Faulkner with "a solution to crucial problems in characterization that had plagued him in his first three novels" (266). The interior monologue combined, as it is in the first three chapters of the novel, with first person narration, provides an intimate view of the narrator's thoughts, attitudes, feelings, and impressions, although it may also pose for readers serious interpretative challenges; the first chapter in particular may be the most problematic of all. One of the most baffling and troubling experiences many readers may have when confronting the novel for the first time is that of narrative indeterminacy. "The reader's movement through the book," however, as CLEANTH BROOKS observes, "is a progression from murkiness to increasing enlightenment, and this is natural, since we start with the

mind of an idiot, go on next through the memories and reveries of the Hamlet-like Quentin, and come finally to the observations of the brittle, would-be rationalist Jason. Part of the sense of enlightenment comes simply from the fact that we are traversing the same territory in circling movements . . ." (*William Faulkner: The Yoknapatawpha Country*, 325–326).

Even after readers progress through the novel, they may still wonder whether the first chapter could have actually been narrated by someone like Benjy, by someone who lacks language. In his assessment of the issue, Noel Polk mentions that Benjy is "*nonlingual*" and in the strict sense "not a narrator at all"; the language of the first chapter then is not his but Faulkner's. Benjy's experience of the world around him is immediate, and, as Polk rightly observes, the narrative account of his awareness at any one give moment "is almost completely visual, cinematic, and what rolls through his mind is not 'memory,' although it is convenient to call it that . . . , but rather more nearly different reels, perhaps, from a movie of his life." Polk also suggests that the words throughout the chapter "are Faulkner's visual representation of what Benjy sees, at the precise moment of seeing; he does not actually verbalize that the golfers are 'going away,' he just registers visually that they are doing so" ("Trying Not to Say: A Primer on the Language of *The Sound and the Fury*," 144–145). By representing Benjy's sense perceptions, especially the visual, Faulkner adeptly exploits the technique of the interior monologue and overcomes the difficulty of casting into the medium of language nonverbal experience.

The narrative strategies that Faulkner employed in writing *The Sound and the Fury* can rightly place the work within the modernist tradition (*see* MODERNISM). In his introduction to *New Essays in The Sound and the Fury*, Noel Polk considers the novel "the quintessential American high modernist text" (1). This novel can also rightly be ranked as Faulkner's first great literary achievement, an achievement significantly dependent on the narrative devices Faulkner employed. In *William Faulkner: An Introduction and Interpretation*, Lawrance Thompson contends that *The Sound and the Fury* "combines so many important Faulknerian techniques which will be found operative in different ways throughout his later novels" that readers who have been "initiated into the mysteries by way of *The Sound and the Fury* should be able to avoid getting lost in some of the elaborate Faulknerian labyrinths which occur in *Absalom, Absalom!* and even in *Light in August*" (29). Whether one judges *The Sound and the Fury* Faulkner's greatest novel—and many do not—one cannot minimize the pivotal role it plays in the development of his craft as a writer.

The novel opens as a tale literally told by an idiot, Benjy Compson. Faulkner adapted the title of the novel from Shakespeare's *Macbeth* (5.5.26–28), where Macbeth describes life as "a tale/Told by an idiot, full of sound and fury,/Signifying nothing." At a meeting in Nagano, Japan, Faulkner in response to a question regarding the addition of the definite article to the title explained that he added it "For emphasis: Sound and fury wasn't quite enough for the ear. The ear said it needs rhythm, emphasis— *The* Sound and *the* Fury" (*Faulkner at Nagano*, 144). Though the title easily relates to Benjy's section and applies especially to him, the more Faulkner worked on the novel, as he pointed out, "the more elastic the title became, until it covered the whole family" (*Faulkner in the University*, 87).

On one level, the novel concerns the collapse of the Compson family and portrays among other things a sense of loss, longing, discontent, and despair. With the exception of Dilsey, the Compsons' black maid, who by the end of the novel appears to have achieved a profound religious insight and a spiritual freedom that transcend the delimitations circumscribing her life, each Compson brother is caught within a debilitating web of memories and unfulfilled longings. Benjy is trapped within the limits of immediate impressions and associations, Quentin within an unrealized sexuality and an incest complex, and Jason within a resentment and anger that dominate his thoughts and provide no relief. Caddy too is caught, but as Michael Millgate has observed, she "finds an outlet from family repression in sexual activity" (*The Achievement of William Faulkner*, 97), and the same may be said of Caddy's daughter. The emotional power with which Faulkner casts the three brothers has a tragic counterpoint in their sister and niece.

In an interview with JEAN STEIN in early 1956 originally published in the *Paris Review*, Faulkner explained that *The Sound and the Fury*, which he said he wrote "five separate times," is "a tragedy of two lost women: Caddy and her daughter" and that its beginning—the image of the muddy drawers on a girl climbing a tree—had a symbolic value which he did not at first realize; this initial "image was replaced by the one of the fatherless and motherless girl climbing down the rainpipe to escape from the only home she had, where she had never been offered love or affection or understanding" (*William Faulkner: Three Decades of Criticism*, ed. Frederick J. Hoffman and Olga W. Vickery, 73).

For further information regarding *The Sound and the Fury*, see *Faulkner in the University*, *Selected Letters of William Faulkner*, and *Faulkner at Nagano*, 9, 69, 80, 103–106, 107, 142–144, and 162.

EXCERPTS FROM CONTEMPORARY REVIEWS OF *THE SOUND AND THE FURY*

Excerpt from Frances Lamont Robbins' review, published in Outlook and Independent, *16 October 1929, 268:*

Judging from *The Sound and the Fury*, . . . we should say that William Faulkner is Joyce's most able and most consistent American disciple. He is by no means a slavish imitator of Joyce's style, and only in the second section of *The Sound and the Fury* does his effort to follow it seem labored and unoriginal. But the discontinuity which is the outward evidence of the Joycean viewpoint is present in Mr. Faulkner's work, and Joyce's search for a clear way to investigate and express the broken motive patterns of human behavior is Mr. Faulkner's search, too. It seems to us, however, that his work is still no more than an exciting promise. For one thing, it is overstrongly marked by a juvenile preoccupation with the *melodramatic* aspects of tragedy, and by the distrust of familiar values which characterizes the work of so many writers of the present generation and limits understanding of life. Mr. Faulkner has strong creative talent, and is richly sensitive to poetic emotion. *The Sound and the Fury* is a tragedy of disintegration. . . . An unusual method of presentation is used in telling the story. It appears at first to require a key, as *Ulysses* does; but careful reading discloses the plot. . . .

Excerpt from M. L. S.'s review, "The Tumult in a Southern Family," published in the Boston Evening Transcript, *October 23, 1929, Section III, 2:*
Here is the very substance of Greek tragedy in the heart of modern Mississippi, and presented after the fashion of James Joyce. It is tragedy in four acts, three of them recorded by the stream of consciousness method, and let no one who takes the trouble to study that method as displayed in this appalling chronicle of the Nemesis that overtakes a decayed Southern family deny its tremendous power.

Excerpt from an anonymous review, "Decayed Gentility," published in The New York Times Book Review, *November 10, 1929, 28:*
The author has chosen an unusual medium for his story in not one but four styles. Yet the four are welded together in perfect unity. The objective quality of the novel saves it from complete morbidity.

Excerpt from Howard Rockey's review, "Fiction, Largely European and Very Good in the Average," published in the Philadelphia Inquirer, *November 30, 1929, 18:*
The publisher does not state whether the entire 400 pages of the volume are intended as autobiography, but as an example of perfection in idiotic expressions, it deserves to be ranked as such. After reading a few pages the reader feels tempted to apply for admission to the nearest insane asylum.

Excerpt from Basil Davenport's review, published in the Saturday Review of Literature, *December 28, 1929, 601–602:*
This is an original and impressive book. In manner it is a new departure in the stream-of-consciousness school. . . .

Excerpt from Clifton Fadiman's review, "Hardly Worth While," published in The Nation, *January 15, 1930, 74–75:*
Probably someone has already remarked that the perfect enjoyment of great literature involves two factors. The reader should make an analysis of the methods employed by the artist to produce a given effect; and at the same time he should experience a synthetic appreciation of that effect in its emotional totality. The analysis must be almost instantaneous, almost unconscious. Otherwise the reader may become enmeshed in a tangle of aesthetic judgments, and experience difficulty in feeling the work of art as a whole.

Here, perhaps, lies the problem of comprehending the present-day revolutionary novelist. Frequently the intelligent reader can grasp the newer literary anarchies only by an effort of analytical attention so strained that it fatigues and dulls his emotional perception. He is so occupied in being a detective that by the time he has to his own satisfaction clarified the artist's intentions and technique he is too worn out to feel anything further. This is why the Joycean method of discontinuity has been entirely successful only when applied to materials of Joycean proportions. For it is obvious that if the theme is sufficiently profound, the characters sufficiently extraordinary, the plot sufficiently powerful, the reader is bound to absorb some of all this despite the strain on his attention. But if after an interval of puzzle-solving, it dawns upon him that the action and characters are minuscule, he is likely to throw the book away in irritation. The analysis has taken too long for the synthesis to be worth the trouble.

This seems to me to be the case with *The Sound and the Fury*, a novel by an extremely talented young writer dealing with the mental and physical disintegration of a Southern family. Mr. Faulkner's work has been magnificently praised by Evelyn Scott and other critics for whose opinions one must have respect. It is in all humility, therefore, that I record the feeling that the theme and the characters are trivial, unworthy of the enormous and complex craftsmanship expended on them. . . .

Excerpt from Dudley Fitts's review, "Two Aspects of Telemachus," published in Hound and Horn 3 *(April–June 1930), 445–450:*
It is the study of Mr. Faulkner's style, the consideration of the book as a rhetorical exercise, as a declamation, that repays the reader. Joyce is the ultimate source, obviously; but the Joycean technic has been pretty thoroughly absorbed, integrated with the author's sensibility. Much of the time the writing is on two or more concurrent planes; and Mr. Faulkner's skill in avoiding the clash, while

preserving the identity, of each tone is noteworthy. . . . *The Sound and the Fury* is an experiment in prose atonality, and as such, is memorable.

Excerpt from Howard Marshall's review,
"Modern Experimenters in the Art of Novel
Writing," published in the **Daily Telegraph,**
April 21, 1931, 17:
Here, then, is a curious position—a writer of genuine talent producing a strange farrago of a book which even intelligent readers will find most tedious and obscure. . . . *The Sound and the Fury*, in short, is an experiment in technique which may be appreciated by a few of Mr. Faulkner's more advanced fellow-writers, but I should not advise the ordinary reader, or even those interested in the art of the novel, to waste any time over it.

Excerpt from Frank Swinnerton's review, "Writers
Who Know Life," published in **The Evening**
News, May 15, 1931, 8:
The dialogue in this book is racy and overwhelmingly convincing. All sounds, sights and memories are so wonderfully indicated that they electrify the reader into attentive belief. . . . Clearly the difficult technique is not a smoke-cloud to hide poverty of any kind. But the book is a teaser, and I fear that, in spite of all its qualities, it may delay general appreciation of a talent which I believe to be really outstanding in our time.

Excerpt from Frank Kendon's review, published in
John O' London's Weekly, May 2, 1931, 130:
Language was invented that one man might communicate his thoughts to another. New powers and reaches of speech have been continually perfected by bold experimenters. The Elizabethans doubled their vocabulary, until through Lyly to Donne, to Milton and Sir Thomas Browne, language curdled with its own richness. Then Waller and Dryden set to work to clear away the tangles. But again, as years went by, new *clichés* took their place, until language became a frozen gentility, from which Wordsworth set out with shears to save it.

We can see the process in the past; it is not quite so easy to recognize that it is going on to-day. If it were not so English would be dying.

When William Faulkner's earlier novel, *Soldiers' Pay*, was published in England, there were in it many signs that he was an experimenter in words too. But his novel could be read—it asked effort, but it could be apprehended. His new book, *The Sound and the Fury*, asks more than effort. It asks faith in the face of an unconquerable incoherence. . . .

Excerpt from an anonymous review, published in **The**
Times Literary Supplement, May 14, 1931, 386:
It is not to be denied that the skill is there, but it is hard to agree that the method is successful in any but a limited sense. . . . For those who feel an attraction in the portrayal of pathological delinquency or find some really tragic effect in the negation, through a hereditary taint, of all the fine and kind elements in young minds no doubt the horrors of this picture will seem poetical: to others, however, they will appear to be of a kind to which no skill can add any compensating merit.

Excerpt from G. W. Stonier's review, published
in **The Fortnightly Review** 129 *(June 1931):*
842–843:
The Sound and the Fury is a difficult book. I have conscientiously read every word of it, partly because I know Mr. Faulkner to be a good writer, and partly because his obscurity seems to be essential to the genuine original beauty of his work. . . . I cannot do justice in a short space to the beauty which Mr. Faulkner has been able to find in these lives of imbeciles, criminals, and unfortunates. The beauty is there, original, and rather disturbing. It is a book which should be read more than once; and yet I hesitate to read it again.

Excerpt from an anonymous review, published in
Life and Letters 7 *(July 1931): 67–68:*
This is a truly horrible book, conveying a frightening sense of disintegration. It is, moreover, an example of the literature of experiment. . . . Skilful in parts it undoubtedly is, but it belongs more properly to the realm of pathology than to art.

CHARACTERS

Ames, Dalton He is Caddy's lover. Ames is unsuccessfully threatened by Caddy's brother Quentin, who is obsessed with the ideal of honor and troubled by incestuous desires. Self-possessed and physically strong, Ames easily defends himself against Quentin's ineffective assault, and knowing that Quentin is incapable of beating him up, he hands him his pistol, which Quentin is unable to fire. Ames is the probable father of Caddy's daughter, named Quentin by Caddy in memory of her brother who committed suicide before the child was born.

Anse   He is the marshal of a town near Cambridge, Massachusetts, who arrests Quentin. On the day of his suicide, Quentin is wrongly accused of kidnapping a little girl from an immigrant Italian family. Anse takes Quentin in for a hearing, which ends in his favor.

Bascomb, Maury L. (Uncle Maury)   Mrs. Caroline Compson's brother and an uncle to Quentin, Caddy, Jason, and Benjy. A freeloader off the Compson family who unscrupulously drinks his brother-in-law's whiskey, he is described by Faulkner in the appendix to the novel as "a handsome flashing swaggering workless bachelor who borrowed money from almost anyone, even Dilsey." He is romantically involved with Mrs. Patterson, to whom he sends love letters until her husband finds out and beats him up. (For further details, *see* the entry for Benjamin in Faulkner's appendix to the novel in Appendix.)

Beard   A minor character, who rents his lot to the visiting circus to pitch its tents.

Bland, Gerald   A Harvard student from Kentucky, he is one of Quentin's classmates. At the picnic his wealthy mother has for him when she is visiting, Bland beats Quentin up when the latter starts a fight. (The picnic is on the afternoon of Quentin's suicide; his mental state impaired, Quentin momentarily confuses Bland with his sister Caddy's seducer, Dalton Ames. Quentin failed in his attempt to defend Caddy's honor when he fought Ames.)

Bland, Mrs.   The wealthy mother of Gerald Bland, she is proud of her son's looks and boastful of the women in his life. Mrs. Bland is present when Anse places Quentin Compson in custody.

Burgess   He is the father of the girl whom Benjy Compson almost violates. Burgess hits Benjy with a fence picket and knocks him out.

Burgess, Mrs.   She is Burgess's wife and the mother of the girl whom Benjy Compson apparently tries to molest.

Charlie   He is one of Caddy Compson's boyfriends. Charlie appears in the first chapter of the novel, narrated by Benjy.

Clay, Sis Beulah   She is an offstage character; Dilsey's daughter Frony mentions that Sis Beulah Clay was mourned for two days at her funeral.

Compson, Benjamin (Benjy)   Called Benjamin by his mother, Benjy is the idiot son and the fourth and youngest child of Jason Richmond Compson and his wife, Caroline Bascomb Compson. Born on April 7, 1895, Benjy was named Maury, after Mrs. Compson's brother Maury Bascomb, but his name was changed when it became evident that he was retarded. He narrates the first chapter of the novel, which takes place on his 33rd birthday. Circumscribed by present sensations, Benjy's world is virtually timeless. Although he does not differentiate between the present and the past, he is able to represent the past through associations in the present; for example, the smell of leaves and trees recalls his sister Caddy, who, no longer physically present, is very much a real part of his life. To help the reader distinguish time shifts in Benjy's narrative, Faulkner intended to use different colors of ink, but his publisher thought it too costly; italics were used instead (*see Selected Letters of William Faulkner*, 71 and 74).

After breaking loose from his yard one afternoon and chasing a few neighbor school girls who are passing by, one of whom he tries to molest, Benjy is castrated. This time period is right after Caddy's wedding, April 25, 1910, when Benjy is 15. When Benjy sees himself naked, he becomes aware that his his testicles are missing and he cries. Benjy's impatient and self-centered brother Jason wants to have him institutionalized in Jackson after their brother Quentin commits suicide and their father dies, but their mother will not allow it. (In Faulkner's appendix to *The Sound and the Fury* [*see* Appendix], Benjy is committed to the state asylum in Jackson in 1933, the year that Mrs. Compson dies. However, in *The* MANSION, Mrs. Compson is still alive when Benjy is sent to the asylum; she insists that her son Jason have Benjy brought home. According to Jason, "his mother whined and wept" until he gave in [*The Mansion*, 322]. Not quite two years later, Benjy burns the house down.)

In 1928, (the year in which three of the four chapters of *The Sound and the Fury* are set), Benjy is 33 years old. Because of his age and because the last chapter occurs on Easter Sunday, some readers may be inclined to interpret Benjy as a Christ-figure. (For further information, *see Faulkner in the University*, 17, 18, 84, 87, 95, 139; and *Faulkner at Nagano*, 103–104.)

Compson, Candace (Caddy)   The second child and only daughter of Jason Richmond Compson and his wife, Caroline Bascomb Compson. Although she is an off-stage character in much of the novel, she very much dominates the thoughts of her three brothers—Benjy, Quentin, and Jason, who narrate the first three chapters of the novel, respectively. In one of Faulkner's explanations regarding the initial idea behind *The Sound and the Fury*, he states that the concept for the novel began with the image of Caddy, in muddy drawers, climbing a tree to look in the window at her grandmother's funeral taking place inside the house (*Faulkner in the University*, 1, 17, and 31; for a slightly different account, *see Faulkner at Nagano*, 103–104). For Faulkner, "the symbolism of the muddy bottom of the drawers became the lost Caddy, which caused one brother [Quentin] to commit suicide and the other brother [Jason] had misused her money that she'd send back to the child, the daughter" (*Faulkner in the University*, 31–32).

Caddy is a lively, independent, and strong-willed person whose behavior is often at odds with her parents and in contradiction to what her brothers, Quentin and Jason, expect of her. Her sexual activity disarms Quentin's fragile mental state and leads him to incestuously covet her. Each brother

perceives and responds to Caddy very differently. Benjy sees her partly as a maternal figure who loves and comforts him and partly as a considerate and compassionate older sister who plays and spends time with him. Quentin sees her as a romantic ideal and an image of Southern womanhood whose chastity must be preserved. Jason views Caddy as a means to an end, to be exploited by his selfish tendencies. He forever disdains her when the bank position promised him by her fiancé, Sydney Herbert Head, falls through after Caddy's short-lived marriage ends in divorce. When Head realizes that the child to whom Caddy gives birth was fathered by another man before their marriage, he divorces her and never gives Jason the job.

Although her child is a girl, Caddy names her Quentin, after her brother who committed suicide. She leaves her child with her parents to rear and leaves JEFFERSON, MISSISSIPPI. Throughout the years, she is diligent in sending her daughter money every month, but Jason intercepts this money and misuses it.

Caddy appears as a young inquisitive child in "THAT EVENING SUN" and very briefly in the short story "A JUSTICE"; she is referred to in *The* MANSION. For further information, *see* Faulkner's appendix to *The Sound and the Fury* and *Faulkner in the University*, 1–2, 6, 74, 148, 247, 262–63, and 274.

Compson, Caroline Bascomb (Mrs. Compson) She is the hypochondriacal wife of Jason Richmond Compson and mother of Quentin, Caddy, Jason, and Benjy Compson. Of her four children, she favors Jason, for in her mind he is more a Bascomb than a Compson; she leaves Benjy, whose name she changes once it is known that he is severely retarded, to the care of others. (At birth, Benjy was named after Mrs. Compson's brother Maury.) A self-indulgent and self-pitying woman, she takes an unwarranted pride in her side of the family, which she believes is more genteel and sophisticated than her husband's. Mrs. Compson's negative effect on her immediate family is evident throughout *The Sound and the Fury*, especially in the second chapter, which Quentin narrates. In an insightful critical essay on the novel, CLEANTH BROOKS discusses

Mrs. Compson's devastating impact on her family and argues that she is a source of their spiritual sickness (see *William Faulkner: The Yoknapatawpha Country*, 333–335).

Mrs. Compson also appears in Faulkner's appendix to *The Sound and the Fury* (see Appendix) and in the short story "THAT EVENING SUN"; she is referred to in *The MANSION*.

Compson, Jason IV   The third child (and second son) of Jason Richmond Compson and his wife, Caroline Bascomb Compson, and brother of Quentin, Caddy, and Benjy. He narrates chapter 3 and he is a major character in the novel.

Jason is an insensitive and selfish person whose logic reflects a cold, calculating mind. In the short story "THAT EVENING SUN," in which he is a young child, the person he will become begins to shine through in his comments and behavior. The cliché-ridden style of his section of *The Sound and the Fury* reflects from the very opening line—"Once a bitch always a bitch" (180)—an uncreative and shallow thought process tainted by common prejudices and stock phrases. As head of the Compson family in *The Sound and the Fury* (his father and older brother have died by the time he narrates chapter 3), he is accountable to virtually no one for his actions. Jason is a compassionless man whose relations with the world are seen in terms of business and what he can get for himself. His dealings with his mistress, Lorraine, for example, show an uncaring man, detached from any emotional or romantic life. His treatment of Dilsey, Benjy, his niece (Miss) Quentin especially, and even his mother, who favors him and whose side of the family, according to her, he takes after, is at times cruel, usually intolerant, at best indifferent. Jason thinks of himself as rational, level-headed, and justified in his resentment and anger for having been cheated of opportunities. He reasons that the money his father got by selling the pasture adjacent to their home was wasted on sending his brother Quentin to Harvard, where he committed suicide, and on Caddy's wedding celebrating a marriage that lasted not even a year. Because Caddy was divorced by her husband, Sydney Herbert Head, for bearing another man's child, Jason was denied a bank position that Head had prom-

ised him. His lingering anger over having lost this job justifies in his own mind the way he treats his niece, Caddy's daughter, who is being reared by the self-pitying Mrs. Compson. He steals the monthly stipend Caddy sends him for her daughter.

According to Faulkner's appendix, Jason commits Benjy to an asylum when their mother dies in 1933. He moves out of the family house and lives above his store. A slightly different version is recounted in *The MANSION*. He appears in *The Mansion*, "THAT EVENING SUN," and "A JUSTICE." He is also described by Faulkner in the appendix to *The Sound and the Fury* (see Appendix) and is referred to in *The TOWN*.

Compson, Jason Richmond (Mr. Compson; Jason III)   He is the son of General Jason Lycurgus Compson II (see ABSALOM, ABSALOM!) and the father of Quentin, Caddy, Jason (IV), and Benjy Compson. An attorney and a Southern gentleman, Mr. Compson is disillusioned and cynical. Quentin, on the day of his suicide, recalls his father saying that "a man is the sum of his misfortunes." Mr. Compson is an individual more inclined to philosophize about life than to practice law. He is sensitive and attentive, especially to his son Quentin, whose thinking and judgment he has heavily influenced, and he is very much adversely affected by his daughter Caddy's sexual behavior and Quentin's death. Against his doctor's advice he drinks heavily, which eventually causes his death in 1912. He also appears in the novel's appendix (see Appendix), *Absalom, Absalom!*, "THAT EVENING SUN," and "A JUSTICE"; he is referred to in *GO DOWN, MOSES* ("The BEAR").

Compson, (Miss) Quentin   She is the daughter of Caddy and probably Dalton Ames. Named after her uncle, who committed suicide, (Miss) Quentin is a rebellious 17-year-old who lives with the Compsons. As an infant, she was left in the care of her self-pitying grandmother when Caddy departed JEFFERSON, MISSISSIPPI. Throughout her young life, her uncle Jason mistreats her and robs her of the money Caddy sends monthly for her welfare. Jason's behavior toward his niece stems in part from the anger he harbors against his sister, whose former husband had promised Jason a bank job that

Jason never got because of Caddy's divorce and the paternity of her daughter. Before running off with a carnival worker, (Miss) Quentin breaks into Jason's locked room through a window and takes almost $7,000 (according to Faulkner's appendix to the novel; *see* Appendix), much of which really belongs to her. When Jason realizes what happened, he tries in vain to find her. (Miss) Quentin appears in Faulkner's appendix to the novel and is referred to in The MANSION.

Compson, Quentin He is the son and oldest child of Jason Richmond Compson and his wife, Caroline Bascomb Compson. Quentin narrates chapter two of *The Sound and the Fury* and appears in the novel's appendix (*see* Appendix). His philosophy of life appears to be heavily influenced by his father. Quentin is a romantic idealist with chivalrous notions of womanhood and he is obsessed with protecting and defending his sister Caddy's virginity and honor. In the appendix to the novel, Faulkner writes that Quentin "loved not his sister's body but some concept of Compson honor." Yet, at the same time, Quentin has incestuous longings for Caddy, longings that he could never act on. In a conversation with his father that Quentin narrates (thus its reliability may be questioned by some readers), Quentin says that he has committed incest with her, a lie he tells perhaps in hope that he and Caddy together will be forced into exile; in this way, he would achieve his goal of protecting her. Quentin can also be seen as a Hamlet-like figure; Caddy, for example, wants him either to act boldly (as when Quentin offers to kill her and then himself, but is unable to do so) or to leave her alone. He is also ineffective when confronting Dalton Ames, Caddy's lover. Ames contemptuously hands his pistol to Quentin and dares him to shoot, but Quentin cannot.

Faulkner develops Quentin's character with great consistency. In ABSALOM, ABSALOM! (much of which he narrates), the themes of sexuality, brother-sister relationship, and death are major concerns seen through Quentin's eyes. When retelling the story of the Sutpens to his roommate Shreve McCannon, Quentin reflects especially on Henry Sutpen's killing of his sister Judith's fiancé, Charles Bon, who without her knowing, is her half brother

(*see* Characters under *Absalom, Absalom!* In the genealogy of *Absalom*, Shreve's last name appears as McCannon and not MacKenzie.). Quentin is aware that Henry is compelled to commit this act to defend the Southern notion of womanly honor and uphold Southern notions of racial correctness, for Charles also has a trace of black blood. However, it is not the incest that forces Henry's hand, but miscegenation. Even though Charles passes as a white man, he cannot be one. These themes resonate in Quentin's mind. On June 2, 1910, at the end of his freshman year at Harvard, Quentin drowns himself in the Charles River in Cambridge, Massachusetts.

Quentin also narrates the short stories "THAT EVENING SUN," "A JUSTICE" and "LION." He is referred to in *The* MANSION. For further information, *see Faulkner in the University*, 2–3, 5, 17–18, 32, 71, 75, 77, 84, 94–95, 121, 135, 141, 247, 262–263, 274–275.

Daingerfield, Miss She is one of the two young women at Mrs. Bland's picnic that Quentin Compson also attends before committing suicide on June 2, 1910. *See also* Holmes, Miss.

Damuddy She is the maternal grandmother of the Compson children who died in 1898. "Damuddy" is the nickname the children gave her. Although they were not immediately informed of her death, the three-year-old Benjy, according to Quentin's reminiscences, intuitively knew of it and cried (*The Sound and the Fury*, 90). In *Faulkner at Nagano*, Faulkner explains that the idea for the novel started with the image of the children "being sent away from the house during the grandmother's funeral" because "[t]hey were too young to be told what was going on" (103). Faulkner credits Caddy with being brave enough to climb a tree and peek through a window in order to find out what was happening (*Faulkner in the University*, 31).

Deacon He is an elderly black man living near HARVARD UNIVERSITY who is fascinated with parades and would take part in any one that came along. Deacon appears in the second chapter of the novel narrated by Quentin. Urban legend has it that for 40 years at the beginning of each school year Deacon never missed an incoming train with arriving students. It is also said that he could always detect Southerners and even identify their home state by their accents. Employing a white boy of about 15, Deacon has the students' luggage carried from the station to their rooms. On the day of his suicide, Quentin gives Deacon a letter to deliver the next day to Shreve MacKenzie, Quentin's Harvard roommate.

Dilsey   *See* Gibson, Dilsey.

Earl   He runs the hardware store in JEFFERSON where Jason has been working since high school. Though his relationship with Jason is less than congenial, Earl puts up with him out of respect for Mrs. Compson, and he does not divulge to her the fact that Jason bought a car with the money she gave him to invest in the business. In *The Sound and the Fury,* only his first name is used; he also appears in *The* MANSION as Earl Triplett.

Frony (Gibson)   She is Dilsey and Roskus Gibson's daughter, T. P. and Versh Gibson's sister, and Luster's mother. Frony also appears in the novel's appendix (*see* Appendix) and is referred to in the short story "THAT EVENING SUN." In the fourth chapter of *The Sound and the Fury,* Frony attends Easter services with her mother, Luster, and Benjy. Because she knows that both white and black people gossip, Frony objects to Dilsey, a black woman, taking the idiot Benjy to her church, but Frony's protest does not faze Dilsey at all.

Gibson, Dilsey   She is the Compsons' black cook in *The Sound and the Fury* and in the short story "THAT EVENING SUN." Kindhearted, considerate, compassionate, and loving, Dilsey is one of Faulkner's most significant and humane characters, and the one who holds the Compson family together. She shows special kindness to Benjy whose 33rd birthday she celebrates with a cake purchased with her own money. She defends Miss Quentin against the mean-spirited Jason and at one time even suggests that he hit her instead of Quentin. Although not narrated by Dilsey, a major portion of the last chapter of *The Sound and the Fury*

is seen through her eyes. As the preacher nears the end of his sermon on Easter Sunday (the time frame of the last chapter), tears come to her eyes, and when she leaves the church with Frony, Luster, and Benjy, Dilsey says, "I seed de beginnin, en now I sees de endin" (297). Though it is uncertain as to what Dilsey specifically has in mind, her statement appears to reflect an eschatological vision echoing the Book of Revelation (Rev 21:1–6).

The excerpt from *The Sound and the Fury* reprinted in *The* PORTABLE FAULKNER is titled "Dilsey." For further information, *see Faulkner in the University,* 5, 85, 119; *Faulkner at Nagano,* 69; and Appendix.

Gibson, Roskus (Rocius)   He is Dilsey's husband and the father of T. P., Versh, and Frony. Roskus suffers from rheumatism, which prevents him from driving the carriage and milking. He is convinced that the Compsons, for whom he works, are bad luck. His presence in the first chapter that Benjy narrates indicates a time period a decade or more before the present (1928), for he died in 1915. Roskus also appears in the short story "A JUSTICE."

Gibson, T. P.   He is Dilsey and Roskus Gibson's son, brother of Versh and Frony. T. P. also appears in Faulkner's appendix to the novel and in the short story "THAT EVENING SUN." Since he is Benjy's caretaker before Luster, his presence in the novel indicates a time period prior to 1928 and sometime in Benjy's mid-teens. At Caddy's wedding (April 25, 1910), T. P. and Benjy get drunk drinking too much champagne. When his father is laid up with rheumatism, T. P. helps with the milking and other chores for the Compsons. For further information, *see Faulkner in the University,* 261–262.

Gibson, Versh   He is Dilsey and Roskus Gibson's oldest child, brother of T. P. and Frony. When Benjy is a child, Versh takes care of him. For further information, *see Faulkner in the University,* 262–262.

Hatcher, Louis   He is a superstitious black man in *The Sound and the Fury.* Quentin and Versh hunt possums with him in the woods.

Hatcher, Martha   She is Louis Hatcher's wife.

Head, Sydney Herbert Caddy Compson's husband, a wealthy northerner from South Bend, Indiana. As a wedding gift, he gives Caddy a car. Head, however, is not the father of the baby Caddy gives birth to seven months after their wedding. An unsavory character, Head was expelled from HARVARD UNIVERSITY for cheating on exams and was blackballed by his club in Cambridge, Massachusetts, for cardsharping. He is arrogant and supercilious toward Caddy's brother Quentin, leading Quentin to beg Caddy not to marry him, but Jason is in favor of the match, primarily because he was promised a position in the bank the Head family owns. When Head divorces Caddy after he realizes that her baby is another man's child, the bank position promised Jason falls through and Jason is forever resentful.

Henry He is one of Quentin's classmates in grade school. Quentin refers to Henry as a boy who paid better attention in school than he did. One time when Quentin is preoccupied in class, Henry answers a question for him.

Holmes, Miss With Miss Daingerfield, she is one of the two young women at Mrs. Bland's picnic, which Quentin also attends. The picnic is on the same day Quentin commits suicide (June 2, 1910).

Hopkins He is a cotton speculator, who frequents the telegraph office in JEFFERSON to keep informed of how the stock market is doing. He is especially interested in what Jason Compson is buying and selling.

Job (Uncle Job) He is a minor character in the novel. An easy-going African American, Job is one of Earl's employees at the supply store in JEFFERSON, where Jason Compson works. Jason is tends to be curt and nasty toward him.

Julio He is an Italian immigrant whose little sister meets Quentin Compson in a bakery and starts following him. Although Quentin attempts to take the little girl to her home, Julio thinks he is kidnapping her. He springs upon Quentin, knocks him to the ground, and has him arrested.

Junkin, Professor He is Miss Quentin Comspon's high school principal (or teacher). He calls Jason to inform him that if Quentin is absent once more, she will have to leave school.

Kenny He is one of the three fellows Quentin sees fishing on the day he commits suicide (June 2, 1910).

Laura, Miss She is one of Quentin's teachers in school at JEFFERSON, MISSISSIPPI.

Lorraine A minor, offstage character, she is a prostitute in MEMPHIS and Jason's mistress. Lorraine is also referred to by Faulkner in his appendix to the novel; she visits Jason in JEFFERSON sometime after his mother's death in 1933 (*see* Appendix).

Luster He is the 14-year-old black youth who watches Benjy. Luster is Frony's son and Dilsey's grandchild. His presence in the novel's first chapter, narrated by Benjy, is the present time, April 1928. As the novel opens, Luster is looking for a lost quarter, which he needs in order to go to a show later that night. Not very patient with Benjy, Luster at times is mean and threatening to him. Luster also appears in Faulkner's appendix to *The Sound and the Fury* (*see* Appendix). (This character would be too young to be the Luster who appears in ABSALOM, ABSALOM!.)

Mac A minor character, who chats about baseball—in particular, the pennant race, the Yankees, and Babe Ruth—with a disagreeable Jason Compson.

MacKenzie, Shrevlin (Shreve) A Canadian, he is Quentin Compson's roommate at HARVARD UNIVERSITY. He appears in both *The Sound and the Fury* and ABSALOM, ABSALOM!. (Though referred to only as Shreve in *Absalom, Absalom!,* his last name appears as McCannon in that novel's genealogy.) In *The Sound and the Fury*, he accompanies Quentin to court on false charges of kidnapping and is later one of the guests at Mrs. Bland's picnic for her son, Gerald. When at the picnic Quentin gets into a fight with Gerald and is beaten up, Shreve ministers to him.

Mike   He is an offstage character who runs a gym in Cambridge where Gerald Bland is learning to box.

Mink   He drives the hack that Jason rides in when showing Caddy her infant daughter, Quentin. Jason holds the infant to the window but as Caddy leaps forward to see her, Jason orders Mink to speed up the carriage leaving Caddy frustrated and angered. Caddy had paid Jason $100 in advance. For Mink's service, Jason buys him a couple of cigars.

Myrtle   She is the married daughter of the sheriff in JEFFERSON. Myrtle and her husband, Vernon, are present when Jason comes to the sheriff's house to report that (Miss) Quentin and her boyfriend have stolen his money and taken off together.

Natalie   She is a girl whom Quentin kisses in the barn when they are children. Caddy catches them and teases Quentin.

Patterson   He is the husband of the woman with whom Maury Bascomb is having an affair and to whom he sends love letters delivered by Caddy and Benjy. When he catches Benjy, who is around 13 years old, delivering a letter by himself, Patterson confronts Maury and beats him up.

Patterson, Mrs.   She is the woman with whom Uncle Maury (Bascomb) is having an affair. He sends her love letters delivered by Caddy and Benjy. When her husband finds out, he gives Maury a black eye and bloody mouth.

the Patterson boy   He is one of Jason Compson's childhood friends. Together they make kites which they sell for a nickel apiece; Jason is treasurer. (Presumably this boy is Patterson's son.)

Peabody, Doctor Lucius Quintus   He is an elderly, overweight YOKNAPATAWPHA COUNTY physician. In *The Sound and the Fury*, Doc Peabody lets the Compson children hang onto his buckboard for a ride. He also appears in SARTORIS, AS I LAY DYING, The HAMLET, The TOWN, The REIVERS, and in the short story "Beyond."

Russell, Ab   He is a farmer outside JEFFERSON from whom Jason borrows an air pump. When searching for his niece Quentin and the carnival worker she is with, Jason stops near Russell's farm to look for them. Before they drive away, they let the air out of one of Jason's tires to prevent him from catching them.

Sartoris, Colonel   An offstage character in the novel. Colonel Sartoris is a legendary figure in YOKNAPATAWPHA COUNTY (*see* characters under *The* UNVANQUISHED *and* REQUIEM FOR A NUN). His first name is John although it is not used in *The Sound and the Fury*. Quentin Compson refers to Colonel Sartoris, when thinking about death, as a friend of his (Quentin's) grandfather and the two—death and his grandfather—as being together and waiting for Colonel Sartoris to come down to them from a higher place.

Shegog, Reverend   He is the black preacher from St. Louis who gives the Easter Sunday sermon at the church Dilsey, Frony, Luster, and Benjy attend. He is a small man but a powerful preacher. His sermon, which begins almost dispassionately, becomes more and more emotionally charged as he proceeds, and by the time he finishes, Dilsey begins to cry and later utters: "I seed de beginnin, en now I sees de endin" (297).

Shreve   *See* MacKenzie, Shrevlin.

Simmons   Referred to by Jason as old man Simmons, he has a key to the old opera house in JEFFERSON where someone stored papers of the failed Merchants' and Farmers' Bank. Jason finds a pad of blank checks there from a St. Louis bank and uses one of them to fool his mother concerning the money that his sister Caddy sends monthly in support of her daughter Quentin. Each month Mrs. Compson burns what she thinks is the check from Caddy, but in fact it is a phony check that Jason makes up.

Snopes, I. O.   He is a minor character in several of Faulkner's works. In *The Sound and the Fury*, I. O.

appears as a cotton speculator and is present at the Western Union office when Jason places his bids. *Also see* characters under *The* HAMLET, *The* TOWN, FATHER ABRAHAM (fragment of a novel incorporated into *The Hamlet*), and the short stories "SPOTTED HORSES" (revised for *The Hamlet*) and "MULE IN THE YARD" (revised for *The Town*). He is also referred to in *The* MANSION.

Spoade   He is a college student from Charleston, South Carolina, who is at HARVARD UNIVERSITY with Quentin Compson in 1910 (and with Gavin Stevens in 1909; *see* characters under *The* MANSION). A senior when Quentin is a freshman, he is known for never missing chapel or his first lecture. Aware of Quentin's lack of interest in girls, Spoade humorously labels Quentin's roommate, Shreve MacKenzie, Quentin's husband. Present at Quentin's hearing on the false kidnapping charges, Spoade, in Quentin's defense, says to the judge that Quentin's father is a congregational minister, which, of course, he is not.

Spoade's son, also referred to as Spoade in *The Mansion*, attends Harvard with Chick Mallison, whom he invites to Charleston during a Christmas break.

Turpin, Buck   According to Jason, he is paid $10 from the traveling carnival for the privilege of putting the show on in JEFFERSON.

Vernon   He is Myrtle's husband and, the son-in-law of JEFFERSON's sheriff. Vernon and his wife are present when Jason arrives at the sheriff's house to report a theft and accuse his niece Quentin of running off with the money.

Walthall, Parson   He is the Methodist minister in JEFFERSON, who objects to the shooting of pigeons that flock around the courthouse. Seeing the pigeons as annoyances, Jason and others want to rid the town of them, but Parson Walthall actively protests and prevents the men from further executing their plan.

Wilkie   He is a servant (most likely a black man) of Gerald Bland's grandfather referred to by Mrs. Bland. Very particular about his mint juleps, the grandfather would not allow Wilkie to pick the mint leaves for them but instead gathered them himself before breakfast while the dew was still on them.

Wright, Doc   He is one of the cotton speculators in the telegraph office in JEFFERSON. Doc Wright and others are very curious about what Jason buys and sells.

RELATED PERSONS AND PLACES

Compson, Charles Stuart   He was a British soldier during the Revolutionary War who was left for dead in a swamp in Georgia. Charles Stuart is the father of Jason Lycurgus Compson I; he appears in Faulkner's appendix to *The Sound and the Fury*. (*See* Appendix.)

Compson Mile   Fictional place in JEFFERSON, the original domain of the Compson family. Jason Lycurgus Compson I acquired the square mile of virgin land in about 1811 from the Chickasaw chief Ikkemotubbe in exchange for a race horse. The Compson holdings were mortgaged after the Civil War and sold piecemeal. In *The Sound and the Fury*, Jason Richard Compson (Mr. Compson) sells the pasture to a golf club to pay for his son Quentin's tuition at Harvard University and his daughter Caddy's wedding. By then, all that remained of the Compson land, according to Faulkner in his appendix to *The Sound and the Fury*, was "the house and the kitchengarden and the collapsing stables and one servant's cabin."

Compson, Jason Lycurgus I   He is referred to in Faulkner's appendix to *The Sound and the Fury* and in REQUIEM FOR A NUN (Act One, "The Courthouse"). Jason is the son of Charles Stuart Compson, a British soldier during the Revolutionary War, and the father of General Jason Lycurgus Compson II. According to Faulkner's appendix to *The Sound and the Fury*, Jason (I) was the grandfather of General Compson. In 1779, Jason (I) is taken by his grandfather, Quentin MacLachan, from Carolina to Kentucky. In 1811, he becomes a clerk in the Chickasaw Agency at Okatoba in Mississippi, and later is the agent's partner. He trades his swift mare with Ikkemotubbe for a square mile of land where he builds his home, known as the Compson place. (In The MANSION, however, in 1821 Quentin (MacLachan) Compson (II) was granted land from the Chickasaw matriarch Mohataha.)

He is one of the founders of JEFFERSON, and this Jason Compson's square mile "was to be the most valuable land in the future town of Jefferson" (*Requiem*, 12). (For Faulkner's descriptions of the Compsons, *see* Appendix.)

Compson, Quentin MacLachan He appears in Faulkner's appendix to *The Sound and the Fury* (*see* Appendix). Quentin MacLachan Compson is the orphaned son of a Glasgow printer. A Jacobite supporter of Bonnie Prince Charlie's failed attempt (1645–46) to regain the British throne for the deposed Stuarts, he fled Culloden Moor for Carolina.

FURTHER READING

Especially helpful are Stephen M. Ross and Noel Polk's *Reading Faulkner: The Sound and the Fury* and the Web site: http://www.usask.ca/english/faulkner.

Backman, Melvin. "*The Sound and the Fury*." In *Faulkner: The Major Years*, 13–40. Bloomington: Indiana University Press, 1966.

Bleikasten, André. *The Most Splendid Failure: Faulkner's The Sound and the Fury*. Bloomington: Indiana University Press, 1976.

Bloom, Harold, ed. *Modern Critical Interpretations of William Faulkner's The Sound and the Fury*. Philadelphia: Chelsea House, 1998.

Brooks, Cleanth. "Man, Time, and Eternity (*The Sound and the Fury*). In *William Faulkner: The Yoknapatawpha Country*, 325–348. Baton Rouge: Louisiana State University Press, 1990.

———. "*The Sound and the Fury*." In *William Faulkner: First Encounters*, 43–77. New Haven: Yale University Press, 1983.

Cowan, Michael H., ed. *Twentieth Century Interpretations of The Sound and the Fury*. Englewood Cliffs, N.J.: Prentice Hall, 1968.

Faulkner, William. *The Sound and the Fury*. 2nd Norton Critical Edition, edited by David Minter. New York: Norton, 1994.

Hahn, Stephen, and Arthur F. Kinney, eds. *Approaches to Teaching Faulkner's The Sound and the Fury*.

New York: Modern Language Association of America, 2000.

Howe, Irving. "*The Sound and the Fury*." In *William Faulkner: A Critical Study*, 157–174. Chicago: University of Chicago Press, 1957.

Kinney, Arthur. *Critical Essays on Faulkner: The Compson Family*. Boston: G. K. Hall, 1982.

Matthews, John T. "The Discovery of Loss in *The Sound and the Fury*." In *The Play of Faulkner's Language*, 63–114. Ithaca: Cornell University Press, 1982.

———. *The Sound and the Fury: Faulkner and the Lost Cause*. New York: Twayne, 1990.

Millgate, Michael. "*The Sound and the Fury*." In *The Achievement of William Faulkner*, 86–103. Lincoln: University of Nebraska Press, 1978.

Polk, Noel, ed. "Trying Not to Say: A Primer on the Language of *The Sound and the Fury*." In *New Essays on* The Sound and the Fury, 139–175. New York: Cambridge University Press, 1993.

Sartre, Jean-Paul. "Time in Faulkner: *The Sound and the Fury*." In *William Faulkner: Three Decades of Criticism*, edited by Frederick J. Hoffman and Olga W. Vickery, 225–232. New York: Harbinger, 1963.

Sundquist, Eric J. "The Myth of *The Sound and the Fury*." In *Faulkner: The House Divided*, 3–27. Baltimore: Johns Hopkins University Press, 1985.

Thompson, Lawrence. "Mirror Analogues in *The Sound and the Fury*." In *William Faulkner: Three Decades of Criticism*, edited by Frederick J. Hoffman and Olga W. Vickery, 211–225. New York: Harbinger, 1963.

"Spotted Horses" (Uncollected Stories)

First published in the June 1931 issue of SCRIBNER'S MAGAZINE (89), 585–597. An expanded revision of the story is included in the first part of chapter 1 of book 4, "The Peasants," of *The HAMLET* (1940); it is reprinted as a novella in *The Faulkner Reader* (1954) and in *Three Famous Short Novels* (1958). The original version appears in UNCOLLECTED STORIES OF WILLIAM FAULKNER (1979). In an August 1945 letter to MALCOLM COWLEY, Faulkner mentioned that

"Spotted Horses" created the character V. K. Suratt that he "fell in love with" (*Selected Letters of William Faulkner*, 197). The story's origin goes back to the 1926 novel fragment FATHER ABRAHAM; it was later revised several times with different titles: "As I Lay Dying," "Abraham's Children," "The Peasants," "Aria Con Amore" and "Horses."

For more information, *see Selected Letters of William Faulkner*, 49–50, 115, 197, 202, 208, 233, 359; *Uncollected Stories of William Faulkner*, 689–690; and *Faulkner in the University*, 29–31 and 66. The film, *The Long, Hot Summer* (Twentieth Century-Fox, 1958), directed by Martin Ritt and starring Paul Newman, Joanne Woodward, Anthony Franciosa, Orson Welles, Lee Remick, Angela Lansbury, and Richard Anderson, was partly based on "Spotted Horses"; the screenplay, written by Irving Ravetch and Harriet Frank, Jr., also drew upon *The Hamlet* and the short story "BARN BURNING."

SYNOPSIS

"Spotted Horses" is a story about the auctioning off of the wild ponies that Flem Snopes and Buck—"the Texas man"—drove up from Texas to FRENCHMAN'S BEND. Told from the first person singular point of view (from V. K. Suratt's), "Spotted Horses" is a humorous tale about the sale and purchase of intractable horses impossible to catch and the damage they cause after they escape from Mrs. Littlejohn's lot. A good portion of the story centers on the poor farmer Henry Armstid's obsession with buying a horse he cannot afford. Henry takes money from his wife and against her will bids on a horse, which the Texas man, who realizes Mrs. Armstid's predicament, refuses to sell to him. Determined to buy a horse, Henry hands the money to Flem, who keeps it even though Buck assures Mrs. Armstid that she can get it back. When Henry attempts to capture the horse he thinks he bought, he breaks his leg and is knocked out. The next day, when Mrs. Armstid tries to get the money from Flem, he lies to her when he says that the Texan took it with him when he left.

CRITICAL COMMENTARY

"Spotted Horses," one of Faulkner's finest stories, belongs in the tall tale tradition employed by the southwestern humorists and continued by Mark Twain. However, Faulkner's narrative is more than just a short story about a horse dealer who comes to the rural hamlet of Frenchman's Bend to dupe farmers into bidding on wild ponies that are virtually impossible to catch. It is a model of the humorous tale of chicanery and depicts the heartlessness of emerging SNOPESISM in the unscrupulous figure of Flem. As Suratt understands (and as will be demonstrated even more thoroughly by the eventual SNOPES TRILOGY of which "Spotted Horses" supplies a key episode), horse-flesh is not the only trading commodity in which Flem Snopes deals. He also deals in human flesh, trading his own to Will Varner as a husband to the pregnant Eula in order to get a financial foothold in Frenchman's Bend, as he will later, in JEFFERSON, trade his wife's favors to Manfred De Spain in exchange for a promotion at the bank. Thus beneath the rollicking humor of "Spotted Horses" lies a view of cynical, self-serving, and amoral human behavior that is captured in the brilliantly homonymic name, Flem (*cf.* phlegm) Snopes (*cf.* snake, sneer, etc.).

"Spotted Horses" is also noteworthy for its superb use of poetic imagery, blending wildly imaginative similes with vivid, realistic detail. For example, one of the wild horses, in Suratt's words, "come swurging up outen the bushes and jumped the road clean, without touching hoof to it. It flew right over my team, big as a billboard and flying through the air like a hawk" (*Uncollected Stories*, 165). At the auction, when Buck attempts to exercise control of one of the untamed animals, "Then it was all dust again, and we couldn't see nothing but spotted hide and mane, and that ere Texas man's boot-heels like a couple of walnuts on two strings, and after a while that two-gallon hat come sailing out like a fat old hen crossing a fence" (169).

CHARACTERS

Ad *See* Snopes, Ad.

Armstid, Henry A poor and foolish farmer intent on buying one of the horses at the auction. Although he has no money to spare, he takes his wife's hard-earned $5 to bid on a horse that he cannot catch and eventually breaks his leg attempting.

Also see As I Lay Dying, Light in August, *The* Hamlet, "Shingles for the Lord," *The* Town, and *The* Mansion.

Armstid, Ina An offstage character in the short story, the Armstids' oldest child. According to Mrs. Armstid, Ina bars the door when she is left alone at night and sleeps with an ax for protection.

Armstid, Mrs. Henry Armstid's wife. Mistreated by Henry, Mrs. Armstid does everything she can to stop her husband from bidding on a horse which they cannot afford. Against her pleas, he takes her hard-earned money ($5) and buys a horse that he cannot even catch. When she repeatedly fails to corner the wild pony that Henry bought, her husband hits her several times with the rope he is holding. Two days after the auction, Mrs. Armstid approaches Flem Snopes to get her money back—money that Buck himself was willing to return to her, but dishonest Flem tells her that Buck took it with him when he left. *Also see The* Hamlet, Light in August *(where her first name is Martha)*, As I Lay Dying *(where she is called Lula)*, and "Shingles for the Lord" *(where, as in "Spotted Horses" and* The Hamlet, *no first name is given)*. (For further information, *see Faulkner in the University*, 30–31).

Buck Referred to as "the Texas man" in the short story, Buck auctions off the wild ponies that he and Flem Snopes brought up from Texas to Frenchman's Bend. Sympathetic toward Mrs. Armstid and her plight, Buck refuses to accept her husband's bid on a horse and tells her to take him home, but to no avail. *Also see* Father Abraham *and Buck Hipps in* The Hamlet.

Bundren, Mrs. An offstage character referred to as a potential customer by the first person narrator (Suratt) of the short story. *Also see* As I Lay Dying.

Durley Minor character in the short story. When talking with Lon Quick and Winterbottom, Durley suggests that Ernest fetch Henry Armstid's wife to tell her that her husband was injured attempting to catch the wild pony he supposedly bought at the auction.

Ernest Minor character in the short story. Ernest finds Mrs. Armstid and informs her that her husband injured himself trying to catch the wild pony he thought he bought at the auction.

Eula *See Snopes, Eula Varner.*

Freeman A minor character in the short story. Suratt, the narrator, sees Freeman coming into town on his wagon. *Also see The* Hamlet.

Littlejohn, Mrs. Owner of the barn where Buck keeps the wild ponies the night before he auctions them off. A sensible and practical woman, she looks out for the welfare of others during the hectic sale of the horses and is especially solicitous toward Mrs. Armstid after the latter's husband is injured trying to catch the horse he bids on, and encourages her to get the money back from Flem Snopes. *Also see The* Hamlet, *The* Town, *and* "Lizards in Jamshyd's Courtyard."

Quick, Lon Bids on one of the wild ponies at the auction in Frenchman's Bend. When the horse he buys runs off toward Samson's Bridge, Quick chases after it. *See The* Hamlet; *a Lon Quick (big Lon) also appears in* As I Lay Dying.

Snopes, Ad (Admiral Dewey) Eck Snopes's young son. He is with his father when Eck tries to catch his wild pony running down the hallway of Mrs. Littlejohn's boardinghouse. On its way out of the house, the horse jumps over the three-foot tall boy. *Also see The* Town *and* The Mansion.

Snopes, Eck He is given one of the wild horses by the Texas man to start the bidding. The night before the thoughtful Eck Snopes had helped the auctioneer barn and feed them. Eck's horse runs in and out of Mrs. Littlejohn's boardinghouse, but is eventually trapped in a dead-end lane where it breaks its neck on the rope that Eck and his son tie across the lane. Eck also appears in *The* Hamlet,

The TOWN, and FATHER ABRAHAM; he is referred to in *The* MANSION.

Snopes, Eula Varner Uncle Billy Varner's youngest child, Jody Varner's sister, and Flem Snopes's wife. Described in earthy terms, Eula attracted young men from miles around and becomes pregnant by one of them. Once her father finds out, he arranges her marriage to Flem. A few weeks after the wedding, the couple goes off to Texas for about a year. When she returns to FRENCHMAN'S BEND with her three-month-old baby, the townsfolk realize what occurred. *Also see The* HAMLET, *The* TOWN, *The* MANSION, and FATHER ABRAHAM.

Snopes, Flem The clerk in Uncle Billy Varner's store and the mastermind behind the auction of the wild ponies. Married to Varner's pregnant daughter, Eula, Flem goes off with his new wife to Texas for almost a year. About a month after Eula returns with her baby to FRENCHMAN'S BEND, Flem arrives with Buck and the wild horses that are to be auctioned off. Ruthless in business, Flem, a man of few words, shows no sympathy toward Mrs. Armstid's plight. Flem is a central figure throughout the SNOPES TRILOGY (*The* HAMLET, *The* TOWN, and *The* MANSION). *Also see* FATHER ABRAHAM, "CENTAUR IN BRASS," "LIZARDS IN JAMSHYD'S COURTYARD," and "BY THE PEOPLE"; Flem is referred to in *As I* LAY DYING and *The* REIVERS.

Snopes, I. O. One of Flem Snopes's cousins. Flem eventually turns over his clerking job at Uncle Billy Varner's store to I. O. Protective and proud of his relative, I. O. is willing to lie to Mrs. Armstid when she arrives at the store rightfully to get her money back from Flem. *Also see The* SOUND AND THE FURY, *The* HAMLET, *The* TOWN, FATHER ABRAHAM, and the short story "MULE IN THE YARD"; I. O. is also referred to in *The* MANSION.

Suratt, V. K. The unidentified narrator of the short story. Suratt is an itinerant salesman, a keen observer of human nature, a natural storyteller, and a genial person. *Also see* SARTORIS, *As I* LAY DYING, and the short stories "LIZARDS IN JAMSHYD'S COURTYARD" and "CENTAUR IN BRASS," (in the last three works his initials are not used). Faulkner later changed Suratt's name to V. K. Ratliff; *see Selected Letters of William Faulkner,* 197. For a discussion of V. K. Ratliff, *see The* HAMLET, *The* TOWN, *The* MANSION, and *Big Woods* ("A BEAR HUNT").

the Texas man *See* Buck.

Tull, Mrs. Vernon Tull's wife, who with her husband, three daughters, and aunt were in the wagon that overturned on the one-way bridge. As they were crossing, one of the loose wild horses coming from the opposite direction frightened Tull's mules, causing them to upset the wagon. *Also see* AS I LAY DYING, *The* HAMLET, *The* TOWN, and *The* MANSION.

Tull, Vernon A minor character in the short story. Unaware of the auction and the wild horses running through the countryside, Tull and his family cross a one-way bridge at the same time one of the ponies comes running toward their wagon. Their frightened mules in panic start turning around, cause the wagon to tip over, and drag Tull until the reins, wrapped around him, break. *Also see* AS I LAY DYING, *The* HAMLET, *The* TOWN, *The* MANSION, SANCTUARY, and the short stories "LIZARDS IN JAMSHYD'S COURTYARD," "SHINGLES FOR THE LORD," "The HOUND," and "TWO SOLDIERS."

Varner, Jody Uncle Billy Varner's ineffectual son and Eula's brother whom Flem Snopes supersedes in Varner's store. *Also see* AS I LAY DYING, LIGHT IN AUGUST, *The* HAMLET, *The* TOWN, *The* MANSION, and "FOOL ABOUT A HORSE."

Varner, Uncle Billy (Will) Owner of Varner's store; Jody and Eula's father. When he finds out that his teenage daughter is pregnant, he arranges to have her marry Flem Snopes. For more information regarding this character, *see The* HAMLET, *The* TOWN, *The* MANSION, AS I LAY DYING, LIGHT IN AUGUST, INTRUDER IN THE DUST, KNIGHT'S GAMBIT ("Tomorrow"), and the short stories "LIZARDS IN JAMSHYD'S COURTYARD," "SHINGLES FOR THE LORD" and "BY THE PEOPLE"; he is sometimes referred to as Will Varner.

Winterbottom   One of the men standing around Mrs. Littlejohn's the evening of the auction. When Mrs. Littlejohn requests that one of the men get Mrs. Armstid to come to her injured husband, he, Quick, and Durley pass the responsibility on to Ernest. *Also see* LIGHT IN AUGUST. A Winterbottom also appears in *The* HAMLET; these characters may not be the same.

FURTHER READING

Eddins, Dwight. "Metahumor in 'Spotted Horses.'" *Ariel* 13.1 (1982): 23–31.

Heck, Francis S. "Faulkner's 'Spotted Horses': A Variation of a Rabelaisian Theme." *Arizona Quarterly* 37.2 (1981): 166–172.

Matthews, John T. "Shortened Stories: Faulkner and the Market." In *Faulkner and the Short Story*, edited by Evans Harrington and Ann J. Abadie, 3–37. Jackson: University Press of Mississippi, 1992.

"Tall Men, The" (Collected Stories)

Short story first published in the *Saturday Evening Post* (May 31, 1941).

SYNOPSIS

Mr. Pearson, a young state draft investigator, seeking to arrest two young men for failing to register for the World War II draft, finds a family both opposed to the government and highly patriotic. Old Deputy Marshal Gombault accompanies Pearson, who contemptuously assumes the McCallums are typical of those who take advantage of New Deal relief and farm subsidy programs. When the two officials arrive to serve the warrant, they find a medical emergency. Buddy McCallum, the boys' father, has mangled his leg in a mill accident. Attended by the doctor and surrounded by his older brothers, he orders his twins, Anse and Lucius McCallum, to go to MEMPHIS to enlist. The two immediately leave to do so, ignoring Pearson's protests. Gombault helps the inexperienced Pearson grasp the hardworking clan's strong individu-

alism and sense of responsibility. After Buddy's leg is amputated, Gombault buries it and is himself revealed as one of the "tall" men.

CRITICAL COMMENTARY

This story, written at the tail end of the Great Depression, reflects Faulkner's strong belief in individualism and his skepticism about bureaucratic agencies and programs. The fiercely independent but highly honorable McCallums will not be ordered into military service by the draft board, but they willingly volunteer to perform their patriotic duty. Most critics agree with James B. Carothers, who finds the story overly didactic and thus one of Faulkner's "least successful" narratives (*William Faulkner's Short Stories*, 68).

CHARACTERS

Gombault   The marshal who escorts the draft board investigator to the McCallum place and tactfully handles the matter of the boys' failure to register for the draft.

McCallum, Anse (old)   Anse, who has been dead for 15 years, is remembered for having walked all the way from Mississippi to Virginia to enlist in Stonewall Jackson's army. Anse was 16 when the Civil War broke out.

McCallum, Anse (young)   Buddy McCallum's son, he and his brother Lucius are sought by a U.S. draft investigator (Mr. Pearson) from Jackson for failing to register for the draft during World War II. In the presence of the marshal, their father tells them to pack, go to MEMPHIS, and enlist.

McCallum, Buddy   The youngest of old Anse McCallum's sons and the father of young Anse and Lucius McCallum. Buddy catches his leg in a hammer mill and has to have it amputated. He mortifies his father, who still has sentiment for the Confederacy, by serving in the "Yankee" army during World War I. He also appears as a character in *SARTORIS*, INTRUDER IN THE DUST, and *The* TOWN.

McCallum, Lee   Another of (old) Anse McCallum's sons.

McCallum, Lucius Buddy McCallum's son. When Mr. Pearson, a U.S. draft investigator, appears to arrest him and his brother young Anse McCallum for avoiding the draft during World War II, their father orders them to go to MEMPHIS and enlist.

McCallum, Rafe Another son of (old) Anse McCallum, he is Stuart's twin. Rafe greets the marshal, Gombault, and the draft investigator, Pearson, when they arrive to arrest his two nephews for failing to register for the draft. He also appears in *SARTORIS* and *KNIGHT'S GAMBIT* and is referred to in *AS I LAY DYING* and *The MANSION*.

McCallum, Stuart Rafe McCallum's twin.

Pearson, Mr. A government draft board investigator who serves warrants on Buddy McCallum's twin sons, Anse and Lucius, for failing to register for the draft.

Schofield, Dr. A physician, he amputates Buddy McCallum's leg, injured in an accident at the hammer mill.

"That Evening Sun" (Collected Stories)

Frequently anthologized, this short story was first published under a slightly different title, "That Evening Sun Go Down," in the March 1931 issue of the *American Mercury* (22), 257–267; a revision titled "That Evening Sun" was reprinted in *These 13* (1931), *A Rose for Emily and Other Stories by William Faulkner* (1945), *The PORTABLE FAULKNER* (1946), *COLLECTED STORIES OF WILLIAM FAULKNER* (1950), *The Faulkner Reader* (1954), *A Rose for Emily* (1956), and *Selected Short Stories of William Faulkner* (1962). For more information, *see Selected Letters of William Faulkner*, 48–49, 91, 208, 278, and *Faulkner in the University*, 21, 79.

SYNOPSIS

"That Evening Sun" is about the Compsons' sometime black replacement cook, Nancy, who is neurotically frightened of the dark because she is convinced that Jesus, her absent husband, will come and kill her during the night for having been unfaithful to him. The story's title is taken from the first lines of W. C. HANDY's song "St. Louis Blues": "I hates to see that evening sun go down." Nancy has prostituted herself to Mr. Stovall, a bank cashier and deacon in the Baptist Church, and is pregnant with his child. Frightened to be alone and knowing that she cannot sleep at the Compsons' where she will be out of danger and where she once slept in the kitchen, she talks the Compson children—Quentin, Caddy, and Jason—into accompanying her to her cabin, where she vainly tries to entertain them with stories and popcorn. When Mr. Compson realizes that his children are at Nancy's, he fetches them home and attempts to persuade the nervous and apprehensive Nancy to go to Aunt Rachel's for the night, where she will be safe, but she refuses.

Narrated by Quentin 15 years after the event took place (at the time of the story he was nine), "That Evening Sun" also portrays the Compson children at a young age; these three characters were previously introduced as adults in *The SOUND AND THE FURY* (1929). Although he and his seven-year-old sister, Caddy, sense Nancy's fears and anxieties, they have only a vague idea of what is happening in her life and virtually no understanding of the details. The five-year-old Jason is even less aware. In the short story, Faulkner skillfully portrays the children's personalities, anticipating the kind of adults they eventually become. Their parents' personalities are also vividly drawn.

CRITICAL COMMENTARY

"That Evening Sun" is an adept and convincing presentation of the overwhelming effect of terror on a person troubled with guilt and convinced that she is about to be vindictively killed by her estranged husband. But despite the evocation of what IRVING HOWE called "an aura of primitive fear," the story, according to Howe, is not ultimately about the drama between Nancy and her husband, but instead about "the moral stamina of the Compsons" and "their reactions to the closeness of death" (*William Faulkner: A Critical Study*,

266). "That Evening Sun" and "Red Leaves," Howe suggests, are Faulkner's best stories and can arguably be called great.

In his discussion of the story's point of view, James Ferguson argues that the story may be as much about the narrator, Quentin Compson, as it is about Nancy and her fears. According to Ferguson, as Quentin narrates the story 15 years later, he relives it, and the language Faulkner uses becomes more and more that of a child as the storyteller recaptures his memories of the past; among other things, such a technique strengthens the story's theme of "the conflict between youth and maturity, and innocence and corruption" and demonstrates "Faulkner's concern with the storytelling process itself: as a means of reliving the past, revenging oneself on time, trying to come to terms with temporal realities through narration" (Ferguson, *Faulkner's Short Fiction*, 112).

CHARACTERS

Compson, Caddy (Candace) The narrator Quentin's inquisitive seven-year-old younger sister. During the course of the story, Caddy comes across as a lively and independent child who is not hesitant to speak her mind or to confront (or tease) her little brother, Jason. *See The Sound and the Fury* and the short story "A Justice"; she is also referred to in *The Mansion*.

Compson, Mrs. The self-consumed wife of Jason Compson, Sr., and the mother of Quentin (the narrator of the story), Caddy, and Jason. Disagreeable and impatient, she shows no compassion toward Nancy. *Also see The Sound and the Fury*; Mrs. Compson is referred to in *The Mansion*.

Compson, Jason (Jr.) The narrator Quentin's five-year-old younger brother. Of the three siblings, Jason, the youngest, reflects an incipient discriminatory social consciousness toward African Americans indicative of the time period and setting of the story. The short story also shows friction between Jason and his sister Caddy that is to continue in *The Sound and the Fury*. Jason also appears in *The Mansion* and the short story "A Justice", and is referred to in *The Town*.

Compson, Jason (Sr.; Mr. Jason) The narrator Quentin's father. Unlike his wife, Mr. Compson shows concern for Nancy's welfare, although he is not able to persuade her to stay with Aunt Rachel. *Also see The Sound and the Fury, Absalom, Absalom!*, and the short story "A Justice."

Compson, Quentin The short story's narrator. The Compsons' oldest child, Quentin is Caddy and Jason's brother. Although he was nine when the events occurred, he narrates the story 15 years later. Although not cognizant of the full significance of the events he narrates, Quentin, nonetheless, shows an astute awareness of what is happening. *Also see The Sound and the Fury* and *Absalom, Absalom!* (much of which he narrates); Quentin also narrates "A Justice" and "Lion" and is referred to in *The Mansion*.

Dilsey The Compsons' African-American cook. Nancy temporarily replaces Dilsey when she is sick. A genuinely kind person, Dilsey offers to let the frightened and confused Nancy stay in her cabin, but Nancy declines. *Also see The Sound and the Fury*.

Frony Dilsey's daughter, an offstage character. *Also see The Sound and the Fury*.

Jason, Mr. *See* Compson, Jason (Sr.).

Jesus A short black man with a scar on his face, Jesus is the husband of the drug-addicted and promiscuous Nancy (Mannigoe), who cooks for the Compsons when Dilsey is indisposed. Nancy is afraid that Jesus will kill her with his razor during the night, but he does not.

For more information, *see Faulkner in the University*, 21 and 79.

Lovelady, Mr. An insurance salesman. On Saturday mornings, he collects on the policies he sells to African Americans. A short, dirty man whose wife committed suicide, he is the father of one daughter. Through him, Dilsey saves up money to buy her coffin.

Nancy The central character in the short story. She takes in white people's laundry and is sometime kitchen help for the Compsons when their maid Dilsey is sick. A drug addict and occasional prostitute, she is pregnant, probably by the bank cashier and deacon in the Baptist church, Mr. Stovall, who one day knocks her down in the street and kicks several of her teeth out when she publicly embarrasses him by asking for payment. She is taken to jail, where the next morning she tries to hang herself but is cut down and revived by the jailer. The short story revolves around the Compson children's witnessing Nancy's delusional fear of the dark and of her absent husband, Jesus, who, she believes, will come back at night to kill her because of her marital infidelity and pregnancy. *Also see* Nancy Mannigoe in REQUIEM FOR A NUN.

Mother *See* Compson, Mrs.

Rachel, Aunt Offstage character in the story. She is said to be the mother of Jesus, Nancy's husband, though she sometimes denies it. An old woman with white hair, Aunt Rachel lives in a cabin beyond Nancy's where she smokes a pipe all day. Nancy is terrified that her absent husband will come during the night to kill her for being unfaithful, and when she begins to panic, Mr. Compson urges her to spend the night at Aunt Rachel's. Nancy, however, declines.

Stovall, Mr. A bank cashier and Baptist deacon, he is a sometime client of Nancy's. Stovall beats her when she accuses him in public of failing to pay for her services. Nancy is pregnant with his child.

T. P. An offstage character referred to by Caddy. Although his identity is not made explicit, he is Dilsey's son and Frony's brother; *see* The SOUND AND THE FURY.

FURTHER READING

Brooks, Cleanth. "Short Stories." In *William Faulkner: First Encounters*, 7–42. New Haven: Yale University Press, 1983.

Johnston, Kenneth G. "The Year of Jubilee: Faulkner's 'That Evening Sun.'" *American Literature* 46 (1974): 93–100.

Jones, Diane Brown. *A Reader's Guide to the Short Stories of William Faulkner*, 267–316. New York: G. K. Hall, 1994.

Kuyk, Dirk, Jr., Betty M. Kuyk, and James A. Miller. "Black Culture in William Faulkner's 'That Evening Sun.'" *Journal of American Studies* 20 (April 1986): 33–50.

Toker, Leona. "Rhetoric and Ethical Ambiguities in 'That Evening Sun.'" *Women's Studies* 22 (1993): 429–439.

Towner, Theresa M. and James B. Carothers. *Reading Faulkner: Collected Stories*, 150–158. Jackson: University of Mississippi Press, 2006.

"That Will Be Fine"
(Collected Stories)

First published in the July 1935 issue of the *American Mercury* (35), 264–276, this short story is reprinted in *Collected Stories of William Faulkner*; for further information, *see Selected Letters of William Faulkner*, 91, 95–96, 274, 278.

SYNOPSIS

"That Will Be Fine" deals with the deadly effects of Uncle Rodney's womanizing and thievery. Narrated by his seven-year-old nephew, Georgie, Uncle Rodney has a reputation in his family for borrowing money he does not repay and for making promises he does not keep. He also has a reputation around MOTTSTOWN as a lady's man, which proves fatal by the end of the story. The family's Christmas holiday at Uncle Rodney's father's house in Mottstown is upset by the looming revelation of Uncle Rodney's misdeeds. Uncle Rodney's sister (Georgie's mother) and brother-in-law (George, Georgie's father) are all expected at Grandpa's home for the holiday. Uncle Rodney's other sister, Aunt Louisa, and her husband, Uncle Fred, live with Grandpa. At the beginning of the story, Uncle Rodney has an urgent need to raise $2,000 to cover his theft of that amount from the Compress Association, where he has been working. Mr. Pruitt, president of the association, comes with a sheriff to the household to have Uncle Rodney arrested on the charge of theft and forgery. The family persuades Pruitt to give them until Christmas to make good the theft.

Georgie is an ill-tempered and greedy boy who expects to earn something for every deed he does. His focus on making dimes, quarters, and multiples of quarters keeps him from noticing the ethics of what Uncle Rodney is paying him to do, making him a miniature Uncle Rodney. The uncle has been paying Georgie to help him conduct an affair with Mrs. Tucker by being the lookout for her husband. Uncle Rodney has also given Georgie money for helping him pry open Grandpa's desk to get whiskey, and Georgie helps his uncle escape in the expectation of being paid 20 quarters. However, the boy is unaware of the gravity of the situation, and he unwittingly leads his uncle into an ambush at Mrs. Tucker's house. Uncle Rodney expects to leave town with Mrs. Tucker and her jewelry, but Mr. Tucker and five friends wait in the bushes outside the house. When Uncle Rodney goes to fetch her, the men shoot him and carry him off on a window shutter. Ironically, Georgie believes the body, covered with a quilt, is a side of beef intended as a present to his grandfather.

CRITICAL COMMENTARY

There is grotesque comedy or, more precisely, black humor in "That Will Be Fine." In his assessment of the story, James Ferguson comments: "Our laughter at the young narrator's unknowing allusion to the body of is uncle as 'a side of beef' . . . is hardly the laughter of delight; this is clearly an instance of very black humor. Moreover, the central ironies of the story derive from the appallingly mercenary and self-centered character of the narrator" (*Faulkner's Short Fiction*, 77).

HELPFUL RESOURCES

Theresa M. Towner and James B. Carothers, *Reading Faulkner: Collected Stories*, 140–149; and Diane Brown Jones, *A Reader's Guide to the Short Stories of William Faulkner*, 260–267.

CHARACTERS

Church, Mrs. A Jefferson lady, she calls on Mrs. Pruitt, the wife of the president of the Compress Association, and spreads the word that Mrs. Pruitt does not wear corsets and has liquor on her breath, outraging Jefferson's values.

Emmeline Nurses Aunt Louisa's baby and complains of being asked to take on extra work at Christmas.

Fred, Cousin The cousin of Georgie, the seven-year-old narrator of the story.

Fred, Uncle The husband of Georgie's Aunt Louisa.

George Georgie's father. Married to Uncle Rodney's sister, George manages the family's livery stable in Jefferson. George has a cynical attitude toward his brother-in-law, who he says will use any means to raise money except working.

Georgie The seven-year-old narrator of the story who abets his thieving, adulterous Uncle Rodney. Georgie is too young to understand his uncle's actions, but old enough to attempt to extract a fee of 20 quarters for his services; his greed and unwitting complicity contribute to Uncle Rodney's death.

John Paul An African-American servant of Georgie's family. John Paul tells Georgie his father would like to make the trouble-prone Uncle Rodney a Christmas present without waiting for Christmas, namely, a job.

Jordon, Mrs. She takes in Georgie for the night when his Uncle Rodney is killed.

Louisa, Aunt Uncle Rodney's sister and the aunt of the narrator, the seven-year-old Georgie. Louisa is protective of her ne'er-do-well brother. In her attempt to prevent his arrest, however, she does so less out of affection for him than out of concern for her father and for the reputation of the family.

Louisa, Cousin Georgie's cousin.

Mandy Georgie's grandfather's cook. Uncle Rodney hides in Mandy's cabin for a time when he is evading the authorities and an irate husband.

Pruitt The president of the Compress Association in MOTTSTOWN. Pruitt gives Uncle Rodney a job to please his duplicitous wife, who is carrying on an affair with Rodney. When Rodney steals the association's bonds, Pruitt generously offers not to prosecute until after Christmas.

Rodney, Uncle The central character in the short story, a thief and adulterer. His seven-year-old nephew, Georgie, the narrator of the short story, abets him in his schemes. Uncle Rodney is a ne'er-do-well who borrows money he does not intend to repay, carries on affairs with married women, and steals from his employer. After being caught embezzling and forging his father's name on a bad check, Uncle Rodney attempts to leave town with Mrs. Tucker and her jewelry. Mr. Tucker and five other MOTTSTOWN men intercept Rodney and shoot him dead for one of the husbands he has cuckolded. (An Uncle Rodney also appears in the short story "SEPULTURE SOUTH: GASLIGHT"; Uncle Rodney's character prefigures that of Maury Bascomb in *The* SOUND AND THE FURY.)

Rosie The black servant who looks after Georgie, the seven-year-old narrator of the story.

Sarah The mother of the seven-year-old narrator, Georgie, and the sister of the thieving, adulterous Uncle Rodney.

Tucker, Mr. A MOTTSTOWN man, he is the husband of one of the women with whom Uncle Rodney has an affair. When he discovers that his wife is planning to run off with her lover, Mr. Tucker and five of his friends ambush and kill him.

Tucker, Mrs. One of Uncle Rodney's amorous conquests.

Watts, Mr. The sheriff in JEFFERSON. He questions Georgie as to the whereabouts of his Uncle Rodney.

"There Was a Queen" (Collected Stories)

This short story first appeared in SCRIBNER'S MAGAZINE (January 1933) and later included in DOCTOR MARTINO AND OTHER STORIES (1934).

SYNOPSIS

"There Was a Queen" concerns three generations of Sartoris women, white and black, who consider the past and cope with disturbing events in the present (1929). The black cook and family pillar Elnora reflects on those now dead and gone, and on those left in the big house—the wheelchair-bound 90-year-old Miss Jenny Du Pre; Narcissa Benbow Sartoris, the widow of Miss Jenny's great grandnephew; and Narcissa's 10-year-old son, Benbow Sartoris.

Elnora's usual contempt toward Narcissa is fueled by Narcissa's mysterious trip to MEMPHIS. Later Elnora prepares supper while repeating the family history yet one more time to her daughter and son, who skeptically interrupt her. Meanwhile Narcissa tells Miss Jenny that she went to Memphis to buy back, with her body, anonymous letters that she had received before her marriage and which, if made public, might damage the family's reputation. Miss Jenny reacts nonjudgmentally, asking to be left alone. As Narcissa and her son dine, Elnora finds Miss Jenny dead by the library window.

CRITICAL COMMENTARY

Many readers resolve the story's ambiguities with the explanation that Narcissa's immoral, self-serving behavior has shocked Miss Jenny to death and has contributed to the final, irreversible decline of the Sartoris family. Attention to the story's rich symbolic subtext, both pagan and biblical, offers an alternative view. The imagery of rebirth and renewal suggests that Narcissa has passed a test of her resilience; Miss Jenny finally can pass on the torch to a new family guardian and die peacefully.

CHARACTERS

Bory *See* Sartoris, Benbow.

Caspey The husband of the Sartoris family cook Elnora, he is in prison for theft.

Du Pre, Virginia (Miss Jenny) She is the strong-minded 90-year-old sister of the late Colonel John Sartoris. In this short story, she is wheelchair-bound. Miss Jenny had been married for only two years when her husband died in a battle during the Civil War. In 1869, seven years after his death, she left Carolina—"the last of the Carolina family" (728)—to live with her brother in Mississippi. *Also see* Characters under SARTORIS, THE UNVANQUISHED, and SANCTUARY; she is referred to in *The* TOWN and *The* MANSION, and as Aunt Jenny Sartoris in the short story "ALL THE DEAD PILOTS," and as Mrs. Virginia Depre in REQUIEM FOR A NUN.

Elnora Colonel John Sartoris's daughter by a slave; she is the cook for the family. Old Bayard is her half-brother, "though possibly but not probably neither of them knew it, including Bayard's father" (p. 727). *Also see* SARTORIS, where she is the African-American daughter of Simon Strother and a servant in the home of old Bayard Sartoris, and "ALL THE DEAD PILOTS," where she is referred to as having knitted socks for Johnny Sartoris.

Joby Elnora's son; he migrates to Beale Street in MEMPHIS.

Miss Jenny *See* Du Pre, Virginia

Saddie Elnora's daughter, who looks after 90-year-old, wheel-chair bound Miss Jenny.

Sartoris, Bayard (old) Colonel John Sartoris's son. *Also see* SARTORIS, *The* HAMLET, *The* TOWN, *The* UNVANQUISHEd, GO DOWN, MOSES ("The Bear"), REQUIEM FOR A NUN, *The* MANSION, *The* REIVERS, and the short story "A ROSE FOR EMILY."

Sartoris, Bayard (young) Narcissa Benbow Sartoris's deceased husband and Bory's father. Young Bayard was killed in an airplane crash before his son was born. *Also see* SARTORIS where he dies the day his son is born.

Sartoris, Benbow (Bory) Narcissa Benbow Sartoris's young son. *Also see* SARTORIS, SANCTUARY, *The* MANSION, KNIGHT'S GAMBIT, and *The* TOWN.

Sartoris, Colonel John Miss Jenny's brother and (old) Bayard Sartoris's father. A Civil War hero, Colonel Sartoris built the house referred to in the opening paragraph of the story. Colonel Sartoris is modeled on Faulkner's great-grandfather, WILLIAM CLARK FALKNER. *Also see* SARTORIS, *The* UNVANQUISHED, *The* SOUND AND THE FURY, LIGHT IN AUGUST, ABSALOM, ABSALOM!, *The* HAMLET, *The* TOWN, *The* MANSION, GO DOWN, MOSES ("The Bear"), REQUIEM FOR A NUN, *The* REIVERS, and the short stories "BARN BURNING," "SHALL NOT PERISH," and "MY GRANDMOTHER MILLARD AND GENERAL BEDFORD FORREST AND THE BATTLE OF HARRYKIN CREEK."

Sartoris, John Old Bayard Sartoris's son and father of the twins, (young) Bayard and John. *Also see* SARTORIS.

Sartoris, John (Johnny) Young Bayard Sartoris's twin brother. Johnny died in France during World War I. *Also see* SARTORIS, "ALL THE DEAD PILOTS," and "WITH CAUTION AND DISPATCH." He is referred to in *The* TOWN and *The* MANSION.

Sartoris, Narcissa Benbow Young Bayard Sartoris's widow and Bory's mother. Narcissa meets with a Federal agent in MEMPHIS to get back the obscene letters that the unnamed book-keeper in Colonel Sartoris's bank had anonymously sent to her and had later stolen from her house; he left them behind at the bank the night he ran off with its money. Though she could not have bought the letters back with money, she did so with her flesh. *Also see* SARTORIS and SANCTUARY; in *The* TOWN and *The* MANSION, she is referred to by her maiden name, Narcissa Benbow. (In *Sartoris*, the letters are attributed to Byron Snopes.)

Simon The late husband of the mother of Elnora; he worked for the Sartoris family. (Simon is probably the Simon Strother of SARTORIS and *The* UNVANQUISHED.)

"Thrift" (Uncollected Stories)

First published on September 6, 1930, in the SAT-URDAY EVENING POST 203, 16–17, 78, 82, "Thrift" was reprinted in *O. Henry Memorial Award Prize Stories of 1931*, edited by Blanche Colton Williams (Garden City: Doubleday, Doran & Co., 1931) and in UNCOLLECTED STORIES OF WILLIAM FAULKNER. For more information, *see Selected Letters of William Faulkner*, 274, and *Uncollected Stories of William Faulkner*, 700–701. For further information about aircraft and flyers of World War I, *see* the Web site http://www.theaerodrome.com.

SYNOPSIS

"Thrift" concerns MacWyrglinchbeath, a Scotsman of profound thriftiness, who decides early in his army career during World War I that he will make as good a profit as possible out of being a soldier. When he discovers that Royal Flying Corps personnel are paid a higher rate than infantrymen, he engineers a transfer into the flying corps by deliberately burning his foot. As a mechanic in the RFC, he learns that he can get additional pay by getting flight time, so he attempts to teach himself to fly, wrecking an aircraft in the process. He is so obdurate in his purpose that the RFC officers send him back to England to flight school. He becomes the pilot of an artillery observation airplane, and, in a device Faulkner later uses in the novel *A FABLE*, MacWyrglinchbeath also becomes a kind of insurance agent for another flyer. His pecuniary interest in keeping alive this other unnamed officer causes MacWyrglinchbeath to get into a dogfight with two German fighters; he shoots them down, but his own observer, Robinson, is killed. MacWyrglinchbeath becomes famous for his parsimony, which extends to his refusing a commission as a second lieutenant because he has figured out that he will make more money as a warrant officer. The story ends with MacWyrglinchbeath returning to his Highlands farm, where the bulk of his RFC pay awaits him.

CRITICAL COMMENTARY

The themes of shrewdness and avarice used by Faulkner here and elsewhere (in particular in certain episodes dealing with Flem Snopes) are often presented in a humorous or comic context; and often the humor is allied with the tall tale. Faulkner himself did not think highly of this short story; *see Selected Letters*, 274.

CHARACTERS

Ffollansbye   A British pilot. Ffollansbye recommends MacWyrglinchbeath for a commission. Much of what the reader learns about MacWyrglinchbeath comes through Ffollansbye. This character also appears in the short story "All the Dead Pilots."

MacWyrglinchbeath   Central character in the short story. He is a Scotsman whose main motivation is the amassing of wealth. Because he learns that the flyers in the Royal Flying Corps are better paid than infantrymen, he transfers into the RFC and later becomes a pilot. MacWyrglinchbeath becomes famous for his parsimony, which extends to his refusing a commission as a second lieutenant because, after figuring out that with the expenses associated with being an officer, he reckons he will make more money as a sergeant.

Robinson   The artilleryman who is assigned to MacWyrglinchbeath's aircraft as observer. Robinson is killed during a dogfight.

Whiteley   The officer who processes MacWyrglinchbeath's transfer into the Royal Flying Corps. He is presented in a comic scene involving the spelling and pronunciation of the Scotsman Mac-Wyrglinchbeath's name.

Town, The

The second novel of the SNOPES TRILOGY, published on May 1, 1957, 17 years after the first volume, The HAMLET, and two years before the third volume, The MANSION. As with the first and third volumes, *The Town* is dedicated to Faulkner's close friend PHILIP AVERY STONE, but here with the designation: "He did half the laughing for thirty years." Two of the novel's chapters (1 and 16) are revisions of two short stories Faulkner previously published. "CENTAUR IN BRASS," revised as chapter 1, first appeared in the *American Mercury* 25 (February 1932), 200–210; "MULE IN THE YARD," revised as chapter 16, was first published in SCRIBNER'S MAGAZINE 96 (August 1934): 65–70. In Faulkner's original outline of the novel, this second volume of the trilogy was titled *Rus in Urbe* (*see Selected Letters of William Faulkner*, 107).

SYNOPSIS

The plot of the novel is fairly simple. Flem and his family (Eula Varner Snopes and her daughter, Linda) arrive in JEFFERSON, where, as Faulkner himself explained in a December 1938 letter to ROBERT K. HAAS, Flem in due time exploits his wife's adultery to blackmail her lover, Manfred de Spain, rises little by little from being a half owner of a back street restaurant to various city jobs to the presidency of a bank, and fills "each post he vacates with another Snopes from the country" (*Selected Letters of William Faulkner,* 107). The exploitative Flem, however, would just as soon rid Jefferson of any Snopes who would impede his progress or expect assistance from him. In *The Hamlet,* for instance, Flem's indifference to the plight of his kinsman Mink for having murdered Jack Houston is a calculated decision to avoid any contact with a relative charged with a crime. In chapter 10 of *The Town,* Flem goes one step further when he discovers that Montgomery Ward Snopes's photography studio, the Atelier Monty, is a front for peep shows. For the sake of respectability and the Snopes name, Flem sees to it that Montgomery goes out of business by having him prosecuted for possessing bootleg whiskey, which Flem has planted in Montgomery's studio. This offense is less embarrassing to Flem than having his cousin arrested for showing slides of indecent French postcards. Flem returns Montgomery's studio key, which he took from sheriff Hub Hampton's desk drawer, to Gavin's office, and on his way out, the philosophic Gavin comments that Flem clearly cares about justice. But Flem's retort undercuts any virtuous motive behind his actions: "I'm interested in Jefferson. . . . We got to live here" (176).

In accepting his wife's affair with the town's mayor, the bachelor Manfred de Spain, Flem, who is sexually impotent, is attending not vicariously to his wife's sexual gratification but instead to his own manipulative intentions. The whole of Jefferson becomes spectator to a fate beyond its control and can do nothing to prevent the course of events, as Chick Mallison explains midway through chapter 1.

Gavin Stevens, in his Don Quixote role as defender of woman's virtue and chastity, unsuccessfully attempts to protect Eula—whom he loves, without admitting it to himself—from Manfred de Spain at the Cotillion Ball. But he is no match for Manfred, who easily defends himself and bloodies Gavin's face. Earlier in this same chapter (3), his twin sister, Margaret Stevens Mallison, sarcastically and almost prophetically remarks to Gowan: "You dont marry Semiramis: you just commit some form of suicide for her" (50). (Semiramis is the legendary founder and queen of Babylon, known for her beauty and sexuality.) Gavin's romanticized love for Eula—he sees her as Helen of Troy, Venus, and Lilith all in one—becomes an obstacle to any sexual relationship they possibly could have had together, and when one night in his office she offers her body to him he refuses. He does not want to be pitied. At first, however, he assumes that her offer is a ploy to sway him as city attorney to drop the suit against de Spain and to stop investigating the theft of the brass safety valves at the city's power plant. During his superintendency (a position de Spain arranged while mayor), Flem stole these valves, but the scheme backfired. At the moment of Eula's seduction (and at other times throughout the novel), the emotionally complicated Gavin is a gallant knight in search of an idealized, virtuous love and, to use CLEANTH BROOKS's phrase, is treated by Faulkner "as a figure of fun" (*see* "Passion, Marriage, and Bourgeois Respectability" in *William Faulkner: The Yoknapatawpha Country,* 192–218).

The day after Eula's visit, Gavin withdraws the suit against de Spain and later on withdraws himself from Jefferson itself for several years to study at Heidelberg and to serve as a YMCA secretary during World War I. After his return from Europe, Gavin's romanticized crusade continues by taking an active role in the education of Eula's 14-year-old daughter, Linda, and by protecting her against SNOPESISM. His love for Linda is avuncular, although those around him think otherwise, including Eula herself, who at her last meeting with Gavin has him promise that he will marry her. Eula's motive is not totally altruistic; she is also thinking of herself. By having Linda married, Eula would be free to leave Flem for de Spain and would no longer need to maintain the appearance of a stable home life.

In the end, however, Eula kills herself, an act brutally practical for her. When Faulkner was asked his thoughts on Eula's suicide, he said that she did it for Linda's sake, that Eula believed that it was worse to run off with a lover than to kill herself (*Faulkner at the University*, 195). On the day of the funeral, de Spain leaves Jefferson for good.

Prior to Eula's death, Flem gains control over the Sartoris Bank by exposing the long-term affair between Eula and de Spain to Eula's father, Will Varner. The outraged Varner rushes from his home in FRENCHMAN'S BEND to Jefferson at 4:00 A.M. to run them all out of town—de Spain, Eula, and Flem. However, Flem proposes a much different tactic, a self-rewarding one that fits his design. He prefers that Eula and her lover leave Jefferson for good and that de Spain be forced to sell his bank stock to Flem so that he (Flem) can take over as president. Reluctantly, Varner agrees to the deal. In between time, Flem, who all along had refused to send Linda away to college, fearing that she would get married and no longer be under his authority, eventually gives her his permission to attend the state university in nearby OXFORD. Soon after, Linda, duped by Flem's apparent kindness, signs an agreement handing over to him any inheritance money she would get from her mother. "This act, which is crucial to the plot," Edmond L. Volpe writes, echoing the sentiments of many critics, "is contrived and implausible, but it is typical of the plot and character breakdowns in *The Town*" (*A Reader's Guide to William Faulkner*, 327). After her mother's suicide, Linda leaves for New York on her own. In the penultimate chapter (chapter 23) of the novel, Ratliff offers an ironic commentary on the events in *The Town*. (Chapter 24 was reprinted as "The Waif" in the *Saturday Evening Post* on May 4, 1957.)

CRITICAL COMMENTARY

The early reviews of *The Town* that appeared in prominent journals were at best tepid. Alfred Kazin's assessment of the novel in the *New York Times Book Review* suggested that Faulkner was tired of the YOKNAPATAWPHA COUNTY chronicle, although Faulkner claimed otherwise (*Faulkner in the University*, 107).

Despite the view by some critics that the characters in the novel are more symbolic than flesh and blood, to Faulkner his characters were real people who grew and changed over time as he himself grew older. In response to this objection, Faulkner at the University of Virginia in 1957 said: "I know more about people than I knew when I first thought of them, and they have become more definite to me as people and that may be what seems like staleness gets into it" (*Faulkner in the University*, 108). Faulkner's personal or emotional involvement in the novel is evident from his August 12, 1956, letter to JEAN STEIN, in which he writes that he "almost cried" when he wrote one scene, presumably Eula Snopes's suicide (*Selected Letters*, 402).

Whether Faulkner was tired of the Yoknapatawpha County chronicle or not is debatable. Of greater importance is the question of the novel's thematic unity. Although Faulkner's work can at times appear episodic, as in LIGHT IN AUGUST, his novels are thematically unified even when he uses the technique of multiple narrators, a device particularly characteristic of his fictional style. In *The Town*, the distinct perspectives the three narrators give on the events they relate also make the novel convincingly realistic. The diversity of seemingly unrelated incidents finds common ground in the narrators' opposition to the invasive force of Snopesism, but more significantly in their delineation of the adverse effects of Flem's character. Their concentration on his character and its impact on others provides a unity to the narrators' accounts and diversity of views. In this respect, *The Town* is a novel of character, centered on Flem's, and the ethics of greed. The novel also displays Flem's preoccupation with his attempt to gain respectability.

Although the locus of the work is Flem's character as it is revealed through his schemes and dealings with others, the novel equally portrays the characters of others as they react to him—especially those of the narrators, whose knowledge of the events they retell is conditioned by hearsay, individual bias, and personal speculation. There are 24 chapters that cover a period from 1909—the year when Flem Snopes with his wife and her daughter arrives in Jefferson—to about a year after Eula shoots herself in 1927. The youngest narrator, Charles Mallison, an attentive and imaginative child, is not born until 1915, but he narrates the majority of the chapters, 10 in all (1, 3, 7, 10, 12, 14, 16, 19, 21, 24). Most of the information he receives is from his cousin Gowan Stevens, who is 13 years old at the beginning of the novel, and from the other two narrators, his uncle Gavin Stevens and the observant sewing machine agent V. K. Ratliff. In many respects, then, Mallison is closest to the collective impression of the town itself, as he himself says on the opening page: "So when I say 'we' and 'we thought' what I mean is Jefferson and what Jefferson thought." Gavin, who narrates eight chapters (2, 5, 8, 13, 15, 17, 20, 22), is a romantically idealistic attorney, quixotic in his defense of honor and decency, and indefatigably engrossed in his opposition to Snopesism. With a HARVARD M.A. and Heidelberg Ph.D., he is the town's intellectual—sensitive, analytic, and nurturing to Eula's teenage daughter, Linda. The discerning Ratliff, perhaps the most detached and objective of the three, narrates six chapters (4, 6, 9, 11, 18, 23). Together the three narrators provide the filters through which the events of *The Town* are retold and in some cases retold comically.

For more details, *see Selected Letters of William Faulkner* and *Faulkner in the University.*

EXCERPTS FROM CONTEMPORARY REVIEWS OF *THE TOWN*

Excerpt from an anonymous review of The Town, *published in* The Booklist, *July 1, 1957, 500:*
Couched in Faulknerese, numerous outrageous anecdotes concerning the incredible Snopeses take on a folklore quality.

Excerpt from Frederick J. Hoffman's review, "The Snopes Balance: 1940 and 1957," published in The Progressive, *September 1957, 33–35:*
In his new novel, *The Town . . .* , William Faulkner returns to a world he has not looked into since 1940. It is difficult to define that world exactly. Superficially it is dominated by the Snopes tribe, a proliferating, plundering, amoral, and scrupulously canny lot, whom Faulkner chose to represent a special form of villainy. In his first full display of Snopeses, *The Hamlet,* he generalized from particular instances and set up a type of human aberration, Snopesism or Snopeishness. . . .

The principal deficiency of *The Town* seems to me to lie in its failure to give its characters status as persons. They are all on the way to becoming public symbols. Faulkner has become rhetorically anxious. It is as though he now feels that no human representation of human good or evil can any longer adequately serve him. He is too concerned to have his people symbolize something other than themselves before they have had the chance properly to become themselves—which is perhaps to say that he has found Snopesism a far less rewarding theme that it was for him in *The Hamlet.* In that earlier novel, the lines were drawn so remarkably well (and Faulkner was so freshly aware of them) that one could be aware simultaneously of the comedy, pathos, and anger which animate that novel.

By comparison, *The Town* often seems a drudging précis of its predecessor, done from the perspective of too many years and too many public honors. Partly this impression is caused by Faulkner's indifference in purpose. In *The Hamlet* the characters were what they were, with the necessary addition of fallibility and contumacy and irrational desire to their natures; in their presences they communicated what they "meant" without too overtly meaning what they should be. *The Town* is crowded with rhetorical feelings (Mallison's, Ratliff's, Stevens') over what human acts symbolically attest or aver or vehemently assert. At the same time the behavior of Snopeses continues, almost in the manner of comic interludes, to "entertain," while Snopesism is itself being considered at the level of the moral editorial. Vigor has departed; in its place we have a nervous energy stimulated by both anxiety and distrust. . . .

Excerpt from Louis Dollarhide's review, "Rich Detail, Energy, Humor; One of His Strongest Books," published in the Clarion-Ledger–Jackson (Miss.) Daily News, *April 28, 1957, 11-C:*

. . . *The Town* illustrates one aspect of Faulkner's writing which has not been sufficiently emphasized by his commentators, the fact that he is a supremely great humorist. A reader would have to go all the way back to Chaucer to find writing comparable in richness of humor and tone to at least episodes in the book—the episode of the stolen brass, the Rouncewell panic, and the episode involving Miss Mamie Hait, Old Het, and I. O. Snopes's mule, which has appeared earlier as a short story called "Mule in the Yard."

In many ways, *The Town* is one of Faulkner's strongest novels. *The Hamlet* is more directly told and is less complex. But what *The Town* may lose in directness of narrative it gains immeasurably in richness of detail, energy and variety of character.

It has the strength of the great English Renaissance writing, which, like Faulkner's, was a deeply traditional art. It may well prove to be one of the most acceptable of Faulkner's novels with readers at large, not because it is more removed from life as the writer sees it (which is often what readers require of artists), but because in moving from hamlet to town he presents, with the exception of the Snopeses, characters of a social order with which most people who read novels can identify. The Snopeses, whoever they are, do not read novels.

Excerpt from Harrison Smith's review, "Story of Greedy, Indomitable Men Told in Humorous Not Grim Fashion," published in the Hartford Times, *May 4, 1957;* St. Petersburg (Fla.) Times, *May 5, 1957;* Toledo Blade, *May 12, 1957, 4:*

. . . [*The Town*] is a humorous and even hilarious, rather than grim novel. The Snopeses were never hostile: they acted like poor folk, and their wives and daughters were occasionally available for amorous aristocrats who were slowly loosening their hold on reality. Apparently humble, Flem Snopes conquered the town, slowly penetrating the power plant, the bank, the ramshackle boarding house which turned into Snopes's Hotel. Mayor de Spain fell under his spell. . . .

The Town must be rated as one of Faulkner's greatest books. His central theme, "Snopesism," goes to the core of the matter, the gradual erosion of the Deep South at the hands of remorseless and avid men; but the novel is enriched with living characters, good or evil, and by the author's knowledgment of the human mind and heart.

CHARACTERS

Adams Mr. The mayor of JEFFERSON before losing to Manfred de Spain in the 1904 election. Mayor Adams has "a long patriarchal white beard" (11) and is married to a fat woman whom some young boys refer to as "Miss Eve Adam."

(Adams, Mrs.) The old fat wife of Mayor Adams jokingly referred to by Cousin Gowan (*see* Stevens, Gowan) and other boys of 12 or 13 as "Miss Eve Adam," with the final s intentionally left off.

Adams, Theron The youngest son of Mayor Adams. When running for reelection, the mayor and his cronies attempt to smear their rival's (Manfred de Spain's) character. As a way of defending his reputation, de Spain challenges Theron to an axe fight. The elderly mayor would not be up to the contest. Theron, however, concedes.

Armstid, Henry A poor farmer in the vicinity of FRENCHMAN'S BEND who had been tricked by Flem Snopes into buying worthless property (*see The HAMLET*). In *The Town* (and in *The MANSION*), Armstid is an off-stage character living in the Jackson asylum. *Also see As I LAY DYING, LIGHT IN AUGUST, "SPOTTED HORSES," and "SHINGLES FOR THE LORD."*

Backus, Melisandre The woman Gavin Stevens's twin sister Margaret (Maggie Mallison) thinks he should marry. Although in different years, Melisandre and Maggie were in school together. Melisandre lives with her father on a cotton farm about six miles from JEFFERSON and marries a rich NEW

ORLEANS bootlegger, who transforms the farm into something that looks "like a cross between a Kentucky country club and a Long Island race track" (178; his name, Harriss, is given in *The* MANSION). They have two children before he is killed gangland style, with a bullet in the middle of his forehead. (In *The Mansion*, the widowed Melisandre marries Gavin; *also see* Mrs. Harriss in KNIGHT'S GAMBIT ("Knight's Gambit").

Beauchamp, Tomey's Turl   A minor character in the novel. He is one of two African-American firemen at the power plant in JEFFERSON in 1910. Tomey's Turl works at night under Mr. Harker and his counterpart, Tom Tom Bird, works during the day. When Flem Snopes becomes superintendent of the plant, he exploits both men in his attempt to steal the solid brass safety valves. When Flem orders Tomey's Turl to retrieve the brass that Tom Tom is hiding on his property, the 30-year-old Tomey's Turl begins an affair with Tom Tom's much younger wife and is caught. After a struggle between Tomey's Turl and Tom Tom, both men realize what Flem is up to and decide to throw the brass into the water tank. (*Also see* the short story "CENTAUR IN BRASS," where he is referred to as Turl.)

Benbow, Miss Narcissa   *See* Sartoris, Narcissa Benbow.

Best, Henry   Minor character in *The Town*. Best is an alderman in JEFFERSON and present at the board meeting investigating the missing brass fittings at the power plant.

Binford, Dewitt   Minor character in the novel. Married to a Snopes, he and his wife take in Byron Snopes's four wild and unruly children until Binford fears for his own life. The children are sent back to Byron.

Binford, Mrs.   Called Miz Dee-wit in the novel, she is Dewitt Binford's wife.

Bird, Tom Tom   The African-American fireman who reads the gauges at the power plant in JEF-FERSON on the day shift. He is married to a young woman, his fourth wife, whom he keeps in seclusion. When he catches his night-shift counterpart, Tomey's Turl Beauchamp, sneaking into his house, he chases him with a butcher knife until the two fall into a ditch. Once they realize their unwitting role in Flem Snopes's scheme to steal the solid brass fittings at the power plant, Tom Tom and Tomey's Turl put the fittings into the town's water tank. (This character also appears as Tom-Tom with no last name in the short story "CENTAUR IN BRASS," where he is married to a third wife, whom he keeps in seclusion.)

Birdsong, Preacher   Minor character in the novel. He learned to box in France during World War I, and is good enough to fight Linda Snopes's beau, Matt Levitt, who won the Golden Gloves in Ohio.

(Bookwright, Cal)   Letty Bookwright's father. His name is found in editions prior to the 1961 Vintage paperback edition of *The Town*; in the Vintage edition, his name is not used and Letty's name is changed to Lucy Pate. *See* Calvin Bookwright in *The* MANSION and Uncle Cal Bookwright in *The* REIVERS.

(Bookwright, Letty)   *See* Pate, Lucy.

Buffaloe, Mr.   Also referred to as Joe Buffaloe, he is the city electrician of JEFFERSON who keeps the steam-driven electric plant running. A mechanical genius, Mr Buffaloe, in 1904, builds a "self-propelled buggy" (12), an automobile, the first in Jefferson. One afternoon, he drives the noisy buggy into the town square causing the horses of Colonel Sartoris's surrey to bolt. An edict, initiated by Colonel Sartoris, to ban all gasoline-propelled vehicles from operating in Jefferson is passed by the board of aldermen and lasts until the new mayor, Manfred de Spain, is elected. Although never officially repealing the edict, the mayor makes a mockery of it. *Also see The* MANSION and *The* REIVERS.

Christian, Uncle Willy   A bachelor about sixty years old, Uncle Willy is the proprietor of a drugstore. He uses morphine, which greatly improves his otherwise misanthropic personality. When the drugstore is burglarized, the morphine stock is taken leaving him in a pinch. *Also see The* MANSION, *The* REIVERS, and the short story "UNCLE WILLY."

Christian, Walter The African-American janitor in Uncle Willy Christian's pharmacy. The grandson of a slave who belonged to Uncle Willy's grandfather, Walter helps himself to the alcohol locked in the store cabinet whenever Uncle Willy turns his back after putting the key down. About the same age as Uncle Willy, Walter is very much like him but a bit more short-tempered and irascible.

Clefus Very minor African-American character in the novel; he sweeps the law office of Gavin Stevens.

Compson, General An offstage character referred to in the novel. General Compson was a Confederate brigadier general during the Civil War and for two days the governor of Mississippi. *Also see* ABSALOM, ABSALOM!, REQUIEM FOR A NUN, *The* UNVANQUISHED, the Appendix to *The* SOUND AND THE FURY (*see* Appendix), INTRUDER IN THE DUST, *The* REIVERS and GO DOWN, MOSES, and the short stories "A BEAR HUNT" and "MY GRANDMOTHER MILLARD AND GENERAL BEDFORD FORREST AND THE BATTLE OF HARRYKIN CREEK."

Compson, Jason Referred to in the novel in reference to collecting rent for his mother from Montgomery Ward Snopes, who runs a photography gallery, a front for peep shows. For other details regarding Jason, *see The* SOUND AND THE FURY, where he is a major character, and the short story "THAT EVENING SUN"; *also see* the Appendix to *The* SOUND AND THE FURY (reprinted in Appendix), *The* MANSION, and "A JUSTICE."

Compson, Mrs. General Compson's wife. Like her husband, she is an offstage character referred to in the novel. Fifty years before the setting of the novel, Mrs. Compson had given old Het a coat and a purple toque. *Also see The* UNVANQUISHED and "MY GRANDMOTHER MILLARD AND GENERAL

BEDFORD FORREST AND THE BATTLE OF HARRYKIN CREEK."

Connors, Buck JEFFERSON's city marshal; he is referred to as Mr. Buck Connor by Tomey's Turl Beauchamp and as Mr. Buck by Otis Harker. Connors investigates the brass fittings missing from the town's power plant. *Also see* "CENTAUR IN BRASS" (which Faulkner revised for *The Town*) and LIGHT IN AUGUST; in both works his last name appears as Connor.

Crenshaw, Jack Revenue field agent, who informs Sheriff Hampton of the whiskey found in the photography studio that Montgomery Ward Snopes operates; the studio is actually a front for peep shows. The discovery leads to Montgomery Ward's arrest and imprisonment at the state penitentiary in PARCHMAN and serves the machinations of Flem Snopes, who had planted the liquor in the first place.

Dee-wit, Miz *See* Binford, Mrs.

de Spain, Major (sometimes De Spain) Manfred de Spain's father. Major de Spain's stock holdings—two of the three biggest blocks—in JEFFERSON's Sartoris Bank make it possible for his son to become president of the bank. In the BIG BOTTOM, Major de Spain established an annual hunting camp soon after the Civil War ended. One of the members of the group was Colonel Sartoris. *Also see* ABSALOM, ABSALOM!, *The* MANSION, INTRUDER IN THE DUST, *The* REIVERS, BIG WOODS, GO DOWN, MOSES ("The OLD PEOPLE," "The BEAR," and "DELTA AUTUMN"), and the short stories "BARN BURNING," "LION," "A BEAR HUNT" and "SHALL NOT PERISH," and "WASH" (where he is referred to not by name but by his title).

de Spain, Manfred (sometimes De Spain) One of the main characters in the novel, Manfred de Spain is the mayor of JEFFERSON, the owner of a car agency, and Eula Varner Snopes's lover. After graduating from West Point, de Spain served as a second lieutenant in Cuba during the Spanish-American War. In deference to his father, Major de Spain, Manfred on occasion is also called Major. Because of his father's stock holdings in Jefferson's Sartoris Bank, Manfred becomes its president when old Bayard Sartoris dies, and serves in this position until Eula's husband, Flem, forces him out by divulging to Eula's father, Will Varner, the adulterous relationship that Manfred and Eula have been carrying on for 18 years. During that time, Manfred had rewarded Flem, who supposedly was unaware of his wife's adultery, by creating for him the new position of superintendent of Jefferson's power plant. Later on, the ever-crafty Flem maneuvers to become the vice president of the bank.

Throughout *The Town*, the sensitive and romantically idealistic attorney Gavin Stevens opposes Manfred and Eula's relationship, but he is unsuccessful in ending it. Eventually, Varner forces Manfred to resign from the bank and sell his bank stock to Flem. Manfred expects to leave Jefferson with Eula, but she commits suicide. After her funeral, de Spain, who, in the words of the narrator Charles Mallison Jr., "flouted the morality of marriage" (*The Town*, 338), leaves Jefferson for good under the pretense of business and health. Although he does not appear as a character in *The* MANSION and *The* REIVERS, he is referred to in these two novels.

Dukinfield, Judge   Called on by Henry Best, one of the aldermen, to preside over the hearing on the brass fittings that were stolen from JEFFERSON's power plant. On the morning of the hearing, however, Judge Dukinfield recuses himself and has Judge Stevens preside. The attorney Gavin Stevens, Judge Stevens's son, had planned to use the hearing as a legal basis to remove Mayor Manfred de Spain from office.

Du Pre, Mrs. Jennie (sometimes Miss Jenny Du Pre)   Colonel (Bayard) Sartoris's sister. In *The Town*, she is an offstage character. *See* SARTORIS, *The* UNVANQUISHED, SANCTUARY, and the short story "THERE WAS A QUEEN"; she is also referred to in *The* MANSION; and as Aunt Jenny Sartoris in "All the Dead Pilots," and as Mrs. Virginia Depre in REQUIEM FOR A NUN. (On some occasions, her name appears as Genevieve Du Pre and Virginia Sartoris.)

Edmonds, McCaslin   The father of Roth Edmonds. An offstage character, McCaslin Edmonds was a member of Major de Spain's hunting camp. For further details, *see* BIG WOODS, *The* REIVERS and the entry for Carothers McCaslin Edmonds (old Cass) in GO DOWN, MOSES, where he is the grandfather of Carothers (Roth) Edmonds.

Edmonds, Roth   An offstage character, Roth Edmonds, the son of McCaslin Edmonds, signs a note to help Lucius Hogganbeck buy a Ford Model T. *Also see* GO DOWN, MOSES, where Roth (Carothers Edmonds) is the son of Zachary (Zack) Edmonds and the grandson of Carothers McCaslin Edmonds (old Cass) and the short story "RACE AT MORNING" (revised for BIG WOODS).

Elma, Miss   Sheriff Hampton's office deputy and the previous sheriff's widow.

Garraway, Mr.   A minor character, he is the owner of a store at SEMINARY HILL and an "inflexible unreconstructible Puritan" (312). In protest over Mayor Manfred de Spain's affair with Eula Varner Snopes, he is the first to transfer his account from Colonel John Sartoris's bank, when de Spain is appointed president to the Bank of Jefferson.

Gatewood, Jabbo   A minor African-American character in the novel. Jabbo is Uncle Noon Gatewood's son and the best auto mechanic in the county. When he is arrested for drunkenness, he never spends more than a night in jail because he is in such demand as a mechanic.

Gatewood, Uncle Noon   A minor African-American character in the novel, Uncle Noon runs a blacksmith shop where Gavin Stevens, with the help of Little Top Sander, goes to sharpen a rake used to puncture the tires of Manfred de Spain's car. Uncle Noon helps V. K. Ratliff turn his Model T into "what they call pickup trucks now" (113).

Gombault Mr.   The U.S. marshal called in to JEFFERSON to investigate Montgomery Ward Snopes and his photography shop. *Also see* the short story

"The TALL MEN" and "Uncle Pete" Gombault following the entry on REQUIEM FOR A NUN.

Gowrie, Mr. A minor offstage character who provides liquor to Chick Mallison's father and to others in JEFFERSON. The name also appears in INTRUDER IN THE DUST.

Grenier, Louis One of the founders of JEFFERSON; he is referred to in the novel. *Also see* REQUIEM FOR A NUN, INTRUDER IN THE DUST, KNIGHT'S GAMBIT ("Hand Upon the Waters"), and *The* REIVERS. In *The* HAMLET, Grenier County is mentioned, a county probably derived from his name.

Habersham, Doctor Referred to in the novel as one of the founders of JEFFERSON. *Also see* REQUIEM FOR A NUN and INTRUDER IN THE DUST.

Habersham, Miss Eunice A minor character in the novel, Miss Habersham uses her home-made truck to deliver orchids for the florist Mrs. Rouncewell. She calls the Travellers' Aid in NEW ORLEANS to assist in getting Byron Snopes's unruly children onto the train bound for El Paso and calls the El Paso Aid to assist in making sure that the children get to the Mexican police so that they can be returned to their father or to wherever they came from. She also calls a train company official to alert the conductor and porter of the children to be picked up in JEFFERSON. *Also see* INTRUDER IN THE DUST for other details regarding this character. (In editions of *The Town* prior to the 1961 Vintage edition, the first name of the Eunice Habersham who calls about Byron Snopes's children is Emily and that of the woman who helps deliver the flowers is Eunice.)

Hait, Lonzo A minor offstage character. With I. O. Snopes, Hait participates in a scheme to have mules killed on train tracks in order to collect damages from the railroad companies. In *The Town*, Hait has been dead for three years; he was killed by a train as he tied five mules to the tracks. *Also see The* MANSION and the short story "MULE IN THE YARD," which Faulkner extensively revised for this novel.

Hait, Mrs. (Miss Mannie) Lonzo Hait's widow. Although a minor character in the novel, she is an example of the rugged and self-reliant individual and of the strong-minded woman found in Faulkner's works. She chops her own firewood, plows her own field, and works her own vegetable garden, and when her husband is hit and killed by a train she collects $8,000 in damages from the railroad company and outwits I. O. Snopes, who thinks he is entitled to some of the money because the mules were his. Because of the continuing dispute between the two, Snopes is eventually forced by his kinsman, Flem, to leave JEFFERSON.

Hampton, Hub (Mr.) YOKNAPATAWPHA COUNTY's sheriff. He figures out that Flem Snopes has a hand in changing Montgomery Ward Snopes's offense from running a pornographic picture shop to bootlegging, a less serious offense that has Montgomery sent to the state penitentiary at PARCHMAN. *Also see The* MANSION, INTRUDER IN THE DUST (where his first name is Hope), *The* HAMLET and *The* REIVERS (where in both novels no first name is given).

Hampton, Sally *See* Parsons, Sally Hampton.

Handy, Professor Minor African-American character in the novel. A musician from Beale Street in MEMPHIS, Professor Handy (possibly named after W. C. HANDY) and his band come to JEFFERSON to play for the Cotillion Ball at Christmas time.

Harker, Mr. A minor character in the novel. A veteran sawmill engineer, Mr. Harker runs the power plant in JEFFERSON. *Also see* the short story "CENTAUR IN BRASS," which Faulkner revised for *The Town*.

Harker, Otis A minor character in *The Town*, he is Mr. Harker's relative who runs the sawmill, a job Mr. Harker gave up for the job at the power plant. On occasion, Otis comes in to the plant when Harker wants a night off. Otis succeeds Grover Cleveland Winbush as night marshal.

Het (old Het) A minor African-American character in the novel. Het sleeps in the poorhouse during the night and travels from house to house for food scraps during the day. After the death of Mrs. Hait's husband, old Het establishes "a kind of local headquarters or advanced foraging post in Mrs. Hait's kitchen" (232). Old Het also appears in the short story "MULE IN THE YARD," which Faulkner extensively revised for *The Town*.

Hogganbeck, Boon Referred to in the novel as Lucius Hogganbeck's father and the Johannes factotum or man Friday at Major de Spain's hunting camp. *Also see* GO DOWN, MOSES ("The OLD PEOPLE," "The BEAR," and "DELTA AUTUMN"), *The REIVERS*, INTRUDER IN THE DUST, and BIG WOODS ("A BEAR HUNT").

Hogganbeck, Lucius The owner of JEFFERSON's, first Model T Ford. Roth Edmonds and perhaps Manfred de Spain sign the note that finances the car's purchase and to set up an automobile jitney service. For other details, *see The* MANSION, *The REIVERS*, and BIG WOODS ("A BEAR HUNT") where he is also referred to as Luke.

Hogganbeck, Miss Melissa Teacher of history at the Academy in JEFFERSON where Linda Snopes is a student for a year and a half, until her stepfather Flem allows her to enter the state university 50 miles away. A die-hard Confederate in whose courses history does not reach Christmas Day, 1865, Miss Melissa Hogganbeck is unwilling to admit that the South was ever defeated. *Also see* KNIGHT'S GAMBIT ("Knight's Gambit").

Holcomb, Ashley A minor character in the novel. He is one of Chick Mallison's boyhood friends. In exchange for the dollar he owes Aleck Sander, Ashley jumps from a tree.

Holston, Alexander Along with Doctor Habersham, Louis Grenier, and Vladimir Kyrilytch Ratcliffe, Alexander Holston is referred to in the novel as one of the founders of JEFFERSON. He was the proprietor of the Holston House (or Hotel) mentioned in the novel. *Also see* REQUIEM FOR A NUN, ABSALOM, ABSALOM!, *The* MANSION, INTRUDER IN THE DUST, and KNIGHT'S GAMBIT ("Hand Upon the Waters").

Houston, Jack Referred to as Zack Houston in chapter 2 of the novel, a chapter narrated by Gavin Stevens, and as Jack Houston in chapter 4 narrated by V. K. Ratliff. In the other two novels of the SNOPES TRILOGY (*The* HAMLET and *The* MANSION), the first name of this character is Jack.

Houston throws the would-be blacksmith I. O. Snopes into the cooling tub when Snopes smarts Houston's stallion with a nail as he was attempting to shoe the horse. According to Ratliff, Houston is a self-assured, proud, overbearing and morose widower. His wife, Lucy Pate, died in the first year of their marriage, killed by a stallion that Houston gave her as a wedding present. Houston was killed by Mink Snopes, one of the meanest of all Snopeses. For other details of this character, *see* especially *The Hamlet; also see* the short story "The HOUND."

Hovis, Mr. A minor character in the novel. Mr. Hovis is the cashier at Sartoris's bank where Manfred de Spain is president.

Ikkemotubbe The son of the sister of the Chickasaw chief, Issetibbeha; he is also called Doom, a corruption of *l'Homme* or *de l'Homme* (see Faulkner's appendix to *The* SOUND AND THE FURY in Appendix) or of *du homme* (see the short story "RED LEAVES"; *Du Homme* in "The OLD PEOPLE" in GO DOWN, MOSES). Doom murdered his way to becoming the Chickasaw king and, to complement his position, had a steamboat, stolen and moved 11 miles overland, remodeled as a palace. *Also see* "A JUSTICE," "A COURTSHIP," and REQUIEM FOR A NUN. He is an offstage character in *The* TOWN and in ABSALOM, ABSALOM!, Go Down, Moses, and *The REIVERS*.

Issetibbeha Referred to in the novel as the wild Chickasaw king with Negro slaves. He is Ikkemotubbe's uncle. *Also see* REQUIEM FOR A NUN, *The REIVERS*, GO DOWN, MOSES ("The OLD PEOPLE" and "The BEAR"), and the short stories "RED LEAVES" (where an Issetibbeha is Ikkemotubbe's son) and "A COURTSHIP."

Jabbo *See* Gatewood, Jabbo.

Job (old man) Referred to in the novel as being Judge Dukinfield's janitor for longer than anyone in JEFFERSON remembers. *Also see* KNIGHT'S GAMBIT ("Smoke") where he is referred to as Uncle Job.

Killegrew, Miss A minor character in the novel. She is the teller at Sartoris's bank in JEFFERSON.

Kneeland, Mr. An offstage character in *The Town*. He owns the tailor shop in JEFFERSON where the men who are going to the annual Cotillion Ball at Christmas rent their dress suits.

Ledbetter, Miz A minor offstage character in the novel. She lives in Rockyford and buys a sewing machine from V. K. Ratliff. She is also referred to in *The* MANSION.

Levitt, Matt A minor character in the novel. He is a boxer from Ohio with the reputation of having won the Golden Gloves, a reputation which, according to Gavin Stevens, is either true or invented by Levitt. After coming to JEFFERSON as a mechanic sent by Ford, he meets the 16-year-old Linda Snopes and drives her around in his racer. Jealous of any rival, Matt interprets Gavin Stevens's avuncular affections toward Linda as a threat and beats him up. After fighting Anse McCallum, whom he also beats up, he loses his job and is told by Sheriff Hamptom, who has impounded his car because of the noise it makes with the cut-out open, to leave town for good, which he does.

Littlejohn, Miz (Mrs.) The proprietor of Littlejohn's Hotel in FRENCHMAN'S BEND. The story of her fearlessly breaking a washboard over one of the escaped wild ponies auctioned off in Frenchman's Bend is retold by V. K. Ratliff in *The Town*. (For other details *see* The HAMLET; this episode is also found in FATHER ABRAHAM and "SPOTTED HORSES.") Mrs. Littlejohn also appears in "LIZARDS IN JAMSHYD'S COURTYARD." (For more information, *see Faulkner in the University*, 66.)

Long, Judge A minor character in the novel, Judge Long is the federal judge of the district that includes JEFFERSON. He sent the bootlegger Wilbur Provine of FRENCHMAN'S BEND to prison not for making whiskey but instead for letting his wife carry water over a mile from a spring to their home. *Also see The* MANSION where he sentences Montgomery Ward Snopes.

McCallum, Anse Mr. Buddy McCallum's son and a minor character in the novel. Anse twice fights the Golden Glove boxer, Matt Levitt, and loses both times. In the first fight, Anse resorts to using a fence rail but the bystanders hold them apart until Sheriff Hampton comes and puts them in jail for the night. The next day, at the insistence of his father, Anse faces Matt in a fair fight and again loses. *Also see* "The TALL MEN."

McCallum, Buddy, Mr. A minor character in the novel, he is Anse McCallum's father. Mr. Buddy McCallum becomes angry with his son for attempting to use a fence rail to fight Matt Levitt and threatens to beat him up with "his cork leg" if he does not fight fairly. When Anse gets the worst of it, Buddy ends the fight. *Also see* "The TALL MEN," INTRUDER IN THE DUST, and Buddy Mac-Callum (Virginius MacCallum, Jr.) in SARTORIS.

McCarron Referred to in the novel, McCarron is Linda Snopes's biological father. V. K. Ratliff retells the story of the night five FRENCHMAN'S BEND boys attacked McCarron when he and Eula Varner were riding together in his buggy. Rivals for her affection, they did not succeed in winning her, but they did succeed in fracturing McCarron's arm. It was that same night, according to Ratliff, that Eula conceived Linda. For other details, *see The* HAMLET and *The* MANSION.

McCaslin, Uncle Ike An offstage character in the novel, McCaslin owns the hardware store in JEFFERSON that Manfred de Spain refers to when challenging Mayor Adams and his son, Theron, to defend their desperate accusations about how de Spain got the scar on his face. McCaslin is also referred to as Roth Edmonds's uncle and as one of the men who frequented Major de Spain's old hunting camp. *Also see* GO DOWN, MOSES, *The* HAMLET, *The* MANSION, INTRUDER IN THE DUST, *The* REIVERS, "A BEAR HUNT," *and* "RACE AT MORNING"; in these works, he is referred to as Isaac McCaslin, Uncle Isaac McCaslin, Cousin Isaac, or Cousin Ike.

McGowan, Skeets A minor character in the novel, Skeets is the clerk and soda-jerker in Uncle Willy Christian's drugstore in JEFFERSON. *Also see* AS I LAY DYING (where his name appears as Skeet Mac-Gowan), *The* MANSION, *and* INTRUDER IN THE DUST.

McLendon, Jackson (Captain McLendon) Referred to in the novel as having organized a JEFFERSON company of soldiers during World War I. *Also see* LIGHT IN AUGUST, *The* MANSION, *and the short story* "DRY SEPTEMBER."

Mallison, Chick (Charles Mallison, Jr.) Gavin Stevens's young nephew and an emerging opponent of SNOPESISM. Chick narrates nine of the 24 chapters of *The Town* (1, 3, 7, 10, 12, 14, 16, 19, 24), all of which contain the heading Charles Mallison. An astute and attentive listener, some of what he recounts occurred before he was even born but was heard secondhand from either his uncle Gavin or cousin Gowan Stevens. In a few passages, Chick provides insights—at times humorous—into his uncle's personality. *Also see* INTRUDER IN THE DUST, KNIGHT'S GAMBIT, *The* MANSION, *and the short stories* "HOG PAWN" (revised for *The Mansion*), *and* "A Name for the City" (revised for REQUIEM FOR A NUN).

Mallison, Charles, Sr. A minor character in the novel, he is Chick Mallison's father and Gavin Stevens's brother-in-law, whom he often kids. Charles questions the motive behind the invitation sent by his wife and the Cotillion Club committee to Manfred de Spain to attend the Christmas Ball. Knowing that a problem will most likely occur, Charles blames his wife and the other women for instigating it. *Also see* INTRUDER IN THE DUST.

Mallison, Margaret (Maggie) Married to Charles Mallison, Sr., Maggie is Chick's mother and Gavin Stevens's twin sister. Over her brother's objection, Maggie and the committee members of the Cotillion Club send Manfred de Spain an invitation to the Christmas Ball. *Also see* INTRUDER IN THE DUST, KNIGHT'S GAMBIT, *and* REQUIEM FOR A NUN.

Nunnery, Cedric A minor character in the novel. He is a five-year-old child who gets lost. With a lighted lantern, Eck Snopes foolishly looks for him in an empty oil tank. Though the child is not there, Eck kills himself when the tank containing gaseous fumes blows up.

Nunnery, Mrs. A minor character in the novel, she is Cedric Nunnery's mother.

Parsons, Maurice A minor character in the novel, he gives both his wife (Sally Hampton Parsons) and Grenier Weddel a black eye because of the corsage Grenier sent to Sally for the Cotillion Ball at Christmas time. (In the 1957 RANDOM HOUSE edition of *The Town*, this character's name is Maurice Priest, but it was changed to Parsons in the 1961 Vintage edition.)

Parsons, Sally Hampton (Mrs. Maurice Parsons) A minor character, she receives a black eye from her husband after accepting a corsage from Grenier Weddel for the Cotillion Ball at Christmas. (In the 1957 RANDOM HOUSE edition of *The Town*, this character's last name is Priest, but it was changed to Parsons in the 1961 Vintage edition.)

Pate, Lucy A minor offstage character referred to in the novel. She died within the first year of her marriage to Jack Houston, killed by the stallion he gave her as a wedding gift. *Also see The* HAMLET. (In editions prior to the 1961 Vintage paperback edition of *The Town*, her name is Letty Bookwright, the youngest daughter of Cal Bookwright.)

Peabody, Doctor (Doc Peabody) A minor character in the novel, Doctor Peabody is a long-time physician in JEFFERSON, with an office above

Uncle Willy Christian's drugstore. When the drugstore is robbed and, among other things, all of Uncle Willy's morphine taken, Doctor Peabody is immediately called to give him an injection that settles him down. For other details regarding Doctor Peabody, *see* SARTORIS, *The* SOUND AND THE FURY, *As I* LAY DYING, *The* HAMLET, *The* REIVERS, and "Beyond." (Because of an age discrepancy, the Doctor Peabody who appears in REQUIEM FOR A NUN cannot be the same character who appears in *The Town*.)

Provine, Wilbur   A minor character in the novel. Not able to prove that Provine makes whiskey illegally, Judge Long instead sends him to prison for making his wife walk a mile and a half for water.

Quistenbery, Dink   A minor character in the novel. Dink married one of Flem Snopes's sisters or relatives from FRENCHMAN'S BEND. When Flem sends I. O. Snopes back to the country for his dealings with Mrs. Hait, Dink and his wife take over the Jefferson Hotel, which was formerly called the Snopes Hotel. Dink puts Byron Snopes's wild children up at this hotel for a brief time.

Ratliff, V. K. (Vladimir Kyrilytch)   One of the major characters and narrators in *The Town* and in the other two novels that comprise the SNOPES TRILOGY, *The* HAMLET and *The* MANSION. In *The Town*, Ratliff narrates chapters 4, 6, 9, 11, 18, and 23, and along with the idealistic Gavin Stevens opposes SNOPESISM, although neither he nor Stevens can do much to stop Flem Snopes's financial success at the expense of others and his rise to the presidency of the Sartoris Bank. The ever-perceptive Ratliff is well aware of the motive behind Flem's rapacity is, a relentless desire to gain respectability. Ratliff is the amiable itinerant sewing machine salesman who travels throughout the region, a keen observer of human nature, and a source of news throughout YOKNAPATAWPHA and the surrounding counties. His narrative is punctuated with local color and humor. *Also see* BIG WOODS ("A BEAR HUNT").

Ratliff appears under an earlier name, V. K. Suratt, in "LIZARDS IN JAMSHYD'S COURTYARD,"

"CENTAUR IN BRASS," SARTORIS, and *As I* LAY DYING. For other details regarding Ratliff, *see* especially *The Hamlet* and *The Mansion*.

Renfrow   A minor character in the novel. After being fired from the restaurant by Flem Snopes, Eck Snopes becomes the night watchman at Renfrow's oil tank at the depot.

Riddell   A family name referred to in *The Town*. The Riddell boy is an offstage character who catches polio, causing the school to be closed. His father is one of the engineers or contractors who helped pave the streets in JEFFERSON.

Roebuck, John Wesley   A minor character in the novel. He is one of young Chick Mallison's boyhood friends. For breaking into Ab Snopes's watermelon patch, John Wesley was shot in the back. Later, as a game he puts on two hunting coats and wraps a sweater around his neck to see if he can outrun the Number Six shot from Aleck Sander's gun. Although John Wesley is not hurt, Chick's hunting jacket is ruined.

Rouncewell, Mrs.   She runs the florist shop in JEFFERSON and does very well selling flowers for the Cotillion Club Christmas Ball. *Also see The* MANSION, *The* REIVERS, and KNIGHT'S GAMBIT ("Tomorrow").

Rouncewell, Whit   The boy who saw two fellows robbing Uncle Willy Christian's drugstore. *Also see The* MANSION where he is referred to as "the Rouncewell boy"; he may be Mrs. Rouncewell's son.

Samson   A minor character in the novel. Samson is the hotel porter who carries the small valise (or "grip," as it is referred to in the novel) belonging to one of the bondsmen present at Gavin Stevens's suit against Mayor de Spain.

Sander, Aleck   Chick Mallison's friend. An African American, Aleck is the son of Big Top and Guster Sander. *Also see* INTRUDER IN THE DUST.

Sander, Big Top A minor African-American character in the novel. Married to Guster, Big Top is Little Top and Aleck's father.

Sander, Guster Big Top's wife and Aleck and Little Top's mother. She is a minor African-American character in the novel. Guster cooks for Chick Mallison's mother.

Sander, Little Top A minor African-American character in the novel. Little Top is Aleck's older brother. Together with Gowan Stevens, Little Top scatters tacks on the street to puncture Manfred de Spain's car tires, a ploy designed by Gowan's older cousin, Gavin, who is annoyed by the noise that de Spain intentionally makes with his car as he races by Stevens's home.

Sartoris, Bayard (young) Colonel (Bayard) Sartoris's restless grandson. Bayard's fast and reckless driving through the YOKNAPATAWPHA COUNTY countryside leads to the death of his grandfather, whose weak heart gives out during the ride. For more information regarding young Bayard Sartoris *see* especially SARTORIS; *also see The* MANSION and the short stories "AD ASTRA" and "THERE WAS A QUEEN."

Sartoris, Benbow The son of (young) Bayard Sartoris and Narcissa Benbow Sartoris. He is a minor offstage character referred to in the novel. *Also see* SARTORIS, *The* MANSION, SANCTUARY, KNIGHT'S GAMBIT, and the short story "THERE WAS A QUEEN."

Sartoris, Colonel A banker, Colonel Sartoris (old Bayard Sartoris) is Colonel John Sartoris's son. Though not literally a colonel, Sartoris received the title out of deference to his father. When the first auto in JEFFERSON frightens Colonel Sartoris's team of horses, he has Mayor Adams pass an edict against the use of "gasoline-propelled vehicles." Change triumphs, however, and, ironically, Colonel Sartoris dies of a heart attack while riding in a car recklessly driven by his grandson, young Bayard. *Also see* SARTORIS, *The* UNVANQUISHED, *The* HAM-

LET, GO DOWN, MOSES ("The BEAR"), REQUIEM FOR A NUN, *The* MANSION, *The* REIVERS, and the short stories "A ROSE FOR EMILY" and "THERE WAS A QUEEN."

Sartoris, Colonel, John An offstage character, he is Colonel (Bayard) Sartoris's father. His first name, John, is not used in *The Town*. The horse thief Ab Snopes was in Colonel (John) Sartoris's cavalry command in 1864. For other details concerning Colonel (John) Sartoris, *see* SARTORIS, *The* SOUND AND THE FURY, LIGHT IN AUGUST, ABSALOM, ABSALOM!, *The* UNVANQUISHED, *The* HAMLET, GO DOWN, MOSES ("The BEAR"), REQUIEM FOR A NUN, *The* MANSION, *The* REIVERS, and the short stories "BARN BURNING," "SHALL NOT PERISH," "MY GRANDMOTHER MILLARD AND GENERAL BEDFORD FORREST AND THE BATTLE OF HARRYKIN CREEK," and "THERE WAS A QUEEN."

Sartoris, Narcissa Benbow An offstage character referred to in the novel, she is (young) Bayard Sartoris's wife. Hoping that marriage would settle Bayard down, Bayard's grandfather, Colonel (Bayard) Sartoris, and great-aunt, Mrs. Du Pre, persuade Narcissa to marry him, but their ploy was not successful. For other information regarding this character, *see* SARTORIS, SANCTUARY, and the short story "THERE WAS A QUEEN."

Snopes Described as looking like John Brown, he is the father of two sons, Byron and Virgil, and the schoolmaster I. O. Snopes replaces. He did not last long as schoolmaster; he came and went during the same summer. An active participant in Sunday revival services that take place throughout the countryside, he was tarred, feathered, and run out by enraged fathers who caught him with a 14-year-old girl in a cotton house. (*See The* MANSION where this character appears as Wesley Snopes.)

Snopes, Ab Flem Snopes's father and one of the first Snopeses to move into FRENCHMAN'S BEND. Before moving on to the JEFFERSON area, Ab (a tenant farmer) and his son rented a little farm from Will Varner. In *The Town*, Ab lives near Jefferson and tries to keep boys away from his watermelon patch. One night, in his spiteful determination to protect his watermelons, Ab shoots a boy named John Wesley Roebuck with squirrel shot. The next morning, Sheriff Hub Hampston tells Snopes he will go to jail if he ever uses the shotgun again. During the Civil War, Ab, a member of the cavalry command of Colonel (John) Sartoris, was a horse thief who stole from both the Union and Confederate armies. Reputedly, Ab had been hanged. For other details relating to Ab Snopes, *see The* HAMLET, *The* UNVANQUISHED, *The* MANSION, and the short stories "BARN BURNING" and "MY GRANDMOTHER MILLARD AND GENERAL BEDFORD FORREST AND THE BATTLE OF HARRYKIN CREEK"; *also see Faulkner in the University*, 250.

Snopes, Admiral Dewey Eck Snopes's son and Wallstreet Panic's younger brother. These three are non-typical Snopeses in the sense that they are not greedy but kindhearted. *Also see The* MANSION and *FATHER* ABRAHAM.

Snopes, Bilbo A minor character in the novel. He is one of I. O. Snopes's twin sons by his second wife, although I. O. is not divorced from his first wife. Vardaman is Bilbo's twin and Clarence his older brother. *Also see The* MANSION.

Snopes, Byron A minor character in the novel. The brother of Virgil Snopes, Byron is the son of a Snopes said to look like a schoolmaster or John Brown (*see* above the entry on Snopes without a first name). With the approval and support of Colonel (Bayard) Sartoris, Byron attends a business college in MEMPHIS and then gets a job as a bookkeeper in the Sartoris Bank. During World War I, Byron was drafted but within a few weeks at the request of the army physicians was discharged because of an accelerated heartbeat that he caused by taping chewing tobacco into his left armpit every night before going to bed. After returning to his job as a bookkeeper, Byron robs the bank and flees to Mexico where he lives for several years before sending his four wild children to Flem Snopes in JEFFERSON. Flem takes the children to FRENCHMAN'S

BEND where they stay for about a week with Dewitt Binford, the husband of a Snopes. The children's wild behavior is so intolerable that they are sent back to Byron. This episode is mentioned in *The* MANSION. Although his name is not used, Byron's theft is referred to in "THERE WAS A QUEEN" when, years later, Narcissa is relating the story (*Collected Stories*, 739). *Also see* SARTORIS.

Snopes, Clarence Eggleston A minor character in the novel, Clarence is I. O. Snopes's oldest son by his second wife (although he was not at the time divorced from his first wife) and brother of twins, Bilbo and Vardaman, and Doris. He is a state senator from YOKNAPATAWPHA COUNTY—Senator C. Eggleston Snopes, as Chick Mallison (in the 1961 Vintage edition of *The Town*) refers to him at one point in chapter 24. (In the 1957 Random House edition of the novel, Clarence attempts to train his brother Byron's four wild children and treats them like dogs until one day they tie him to a sapling and almost roast him alive. In the 1961 Vintage edition of *The Town*, Doris Snopes, Clarence's younger brother, tries to train Byron's wild children and is the one who is almost burned alive; *The* MANSION contains this account of the details.) Clarence also appears in SANCTUARY and the short story "BY THE PEOPLE" (which Faulkner revised for *The Mansion*).

Snopes, Doris A minor character in the novel, Doris is the 17-year-old younger brother of Clarence Eggleston Snopes, who lives in FRENCHMAN'S BEND. He is described as looking almost exactly like Clarence, but with a child's mentality and an animal's moral sense. When he takes in Byron Snopes's four unruly children he intends to train them to hunt in a pack, but does not succeed. The children, however, almost succeed in burning Doris alive when they tie him to a sapling and set ablaze a cord of wood stacked around him. He is rescued at the last minute when his mother runs for help after hearing his screams. This episode is also recounted in *The* MANSION. (Prior to the 1961 Vintage edition of *The Town*, it is Clarence, and not Doris, who is tied to the sapling and almost burned to death.)

Snopes, Eck One of the only three or four honest, kindhearted, and considerate Snopeses. According to Gavin Stevens, without a doubt Eck is not a Snopes because he does not share the Snopeses' dishonesty and rapacious traits. (*Also see* Montgomery Ward Snopes's comment in *The* MANSION, 83, where he does not consider Eck and his two sons, Wallstreet and Admiral Dewey, to be real Snopeses.) In *The Town*, Eck arrives in JEFFERSON wearing a neck brace because of an accident at Will Varner's sawmill, the result of preventing a cypress log from falling on a black man. He first takes Flem's place in Flem's sidestreet restaurant, and then, after he is fired for being honest, he works as the night watchman of an oil tank until he blows himself up looking for the five-year-old Cedric Nunnery. Eck foolishly lowers a lighted lantern into an oil tank that he thinks is fully emptied of its gas. The only part of him that was ever found was the neck brace. *Also see* FATHER ABRAHAM, *The* HAMLET, *The* MANSION, and "SPOTTED HORSES."

Snopes, Eula Varner One of the main characters in the novel. Eula is Flem Snopes's wife and, by another man, (Hoake) McCarron, Linda Snopes's mother. After marrying Flem and moving from FRENCHMAN'S BEND to JEFFERSON with her daughter (*see The* HAMLET), Eula becomes Mayor Manfred de Spain's mistress, and each year she and her daughter vacation together with him. In her 18-year affair with de Spain, Eula is faithful until she attempts to bribe the city attorney, Gavin Stevens, by offering herself to him in an attempt to stop a city investigation of her husband's guilt in the theft of the missing brass fittings from Jefferson's power plant. But the honorable and innocent Gavin Stevens rejects the advance. Although Eula may have been sent by her husband, her motive for offering the bribe—and later, for her suicide—is to protect her daughter from shame. To spare Linda from the disgrace that would have been caused by running off with de Spain, Eula kills herself. The inscription on her ornate tombstone, an adaptation from the Book of Proverbs (12:4 and 31:28), was chosen by Flem and reads:

A Virtuous Wife Is a Crown to Her Husband
Her Children Rise and Call Her Blessed.

In *The Town*, Eula's relationship with Gavin Stevens is at once honest and complicated. Knowing that he is a gentleman, an intelligent, cultured man of high principles and morals, she confides in him on several occasions, and at one point even asks him to promise to marry Linda. Gavin assures her that he will, if things do not work out for her daughter. In these conversations with Stevens, Eula also tells him about Flem's impotence and about his manipulative plans to fleece money from Linda's inheritance.

Eula is a complex and beautiful woman, tragically confined by circumstances that overcome her will to live. In this novel, she is referred to as Helen, Semiramis, and Lilith, figures of immense attraction, sexual power, and beauty. She is "larger than life," Faulkner once commented, and no one place could hold her, neither Frenchman's Bend nor Jefferson (*see Faulkner in the University*, 31; for other details concerning Eula, see 108, 115–116, and 118–119). *Also see The Hamlet*, FATHER ABRAHAM and the short story "SPOTTED HORSES"; Eula is referred to in the third novel of the SNOPES TRILOGY, *The* MANSION.

Snopes, Flem A central figure in this and the other two novels, *The* HAMLET and *The* MANSION, that make up the SNOPES TRILOGY. Married to Eula Varner, the sexually impotent, and the most financially successful Snopes, Flem exploits his wife's 18-year love affair with Manfred de Spain to achieve his greedy ambitions. Much of the novel's narrative focus concentrates on Flem and his schemes. The son of the sharecropper Ab Snopes, Flem begins his rise to power in FRENCHMAN'S BEND (*see The Hamlet*). After marrying Eula, he moves with her and her infant daughter, Linda, a child by another man, (Hoake) McCarron, to JEFFERSON where he advances from working in the sidestreet restaurant that he owns in partnership with Grover Cleveland Winbush to the presidency of the Sartoris Bank. After leaving the restaurant, he becomes the superintendent of the town's power plant, a job created for him by de Spain, and stays in that position until auditors find that the brass safety valves for the boilers are missing. Flem ends up having to pay for them. All along Flem is purchasing stock in the Sartoris Bank, and when Colonel (Bayard) Sartoris dies, Flem becomes the bank's vice president. At this point, as Ratliff perceptively suspects, Flem is eyeing the president's job. In order to secure that position, and to take revenge on his wife and her lover, Flem reveals to Eula's father the affair she is having with Manfred. Eula's daughter, Linda, is not beyond the pale of Flem's rapacity; he succeeds in gaining her affections and in having her sign over to him her inheritance. Eula's father, Will Varner, is outraged by his daughter's behavior and, holding much of the bank stock, agrees to force Manfred out as president to be replaced by Flem. *Also see* SARTORIS, *The Hamlet, The Mansion,* FATHER ABRAHAM, "SPOTTED HORSES," "CENTAUR IN BRASS," and "LIZARDS IN JAMSHYD'S COURTYARD." Flem is also referred to in As I LAY DYING and *The* REIVERS.

Snopes, I. O. A minor character in the novel, I. O. looks like a weasel and talks incessantly, mostly in garbled and worn out proverbs. He fails in working behind the counter in Flem Snopes's restaurant; he fails as a blacksmith, angering Zack Houston to the point of throwing him into the cooling tub, and he fails as a schoolmaster. But he is successful at being a bigamist. I. O. is the father of several children, a five-year-old boy by his "first" wife, Montgomery Ward, and of Clarence, the twins Vardaman and Bilbo, and Doris by his "second" wife. Like other Snopeses, I. O. is a conniver; his scheme to have mules killed on the railroad tracks to collect insurance money lasts until his partner Lonzo Hait is also killed. Thinking he should be compensated by Hait's widow for lost money, I. O. expects to be paid, but she outwits him. Flem, to preserve his own respectability, gives I. O. some money under the condition that he leave Jefferson for good. *Also see The* SOUND AND THE FURY, *The* HAMLET, FATHER ABRAHAM, and the short stories "SPOTTED HORSES" and "MULE IN THE YARD." He is also referred to in *The* MANSION.

Of I. O.'s two wives only his second wife is referred to as Miz I. O. Snopes. The first wife arrives in FRENCHMAN'S BEND when I. O. is schoolmaster and married to his second wife, a Frenchman's Bend belle and niece of Mrs. Vernon Tull's sister. Miz Snopes, the second wife, calls for help when Doris, tied to a sapling, is almost burned alive by Byron Snopes's unruly children.

Snopes, Linda The daughter of Eula Varner Snopes and (Hoake) McCarron (*see The* HAMLET). Linda was born after her mother married Flem Snopes and grows up in JEFFERSON, assuming until her late teens that Flem is her father. During her high school days, the romantic Gavin Stevens, in an ostensibly avuncular manner, treats Linda to ice-cream sodas after school and takes a strong interest in her education and reading, especially in the area of poetry. When graduating from high school, she is the valedictorian of her class. At first Flem forbids her to go away to college, allowing her only to attend the Academy in Jefferson. When he later permits her to attend the university 40 miles away, she is so grateful that she cries in his arms and for the first time calls him "Daddy"; she also signs over her inheritance to him. Soon after her mother commits suicide in 1927, Linda moves to Greenwich Village. *Also see The* MANSION and *The Hamlet* where she is an infant.

Snopes, Mink The meanest of all Snopeses, according to V. K. Ratliff, and his meanness was for no gain. After killing Jack Houston and before being sent off to the state penitentiary at PARCHMAN, Mink spends eight months in jail in JEFFERSON vainly waiting for his kinsman Flem to come to his rescue, but Flem avoids him. (For other details relating to Mink, *see The* HAMLET and *The* MANSION; and *also see* Faulkner's comment in *Faulkner in the University*, 262).

Snopes, Miz I. O. *See* Snopes, I. O.

Snopes, Montgomery Ward He is the eldest child of the bigamist I. O. Snopes and his first wife. (I. O. is not divorced before marrying a second wife.) While in France during World War I, Montgomery Ward runs a YMCA canteen, part of which he converts into a night club and employs a French woman to entertain the troops. When he comes back from the war, he opens a photography shop that is a front to show French pornographic postcards. To protect his family name, Flem Snopes has Montgomery Ward arrested, but not for pornography; Flem plants moonshine liquor in the photography shop for which Montgomery Ward is arrested and sent to the prison at PARCHMAN. *Also see The* MANSION *and* SARTORIS; in the latter novel Montgomery Ward leaves for France with Horace Benbow, but in *The Town* he leaves with Gavin Stevens.

Snopes, Mrs. Eck A minor character in the novel, she is Eck Snopes's wife and the landlady of a boardinghouse in JEFFERSON. After her husband Eck dies by accidently blowing himself up in an oil tank, the oil company pays her $1,000 which she uses to help her son Wallstreet buy a half interest in a grocery store.

Snopes, Mrs. Flem *See* Snopes, Eula Varner.

Snopes, Vardaman A minor character in the novel, Vardaman is I. O. Snopes's son by his second wife. (I. O. is still married to his first wife at the time.) Vardaman is Bilbo's twin, Clarence's younger brother, and Doris's older brother. *Also see The* MANSION.

Snopes, Virgil An offstage character referred to in the novel. Byron's brother, Virgil is the son of the schoolmaster Snopes, who looks like John Brown (*see* the entry on Snopes without a first name). *Also see* SANCTUARY *and The* MANSION.

Snopes, Wallstreet Panic (Wall) Eck Snopes's son and, like his father, he is not a typical Snopes, mean, exploitative, or greedy. Wallstreet, however, is ambitious and also studious. With the help of his teacher, Miss Vaiden Wyott, who had explained the meaning of his name and mentioned that he did not have to keep it, Wallstreet changes his name simply to Wall Snopes by the time he enters the fourth grade. With the money he received from the oil company, as compensation for his father's death ($1,000), Wallstreet, through hard work, determination and honesty, becomes part owner of a backstreet grocery store where he has been a clerk and errand boy. He saves his money, and after the original owner's death, buys the store, which he runs very successfully with his wife. Although one time he almost loses the business when he overbuys, he and his wife both know enough not to borrow from the manipulative Flem Snopes. Eventually they own a small chain of grocery stores throughout north Mississippi. *Also see The* HAMLET *and The* MANSION.

Spilmer, Mr. A minor character in the novel. Mr. Spilmer is a farmer and one of Mrs. Hait's neighbors. Mrs. Hait ties a mule to a tree in a ravine behind his house. *Also see* the short story "MULE IN THE YARD," which Faulkner extensively revised for chapter 16 of *The Town*.

Stevens, Gavin A major character in the novel. Partly modeled on Faulkner's longtime friend PHILIP AVERY STONE, Gavin is an attorney from a prominent family in JEFFERSON and after his return from World War I becomes county attorney. He is Judge Lemuel Stevens's son, Margaret Stevens Mallison's twin, and Chick Mallison's uncle, on whom Gavin has a considerable influence. Jefferson's "intellectual," Gavin is a Phi Beta Kappa with a master's degree from HARVARD UNIVERSITY, a doctorate from Heidelberg University in Germany, and a law degree from the UNIVERSITY OF MISSISSIPPI. During World War I, he served in the American Field Service and YMCA in France from 1915 through 1918, and his professional positions at one time or another also include city attorney (after his father retired from the position) and district attorney. Gavin narrates chapters 2, 5, 8, 13, 15, 17, 20 and 22 of the novel.

A romantic and an idealist, Gavin can at times appear foolish to those around him, especially to his sister. For example, when he defends the honor of the married Eula Varner Snopes, whose dancing with Manfred de Spain shocks onlookers, he gets his face bloodied by Manfred. What Gavin seems to be doing here, according to his nephew Chick, is defending the ideal of women's chastity and virtue. Throughout *The Town* (and *The* MANSION)

Gavin is preoccupied with preventing the spread of SNOPESISM. As part of this mission, he takes an active interest in the education of Eula's teenage daughter Linda by discussing poetry with her and giving her college catalogues to help her choose a college to attend. Although Gavin's interest in Linda may be an unconscious sublimation of his romantic feelings for her mother, he shows such genuine and singular kindness toward the daughter that after Eula's suicide his friend and ally against Snopesism, V. K. Ratliff, half-jokingly suggests that he marry Linda. Gavin, of course, does not.

Also see KNIGHT'S GAMBIT, INTRUDER IN THE DUST, REQUIEM FOR A NUN, and *The Mansion;* Gavin Stevens also appears in LIGHT IN AUGUST, "HAIR," GO DOWN, MOSES ("Go Down, Moses"), "The TALL MEN," "HOG PAWN," and "BY THE PEOPLE." Some readers may see Gavin Stevens as Faulkner's mouthpiece, particularly in *Intruder in the Dust,* but such an assumption cannot be justified. Faulkner was too skilled an artist to identify with his characters, even though some of their sentiments may echo his. For more information regarding Gavin Stevens, *see Faulkner in the University,* 25, 72, 118, 140–141 and 201; and James Farnham's "Faulkner's Unsung Hero: Gavin Stevens" in *Arizona Quarterly* (summer 1965), 115–132, where Farnham discusses Stevens's significance in the SNOPES TRILOGY and how, by the end of *The Mansion,* he becomes a realist in his view of humanity. Horace Benbow, Gavin's precursor, shares a similar educational background and other personal characteristics.

Stevens, Gowan Chick Mallison's first cousin once removed (their grandfathers are brothers) and Gavin Stevens's 13-year-old cousin. For a time growing up, Gowan lives with the Mallisons and goes to school in JEFFERSON; this period in his life is when his father, who works for the State Department, is sent to the Far East. Gowan is one of Chick's primary sources of information on the early events surrounding Flem Snopes and his wife Eula; these events, which took place before Chick was born, are recounted by him in *The Town.* (In the opening lines of the novel, Chick explains his indebtedness to Gowan and to his uncle Gavin.) *Also see* SANCTUARY and REQUIEM FOR A NUN. In *Requiem* Gowan is Gavin's nephew; Faulkner is not always consistent with some of his characters.

Stevens, Judge Lemuel Father of the twins Gavin Stevens and Margaret (Maggie) Stevens Mallison. A minor character in the novel, Judge Stevens is designated by Judge Dukinfield, who recuses himself, to preside over the case of the missing brass fittings that Gavin, the city attorney, brings against Mayor Manfred de Spain. (This episode is also referred to in *The* MANSION, the third volume of the SNOPES TRILOGY.) *Also see* Judge Stevens in *The Mansion* and *The* REIVERS and Captain Stevens in KNIGHT'S GAMBIT ("Tomorrow").

Stone, Mr. The OXFORD, MISSISSIPPI, attorney whom Linda Snopes consults to relinquish her inheritance to Flem Snopes.

Thorndyke, Mr. An Episcopal clergyman in JEFFERSON. With three other preachers (a Methodist, a Baptist, and a Presbyterian), he visits Gavin Stevens. The oldest of the four men, the Presbyterian, who does the talking, suggests that either one or all four ministers conduct Eula Varner Snopes's funeral service. The offer, which angers Stevens, who sees through it as a gesture of self-righteousness to forgive Eula of her suicide, is adamantly turned down. Stevens says point blank that their mission is not to bury but to forgive Eula and says that he plans to conduct the funeral service himself.

Tom A farmer briefly referred to in the novel. Tom is one of Colonel (old Bayard) Sartoris's customers at the bank. Legend has it that Tom gave the colonel an undecipherable note that the colonel himself had previously drawn up. Since neither one of them could read what was scribbled on it, the colonel ripped it up and wrote out another note.

Trumbull An old blacksmith in FRENCHMAN'S BEND. For 50 years, he ran Will Varner's blacksmith shop until it was taken over by Eck Snopes and the incompetent I. O. Snopes, the bigamist. When I. O. departs Frenchman's Bend, Flem Snopes gets Trumbull to go back to Varner to run the blacksmith shop. *Also see The* HAMLET.

Tull, Miz Vernon   Vernon Tull's wife. Her sister's niece by marriage is the bigamist I. O. Snopes's "second" wife. *Also see The* HAMLET and Cora Tull in *As I Lay Dying,* and the short story "SPOTTED HORSES."

Tull, Vernon   A farmer in the FRENCHMAN'S BEND area. Dewitt Binford borrows a flashlight from Tull to spy on Byron Snopes's four unruly children whom Dewitt took into his house. *Also see As I Lay Dying, Sanctuary, The Hamlet, The Mansion,* and the short stories "SPOTTED HORSES," "THE HOUND," "LIZARDS IN JAMSHYD'S COURTYARD," "TWO SOLDIERS," and "SHINGLES FOR THE LORD."

Varner, Jody   Will Varner's son and Eula Varner Snopes's older brother. *Also see As I Lay Dying, Light in August, The Hamlet, The Mansion,* and the short stories "FOOL ABOUT A HORSE" and "SPOTTED HORSES."

Varner, Mrs. (Miz)   Will Varner's wife, the mother of Jody and Eula Varner Snopes, and Linda Snopes's grandmother. *Also see The* HAMLET and *Father Abraham.*

Varner, Will (Uncle Billy)   Eula Varner Snopes's father and the grandfather of Linda Snopes; Jody Varner is his son. A landowner and business man, Varner, among other things, owns the country store in FRENCHMAN'S BEND where Flem Snopes was a clerk and got his start, the farm that Flem's father Ab rented, and the blacksmith shop. (For other details regarding Varner's business and county activities, *see* his entry under *The* HAMLET.) Varner owns one of the three biggest blocks of stock in Colonel (old Bayard) Sartoris's bank in JEFFERSON, making it possible for his son-in-law Flem to become the bank's president when Manfred de Spain is forced to resign. When Varner learns that Manfred and Eula have had a long-term love affair and that his granddaughter Linda has

signed over her inheritance to Flem (whom Varner has purposely kept out of his will), he becomes so enraged that at four o'clock in the morning he charges into Jefferson to have it out with Eula, Flem, and de Spain. Although he never forgives Flem for the large profit he had made with the OLD FRENCHMAN PLACE (a motive to leave Flem out of his will), Varner, for practical reasons, agrees to having Flem become president of the bank. But Manfred's intention to leave Jefferson with Eula comes to naught when she commits suicide. *Also see The* MANSION, LIGHT IN AUGUST, INTRUDER IN THE DUST, KNIGHT'S GAMBIT ("Tomorrow"), *As I Lay Dying,* and the short stories "SPOTTED HORSES," "LIZARDS IN JAMSHYD'S COURTYARD," "SHINGLES FOR THE LORD," and "BY THE PEOPLE"; his store is referred to in "FOOL ABOUT A HORSE" and "THE HOUND."

Weddel, Grenier   A bachelor whose marriage proposal is rejected by Sally Hampton. She marries Maurice Parsons instead. Grenier, nonetheless, sends married Sally a large corsage for the annual Christmas dance. Although she does not wear it, her husband is perturbed enough to give Grenier, and later his wife, a black eye.

Widrington, Mrs.   A minor character in the novel. She comes to JEFFERSON with her wealthy contractor husband and an expensive Pekinese with a gold nameplate on its collar. When the dog is missing, Mrs. Widrington offers a reward in the newspapers. The dog is stolen and killed by Byron Snopes's four half-breed Jircarill Apache Indian children.

Wildermark   Owns the department store in JEFFERSON where Gavin Stevens buys a suitcase for Linda Snopes, who is graduating from high school. Mrs. Mannie Hait buys old-fashioned shoes from Wildermark, which he orders once a year for her.

Wildermark, Mr. (senior)   Referred to as the senior Mr. Wildermark in the novel. The relationship between him and the owner of the department store is not specified. This Wildermark is beaten in chess by Doctor Wyott.

Winbush, Grover Cleveland   Part owner of a sidestreet restaurant in JEFFERSON. He becomes Jefferson's night marshal after his partner Flem Snopes forces him out of the business. When the town's drugstore is robbed, Grover Cleveland Winbush is fired for not being on duty. Instead of patrolling the streets, he was at one of Montgomery Ward Snopes's peep shows. He later becomes a night watchman at a brick yard. *Also see The MANSION.* (In *The HAMLET*, Aaron Rideout, and not Grover Cleveland Winbush, owns half the restaurant with his cousin V. K. Ratliff before the latter is compelled to sell his portion to Flem.)

Wyott, Doctor   The 80-year-old president emeritus of the Academy in JEFFERSON founded by his grandfather. Doctor Wyott is able to read Greek, Hebrew, and Sanskrit. An atheist for more than 60 years, he wears two foreign decorations to publicly display his beliefs. Doctor Wyott has beaten the senior Mr. Wildermark, an apparently accomplished chess player, at the game.

Wyott, Miss Vaiden   A minor character in the novel. Wallstreet Panic Snopes's elementary school teacher in JEFFERSON, Miss Wyott—Miss Vaiden as the children address her—helps Wallstreet during the summer to pass the third grade, and at her suggestion, he changes his name to Wall Snopes upon entering the fourth grade. Grateful for her help, he asks her to marry him after he graduates from high school, but, sensitive to his feelings, she declines, telling him she is already engaged. Before she leaves to teach in a school in Bristol, Virginia, Miss Vaiden arranges for him to meet the girl he later marries.

FICTIONAL PLACES

Sartoris Station   Fictional name of College Hill Station, a flag stop on the railroad four miles north of OXFORD, MISSISSIPPI. Lying two and a half miles from SEMINARY HILL (Faulkner's name for College Hill), Sartoris Station figures in *The Town.*

Seminary Hill   Faulkner's name for the hamlet of College Hill, a once exclusively Presbyterian settlement five miles north of OXFORD, MISSISSIPPI.

Faulkner peoples Seminary Hill with Baptists and Methodists. In *The Town,* Gavin Stevens drives out to Seminary Hill to Mr. Garraway's store to eat cheese and crackers and listen to old Garraway abuse Calvin Coolidge.

FURTHER READING

Beck, Warren. *Man in Motion: Faulkner's Trilogy.* Madison: University of Wisconsin Press, 1961.
Brooks, Cleanth. "Passion, Marriage, and Bourgeois Respectability (*The Town*)." In *William Faulkner: The Yoknapatawpha Country,* 192–218. Baton Rouge: Louisiana State University Press, 1990.
Horton, Merrill. *Annotations to William Faulkner's* The Town. New York: Garland, 1996.
Marcus, Steven. "Snopes Revisited." In *William Faulkner: Three Decades of Criticism,* edited by Frederick J. Hoffman and Olga W. Vickery, 282–391. New York: Harbinger, 1963.
Millgate, Michael. "*The Town.*" In *The Achievement of William Faulkner,* 234–244. Lincoln: University of Nebraska Press, 1978.
Polk, Noel. "Faulkner and Respectability." In *Fifty Years of Yoknapatawpha: Faulkner and Yoknapatawpha, 1979,* edited by Doreen Fowler and Ann J. Abadie, 110–133. Jackson: University Press of Mississippi, 1980.
Watson, James G. *The Snopes Dilemma: Faulkner's Trilogy.* Coral Gables, Fla.: University of Miami Press, 1968.

"Turnabout" (Collected Stories)

This story was first published in the SATURDAY EVENING POST (March 5, 1932) and later in DOCTOR MARTINO AND OTHER STORIES (1934). It also was the basis for the 1933 HOWARD HAWKS film, *Today We Live,* for which Faulkner was co-scriptwriter.

SYNOPSIS

"Turnabout" concerns a World War I contest of combat in the air and on the sea. In a French port town (possibly Dunkirk), an American aviator,

Captain Bogard, encounters a young drunken British seaman, Claude Hope, whom he takes to his air base. There the other Americans contemptuously judge Hope, who exhibits the breezy, self-effacing humor typical of his upper-class background, as weak and naive.

When Bogard takes him along as gunner on a bombing raid, Hope performs competently and is impressed by the coolness of the American crew as they safely land the plane with a bomb precariously dangling from a wing; the flyers had been unaware of this mishap. Hope returns the favor by inviting Bogard along on a daytime raid by his small torpedo boat. Bogard sees that this dangerous mission demands as much, if not more, courage and expertise as his own raids. He becomes sick when, under fire, the torpedo initially fails to disengage and the boat must keep circling its prey, an Argentine wheat freighter in a harbor protected by a German cruiser. At the very last moment, the British blow up the ship. Bogard comes to a disquieting truth: Combatants are constantly at risk of being betrayed by mechanical malfunctions. A month later, Hope's torpedo boat is reported missing. Shortly afterward, Bogard and his crew are cited for valor for executing a daring daylight raid to destroy an ammunition depot and damage enemy headquarters. Perhaps inspired by Hope or perhaps avenging his death, Bogard imitates torpedo boat tactics in diving close to the target before releasing his bombs. As he does so, he fantasizes that all the military and political leaders from both sides are in the chateau he is attacking.

CRITICAL COMMENTARY

The ending of "Turnabout" has caused some readers to question the merits of the story. But however readers judge the last two paragraphs, "Turnabout," as Hans H. Skei observes, "seems to be a story relying on the myths about courage and loyalty and honour as essential qualitites displayed in a war. All through the story laughter, youthful courage, honourable behaviour, and even patriotism replace the extremely negative tone in the earlier stories; except for the final paragraphs where Faulkner's more genuine moral concerns slip into the story" (*William Faulkner: The Novelist as Short Story Writer* 137).

CHARACTERS

Albert A British military policeman in France in 1918, he takes charge of Midshipman L. C. W. Hope from the American MPs who have picked him up out of the street.

Bogard, Captain H. S. An American aviator in France during World War I, he takes a young British naval officer, L. C. W. Hope, aloft and impresses him with his coolness and courage. In turn, Bogard then accompanies Hope on a torpedo boat mission and is likewise impressed.

Burt A boatswain's mate in the British Royal Navy's torpedo boat *X001*. He is killed in a World War I action, along with the rest of the crew.

Collier He is a mandolin-playing American aviator in France in 1918. Lieutenant McGinnis suggests that Collier provide the music on one of Midshipman L. C. W. Hope's torpedo boat missions, which he wrongly regards as pleasure cruises.

Harper He is Captain Bogard's aerial gunner. Midshipman L. C. W. Hope replaces him for one mission over France in 1918 and is deeply impressed by the steady nerves required for the job.

Hope, L. C. W. (Claude) A young officer in the Royal Navy, he is the second-in-command of a torpedo boat based in France during World War I. Homeless (he sleeps in the street), drunken, and infantile, he is deeply impressed with the dangers of flying when he accompanies Captain Bogard on a bombing mission. Bogard is later equally impressed with the dangers of Hope's raids into German waters. The young midshipman dies in action at sea, along with the other three men in his crew.

Jerry An American flyer in France, he is dismissive of Midshipman Hope because of Hope's immature way of expressing himself. Captain Bogard takes Jerry aside and tells him to leave the young Englishman alone.

McGinnis, Darrell (Mac) An American flyer in France during World War I, he misinterprets

Midshipman Hope's infantile chatter and openly questions his courage.

Reeves   A crewman aboard the torpedo boat *X001*, he is killed in action when the boat is sunk in German-controlled waters.

Smith, R. Boyce (Ronnie)   The commanding officer of torpedo boat *X001*, he is killed in action with the three men in his crew.

Watts   He is an aerial gunner in Captain Bogard's crew in France during World War I.

Wutherspoon, Jamie   An acquaintance of the British naval officer Midshipman Hope, he uses a neighboring street in the French port town for his "home."

FURTHER READING

Theresa M. Towner and James B. Carothers, *Reading Faulkner: Collected Stories*, 260–274.

"Two Dollar Wife"

Originally titled "Christmas Tree," "Two Dollar Wife" was first published in *College Life* 18 (January 1936), 8–10, 85, 86, 88, 90. This short story is reprinted in *Uncollected Stories of William Faulkner*. For more information, *see Selected Letters of William Faulkner*, 77, and *Uncollected Stories*, 701–702.

SYNOPSIS

"Two Dollar Wife" deals with irresponsible youth on a spree one New Year's Eve and the consequences of self-absorption. Reminiscent of the flappers and swells of the Prohibition era, Doris Houston and her date, Maxwell Johns, spend the night out with friends drinking and gambling. The two get married using a marriage license obtained on a dare a month before, but Doris at that time had changed her mind. Coming back to the Houston house to announce their marriage, they discover that Doris's

young brother had almost died from swallowing the needle Maxwell carelessly threw on a chair. The short story ends with Doris's angered mother forcing Maxwell out of the house.

CRITICAL COMMENTARY

Doris Houston and Maxwell Johns are part of a group of irresponsible and unlikable young people. In his discussion of Faulkner's short stories, James Ferguson considers "Two Dollar Wife" a failed potboiler, and "without question one of the worst pieces of fiction ever produced by a major American writer" (*Faulkner's Short Fiction*, 39).

CHARACTERS

Carberry, Dr.   The physician who saves the life of Mrs. Houston's son, Doris's baby brother. The child almost died after swallowing the needle Maxwell Johns thoughtlessly threw on a chair.

Houston, Doris   One of the main characters in the short story. A naive 18-year-old and, like her beau, Maxwell Johns, Doris is thoughtless and self-indulgent. On a whim, she agrees to marry Maxwell, but she regrets the notion immediately and reneges. A month later, however, on New Year's Eve—the time of the short story—she marries Maxwell, who in his determination to marry her bribes a justice of the peace. Doris's mother angrily sends Maxwell off when the couple arrives at Doris's home to announce their marriage.

Houston, Mrs.   Doris Houston's mother. On New Year's Eve, Doris and her beau, Maxwell Johns, stay out far later than Mrs. Houston had indicated was allowed. When the young couple returns to Doris's home the next morning and announce that they got married, the angry Mrs. Houston is more concerned with the fate of her son, who swallowed the needle that Maxwell threw on a chair, than with the marriage. She demands that Maxwell leave the house.

Johns, Maxwell   One of the major characters in the short story. Suspended from Sewanee, Maxwell is careless and self-indulgent. The title refers to the cost of a marriage license, which Maxwell and his girl, Doris Houston, who on occasion calls him Unconscious, obtain on a dare by their friend Walter Mitchell. Doris refuses to elope, however, and Maxwell carries the license with him as a kind of talisman. On New Year's Eve, the pair use the license to get married before a justice of the peace. When they return to Doris's home around nine o'clock in the morning, the couple discover that her baby brother has almost died from swallowing the sewing needle that Maxwell threw on a chair right before they left for the evening. Maxwell is asked to leave immediately by Doris's angry mother. Oblivious of the cars around him, he drives off erratically, an indication of the emotional and physical condition that he is in after a night of drinking.

Jornstadt The handsome Princeton man girls are crazy about. He is from Minnesota visiting his aunt. Although he is not familiar with shooting craps, he is asked to roll against Maxwell Johns and bests him two out of three times. Jornstadt's friend Hap White collects the winnings: Jornstadt's flask and Maxwell's marriage license. Before leaving the country club, Maxwell challenges him to drinking corn liquor that certainly will inebriate him. He passes out on the drive to Marley where Maxwell and Doris get married by a justice of the peace.

Lucille A minor character in the short story, she accompanies Walter Mitchell to the New Year's Eve party at the country club. She is a witness to the impromptu wedding of Doris Houston and Maxwell Johns. Convincing Doris that forgery is worse than bigamy, Lucille eggs her on to get married.

Mitchell, Walter A minor character in the short story. He originally dares Maxwell Johns and Doris Houston to get married, eventually the two do so a month later on New Year's Eve. With his date, Lucille, Walter drives Doris and Maxwell to the country club and later to the justice of the peace in Marley.

Peter (Pete) A black man at the country club whose dice Maxwell Johns and Jornstadt use in their crap game. To get even with Jornstadt, Maxwell has Peter get some extremely potent corn

liquor that Maxwell challenges Jornstadt to drink; it eventually causes him to pass out.

White, Hap Minor character in the short story. Hap brings the Princeton man Jornstadt to the New Year's Eve party at the country club. Unlike the attractive Jornstadt, Hap is heavy set with an ingratiating look. He shows Jornstadt how to play dice.

"Two Soldiers" (Collected Stories)

First published on March 28, 1942, in the SATURDAY EVENING POST 214, 9–11, 35–36, 38, 40, "Two Soldiers" is reprinted in the *Collected Stories of William Faulkner* and in *Selected Short Stories of William Faulkner*. For more information, *see Selected Letters of William Faulkner*, 169, 184, 191–192, 274, 278.

SYNOPSIS

Set at the very beginning of World War II, "Two Soldiers" concerns a young boy, the unnamed protagonist and narrator of the story, and his ingenuous intent to be with his older brother, Pete Grier, when the latter enlists in the army following the Japanese attack on Pearl Harbor. Not quite nine years old and having no inkling of the seriousness of war or the workings of the army, the young boy understands only that his brother is gone and that he must be with him. The day after Pete leaves to sign up, the narrator makes his way, alone, from his home in FRENCHMAN'S BEND to MEMPHIS with the plan to enlist so that he can act as his brother's helper. After finding the army enlistment office, he demands to be allowed to join his brother but is prevented, of course, from doing so by the authorities. Pete is called into the office to talk to his younger brother and impresses upon him the need to take care of the farm and their parents. The narrator's earnestness touches everyone he meets. He is fed lunch by Mrs. McKellogg, the wife of an army officer, and later in the day is driven back to

Frenchman's Bend by a soldier. During the car ride, the young narrator breaks down and cries, without ever knowing quite why, perhaps a mute premonition of what will happen to his brother. (*See* the companion story, "SHALL NOT PERISH," in which the Grier family receives the news that Pete has been killed in the war.)

CRITICAL COMMENTARY

In "Two Soldiers," Faulkner undoubtedly was expressing some of his own sentiments about Pearl Harbor and the war effort to such an extent that some readers may consider the story too patently patriotic to be good literature and the young narrator's voice, as JOSEPH BLOTNER mentions, "overwrought and artificial" (*Faulkner: A Biography,* 436). In a May 1944 letter to his literary agent HAROLD OBER, Faulkner explained, at Ober's request, why he liked this short story. Faulkner replied: "I like it because it portrays a type which I admire—not only a little boy, and I think little boys are all right, but a true American: an independent creature with courage and bottom and heart—a creature which is not vanishing, even though every articulate medium we have—radio, moving pictures, magazines—is busy day and night telling us that it has vanished, has become a sentimental and bragging liar" (*Selected Letters,* 184).

CHARACTERS

Foote, Mr. A police officer in JEFFERSON. While on his way to MEMPHIS to enlist in the army to be with his older brother, Pete Grier, the nine-year-old unnamed narrator of the short story meets Mr. Foote, whom he refers to as the Law. After leaving the young boy in the custody of the ticket agent at the bus depot, Mr. Foote seeks the assistance of two Jefferson women who question the boy about his brother and decide to send him on to Memphis in search of him.

(the young Grier boy) *See* unnamed narrator.

Grier, Pete The 18-year-old brother of the young unnamed narrator of the short story. Pete and his younger brother listen to the news each night over Old Man Killegrew's radio and hear of the Japanese

attack on Pearl Harbor. Resolved to fight for his country, Pete leaves home in FRENCHMAN'S BEND for MEMPHIS to enlist in the army. The next morning, Pete's little brother sneaks off to Memphis, where he tries to enlist too, but he is sent back. *Also see* the short story "SHALL NOT PERISH," which opens with the news of Pete's death.

Habersham, Mrs. An elderly woman and social worker in JEFFERSON. She and a younger colleague are called on by the police officer Mr. Foote to deal with the nine-year-old narrator of the story, who is trying to reach MEMPHIS to join his older brother Pete Grier at the enlistment office. After questioning the boy, Mrs. Habersham agrees to let him travel on to Memphis in search of his brother.

Killegrew, Old Man Pete Grier and his little brother stand outside Killegrew's house after supper to listen to the war news coming over Killegrew's radio, which he turns up for his deaf wife to hear. *Also see* "SHINGLES FOR THE LORD" and "SHALL NOT PERISH."

McKellogg, Colonel An army officer in MEMPHIS. Colonel McKellogg arranges for a car and driver to take the enlistee Pete Grier's little brother (the unnamed narrator of the story) back home to FRENCHMAN'S BEND.

McKellogg, Mrs. Colonel McKellogg's wife. She takes in the enlistee Pete Grier's little brother (the unnamed narrator of the story) and arranges for his safe return from MEMPHIS to his family in FRENCHMAN'S BEND. Before sending the boy back home, she feeds him lunch.

Marsh, Uncle Pete Grier's uncle on his mother's side. He was was wounded in France during World War I.

Maw (Mrs. Grier) Referred to as Maw in the short story, she is the mother of Pete Grier and his young brother, the unnamed narrator. She cried when she found out that Pete was going to MEMPHIS to enlist after the attack on Pearl Harbor. After making an early breakfast for Pete, she finishes packing his grip (a suitcase). *Also see* "SHALL NOT PERISH" and "SHINGLES FOR THE LORD."

Pap (Mr. Grier) The young unnamed narrator's father. He is referred to as Father in "SHALL NOT PERISH"; *see* Res Grier in "SHINGLES FOR THE LORD." He is also referred to in *The MANSION.*

Tull The father of Pete Grier's girlfriend. (The surname Tull appears in several other works.)

unnamed narrator Pete Grier's young brother, almost nine years old. Intent on being with his older brother, the boy on his own leaves FRENCHMAN'S BEND for MEMPHIS the day after Pete travels there to enlist. Although he finds the enlistment office and speaks with Pete, the boy is persuaded to return home to look after his parents and the farm. Before a soldier drives him back to Frenchman's Bend, the boy is fed lunch by an army officer's wife. During the drive home, the boy's emotions momentarily overcome him and he breaks down and cries. *Also see* "SHALL NOT PERISH."

FURTHER READING

Theresa M. Towner and James B. Carothers, *Reading Faulkner: Collected Stories*, 47–53; and Diane Brown Jones, *A Reader's Guide to the Short Stories of William Faulkner*, 64–72.

"Uncle Willy"
(*Collected Stories*)

Story first published in *American Mercury* (October 1935).

SYNOPSIS

JEFFERSON, MISSISSIPPI, do-gooders try to reform the town ne'er-do-well, who is aided in his escape by a 14-year-old boy, who narrates the story. Uncle Willy Christian is a morphine addict who indulges his habit in front of the town boys he befriends. After church members force him to give up his addiction, he switches to alcohol. He returns from a MEMPHIS drinking spree with a prostitute as a wife. After she is paid off and sent away, Uncle Willy is confined to an institution. While there, he manages to sell his holdings for cash, which he spends on an airplane. His plan is to set out for California with his black employees, the old handyman Job and the driver Secretary. The flight instructor will not teach him without a medical certificate, so Uncle Willy has Secretary take the lessons in order to then teach him. Summoned by Uncle Willy, the boy runs away to join the trio as they set out from Memphis. Job, alarmed by the foolhardiness of the scheme, phones Jefferson for help to stop Uncle Willy. Before the rescuers arrive, Uncle Willy dies while trying to fly solo in the plane.

CRITICAL COMMENTARY

This contest of small-town values with the individual rights of an eccentric, resolute nonconformist appears to yield no clear winner. James Ferguson asserts that the story demonstrates "how the concept of community, in spite of its often very positive values, can become destructive when it is pitted against the integrity of the individual" (*Faulkner's Short Fiction*, 81–82). However, in defense of the community, readers should note that the romanticized view of Uncle Willy as admirable and heroic is presented by an innocent and somewhat naive youngster. Thus, as is often the case with Faulkner's fiction, the meaning one draws from the story turns on the question of the reliability of the narrator.

CHARACTERS

Barbour Uncle Willy Christian's Sunday school teacher.

Barger, Sonny A storekeeper.

Bean, Captain A flying instructor at the JEFFERSON airport, he refuses to give Willy Christian flying lessons without permission from his doctor.

Callaghan, Miss A schoolteacher, she leaves her desk and takes a seat as a pupil for an April Fool's joke.

Christian, Mrs. A MEMPHIS prostitute, she is briefly Uncle Willy Christian's wife. The townspeople persuade her to leave by giving her Uncle

Willy's car and a thousand dollars, and she returns to her MANUEL STREET brothel.

Christian, Uncle Willy An old JEFFERSON, MISSISSIPPI, drugstore proprietor, a great favorite of the local boys, with a drug habit and an affinity for airplanes. When meddlesome church people try to cure him of his addiction, he takes to his airplane in a bid to escape them and perishes in a crash near Jefferson. He also appears as a minor character in *The* TOWN, *The* MANSION, and *The* REIVERS.

Hovis, Mrs. One of the ladies intent on breaking Uncle Willy Christian of his drug habit. She alternates with Mrs. Merridew in standing watch over him until his sister arrives from Texas.

Merridew, Mrs. The leader of the group of JEFFERSON, MISSISSIPPI, townspeople that try to cure Uncle Willy Christian of his dependence on drugs. Mrs. Merridew's lemonade, fried chicken, and ice cream fail to cure the addicted druggist.

Miller, Brother He teaches the adult Bible classes the drug-addicted Uncle Willy Christian is forced to attend.

Robert, Uncle He is the uncle of the boy who narrates Uncle Willy Christian's story.

Schultz, Reverend The preacher at Uncle Willy Christian's church, he helps the ladies coerce Willy into leading a drug-free life. Reverend Schultz and Mrs. Merridew arrange for a clerk to take over Willy's drugstore.

Schultz, Sister She is the wife of Reverend Schultz, the preacher at Uncle Willy Christian's church.

Secretary Uncle Willy Christian's African-American driver who regularly chauffeurs Willy to MEMPHIS.

Wylie, Job He works in Uncle Willy Christian's drugstore and refuses to leave when the clerk brought in to replace Willy fires him.

Uncollected Stories of William Faulkner

A collection of 45 stories published by RANDOM HOUSE in 1979, and reissued as a centenary edition by Vintage International in 1997. Edited with an introduction, notes, and bibliography by JOSEPH BLOTNER, the volume contains uncollected stories (i.e., those not found in COLLECTED STORIES OF WILLIAM FAULKNER), never-before-published stories, and stories Faulkner revised for books (*The* UNVANQUISHED, *The* HAMLET, GO DOWN, MOSES, BIG WOODS, and *The* MANSION). (*See* Appendix for titles and *see* entries for individual stories.)

In his introduction to the collection, Blotner rightly points out that the stories taken as a whole "present a view of Faulkner's developing art over a span of thirty years" (xv). Although some of the stories differ remarkably from one another and show an apprentice at work, others clearly demonstrate Faulkner's strengths and success at writing short stories. The collection readily makes accessible to readers and students of Faulkner stories that would otherwise be difficult to track down.

"Unvanquished, The" (Uncollected Stories)

Short story first published in the SATURDAY EVENING POST (November 14, 1936) and included as "Riposte in Tertio" in *The* UNVANQUISHED (1938).

SYNOPSIS

At the height of the Civil War Miss Rosa Millard ("Granny"), the mistress of Sartoris plantation, and Ab Snopes, with the assistance of young Bayard Sartoris and his black friend Ringo, engage in a scheme to defraud the Union army. Miss Rosa uses forged documents to obtain mules from the Federals, and then Ab sells the animals back to the Federals, eventually turning a profit for Miss Rosa of nearly $7,000. Though Granny uses some of the money to help out those the war has made destitute, the questionable business dealings have corrupted her and made her arrogant. Her explanation to God is more defiant than penitent as she explains that she has sinned to help the less fortunate. Snopes persuades Granny to use a forged federal order to seize four horses from a bushwhacker gang known as Grumby's Independents. Bayard and Ringo try to stop her, but she insists on going through with this last crooked deal. Grumby sees through the con and murders her at the appointed meeting place, an abandoned cotton compress.

CRITICAL COMMENTARY

Like the closely-related "VENDÉE," this story reflects the difficult and often tragic circumstances on the Confederate home front. With most of the men, like Colonel Sartoris, away at war, the women and children must fend for themselves, having to cope not only with hardship, poverty, and the Union army but also with scalawags like Ab Snopes and the bushwhacker Grumby, whose loyalty is only to their own self-interest. In her conflict with all of these opponents, Miss Rosa exhibits considerable tenacity, courage, and shrewdness, but her willingness to compromise her moral and ethical principles—even if pragmatically justified—eventually leads to her violent death at the hands of Grumby. The contradictions in her behavior are not lost on her young grandson Bayard, the narrator of the story.

When Faulkner incorporated the story into *The UNVANQUISHED*, he changed its title to free the original one for use as the title of the book. The new title he settled on, "Riposte in Tertio," is a term that describes a defensive move in fencing. The phrase is a telling and appropriate description of Granny's actions in the story—actions that typically would be undertaken by men and that parallel those of soldiers on the battlefield. In fact, Snopes remarks, "When Kernel Sartoris left here, he told me to look out for you against General Grant and them. What I wonder is, if somebody hadn't better tell Abe Lincoln to look out for General Grant against Miz Rosa Millard." Like Drusilla Hawk in "An Odor of Verbena," Charlotte Rittenmeyer in *The WILD PALMS*, and Caddy Compson in *The SOUND AND THE FURY*, Rosa Millard appropri-

ates attitudes and behavior that are traditionally reserved for males.

CHARACTERS

For a list of the characters in this story *see* the entry on *The UNVANQUISHED*.

Unvanquished, The

A cycle of short stories fabricated into a novel, part of the YOKNAPATAWPHA COUNTY cycle, *The Unvanquished* is set in northern Mississippi during the Civil War and Reconstruction. Published in 1938, the novel fills out the Sartoris family history that Faulkner introduced in *SARTORIS* (1930). Some critics dismiss *The Unvanquished* as a set of conventionally romantic Civil War tales peopled with stereotypical brave Confederate cavalrymen, indomitable women back home on the plantation, and loyal, self-sacrificing African-American servants—not an unfair characterization, though as ever with Faulkner there are passages of great power.

The novel is the first of three—*The HAMLET* (1940) and *GO DOWN, MOSES* (1942) were to follow—to be spun out of material Faulkner had developed earlier. It consists of a sequence of six stories published in magazines between September 1934 and December 1936, with a seventh, "An Odor of Verbena," written specifically to close out the volume. All seven sections are told from the point of view of young Bayard Sartoris (3). Most commentators agree there is sufficient continuity of characters, situations, and themes to classify *The Unvanquished* as a novel.

RANDOM HOUSE showed interest in publishing the Bayard-Ringo stories (so called after young Sartoris and his African-American childhood friend Ringo Strother) as a set in the spring of 1937. Two major thematic lines link the pieces: the war and its shattered aftermath, and the growing up of two boys. In a July 1938 letter to ROBERT K. HAAS at Random House, Faulkner identified "Granny's struggle between her morality and her children's needs" as the central and unifying theme of the novel.

The publisher probably reasoned, too, that the stories would have broad sales appeal, since all but one of the first six had been published in the mass-circulation SATURDAY EVENING POST.

In Hollywood writing for films, Faulkner re-read the previously published stories and began the task of synthesis and revision, toning down comic or farcical elements and making other changes with a view to turning the collection into serious literature. The new story, "An Odor of Verbena," the longest of the seven at 12,500 words, carried the action into Reconstruction and the adulthood of Bayard and Ringo, tying the strands of the earlier stories together and providing the novel's climax. Faulkner hoped to sell "Verbena" to a magazine before its publication as part of the novel. "If the *Post* don't want it, try someone else," he wrote his agent, MORTON GOLDMAN. He continued the work on his return to OXFORD, MISSISSIPPI, in mid-August 1937, and put his final touches on the manuscript in an office at Random House in New York in October.

SYNOPSIS

The first story, "Ambuscade," published in the *Post* in September 1934, introduces Bayard and Ringo, both 12 years old, just after the fall of the strategic fortress of Vicksburg in July 1863. The setting is the SARTORIS plantation; Colonel John Sartoris's mother-in-law, Rosa Millard, manages the place while he is off fighting in the war. The action involves the boys' firing at a Yankee officer, then hiding under the flowing skirts of Granny Millard when the enemy comes to investigate. For the novel, Faulkner added clarifying passages and filled out the portrait of Colonel Sartoris, with the aim of building him into a more imposing figure.

In "Retreat," the second story, the Confederate cause is nearly lost, the Yankees are swarming, and Granny Rosa is worried about the family silver. A Union patrol confiscates two Sartoris mules, Old Hundred and Tinny; the boys help Colonel Sartoris's partisans capture some Yankees; the enemy in retribution burns the Sartoris plantation; the slave Loosh Strother leads the Yankees to the treasure and walks away from

Sartoris a free man. In revising, Faulkner added six pages limning two characters who will figure prominently in GO DOWN, MOSES, the twins Buck and Buddy McCaslin.

"Raid," the third story, finds Granny and the boys pursuing the federal troops into Alabama in search of compensation for the mules, the silver, and two "runaways," Loosh and Philadelphia Strother. They stop over briefly at Hawkhurst plantation, where cousin Drusilla Hawk (Sartoris), whose fiancé has been killed at SHILOH, burns for revenge. Drusilla dresses like a man, rides well, is willing to learn to shoot, and wants to enlist in Colonel Sartoris's partisan cavalry command. Miss Rosa tracks down the Union Colonel Nathaniel Dick, who agrees to pay for the livestock. Through a comedy of errors involving a play on the mules' names, he gives Miss Rosa a chit for 110 mules, 110 runaways, and 10 chests of silver. Here Granny, accepting the Yankees' overpayment, takes her first steps in straying from the strict code of behavior that has governed her life.

The first three stories appeared in the *Post* in the autumn of 1934. By then, Faulkner had written and sent on to the magazine the fourth and fifth stories in the series. The fourth, "Riposte in Tertio" (originally titled "The Unvanquished"), introduces Ab Snopes, the father of the imperishable Flem Snopes of the SNOPES TRILOGY. Ab sells the compensatory mules and horses back to the Federals, eventually turning a profit for Miss Rosa of nearly $7,000. Though Granny uses some of the money to help out those the war has made destitute, it has corrupted her and made her arrogant. Her explanation to God is more defiant than penitent as she explains that she has sinned to help the less fortunate.

Ab Snopes persuades Granny to use a forged federal order to seize four horses from a bushwhacker gang known as Grumby's Independents. Bayard and Ringo try to stop her, but she insists on going through with this last crooked deal. Grumby sees through the con and murders her at the appointed meeting place, an abandoned cotton compress.

Revenge is the theme and plot of the fifth story, "Vendée." Bayard and Ringo track down Grumby; Bayard shoots him. The boys stake his corpse to the door of the cotton compress, cut off his right hand, and nail it to Granny's wooden grave marker. Then they burst into tears.

"Skirmish at Sartoris" (originally titled "Drusilla" and first published in SCRIBNER'S MAGAZINE in 1935), the sixth story, recounts Colonel Sartoris's election-day shooting of the carpetbagger Calvin Burden and his grandson, a double homicide first related in LIGHT IN AUGUST (1932). By now, the ex-soldier Drusilla has come to live platonically at Sartoris and help the colonel restore the plantation. As a comic counterpoint, the ladies of JEFFERSON, MISSISSIPPI, believing Drusilla's virtue compromised, force her into marriage with the colonel. The ending is conventionally happy: the interfering carpetbaggers are confounded, and Drusilla and Sartoris are joined.

The mood darkens in the concluding story, "An Odor of Verbena," which recounts the killing of John Sartoris and the demand for revenge that falls on Bayard, now 24 years old. Ben Redmond, Sartoris's business and political rival, shoots the colonel in the Jefferson square, an incident modeled on the murder in 1889 of Faulkner's great-grandfather, WILLIAM CLARK FALKNER.

Here Faulkner alludes to events in earlier stories and shows Bayard contemplating his violent, driven father's war career, his railroad-building, his forays into politics. Right or wrong, Colonel Sartoris acts for the good of the community as he sees it, he and his admirers claim. But unlike Thomas Sutpen, who makes a brief appearance in the story, Sartoris is no innocent; he recognizes he has done wrong to Redmond and others. Sensing the approach of death, he hints at as much to his son.

Drusilla, with her "rapport for violence," insists that Bayard kill his father's murderer, just as he had killed Grumby to revenge his grandmother; so too does George Wyatt, one of his father's veterans and a sort of spokesman for Jefferson manhood. Even Aunt Jenny Du Pre, who rejects the old Southern eye-for-an-eye code, understands finally that Bayard must face Redmond.

But he takes his revenge in his own way. Like his father, Bayard decides to approach Redmond unarmed. Like Aunt Jenny, he has rejected the code. He climbs the wooden stairs up to Redmond's second-floor office and stares him down. Redmond fires twice, missing intentionally, then rises, closes up the office, walks down to the depot, boards the southbound train, and leaves Jefferson forever. The widow Drusilla exits too, to live with relatives in Alabama. Drusilla leaves behind for Bayard a sprig of verbena, symbolic of optimism and renewal. In Faulkner's own words, the sprig "meant that she realized that [confronting Redmond] took courage too and maybe more moral courage than to have drawn blood."

CRITICAL COMMENTARY

Readers new to Faulkner's work often are advised to begin with *The Unvanquished*. Though admitting it was hardly the novel he liked best (he reserved that tribute for *The Sound and the Fury*), Faulkner himself recommended the reader new to him start with the Bayard-Ringo stories.

MALCOLM COWLEY called *The Unvanquished*, along with *Go Down, Moses*, representative "of a hybrid form between the random collection and the unified novel," and he did not hold it in high regard. By contrast, CLEANTH BROOKS considers *The Unvanquished* undervalued. The stories "are simple, yet beautifully crafted, and show off the author's narrative skills in a very clear light," he told the biographer Jay Parini in a 1985 interview. "They have been unfairly dismissed as minor Faulkner. . . . They are much finer than that." Brooks saw unity in the work, which he characterized as "a novel about growing up—it is the story of an education." The final story draws together the themes of the preceding ones and confirms Bayard's passage into adulthood. The confrontation with Redmond, in Brooks's words, "is the concluding act in his long initiation into the moral responsibility that goes with manhood."

That said, most later critics grade *The Unvanquished* minor Faulkner. IRVING HOWE thought it betrayed its origin as a set of stories for magazines, despite the undoubted narrative power of some of the episodes: blacks trailing in the wake of the Union army in a mass movement toward freedom, for example, or Bayard's rejection of the southern code of violence. "When so much of the action is presented in a slick and jolly manner, no adequate treatment is possible of such themes as civil war, the disruption of a society, and the cost of immoral behavior in behalf of urgent human needs," Howe wrote.

CRITICAL RECEPTION

Random House published *The Unvanquished*, with black-and-white drawings by Edward Shenton, on February 15, 1938. The early notices were more favorable than usual with a new Faulkner work, perhaps because the book made fewer demands on the reviewer. *Time* saw in the novel "something of the air of Two Little Confederates as it might have been rewritten by an author aware of the race problem, economics and Freudian psychology." *Time's* unsigned review liked *The Unvanquished* for the action—and for the absence of "the involved Proustian passages that made *Absalom, Absalom!* almost unreadable." Writing in *The New York Times*, Ralph Thompson found the matter of the novel "unFaulknerian—no corruption, miscegenation or corncobs." Thompson especially admired the boy characters and Miss Rosa, in his view among "the most successful Mr. Faulkner has ever drawn."

The reviewer for the hometown OXFORD EAGLE expressed undisguised relief: "Oxonians who . . . have found his writing too involved for their minds to follow or his subjects too revolting for them to stomach, will find here a book that they can understand, can enjoy, can leave lying on their living room tables," Dale Mullen wrote.

Random House's hopes that *The Unvanquished* would have mass appeal were unrealized, at least initially. METRO-GOLDWYN-MAYER did, however, buy the film rights for $25,000. But by June 1940, nearly two and a half years after its publication, sales of the novel had earned Faulkner only $2,327.

CHARACTERS

Benbow, Cassius Q. (Uncle Cash) ("Skirmish at Sartoris") A former slave, he flees to the Yankees in 1863 during the Civil War. When he seeks election to the post of marshal of JEFFERSON, MISSISSIPPI, after the war, Colonel John Sartoris and his white associates violently oppose him.

Benbow, Judge ("An Odor of Verbena") Judge Benbow handles the legal work when Colonel John Sartoris buys Ben Redmond's share of the railroad the two jointly own, dissolving their partnership.

Bowden, Matt ("Vendée") A member of Major Grumby's bushwhacker group, he turns against Grumby after the killing of Granny Rosa Millard and helps Bayard Sartoris and Ringo Strother exact their revenge. Faulkner describes him as a dark man with an ink-colored beard and "little black-haired hands."

Breckbridge, Gavin ("Raid") The fiancé of Drusilla Hawk (Sartoris), he gave Drusilla a blood horse, Bobolink, just before the Civil War broke out in 1861. Breckbridge was killed at the BATTLE OF SHILOH in April 1862.

Bridger ("Vendée") An accomplice of Matt Bowden, he falls out with Grumby over the bushwhacker's murder of Rosa Millard, saying the unnecessary killing of the old lady forced the guerrilla band to leave a profitable area of operations.

Burden ("Skirmish at Sartoris") A Missouri carpetbagger, he came to Mississippi "with a patent from Washington to organize the niggers into Republicans." Though he is given no first name, he is one of the Burdens of LIGHT IN AUGUST.

Compson, Jason Lycurgus II (General) ("An Odor of Verbena") A prominent citizen of JEFFERSON, he lifts his hat in salute to Bayard Sartoris (2) as he sets off to confront his father's killer, Redmond. General Compson, the grandfather of Quentin Compson, who narrates the Sutpen story in ABSALOM, ABSALOM!, is a recurrent figure in the YOKNAPATAWPHA cycle.

Compson, Mrs. ("Retreat," "Raid," and "Vendée") She loans Granny Rosa Millard a hat and a parasol as she sets out on her adventures in Yankee-occupied north Mississippi in 1863; Rosa asks her to "drive out home now and then and look after the flowers." After Rosa's death, she invites Bayard Sartoris (2) and Ringo Strother to live with her till Bayard's father, John Sartoris, returns from the war.

Cook, Celia ("Ambuscade") As a young girl, she watches the Confederate cavalry commander NATHAN BEDFORD FORREST ride down South Street in OXFORD, MISSISSIPPI; she commemorates the event by etching her name into a windowpane with a diamond ring.

Dick, Nathaniel ("Ambuscade" and "Raid") An Ohio officer in the Union army, he feigns not knowing that the fugitives Bayard Sartoris (2) and Ringo Strother are hiding under Granny Rosa Millard's skirts when he comes to Sartoris plantation to investigate an ambush attempt.

Later, Miss Rosa appeals to the benevolent Colonel Dick to restore her stolen silver and mules. He repays her many times over when he gets his general to sign an order turning captured livestock over to her. She exploits the order to rustle a small fortune in enemy horses and mules.

Du Pre, Virginia (Genevieve Du Pre; Virginia Sartoris) ("An Odor of Verbena") The strong-minded sister of Colonel John Sartoris, "Aunt Jenny" is an admired type of traditional Southern woman, slender, with a weary expression. She resembled her brother in many ways, though her eyes were "wise instead of intolerant."

Aunt Jenny had been married only two years when her South Carolinian husband was killed at Fort Moultrie in Charleston harbor at the outbreak of the Civil War. She comes to her brother's home seven years a widow in 1868 and lives to see many of the male Sartorises die violently.

John Sartoris names his first locomotive for her. Jenny fiercely approves of her nephew Bayard Sartoris (2)'s decision not to take revenge on his father's killer, his railroad partner Ben Redmond.

Fortinbride, Brother ("Riposte in Tertio") Wounded serving as a private in Colonel John Sartoris's regiment at the first Battle of Manassas early in the Civil War, he comes home to die but recovers miraculously to preach at the colonel's church, even though he is not a minister. He used to stand in the pre-war rector Doctor Worsham's place "and talk quiet about God."

A gaunt-faced man whose frock coat is patched with Yankee tent canvas, Brother Fortinbride helps Rosa Millard distribute money and stolen Yankee mules to the YOKNAPATAWPHA COUNTY hill folk, and he officiates at Miss Rosa's funeral.

Grumby, Major ("Riposte in Tertio" and "Vendée") He is the vicious, cowardly leader of a band of 60 or so bushwhackers who terrorize north Mississippi civilians, "raiding smokehouses and stables, and houses where they were sure there were no men." When Miss Rosa Millard, Colonel John Sartoris's mother-in-law, confronts Grumby about some stolen horses he has hidden away at an abandoned cotton compress, Grumby shoots and kills her. Bayard Sartoris (3) and his friend Ringo Strother track Grumby down and exact their revenge, nailing his body to the door of the compress and attaching his severed hand to Miss Rosa's wooden gravemarker.

Habersham ("Skirmish at Sartoris") He is the JEFFERSON, MISSISSIPPI, bank clerk who signs Colonel John Sartoris's peace bond after he shoots and kills the carpetbagger Burdens in a dispute over black voting rights.

Habersham's wife, Martha Habersham, helps arrange the marriage of Sartoris and Drusilla Hawk (Sartoris).

Habersham, Martha ("Skirmish at Sartoris") The meddlesome wife of a JEFFERSON, MISSISSIPPI, bank clerk, one of those Jefferson women who had never accepted the outcome of the Civil War, she acts as a surrogate for Aunt Louisa Hawk, whose daughter Drusilla, an ex-Confederate soldier, is living platonically at Sartoris with her former regimental commander, Colonel John Sartoris.

With other Jefferson ladies, Mrs. Habersham, assuming incorrectly that Sartoris has taken sexual advantage of Drusilla, pressures the couple into marrying.

Harris, Plurella ("Rispose in Tertio") This is a nom de guerre for Rosa Millard, invented by Ringo Strother for Miss Rosa's use in her campaign to inveigle the Yankees out of horses and mules.

Harrison ("Ambuscade") A Union army sergeant, he searches SARTORIS plantation after Bayard Sartoris (3) and Ringo Strother shoot at a Yankee scout from ambush.

Hawk, Dennison ("Raid") The father of Drusilla Hawk (Sartoris) and Dennison Hawk, Jr., he is dead at the time of the novel's action, killed in an early Civil War battle. He lies buried among cedars on a knoll overlooking his plantation, Hawkhurst.

Hawk, Dennison, Jr. (Cousin Denny) ("Raid" and "An Odor of Verbena") He is Drusilla Hawk's (Sartoris) younger brother, only 10 years old during the war that engulfs his home, Hawkhurst.

Later, Cousin Denny studies law in Montgomery, Alabama. Drusilla goes to live with him there after she leaves SARTORIS.

Hawk, Drusilla *See* Sartoris, Drusilla Hawk.

Hawk, Louisa ("Raid" and "Skirmish at Sartoris") A war widow, the mother of Drusilla Hawk (Sartoris) and Dennison Hawk, Jr., she is Rosa Millard's sister. From her home in Alabama, she becomes convinced that Drusilla and Colonel John Sartoris are living in sin, and she goes to JEFFERSON, MISSISSIPPI, to confront the situation. With assistance from Mrs. Compson and Martha Habersham, she pressures the couple into marriage.

Hilliard ("An Odor of Verbena") A livery stable hand in OXFORD, MISSISSIPPI, he supplies Ringo Strother with a horse when he comes to the university to tell Bayard Sartoris (3) of his father's death.

Holston, Mrs. ("Skirmish at Sartoris") She is the elderly lady whose black porter witnesses Colonel John Sartoris's killing of the carpetbagging Burden at a polling station in JEFFERSON, MISSISSIPPI.

Jingus ("Raid") He is an African-American slave of the Hawks, who move into his cabin after federal troops burn HAWKHURST.

Lena, Missy ("Raid" and "Retreat") She is a black servant of the Hawks. Ringo Strother sleeps in her cabin when Rosa Millard and her grandson Bayard Sartoris (3) come to visit Hawkhurst.

Louvinia *See* Strother, Louvinia.

McCaslin, Amodeus (Uncle Buddy) ("Retreat") The bachelor twin brother of Theophilus McCaslin (Uncle Buck) and co-proprietor of a YOKNAPATAWPHA COUNTY plantation, he and his brother have ideas about land ownership and responsibility that their younger friend Colonel John Sartoris regards as 50 years ahead of the times: "They believed that land did not belong to people but that people belonged to land."

The McCaslins were past seventy in 1861 and Sartoris insisted he would take only one of them into his volunteer infantry regiment. They played head-to-head poker to decide; Buddy won, and 1864 finds him serving as a sergeant in Tennant's brigade in the Army of Northern Virginia.

McCaslin, Theophilus (Filus, Uncle Buck) ("Retreat" and Vendée") The twin brother of Amodeus (Uncle Buddy) McCaslin, he and his brother are the inheritors of old Lucius Quintus Carothers McCaslin's vast YOKNAPATAWPHA COUNTY plantation holdings.

Left at home when the cards fall for his twin brother, who wins a poker hand and joins the Confederate army, Uncle Buck helps bury Granny Rosa Millard, refusing to let anyone spell him at the shovel. After the funeral, he asks Bayard Sartoris (2) and Ringo Strother: "What you boys going to do now?" Buck then accompanies the boys as they attempt to track down the bushwhackers who killed Granny Rosa.

Millard, Miss Rosa (Granny) ("Ambuscade," "Retreat," "Raid," "Riposte in Tertio" and "Vendée") The canny and indomitable mother-in-law of Colonel John Sartoris and the grandmother of young Bayard Sartoris (2), she manages the SARTORIS plantation during the Civil War, when the master is away with the Confederate army. When the Yankees put a price on Sartoris's head, she flees with Bayard and the house servants.

As the fighting engulfs north Mississippi, Miss Rosa is forced to bend her notions of right and wrong, though seldom for her own benefit. With Ab Snopes, she tricks the Federals into supplying her with a small fortune in horses and mules, then effaces the U.S. brands and sells them back to the enemy. With the proceeds, she aids the poor hill folk of YOKNAPATAWPHA COUNTY.

The bushwhacker Grumby kills her in a dispute over stolen horses. Young Bayard avenges her by tracking down and killing Grumby and nailing his severed hand to his grandmother's wooden grave marker.

Mitchell, Unc Few ("Retreat") He is a local figure, "born loony," according to Louvinia Strother, who likens Colonel John Sartoris to him. When the Yankees question Sartoris, asking him where the wanted man Sartoris lives, he pantomimes deafness, fooling the enemy long enough to make his escape.

Newberry, Colonel ("Ripose in Tertio") A Union colonel commanding an Illinois regiment garrisoned in Mottstown, he authorizes the last handover of mules to Rosa Millard before the Yankees catch on to her trickery.

Redmond, Ben ("An Odor of Verbena) A lawyer, he is the railroad business partner and later the bitter business and political rival of Colonel John Sartoris. Redmond is an honest man, but he lacks Sartoris's cachet as a Confederate veteran; he'd "had something do with cotton for the Government" during the Civil War, and Sartoris used to taunt him for not having smelled powder.

When their differences become irreconcilable, Redmond sells his share of the road to Sartoris. Escalating the feud, Sartoris challenges him in an election for a seat in the Mississippi legislature and wins; this and Sartoris's incessant taunting ultimately drive Redmond to violence. Even Sartoris loyalists wish that the colonel would leave Redmond alone.

Redmond shoots and kills the unarmed Sartoris on the square in JEFFERSON, MISSISSIPPI. When Sartoris's son Bayard Sartoris (2), unarmed, confronts Redmond in his law office, he fires two shots at nothing, exits the office, walks down to the station, boards the just-arriving southbound train, and leaves Jefferson forever.

Faulkner narrated the story of the killing previously in SARTORIS, where Redmond appears under the name of Redlaw.

Sartoris, Bayard (1) ("An Odor of Verbena") The brother of Colonel John Sartoris. General J. E. B. STUART's aide-de-camp in 1862, he is killed just before the Second Battle of Manassas in a cavalry raid on the headquarters of the Yankee general Pope.

Sartoris, Bayard (2) (old) ("Ambuscade," "Retreat," "Raid," "Riposte in Tertio," "Vendée" and "An Odor of Verbena") The son of Colonel John Sartoris, founder of the prominent JEFFERSON, MISSISSIPPI, family, he is the boy hero, with his black friend Ringo Strother, of a series of picaresque adventures set in Civil War and Reconstruction-era YOKNAPATAWPHA COUNTY. He and Ringo follow war events closely, and he glories in his father's violent exploits. In "Vendée, he revenges himself on the bushwhacker who murders his grandmother, shooting him down and nailing his mutilated hand to her wooden grave marker.

As a young man, Bayard renounces his father's violent ways. Though he is expected to take revenge on the colonel's killer, Ben Redmond (called Redlaw in the novel SARTORIS), he instead faces him down unarmed and forces him to leave Jefferson forever.

Bayard is a key figure in *Sartoris*, and also appears in *The* HAMLET, GO DOWN, MOSES, ("The BEAR"), *REQUIEM FOR A NUN, The MANSION, The REIVERS*, and the short stories "A ROSE FOR EMILY" and "THERE WAS A QUEEN."

Sartoris, Colonel John ("Ambuscade," "Retreat," "Raid," "Skirmish at Sartoris," and "An Odor of Verbena") Head of the founding family of Faulkner's YOKNAPATAWPHA COUNTY cycle, this hard, violent, and imaginative man is said to have been modeled on Faulkner's great-grandfather, the soldier and railroad builder WILLIAM CLARK FALKNER.

Sartoris serves as an officer in Lee's army in the Civil War and later as the commander of a unit of partisan cavalry in northern Mississippi. He is presented as a soldier hero who causes so much grief for the Yankees that they put up a reward for his capture. "He was not big; it was just the things he did, that we knew he was doing, had been doing in Virginia and Tennessee, that made him seem so big to us," says his young son Bayard, who idolizes him. The colonel carries violence with him into postwar life, sallying forth on his wedding day in 1872 to shoot down two Yankees and so prevent a black candidate from winning election as JEFFERSON, MISSISSIPPI, marshal.

Along with violently opposing Yankee "carpetbaggers," Sartoris rebuilds his ruined plantation, develops a railroad, and defeats his bitter business rival to win election to the Mississippi legislature. Sartoris tires of violence at the last, however. He faces his rival Redmond alone and unarmed and is shot to death.

Colonel Sartoris, though long dead, is a palpable spirit in SARTORIS. His legendary wartime exploits form part of the background of The SOUND AND THE FURY. Faulkner narrates his killing of the two Burdens, New England carpetbaggers by way of Missouri, in LIGHT IN AUGUST. In ABSALOM, ABSALOM!, Thomas Sutpen rebuffs Sartoris in his effort to mobilize Yoknapatawpha planters against Reconstruction.

In the larger context of the Yoknapatawpha cycle, Colonel Sartoris stands at the head of an aristocratic family of the type that will pass from the scene with the rise of the Snopeses. Faulkner saw in his own family history a pattern of slow decline, and acknowledged similarities in character and experience between the founder of the Sartoris clan and his great-grandfather (*Faulkner in the University*, 254).

Sartoris, Drusilla Hawk ("Raid," "Skirmish at Sartoris," and "An Odor of Verbena") The daughter of Dennison Hawk Sr. and Louisa Hawk, she cuts her hair, alters her mode of dress, and enlists in Colonel John Sartoris's regiment after her

fiancé, Gavin Breckbridge, is killed at the BATTLE OF SHILOH. She is said to be the best woman rider in the country.

Drusilla survives the war and settles at Sartoris plantation with the colonel and his family. Though she and Sartoris are not lovers, her mother and the elderly ladies of JEFFERSON, MISSISSIPPI, pressure the couple to marry. They acquiesce, even though they are probably not in love.

When his business rival Redmond shoots and kills the colonel, Drusilla insists that Bayard Sartoris (2) seek revenge. But Bayard no longer glorifies his father's violent ways and he does not respond to the hysterical Drusilla's goading.

Drusilla eventually accepts young Bayard's conduct in the Redmond matter. By the time she leaves Jefferson for good to join her lawyer brother in Alabama, they are reconciled.

Sartoris, Virginia *See* Du Pre, Virginia.

Snopes, Ab(ner) ("Riposte in Tertio") An unscrupulous scavenger, "a sort of jackal" in Faulkner's phrase, he is one of the first of the poor white Snopeses in YOKNAPATAWPHA COUNTY.

Snopes avoids service in the Confederate army during the Civil War, and stays on at Colonel John Sartoris's plantation. Sartoris asks Snopes to keep an eye on his mother-in-law, Miss Rosa (Granny) Millard; he asks his son Bayard Sartoris (2) and Bayard's friend Ringo Strother to keep an eye on Snopes. Showing a lack of respect for him, Ringo, a slave, calls him "Ab Snopes"; Miss Rosa corrects him.

In collaboration with Miss Rosa, he steals horses and mules from the Union army and sells them back to the Yankees; Rosa believes, probably correctly, that he is cheating her out of some of the profits. After her killing, he goes into partnership with Rosa's murderer, the horse thief and bushwhacker Grumby. Snopes's connection with Grumby leads young Bayard and others to give him a severe beating.

Strother, Joby ("Ambuscade" and "Retreat") A slave of the Sartoris family, he is Ringo Strother's grandfather. Though he complains about being overworked, he remains loyal to the family when the Yankees arrive. Joby came from Carolina with John Sartoris and had been his bodyservant until he trained his son Simon for the task.

Strother, Loosh (Lucius) ("Ambuscade" and "Raid") A slave of the Sartorises, he has a strong desire for freedom. Loosh travels at night toward the Yankee lines, then returns to Sartoris plantation to announce: "Ginral Sherman gonter sweep the earth and the Race gonter all be free." When federal troops finally arrive, Loosh shows them where the family silver is hidden.

Strother, Louvinia ("Ambuscade" and "Raid") The wife of Joby Strother, she equips Colonel John Sartoris with his boots and pistols so he can escape from the Yankees. The faithful Louvinia is mortified by the betrayal of her son Loosh, who shows the Yankees where the Sartoris silver is hidden.

Strother, Philadelphia (Philadelphy) ("Ambuscade" and "Raid") One of the Sartoris slaves, she reluctantly goes off with her husband, Loosh, who during the Civil War follows the Federal forces in search of freedom. Loosh later leads the Yankees to the hiding place of the Sartoris family silver.

Strother, Ringo (Marengo) ("Ambuscade," "Retreat," "Raid," "Riposte in Tertio," Vendée," "An Odor of Verbena") One of the Sartoris slaves, he is the boyhood friend and companion of Bayard Sartoris (2). Born the same month, nursed together, raised eating and sleeping together, they are inseparable in a series of adventures in northern Mississippi during the Civil War, among them an ambush of a Yankee patrol.

Resourceful and intelligent, Ringo is the first to recognize the money-making potential of a federal order for the restitution of stolen goods that Bayard's grandmother, Rosa Millard, extracts from Colonel Nathaniel Dick. With Ringo's canny advice, she develops the order into a lucrative scheme of selling the Yankees their own horses and mules.

Later, when the bushwhacker Grumby murders Miss Rosa over a question of stolen horses, Ringo helps Bayard track him down and exact his revenge. The boys nail Grumby's corpse to a cotton compress door and attach his severed hand to Miss Rosa's grave marker.

After the war, Ringo volunteers to help Bayard avenge his father's death at Ben Redmond's hands. He is perplexed at first when Bayard allows Redmond to leave JEFFERSON, MISSISSIPPI, unscathed, but he accompanies Bayard home after the encounter and remains at his side in silent companionability through the long afternoon.

Strother, Simon ("An Odor of Verbena") A son of Joby Strother, a slave of Colonel John Sartoris, he is the father of Ringo Strother, the boyhood friend and companion of Bayard Sartoris (2). Simon came out of the Civil War with "a Confederate private's coat with a Yankee brigadier's star on it."

Sutpen, Thomas ("An Odor of Verbena") Colonel John Sartoris's regimental second-in-command at the start of the Civil War, he succeeds Sartoris as colonel when the troops vote out Sartoris as their commander; Sartoris never forgives him. Sartoris's son Bayard sketches Sutpen as "underbred, a cold, ruthless man" with a mysterious past. During the Reconstruction troubles, he refuses to have anything to do with Sartoris's night-rider terrorists.

Sutpen is a central figure in ABSALOM, ABSALOM!

White, Jed ("An Odor of Verbena") On George Wyatt's order, he rides out to Sartoris plantation to report that young Bayard Sartoris (2) is all right after his encounter with Ben Redmond in Redmond's JEFFERSON, MISSISSIPPI, law office.

Wilkins, Mrs. ("An Odor of Verbena") She is the small, thin, and gray wife of Professor Wilkins, one of Bayard Sartoris (2)'s law teachers at the university in OXFORD, MISSISSIPPI, and an acquaintance of Bayard's grandmother, Rosa Millard. Bayard lives with the Wilkinses while he is studying law. Mrs. Wilkins reminds him of his grandmother.

Wilkins, Professor ("An Odor of Verbena") He is one of Bayard Sartoris (2)'s law instructors at the university in OXFORD, MISSISSIPPI, and Bayard lives with the professor and his wife during the university term.

Ringo Strother carries word of Colonel John Sartoris's killing to Wilkins, who interrupts Bayard at his law books to break the news of his father's death to him, then offers Bayard a horse and a pistol.

Worsham, Doctor ("Riposte in Tertio") He is the Episcopal rector of Colonel John Sartoris's church before the Civil War.

Wyatt, George ("An Odor of Verbena") He serves in Colonel John Sartoris's troop during the war and afterward is an ally in Sartoris's schemes to suppress the black vote in JEFFERSON, MISSISSIPPI.

Wyatt attempts, through Drusilla Hawk Sartoris, to persuade the colonel to leave off the taunting of Ben Redmond that ultimately leads Redmond to shoot him. Failing to talk Bayard Sartoris (2) out of confronting Redmond after his father's killing, Wyatt gathers a group of six veterans to wait in the street as Bayard mounts the steps to Redmond's law office. After the encounter, he orders Jed White to ride out to SARTORIS plantation and report that Bayard is all right.

FURTHER READING

Brooks, Cleanth. "The Old Order (*The Unvanquished*)." In *William Faulkner: The Yoknapatawpha Country*, 75–99. Baton Rouge: Louisiana State University Press, 1990.

Backman, Melvin. "*The Unvanquished*." In *Faulkner: The Major Years*, 113–128. Bloomington: Indiana University Press, 1966.

Clarke, Deborah. "Gender, War, and Cross-Dressing in *The Unvanquished*." In *Faulkner and Gender: Faulkner and Yoknapatawpha, 1994*, edited by Donald M. Kartiganer and Ann J. Abadie, 228–251. Jackson: University Press of Mississippi, 1996.

Donaldson, Susan V. "Dismantling the *Saturday Evening Post* Reader: *The Unvanquished* and Changing 'Horizons of Expectation.'" In *Faulkner and Popular Culture: Faulkner and Yoknapatawpha, 1988*, edited by Doreen Fowler and Ann J. Abadie, 179–195. Jackson: University Press of Mississippi, 1990.

Dwyer, June. "Feminization, Masculinization, and the Role of the Woman Patriot in *The Unvanquished*." *Faulkner Journal* 6.2 (spring 1991): 55–64.

Hinkle, James, and Robert McCoy. *Reading Faulkner: The Unvanquished*. Jackson: University Press of Mississippi, 1995.

Kinney, Arthur F., ed. *Critical Essays on William Faulkner: The Sartoris Family*. Boston: G. K. Hall, 1985.

Millgate, Michael. "*The Unvanquished*." In *The Achievement of William Faulkner*, 165–170. Lincoln: University of Nebraska Press, 1978.

Roberts, Diane. "A Precarious Pedestal: The Confederate Woman in Faulkner's *Unvanquished*." *Journal of American Studies* 26.2 (August 1992): 233–246.

Taylor, Walter. *Faulkner's Search for the South*. 90–98. Urbana: University of Illinois Press, 1983.

"Vendée" (Uncollected Stories)

Short story first published in the December 5, 1936 issue of the SATURDAY EVENING POST, extensively revised for its appearance as chapter 5 of The UNVANQUISHED (1938).

SYNOPSIS

Narrated by a teenage Bayard Sartoris, the son of a Confederate colonel, John Sartoris, "Vendée" is a story of revenge set during the final days of the Civil War. Bayard's grandmother, Rosa Millard, has been murdered by Grumby, her erstwhile partner in stealing mules from the Union army. After Granny's funeral Bayard and Ringo, his black companion, vow revenge against the murderer. With the assistance of Uncle Buck McCaslin, the boys track down Grumby, and Bayard shoots him. The boys skin his corpse and nail the pelt to the door of an old cotton compress, cut off his right hand, and tie it to Granny's grave marker. Then the boys burst into tears. The story ends with Colonel Sartoris' return home from the war. As the soldier embraces his son, Uncle Buck boasts of the boy's courage: "Ain't I told you he is John Sartoris' boy? Hey? Ain't I told you?"

CRITICAL COMMENTARY

The Vendée is a geographical region of west-central France, located on the Bay of Biscay. Associated with a long history of rebellion against central authority, it was the site of religious wars in the 1500s and a peasants' revolt against the French government in the 1790s. The latter conflict, known as the Revolt in the Vendée, provides the subject for Victor Hugo's novel, *Ninety-Three*, as well as Honore de Balzac's novel, *The Chouans*. (Faulkner was heavily influenced by Balzac's "human comedy," and he considered titling the "Peasants" section of *The HAMLET* "The Chouans.") Karl Marx employs the term "a Vendée" to mean "a focus of persistent counter-revolutionary activities."

Faulkner's "Vendée" describes the counteractions of Rosa Millard and her two young compatriots, Bayard Sartoris and Ringo, against a treacherous enemy, Grumby. CLEANTH BROOKS argues that the undertaking by an old woman and two young boys of defensive actions that would typically be conducted by men demonstrates the breakup of traditional Southern society caused by the Civil War (*Yoknapatawpha Country*, 92). John Pilkington agrees that the gruesome details of the story "serve as a rendering of the depths to which ordinarily law-abiding persons may sink in a society that has fallen apart," yet he still finds the story melodramatic and incredulous (*Heart of Yoknapatawpha*, 206). The narrative seems to be improved by its context within *The Unvanquished*, in which it serves as just one of several stages in the coming-of-age story of Bayard Sartoris.

CHARACTERS

For a list of the characters in this story *see* the entry on *The Unvanquished*.

"Wash" (Collected Stories)

Story that first appeared in *Harper's* (February 1934) and was included in *DOCTOR MARTINO AND OTHER STORIES* (1934) and later reworked as a key episode in the novel *ABSALOM, ABSALOM!* (1936).

SYNOPSIS

This short story dramatizes the extreme disillusionment of Wash Jones, a poor white man, by Thomas Sutpen, his hero and benefactor, which results in violence and tragedy. In the opening scene, Wash's 17-year-old granddaughter Milly gives birth to a baby fathered by the 60-year-old Sutpen; disappointed that the child is not a son, Sutpen speaks to her callously. A flashback recalls how Sutpen fought in and lost his son in the Civil War, from which he returned to find his plantation in ruins. A squatter in Sutpen's old fishing shack, Wash is held in contempt by nearly everyone. Later he helps Sutpen in his store, and the two drink together despite their social distance. When Sutpen becomes interested in Milly, Wash mistakenly trusts that he will do right by her. Overhearing Sutpen's cruel remarks to Milly, he is enraged and slays Sutpen with a scythe. He then retreats to the cabin to tend to Milly and to await the law. When the sheriff finally arrives, Wash takes a butcher knife to Milly and the baby, sets the cabin on fire, and charges out with the scythe, ignoring the order to stop or to be shot.

CRITICAL COMMENTARY

"Wash" is one of Faulkner's most perceptive treatments of class consciousness and the conflicts and contradictions contained therein. Initially Jones considers Sutpen, riding about his plantation astride his black stallion, as a deity: "If God Himself was to come down and ride the natural earth, that's what He would aim to look like." Despite their extreme differences in social status and wealth, Jones, who is considered "white trash" even by the Negro slaves, interprets his intimacy with Sutpen—helping him in the store, reminding him of his wartime exploits, drinking liquor from the same jug with him in the scuppernong arbor behind the house, escorting the old man home when he is too drunk to walk by himself—as a kind of acceptance and an endorsement of his own self-worth. But such thoughts prove illusionary, no less a lie than when, during the war, Jones had told people he was "looking after the Kernel's place" while Sutpen was away at war. The moment of self-awareness comes when Jones overhears Sutpen callously say to Milly, who has just given birth to Sutpen's daughter: "Too bad you're not a mare. Then I could give you a decent stall in the stable." Hearing his granddaughter characterized as a brute animal leads to Jones's even more brutish treatment of Sutpen: he murders him with a scythe, a field hand's tool. Yet, ironically, even in Wash's bold act of murder and the subsequent courage with which he faces the arresting officers, he is desperately asserting a dignity and self-worth that he had previously and mistakenly identified in his idealized view of a besotted, lecherous old man.

As Diane B. Jones has stated, for many readers "it is nearly impossible to read 'Wash' without superimposing Sutpen's fuller story [from ABSALOM, ABSALOM!] on the action." Yet, as she further notes, such an approach is most unfortunate, since the story "merits attention as an independent text" (398–399). Those critics who do consider the story as a self-contained work generally regard it as one of Faulkner's more powerful stories. For Jack F. Stewart it is his "most concentrated parable of Southern degeneracy in the aftermath of the Civil War." For Neil Isaacs it represents a "mythic archetype of the death of the gods." For H. R. Stoneback "Wash" is "the moving epiphany and powerful tragedy of Wash Jones." As such, Stoneback asserts, the story deserves to be commended "for its handling of the basic theme of the discovery of evil, for its skillful presentation of disillusionment and loss of innocence, and for its commentary on an important thematic concern in Faulkner, the dangers of the abstraction of social status and class" (*A William Faulkner Encyclopedia*, 432–433).

CHARACTERS

For the list of characters in this story *see* the entry on ABSALOM, ABSALOM!.

Wild Palms, The [If I Forget Thee, Jerusalem]

A novel in the form of two alternating stories titled "Wild Palms" and "Old Man"; published by RANDOM HOUSE in 1939 as *The Wild Palms*. A "corrected text" issued in 1990 used Faulkner's original choice of title, *If I Forget Thee, Jerusalem*. However, objections from Faulkner's estate led to the restoration of *The Wild Palms* as the title in 2003.

SYNOPSIS

The novel opens in present time with Charlotte Rittenmeyer hemorrhaging in the bedroom of a rented beach cottage in a town modeled upon the Gulf Coast resort of Pascagoula, Mississippi. She is near death from complications of a botched abortion by her lover, Harry Wilbourne.

Faulkner introduces the tall convict, Harry Wilbourne's foil, in the second section. He is serving a 15-year prison sentence for a train robbery, the plans for which he took from a pulp detective magazine. Rain falls incessantly, and news of a flood seeps into the prison. Finally a levee breaks nearby, and the inmates are evacuated.

Section 3 is a flashback. Close to the end of an internship in a NEW ORLEANS hospital, Harry meets Charlotte, a sculptor married to the humdrum businessman Francis Rittenmeyer and the mother of two little girls, at a Vieux Carré party. They fall in love at once. Even more improbably, the impecunious Harry finds $1,278 in a lost wallet to fund their flight on what Charlotte fiercely insists will be a perpetual honeymoon. The lovers—Charlotte driven, insistent and uncompromising, Harry pliant—set off for Chicago, leaving Francis Rittenmeyer, the girls, and Harry's medical career behind.

In the fourth section, the convict is turned loose during the flood with instructions to search for a woman trapped in a tree and a man stranded on the roof of a cottonhouse. The prison authorities later report the convict drowned, but in fact he and the woman, also unnamed, are adrift on the surging waters.

In section 5, Harry and Charlotte find shelter in Chicago. He gets work as an intern but loses the job; she lands a temporary job dressing windows in a department store. Gradually their money runs out. A sympathetic newspaper friend, McCord, provides them a haven in a cottage on a Wisconsin lake. With the approach of winter, the idyll ends and they return to Chicago. Harry senses a descent into domesticity and realizes they must take flight again. He accepts the offer of a job as doctor in a Utah mining camp, and they strike out for the mountains.

Section 6 finds the convict and the rescued woman, who is pregnant, swept along with the flood. It carries them up the Yazoo River and into the Mississippi—the "Old Man" river of the story's title. They pass Vicksburg, then Baton Rouge. The woman goes into labor. The convict grounds the skiff on a snake-infested Indian mound and delivers her baby, cutting the umbilical cord with the jagged edge of a tin-can lid.

In section 7, set in the frozen waste of the Utah mining camp, Faulkner introduces two new characters, "Buck" and Billie Buckner. The four become friends and even share quarters and an inefficient gasoline heater as bitter cold clamps down on the mountains. Eventually Buck asks Harry to perform an abortion on Billie. At first he refuses, but Charlotte talks him into it and he carries out the procedure successfully. Not long afterward, Charlotte tells Harry that she, too, is pregnant.

In section 8, the convict finds haven in a Louisiana swamp. He goes into partnership with an alligator hunter known as the Cajan and, for a time, experiences fulfillment in freedom. But the flood finally reaches the bayou and he and the woman, with her child, are forced to flee. The convict eventually returns to his starting point and reports back to the prison officials, delivering the skiff and its passenger.

Section 9 returns to the present. Harry has sent for his landlord, who happens to be a physician; the doctor promptly sends for the authorities. An ambulance carries Charlotte to the hospital, and Harry is taken to jail. Charlotte dies in surgery; Harry is convicted of manslaughter and sentenced to 50 years in prison. Before her death, Charlotte had asked her husband to plead for Harry, and he obediently turns up to ask the court for mercy. Later, Rittenmeyer offers Harry bail bond money and the chance to escape to Mexico; when he refuses, Rittenmeyer presents him with a cyanide capsule. Harry turns this down too, opting for

prison and the memory of his love for Charlotte: he decides, "*between grief and nothing I will take grief*" (324).

Section 10 concludes the novel on an antiromantic and farcical note. The tall convict is back in PARCHMAN prison with 10 years added to his sentence for attempted escape. His one-time girlfriend, the woman for whom he planned and attempted the low comedy train robbery, visits him in prison. Then the visits stop, and he learns she has married a prison guard. On her honeymoon, she sends him a postcard signed, "*Your friend (Mrs) Vernon Waldrip*" (339).

CRITICAL COMMENTARY

Most early critics regarded *The Wild Palms* as a minor work. Some judged it a failure for its pairing of two essentially separate tales; others devalued the work because it is only tangentially related to Faulkner's Yoknapatawpha series. More recently, however, the novel has been accorded much more favorable recognition. A major turning point came with the publication of Thomas McHaney's admiring and insightful book-length study of the novel in 1975.

MICHAEL MILLGATE describes the book as "a double novel" (*Achievement*, 175). It begins with the first of five sections of "Wild Palms," the story of Harry Wilbourne and Charlotte Rittenmeyer, who sacrifice everything for love. The five sections of "Old Man," in which an unnamed prison convict is caught up in a great Mississippi River flood, are a counterpoint to the tale of Harry and Charlotte, as the convict is a loner, rejecting love and relationship.

The only direct connection between the two stories is the Mississippi state prison at PARCHMAN. "Old Man" takes place in 1927; "Wild Palms" is set a decade later. Though Harry will eventually serve hard time at the convict's prison, none of the characters in the two stories meet or cross paths.

Faulkner offered at least two explanations for his decision to alternate the stories. "When I reached the end of what is now the first section of *The Wild Palms*, I realized suddenly that something was missing, it needed emphasis, something to lift it like counterpoint in music," he said in the PARIS REVIEW interview of 1955. On another occasion, though, he seemed to suggest he joined the two tales simply because he needed to fill out a book: each story alone was too short.

IRVING HOWE gives Faulkner the benefit of the doubt, arguing that more than whim or the exigencies of the bookmaking trade led him to the pairing. "[T]he correspondences and joined oppositions between the two stories are so numerous and suggestive that we are obliged to take them seriously, as elements of a literary design," he wrote (*William Faulkner: A Critical Study*, 239). NOEL POLK, who edited the Library of America edition of *If I Forget Thee, Jerusalem*, concluded from typescript and manuscript analysis that Faulkner did not interleave existing stories, but wrote "Wild Palms" and "Old Man" together.

Following McHaney's detailed examination of the structural affinities of the two sections of the book, other critics have continued to argue that the situations and themes of the paired stories unify *The Wild Palms*. The theme of flight and refuge is an obvious link. Harry and Charlotte sacrifice all in their bid for freedom and love; the tall convict, offered his freedom and a sort of love as well, wants only to return to the safe haven of prison. Each story details an escape from confinement to a provisional freedom and then to an ultimate, still more circumscribed confinement. Harry, in aborting Charlotte's pregnancy, takes life; the convict, in delivering the flood refugee's baby, gives it.

William H. Rueckert calls *The Wild Palms* "Faulkner's most profound fiction on a potentially generative idealism (love, passionate romantic love) which is ironically destructive." The challenge, Rueckert goes on to say, "is to have the wildness without the destruction." Here as elsewhere in Faulkner's works, Rueckert believes, resolving that conflict is virtually impossible because of "the polarity and antagonism between the values of passionate romantic love and society" (*Faulkner from Within*, 134–135). Rueckert draws an interesting parallel between Harry Wilbourne and Ike McCaslin of GO DOWN, MOSES: both have experienced and lost a wilderness life bordering on the transcendent, and that experience now lives on in their memories. By contrast, the convict will never know such an experience, since "'between grief and nothing' he takes nothing" (140).

Understandably, feminist critics have found *The Wild Palms* an especially engaging text to study, particularly in its characterization of Charlotte Rittenmeyer. Deborah Clark notes how Charlotte's independence, aggressiveness, and creativity push against the gender boundaries of her day (*Robbing the Mother*, 109–117); and Anne Goodwyn Jones believes that Faulkner accords Charlotte "a respect . . . that is absent from his treatment of other sexually active and assertive and intelligent women" (in *Faulkner and Popular Culture*, edited by Doreen Fowler and Ann J. Abadie, 145). These and other commentators are particularly interested in the link Faulkner establishes with Charlotte between the feminine and creativity.

The tall convict is physically adept but limited in intelligence. The critic MALCOLM COWLEY once characterized him as "the ideal soldier for a fascist army." Others have found him more timid than alarming, so afraid of the world that he gratefully returns to his haven behind bars.

CHARACTERS

Bledsoe ("Old Man") He looks after the mules at Parchman penitentiary in Mississippi.

Buckworth ("Old Man") The deputy warden at Parchman, he reports the convict dead, drowned in the flood. The convict's eventual voluntary return poses a paperwork problem that threatens to embarrass the warden; he resolves it by transferring Buckworth to the highway patrol.

Cajan, the ("Old Man") An alligator hunter who lives deep in a Louisiana bayou, he befriends the convict and the woman and her child. He and the convict become hunting partners even though they cannot communicate in words. The men work together for 10 days, and the convict temporarily abandons his goal of returning to prison. But the Cajan's alligator hide business is flooded out when a levee is blown up for flood control, and the convict resumes his prisonward journey.

Convict, the ("Old Man") A young innocent from the Mississippi hill country, his reading of paperback crime novels inspires him to attempt a train robbery, more for the satisfaction of carrying out a well-conceived scheme than for the money. The robbery misfires, and he is arrested and sentenced to 15 years in prison. The tall convict, as he is usually styled, resents not the police and courts but instead the crime-story writers who misled him. He is a model prisoner. As a result, he is taken from the prison during the Great Mississippi Flood of 1927, given a skiff, and asked to rescue a man on a cotton house and a pregnant woman who has taken refuge in a tree. He finds the woman but not the man. The flood carries them far downstream and he fights against impossible odds for their lives. The prison officials give him up for drowned, but he heroically pursues his goals to deliver the woman and her newborn baby to safety and return to his place of security in prison. Since the prison warden has long since reported the tall convict dead, his eventual return is an embarrassment. To cover it, the warden adds 10 years to the convict's sentence for attempted escape. Relieved to be free of the woman and back in prison, the convict hardly cares.

Hamp ("Old Man") He impersonates a judge at the warden's request and adds 10 years to the convict's sentence for attempted escape.

Hogben ("Wild Palms") The engineer who operates the ore train at the Utah mine, he explains to Harry Wilbourne that he must make a trip every 30 days in order to keep the franchise.

Louisa ("Wild Palms") A maid in the San Antonio brothel where Harry Wilbourne asks for medicine that will cause Charlotte Rittenmeyer to abort.

McCord (Mac) ("Wild Palms") A Chicago newspaperman, he befriends Harry Wilbourne and Charlotte Rittenmeyer even though he is skeptical of their notions of love and commitment. McCord lends Harry and Charlotte the lake cabin he co-owns. He helps Charlotte find a job in Chicago. Later, McCord tries to talk Harry out of taking a job in a Utah mine that turns out to be a sham.

Martha ("Wild Palms") The wife of the doctor whose Gulf Coast beach house Harry Wilbourne and Charlotte Rittenmeyer rent, she is more interested in her tenants' ability to pay the rent than in whether they are married. While her husband rages at Harry for what he regards as his immortality, Martha matter-of-factly brews and offers him a cup of coffee.

Pete ("Wild Palms") He works in the San Antonio brothel where Harry Wilbourne goes in search of a drug that will cause Charlotte Rittenmeyer to have an abortion. Pete advises the brothel bouncer to "sock" (punch) Wilbourne.

Richardson, Dr. ("Wild Palms") A skilled surgeon, he attends Charlotte Rittenmeyer in the hospital emergency room, where she dies.

Rittenmeyer, Ann ("Wild Palms") The younger daughter of Charlotte and Francis Rittenmeyer.

Rittenmeyer, Charlotte (1) ("Wild Palms") A sculptor, fiercely independent, aggressive, and strong-willed, she meets Harry Wilbourne, a poverty-stricken medical intern, at a party in the Vieux Carré in NEW ORLEANS and eventually leaves her well-to-do husband and two daughters for him. With $1,278 in cash that Harry finds in a lost wallet, they set out for Chicago. The money begins to run low and they find jobs. Charlotte sells little sculpted figures, then works as a display designer in a department store. She believes that marriage, children, and concern for comfort and security are the death of love. When money worries encroach, she and Harry move on—to a friend's lake cottage, back to Chicago, to a mine in the frozen Utah wilderness, to San Antonio, to a small town on the Mississippi Gulf Coast. She has no use for Harry's anxieties and misgivings about their irregular life, but her pregnancy threatens her notion of love and she browbeats Harry into agreeing to perform an abortion on her. He is afraid; he wants her to carry the baby to term, even if it means applying to a charity ward. Charlotte refuses. Something goes wrong with the procedure, and Charlotte fails to heal. She dies on the operating table of a Mississippi hospital.

Rittenmeyer, Charlotte (2) ("Wild Palms")
The older daughter of Charlotte and Francis
Rittenmeyer.

Rittenmeyer, Francis (Rat) ("Wild Palms")
Charlotte Rittenmeyer's abandoned husband,
rigid but devoted after his fashion, he is an observant Roman Catholic and refuses to grant his wife
a divorce when she leaves him and their children
for Harry Wilbourne. Rittenmeyer allows Charlotte to live without harassment so long as she
gets in touch with him once a month, and he
gives Wilbourne a check to cover her fare home
in an emergency. At their last meeting, Charlotte
tells him about her illness and makes him promise
not to take action against Wilbourne if she dies.
After her death, Rittenmeyer fulfills his pledge.
He offers to pay Wilbourne's bond and urges him
to flee to Mexico. When Wilbourne refuses, he
rises to make a plea for him in court. As a final
effort, he brings cyanide to Wilbourne's cell; the
convict refuses it.

Waldrip, Mrs. Vernon ("Old Man") The convict's former girlfriend, she dreams of being the
consort of a successful criminal. She visits the convict in prison once, and later sends him a postcard
showing the hotel where she and her husband are
spending their honeymoon.

Warden, the ("Old Man") The callous, self-serving head of Parchman penitentiary, he charges
the tall convict with attempted escape and adds 10
years to his sentence.

Wilbourne, Dr. ("Wild Palms") Harry Wilbourne's father, he married Harry's much-younger
mother late in life. Dr. Wilbourne died of toxemia
from sucking a snake bite on a child's hand, leaving
Harry an orphan at age 2. He provided $2,000 in
his will for his son's medical education.

Wilbourne, Henry ("Harry") ("Wild Palms")
A young, penniless, and pliant medical intern
who lives a monastic life and has no experience of
women, he falls deeply in love with Charlotte Rittenmeyer. After finding $1,278 in a New Orleans

street, he quits his internship only a few months
before he would have taken his medical degree
and leaves for Chicago with Charlotte. They exist
precariously for the next two years. Charlotte's
principles regarding love seem to bar security and
routine. Harry finds a job doing laboratory work
in a charity hospital in the black ghetto, but loses
it after a few weeks. The two move from job to
marginal job. Gradually their money runs out.
They retire for a time to the lake cottage of their
journalist friend McCord; then, against McCord's
advice, Harry accepts an appointment as company
physician at a spurious mine in the mountains of
Utah. Charlotte becomes pregnant in Utah and
tries to talk Harry into performing an abortion
on her. He resists and offers to make whatever
sacrifices are necessary for the child. Charlotte is
adamant. Children do not fit her notions of love;
after all, she has left two daughters behind with
her husband in New Orleans. Harry finally agrees
to do the abortion but bungles the job, and Charlotte becomes seriously ill. She dies in a Mississippi
Gulf Coast hospital, and Harry is charged with
manslaughter for her death. He pleads guilty and is
sentenced to 50 years in prison. In jail, he refuses
Charlotte's husband's offer to help him escape
or, finally, to commit suicide. One must live to
remember, he tells himself; he refuses to give up
the memory of his life with Charlotte. "Yes," he
decides. "Between grief and nothing I will take
grief" (*The Wild Palms*, 324).

the woman ("Old Man") An unnamed victim
of the Great Mississippi Flood of 1927, she takes
refuge in a cypress tree when the waters rise and
the convict rescues her there. The floodwaters
carry them far downstream; she gives birth; and
after weeks of desperate effort, the convict returns
her safely to dry land.

FURTHER READING

Bernhardt, Laurie A. "'Being Worthy Enough': The
Tragedy of Charlotte Rittenmeyer." *Mississippi
Quarterly* 39.3 (summer 1986): 351–364.

Brooks, Cleanth. "The Tradition of Romantic Love
and *The Wild Palms*." *Mississippi Quarterly* 25 (summer 1972): 265–287.

Eldred, Joyce Carey. "Faulkner's Still Life: Art and Abortion in *The Wild Palms*." *Faulkner Journal* 4.1–2 (1988–1989): 139–158.

Fowler, Doreen A. "Measuring Faulkner's Tall Convict." *Studies in the Novel* 14 (fall 1982): 280–284.

Hamblin, Robert W. "Beyond the Edge of the Map: Faulkner, Turner, and the Frontier Line." In *Faulkner in the Twenty-First Century: Faulkner and Yoknapatawpha, 2000*, edited by Robert W. Hamblin and Ann J. Abadie, 154–171. Jackson: University Press of Mississippi, 2003.

Jones, Anne Goodwyn. "'The Kotex Age': Women, Popular Culture, and *The Wild Palms*." In *Faulkner and Popular Culture: Faulkner and Yoknapatawpha, 1988*, edited by Doreen Fowler and Ann J. Abadie, 142–162. Jackson: University Press of Mississippi, 1990.

McHaney, Thomas L. *William Faulkner's* The Wild Palms: *A Study*. Jackson: University Press of Mississippi, 1975.

Meindl, Dieter. "Romantic Idealism and *The Wild Palms*." In *Faulkner and Idealism: Perspectives from Paris*, edited by Michel Gresset and Patrick Samway, 86–96. Jackson: University Press of Mississippi, 1983.

Mortimer, Gail L. "The Ironies of Transcendent Love in Faulkner's *The Wild Palms*." *Faulkner Journal* 1.2 (spring 1986): 30–42.

Parini, Jay. *One Matchless Time: A Life of William Faulkner*, 234–241. New York: Harper Collins, 2004.

Turner, W. Craig. "Faulkner's 'Old Man' and the American Humor Tradition." *University of Mississippi Studies in English* 5 (1984–1987): 149–157.

Urgo, Joseph R. "Faulkner Unplugged: Abortopoesis and *The Wild Palms*." In *Faulkner and Gender: Faulkner and Yoknapatawpha, 1994*, edited by Donald M. Kartiganer and Ann J. Abadie, 252–272. Jackson: University Press of Mississippi, 1996.

"With Caution and Dispatch" (Uncollected Stories)

Written sometime in the early 1930s, this short story was first published posthumously in UNCOL-LECTED STORIES OF WILLIAM FAULKNER. For further information, *see Selected Letters of William Faulkner*, 63 and 274; *Uncollected Stories*, 711; and Diane Brown Jones, *A Reader's Guide to the Short Stories of William Faulkner*, 210, 403, and 404. See also FLYING, FAULKNER AND.

SYNOPSIS

"With Caution and Dispatch" is a tall tale-like short story dealing with the misadventures of Second Lieutenant (Johnny) Sartoris, a World War I aviator born in YOKNAPATAWPHA COUNTY. When Sartoris's squadron is ordered to fly their Sopwith Camel fighter planes to France, Sartoris manages to crash three times, destroying his aircraft but miraculously surviving the crashes. His first accident was the result of a mechanical malfunction caused by Sartoris's skylarking. This crash takes place in England. Sartoris is issued a second Camel, and he rushes to catch up with his group. While flying low over the English Channel, however, he manages to crash onto the deck of a supposedly neutral freighter. He is held a prisoner for a while, then taken off that ship and escorted onto a British man-of-war vessel, where he is told he has interfered with a top-secret operation and commanded to tell no one what he saw. In France, he is given a third Camel, which he crash-lands at his own aerodrome. Sartoris seems more afraid of being thought cowardly by his squadron mates than he is of his near-brushes with death.

In "With Caution and Dispatch"—one of several stories dealing with World War I and aviatorial courage (*also see* "ALL THE DEAD PILOTS" and "DEATH DRAG")—Faulkner mocks both the folly and courage of young aviators and the wastefulness and secretiveness of war. In the later novel A FABLE, he uses similar themes but to a much darker effect.

CHARACTERS

Atkinson One of the four flight commanders in the story. Atkinson is to meet (John) Sartoris at Candas to take him back to the squadron, but Sartoris crashes before getting there.

Britt One of the four flight commanders in the story. His flight squadron includes Second

Lt. (John) Sartoris, who is apprehensive that his squadron mates will suspect him of cowardice. Britt relieves him of that fear when he greets Sartoris after his third crash at the French aerodrome. As Sartoris emerges from his fighter, which is on its back near the mess tent, Britt hands a pair of flying goggles and wryly tells him to get another Camel and see if he can crash it before teatime.

Haig, General (Douglas) A British general referred to in the story. He was part of the command in Ypres, Belgium, where several battles took place.

Harry An adjutant who assists the major in calling Pool to inform him of (John) Sartoris's crash landing.

Immelman (Max) A German aviator referred to in the short story. *Also see* A FABLE; as in the novel his name appears with only one *n* in "With Caution and Dispatch."

Johnson, Jack Referred to in the short story, he is the first African-American heavyweight champion of the world.

Ludendorff, General (Erich) A German general referred to in the short story.

Pool The colonel whom Harry is asked by the major to call after (John) Sartoris's crash landing.

Sartoris, (Johnny) A second lieutenant in the Flying Corps, he is the central character in the short story. A supposedly skillful pilot, Sartoris crashes three different Camel fighters on what should have been a simple short flight across the English Channel to France. *Also see* SARTORIS and "ALL THE DEAD PILOTS"; he is referred to in *The Mansion* and in the short story "THERE WAS A QUEEN."

Sibleigh One of the four flight commanders and one of the best Camel pilots. *Also see* SARTORIS and A FABLE.

Tate One of the four flight commanders in the short story.

Vision in Spring

A sequence of 14 love poems Faulkner wrote in 1921 and hand-bound to give to Estelle Franklin, whom he married in 1929 (*see* FAULKNER, LIDA ESTELLE OLDHAM). *Vision in Spring*, edited with an introduction by Judith L. Sensibar, was published posthumously in 1984. Though there is a single narrator of the poems named Pierrot, the sequence contains several distinct voices. In her introduction, Sensibar argues that in Faulkner's poems, and especially in *Vision in Spring*, Faulkner learned "ways to cast off the mask while retaining in his writing those qualities that made it so imaginatively compelling. . . . The protean poet-dreamer resurfaces in his tragic and comic fictional protagonists" (xiii–xiv). *Vision in Spring*, like Faulkner's poetry in general, is derivative and shows the influence of writers such as T. S. Eliot, Keats, Swinburne, and the symbolist poets.

William Faulkner: Early Prose and Poetry

A collection of poems, prose pieces, and pen-and-ink drawings that Faulkner published between 1917 and 1925, the early period of his literary career. Compiled with an introduction by CARVEL COLLINS, the collection was published in 1962 by Little, Brown and Co. (For titles, *see* Appendix.)

William Faulkner's University Pieces

A collection of Faulkner's poetry, prose, and drawings between 1916 and 1925 that first appeared in several UNIVERSITY OF MISSISSIPPI publications.

Compiled with an introduction by CARVEL COLLINS, *William Faulkner's University Pieces* was published in 1962 by Kendyusha Press in Japan to pay tribute to Faulkner's successful visit to Nagano (*see* FAULKNER AT NAGANO) and to the reception of his works by the Japanese academic community. The collection also contains Faulkner's first published short story, "Landing in Luck," a story about a cadet's first solo flight, which appeared in the November 1919 issue of the student newspaper, *The* MISSISSIPPIAN.

Wishing Tree, The

Posthumously published children's story, written in 1927 for Faulkner's stepdaughter, VICTORIA FRANKLIN. The author typed and bound the story and presented it to Victoria on her eighth birthday. "Bill he made this book," the inscription read.

The Wishing Tree is a fairy story that promises good things. For children who are good, though, the tree is not necessary for good things to come to pass. Faulkner hand-produced at least two copies of the tale. *The Wishing Tree* was published posthumously in the SATURDAY EVENING POST 240 (8 April 1967), 48–53, 57–58, 60–63. In April 1967, RANDOM HOUSE published the story in book form, with illustrations by Dan Bolognese.

PART III

Related People, Places, and Topics

A

Aiken, Conrad (1889–1973) Poet and writer, born in Savannah, Georgia, and reared in Cambridge, Massachusetts. Aiken's work was an early influence on Faulkner, particularly his verse novel *The Jig of Forslin* (1917) and the collection of tone poems titled *The House of Dust* (1920).

Faulkner praised Aiken's experimental *Turns and Movies* (1916) in an essay in THE MISSISSIPPIAN for February 16, 1921: "He, alone of the entire yelping pack, seems to have a definite goal in mind."

Aiken helped build Faulkner's literary reputation with a favorable review of his second novel, MOSQUITOES, in the *New York Evening Post* in 1927. "Mr. Faulkner has a sense of character; he has a sense of humor; he has a sense of style," he wrote. Aiken published an appreciation of Faulkner's much-criticized style in The ATLANTIC MONTHLY in November 1939. He conceded Faulkner's obscurity; "Each time," he wrote, "one must learn all over again *how* to read this strangely fluid and slippery and heavily mannered prose." That said, Aiken went on to observe that readers willing to tackle his intricacies and patches of overwriting were in for great rewards.

alcoholism, Faulkner and The affliction of alcoholism came to Faulkner through his father and grandfather. JOHN WESLEY THOMPSON FALKNER, the novelist's paternal grandfather, periodically drank himself into a stay at the KEELEY INSTITUTE in MEMPHIS. His father, MURRY CUTHBERT FALKNER, continued the family pattern of heavy drinking. He too checked into Keeley's at intervals to purge himself of alcohol.

Doctors and biographers have offered physiological and psychological explanations for Faulkner's regular, often predictable, and always prodigious bouts of drinking. In 1953, a New York psychiatrist, Dr. S. Bernard Wortis, concluded after examining Faulkner that increased worry, strain, or misery lessened his naturally low tolerance for alcohol. Wortis theorized that Faulkner drank in an attempt to narcoticize intense and ever-present emotional pain.

Alcohol troubles were familiar—though evidently not especially terrifying—to Faulkner from his early childhood in OXFORD, MISSISSIPPI. He knew about the Young Colonel's trips to the Keeley Institute, where Dr. Leslie E. Keeley treated his patients with injections of double chloride of gold, a potion said to leave an extreme distaste for liquor in an alcoholic's mouth. In his 1896 study *The Non-Heredity of Inebriety*, Keeley classified alcoholism as a disease susceptible to treatment, not a fault of character, and argued that every alcoholic has within himself the power to recover.

Murry Falkner's appearances at the clinic must have shaken the doctor's faith in his theories about heredity, alcoholism, and the primacy of the will. Falkner's teetotalling wife, MAUD BUTLER FALKNER, used to pack him off to the Keeley Institute when his drinking became unbearable. She hated liquor, and to emphasize her point she sometimes brought the boys along on the trip to Memphis. In the boys' recollections, though, the trips do not sound unpleasant. While their father submitted to the cure, Billy and his brothers amused themselves with streetcar excursions into the city. On one such journey, they caught their first glimpse of the Mississippi River.

Faulkner seems to have taken up drinking in the first instance out of boredom. In 1915 the family, concerned about his apparent aimlessness, put him to work at the Young Colonel's bank, an apprenticeship he found intolerable. To pass the time, he dipped into his grandfather's brand whiskey.

"Learned the medicinal value of his liquor," Faulkner remarked later. "Grandfather thought it was the janitor. Hard on the janitor."

As time went on, Faulkner's drinking became a cause for alarm. His friend STARK YOUNG, who saw a good deal of the aspiring novelist in New York City in 1921, expressed astonishment at the amount of alcohol—whiskey and sometimes cheap gin—he could put away. Faulkner was, after all, a small man, and slightly built. In the autumn of 1928, after he finished correcting proofs of *The Sound and the Fury,* he locked himself in his room on Macdougal Street in New York and drank himself into unconsciousness.

Faulkner called alcoholism "the chemistry of craving." The drinking bouts became a recurring pattern in the last stages of his creative work: Tired, emotionally spent, prone to feelings of depression and emptiness, Faulkner would enscript a date neatly on the last page of a manuscript, or finish correcting the last page of proofs, and then begin to drink.

The publication of *Sanctuary* in 1931 brought him a degree of celebrity, and he made the rounds of literary parties during a seven-week interval in New York that autumn. But what he really enjoyed were evenings drinking with Dashiell Hammett, a master of the detective novel and a formidable alcoholic himself. The good times with Hammett ended in Faulkner's disappearance for several days on a lonely binge in his hotel room.

The completion of *Absalom, Absalom!* in 1936, coupled with Faulkner's all but chronic money troubles and his enduring grief over his youngest brother's death in an airplane crash, touched off another bout of self-destructive drinking. His mother and

his stepson MALCOLM FRANKLIN took turns sitting by his "drunk bed," but the episode grew so prolonged that they decided to send Faulkner off for the first of what would be several stays at Wright's Sanatorium, a small private hospital in BYHALIA, MISSISSIPPI.

On many occasions, Faulkner himself would conclude an episode before it reached headline category. His daughter JILL FAULKNER recalled the invariable signal for the end: Faulkner coming into the kitchen to mix and drink down a concoction of Worcestershire sauce and a raw egg.

Faulkner's love affairs, especially his long-running association with META CARPENTER, would sometimes trigger a binge. Carpenter's marriage to another man sent him into a spin in the autumn of 1937. In a drunken stupor, he fell against a steampipe in the bathroom of his room at the ALGONQUIN HOTEL in New York and seared his back. A doctor treated him for severe burns and dosed him with paraldehyde to kill his craving for alcohol. The burn required a skin graft which became infected; pain and discomfort from the injury troubled Faulkner long afterwards.

Faulkner's work for WARNER BROTHERS in Hollywood in the 1940s drove him to a despair that regularly ended in a drinking episode. His studio friends would intervene, making excuses for him, warning him against drinking on the job, finally cutting off his supply of liquor. At such times Faulkner would try to negotiate. The novelist was famously sparing with his signature. But on one occasion he signed a stack of his books piled on the coffee table of his movie friend A. I. (Buzz) BEZZERIDES, with whom he happened to be living, and then pleaded for a drink.

The approaching end of his strange affair with JOAN WILLIAMS, a girl thirty years his junior, coupled with recurring back pain (the result of falls from a horse), landed Faulkner in the Gartley-Ramsay Hospital, a private psychiatric institute in Memphis, in fall 1952. He resumed drinking, mixing whiskey and beer with the sedative Seconal, when he returned home to ROWAN OAK, and narrowly missed serious injury when he tumbled down the stairs there. His wife, ESTELLE OLDHAM FAULKNER, desperate, phoned Faulkner's friend and editor, SAXE COMMINS, who traveled down to Oxford from New York at her summons. Commins found the novelist semiconscious on a couch, battered, incontinent, and near delirium; he wrote to his wife that he was witnessing "the complete disintegration of a man."

Commins saw Faulkner back into the Gartley-Ramsay Hospital. He returned two weeks later to find Estelle launched on a prolonged drinking spell of her own, having discovered Joan Williams's letters to Faulkner.

The critic and biographer Federick Karl regards Faulkner's drinking as suicidal. The episodes were "virtually acts of self-destruction," Karl wrote, "since he needed to be saved by others"—his mother, Estelle, friends such as Commins. "With alcohol, he had found the middle ground or perfect balance between life and death," Karl continued. "Suicide by direct means was out, but suicide through drinking was a way of dealing with life."

Karl speculates, too, that Faulkner may have prized alcohol as the fuel for his artistic flame, much as had the romantic and symbolist poets he admired as a young man.

Faulkner himself used to make light of what was patently an unalloyed private horror, as though offering a handout for public consumption. It is true that he actually liked whiskey, preferring Jack Daniel's when he could afford it.

In a PARIS REVIEW interview with JEAN STEIN in 1956, Faulkner observed that all a writer needed for his work were paper, tobacco, a little food, and whiskey.

"Bourbon, you mean?" she asked.

"No, I ain't that particular," Faulkner answered. Then, parodying his famous line in the 1939 novel THE WILD PALMS and satirizing his own tortured emotional life, he went on, "Between scotch and nothing I'll take scotch."

Critics have noted that alcoholics in Faulkner's fiction are rarely aggressive or dangerously violent. Some are quiet, almost gentle, and defeated, like the elder Jason Compson in *The Sound and the Fury.* Boon Hogganbeck in "The BEAR" (*see* GO DOWN, MOSES), *The* REIVERS, and other works is a rare example of a riotous drinker in Faulkner's fiction. Rider, a character in the short story "PANTALOON IN BLACK" (in *Go Down, Moses*), consumes vast quantities of moonshine in cold, furious despair, hoping to dull the pain of his wife's death.

Faulkner's last binge began with bourbon, taken along with doses of prescription painkillers for his back, which he had reinjured in a fall from a horse. His nephew JAMES MURRY (Jimmy) FAULKNER raised the subject of the cure, even though the novelist had gone through only about a fifth and a half of whiskey and it was early yet in the drinking cycle. To Jimmy's surprise, Faulkner agreed to return to Wright's Sanatorium in Byhalia, where he died early in the morning of July 6, 1962.

Algonquin Hotel Faulkner's usual stopping-place in New York City, this medium-sized, unpretentious hotel at 59 West 44th Street attracted a loyal clientele of actors, writers, and others associated with the arts. It was famous in the 1920s and 1930s for its Round Table gatherings of Franklin P. Adams, Robert Benchley, Heywood Broun, Dorothy Parker, Alexander Woollcott, and other writers. The host, Frank Case, went out of his way to cater to artistic types.

Faulkner began staying at the Algonquin in the early 1930s, after he had made a name for himself with *The* SOUND AND THE FURY and SANCTUARY. He badly injured himself there in 1937 when, in a drunken stupor, he fell against a scalding steampipe, an injury that required a long period of recuperation.

Faulkner remained loyal to the Algonquin through the 1940s and 1950s. He worked on the final typescript of *The* REIVERS at the Algonquin in late 1961 and put up there for the last time in May 1962, when he traveled to New York to accept the National Institute of Arts and Letters' Gold Medal for fiction.

Anderson, Elizabeth Prall See PRALL, ELIZABETH.

Anderson, Sherwood (1876–1941) Ohio-born author of *Winesburg, Ohio,* a well-regarded collection of short stories; the novel *Dark Laughter;* and other works. Faulkner was already an admirer of Anderson's stories when Anderson's wife, ELIZABETH PRALL, introduced them in NEW ORLEANS in the autumn of 1924. The two men hit it off at first, in spite of the more than 20-year difference in their ages.

Anderson used Faulkner for the basis of the main character in his short story "A Meeting South," in which a bordello madam befriends a young southerner.

The friendship cooled quickly. Faulkner wrote a parody highly critical of aspects of Anderson's work in 1925; perhaps the older writer read and resented it. Faulkner came to regard Anderson as "a one- or two-book man" who ought to have stopped writing after *Dark Laughter* (1925), a judgment that many critics share.

All the same, Anderson treated Faulkner generously. He read at least part of Faulkner's first novel in progress, SOLDIERS' PAY, and recommended it to his publisher, BONI & LIVERIGHT, although Faulkner retold the story, which he claimed to have heard from Elizabeth Prall, that Anderson only agreed to recommend the book as long as he didn't have to read it.

In any case, Boni & Liveright published *Soldiers' Pay* in February 1926. Anderson told his editor at Boni & Liveright that he hadn't congratulated Faulkner on seeing the book into print. "I do not like the man very much," Anderson wrote. "He was so nasty to me personally that I don't want to write him myself."

Faulkner dedicated SARTORIS to Anderson in 1929. "TO SHERWOOD ANDERSON," the dedication read, "through whose kindness I was first published, with the belief that this book will give him no reason to regret that fact."

Faulkner and Anderson finally effected a reconciliation of sorts when they met at a party in New York City in 1937.

Annual Faulkner and Yoknapatawpha Conference   Yearly Faulkner conference sponsored by the Center for the Study of Southern Culture and the English Department at the University of Mississippi. Held in Faulkner's home town of OXFORD, MISSISSIPPI, the conference is normally scheduled for the last week of July. It was first held in 1974.

In addition to papers and panel discussions on various issues related to Faulkner studies, there are tours of Oxford and the surrounding area including NEW ALBANY (where Faulkner was born), RIPLEY, the MISSISSIPPI DELTA, and other places. The winner of the Faux Faulkner contest for the best imitation of Faulkner's stylistic mannerisms is also announced at this time (for examples, *see The Best of Bad Faulkner: Choice Entries from the Faux Faulkner Competition,* edited with a preface by Dean Faulkner Wells [San Diego: A Harvest/HBJ Original, 1991]). Conference proceedings are published each year and are on a wide range of topics that have included race, women, humor, religion, culture, gender, POSTMODERNISM, and sexuality.

Atlantic Monthly, The   Long-running and still prominent monthly magazine of literature, the arts, and politics, established in Boston in 1857. Initially reflective of New England regional culture, it later published a wide spectrum of authors and became national in content.

Faulkner in the 1920s attempted without success to sell short stories to the *Atlantic.* The poet and critic CONRAD AIKEN introduced Faulkner to the magazine's readership in November 1939 with his highly appreciative essay "William Faulkner: The Novel as Form."

In September 1940, the *Atlantic* accepted the Faulkner short story "Gold Is Not Always," paying $300 for it. In the magazine's August 1946 issue, an essay by the French philosopher and writer Jean-Paul Sartre, "American Novelists in French Eyes," assessed the impact of American fiction, particularly that of Faulkner and John Dos Passos, on French culture.

Faulkner sold an essay on SHERWOOD ANDERSON ("Sherwood Anderson: An Appreciation") to the *Atlantic* for $300; the piece appeared in June 1953. In August of that year, the magazine published Faulkner's speech to his daughter Jill's graduating class at Pine Manor Junior College in Massachusetts. The *Atlantic* paid $250 for the speech, titled "Faith or Fear."

B

Baird, Helen (n.a.) Faulkner met this Tennessee-born artist and sculptor in NEW ORLEANS in 1925. She was 21 years old, barely five feet tall, and dark. Faulkner seems to have fallen in love with her right away. She barely responded, and sometimes appeared merely to tolerate his company.

Faulkner courted Baird, in his words "a sullen-jawed yellow-eyed humorless gal in a linen dress," during the summer of 1926 in PASCAGOULA, MISSISSIPPI, where the family of his friend PHILIP AVERY STONE kept a summer place. Despite her mother's objections, Baird encouraged Faulkner's attentions, at least to the point of accepting poems and other gifts from him, including HELEN: A COURTSHIP, a series of poems. The volume was published after Faulkner's death.

Faulkner resumed the courtship in Pascagoula in the summer of 1927. While staying with the Stones, he worked on the manuscript of his novel MOSQUITOES, modeling the character of Patricia Robyn on Helen Baird. She also shared some of the physical characteristics of Charlotte Rittenmeyer in *The WILD PALMS*.

Mosquitoes, published in April 1927, carried a dedication "To Helen." In early May, Helen Baird married Guy Lyman, a longtime suitor, in New Orleans. In later years, Faulkner and the Lymans met occasionally as old friends.

Ballenbaugh's Ferry Fictional place, the successor to Wyott's Crossing, on the TALLAHATCHIE RIVER in northern YOKNAPATAWPHA COUNTY on the wagon road to MEMPHIS. An "ancestryless giant" named Ballenbaugh took the ferry over from Wyott before the Civil War. His son succeeded him in the enterprise, converting it into a roaring dormitory, eating place, distillery, casino, and dance hall. A Baptist minister named Hiram Hightower shuts the resort down in 1886, and by 1905 the younger Ballenbaugh's only child, a prim, severe 50-year-old spinster, runs a small store and resort for hunters and fishermen there.

Barnett, Ned (1865?–1947) By Falkner family tradition and Barnett's own possibly fanciful account, Ned Barnett had been born into slavery and served Faulkner's great-grandfather, WILLIAM CLARK FALKNER. Barnett later came to OXFORD, MISSISSIPPI, to work for the "Young Colonel," J. W. T. FALKNER, as butler, factotum and chief of staff— or so the story ran. More probably, Barnett was born in August 1865, after Emancipation and Confederate defeat, and he passed most of his life as a Tippah County tenant farmer.

As an elderly man, Barnett was a tenant on Faulkner's GREENFIELD FARM, where he looked after Faulkner's horses. In the Last Will and Testament that Faulkner executed in 1940, Barnett was granted the use of the tenant house at Greenfield Farm until his death. He also served as butler and waiter at table in the Faulkner household at ROWAN OAK. Faulkner paid Barnett and the other servants little or nothing, but provided food and shelter and covered medical expenses.

Faulkner's stable on his Rowan Oak property. *(Harriett and Gioia Fargnoli)*

The Faulkners referred to Barnett as Uncle Ned. He regarded himself as an adviser to Faulkner as well as a retainer. "He's a cantankerous old man, who approves of nothing I do," the novelist once said of him.

Ned Barnett died in 1947 in RIPLEY, MISSISSIPPI, his native place. Something of him seems to have gone into the character of Simon, old Bayard Sartoris's coachman in SARTORIS. *Also see* Simon in "THERE WAS A QUEEN" and Simon Strother in *The UNVANQUISHED.*

Barr, Caroline (184?–1940)   Faulkner's "second mother," born into slavery in Mississippi. Small, thin, and neat, four times married, she came to OXFORD, MISSISSIPPI, to help MAUD BUTLER FALKNER with her three young sons in 1902. The boys knew her as Mammy Callie; and she lived to inhabit a cottage behind the Faulkner house, ROWAN OAK, and help raise Faulkner's daughter, JILL FAULKNER.

Faulkner's brother Johncy (see FALKNER, JOHN WESLEY THOMPSON III) left this description of Callie Barr: "I remember her small and black (she weighed only ninety-eight pounds), standing unobtrusively to the side, always with a head rag and some sort of bonnet on, a snuff stick in her mouth, and always in a fresh-starched dress and apron and soft-toed black shoes" (*My Brother Bill*, 48). She could not read or write, but had a rich mental library of stories about pre-Civil War Lafayette County and about the Ku Klux Klan terror in the war's aftermath.

Elements of Caroline Barr appear in several memorable Faulkner characters: as Mammie Cal'line Nelson in SOLDIERS' PAY; as Dilsey Gibson, the Compsons' cook, in *The SOUND AND THE FURY*; and as Molly Beauchamp in GO DOWN, MOSES.

Barr died at ROWAN OAK in January 1940 at close to 100 years of age. Faulkner organized the funeral and delivered Caroline Barr's eulogy, remembering her as "a fount not only of authority and information, but of affection, respect and security." Afterward, at his request, a black choral group sang "Swing Low, Sweet Chariot." Faulkner wrote this epitaph for her gravestone:

Callie Barr Clark, 1840–1940, MAMMY Her
white children bless her

Faulkner dedicated *Go Down, Moses* to Caroline Barr in 1942:

To MAMMY Mississippi [1840–1940]

Who was born in slavery and who gave to my family a fidelity without stint or calculation of recompense and to my childhood an immeasurable devotion and love

Battenburg Fictional place on the road between JEFFERSON, MISSISSIPPI, and MEMPHIS. In KNIGHT'S GAMBIT, a Memphis gangster runs down a child in Battenburg on his way back to Memphis from a "job" in Jefferson.

Beat Four Fictional district in YOKNAPATAWPHA COUNTY northeast of JEFFERSON, MISSISSIPPI. (Mississippi counties are divided into "beats" for administrative purposes; the actual LAFAYETTE COUNTY has five.) Beat Four is "a region of lonely pine hills dotted meagerly with small tilted farms and peripatetic sawmills and contraband whiskey kettles" peopled by white hill clans such as the Gowries of INTRUDER IN THE DUST.

In *Intruder*, Lucas Beauchamp, an African American, is alleged to have killed Vinson Gowrie at Fraser's Store in Beat Four.

Beck, Warren (n.a.) Writer, critic, and teacher. Beck was one of the first academic admirers of Faulkner's work. In the spring of 1941 he published three essays that acknowledged Faulkner's ethical perspective as well as his daring narrative technique and prose style.

In a 1941 correspondence, Faulkner wrote candidly to Beck about his stylistic excesses and shortcomings, confessing that he was "an old 8th grade man"—that is, largely self-taught.

Beck's *Man in Motion*, a book-length appraisal of Faulkner's fiction, appeared in 1962.

Bezzerides, Albert Isaac (1908–2007) Scriptwriter. Born in Samsun, Turkey, of Greek-Armenian parents, Bezzerides studied engineering at the University of California at Berkeley before finding his way into motion pictures. WARNER BROTHERS filmed his novel of truck drivers, *The Long Haul*, as *They Drive By Night*, starring HUMPHREY BOGART.

Warm and emotional, Buzz Bezzerides proved a good friend to Faulkner in Hollywood during the 1940s. He and his wife put Faulkner up for a long stretch at their house near Santa Monica. Bezzerides often drove him to work at the studio and kept a protective eye on him while there. He also curtailed more than one of Faulkner's self-destructive drinking binges.

Bezzerides moved into television in the 1950s and 1960s, writing scripts for such popular series as *Rawhide* and *The Virginian*. He authored the script of *William Faulkner: A Life of Paper*, the 1979 PBS documentary on Faulkner's life and career.

Big Bottom Fictional place. Modeled on the jungly bottoms of the actual TALLAHATCHIE RIVER, it is a wilderness of gum, cypress, and oak trees. The Big Bottom is the site of the decrepit hunting and fishing cabin Wash Jones and his granddaughter inhabit in ABSALOM, ABSALOM! Jones murders Thomas Sutpen there, cutting him down with a rusty scythe. Major Cassius De Spain eventually acquires the camp and the scenes of "The BEAR" (in GO DOWN, MOSES) are enacted there.

SARDIS LAKE, a reservoir filled in the 1930s, now covers most of the Big Bottom country.

Bilbo, Theodore Gilmore (1877–1947) A Mississippi-born politician, a one-time Baptist minister, he served as governor of Mississippi (1916–20 and 1928–32) and United States senator (1935–47). A champion of the state's rural white population, he came to power on the tide of Mississippi's "redneck revolt" of populist hill country small farmers, winning the lieutenant governorship in 1911 before following his ambition to higher office.

Bilbo captured the nomination for the governorship in 1915 and won office with LEE M. RUSSELL, J. W. T. FALKNER's law protegé, as his running mate. "A slick little bastard," in the pungent phrase of one political opponent, Bilbo had a highly developed ability to look after his own political interests. His successful effort to control UNIVERSITY OF MISSISSIPPI patronage cost MURRY FALKNER his job as business manager there in 1930.

Bilbo was corrupt and opportunistic, a virulent racist and white supremacist, a supporter of the liberal New Deal who violently opposed legislation aiding blacks. A hero to the state's poor whites, he was an anathema to his enemies.

The fictional Flem Snopes is the Faulknerian apotheosis of the Bilbo man. Faulkner modeled the corrupt governor in the short story "Monk" (*see* KNIGHT'S GAMBIT) after Bilbo; one of the redneck Gowrie brothers in INTRUDER IN THE DUST is named for him.

Blotner, Joseph (1923–) Scholar and Faulkner biographer, born in Plainfield, New Jersey. An Army Air Force veteran of World War II, he was educated at Drew University, Northwestern University, and the University of Pennsylvania. He and Faulkner met in 1957 at the University of Virginia, where Blotner was an assistant professor of English and head of the Balch Committee, which brought the novelist to Charlottesville as writer-in-residence.

With a colleague, Frederick Gwynn, Blotner acted as Faulkner's gatekeeper. A close friendship developed between Blotner and Faulkner, and they were much together during Faulkner's later years.

The family chose Blotner as Faulkner's authorized biographer shortly after the novelist's death in 1962. His two-volume *Faulkner: A Biography* appeared in 1974. Blotner published a revised one-volume edition of the biography in 1984.

"Faulkner could hardly have left his reputation as a writer and as a man in better hands," the historian and later Faulkner biographer Joel Williamson wrote.

Faulkner's biographer, Joseph Blotner (left), pictured with Faulkner (center) and Frederick Gwynn. Blotner and Gwynn edited *Faulkner in the University*. *(William Faulkner Collection, Special Collections Department, Manuscripts Division, University of Virginia Library. Photo by Ralph Thompson.)*

With Gwynn, Blotner edited FAULKNER IN THE UNIVERSITY (1959), a record of the novelist's views on literature as expressed to University of Virginia students. He also published *Selected Letters of William Faulkner* in 1977. Blotner moved from Virginia to the University of North Carolina at Chapel Hill (1968–71) and the University of Michigan (1971–93). His biography of poet and novelist ROBERT PENN WARREN appeared in 1997.

Bogart, Humphrey (1899–1957) American actor, best known for his role as a cynical, heroic loner in *Casablanca* (1942) and other films. Faulkner met Bogart in Hollywood in the 1940s when Faulkner wrote film scripts for the WARNER BROTHERS story department.

Faulkner and Bogart became friends on the set of *To Have and Have Not* in early 1944. Bogart played the lead role in the adaptation of the ERNEST HEMINGWAY novel opposite 20-year-old Lauren Bacall, whose photograph on a magazine cover impressed the studio's talent scouts. Bogart, then rising 45, and Bacall soon married.

At one stage of the filming of *To Have and Have Not* Faulkner, whose scriptwriting instincts were ahead of his time, prepared a six-page-long speech for Bogart. The actor balked at this, plaintively asking Faulkner whether he would be expected to deliver all the lines.

Boni & Liveright Publishing firm, based in New York City, an early publisher of Faulkner's works. Founders Albert Boni and HORACE LIVERIGHT established the Modern Library with $25,000 in 1917. During the 1920s, from its office on 48th Street between Fifth and Sixth Avenues, Boni & Liveright published such authors as Sigmund Freud, Ezra Pound, Eugene O'Neill, T. S. Eliot, ERNEST HEMINGWAY, and Theodore Dreiser.

On SHERWOOD ANDERSON's recommendation, the firm brought out Faulkner's first novel, SOLDIERS' PAY, on February 25, 1926, paying a $200 advance, and followed up with his second novel, MOSQUITOES, in 1927. Saying it lacked plot and character development, Boni & Liveright rejected Faulkner's third offering, FLAGS IN THE DUST, and urged him to withdraw it altogether. "We're very much disappointed by it," Liveright wrote. "The story really doesn't get anywhere and has a thousand loose ends." HARCOURT, BRACE AND COMPANY published a heavily revised *Flags in the Dust* in 1929 as *SARTORIS*.

With the rejection of *Flags in the Dust,* Faulkner broke off relations with the firm.

Brodsky, Louis Daniel (1941–) Poet, scholar, and curator of the Brodsky Collection at Southeast State Missouri University. The collection, which Brodsky acquired over a period of about three decades before transferring ownership to the university in 1988, is one of the major collections of Faulkner material. It includes books, letters, holograph and typescript manuscripts, galley proofs, art work, movie scripts, photographs, and biographical material. In addition to publishing his own poetry, Brodsky is the author of *William Faulkner: Life Glimpses* (Austin: University of Texas Press, 1990) and, with Robert W. Hamblin, has edited the five-volume work *Faulkner: A Comprehensive Guide to the Brodsky Collection* (Jackson: University Press of Mississippi, 1982–88).

Brooks, Cleanth (1906–1994) Literary critic. Born in Murray, Kentucky, Brooks was a professor at Yale University from 1945 to 1976 and a leading practitioner of the New Criticism of the 1940s and 1950s. Among other features, the New Criticism emphasizes a literary text's autonomy and rhetorical structure; *see* especially Brooks's essay, "In Search of the New Criticism," published in *The American Scholar* 53 (1983/1984), 41–53.

Brooks published *The Well Wrought Urn,* probably his best known work of criticism, in 1947. He followed this in 1950 with the influential *Understanding Poetry: An Anthology for College Students,* written with his friend ROBERT PENN WARREN. Brooks's works on Faulkner are important and he was a lifelong admirer of Faulkner's work. Notable are *William Faulkner: First Encounters* (1983), *William Faulkner: Toward Yoknapatawpha and Beyond* (1978), and *William Faulkner: The Yoknapatawpha Country* (1963).

In *Faulkner: First Encounters,* Brooks asserts that Faulkner's vision of reality is large enough to encompass both tragedy and comedy, and that a reader will often find both in the same novel. "What the reader will not find," Brooks observes, "is mawkish sentimentality or mere farce, nor will he find special pleading for a thesis or a cause." Brooks also wrote important works on Milton and Thomas Percy.

Bull Run, first battle of   The first major clash of the Civil War, known to Confederates as the first battle of Manassas. Union and Confederate forces massed near the sluggish stream of Bull Run in mid-July 1861. The battle opened early in the morning of July 21 with a Union attack on the Confederates near Sudley Spring.

After several hours of hard but inconclusive fighting, a Confederate attack forced a Union withdrawal toward Washington that rapidly turned into a rout. Federal casualties for the day were 2,645 killed, wounded, and missing. The Confederates lost 1,981 men and claimed a great victory.

Colonel WILLIAM C. FALKNER, Faulkner's great-grandfather, commanded the second Mississippi regiment of infantry with distinction at Bull Run. In the thick of the fight, the Old Colonel had two horses shot out from under him; around 100 of his men were killed or wounded. Dispatches credited the second Mississippi with capturing four guns from a Union battery, and in his after-battle report the Confederate cavalry commander J. E. B. STUART commended Falkner for his gallantry. All the same, Falkner's regiment voted him out of the colonelcy in April 1862, perhaps in response to his iron and unpopular disciplinary measures. His appeals were ignored, and he returned embittered to Mississippi.

Butler, Charles Edward   (1848–unknown) Faulkner's maternal grandfather, descended from one of the earliest settler families of LAFAYETTE COUNTY, MISSISSIPPI. Butler married LELIA DEAN SWIFT (BUTLER) in 1868. They produced two children: a son, Sherwood, and a daughter, Maud (*see* FALKNER, MAUD BUTLER), both born in OXFORD, MISSISSIPPI.

In April 1876, Butler won election to the office of Oxford town marshal, a paid post involving police work and tax collection. In May 1883, he shot and killed S. M. Thompson, the editor of the OXFORD EAGLE, on the town square as he attempted to arrest him for drunkenness. A jury acquitted Butler of manslaughter in May 1884.

Butler served as town marshal for 12 years. In December 1887 he disappeared, taking as much as $3,000 in town funds with him and leaving his wife and children without means of support. According to family legend, the stolen money financed his elopement with the "beautiful octoroon" companion of a prominent local woman.

Maud Butler was 16 at the time of her father's disappearance. Faulkner never knew him.

Butler, Lelia Dean Swift (1849–1907) Faulkner's pious, stern maternal grandmother, known to him as "Damuddy." Born in Arkansas, she married CHARLES BUTLER of LAFAYETTE COUNTY, MISSISSIPPI, and came to live in OXFORD, MISSISSIPPI. Her husband abandoned the family, which included their grown son, Sherwood, and their daughter, Maud, in 1887 and never returned.

Lelia Butler painted well enough to be offered a scholarship in 1890 to study art in Rome but she declined, saying she couldn't leave her daughter. She came to live with the Murry Falkners after their move to Oxford in 1902. Clever with her hands, she made Billy Falkner a nine-inch doll dressed as a policeman. He named it Patrick O'Leary.

Lelia Butler's grandsons visited her often in her sickroom as she lay dying through 1907. Thin, shrunken and dosed with morphine, she nevertheless struck the boys as invariably gentle and patient with them right to the end. She died in June after a long, painful illness, probably uterine cancer.

Damuddy is the nickname the Compson children use for their grandmother in The SOUND AND THE FURY. The harrowing opening scene in the novel is drawn from Faulkner's recollection of Damuddy's—Lelia Butler's—funeral.

Byhalia, Mississippi North Mississippi town 50 miles from OXFORD, MISSISSIPPI. Byhalia was the home of Wright's Sanatorium, a small, private hospital where Faulkner sometimes went to recover from severe alcoholic poisoning.

Dr. Leonard Wright, a Tennessean, operated the sanatorium in three white clapboard houses a mile outside of town. Estelle Faulkner (see FAULKNER, ESTELLE OLDHAM) first took her husband there in January 1936 when money pressures, his brother Dean's death, and the completion of ABSALOM, ABSALOM! touched off a major drinking bout that ended in alcoholic collapse.

Faulkner returned to Byhalia and its regimen of vitamins, drugs, nourishment, and rest in October 1953, after a series of frustrations in the writing of his Great War novel A FABLE. He checked in again in January 1960. Dr. Wright admitted Faulkner to the sanatorium for the last time at 6 P.M. on July 5, 1962. He died there of heart failure in the early hours of July 6.

C

Caledonia Chapel Fictional place in rural BEAT FOUR in northeastern YOKNAPATAWPHA COUNTY, nine miles from JEFFERSON, MISSISSIPPI. The name suggests the Scots or Scots-Irish background of the hill people of Beat Four. In INTRUDER IN THE DUST, the Gowrie clan bury its dead in the graveyard at Caledonia Chapel.

Callicoat, Buster (n.a.) A stablehand who worked in MURRY FALKNER's livery stable around 1909, he was a member of a large OXFORD, MISSISSIPPI, family. Young Billy Falkner sought out his company, drawn to the colorful stories and antics of this large, boisterous man with, as the novelist recalled a half-century later, a mental age of about ten.

Faulkner reportedly modeled the character of Boon Hogganbeck, who appears in GO DOWN, MOSES, The REIVERS, and elsewhere, on Buster Callicoat.

Like the fictional Boon, Callicoat drew the errand of journeying to MEMPHIS to replenish the whiskey supply of the autumn hunting camp in the Delta. Billy Falkner accompanied him on that urgent mission on one occasion.

Camus, Albert (1913–1960) French novelist, playwright, and essayist. Born in Algiers, capital of the French colony of Algeria, and educated at the University of Algiers, he migrated to Paris in 1939 and was active in the Resistance during World War II. After liberation in 1944, he wrote for and helped edit the journal *Combat*. In his postwar work, Camus became an existentialist exponent of disillusion.

Faulkner's style influenced the young Camus, who remained an admirer of the American's fiction. He once called Faulkner "the greatest writer in the world." Camus's novels include *The Stranger* (1942) and *The Plague* (1947); *The Rebel* (1951) is a collection of philosophical essays. He won the Nobel Prize in literature in 1957.

Faulkner and Camus met in Paris in 1955 but did not manage to connect: Faulkner shook Camus's hand rather distantly at a reception, and Camus shyly withdrew. Drawn to the theatre, Camus adapted a number of works for the stage, including Faulkner's experimental play embedded in a novel, REQUIEM FOR A NUN, performed in Paris on September 20, 1956.

In a tribute published after Camus's death in an automobile accident, Faulkner wrote that in spite of denying the existence of God, the French writer had spent his life "searching himself and demanding of himself answers which only God could know" (Blotner, *Faulkner: A Biography*, Volume 2, 1,756).

Cape & Smith New York City publishing firm, Faulkner's fourth publisher. HARRISON SMITH, Faulkner's editor at HARCOURT, BRACE AND COMPANY left Harcourt in late 1928 to found his own firm, forming an alliance with Jonathan Cape, the English publisher. Cape & Smith brought out the works of an impressive group of authors, among them H. G. Wells, T. E. Lawrence, H. L. Mencken,

Eugene O'Neill—and, beginning in 1929, William Faulkner.

On February 28, 1929, Cape & Smith signed a contract to publish *The SOUND AND THE FURY*, giving Faulkner a $200 advance. The new house released what would become Faulkner's best-known novel on October 7, 1929.

Cape & Smith published *AS I LAY DYING* in 1930 and *SANCTUARY* in 1931. Financial strains caused the breakup of the firm in 1931; the partners went into bankruptcy owing the chronically hard-up Faulkner some $4,000 in royalties from *Sanctuary*. With ROBERT K. HAAS, Smith went on in 1932 to found SMITH & HAAS, with Faulkner as one of the house's prize authors.

Carpenter, Meta (1908–1994) A native of MEMPHIS, Carpenter was working in Hollywood as secretary and "script girl" to the director HOWARD HAWKS when she met Faulkner in late 1935. She was 28 years old, ten years younger than Faulkner, recently divorced, tall, thin and blonde, and within a few weeks she and the novelist were involved in a love affair that would endure, on and off, for 15 years.

When they met, Faulkner was still grieving for his brother DEAN FALKNER, who had been killed in a plane crash, and had suspended work on *ABSALOM, ABSALOM!* to make money in Hollywood. He fell deeply in love and began to contemplate the breakup of his marriage. There was a powerful physical element too; Faulkner told her he and Estelle had not had sexual relations for three years.

Estelle Faulkner (*see* FAULKNER, ESTELLE OLDHAM) defended the marriage tenaciously, and Faulkner ultimately abandoned the idea of leaving her and their daughter Jill. "The pull of Oxford and the Faulkner way of life was greater than to me," Carpenter recalled. "Everything at Rowan Oak, even the wife . . . whose weaknesses bound him to her, drew him away from me." She ultimately broke off the affair and married the Austrian concert pianist Wolfgang Rebner.

Carpenter divorced Rebner and became Faulkner's lover again when Faulkner returned to Hollywood in 1942. They parted for a third time in 1945. She remarried Rebner, but they were no

Meta Carpenter met Faulkner in late 1935 while working as a secretary in Hollywood.

happier together than before, and she and Faulkner restarted their long affair in 1951. It ended after only a few weeks, and Faulkner never saw her again.

Her memoir, *A Loving Gentleman: The Love Story of William Faulkner and Meta Carpenter* (1976), chronicled their long, sometimes tortured relationship.

Catalpa Street Fictional street in MEMPHIS, site of Miss Reba's brothel in *The REIVERS*. (The actual Catalpa Avenue is several miles distant from the Memphis Tenderloin district.) In Lucius Priest's description, Catalpa is "a sidestreet, almost a back alley, with two saloons at the corner and lined with houses that didn't look old or new either, all very quiet" (97).

Cerf, Bennett (1898–1971) Publisher, born in New York City. A marketer of the classics under the Modern Library imprint, he cofounded RANDOM HOUSE with DONALD KLOPFER in 1927. "I've got the name for our publishing operation," he told a colleague. "We just said we were going to publish a few books on the side at random. Let's call it Random House." Cerf went on to head this leading American publisher for 40 years.

Cerf became interested in Faulkner after reading SANCTUARY in 1931. He pursued Faulkner for several years, first publishing a limited edition of The SOUND AND THE FURY in 1933, for which the author received $750. In the autumn of 1935 Cerf met with Faulkner and suggested that the author could name his terms with Random House.

Random House absorbed Faulkner's former publisher SMITH & HAAS in 1936, taking on HARRISON SMITH and ROBERT K. HAAS as partners. On October 26, Cerf and company published ABSALOM, ABSALOM! in a first printing of 6,000 copies.

Random House was reasonably generous with advances when Faulkner found himself short of money in the 1940s. By 1954, his works were making money. Cerf tried to persuade him to be the subject of a cover story in *Time* magazine (he first appeared on *Time's* cover in 1939), saying it would boost sales of his new novel, A FABLE. The intensely publicity shy author replied with a telegram: "I protest whole idea but will never consent to my picture on cover. Estimate what refusal will cost Random House and I will pay it."

Along with running a major American publishing house, Cerf compiled humor anthologies, wrote a syndicated newspaper column, judged the Miss America pageant and, as a far more outgoing personality than his most celebrated author, appeared regularly on television.

Chatto & Windus English publishing house, the publisher of Faulkner's works in the United Kingdom. The Welsh novelist Richard Hughes brought Faulkner to the attention of the London firm, which published SOLDIERS' PAY in June 1930 (with an introduction by Hughes), The SOUND AND THE FURY in 1931, and other works as they appeared.

In later years, Faulkner customarily called on this venerable publisher whenever he traveled in Europe. Faulkner liked his editor there, the former British army officer Harold Raymond, responding perhaps to Raymond's military bearing.

Chickasaw Indians A Native American hunter and warrior tribe with permanent settlements in northeast Mississippi, the Chickasaw ranged over hunting grounds in Mississippi, Alabama, Tennessee, and Kentucky. By the beginning of the 19th century, with most of the game driven out of the country, the Chickasaw had turned to farming, growing cotton with the forced labor of as many as 1,000 black slaves.

With the Cherokee, Choctaw, Creek, and Seminole, the Chickasaw were one of the so-called Five Civilized Tribes removed to Indian Territory (now Oklahoma) in the 1830s. King Ishtehotopah signed the Treaty of Pontotoc on October 22, 1831, ceding six million acres of Chickasaw lands in northern Mississippi to the United States government. The tribe began the westward migration in 1835, opening the way for mass white settlement of the region.

Chickasaw Indians resettled in Oklahoma fought for the CONFEDERATE STATES OF AMERICA during the Civil War, 1861–65.

Colonel Robert Shegog of OXFORD, MISSISSIPPI, built his house, later Faulkner's ROWAN OAK, on land purchased from a Chickasaw Indian. In the short story "RED LEAVES" (1930), Faulkner explored Chickasaw history and culture through the fictional characters Issetibbeha and Moketubbe. Sam Fathers in "The OLD PEOPLE" (published in 1940, reprinted in GO DOWN, MOSES, 1942) is the son of the Chickasaw chief Ikkemotubbe and a slave mother. In the same story, Jobaker is a full-blooded Chickasaw leading a solitary life deep in the big woods.

In "The BEAR" (1942, included in *Go Down, Moses*), Ikkemotubbe sells one hundred square miles of the BIG BOTTOM wilderness to the empire-building planter Thomas Sutpen, the principal character in the novel ABSALOM, ABSALOM! (1936).

Faulkner borrowed from the Chickasaw language when deciding on the name of his fictional county; see YOKNAPATAWPHA COUNTY.

Chilton's Drug Store A shop in downtown OXFORD, a popular gathering place for young people when Faulkner was an adolescent. Ice cream sundaes were available at Chilton's. The proprietors were two brothers, Uncle Bob and Uncle Top Chilton.

Coindreau, Maurice Edgar (1892–1990) A French-born professor at Princeton. After reading As I Lay Dying and The Sound and the Fury, Coindreau introduced literary France to Faulkner's work in 1931 with an favorable article in the Nouvelle Review Française. The piece touched off a Faulkner boomlet; his work later would become widely admired in France. He translated Faulkner's work for the French publisher Gallimard. In 1934, his translation of As I Lay Dying (Tandis que j'agonise), with a preface by Valéry Larbaud, was published. Coindreau traveled to Los Angeles in June 1937 to consult with Faulkner on his translation of The Sound and the Fury.

Collins, Carvel (1912–1990) Professor of English, critic, and editor. Collins taught at Harvard, Massachusetts Institute of Technology, and the University of Notre Dame, among other colleges and universities. One of the first important figures in Faulkner scholarship, Collins edited and introduced several of Faulkner's works: New Orleans Sketches (1958; revised and expanded, 1968), William Faulkner's University Pieces (1962), William Faulkner: Early Prose and Poetry (1962), Mayday (1977; revised, 1980), and Helen: A Courtship (1981). Collins also wrote introductions to The Unvanquished (Signet Books, 1959), William Faulkner: The Cofield Collection (a collection of photos, 1980), and other works.

Commercial Hotel Fictional place, established around the time of the Civil War as rival to Jefferson, Mississippi's, leading hostelry, the Holston House. It did not quite rise to the handsomely turned-out Holston. It later becomes the Snopes Hotel; in The Reivers, set in 1905, Boon Hogganbeck lives in a rented room there.

Commins, Saxe (1892–1958) Faulkner's sometime editor at Random House beginning in 1937, and a loyal friend to the author and his wife. A nephew of the political radical Emma Goldman, Commins practiced as a dentist for a time; the playwright Eugene O'Neill, one of his patients, helped lead him into a new career as an editor.

Commins knew Faulkner's work before they met. He had written a volume titled Psychology: A Simplification in the 1920s, and when a package that should have contained his author's copies arrived from his publisher, Horace Liveright, he found copies of Faulkner's Mosquitoes inside. Some scholars believed Commins may have worked on Absalom, Absalom!, which would date their first association to 1936.

As an editor, Commins was solicitous and unfailingly encouraging. The two men were friends as well as literary associates, and Faulkner often visited Commins at his home on Elm Road in Princeton, New Jersey. Working with measurements from Estelle Faulkner, Commins bought the dress suit the novelist wore for his Nobel Prize acceptance in 1950. He also made travel arrangements and booked hotels for Faulkner, helped him to recover from his alcoholic binges, and listened to his troubles with Estelle. In a harrowing episode, Commins after a Faulkner drinking binge at Thanksgiving 1952 checked the novelist into a Bronx sanitorium where he underwent electroshock therapy. There is no evidence the shock treatments had any effect on his drinking or its causes.

Faulkner used Commins's Random House office to approach the finish of the slowly developing Great War novel A Fable in the winter and spring of 1953. Commins put in hard editorial work on A Fable and on The Town, the second novel in the Snopes trilogy, reconciling discrepancies between that book and the opening volume, The Hamlet. He died of a heart attack at home in Princeton in July 1958, age 66.

Compson Family name in Yoknapatawpha County. A Compson with no first name is referred to in "Skirmish at Sartoris" (The Unvanquished) as the crazy husband of Mrs. Compson. Sometime during the Civil War, he was locked up for shooting sweet potatoes off the heads of little black children. (See Appendix.)

Compson Mile Fictional place in Jefferson, Mississippi, the original domain of the Compson family. Jason Lycurgus Compson I acquired the square mile of virgin land about 1811 from the Chickasaw chief Ikkemotubbe in exchange for a race horse.

The Compson holdings were mortgaged after the Civil War and sold piecemeal. In *The SOUND AND THE FURY*, Jason Richard Compson sells the pasture to a golf club to pay for his daughter Caddy's wedding and his son Quentin's Harvard tuition. By then, all that remained of the Compson land, according to Faulkner in his appendix to *The Sound and the Fury*, was "the house and the kitchengarden and the collapsing stables and one servant's cabin."

Compson's Creek Fictional name for Burney's Branch, a creek that flows less than a mile east of the courthouse in OXFORD, MISSISSIPPI. In *REQUIEM FOR A NUN*, CHICKASAW INDIANS bathe their legs in the stream before going to Compson's store.

Confederate States of America A league of 11 southern states, including Mississippi, that seceded from the United States in 1860–61 over issues of slavery and states' rights and that fought an unsuccessful four-year civil war for independence.

Faulkner used incidents and issues from the War Between the States, as many southerners call the Civil War, in a number of works, including *ABSALOM, ABSALOM!* and *The UNVANQUISHED*. His great-grandfather WILLIAM CLARK FALKNER briefly commanded the 2nd Mississippi Infantry in Virginia and later led a partisan cavalry unit in northern Mississippi.

The defeated South loomed large in Faulkner's tragic vision, yet he was no lost-cause sentimentalist. A reporter once asked him what part of the Southern tradition he hoped his grandson would continue, and what part he would reject. "I hope that his mother and father will try to raise him without bigotry as much as can be done," Faulkner answered. "He can have a Confederate battleflag if he wants it, but he shouldn't take it too seriously" (Blotner, *Faulkner: A Biography*, volume 2).

Coughlan, Robert (n.a.) Journalist and profiler of Faulkner. *Life* magazine assigned Coughlan to do a 6,000-word piece on Faulkner in spite of the novelist's notorious distaste for publicity. He inter-

The Confederate Monument, a tribute to the county's Confederate heroes, in Courthouse Square, Oxford, Mississippi. Erected on the south side of the County Courthouse in 1907 by the Patriotic Daughters of Lafayette County, the monument's soldier faces the south, with his back to the north. *(Harriett and Gioia Fargnoli)*

viewed Faulkner and others in OXFORD, MISSISSIPPI, over a ten-day span in August 1951; the novelist grudgingly met with him for about an hour. The result, a two-part article titled "The Private World of William Faulkner," appeared in the September 28 and October 5 issues of 1953.

Coughlan's profile was the first substantial biographical treatment of Faulkner. Henri Cartier-Bresson's photographs accompanied the piece: Faulkner in front of ROWAN OAK with two fox terriers; scenes from Oxford's Courthouse Square; the YOCONA RIVER; a ramshackle farmstead; and a decaying antebellum mansion, "the old Carter-Tate House," according to *Life*, "built about 1840."

Coughlan included a good deal of personal detail, including details of Faulkner's heavy drinking. "His is not a split personality, but rather a fragmented one, loosely held together by some strong inner force, the pieces often askew and sometimes painfully in friction," he wrote. "It is to ease these pains, one can guess, that he escapes periodically and sometimes for periods of weeks into alcoholism, until his drinking has become legendary in the town and in his profession, and hospitalization and injections have on occasion been necessary to save his life."

This sounds rather tame by the intrusive standards of our own day, but all the same Faulkner's mother, MAUD BUTLER FALKNER, disliked the pieces so intensely that she canceled her *Life* subscription. The journalist offered the standard justification for the intrusion: "Because he has created [the books], he does not belong entirely to himself."

Coughlan expanded the material into a book, *The Private World of William Faulkner*, published in 1954.

Cowley, Malcolm (1898–1989) Editor and literary critic, born in Belasco, Pennsylvania. His influential *Exile's Return* (1934; revised 1951) analyzed the American expatriate writers he had known in Paris in the 1920s—the "Lost Generation." Cowley served as associate editor of the *New Republic* from 1929 to 1944 and as literary advisor to the VIKING PRESS from 1948 to 1985.

Cowley edited the anthology *The PORTABLE FAULKNER*, published in 1946, which confirmed Faulkner's reputation as a serious literary artist. In early 1944, at a time when all but one of Faulkner's 17 books were out of print, Cowley had taken stock of Faulkner's standing.

The critic proposed a long essay on Faulkner to "redress the balance between his worth and his reputation." A portion of it appeared in the *New York Times Book Review* of October 29, 1944, as "William Faulkner's Human Comedy." Cowley followed up with essays in the *Saturday Review* (April 1945) and the *Sewanee Review* (summer 1945), and capped his reclamation project with the anthology for Viking.

He worked closely with Faulkner to arrange and explicate the material and wrote the introduction and prefaces to the book's seven sections. Faulkner supplied character genealogies and a map of YOKNAPATAWPHA COUNTY. The final product pleased Faulkner with its clear exposition of his artistic aims.

"I wonder whether the reviewers will really *read* you this time instead of judging by their preconceived ideas and their memories of what Clifton Fadiman [a harsh and consistent Faulkner critic] said in the days when he was writing in the *New Yorker*," Cowley wrote the novelist in November 1945 (Cowley, *The Faulkner-Cowley File*, 60).

Cowley's book and his private lobbying had the effect, too, of bringing Faulkner's work back into the marketplace. At his suggestion, RANDOM HOUSE published a Modern Library edition of *The SOUND AND THE FURY* and *As I LAY DYING*. Yet despite his debt to Cowley, Faulkner denied his 1948 request to be profiled for the mass-market *Life* magazine, a piece projected as a companion to a *Life* profile of ERNEST HEMINGWAY.

"The only plan I can accept," Faulkner wrote Cowley, "is one giving me the privilege of editing the result. Which means I will want to blue pencil everything which even intimates that something breathing and moving sat behind the typewriter which produced the books" (Cowley, *The Faulkner-Cowley File*, 121–122).

criticism, Faulkner and Faulkner's reputation as an important writer—innovative, technically adept, and provocative—began to emerge shortly after World War II and coincided with the publication in 1946 of *The PORTABLE FAULKNER*, edited with an introduction by MALCOLM COWLEY. ROBERT PENN WARREN considered this publication "the great watershed for Faulkner's reputation in the United States" ("Introduction: Faulkner: Past and Present," in *Faulkner: A Collection of Critical Essays*, edited by Robert Penn Warren, 10), published at a time when all of Faulkner's works except SANCTUARY (1931) were out of print. Faulkner's status was significantly bolstered in 1950 when he was awarded the 1949 NOBEL PRIZE IN LITERATURE. From this period on, serious Faulkner crit-

criticism, Faulkner and 377

icism began in the United States. (It should be noted that outside this country, and especially in France as early as the 1930s, Faulkner was highly regarded by such writers as Jean-Paul Sartre; André Malraux; MAURICE COINDREAU, one of Faulkner's first French translators; and Valéry Larbaud. (For further information about Faulkner's international status, *see* the fine collection of essays in *Faulkner: International Perspectives*, edited by Doreen Fowler and Anne J. Abadie.)

Prior to Faulkner's Nobel Prize award and the publication of *The Portable Faulkner*, most critics in one way or another attacked Faulkner and his perplexing style. One commentator, Henry Seidel Canby, clearly showed his disgust of Faulkner in the very title of his review of *Sanctuary*, "The School of Cruelty," which appeared in the *Saturday Review of Literature* in May 1931. Other critics, however—Robert Penn Warren, CONRAD AIKEN, George Marion O'Donnell, and Warren Beck—voiced favorable responses to Faulkner's writings. As close readers attempting to see beyond the disparaging assessment of Faulkner's style and charges that he exploited violence and sex, these critics began to judge Faulkner on his own terms and virtually laid a foundation for later commentators. Cowley, for example, in his introduction to *The Portable Faulkner*, expands upon an interpretation regarding the overall unity in Faulkner's works first touched upon by O'Donnell in his essay "Faulkner's Mythology," published in the summer 1939 issue of the *Kenyon Review*. Others, too, had picked up on the thematic integrity of Faulkner's work and the value of his achievement in relation to the whole of his writings, as Kay Boyle pointed out in her March 1938 review of *The UNVANQUISHED* that appeared in the *New Republic*.

By the late 1940s and early 1950s, Faulkner criticism began to come into its own. Studies of individual novels started to appear. The summer 1949 and autumn 1950 issues of *Perspective*, both of which were devoted to Faulkner, included Summer Powell's discussion of *The SOUND AND THE FURY* and OLGA W. VICKERY's study of *AS I LAY DYING*, among others. Although Evelyn Scott published a study of *The Sound and the Fury* in 1929 when the novel first came out, a study Fred-

erick J. Hoffman called "a landmark in Faulkner criticism" for its thorough discussion of form and point of view ("An Introduction," in *William Faulkner: Three Decades of Criticism*, edited by Frederick J. Hoffman and Olga W. Vickery, 17), it was really not until the late 1940s and after that critics began in earnest to concentrate on specific works, including the short stories, and on such varied topics as the coherence of the works, individually and collectively; rhetorical and stylistic devices; Faulkner's profound sense of place and time; biographical and historical interests; textual concerns; and specialized issues like gender, race, popular culture, religion, and films. With his published interviews, FAULKNER AT NAGANO (1956) and FAULKNER IN THE UNIVERSITY (1959), both following the published version (1951) of his Nobel Prize acceptance speech in December 1950, Faulkner himself added his own voice to Faulkner criticism. A few noteworthy studies chosen at random include IRVING HOWE's *William Faulkner: A Critical Study* (1951); Vickery's *The Novels of William Faulkner: A Critical Interpretation* (1959, 3rd edition 1995); CLEANTH BROOKS's *William Faulkner: The Yoknapatawpha Country* (1963); Melvin Backman's *Faulkner: The Major Years* (1966); MICHAEL MILLGATE's *The Achievement of William Faulkner* (1966); Brooks's *William Faulkner: Toward Yoknapatawpha and Beyond* (1978), a companion piece on Faulkner's works Brooks did not cover in his earlier volume; John T. Matthews's *The Play of Faulkner's Language* (1982); *New Essays on "Light in August"* (1987), edited by Michael Millgate; André Bleikasten's *The Ink of Melancholy: Faulkner's Novels from "The Sound and the Fury" to "Light in August"* (1990); and *New Essays on "Go Down, Moses"* (1996), edited by Linda Wagner-Martin. An invaluable source of Faulkner information and short critical pieces is *Teaching Faulkner*, published twice annually by the Center for Faulkner Studies, Southeast Missouri State University, edited by Robert W. Hamblin with Charles A. Peek as associate editor.

Character studies, general introductions to Faulkner, and guides and indexes to his characters also started appearing in the late 1950s and early 1960s: John Lewis Longley Jr.'s *The Tragic*

Mask: A Study of Faulkner's Heroes (1957); Lawrence Thompson's *William Faulkner: An Introduction and Interpretation* (1963; 2nd edition 1967); Robert W. Kirk's *Faulkner's People: A Complete Guide and Index to the Characters in the Fiction of William Faulkner* (with Marvin Klotz, 1963); Edmond L. Volpe's *A Reader's Guide to William Faulkner* (1964); and Thomas E. Connolly's *Faulkner's World: A Directory of His People and Synopses of Actions in His Published Works* (1988). In 1999, *A William Faulkner Encyclopedia*, the first encyclopedia of Faulkner's life and work, edited by Robert W. Hamblin and Charles A. Peek was published.

Although a few biographical resources were available relatively early on—for example, the anecdotal account of Faulkner, *My Brother Bill: An Affectionate Reminiscence* (1963), by Faulkner's brother John; *The Falkners of Mississippi* (1967), by Faulkner's brother Murry (known as Jack); and Millgate's extensive introduction to *The Achievement of William Faulkner* (1966)—the first full-scale biography of Faulkner was published in 1974 by JOSEPH BLOTNER, *Faulkner: A Biography* (2 vols.; revised one-volume edition, 1984). Other lengthy biographies followed, such as Joel Williamson's *William Faulkner and Southern History* (1993), Richard Gray's *The Life of William Faulkner: A Critical Biography* (1994), and Jay Parini's *One Matchless Time: A Life of William Faulkner* (2004).

The important area of textual studies, including concordances, glossaries, and commentaries, started to appear in the early 1980s and is virtually synonymous with the Faulkner scholar NOEL POLK. Under the editorship of Polk and Blotner, the Library of America has published corrected texts of Faulkner's novels: *William Faulkner: Novels 1926–1929; William Faulkner: Novels 1930–1935; William Faulkner: Novels 1936–1940; William Faulkner: Novels 1942–1954;* and *William Faulkner: Novels 1957–1962.* The University Press of Mississippi, under the general editorship of Noel Polk, publishes the Reading Faulkner Series of glossaries and commentaries on Faulkner's works.

For a list of Faulkner's works and for a secondary bibliography, *see* Appendix.

Crossman County Faulkner's fictional PONTOTOC COUNTY MISSISSIPPI, east of LAFAYETTE COUNTY. The murdered timber buyer Jake Montgomery in *INTRUDER IN THE DUST* is from Crossman County.

D

Doane's Mill, Alabama   Fictional place. It is the orphaned Lena Grove's home village in LIGHT IN AUGUST. Lucas Burch, her seducer, worked in the sawmill there, but left when Lena became pregnant. At the start of the novel, Lena Grove leaves Doane's Mill on foot for Mississippi to search for Burch, the father of the child she is carrying. Faulkner notes the village is on the decline as the pinewoods recede with the harvest; Doane's Mill had no listing with the Post Office and once the sawmill was abandoned even its "hookwormridden heirs" would hardly remember it.

The Double Dealer   A literary magazine established in NEW ORLEANS in January 1921, it was an outlet for Faulkner's early work. The founders, Julius Weis Friend and Albert Goldstein, patterned their journal after H. L. Mencken's magazine *The Smart Set* and named it for a William Congreve play in which a character declares he can deceive people by speaking the truth. They subtitled *The Double Dealer* "A National Magazine from the South."

The editors admired the modernist revolt of JAMES JOYCE, Ezra Pound, and others (*see* MODERNISM). They published the poetry of Hart Crane, John Crowe Ransom, Allen Tate, and ROBERT PENN WARREN, and prose by SHERWOOD ANDERSON, ERNEST HEMINGWAY, and Thornton Wilder. The magazine rarely could afford to pay contributors, although Faulkner wrote home excitedly in February 1925 that he had become only the second writer ever to see cash from *The Double Dealer*—the other being Anderson, or so Faulkner claimed. "Fame, stan' by me," he added. "It's him and me fum now on."

Friend kept the periodical going with money from his own pocket. *The Double Dealer* published Faulkner's poem "Portrait" in June 1922 and more of his poems, prose sketches, and critical articles over the following three years.

E

Erskine, Albert (n.a.) A Tennessean, Erskine edited the *Southern Review* with ROBERT PENN WARREN and CLEANTH BROOKS before moving on to RANDOM HOUSE in 1947.

Erskine helped SAXE COMMINS edit Faulkner's novel *INTRUDER IN THE DUST,* and later worked with Commins to put together the hefty volume of short fiction published as COLLECTED STORIES OF WILLIAM FAULKNER (1950).

After Commins's death, Erskine handled the editing of *The* MANSION, the third novel in the SNOPES TRILOGY. He was troubled, as Commins had been, by the discrepancies among *The* HAMLET, *The* TOWN, and *The Mansion.*

Faulkner liked Erskine, and he made no objection to his efforts to sort out the details, although he did offer this observation: "What I am trying to say is, the essential truth of these people and their doings is the thing; the facts are not too important" (*Selected Letters,* 422).

Erskine and Warren later collaborated as co-editors on highly regarded short story and poetry anthologies.

F

Fadiman, Clifton (1904–1999) Literary critic and sometimes unfriendly reviewer of Faulkner's work. Fadiman had qualified praise for Faulkner's early fiction, and with the publication of SANCTU-ARY in 1931 he placed Faulkner in the front rank of younger American novelists.

In a famously scathing review in the *New Yorker* in 1936, he called ABSALOM, ABSALOM! "the most consistently boring novel by a reputable writer to come my way during the last decade."

Four years later, Fadiman's notice of *The* HAM-LET, the first of the Snopes novels, was even nas-

William Faulkner (left) with an unidentified woman and his editor, Saxe Commins, at the National Book Award presentation in New York on January 25, 1955. *(Brodsky Collection, Center for Faulkner Studies, Southeast Missouri State University)*

tier. "All in the line of duty," he wrote in the *New Yorker*, "I have spent part of this week weaving through 'The Hamlet.' From the intense murk of its sentences I emerge, somewhat shaken, to report that the author apparently continues to enjoy as lively a case of the 'orrors as you are apt to find outside a Keeley-cure hostelry."

By coincidence, Fadiman drew the assignment of presenting Faulkner with his second National Book Award, for *A* FABLE, at a ceremony in New York City in January 1955.

Falkner/Faulkner Faulkner created an elaborate new biography for his enlistment in the ROYAL AIR FORCE in June 1918. Among the fictional details he concocted for Canadian recruiters in New York City was a *u* added to the family name. From then on, the world knew him as William Faulkner. His brother Dean (who died in 1935) followed suit, also becoming a Faulkner. His other brothers retained the Falkner spelling.

Some scholars regard the name change, though slight, as not only an expression of independence on Faulkner's part but also as an act of hostility toward his family, a way of distancing himself from a family in decline.

Faulkner explained it this way in a letter to MALCOLM COWLEY: "Maybe when I began to write, even though I thought then I was writing for fun, I was secretly ambitious and did not want to rise on grandfather's coat-tails, and so accepted the 'u,'

381

Gravesite of Faulkner's parents and brothers in Oxford, Mississippi. When enlisting in the Royal Air Force in 1918, Faulkner added the "u" to the spelling of Falkner. *(Harriett and Gioia Fargnoli)*

was very glad of such an easy way to strike out for myself" (Cowley, *The Faulkner-Cowley File*, 66).

Falkner, John Wesley Thompson (1848–1922) Faulkner's paternal grandfather, a lawyer, banker, and politician. The son of WILLIAM CLARK FALKNER, he graduated from the UNIVERSITY OF MISSISSIPPI and gained admission to the state bar in 1869. He established what would soon become a successful law practice in RIPLEY, MISSISSIPPI, and married SALLIE MCALPINE MURRY (FALKNER), the daughter of a leading Tippah County family. They raised three children, MURRY CUTHBERT FALKNER (born 1870), MARY HOLLAND FALKNER WILKINS (born 1872) and JOHN WESLEY THOMPSON FALKNER Jr. (born 1882).

Known by courtesy as the Young Colonel, Falkner moved his family from Ripley to OXFORD,

MISSISSIPPI, 40 miles to the southeast, in late 1885, and there went into practice with the prominent, politically connected lawyer Charles Bowen Howry. While he immersed himself in business and Democratic party politics, Sallie Murry devoted her considerable energies to Women's Christian Temperance Union activities and the Women's Book Club of Oxford. In 1886 Falkner won appointment as deputy U.S. attorney for the Northern District of Mississippi.

Friends talked him out of revenging himself on RICHARD THURMOND for the 1889 murder of his father. His legal and political affairs continued to prosper into the 1890s. In 1895 the voters of LAFAYETTE COUNTY sent him to the state senate, and the governor appointed him to the University of Mississippi board of trustees. He sold the "family" railroad, the GULF & CHICAGO RAILROAD, in 1902 to concentrate his efforts on law and politics. In 1910, he founded the First National Bank of Oxford, the third of the town's three banks, and a profitable business almost from the start.

A legendary drinker, Falkner, at his wife's insistence, submitted to periodic cures at the KEELEY INSTITUTE of MEMPHIS—the foundation of a family tradition that would pass through his son to his novelist grandson. He took leave of his business affairs once or twice a year to join hunting expeditions for bear, deer, and lesser game in the near-wilderness of the MISSISSIPPI DELTA.

William Faulkner saw a lot of the Young Colonel, for his home after 1900, known as "The Big Place," was the center of family activity. The novelist used elements of his grandfather's experience to form the fictional character of Bayard Sartoris, Colonel John Sartoris's son. In *The UNVANQUISHED*, Bayard is an adolescent witness to episodes of the Civil War in north Mississippi; in *SARTORIS* and *FLAGS IN THE DUST*, he is an irascible, imposing old banker, much like the patriarchal figure young Billy Falkner had known.

Sallie Murry Falkner died in 1906. Her husband missed her terribly; his grandsons recalled seeing him seated in the square, tracing her name in the air with his walking stick. Overcoming a last-minute hesitation, the Young Colonel married Mary Kennedy, the widow of a ship's cabinetmaker, in San

Jose, California, in 1912. She was a large woman, chatty, "with big teeth and bad breath," according to a Falkner family source. They separated and she returned to California after less than a year of married life.

Falkner's, and the family's, decline began, perhaps, around 1910 with a seismic shift in Mississippi Democratic politics—the rise of JAMES K. VARDAMAN and THEODORE BILBO on the populist tide—the so-called revolt of the rednecks. One early ramification: The Young Colonel lost his bid for re-election as Oxford city attorney. A decade later, younger stockholders forced the increasingly deaf, irascible, and forgetful Falkner out of the First National Bank. He died of heart failure in March 1922, the last of Faulkner's grandparents to go.

Falkner, John Wesley Thompson, Jr. (1882–1962)

Faulkner's uncle. The ambitious and capable youngest child of JOHN WESLEY THOMPSON and SALLIE MURRY FALKNER, he studied law at the UNIVERSITY OF MISSISSIPPI, became a partner in a grocery, managed the family-owned Opera House in OXFORD, MISSISSIPPI, and eventually joined the law, banking, and Democratic Party political enterprises of his father.

The family knew him as "John, honey." Faulkner spent considerable time with Judge Falkner in the 1920s, acting as his chauffeur in at least two of his unsuccessful campaigns for political office. The experience provided Faulkner with a fund of anecdotes, including material for the wild ponies episode in book 4 of The HAMLET.

Though unable to win political office for himself, John Falkner Jr. proved a talented political organizer and campaign manager. In business as in politics, he succeeded in most of what he attempted, in contrast to his feckless older brother, MURRY CUTHBERT FALKNER, the novelist's father.

Uncle John had scant regard for Faulkner as a young man, regarding him as the black sheep of the family. As he told journalist Robert Coughlan in the early 1950s, his nephew in those years "just *wouldn't* work."

Falkner, John Wesley Thompson III ("Johncy") (1901–1963)

Faulkner's younger brother, the third of four Falkner children, known as Johncy. He studied engineering at the UNIVERSITY OF MISSISSIPPI and married his childhood sweetheart, Lucille (Dolly) Ramey. They had two children, JAMES (Jimmy) MURRY FAULKNER (born 1923), a favorite of his novelist uncle, and Murry Cuthbert II (born 1928), known as Chooky.

In the early 1930s, Johncy took flying lessons from an aviator and preacher whose airplane carried the legend "Jesus Saves" on the fuselage. He later worked as a manager at a MEMPHIS airport and oversaw a LAFAYETTE COUNTY, MISSISSIPPI, farm Faulkner owned.

Clever and imaginative, he followed his mother's example and took up painting; he was so good at telling stories to his children that he decided to write them down for sale to the magazines. Faulkner grudgingly supplied editorial introductions, but the SATURDAY EVENING POST rejected the first two stories Johncy sent in. In 1941, he published a novel, *Men Working,* set in the Mississippi hill country. Faulkner biographer Jay Parini saw echoes of As I LAY DYING and Erskine Caldwell's best seller *Tobacco Road.* Whatever its merits, *Men Working* sank without a trace.

Johncy Falkner's *My Brother Bill: An Affectionate Memoir* was published in 1963. For this book, Johncy added a *u* to his last name.

Falkner, Maud Butler (1871–1960)

Faulkner's proud, determined, iron-willed mother. The daughter of CHARLES and LELIA SWIFT BUTLER, she grew up in straitened circumstances in OXFORD, MISSISSIPPI. Her mother was a gifted amateur painter, and clever with her hands. Her father, the town marshal for a dozen years, vanished with town funds late in 1887, leaving a penniless family behind.

Maud Butler overcame poverty and distress to graduate from the Mississippi Women's College. She held a secretarial job to support herself and her mother and indulged literary and artistic interests as a member of the town's Browning Club. After a short courtship, she married MURRY CUTHBERT FALKNER, the son of the prominent Oxford lawyer JOHN WESLEY THOMPSON FALKNER and brother of her friend MARY HOLLAND FALKNER WILKINS, in a quiet ceremony in a Methodist parsonage on October 29, 1896. The newlyweds settled in a plain one-story clapboard house at Cleveland and Jefferson Streets in NEW ALBANY, MISSISSIPPI, where Murry worked for the family-owned GULF & CHICAGO RAILROAD. Their first child, William Cuthbert, was born in New Albany on September 25, 1897. Maud reported him as a colicky baby who kept her up nearly every night during the first year of his life.

With Murry Falkner's promotion to treasurer of the railroad, the family moved up the line to RIPLEY, MISSISSIPPI. The Falkners' second and third children, MURRY C. FALKNER JR. (born 1899; known as Jack), and JOHN WESLEY THOMPSON FALKNER III (born 1901; known as Johncy) were born there.

The Falkners moved to Oxford in 1902 when Maud's father-in-law, the Young Colonel, sold the railroad that had employed her husband. With the loss of his job, Murry wanted to strike out for Texas and become a rancher. Maud refused to consider the idea. They stayed on in "the old Johnny Brown place," a gift of the Young Colonel, on Second South Street, a few blocks from the Courthouse Square.

The marriage was difficult. Maud and Murry Falkner were temperamentally at odds—she interested in books and painting, he a bluff, liquorish outdoorsman. She hated his drinking, which sometimes took a serious turn: When that happened, she and the children escorted him to the KEELEY INSTITUTE near MEMPHIS for a several days' "cure."

The family moved into the Rowsey house on South Street three blocks from the Square in 1905. Maud delivered the couple's fourth and last child, DEAN SWIFT (FAULKNER), there in 1907.

Maud Falkner assumed full responsibility for the children's physical and spiritual welfare. When she saw first-born Billy walking with a stoop, she laced him tight in a canvas vest every day for two years. That straightened his posture—and kept it straight for the rest of his life. She saw to the boys' religious training, raising them as Methodists (though she had grown up a Baptist) and taking them to revivalist camp meetings every summer. She also passed along her love of literature to them.

Billy was her clear favorite. She tolerated his youthful eccentricities (and they were almost without number), for she suspected him of being a "genius." She defended him when Oxford expressed outrage over the violence and perversion in some of his early work, particularly SANCTUARY.

She was small, barely five feet tall, with fine features and dark eyes. She could be stern and inflexible; she met hardship and disappointment with courage. The motto "Never Complain, Never Explain" hung over the stove in her kitchen, and she practiced it faithfully. She never completely accepted Faulkner's wife, ESTELLE OLDHAM (FAULKNER), a divorcée who drank whiskey, and she quarreled with other daughters-in-law too. To the end of her life, Faulkner visited her every day when he was in Oxford; he usually called alone, knowing how his mother felt about Estelle.

Her youngest son Dean's death in an airplane crash in 1935 nearly destroyed her; she talked of suicide for a time. Murry Falkner's passing three years earlier had left her strangely unmoved, however.

In spite of some misgivings she remained fiercely proud of her son's work, and she lived to see him recognized as perhaps the leading American novelist of the 20th century. She joined Faulkner on the set to observe the filming of INTRUDER IN THE DUST in Oxford in the spring of 1949, and the following year he took her with him to the French consulate in NEW ORLEANS in 1951 to accept the award of the French Legion of Honor.

Maud Butler Falkner died in the Oxford Hospital on October 16, 1960. She had kept up her interest in books to the end: a copy of Lawrence's *Lady Chatterley's Lover* lay on the stand next to her bed the night she suffered a cerebral hemorrhage and lapsed into a coma.

Falkner, Murry Charles, Jr. (1899–1975) Faulkner's younger brother, nearest him in age, known as Jack. The brothers were only two years apart in age and they were much together as children, with Billy, as the elder, usually taking the lead in amusements and mischief. While Faulkner's military ambitions went unrealized (he trained briefly in Canada as an air cadet), Jack saw active service in both world wars—contributions Faulkner certainly admired and probably envied.

Jack Falkner enlisted in the U.S. Marines near the end of World War I, went to France with the 5th Marine Regiment, and fought in the late summer of 1918 at Belleau Wood. Severely wounded in the knee and head near the Argonne Forest on November 1, 1918, Jack returned home to OXFORD, MISSISSIPPI, after several months' convalescence and entered the UNIVERSITY OF MISSISSIPPI. He took a law degree from Ole Miss, worked in his uncle JOHN WESLEY THOMPSON FALKNER Jr.'s law office, obtained a position in the U.S. Treasury Department, and went on to become an agent in the newly organized Federal Bureau of Investigation.

Like his brothers, Jack Falkner loved to fly. He bought his own airplane in the late 1930s, an 85-horsepower Aeronca that he loaned to Faulkner in 1940 when the FBI transferred him to Alaska.

Falkner served in U.S. Army counterintelligence during World War II and saw action in North Africa. He came home in 1945 with a French bride, Suzanne (he had married and divorced an Oxford woman, Cecile Hargis), and returned to the FBI. He was a godparent to Faulkner's only child, JILL FAULKNER.

A large, bluff man who greatly resembled his father, Jack got along well with his novelist brother, though there were constraints in their relationship and they were not intimate. His memoir *The Falkners of Mississippi* (1967) is a valuable source of Falkner (and Faulkner) lore.

Falkner, Murry Cuthbert (1870–1932) Faulkner's hapless, inebriate father, the son of JOHN WESLEY THOMPSON and SALLIE MURRY FALKNER. Raised in his parents' prosperous households in RIPLEY and OXFORD, MISSISSIPPI, he was restless at school and dropped out of the UNIVERSITY OF MISSISSIPPI after two undistinguished years to go to work on the family railroad, a merger of three small lines rechristened the GULF & CHICAGO RAILROAD, where he did duty as fireman, engineer, and conductor.

Murry Falkner inherited the family propensity to violent encounters. A gambler and grocer named Elias Walker once approached him at a lunch counter after an argument over a girl and discharged a 12-gauge shotgun into his back at close range. He dropped to the floor and Walker

shot him with a pistol, wounding Falkner in the mouth and shattering several teeth. Falkner survived to make a full recovery and returned to the Gulf & Chicago. (A jury acquitted Elias Walker.) A promotion to general passenger agent at the NEW ALBANY, MISSISSIPPI, depot in 1896 gave him the wherewithal to seek a wife. He married MAUD BUTLER (FALKNER), the daughter of a one-time LAFAYETTE COUNTY sheriff who had deserted his family, in October 1896 after a secretive courtship. She bore their first child on September 25, 1897: William Cuthbert, named for his great-grandfather, the Old Colonel, and his father. Three more boys followed: MURRY CHARLES FALKNER Jr., known as Jack, in 1899; JOHN WESLEY THOMPSON FALKNER III, called Johncy, in 1901; and DEAN SWIFT FAULKNER, born in 1907.

Strains appeared early in the marriage. Murry Falkner read Western adventure novels, liked to hunt and fish, raised bird dogs, drank hard, lacked ambition and self-confidence, and resented his over-dependence on his powerful father. Maud knew something of literature and art, was energetic and determined, and detested her husband's drinking. Though William Faulkner never broke openly with his father, he plainly took his mother's side. He regarded his father as dull, uninteresting, a failure. In turn, Murry Falkner claimed never to have read anything his novelist son wrote.

Falkner rose to become treasurer of the Gulf & Chicago and expected to succeed his father as president. It was not to be. The Young Colonel sold the Gulf & Chicago in 1902, turning Murry out of a job he loved. Circumstances forced him to move to Oxford and live in a house of his father's. Murry Falkner's long decline and defeat, compounded by alcoholism, had begun.

He ran a livery stable for a time, but business fell off rapidly with the coming of the automobile. A coal-oil agency was no more successful. In 1912, he bought a hardware store on the square in Oxford. But Falkner proved a poor salesman—none of the Falkners could "sell a stove to an Eskimo or a camel to an Arab," he once said—and he chafed at a merchant's sedentary life. In 1918, through his father's influence, he obtained a position in the University of Mississippi's business office, rising to become business manager and secretary of the university. The job came with a house on campus and other perquisites; besides, in the words of Faulkner biographer Jay Parini, "it meant that Murry would no longer have to depend on the local free market economy for a living." But he ultimately lost the Ole Miss job, his last, in a political shuffle.

Faulkner came to regard his great-grandfather, the legendary Old Colonel, as his true father. As critics have noted, key Faulkner characters are boys or men with absent or inadequate fathers: Quentin Compson in *The SOUND AND THE FURY,* Joe Christmas in *LIGHT IN AUGUST,* Charles Bon in *ABSALOM, ABSALOM!* The theme of family decline runs through much of Faulkner's fiction. Yet not all of Murry Falkner's influence was negative. There were regular Sunday afternoon rides in the trap. Murry taught his sons to ride and shoot. Faulkner probably got along best with his father at the Club House, the Falkners' cabin in the woods along the TALLAHATCHIE RIVER, where Murry used to go to hunt, fish, and drink. Faulkner drew on these experiences for descriptions and events of "the big woods"—the Delta country of the novella "The BEAR" (*see GO DOWN, MOSES*) and other works. Murry also formed the basis for an affectionate portrait of the livery stable owner Maury Priest in *The REIVERS.*

Murry Falkner died of a heart attack 10 days short of his 62nd birthday. His doctor had warned that heavy drinking would kill him; he ignored the warning. William Faulkner at once assumed the role of head of the family.

Falkner, Sallie McAlpine Murry (1850–1906)
Faulkner's paternal grandmother. The daughter of a Tippah County, Mississippi, doctor, she married JOHN WESLEY THOMPSON FALKNER in 1869. They reared three children: MURRY CUTHBERT FALKNER (Faulkner's father, born 1870); Mary Holland (Auntee) Falkner, (born 1872); and JOHN WESLEY THOMPSON FALKNER Jr. (born 1882).

An evangelical, Sallie Falkner was a teetotaling counterpoint to her hard-drinking hurband; for some years, she served as president of the Oxford Temperance League. She was capable, decisive, and quick-thinking. When the doctors had all but

given up on her son Murry, near death from a bullet wound to the mouth, she dosed him with the evil-smelling resin asafetida, causing him to vomit up the imbedded slug. He made a full recovery.

Sallie Murry Falkner may have formed a partial basis for the character of Granny Rosa Millard, the indomitable matriarch in *The UNVANQUISHED.* She died after a long, wasting illness on December 21, 1906. Billy Falkner, aged nine, attended her funeral.

Falkner, William Clark (1825–1889)
Faulkner's paternal great-grandfather, a Confederate soldier, lawyer, railroad developer, and author. Faulkner told the literary critic MALCOLM COWLEY that he had used his great-grandfather as the model for the violent, impulsive, and energetic fictional character of Colonel John Sartoris. But some critics suggest a lot of the Old Colonel, as he was known, went into

Colonel W. C. Falkner (c. 1889), William Faulkner's great-grandfather and model for the fictional John Sartoris. *(Brodsky Collection, Center for Faulkner Studies, Southeast Missouri State University)*

the grasping, amoral Flem Snopes too; he was, after all, a town businessman rather than a planter.

The son of Caroline and Joseph Falkner, he was born in Knox County, Tennessee, where his parents paused in their migrant journey from North Carolina to the Mississippi River town of Ste. Genevieve, Missouri. He moved to his aunt Justiana Word Thompson's home in RIPLEY, MISSISSIPPI, in 1841 or 1842; she and her husband, John Wesley Thompson, eventually adopted him. Falkner acquired an informal and rudimentary education and read law. He served in the Mississippi militia during the Mexican War; in a mysterious incident, he was wounded in the hand and foot before he saw any actual fighting and returned home to convalesce. A brawler, he killed two men (Robert Hindman and Erasmus W. Morris) in separate incidents, claiming self-defense both times; in each case, the jury agreed. He married Holland Pearce, the daughter of a wealthy slaveowner, in 1847; this was Falkner's entrée into the planter class. She delivered their son, JOHN WESLEY THOMPSON FALKNER, in September 1848. Holland Pearce Falkner died of tuberculosis in 1849, and Falkner married Elizabeth Houston Vance in 1851. Four of their children lived to adulthood: William Henry, Willie Medora, Effie Dun, and Alabama Leroy. There is circumstantial evidence that he also produced a shadow family, the result of miscegenation with slaves he owned (see Joel Williamson, *Faulkner and Southern History*).

Falkner bought and sold slaves, farmed, and practiced law. With the coming of the Civil War, he raised a volunteer rifle company, the MAGNOLIA RIFLES, and won election in April 1861 as colonel of the 2nd Mississippi infantry. He fought at First Manassas (see BULL RUN, FIRST BATTLE OF) in July 1861; two horses were shot from under him during the battle, and senior officers singled him out for bravery.

His men, however, were less impressed, perhaps because he tended to be a harsh disciplinarian. They voted him out of the colonelcy in April 1862. Falkner returned home to Mississippi, raised the irregular cavalry unit known as the 1st Mississippi Partisan Rangers, and carried on intermittent guerrilla warfare—horse-stealing, bridge-burning, tear-

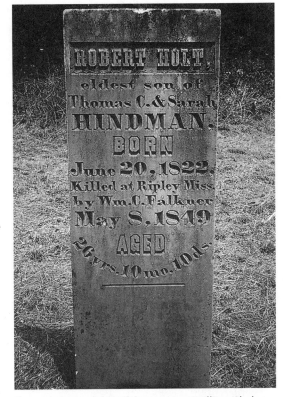

The gravestone of one of the two men William Clark Falkner killed; in both cases Falkner was acquitted of murder. *(Harriett and Gioia Fargnoli)*

ing up railroad track, occasional skirmishing—in north Mississippi through the middle of 1863. The Partisans accomplished little militarily, though, and at the cost of a long list of dead and wounded. Falkner resigned in October 1863, citing poor health, and by family report passed the rest of the war running cotton through the Yankee lines into MEMPHIS. Federal troops burned his home in Ripley in July 1864.

He rebuilt on the ruins of his law practice after the war and, as the fictional Colonel John Sartoris would do, participated in the postwar boom of railroad construction (and reconstruction) in the South. He became a principal in the Ripley Railroad Company, which built a 25-mile narrow gauge line from Ripley to Middleton, Tennessee, for a connection with the long-haul Charleston & Memphis. By 1886 he had gained full control of the railroad, now rather grandly named the GULF & SHIP ISLAND RAILROAD (the locals called it the "Doodlebug" line), from his partner RICHARD J. THURMOND. Exploiting Mississippi's notorious convict labor system (prisoners could be leased from the state for $50 per man per year), he extended the line 40 miles south of Ripley to NEW ALBANY and PONTOTOC, Mississippi.

Falkner privately published his first literary effort in 1851, a long poem titled *The Siege of Monterrey*, based on his Mexico experiences. He enjoyed considerable success, or at least sales, with his postwar work: The melodramatic novel *The White Rose of Memphis* (1880) reportedly remained in print for 30 years and sold 160,000 copies. He followed with a novel called *The Little Brick Church* (1882) and the travel book *Rapid Ramblings in Europe* (1884).

Falkner won election to a seat in the Mississippi legislature on November 5, 1889. Late that afternoon his bitter rival, Thurmond, approached him in front of the courthouse on the square in Ripley and shot him once in the head with a .44-caliber pistol. He died of the wound late the following night. A jury acquitted Thurmond of manslaughter in February 1890.

Farmington Hunt Club   An Albemarle County, Virginia, social and sporting organization, the Farmington Hunt Club followed the traditions of the British hunt: pink coats, white stocks, black top-boots, and derbies. Fox hunting over Albemarle's rolling hills with the Farmington club and the KESWICK HUNT CLUB became a passion of Faulkner's last years.

The novelist was nearly 60 when he sought jumping instruction from the Farmington's huntsman, Grover Vandevender. He first took to the field with the hunt in the autumn of 1958. The club killed a fox only four or five times a year; that suited Faulkner, who enjoyed the chase far more than the kill.

A daring but accident-prone rider, he suffered serious shoulder and back injuries in falls. But he never let a mishap slow him down. "He was all nerve," Vandevender said of Faulkner. "It could rain or snow, but he stayed out to the last hound bark."

Faulkner rode with both hunts, sometimes four or five times a week in season. He became a member of the Farmington club in the winter 1959.

Faulkner, Dean Swift (1907–1935)   Faulkner's high-spirited, restless youngest brother. His father's favorite, Dean Faulkner (who adopted his novelist brother's spelling of the surname) was a star athlete at the UNIVERSITY OF MISSISSIPPI who evidently did not find grown-up life to his taste. Wild and unstable, he seemed incapable of settling down. Faulkner became a sort of guardian to him. He loaned Dean money to pay for flying lessons, and flying paradoxically seemed to bring Dean back to earth. He turned out to be a skilled, responsible, and careful pilot.

Dean Swift Faulkner died in a crash at an air show in PONTOTOC, MISSISSIPPI, on November 10, 1935. Only 28 years old, he left his wife, Louise Hale, pregnant with their first child. (She delivered a daughter, Dean, the following March.) For an inscription on his gravestone, Faulkner borrowed the epitaph he had given John Sartoris in SARTORIS: "I bare him on eagles' wings and brought him unto Me."

Faulkner, as head of the family, assumed responsibility for the infant Dean. She was married under the eye of her surrogate father at ROWAN OAK in 1958.

Faulkner, Estelle Oldham (Lida) (1896–1972) Faulkner's wife, born in OXFORD, MISSISSIPPI, the daughter of LEMUEL EARLY OLDHAM, a prominent lawyer, and LIDA ALLEN OLDHAM. Billy Falkner and Estelle Oldham lived within a few blocks of each other as children.

Estelle had a conventional Southern girl's upbringing. She became an accomplished pianist, a good dancer, and an amusing light conversationalist. She attended Mary Baldwin College in Virginia for a year before returning, homesick, to enroll as a special student at the UNIVERSITY OF MISSISSIPPI.

She was a petite, popular girl, "pretty as a partridge," Faulkner's brother wrote, and she never lacked for suitors. As teenagers, she and Billy read Swinburne together, and over time she came to a sort of understanding with the unprepossessing Faulkner. Her parents strongly disapproved of him, however, and her mother maneuvered her into an engagement to the young Ole Miss law graduate CORNELL FRANKLIN. Estelle offered to elope with Faulkner; he insisted that they seek her father's permission. Lemuel Oldham categorically refused to grant it, and Estelle and Franklin were married in April 1918. She accompanied her husband to Honolulu, where he had set up as a lawyer, and later went with him to China. Faulkner was devastated.

Estelle and Franklin produced two children, MELVINA VICTORIA and MALCOLM FRANKLIN, but the marriage foundered, partly as a consequence of Franklin's dissipations, though Estelle was rumored to have had lovers too. She spent long periods on furlough at home in Oxford, where she again took up with Faulkner.

She returned to Mississippi for good in 1928 and her divorce became final the following year. Desperate and unhappy, an anomaly as a divorcée in conservative Oxford, she evidently pressured Faulkner to provide her a way out of her troubles. With a push from Estelle's Aunt Dot (DOROTHY OLDHAM), he overcame his ambivalence and they decided to marry, Faulkner writing his publisher to ask for a $500 advance to meet the expenses of the ceremony and honeymoon.

Again, Faulkner insisted on Estelle's father's blessing. Lem Oldham's daughter was 33 and alone with two children, but he still hesitated before agreeing to his daughter's second marriage. Faulkner, Estelle, and the children set off for a honeymoon in PASCAGOULA, MISSISSIPPI, after a brief ceremony in the parsonage of the College Hill Presbyterian Church on June 20, 1929. Faulkner corrected proofs of The SOUND AND THE FURY there. On edge, displeased with the editing of the novel, he became uncommunicative and withdrawn—an early taste for Estelle of what married life with the artist would be like. Estelle soon signaled she had had enough; one evening she waded out into Pascagoula Bay to a point where the bottom dropped off steeply and might have drowned had not a neighbor heard Faulkner's shout and pulled her from the water.

The marriage seems to have been a failure from the start. Estelle was voluble, Faulkner silent; she

was shallow, he was utterly committed to his art. Estelle liked to dance and party; her husband preferred solitude, time with the children, hunting, fishing or riding. They both were self-destructive drinkers, and their alcoholism caused incalculable grief. Estelle developed a habit of making public threats of suicide. Her extravagance—she had been used to luxury as Franklin's wife—infuriated her husband. Faulkner once threw out several pieces of expensive furniture she had imported into ROWAN OAK in his absence and then placed a personal notice in the Oxford and Memphis newspapers denying responsibility for any debts Mrs. William Faulkner or Mrs. Estelle Oldham Faulkner might incur.

The Faulkners' first child, a girl named Alabama, was born two months premature in January 1931 and lived only 10 days. The ordeal drew the two together briefly. But both resumed their drinking shortly thereafter. Estelle had bouts of ill health too. The birth of their only surviving child, JILL (FAULKNER), in June 1933 did little to heal the rifts.

From the mid-1930s on, Estelle had to deal with her husband's affairs with a succession of young women: META CARPENTER, JOAN WILLIAMS, JEAN STEIN. Faulkner once cruelly threw Estelle together with Carpenter at a harrowing Hollywood dinner party, so it may be understandable that she sometimes reacted irrationally and violently. When Faulkner showed up at the studio one day with

The Faulkner gravesite in Oxford, Mississippi, where he and his wife, Estelle Oldham Faulkner, are buried. *(Harriett and Gioia Fargnoli)*

At Faulkner's funeral, Estelle Faulkner (standing) is assisted by her son, Malcolm Franklin. Seated at left are Faulkner's daughter, Jill, and her husband, Paul Summers. *(AP/Wide World Photos)*

an angry bruise on his forehead, he explained it this way to a scriptwriting colleague: "I was just reading a magazine, and she came at me with a croquet mallet." In the early 1950s, in the midst of Faulkner's involvement with Williams, Estelle considered divorcing him. When Faulkner took up with Stein in the late 1950s, Estelle again offered him a divorce, this time more forcefully, but Faulkner turned her down. The affair with Jean Stein ended; it was his last. Estelle curbed her drinking and began attending Alcoholics Anonymous meetings, although this too proved a source of trouble, for Faulkner made no effort to check his intake of Jack Daniel's.

In spite of everything, the Faulkners remained together. Estelle Faulkner survived the novelist by 10 years.

Faulkner, James Murry (Jimmy) (1923–2001) Faulkner's nephew, the son of John III and Dolly Falkner, known as Jimmy. Faulkner liked to play with the toddler Jimmy and, as he grew older, would take him hunting or aloft in one of the Waco aircraft he used to fly. Jimmy called Faulkner "Brother Will," and became a surrogate son to him.

Jimmy Faulkner volunteered as a Marine aviation cadet in 1943 and carried his uncle's goggles and leather flying jacket into the service with him.

He saw combat action in the Pacific during World War II, surviving a crash at sea off Okinawa. He returned to active duty during the Korean War and stayed on afterward in the Marine reserves, rising to the rank of lieutenant colonel.

They remained close to the end of Faulkner's life. "I think that Jim is the only person who likes me for what I am," Faulkner once said of him. A few months before his death, Faulkner told Jimmy of his premonition of the end and asked him to take care of some things after he had gone. In July 1962, Jimmy Faulkner drove the novelist to Wright's Sanitarium in BYHALIA, MISSISSIPPI, for the last of his visits there.

In the 1985 film version of the short story "BARN BURNING," Jimmy Faulkner played the minor role of Major de Spain; the film, part of an educational series hosted by Henry Fonda, stars Tom Lee Jones, Diane Kagan, and Shawn Wittington.

Faulkner, Jill (Jill Faulkner Summers) (1933–)

Faulkner's only child, his "heart's darling" (supplanting the fictional Candace (Caddy) Compson of *The SOUND AND THE FURY*), born in OXFORD, MISSISSIPPI, on June 25, 1933. Caroline Barr, "Mammy," took care of Jill in her infancy. With two troubled parents—a drunken mother and a drunken, often absent father—she had a difficult childhood.

Jill called him "Pappy." Father and daughter had a good relationship in the early years, at least when Faulkner was in residence at ROWAN OAK. He sang

Jill Faulkner's bedroom at Rowan Oak. *(Harriett and Gioia Fargnoli)*

to her, read to her, and invented stories for her about the escapades of Virgil Jones, a guitar-strumming squirrel.

Faulkner brought Jill out to Hollywood in 1943, arranged horseback riding lessons for her, introduced her to his lover, META CARPENTER, and sent her back home to Mississippi in the autumn with a prized possession—a gentle mare named Lady Go-Lightly.

Jill probably saved Faulkner's marriage to ESTELLE OLDHAM FAULKNER, such as it was; he dreaded the estrangement from his daughter a divorce would make inevitable. But she clearly suffered from her parents' troubles and often upbraided her father about his drunkenness.

Like her father, Jill had a streak of stoicism. Growing up the child of the dysfunctional Faulkners "was exhausting," she told the biographer Jay Parini simply, "but I survived it."

Faulkner proved a stern father as Jill grew older. He seemed to encourage her tomboy tendencies, but once, when he saw her on the Courthouse Square wearing shorts, he passed her by without a word. He told her later that ladies did not dress that way in public. Nor, for a long time, would he allow her a radio, a phonograph, or, later, a television.

At Estelle's suggestion, Jill accompanied the novelist to Stockholm in December 1950 to accept his Nobel Prize. Faulkner spoke at Jill's graduation from Oxford High School in May 1951 and at her graduation from Pine Manor Junior College in Wellesley, Massachusetts. He dedicated the novel *A FABLE* (1954) to Jill, explaining that it was his way of saying farewell to her childhood.

Faulkner gave her away to PAUL D. SUMMERS Jr. at her wedding at Rowan Oak in August 1954. Jill and Summers became the parents of three sons. They named the middle boy, born in 1958, William Cuthbert Faulkner.

From the late 1950s onward, Faulkner spent as much time as possible in Charlottesville, Virginia, where Jill and her lawyer husband had settled. By then, he and Estelle had negotiated the armistice that quieted their long-running marital war. Still, when all was said, being Faulkner's child had been a difficult business. "Given his independent personality," Jill said of him, "he shouldn't have burdened himself with a family" (Joel Williamson, *William Faulkner and Southern History*, 294).

Faulkner and Yoknapatawpha Conference   *See* ANNUAL FAULKNER AND YOKNAPATAWPHA CONFERENCE.

film, Faulkner and   On a recommendation from Leland Hayward, BEN WASSON's superior at the American Play Company, Faulkner was invited by Sam Marx at METRO-GOLDWYN-MAYER Studios to Hollywood where he arrived in May 1932 to work as a screenwriter for MGM. In that same year his father died and LIGHT IN AUGUST was published. Faulkner continued to work on and off in Hollywood for MGM, Twentieth Century–Fox, and WARNER BROTHERS for the next 22 years, an opportunity that provided him with a much-needed income to supplement his sparse earnings as a fiction writer. In late 1935, Faulkner met META CARPENTER, also a native of Mississippi, who was working as a secretary for the director-producer HOWARD HAWKS. The two developed an intimate relationship over the next 15 years.

Although Faulkner's reputation as a novelist was not universally acclaimed in 1932, he was known and respected. Hawks, with whom Faulkner became friends, had been favorably impressed with SOLDIERS' PAY (1926), Faulkner's first novel. Hawks also purchased the rights to Faulkner's "Turn About" (*see* "TURNABOUT"), a short story dealing with air and sea combat in World War I, and requested that Faulkner write the screenplay. He did so with Edith Fitzgerald and Dwight Taylor. The story was the basis for Hawks's 1933 film *Today We Live.*

Though Faulkner was not enamored with Hollywood, his personal biases never interfered with his professional responsibilities. As JOSEPH BLOTNER comments in his biography of Faulkner, the short story "GOLDEN LAND" clearly reveals Faulkner's attitude toward Hollywood: "Set in Beverly Hills, its every page seemed imbued with the distaste and unhappiness he had felt. The terrain, the climate, the architecture, the people, their behavior, their dress—all displeased him" (342). During his association with Hollywood, Faulkner worked or collaborated on well over 40 films, including the

following six, which he coauthored and for which he received screen credit: *Today We Live* (1933), *The Road to Glory* (1936), *Slave Ship* (1937), *To Have and Have Not* (1944), *The Big Sleep* (1946), and *Land of the Pharaohs* (1955). *To Have and Have Not,* loosely based on ERNEST HEMINGWAY's novel of the same title, is, as Gene D. Phillips observes in *Fiction, Film, and Faulkner: The Art of Adaptation,* the only film in history "to be the creative product of two Nobel Prize winners" (43).

Faulkner invested much time, energy, and creative talent on other scripts, none of which ever made it to the big screen. These screenplays included, for example, *Manservant* (1932), *The College Widow* (1932), and those dealing particularly with the war effort, such as *The Life and Death of a Bomber/Liberator Story* (1942/1943), *The De Gaulle Story* (1942), and *Battle Cry* (1943).

In addition to "Turn About," many other Faulkner works have been adapted to film. One critic, Bruce F. Kawin, observes that Faulkner is "the most cinematic of novelists. Such techniques as montage, freeze-frame, slow motion and visual metaphor abound in his fiction" (*Faulkner and Film,* 5). Faulkner's works adapted by other screenwriters include INTRUDER IN THE DUST (film by same title, 1949), PYLON (film titled *The Tarnished Angels,* 1957), *The* HAMLET (film titled *The Long Hot Summer,* 1958), *The* SOUND AND THE FURY (film by same title, 1959), SANCTUARY and REQUIEM FOR A NUN (film titled *Sanctuary,* 1961), and *The* REIVERS (film by same title, 1969).

Perhaps because Faulkner himself typically disparaged his Hollywood work, the study of his contributions to film continues to be dwarfed by the examinations of his fiction. Bruce Kawin was the first scholar to take Faulkner's screenwriting seriously, with his pioneering study, *Faulkner and Film* (1977), and his edition of *Faulkner's MGM Screenplays* (1982). The 1978 Faulkner and Yoknapatawpha Conference examined the topic of "Faulkner, Modernism, and Film"; and Tom Dardis devoted a chapter of *Some Time in the Sun* (1981), his story of American authors in Hollywood, to Faulkner. Gene B. Phillips extended Kawin's explorations in *Fiction, Film, and Faulkner* (1988). Louis Daniel Brodsky and Robert W. Hamblin have edited a number of the screenplays that Faulkner wrote for WARNER BROS. in the 1940s, including *The De Gaulle Story* (1984), *Battle Cry* (1985), *Country Lawyer and Other Stories for the Screen* (1987), and *Stallion Road* (1989). Still, a definitive treatment of Faulkner's Hollywood career has yet to be written.

Also see BOGART, HUMPHREY.

flying, Faulkner and The notion of flight long fascinated Faulkner. His simple boyhood curiosity grew into a complex involvement, an obsession perhaps, when he chose the persona of aviator-hero as one of the many fronts he presented to the world. Later, flying itself provided opportunities for a brush with the ultimate that Faulkner seemed to crave.

As a boy, Billy Falkner led his brothers and their cousin Sally Murry in building an airplane from a pattern in *American Boy* magazine. Setting up shop in a barn on the Falkner place, the boys used their mother's bean poles for the frame and old newspapers stuck on with flour paste for the skin.

The final product was close to full scale. Billy took the first test flight, launched from the lip of a 10-foot-deep sand ditch in the Falkners' back lot. The plane came apart in midair.

The air war over France in 1914–18 caught Faulkner's imagination; in early 1918, at age 20, he tried to join the U.S. Army Flying Corps. The army judged him too short and too light of weight. In the spring, Faulkner and his friend PHILIP AVERY STONE plotted a scheme to infiltrate him into the ROYAL AIR FORCE as a flying cadet. Faulkner invented an English background (he claimed his birthplace as Finchley in Middlesex) and added the *u* to his last name. He and Stone even forged reliable-looking references from England. Faulkner successfully enlisted in the RAF in New York City on June 18, 1918.

Faulkner's hometown newspaper, the *Oxford EAGLE* reported on June 27: "Mr. William Falkner who has been spending a few months in New York is visiting his parents Mr. and Mrs. Murry Falkner. He has joined the English Royal Flying Corps and leaves the eighth of July for Toronto, Canada, where he will train."

Faulkner later invented an immodestly eventful flying career, essentially creating a fictional character for himself: British flying officer and wounded war hero. As late as 1932, a UNIVERSITY OF MISSISSIPPI professor writing about Faulkner remarked approvingly of the novelist's modesty about his war career, even though he had "two enemy planes to his credit and several times barely escaped death." In NEW ORLEANS in the 1920s, Faulkner walked with a manufactured limp, claimed he wore a silver plate in his head, and explained that he drank immoderately to dull the pain of his war injuries.

"During the war he was with the British Air Force and made a brilliant record," the New Orleans little magazine *DOUBLE DEALER* wrote in introducing the aspiring poet and critic in the mid-1920s. "He was severely wounded."

Faulkner was somewhat more truthful with his family; after all, his brother Jack, a Marine, actually had been seriously wounded, and in the head too, fighting on the Argonne front in northern France in November 1918. Faulkner claimed he had flown solo, and had cracked up a couple of aircraft in the service of the Crown.

In fact, Faulkner never got out of ground school. He turned up at the RAF recruits' depot in Toronto in July 1918 carrying a suitcase labeled "William Faulkner, Oxford, Mississippi," and gained an indoctrination into military life. By November, he claimed to have been flying for three months, and to have logged four hours' solo time aloft.

There is no evidence that Faulkner flew at all, let alone banged up any aircraft. And his ground school marks were mediocre—around 70 percent, according to his service record. With the armistice of November 11, 1918, the British government moved rapidly to discharge surplus air cadets. Faulkner was home in Oxford by late December, with $42.58 in demobilization pay and a promise that he eventually would be made an honorary second lieutenant.

Faulkner anticipated the honorary designation, posing at home in his British officer's uniform, with second lieutenant's pips affixed to the shoulder straps, unearned pilot's wings on the tunic, a swagger stick under his arm. Frederick Karl, a Faulkner biographer, suggests that the elegant uniform and the imposture gave him an edge over the authentically wounded Jack and over their shambling and most unmilitary father. Karl regards the brief RAF experience, and Faulkner's use of it, as crucial in the artist's development because it turned him into a storyteller.

The military experience, real and imagined, informed Faulkner's novels SOLDIERS' PAY (1926), SARTORIS (1929) and A FABLE (1954), as well as several short stories, including "Ad Astra" and "ALL THE DEAD PILOTS."

Faulkner finally earned a pilot's license in 1933 under the instruction of the veteran aviator VERNON C. OMLIE. He told Omlie that he had become afraid after crashing as an RAF pilot and wanted to recover his courage as well as his skills. Though Omlie reported him as a slow learner and dangerously clumsy on landings, Faulkner lifted off for his first solo flight on April 20, 1933.

Omlie introduced Faulkner to the world of aerial circuses, with their stunt flyers, wingwalkers, and parachutists. These performers caught Faulkner's imagination. He saw them as the gypsies of the industrial age, misfits driven by an urge to escape the earthbound world. Much of the barnstormer material made its way into the novel PYLON (1935), whose main characters, Roger and Laverne Shumann, were partly modeled on Vernon Omlie and his wife, Phoebe.

"To me [the barnstormers] were a fantastic and bizarre phenomenon on the face of a contemporary scene," Faulkner explained. "That is, there was really no place for them in the culture, in the economy, yet they were there, at that time, and everyone knew they wouldn't last very long, which they didn't" (*Faulkner in the University*, 36).

Faulkner used money from the sale of the film rights for his novel SANCTUARY to buy his own airplane, a 210-horsepower Waco cabin cruiser, in the autumn of 1933. He eventually turned the machine over to his younger brother DEAN FAULKNER, who had learned to fly—and had developed a career out of it—at Faulkner's suggestion. Dean died in a crash during an airshow at PONTOTOC, MISSISSIPPI, in November 1935. Faulkner blamed himself for the tragedy and had nightmares about it long afterward.

Horses eventually supplanted airplanes as one of Faulkner's means (drinking was another) of risking himself. Reckless riding over rough country aboard powerful mounts supplied some of the danger that doubtless formed a necessary part of flying's appeal—no exaggerated danger, so it happened, for Faulkner suffered painful back injuries in a series of falls from horses.

Faulkner biographer Joel Williamson argues that horses were an explicit extension of the novelist's earlier role as a wounded flyer, that there was an essential similarity between the man and his airplane and the man and his horse: "Both attempted to assert mastery over awesome power that gave amplitude to themselves," Williamson wrote. "More important, that power was dangerous, capricious, and liable to go out of control for no discernable reason—with hardly a second's warning and with devastating and often fatal results."

By the 1940s, fame forced the novelist to correct his heavily fictionalized military biography, or anyway attempt to erase it from the record. MALCOLM COWLEY planned to use the 1920s war hero story, including the fiction of his having been in combat over France, as part of his biographical sketch for *The* PORTABLE FAULKNER (1946). He dropped it on Faulkner's strong protest.

Johncy Falkner either believed his brother's fictions about his RAF service or decided to repeat them out of family loyalty. In his memoir *My Brother Bill*, published in 1963, a year after Faulkner's death, he noted that Billy was the first of the Falkner boys to learn to ride a bicycle. "I think it was his sense of balance that helped him live through flying Camels in the First War, for there was never a more tricky airplane built than a Sopwith Camel," Johncy wrote.

Foote, Shelby (1916–2005) Novelist and historian, born in Greenville, Mississippi. He wrote five well-received novels before turning to the work for which he is best known, his three-volume history *The Civil War: A Narrative* (1958–74), the work of 20 years.

Faulkner's friend BEN WASSON introduced the admiring Foote to the novelist in June 1941. Foote later sent him signed copies of his own novels. Like Foote, Faulkner had a deep interest in the Civil War. In April 1952, on the 90th anniversary of the BATTLE OF SHILOH in southwestern Tennessee, Foote escorted Faulkner around the battlefield.

They talked about writing that day, and Foote recalled later that Faulkner there had delivered the only piece of writerly advice he ever offered him: Don't work when you're tired.

Commenting on Foote's fiction, Faulkner once remarked that he would "like Foote more if he sounded less like Faulkner and more like Foote."

Ford, Ruth (1915–) Mississippi-born actress and friend of Faulkner, a slightly built woman with dark hair and eyes. Faulkner found her attractive and usually met her on trips to New York City. On one visit, in the late 1940s, he suggested they become lovers. They had been friends a long time, he reminded her; "Ain't it time I was promoted?" She brushed him off (Jay Parini, *One Matchless Time*, 299–300).

Ford helped advise Faulkner on the stage version of his novel REQUIEM FOR A NUN. She eventually married the actor Zachary Scott. Ford and Scott played the lead roles in both the London and New York stage productions of *Requiem for a Nun*.

Forrest, Nathan Bedford (1821–1877) Confederate soldier, born in Bedford, Tennessee. A prewar livestock dealer and slave trader with scant formal education, Forrest became the most feared Confederate cavalry commander of the Civil War. After the war, he was a leader of the Ku Klux Klan terror organization.

Forrest's cavalry operated extensively from 1862 to 1865 in northern Mississippi and western Tennessee—the home country of Faulkner's great-grandfather, Colonel WILLIAM C. FALKNER, and his 1st Mississippi Partisan Rangers. Family legend held that the Old Colonel rode with Forrest, though that was almost certainly a fiction.

Union troops passed through RIPLEY, MISSISSIPPI, Falkner's hometown, early in June 1864 in pursuit of Forrest's command. Faulkner's great-grandmother allegedly supplied false information to a Yankee officer who sought information on Confederate movements. Forrest inflicted a sharp defeat on the Union forces at Brice's Cross Roads, Mississippi, on June 10. On General WILLIAM TECUMSEH SHERMAN's order, Union troops set fire to public buildings in Ripley later in the summer. The blaze spread and destroyed several homes, including Colonel Falkner's.

Faulkner reworked the family tale of the encounter between the Yankee officer and his great-grandmother into a scene featuring Granny Rosa Millard in his Civil War novel, *The* UNVANQUISHED. In *The* REIVERS, he retold the story, possibly apocryphal, of Forrest's brother's riding into the lobby of the GAYOSO HOTEL in Yankee-occupied MEMPHIS, sending the fictional Theophilus McCaslin along as one of Forrest's escorts.

Four Seas Company This small Boston publishing house, specializing in young unknown poets (including William Carlos Williams in 1922), was Faulkner's first book publisher. Faulkner approached the firm in June 1923 to offer a collection of his verse, which Four Seas rejected.

In May 1924, Faulkner's friend PHILIP AVERY STONE proposed to pay publication costs if Four Seas would publish Faulkner's poem cycle the *The* MARBLE FAUN. The house offered to do a first edition of 1,000 copies for $400, payable in two equal installments.

Stone and Faulkner raised the money. Four Seas duly published *The Marble Faun*, a 51-page volume between green covers dedicated to Faulkner's mother and with an introduction by Stone, on December 15, 1924.

Franklin, Cornell Sidney (c. 1889–1959) The first husband of ESTELLE OLDHAM FAULKNER. A UNIVERSITY OF MISSISSIPPI graduate and a lawyer, Franklin settled in Hawaii and did well there, becoming assistant district attorney in Honolulu. After a long, curious courtship, much promoted by the Franklin and Oldham families, he and Estelle Oldham were married on April 18, 1918.

Before the ceremony, Estelle had offered to elope with Billy Falkner. He insisted on obtaining their families' permission. When the Oldhams and the Falkners strongly disapproved, Estelle went ahead with the Franklin wedding, a lavish affair which Billy declined to attend.

She moved to Hawaii with her husband and later to Shanghai. They had two children, MELVINA VICTORIA and MALCOLM ARGYLE FRANKLIN, but increasingly became estranged, Franklin pursuing his business interests and his private pastime of gambling and Estelle spending increasing amounts of time back home in Oxford, where she saw much of Faulkner.

Cornell Franklin and Estelle Oldham were divorced in April 1929. Franklin died in 1959.

Franklin, Malcolm Argyle (1923–1977) Son of CORNELL SIDNEY FRANKLIN and ESTELLE OLDHAM Franklin (later FAULKNER). Faulkner assumed a parent's role with young Malcolm (known as Mac), whom he came to know well before he married Estelle in 1929. Jay Parini, a Faulkner biographer, raises the possibility Mac may not have been Franklin's son and may in fact have been Faulkner's.

As children, Mac and his older sister, MELVINA VICTORIA FRANKLIN, viewed their mother's friend as a glamorous figure—a free spirit and an airman. Faulkner used to tell them elaborate stories and supply them with candy. They looked forward to his visits during his long courtship of their mother.

Faulkner took his stepson hunting and for walks in the woods, encouraged his interests in natural history and archeology, and taught him to play chess. When he grew older, Malcolm helped his mother manage the novelist during his alcoholic illnesses.

Mac Franklin served as an army medic in Europe during World War II, and after the war took a biology degree from the UNIVERSITY OF MISSISSIPPI. As an adult, he generously attributed his good qualities to his stepfather's influence. Still, their relationship was sometimes difficult. Mac admired his stepfather, but Faulkner often neglected him for his work as he neglected other family relationships.

Mac Franklin's marriage ended in divorce, and his ex-wife remarried in 1957 without informing him. He began to drink heavily and threaten violence. An unsigned letter advising Mac to "act like a man" in the situation touched off a family crisis. Mac thought Faulkner had written it; in fact it came from his aunt DOROTHY OLDHAM, who simply had neglected to sign it.

Mac's friends blamed the Faulkners—particularly the novelist—for his troubles. Mac realized finally that Faulkner had not sent the offending letter, although he resented him still for endorsing its contents.

Malcolm Franklin published a memoir, *Bitterweeds: Life with William Faulkner at Rowan Oak,* in 1977, the year he died.

Franklin, Melvina Victoria de Graffenreid (1919–) Daughter of CORNELL SIDNEY FRANKLIN and ESTELLE OLDHAM Franklin (later FAULKNER). Faulkner met her for the first time when her mother brought her to OXFORD, MISSISSIPPI, from Hawaii as an infant. Victoria's Chinese nurse bestowed the nickname Cho-Cho—butterfly—on her.

Faulkner actively parented Cho-Cho and her younger brother Malcolm. When her husband, Claude Selby, left not long after their marriage in 1936 and the birth of their daughter, Faulkner gave her typing work to keep her occupied and was solicitous in other ways.

Victoria Franklin had a successful second marriage. She and William Fielden, an executive with the British-American Tobacco Company in China, were married at her father's home in Shanghai in 1940. They returned to Mississippi for the duration of the war, went back to China after 1945, and later settled in Manila, the Philippines.

Faulkner and Victoria enjoyed a reunion in 1955 during the novelist's visit to Japan, where he was star turn at a writers' conference, and the Philippines.

Frenchman's Bend Fictional place, a settlement on the Yoknapatawpha River in southeastern YOKNAPATAWPHA COUNTY 20 miles southeast of Jefferson, peopled mostly by poor white farmers who raise cotton and corn and live precariously in broken-backed "dogtrot" houses.

In *As I LAY DYING,* a washed-out bridge at Frenchman's Bend prevents Anse Bundren from crossing the flooded river to carry his wife's body to JEFFERSON, MISSISSIPPI, for burial. The settlement figures prominently in *The HAMLET,* the first novel in the SNOPES TRILOGY, and is mentioned in other works.

A description of Frenchman's Bend opens *The Hamlet*. At this time (1907), Will Varner owns most of the original plantation granted to the French settler Grenier, having systematically bought up the small farms parcelled out of the abandoned OLD FRENCHMAN PLACE. His son Jody Varner runs VARNER'S STORE, the chief enterprise and gathering place in Frenchman's Bend. Other landmarks are a cotton gin and a derelict antebellum plantation house with ruined stables and fallen-in slave cabins.

G

Gallimard Editions Faulkner's French publisher. The firm's head, Gaston Gallimard, moved to acquire the French rights to Faulkner's fiction in April 1931 on the recommendation of the translator MAURICE COINDREAU. Coindreau first translated AS I LAY DYING and continued with other Faulkner works. Faulkner's novels sold well in France, and he enjoyed a high literary reputation there even as his stock slumped in the United States.

Gayoso Hotel A Civil War–era MEMPHIS hostelry named for an 18th-century Spanish governor. The hotel is famous in Southern lore for cavalry commander NATHAN BEDFORD FORREST's surprise raid in August 1864. Forrest's brother and his escorts allegedly rode into the Gayoso and terrorized the Yankee officers gathered there. When Forrest retreated from the Union-held city, he left behind 62 of his troopers dead or wounded.

Faulkner's narrator in The REIVERS muses about the Gayoso as a "family shrine" because Theophilus McCaslin was one of Forrest's horsemen.

Once the city's leading hotel, the Gayoso fell into dilapidation and closed around 1960.

Gihon County, Alabama Fictional place. In The UNVANQUISHED, Granny Rosa Millard, Bayard Sartoris, and Ringo Strother travel during the Civil War to HAWKHURST in Gihon County, home of Miz Millard's sister, the war widow Louisa Hawk. They find Hawkhurst a ruin, burned out by Union forces, and Aunt Louisa and her children living in the slave quarters.

Goldman, Morton Faulkner's literary agent, successor to the novelist's Mississippi friend BEN WASSON. When in low water, Faulkner leaned hard on Goldman to seek out money-making opportunities. "I can use money right now to beat hell," the novelist wrote him in 1935—a typical extract from a letter to Goldman.

Glasgow Fictional town in CROSSMAN COUNTY, an eastern neighbor of YOKNAPATAWPHA COUNTY. In INTRUDER IN THE DUST, Jake Montgomery steals sawed lumber from his partner, Vinson Gowrie, and hauls it away to Glasgow or HOLLYMOUNT at night. Montgomery's father farms just outside Glasgow.

Grant, Ulysses S. (1822–1885) Soldier and 18th president of the United States, born in Point Pleasant, Ohio. As commander of the Union Army of the Tennessee and later as senior Union commander in the West, Grant defeated Confederate forces at SHILOH in 1862 and captured the strategic fortress of Vicksburg on the Mississippi River in 1863 (see VICKSBURG CAMPAIGN).

Grant's troops campaigned in northern Mississippi, including RIPLEY and OXFORD, MISSISSIPPI, both of which were Falkner hometowns, in 1862–63. The general was alleged to have looked down South Street in Oxford and declared it one of the prettiest streets in America.

In 1864–65, he was commander in chief of all Union forces, with headquarters in the field in Virginia. Grant accepted Confederate General Robert E. Lee's surrender of the Army of Northern Virginia at Appomattox Courthouse on April 9, 1865. The surrender effectively brought the Civil War to a close.

Greenfield Farm   Faulkner bought a run-down, 320-acre hill farm in LAFAYETTE COUNTY, MISSISSIPPI, 17 miles northeast of OXFORD, MISSISSIPPI, in February 1938, borrowing $2,000 from the New Orleans Land Bank for the purpose. He named it Greenfield Farm, and his brother JOHN WESLEY THOMPSON FALKNER III ("Johncy") managed it for him for the first few years.

Under Faulkner's supervision, Johncy refurbished the farmhouse and bought a used tractor to clear the Puskus Creek bottomlands, though he and Faulkner's four black tenant families used mules for the actual cultivation of the crops. The brothers raised corn and cotton and hogs at Greenfield Farm, and kept a stable of brood mares with a stud horse named Big John. The farm had a commissary that sold flour, meal, sugar, lard, soap, corn, tobacco, clothing, and farm gear. Faulkner himself presided over an annual Fourth of July barbecue there. The novelist fancied himself a farmer, and a sort of seigneur too. His baronial manner led to tension with Johncy. After they made their first crop, a bountiful one, Faulkner surveyed the scene and said only, "I don't see anything here to complain of."

He loved the place, though it arguably represented a financial drain for him, and he poured his farming experiences directly into his fiction, particularly when he wrote about the small farmer class, white and black, as in GO DOWN, MOSES, the SNOPES trilogy, and INTRUDER IN THE DUST.

Faulkner used to take his daughter, Jill, out to Greenfield Farm for a few days at hog-killing time in late autumn. They stayed in The Lodge, a large

cabin on the place, while he checked the commissary accounts, supervised the slaughter, and saw to the mending of the fences.

Faulkner deeded Greenfield Farm (along with ROWAN OAK, his Oxford house) to Jill on her 21st birthday in 1954.

Grenier County   Fictional place, sharing a southern border with YOKNAPATAWPHA COUNTY. In *The HAMLET*, Ab Snopes burns the barn of a Grenier County farmer named Harris (4).

Gulf & Chicago Railroad   WILLIAM C. FALKNER, Faulkner's great-grandfather, formed this grandly named branch railroad line in 1888. The Gulf & Chicago offered service from Middleton, Tennessee, to PONTOTOC, MISSISSIPPI—a distance of 63 miles. By the autumn of 1888 the line was carrying enough traffic to persuade the Old Colonel to operate two trains a day.

Faulkner's father, MURRY C. FALKNER, worked for the Gulf & Chicago as a young man, first as a mail agent, later as a general passenger agent, and finally as treasurer and auditor.

Faulkner's grandfather, JOHN WESLEY THOMPSON FALKNER, decided to sell the line to the Mobile, Jackson and Kansas City Railroad Company in 1902, putting the future novelist's father out of a job.

Faulkner fictionalized his great-grandfather's railroad experiences in *The UNVANQUISHED*; John Sartoris himself is in the engine cab, tugging furiously on the steam whistle, when the first train on the newly built line steams into JEFFERSON in 1874.

Gulf & Ship Island Railroad   In his second railroad venture, WILLIAM C. FALKNER, Faulkner's great-grandfather, and a partner obtained a legislative charter in February 1882 for a line to extend southward for an eventual link with a line building to the north from Hattiesburg, Mississippi. This initiative grew out of his first venture, the Ripley Railroad Company, a 25-mile narrow gauge line—the "Doodlebug line," so called—from RIPLEY, MISSISSIPPI, to Middleton, Tennessee.

Falkner pushed the railroad from Ripley, the terminus of his SHIP ISLAND, RIPLEY & KENTUCKY

RAILROAD, 37 miles south to PONTOTOC, MISSISSIPPI, over the next four years. He also bought out his partner RICHARD J. THURMOND's share of the Ship Island, Ripley & Kentucky.

In 1888, he merged the Gulf & Ship Island into a new, larger company, the GULF & CHICAGO RAILROAD, which eventually absorbed the Ship Island, Ripley & Kentucky. (*Also see* the entry on GULF & CHICAGO RAILROAD.)

H

Haas, Robert K. (1890–1964) Faulkner's editor and publisher. He graduated from Yale and fought in France during World War I before going into publishing. A founder of the Book-of-the Month Club, he came out of retirement in 1932 to join HARRISON SMITH in the firm of SMITH & HAAS.

Haas moved to RANDOM HOUSE as a partner when the larger firm absorbed Smith & Haas early in 1936. Haas worked with Faulkner there for more than two decades—long enough to see him mature and then pass his peak as an artist.

Faulkner first proposed the idea that grew into *The REIVERS* (1962) to Haas as far back as 1940, calling it a "sort of Huck Finn" story.

Haas quite often entertained Faulkner when he came to New York. MALCOLM COWLEY recalls two rather formal occasions, one on which Haas hired two butlers to manage the affair and a second in November 1950 on the night before Faulkner left for Stockholm to accept the NOBEL PRIZE IN LITERATURE. Cowley found the novelist "abstracted" that evening, "as if reserving his strength for a supreme ordeal" (*The Faulkner-Cowley File*, 129).

Handy, W. C. (1873–1958) Alabama-born musician and composer of such famous songs as "St. Louis Blues" and "Beale Street Blues," and widely regarded as "the father of the Blues." Trained as a schoolteacher, he soon tired of that life and devoted himself full time to music. By 1909, he had his own band, based in MEMPHIS.

Handy used to come down from Memphis to perform with his band at OXFORD, MISSISSIPPI, dances the teenage Billy Falkner attended. Estelle Oldham, Faulkner's future wife, danced to Handy's music when he played at UNIVERSITY OF MISSISSIPPI parties and balls. It is from the first line of "St. Louis Blues"—"I hates to see that evening sun go down"—that Faulkner got the title of his short story "THAT EVENING SUN."

Harcourt, Brace and Company New York City publisher, founded in 1920. Harcourt, Brace published Faulkner's third novel, *SARTORIS,* in January 1929 after BONI & LIVERIGHT had rejected the manuscript (then titled *FLAGS IN THE DUST.*)

Alfred Harcourt had grave doubts about Faulkner's next submission, *The SOUND AND THE FURY.* He allowed one of his editors, HARRISON SMITH, to take the manuscript with him when Smith left to establish his own firm; CAPE & SMITH published *The Sound and the Fury* in October 1929.

Harcourt, Brace published *By Their Fruits,* a novel by Faulkner's brother Johncy (JOHN WESLEY THOMPSON FALKNER III), in 1941.

Harper's Magazine Venerable literary periodical, founded as *Harper's Monthly Magazine* by the publisher Harper & Bros. in New York City in 1850. By Faulkner's time, *Harper's* had changed from a strictly literary format to a mix that included politics and social issues.

The magazine published a half-dozen or more Faulkner short stories in the 1930s, beginning with "The HOUND" in August 1931. Payment usually ran $350 to $400 per story, not the top magazine rate, but important income nevertheless to the financially hard-pressed writer.

In 1944, when Faulkner's reputation was at low ebb, *Harper's* turned down MALCOLM COWLEY's proposal for a lengthy essay on Faulkner's merits and his place in contemporary literature.

Faulkner's "On Fear: The South in Labor," an essay on race relations, appeared in *Harper's* in June 1956, part of a series of Faulkner essays called "The American Dream: What Happened to It?" Faulkner expressly directed his agent to place the piece on race in *Harper's* or in the ATLANTIC MONTHLY rather than in *Life* or another of the "slick" magazines, which he believed were biased against the South. In this passionate essay, Faulkner urged the white South to rise above the region's tortured racial history. "To live anywhere in the world today and be against equality because of race or color," he wrote, "is like living in Alaska and being against snow."

Harper's paid $350 for "On Fear."

Harvard University The first North American institution of higher learning, founded in 1636 in Cambridge (then New Towne), Massachusetts, near Boston. It remains one of the two or three best-known and most prestigious American universities.

Faulkner's fictional Quentin Compson is a student at Harvard in 1909–10 in *The SOUND AND THE FURY* and *ABSALOM, ABSALOM!* At the end of his first year at Harvard Quentin commits suicide by drowning himself in the Charles River. Gavin Stevens and his nephew Charles (Chick) Mallison, Jr., who appear in several of Faulkner's works, are educated at Harvard.

In the fall of 1948, Professor CARVEL COLLINS taught a seminar at Harvard on Faulkner's work—the first such course anywhere. In 1959, Faulkner told the University of Texas scholar JAMES B. MERIWETHER that he wanted to see his manuscripts go to Harvard because it was the nation's oldest university.

Hawkhurst Fictional place, the GIHON COUNTY, ALABAMA, home of Rosa Millard's widowed sister, Louisa Hawk, and Louisa's children Drusilla Hawk (Sartoris) and Dennison Hawk Jr. In *The UNVANQUISHED,* the place is a ruin when Granny Millard, Bayard Sartoris, and Ringo Strother arrive as refugees in 1863. Yankee raiders had burned it, just as they had burned Sartoris plantation, and Granny found her sister's family resettled in the slave quarters.

Hawks, Howard (1896–1977) Movie director, born in Goshen, Indiana, educated at Phillips Exeter Academy and Cornell University. He served with the Army Air Corps during World War I and later drove racing cars. His *Dawn Patrol* (1930), a classic film of World War I air warfare, established Hawks as one of Hollywood's leading directors.

Hawks and Faulkner became friends in the early 1930s, during Faulkner's first scriptwriting sojourns in Hollywood. He met his lover META CARPENTER through Hawks, for whom she worked as an assistant.

Hawks's film *Today We Live,* based on the Faulkner short story "Turn About" (see "TURNABOUT"), had its premiere in OXFORD, MISSISSIPPI, in April 1933; Faulkner had helped with the script. In the 1940s, they collaborated on the WARNER BROTHERS movies *To Have and Have Not* and *The Big Sleep.* Hawks brought Faulkner to Egypt in the early 1950s to work on the script of *Land of the Pharaohs.*

Hawks and Faulkner had flying and hunting in common and got along well together. Each had a high regard for the other's craftsmanship.

Hell Creek Fictional name for Spring Creek, which flows into the TALLAHATCHIE RIVER north of OXFORD, MISSISSIPPI. The road from Oxford to MEMPHIS crosses Spring Creek between the Tallahatchie and the town of Waterford.

In *The REIVERS,* Boon Hogganbeck darkly warns Lucius Priest and Ned McCaslin of the difficulties he expects to encounter in taking Grandfather Priest's automobile through boggy Hell Creek bottom.

The car becomes hopelessly stuck in the mire. A farmer with two mules stationed at the bridge rapaciously charges Boon six dollars to free the car and tow it to high ground on the far side of the creek.

Hemingway, Ernest (1899–1961) Writer and celebrity, a medical doctor's son, born in Oak Park, Illinois. After serving with a Red Cross ambulance unit in Italy (1917–18) during World War I, he worked as a journalist, and as an expatriate in Paris in the 1920s established himself with *In Our Time* (1925), *The Sun Also Rises* (1926), and *A Farewell to Arms* (1929) as one of the leading American writers of his generation.

In this early work, Hemingway perfected his distinctive and much-imitated style, so different from Faulkner's: simple sentences, exact description, terse, highly suggestive dialogue. He returned to the United States in 1927 but never settled down, moving restlessly from Florida to Cuba to Europe and back again. He sought release (and material for his work) in hunting and fishing, bullfighting, and war. *Death in the Afternoon* (1932) grew out of his passion for the bullring; he based *For Whom the Bell Tolls* (1940), regarded as one of his better novels, on his journalistic and other experiences in Spain during the Spanish civil war of 1936–39. He won critical and popular acclaim for *The Old Man and the Sea* in 1952, and was awarded the NOBEL PRIZE IN LITERATURE in 1954.

Faulkner and Hemingway were sometimes admiring but more often wary of each other. Hemingway praised Faulkner as the most talented writer of his time, admitting, according to the critic MALCOLM COWLEY, that he ranked Faulkner above himself. But he also regarded Faulkner's work as uneven and undisciplined; he wrote too much, according to Hemingway, and he wrote carelessly.

Faulkner did not hold Hemingway in such high esteem, though he did have one of his characters, Temple Drake (Stevens) in REQUIEM FOR A NUN (1951), quote the character Maria in *For Whom the Bell Tolls*. Nor was Faulkner much impressed with Hemingway's carefully cultivated image as a man of action. He once remarked dismissively that of all the ways of dying, "Hemingway would like most to be gored by a bull."

At a UNIVERSITY OF MISSISSIPPI seminar on the novel in 1947, Faulkner extemporaneously listed

Faulkner and John Dos Passos attended a reception at the University of Virginia, where Faulkner was writer-in-residence during 1957–58. *(William Faulkner Collection, Special Collections Department, Manuscripts Division, University of Virginia Library. Photo by Ralph Thompson.)*

Hemingway fourth of the five major novelists of his generation, after Thomas Wolfe, himself, and John Dos Passos, and just ahead of John Steinbeck. Hemingway never overreached his talent, Faulkner said; he never tried anything he was not sure he could pull off. "He has no courage, has never climbed out on a limb," Faulkner famously said.

The comment got back to Hemingway in Cuba and deeply wounded him. Altogether missing the point, he started a letter to Faulkner listing his combat actions, then asked a soldier familiar with his war record to set Faulkner straight. The Mississippian tried to make it clear and he meant only to question Hemingway's courage as a writer, but the remark followed him for the rest of his life. Certainly Hemingway never forgot it.

Faulkner's main criticism of Hemingway was of the latter's values rather than his technique; he admired Hemigway as a stylist, but found the ideas that underpinned his work thin. In much of Hemingway's work, Faulkner believed, God, a Creator, was absent, except in *The Old Man and the Sea*.

"They had to differ," the critic Malcolm Cowley remarked, "for the simple reason that they were rivals who—partly by the influence on both of them of their time—resembled each other in many fashions, great and small." They differed in no area more strikingly than in their attitude toward writing, Cowley went on: "Hemingway kept his inspiration in check, for he liked to know what he was doing at every moment. Quite the opposite of Faulkner in this respect, he sometimes sacrificed his genius to his talent" (*The Faulkner-Cowley File*, 159–160).

Hemingway produced little of enduring value in his last years. Deeply depressed and apparently afraid he had written himself out, he took his own life in an Idaho hunting lodge in 1961. *A Moveable Feast*, a memoir of his Paris years, appeared three years after his death.

history, Faulkner and   Past and present clash eternally in Faulkner's fiction. In his use of the past he is, in the words of the critic and biographer Frederick Karl, "the most historical of our important writers: one who broke away from the past in his techniques even while the past meant so much to him." As a child, he absorbed a living history in the tales of aging Civil War veterans; he witnessed as a young man the final destruction of the wilderness of the Mississippi CHICKASAW INDIANS; he died only a few weeks before a young African American defied race, class, and the legacy of Southern history and enrolled in the UNIVERSITY OF MISSISSIPPI.

For Faulkner, the past was a palpable presence. "He was steeped in the legends of the Highlanders, reports by old hunters of the original wilderness, the primitive isolation of Mississippi before 'the Wawh,' [the Civil War] the violent separation of the races ordained by God," the critic ALFRED KAZIN wrote in *An American Procession* (1984). "Faulkner lived with sacred history like a character in the Bible." Biblical, too, is a powerful sense in all of Faulkner's work of the South's, and of America's, sins. For him, slavery and despoliation of the natural world are facets of original sin.

Faulkner exploited the past in some of his most important fiction, most notably in ABSALOM, ABSALOM! (1936), but also in *The SOUND AND THE FURY* (1929), GO DOWN, MOSES (1942), and the SNOPES TRILOGY—*The HAMLET* (1940), *The TOWN* (1957) and *The MANSION* (1959). One of Faulkner's biographers, Jay Parini, suggests the incest theme in

The Sound and the Fury "becomes a metaphor for the South after the Civil War, a region ingrown, self-destructive, self-cannibalizing."

Faulkner's fictional reach extends back to the 1790s, when a few thousand Native Americans and their black slaves peopled his YOKNAPATAWPHA COUNTY region. By the 1830s, the new world encroaches and the elements are assembled for the great conflict that echoes through all of Faulkner's work: the conflict of man in nature and in society. Settlers arrive from east of the Appalachians with their slaves and their notions of land ownership. Thomas Sutpen buys a hundred square miles of land from an old Chickasaw chief who has no right to sell and implements his grand design, creating "a country all divided and fixed and neat with a people living on it all divided and fixed and neat because of what color their slaves happened to be and what they happened to own" (*Absalom, Absalom!*, 221). The Civil War destroys Sutpen and brings his design to nothing. The sins live on, though: the legacy of slavery, the destruction of the Big Woods. Sutpen, near ruin, sells off tracts of wilderness to the planter and businessman Major De Spain, who first opens the Delta bottoms to the logging companies.

The old, proud South found itself reduced to the status of an economic dependent of the North after the war, exporting low-cost raw materials—cotton, forest products—in return for expensive manufactured goods. The North imposed high tariffs and railroad freight charges. Money was scarce, the cost of borrowing high. Those who adapted to modern, Northern ways stood the best chance of survival: Jason Compson, the cotton speculator in *The Sound and the Fury*; and Flem Snopes in *The Hamlet, The Town* and *The Mansion*. Descending from the Civil War–era bushwhacker class of landless whites, Snopes displaces the crumbling planter aristocracy, ruthlessly trampling their antique codes and values in the process.

Jason Compson pays out $10 a month to a New York advisory firm for daily information on the cotton market. The Compsons, once powerful planters and masters of all they surveyed, are reduced in three generations to a state of dependency on an anonymous Northern cotton tipster. And it doesn't even work: Compson's $10 a month of inside information proves worthless.

In *Go Down, Moses* and other works, Faulkner linked the destruction of the wilderness to the loss of values that bring on decline and ultimate fall. Isaac McCaslin, the hunter of the "The BEAR" (in *Go Down, Moses*) turns 21 and renounces his plantation inheritance, claiming that man had "cursed and tainted" what God created. Ike learns early that the bear, the quarry of the annual autumn hunting parties into the vanishing woods, may seem indestructible but in truth is too big for the country it inhabits. The hunters finally bring down the old two-toed bear. Within a few years, as Major de Spain sells off timber rights, the industrialists—the modernizers—effect an astonishing change.

Faulkner's fictional history closely paralleled his family's history. The Civil War ended 32 years before Faulkner's birth, but it lived on still in turn-of-the century OXFORD, MISSISSIPPI, in the bitter legacy of defeat and, in Shreve MacKenzie's phrase in *Absalom, Absalom!*, "of never forgiving General Sherman. . . ."

Shreve continues his colloquy with Quentin Compson in their Harvard dormitory room: ". . . so that forever more as long as your children's children's children produce children you won't be anything but a descendant of a long line of colonels killed in Pickett's charge at Manassas?"

"'Gettysburg,' Quentin said. 'You cant understand it. You would have to be born there." (*Absalom*, 289)

"Lying behind nearly everything he wrote was the great American divide, the Civil War," Frederick Karl observed. "Little can be understood in Faulkner without an awareness of that great hovering presence, the shadow of courage and debacle."

Faulkner's paternal great-grandfather, WILLIAM CLARK FALKNER, commanded the 2nd Mississippi Volunteers at BULL RUN in 1861. Returning home a year later, he raised a unit of irregular cavalry for operations in north Mississippi. In 1864, Federal troops burned Falkner's home in RIPLEY, MISSISSIPPI, and the Oxford hotel of Burlina Butler, the future novelist's maternal great-grandmother. Burlina's son Henry died in a Georgia hospital of wounds received in the fighting around Atlanta in 1864.

The stories and novels mirror this. The husband of Aunt Virginia (Jenny) Du Pre (in *SARTORIS* and *The UNVANQUISHED*) is killed in Charleston at the beginning of the war. Her brother Bayard Sartoris dies in a raid on a Yankee headquarters in Virginia. Henry Sutpen (in *Absalom, Absalom!*) is wounded at SHILOH. Quentin Compson's grandfather loses his right arm there. In *The Unvanquished*, Drusilla Hawk's father and her fiancé are killed in battle.

Like the fictional Snopeses, the Falkners adapted to postwar conditions. W. C. Falkner, the Old Colonel, built railroads using methods as ruthless as those of any Flem Snopes. His son, JOHN WESLEY THOMPSON FALKNER, the Young Colonel, maintained the family position for another generation through banking and the law. Younger rivals eventually drove him out of his bank. Circumstances forced him to break up the family mansion, the Big Place, into apartments and sell off the corner lot to a gasoline retailer. The Falkners were slipping. The novelist's hapless father, the Old Colonel's grandson, lacked the wherewithal to arrest the decline.

As an artist, Faulkner stood somewhat outside this pattern of failure and slow disintegration. Even so, it is suggestive that he chose for a dwelling place a deteriorated antebellum mansion, a Compson sort of place, built on land purchased from a Chickasaw chief. When he could afford it, he bought a run-down LAFAYETTE COUNTY hill farm of the type the marginal people, white and black, of his Yoknapatawpha fiction worked on shares.

Faulkner remarked in a 1933 letter that southern writers tended either "to draw a savage indictment of the contemporary scene" or to create, as an escape, "a make-believe region of swords and magnolias and mockingbirds." His *Absalom, Absalom!* appeared the same year as Margaret Mitchell's Civil War fantasy *Gone with the Wind*, the apotheosis of make-believe. Faulkner's issues were race and history, not gallantry in battle; his South was not noble—it was morally corrupt.

Still, Faulkner himself approached the "hoop skirts and plug hat" (his phrase) school of historical fiction in a series of stories originally written for magazine publication. In 1938, he linked them to form the novel *The Unvanquished*, in which young Bayard Sartoris and his black friend Ringo Strother experience a series of adventures in north Mississippi during the Civil War and early Reconstruction. The South may have been losing the war, but the boys and Bayard's indomitable grandmother consistently outwit the invading Yankees.

For all its picturesqueness, *The Unvanquished* takes up serious themes too. In a moving passage, Faulkner shows the impact of the promise of freedom on north Mississippi slaves. In their thousands, they put themselves in motion toward the Yankees and tell the narrator Bayard that they are "Going to cross the Jordan."

In the violent aftermath of the war, Bayard's father, John Sartoris, the ruthless, intolerant and homicidal fictional counterpart of W. C. Falkner, attempts to restore the antebellum order, challenging the carpetbagging Burdens, interlopers from Missouri who have taken up the case of black political freedom. Sartoris shoots down two of the Burdens at the voting hall and carries the ballot box away to his plantation, where he strictly supervises the voting to deny election to a black candidate for town marshal.

There is little nostalgia for the past in Faulkner. The modern world overwhelms a society that deserves to collapse. "The Old Order, he clearly indicates, did *not* satisfy human needs, did *not* afford justice, and therefore was 'accurst' and held the seeds of its own ruin," the novelist and critic ROBERT PENN WARREN wrote in *New and Selected Essays*. Faulkner's fiction is a critique of what has gone before and what is; it is also, as Warren suggests, a parable. "From the land itself, from its rich soil yearning to produce, and from history, from an error or sin committed long ago and compounded a thousand times, the doom comes," Warren remarked. "That is, the present is to be understood, and fully felt, only in terms of the past."

Modernity chews up the landscape as it chews up the past. In "DELTA AUTUMN," one of the stories that make up *Go Down, Moses*, the process is nearly complete. The axes and plows have gnawed away till barely a patch of the Big Woods survives. The hunters used to make their way slowly into the nearby wilderness in mule-drawn wagons; now they must drive a hundred miles to find a wilderness in which to hunt.

With the Civil Rights movement of the 1950s, the past caught up to the South, and to America. Faulkner played an equivocal part in the struggle. All the same, the crisis fulfilled the prophecy and the historical vision of his fiction. In the end, the issues he addressed are common to all, "a general plight and problem," as Warren observed. His concerns were not ultimately with the South, but with the general philosophical question of the interrelationship of man and nature.

Hoke's Station   Fictional place, a "tiny log-line junction" with sidetracks, a loading platform and a commissary store in Major De Spain's hunting preserve in the MISSISSIPPI DELTA wilderness. In Go DOWN, MOSES, Isaac (Ike) McCaslin returns after a long absence to find the loggers have transformed the little wilderness outpost.

Holiday   Glossy travel and leisure magazine. The editors approached Faulkner in 1952 with an offer of $2,000 for a piece on his native country; his 10,500-word fictional memoir "Mississippi" appeared in *Holiday* in April 1954.

The magazine in 1954 asked Faulkner for an article on Vicksburg, Mississippi. He declined on account of unfamiliarity with the place.

Hollymount   Fictional town in CROSSMAN COUNTY, east of YOKNAPATAWPHA COUNTY. Jake Montgomery runs stolen timber into Hollymount and neighboring GLASGOW in *INTRUDER IN THE DUST*.

Holly Springs   A market town and railroad junction in a cotton-growing region of northern Mississippi. Faulkners bound from OXFORD, MISSISSIPPI, to MEMPHIS used to change trains in Holly Springs.

The Confederate general Earl Van Dorn raided the Union supply depot at Holly Springs on December 20, 1862. Faulkner used the operation as a model for the engagement that cost Charley Gordon his life in the posthumously published short story "Rose of Lebanon" (*see* "A RETURN"). In the story, Gordon is killed not in the attack on Grant's warehouses but ingloriously in a raid on a henhouse.

Faulkner reworked the material, changing the location and other particulars, for the novel LIGHT IN AUGUST, in which Gail Hightower broods on his grandfather's death in an operation much like the Holly Springs raid.

In the early 1950s, Faulkner occasionally arranged to rendezvous in Holly Springs with the young Memphis writer JOAN WILLIAMS, with whom he had a rather plaintive affair.

Holston House   Fictional place, the leading hotel in JEFFERSON, MISSISSIPPI, dating from the days when Jefferson was a mere village of a few stores, a blacksmith and livery stable, and a saloon. It is named for YOKNAPATAWPHA COUNTY's first tavern-keeper, Alexander Holston.

The Holston House figures in ABSALOM, ABSALOM!, The UNVANQUISHED, and other works. In The Unvanquished, patrons with their feet on the gallery rail silently observe young Bayard Sartoris as he passes en route to the law office of his father's killer. In The REIVERS, Lucius Priest describes it as well-appointed, with carpets, leather chairs, brass cuspidors, and linen tablecloths in the dining room.

Hotel Peabody   A stately house on Main Street in MEMPHIS. Faulkner and his wife, ESTELLE OLDHAM FAULKNER, usually took a room at the Peabody for overnight and occasional weekend visits to Memphis.

In The REIVERS, Lucius Priest, looking back on a long-ago trip to Memphis, mentions passing the Peabody ("they have moved it since") with Boon Hogganbeck and Ned McCaslin in Grandfather's car, though he notes that his family always patronized the GAYOSO.

Housman, A. E.   (1859–1936)   English poet and classical scholar, professor of Latin at Cambridge University. Housman published three volumes of lyric verse: A Shropshire Lad (1896), Last Poems (1922), and More Poems (1936).

As a young man Billy Falkner deeply admired A Shropshire Lad and patterned some of his own early verse on Housman's melancholy, sometimes cynical ballads. Into the late 1940s, Faulkner continued to admire Housman; he recommended his mildly erotic lyrics to JOAN WILLIAMS as part of his courtship (perhaps seduction would be a better word) of her.

Howe, Irving   (1920–1993)   Writer, literary and social critic, born in New York City. Influential in the left-leaning New York literary world of the 1950s, he cofounded the journal Dissent and contributed frequently to Partisan Review and the New Republic.

Howe published William Faulkner: A Critical Study, an important survey of major Faulkner novels and short works, in 1952. A revised and expanded edition appeared in 1975. Other Howe works include Politics and the Novel (1957) and World of Our Fathers (1976).

I

interior monologue   A narrative technique that presents to the reader the flow of a character's inner thought processes and impressions. First exploited by the French writer Edouard Dujardin (1861–1949) in his novel *Les Lauriers Sont Coupés* (1887; English title, *We'll to the Woods No More*), this technique was used by JAMES JOYCE, Virginia Woolf, and others, including William Faulkner. It is similar to, but not identical with, the stream-of-consciousness technique in that it represents the fluency and disconnectedness of ideas, memories, and sensations that comprise one's conscious thoughts. It is different in that the interior monologue tends to disregard basic grammatical and syntactical rules. Although it sometimes causes interpretative obstacles for the reader, the interior monologue can give a much richer and a much more penetrating portrait of a character's intimate thoughts than traditional narrative techniques.

Joyce's use of the interior monologue in *Ulysses* was an influence on Faulkner, particularly on *The SOUND AND THE FURY* and *AS I LAY DYING*. The Joyce scholar Michael Groden has observed that with the interior monologue technique Faulkner was able to resolve serious characterization problems that he confronted when writing the earlier novels *SOLDIERS' PAY* and *MOSQUITOES* (see "Criticism in New Composition: *Ulysses* and *The Sound and the Fury*," *Twentieth Century Literature* 21 [October 1975], 266).

According to James Joyce, the first to use the term interior monologue was the French novelist and translator Valéry Larbaud, in reference to *Ulysses* (see *Letters of James Joyce*, vol. 3, edited by Richard Ellmann, New York: Viking Press, 83).

Iron Bridge   Fictional place, carrying the highway from YOKNAPATAWPHA COUNTY to MEMPHIS over the TALLAHATCHIE RIVER. In *The REIVERS*, Faulkner places it at Wyott's Crossing, an old ferry site.

J

Jefferson, Mississippi Fictional place, seat of Faulkner's imaginary YOKNAPATAWPHA COUNTY, Mississippi. It is based on the actual OXFORD, MISSISSIPPI, and perhaps in part on RIPLEY, MISSISSIPPI, but with significant changes. In his fiction, Faulkner kept the UNIVERSITY OF MISSISSIPPI in "Oxford," which he sited 50 miles (and in *The Unvanquished*, 40 miles) from Jefferson. Many of the houses described in the fictional Jefferson have no exact counterpart in the real Oxford.

Many Oxford landmarks are, however, used in Jefferson: the Courthouse Square, the center of community life and the Saturday afternoon destination of Yoknapatawpha country people; the courthouse, with its four-faced clock; the jail; and the railroad depot down the hill and to the west of the square.

Faulkner describes the Jefferson square in *REQUIEM FOR A NUN*. The centerpiece is the courthouse in a grove in the square "quadrangular around it." The novelist moved the cemetery, which lies northeast of the square in Oxford, to a point northwest of the Jefferson square so the statue of the fictional "Colonel John Sartoris, CSA," could overlook the railroad Sartoris built. A statue of John Sartoris's model, WILLIAM C. FALKNER, the novelist's great-grandfather, gazes out at the Falkner railroad from the cemetery in Ripley.

Oxford's history and Jefferson's correspond roughly, as well. The first settlers arrive about 1815. The prosperous town of the 1850s withers during the Civil War; Sherman's forces burn the square in 1864. The Sartorises and the Compsons and the de Spains rebuild on the ruins, but by the turn of the new century the Snopeses are encroaching, threatening the continued social and economic leadership of Jefferson's leading families. The elms and the horse troughs and the hitching posts will disappear with the arrival of automobiles and paved roads; Flem Snopes and his kin will become Jefferson's new dominant clan.

By the end of the Yoknapatawpha saga, Jefferson's big old wooden houses with their shaggy lawns and great trees are decayed, and characterless new neighborhoods, "neat small new one-storey houses designed in Florida or California set with matching garages," proliferate (*Intruder*, 118).

Faulkner's sketch map in *ABSALOM, ABSALOM!* shows some of Jefferson's landmarks: a statue of John Sartoris, from *SARTORIS*; the cemetery where Addie Bundren is buried in *AS I LAY DYING*; the Courthouse from *SANCTUARY* and *The SOUND AND THE FURY*; the Burden place from *LIGHT IN AUGUST*; and the bank from *Sartoris* and *The TOWN*.

The jail where Lucas Beauchamp is held in *INTRUDER IN THE DUST* is shown too, as are the dwelling places of Miss Rosa Coldfield (*Absalom*), Gail Hightower (*Light in August*), the Compsons (*The Sound and the Fury*), and Horace and Narcissa Benbow (*Sartoris*).

Jonsson, Else The widow of a Swedish translator of Faulkner's works, she met the novelist in Stockholm in December 1950 when he turned up to claim his 1949 NOBEL PRIZE IN LITERATURE. Faulkner and Else Jonsson managed several secret rendezvous in Europe in the early 1950s.

Some of Faulkner's letters to Jonsson were published in *Faulkner: After the Nobel Prize*, Michel Gresset and Kenzaburo Ohashi, eds. (1987).

Joyce, James (1882–1941)   Self-exiled Irish novelist and poet whose influence on 20th-century literature is immeasurable. Having shaped both the modernist and postmodernist canon with his publications of *A Portrait of the Artist as a Young Man* (1916), *Ulysses* (1922), and *Finnegans Wake* (1939), Joyce has had one of the most enduring influences not only in English but also on the whole of 20th-century literature. With T. S. Eliot and Virginia Woolf, he is considered one of the principal modernist writers. (*See* MODERNISM and POSTMODERNISM.)

The eldest child of John Stanislaus and Mary Jane (May) Murray Joyce, James Joyce was born in Rathgar, a fashionable suburb of Dublin, on February 2, 1882. In 1888 he entered Clongowes Wood College, one of the best Jesuit schools in Ireland, located in Sallins, County Kildare, and remained a student there until June 1891, when he withdrew because of his family's financial difficulties. After a brief interruption in his formal education, Joyce resumed his studies in 1893 at Belvedere College, a Jesuit school in Dublin, and graduated five years later. He attended University College, Dublin, founded as Catholic University by John Henry Cardinal Newman in 1853, and graduated with a degree in modern languages in 1902. In June 1904, Joyce met for the first time Nora Barnacle. By October they left Ireland and eventually settled in Trieste, where he taught at the Berlitz School and where his two children, Giorgio and Lucia, were born. While in Trieste, Joyce published *Chamber Music* (1907), *Dubliners* (1914), and *A Portrait of the Artist as a Young Man;* he also wrote his only play, *Exiles* (1918), and began *Ulysses*. With the outbreak of World War I, Joyce and his family moved to Zurich, where he continued writing *Ulysses*. After the war they returned to Trieste for a brief time before moving to Paris in 1920. With the outbreak of World War II, a few months after the publication of *Finnegans Wake* in May 1939, the Joyces moved from Paris to Saint-Gérand-le-Puy, a small village near Vichy, where they stayed for a year before departing for Zurich, where Joyce died on January 13, 1941, two days after what appeared to be successful abdominal surgery. Two days later he was buried in Fluntern cemetery.

Joyce's works reflect the 20th-century's major movements in literature from symbolism and realism to modernism and postmodernism. His use of the INTERIOR MONOLOGUE and the STREAM OF CONSCIOUSNESS techniques, along with other innovative narrative strategies, have influenced generations of writers including William Faulkner, who on several occasions mentioned his debt to Joyce. In a 1958 interview with Richard Ellmann, Joyce's biographer, Faulkner said he thought of himself as Joyce's heir when writing *The* SOUND AND THE FURY (*see James Joyce* [New York: Oxford University Press, 1982], 297, asterisked note). Although Faulkner, according to Ellmann, did not read *Ulysses* in its published form as a book until 1930, he did read portions of the novel as they were serialized in the *Little Review* between 1918 and 1920 and discussed the work at length with his close friend PHILIP AVERY STONE. There is evidence, however, that Faulkner in fact read *Ulysses* as early as 1924 when he received a copy of the novel from Stone (*see William Faulkner: The Carl Petersen Collection*, Berkeley, Calif.: Serendipity Books, 1991, 70); and in *Faulkner at Nagano*, edited by Robert A. Jelliffe (Tokyo: Kenkyusha Ltd., 1962), Faulkner, in response to a question of whether he read *Ulysses* before or after he began to write, said, "No, I began to write before I read *Ulysses*. I read *Ulysses* in the middle 20's and I had been scribbling for several years" (*Faulkner at Nagano*, 203). He had never met Joyce but knew of him and, when in Paris in 1925, "would go to some effort to go to the café that [Joyce] inhabited to look at him" (*Faulkner in the University*, 58). Joyce was "the only literary man" Faulkner remembered seeing while in Europe.

Critics have readily recognized the influence of *Ulysses* on Faulkner's *The Sound and the Fury* and AS I LAY DYING, two novels that very skillfully incorporate the narrative technique of the interior monologue that Joyce pioneered, and to a lesser degree employed in SOLDIERS' PAY and MOSQUI-

TOES. "With this technique," as Michael Groden observes in "Criticism in New Composition: *Ulysses* and *The Sound and the Fury*" published in *Twentieth Century Literature* 21 (October 1975), "Faulkner discovered a solution to crucial problems in characterization that had plagued him in his first three novels [*Soldiers' Pay, Mosquitoes,* and *SARTORIS*]" (266). Faulkner was familiar with other works by Joyce, including his poetry. For instance, one of the poems that Faulkner would recite from memory was "Watching the Needleboats at San Sabba," first published by Joyce in 1913 in the *Saturday Review* and later reprinted in *Pomes Penyeach* (1927). Faulkner presented a copy of *Pomes Penyeach* to Meta Carpenter in Hollywood in 1935 or 1936 (Brodsky and Hamblin, *Faulkner and Hollywood* [10]); and a discarded fragment of Faulkner's story, "Weekend Revisited," contains an exact quotation from Joyce's short story, "Counterparts" (Brodsky and Hamblin, *Faulkner: A Comprehensive Guide to the Brodsky Collection,* I, 193). In "Faulkner's 'Portrait of the Artist'" published in *The Mississippi Quarterly* 19 (Summer 1966), 121–31, Joyce W. Warren closely examines the parallels between Faulkner's second novel, *Mosquitoes,* and Joyce's *A Portrait of the Artist as a Young Man.* Richard P. Adams also touches upon Faulkner's reading of Joyce in "The Apprenticeship of William Faulkner," *Tulane Studies in English* 12 (1962), 138–140.

Two comments that Faulkner made about James Joyce on two separate occasions recorded in *Faulkner in the University* may be misleading to readers who have not studied Joyce's compositional methods. The first, that Joyce was "a genius who was electrocuted by the divine fire" (53)—or "touched by the divine [afflatus]," as he phrased it in an interview recorded in *Faulkner at Nagano* (44)—and the second, that he "had more talent than he could control" (280), can give the impression that Joyce himself wrote under the spell of the stream of consciousness or under a wild dadaist inspiration. Nothing can be further from the truth. Joyce was one of the most meticulous writers of his age; he carefully controlled and shaped his works word by word and would revise even up to the last moments before publication. (For a few examples of Joyce's influence on Faulkner, *see* CLEANTH BROOKS's brief comments in *William Faulkner: Toward Yoknapatawpha and Beyond* [Baton Rouge: Louisiana State University Press, 1990, 370–372].)

K

Kazin, Alfred (1915–1998)   Literary critic and teacher, born in New York City. His *On Native Grounds* (1942) is a classic study of modern American prose fiction from late 19th century novelist William Dean Howells through Faulkner. In the 1940s and 1950s Kazin was an influential and widely read book reviewer, and his memoir *A Walker in the City* (1951) won critical and popular acclaim.

Kazin did not greatly admire Faulkner's later work. In a review of *The* UNVANQUISHED (1938) in the *New York Herald Tribune*, Kazin charged that Faulkner wrote "like a wilful sullen child in some gaseous world of his own, pouting in polysyllabics, stringing truncated paragraphs together like dirty wash, howling, stumbling, losing himself in verbal murk." But along with CLEANTH BROOKS and others, he wrote a critical appreciation of the novelist for a Faulkner issue of the *Harvard Advocate* in 1951.

The critic found *The* TOWN (1957), the second of the three Snopes novels, deeply disappointing: "The truth is not merely that *The Town* is a bad novel by a great writer, but also that Faulkner has less and less interest in writing what are called 'novels' at all."

In a more considered judgment in *An American Procession* (1982), Kazin linked Faulkner to Hawthorne and Melville and elaborately praised *The* SOUND AND THE FURY (1929), setting it above the seminal work that may have influenced its experimental technique, JAMES JOYCE's *Ulysses* (1922).

"*The Sound and the Fury* is a greater *novel*" than *Ulysses*, Kazin wrote, "more dramatic, more universally representative through the interior life of everyone in it."

Keeley Institute   A treatment center for alcoholics located 15 miles from MEMPHIS, the Keeley Institute was much frequented by Faulkner's paternal grandfather, J. W. T. FALKNER, and his father, MURRY C. FALKNER. The institute's founder, Dr. Leslie E. Keeley, claimed in *The Non-Heredity of Inebriety* (1896) that alcoholism was a disease, not a vice.

The Keeley cure involved injections of double chloride of gold, said to give a patient an extreme distaste for whiskey. Dr. Keeley reported a relapse rate of only 5 percent; Falkner father and son were among that small minority of returnees.

MAUD FALKNER, the future novelist's mother, used to deliver her husband to the Keeley Institute when his drinking became unbearable. Sometimes she brought the children along. While their father took the cure, Billy and his brothers amused themselves by exploring the institute grounds and riding the streetcar to Memphis and back.

Keswick Hunt Club   Faulkner rode as a guest with this hunt club, established in the late 19th century and the oldest in Albemarle County, Virginia, beginning in late 1958.

The Keswick, better known locally than its younger rival, the FARMINGTON HUNT CLUB, had a reputation as a rough-riding, hard-drinking band more interested in hunting than show. By Faulkner's time, though, the differences between the two clubs had blurred. Faulkner rode with one or the other as often as four or five times a week in season.

Klopfer, Donald (n.a.) Publisher. He cofounded RANDOM HOUSE, Faulkner's publisher, with BENNETT CERF in 1927. Along with Cerf, he was a strong supporter of Faulkner's work, and he sometimes acted as an informal financial adviser to the novelist.

Klopfer and his wife, Pat, entertained Faulkner at their Lebanon, New Jersey, country house and in their New York City apartment. Faulkner appreciated Klopfer's quiet, low-key manner, so different from the extrovert Cerf's.

Faulkner hand-delivered the 175,000-word manuscript of *A FABLE* to Klopfer at Random House in November 1953. Klopfer also performed editing chores, mostly reconciling inconsistencies, on *The MANSION*, the last novel in the SNOPES TRILOGY.

Knopf, Alfred A. (1892–1984) Publisher. He established his own firm in 1915 and, with his wife, made it one of the leading literary houses in America. Among Knopf's authors were 16 Nobel laureates and 26 Pulitzer Prize winners, and the firm's Borzoi trademark became a byword for excellence.

In the early 1930s, Knopf showed interest in publishing Faulkner. They met at a party at Knopf's New York City apartment in late 1931. Faulkner, in company with the writer Dashiell Hammett, fell to the floor drunk.

Knopf and Faulkner met again at a gathering at BENNETT CERF's not long afterward. As the biographer JOSEPH BLOTNER tells the anecdote, Knopf approached Faulkner with a request for his signature on several first editions of his works. Faulkner was reluctant, explaining that special signed editions were a source of income, but at Bennett Cerf's prompting he agreed to sign one, because "Mrs. Knopf has been very kind to me."

Knopf headed the firm, which became a division of RANDOM HOUSE in 1960, until his death.

L

Lafayette County, Mississippi A 679-square-mile county in north-central Mississippi, organized in 1836, it was the model for Faulkner's fictional YOKNAPATAWPHA COUNTY.

The TALLAHATCHIE RIVER, with its rich bottomlands, forms part of the county's northern boundary; the YOCONA RIVER (given on old maps as Yocanapatafa, the origin of the name of Faulkner chose for his fictional Lafayette) drains the southern portion. OXFORD, MISSISSIPPI, at the county's center is the seat, with a courthouse and the UNIVERSITY OF MISSISSIPPI; other towns include College Hill to the northwest, Taylor to the southwest, and Lafayette Springs to the east. CHICKASAW INDIAN burial mounds are found at scattered sites.

Faulkner's grandfather, J. W. T. FALKNER, won election as state senator from Lafayette County in 1895. In the novelist's childhood, the county had a population of around 22,000. Nearly half the inhabitants were black, the descendants of slaves; before the Civil War, fully 40 percent of the county's white families owned slaves. White or black, most were small farmers dependent on cotton. Decades of reliance on a single crop marked the landscape of the novelist's youth: Cotton depleted the soil and overcultivation left the county nearly treeless, its hills and ravines scored by erosion.

African-American northward migration since World War II has altered Lafayette County's racial balance; blacks today make up about a quarter of the population. The county remains comparatively poor, with per capita personal income at about 75 percent of the national average.

Library of America A book imprint, the Library of America was established in 1979 with a self-proclaimed mission to publish the country's most significant writing in authoritative, durable editions. The first volumes appeared in 1982.

Five individual volumes republish all of Faulkner's novels. All were edited by the leading Faulkner scholars JOSEPH BLOTNER and NOEL POLK.

William Faulkner: Novels 1926–1929 (2006) contains SOLDIERS' PAY, MOSQUITOES, FLAGS IN THE DUST (published in an edited-down version as SARTORIS), and THE SOUND AND THE FURY.

William Faulkner: Novels 1930–1935 (1985) contains AS I LAY DYING, SANCTUARY, LIGHT IN AUGUST, and PYLON.

William Faulkner: Novels 1936–1940 (1990) contains ABSALOM, ABSALOM!, The UNVANQUISHED, IF I FORGET THEE, JERUSALEM, and The HAMLET.

William Faulkner: Novels 1942–1954 (1994) contains GO DOWN, MOSES, INTRUDER IN THE DUST, REQUIEM FOR A NUN, and A FABLE.

William Faulkner: Novels 1957–1962 (1999) contains The TOWN, The MANSION, and The REIVERS.

Liveright, Horace Publisher. A one-time toilet paper manufacturer, he and his newspaperman partner, Albert Boni, founded the Modern Library in 1917; their firm, BONI & LIVERIGHT, published works by Ezra Pound, T. S. Eliot, Eugene O'Neill, ERNEST HEMINGWAY, and Theodore Dreiser.

Liveright accepted Faulkner's first novel, SOL-DIERS' PAY, on SHERWOOD ANDERSON's recommendation in 1925 and published it the following year. He published Faulkner's second novel, MOSQUI-TOES, in 1927. To the novelist's chagrin, Liveright in November 1927 turned down FLAGS IN THE DUST (eventually published as SARTORIS in 1929), saying the novel was so poorly put together that Faulkner should withdraw it altogether.

"It's too bad you don't like Flags in the Dust," Faulkner wrote him in November 1927. "I'd like you to fire it on back to me, as I shall try it on someone else. I still believe it is the book which will make my name for me as a writer." (*Selected Letters*, 39)

Faulkner resolved to offer the book to another publisher, and he plotted to sever his contractual tie to Boni & Liveright. It seemed a risky move at the time, but in the end, Liveright let Faulkner go without penalty. Harcourt, Brace published *Sartoris* in January 1929 and brought out The SOUND AND THE FURY in October of that year, paying its author a $200 advance against royalties.

The Long, Hot Summer

In 1958, a film version of *The* HAMLET, directed by Martin Ritt and starring Paul Newman, Joanne Woodward, Anthony Franciosa, Orson Welles, Lee Remick, Angela Lansbury, and Richard Anderson, was released by Twentieth Century-Fox. The screenplay was written by Irving Ravetch and Harriet Frank, Jr., and based on book 3 ("The Long Summer") of the novel and on the short stories "BARN BURNING" and "SPOTTED HORSES."

Loos, Anita (1893–1981)   Novelist, playwright, and screenwriter. Her novel *Gentlemen Prefer Blondes* (1925), subtitled *The Illuminating Diary of a Professional Lady*, satirized naive, gold-digging women of the Jazz Age and became a great success. Loos later wrote satires of Hollywood and a series of autobiographical works, including *This Brunette Prefers Work* (1956).

Faulkner met Loos in the Vieux Carré in NEW ORLEANS in the mid-1920s through SHERWOOD ANDERSON, an Ohio friend of Loos's husband, John Emerson. Faulkner was impersonating a wounded war hero at the time, and was said to have a metal plate in his head.

Faulkner liked *Gentlemen Prefer Blondes* and wrote to Loos in admiration of the main character Lorelei Lee's friend Dorothy. "I am still rather Victorian in my prejudices regarding the intelligence of women," he wrote her. "But I wish I had thought of Dorothy first" (*Selected Letters*, 32)

After a long lapse, Faulkner and Loos became reacquainted in Hollywood in the 1950s.

M

MacCullum Faulkner's early spelling of McCallum, a fictional family name in YOKNAPATAWPHA COUNTY. The name appears as MacCallum in Faulkner's third novel, SARTORIS (1929), and in AS I LAY DYING (1930), but the spelling changed; some characters have both spellings. In the appropriate character entries, the spelling of this family name matches that found in the work under discussion.

Magnolia Rifles William Clark FALKNER, Faulkner's great-grandfather, raised this volunteer infantry company in Ripley County, Mississippi, at the beginning of the Civil War in 1861.

The company became part of the 2nd Mississippi infantry regiment; Falkner won election as colonel of the regiment in May 1861. The 2nd Mississippi saw action at the FIRST BATTLE OF BULL RUN (Manassas) in July 1861.

Manuel Street Fictional street in the red-light district of MEMPHIS. Miss Reba Rivers's brothel is on Manuel Street in SANCTUARY. (Faulkner moves Reba's place to CATALPA STREET in The REIVERS.) Manuel Street also figures as the tenderloin district in REQUIEM FOR A NUN.

Massey, Linton R. (n.a.) A Virginian of the country squire class, he admired Faulkner and began collecting his work in 1930. Massey, his wife Mary, and the Faulkners became close friends during Faulkner's UNIVERSITY OF VIRGINIA years in the 1950s.

In 1959, Massey organized a comprehensive exhibit in Charlottesville, Virginia, of Faulkner's works over a period of 40 years. Faulkner himself gave the exhibit its title: "Man Working." In 1962, shortly before Faulkner's death, Massey offered the novelist a $50,000 interest-free loan so he could buy Red Acres, a country estate near Charlottesville.

McLean, Alabama Leroy Falkner (1874–1968) Faulkner's imposing, imperious great-aunt, the youngest child of WILLIAM C. FALKNER, the Old Colonel, and his second wife Lizzie Vance, known to the family as Aunt 'Bama.

The Old Colonel called her Baby Roy, and she was his favorite. She used to fascinate her young nephew with stories of her near-legendary father: Confederate soldier, railroad builder, novelist. Faulkner corresponded regularly with her throughout his life ("You are a good letter writer," he once wrote her. "A stranger could even tell the color of your eyes from your letters"), and she responded with interest and intense pride in his literary career. She was frugal, but she made Faulkner a gift of $20 just before he set off for Europe in 1925.

Faulkner named his first child, a daughter, after Aunt 'Bama. The baby lived only a few days. Aunt 'Bama herself survived her novelist grandnephew by six years.

Memphis City in southwestern Tennessee, the state's largest. It is an important river port, and a leading cotton, livestock, manufacturing and transportation center of the mid-South. Andrew Jackson and others founded the settlement on a bluff overlooking the Mississippi River in 1819, and it was an important commercial center by the time of the Civil War. Union forces occupied Memphis in June 1862.

Corrupt Yankees and Southerners traded in contraband cotton during the Civil War; Faulkner's great-grandfather, WILLIAM C. FALKNER, was alleged to have sought his fortune by running cotton through the Union lines. Memphis served as a base for federal offensives into northern Mississippi. The Confederate General NATHAN BEDFORD FORREST carried out a famous raid into Memphis in August 1864.

Faulkner's grandfather and father were treated for alcoholism at the KEELEY INSTITUTE near the city. As a boy, Billy Falkner had his first glimpse of the Mississippi River from a Memphis streetcar.

Mississippians regarded Memphis, only 70 miles northwest of OXFORD, MISSISSIPPI, as a center of sophistication. Faulkner went there as a young man to gamble, drink, and to visit blues clubs along Beale Street. His friend PHILIP AVERY STONE introduced him to the city's bordellos and its colorful gangster underworld, material he exploited later in SANCTUARY and The REIVERS.

Memphis became notorious in the 1920s as "the Murder Capital of the U.S.A." Parts of Sanctuary are set in the city's violent and colorful tenderloin. The fictional Popeye Vitelli is modeled partly on John Revinsky, who went to prison for the murder of a Memphis brothel madam, and partly on Popeye Pumphrey, a well-known Memphis gambler and bootlegger of the Prohibition era. In The REIVERS, Lucius (Loosh) Priest describes his first view of a section the city's red light district, which ran along Gayoso and Mulberry Streets (97).

Faulkner took flying lessons at the Memphis airport beginning in 1933. Later in the 1930s, he regularly took his wife Estelle and daughter Jill to Memphis, where they would stay in a suite at the Peabody Hotel after an exhilarating day of flying in the novelist's Waco cabin cruiser.

Memphis Commercial Appeal Leading daily newspaper of southwestern Tennessee and northern Mississippi. The Falkners read the Commercial Appeal regularly in OXFORD, MISSISSIPPI; Faulkner could read and thoroughly understand the paper's sports page before he went to school. He used to read the Commercial Appeal's comics aloud to his daughter Jill at breakfast.

The newspaper covered the novelist's rise in the 1930s and chronicled his doings thereafter. Faulkner published a series of letters to the editor—actually, short essays—on racial issues in the Commercial Appeal in the 1950s.

In a letter dated March 26, 1950, he protested a Mississippi court's decision to sentence a white man to life in prison for the murder of three black children, arguing that the killer would have been put to death had the children been white.

An early version of Faulkner's essay "On Fear: The South in Labor" first appeared as a letter to the editor of the Memphis paper on April 3, 1955. Another important topical essay, "To Claim Freedom is Not Enough," saw print first in the Commercial Appeal on November 11, 1955.

The letters, with their liberal (for the South) views on racial issues, brought widespread condemnation of "Weeping Willie Faulkner"—an appellation a Faulkner critic coined in a letter to the Commercial Appeal—in his home region.

Meriwether, James B.   Teacher. As a professor at the University of Texas in the 1950s, he established himself as a leading Faulkner bibliographer and textual scholar. Meriwether assisted RANDOM HOUSE editors in reconciling discrepancies between The HAMLET and The TOWN, the first two novels in the SNOPES TRILOGY, in 1957. He performed the same service for the third Snopes novel, The MANSION, in 1959.

Meriwether built up the University of Texas library's holdings in Faulkner manuscripts and other material. He negotiated the purchase of typescripts and other material from the novelist's longtime friend PHILIP AVERY STONE, a transaction that left Faulkner angry and embittered. Meriwether published the first book-length biography of Faulkner, The Literary Career of William Faulkner, in 1972.

With MICHAEL MILLGATE, he coedited Lion in the Garden: Interviews with William Faulkner, 1926–1962 (1980).

Metro-Goldwyn-Mayer Hollywood movie studio. Samuel Goldwyn (1882–1974) and Louis B. Mayer (1885–1957) merged their independent production companies in 1925 to form MGM. Faulkner went to work as a scriptwriter at the Culver City studio in May 1932 on a six-week contract paying $500 a week.

> I have written one scenario," he wrote home to his wife, "and am now writing one for Wallace Beery and Robt. Montgomery, in collaboration with an actor-author named Ralph Graves. I am a sort of doctor, to repair the flaws in it. (*Selected Letters*, 64)

Faulkner had great difficulty adapting his talents to writing for the screen, nor did he care for California. The director HOWARD HAWKS tutored Faulkner in the film arts, and on his recommendation MGM renewed the novelist's initial contract.

The studio bought the film rights to Faulkner's novel *The UNVANQUISHED* in 1938 for $25,000, with $19,000 going to Faulkner. In July 1948, MGM paid $50,000 for the rights to INTRUDER IN THE DUST. Faulkner's share came to $40,000—sufficient to free him from his detested association with the WARNER BROTHERS studio.

MGM came to Oxford in the winter of 1949 to film *Intruder*. The movie had its premiere in the Lyric Theater in Oxford in October of that year.

In 1957, HAROLD OBER, Faulkner's agent, learned that MGM had decided to exercise its option on *The Unvanquished*. Ober told Faulkner he could probably get him $50,000 to $75,000 for writing the screenplay. Now financially secure, Faulkner declined to pursue the matter.

Midnight, Arkansas Fictional place in "The Bear" in GO DOWN, MOSES. Fonsiba Beauchamp, the daughter of the slaves Tomey's Turl and Tennie Beauchamp, settles on a small farm in this backwater village with her inept, displaced husband, whose exposure to Yankee ways has rendered him unfit for agricultural life. The village has a tavern, a livery stable, two stores, a saloon, a blacksmith shop and a bank.

Millgate, Michael (n.a.) Scholar. He is the author of the critical studies *William Faulkner* (1961), *The Achievement of William Faulkner* (1966), and *Faulkner's Place* (1997). In other works, he has painstakingly detailed Faulkner's seriocomic military career as a ROYAL AIR FORCE cadet in Canada in 1918. With JAMES B. MERIWETHER, he coedited *Lion in the Garden: Interviews with William Faulkner, 1926–1962* (1980).

Millgate also is an authority on the life and works of the English novelist Thomas Hardy. His *Thomas Hardy: A Biography* appeared in 1982, and he edited with others a multivolume collection of Hardy's letters published between 1978 and 1988.

The Mississippian Student newspaper at the UNIVERSITY OF MISSISSIPPI, an early outlet for Faulkner's poetry, prose fiction, and criticism. His revised poem "L'Apres-Midi d'un Faune" appeared in the student paper in October 1919. Faulkner published his first piece of fiction, the short story "Landing in Luck," in *The Mississippian* on November 26, 1919; the same issue carried a Faulkner poem, "Sapphics," after the manner of Swinburne.

Nine Faulkner poems appeared in the paper during the spring semester of 1920. The poems provoked student rivals to produce a series of parodies of Faulkner's literary style and personal manner, among them "Une Ballade d'une Vache Perdue," describing the lost and wandering heifer Betsey.

The ballad inspired Faulkner's delayed-reaction joke short story "AFTERNOON OF A COW," attributed to the fictional author-critic Ernest V. Trueblood. Written in 1937, it was published a decade later.

Mississippi Delta A flat, alluvial plain between the Mississippi and Yazoo Rivers and the most distinctive geographical region of Mississippi. Big cotton planters in the Delta counties dominated the state's political life until the early 20th century, which saw the rise of the hill country small farmer class. Faulkner's paternal grandfather, J. W. T. FALKNER, aligned himself politically with these populist challengers of Delta power.

During Faulkner's youth, patches of Delta wilderness still survived within 30 miles of OXFORD,

MISSISSIPPI: flat, low-lying, densely forested country that sustained populations of deer, bear, and other game. His friend PHILIP AVERY STONE introduced him to the Delta wilderness. For a number of years Faulkner took part in the regular November deer hunt from Stone's father's hunting camp near Batesville on the edge of the wilderness.

By the late 1930s the elder Stone had sold off his several-thousand-acre hunting reserve to the timber companies, which had clear-cut the land and sold it off to farmers. The annual deer hunt moved 120 miles southwest to the Big Sunflower River in the Delta near Anguilla, Mississippi.

Faulkner translated his experiences in the Delta wilderness into fiction in a series of hunting stories. In "The BEAR" (*see* GO DOWN, MOSES) Faulkner records Ike McCaslin's memory of his first experience of the BIG BOTTOM, the wilderness area along the TALLAHATCHIE RIVER, at the age of 10. Later in the story, Major De Spain sells off the timber rights to his wilderness kingdom to a Memphis lumber company. On that year's hunt, an older Ike sees "with shocked and grieved amazement" the first consequences of the sale: a nearly finished planing mill, vast stacks of steel rails and crossties, a complex of corrals for mules, and a tent city for the crews that would clear the woods.

In *The REIVERS*, the site of de Spain's camp is described as a drainage district, a one-time wilderness now "tame with corn and cotton."

"The OLD PEOPLE," "A BEAR HUNT," "RACE AT MORNING," and a revised version of "The Bear" were repackaged and published as BIG WOODS in 1954.

modernism   A term that identifies the general characteristics of a movement in the arts that began in the late 19th century as a reaction against traditional art forms and became prominent in the first part of the 20th century. In literature, modernism is identified with a sense of historical discontinuity, cultural relativism, and continuing experimentation

that includes the STREAM-OF-CONSCIOUSNESS technique, the device of the INTERIOR MONOLOGUE, and narrational uncertainty. Influenced by discoveries in the social sciences—psychology in particular—modernism questions the role of social institutions such as religion and the family to effect norms of behavior. Modernist writers include Ezra Pound, JAMES JOYCE, T. S. Eliot, Virginia Woolf, and D. H. Lawrence. Many critics consider Faulkner's *The SOUND AND THE FURY,* with its unusual narrative strategies and unreliable multiple narrators, the classic American modernist work.

Mott County   Fictional place, corresponding to Calhoun County, Mississippi, south of LAFAYETTE COUNTY, and lying south of Faulkner's YOKNAPATAWPHA COUNTY.

Mottson   *See* MOTTSTOWN.

Mottstown   Fictional town. The seat of Faulkner's Okatoba County, Mottstown is 45 minutes by train from fictional JEFFERSON, MISSISSIPPI, and corresponds to Water Valley, Mississippi, 20 miles southwest of OXFORD, MISSISSIPPI. It is called Mottson in *The SOUND AND THE FURY* and *As I LAY DYING*.

In *LIGHT IN AUGUST,* the fugitive Joe Christmas accepts a ride with a black wagoner bound for Mottstown. Christmas is later captured and held briefly in the jail there. Jason Compson IV in *The Sound and the Fury* loses the trail of his niece (Miss) Quentin Compson in Mottson. In *As I Lay Dying,* floods force the Bundrens to detour through Mottson on their way to Jefferson.

Mount Vernon   Fictional place. Described as 18 miles from JEFFERSON, MISSISSIPPI, in *As I LAY DYING,* Mount Vernon is possibly Faulkner's name for Abbeville, a village north of OXFORD, MISSISSIPPI. The road to Mount Vernon is offered as an alternate route for the flood-harassed Bundrens in *As I Lay Dying.*

N

New Albany, Mississippi   Town in Union County, Mississippi, on the TALLAHATCHIE RIVER northeast of OXFORD, MISSISSIPPI, and a trading center for a cotton, corn, and dairy region. In the 1890s, New Albany had a population of about 600 and was the midpoint station on Colonel WILLIAM C. FALKNER's GULF & CHICAGO RAILROAD.

MURRY FALKNER, Faulkner's father, moved to New Albany in September 1896 to take up his duties as general passenger agent of the Gulf & Chicago. William Cuthbert Falkner was born in a plain one-story clapboard house at Cleveland and Jefferson Streets there on September 25, 1897.

New Hope Church   Fictional place in AS I LAY DYING. It is an intermediate destination in the Bundren odyssey in the novel. In Faulkner's time, there were four churches of that name in the vicinity of OXFORD, MISSISSIPPI.

New Orleans, Louisiana   Situated in southeastern Louisiana on a great bend of the Mississippi River 107 miles from the river's mouth, New Orleans is a cultural and economic center of the South, one of its largest cities, and a leading port of entry.

Developed by the French, at times under Spanish rule, New Orleans became part of the United States with the Louisiana Purchase of 1803. The cosmopolitan city's great age ended during the Civil War with the arrival of Union occupation forces in 1862. Long afterward, artists, writers, and musicians were attracted to the picturesque French Quarter, also known as the Vieux Carré, the historic district bounded by Canal Street, the Esplanade, North Rampart Street, and the river. Jazz had its origin among the black musicians of late 19th-century New Orleans.

Eight hours from OXFORD, MISSISSIPPI, by train, New Orleans provided an escape and an opportunity for young Faulkner in the early 1920s. He and PHILIP AVERY STONE ventured there for uproarious weekends and for discussions of art and artists. Young writers flourished in the Vieux Carré and found an outlet for their work in the little magazine DOUBLE DEALER, founded in New Orleans in 1921. The magazine published poetry by Hart Crane, Allen Tate, and ROBERT PENN WARREN, stories by SHERWOOD ANDERSON, and sketches and short literary essays by Faulkner.

Faulkner met Anderson, whose early work he admired, in New Orleans in 1924. The older writer tirelessly promoted the city as a haven for writers. Faulkner stayed in Anderson's apartment at 540B St. Peter Street in the Vieux Carré for several weeks in 1925 before moving on to WILLIAM SPRATLING's attic at 624 Orleans Alley. He and Spratling sailed together from New Orleans to Europe in July 1925.

Faulkner published sketches of the city and its denizens for the *Double Dealer* and the NEW ORLEANS TIMES-PICAYUNE daily newspaper. He exploited his New Orleans experiences in his second novel, MOSQUITOES (1927), likening the city to "an aging yet still beautiful courtesan." He set the novel's early scenes in the Vieux Carré, the main action in a yacht adrift on Lake Ponchartrain, and the concluding sequences in the red light district.

In PYLON (1935), Faulkner opens with a fictional version of the dedication of Shushan Airport, built on land reclaimed from Lake Ponchartrain. Faulkner renames it Feinman Airport of the city of New Valois, built on filled land taken from Lake Rambaud.

In ABSALOM, ABSALOM! (1936), Thomas Sutpen travels from JEFFERSON, MISSISSIPPI, to New Orleans to seek out the mistress and child of Charles Bon, his daughter Judith's suitor. The unsophisticated Henry Sutpen, Judith's brother, makes the same journey a little later to investigate Bon's background.

New Orleans has fallen on hard times since a hurricane struck in August 2005, with devastating results. Low-lying areas of the city were destroyed by floodwaters, though much of the Vieux Carré escaped serious damage.

New Orleans Times-Picayune Leading daily newspaper of NEW ORLEANS, LOUISIANA, and an early paying outlet for Faulkner's work. He became friends with the newspaper's literary editor, John McClure, and other staffers and produced a series of New Orleans sketches for the *Times-Picayune* in 1925 (*see* NEW ORLEANS SKETCHES).

The first in the series, "Mirrors of Chartres Street," appeared on February 8, 1925. Others followed at intervals during the year. Faulkner also produced short stories, poems, and essays for the paper. "I am like John Rockefeller," he wrote his mother, "whenever I need money I sit down and dash off ten dollars worth for them. (Quoted in Parini, *One Matchless Time*, 74).

The *Times-Picayune* pieces helped finance Faulkner's sojourn in Italy, France, and England from August to November 1925.

Nine-Mile Branch Fictional stream running through willow and cypress bottoms in YOKNAPA-

TAWPHA COUNTY. In INTRUDER IN THE DUST, it leads to the Gowrie clan's burial ground at CALEDONIA CHAPEL.

Nobel Prize in literature Prestigious international award, established by the bequest of the Norwegian explosives manufacturer Alfred B. Nobel (1833–96). Sinclair Lewis (1930), Eugene O'Neill (1936), and Pearl S. Buck (1938) were the first American recipients.

The Swedish Academy failed to agree on a winner for 1949 and withheld the prize; the committee decided later to award two literature Nobels in 1950. In early November 1950, the wire services reported Faulkner and the British philosopher BERTRAND RUSSELL as the leading candidates.

The academy selected Faulkner for the 1949 award on November 10, 1950, citing his "powerful

Faulkner and his 17-year-old daughter, Jill, prepare to board a plane from New York to Stockholm, Sweden where Faulkner would receive the Nobel Prize in literature in December 1950. *(AP/Wide World Photos)*

and independent artistic contribution in America's new literature of the novel." Fifteen of the 18 members voted to award him the prize, which carried a cash grant of around $30,000. The next day, a Swedish journalist in New York called Faulkner at home in OXFORD, MISSISSIPPI, to tell him he had won.

Faulkner at first refused to travel to Sweden to accept. Nor did the honor seem to impress him, anyway at first. "They gave it to Sinclair Lewis and Old China Hand Buck," he told an Oxford reporter, "and they passed over Sherwood Anderson and Theodore Dreiser."

Political pressures were brought to bear; friends tried to talk Faulkner around. His wife suggested this would be an opportunity for their daughter JILL (FAULKNER) to see something of Europe. That persuaded Faulkner, and he and Jill left for Stockholm on December 6, Faulkner shaky from another drinking binge.

The Nobel presentation speech graded Faulkner as "the unrivaled master of all living British and American novelists as a deep psychologist" and as "the greatest experimentalist among 20th-century novelists."

Faulkner then gave a memorable "Address upon Receiving the Nobel Prize in Literature"—a good deal more memorable in the printed version, actually, for Faulkner, nervous and deeply ill at ease, raced through a barely audible delivery (*see* Appendix).

The novelist ended the address with a moving affirmation of faith: "I believe that man will not merely endure: he will prevail. He is immortal, not because he alone among creatures has an inexhaustible voice, but because he has a soul, a spirit capable of compassion and sacrifice and endurance."

With a check for $30,171 in his pocket, Faulkner left for home after only 72 hours in Sweden. He and Jill spent five days in Paris and stopped briefly in England and Ireland. A high school band playing a Sousa march greeted them on their return to Oxford.

Faulkner ended up giving away the Nobel cash award in scholarships and other bequests. "I haven't earned it and I don't feel like it's mine," he explained.

O

Ober, Harold (1881–1959) Faulkner's literary agent. A native of Nashua, New Hampshire, he graduated from Harvard University in 1905 with ambitions to write, but decided he lacked the talent and went into the business of representing writers instead.

Ober founded his own agency in 1929. His client list included Paul Gallico, Catherine Drinker Bowen, and Agatha Christie; he loaned $20,000 to the chronically troubled F. Scott Fitzgerald and took Fitzgerald's daughter into his family for a time.

Faulkner and Ober met through ROBERT K. HAAS, Faulkner's editor and publisher and a Scarsdale neighbor of Ober's. In Ober's first effort for Faulkner, he sold the short story "BARN BURNING" to HARPER'S MAGAZINE in March 1938. He later negotiated lucrative film rights deals for Faulkner.

Both men were reserved and formal—so much so that they began calling each other Bill and Harold only after working together for four years. Ober died of a heart attack in September 1959.

Okatoba County Fictional name for Yalobusha County, Mississippi, lying southwest of LAFAYETTE COUNTY. Miss Habersham's fantasy car trip in INTRUDER IN THE DUST takes her into Okatoba County before she turns northward to return to YOKNAPATAWPHA COUNTY. Okatoba is also mentioned in KNIGHT'S GAMBIT.

Faulkner and several associates established the OKATOBA HUNTING AND FISHING CLUB in 1937.

Okatoba Hunting and Fishing Club With R. L. Sullivan and Whitson Cook, Faulkner founded this sporting club in 1937. General James Stone, the father of Faulkner's friend PHILIP AVERY STONE, gave the club hunting rights on his several thousand acres of MISSISSIPPI DELTA wilderness near Batesville. Faulkner wrote a state game warden that the club intended to protect the game from extermination.

Faulkner used these circumstances in "The BEAR" (GO DOWN, MOSES). After selling off the timber rights to his share of the big woods, Major De Spain offers Ike McCaslin and his hunting companions use of the house and hunting lands anytime. De Spain himself never goes there again, and loggers carry out a swift destruction of the wilderness.

Old Frenchman Place (sometimes referred to as Old Frenchman's Place) Fictional place near FRENCHMAN'S BEND in YOKNAPATAWPHA COUNTY. Flem Snopes "unloads" the ruined plantation, rumored to be the site of buried treasure, on Henry Armstid, Odum Bookwright, and the usually level-headed V. K. Ratliff in The HAMLET, the first novel in the SNOPES TRILOGY. (This episode of the novel is a revision of the short story "LIZARDS IN JAMSHYD'S COURTYARD.")

Faulkner introduced the Old Frenchman Place in SANCTUARY. Built before the Civil War, it had deteriorated into a wreck, pulled apart for firewood, amid ruined cotton fields and gardens. The gangster Popeye murders Tommy and brutally rapes Temple Drake there. According to REQUIEM

FOR A NUN, Old Frenchman Place was built by the wealthy Frenchman Louis Grenier. In grandeur and size, it rivaled Thomas Sutpen's mansion in ABSALOM, ABSALOM!

Oldham, Dorothy (Dot) (1905–1968) Younger sister of Faulkner's wife, ESTELLE OLDHAM FAULKNER. Dot Oldham and Billy Falkner spent much time together in OXFORD, MISSISSIPPI, in 1919, when Estelle was married to CORNELL FRANKLIN and living in Honolulu. They used to play golf together.

She earned a master's degree in history from the UNIVERSITY OF MISSISSIPPI, ran soft drink and beer wholesaling businesses, and eventually became a librarian at Ole Miss, where she was curator of the Mississippi Collection. In May 1929, with Faulkner in a state of exhaustion after finishing SANCTUARY, she suggested he overcome his ambivalence and propose marriage to Estelle, who promply accepted.

Oldham, Lemuel Earl (1870–1945) Faulkner's father-in-law. He graduated from the UNIVERSITY OF MISSISSIPPI and practiced law in Bonham, Texas, where his first daughter, ESTELLE OLDHAM (FAULKNER), was born. He moved his family to OXFORD, MISSISSIPPI, in 1905 to take up the post of clerk of the U.S. Circuit Court.

A Republican, a rarity in Mississippi in those days, Oldham surmounted this political liability to become a successful businessman and lawyer in Oxford, where he became known by the honorific "the major." He pursued banking and other interests, was general counsel for a railroad, and in 1921 won a patronage appointment as U.S. attorney for the Northern District of Mississippi. Some in Oxford regarded the Oldhams as pretentious; they owned, after all, two grand pianos.

The Oldhams and the Falkners were neighbors in Oxford, and Billy Falkner grew up with Oldhams as friends and playmates—Estelle, her sisters Victoria (Tochie) and DOROTHY OLDHAM, and Estelle's brother Edward (who died in 1916).

In 1918, Lem Oldham refused his consent when Falkner sought to marry Estelle. He was hardly more encouraging in June 1929 when the novelist and Estelle prepared at last to marry.

Oldham's business ventures declined and he fell on hard times in the 1930s; for a time, Faulkner

contributed $100 a month to the support of the major and his wife, Lida.

Oldham formed the basis for the character of the judge in the short story "Beyond the Gate" (*see* "BEYOND") He died in May 1945.

Oldham, Lida Allen (1896–1956) Faulkner's mother-in-law. She claimed Sam Houston and the Confederate general Felix Zollicoffer as ancestors; with a highly developed sense of pride of family, "she never let anyone forget that." One grandfather was killed at the BATTLE OF SHILOH in 1862, and another died in a federal prisoner-of-war camp in Ohio.

The stepdaughter of a prominent federal judge in Mississippi, Miss Lida studied piano at the Cincinnati Conservatory of Music before settling into marriage with a young lawyer, LEMUEL E. OLDHAM. They had four children: ESTELLE (FAULKNER; born 1896), Victoria (Tochie), DOROTHY (OLDHAM), and Edward (died 1916).

She taught her daughters (and later her granddaughter, JILL FAULKNER) to play the piano, and saw to it that all three girls attended college. Young Billy Falkner was deeply fond of Miss Lida. All the same, she opposed his efforts to marry Estelle as forcibly as did her husband.

Omlie, Vernon C. (c. 1896–1936) Faulkner's flying instructor. A North Dakotan, he took up flying in 1916 and served as a flight instructor during World War I. He and his aeronaut wife, Phoebe (1902–75), a pilot, wingwalker and parachute jumper, alit with their flying circus in MEMPHIS in 1922 and established thriving aviation businesses there.

A careful and meticulous instructor, Omlie taught Faulkner to fly in the winter and spring of 1933 from a landing ground south of OXFORD, MISSISSIPPI. Faulkner took Omlie's Waco F biplane up on a solo flight on April 20—the first time he had ever gone aloft alone, in spite of his stories about flying for the ROYAL AIR FORCE. He evidently related some of his fictitious flying adventures to his instructor and asked him to keep quiet about the lessons.

Faulkner and Omlie collaborated in barnstorming and air circuses in Oxford and vicinity, with stunt flying and parachute jumps. Omlie and Faulkner's brother DEAN FAULKNER were business partners before Dean's death in an airplane crash in November 1935.

Much of the aviation experience and lore Faulkner absorbed from the Omlies made its way into the novel PYLON (1935). The characters of Roger and Laverne Shumann were modeled in part on Vernon and Phoebe Omlie.

Omlie died as a passenger in a crash near St. Louis of a Chicago-bound airliner on August 5, 1936. His widow went on to become an official in the research division of the Civil Aeronautics Administration.

Oxford, Mississippi City in north-central Mississippi. The seat of LAFAYETTE COUNTY, Oxford was a farming, manufacturing, and tourist center, site of the UNIVERSITY OF MISSISSIPPI (Ole Miss), lifelong home of Faulkner, and the model for his fictional JEFFERSON, MISSISSIPPI. Oxford was settled in the 1840s on patent lands of the Chickasaw Ho-Kah. In 1962 the city became briefly notorious when whites violently opposed the admission of an African-American student, James Meredith, to the university.

Federal forces under General ULYSSES S. GRANT occupied Oxford briefly in December 1862. The Union commander ANDREW J. SMITH returned in the summer of 1864 in pursuit of NATHAN BEDFORD FORREST's cavalry and set fire to the center of the town on August 22. Where "once stood a handsome little country town, now only remained the blackened skeletons of the houses and smoldering ruins," a *Chicago Times* correspondent wrote in the aftermath of Smith's visit.

Oxford still showed traces of Civil War damage when Faulkner's grandfather JOHN WESLEY THOMPSON FALKNER moved there from RIPLEY, MISSISSIPPI, in late 1885. The Young Colonel pursued banking, railroad, and legal business from his law office on the northeast corner of the Courthouse Square and became active in Democratic politics.

MURRY FALKNER moved his family from Ripley to Oxford in September 1902, when his father sold the railroad that had employed him. In contrast with Ripley, the place struck the Falkner boys, Billy and Jack, as a metropolis.

Oxford in 1902 had a population of around 1,800, making it three times the size of Ripley. The town boasted a courthouse with a four-faced clock; Ole Miss, a mile west of the city center; a nearly new water tower, 140 feet high; a newspaper (the OXFORD EAGLE); and hardware, dry goods, confectioners, and other stores clustered on the square.

This statue of William Faulkner (by sculptor William N. Beckwith) in Courthouse Square, Oxford, Mississippi, was dedicated on the centennial of Faulkner's birth, September 25, 1997. *(Harriett and Gioia Fargnoli)*

The Murry Falkners settled into "the old Johnny Brown place" on Second South Street. Billy Falkner entered the Oxford school in September 1905. He later attended high school there, took classes sporadically at the university, painted houses in Oxford, and worked in the university post office and power plant.

In April 1931, Faulkner and his wife, ESTELLE OLDHAM FAULKNER, bought the old Shegog place on the Old Taylor Road, built in the mid-1840s. Renamed ROWAN OAK, it was Faulkner's permanent residence for the rest of his life.

Oxford had altered considerably by the 1930s. The first automobile arrived in 1908, a red Winton Six touring car. Soon the roads were paved, inviting more cars. The sidewalks and the Square were paved, too, the downtown storefronts "renovated." The Big Place, J. W. T. Falkner's home and the center of Falkner life in the early years of the century, was divided into apartments; a gas station went up on the corner lot. Faulkner and his family mourned the lost Oxford of their youth.

Oxford today is best known to the world as Faulkner's home. Rowan Oak is a museum. The University of Mississippi is a center of Faulkner scholarship.

Faulkner's post oak barn on his Rowan Oak property. Built c. 1844, the barn was restored in the 1990s. *(Harriett and Gioia Fargnoli)*

Oxford is also a fictional place about 40 miles from Jefferson and FRENCHMAN'S BEND. In Faulkner's fiction, it serves as the location of the University of Mississippi, where in ABSALOM, ABSALOM! Henry Sutpen meets his half brother Charles Bon and where in *The* HAMLET the schoolteacher Labove is a student and football player. In *The* UNVANQUISHED, Bayard Sartoris is a law student in Oxford when he learns of his father's murder in Jefferson.

Oxford Eagle   Weekly newspaper. Established in OXFORD, MISSISSIPPI, in 1877, it recorded the business, social, and literary doings of the Falkners and Faulkners beginning in the 1880s.

The newspaper reported William Faulkner's marriage to ESTELLE OLDHAM (FAULKNER) in 1929 and thereafter made note of his works as they appeared, usually with local reaction and a synopsis of outland critical opinion.

"Faulkner Writes Another Novel" ran the *Eagle*'s headline on the appearance of SANCTU-ARY in 1931. "It is said that in this novel Faulkner looses all the fury of his pen and this is one of the most stirring of the many books written by him," the paper reported, before going on to call the book "disgusting."

Phillip E. Mullen, a son of the *Eagle*'s proprietor, covered Faulkner sympathetically for many years, presenting this strange, exotic, and sometimes infuriating author to local people who knew him only by reputation rather than through his works. "Few Oxford people realize the distinction of having as a native son, William Faulkner," Mullen wrote.

Mullen also defended Oxford's most famous citizen from unfriendly outside criticism. *Time* magazine's 1934 characterization of DOCTOR MARTINO AND OTHER STORIES as "merely potboilers" moved Mullen to remark, "As the Greek philosophers have so aptly put it, a guy's gotta eat."

Faulkner gave his only extended interview after winning the NOBEL PRIZE to Phil Mullen. Faulkner's daughter, JILL FAULKNER, worked as an editor at the *Eagle* for a brief period in 1954.

The *Eagle* today is a daily newspaper, published Monday through Friday.

P

Parchman Mississippi state penitentiary and penal farm. Faulkner uses Parchman as a locale in the short story "Monk" and sets the opening scene of "Old Man" there. The "tall convict" of the latter story is assigned to a Parchman chain gang. Faulkner later wove the two stories together to create "The WILD PALMS" (1939).

In *The* HAMLET, the first volume of the SNOPES TRILOGY, V. K. Ratliff speculates that Mink Snopes is Parchman-bound for the killing of Jack Houston; he ultimately serves 38 years for the murder. The time Mink spends at Parchman is covered in the first section of *The* MANSION, the third novel of the trilogy.

Paris Review Quarterly journal of poetry, prose fiction, and art and literary criticism, founded in 1953. With George Plimpton as editor, the *Paris Review* published a notable series of interviews with authors, including JEAN STEIN's interview with Faulkner in May 1956. The critic MALCOLM COWLEY collected some of them in *Writers at Work: The Paris Review Interviews* (1959).

Biographer JOSEPH BLOTNER regards Stein's piece as the best and most comprehensive Faulkner interview ever published. In it, Faulkner explained how he came to develop the YOKNAPATAWPHA COUNTY cycle. "I like to think of the world I created as being a kind of keystone in the universe; that, as small as that keystone is, the universe itself would collapse. My last book will be the Doomsday Book, the Golden Book, of Yoknapatawpha County. Then I shall break the pencil and I'll have to stop."

He also identified *The* SOUND AND THE FURY as his favorite work, because it had given him the most "grief and anguish." He loved it, he told Stein, "as the mother loves the child who became the thief or murderer more than the one who became the priest."

Parsham, Tennessee Faulkner's name for Grand Junction, Tennessee, a railroad town 65 miles northwest of OXFORD, MISSISSIPPI. The National Field trials for bird dogs have been conducted there since 1900. Oxford rail passengers bound for MEMPHIS changed trains at Grand Junction.

The horse race in *The* REIVERS takes place in Parsham, pronounced "Possum" in the dialect of some of the characters.

Pascagoula, Mississippi City in southeastern Mississippi, a resort, fishing and shipbuilding center, and port of entry on the Gulf of Mexico.

Faulkner spent parts of the summers of 1925, 1926, and 1927 in Pascagoula. He wrote, swam, wandered about, and conducted an unsuccessful courtship of HELEN BAIRD. Faulkner worked on his first novel, SOLDIERS' PAY, in Pascagoula in June 1925; started his second novel, MOSQUITOES, there in June 1926; and finished FLAGS IN THE DUST (published as SARTORIS) in the Gulf city in late September 1927.

Faulkner and his wife, ESTELLE OLDHAM FAULKNER, spent their honeymoon in Pascagoula in June 1929. The novelist returned to Pascagoula with JEAN STEIN in November 1955. Among other sights, he showed her the circular bench where he had worked on *Mosquitoes*. They encountered only one other figure on the cold, windswept beach—Helen Baird.

Pascagoula also figures as a location in Faulkner's writing. In *The* MANSION, Linda Snopes Kohl works for the war effort in Pascagoula for a time during World War II.

Pemberton, John C. (1814–1881) Pennsylvania-born Confederate soldier. Commanding Confederate forces in Mississippi in 1862–63, he retreated into the river fortress of Vicksburg under pressure from the Union General ULYSSES S. GRANT. After a six-week siege, Pemberton surrendered Vicksburg to Grant on July 4, 1863 (*see* VICKSBURG CAMPAIGN).

Vicksburg was one of the decisive Union victories of the war, and the South never forgave Pemberton for his ineptitude in defending the place. In Faulkner's novel *The* UNVANQUISHED (1938), young Bayard Sartoris and his enslaved friend Ringo Strother made a "living map" behind the smokehouse in the summer of 1863, using wood-chips to fight Pemberton's Vicksburg battles to a favorable conclusion.

Pickett, George C. (1825–1875) Confederate soldier. On Gen. Robert E. Lee's orders, at a little after two o'clock in the afternoon of July 3, 1863, he led the doomed assault at Gettysburg, known ever after—and known more familiarly to Southerners of Faulkner's generation than ever Lexington and Concord were—as Pickett's charge. Faulkner refers to Pickett's charge in *The* UNVANQUISHED.

OXFORD, MISSISSIPPI, claimed later that a locally raised infantry company, the UNIVERSITY GREYS of the UNIVERSITY OF MISSISSIPPI, "reached the highest point of the Confederacy." during Pickett's charge, "forty-seven yards beyond the farthest" advance of any other of General Pickett's troops.

Pittsburgh Landing Tennessee town. *See* SHI-LOH, BATTLE OF.

Polk, Noel (1943–) Noted Faulkner textual scholar, critic, and professor of English at Missis-

sippi State University in Starkville. Among his critical writings, the Mississipi-born Polk has published *Faulkner's "Requiem for a Nun": A Critical Study* (1981); *An Editorial Handbook for William Faulkner's "The Sound and the Fury"* (1985); and *Children of the Dark House: Text and Context in Faulkner* (1996).

With JOSEPH BLOTNER, Polk edited all five volumes of Faulkner's works in the LIBRARY OF AMERICA edition: *William Faulkner: Novels 1926–1929*; *William Faulkner: Novels 1930–1935*; *William Faulkner: Novels 1936–1940*; *William Faulkner: Novels 1942–1954*; and *William Faulkner: Novels 1957–1962*. Polk is also a founding member of the Mississippi Institute of Arts and Letters.

Pontotoc, Mississippi Northern Mississippi town, 30 miles southeast of OXFORD, MISSISSIPPI, the native place of Colonel WILLIAM C. FALKNER's first wife, Elizabeth Vance, and the southern terminus of the Old Colonel's GULF & SHIP ISLAND RAILROAD—"the Doodlebug Line." Several fine antebellum houses still stand.

MURRY FALKNER, Faulkner's father, lived there in 1891 as an employee of the railroad and was shot and badly injured in a dispute with a local man. Faulkner's brother DEAN SWIFT FAULKNER, flying in an air show, died in the crash of his airplane near Pontotoc in November 1935.

postmodernism A movement in the arts stemming directly from and in reaction to MODERNISM. Although sharing certain characteristics or tendencies with modernism (such as textual strategies and the questioning of the authority of social institutions), postmodernist fiction interrogates the legitimacy of the ontology of the text itself (or the ontology of the world which a text projects), but it does not, like modernism, substitute the moral authority of social institutions with that of the individual. Literary postmodernism also encourages extensive experimentation in narrative presentation and rhetorical and stylistic devices. An observation by CONRAD AIKEN on the extraordinary effectiveness of Faulkner's style when seen as a whole, first published in the ATLANTIC MONTHLY in November 1939, is apropos of a discussion of Faulkner and postmodernism. If one views Faulkner's "sentences not simply by themselves . . . but in their relation to the book as a whole, one sees a functional reason and necessity for their being as they are. They parallel in a curious and perhaps inevitable way, and not without aesthetic justification, the whole elaborate method of *deliberately withheld meaning*, of progressive and partial and delayed disclosure, which so often gives the characteristic shape to the novels themselves. It is a persistent offering of obstacles, a calculated system of screens and obtrusions, of confusions and ambiguous interpolations and delays, with one express purpose; and that purpose is simply to keep the form—and the idea—fluid and unfinished, still in motion, as it were, and unknown, until the dropping into place of the very last syllable" ("William Faulkner: The Novel as Form" in *William Faulkner: Three Decades of Criticism*, 137–138).

Faulkner, along with JAMES JOYCE and Samuel Beckett, has long been seen as one of the precursors to the postmodernist movement. In *Postmodernist Fiction* (New York: Methuen, 1987), Brian McHale points to chapter 8 of ABSALOM, ABSALOM!, in which Quentin Compson and Shreve McCannon reconstruct the Sutpen murder mystery, as the precise moment when postmodernism took its bow. This chapter, according to McHale, "dramatizes the shift of dominant from problems of *knowing* to problems of *modes of being*—from an epistemological dominant to an *ontological one*. At this point Faulkner's novel touches and perhaps crosses the boundary between modernist and postmodernist writing" (10). Modernism and postmodernism share the common characteristic of textual positioning and the role of the text for both narrator and reader.

Prall, Elizabeth (Elizabeth Prall Anderson) (n.a.)

Faulkner met this former teacher of Greek in New York City in the autumn of 1924, when she gave him a job clerking in the Doubleday bookstore she managed at 38th Street and Fifth Avenue.

Prall married the writer SHERWOOD ANDERSON as his third wife and settled with him in NEW ORLEANS. Faulkner renewed his acquaintance with her and met her husband there. At Prall's invitation, he stayed in the couple's Vieux Carré apartment for several weeks in early 1925.

The Andersons moved to Marion, Virginia, in 1927 and were divorced the following year. By then Faulkner's initial friendship with Anderson had cooled to the point of rancor.

R

race, Faulkner and Faulkner's attitudes on white and black relations in a South cursed with the legacy of slavery were complex and profoundly ambiguous. A Mississippian, a traditionalist, and a literary artist of the first rank, Faulkner created a powerfully liberal body of fiction, yet his public pronouncements on race were confused, contradictory, and ill-judged. More than any white writer of his time, he invented fully realized and sympathetic black characters. Yet a reflexive racism pervaded Faulkner's thought, his actions, and his literary works.

The Falkners of OXFORD, MISSISSIPPI, employed blacks as servants and had blacks as near neighbors. The Falkner boys had black playmates. Circumstantial evidence suggests that WILLIAM CLARK FALKNER, the Old Colonel, Faulkner's great-grandfather, produced a "shadow family" of at least two children with one of his former slaves. The future novelist would weave miscegenation themes into his fiction: A number of memorable characters, among them Clytemnestra Sutpen, Joe Christmas, Sam Fathers and Lucas Beauchamp, are of mixed parentage. Blacks lived in every section of Oxford in the early 1900s, though the largest concentration lay in the black quarter known as Freedmantown.

For all this familiarity, hysteria about racial matters convulsed the Mississippi of Faulkner's childhood. Demagogic politicians and popular fiction such as Thomas Dixon's The Clansman (1908)

portrayed blacks, especially black men, as retrogressing into savagery since the end of slavery in 1865. Lynching became a terrible symptom of white hysteria. More than 200 blacks died at the hands of white mobs in Mississippi between 1889 and 1909—more than in any other state.

Billy Falkner absorbed this atmosphere as a boy. In October 1908, a 2,000-strong mob lynched a black bootlegger named Nelse Patton on the square in Oxford within earshot of the Falkner home. He had been accused of assaulting a white woman; the mob broke into the jail, dragged Patton to the square and strung him up naked on a telephone pole, fired a fusillade at him, and left him hanging through the night. Faulkner may have used the memory of the Patton murder in "DRY SEPTEMBER," a 1931 short story in which a middle-aged white woman's accusation touches off the lynching of an innocent black man. In the novel INTRUDER IN THE DUST (1948), a mob forms outside the jail where Lucas Beauchamp awaits trial on a murder charge.

Billy's first teacher owned a copy of The Clansman, and somehow the book eventually passed into his library. The stage version of the novel played in the Opera House in Oxford only a few weeks after Patton's murder. JOHN WESLEY THOMPSON FALKNER, Billy's grandfather, owned the theater.

Strict subordination of black to whites governed racial relations in the Oxford of Faulkner's childhood. Billy and his brothers attended the all-white grade school. Their black playmates made do with dramatically inadequate schools. Faulkner's family—his parents, his brothers, his wife—accepted segregation as though it were the natural order of things. In this, as in so much else, Faulkner stood apart. He came to be deeply troubled over the South's racial past and present.

His attitudes toward individual African Americans were a blend of paternalism, generosity, gratitude, and real affection, even love. He regarded the longtime Falkner servant CAROLINE BARR, known to the family as Mammie Callie, as a second mother. She lived for nearly a century, long enough to help rear Faulkner's own daughter, JILL FAULKNER, born in 1933. He maintained close and affectionate relations, too, with the elderly retainer NED BARNETT.

Faulkner purchased GREENFIELD FARM, a run-down 320-acre farm in LAFAYETTE COUNTY, in 1938 and, in the face of advice to convert it into a modern cattle operation with minimal labor requirements, peopled the place with black tenants. He probably lost money on the farm, and he liked to complain of having to support the tenants he had settled there. All the same, the farm filled a need in Faulkner. He could play the role of planter there—and of seigneur, too, patron of the black families who worked the place under his benign supervision. He could draw satisfaction from doing his best for individual black people.

Callie Barr, Ned Barnett, and the Greenfield farmers were, of course, in a familiar and accepted social position: They were servants and tenants, clearly subordinate to whites. Faulkner's attitudes toward such people may reflect what the biographer Frederick Karl diagnoses as his unconscious racism. In the early 1940s, a time when racial questions had begun to claim Faulkner's attention, he consistently used the epithet "nigger" in correspondence with his friend and editor ROBERT K. HAAS, a northerner and a Jew who, as Karl notes, almost certainly would not have used it himself.

"For a man so alert to language and to nuance . . . it is inconceivable he did not know what he was doing or thought he was using the word neutrally," Karl wrote. "At its deepest levels, his continued use of the word indicates a racism so unconsciously insistent it becomes a force in his personal assessment of racial issues and racial justice."

But Faulkner was no bigot, even if he did lapse into the use of racial slurs. That sort of crudeness did not seep into his art. As Karl observed, "Faulkner's views on race *in his fiction* were highly sophisticated."

Faulkner characters learn their racial lessons early. In "The Fire and the Hearth," one of the linked stories in GO DOWN, MOSES, Henry Beauchamp's white McCaslin "foster-brother" shows a sudden, unexpected change in their relationship. They will no longer sleep in the same bed, eat at the same table. Henry's mother understands. She lays a single plate at the table for the McCaslin boy. "So he entered his heritage," the narrator comments. "He ate its bitter fruit" (*Go Down, Moses*, 110).

Caroline Barr is commonly regarded as a model for one of Faulkner's best-known characters, white or black, Dilsey Gibson of *The SOUND AND THE FURY* (1929). Struggling heroically to keep the disintegrating Compson family together, she represents essential qualities of loyalty, fidelity, sacrifice, and endurance. She is, said the novelist and critic ROBERT PENN WARREN, "the very ethical center of the book, the vessel of virtue and compassion." Yet Dilsey retains the traditional role of service to white folks and dependence on them. So do Clytie Sutpen in ABSALOM, ABSALOM! (1936) and Molly Beauchamp in *Go Down, Moses* (1942) and *Intruder in the Dust*.

Faulkner does not, however, restrict himself altogether to this pattern. Joe Christmas in LIGHT IN AUGUST (1932) is anything but subservient, though he is deeply wounded. Wrote Warren, "With his mixed blood, he is the lost, suffering, enduring creature, and even the murder he commits at the end is a fumbling attempt to define his manhood, an attempt to break out of the iron ring of mechanism." There is no actual proof that Christmas has black blood, but he thinks he does, and so do others. He is a marginal figure, uncertain of his identity: a paradigm, so it seems, for the *human* dilemma.

Lucas Beauchamp is fiercely proud both of his descent from the white McCaslins and of his blackness. In the character of Beauchamp, Faulkner seems to suggest the South is a single race, white and black. Like Sam Fathers, the sage of the forest in *Go Down, Moses* and elsewhere, Beauchamp is a stoical hero, "a focus of dignity and integrity," in Warren's words, a man prepared to stand on his principles no matter what the cost. *"We got to make him be a nigger first,"* outraged whites say of him. *"He's got to admit he's a nigger. Then maybe we'll accept him as he seems to intend to be accepted"* (*Intruder*, 18; italics Faulkner's). But Beauchamp refuses to be intimidated. He defiantly refuses to follow white strictures on how blacks should behave.

World War II focused Faulkner's attention on race as never before. In a letter to his stepson MALCOLM FRANKLIN in 1943, he remarked on the irony of an all-black fighter squadron flying combat missions in North Africa on the same day 20 blacks were killed in a race riot in Detroit. He predicted that the war would bring necessary changes.

Intruder in the Dust, a call for southern whites to do justice to blacks, grew out of this pattern of thinking. More tract than novel, with a creaky murder-mystery plot, it is a powerful expression nevertheless of Faulkner's concern. Gavin Stevens, the white lawyer who defends Lucas Beauchamp on a charge of murder, exhorts white southerners to do justice to blacks without northern prodding (or, for that matter, northern interference).

Faulkner's views sound wholly inadequate today, but in 1948 they set Faulkner apart from all but a few white southerners. In protest of tentative federal government moves toward integration, white southern Democrats bolted from the national party to form the segregationist "Dixiecrats." Their presidential candidate, Strom Thurmond of South Carolina, polled more than 1.1 million votes in the 1948 election. Faulkner's family utterly rejected his comparative liberalism on race. Someone once suggested to his uncle JOHN WESLEY THOMPSON FALKNER Jr., an Oxford lawyer, that he had served as the model for the Stevens character. His response summarizes the Falkners' attitude on the matter, and on their famous kinsman's work as well: "Me, that nigger-lovin' Stevens? Naw, I don't read Billy's books much. But he can write them if he wants to. I guess he makes money at it—writing those dirty books for Yankees."

Intruder is a faithful reflection of Faulkner's confusion about racial questions. He seems to have drawn back from the implications of his beliefs, perhaps partly because he was a man of his time and place after all, and partly too because he dreaded changes in the pattern of southern life. For Faulkner, change all too often meant destruction—as in the lumber companies' clear-cutting of the Big Woods of the MISSISSIPPI DELTA, the last wilderness of the novelist's home country.

Confused or not, Faulkner became increasingly drawn into racial politics, usually in response to white atrocities against blacks. In a letter to the Memphis *Commercial Appeal* in 1950, he protested a Mississippi court's decision to sentence a white man to life in prison for the killing of three black children. The killer surely would have been put to death had the children been white, Faulkner argued. In 1951, on the urging of northern civil rights groups, he challenged the conviction and execution of a black man, Willie McGee, accused of raping a white woman. There was no evidence McGee had forced himself on the woman, Faulkner observed, and besides execution would make a martyr of McGee and "create a long-lasting stink in my native state." The local prosecutor suggested Faulkner had "aligned himself with the communists" in speaking out for McGee.

The conflict escalated with the U.S. Supreme Court's May 1954 ruling in *Brown v. Board of Education* that segregated schools were unconstitutional. A year later, the high court instructed federal district courts to require a start toward desegregation; the court eventually extended the ruling to apply to public gathering places, transportation, and state-supported colleges and universities.

In the spring of 1955, Faulkner sent a series of letters to the *Commercial Appeal* attacking Mississippi's segregated schools. "Our present schools are not even good enough for white people ...."

he wrote. "So what do we do? Make them good enough, improve them to the best possible? No, we beat the bushes, rake and scrape to raise additional taxes to establish another system at best only equal to that one which is already not good enough." Such comments earned Faulkner the epithet of "Weeping Willie" in Oxford. Nor could he turn to his family for support. With the *Brown* ruling, his brother Johncy announced he would stand at the schoolhouse door with a gun to block the integration of Oxford's schools.

Faulkner expanded his views on race in an essay in HARPER'S MAGAZINE in June 1956, suggesting white southerners meant to halt black advances because they were afraid of competition—were afraid of losing their place in the social and economic order. "To live anywhere in the world today and be against equality because of race or color," he went on, "is like living in Alaska and being against snow."

With Faulkner's celebrity (he had won the 1949 NOBEL PRIZE IN LITERATURE), journalists eagerly sought out his views on controversial issues. Faulkner himself initiated the contact in Rome in the summer of 1955 with a statement on the EMMETT TILL lynching in Mississippi. Whites accused the 14-year-old Till, a Chicagoan visiting relatives in Greenwood, Mississippi, of whistling at a white woman and making an obscene remark to her. The boy disappeared and was later found dead; two of the woman's relatives were charged with his murder. The killing revolted Faulkner. "Perhaps the purpose of this sorry and tragic error committed in my native Mississippi by two white adults on an afflicted Negro child is to prove to us whether or not we deserve to survive," he said in a broadside released through the U.S. Information Service. "Because if we in America have reached that point in our desperate culture when we must murder children, no matter for what reason or what color, we don't deserve to survive, and probably won't."

Mississippi juries acquitted the two white men accused of the abduction and murder of Emmett Till. Faulkner's comments on these and other racial matters brought him hate mail and threatening phone calls in the night. Possibly the threats frightened him; more probably, they made clear to him the full fury of southern resistance. For whatever reason, the Autherine Lucy case threw him off his balance. In early 1956, a federal judge ordered the University of Alabama to admit this young black woman. Though Faulkner remained broadly sympathetic to her aims, he urged her to abandon the attempt to enroll. He thought enraged whites would murder her, and that the incident would touch off a race war in the South.

In "A Letter to the North" published in the mass-circulation *Life* magazine on March 5, 1956, Faulkner argued for a gradual approach to integration and for the South to be allowed to work out the problem undisturbed. Elaborating on the Gavin Stevens argument in *Intruder in the Dust*, he asserted that only the South alone could find a way out of the dilemma. The issues were spiritual and moral; the solution was understanding and conversion, not legislation.

"I have been on record as opposing the forces in my native country which would keep the condition out of which this present evil and trouble has grown," he wrote. "Now I must go on record as opposing the forces outside the South which would use legal or police compulsion to eradicate that evil overnight."

Faulkner's advice to civil rights groups, northern liberals and the federal government: "'Go slow now. Stop now for a time, a moment.'"

Unfortunately, Faulkner had more to say on the subject of Autherine Lucy. The Lucy case worried him deeply. In an attempt to amplify his warnings, he offered an interview to a British journalist, Russell Warren Howe, for publication in the public affairs periodical *The Reporter*. He had been drinking steadily before the interview, perhaps a partial explanation for the noxious remarks Howe attributed to him. "A Talk with William Faulkner" appeared on March 22, 1956. "If that girl goes back to Tuscaloosa she will die," Faulkner said. "Then the top will blow off. The government will send its troops and we'll be back at 1860. They must stop pushing these people. The trouble is the North doesn't know that country. They don't know the South will go to war."

Faulkner continued, "If it came to fighting I'd fight for Mississippi against the United States even if it meant going out into the streets and shooting Negroes. I will go on saying that the Southerners are wrong and that their position is untenable, but if I have to make the same choice Robert E. Lee made then I'll make it."

Astonishingly, Faulkner went on to say that his black tenant farmers would align with him. "My Negro boys down on the plantation would fight against the North with me," he told Howe. "If I say to them, 'Go get your shotguns, boys,' they'll come."

Faulkner tried afterward to repudiate the comments about shooting down blacks, saying they were "foolish and dangerous." He also claimed he had been misquoted. Howe responded that he had transcribed the interview verbatim from shorthand notes.

Autherine Lucy ignored Faulkner's advice and entered the University of Alabama, igniting three days of white rioting. When she accused university officials of conspiring with the rioters, the trustees expelled her. The Lucy matter seemed to mark a turning point in Faulkner's attitudes about race, or perhaps a reversion to earlier views. From then onward he fully aligned himself with the forces of gradualism. His later utterances had a lecturing, patronizing tone, sometimes offensive and always in sad contrast to the subtlety and empathy of much of his literary output.

In his last public effort on the race question, Faulkner invited his adopted state of Virginia to lead the way to racial justice. Once again, though, his comments sounded unworthy of an important writer. Whites, he said, "must teach the negro the responsibility of personal morality and rectitude—either by taking him into our own white schools or giving him white teachers in his own schools until we have taught the teachers of his own race to teach and train him in these hard and unpleasant habits."

Faulkner had little to say about race during his last years. In any event, a temporary lull had fallen on the racial battlefield. Segregation remained largely intact in the South when Faulkner died in July 1962. Some weeks later, when a black student named James Meredith enrolled at the UNIVERSITY OF MISSISSIPPI, the battle flared again in all its ferocity.

Rainey, Paul   New York City millionaire sportsman, the squire of Cotton Plant, with a restored plantation house and the largest game preserve in Mississippi. MURRY FALKNER, the novelist's father, advised Rainey on the stables at Cotton Plant.

Rainey lent something to the character of Harrison Blair in the short story "FOX HUNT." He appears in modified form as Sells Wells, "owner of a plantation measured not in acres but in miles," in Faulkner's fictionalized memoir "Mississippi" (1953) and under his own name in *The REIVERS*.

Random House   Leading American publisher, based in New York City. BENNETT CERF and DONALD KLOPFER founded the firm in 1927; Cerf served as its head for 40 years.

Cerf pursued Faulkner for the Random House lists for several years. In 1935, he invited Faulkner to name his terms, saying he would rather publish Faulkner than "any other fiction writer living in America."

Random House absorbed Faulkner's publishers, SMITH & HAAS, in 1936. On October 26, the firm published *ABSALOM, ABSALOM!* in an edition of 6,000 copies; Random House published every Faulkner work thereafter.

Random House never expected substantial sales of Faulkner's works, and during a period of the mid-1940s all his books were out of print. A postwar critical and popular resurgence led by MALCOLM COWLEY culminated in Faulkner's NOBEL PRIZE IN LITERATURE for 1949, and sales soared. The firm reported in late 1950 that four Faulkner novels had sold a total of 140,000 copies in hardcover and that nearly 2.5 million copies of three novels were in print in paperback.

In a marketing coup in 2005, television superstar Oprah Winfrey's Book Club packaged the Vintage paperback editions of three novels, *As I Lay Dying*,

The SOUND AND THE FURY and LIGHT IN AUGUST, in a "Summer of Faulkner" promotion. Vintage is a division of Random House.

Reed, W. M. (n.a.) Proprietor of the Gathright-Reed drugstore on the square in OXFORD, MISSISSIPPI, known as "Mac." In 1929, he helped Faulkner distribute campaign literature for his uncle JOHN WESLEY THOMPSON FALKNER Jr., which began a lifelong friendship.

Mac Reed sold Faulkner's novels in his store, even SANCTUARY (1931), which most of Oxford regarded as obscene. Faulkner in 1960 appointed his old friend a director of the William Faulkner Foundation.

The Reporter Journal of social and political affairs. On March 22, 1956, it published a notorious interview with Faulkner on race.

Deeply worried about an explosion of racial violence in the segregated South, Faulkner himself pushed for the interview, which took place in SAXE COMMINS's office at RANDOM HOUSE in New York City. Faulkner had been drinking heavily, perhaps a partial explanation for the incendiary comments attributed to him.

"I would wish now that the liberals would stop—they should let us sweat in our own fears for a little while," he began, mildly enough. "Our position is wrong and untenable but it is not wise to keep an emotional people off balance."

Then he hit his stride. Though broadly sympathetic to her aims, he urged a young black woman named Autherine Lucy to abandon her attempt to enter the University of Alabama, an NAACP-backed bid that had touched off white rioting in the university town of Tuscaloosa.

"If that girl goes back to Tuscaloosa she will die," Faulkner told the interviewer, Russell Howe. "Then the top will blow off. The government will send its troops and we'll be back at 1860. They must stop pushing these people. The trouble is the North doesn't know that country. They don't know the South will go to war."

Shockingly, Faulkner went on: "As long as there's a middle of the road, all right, I'll be on it.

But if it came to fighting I'd fight for Mississippi against the United States even if it meant going out into the streets and shooting Negroes. I will go on saying that the Southerners are wrong and that their position is untenable, but if I have to make the same choice Robert E. Lee made then I'll make it."

Faulkner collapsed from the effects of alcohol shortly after the interview. By the time of publication he had recovered sufficiently to repudiate the statements about fighting for Mississippi and shooting down blacks, calling his words "foolish and dangerous." He also complained of having been misquoted.

"These are statements which no sober man would make, nor, it seems to me, any sane man believe," he said.

Howe responded that he had transcribed the interview verbatim from shortland notes. "If the more Dixiecrat remarks misconstrue his thoughts, I, as an admirer of Mr. Faulkner, am glad to know it. But what I set down is what he said," Howe insisted.

Ripley, Mississippi Northern Mississippi town, the seat of Tippah County, 35 miles northeast of OXFORD, MISSISSIPPI. WILLIAM C. FALKNER, Faulkner's great-grandfather, migrated to Ripley from Missouri in 1839 and eventually established himself as a leading citizen of the place.

Falkner helped raise an infantry company, the MAGNOLIA RIFLES, in Ripley in 1861. In July 1864, Union forces under A. J. SMITH burned the courthouse and other buildings, including Falkner's house.

Falkner prospered in the law and in railroad development in Ripley after the Civil War, building his GULF & SHIP ISLAND RAILROAD line south to Pontotoc, 37 miles distant. Faulkner's father, MURRY C. FALKNER, lived and worked in Ripley as a railroad official from 1898 to 1902. William Faulkner lived in Ripley from age one to five. The Falkners' second child, Jack (JOHN WESLEY THOMPSON FALKNER III), was born there in May 1899.

A statue of Falkner, 8 feet tall atop a 14-foot tall pedestal, towers over the cemetery in Ripley.

Ripley Railroad Company *See* Gulf & Ship Island Railroad.

Rockyford Fictional village in Yoknapatawpha County, east of Jefferson, Mississippi. In *The Town*, V. K. Ratliff sells a sewing machine to a Miz Ledbetter of Rockyford. The village is mentioned in *The Mansion*, the third novel of the Snopes trilogy.

Rowan Oak Faulkner's home of 32 years, in Oxford, Mississippi. An English architect designed and built the house, set in rugged grounds three-quarters of a mile south of the Oxford square on the Old Taylor Road, for Robert Shegog in 1844. A winding cedar-lined drive leads to the L-shaped, two-story house. In the front, four tall columns support a Grecian roof and a balcony projects over the Georgian front doors.

Mrs. Julia Bailey bought the house and most of the land from Shegog in 1872. The grounds, known thereafter as Bailey's Woods, were a favorite haunt of Oxford children; young Billy Falkner and his future wife, Estelle Oldham (Faulkner) both played there in the early years of the 20th

Faulkner named his home Rowan Oak after the rowan tree, a symbol of strength and tranquility. Built in the late 1840s, the house needed major repairs when Faulkner purchased it in 1930. Faulkner restored and renovated the house over the next quarter-century. It is now maintained by the University of Mississippi. *(Harriett and Gioia Fargnoli)*

century. By the late 1920s the old place had fallen into disrepair. Faulkner bought the house and four acres from a Bailey descendant for $6,000 in April 1930.

When the novelist and Estelle and her children moved into the Shegog place in June 1930, they found rotted beams, a leaky roof, cracking plaster, and a mice- and squirrel infestation in the attic. The ghost of Judith Shegog, killed in a fall while trying to elope with one of the Yankee general A. J. Smith's officers, supposedly haunted the house.

There was no electricity or plumbing. The Faulkners used oil lamps at first and carried water up from the wellhouse. Faulkner himself undertook much of the initial restoration, even the heaviest structural work, which involved jacking up the house to replace the rotted foundation sills. Within a few months, he had introduced wiring and running water, replaced the roof, and begun restoration of the lawn and gardens. In September 1937, to protect Rowan Oak from the encroachment of Oxford, he bought the contiguous 30-acre Bailey's Woods.

"It wasn't just land," his brother Jack (John Wesley Thompson Falkner III) wrote. "It was a sense of himself, extended into the land."

Faulkner renamed the property Rowan Oak, after a Scottish tree that signified peace and security. He wrote much of his best work there and loved the place, but outsiders sometimes found it disheartening. Saxe Commins, who came to Oxford in 1952 to nurse Faulkner through an alcoholic episode, set down his reaction to Rowan Oak in a letter to his wife: "It is a rambling Southern mansion, deteriorated like its owner, built in 1838 and not much improved since. The rooms are bare and what they do contain is rickety, tasteless, ordinary. There is none of the charm and orderliness and comfort that you give to a home."

Faulkner prepared to leave Rowan Oak and move permanently to Virginia in the spring of 1962, but he lapsed into his final illness there in early July.

The house today is a Faulkner museum.

Pathway in Bailey's Woods, over 30 acres of land that Faulkner owned adjacent to Rowan Oak. *(Harriett and Gioia Fargnoli)*

Royal Air Force (RAF)   The air service of the British military, known as the Royal Flying Corps before April 1, 1918. William Cuthbert Falkner enlisted in the RAF, then in process of training squadrons in Canada, in New York City in June 1918, signing on as a cadet with a fictitious English background and using the name *Faulkner*.

He reported to the RAF depot in Toronto in July and trained for five months, until the armistice of November 11, 1918, brought his military career to a close. Though Faulkner never managed a training flight, he subsequently embroidered his record, first claiming to have graduated as a solo pilot and later promoting himself to wounded war hero with a steel plate in his head.

Russell, Bertrand (1872–1970)   English mathematician and philosopher, the third earl Russell.

Known particularly for his work in mathematical logic, he also wrote widely on education, economics, and politics. His major works include *The Analysis of Mind* (1921) and *Human Knowledge: Its Scope and Limits* (1948).

Russell and Faulkner briefly shared a publisher—BONI & LIVERIGHT, which brought out Faulkner's first novel. As the winner of the 1950 NOBEL PRIZE IN LITERATURE, Russell sat next to Faulkner at the ceremony in Stockholm honoring the American novelist as the winner of the 1949 prize. Russell later reported that Faulkner seemed reserved and shy.

Russell, Lee M. (1875–1943)   A Mississippi lawyer and politician, born in Dallas, LAFAYETTE COUNTY, into the poor farmer class, he obtained an education by dint of hard work and earned a law degree from the UNIVERSITY OF MISSISSIPPI, although his social status barred him from membership in a university fraternity.

J. W. T. FALKNER, Faulkner's grandfather, took Russell into his firm as a junior partner in 1903 and he prospered there. He also built connections among the small farmer class that helped him with election successively to the state legislature and state senate. In 1914, Mississippi voters elected him lieutenant governor.

On the tide of the populist political surge known as the redneck revolt, Russell went on to win election as governor in 1919. One of his initiatives as governor involved the shutting down of fraternities and social clubs at Ole Miss.

S

Samson's Bridge   Fictional place, spanning a major river (either the TALLAHATCHIE or the YOCONA) in YOKNAPATAWPHA COUNTY.

In LIGHT IN AUGUST, someone at Samson's tells Lena Grove that she will find Lucas Burch at a planing mill in JEFFERSON, MISSISSIPPI. Floods have washed the bridge away in AS I LAY DYING. It is also referred to in the short story "SPOTTED HORSES."

Sardis Lake   Twenty-mile-long reservoir in Panola County and LAFAYETTE COUNTY in northern Mississippi, northwest of OXFORD, MISSISSIPPI, formed by the damming of the TALLAHATCHIE RIVER. Faulkner liked to camp, fish, and hunt along its shores.

In the late 1940s, he used to cruise the lake aboard the houseboat *Minmagary,* which he and several friends built. Through trial and error in his sloop-rigged dory *Ring Dove* during the summer of 1949, Faulkner became a skilled freshwater sailor.

Sartoris   Fictional place in YOKNAPATAWPHA COUNTY. Four miles north of JEFFERSON, MISSISSIPPI, Sartoris is the plantation home of John Sartoris. Yankee troops searching for Colonel Sartoris, a Confederate cavalry raider, burned the house in 1863. Sartoris's son Bayard Sartoris (*see* SARTORIS and *The* UNVANQUISHED) witnessed the episode with his grandmother, Rosa Millard. Colonel Sartoris rebuilt on the ruins of the old place after the war. By the 1920s Bayard, now an old man, is farming the place on shares.

Sartoris Station   Fictional name of College Hill Station, a flag stop on the railroad four miles north of OXFORD, MISSISSIPPI. Lying two and a half miles from SEMINARY HILL (Faulkner's name for College Hill), Sartoris Station figures in *The* TOWN, the second novel in the SNOPES TRILOGY.

Saturday Evening Post   Weekly magazine, established in 1821 to provide light weekend reading for Philadelphians. In 1897, a new owner converted the *Post* into a middlebrow national publication and eventually built circulation to 3 million. The old magazine failed in 1969 and reappeared two years later as a quarterly.

Faulkner began submitting work to the *Post* in the mid-1920s; the *Post* routinely returned it. He made his first sale to the magazine in 1930 with the short story "THRIFT," published on September 6 of that year. The *Post* paid $750 for its second Faulkner story, "RED LEAVES," which appeared October 25, 1930. From then on Faulkner found the magazine a generally steady, always lucrative outlet for his short fiction. The *Post* offered $900 for "A BEAR HUNT" and published the story on February 10, 1934.

The magazine sometimes exasperated Faulkner, and he rather illogically resented it for tempting him to write lesser work for money. In negotiations over one set of stories, he wrote his sometime agent MORTON GOLDMAN that he didn't care who bought "trash" as long as he received the best possible price for it (*Selected Letters,* 84).

Faulkner sold several of the stories that became the novel *The* UNVANQUISHED to the *Post* in 1934 and 1936. The magazine published a version of the novella "The BEAR" on May 9, 1942.

In 1957, Faulkner's agent HAROLD OBER sold the last chapter of *The* TOWN, the third novel in the SNOPES TRILOGY, to the *Post*. It appeared as "The Waifs" on May 4.

Scribner's Magazine Distinguished American literary monthly magazine, a sometime publisher (after many rejections) of Faulkner's fiction. The younger Charles Scribner (1854–1930) established the magazine in 1887 after his father sold *Scribner's Monthly*. Contributors included Robert Louis Stevenson, Henry James, Rudyard Kipling, Edith Wharton, and Stephen Crane.

In the 1920s, *Scribner's* became the first literary magazine to publish the work of ERNEST HEMINGWAY and Thomas Wolfe. The editors rejected several Faulkner stories in the late 1920s. On one rejection, editor Alfred Dashiell wrote that in "ONCE ABOARD THE LUGGER" Faulkner supplied too much atmosphere and not enough story. "It would seem that in the attempt to avoid the obvious you have manufactured the vague," Dashiell commented.

Faulkner continued to submit pieces to Dashiell, and the author's persistence paid off. *Scribner's* accepted "DRY SEPTEMBER" in May 1930, paying $200 for it; the short story appeared in January 1931. The magazine also published "SPOTTED HORSES" (1931), "MULE IN THE YARD" (1934), "SKIRMISH AT SARTORIS" (1935), and other stories.

Scribner's ceased publication in 1939.

Seminary Hill Faulkner's name for the hamlet of College Hill, a once exclusively Presbyterian settlement five miles north of OXFORD, MISSISSIPPI. Faulkner peoples Seminary Hill with Baptists and Methodists.

In *The* TOWN, the second novel in the SNOPES TRILOGY, Gavin Stevens drives out to Seminary Hill to Mr. Garraway's store to eat cheese and crackers and listen to old Garraway abuse Calvin Coolidge.

Sewanee Review Literary quarterly, the oldest journal of its kind in the United States. Founded in 1892 and published by the University of the South in Sewanee, Tennessee, the review's chief aim is to interpret the role of the South in American culture.

The third installment of the critic MALCOLM COWLEY's important essay on Faulkner's fiction, "William Faulkner's Human Comedy," appeared in the *Sewanee Review* in the summer of 1945. The essay helped achieved Cowley's object, as he explained it, of righting "the balance between [Faulkner's] worth and his reputation."

Faulkner in 1948 sold the oft-rejected short story "A COURTSHIP," written in 1942, to the Tennessee quarterly for $200. He instructed the editors to change a character's name from Callicoat to Hogganbeck to be consistent with what Faulkner called his "Yoknapatawpha genealogy."

"A Courtship" won a 1949 O. Henry Memorial Award, given annually to the best short stories published in magazines.

Sherman, William Tecumseh (1820–1891) Soldier. With ULYSSES S. GRANT, he was one of the leading Union commanders of the Civil War. He distinguished himself at the BATTLE OF SHILOH (1862) and in the VICKSBURG CAMPAIGN (1863) before succeeding Grant in command in the West. His campaigns in Georgia and the Carolinas in 1864–65 sealed the Confederacy's fate.

Sherman loomed large in Falkner family lore. Colonel WILLIAM C. FALKNER's 2nd Mississippi Regiment captured four cannon from Sherman's command at the FIRST BATTLE OF BULL RUN (Manassas) in 1861. In December 1862, Sherman, with 30,000 men, devastated the northern Mississippi countryside from a base at College Hill near OXFORD, burning gins, mills, barns, and houses, and confiscating or destroying livestock.

In 1864, General ANDREW J. SMITH, with orders from Sherman to pursue the Confederate raider NATHAN BEDFORD FORREST, burned public buildings and homes in RIPLEY and Oxford, including the Ripley residence of Colonel Falkner.

Shiloh, battle of A two-day engagement, April 6 and 7, 1862, near Pittsburgh Landing in southwestern Tennessee, between the Union army of ULYSSES

S. GRANT and Confederate forces under Albert Sidney Johnston and Pierre G. T. Beauregard.

Grant recovered from a surprise Confederate assault on the first day, regrouped overnight, and forced a Confederate withdrawal after hard fighting on the second day of the battle. One of the bloodiest of Civil War encounters, Shiloh claimed more than 23,000 total casualties, including 3,477 Union and Confederate dead.

Some 2,000 Confederate casualties were taken to hospitals in OXFORD, MISSISSIPPI, 80 miles to the southwest; more than a third of the wounded died there and were buried in a cemetery near the UNIVERSITY OF MISSISSIPPI campus.

Faulkner's character Gavin Breckbridge, Drusilla Hawk (Sartoris)'s fiancé in The UNVANQUISHED, was killed at Shiloh. In ABSALOM, ABSALOM!, Charles Bon carries the wounded Henry Sutpen off the Shiloh battlefield. The novelist and historian SHELBY FOOTE escorted Faulkner over the Shiloh ground (as Southerners, Faulkner and Foote would have referred to the battle as Pittsburgh Landing) on April 6, 1952, the 90th anniversary of the battle.

Ship Island, Ripley & Kentucky Railroad   In his first railroad venture, Faulkner's great-grandfather, WILLIAM C. FALKNER, won a legislative charter for the Ripley Railroad Company, a narrow-gauge line connecting RIPLEY, MISSISSIPPI, with Middleton, Tennessee, on the Memphis & Charleston Railroad.

In January 1872, the legislature authorized a change of name to the far grander Ship Island, Ripley & Kentucky. The first train on the Old Colonel's railroad ran in August 1872. The locals dubbed it "the Doodlebug line."

Smith, Andrew J. (1815–1897)   Soldier. One of General WILLIAM T. SHERMAN's subordinate commanders, he led several expeditions into northern Mississippi in 1864 in pursuit of the elusive Confederate cavalry commander NATHAN BEDFORD FORREST.

On August 22, 1864, Smith's command burned the town center and several homes in OXFORD, MISSISSIPPI, including the 20-room mansion of Jacob Thompson, a high Confederate official who

fomented sedition in the United States from his envoy's post in Canada.

According to legend, Judith Shegog of Oxford had fallen in love with one of Smith's young officers. She fell to her death from a second-floor balcony of the Shegog place in an attempt to elope with her Yankee. Faulkner acquired the house in 1930 and renamed it ROWAN OAK. Nearly 70 years after her death, Judith's ghost still supposedly haunted the place.

Smith, Harrison (Hal) (n.a.)   Publisher. Faulkner and Smith met after Faulkner's friend BEN WASSON delivered the manuscript of the rejected FLAGS IN THE DUST to Smith, an editor at HARCOURT, BRACE, in August 1928. Smith liked the novel and persuaded Alfred Harcourt to publish it as SARTORIS (1929).

Hal Smith left Harcourt in 1929 to start his own firm. With the English publisher Jonathan Cape, he formed CAPE & SMITH; he took the manuscript of The SOUND AND THE FURY along with him.

Cape & Smith thus became Faulkner's fourth publisher in four years. The firm soon ran into financial trouble, however, and Smith split with Cape in 1931. ROBERT K. HAAS joined him in 1932 to form SMITH & HAAS.

Partly on account of his own money troubles, Faulkner became disenchanted with Smith & Haas in 1935 and cast about for a new publisher. His opportunity came in January 1936, when RANDOM HOUSE bought Smith & Haas, hiring Smith for a one-year trial period. Smith continued to act as Faulkner's editor on ABSALOM, ABSALOM! Random House published the novel later in 1936.

Smith resigned from Random House, feeling he had been forced out, in January 1937. He remained friends with Faulkner long after his departure from Random House, and Faulkner sometimes joined him on his 38-foot ketch, Cossack II.

As editor of the Saturday Review, Smith in April 1945 published a section of the serial long essay by MALCOLM COWLEY that helped restore Faulkner's literary reputation, which had slumped badly during the war years. In this piece, Cowley judged Faulkner's career "a labor of imagination that has not been equaled in our time."

Smith & Haas   Publishing firm, founded by HAR-RISON SMITH and ROBERT K. HAAS in 1932. Smith split with Jonathan Cape, with whom (under the aegis of CAPE & SMITH) he had published Faulkner's *The SOUND AND THE FURY* in 1929, to establish the partnership with Haas.

The new firm published the novel *LIGHT IN AUGUST* in October 1932, followed by *A GREEN BOUGH,* a collection of 44 of Faulkner's poems (13 of them previously published), in April 1933.

Smith and Haas brought out *DOCTOR MARTINO AND OTHER STORIES* in 1934 and the novel *PYLON* in 1935 before selling the firm to RANDOM HOUSE. Both the principals went on to Random House, with Smith, who remained only a short time before moving on to become editor of the *Saturday Review,* serving as editor of Faulkner's novel *ABSALOM, ABSALOM!* in 1936.

Snopes   The name Faulkner gives to a rapacious group of kinsfolk who encroach upon the FRENCHMAN'S BEND area and the town of JEFFERSON for personal gain. In chapter 2 of *The TOWN,* Gavin Stevens momentarily reflects on their traits: "[T]hey none of them seemed to bear any specific kinship to one another; they were just Snopeses, like colonies of rats or termites are just rats and termites" (40). *See* SNOPESISM.

Snopesism   In reference to the SNOPES TRILOGY—*The HAMLET, The TOWN,* and *The MANSION*—a term designating the disruptive and invasive force embodied in the SNOPES clan. Identified with the predatory activities of the Snopeses, and especially with those of the rapacious Flem Snopes, the clan's ostensive leader, Snopesism is an encroachment upon the innocent and unsuspecting citizens of FRENCHMAN'S BEND and the town of JEFFERSON, MISSISSIPPI. Although the term does not apply to every Snopes (see, for example, Colonel Sartoris Snopes and Eckrum Snopes), the Snopeses tend to be scoundrels of one type or another. Montgomery Ward Snopes parodies himself and his family when he says: "I was probably pretty young, when I realized that I had come from what you might call a family, a clan, a race, maybe even a species, of pure sons of bitches" (*The Mansion,* 87).

Snopesism, however, is not without its opponents. Gavin Stevens, V. K. Ratliff, and Linda Snopes Kohl, in particular, are very much its foes.

Snopes trilogy   The name given, collectively, to three interrelated novels: *The HAMLET* (1940), *The TOWN* (1957), and *The MANSION* (1959). Two years after Faulkner's death on July 6, 1962, RANDOM HOUSE published a three-volume set under the title *Snopes,* as Faulkner had intended. The initial idea behind the trilogy goes back as far as the late 1920s, when Faulkner began *FATHER ABRAHAM.* Although he abandoned this work and turned his attention to writing about the Sartoris family, his interest in the Snopeses never waned. At first, Faulkner worked on related short stories and novel fragments that he would eventually incorporate into the trilogy. In a 1957 interview at the UNIVERSITY OF VIRGINIA shortly before the publication of *The Town,* Faulkner explained that the story behind the trilogy came to him in a flash: "I thought of the whole story at once like a bolt of lightning lights up a landscape and you see everything but it takes time to write it" (*Faulkner in the University,* 90).

With a few flashbacks—for example, the story of Eula Varner's childhood and the account of Jack Houston's life before his short-lived marriage to his childhood sweetheart, Lucy Pate—the Snopes trilogy covers a period of almost 50 years: Flem Snopes's arrival in FRENCHMAN'S BEND in 1902; his manipulation of Will Varner and marriage to Varner's daughter Eula, pregnant by another man; his departure for JEFFERSON, MISSISSIPPI, where he trades on his wife's adulterous relations with Manfred de Spain to promote his ambition to become bank president; and Flem's murder by his kinsman Mink Snopes in 1946. The trilogy's diversity of character, episodes, points of view, and themes are held together by its basic story or subject matter, the rise of SNOPESISM—an invasive and corrupting force in the life of a community. The central character behind the encroachment of the Snopes family is Flem, a quiet, scheming man, ruthless and motivated by greed.

The novels contain episodes both humorous and tragic, sometimes both at once, as in the stories surrounding the innocent Ike Snopes, a 21-year-old idiot. The multiple narrative perspective throughout the three novels adds to their vitality and enhances the individuality of storytelling. At times the fragmented, and perhaps even unreliable (*see* MODERNISM) points of view provide readers with a lively complexion of the society or world in which people live and struggle with one another. Because the novels were written over a 30-year period, discrepancies were bound to occur, and Faulkner himself acknowledged this in a brief comment in *The Mansion*. JAMES B. MERIWETHER, a textual critic, assisted the publisher Random House in correcting some of these discrepancies. For further details, *see Selected Letters of William Faulkner*, 107–108, 197, and James B. Meriwether, "Sartoris and Snopes: An Early Notice," *Library Chronicle of the University of Texas* 7 (summer 1962): 36–39.

Sons of Confederate Veterans

A southern fraternal organization, with many chapters in the former Confederate states, established to keep memories of the Civil War fresh. JOHN WESLEY THOMPSON FALKNER, Faulkner's grandfather, helped organize and served as commander of the northern Mississippi Lamar Camp of the Sons of Confederate Veterans.

The organization remains active and is open to all male descendants of Confederate veterans.

Spratling, William

(1900–1967) Artist, architect, and instructor. Born in Sonyea, New York, and reared in Alabama, a raffish and openly homosexual member of the literary colony in NEW ORLEANS, he befriended Faulkner in 1925, taking him into his apartment in Orleans Alley in the Vieux Carré. Faulkner worked on SOLDIERS' PAY there.

Faulkner and Spratling traveled to Europe together in the summer of 1925, landing at Genoa on August 2. Spratling became involved in a café fight and spent the night in a Genoese jail, an experience Faulkner borrowed for his unfinished novel ELMER and the short story "Divorce in Naples."

Spratling returned to his teaching post at Tulane University in September. On the way home to New Orleans, he called on the publisher HORACE LIVERIGHT; in October he wrote Faulkner with the news that Liveright had agreed to publish *Soldiers' Pay*.

Faulkner moved into Spratling's apartment on St. Peter Street when he returned to New Orleans in December 1925. They collaborated the following year on a book of sketches of Vieux Carré personalities called *Sherwood Anderson and Other Creoles*: Faulkner supplied the text, a parody of SHERWOOD ANDERSON's style. The authors paid a printer to strike off 400 copies, and sold every one at $1.50 each. The parody offended Anderson, however, and contributed to the chill that fell over his relationship with Faulkner.

Spratling taught architecture at Tulane before settling permanently in Taxco, Mexico, where he became a noted jewelry designer. He was killed in an automobile accident in Mexico in August 1967.

Stallings, Lawrence

(1894–1968) Georgia-born author and screenwriter. He served in France with the U.S. Marines in World War I and was seriously wounded (he lost a leg) at Belleau Wood in 1918. His war experiences provided the background for his novel *Plumes* (1924) and for the bitter and highly successful play *What Price Glory?* (1924), written with Maxwell Anderson.

Stallings and Faulkner met in New York, where Stallings was a member of the writers' circle that gathered at the Algonquin Hotel, and in Hollywood. Faulkner credited him with helpful advice about dealing with movie people.

Stein, Jean

(b. c. 1935) A companion and lover of Faulkner's in the mid-1950s, she was a 19-year-old student at the Sorbonne when they met at a party in St. Mortiz, Switzerland, on Christmas Eve 1953. The tall, thin, dark-haired daughter of the founder of the Music Corporation of America, Stein seems to have restored Faulkner's morale, shattered by the end of his affair with JOAN WILLIAMS. The novelist, working in Egypt with HOWARD HAWKS on the movie *Land of the Pharaohs*, saw Stein in Paris and Rome that winter. Despite the 37-year difference in their ages, the affair lasted four years.

Stein kept notes of their conversations and, with Faulkner's help, published them in a famous *PARIS REVIEW* interview in May 1956. She broke off the affair with the aging novelist in 1957. The action devastated Faulkner, touching off a serious drinking bout that landed him in the University of Virginia Medical Center in Charlottesville.

Stone, Philip Avery (1893–1967) ˙ A member of a prominent OXFORD, MISSISSIPPI, law and banking family, Faulkner's friend, mentor and fiercely protective early supporter. He took a bachelor's degree in Latin and Greek from the UNIVERSITY OF MISSISSIPPI and law degrees from Ole Miss and Yale University. He joined his father's law practice, but his first love was literature.

The Falkner and Stone families were acquainted, but Stone and Faulkner did not become close until 1914, when Phil Stone, older by four years and just returned from Yale, read some of Faulkner's early poetry. He encouraged Faulkner, talked to him in great detail about literature's aims and methods, introduced him to the work of Yeats, Eliot and Pound, and loaned him books. Stone offered the apprentice artist a kind of conversation hard to find elsewhere in Oxford.

The relationship waxed in 1914–16, formative years for Faulkner. Stone filled Faulkner with anecdotes about LAFAYETTE COUNTY hill people and with lore about hunting. At age 12, Stone had killed a bear at his father's camp in the MISSISSIPPI DELTA wilderness; Faulkner would rework Stone's experience in the novella "The BEAR." Faulkner drew one of the themes of "The Bear," the timber companies' gradual destruction of the wilderness, from Stone's father's selling off portions of his hunting reserve to the clear-cutters.

Stone's uncles Theophilus and Amodeus Potts gave their first names and something of their experiences to the McCaslin twins, Theophilus and Amodeus McCaslin, respectively nicknamed Uncle Buck and Uncle Buddy, in GO DOWN, MOSES. Something of Stone himself went into the character of Gavin Stevens, the JEFFERSON, MISSISSIPPI, lawyer of INTRUDER IN THE DUST. Stone also introduced Faulkner to the gambling, roadhouse, and bordello culture of northern Mississippi and MEMPHIS, Tennessee, raw material the novelist exploited for many works, from SANCTUARY (1931) to The REIVERS (1962). They used to tool around in a convertible Ford Stone dubbed "Drusilla," a

name Faulkner chose for the redoubtable female cavalry trooper in The UNVANQUISHED.

Faulkner joined Stone in New Haven, Connecticut, in the spring of 1918, marking a new phase in his life. With Stone's encouragement and connivance he finagled his enlistment in the ROYAL AIR FORCE as a cadet. When he returned to Mississippi later in 1918, he and Stone were much together. Stone acted as his agent and promoter, having his poems and stories typed at his law office, fixing punctuation, sending manuscripts off to magazines, and negotiating with publishers on Faulkner's behalf.

To give Faulkner an income to support his writing, Stone in late 1921 used his family's influence to help him land him a job as postmaster of the University of Mississippi post office. In 1924, he oversaw the publication of Faulkner's first book, the collection of poems titled The MARBLE FAUN. Stone wrote a preface for the book, arranged for its promotion and sale, and may have paid for part of the $400 printing charge.

"This poet is my personal property," he wrote the Yale *Alumni Weekly*, "and I urge all my friends and classmates to buy the book."

By the late 1920s the relationship had begun to change. Faulkner evidently resented Stone's proprietorial attitude toward his work. A loan of several hundred dollars from Stone may have fueled the resentment. Whatever the cause, Faulkner no longer discussed everything he was working on with Stone, and he began typing out his own fair copies of manuscripts, beginning with SARTORIS (1929).

They drifted further apart during the depression years of the 1930s. Beset with his own problems, Stone no longer seemed interested in Faulkner's literary work. At age 42, he stunned his friends by going off to New Orleans to marry a much younger woman, Emily Whitehurst. When his father's bank failed, Stone took on $50,000 in family debt, vowing to pay it off. Faulkner loaned him $6,000 for this purpose in 1939. Increasingly hard up, Stone never paid the money back—a fresh cause of estrangement between the two old friends. During the 1950s Faulkner's comparatively liberal views on racial matters led to further alienation. Stone became increasingly critical, not to say dismissive, of Faulkner's oeuvre.

Stone claimed to have suggested to Faulkner the theme of the SNOPES TRILOGY, the rise and triumph of the rednecks at the expense of the old planter class. Faulkner dedicated all three of the Snopes novels—The HAMLET, The TOWN, and The MANSION—"To Phil Stone."

stream of consciousness A phrase that describes the fluency of conscious thoughts, perceptions, and sensations. It was first used by William James in *Principles of Psychology* (1890) and subsequently employed by writers and critics to describe a literary technique that expresses either the manner in which a character's thoughts are (directly or indirectly) represented to the reader or, less frequently, the manner an author uses to write a specific passage. Similar to but not identical with the INTERIOR MONOLOGUE, the stream-of-consciousness technique differs in that it normally adheres to syntactical and grammatical rules, whereas the interior monologue tends to disregard them. Faulkner is one of several writers associated with the stream-of-consciousness technique (and with the interior monologue); other celebrated writers include Henry James, JAMES JOYCE, and Virginia Woolf.

Stuart, James Ewell Brown (Jeb) (1833–1864) Virginia-born Confederate soldier. A flamboyant, gaudily attired cavalier, Robert E. Lee's "eyes of the army," he carried out a series of famous cavalry operations, including an 1862 ride around the Union army, that were sometimes more spectacular than productive. He was killed in action at Yellow Tavern in Virginia on May 11, 1864.

Bayard Sartoris of Faulkner's fictional clan rides with General Stuart in SARTORIS. Sartoris's foolhardy behavior leads to his death: On a raid with Stuart, he rides into the Yankee General Pope's camp in search of anchovies and is shot for his trouble.

Summers, Paul D. Jr. Faulkner's son-in-law. A 1951 West Point graduate from a well-to-do background and a veteran of the Korean War, he met JILL FAULKNER at a wedding at Fort Leavenworth in early 1954.

They were married in St. Peter's Episcopal Church in OXFORD, MISSISSIPPI, in August 1954, with dinner at ROWAN OAK, the Faulkner home. Summers left the army for law school at the UNIVERSITY OF VIRGINIA and set up a practice in Charlottesville in 1957. He and Jill named the second of their three sons, William Cuthbert Faulkner Summers, for her father.

Sutpen's Hundred Fictional place in ABSALOM, ABSALOM!, Sutpen's Hundred is Thomas Sutpen's plantation in YOKNAPATAWPHA COUNTY, 12 miles northwest of JEFFERSON, MISSISSIPPI. Sutpen acquired the land from the CHICKASAW INDIANS in 1833, tore a plantation out of the wilderness and, with the unwilling assistance of a French architect, built an enormous house.

The mansion falls into disrepair after the Civil War. When Miss Rosa Coldfield takes Quentin Compson to Sutpen's Hundred in September 1910, the roofline sags, the chimneys are half-toppled, and the steps are rotting away. In December 1910, Clytemnestra Sutpen, Sutpen's daughter by a slave woman, sets fire to the rotted shell, destroying Thomas Sutpen's creation utterly.

T

Tallahatchie River   The stream rises in southern Tippah County in northern Mississippi and flows 230 miles south and southwest, joining the Yalobusha to form the Yazoo River. The dark, slow-moving Tallahatchie forms all but a few miles of the northern border of LAFAYETTE COUNTY.

The Faulkners and other families cooperatively shared a resort dubbed the "Club House," a large two-story cabin in the bottomlands where the Tippah River flows into the larger Tallahatchie. Faulkner used to hunt and fish there as a boy.

On Faulkner's hand-drawn map of his fictional Mississippi geography (see ABSALOM, ABSALOM!), the Tallahatchie forms the northern boundary of YOKNAPATAWPHA COUNTY. The BIG BOTTOM, the wilderness site of Major de Spain's hunting camp in GO DOWN, MOSES and The TOWN, is in the Tallahatchie region.

Thurmond, Richard J.   Business partner of Faulkner's great-grandfather, WILLIAM C. FALKNER. Thurmond and the Old Colonel quarreled over management and ownership of railroads, and their collaboration broke up in enmity.

Falkner accused Thurmond of cheating him in various business deals; Thurmond hated the noisy and violent Old Colonel. On election day 1889, Thurmond approached him on the square in RIPLEY, MISSISSIPPI, aimed a .44 caliber pistol at his head, and fired. Falkner died the next night. A jury acquitted Thurmond in February 1890.

Thurmond appears as Redlaw in SARTORIS and as Ben Redmond in The UNVANQUISHED. Faulkner fictionalizes the killing of the Old Colonel in both novels. In The Unvanquished, young Bayard Sartoris agonizes over whether he should exact revenge for his father's death at Redmond's hands and finally confronts Redmond in his JEFFERSON, MISSISSIPPI, law office. Redmond fires twice at young Bayard, aiming to miss, then leaves Jefferson forever.

Till, Emmett (1941–1955)   In August 1955, whites accused this 14-year-old black youth from Chicago, who was visiting relatives in Greenwood, Mississippi, of whistling at a white woman and making an obscene remark to her. The boy disappeared on August 24; his body was found in the TALLAHATCHIE RIVER three days later. The woman's husband and brother-in-law were charged with Till's kidnapping and murder.

Faulkner read reports of the lynching while in Rome and immediately issued a statement condemning it. Mississippi juries acquitted the two whites accused of Till's murder. Faulkner called the verdict "a sorry and tragic error," and added in a statement: "If we in America have reached that point in our desperate culture when we must murder children, no matter for what reason or what color, we don't deserve to survive, and probably won't."

Faulkner later revised his attitude on the Till case, another example of his sometimes contradictory public pronouncements on racial issues.

In a 1956 radio interview, he said, "The Till boy got himself into a fix, and he almost got what he deserved. But even so you don't murder a child."

time, Faulkner and   One of the first impressions readers may have when encountering Faulkner is wonderment at his intricate use of time. In the plots, in the lives of characters, and in the stylistic devices of the narratives—especially the device of the INTERIOR MONOLOGUE—time is a formidable presence. Time is not a static dimension disassociated from the world of Faulkner's fiction. It plays a significant role in the depiction of characters seen within a context larger than that of individual experience, a context that often includes the effects of the past and of historical reminiscences. Faulkner's notion of time is also a part of the dynamic of his storytelling. It integrates different time periods in his narrative, a stylistic device indentifiably Faulknerian. Time in Faulkner is not merely chronological; it is more akin to the Greek notion of *kairos* (time as memorable event) than *chronos* (time that can be measured). History and the remembrance of the past, both immediate and distant, can be a formidable force in the present. If Faulkner's sense of time poses difficulties for the reader by demanding special attentiveness, it also engages the reader in the dynamics of storytelling.

On a few occasions, Faulkner commented on his understanding of time. In one interview, he stated, "I agree pretty much with [the French philosopher Henri] Bergson's theory of the fluidity of time. There is only the present moment, in which I include both the past and the future, and that is eternity. In my opinion time can be shaped quite a bit by the artist; after all, man is never time's slave" (*Lion in the Garden: Interviews with William Faulkner, 1926–1962*, edited by James B. Meriwether and Michael Millgate, 70). In another interview recorded by Meriwether and Millgate, Faulkner said that "time is a fluid condition which has no existence except in the momentary avatars of individual people. There is no such thing as *was*—only *is*" (255). In his chapter titled "Faulkner on Time and History" in *William Faulkner: Toward Yoknapatawpha and Beyond*, CLEANTH BROOKS

examines these passages and Bergson's possible influence on Faulkner and concludes that for the novelist "time does not exist apart from the consciousness of some human being. Apart from that stream of living consciousness, time is merely an abstraction. Thus, *as actually experienced,* time has little to do with the time that is measured off with the ticking of the chronometer. . . . Though clock time, as an abstraction, might be deemed to be in some sense unreal, Faulkner, like Bergson himself, conceded that clock-and-calendar time had its uses and that no human life of the slightest complexity could get along without constant reference to it" (254). If time in Faulkner's narratives jumps from one tense to another, it does so to underline an aesthetic or artistic claim. The integrity or wholeness of art is not constrained by the dimension of time. In this respect, in the act of reading itself, time is momentarily suspended and subordinate to art.

The French philosopher and writer Jean-Paul Sartre also discusses Faulkner's concept of time. When in *Literary and Philosophical Essays* Sartre observes that it becomes "immediately obvious that Faulkner's metaphysics is a metaphysics of time" and that humanity's misfortune lies in "being time-bound" (85), he quotes a statement that Quentin Compson, on the day of his suicide in *The SOUND AND THE FURY*, remembers his father saying "a man is the sum of his misfortunes. One day you'd think misfortune would get tired, but then time is your misfortune" (104). Sartre considers time the real subject of the novel. In fact, time is the key to understanding many of Faulkner's characters and themes. The thoughts of Quentin's idiot brother Benjy (*see* Compson, Benjamin in character entries under *The Sound and the Fury*) while apparently free from the rational burden of time, are bound to sensations and perceptions of the present. The fluidity of time runs through one's consciousness; thus, as in the case of Benjy the past (or the future) can become the present. This sentiment is not dissimilar to what Gavin Stevens says in *REQUIEM FOR A NUN:* "The past is never dead. It's not even past" (80).

The Bundrens in *As I LAY DYING* take a different tack. Hearkening back to a promise he made to his wife, Addie, Anse Bundren is determined to take her body to JEFFERSON, MISSISSIPPI, for interment with her family. Through their actions in delaying Addie's burial for 10 hot summer days after her death, the Bundrens are, in effect, denying the effects of the passage of time. Dewey Dell's progressing pregnancy and Addie's putrefaction, of course, counter the stoppage of time. Anse's unseemly remarriage on the same day as Addie's burial again is a denial of time, as he leapfrogs the traditional mourning period.

Clock time, however, also has its place in Faulkner's works and in the lives of his characters. He carefully crafted the time schemes of his fiction, though not in a way as apparent as in the works of someone like JAMES JOYCE. References to particular days, years, and seasons are found throughout Faulkner's works and give the reader the necessary time-markers to understand a work's chronology. For characters such as Henry Sutpen in ABSALOM, ABSALOM!, Mink Snopes in The MANSION, and even for Dal Martin in the short story "The BIG SHOT," chronological time is very much a part of their consciousnesses as something to be endured in order to execute their designs. In this respect, the characters transcend the limits of time through sheer determination.

Finally, Faulkner puts historical time to work in his novels. In the introduction to his study of the uses of the past in Faulkner's novels, Carl Rollyson comments, "Faulkner's novels are historical in the sense that their concern is frequently with characters who are obsessed with a personal, family, or regional past" (*Uses of the Past in the Novels of William Faulkner*, 1). The Yoknapatawpha novels especially create an informal history of this fictional region of northern Mississippi, weaving actual events and people into the lives of Faulkner's characters. In *Requiem for a Nun*, however, Faulkner employs history as a symbolic underpinning to events in the present. He uses what has happened over the passage of years in social and political spheres to illuminate what is happening in the moral realm of the novel. In several ways, then, this novel brings together Faulkner's stylistic experimentation with his philosophical understanding of time to pin his characters into their fates. To Faulkner, "no man is himself, he is the sum of his past. There is no such thing really as was because the past is. It is a part of every man, every woman, and every moment" (*Faulkner in the University*, 84).

U

United Daughters of the Confederacy An organization, still existant, of southern women formed to nurture memories of the Civil War. Local chapters sponsored aid programs for ex-soldiers and widows, arranged celebrations of Confederate heroes, and campaigned for memorial monuments.

Faulkner's grandmother, SALLIE MURRY FALKNER, served a term as president of the Albert Sidney Johnston Chapter. She quit the UDC in 1910 in a disagreement over the placement of the OXFORD, MISSISSIPPI, Confederate monument. Miss Sallie favored the Courthouse Square; the committee opted for a site on the UNIVERSITY OF MISSISSIPPI campus.

University Greys A volunteer infantry company composed of students of the UNIVERSITY OF MISSISSIPPI, formed at the outset of the Civil War in 1861. In ABSALOM, ABSALOM!, Henry Sutpen and Charles Bon join the Greys after the FIRST BATTLE OF BULL RUN.

The Confederate diehards of OXFORD, MISSISSIPPI, later boasted that the University Greys reached the high point of the Confederacy, about 50 yards beyond the advance of any other of GENERAL GEORGE C. PICKETT's troops at Gettysburg on July 3, 1863.

University of Mississippi A state university, founded in OXFORD, MISSISSIPPI, in 1848, known as Ole Miss, and a center of Faulkner scholarship. Falkners attended Ole Miss beginning with Faulkner's grandfather, J. W. T. FALKNER. ESTELLE OLDHAM (FAULKNER), the novelist's future wife,

enrolled as a special student in 1915, and Faulkner attended classes sporadically in 1919–20.

Faulkner's father, MURRY C. FALKNER, an Ole Miss dropout, became university secretary and business manager in December 1918. Faulkner's first published works—two drawings—appeared in the Ole Miss yearbook around that time. Faulkner himself enrolled as a nondegree student in English and foreign languages at age 22. There he acquired his Oxford nickname "Count No 'count," a reference to his notorious dandyism.

Faulkner's short story "Landing in Luck," about an air cadet's first solo flight, appeared in the student newspaper, The MISSISSIPPIAN, in November 1919, and he published critical articles there. But the university refused a copy of his first novel, SOLDIERS' PAY, in 1926.

Though Faulkner dropped out of Ole Miss for good in November 1920, his connection with the university did not cease. In the late 1920s, he worked the night shift in the university's power plant and wrote most of AS I LAY DYING (1930) on the job. In the late 1920s, the university named a new dormitory Falkner Hall, after Faulkner's grandfather.

Faulkner reluctantly agreed in the spring of 1947 to address English classes at Ole Miss. On a promise that no faculty would be present and no notes would be taken, he spoke to six classes in April, talking about his writing and his contemporaries' achievement. In one session, he rated the leading writers of his generation, placing ERNEST HEMINGWAY near the bottom of the list of five or six for an

Faulkner conducted a series of question-and-answer sessions at the University of Virginia, later collected in *Faulkner in the University*. *(William Faulkner Collection, Special Collections Department, Manuscripts Division, University of Virginia Library. Photo by Ralph Thompson.)*

alleged lack of artistic courage. Faulkner's musings became public, deeply wounding Hemingway when they reached him.

Racial conflict convulsed Ole Miss during the Civil Rights era. Serious rioting erupted there in the autumn of 1962 when James Meredith, an African American, attempted to enroll. Two people were killed and more than 300 injured, and university buildings were damaged when white opponents of integration went on a rampage.

The university today maintains an important collection of Faulkner manuscripts and other material, and for more than a quarter century has been the site of an ANNUAL FAULKNER AND YOKNAPATAWPHA CONFERENCE. It owns and maintains ROWAN OAK.

University of Texas   A major research university in Austin, Texas. The university library built up a collection of Faulkner material in the 1950s at the instigation of JAMES MERIWETHER, a faculty member and leading Faulkner textual scholar.

Faulkner made it clear, however, that he did not want his manuscripts to go to Texas, preferring HARVARD UNIVERSITY—as the country's oldest and most prestigious university—instead. Texas also houses the papers of CARVEL COLLINS, one of the first Faulkner scholars, along with some of JOSEPH BLOTNER and JAMES MERIWETHER.

University of Virginia   A state university and a major research center in Charlottesville, founded by Thomas Jefferson and others in 1825. Faulkner was writer in residence there in 1957–58, and the university maintains an important Faulkner archive.

Faulkner got his first view of the university in October 1931 at a southern writers' conference, where he was treated as a major figure on the strength of *The SOUND AND THE FURY* (1929) and *SANCTUARY* (1931). Always ill at ease in such gatherings, he drank heavily through this one before his publisher, HARRISON SMITH, could spirit him away to New York.

The university offered Faulkner the writer in residence post in 1956 with a salary of $2,500. He accepted at once, in part because his daughter, JILL FAULKNER, her husband, and their first child were established in Charlottesville. He arrived to take up his duties in February 1957.

Faulkner met with graduate and undergraduate classes, mostly in question-and-answer sessions. Asked at one session to describe his aims, he replied: "A writer wants to make something that he knows that a hundred or two hundred or five hundred, a thousand years later will make people feel what they feel when they read Homer, or read Dickens or Balzac, Tolstoy" (*Faulkner in the University*, 61).

Two University of Virginia faculty members, Frederick L. Gwynn and JOSEPH BLOTNER, recorded many of the sessions. Their edited transcripts were published as *Faulkner in the University* in 1959.

V

Vardaman, James K. (1861–1930) Lawyer, newspaper editor, and politician. He led the "revolt of the rednecks" against Mississippi's planter-dominated Democratic Party machine during the first decade of the 20th century.

A flamboyant demagogue, Vardaman sprang from the small-farmer class of the Mississippi hill country. He had reforming instincts as governor from 1904 to 1908, but the reforms he supported were for whites only. He opposed even rudimentary state aid for black schools, saying education would "spoil a good field hand and make an insolent cook." He closed down the state's teacher training school for blacks, literally padlocking the doors.

An observer said of Vardaman, "He stood for the poor white against the 'nigger'—those were his qualifications as a statesman."

J. W. T. FALKNER Jr., Faulkner's paternal grandfather, supported Vardaman. Falkner headed OXFORD, MISSISSIPPI's, Vardaman Club and campaigned for him during his successful run for the U.S. Senate, where he served from 1913 to 1919. A Vardaman Bundren appears in AS I LAY DYING, and the novelist names one of the extensive poor white Gowrie clan of INTRUDER IN THE DUST after the Mississippi politician.

Varner's Store Fictional place, in southern YOKNAPATAWPHA COUNTY near FRENCHMAN'S BEND, 12 miles from JEFFERSON, MISSISSIPPI. In *The HAMLET* its "heel-gnawed porch" is a gathering place for local men with time on their hands.

In *LIGHT IN AUGUST*, storekeeper Jody Varner sells Lena Grove crackers, cheese, and a 15-cent box of "sour-deans" (sardines), and she catches a ride into Jefferson from the store. In Faulkner's hand-drawn map of Yoknapatawpha County in *ABSALOM, ABSALOM!*, Varner's Store is identified as the place "where Flem Snopes got his start."

Vickery, Olga W. (1925–1970) Polish-born American professor and critic. Vickery taught literature at several colleges and universities, including Mount Holyoke, Lake Forest, Purdue, and the University of Southern California. She received her doctorate from the University of Wisconsin in 1953.

Among her better known contributions to Faulkner studies are her article on *AS I LAY DYING* in *Perspective* (1950); *The Novels of William Faulkner* (1959; 3rd ed. 1995), based on her doctoral dissertation; and *William Faulkner: Three Decades of Criticism* (edited with Frederick J. Hoffman, 1960). *The Novels of William Faulkner* is an insightful and worthwhile study that preceded critical works by CLEANTH BROOKS (*William Faulkner: The Yoknapatawpha Country*, 1963), Melvin Backman (*Faulkner: The Major Years*, 1966), and MICHAEL MILLGATE (*The Achievement of William Faulkner*, 1966).

Vicksburg campaign Union General Ulysses S. Grant carried out operations against this strategic Mississippi River fortress from October 1862 to July 1863. A series of battles and a six-week siege ended in the Confederate surrender of the city and fortress on July 4, 1863.

One of the decisive Union victories of the war, the Vicksburg campaign forms a backdrop to part of Faulkner's Civil War novel The UNVANQUISHED. The two young protagonists, Bayard Sartoris and Ringo Strother, execute their own military operations on a "living map" behind the smokehouse at Sartoris, the family plantation.

Viking Press   Publishing firm, founded in 1925 by Harold Guinzburg and George Oppenheimer. In 1945, Viking contracted with MALCOLM COWLEY to edit a collection of Faulkner's fiction for the Viking Portable Library series. At the time, all of Faulkner's books except SANCTUARY were out of print, and Cowley suggested to the author that this project would be "a bayonet prick in the ass of Random House to reprint the others."

Cowley and Faulkner worked closely on the anthology. Viking published The PORTABLE FAULKNER in 1946 with an introduction by Cowley.

Faulkner professed to be delighted with the outcome. "The job is splendid," he wrote Cowley in April 1946. "Damn you to hell anyway. By God, I didn't know myself what I had tried to do, and how much I succeeded" (The Faulkner-Cowley File, 90–91).

W

Warner, Jack (1892–1978) Born in London, Ontario, Canada, the son of Polish immigrants named Eichelbaum, he and his three brothers built one of Hollywood's great movie empires after introducing sound to film with *The Jazz Singer* in 1927.

Faulkner went to work as a $300 a week contract scriptwriter for Warner Brothers in 1942. By then Jack handled the studio's "talent"—actors, directors, writers. There was mutual antipathy. "A lot of him wasn't that nice to know," Jack Warner Jr. said of Warner. "At times he gloried in being a no-good sonofabitch." The talent detested the bullying Warner; he expressed his own views in a famous slur on writers. "You're all schmucks with Underwoods," he once said. (Underwood was a well-known brand of typewriter.) Faulkner's relations with Warner were difficult, and the studio head repeatedly denied his request for release from his contract in the later 1940s.

Warner Brothers (Warner Bros.) Hollywood movie studio, established in 1919 by Harry, Albert, Samuel, and JACK WARNER. The company emerged as a major studio with the release of the first feature movie with sound, *The Jazz Singer,* in 1927. All the same, Warner Brothers prided itself not on innovation but instead on turning out a steady stream of moderately budgeted, profitable movies.

Faulkner had a miserable career as a screenwriter for Warner Brothers in the 1940s. He blundered into an ironclad seven-year contract in 1942 for a pedestrian $300 a week at a time when top Hollywood writers were pulling down weekly wages of $2,500. Jack Warner reputedly boasted that he kept America's best writer on his payroll for $300 a week.

Faulkner worked on a succession of forgettable production-line films until his director friend HOWARD HAWKS rescued him to work on the war movie *Battle Cry* (later canceled) and the adaptation of ERNEST HEMINGWAY's novel *To Have and Have Not,* starring HUMPHREY BOGART and Lauren Bacall. He also worked on the Bogart film *The Big Sleep,* an adaptation of Raymond Chandler's novel of the same title.

Warner routinely denied Faulkner's request to be let out of his long contract. Faulkner resisted passively, taking extended leaves from the studio. In November 1953, Hawks asked him to write the screenplay for *Land of the Pharaohs.* Faulkner agreed, but only to oblige Hawks. It was his last work for Warner Brothers.

Warren, Robert Penn (1905–1989) A Kentucky-born poet, novelist, and critic, he was associated with Allen Tate and other writers steeped in the issues and traditions of the South. A founder and editor of the *Southern Review* (1935–42), Warren taught at Yale (1961–73) and in 1986 became the first official poet laureate of the United States.

Warren's best-known work is the novel *All the King's Men* (1946), based on the career of the populist Louisiana politician Huey Long. In May 1946 HARCOURT, BRACE & COMPANY sent an advance copy of the novel to Faulkner, hoping for a comment suitable for the jacket blurb. Faulkner responded that he was not greatly impressed, although he found a relatively short historical sequence involving an ancestor of the narrator "beautiful and moving" (*Selected Letters*, 239). He went on to say that Willie Stark, the main character in Warren's novel, left him cold. "I didn't mind neither loving him nor hating him," he wrote, "but I did object to not being moved to pity. . . . He was neither big enough nor bad enough."

Warren held Faulkner in high but not uncritical regard. "For range of effect, philosophical weight, originality of style, variety of characterization, humor and tragic intensity [Faulkner's works] are without equal in our time and country," he wrote. But he went on to assert that there are "grave defects" in Faulkner's fiction (Warren, *New and Selected Essays*, 197).

Warwick Plantation of Hubert Beauchamp in GO DOWN, MOSES. Miss Sophonsiba Beauchamp, Beauchamp's spinster sister, rather pretentiously named the place after the English great house. Not everyone humored her whim.

Wasson, Ben (n.a.) Faulkner's friend and sometime agent and editor, born in Greenville, Mississippi. They met in OXFORD, MISSISSIPPI, where Wasson studied law at the UNIVERSITY OF MISSISSIPPI. At their first meeting, Wasson recalled, Faulkner recited the poet A. E. HOUSMAN. "I had never known anyone who loved poetry enough to be so bold as to quote it," he said. Later, Wasson sold handbound copies of The MARIONETTES, young Faulkner's poetic drama, for $5 apiece.

Wasson moved to New York City and entered the publishing world, taking a job at the American Play Company, a literary agency that specialized in dramatists. In 1928, he placed FLAGS IN THE DUST with HARCOURT, BRACE & COMPANY, negotiating a $300 advance for Faulkner. With Wasson's extensive cuts, the novel was published as SARTORIS in 1929.

Wasson joined the firm of CAPE & SMITH in 1929 and became Faulkner's editor on The SOUND AND THE FURY. He helped the novelist land a screenwriting job with MGM in Hollywood in 1932.

Faulkner and Wasson saw each other frequently in Hollywood. The novelist arranged a bizarre episode in which Wasson escorted Faulkner's mistress, META CARPENTER, to dinner with Faulkner and his wife, Estelle. Faulkner pretended that Meta was Wasson's girlfriend, and his wife went along with the charade, but she later expressed her anger at Wasson.

Faulkner inexplicably cut Wasson in an encounter at RANDOM HOUSE in New York one day in 1957, abruptly ending 40 years of friendship. Wasson never learned why Faulkner had snubbed him, and they never saw each other again.

Webb, James (n.a.) Chairman of the English department at the UNIVERSITY OF MISSISSIPPI, he persuaded the notoriously image-shy Faulkner to have his portrait painted in March 1962. The portrait would augment the expanding Faulkner collection at the university.

Faulkner agreed to sit for a series of photographs from which artist Murray Goldsborough would paint the portrait. Faulkner posed in a tweed jacket with a pipe. He admitted to Webb later that he liked Goldsborough's work.

Whiteleaf Bridge Fictional place in southeastern YOKNAPATAWPHA COUNTY. It carries the road to FRENCHMAN'S BEND across fictional Whiteleaf Creek. The bridge figures in The HAMLET and INTRUDER IN THE DUST.

Wilkins, Mary Holland Falkner (1872–1946) Faulkner's aunt, the second child of JOHN WESLEY THOMPSON FALKNER and SALLIE MURRY FALKNER, known to the family as Huldy and to the novelist and his brothers as Auntee.

She introduced her brother MURRY FALKNER to his future wife, MAUD BUTLER (FALKNER), and Huldy and Miss Maud remained close friends all their lives. She married James Porter Wilkins, a physician, in 1898, and they settled in OXFORD, MISSISSIPPI. Their daughter Sallie Murry, a childhood playmate of the Falkner boys, was born in 1899.

Widowed in the early years of the new century, she took over the management of her parents' house, the Big Place, as her mother began to fail in health. Auntee often entertained the Falkner boys there. She took them all to the university observatory in 1910 to observe the transit of Halley's Comet.

In their later years, she and Faulkner's mother went to the movies together nearly every night, taking in the pictures at the Ritz and the Lyric on alternate evenings.

Brisk, outspoken, an accomplished horsewoman, and intensely family-proud, Auntee was a partial model for Granny Rosa Millard in The UNVAN-QUISHED and for Aunt Jenny Du Pre in SARTORIS and The Unvanquished.

Williams, Joan (1928–2004) In August 1949, Joan Williams turned up uninvited at ROWAN OAK for a glimpse of Faulkner, by then a famous author. A student at Bard College in New York, she was interested in Faulkner's work and wanted to become a writer herself.

Joan Williams was 20; Faulkner was 52. They exchanged letters and met surreptitiously in MEMPHIS in January 1950, where Faulkner made it evident he wished her to be his lover. But she wanted a mentor, and she tried to fend him off.

Still, they continued to meet and correspond. Faulkner looked over Joan's short stories and encouraged her ambition. ESTELLE FAULKNER got wind of the relationship, met Joan at the PEABODY HOTEL in Memphis to discourage it, and afterward telephoned Joan's parents to enlist their help in breaking it off. In a hopeless dodge, Faulkner asked her, in future, to write him in care of Quentin Compson, General Delivery, Oxford.

Faulkner and Joan Williams continued to see one another. He gave her the original manuscript of The SOUND AND THE FURY, which she did not keep. He asked his agent, HAROLD OBER, to place her short stories. She finally relented and slept with him, though she wrote later that she never felt comfortable with him as an older man—and married at that.

Joan drifted steadily away from Faulkner and in early 1954 wrote that she intended to marry. They continued to correspond after her marriage to Ezra Bowen, son of the biographer Catherine Drinker Bowen.

Faulkner suggested The Morning and the Evening as the title for her first novel, finally accepted for publication in 1959. She visited Faulkner at Rowan Oak in late June 1962, only 10 days or so before his death.

Williams's second novel, The Wintering, appeared in 1971. It is a fictional account of her involvement with Faulkner, who is called Jeff Almoner in the novel.

Y

Yocona River Rising in western Pontotoc County, it flows westward for 130 miles, draining southern LAFAYETTE COUNTY, before emptying into the TALLAHATCHIE RIVER in Quitman County. As a boy, Faulkner used to hunt in its bottoms.

The Yocona (pronounced Yock-nee) is shown on old maps as the Yocanapatafa. Faulkner used a version of the name for his fictional YOKNAPA-TAWPHA COUNTY. In the second decade of the 20th century, the state established the Yoknapatawpha Drainage District to control flooding in southern Lafayette County.

This historical marker was placed near Faulkner's gravesite by the Oxford Rotary in 1990. *(Harriett and Gioia Fargnoli)*

Yoknapatawpha County Fictional place, Faulkner's "intact world" of north-central Mississippi, corresponding to the actual LAFAYETTE COUNTY, though differing in some details. Yoknapatawpha has given its name to a cycle of interconnected major novels (and some minor works) set there, beginning with SARTORIS (1929) and continuing through The SOUND AND THE FURY (1929), AS I LAY DYING (1930), LIGHT IN AUGUST (1932), ABSALOM, ABSALOM! (1936), The HAMLET (1940), GO DOWN, MOSES (1942), The TOWN (1957), The MANSION (1959), and The REIVERS (1962).

Yoknapatawpha is a self-contained world of rich bottomlands, broad cotton fields, eroded hills, and pine barrens peopled by CHICKASAW INDIANS and African-American slaves, plantation masters, defeated Confederates, indomitable spinsters, and poor, white hill farmers. Charlatans, thieves, and rascals jostle with honest, hard-working folk. In time, the Yoknapatawpha saga spans roughly 170 years, from the establishment of a Chickasaw agency and trading post on the future site of JEFFERSON, MISSISSIPPI, before 1800, to 1961. In content, it deals with the Native American tradition, early exploration and settlement, the rise of the plantation system, the Civil War, the emancipation of slaves and Reconstruction, the decline of the planter aristocracy, and the machine and commercial culture of the modern era—the transformation of the COMPSON MILE of the 1830s into the Eula Acres subdivision of the decade following World War II.

According to the critic MALCOLM COWLEY, writing in the *Saturday Review* in April 1946, "Faulkner performed a labor of imagination that has not been equaled in our time, and a double labor: first, to invent a Mississippi county that was like a mythical kingdom, but was complete and living in all its details; second, to make his story of Yoknapatawpha stand as a parable or legend of all the Deep South."

Though Faulkner developed his grand design over 30 years, he sketched the outlines of his legendary place in *Sartoris,* his third novel. Signing himself "William Faulkner, sole owner and proprietor," the novelist drew a map of his fictional county for *Absalom, Absalom!* and prepared a second map for the Viking Press's *The PORTABLE FAULKNER* (1946). The *Absalom* sketch gives Yoknapatawpha County an area of 2,400 square miles, with a population of 6,298 whites and 9,313 Negroes. The fictional county is more than three times larger than Lafayette County, with only two-thirds of its model's population; nor did the real place ever have a black majority. The TALLAHATCHIE RIVER forms the northern boundary of Faulkner's Yoknapatawpha; the YOCONA RIVER delimits the county on the south. There are no formal eastern or western boundaries.

The geography of Yoknapatawpha is substantially consistent throughout the chronicle, with the exception of *As I Lay Dying.* For some reason, the routes the Bundrens follow and the landmarks they pass in that novel as they carry Addie Bundren's body to Jefferson for burial do not conform to those of the other novels. In other works, minor details do not always agree, a fact that troubled Faulkner's editors far more than it troubled Faulkner himself.

Faulkner's scratch maps place the county seat, Jefferson, near the center of Yoknapatawpha. "John Sartoris' railroad" bisects the county north and south. A road leads from Jefferson northwest 12 miles to the mansion of SUTPEN'S HUNDRED, set in "Issetibbeha's Chickasaw Grant." Just beyond, on the Tallahatchie, is the "fishing camp where Wash Jones killed Sutpen, later bought and restored by Major Cassius de Spain." The road out of Jefferson to the northeast passes "McCallum's [sic], where young Bayard Sartoris went when his grandfather's heart failed in the car wreck." Beyond the MacCallum farm is the large McCaslin plantation, which figures in *The Unvanquished, Go Down, Moses* and *Intruder in the Dust.* Southeast of the county seat, at a distance variously given as 12 or 20 or 22 miles, lies the hamlet of FRENCHMAN'S BEND, with VARNER'S STORE and the OLD FRENCHMAN PLACE.

Faulkner's Yoknapatawpha is a social microcosm of the American South, and it is far more than that. The novelist once called his imaginary Mississippi county "a kind of keystone of the universe." If it were taken away, he went on to say, "the universe itself would collapse."

In response to a question about his fictional county, during a class session at the UNIVERSITY OF VIRGINIA where he was writer in residence, Faulkner mentioned that Yoknapatawpha is "a Chickasaw Indian word meaning water runs slow through flat land" (*Faulkner in the University,* 74). But the term, a combination of two Chickasaw words—*Yaakni'* and *patafa*—means land or earth that has been ripped or cut open for disemboweling (Pamela Munro and Catherine Willmond, *Chickasaw: An Analytical Dictionary*). Faulkner, however, who is the sole creator of this fictional land, can make of the term what he likes. He first identifies Yoknapatawpha County by name in *As I Lay Dying.*

Young, Stark (1881–1963) Poet, novelist, and critic. Born in Como, Mississippi, he moved to OXFORD with his family in 1895, graduated from the UNIVERSITY OF MISSISSIPPI in 1901, published his first collection of verse in 1906, and taught drama and English at the University of Texas and Amherst College until 1921.

Faulkner first met Young in the summer of 1914, introduced by Young's protégé PHILIP AVERY STONE. Young encouraged and befriended Faulkner and read his poems.

Young invited Faulkner to come to New York and sleep on his sofa until he landed a job. In the autumn of 1921 Faulkner took him up on the offer, and Young found work for him at a bookshop.

Young and Faulkner continued to meet when Young returned to Oxford for visits with his family, but they followed divergent literary paths. Young's novel *So Red the Rose* (1934), a family chronicle set in Mississippi, is a conventional idealized account of the Old South in the Civil War, far different from the picture of the region Faulkner created in his YOKNAPATAWPHA COUNTY novels.

PART IV

Appendixes

CHRONOLOGICAL BIBLIOGRAPHIES OF FAULKNER'S WORKS AND ADAPTATIONS

1. Chronology of Faulkner's Writings, Interviews, Addresses, and Publications (Note: Roman numerals refer to volume numbers, Arabic numerals to page numbers.)

See below for a chronology of works by category.

"L'Après-midi d'un Faune" (August 6, 1919; poem, first published in *New Republic*, XX, 24; reprinted in *Mississippian*, IX [October 29, 1919] 4, in *Salmagundi* [see below], and in *William Faulkner: Early Prose and Poetry* [see below]).

"Cathay" (November 12, 1919; poem, first published in *Mississippian*, IX, 8; reprinted in *William Faulkner: Early Prose and Poetry* [see below]).

"Sapphics" (November 26, 1919; poem, first published in *Mississippian*, IX, 3; reprinted in *William Faulkner: Early Prose and Poetry* [see below]).

"Landing in Luck" (November 26, 1919; short story, first published in *Mississippian*, IX, 2, 7; reprinted in *William Faulkner: Early Prose and Poetry* [see below]).

"After Fifty Years" (December 10, 1919; poem, first published in *Mississippian*, IX, 4; reprinted in "Faulkner Juvenilia" by Martha Mayes, *New Campus Writing No. 2*, edited by Nolan Miller [New York: Bantam, 1957], and in *William Faulkner: Early Prose and Poetry* [see below]).

"Moonlight" (c. 1919–21; short story published posthumously in *Uncollected Stories of William Faulkner* [see below]).

"Une Ballade des Femmes Perdues" (January 28, 1920; poem, first published in *Mississippian*, IX, 3; reprinted in "Faulkner Juvenilia" by Martha Mayes, *New Campus Writing No. 2*, edited by Nolan Miller [New York: Bantam, 1957], and in *William Faulkner: Early Prose and Poetry* [see below]).

"Naiad's Song" (February 4, 1920; poem, first published in *Mississippian*, IX, 3; reprinted in *William Faulkner: Early Prose and Poetry* [see below]).

"Fantouches" (February 25, 1920; poem, first published in *Mississippian*, IX, 3; reprinted in "Faulkner Juvenilia" by Martha Mayes, *New Campus Writing No. 2*, edited by Nolan Miller [New York: Bantam, 1957]; reprinted as "Fantoches" in *William Faulkner: Early Prose and Poetry* [see below]).

"Clair de Lune" (March 3, 1920; poem, first published in *Mississippian*, IX, 6; reprinted in *William Faulkner: Early Prose and Poetry* [see below]).

"Streets" (March 17, 1920; poem, first published in *Mississippian*, IX, 2; reprinted in *William Faulkner: Early Prose and Poetry* [see below]).

"The Ivory Tower" (March 17, 1920; critical essay, first published in *Mississippian*, IX, 4; reprinted with minor changes in "Faulkner Juvenilia" by Martha Mayes, *New Campus Writing No. 2*, edited by Nolan Miller [New York: Bantam, 1957]).

"A Poplar" (March 17, 1920; poem, first published in *Mississippian*, IX, 7; reprinted in "Faulkner Juvenilia" by Martha Mayes, *New Campus Writing No. 2*, edited by Nolan Miller [New York: Bantam, 1957], and in *William Faulkner: Early Prose and Poetry,* [see below]).

To the Editor (April 7, 1920; letter, first published in *Mississippian*, IX, 1; reprinted in "Faulkner Juvenilia" by Martha Mayes, *New Campus Writing No. 2*, edited by Nolan Miller [New York: Bantam, 1957].

"A Clymene" (April 14, 1920; poem, first published in *Mississippian*, IX, 3; reprinted in *William Faulkner: Early Prose and Poetry*, [see below]).

"Study" (April 24, 1920; poem, first published in *Mississippian*, IX, 4; reprinted in "Faulkner Juvenilia" by Martha Mayes, *New Campus Writing No. 2*, edited by Nolan Miller [New York: Bantam, 1957], and in *William Faulkner: Early Prose and Poetry* [see below]).

"Alma Mater" (May 12, 1920; poem, first published in *Mississippian*, IX, 3; reprinted in *William Faulkner: Early Prose and Poetry* [see below]).

The Marionettes (fall 1920; one-act verse play; published posthumously in 1977 [see below]).

Review of *In April Once* by W. A. Percy (November 10, 1920; book review, first published in *Mississippian*, IX, 5; reprinted in *William Faulkner: Early Prose and Poetry* [see below]).

"To a Co-ed" (1920; poem, first published in *Ole Miss, the Yearbook of the University of Mississippi*, XXIV [1919–20]; reprinted in *Memphis Commercial Appeal*, November 6, 1932 [Magazine Section], in *The Literary Career of William Faulkner* by James B. Meriwether [Princeton University Library, 1961], and in *William Faulkner: Early Prose and Poetry* [see below]).

Review of *Turns and Movies* by Conrad Aiken (February 16, 1921; book review, first published in *Mississippian*, X, 5; reprinted in *William Faulkner: Early Prose and Poetry* [see below]).

"Co-Education at Ole Miss" (May 4, 1921; poem, first published in *Mississippian*, X, 5; reprinted in *William Faulkner: Early Prose and Poetry* [see below]).

"Nocturne" (1921; poem, first published in *Ole Miss, the Yearbook of the University of Mississippi*, XXV [1920–21]; facsimile published in *The Literary Career of William Faulkner* by James B. Meriwether [Princeton University Library, 1961], and in *William Faulkner: Early Prose and Poetry* [see below]).

Vision in Spring (1921–23; cycle of 14 love poems [earlier version contained eight poems]; posthumously published in 1984, edited by Judith L. Sensibar, University of Texas Press, Austin).

"Love" (fall 1921; short story unpublished and basis of film scenario *Manservant* [see below]).

"Adolescence" (c. 1922; short story published posthumously in *Uncollected Stories of William Faulkner* [see below]).

Review of *Aria da Capo* by Edna St. Vincent Millay (January 13, 1922; book review, first published in *Mississippian*, XI, 5; reprinted in *William Faulkner: Early Prose and Poetry* [see below]).

"American Drama: Eugene O'Neill" (February 3, 1922; article, first published in *Mississippian*, XI, 5; reprinted in *William Faulkner: Early Prose and Poetry* [see below]).

"The Hill" (March 10, 1922; prose poem, first published in *Mississippian*, XI, 1–2; reprinted in *William Faulkner: Early Prose and Poetry* [see below]).

"American Drama: Inhibitions" (March 17 and 24, 1922; article, first section published in *Mississippian*, XI, 5 [March 17, 1922], and second section in *Mississippian*, XI, 5 [March 24, 1922]; reprinted in *William Faulkner: Early Prose and Poetry*, [see below]).

"Portrait" (June 1922; poem, first published in *Double Dealer*, II, 337; reprinted in *Salmagundi* [see below], and in *William Faulkner: Early Prose and Poetry* [see below]).

Review of *Linda Condon, Cytherea*, and *The Bright Shawl* by Joseph Hergesheimer (December 15, 1922; review of 3 books, first published in *Mississippian*, XII, 5; reprinted in *William Faulkner: Early Prose and Poetry* [see below]).

"Mississippi Hills" (October 1924; poem, revised as "My Epitaph" [see below]; slightly altered and retitled as "Mississippi Hills: My Epitaph," reproduced in *William Faulkner: "Man Working," 1919–1962, A Catalogue of the William Faulkner Collections at the University of Virginia*, compiled by Linton R. Massey [Charlottesville: Bibliographical Society, University of Virginia, 1968]).

The Marble Faun (December 15, 1924; poem of 806 lines with prologue and epilogue; preface by Phil Stone; published by Four Seas Company, Boston; republished with *A Green Bough* [photographically reproduced from original editions], by Random House, New York, 1965).

Mississippi Poems (December 30, 1924; typescript of 12 poems presented by Myrtle Ramey; eight of which revised for *A Green Bough* [1933]; posthumously published in 1979 [see below]).

Helen: A Courtship (1925; poems for Helen Baird; published posthumously in 1981 [see below]).

"Mirrors of Chartres Street" (February–September 1925; 11 of 16 prose sketches appearing in the

New Orleans Times-Picayune, with introduction by William Van O'Connor [Minneapolis: Faulkner Studies, 1953]; also see two separate references below titled *New Orleans Sketches*).

"Dying Gladiator" (January/February 1925; poem, first published in *Double Dealer*, VII, 85; reprinted in *Salmagundi* [see below] and in *William Faulkner: Early Prose and Poetry* [see below]).

"On Criticism" (January/February 1925; article, first published in *Double Dealer*, VII, 83–84; reprinted in *Salmagundi* [see below] and in *William Faulkner: Early Prose and Poetry* [see below]).

"New Orleans" (January/February 1925; prose sketch, first published in *Double Dealer*, VII, 102–07; reprinted in *Salmagundi* [see below] and in *New Orleans Sketches*, edited by Carvel Collins [see below]).

"Mirrors of Chartres Street" (February 8, 1925; sketch, first published in the *New Orleans Times-Picayune*, pp. 1, 6; reprinted in *Mirrors of Chartres Street* [Minneapolis: Faulkner Studies, 1953], in *New Orleans Sketches*, edited by Ichiro Nishizaki [see below], and in *New Orleans Sketches*, edited by Carvel Collins [see below]).

"Damon and Pythias Unlimited" (February 15, 1925; sketch, first published in the *New Orleans Times-Picayune*, p. 7; reprinted in *Mirrors of Chartres Street* [Minneapolis: Faulkner Studies, 1953], in *New Orleans Sketches*, edited by Ichiro Nishizaki [see below], and in *New Orleans Sketches*, edited by Carvel Collins [see below]).

"Home" (February 22, 1925; sketch, first published in the *New Orleans Times-Picayune*, p. 3; reprinted in *Mirrors of Chartres Street* [Minneapolis: Faulkner Studies, 1953], in *New Orleans Sketches*, edited by Ichiro Nishizaki [see below], and in *New Orleans Sketches*, edited by Carvel Collins [see below]).

"Nympholepsy" (1925; short story published posthumously in *Mississippi Quarterly*, XXVI (Summer 1973): 403–409, edited with an introduction by James B. Meriwether; reprinted in *Uncollected Stories of William Faulkner*, [see below]).

"Frankie and Johnny" (c. 1925; short story published posthumously in *Mississippi Quarterly*, XXXI (Summer 1978): 453–464, edited with an introduction by James B. Meriwether; reprinted in *Uncollected Stories of William Faulkner*, [see below]).

"Jealousy" (March 1, 1925; sketch, first published in the *New Orleans Times-Picayune*, p. 2; reprinted in *Faulkner Studies*, III (Winter 1954): 46–50; in *Jealousy and Episode: Two Stories by William Faulkner*, [Minneapolis: Faulkner Studies, 1955]; in *New Orleans Sketches*, edited by Ichiro Nishizaki [see below]; and in *New Orleans Sketches*, edited by Carvel Collins [see below]).

"The Priest" (1925; short story published posthumously in *Mississippi Quarterly*, XXIX (Summer 1976): 445–450, edited with an introduction by James B. Meriwether; reprinted in *Uncollected Stories of William Faulkner* [see below]).

"The Faun" (April 1925; poem, first published in *Double Dealer*, VII, 148; reprinted in *Salmagundi* [see below] and in *William Faulkner: Early Prose and Poetry* [see below]).

"Verse Old and Nascent: A Pilgrimage" (April 1925; article, first published in *Double Dealer*, VII, 129–131; reprinted in *Salmagundi* [see below] and in *William Faulkner: Early Prose and Poetry* [see below]).

"Cheest" (April 5, 1925; sketch, first published in the *New Orleans Times-Picayune*, p. 4; reprinted in *Mirrors of Chartres Street* [Minneapolis: Faulkner Studies, 1953]; in *New Orleans Sketches*, edited by Ichiro Nishizaki [see below]; and in *New Orleans Sketches*, edited by Carvel Collins [see below]).

"Out of Nazareth" (April 12, 1925; sketch, first published in the *New Orleans Times-Picayune*, p. 4; reprinted in *Mirrors of Chartres Street* [Minneapolis: Faulkner Studies, 1953]; in *New Orleans Sketches*, edited by Ichiro Nishizaki [see below]; and in *New Orleans Sketches*, edited by Carvel Collins [see below]).

"Sherwood Anderson" (April 26, 1925; article, first published in the *Dallas Morining News*, Part III, p. 7; reprinted in *Princeton University Library Chronicle*, XVIII (Spring 1957): 89–94, and in *William Faulkner: New Orleans Sketches* [1968 Random House edition, see below], edited by Carvel Collins).

"The Kingdom of God" (April 26, 1925; sketch, first published in the *New Orleans Times-Picayune*, p. 4; reprinted in *Mirrors of Chartres Street* [Minneapolis: Faulkner Studies, 1953]; in *New Orleans Sketches*, edited by Ichiro Nishizaki [see below];

and in *New Orleans Sketches*, edited by Carvel Collins [see below]).

"The Rosary" (May 3, 1925; sketch, first published in the *New Orleans Times-Picayune*, p. 2; reprinted in *Mirrors of Chartres Street* [Minneapolis: Faulkner Studies, 1953]; in *New Orleans Sketches*, edited by Ichiro Nishizaki [see below]; and in *New Orleans Sketches*, edited by Carvel Collins [see below]).

"The Cobbler" (May 10, 1925; sketch, first published in the *New Orleans Times-Picayune*, p. 7; reprinted in *Mirrors of Chartres Street* [Minneapolis: Faulkner Studies, 1953]; in *New Orleans Sketches*, edited by Ichiro Nishizaki [see below]; and in *New Orleans Sketches*, edited by Carvel Collins [see below]).

"Chance" (May 17, 1925; sketch, first published in the *New Orleans Times-Picayune*, p. 7; reprinted in *Mirrors of Chartres Street* [Minneapolis: Faulkner Studies, 1953]; in *New Orleans Sketches*, edited by Ichiro Nishizaki [see below]; and in *New Orleans Sketches*, edited by Carvel Collins [see below]).

"Sunset" (May 25, 1925; sketch, first published in the *New Orleans Times-Picayune*, p. 7; reprinted in *Mirrors of Chartres Street* [Minneapolis: Faulkner Studies, 1953]; in *New Orleans Sketches*, edited by Ichiro Nishizaki [see below]; and in *New Orleans Sketches*, edited by Carvel Collins [see below]).

"The Kid Learns" (May 31, 1925; sketch, first published in the *New Orleans Times-Picayune*, p. 2; reprinted in *Mirrors of Chartres Street* [Minneapolis: Faulkner Studies, 1953]; in *New Orleans Sketches*, edited by Ichiro Nishizaki [see below]; and in *New Orleans Sketches*, edited by Carvel Collins [see below]).

"The Lilacs" (June 1925; poem, first published in *Double Dealer*, VII, 185–187; reprinted in *Salmagundi* [see below], in *A Green Bough* [revised as I], and in *Anthology of Magazine Verse for 1925 and Yearbook of American Poetry*, edited by William Stanley Braithwaite [Boston: B. J. Brimmer Co., 1925]).

"The Liar" (July 26, 1925; sketch, first published in the *New Orleans Times-Picayune*, pp. 3, 6; reprinted in *New Orleans Sketches*, edited by Carvel Collins [see below]).

"Episode" (August 16, 1925; sketch, first published in the *New Orleans Times-Picayune*, p. 2; reprinted in *Eigo Seinen* [Tokyo] on December 1, 1954; in *Faulkner Studies*, III [Winter 1954], 51–53; in *Jeal-*

ousy and Episode: Two Stories by William Faulkner [Minneapolis: Faulkner Studies, 1955]; in *New Orleans Sketches*, edited by Ichiro Nishizaki [see below]; and in *New Orleans Sketches*, edited by Carvel Collins [see below]).

"Country Mice" (September 20, 1925; sketch, first published in the *New Orleans Times-Picayune*, p. 7; reprinted in *New Orleans Sketches*, edited by Carvel Collins [see below]).

"Yo Ho and Two Bottles of Rum" (September 27, 1925; sketch, first published in the *New Orleans Times-Picayune*, pp. 1–2; reprinted in *New Orleans Sketches*, edited by Carvel Collins [see below]).

Elmer (1925; unfinished novel; typescript posthumously published in *Mississippi Quarterly*, 36 [Summer 1983]: 343–447, and by Seajay Press, Northport, Alab., in 1983; see "A Portrait of Elmer" below).

"Al Jackson" (1925; short story published posthumously in *Uncollected Stories of William Faulkner* [see below]).

"Don Giovanni" (c. 1925; short story published posthumously in *Uncollected Stories of William Faulkner* [see below]).

"Peter" (c. 1925; short story published posthumously in *Uncollected Stories of William Faulkner* [see below]).

Mayday (January 27, 1926; fable [hand-lettered, illustrated, and bound by Faulkner] given to Helen Baird; facsimile reproduction with a companion essay by Carvel Collins published by University of Notre Dame Press, Notre Dame, Ind., 1977; published with text set in type and illustrations reproduced, with revised essay as an introduction, by University of Notre Dame Press, Notre Dame, Ind., 1980).

Soldiers' Pay (February 25, 1926; novel, first published by Boni & Liveright, New York; elsewhere since; re-edited by Noel Polk, notes by Joseph Blotner and Noel Polk, published by Library of America: *William Faulkner: Novels 1926–1929*, New York, in 2006).

Foreword to *Sherwood Anderson & Other Famous Creoles: A Gallery of Contemporary New Orleans* by William Spratling (1926; published by Pelican Bookshop Press, New Orleans; reprinted in *The Tangled Fire of William Faulkner* by William Van O'Connor, Minneapolis: University of Minnesota Press, 1954).

Father Abraham (1926–27; unfinished story, edited and with an introduction and textual notes by James B. Meriwether and published posthumously by Red Ozier Press, New York, in 1983 [limited edition of 210 copies] and by Random House, New York, in 1984 [a facsimile edition]; forms the beginning of *The Hamlet* [see below]; also recast as "Spotted Horses" [see below]).

"The Wishing Tree" (c. January/February 1927; fairy tale, published posthumously in *Saturday Evening Post* 240 [April 8, 1967]: 48–53, 57–58, 60–63; and published in book form by Random House, New York, on April 10, 1967).

Mosquitoes (April 30, 1927; novel, first published by Boni & Liveright, New York; elsewhere since; re-edited by Noel Polk, notes by Joseph Blotner and Noel Polk, published by Library of America: *William Faulkner: Novels 1926–1929*, New York, in 2006).

"Hermaphroditus" (April 1927; poem, first appeared in Faulkner's novel *Mosquitoes* [see above], p. 252; revision reprinted XXX in *A Green Bough* [see below]).

"The Big Shot" (c. 1929; short story, published posthumously in *Mississippi Quarterly*, XXVI (Summer 1973): 313–324, and in *Uncollected Stories of William Faulkner* [see below]).

"A Dangerous Man" (c. 1929; short story, published posthumously in *Uncollected Stories of William Faulkner* [see below]).

Sartoris (January 31, 1929; novel; published by Harcourt, Brace, New York; elsewhere since; also see below, *Flags in the Dust*; re-edited text by Noel Polk, notes by Joseph Blotner and Noel Polk, published by Library of America: *William Faulkner: Novels 1926–1929*, New York, in 2006).

The Sound and the Fury (October 7, 1929; novel, first published by Jonathan Cape and Harrison Smith, New York; elsewhere since; most of the last chapter, "April Eighth, 1928," published under the title "Dilsey" in *The Portable Faulkner* [see below]; published in 1946 by Modern Library, New York, with an appendix as a foreword titled "Compson 1699–1945" and together with *As I Lay Dying* [see below]; complete novel published with the appendix at the end in *The Faulkner Reader* [see below]; film adaptation with same title released in 1959 [see below]; corrected text by Noel Polk published

by Random House, New York, in 1984; re-edited by Noel Polk, notes by Joseph Blotner and Noel Polk, published by Library of America: *William Faulkner: Novels 1926–1929*, New York, in 2006).

"Dull Tale" (c. 1929–30; short story published posthumously in *Uncollected Stories of William Faulkner* [see below]).

"A Return" (c. 1929–30; short story, published posthumously in *Uncollected Stories of William Faulkner* [see below]).

As I Lay Dying (October 6, 1930; novel, first published by Jonathan Cape and Harrison Smith, New York; elsewhere since; published together with *The Sound and the Fury* [see below]; new edition published in 1964 by Random House, New York; re-edited text by Noel Polk published in 1985 by the Library of America: *William Faulkner: Novels 1930–1935*], New York, and the corrected text by Vintage International, New York, in October 1990).

"A Rose for Emily" (April 1930; short story, first published in *Forum*, LXXXIII, 233–238; reprinted revision in *These 13*, in *A Rose for Emily and Other Stories* [see below], in *The Portable Faulkner* [see below], in *Collected Stories* [see below], in *The Faulkner Reader* [see below], in *A Rose for Emily* [see below], and in *Selected Short Stories of William Faulkner* [see below]).

To the editor (April 1930; letter, published in *Forum*, LXXXIII, lvi).

"Honor" (July 1930; short story, first published in *American Mercury*, XX, 268–274; reprinted in *Doctor Martino and Other Stories* [see below], in *Collected Stories* [see below], and in *Selected Short Stories of William Faulkner* [see below]).

"Thrift" (September 6, 1930; short story, first published in *Saturday Evening Post*, CCIII, 16–17, 78, 82; reprinted in *O. Henry Memorial Award Prize Stories of 1931*, edited by Blanche Colton Williams [Garden City: Doubleday, Doran, 1931] and in *Uncollected Stories of William Faulkner* [see below]).

"Red Leaves" (October 25, 1930; short story, first published in *Saturday Evening Post*, CCIII, 6–7, 54, 56, 58, 60, 62, 64; revision published in *These 13* [see below], in *The Portable Faulkner* [see below], in the edition of *A Rose for Emily and Other Stories* edited and annotated by Kenzaburo Ohashi [see below], in *Collected Stories of William Faulkner* [see below], and in *Selected Short Stories of William Faulkner* [see below]; a portion again revised and included in *Big Woods*, pp. 99–109 [see below]).

"Evangeline" (c. 1930–31; short story published posthumously in *Uncollected Stories of William Faulkner* [see below]).

"Dry September" (January 1931; short story, first published in *Scribner's Magazine*, LXXXIX, 49–56; reprinted revision in *These 13* [see below], in *A Rose for Emily and Other Stories by William Faulkner* [see below], in *Collected Stories of William Faulkner* [see below], in *The Faulkner Reader* [see below], and in *Selected Short Stories of William Faulkner* [see below]).

Sanctuary (February 9, 1931; novel, first published by Jonathan Cape and Harrison Smith, New York; elsewhere since; published with an introduction by Faulkner [see below] by Modern Library, New York, on March 25, 1932; film adaptation titled *The Story of Temple Drake* released in 1933 [see below]; chapter 25 published under the title "Uncle Blud and the Three Madams" in *The Portable Faulkner* [see below]; published together with *Requiem for a Nun* [see below]; film adaptation based on *Sanctuary* and *Requiem for a Nun* titled *Sanctuary* released in 1961 [see below]; re-edited text by Noel Polk published in 1985 by the Library of America: *William Faulkner: Novels 1930–1935*, New York; the corrected text with Faulkner's introduction in the Editors' Note published by Vintage International, New York, in December 1993).

"That Evening Sun Go Down" (March 1931; short story, first published in *American Mercury*, XXII, 257–267; revision titled "That Evening Sun" reprinted *These 13* [see below], in *A Rose for Emily and Other Stories by William Faulkner* [see below], in *The Portable Faulkner* [see below], in *Collected Stories of William Faulkner* [see below], in *The Faulkner Reader* [see below], in *A Rose for Emily* [see below], and in *Selected Short Stories of William Faulkner* [see below]).

"Ad Astra" (March 27, 1931; short story, first published in *American Caravan*, IV, 164–181; reprinted revision in *These 13* [see below], in *The Portable Faulkner* [see below], and in *Collected Stories of William Faulkner* [see below]).

"Hair" (May 1931; short story, first published in *American Mercury*, XXIII, 53–61; reprinted revision in *These 13* [see below] and in *Collected Stories of William Faulkner* [see below]).

"Beyond the Talking" (May 20, 1931; review of *The Road Back* by Erich Maria Remarque, published in *New Republic*, LXVII, 23–24).

"Spotted Horses" (June 1931; short story, first published in *Scribner's Magazine*, LXXXIX, 585–597; expanded revision included in chapter 1 of book 4 of *The Hamlet* [see below], reprinted as a novella in *The Faulkner Reader* [see below], and in *Three Famous Short Novels* [see below]; original version reprinted in *Uncollected Stories of William Faulkner* [see below]).

"The Hound" (August 1931; short story, first published in *Harper's Magazine*, CLXIII, 266–274; reprinted in *Doctor Martino and Other Stories* [see below] and in *A Rose for Emily and Other Stories by William Faulkner* [see below]; revision included in book 3 of *The Hamlet* [see below]; original version reprinted in *Uncollected Stories of William Faulkner* [see below]).

"Fox Hunt" (September 1931; short story, first published in *Harper's Magazine*, CLXIII, 392–402; reprinted in *Doctor Martino and Other Stories* [see below] and in *Collected Stories of William Faulkner* [see below]).

"All the Dead Pilots" (September 21, 1931; short story, first published in *These 13* [see below]; reprinted in *Collected Stories of William Faulkner* [see below]).

"Carcassonne" (September 21, 1931; short story, first published in *These 13* [see below] and in *Collected Stories of William Faulkner* [see below]).

"Crevasse" (September 21, 1931; short story, first published in *These 13* [see below], in *Collected Stories of William Faulkner* [see below], and in *A Rose for Emily* [see below]).

"Divorce in Naples" (September 21, 1931; short story, first published in *These 13* [see below] and in *Collected Stories of William Faulkner* [see below]).

"A Justice" (September 21, 1931; short story, first published in *These 13* [see below]; reprinted in *The Portable Faulkner* [see below], in *Collected Stories of William Faulkner* [see below], and in *The Faulkner Reader* [see below]); revised portion included in *Big Woods*, pp. 139–142 [see below]).

"Mistral" (September 21, 1931; short story, first published in *These 13* [see below] and in *Collected Stories of William Faulkner* [see below]).

"Victory" (September 21, 1931; short story, first published in *These 13* [see below] and in *Collected Stories of William Faulkner* [see below]).

These 13 (September 21, 1931; collection of 13 short stories [see above]; published by Jonathan Cape and Harrison Smith, New York, 1931; stories reprinted in *Collected Stories of William Faulkner* [see below]).

"Doctor Martino" (November 1931; short story, first published in *Harper's Magazine*, CLXIII, 733–743; reprinted in *Doctor Martino and Other Stories* [see below] and in *Collected Stories of William Faulkner* [see below]).

Night Bird (c. November 1931; scenario of unwritten screenplay and basis of *The College Widow* [see below]; published posthumously in *Faulkner's MGM Screenplays*, pp. 32–33, edited with introduction and commentaries by Bruce F. Kawin, University of Tennessee Press, Knoxville, 1982).

Idyll in the Desert (December 1931; short story, first published separately by Random House, New York, in 1931; reprinted in *Uncollected Stories of William Faulkner* [see below]).

"With Caution and Dispatch" (c. 1932; short story, published posthumously in *Uncollected Stories of William Faulkner* [see below]).

"Death-Drag" (January 1932; short story, first published in *Scribner's Magazine*, XCI, 34–42; reprinted with minor revisions as "Death Drag" in *Doctor Martino and Other Stories* [see below], in *The Portable Faulkner* [see below], and in *Collected Stories of William Faulkner* [see below]).

"Centaur in Brass" (February 1932; short story, first published in *American Mercury*, XXV, 200–210; reprinted in *Collected Stories of William Faulkner* [see below]; revised for first chapter of *The Town* [see below]).

"Once Aboard the Lugger" (February 1, 1932; title for two short stories, the first of which was first published in *Contempo*, I, 1, 4, and reprinted in *Uncollected Stories of William Faulkner* [see below]; the second, first published in *Uncollected Stories of William Faulkner* [see below]).

"I Will Not Weep for Youth" (February 1, 1932; poem, first published in *Contempo*, I, 1; reprinted in *An Anthology of the Younger Poets*, edited by Oliver Wells and with a preface by Archibald MacLeish [Philadelphia: Centaur Press, 1932]).

"Knew I Love Once" (February 1, 1932; poem, first published in *Contempo*, I, 1; reprinted in *A Green Bough* [revised as XXXIII] and in *An Anthology of the Younger Poets*, edited by Oliver Wells [Philadelphia: Centaur Press, 1932]).

"Twilight" (February 1, 1932; poem, first published in *Contempo*, I, 1; reprinted in *A Green Bough* [revised as X], and in *An Anthology of the Younger Poets*, edited by Oliver Wells [Philadelphia: Centaur Press, 1932]).

"Visions in Spring" (February 1, 1932; poem, published in *Contempo*, I, 1).

"Spring" (February 1, 1932; poem, first published in *Contempo*, I, 2; reprinted in *A Green Bough* [revised as XXXVI]).

"April" (February 1, 1932; poem, published in *Contempo*, I, 2).

"To a Virgin" (February 1, 1932; poem, first published in *Contempo*, I, 2; reprinted in *A Green Bough* [revised as XXXIX], and in *An Anthology of the Younger Poets*, edited by Oliver Wells [Philadelphia: Centaur Press, 1932]).

"Winter Is Gone" (February 1, 1932; poem, first published in *Contempo*, I, 2; reprinted in *An Anthology of the Younger Poets*, edited by Oliver Wells [Philadelphia: Centaur Press, 1932]).

"My Epitaph" (February 1, 1932; poem, first published in *Contempo*, I, 2; revised and reprinted as *This Earth*, 1932 [see below]; reprinted in *A Green Bough* [revised as XLIV]; reprinted in *An Anthology of the Younger Poets*, edited by Oliver Wells [Philadelphia: Centaur Press, 1932]; retitled as "If There Be Grief" and published in *Mississippi Verse*, edited by Alice James [Chapel Hill: University of North Carolina Press, 1934]; reprinted in *Life*, LlII [20 July 1952]: 42).

"Lizards in Jamshyd's Courtyard" (February 27, 1932; short story, first published in *Saturday Evening Post*, CCIV, 12–13, 52, 57; revision included in book 4 of *The Hamlet* [see below]; original version reprinted in *Uncollected Stories of William Faulkner* [see below]).

"Turn About" (March 5, 1932; short story, first published in *Saturday Evening Post*, CCIV, 6–7, 75–76, 81, 83; revision reprinted in *Doctor Martino and Other Stories* [see below] and in *A Rose for Emily and Other Stories by William Faulkner* [see below];

reprinted as "Turnabout" in *Collected Stories of William Faulkner* [see below], in *The Faulkner Reader* [see below], and in *Selected Short Stories of William Faulkner* [see below]; basis of screenplay of same title and film titled *Today We Live* [see below]).

"Introduction" to *Sanctuary* by William Faulkner (March 25, 1932; first published with the Modern Library edition of the novel [see above, *Sanctuary*]; reprinted in the editors' note of the Vintage International Edition, 1993 [see above, *Sanctuary*]).

"Smoke" (April 1932; short story, first published in *Harper's Magazine*, CLXIV, 562–578; reprinted with minor changes in *Doctor Martino and Other Stories* [see below] and in *Knight's Gambit* [see below]).

To Maurice Edgar Coindreau (April 14, 1932; letter, published in facsimile in *Princeton University Library Chronicle*, XVIII [spring 1957], Plate 2).

Salmagundi (April 30, 1932; reprinted prose pieces and poems [see above]; edited with an introduction by Paul Romaine; published by Casanova Press, Milwaukee).

Manservant (May 24, 1932; scenario of unwritten screenplay based on the unpublished short story "Love" [see above]; published posthumously in *Faulkner's MGM Screenplays*, pp. 7–28, edited with introduction and commentaries by Bruce F. Kawin, University of Tennessee Press, Knoxville, 1982).

"A Child Looks for His Window" (May 25, 1932; poem, published in *Contempo*, II, 3).

The College Widow (May 26, 1932; scenario of unwritten screenplay based on *Night Bird* [see above]; published posthumously in *Faulkner's MGM Screenplays*, pp. 40–53, edited with introduction and commentaries by Bruce F. Kawin, University of Tennessee Press, Knoxville, 1982).

Absolution (June 1, 1932; scenario of unwritten screenplay; published posthumously in *Faulkner's MGM Screenplays*, pp. 60–69, edited with introduction and commentaries by Bruce F. Kawin, University of Tennessee Press, Knoxville, 1982).

Flying the Mail (June 3, 1932; scenario of unwritten screenplay; published posthumously in *Faulkner's MGM Screenplays*, pp. 83–99, edited with introduction and commentaries by Bruce F. Kawin, University of Tennessee Press, Knoxville, 1982).

"Miss Zilphia Gant" (June 27, 1932; short story, first published separately by Book Club of Texas (Dallas), with a preface by Henry Smith; reprinted in *Uncollected Stories of William Faulkner* [see below]).

Light in August (October 6, 1932; novel; first published by Smith & Haas, New York; elsewhere since; excerpt from novel published under title of "Percy Grimm" in *The Faulkner Reader* [see below]; re-edited text by Noel Polk, notes by Joseph Blotner and Noel Polk published in 1985 by Library of America: *William Faulkner: Novels 1930–1935*, New York, and in October 1990 by Vintage International, New York).

This Earth (December 1932; revision of poem "My Epitaph" [see above]; published by Equinox Cooperative Press, New York).

"A Mountain Victory" (December 3, 1932; short story, first published in *Saturday Evening Post*, CCV, 6–7, 39, 42, 44–46; reprinted revision as "Mountain Victory" in *Doctor Martino and Other Stories* [see below], in *Collected Stories of William Faulkner* [see below], and in *Selected Short Stories of William Faulkner* [see below]).

"There Was a Queen" (January 1933; short story, first published in *Scribner's Magazine*, XCIII, 10–16; reprinted in *Doctor Martino and Other Stories* [see below], in *Collected Stories of William Faulkner* [see below], and in *Selected Short Stories of William Faulkner* [see below]).

War Birds (January 12, 1933; screenplay unproduced, published posthumously in *Faulkner's MGM Screenplays*, pp. 275–420, edited with introduction and commentaries by Bruce F. Kawin, University of Tennessee Press, Knoxville, 1982).

Today We Live (April 12, 1933 [advance showing]; screenplay [originally titled "Turn About"] with Edith Fitzgerald and Dwight Taylor, based on Faulkner's short Story "Turn About" [see above]; directed by Howard Hawks and released on April 21, 1933 by MGM; original script titled "Turn About," published posthumously in *Faulkner's MGM Screenplays*, pp. 128–255, edited with introduction and commentaries by Bruce F. Kawin, University of Tennessee Press, Knoxville, 1982).

"The Race's Splendor (April 12, 1933; poem, first published in *New Republic*, LXXIV, 253; reprinted in *A Green Bough* [as XXXVII, and in *New Republic*, CXXXI [November 22, 1954]: 82).

"Night Piece" (April 12, 1933; poem, first published in *New Republic*, LXXIV, 253; reprinted in *A Green Bough* [as VII]).

"Gray the Day" (April 12, 1933; poem, first published in *New Republic*, LXXIV, 253; reprinted in *A Green Bough* [as XXX]).

"Over the World's Rim" (April 12, 1933; poem, first published in *New Republic*, LXXIV, 253; reprinted in *A Green Bough*, as XXVIII]).

"The Ship of Night" (April 19, 1933; poem, first published in *New Republic*, LXXIV, 272; reprinted in *A Green Bough* as XXXIV]).

A Green Bough (April 20, 1933; 44 poems [13 previously published; see above]; illustrations by Lynd Ward; published by Smith & Haas, New York; seven poems reprinted with titles—XIV ["Mother and Child"], XVI ["Mirror of Youth"], XVIII ["Boy and Eagle"], XIX ["Green Is the Water"], XX ["Here He Stands"], XXXV ["The Courtesan is Dead"], and XLIV ["If There Be Grief," also see above: "My Epitaph"]—in *Mississippi Verse*, edited by Alice James [Chapel Hill: University of North Carolina Press, 1934]; republished with *The Marble Faun* [photographically reproduced from original editions], by Random House, New York, 1965).

Louisiana Lou (April/May 1933; screenplay unproduced [later version without contribution from Faulkner was released by MGM in 1934 under the title *Lazy River*]).

"Man Comes, Man Goes" (May 3, 1933; poem, first published in *New Republic*, LXXIV, 338; reprinted in *A Green Bough* [as VI], in *The New Republic Anthology: 1915–1935*, edited by Groff Conklin [New York: Dodge, 1936], and in *Fiction Parade*, V [October 1937]: 740).

The Story of Temple Drake (May 12, 1933; film adaptation of the novel, *Sanctuary* [see above]; screenplay by Oliver H. P. Garret and directed by Stephen Roberts; released by Paramount).

"The Flowers That Died" (June 25, 1933; poem, published in *Contempo*, III, 1).

"Artist at Home" (August 1933; short story, first published in *Story*, III, 27–41; reprinted in *Collected Stories of William Faulkner* [see below]).

Mythical Latin-American Kingdom Story (August 26, 1933; tentative title of screenplay unproduced; published posthumously in *Faulkner's MGM Screenplays*, pp. 449–543, edited with introduction and commentaries by Bruce F. Kawin, University of Tennessee Press, Knoxville, 1982).

"Beyond" (September 1933; short story, first published in *Harper's Magazine*, CLXVII, 394–403; reprinted in *Doctor Martino and Other Stories* [see below], in *Collected Stories of William Faulkner* [see below], and in *Selected Short Stories of William Faulkner* [see below]).

"Elly" (February 1934; short story, first published in *Story*, IV, 3–15; reprinted in *Doctor Martino and Other Stories* [see below] and in *Collected Stories of William Faulkner* [see below]).

"Pennslyvania Station" (February 1934; short story, first published in *American Mercury*, XXXI, 166–174; reprinted in *Collected Stories of William Faulkner* [see below]).

"Wash" (February 1934; short story, first published in *Harper's Magazine*, CLXVIII, 258–266; reprinted in *Doctor Martino and Other Stories* [see below], in *The Portable Faulkner* [see below], in *Collected Stories of William Faulkner* [see below], and in *The Faulkner Reader* [see below]; included, with major revisions, in the latter part of chapter 7 of *Absalom, Absalom!* [see below]).

"A Bear Hunt" (February 10, 1934; short story, first published in *Saturday Evening Post*, CCVI, 8–9, 74, 76; reprinted in *Collected Stories of William Faulkner* [see below]; reprinted, in revised version, in *Big Woods* [see below]).

"Black Music" (April 16, 1934; short story, first published in *Doctor Martino and Other Stories* [see below]; reprinted in *Collected Stories of William Faulkner* [see below]).

"Leg" (April 16, 1934; short story, first published in *Doctor Martino and Other Stories* [see below]; reprinted as "The Leg" in *Collected Stories of William Faulkner* [see below]).

Doctor Martino and Other Stories (April 16, 1934; collection of 14 stories [see above], published by Smith & Haas, New York).

"Mule in the Yard" (August 1934; short story, first published in *Scribner's Magazine*, XCVI, 65–70; reprinted in *Collected Stories of William Faulkner* [see below]; with major revisions incorporated in chapter 16 of *The Town* [see below]).

"Ambuscade" (September 29, 1934; short story, first published in *Saturday Evening Post*, CCVII, 12–13, 80–1; reprinted revision as chapter 1 of *The Unvanquished* [see below]; original version reprinted in *Uncollected Stories of William Faulkner* [see below]).

"Retreat" (October 13, 1934; short story, first published in *Saturday Evening Post*, CCVII, 16–17, 82, 84–85, 87, 89; reprinted revision as chapter 2 of *The Unvanquished* [see below]; original version reprinted in *Uncollected Stories of William Faulkner* [see below]).

"Lo!" (November 1934; short story, first published in *Story*, V, 5–21; reprinted in *Collected Stories of William Faulkner* [see below] and in *Selected Short Stories of William Faulkner* [see below]).

"Raid" (November 3, 1934; short story, first published in *Saturday Evening Post*, CCVII, 18–19, 72–73, 75, 77–78; reprinted revision as chapter 3 of *The Unvanquished* [see below]; original version reprinted in *Uncollected Stories of William Faulkner* [see below]).

"A Portrait of Elmer" (c. 1934–35; short story, posthumously published in *Uncollected Stories of William Faulkner* [see below]).

Pylon (March 25, 1935 [copyright page reads "First Printing, February, 1935"]; novel, first published by Smith & Haas, New York; elsewhere since; film adaptation titled *The Tarnished Angels* released in 1957 [see below]; re-edited text by Noel Polk with notes by Joseph Blotner and Noel Polk, published in 1985 by Library of America: *William Faulkner: Novels 1930–1935*, New York; corrected text by Noel Polk with illustrations by David Tamura published in February 1987 by Vintage, New York).

"Skirmish at Satoris" (April 1935; short story, first published in *Scribner's Magazine*, XCVII, 193–200; reprinted revision as chapter 6 of *The Unvanquished* [see below]; original version reprinted in *Uncollected Stories of William Faulkner* [see below]).

"Folklore of the Air" (November 1935; review of *Test Pilot* by Jimmy Collins, published in *American Mercury*, XXXVI, 370–372).

"Golden Land" (May 1935; short story, first published in *American Mercury*, XXXV, 1–14; reprinted in *Collected Stories of William Faulkner* [see below]).

"That Will Be Fine" (July 1935; short story, first published in *American Mercury*, XXXV, 264–276; reprinted in *Collected Stories of William Faulkner* [see below]).

"Uncle Willy" (October 1935; short story, first published in *American Mercury*, XXXVI, 156–168; reprinted in *Collected Stories of William Faulkner* [see below]).

"Lion" (December 1935; short story, first published in *Harper's Magazine*, CLXXI, 67–77; revised and included in "The Bear" in *Go Down, Moses and Other Stories* [see below]; original version reprinted in *Uncollected Stories of William Faulkner* [see below]).

"Two Dollar Wife" (1936; short story, first titled "Christmas Tree" and first published in *College Life*, XVIII (January 1936): 8–10, 85, 86, 88, 90; reprinted in *Uncollected Stories of William Faulkner* [see below]).

"The Brooch" (January 1936; short story, first published in *Scribner's Magazine*, XCIX, 7–12; reprinted in *Collected Stories of William Faulkner* [see below]).

The Road to Glory (June 1936; screenplay with Joel Sayre; directed by Howard Hawks and released by Twentieth Century-Fox).

"Fool About a Horse" (August 1936; short story, first published in *Scribner's Magazine*, C, 80–86; revision included in book 1 of *The Hamlet* [see below]; original version reprinted in *Uncollected Stories of William Faulkner* [see below]).

"Absalom, Absalom!" (August 1936; excerpt [chapter 1] from novel of same title [see below], published in *American Mercury*, XXXVIII, pp. 466–474).

Absalom, Absalom! (October 26, 1936; novel (with map of Yoknapatawpha County), first published by Random House, New York; elsewhere since; chapter 2 published in *The Portable Faulkner* [see below]; corrected text by Noel Polk, published by Random House, New York, in 1986 and by Vintage in 1990; re-edited text by Noel Polk, and notes by Joseph Blotner and Noel Polk, published by Library of America: *William Faulkner: Novels 1936–1940*, New York, in 1990).

"The Unvanquished" (November 14, 1936; short story, first published in *Saturday Evening Post*, CCIX, 12–13, 121–122, 124, 126, 128, 130; retitled and revised as "Riposte in Tertio," chapter 4 of *The Unvanquished* [see below]; original version and title reprinted in *Uncollected Stories of William Faulkner* [see below]).

"Vendée" (December 5, 1936; short story, first published in *Saturday Evening Post*, CCIX, 16–17, 86, 87, 90, 92, 93, 94; revised as chapter 5 in *The Unvanquished* [see below]; original version reprinted in *Uncollected Stories of William Faulkner* [see below]).

To Maurice Edgar Coindreau (February 26, 1937; letter, published in facsimile in *Princeton University Library Chronicle*, XVIII [spring 1957], plate 2).

"Monk" (May 1937; short story, first published in *Scribner's Magazine*, CL, 16–24; reprinted in *Knight's Gambit* [see below]).

Slave Ship (June 1937; screenplay with Sam Hellman, Lamar Trotti, and Gladys Lehman; directed by Tay Garnett and released by Twentieth Century-Fox).

To the President of the League of American Writers (1938; letter, published in *Writers Take Sides: Letters about the War in Spain from 418 American Authors* [New York: League of American Writers]).

"An Odor of Verbena" (February 15, 1938; short story, first published as chapter 7 of *The Unvanquished* [see below]; reprinted in *A Rose for Emily and Other Stories by William Faulkner* [see below] and in *The Faulkner Reader* [see below]).

The Unvanquished (February 15, 1938; series of seven interrelated stories, first published by Random House, New York; first six are revisions of previously published short stories [see above]; stories III, "Raid," and VII, "An Odor of Verbena," published in *The Portable Faulkner* [see below]; basis of unproduced screenplay of same title by Sidney Howard for MGM, 1938; re-edited text by Noel Polk, notes by Joseph Blotner and Noel Polk, published in 1990 by Library of America: *William Faulkner: Novels 1936–1940*, New York, and a corrected text by Noel Polk in October 1991 by Vintage International, New York).

The Wild Palms (January 19, 1939; novel with two interwoven narratives ("Wild Palms" and "Old Man"), first published by Random House, New York; the parts designated "Old Man" published under the title "Old Man" in *The Portable Faulkner* [see below] and as a novella in *The Faulkner Reader*

[see below]; elsewhere since; also see below: *The Wild Palms and The Old Man* and *The Old Man*; re-edited text by Noel Polk with notes by Joseph Blotner and Noel Polk, published as *If I Forget Thee, Jerusalem* in 1990 by Library of America: *William Faulkner: Novels 1936–1940*, New York; and by Vintage International in 1995).

"Barn Burning" (June 1939; short story, first published in *Harper's Magazine*, CLXXIX, 86–96; reprinted in *A Rose for Emily and Other Stories* [see below], in *Collected Stories of William Faulkner* [see below], in *The Faulkner Reader* [see below], and in *Selected Short Stories of William Faulkner* [see below]; revised portions included in book 1 of *The Hamlet* [see below]; television adaptation with same title telecast in 1954 and another in 1980; film version on videocassette released in 1985 [see below]).

"Hand Upon the Waters" (November 4, 1939; short story, first published in *Saturday Evening Post*, CCXII, 14–15, 75–76, 78–79; reprinted in *Knight's Gambit* [see below]).

The Hamlet (April 1, 1940; novel [first in the Snopes trilogy—see *The Town* and *The Mansion* below], first published by Random House, New York; chapter 1 of book 4, "The Peasants," published in *The Portable Faulkner* [see below]; also see "Spotted Horses," above]; reset text published by Modern Library on March 20, 1950; film adaptation titled *The Long, Hot Summer* released in 1958 [see below] and television adaptation titled *The Long, Hot Summer* telecast in 1985 [see below]; re-edited text by Noel Polk, notes by Joseph Blotner and Noel Polk, published in 1990 by Library of America: *William Faulkner: Novels 1936–1940*, New York; and by Vintage International, New York, in October 1991).

"A Point of Law" (June 22, 1940; short story, first published in *Collier's Magazine*, CV, 20–21, 30, 32; reprinted revision included in "The Fire and the Hearth" in *Go Down, Moses and Other Stories* [see below]; original version reprinted in *The Uncollected Stories of William Faulkner* [see below]).

"Almost" (July 1940; short story, revised and retitled "Was"; first published in *Go Down, Moses and Other Stories* [see below]).

"The Old People" (September 1940; short story, first published in *Harper's Magazine*, CCXXXI, 418–425, revision included in *Go Down, Moses* and *Other Stories* [see below]) and reprinted in *Big Woods* [see below]; original version reprinted in *Uncollected Stories of William Faulkner* [see below]).

"Pantaloon in Black" (October 1940; short story, first published in *Harper's Magazine*, CLXXXI, 503–513, revised for *Go Down, Moses and Other Stories* [see below]; original version reprinted in *Uncollected Stories of William Faulkner* [see below]).

"Gold Is Not Always" (November 1940; short story, first published in *Atlantic Monthly*, CLXVI, 563–570; revision incorporated in "The Fire and the Hearth" in *Go Down, Moses and Other Stories* [see below]; original version reprinted in *Uncollected Stories of William Faulkner* [see below]).

"Tomorrow" (November 23, 1940; short story, first published in *Saturday Evening Post*, CCXIII, 22–23, 32, 35, 37, 38, 39; reprinted in *Knight's Gambit* [see below]; television adaptation with same title telecast in 1960 [see below] and film adaptation with same title released in 1972 [see below]).

"Go Down, Moses" (January 25, 1941; short story, first published in *Collier's Magazine*, CVII, 19–20, 45, 46; revision reprinted in *Go Down, Moses and Other Stories* [see below]; original version reprinted in *Uncollected Stories of William Faulkner* [see below]).

"The Tall Men" (May 31, 1941; short story, first published in *Saturday Evening Post*, CCXIII, 14–15, 95–96, 98–99; reprinted in *Collected Stories of William Faulkner* [see below]).

To the Editor (July 12, 1941; letter, published in *Memphis Commercial Appeal*, p. 4).

"Snow" (c. 1942; short story published posthumously in *Mississippi Quarterly*, XXVI (Summer 1973), 325–330, and in *Uncollected Stories of William Faulkner* [see below]).

"Two Soldiers" (March 28, 1942; short story, first published in *Saturday Evening Post*, CCXIV, 9–11, 35–36, 38, 40; reprinted in *Collected Stories of William Faulkner* [see below] and in *Selected Short Stories of William Faulkner* [see below]).

"The Bear" (May 9, 1942; short story, first published in *Saturday Evening Post*, CCXIV, 30–31, 74, 76–77; with major revisions included in "The Bear" in *Go Down, Moses and Other Stories* [see below], and reprinted in *The Portable Faulkner* [see below] and as a novella in *The Faulkner Reader* [see below];

reprinted without part 4 in *Big Woods* [see below]; the shorter first published version reprinted in *Uncollected Stories of William Faulkner* [see below]).

"Delta Autumn" (May/June 1942; short story, first published in *Story*, XX, 46–55; reprinted revision in *Go Down, Moses and Other Stories* [see below], in *A Rose for Emily and Other Stories by William Faulkner* [see below], and in *The Portable Faulkner* [see below]; section of reprinted revision again revised and included as epilogue in *Big Woods* [see below]; first version reprinted in *Uncollected Stories of William Faulkner* [see below]).

"Was" (May 11, 1942; short story, retitled revision of the story "Almost" [see above] and first published as the first story in *Go Down, Moses and Other Stories* [see below]; reprinted in *The Portable Faulkner* [see below]).

Go Down, Moses and Other Stories (May 11, 1942; novel containing seven interrelated stories, six of which previously published [see above], first published by Random House, New York; title changed for second edition published by Random House on January 26, 1949, and for all subsequent editions to *Go Down, Moses* [see below]).

The De Gaulle Story (July–November 1942; screenplay unproduced; published posthumously in *Faulkner: A Comprehensive Guide to the Brodsky Collection*, Vol III: *The De Gaulle Story*, edited Louis Daniel Brodsky and Robert W. Hamblin [Jackson: University Press of Mississippi, 1984]).

"Shingles for the Lord" (February 13, 1943; short story, first published in *Saturday Evening Post*, CCXV, 14–15, 68, 70–71; reprinted in *Collected Stories of William Faulkner* [see below] and in *The Faulkner Reader* [see below]).

Country Lawyer (March–April 1943; story treatment; published posthumously in *Country Lawyer and Other Stories for the Screen*, edited Louis Daniel Brodsky and Robert W. Hamblin [Jackson: University Press of Mississippi, 1987]).

"My Grandmother Millard and General Bedford Forrest and the Battle of Harrykin Creek" (March/April 1943; short story, first published in *Story*, XXII, 68–86; reprinted in *Collected Stories of William Faulkner* [see below]).

"L'Après-midi d'une Vache" (June/July 1943; short story, French translation of "Afternoon of a Cow" [see below]; first published in Maurice Edgar Coindreau's French translation in *Fontaine*, pp. 27–28).

"Shall Not Perish" (July/August 1943; short story, first published in *Story*, XXIII, 40–47; reprinted in *Collected Stories of William Faulkner* [see below] and in *A Rose for Emily* [see below]).

Battle Cry (April–August 1943; screenplay unproduced; published posthumously in *Faulkner: A Comprehensive Guide to the Brodsky Collection*, Vol IV: *Battle Cry: A Screenplay by William Faulkner*, edited Louis Daniel Brodsky and Robert W. Hamblin [Jackson: University Press of Mississippi, 1985]).

To Have and Have Not (October 1944; screenplay with Jules Furthman; directed by Howard Hawks and released by Warner Brothers).

A Rose for Emily and Other Stories by William Faulkner (April 1945; eight selected stories [see above] with foreword by Saxe Commins, Editions for the Armed Services, New York; work with same title but containing only four stories [three of which appear in the Armed Services edition but here with "Red Leaves" as the fourth story; see above], edited with annotations by Kenzaburo Ohashi and published by Kairyudo, Tokyo, n.d.).

Stallion Road (June–September 1945; screenplay unproduced; published posthumously in *Stallion Road: A Screenplay*, edited Louis Daniel Brodsky and Robert W. Hamblin [Jackson: University Press of Mississippi, 1989]).

The Portable Faulkner (April 29, 1946; selection of Faulkner's work [see above] with a new map of Yoknapatawpha County [see above, *Absalom, Absalom!*] and first appearance of the appendix on the Compsons [see below]; edited by Malcolm Cowley; first published by Viking Press, New York).

"Compson: 1699–1945" (April 29, 1946; appendix to *The Sound and the Fury* first published as "1699–1945 The Compsons" in *The Portable Faulkner* [see above]).

"An Error in Chemistry" (June 1946; short story, first published in *Ellery Queen's Mystery Magazine*, VII, 5–19; reprinted in *Knight's Gambit* [see below]).

The Big Sleep (August 1946; screenplay adaptation (with Leigh Brackett and Jules Furthman) of novel by Raymond Chandler; directed by Howard Hawks and released by Warner Brothers).

"His Name Was Pete" (August 15, 1946; article, first published in *Oxford* [Mississippi] *Eagle*, p. 1; reprinted with minor changes in *Oxford Eagle* December 21, 1950, p. 25, in *Magazine Digest*, XXVI (January 1953), 93–94, and in *Milwaukee Journal*, January 28, 1953, p. 24).

The Sound and the Fury and *As I Lay Dying* (December 20, 1946; two novels previously published separately [see above], published by Modern Library, New York, with a new appendix as a foreword by the author titled "Compson: 1699–1945" [see above]).

To the Editor (March 13, 1947; letter, first published in the *Oxford* [Mississippi] *Eagle*, p. 5; reprinted with minor changes in the *Oxford Eagle* [December 21, 1950], p. 25).

"Afternoon of a Cow" (Summer 1947; short story, first published in *Furioso*, II, 5–17; reprinted in *Parodies: An Anthology from Chaucer to Beerbohm—and After*, edited by Dwight Macdonald, published by Random House, New York, 1960; first published in 1943 in a French translation as "L'Après-midi d'une Vache" [see above]; reprinted in *Uncollected Stories of William Faulkner* [see below]).

"Lucas Beauchamp" (1948; short story, published posthumously with an introduction by Patrick Samway, S. J., in *Virginia Quarterly*, 75 (summer 1999): 417–437; with slight changes extracted from the first two chapters of *Intruder in the Dust* [see below]).

Intruder in the Dust (September 27, 1948; novel, first published by Random House, New York; film adaptation with same title released in 1949 [see below]; elsewhere; by Vintage International in October of 1991, and re-edited by Noel Polk, notes by Joseph Blotner and Noel Polk, by Library of America: *Faulkner: Novels 1942–1954*, New York, in 1994).

"A Courtship" (Autumn 1948; short story, first published in *Sewanee Review*, LVI, 634–653; reprinted in *Collected Stories of William Faulkner* [see below]).

The Old Man (November 1948; reprint of the chapters designated "Old Man" from the novel *The Wild Palms* [see above], published by New American Library, New York [also see *The Wild Palms and The Old Man* and *If I Forget Thee, Jerusalem*, below]).

Go Down, Moses (January 26, 1949; novel containing seven interrelated stories, published by Random

House, New York; previously published under the title *Go Down, Moses and Other Stories* [see above]; elsewhere; published in November 1990 by Vintage International, New York, and a re-edited text by Noel Polk with notes by Joseph Blotner and Noel Polk by Library of America: *William Faulkner: Novels 1942–1954*, New York, in 1994).

Intruder in the Dust (October 11, 1949; film adaptation with same title [see above]; directed by Clarence Brown and released by MGM).

Knight's Gambit (November 27, 1949; six mystery stories [five of which previously published, see above], first published by Random House, New York; published by Vintage Books, New York, in October 1978, elsewhere).

"Knight's Gambit" (November 27, 1949; mystery story published in *Knight's Gambit* [see above]).

"To the Voters of Oxford" (1950; broadside, first printed in Oxford, Mississippi; reprinted with minor changes in *The New Yorker*, XXVI [November 25, 1950], 29; original reprinted in "Faulkner and His Folk," by Hodding Carter, in *Princeton University Library Chronicle*, XVIII [spring 1957], 98–99).

To the Editor (March 26, 1950; letter, published in *Memphis Commercial Appeal*, Section IV, p. 4).

To the Editor (April 9, 1950; letter, published in *Memphis Commercial Appeal*, Section IV, p. 4).

To the Secretary of the American Academy of Arts and Letters (June 12, 1950; letter, published in *Proceedings of the American Academy of Arts and Letters and the National Institute of Arts and Letters*, second series, no. 1, 1951).

Collected Stories of William Faulkner (August 21, 1950; 42 previously published stories [see above], Random House, New York; republished in November 1995 by Vintage International, New York).

To the Editor (September 14, 1950; letter, first published in *Oxford* [Mississippi] *Eagle*, p. 13; reprinted in *Oxford Eagle* on December 21, 1950, p. 25, and in "Faulkner and His Folk," by Hodding Carter, in *Princeton University Library Chronicle*, XVIII [Spring 1957], 100–01).

"A Name for the City" (October 1950; fictional essay, first published in *Harper's Magazine*, CCI, 200–214; revision included in first section of the prologue to act 1 of *Requiem for a Nun* [see below]).

To the Editor (November 13, 1950; letter, published in *Time* LVI, 6).

Nobel Prize Acceptance Speech (December 10, 1950; address delivered in Stockholm, Sweden, upon receiving the Nobel Prize in literature; published in *Les Prix Nobel en 1950*, Stockholm, 1951; reprinted with minor changes as a pamphlet by Spiral Press, New York, 1951, and elsewhere; reprinted in *The Faulkner Reader* [see below], and in *Faulkner at Nagano* [see below]; recorded by Faulkner on Caedmon records [TC-1035]).

Notes on a Horsethief (February 1951 [though dated 1950]; novella with decorations by Elizabeth Calvert; published by Levee Press, Greenville, Mississippi; revised and incorporated into *A Fable* [see below]).

Address to graduating class of University High School (May 28, 1951; address delivered in Oxford, Mississippi; printed in *Oxford* [Mississippi], *Eagle*, May 31, 1951, p. 1; reprinted with minor changes as "Never Be Afraid" in *Harvard Advocate*, CXXXV [November 1951]: 7).

"An Interview with William Faulkner" (Summer 1951; interview with Lavon Rasco, published in *Western Review*, XV, 300–304).

Requiem for a Nun (September 27, 1951; novel in the form of a three-act play with a prose narrative preceding each act [sequel to *Sanctuary*, see above], first published by Random House, New York; excerpt from the novel, "The Courthouse (A Name for the City)" [act 1], published in *The Faulkner Reader* [see below]; also published by Vintage Books in April 1975, and a re-edited text by Noel Polk with notes by Noel Polk and Joseph Blotner, by Library of America: *William Faulkner: Novels 1942–1954*, New York, in 1994).

"The Jail" (September/October 1951; excerpt [preface to act 3, "The Jail" [from *Requiem for a Nun* [see above], published in *Partisan Review*, XVIII, pp. 496–515).

Address upon being made an Officer of the Legion of Honor (October 26, 1951; address delivered in New Orleans, Louisiana; facsimile of manuscript [in French] reproduced in *Princeton University Library Chronicle*, XVIII [spring 1957]).

Address to the Annual Meeting of the Delta Council (May 15, 1952; address delivered in Cleveland,

Mississippi; printed in the Greenville, Mississippi, *Delta Democrat-Times* [May 18, 1952], p. 9; reprinted in 1952 by the Delta Council in pamphlet form as *An Address Delivered by William Faulkner*, and as "Man's Responsibility to Fellow Man" in *Vital Speeches of the Day*, XVIII [September 15, 1952]: 728–730).

Review of Ernest Hemingway, *The Old Man and the Sea* (Autumn 1952; book review, published in *Shenandoah* III: 55).

"Mr. Acarius" (February 1953; short story posthumously published in *Saturday Evening Post*, CCXXXVIII (October 9, 1965): 26–27, 29, 31, and reprinted in *Uncollected Stories of William Faulkner* [see below]).

To Richard Walser (1953; letter, published in *The Enigma of Thomas Wolfe*, edited by Richard Walser, Cambridge: Harvard University Press, 1953, p. vii).

"Sherwood Anderson: An Appreciation" (June 1953; article, published in *Atlantic Monthly*, CXCI, 27–29).

Address to the graduating class of Pine Manor Junior College (June 8, 1953; addressed delivered in Wellesley, Massachusetts; printed as "Faith or Fear" in *Atlantic Monthly*, CXCII [August 1953]: 53–55).

"Conversation with William Faulkner" (January 1954; interview with Loic Bouvard, published in *Bulletin de l'association amicale universitaire France-Amérique*, pp. 23–29; translated from the French by Henry Dan Piper and published in *Modern Fiction Studies*, V [winter 1959–60]: 361–364).

"An Interview with Faulkner" (February 14, 1954; interview with A. M. Dominicus, published in *La Fiera Letteria* [Rome]; translated from the Italian by Elizabeth Nissen and published in *Faulkner Studies*, III [summer–autumn 1954]: 33–37).

"A Guest's Impression of New England" (1954; article, first published in *New England Journeys 2* (Ford Times special edition): 6–8; reprinted in *The Ford Times Guide to Travel in USA*, edited by C. H. Dykeman [New York: Golden Press, 1962]).

The Faulkner Reader (April 1, 1954; anthology containing a foreword by Faulkner, the Nobel Prize Address, the whole of *The Sound and the Fury*, three "novellas" from three novels; eight short stories, and excerpts from three novels; Random

House, New York; republished in 1959 by Modern Library, New York).

"Mississippi" (April 1954; article, first published in *Holiday*, XV, 33–47; excerpted in *Big Woods* [see below]).

"Foreword" to *The Faulkner Reader* (1954; published by Random House, New York; [see above]).

"Percy Grimm" (April 1, 1954; excerpt from *Light in August* [see above] reprinted in *The Faulkner Reader* [see above]).

"Notes on a Horsethief" (July 1954; excerpt from *A Fable* [see below], published in *Vogue*, CXXIV, pp. 46–51, 101–107; abbreviated version published with minor changes in *Perspectives USA 9* [autumn 1954]: 24–59; earlier 1951 version as novella with same title [see above]).

A Fable (August 2, 1954; novel, first published by Random House, New York; also published by New American Library in September 1958, Vintage in January 1978, and a re-edited text by Noel Polk with notes by Joseph Blotner and Noel Polk, by Library of America: *William Faulkner: Novels 1942–1954* in 1994).

The Wild Palms and The Old Man (September 1954; novel, rearranged version of *The Wild Palms* [see above] dividing the originally intended interwoven narratives into two separate sections: "The Wild Palms" and "Old Man"; published by New American Library, New York [also see below, *If I Forget Thee, Jerusalem*]).

"Hog Pawn" (c. October 1954; short story, first published posthumously in *Uncollected Stories of William Faulkner* [see below]; refashioned and included in chapter 14 of book 3, "Flem," of *The Mansion* [see below]).

"Sepulture South: Gaslight" (December 1954; short story, published in *Harper's Bazaar*, LXXXVIII, 84–85, 140–141; reprinted in *Uncollected Stories of William Faulkner* [see below]).

To the Editor (December 26, 1954; letter, *New York Times*, Section IV, p. 6).

"To the Youth of Japan" (1955; pamphlet [text in English with Japanese translation], first published by the U.S. Information Service [Tokyo]; English text reprinted in *Faulkner at Nagano* [see below]).

"An Innocent at Rinkside" (January 24, 1955; article, published in *Sports Illustrated*, II, 15).

Address upon receiving the National Book Award for Fiction (January 25, 1955; address delivered in New York; printed in *New York Times Book Review* [February 6, 1955], pp. 2, 4).

"A Walk with Faulkner" (January 30, 1955; interview with Harvey Breit, published in *New York Times Book Review*, pp. 4, 12; reprinted in Harvey Breit's *The Writer Observed*, World, Cleveland, 1956, pp. 281–284).

To the Editor (February 20, 1955; letter, first published in the *Memphis Commercial Appeal*, Section V, p. 3; reprinted in *New York Times Book Review* [March 13, 1955], p. 8).

"Race at Morning" (March 5, 1955; short story, first published in *Saturday Evening Post*, CCXXVII, 26, 103–104, 106; revision reprinted in *Big Woods* [see below] and in *Selected Short Stories of William Faulkner* [see below]; original version reprinted in *Uncollected Stories of William Faulkner* [see below]).

To the Editor (March 20, 1955; letter, first published in the *Memphis Commercial Appeal*, Section V, p. 3; reprinted with changes in "On Fear: The South in Labor" [see below]; reprinted in full in "Faulkner and His Folk," by Hodding Carter, in *Princeton University Library Chronicle*, XVIII [Spring 1957]: 102–103).

To the Editor (March 25, 1955; letter, published in *New York Times*, p. 22).

New Orleans Sketches by William Faulkner (April 1, 1955; thirteen of sixteen prose sketches from the *New Orleans Times-Picayune* [see above], edited with notes in Japanese and English by Ichiro Nishizaki, Hokuseido Press, Tokyo; eleven reprinted in *Mirrors of Chartres Street* [see above]).

To the Editor (April 3, 1955; letter, first published in the *Memphis Commercial Appeal*, Section V, p. 3; reprinted in "Faulkner and His Folk," by Hodding Carter, in *Princeton University Library Chronicle*, XVIII [Spring 1957]: 103–104).

To the Editor (April 10, 1955; letter, published in the *Memphis Commercial Appeal*, Section V, p. 3).

Address at the University of Oregon (April 13, 1955; address delivered in Eugene, Oregon; printed as "On Privacy. The American Dream: What Happened to It" in *Harper's Magazine*, CCXI [July 1955]: 33–38).

To the Editor (April 17, 1955; letter, published in the *Memphis Commercial Appeal*, Section V, p. 3).

"Kentucky: May: Saturday" (May 16, 1955; article, first published in *Sports Illustrated*, II, 22–24, 26; reprinted in *Essays Today 2*, edited by Richard M. Ludwig [New York: Harcourt, Brace, 1956]).

Land of the Pharaohs (July 1955; screenplay with Harry Kurnitz and Harold Jack Bloom; directed by Howard Hawks and released by Warner Brothers).

"Impressions of Japan" (September 26 and October 2, 1955; article released by the United States Embassy in Tokyo, first part published in the *Memphis Commercial Appeal*, [September 1955], Section V, p. 14, and second part published in the *Memphis Commercial Appeal*, [October 2, 1955], Section V, p. 10; reprinted in *Faulkner at Nagano* [see below] and in *Esquire*, L [December 1958]: 140).

"By the People" (October 1955; short story, first published in *Mademoiselle*, XLI, 86–89, 130, 131, 132, 133, 134, 135, 136, 137, 138, 139; revision included in chapter 13 of *The Mansion* [see below]).

Address to the annual meeting of the Southern Historical Association (November 10, 1955; address delivered in Memphis, Tennessee; printed in the *Memphis Commercial Appeal*, [November 11, 1955], p. 8; reprinted as "To Claim Freedom Is Not Enough" in *Christian Century*, LXXII [November 30, 1955]: 1,395–1,396; reprinted with additions as "American Segregation and the World Crisis" in the pamphlet, *Three Views of the Segregation Decisions*, pp. 9–12 [Atlanta, Georgia: Southern Regional Council, 1956]).

A Rose for Emily (1956; four stories [see above and also see *A Rose for Emily and Other Stories*], edited with notes by Naotaro Takiguchi and Masao Takahashi, published by Nan 'un-do, Tokyo; two of the stories—"Shall Not Perish" and "Crevasse"—do not appear in *A Rose for Emily and Other Stories*).

"Message Given at Nagano" (1956; statement, published in *Faulkner at Nagano* [see below]).

"A Letter to the North" (March 5, 1956; article, first published in *Life*, XL, 51–52; excerpt reprinted in *Readers' Digest*, LXVIII [May 1956]: 75–78).

"The Art of Fiction XII: William Faulkner" (Spring 1956; interview with Jean Stein, published in *Paris Review* 12: 28–52; reprinted in *Writers at Work: The Paris Review Interviews*, edited by Malcolm Cowley and published by Viking Press, New York, 1958, pp. 119–141).

"A Talk with William Faulkner" (March 22, 1956; interview with Russell Warren Howe, published in *Reporter*, XIV, pp. 18–20).

To the Editor (March 26, 1956; letter, published in *Life*, XL, 19 [also see above, "A Letter to the North"]).

To the Editor (April 19, 1956; letter, published in *Reporter*, XIV, 7).

To the Editor (April 23, 1956; letter, *Time*, LXVII, 12).

"On Fear: The South in Labor" (June 1956; article, published in *Harper's Magazine*, CCXII, 29–34).

"The Art of Fiction: An Interview with William Faulkner" (Summer 1956; interview with Cynthia Grenier, published in *Accent* XVI, pp. 167–177).

Faulkner at Nagano (July 15, 1956; interviews, short written statements and the Nobel Prize Address, edited with a preface by Robert A. Jelliffe; published by Kenyusha, Tokyo; many of the interviews reedited and rearranged, published in *Esquire*, L (December 1958): 139, 141–142).

"If I Were a Negro" (September 1956; article, published in *Ebony*, XI, 70–73).

Big Woods (October 14, 1955; four previously published hunting stories, revised with preludes and epilogue, published by Random House, New York; republished in 1994 by Vintage International, New York).

To the Editor (December 10, 1956; letter, *Time*, LXVIII, 6, 9).

To the Editor (December 16, 1956; letter, *New York Times*, section IV, p. 8).

To the Editor (February 11, 1957; letter, *Time*, LXIX, 8).

Address upon receiving the Silver Medal of the Athens Academy (March 28, 1957; address delivered in Athens, Greece; printed in *The Literary Career of William Faulkner* by James B. Meriwether [Princeton University Library, 1961]).

The Town (May 1, 1957; novel [second in the Snopes trilogy—see *The Hamlet*, above, and *The Mansion*, below], first published by Random House, New York; also published by Vintage Books in January 1961; a re-edited text by Noel Polk with notes by Joseph Blotner and Noel Polk, by Library of America: *William Faulkner: Novels 1957–1962* in 1999).

"The Waifs" (May 4, 1957; excerpt from *The Town* [see above], published in *Saturday Evening Post*, CCXXIX, pp. 27, 116, 118, and 120).

To the Editor (October 13, 1957; letter, published in *New York Times*, Section IV, p. 10).

The Tarnished Angels (January 1958; film adaptation of *Pylon* [see above]; screenplay by George Zuckerman and directed by Douglas Sirk; released by Universal-International).

The Long, Hot Summer (March 1958; film adaptation of *The Hamlet* [see above]; screenplay by Irving Ravetch and Harriet Frank Jr.; directed by Martin Ritt and released by Twentieth Century–Fox; television version with same title, see below).

Three Famous Short Novels (1958; excerpts from three novels: *The Hamlet* ["Spotted Horses"], *The Wild Palms* ["Old Man"], and *Go Down, Moses* ["The Bear"]; published by Random House, New York).

New Orleans Sketches (1958; sixteen prose sketches from the *Times-Picayune* [see above] and eleven short pieces titled "New Orleans" [see above] from the *Double Dealer*; edited with introduction by Carvel Collins; published by Rutgers University Press, New Brunswick, N.J.; republished in 1961 by Grove Press, New York; new edition with additional essay published in 1968 by Random House, New York).

Address to the Raven, Jefferson, and ODK Societies (February 20, 1958; address delivered in Charlottesville, Virginia; printed as "A Word to Virginians" in *University of Virginia Magazine*, II [spring 1958]: 11–14; reprinted in *Faulkner in the University* [see below]).

Address to the English Club of the University of Virginia (April 24, 1958; printed as "A Word to Young Writers" in *Faulkner in the University* [see below]).

The Sound and the Fury (March 1959; film adaption of novel with same title [see above]; screenplay by Irving Ravetch and Harriet Frank Jr.; directed by Martin Ritt and released by Twentieth Century–Fox).

Faulkner in the University (1959; transcribed recordings of class conferences and addresses, edited by Frederick L. Gwynn and Joseph L. Blotner, Charlottesville: University Press of Virginia).

Note to *Requiem for a Nun: a Play* from the novel by William Faulkner, see above (1959; adapted to the stage by Ruth Ford; published by Random House, New York).

Address to the seventh national conference of the U.S. National Commission for UNESCO (October 2, 1959; address delivered in Denver, Colorado; printed as "From Yoknapatawpha to UNESCO, the Dream" in *Saturday Review*, XLII [November 14, 1959]: 21).

"Notice" (October 22, 1959; public notice (an appeal to hunters on Faulkner's land), first published in the *Oxford* [Mississippi] *Eagle*, p. 7; reprinted in *Time*, LXXIV [November 2, 1959]: 29).

The Mansion (November 13, 1959; novel [third in the Snopes trilogy—see *The Hamlet* and *The Mansion* above], first published by Random House, New York; also published by Vintage Books in September 1965, and a re-edited text by Noel Polk with notes by Joseph Blotner and Noel Polk, by Library of America: *William Faulkner: Novels 1957–1962* in 1999).

Note to *The Mansion* by William Faulkner (November 13, 1959; note published with the novel, see above).

"Mink Snopes" (December 1959; excerpt [chapters 1 and 2] from *The Mansion* published in *Esquire*, LII, pp. 226–230, 247–264).

Tomorrow (March 7, 1960; television adaptation of short story of same title [see above]; telefilm by Horton Foote and directed by Robert Mulligan; telecast on CBS; for film version of short story, see below].

To the Editor (August 28, 1960; letter, published in *New York Times*, Section IV, p. 10).

To Sherwood Anderson (1961; letter [undated], facsimile reproduced in *The Literary Career of William Faulkner* by James B. Meriwether, Princeton University Library, plates 27, 28, and 29; also see Faulkner's novel *Mosquitoes* [pp. 277–278] where he incorporates material from this letter).

Sanctuary (February 1961; film adaptation based on novel of same title and *Requiem for a Nun* [see above]; screenplay by James Poe and directed by Tony Richardson; released by Twentieth Century-Fox).

"Albert Camus" (Spring 1961; homage to Albert Camus after his death [1960], published in *Transatlantic Review* 6: 5; French translation published a year earlier in the *Nouvelle Revue française*).

"Hell Creek Crossing" (March 31, 1962; excerpt from *The Reivers* [see below] published in *Saturday Evening Post*, CCXXXV, pp. 22–25).

Selected Short Stories of William Faulkner (1962; thirteen short stories previously published [see above], Modern Library, New York).

The Reivers (June 4, 1962; novel, first published by Random House, New York; also published by Vintage Books in September 1992; a re-edited text by Noel Polk with notes by Joseph Blotner and Noel Polk published by Library of America: *William Faulkner: Novels 1957–1962* in 1999; film adaptation with same title released in 1969 [see below]).

William Faulkner: Early Prose and Poetry (1962; previously published poems, prose pieces, and pen-and-ink drawings [see above]; compiled with an introduction by Carvel Collins; published by Little, Brown, Boston).

"The Education of Lucius Priest" (May 1962; edited excerpt from *The Reivers* [see above] published in *Esquire*, LVII, pp. 109–116).

Address upon receiving the Gold Medal for Fiction of the National Institute of Arts and Letters (May 24, 1962; address delivered in New York; printed in *Proceedings of the American Academy of Arts and Letters and the National Institute of Arts and Letters*, Second Series, No. 13 [New York, 1963]: 226–227).

William Faulkner's University Pieces (1962; edited with an introduction by Carvel Collins, Kendyusha Press).

Essays, Speeches, and Public Lectures by William Faulkner (1966; collection of Faulkner's articles, speeches, forewords, book reviews, and public lectures; edited by James B. Meriwether and published by Random House, New York, 1966).

The Reivers (1969; film adaptation of novel of same title [see above]; screenplay by Irving Ravetch and Harriet Frank Jr.; directed by Mark Rydell and released by National General).

Tomorrow (1972; film adaptation of short story of same title [see above]; screenplay by Horton Foote; directed by Joseph Anthony and released by Filmgroup [for television adaptation of short story, see above]).

Flags in the Dust (August 22, 1973; novel [complete text of the novel *Sartoris*, see above]; edited with an introduction by Douglas Day and published posthumously by Random House, New York).

Uncollected Stories of William Faulkner (1979; forty-five stories [see above], some revised for books and others uncollected or unpublished; edited and notes by Joseph Blotner; first published by Random House, New York; republished in a centenary edition by Vintage International, New York, in September 1997).

The Marionettes: A Play in One Act (1977; edited with an introduction by Noel Polk; published by University Press of Virginia, Charlottesville).

Mississippi Poems (1979; poems published posthumously by Yoknapatawpha Press, Oxford, Miss.).

Barn Burning (March 17, 1980; television adaptation of short story of same title [see above]; telefilm by Horton Foote and directed by Peter Werner; telecast on PBS).

Helen: A Courtship (1981; poems for Helen Baird, published posthumously by Tulane University, New Orleans, and Yoknapatawpha Press, Oxford, Miss.).

The Long, Hot Summer (October 6 and 7, 1985; television adaptation of *The Hamlet* [see above] and its film version titled *The Long, Hot Summer* [see above]; telefilm by Rita Mae Brown and Dennis Turner; directed by Stuart Cooper; telecast by NBC).

If I Forget Thee, Jerusalem (1990; novel, original title of *The Wild Palms* [see above]; corrected text by Noel Polk published in 1990 by Library of America [volume 2 of Faulkner's collected works: *Novels 1936–1940*], New York, and in November 1995 by Vintage International, New York).

Old Man (1998; telefilm version of the "Old Man" section of the novel *Wild Palms* [see above]; telefilm by Horton Foote and directed by John Kent Harrison; telecast on CBS).

The Sound and the Fury (April Seventh, 1928) (2008; dramatic adaptation of the first chapter of *The Sound and the Fury*; produced by Elevator Repair Service theater company.)

2. Categorical Chronology of Faulkner's Writings, Interviews, Addresses, and Publications

Addresses

Nobel Prize Acceptance Speech (December 10, 1950; address delivered in Stockholm, Sweden, upon receiving the Nobel Prize in literature; published in *Les Prix Nobel en 1950*, Stockholm, 1951; reprinted with minor changes as a pamphlet by Spiral Press, New York, 1951, and elsewhere; reprinted in *The Faulkner Reader* and in *Faulkner at Nagano*; recorded by Faulkner on Caedmon records [TC-1035]).

Address to graduating class of University High School (May 28, 1951, address delivered in Oxford, Mississippi; printed in the *Oxford* [Mississippi] *Eagle*, May 31, 1951, p. 1; reprinted with minor changes as "Never Be Afraid" in *Harvard Advocate*, CXXXV [November 1951]: 7).

Address upon being made an Officer of the Legion of Honor (October 26, 1951; address delivered in New Orleans, Louisiana; facsimile of manuscript [in French] reproduced in *Princeton University Library Chronicle*, XVIII [spring 1957]).

Address to the Annual Meeting of the Delta Council (May 15, 1952; address delivered in Cleveland, Mississippi; printed in the Greenville, Mississippi, *Delta Democrat-Times* [May 18, 1952], p. 9; reprinted in 1952 by the Delta Council in pamphlet form as *An Address Delivered by William Faulkner*, and as "Man's Responsibility to Fellow Man" in *Vital Speeches of the Day*, XVIII [September 15, 1952], 728–730).

Address to the graduating class of Pine Manor Junior College (June 8, 1953; addressed delivered in Wellesley, Massachusetts; printed as "Faith or Fear" in *Atlantic Monthly*, CXCII [August 1953]: 53–55).

Address upon receiving the National Book Award for Fiction (January 25, 1955; address delivered in New York; printed in *New York Times Book Review* [February 6, 1955], pp. 2, 4).

Address at the University of Oregon (April 13, 1955; address delivered in Eugene, Oregon; printed as "On Privacy. The American Dream: What Happened to It" in *Harper's Magazine*, CCXI [July 1955]: 33–38).

Address to the annual meeting of the Southern Historical Association (November 10, 1955; address delivered in Memphis, Tennessee; printed in the *Memphis Commercial Appeal* [November 11, 1955], p. 8; reprinted as "To Claim Freedom Is Not Enough" in *Christian Century*, LXXII [November 30, 1955]: 1,395–1,396; reprinted with additions as "American Segregation and the World Crisis" in the pamphlet *Three Views of the Segregation*

Decisions, pp. 9–12 [Atlanta, Georgia: Southern Regional Council, 1956]).

Address upon receiving the Silver Medal of the Athens Academy (March 28, 1957; address delivered in Athens, Greece; printed in *The Literary Career of William Faulkner* by James B. Meriwether [Princeton University Library, 1961]).

Address to the Raven, Jefferson, and ODK Societies (February 20, 1958; address delivered in Charlottesville, Virginia; printed as "A Word to Virginians" in *University of Virginia Magazine*, II [Spring 1958]: 11–14; reprinted in *Faulkner in the University*).

Address to the English Club of the University of Virginia (April 24, 1958; printed as "A Word to Young Writers" in *Faulkner in the University*).

Address to the seventh national conference of the U.S. National Commission for UNESCO (October 2, 1959; address delivered in Denver, Colorado; printed as "From Yoknapatawpha to UNESCO, the Dream" in *Saturday Review*, XLII [November 14, 1959]: 21).

Address upon receiving the Gold Medal for Fiction of the National Institute of Arts and Letters (May 24, 1962; address delivered in New York; printed in *Proceedings of the American Academy of Arts and Letters and the National Institute of Arts and Letters*, Second Series, 13 [New York, 1963]: 226–227).

Articles and Essays

"The Ivory Tower" (March 17, 1920; critical essay, first published in *Mississippian*, IX, 4; reprinted with minor changes in "Faulkner Juvenilia" by Martha Mayes, *New Campus Writing No. 2*, edited by Nolan Miller [New York: Bantam, 1957]).

"American Drama: Eugene O'Neill" (February 3, 1922; article, first published in *Mississippian*, XI, 5; reprinted in *William Faulkner: Early Prose and Poetry*).

"American Drama: Inhibitions" (March 17 and 24, 1922; article, first section published in *Mississippian*, XI [March 17, 1922]: 5, and second section in *Mississippian*, XI [March 24, 1922]: 5; reprinted in *William Faulkner: Early Prose and Poetry*).

"On Criticism" (January/February 1925; article; first published in *Double Dealer*, VII, 83–84; reprinted in *Salmagundi* and in *William Faulkner: Early Prose and Poetry*).

"Verse Old and Nascent: A Pilgrimage" (April 1925; article, first published in *The Double Dealer*, VII, 129–131; reprinted in *Salmagundi* and in *William Faulkner: Early Prose and Poetry*).

"Sherwood Anderson" (April 26, 1925; article, first published in the *Dallas Morning News*, part 3, p. 7; reprinted in *Princeton University Library Chronicle*, XVIII (spring 1957), 89–94, and in *William Faulkner: New Orleans Sketches* [1968 Random House edition], edited by Carvel Collins).

"His Name Was Pete" (August 15, 1946; article, first published in the *Oxford* [Mississippi] *Eagle*, p. 1; reprinted with minor changes in *Oxford Eagle* December 21, 1950, p. 25, in *Magazine Digest*, XXVI (January 1953): 93–94, and in the *Milwaukee Journal*, January 28, 1953, p. 24).

"Sherwood Anderson: An Appreciation" (June 1953; article, published in *Atlantic Monthly*, CXCI, 27–29).

"A Guest's Impression of New England" (1954; article, first published in *New England Journeys Number 2* (*Ford Times* special edition), 6–8; reprinted in *The Ford Times Guide to Travel in USA*, edited by C. H. Dykeman [New York: Golden Press, 1962]).

"Mississippi" (April 1954; article, first published in *Holiday*, XV, 33–47; excerpted in *Big Woods*).

"An Innocent at Rinkside" (January 24, 1955; article, published in *Sports Illustrated*, II, 15).

"Kentucky: May: Saturday" (May 16, 1955; article, first published in *Sports Illustrated*, II, 22–24, 26; reprinted in *Essays Today 2*, edited by Richard M. Ludwig [New York: Harcourt, Brace, 1956]).

"Impressions of Japan" (September 26 and October 2, 1955; article released by the United States Embassy in Tokyo, first part published in the *Memphis Commercial Appeal* [September 26, 1955], Section V, p. 14, and second part published in the *Memphis Commercial Appeal*, [October 2, 1955], Section V, p. 10; reprinted in *Faulkner at Nagano* and in *Esquire*, L [December 1958]: 140).

"A Letter to the North" (March 5, 1956; article, first published in *Life*, XL, 51–52; excerpt reprinted in *Readers' Digest*, LXVIII [May 1956]: 75–78).

"On Fear: The South in Labor" (June 1956; article, published in *Harper's Magazine*, CCXII, 29–34).

"If I Were a Negro" (September 1956; article, published in *Ebony*, XI, 70–73).

Collections

These 13 (September 21, 1931; collection of 13 short stories; published by Cape & Smith, New York, 1931; stories reprinted in *Collected Stories of William Faulkner* [see below]).

Doctor Martino and Other Stories (April 16, 1934; collection of 14 stories, published by Smith & Haas, New York).

A *Rose for Emily and Other Stories by William Faulkner* (April 1945; eight selected stories [see above] with foreword by Saxe Commins, Editions for the Armed Services, New York; work with same title but containing only four stories [three of which appear in the Armed Services edition but here with "Red Leaves" as the fourth story; see above], edited with annotations by Kenzaburo Ohashi and published by Kairyudo, Tokyo, n.d.).

The Portable Faulkner (April 29, 1946; selection of Faulkner's works with a new map of Yoknapatawpha County [see the novel *Absalom, Absalom!*] and first appearance of the appendix on the Compsons; edited by Malcolm Cowley; first published by Viking Press, New York).

Knight's Gambit (November 27, 1949; six mystery stories [five of which previously published, see above], first published by Random House, New York; published by Vintage Books, New York, in October 1978, elsewhere).

Collected Stories of William Faulkner (August 21, 1950; 42 previously published stories, Random House, New York; republished in November 1995 by Vintage International, New York).

The Faulkner Reader (April 1, 1954; anthology containing a foreword by Faulkner, the Nobel Prize Address, the whole of *The Sound and the Fury*, three "novellas" from three novels; eight short stories, and excerpts from three novels; Random House, New York; republished in 1959 by Modern Library, New York).

Big Woods (October 14, 1955; four previously published hunting stories, revised with preludes and epilogue, published by Random House, New York; republished in 1994 by Vintage International, New York).

Three Famous Short Novels (1958; excerpts from three novels: *The Hamlet* ["Spotted Horses"], *The Wild Palms* ["Old Man"], and *Go Down, Moses* ["The Bear"]; published by Random House, New York).

Selected Short Stories of William Faulkner (1962; 13 short stories previously published, Modern Library, New York).

Uncollected Stories of William Faulkner (1979; 45 stories, some revised for books and others uncollected or unpublished; edited and notes by Joseph Blotner; first published by Random House, New York; republished in a centenary edition by Vintage International, New York, in September 1997).

Fable

Mayday (January 27, 1926; fable [hand-lettered, illustrated, and bound by Faulkner] given to Helen Baird; facsimile reproduction with a companion essay by Carvel Collins published by University of Notre Dame Press, Notre Dame, 1977; published with text set in type and illustrations reproduced, with revised essay as an introduction, by University of Notre Dame Press, Notre Dame, 1980).

Fairy Tale

"The Wishing Tree" (c. January/February 1927; posthumously published in *Saturday Evening Post* 240 [April 8, 1967]: 48–53, 57–58, 60–63; published in book form by Random House, New York, on April 10, 1967).

Forewords, Prefaces, Introductions, and Appendixes

"Foreword" to *Sherwood Anderson & Other Famous Creoles: A Gallery of Contemporary New Orleans* by William Spratling (1926; published by Pelican Bookshop Press, New Orleans; reprinted in *The Tangled Fire of William Faulkner* by William Van O'Connor, Minneapolis: University of Minnesota Press, 1954).

The Sound and the Fury and *As I Lay Dying* (December 20, 1946; two novels previously published separately, published by Modern Library, New York, with a new appendix as a foreword by the author titled "Compson: 1699–1945").

The Faulkner Reader (April 1, 1954; anthology containing a foreword by Faulkner, the Nobel Prize Address, the whole of *The Sound and the Fury*, three "novellas" from three novels; eight short stories, and excerpts from three novels; Random House, New York; republished in 1959 by Modern Library, New York).

"Foreword" to *The Faulkner Reader* (1954; published by Random House, New York).

Interviews

"An Interview with William Faulkner" (Summer 1951; interview with Lavon Rasco, published in *Western Review*, XV, pp. 300–304).

"Conversation with William Faulkner" (January 1954; interview with Loic Bouvard, published in *Bulletin de l'association amicale universitaire France-Amérique*, pp. 23–29; translated from the French by Henry Dan Piper and published in *Modern Fiction Studies*, V [winter 1959–60]: 361–364).

"An Interview with Faulkner" (February 14, 1954; interview with A. M. Dominicus, published in *La Fiera Letteria* [Rome]; translated from the Italian by Elizabeth Nissen and published in *Faulkner Studies*, III (summer–autumn 1954]: 33–37).

"A Walk with Faulkner" (January 30, 1955; interview with Harvey Breit, published in *New York Times Book Review*, pp. 4, 12; reprinted in Harvey Breit's *The Writer Observed* [Cleveland: World, 1956], pp. 281–284).

"The Art of Fiction XII: William Faulkner" (spring 1956; interview with Jean Stein, published in *Paris Review* 12: 28–52; reprinted in *Writers at Work: The Paris Review Interviews*, edited by Malcolm Cowley and published by Viking Press, New York, 1958, pp. 119–141).

"A Talk with William Faulkner" (March 22, 1956; interview with Russell Warren Howe, published in *Reporter*, XIV, pp. 18–20).

"The Art of Fiction: An Interview with William Faulkner" (summer 1956; interview with Cynthia Grenier, published in *Accent*, XVI, pp. 167–177).

Faulkner at Nagano (July 15, 1956; interviews, short written statements and the Nobel Prize Address, edited with a preface by Robert A. Jelliffe; published by Kenyusha, Tokyo; many of the interviews reedited and rearranged, published in *Esquire*, L (December 1958): 139, 141–142).

Letters

To the Editor (April 7, 1920; letter, first published in *Mississippian*, IX, 1; reprinted in "Faulkner Juvenilia" by Martha Mayes, *New Campus Writing No.*

2, edited by Nolan Miller [New York: Bantam, 1957]).

To the Editor (April 1930; letter, published in *Forum*, LXXXIII, lvi).

To Maurice Edgar Coindreau (April 14, 1932; letter, published in facsimile in *Princeton University Library Chronicle*, XVIII [spring 1957]: plate 2).

To the President of the League of American Writers (1938; letter, published in *Writers Take Sides: Letters about the War in Spain from 418 American Authors* [New York: League of American Writers]).

To the Editor (July 12, 1941; letter, published in the *Memphis Commercial Appeal*, p. 4).

To the Editor (March 13, 1947; letter, first published in the *Oxford* [Mississippi] *Eagle*, p. 5; reprinted with minor changes in the *Oxford Eagle* [December 21, 1950], p. 25).

To the Editor (March 26, 1950; letter, published in the *Memphis Commercial Appeal*, Section IV, p. 4).

To the Editor (April 9, 1950; letter, published in the *Memphis Commercial Appeal*, Section IV, p. 4).

To the Secretary of the American Academy of Arts and Letters (June 12, 1950; letter, published in *Proceedings of the American Academy of Arts and Letters and the National Institute of Arts and Letters*, Second Series, 1, 1951).

To the Editor (September 14, 1950; letter, first published in the *Oxford* [Mississippi] *Eagle*, p. 13; reprinted in the *Eagle* on December 21, 1950, p. 25, and in "Faulkner and His Folk," by Hodding Carter, in *Princeton University Library Chronicle* XVIII [spring 1957], 100–101).

To the Editor (November 13, 1950; letter, published in *Time*, LVI, 6).

To Richard Walser (1953; letter, published in *The Enigma of Thomas Wolfe*, edited by Richard Walser, Cambridge: Harvard University Press, 1953, p. vii).

To the Editor (December 26, 1954; letter, *New York Times*, Section IV, p. 6).

To the Editor (February 20, 1955; letter, first published in the *Memphis Commercial Appeal*, Section V, p. 3; reprinted in *New York Times Book Review* [March 13, 1955], p. 8).

To the Editor (March 20, 1955; letter, first published in the *Memphis Commercial Appeal*, Section V, p. 3;

reprinted with changes in "On Fear: The South in Labor; reprinted in full in "Faulkner and His Folk," by Hodding Carter, in *Princeton University Library Chronicle*, XVIII [spring 1957]: 102–103).

To the Editor (March 25, 1955; letter, published in *New York Times*, p. 22).

To the Editor (April 3, 1955; letter, first published in the *Memphis Commercial Appeal*, Section V, p. 3; reprinted in "Faulkner and His Folk," by Hodding Carter, in *Princeton University Library Chronicle*, XVIII [spring 1957]: 103–104).

To the Editor (April 10, 1955; letter, published in the *Memphis Commercial Appeal*, Section V, p. 3).

To the Editor (April 17, 1955; letter, published in the *Memphis Commercial Appeal*, Section V, p. 3.).

To the Editor (March 26, 1956; letter, published in *Life*, XL, 19; [also see above, "A Letter to the North"]).

To the Editor (April 19, 1956; letter, published in *Reporter*, XIV, 7).

To the Editor (April 23, 1956; letter, *Time*, LXVII, 12).

To the Editor (December 10, 1956, letter, *Time*, LXVIII, 6, 9).

To the Editor (December 16, 1956, letter, *New York Times*, Section IV, p. 8).

To the Editor (February 11, 1957, letter, *Time*, LXIX, 8).

To the Editor (October 13, 1957, letter, published in *New York Times*, Section IV, p. 10).

To the Editor (August 28, 1960, letter, published in *New York Times*, Section IV, p. 10).

To Sherwood Anderson (1961; letter [undated], facsimile reproduced in *The Literary Career of William Faulkner* by James B. Meriwether, Princeton University Library, plates 27, 28, and 29; also see Faulkner's novel *Mosquitoes* [pp. 277–281] where he incorporates material from this letter).

Selected Letters of William Faulkner (1977; selected letters edited by Joseph Blotner, published by Random House, New York)

Novels

Elmer (1925; unfinished novel; typescript posthumously published in *Mississippi Quarterly* 36 [summer 1983]: 343–447, and by Seajay Press of Northport, Alabama, in 1983; see the short story "A Portrait of Elmer," below).

Soldiers' Pay (February 25, 1926; novel, first published by Boni & Liveright, New York; elsewhere since; re-edited by Noel Polk, notes by Joseph Blotner and Noel Polk, published by Library of America: *William Faulkner: Novels 1926–1929*, New York, in 2006).

Father Abraham (1926–27; an unfinished novel, edited with an introduction and textual notes by James B. Meriwether and published posthumously by Red Ozier Press, New York, in 1983 [limited edition of 210 copies] and by Random House, New York, in 1984 [facsimile edition]; forms the beginning of *The Hamlet*; recast as "Spotted Horses").

Mosquitoes (April 30, 1927; novel, first published by Boni & Liveright, New York; elsewhere since; re-edited by Noel Polk, notes by Joseph Blotner and Noel Polk, published by Library of America: *William Faulkner: Novels 1926–1929*, New York, in 2006).

Sartoris (January 31, 1929; novel; published by Harcourt, Brace, New York; elsewhere since; also see below, *Flags in the Dust*).

The Sound and the Fury (October 7, 1929; novel, first published by Cape & Smith, New York; elsewhere since; most of the last chapter, "April Eighth, 1928," published under the title "Dilsey" in *The Portable Faulkner*; published in 1946 by Modern Library, New York, with an appendix as a foreword titled "Compson: 1699–1945" and together with *As I Lay Dying*; complete novel published with the appendix at the end in *The Faulkner Reader*; film adaptation with same title released in 1959; corrected text by Noel Polk published by Random House, New York, in 1984; re-edited by Noel Polk, notes by Joseph Blotner and Noel Polk, published by Library of America: *William Faulkner: Novels 1926–1929*, New York, in 2006).

As I Lay Dying (October 6, 1930; novel, first published by Cape & Smith, New York; elsewhere since; published together with *The Sound and the Fury*; new edition published in 1964 by Random House, New York; re-edited text by Noel Polk published in 1985 by Library of America: *William Faulkner: Novels 1930–1935*, New York, and by Vintage International, New York, in October 1990).

Sanctuary (February 9, 1931; novel, first published by Cape & Smith, New York; elsewhere since; published with an introduction by Faulkner by Modern Library, New York, on 25 March 1932; film adaptation titled *The Story of Temple Drake* released in 1933; chapter 25 published under the title "Uncle Bud and the Three Madams" in *The Portable Faulkner*; published together with *Requiem for a Nun*; film adaptation based on *Sanctuary* and *Requiem for a Nun*, titled *Sanctuary*, released in 1961; re-edited by Noel Polk with notes by Joseph Blotner and Noel Polk, published in 1985 by Library of America: *William Faulkner: Novels 1930–1935*, New York; the corrected text with Faulkner's introduction in the Editors' Note published by Vintage International, New York, in December 1993).

Light in August (October 6, 1932; novel; first published by Smith & Haas, New York; elsewhere since; excerpt from novel published under title of "Percy Grimm" in *The Faulkner Reader*; re-edited by Noel Polk with notes by Joseph Blotner and Noel Polk, published in 1985 by Library of America: *William Faulkner: Novels 1930–1935*, New York, and in October 1990 by Vintage International, New York).

Absalom, Absalom! (October 26, 1936; novel [with map of Yoknapatawpha County], first published by Random House, New York; elsewhere since; chapter 2 published in *The Portable Faulkner*; re-edited by Noel Polk published by Random House, New York, in 1986, and by Library of America with notes by Joseph Blotner and Noel Polk; *William Faulkner: Novels 1936–1940*, New York, in 1990).

The Unvanquished (February 15, 1938; series of seven interrelated stories, first published by Random House, New York; first six are revisions of previously published short stories; stories III, "Raid," and VII, "An Odor of Verbena," published in *The Portable Faulkner*; basis of unproduced screenplay of same title by Sidney Howard for MGM, 1938; re-edited by Noel Polk with notes by Joseph Blotner and Noel Polk, published in 1990 by Library of America: *William Faulkner: Novels 1936–1940*, New York, and in October 1991 by Vintage International, New York).

The Wild Palms (January 19, 1939; novel with two interwoven narratives ("Wild Palms" and "Old Man"), first published by Random House, New York; the parts designated "Old Man" published under the title "Old Man" in *The Portable Faulkner* and as a novella in *The Faulkner Reader*; elsewhere since; also see below: *The Wild Palms and The Old Man* and *The Old Man*; re-edited by Noel Polk, with notes by Joseph Blotner and Noel Polk, published as *If I Forget Thee, Jerusalem* in 1990 by Library of America: *William Faulkner: Novels 1936–1940* and by Vintage International in 1995).

The Hamlet (April 1, 1940; novel [first in the Snopes trilogy—see *The Town* and *The Mansion*, below], first published by Random House, New York; chapter 1 of book 4, "The Peasants," published in *The Portable Faulkner* [also see "Spotted Horses" under *Short Stories* below]; reset text published by Modern Library on March 20, 1950; film adaptation titled *The Long, Hot Summer* released in 1958; television adaptation titled *The Long, Hot Summer* telecast in 1985; re-edited by Noel Polk with notes by Joseph Blotner and Noel Polk, published in 1990 by the Library of America: *William Faulkner: Novels 1936–1940*, New York, and by Vintage International, New York, in October 1991).

Go Down, Moses and Other Stories (May 11, 1942; novel containing seven interrelated stories, six of which previously published, first published by Random House, New York; title changed for second edition published by Random House on January 26, 1949 and for all subsequent editions to *Go Down, Moses*).

The Sound and the Fury and *As I Lay Dying* (December 20, 1946; two novels previously published separately, published by Modern Library, New York, with a new appendix as a foreword by the author titled "Compson: 1699–1945").

Intruder in the Dust (September 27, 1948; novel, first published by Random House, New York; film adaptation with same title released in 1949; elsewhere; by Vintage International in October of 1991, and re-edited by Noel Polk with notes by Joseph Blotner and Noel Polk, by the Library of America: *William Faulkner: Novels 1942–1954*, New York, in 1994).

Go Down, Moses (January 26, 1949; novel containing seven interrelated stories, published by Random House, New York; previously published under the title *Go Down, Moses and Other Stories*; elsewhere; published in November 1990 by Vintage International, New York, and re-edited by Noel Polk, with notes by Joseph Blotner and Noel Polk, by the Library of America: *William Faulkner: Novels 1942–1954*, New York, in 1994).

Requiem for a Nun (September 27, 1951; novel in the form of a three-act play with a prose narrative preceding each act [sequel to *Sanctuary*, first published by Random House, New York]; excerpt from the novel, "The Courthouse (A Name for the City)" [act 1], published in *The Faulkner Reader*; also published by Vintage Books in April 1975, and re-edited by Noel Polk with notes by Joseph Blotner and Noel Polk, by the Library of America: *William Faulkner: Novels 1942–1954*, New York, in 1994).

A Fable (August 2, 1954; novel, first published by Random House, New York; also published by New American Library in September 1958, Vintage in January 1978, and re-edited by Noel Polk with notes by Joseph Blotner and Noel Polk, by Library of America: *William Faulkner: Novels 1942–1954* in 1994).

The Wild Palms and The Old Man (September 1954; novel, rearranged version of *The Wild Palms* dividing the originally intended interwoven narratives into two separate sections: "The Wild Palms" and "Old Man"; published by New American Library, New York [also see below, *If I Forget Thee, Jerusalem*]).

The Town (May 1, 1957; novel [second in the Snopes trilogy—see *The Hamlet*, above, and *The Mansion*, below], first published by Random House, New York; also published by Vintage Books in January 1961.)

The Mansion (November 13, 1959; novel [third in the Snopes trilogy—see *The Hamlet* and *The Mansion*, above], first published by Random House, New York; also published by Vintage Books in September 1965; re-edited by Noel Polk with notes by Joseph Blotner and Noel Polk, by the Library of America: *William Faulkner: Novels 1957–1962* in 1999).

The Reivers (June 4, 1962; novel, first published by Random House, New York; also published by Vintage Books in September 1966; re-edited text by Noel Polk with notes by Joseph Blotner and Noel Polk, published by the Library of America: *Faulkner: Novels 1957–1962* in 1999; film adaptation with same title released in 1969).

Flags in the Dust (August 22, 1973; novel [complete text of the novel *Sartoris*, see above]; edited with an introduction by Douglas Day and published posthumously by Random House, New York; re-edited text by Noel Polk with notes by Joseph Blotner and Noel Polk, published by the Library of America: *William Faulkner: Novels 1926–1929* in 2006).

If I Forget Thee, Jerusalem (1990; novel, original title of *The Wild Palms* [see above]; re-edited text by Noel Polk with notes by Joseph Blotner and Noel Polk, published in 1990 by the Library of America: *William Faulkner: Novels 1936–1940*, New York, and in November 1995 by Vintage International, New York).

Poems and Verse Play

"L'Après-midi d'un Faune" (August 6, 1919; poem, first published in *New Republic*, XX, 24; reprinted in *Mississippian* IX [October 29, 1919]: 4, in *Salmagundi* and in *William Faulkner: Early Prose and Poetry*).

"Cathay" (November 12, 1919; poem, first published in *Mississippian*, IX, 8; reprinted in *William Faulkner: Early Prose and Poetry*).

"Sapphics" (November 26, 1919; poem, first published in *Mississippian*, IX, 3; reprinted in *William Faulkner: Early Prose and Poetry*).

"After Fifty Years" (December 10, 1919; poem, first published in *Mississippian*, IX, 4; reprinted in "Faulkner Juvenilia" by Martha Mayes, *New Campus Writing No. 2*, edited by Nolan Miller [New York: Bantam, 1957], and in *William Faulkner: Early Prose and Poetry*).

"Une Ballade des Femmes Perdues" (January 28, 1920; poem, first published in *Mississippian*, IX, 3; reprinted in "Faulkner Juvenilia" by Martha Mayes, *New Campus Writing No. 2*, edited by Nolan Miller [New York: Bantam, 1957], and in *William Faulkner: Early Prose and Poetry*).

"Naiad's Song" (February 4, 1920; poem, first published in *Mississippian*, IX, 3; reprinted in *William Faulkner: Early Prose and Poetry*).

"Fantouches" (February 25, 1920; poem, first published in *Mississippian*, IX, 3; reprinted in "Faulkner Juvenilia" by Martha Mayes, *New Campus Writing No. 2*, edited by Nolan Miller [New York: Bantam, 1957]; reprinted as "Fantoches" in *William Faulkner: Early Prose and Poetry*).

"Clair de Lune" (March 3, 1920; poem, first published in *Mississippian*, IX, 6; reprinted in *William Faulkner: Early Prose and Poetry*).

"Streets" (March 17, 1920; poem, first published in *Mississippian*, IX, 2; reprinted in *William Faulkner: Early Prose and Poetry*).

"A Poplar" (March 17, 1920; poem, first published in *Mississippian*, IX, 7; reprinted in "Faulkner Juvenilia" by Martha Mayes, *New Campus Writing No. 2*, edited by Nolan Miller [New York: Bantam, 1957], and in *William Faulkner: Early Prose and Poetry*).

"A Clymene" (April 14, 1920; poem, first published in *Mississippian*, IX, 3; reprinted in *William Faulkner: Early Prose and Poetry*).

"Study" (April 24, 1920; poem, first published in *Mississippian*, IX, 4; reprinted in "Faulkner Juvenilia" by Martha Mayes, *New Campus Writing No. 2*, edited by Nolan Miller [New York: Bantam, 1957], and in *William Faulkner: Early Prose and Poetry*).

"Alma Mater" (May 12, 1920; poem, first published in *Mississippian*, IX, 3; reprinted in *William Faulkner: Early Prose and Poetry*).

The Marionettes (fall 1920; verse play, published posthumously by University Press of Virginia in 1977, edited with an introduction by Noel Polk).

"To a Co-ed" (1920; poem, first published in *Ole Miss, the Yearbook of the University of Mississippi*, XXIV [1919–20]; reprinted in the *Memphis Commercial Appeal*, November 6, 1932 [magazine section], in *The Literary Career of William Faulkner* by James B. Meriwether [Princeton University Library, 1961], and in *William Faulkner: Early Prose and Poetry*).

"Co-Education at Ole Miss" (May 4, 1921; poem, first published in *Mississippian*, X, 5; reprinted in *William Faulkner: Early Prose and Poetry*).

"Nocturne" (1921; poem, first published in *Ole Miss, the Yearbook of the University of Mississippi*, XXV [1920–21]; facsimile published in *The Literary Career of William Faulkner* by James B. Meriwether [Princeton University Library, 1961], and in *William Faulkner: Early Prose and Poetry*).

Vision in Spring (1921–23; cycle of 14 love poems [earlier version contained eight poems]; posthumously

published in 1984, edited by Judith L. Sensibar, University of Texas Press, Austin).

"The Hill" (March 10, 1922; prose poem, first published in *Mississippian*, XI, 1–2; reprinted in *William Faulkner: Early Prose and Poetry*).

"Portrait" (June 1922; poem, first published in *Double Dealer*, II, 337; reprinted in *Salmagundi* and in *William Faulkner: Early Prose and Poetry*).

"Mississippi Hills" (October 1924; poem, revised as "My Epitaph" [see below]; slightly altered and retitled as "Mississippi Hills: My Epitaph," reproduced in *William Faulkner: "Man Working," 1919–1962, A Catalogue of the William Faulkner Collections at the University of Virginia*, compiled by Linton R. Massey [Charlottesville: Bibliographical Society, University of Virginia, 1968]).

The Marble Faun (December 15, 1924; poem of 806 lines with prologue and epilogue; preface by Phil Stone; published by Four Seas Company, Boston; republished with *A Green Bough* [photographically reproduced from original editions] by Random House, New York, 1965).

Mississippi Poems (December 30, 1924; typescript of 12 poems presented to Myrtle Ramey; eight of which were revised for *A Green Bough* [1933]; posthumously published in 1979 [see below]).

Helen: A Courtship (1925; poems for Helen Baird, published posthumously in 1981 [see below]).

"Dying Gladiator" (January/February 1925; poem, first published in *Double Dealer*, VII, 85; reprinted in *Salmagundi* and in *William Faulkner: Early Prose and Poetry*).

"The Faun" (April 1925; poem, first published in *Double Dealer*, VII, 148; reprinted in *Salmagundi* and in *William Faulkner: Early Prose and Poetry*).

"The Lilacs" (June 1925; poem, first published in *Double Dealer*, VII, 185–187; reprinted in *Salmagundi*, in *A Green Bough* [revised as I], and in *Anthology of Magazine Verse for 1925 and Yearbook of American Poetry*, edited by William Stanley Braithwaite [Boston: B. J. Brimmer, 1925]).

"Hermaphroditus" (April 1927; poem, first appeared in Faulkner's novel *Mosquitoes*, p. 252; revision reprinted XXX in *A Green Bough*).

"I Will Not Weep for Youth" (February 1, 1932; poem, first published in *Contempo*, I, 1; reprinted in *An Anthology of the Younger Poets*, edited by Oliver

Wells and with a preface by Archibald MacLeish [Philadelphia: Centaur Press, 1932]).

"Knew I Love Once" (February 1, 1932; poem, first published in *Contempo*, I, 1; reprinted in *A Green Bough* [revised as XXXIII], and in *Anthology of the Younger Poets*, edited by Oliver Wells [Philadelphia: Centaur Press, 1932]).

"Twilight" (February 1, 1932; poem, first published in *Contempo*, I, 1; reprinted in *A Green Bough* [revised as X], and in *An Anthology of the Younger Poets*, edited by Oliver Wells [Philadelphia: Centaur Press, 1932]).

"Visions in Spring" (February 1, 1932; poem, published in *Contempo*, I, 1).

"Spring" (February 1, 1932; poem, first published in *Contempo*, I, 2; reprinted in *A Green Bough* [revised as XXXVI]).

"April" (February 1, 1932; poem, published in *Contempo*, I, 2).

"To a Virgin" (February 1, 1932; poem, first published in *Contempo*, I, 2; reprinted in *A Green Bough* [revised as XXXIX], and in *An Anthology of the Younger Poets*, edited by Oliver Wells [Philadelphia: Centaur Press, 1932]).

"Winter Is Gone" (February 1, 1932; poem, first published in *Contempo*, I, 2; reprinted in *An Anthology of the Younger Poets*, edited by Oliver Wells [Philadelphia: Centaur Press, 1932]).

"My Epitaph" (February 1, 1932; poem, first published in *Contempo*, I, 2; revised and reprinted as *This Earth*, 1932; reprinted in *A Green Bough* [revised as XLIV]; reprinted in *An Anthology of the Younger Poets*, edited by Oliver Wells [Philadelphia: Centaur Press, 1932]; retitled as "If There Be Grief" and published in *Mississippi Verse*, edited by Alice James [Chapel Hill: University of North Carolina Press, 1934]; reprinted in *Life*, LIII [July 20, 1952]: 42).

Salmagundi (April 30, 1932; reprinted prose pieces and poems; edited with an introduction by Paul Romaine; published by Casanova Press, Milwaukee).

"A Child Looks from His Window" (May 25, 1932; poem, published in *Contempo*, II, 3).

This Earth (December 1932; revision of poem "My Epitaph"; published by Equinox Cooperative Press, New York).

"The Race's Splendor" (April 12, 1933; poem, first published in *New Republic*, LXXIV, 253; reprinted in *A Green Bough* [as XXXVII], and in *New Republic*, CXXXI [November 22, 1954]: 82).

"Night Piece" (April 12, 1933; poem, first published in *New Republic*, LXXIV, 253; reprinted in *A Green Bough* [as VII]).

"Gray the Day" (April 12, 1933; poem, first published in *New Republic*, LXXIV, 253; reprinted in *A Green Bough* [as XXX]).

"Over the World's Rim" (April 12, 1933; poem, first published in *New Republic*, LXXIV, 253; reprinted in *A Green Bough* [as XXVIII]).

"The Ship of Night" (April 19, 1933; poem, first published in *New Republic*, LXXIV, 272; reprinted in *A Green Bough* [as XXXIV]).

A Green Bough (April 20, 1933; 44 poems [13 previously published; illustrations by Lynd Ward; published by Smith & Haas, New York; seven poems reprinted with titles—XIV ["Mother and Child"], XVI ["Mirror of Youth"], XVIII ["Boy and Eagle"], XIX ["Green Is the Water"], XX ["Here He Stands"], XXXV ["The Courtesan is Dead"], and XLIV ["If There Be Grief," also see above: "My Epitaph"]—in *Mississippi Verse*, edited by Alice James [Chapel Hill: University of North Carolina Press, 1934]; republished with *The Marble Faun* [photographically reproduced from original editions], by Random House, New York, 1965).

"Man Comes, Man Goes" (May 3, 1933; poem, first published in *New Republic*, LXXIV, 338; reprinted in *A Green Bough* [as VI], in *The New Republic Anthology: 1915–1935*, edited by Groff Conklin [New York: Dodge, 1936], and in *Fiction Parade*, V [October 1937]: 740).

"The Flowers That Died" (June 25, 1933; poem, published in *Contempo*, III, 1).

William Faulkner: Early Prose and Poetry (1962; previously published poems, prose pieces, and pen-and-ink drawings; compiled with an introduction by Carvel Collins; published by Little, Brown, Boston).

Mississippi Poems (1979; poems published posthumously by Yoknapatawpha Press, Oxford, Miss.).

Helen: A Courtship (1981; poems published posthumously by Tulane University, New Orleans, and by Yoknapatawpha Press, Oxford, Miss.).

Prose Sketches

"Mirrors of Chartres Street" (February–September 1925, 11 of 16 prose sketches appearing in the *New Orleans Times-Picayune*, with introduction by William Van O'Connor [Minneapolis: Faulkner Studies, 1953]; also see two separate references below titled *New Orleans Sketches*).

"New Orleans" (January/February 1925; prose sketch, first published in *Double Dealer*, VII, 102–107; reprinted in *Salmagundi* and in *New Orleans Sketches*, edited by Carvel Collins).

"Mirrors of Chartres Street" (February 8, 1925; sketch, first published in the *New Orleans Times-Picayune*, pp. 1, 6; reprinted in *Mirrors of Chartres Street* [Minneapolis: Faulkner Studies, 1953], in *New Orleans Sketches*, edited by Ichiro Nishizaki, and in *New Orleans Sketches*, edited by Carvel Collins).

"Damon and Pythias Unlimited" (February 15, 1925; sketch, first published in the *New Orleans Times-Picayune*, p. 7; reprinted in *Mirrors of Chartres Street* [Minneapolis: Faulkner Studies, 1953], in *New Orleans Sketches*, edited by Ichiro Nishizaki, and in *New Orleans Sketches*, edited by Carvel Collins).

"Home" (February 22, 1925; sketch, first published in the *New Orleans Times-Picayune*, p. 3; reprinted in *Mirrors of Chartres Street* [Minneapolis: Faulkner Studies, 1953], in *New Orleans Sketches*, edited by Ichiro Nishizaki, and in *New Orleans Sketches*, edited by Carvel Collins).

"Jealousy" (March 1, 1925; sketch, first published in the *New Orleans Times-Picayune*, p. 2; reprinted in *Faulkner Studies*, III [winter 1954]): 46–50; in *Jealousy and Episode: Two Stories by William Faulkner*, [Minneapolis: Faulkner Studies, 1955]; in *New Orleans Sketches*, edited by Ichiro Nishizaki; and in *New Orleans Sketches*, edited by Carvel Collins).

"Cheest" (April 5, 1925; sketch, first published in the *New Orleans Times-Picayune*, p. 4; reprinted in *Mirrors of Chartres Street* [Minneapolis: Faulkner Studies, 1953]; in *New Orleans Sketches*, edited by Ichiro Nishizaki; and in *New Orleans Sketches*, edited by Carvel Collins).

"Out of Nazareth" (April 12, 1925; sketch, first published in the *New Orleans Times-Picayune*, p. 4; reprinted in *Mirrors of Chartres Street* [Minneapolis: Faulkner Studies, 1953]; in *New Orleans Sketches*,

edited by Ichiro Nishizaki; and in *New Orleans Sketches*, edited by Carvel Collins).

"The Kingdom of God" (April 26, 1925; sketch, first published in the *New Orleans Times-Picayune*, p. 4; reprinted in *Mirrors of Chartres Street* [Minneapolis: Faulkner Studies, 1953]; in *New Orleans Sketches*, edited by Ichiro Nishizaki; and in *New Orleans Sketches*, edited by Carvel Collins).

"The Rosary" (May 3, 1925; sketch, first published in the *New Orleans Times-Picayune*, p. 2; reprinted in *Mirrors of Chartres Street* [Minneapolis: Faulkner Studies, 1953]; in *New Orleans Sketches*, edited by Ichiro Nishizaki); and in *New Orleans Sketches*, edited by Carvel Collins).

"The Cobbler" (May 10, 1925; sketch, first published in the *New Orleans Times-Picayune*, p. 7; reprinted in *Mirrors of Chartres Street* [Minneapolis: Faulkner Studies, 1953]; in *New Orleans Sketches*, edited by Ichiro Nishizaki; and in *New Orleans Sketches*, edited by Carvel Collins).

"Chance" (May 17, 1925; sketch, first published in the *New Orleans Times-Picayune*, p. 7; reprinted in *Mirrors of Chartres Street* [Minneapolis: Faulkner Studies, 1953]; in *New Orleans Sketches*, edited by Ichiro Nishizaki; and in *New Orleans Sketches*, edited by Carvel Collins).

"Sunset" (May 25, 1925; sketch, first published in the *New Orleans Times-Picayune*, p. 7; reprinted in *Mirrors of Chartres Street* [Minneapolis: Faulkner Studies, 1953]; in *New Orleans Sketches*, edited by Ichiro Nishizaki; and in *New Orleans Sketches*, edited by Carvel Collins).

"The Kid Learns" (May 31, 1925; sketch, first published in the *New Orleans Times-Picayune*, p. 2; reprinted in *Mirrors of Chartres Street* [Minneapolis: Faulkner Studies, 1953]; in *New Orleans Sketches*, edited by Ichiro Nishizaki; and in *New Orleans Sketches*, edited by Carvel Collins).

"The Liar" (July 26, 1925; sketch, first published in the *New Orleans Times-Picayune*, pp. 3, 6; reprinted in *New Orleans Sketches*, edited by Carvel Collins).

"Episode" (August 16, 1925; sketch, first published in the *New Orleans Times-Picayune*, p. 2; reprinted in *Eigo Seinen* [Tokyo] on December 1, 1954; in *Faulkner Studies*, III [winter 1954]: 51–53; in *Jealousy and Episode: Two Stories by William Faulkner* [Minneapolis: Faulkner Studies, 1955]; in *New*

Orleans Sketches, edited by Ichiro Nishizaki; and in *New Orleans Sketches,* edited by Carvel Collins).

"Country Mice" (September 20, 1925; sketch, first published in the *New Orleans Times-Picayune,* p. 7; reprinted in *New Orleans Sketches,* edited by Carvel Collins).

"Yo Ho and Two Bottles of Rum" (September 27, 1925; sketch, first published in the *New Orleans Times-Picayune,* pp. 1–2; reprinted in *New Orleans Sketches,* edited by Carvel Collins).

New Orleans Sketches by William Faulkner (April 1, 1955; 13 of 16 prose sketches from the *New Orleans Times-Picayune,* edited with notes in Japanese and English by Ichiro Nishizaki, Hokuseido Press, Tokyo; 11 reprinted in *Mirrors of Chartres Street*).

New Orleans Sketches (1958; 16 prose sketches from the *New Orleans Times-Picayune,* [see above] and 11 short pieces titled "New Orleans" [see above] from the *Double Dealer;* edited with introduction by Carvel Collins; published by Rutgers University Press, New Brunswick, N.J.; republished in 1961 by Grove Press, New York; new edition with additional essay published in 1968 by Random House, New York).

Short Stories

"Landing in Luck" (November 26, 1919; short story, first published in *Mississippian,* IX, 2, 7; reprinted in *William Faulkner: Early Prose and Poetry*).

"Moonlight" (c. 1919–21; short story published posthumously in *Uncollected Stories of William Faulkner*).

"Love" (fall 1921; short story unpublished and basis of film scenario titled *Manservant*).

"Adolescence" (c. 1922; short story published posthumously in *Uncollected Stories of William Faulkner*).

"Nympholepsy" (1925; short story published posthumously in *Mississippi Quarterly,* XXVI (summer 1973): 403–409, edited with an introduction by James B. Meriwether; reprinted in *Uncollected Stories of William Faulkner*).

"Frankie and Johnny" (c. 1925; short story published posthumously in *Mississippi Quarterly,* XXXI (summer 1978): 453–464, edited with an introduction by James B. Meriwether; reprinted in *Uncollected Stories of William Faulkner*).

"The Priest" (1925; short story published posthumously in *Mississippi Quarterly,* XXIX (summer 1976): 445–450, edited with an introduction by James B. Meriwether; reprinted in *Uncollected Stories of William Faulkner*).

"Al Jackson" (1925; short story published posthumously in *Uncollected Stories of William Faulkner*).

"Don Giovanni" (c. 1925; short story published posthumously in *Uncollected Stories of William Faulkner*).

"Peter" (c. 1925; short story published posthumously in *Uncollected Stories of William Faulkner*).

"The Big Shot" (c. 1929; short story published posthumously in *Mississippi Quarterly,* XXVI (summer 1973): 313–324, and in *Uncollected Stories of William Faulkner*).

"A Dangerous Man" (c. 1929; short story published posthumously in *Uncollected Stories of William Faulkner*).

"Dull Tale" (c. 1929–30; short story published posthumously in *Uncollected Stories of William Faulkner*).

"A Return" (c. 1929–30; short story published posthumously in *Uncollected Stories of William Faulkner*).

"A Rose for Emily" (April 1930; short story, first published in *Forum,* LXXXIII, 233–238; reprinted revision in *These 13,* in *A Rose for Emily and Other Stories,* in *The Portable Faulkner,* in *Collected Stories,* in *The Faulkner Reader,* in *A Rose for Emily,* and in *Selected Short Stories of William Faulkner*).

"Honor" (July 1930; short story, first published in *American Mercury,* XX, 268–274; reprinted in *Doctor Martino and Other Stories,* in *Collected Stories,* and in *Selected Short Stories of William Faulkner*).

"Thrift" (September 6, 1930; short story, first published in *Saturday Evening Post,* CCIII, 16–17, 78, 82; reprinted in *O. Henry Memorial Award Prize Stories of 1931,* edited by Blanche Colton Williams [Garden City: Doubleday, Doran, 1931] and in *Uncollected Stories of William Faulkner*).

"Red Leaves" (October 25, 1930; short story, first published in *Saturday Evening Post,* CCIII, 6–7, 54, 56, 58, 60, 62, 64; revision published in *These 13,* in *The Portable Faulkner,* in the edition of *A Rose for Emily and Other Stories* edited and annotated by Kenzaburo Ohashi, in *Collected Stories of William Faulkner,* and in *Selected Short Stories of William Faulkner;* a portion again revised and included in *Big Woods,* pp. 99–109).

"Evangeline" (c. 1930–31; short story published posthumously in *Uncollected Stories of William Faulkner*).

"Dry September" (January 1931; short story, first published in *Scribner's Magazine*, LXXXIX, 49–56; reprinted revision in *These 13*, in *A Rose for Emily and Other Stories by William Faulkner*, in *Collected Stories of William Faulkner*, in *The Faulkner Reader*, and in *Selected Short Stories of William Faulkner*).

"That Evening Sun Go Down" (March 1931; short story, first published in *American Mercury*, XXII, 257–267; revision entitled "That Evening Sun" reprinted in *These 13*, in *A Rose for Emily and Other Stories by William Faulkner*, in *The Portable Faulkner*, in *Collected Stories of William Faulkner*, in *The Faulkner Reader*, in *A Rose for Emily*, and in *Selected Short Stories of William Faulkner*).

"Ad Astra" (March 27, 1931; short story, first published in *American Caravan*, IV, 164–181; reprinted revision in *These 13*, in *The Portable Faulkner*, and in *Collected Stories of William Faulkner*).

"Hair" (May 1931; short story, first published in *American Mercury*, XXIII, 53–61; reprinted revision in *These 13* and in *Collected Stories of William Faulkner*).

"Spotted Horses" (June 1931; short story, first published in *Scribner's Magazine*, LXXXIX, 585–597; expanded revision included in chapter 1 of book 4 of *The Hamlet*, reprinted as a novella in *The Faulkner Reader* and in *Three Famous Short Novels*; original version reprinted in *Uncollected Stories of William Faulkner*).

"The Hound" (August 1931; short story, first published in *Harper's Magazine*, CLXIII, 266–274; reprinted in *Doctor Martino and Other Stories* and in *A Rose for Emily and Other Stories by William Faulkner*; revision included in book 3 of *The Hamlet*; original version reprinted in *Uncollected Stories of William Faulkner*).

"Fox Hunt" (September 1931; short story, first published in *Harper's Magazine*, CLXIII, 392–402; reprinted in *Doctor Martino and Other Stories* and in *Collected Stories of William Faulkner*).

"All the Dead Pilots" (September 21, 1931; short story, first published in *These 13*; reprinted in *Collected Stories of William Faulkner*).

"Carcassonne" (September 21, 1931; short story, first published in *These 13* and in *Collected Stories of William Faulkner*).

"Crevasse" (September 21, 1931; short story, first published in *These 13*, in *Collected Stories of William Faulkner*, and in *A Rose for Emily*).

"Divorce in Naples" (September 21, 1931; short story, first published in *These 13* and in *Collected Stories of William Faulkner*).

"A Justice" (September 21, 1931; short story, first published in *These 13*; reprinted in *The Portable Faulkner*, in *Collected Stories of William Faulkner*, and in *The Faulkner Reader*; revised portion included in *Big Woods*, pp. 139–142).

"Mistral" (September 21, 1931; short story, first published in *These 13* and in *Collected Stories of William Faulkner*).

"Victory" (September 21, 1931; short story, first published in *These 13* and in *Collected Stories of William Faulkner*).

These 13 (September 21, 1931; collection of 13 short stories; published by Cape & Smith, New York, 1931; stories reprinted *Collected Stories of William Faulkner*).

"Doctor Martino" (November 1931; short story, first published in *Harper's Magazine*, CLXIII, 733–743; reprinted in *Doctor Martino and Other Stories* and in *Collected Stories of William Faulkner*).

Idyll in the Desert (December 1931; short story, first published separately by Random House, New York, in 1931; reprinted in *Uncollected Stories of William Faulkner*).

"With Caution and Dispatch" (c. 1932; short story, published posthumously in *Uncollected Stories of William Faulkner*).

"Death-Drag" (January 1932; short story, first published in *Scribner's Magazine*, XCI, 34–42; reprinted with minor revisions as "Death Drag" in *Doctor Martino and Other Stories*, in *The Portable Faulkner*, and in *Collected Stories of William Faulkner*).

"Centaur in Brass" (February 1932; short story, first published in *American Mercury*, XXV, 200–210; reprinted in *Collected Stories of William Faulkner*; revised for first chapter of *The Town*).

"Once Aboard the Lugger" (February 1, 1932; title for two short stories, the first of which first published in *Contempo*, I, 1, 4, and reprinted in *Uncollected Stories of William Faulkner*; the second, first published in *Uncollected Stories of William Faulkner*).

"Lizards in Jamshyd's Courtyard" (February 27, 1932; short story, first published in *Saturday Evening Post*, CCIV, 12–13, 52, 57; revision included in book 4 of *The Hamlet*; original version reprinted in *Uncollected Stories of William Faulkner*).

"Turn About" (March 5, 1932; short story, first published in *Saturday Evening Post*, CCIV, 6–7, 75–76, 81, 83; revision reprinted in *Doctor Martino and Other Stories* and in *A Rose for Emily and Other Stories by William Faulkner*; reprinted as "Turnabout" in *Collected Stories of William Faulkner*, in *The Faulkner Reader*, and in *Selected Short Stories of William Faulkner*; basis of screenplay of same title and film titled *Today We Live*).

"Smoke" (April 1932; short story, first published in *Harper's Magazine*, CLXIV, 562–578; reprinted with minor changes in *Doctor Martino and Other Stories* and in *Knight's Gambit*).

"Miss Zilphia Gant" (June 27, 1932; short story, first published separately Book Club of Texas (in Dallas), with a preface by Henry Smith; reprinted in *Uncollected Stories of William Faulkner*).

"A Mountain Victory" (December 3, 1932; short story, first published in *Saturday Evening Post*, CCV, 6–7, 39, 42, 44–46; reprinted revision as "Mountain Victory" in *Doctor Martino and Other Stories*, in *Collected Stories of William Faulkner*, and in *Selected Short Stories of William Faulkner*).

"There Was a Queen" (January 1933; short story, first published in *Scribner's Magazine*, XCIII, 10–16; reprinted in *Doctor Martino and Other Stories*, in *Collected Stories of William Faulkner*, and in *Selected Short Stories of William Faulkner*).

"Artist at Home" (August 1933; short story, first published in *Story*, III, 27–41; reprinted in *Collected Stories of William Faulkner*).

"Beyond" (September 1933; short story, first published in *Harper's Magazine*, CLXVII, 394–403; reprinted in *Doctor Martino and Other Stories*, in *Collected Stories of William Faulkner*, and in *Selected Short Stories of William Faulkner*).

"Elly" (February 1934; short story, first published in *Story*, IV, 3–15; reprinted in *Doctor Martino and Other Stories* and in *Collected Stories of William Faulkner*).

"Pennsylvania Station" (February 1934; short story, first published in *American Mercury*, XXXI, 166–174; reprinted in *Collected Stories of William Faulkner*).

"Wash" (February 1934; short story, first published in *Harper's Magazine*, CLXVIII, 258–66; reprinted in *Doctor Martino and Other Stories*, in *The Portable Faulkner*, in *Collected Stories of William Faulkner*, and in *The Faulkner Reader*; with major revisions included in the latter part of chapter 7 of *Absalom, Absalom!*).

"A Bear Hunt" (February 10, 1934; short story, first published in *Saturday Evening Post*, CCVI, 8–9, 74, 76; reprinted in *Collected Stories of William Faulkner*; reprinted revision in *Big Woods*).

"Black Music" (April 16, 1934; short story, first published in *Doctor Martino and Other Stories*; reprinted in *Collected Stories of William Faulkner*).

"Leg" (April 16, 1934; short story, first published in *Doctor Martino and Other Stories*; reprinted as "The Leg" in *Collected Stories of William Faulkner*).

Doctor Martino and Other Stories (April 16, 1934; collection of 14 stories, published by Smith & Haas, New York).

"Mule in the Yard" (August 1934; short story, first published in *Scribner's Magazine*, XCVI, 65–70; reprinted in *Collected Stories of William Faulkner*; with major revisions incorporated in chapter 16 of *The Town*).

"Ambuscade" (September 29, 1934; short story, first published in *Saturday Evening Post*, CCVII, 12–13, 80–81; reprinted revision as chapter 1 of *The Unvanquished*; original version reprinted in *The Uncollected Stories of William Faulkner*).

"Retreat" (October 13, 1934; short story, first published in *Saturday Evening Post*, CCVII, 16–17, 82, 84–85, 87, 89; reprinted revision as chapter 2 of *The Unvanquished*; original version reprinted in *Uncollected Stories of William Faulkner*).

"Lo!" (November 1934; short story, first published in *Story*, V, 5–21; reprinted in *Collected Stories of William Faulkner* and in *Selected Short Stories of William Faulkner*).

"Raid" (November 3, 1934; short story, first published in *Saturday Evening Post*, CCVII, 18–19, 72–73, 75, 77–78; reprinted revision as chapter 3 of *The Unvanquished*; original version reprinted in *Uncollected Stories of William Faulkner*).

"A Portrait of Elmer" (c. 1934–35; short story, posthumously published in *Uncollected Stories of William Faulkner*).

"Skirmish at Satoris" (April 1935; short story, first published in *Scribner's Magazine*, XCVII, 193–200; reprinted revision as chapter 4 of *The Unvanquished*; original version reprinted in *Uncollected Stories of William Faulkner*).

"Golden Land" (May 1935; short story, first published in *American Mercury*, XXXV, 1–14; reprinted in *Collected Stories of William Faulkner*).

"That Will Be Fine" (July 1935; short story, first published in *American Mercury*, XXXV, 264–276; reprinted in *Collected Stories of William Faulkner*).

"Uncle Willy" (October 1935; short story, first published in *American Mercury*, XXXVI, 156–168; reprinted in *Collected Stories of William Faulkner*).

"Lion" (December 1935; short story, first published in *Harper's Magazine*, CLXXI, 67–77; revised and included in "The Bear" in *Go Down, Moses and Other Stories*; original version reprinted in *Uncollected Stories of William Faulkner*).

"Two Dollar Wife" (1936; short story first titled "Christmas Tree" and first published in *College Life*, XVIII [January 1936]: 8–10, 85, 86, 88, 90; reprinted in *Uncollected Stories of William Faulkner*).

"The Brooch" (January 1936; short story, first published in *Scribner's Magazine*, XCIX, 7–12; reprinted in *Collected Stories of William Faulkner*).

"Fool About a Horse" (August 1936; short story, first published in *Scribner's Magazine*, C, 80–86; revision included in book 1 of *The Hamlet*; original version reprinted in *Uncollected Stories of William Faulkner*).

"The Unvanquished" (November 14, 1936; short story, first published in *Saturday Evening Post*, CCIX, 12–13, 121–122, 124, 126, 128, 130; retitled and revised as "Riposte in Tertio," chapter 4 of *The Unvanquished*; original version and title reprinted in *Uncollected Stories of William Faulkner*).

"Vendée" (December 5, 1936; short story, first published in *Saturday Evening Post*, CCIX, 16–17, 86, 87, 90, 92, 93, 94; revised as chapter 5 in *The Unvanquished*; original version reprinted in *Uncollected Stories of William Faulkner*).

"Monk" (May 1937; short story, first published in *Scribner's Magazine*, CL, 16–24; reprinted in *Knight's Gambit*).

"An Odor of Verbena" (February 15, 1938; short story, first published as chapter 7 of *The Unvanquished*; reprinted in *A Rose for Emily and Other Stories by William Faulkner* and in *The Faulkner Reader*).

The Unvanquished (February 15, 1938; series of seven interrelated stories, first published by Random House, New York; first six are revisions of previously published short stories; stories III, "Raid," and VII, "An Odor of Verbena," published in *The Portable Faulkner*; basis of unproduced screenplay of same title by Sidney Howard for MGM, 1938; corrected text by Noel Polk published in 1990 by Library of America [volume 2 of Faulkner's collected works: *Novels 1936–1940*], New York, and in October 1991 by Vintage International, New York).

"Barn Burning" (June 1939; short story, first published in *Harper's Magazine*, CLXXIX, 86–96; reprinted in *A Rose for Emily and Other Stories*, in *Collected Stories of William Faulkner*, in *The Faulkner Reader*, and in *Selected Short Stories of William Faulkner*; revised portions included in book 1 of *The Hamlet*; television adaptation with same title telecast in 1954 and another in 1980; film version on videocassette released in 1985).

"Hand Upon the Waters" (November 4, 1939; short story, first published in *Saturday Evening Post*, CCXII, 14–15, 75–76, 78–79; reprinted in *Knight's Gambit*).

"A Point of Law" (June 22, 1940; short story, first published in *Collier's Magazine*, CV, 20–21, 30, 32; reprinted revision included in "The Fire and the Hearth" in *Go Down, Moses and Other Stories*; original version reprinted in *Uncollected Stories of William Faulkner*).

"Almost" (July 1940; short story, revised and retitled "Was"; first published in *Go Down, Moses and Other Stories*).

"The Old People" (September 1940; short story, first published in *Harper's Magazine*, CLXXXI, 418–425; revision included in *Go Down, Moses and Other Stories*) and reprinted in *Big Woods*; original version reprinted in *Uncollected Stories of William Faulkner*).

"Pantaloon in Black" (October 1940; short story, first published in *Harper's Magazine*, CLXXXI, 503–513; revised for *Go Down, Moses and Other Stories*;

original version reprinted in *Uncollected Stories of William Faulkner*).

"Gold Is Not Always" (November 1940; short story, first published in *Atlantic Monthly*, CLXVI, 563–570; revision incorporated in "The Fire and the Hearth" in *Go Down, Moses and Other Stories*; original version reprinted in *Uncollected Stories of William Faulkner*).

"Tomorrow" (November 23, 1940; short story, first published in *Saturday Evening Post*, CCXIII, 22–23, 32, 35, 37, 38, 39; reprinted in *Knight's Gambit*; television adaptation with same title telecast in 1960 and film adaptation with same title released in 1972).

"Go Down, Moses" (January 25, 1941; short story, first published in *Collier's Magazine*, CVII, 19–20, 45, 46; revision reprinted in *Go Down, Moses and Other Stories*; original version reprinted in *Uncollected Stories of William Faulkner*).

"The Tall Men" (May 31, 1941; short story, first published in *Saturday Evening Post*, CCXIII, 14–15, 95–96, 98–99; reprinted in *Collected Stories of William Faulkner*).

"Snow" (c. 1942; short story published posthumously in *Mississippi Quarterly*, XXVI [summer 1973]: 325–330, and in *Uncollected Stories of William Faulkner*).

"Two Soldiers" (March 28, 1942; short story, first published in *Saturday Evening Post*, CCXIV, 9–11, 35–36, 38, 40; reprinted in *Collected Stories of William Faulkner* and in *Selected Short Stories of William Faulkner*).

"The Bear" (May 9, 1942; short story, first published in *Saturday Evening Post*, CCXIV, 30–31, 74, 76–77; with major revisions included in "The Bear" in *Go Down, Moses and Other Stories*, and reprinted in *The Portable Faulkner* and as a novella in *The Faulkner Reader*; reprinted without part 4 in *Big Woods*; the shorter first published version reprinted in *Uncollected Stories of William Faulkner*).

"Delta Autumn" (May/June 1942; short story, first published in *Story*, XX, 46–55; reprinted revision in *Go Down, Moses and Other Stories*, in *A Rose for Emily and Other Stories by William Faulkner*, and in *The Portable Faulkner*; section of reprinted revision again revised and included as epilogue in *Big Woods*; first version reprinted in *Uncollected Stories of William Faulkner*).

"Was" (May 11, 1942; short story, retitled revision of the story "Almost" and first published as the first story in *Go Down, Moses and Other Stories*; reprinted in *The Portable Faulkner*).

"Shingles for the Lord" (February 13, 1943; short story, first published in *Saturday Evening Post*, CCXV, 14–15, 68, 70–71; reprinted in *Collected Stories of William Faulkner* and in *The Faulkner Reader*).

"My Grandmother Millard and General Bedford Foffest and the Battle of Harrykin Creek" (March/April 1943; short story, first published in *Story*, XXII, 68–86; reprinted in *Collected Stories of William Faulkner*).

"L'Après-midi d'une Vache" (June/July 1943; short story, French translation of "Afternoon of a Cow"; first published in Maurice Edgar Coindreau's French translation in *Fontaine*, pp. 27–28).

"Shall Not Perish" (July/August 1943; short story, first published in *Story*, XXIII, 40–47; reprinted in *Collected Stories of William Faulkner* and in *A Rose for Emily*).

A Rose for Emily and Other Stories by William Faulkner (April 1945; eight selected stories with foreword by Saxe Commins, Editions for the Armed Services, New York; work with same title but containing only four stories [three of which appear in the Armed Services edition, but here with "Red Leaves" as the fourth story], edited with annotations by Kenzaburo Ohashi and published by Kairyudo, Tokyo, n.d.).

"An Error in Chemistry" (June 1946; short story, first published in *Ellery Queen's Mystery Magazine*, VII, 5–19; reprinted in *Knight's Gambit*).

"Afternoon of a Cow" (Summer 1947; short story, first published in *Furioso*, II, 5–17; reprinted in *Parodies: An Anthology from Chaucer to Beerbohm—and After*, edited by Dwight Macdonald, published by Random House, New York, 1960; first published in 1943 in a French translation as "L'Après-midi d'une Vache"; reprinted in *Uncollected Stories of William Faulkner*).

"Lucas Beauchamp" (1948; short story, published posthumously with an introduction by Patrick Samway, S.J., in *Virginia Quarterly*, 75 (summer 1999): 417–437; with slight changes extracted from the first two chapters of *Intruder in the Dust* [see below]).

"A Courtship" (autumn 1948; short story, first published in *Sewanee Review*, LVI, 634–653; reprinted in *Collected Stories of William Faulkner*).

Knight's Gambit (November 27, 1949; six mystery stories [five of which previously published], first published by Random House, New York; published by Vintage Books, New York, in October 1978; elsewhere).

"Knight's Gambit" (November 27, 1949; mystery story published in *Knight's Gambit*).

Collected Stories of William Faulkner (August 21, 1950; 42 previously published stories, Random House, New York; republished in November 1995 by Vintage International, New York).

"A Name for the City" (October 1950; fictional essay, first published in *Harper's Magazine*, CCI, 200–214; revision included in first section of the prologue to act 1 of *Requiem for a Nun*).

"Mr. Acarius" (February 1953; short story, posthumously published in *Saturday Evening Post*, CCXXXVIII (October 9, 1965): 26–27, 29, 31, and reprinted in *Uncollected Stories of William Faulkner*).

"Hog Pawn" (c. October 1954; short story, first published posthumously in *Uncollected Stories of William Faulkner*; refashioned and included in chapter 14 of book 3, "Flem," of *The Mansion*).

"Sepulture South: Gaslight" (December 1954; short story, published in *Harper's Bazaar*, LXXXVIII, 84–85, 140–141; reprinted in *Uncollected Stories of William Faulkner*).

"Race at Morning" (March 5, 1955; short story, first published in *Saturday Evening Post*, CCXXVII, 26, 103–104, 106; revision reprinted in *Big Woods* and in *Selected Short Stories of William Faulkner*; original version reprinted in *Uncollected Stories of William Faulkner*).

"By the People" (October 1955; short story, first published in *Mademoiselle*, XLI, 86–89, 130, 131, 132, 133, 134, 135, 136, 137, 138, 139; revision included in chapter 13 of *The Mansion*).

A Rose for Emily (1956; four stories [see above; also see *A Rose for Emily and Other Stories*], edited with notes by Naotaro Takiguchi and Masao Takahashi, published by Nan 'un-do, Tokyo; two of the stories—"Shall Not Perish" and "Crevasse"—do not appear in *A Rose for Emily and Other Stories*).

Big Woods (October 14, 1955; four previously published hunting stories, revised with preludes and epilogue, published by Random House, New York; republished in 1994 by Vintage International, New York).

Selected Short Stories of William Faulkner (1962; 13 short stories previously published, Modern Library, New York).

Uncollected Stories of William Faulkner (1979; 45 stories, some revised for books and others uncollected or unpublished; edited and notes by Joseph Blotner; first published by Random House, New York; republished in a centenary edition by Vintage International, New York, in September 1997).

Reviews

Review of *In April Once*, by W. A. Percy (November 10, 1920; book review, first published in *Mississippian*, IX, 5; reprinted in *William Faulkner: Early Prose and Poetry*).

Review of *Turns and Movies*, by Conrad Aiken (February 16, 1921; book review, first published in *Mississippian*, X, 5; reprinted in *William Faulkner: Early Prose and Poetry*).

Review of *Aria da Capo*, by Edna St. Vincent Millay (January 13, 1922; book review, first published in *Mississippian*, XI, 5; reprinted in *William Faulkner: Early Prose and Poetry*).

Review of *Linda Condon, Cytherea*, and *The Bright Shawl*, by Joseph Hergesheimer (December 15, 1922; review of three books, first published in *Mississippian*, XII, 5; reprinted in *William Faulkner: Early Prose and Poetry*).

"Beyond the Talking" (May 20, 1931; review of *The Road Back*, by Erich Maria Remarque, published in *New Republic*, LXVII, 23–24).

"Folklore of the Air" (November 1935; review of *Test Pilot*, by Jimmy Collins, published in *American Mercury*, XXXVI, 370–372).

Review of *The Old Man and the Sea*, by Ernest Hemingway (autumn 1952; book review, published in *Shenandoah*, III, 55).

Screenplays

Night Bird (c. November 1931; scenario of unwritten screenplay and basis of *The College Widow*; published posthumously in *Faulkner's MGM Screenplays*, pp. 32–33, edited with introduction and commentaries by Bruce F. Kawin, University of Tennessee Press, Knoxville, 1982).

Manservant (May 24, 1932; scenario of unwritten screenplay based on the unpublished short story "Love"; published posthumously in *Faulkner's MGM Screenplays,* pp. 7–28, edited with introduction and commentaries by Bruce F. Kawin, University of Tennessee Press, Knoxville, 1982).

The College Widow (May 26, 1932; scenario of unwritten screenplay based on *Night Bird;* published posthumously in *Faulkner's MGM Screenplays,* pp. 40–53, edited with introduction and commentaries by Bruce F. Kawin, University of Tennessee Press, Knoxville, 1982).

Absolution (June 1, 1932; scenario of unwritten screenplay; published posthumously in *Faulkner's MGM Screenplays,* pp. 60–69, edited with introduction and commentaries by Bruce F. Kawin, University of Tennessee Press, Knoxville, 1982).

Flying the Mail (June 3, 1932; scenario of unwritten screenplay; published posthumously in *Faulkner's MGM Screenplays,* pp. 83–99, edited with introduction and commentaries by Bruce F. Kawin, University of Tennessee Press, Knoxville, 1982).

War Birds (January 12, 1933; screenplay unproduced, published posthumously in *Faulkner's MGM Screenplays,* pp. 275–420, edited with introduction and commentaries by Bruce F. Kawin, University of Tennessee Press, Knoxville, 1982).

Today We Live (April 12, 1933 [advance showing]; screenplay [originally titled "Turn About"] with Edith Fitzgerald and Dwight Taylor, based on Faulkner's short story "Turn About" [see above]; directed by Howard Hawks and released on April 21, 1933, by MGM; original script titled "Turn About," published posthumously in *Faulkner's MGM Screenplays,* pp. 128–255, edited with introduction and commentaries by Bruce F. Kawin, University of Tennessee Press, Knoxville, 1982).

Louisiana Lou (April/May 1933; screenplay unproduced [later version without contribution from Faulkner was released by MGM in 1934 under the title *Lazy River*]).

The Road to Glory (June 1936; screenplay with Joel Sayre; directed by Howard Hawks and released by Twentieth Century-Fox).

Slave Ship (June 1937; screenplay with Sam Hellman, Lamar Trotti, and Gladys Lehman; directed by Tay Garnett and released by Twentieth Century-Fox).

The De Gaulle Story (July–November 1942; screenplay unproduced; published posthumously in *Faulkner: A Comprehensive Guide to the Brodsky Collection, Vol III: The De Gaulle Story,* edited Louis Daniel Brodsky and Robert W. Hamblin [Jackson: University Press of Mississippi, 1984]).

Country Lawyer (March–April 1943; story treatment; published posthumously in *Country Lawyer and Other Stories for the Screen,* edited Louis Daniel Brodsky and Robert W. Hamblin [Jackson: University Press of Mississippi, 1987]).

Battle Cry (August 16, 1943; unproduced screenplay; edited by Louis Daniel Brodsky and Robert W. Hamblin; published in 1985 by University Press of Mississippi, Jackson).

To Have and Have Not (October 1944; screenplay with Jules Furthman, adapted from the novel of the same title by Ernest Hemingway; directed by Howard Hawks and released by Warner Brothers).

Stallion Road (June–September 1945; screenplay unproduced; published posthumously in *Stallion Road: A Screenplay,* edited Louis Daniel Brodsky and Robert W. Hamblin [Jackson: University Press of Mississippi, 1989]).

The Big Sleep (August 1946; screenplay with Leigh Brackett and Jules Furthman, adapted from the novel of the same title by Raymond Chandler; directed by Howard Hawks and released by Warner Brothers).

Land of the Pharaohs (July 1955; screenplay with Harry Kurnitz and Harold Jack Bloom; directed by Howard Hawks and released by Warner Brothers).

The Tarnished Angels (January 1958; film adaptation of *Pylon* [see above]; screenplay by George Zuckerman and directed by Douglas Sirk; released by Universal-International).

LIBRARY HOLDINGS; BIBLIOGRAPHIES OF SECONDARY SOURCES; WEB SITES; AND SOCIETIES, CENTERS, AND CONFERENCES

1. Library Holdings and Manuscript Collections

Beinecke Rare Books and Manuscript Library, Yale University, New Haven, Connecticut

Berg Collection, New York Public Library

Louis Daniel Brodsky Collection, Kent Library, Southeast Missouri State University, Cape Girardeau

Humanities Research Center, University of Texas, Austin

Lafayette County Courthouse, Oxford, Mississippi

Mississippi Department of Archives and History, Jackson

Princeton University Library, Princeton, New Jersey

Ripley Public Library, Ripley, Mississippi

Rowan Oak Papers, Special Collections Department, John Davis Williams Library, University of Mississippi, Oxford

Special Collections, University of Virginia, Charlottesville, Virginia

Tippah County Courthouse, Ripley, Mississippi

William B. Wisdom Collection, Howard-Tilton Memorial Library, Tulane University, New Orleans, Louisiana

2. Biographical References

Alexander, Sidney. "The Nobel Prize Comes to Mississippi: How Yoknapatawpha County Sees Its Author," *Commentary* 12 (summer 1951): 176–180.

Bezzerides, A. I. *William Faulkner: A Life on Paper.* Edited by Ann Abadie. Jackson: University Press of Mississippi, 1980.

Blotner, Joseph. *Faulkner: A Biography.* 2 vols. New York: Random House, 1974. One vol. rev. ed., 1984.

———, ed. *Selected Letters of William Faulkner.* New York: Random House, 1977.

Bouvard, Loic. "Conversation with William Faulkner." *Modern Fiction Studies* 5 (winter 1959–60): 361–364.

Bradford, Roark. "The Private World of William Faulkner." *'48, the Magazine of the Year* 2 (May 1948): 83–84, 90.

Breit, Harvey. "A Walk with Faulkner." *New York Times Book Review* (January 30, 1955), 4, 12. Reprinted in *The Writer Observed.* Cleveland: World, 1956, 281–284.

Brennan, Dan. "Journey South." *University of Kansas City Review* 22 (autumn 1955), 11–16.

Brodsky, Louis Daniel. *William Faulkner: Life Glimpses.* Austin: University of Texas Press, 1990.

Brodsky, Louis Daniel, and Robert W. Hamblin. *Faulkner and Hollywood: A Retrospective from the Brodsky Collection.* Cape Girardeau: Southeast Missouri State University, 1984.

———. *Faulkner: A Comprehensive Guide to the Brodsky Collection. Vol. II: The Letters.* Jackson: University Press of Mississippi, 1984.

———. *Selections from the William Faulkner Collection of Louis Daniel Brodsky.* Charlottesville: University Press of Virginia, 1979.

———. *William Faulkner: A Perspective from the Brodsky Collection.* Cape Girardeau: Southeast Missouri State University, 1979.

Buttitta, Anthony. "William Faulkner: That Writin' Man of Oxford." *Saturday Review of Literature* 18 (May 21, 1938): 6–8.

Cantwell, Robert. "The Faulkners: Recollections of a Gifted Family." *New World Writings* 2 (November 1952), 300–315. Reprinted in *William Faulkner: Three Decades of Criticism*, edited by Frederick J. Hoffman and Olga W. Vickery, 51–66. New York: Harcourt, Brace & World, 1963.

Carter, Hodding. "Faulkner and His Folk." *Princeton University Library Chronicle* 18 (spring 1957): 95–107.

Chapsal, Madeleine. "A Lion in the Garden." *Reporter* 13 (November 3, 1955): 40.

Cofield, Jack. *William Faulkner: The Cofield Collection.* Oxford, Miss.: Yoknapatawpha Press, 1978.

Coughlan, Robert. *The Private World of William Faulkner.* New York: Harper, 1954.

Cowley, Malcolm. *The Faulkner-Cowley File: Letters and Memories, 1944–1962.* New York: Viking Press, 1966.

Cullen, John B., and Floyd C. Watkins. *Old Times in the Faulkner Country.* Chapel Hill: University of North Carolina Press, 1961.

Dain, Martin J. *Faulkner's County: Yoknapatawpha.* New York: Random House, 1964.

———. *Faulkner's World: The Photographs of Martin J. Dain.* Edited and with an introduction by Thomas S. Rankin. Jackson: University Press of Mississippi, 1997.

Dominicus, A. M. "An Interview with Faulkner." *Faulkner Studies* 3 (summer–autumn 1954): 33–37.

Doyle, Don H. *Faulkner's County: The Historical Roots of Yoknapatawpha.* Chapel Hill: University of North Carolina Press, 2001.

Evans, Medford. "Oxford, Mississippi." *Southwest Review* 15 (winter 1929): 46–63.

Falkner, Murry C. *The Falkners of Mississippi: A Memoir.* Baton Rouge: Louisiana State University Press, 1967.

Fant, Joseph L., and Robert Ashley, eds. *Faulkner at West Point.* New York: Random House, 1964.

Faulkner, Jim. *Across the Creek: Faulkner Family Stories.* Jackson: University Press of Mississippi, 1986.

———. "Auntee Owned Two," *Southern Review* 8 (October 1972): 836–844.

Faulkner, John. *My Brother Bill: An Affectionate Reminiscence.* New York: Trident Press, 1963.

Franklin, Malcolm A. *Bitterweeds: Life with William Faulkner at Rowan Oak.* Irving, Tex.: Society for the Study of Traditional Culture, 1977.

———. "A Christmas in Columbus." *Mississippi Quarterly* 27 (summer 1974): 319–322.

Gray, Richard. *The Life of William Faulkner: A Critical Biography.* Oxford, England: Blackwell, 1994.

Green, A. Wigfall. "William Faulkner at Home." *Sewanee Review* 40 (summer 1932): 294–306. Reprinted in *William Faulkner: Two Decades of Criticism*, edited by Frederick J. Hoffman and Olga W. Vickery, 33–47. East Lansing: Michigan State University Press, 1951.

Grenier, Cynthia. "An Interview with William Faulkner—September, 1955." *Accent* 16 (summer 1956): 167–177.

Gresset, Michel. *A Faulkner Chronology.* Jackson: University Press of Mississippi, 1985.

Gwynn, Frederick L., and Joseph Blotner, eds. *Faulkner in the University: Class Conferences at the University of Virginia, 1957–1958.* Charlottesville: University of Virginia Press, 1959.

———. "Faulkner in the University: A Classroom Conference." *College English* 19 (October 1957): 1–6.

———. "William Faulkner on Dialect." *University of Virginia Magazine* 2 (winter 1958): 7–13; cont'd. in 2 (spring 1958): 32–37.

Haynes, Jane Isbell. *William Faulkner: His Lafayette County Heritage.* Columbia, S.C.: Seajay Press, 1992.

———. *William Faulkner: His Tippah County Heritage.* Columbia, S.C.: Seajay Press, 1992.

Hickman, Lisa C. *William Faulkner and Joan Williams: The Romance of Two Writers.* Jefferson, N.C.: McFarland and Company, 2006.

Howe, Russell Warren. "A Talk with William Faulkner." *Reporter* 14 (March 22, 1956): 18–20.

Inge, M. Thomas, ed. *Conversations with William Faulkner.* Jackson: University Press of Mississippi, 1999.

Jelliffe, Robert A., ed. *Faulkner at Nagano.* Tokyo, Japan: Kenkyusha, 1956.

Karl, Frederick. *William Faulkner, American Writer: A Biography.* New York: Weidenfeld & Nicolson, 1989.

Lawrence, John, and Dan Hise. *Faulkner's Rowan Oak.* Jackson: University Press of Mississippi, 1995.

Meriwether, James B., and Michael Millgate, eds. *Lion in the Garden: Interviews with William Faulkner, 1926–1962.* New York: Random House, 1968.

Minter, David. *William Faulkner: His Life and Work.* Baltimore, Md.: Johns Hopkins University Press, 1980.

Morris, Willie, and William Eggleston. *Faulkner's Mississippi.* Birmingham, Ala.: Oxmoor House, 1990.

——— (with photos by William Albert Allard). "Faulkner's Mississippi." *National Geographic* 175 (March 1989): 313–339.

Oates, Stephen B. *William Faulkner: The Man and the Artist.* New York: Harper & Row, 1987.

Parini, Jay. *One Matchless Time: A Life of William Faulkner.* New York: HarperCollins, 2004.

Raimbault, R. N. *Faulkner.* Paris, France: Editions Universitaires, 1963.

Rascoe, Lavon. "An Interview with William Faulkner." *Western Review* 15 (summer 1951): 300–304.

Richardson, H. Edward. *William Faulkner: The Journey to Self-Discovery.* Columbia: University of Missouri Press, 1969.

Smith, Bradley. "The Faulkner Country." *'48, the Magazine of the Year* 2 (May 1948): 85–89.

Smith, Marshall J. "Faulkner of Mississippi." *Bookman* 74 (December 1931): 411–417.

Snell, Susan. *Phil Stone of Oxford: A Vicarious Life.* Athens: University of Georgia Press, 1991.

Stein, Jean. "William Faulkner." *Paris Review,* 4 (spring 1956): 28–52. Reprinted in *Writers at Work,* edited by Malcolm Cowley, 119–141. New York: Viking, 1958. Also reprinted in *William Faulkner: Three Decades of Criticism,* edited by Frederick J. Hoffman and Olga W. Vickery, 67–82. New York: Harcourt, Brace & World, 1963.

Stone, Phil. "William Faulkner: The Man and His Work." *Oxford Magazine* (Oxford, Mississippi), copy 1 (1934): 13–14; continued in copies 2 and 3; unfinished. Reprinted in James B. Meriwether, "Early Notices of Faulkner by Phil Stone and Louis Cochran." *Mississippi Quarterly* 17 (summer 1964): 136–164.

Sullivan, Frank. "A Distinguished Commuter." *Saturday Review* 34 (June 9, 1951): 4.

Taylor, Herman E. *Faulkner's Oxford: Recollections and Reflections.* Nashville, Tenn.: Rutledge Hill Press, 1990.

Wagner, Linda W. "William Faulkner." In *Dictionary of Literary Biography: American Novelists, 1910–1945, Part 1: Louis Adamic—Vardis Fisher,* vol. 9, edited by James J. Martine, 282–302. Detroit: Gale, 1981.

Wasson, Ben. *Count No 'Count: Flashbacks to Faulkner.* Jackson: University Press of Mississippi, 1983.

Watson, James G., ed. *Thinking of Home: William Faulkner's Letters to His Mother and Father, 1918–1925.* New York: Norton, 1992.

Webb, James W., and A. Wigfall Green, eds. *William Faulkner of Oxford.* Baton Rouge: Louisiana State University Press, 1965.

Wilde, Meta Carpenter, and Orin Borsten. *A Loving Gentleman: The Love Story of William Faulkner and Meta Carpenter.* New York: Simon & Schuster, 1976.

Williamson, Joel. *William Faulkner and Southern History.* New York: Oxford University Press, 1993.

Wittenberg, Judith Bryant. *Faulkner: The Transfiguration of Biography.* Lincoln: University of Nebraska Press, 1979.

Wolff, Sally, with Floyd C. Watkins, eds. *Talking about William Faulkner: Interviews with Jimmy Faulkner and Others.* Baton Rouge: Louisiana State University Press, 1996.

Young, Stark. "New Year's Craw." *New Republic* 93 (January 12, 1938): 283–284.

3. Bibliographical References

Bassett, John E. *Faulkner: An Annotated Checklist of Recent Criticism.* Kent, Ohio: Kent State University Press, 1983.

———. *Faulkner in the Eighties: An Annotated Critical Bibliography.* Metuchen, N.J.: Scarecrow, 1991.

———. *William Faulkner: An Annotated Checklist of Criticism.* New York: David Lewis, 1972.

Beebe, Maurice. "Criticism of William Faulkner: A Selected Checklist with an Index to Studies of Separate Works." *Modern Fiction Studies* 2 (autumn 1956): 150–164.

Blotner, Joseph. *William Faulkner's Library: A Catalogue.* Charlottesville: University Press of Virginia, 1964.

Blotner, Joseph, Thomas L. McHaney, Michael Millgate, Noel Polk, and James B. Meriwether, eds. *William Faulkner Manuscripts.* 44 vols. New York: Garland, 1985–87.

Bonner, Thomas, Jr., comp. *William Faulkner: The William B. Wisdom Collection: A Descriptive Catalogue.* New Orleans, La.: Tulane University Libraries, 1980.

Brodsky, Louis Daniel, and Robert W. Hamblin, eds. *The Brodsky Faulkner Collection, 1959–1989: The Collector's 101 Favorites.* Southeast Missouri State University: Center for Faulkner Studies, 1989.

———. *Country Lawyer and Other Stories for the Screen.* Jackson: University Press of Mississippi, 1987.

———. *Faulkner: A Comprehensive Guide to the Brodsky Collection.* 5 vols. Jackson: University Press of Mississippi, 1982–88.

Butterworth, Keen. "A Census of Manuscripts and Typescripts of William Faulkner's Poetry." *Mississippi Quarterly* 26 (summer 1973): 333–360.

Capps, Jack L., ed. *The Faulkner Concordances.* 34 vols. Ann Arbor, Mich.: UMI Research Press/The Faulkner Concordance Advisory Board, 1977–90.

Cox, Leland, ed. *William Faulkner: Biographical and Reference Guide: A Guide to His Life and Career.* Detroit, Mich.: Gale, 1982.

Daniel, Robert W. *A Catalogue of the Writings of William Faulkner.* New Haven: Yale University Library, 1942.

Doyle, Don H. *Faulkner's County: The Historical Roots of Yoknapatawpha.* Chapel Hill: University of North Carolina Press, 2001.

Duvall, John N., and Ann J. Abadie, eds. *Faulkner and Postmodernism: Faulkner and Yoknapatawpha, 1999.* Jackson: University Press of Mississippi, 2002.

Hayhoe, George F. "Faulkner in Hollywood: A Checklist of His Film Scripts at the University of Virginia." *Mississippi Quarterly* 31 (summer 1978): 407–419.

Howard, Peter. *William Faulkner: The Carl Peterson Collection.* Berkeley, Calif.: Serendipity Press, 1991.

Kawin, Bruce, ed. *Faulkner's MGM Screenplays.* Knoxville: University of Tennessee Press, 1982.

Massey, Linton, comp. *William Faulkner: "Man Working," 1919–1962: A Catalogue of the William Faulkner Collections at the University of Virginia.* Charlottesville: Bibliographical Society of the University of Virginia, 1968.

Meriwether, James B. *The Literary Career of William Faulkner: A Bibliographical Study.* Princeton, N.J.: Princeton University Library, 1961; revised edition, Columbia, S.C.: University of South Carolina Press, 1972.

———, ed. *A Faulkner Miscellany.* Jackson: University Press of Mississippi, 1974.

Meriwether, James B. *The Merrill Checklist of William Faulkner.* Columbus, Ohio: Merrill, 1970.

———. *William Faulkner: An Exhibit of Manuscripts* (Austin, Texas, 1959).

———. "The Short Fiction of William Faulkner: A Bibliography." *Proof* 1 (1971): 293–329.

———. "William Faulkner: A Check List." *Princeton University Library Chronicle* 18 (spring 1957): 136–158. A bibliography of Faulkner's works.

Perry, Bradley T. "Faulkner Critics: A Bibliography Breakdown." *Faulkner Studies* 2 (spring–summer–winter 1953): 11–13, 30–32, 60–64.

———. "A Selected Bibliography of Critical Works on William Faulkner." *University of Kansas City Review* 18 (winter 1951): 159–164.

Petersen, Carl. *Each in Its Ordered Place: A Faulkner Collector's Notebook.* Ann Arbor, Mich.: Ardis, 1975.

———. *On the Track of the Dixie Limited: Further Notes of a Faulkner Collector.* La Grange, Ill.: Colophon Book Shop, 1979.

Ricks, Beatrice. *William Faulkner: A Reference Guide.* Metuchen, N.J.: Scarecrow, 1981.

Runyan, Harry. "Faulkner's Non-Fiction Prose: An Annotated Checklist." *Faulkner Studies* 3 (winter 1954): 67–69.

Sensibar, Judith. *Faulkner's Poetry: A Bibliographic Guide to Texts and Criticism.* Ann Arbor, Mich.: UMI Research Press, 1988.

Sleeth, Irene Lynn. "William Faulkner: A Bibliography of Criticism." *Twentieth Century Literature* 8 (April 1962): 18–43. Also published separately in *The Swallow Pamphlets,* Number 13. Denver: Alan Swallow, 1962.

Smith, Thelma M., and Ward L. Miner. "Faulkner Checklist and Bibliography." In *Transatlantic Migration: The Contemporary American Novel in France,* 227–235. Durham: Duke University Press, 1955.

Stallman, Robert W. "William Faulkner." In *Critiques and Essays on Modern Fiction, 1920–1951,* edited by John W. Aldridge, 582–586. New York: Ronald Press, 1952.

Starke, Aubrey. "An American Comedy: An Introduction to a Bibliography of William Faulkner." *Colophon* 5 (1934), part 19.

Sweeney, Patricia. *William Faulkner's Women Characters: An Annotated Bibliography of Criticism, 1930–1983.* Santa Barbara, Calif.: ABC-Clio, 1985.

Vickery, Olga W. "A Selective Bibliography." In *William Faulkner: Three Decades of Criticism*, 393–428. East Lansing: Michigan State University Press, 1960. A bibliography of Faulkner criticism.

4. Reference Works, Guides, and Periodicals

Connolly, Thomas E. *Faulkner's World: A Directory of His People and Synopses of Actions in His Published Works.* Lanham, Md.: University Press of America, 1988.

Dasher, Thomas E. *William Faulkner's Characters: An Index to the Published and Unpublished Fiction.* New York: Garland, 1981.

English Institute Essays, 1952 (essays on *The Sound and the Fury*). New York: Columbia University Press, 1954.

The Faulkner Journal, 1985–1988, 1991— (Dawn Trouard, managing editor, Humanities and Fine Arts Building, RM 405, University of Central Florida, Orlando, FL 32816-1346; Web site: http://pegasus.cc.ucf.edu/~faulkner/).

The Faulkner Journal of Japan (see *Faulkner Studies*).

The Faulkner Newsletter & Yoknapatawpha Review, 1981 (Oxford, Mississippi; Web site: http://www.watervalley.net/yoknapatawphapress/news.html).

Faulkner Studies (title given to three separate journals; the two that published in 1952–54 and 1980 are defunct; the third started publishing in 1991 in Japan, also *The Faulkner Journal of Japan*).

Ford, Margaret P., and Suzanne Kincaid. *Who's Who in Faulkner.* Baton Rouge: Louisiana State University Press, 1963.

Hamblin, Robert W., and Charles A. Peek, eds. *A William Faulkner Encyclopedia.* Westport, Conn.: Greenwood Press, 1999.

Harvard Advocate (William Faulkner issue) 135 (November 1951).

Hoffman, Frederick J. *William Faulkner.* 2nd ed. New York: Twayne, 1966.

Kirk, Robert W., with Marvin Klotz. *Faulkner's People: A Complete Guide and Index to Characters in the Fiction of William Faulkner.* Berkeley: University of California Press, 1963.

McHaney, Thomas. *William Faulkner: A Reference Guide.* Boston: G. K. Hall, 1976.

Mississippi Quarterly (summer issues devoted to Faulkner).

Modern Fiction Studies (William Faulkner special number) 2 (autumn 1956). Essays by Melvin Backman, Robert Flynn, David L. Frazier, Roma A. King, W. R. Moses, Karl E. Zink.

Oxford American, 1992 (Web site: http://www.oxfordamericanmag.com/).

Munro, Pamela, and Catherine Willmond. *Chickasaw: An Analytical Dictionary.* Norman: University of Oklahoma Press, 1994.

Peek, Charles A., and Robert W. Hamblin, eds. *A Companion to Faulkner Studies.* Westport, Conn.: Greenwood, 2004.

Perspective (Faulkner) 2 (summer 1949). Essays by Ruel E. Foster, Phyllis Hirshleifer, Sumner C. Powell, Russell Roth, Ray B. West.

Perspective (Faulkner, no. 2) 3 (autumn 1950). Essays by Harry M. Campbell, Tommy Hudson, Olga Westland Vickery, Edgar W. Whan.

Princeton University Library Chronicle (William Faulkner) 18 (spring 1957).

Runyan, Harry. *A Faulkner Glossary.* New York: Citadel, 1964.

Teaching Faulkner, edited by Robert W. Hamblin and Charles A. Peek, published by the Center for Faulkner Studies, Southeast Missouri State University (Web site: http://www.semo.edu/cfs/teaching).

Tuck, Dorothy. *Crowell's Handbook of Faulkner.* New York: Crowell, 1964.

Volpe, Edmond L. *A Reader's Guide to William Faulkner.* New York: Noonday, 1964; San Jose, Calif.: Authors Choice Press, 2001.

Weinstein, Philip, ed. *The Cambridge Companion to William Faulkner.* New York: Cambridge University Press, 1995.

5. Selected General Bibliography

Adams, Richard P. *Faulkner: Myth and Motion.* Princeton, N.J.: Princeton University Press, 1968.

Adams, Robert M. "Poetry in the Novel: or, Faulkner Esemplastic." *Virginia Quarterly Review* 29 (summer 1953): 419–434.

D'Agostino, Nemi. "William Faulkner." *Studia Americani* 1 (1955): 257–308.

Aiken, Conrad. "'Mosquitoes,'" *New York Post* (June 11, 1927): 7. Reprinted in his *A Reviewer's ABC: Collected Criticism from 1916 to the Present*, 197–200. New York: Meridian, 1958.

———. "William Faulkner: The Novel as Form." *Atlantic Monthly* 164 (November 1939): 650–654. Reprinted in his *A Reviewer's ABC: Collected Criticism from 1916 to the Present*, 200–207; New York: Meridian, 1958; in *William Faulkner: Three Decades of Criticism*, edited by Frederick J. Hoffman and Olga W. Vickery, 135–142; New York: Harcourt, Brace & World, 1963; and also in *Faulkner A Collection of Critical Essays*, edited by Robert Penn Warren, 46–52. Englewood Cliffs, N.J.: Prentice Hall, Inc., 1966.

Allen, Charles A. "William Faulkner's Vision of Good and Evil." *Pacific Spectator* 10 (summer 1956): 236–241.

Altman, Meryl. "The Bug That Dare Not Speak Its Name: Sex, Art, Faulkner's Worst Novel, and the Critics." *The Faulkner Journal* 9 (fall 1993/spring 1994): 1–2, 43–68.

Anderson, Charles. "Faulkner's Moral Center." *Etudes Anglaises* 7 (January 1954): 48–58.

Anonymous. "The Worldwide Influence of William Faulkner: Reports from Six Capitols." *New York Times Book Review* 64 (November 15, 1959): 52–53. Statements by Walter Allen, Celia Bertin, Max Frankel, Flora Lewis, Masami Nishkawa, Emilio Cecchi.

Archer, H. Richard. "Collecting Faulkner Today." *Faulkner Studies* 1 (fall 1952): 42–43.

———. "The Writings of William Faulkner: A Challenge to the Bibliographer." *Papers of the Bibliographical Society of America* 50 (3rd quart. 1956): 229–242.

Arnold, Edwin T. *Annotations to Faulkner's Mosquitoes*. New York: Garland Publishing, 1989.

———. "Freedom and Stasis in Faulkner's Mosquitoes." *Mississippi Quarterly: The Journal of Southern Culture* (Mississippi State University) 28 (1975): 281–297.

Arnold, Edwin T., and Dawn Trouard. *Reading Faulkner*: Sanctuary. Jackson: University Press of Mississippi, 1996.

Arthos, John. "Ritual and Humor in the Writing of William Faulkner." *Accent* 9 (autumn 1948): 17–30. Reprinted in *William Faulkner: Two Decades of Criticism*, edited by Frederick J. Hoffman and Olga W. Vickery, 101–118. East Lansing: Michigan State University Press, 1951.

Atkinson, Ted. *Faulkner and the Great Depression: Aesthetics, Ideology, and Cultural Politics*. Athens: University of Georgia Press, 2005.

Aymé, Marcel. "What French Readers Find in William Faulkner's Fiction." *New York Times Book Review* (December 17, 1950): 4. Reprinted in *Highlights of Modern Literature*, edited by Francis Brown, 103–106. New York: Mentor, 1954.

Bache, William B. "Moral Awareness in 'Dry September.'" *Faulkner Studies* 3 (winter 1954): 53–57.

Backman, Melvin. *Faulkner: The Major Years: A Critical Study*. Bloomington: Indiana University Press, 1966.

———. "Faulkner's Sick Heroes: Bayard Sartoris and Quentin Compson." *Modern Fiction Studies* 2 (autumn 1956): 95–108.

———. "Sickness and Primitivism: A Dominant Pattern in William Faulkner's Work." *Accent* 14 (winter 1954): 61–73.

Backus, Joseph M. "Names of Characters in Faulkner's 'The Sound and the Fury.'" *Names* 6 (December 1958): 226–233.

Baker, Carlos. "Cry Enough!" *Nation* 179 (August 7, 1954): 115–118.

———. "William Faulkner: The Doomed and the Damned." In *The Young Rebel in American Literature*, edited by Carl Bode, 145–169. London: Heinemann, 1959.

Baker, James R. "Ideas and Queries." *Faulkner Studies* 1 (spring 1952): 4–7.

———. "The Symbolic Extension of Yoknapatawpha County." *Arizona Quarterly* 8 (autumn 1952): 223–228.

Baldanza, Frank. "Faulkner and Stein: A Study in Stylistic Intransigence." *Georgia Review* 13 (fall 1959): 274–286.

Barth, J. Robert. "A Rereading of Faulkner's Fable." *America* 92 (October 9, 1954): 44–46.

Barth, J. Robert, ed. *Religious Perspectives in Faulkner's Fiction: Yoknapatawpha and Beyond*. Notre Dame, Ind.: University of Notre Dame Press, 1972.

Bassett, John Earl. *Vision and Revisions: Essays on Faulkner.* West Cornwall, Conn.: Locust Hill Press, 1989.

———. "Faulkner's *Mosquitoes:* Toward a Self-Image of the Artist." *Southern Literary Journal* 12, no. 2 (1980): 49–64.

Beach, Joseph Warren. "William Faulkner." In *American Fiction, 1920–1940,* 123–169. New York: Macmillan, 1941.

Beck, Warren. *Faulkner: Essays.* Madison: University of Wisconsin Press, 1976.

———. *Man in Motion: Faulkner's Trilogy.* Madison: University of Wisconsin Press, 1961.

———. "Faulkner and the South." *Antioch Review* 1 (spring 1941): 82–94.

———. "Faulkner's Point of View." *College English* 2 (May 1941): 736–749.

———. "A Note on Faulkner's Style," *Rocky Mountain Review* 6 (spring–summer 1942): 6–7, 14.

———. "William Faulkner's Style." *American Prefaces* 6 (spring 1941): 195–211. Reprinted in *William Faulkner: Three Decades of Criticism,* edited by Frederick J. Hoffman and Olga W. Vickery, 142–156. New York: Harcourt, Brace & World, 1963. Also reprinted in *Faulkner: A Collection of Critical Essays,* edited by Robert Penn Warren, 53–65. Englewood Cliffs, N.J.: Prentice Hall, Inc., 1966.

Bergel, Lienhard. "Faulkner's 'Sanctuary.'" *Explicator* 6 (December 1947): item 20.

Birney, Earle. "The Two William Faulkners." *Canadian Forum* 18 (June 1938): 84–85.

Bledsoe, Erik. *Margaret Mitchell's Review of "Soldiers' Pay."* *Mississippi Quarterly: The Journal of Southern Culture* 49, no. 3 (summer 1996): 591–593.

Bleikasten, André. *Faulkner's As I Lay Dying.* Rev. ed. Translated by Roger Little. Bloomington: Indiana University Press, 1973.

———. *The Ink of Melancholy: Faulkner's Novels from "The Sound and the Fury" to "Light in August."* Bloomington: Indiana University Press, 1990.

Bloom, Harold, ed. *Modern Critical Views: William Faulkner.* New York: Chelsea House, 1986.

———. *William Faulkner's "Sanctuary": Modern Critical Interpretations.* New York: Chelsea House, 1988.

Blotner, Joseph L. "'As I Lay Dying': Christian Lore and Irony." *Twentieth Century Literature* 3 (April 1957): 14–19.

Blum, Irving D. "The Parallel Philosophy of Emerson's 'Nature' and Faulkner's 'The Bear.'" *Emerson Society Quarterly* 13 (4th quarter 1958): 22–25.

Bockting, Ineke. *Character and Personality in the Novels of William Faulkner: A Study in Psychostylistics.* Lanham, Md.: University Press of America, 1995.

Bosha, Francis. *The Textual History and Definitive Textual Apparatus for "Soldiers' Pay": A Bibliographic Study of William Faulkner's First Novel.* Abstract in *Dissertation Abstracts International* 39 (1979): 5509A.

Bowling, Lawrence E. "Faulkner: Technique of 'The Sound and the Fury.'" *Kenyon Review* 10 (autumn 1948): 552–566. Reprinted in *William Faulkner: Two Decades of Criticism,* edited by Frederick J. Hoffman and Olga W. Vickery, 165–179. East Lansing: Michigan State University Press, 1951.

———. "Faulkner and the Theme of Innocence." *Kenyon Review* 20 (summer 1958): 466–487.

Boyle, Kay. "Tattered Banners." *New Republic* 94 (March 9, 1938): 136–137.

Boynton, Percy H. "The Retrospective South." In *America in Contemporary Fiction,* 103–112. Chicago: University of Chicago Press, 1940.

Breaden, Dale G. "William Faulkner and the Land." *American Quarterly* 10 (fall 1958): 344–357.

Breit, Harvey. "A Sense of Faulkner." *Partisan Review* 18 (January–February 1951): 88–94.

———. "William Faulkner." *Atlantic Monthly* 188 (October 1951): 53–56.

Brooks, Cleanth. *On the Prejudices, Predilections, and Firm Beliefs of William Faulkner.* Baton Rouge: Louisiana State University Press, 1987.

———. *William Faulkner: First Encounters.* New Haven, Conn.: Yale University Press, 1983.

———. *William Faulkner: Toward Yoknapatawpha and Beyond.* New Haven, Conn.: Yale University Press, 1978.

———. *William Faulkner: The Yoknapatawpha Country.* New Haven, Conn.: Yale University Press, 1963.

———. "'Absalom, Absalom!' The Definition of Innocence." *Sewanee Review* 59 (autumn 1951): 543–558.

———. "Primitivism in 'The Sound and the Fury.'" In *English Institute Essays 1952,* edited by Alan S. Downer, 5–28. New York: Columbia University Press, 1954.

Brooks, Cleanth, and Robert Penn Warren. *Understanding Fiction*, 409–414. New York: F. S. Crofts, 1943.

Broughton, Panthea Reid. *William Faulkner: The Abstract and the Actual*. Baton Rouge: Louisiana State University Press, 1974.

Brown, Calvin S. *A Glossary of Faulkner's South*. New Haven, Conn.: Yale University Press, 1976.

Brown, James. "Shaping the World of 'Sanctuary.'" *University of Kansas City Review* 25 (winter 1958): 137–142.

Brumm, Ursula. "Wilderness and Civilization: A Note on William Faulkner." *Partisan Review* 22 (summer 1955): 340–350. Reprinted in *William Faulkner: Three Decades of Criticism*, edited by Frederick J. Hoffman and Olga W. Vickery, 125–134. New York: Harcourt, Brace & World, 1963.

Brylowski, Walter. *Faulkner's Olympian Laugh: Myth in the Novels*. Detroit, Mich.: Wayne State University Press, 1968.

Burgum, Edwin Berry. "William Faulkner's Patterns of American Decadence." In *The Novel and the World's Dilemma*, 205–222. New York: Oxford University Press, 1947.

Butterworth, Nancy. *A Critical and Textual Study of Faulkner's "A Fable."* Ann Arbor, Mich.: UMI Research Press, 1983.

——— and Keen Butterworth. *Annotations to Faulkner's A Fable*. New York: Garland, 1989.

Campbell, Harry M. "Experiment and Achievement: 'As I Lay Dying' and 'The Sound and the Fury.'" *Sewanee Review* 51 (spring 1943): 305–320.

———. "Faulkner's 'Absalom, Absalom!'" *Explicator* 7 (December 1948): item 24.

———. "Faulkner's 'Sanctuary.'" *Explicator* 4 (June 1946): item 61.

———. "Structural Devices in the Works of Faulkner," *Perspective* 3 (autumn 1950): 209–226.

Campbell, Harry M., and Ruel E. Foster. *William Faulkner: A Critical Appraisal*. Norman: Oklahoma University Press, 1951.

Canby, Henry Seidel. "The School of Cruelty." *Saturday Review of Literature* 7 (March 21, 1931): 673–674. Reprinted in *Seven Years' Harvest*, 77–83. New York: Farrar & Rinehart, 1936.

Cantwell, Robert. "Faulkner's 'Popeye.'" *Nation* 186 (February 15, 1958): 140–141, 148.

Caraceni, Augusto. "William Faulkner." *Aretusa* 2 (November 1945): 23–28.

Carey, Glenn O., ed. *Faulkner: The Unappeased Imagination: A Collection of Critical Essays*. Troy, N.Y.: Whitston, 1980.

Cargill, Oscar. "The Primitivists." In *Intellectual America*, 370–386. New York: Macmillan, 1941.

Carothers, James B. *William Faulkner's Short Stories*. Ann Arbor, Mich.: UMI Research Press, 1985.

Carpenter, Lucas. "Faulkner's 'Soldiers' Pay': 'Yaphank' Gilligan." *Notes on Modern American Literature* 8, no. 3 (winter 1984): item 17.

Carpenter, Richard C. "Faulkner's 'Sartoris.'" *Explicator* 14 (April 1956): item 41.

Carter, Thomas H. "Dramatization of an Enigma." *Western Review* 19 (winter 1955): 147–158.

Cash, W. J. *The Mind of the South*. New York: Knopf, 1941. Reprint, Garden City, N.Y.: Doubleday, 1954.

Cecchi, Emilio. "William Faulkner." *Pan* 2 (May 1934): 64–70.

Chabrier, Gwendolyn. *Faulkner's Families: A Southern Saga*. New York: Gordian, 1993.

Chamberlain, John. "Dostoyefsky's Shadow in the Deep South." *New York Times Book Review* (February 15, 1931): 9.

Chamier, Suzanne. "Faulkner and Queneau: Raymond Queneau's Preface to 'Mosquitoes'." *The Faulkner Journal* 13 (fall 1997/spring 1998): 1–2, 15–36.

Chapman, Arnold. "Pampas and Big Woods: Heroic Initiation in Güiraldes and Faulkner." *Comparative Literature* 11 (winter 1959): 61–77.

Chappell, Charles. *Detective Dupin Reads William Faulkner: Solutions to Six Yoknapatawpha Mysteries*. San Francisco: International Scholars Publications, 1997.

Chase, Richard. "Faulkner—The Great Years." In *The American Novel and its Tradition*, 205–236. Garden City: Doubleday Anchor Books, 1957.

Claridge, Henry. *William Faulkner: Critical Assessments*. New York: Routledge, 2000.

Clarke, Deborah. *Robbing the Mother: Women in Faulkner*. Jackson: University Press of Mississippi, 1994.

Coanda, Richard. "'Absalom, Absalom!' The Edge of Infinity." *Renascence* 11 (autumn 1958): 3–9.

Coffee, James M. *Faulkner's Un-Christlike Christians: Biblical Allusions in the Novels*. Ann Arbor, Mich.: UMI Research Press, 1983.

Coindreau, Maurice E. *The Time of William Faulkner: A French View of Modern American Fiction.* Edited and translated by George M. Reeves. Columbia: South Carolina University Press, 1971.

———. "On Translating Faulkner." *Princeton University Library Chronicle* 18 (spring 1957): 108–113.

———. "William Faulkner in France." *Yale French Studies* 10 (fall 1952): 85–91.

Collins, Carvel. "Are These Mandalas?" *Literature and Psychology* 3 (November 1953): 3–6.

———. "A Conscious Literary Use of Freud?" *Literature and Psychology* 3 (June 1953): 2–3.

———. "Faulkner and Certain Earlier Southern Fiction." *College English* 16 (November 1954): 92–97.

———. "Faulkner's Reputation and the Contemporary Novel." In *Literature in the Modern World,* edited by William J. Griffin, 65–71. Nashville: George Peabody College for Teachers, 1954.

———. "Faulkner's 'The Sound and the Fury.'" *Explicator* 17 (December 1958): item 19.

———. "The Interior Monologues of 'The Sound and the Fury.'" In *English Institute Essays 1952,* edited by Alan S. Downer, 29–56. New York: Columbia University Press, 1954. Reprinted in *Massachusetts Institute of Technology Publications in the Humanities,* No. 6 (1954).

———. "Nathaniel West's 'The Day of the Locust' and 'Sanctuary.'" *Faulkner Studies* 2 (summer 1953): 23–24.

———. "A Note on 'Sanctuary.'" *Harvard Advocate* 135 (November 1951): 16.

———. "A Note on the Conclusion of 'The Bear.'" *Faulkner Studies* 2 (winter 1954): 58–60.

———. "The Pairing of 'The Sound and the Fury' and 'As I Lay Dying.'" *Princeton University Library Chronicle* 18 (spring 1957): 114–123.

———. "War and Peace and Mr. Faulkner." *New York Times Book Review* (August 1, 1954): 1, 13.

Connolly, Cyril. "'Pylon.'" *New Statesman and Nation* 9 (April 13, 1935): 284–285.

Coughlan, Robert. *The Private World of William Faulkner.* New York: Harper, 1954.

Cowley, Malcolm. "Flem Snopes Gets his Come-Uppance." *New York Times Book Review* (November 15, 1959): 1, 18.

———. "Introduction," *The Portable Faulkner,* 1–24. New York: Viking Press, 1946. Reprinted in *William Faulkner: Three Decades of Criticism,* edited by Frederick J. Hoffman and Olga W. Vickery, 94–109. New York: Harcourt, Brace & World, 1963. Also reprinted in *Faulkner: A Collection of Critical Essays,* edited by Robert Penn Warren, 34–45. Englewood Cliffs, N.J.: Prentice Hall, Inc., 1966.

———. "An Introduction to William Faulkner." In *Critiques and Essays on Modern Fiction, 1920–1951,* edited by John W. Aldridge, 427–446. New York: Ronald Press, 1952.

———. "Poe in Mississippi." *New Republic* 89 (November 4, 1936): 22.

———. "Sanctuary." *New Republic* 97 (January 25, 1939): 349.

———. "William Faulkner's Human Comedy." *New York Times Book Review* (October 19, 1944): 4.

———. "William Faulkner's Legend of the South." *Sewanee Review* 53 (summer 1945): 343–361. Reprinted in *A Southern Vanguard,* edited by Allen Tate, 13–27. New York: Prentice-Hall, 1947.

———. "William Faulkner Revisited." *Saturday Review of Literature* 28 (April 14, 1945): 13–16.

———. "In Which Mr. Faulkner Translates Past into Present." *New York Herald Tribune* (Books) (September 30, 1951): 1, 14.

———. "Voodoo Dance." *New Republic* 82 (April 10, 1935): 284–285.

Cox, Dianne L. *William Faulkner's As I Lay Dying: A Critical Casebook.* New York: Garland, 1985.

Coy, Javier, and Michel Gresset, eds. *Faulkner and History.* Salamanca, Spain: Universidad de Salamanca, 1986.

Cullen, John B. in collaboration with Floyd C. Watkins. *Old Times in the Faulkner Country.* Chapel Hill: University of North Carolina Press, 1961.

Dabney, Lewis M. *The Indians of Yoknapatawpha: A Study in Literature and History.* Baton Rouge: Louisiana State University Press, 1973.

Dain, Martin J. *Faulkner's County—Yoknapatawpha* (photos taken in and around Oxford, Mississippi). New York: Random House, 1964.

Dauffenbach, Claus. *A Portrait of the Modernist as a Young Aesthete: Faulkner's "Mosquitoes."* Amerikastudien–American Studies, Mainz, Germany (Amst). 1997, 42:4, 547–558.

Davis, Thadious M. *Faulkner's "Negro": Art and the Southern Context.* Baton Rouge: Louisiana State University Press, 1983.

De Voto, Bernard. "Faulkner's South." *Saturday Review of Literature* 17 (February 19, 1938): 5.

———. "Witchcraft in Mississippi." *Saturday Review of Literature* 15 (October 31, 1936): 3–4, 14. Reprinted in *Minority Report*, 209–218. Boston: Little, Brown, 1940.

Doran, Leonard. "Form and the Story Teller." *Harvard Advocate* 135 (November 1951): 12, 38–41.

Doster, William C. "The Several Faces of Gavin Stevens." *Mississippi Quarterly* 11 (fall 1958): 191–195.

Douglas, Harold J., and Robert Daniel. "Faulkner and the Puritanism of the South." *Tennessee Studies in Literature* 2 (1957): 1–13.

Dowling, David. *William Faulkner.* New York: St. Martin's Press, 1989.

Downing, Francis. "An Eloquent Man." *Commonweal* 53 (December 15, 1950): 255–258.

Duvall, John N. *Faulkner's Marginal Couple: Invisible, Outlaw, and Unspeakable Communities.* Austin: University of Texas Press, 1990.

Edel, Leon. *The Psychological Novel, 1900–1950,* 147–154. New York: Lippincott, 1955.

Edgar, Pelham. "Four American Novelists." In *The Art of the Novel,* 338–351. New York: Macmillan, 1933.

Edmonds, Irene C. "Faulkner and the Black Shadow." In *Southern Renascence: The Literature of the Modern South,* edited by Louis D. Rubin, Jr. and Robert D. Jacobs, 192–206. Baltimore, Md.: Johns Hopkins University Press, 1953.

Emerson, O. B. *Faulkner's Early Literary Reputation in America.* Ann Arbor, Mich.: UMI Research Press, 1984.

Emmanuel, Pierre. "Faulkner and the Sense of Sin." *Harvard Advocate* 135 (November 1951): 20.

England, Martha Winburn. "Teaching 'The Sound and the Fury.'" *College English* 18 (January 1957): 221–224.

English, H. M., Jr. "'Requiem for a Nun.'" *Furioso* 7 (winter 1952): 60–63.

Everett, Walter K. *Faulkner's Art and Characters.* Woodbury, N.Y.: Barron's Educational Series, 1969.

Fadiman, Clifton. "Mississippi Frankenstein." *The New Yorker* 14 (January 21, 1939): 60–62.

———. "William Faulkner." In *Party of One,* 98–125. Cleveland: World, 1955.

———. "The World of William Faulkner." *Nation* 132 (April 15, 1931): 422–423.

Fargnoli, Nicholas. *William Faulkner: A Literary Companion.* New York: Pegasus Books, 2008.

Farnham, James. "Faullkner's Unsung Hero: Gavin Stevens." *Arizona Quarterly* (summer 1965): 115–132.

Ferguson, James. *Faulkner's Short Fiction.* Knoxville: University of Tennessee Press, 1991.

Fiedler, Leslie A. "William Faulkner: An American Dickens." *Commentary* 10 (October 1950): 384–387.

Flint, R. W. "Faulkner as Elegist." *Hudson Review* 7 (summer 1954): 246–257.

Flynn, Robert. "The Dialectic of 'Sanctuary.'" *Modern Fiction Studies* 2 (autumn 1956): 109–113.

Ford, Dan, ed. *Heir and Prototype: Original and Derived Characterizations in Faulkner.* Conway: University of Central Arkansas Press, 1988.

Foster, Ruel E. "Dream as Symbolic Act in Faulkner." *Perspective* 2 (summer 1949): 179–194.

———. "A Further Note on the Conclusion of 'The Bear.'" *Faulkner Studies* 3 (spring 1954): 4–5.

Fowler, Doreen. *Faulkner: The Return of the Repressed.* Charlottesville: University Press of Virginia, 1997.

———. *Faulkner's Changing Vision: From Outrage to Affirmation.* Ann Arbor, Mich.: UMI Research Press, 1983.

Fowler, Doreen, and Ann J. Abadie, eds. *"A Cosmos of My Own": Faulkner and Yoknapatawpha, 1980.* Jackson: University Press of Mississippi, 1981.

———. *Faulkner: International Perspectives.* Jackson: University Press of Mississippi, 1980.

———. *Faulkner and the Craft of Fiction.* Jackson: University Press of Mississippi, 1989.

———. *Faulkner and Humor.* Jackson: University Press of Mississippi, 1986.

———. *Faulkner and Popular Culture.* Jackson: University Press of Mississippi, 1990.

———. *Faulkner and Race.* Jackson: University Press of Mississippi, 1987.

———. *Faulkner and Religion.* Jackson: University Press of Mississippi, 1991.

———. *Faulkner and the Southern Renaissance.* Jackson: University Press of Mississippi, 1982.

———. *Faulkner and Women.* Jackson: University Press of Mississippi, 1986.

———. *Fifty Years of Yoknapatawpha.* Jackson: University Press of Mississippi, 1980.

———. *New Directions in Faulkner Studies.* Jackson: University Press of Mississippi, 1984.

Frazier, David L. "Gothicism in 'Sanctuary': The Black Pall and the Crap Table." *Modern Fiction Studies* 2 (autumn 1956): 114–124.

Frey, Leonard H. "Irony and Point of View in 'That Evening Sun.'" *Faulkner Studies* 2 (autumn 1953): 33–40.

Friedman, Allen Warren. *William Faulkner.* New York: Ungar, 1984.

Frohock, W. M. "William Faulkner: The Private versus the Public Vision." *Southwest Review* 34 (summer 1949): 281–294. Reprinted in *The Novel of Violence in America*, 101–124. Dallas: Southern Methodist University Press, 1950.

———. "William Faulkner: The Private Vision." In *The Novel of Violence in America*, 2nd ed., 144–165. Dallas: Southern Methodist University Press, 1957.

Galharn, Carl. "Faulkner's Faith: Roots from 'The Wild Palms.'" *Twentieth Century Literature* 1 (October 1955): 139–160.

Garrett, George P., Jr. "An Examination of the Poetry of William Faulkner." *Princeton University Library Chronicle* 18 (spring 1957): 124–135.

———. "Faulkner's Early Literary Criticism." *Texas Studies in Literature and Language* 1 (spring 1959): 3–10.

———. "Some Revisions in 'As I Lay Dying.'" *Modern Language Notes* 73 (June 1958): 414–417.

Geismar, Maxwell. "William Faulkner: Before and After the Nobel Prize." In *American Moderns: From Rebellion to Conformity*, 91–106. New York: Hill and Wang, 1958.

———. "William Faulkner: The Negro and the Female." In *Writers in Crisis*, 143–183. Boston: Houghton Mifflin, 1942.

Gérard, Albert. "Justice in Yoknapatawpha County: Some Symbolic Motifs in Faulkner's Later Writing." *Faulkner Studies* 2 (winter 1954): 49–57.

Giles, Barbara. "The South of William Faulkner." *Masses and Mainstream* 3 (February 1950): 26–40.

Glicksberg, Charles I. "William Faulkner and the Negro Problem." *Phylon* 10 (June 1949): 153–160.

———. "The World of William Faulkner." *Arizona Quarterly* 5 (spring 1949): 46–58.

Glissant, Edouard. *Faulkner, Mississippi.* Chicago: University of Chicago Press, 2000.

Godden, Richard. *Fictions of Labor: William Faulkner and the South's Long Revolution.* Cambridge: Cambridge University Press, 1997.

Goellner, Jack. "A Closer Look at 'As I Lay Dying.'" *Perspective* 7 (spring 1954): 42–54.

Going, William T. "Faulkner's 'A Rose for Emily.'" *Explicator* 16 (February 1958): item 27.

Gold, Joseph. *William Faulkner: A Study in Humanism: From Metaphor to Discourse.* Norman: Oklahoma University Press, 1966.

Gordon, Caroline. "Notes on Faulkner and Flaubert." *Hudson Review* 1 (summer 1948), 222–231. Revised and reprinted in *The House of Fiction*, edited by Caroline Gordon and Allen Tate, 531–534. New York: Scribner's, 1950.

Greene, Graham. "The Furies in Mississippi." *London Mercury* 35 (March 1937): 517–518.

Greet, T. Y. "The Theme and Structure of Faulkner's 'The Hamlet.'" *PMLA* 72 (September 1957): 775–790. Reprinted in *William Faulkner: Three Decades of Criticism*, edited by Frederick J. Hoffman and Olga W. Vickery, 330–347. New York: Harcourt, Brace & World, 1963.

———. "Toward the Light: The Thematic Unity of Faulkner's 'Cycle.'" *Carolina Quarterly* 3 (fall 1950): 38–44.

Gresset, Michel. *Fascination: Faulkner's Fiction, 1919–1936.* Durham, N.C.: Duke University Press, 1989.

Gresset, Michel, and Noel Polk, eds. *Intertextuality in Faulkner.* Jackson: University Press of Mississippi, 1985.

Gresset, Michel, and Patrick Samway, eds. *Faulkner and Idealism: Perspectives from Paris.* Jackson: University Press of Mississippi, 1983.

———. *A Gathering of Evidence: Essays on William Faulkner's* Intruder in the Dust. Philadelphia: Saint Joseph's University Press, 2004.

Griffin, William J. "How to Misread Faulkner: A Powerful Plea of Ignorance." *Tennessee Studies in Literature* 1 (1956): 27–34.

Grimwood, Michael. *Heart in Conflict: Faulkner's Struggles with Vocation.* Athens: University of Georgia Press, 1987.

Groden, Michael. "Criticism in New Composition: *Ulysses* and *The Sound and the Fury*," *Twentieth Century Literature* 21 (October 1975): 265–277.

Guérard, Albert Jr. "'Requiem for a Nun': An Examination." *Harvard Advocate* 135 (November 1951): 19, 41–42.

Gutting, Gabriele. *The Function of Geographical and Historical Facts in William Faulkner's Fictional Picture of the Deep South.* New York: Lang, 1992.

Gwin, Minrose. *The Feminine in Faulkner: Reading (Beyond) Sexual Difference.* Knoxville: University of Tennessee Press, 1990.

Gwynn, Frederick L. "Faulkner's Prufrock—and Other Observations." *Journal of English and Germanic Philology* 52 (January 1953): 63–70.

———. "Faulkner's Raskolnikov." *Modern Fiction Studies* 4 (summer 1958): 169–172.

Hahn, Stephen, and Robert W. Hamblin, eds. *Teaching Faulkner: Approaches and Methods.* Westport, Conn.: Greenwood Publishing, 2000.

Hamblin, Robert W. "Before the Fall: The Theme of Innocence in Faulkner's 'That Evening Sun'." *Notes on Mississippi Writers* 11 (winter 1979): 86–94.

———. "Beyond the Edge of the Map: Faulkner, Turner, and the Frontier Line." In *Faulkner in the Twenty-First Century: Faulkner and Yoknapatawpha, 2000,* edited by Robert W. Hamblin and Ann J. Abadie, 154–171. Jackson: University Press of Mississippi, 2003.

———. "'Carcassonne': Faulkner's Allegory of Art and the Artist." *Southern Review* 15 (spring 1979): 355–365.

———. "'A Casebook on Mankind': Faulkner's Use of Shakespeare." *Teaching Faulkner,* no. 15 (fall 1999): 4–8.

———. "The Curious Case of Faulkner's 'The De Gaulle Story.'" *Faulkner Journal* 16 (fall 2000/spring 2001): 79–86.

———. "'Did You Ever Have a Sister?': Salinger's Holden Caulfield and Faulkner's Quentin Compson." *Teaching Faulkner,* no. 14 (fall 1998): 3–6.

———. "'A Fine Loud Grabble and Snatch of AAA and WPA': Faulkner, Government, and the Individual." *Arkansas Review* 31 (April 2000): 10–15.

———. "Homo Agonistes, or, William Faulkner as Sportswriter." *Aethlon: The Journal of Sport Literature* 13 (spring 1996): 13–22.

———. "'Like a Big Soft Fading Wheel': The Triumph of Faulkner's Art." In *Faulkner at 100: Retrospect and Prospect,* edited by Donald M. Kartiganer and Ann J. Abadie, 272–284. Jackson: University Press of Mississippi, 2000.

———. "*The Marble Faun:* Chapter One of Faulkner's Continuing Dialectic on Life and Art." *Publications of Missouri Philological Association* 3 (1978): 80–90.

———. "*No Such Thing As Was*": William Faulkner and Southern History. Cape Girardeau, Mo.: Center for Faulkner Studies, 1994.

Hamblin, Robert W., and Ann J. Abadie, eds. *Faulkner in the Twenty-First Century: Faulkner and Yoknapatawpha, 2000.* Jackson: University Press of Mississippi, 2003.

Hamblin, Robert W., and Louis Daniel Brodsky. "Faulkner's 'L'Apres-Midi d'une Faun': The Evolution of a Poem." *Studies in Bibliography* 33 (1980): 254–263.

Hamilton, Edith. "Faulkner: Sorcerer or Slave?" *Saturday Review* 35 (July 12, 1952): 8–10, 39–41.

Handy, William J. "'As I Lay Dying': Faulkner's Inner Reporter." *Kenyon Review* 21 (summer 1959): 437–451.

Hannon, Charles. *Faulkner and the Discourses of Culture.* Baton Rouge: Louisiana State University Press, 2005.

Harder, Kelsie B. "Charactonyms in Faulkner's Novels." *Bucknell Review* 8 (May 1959): 189–211.

———. "Proverbial Snopeslore." *Tennessee Folklore Society Bulletin* 24 (September 1958): 89–95.

Hardwick, Elizabeth. "Faulkner and the South Today." *Partisan Review* 15, no. 10 (October 1948): 1,130–1,135. Reprinted in *Faulkner A Collection of Critical Essays,* edited by Robert Penn Warren, 226–230. Englewood Cliffs, N.J.: Prentice-Hall, Inc., 1966.

Hartwick, Harry. "The Cult of Cruelty." In *The Foreground of American Fiction,* 160–166. New York: American Book Co., 1934.

Harrington, Evans B. "Technical Aspects of William Faulkner's 'That Evening Sun.'" *Faulkner Studies* 1 (winter 1952): 54–59.

Harrington, Evans, and Ann J. Abadie, eds. *Faulkner, Modernism, and Film.* Jackson: University Press of Mississippi, 1979.

———. *Faulkner and the Short Story.* Jackson: University Press of Mississippi, 1992.

————. *The Maker and the Myth.* Jackson: University Press of Mississippi, 1978.

————. *The South and Faulkner's Yoknapatawpha: The Actual and the Apocryphal.* Jackson: University Press of Mississippi, 1977.

Harrington, Gary. *Faulkner's Fables of Creativity: The Non-Yoknapatawpha Novels.* Athens: University of Georgia Press, 1990.

Hatcher, Harlan. "Ultimate Extensions." In *Creating the Modern American Novel*, 234–243. New York: Farrar and Rinehart, 1935.

Hayakawa, Hiroshi. "Negation in William Faulkner." In *Studies in English Grammar and Linguistics: A Miscellany in Honor of Takanobu Otsuka.* Edited by Kazuo Araki et al., 103–113. Tokyo: Kenkyusha, 1958.

Heilman, Robert B. "Schools for Girls." *Sewanee Review* 60 (spring 1952): 304–309.

Hemenway, Robert. "Enigmas of Being in *As I Lay Dying*." *Modern Fiction Studies* 16 (1970): 133–146.

Hepburn, Kenneth W. "Faulkner's 'Mosquitoes': A Poetic Turning Point." *Twentieth-Century Literature: A Scholary and Critical Journal* (1971): 17, 19–28.

Hettich, Blaise. "A Bedroom Scene in Faulkner." *Renascence* 8 (spring 1956): 121–126.

Hickerson, Thomas Felix. *The Faulkner Feuds.* Chapel Hill, N.C.: Colonial Press, 1964.

Hicks, Granville. "Faulkner's South: A Northern Interpretation." *Georgia Review* 5 (fall 1951): 269–284.

————. "The Last of the Snopeses." *Saturday Review* 42 (November 14, 1959): 20–21.

————. "The Past and the Future of William Faulkner." *Bookman* 74 (September 1931): 17–24.

Hines, Thomas S. *William Faulkner and the Tangible Past: The Architecture of Yoknapatawpha.* Berkeley: University of California Press, 1996.

Hinkle, James, and Robert McCoy. *Reading Faulkner: The Unvanquished.* University Press of Mississippi, 1995.

Hoadley, Frank M. "Folk Humor in the Novels of William Faulkner." *Tennessee Folklore Society Bulletin* 23 (September 1957): 75–82.

Hoffman, A. C. "Faulkner's 'Absalom, Absalom!'" *Explicator* 10 (November 1951): item 12.

————. "Point of View in 'Absalom, Absalom!'" *University of Kansas City Review* 19 (summer 1953): 233–239.

Hoffman, Daniel. *Faulkner's Country Matters: Folklore and Fable in Yoknapatawpha.* Baton Rouge: Louisiana State University Press, 1989.

————. "Violence and Rhetoric." In *The Modern Novel in America, 1900–1950*, 154–164. Chicago: Henry Regnery, 1951.

Hoffman, Frederick J., and Olga W. Vickery, eds. *William Faulkner: Three Decades of Criticism.* East Lansing: Michigan State University Press, 1960.

Hogan, Patrick G., Jr. "Critical Misconceptions of Southern Thought: Faulkner's Optimism," *Mississippi Quarterly* 10 (January 1957): 19–28.

Holmes, Catherine Denham. *Annotations to William Faulkner's 'The Hamlet'.* Abstract in *Dissertation Abstracts International* 55 (1995): 11.

Holmes, Edward M. *Faulkner's Twice-Told Tales: His Re-Use of Materials.* The Hague, Netherlands: Mouton, 1966.

Hönnighausen, Lothar. *Faulkner: Masks and Metaphors.* Jackson: University Press of Mississippi, 1997.

————. *William Faulkner: The Art of Stylization in His Early Graphic and Literary Work.* Cambridge: Cambridge University Press, 1987.

————, ed. *Faulkner's Discourse: An International Symposium.* Tubingen, Germany: Max Niemeyer Verlag, 1989.

Hopper, Vincent F. "Faulkner's Paradise Lost." *Virginia Quarterly Review* 23 (summer 1947): 405–420.

Horton, Merrill. *Annotations to William Faulkner's "The Town".* New York: Garland, 1996.

Howe, Irving. *William Faulkner: A Critical Study.* 3rd ed, revised and expanded. Chicago: The University of Chicago Press, 1975.

————. "Faulkner: An Experiment in Drama." *Nation* 173 (September 29, 1951): 263–264.

————. "Faulkner: End of a Road." *New Republic* 141 (December 7, 1959): 17–21.

————. "The South and Current Literature." *American Mercury* 67 (October 1948): 494–503.

————. "The Southern Myth and William Faulkner." *American Quarterly* 3 (winter 1951): 357–362.

————. "William Faulkner and the Negro." *Commentary* 12 (October 1951): 359–368.

———. "William Faulkner and the Quest for Freedom." *Tomorrow* 9 (December 1949): 54–56.

Howell, Elmo. "Colonel Sartoris Snopes and Faulkner's Aristocrats." *Carolina Quarterly* 11 (summer 1959): 13–19.

———. "Faulkner's 'Sartoris.'" *Explicator* 17 (February 1959): item 33.

———. "A Note on Faulkner's Negro Characters." *Mississippi Quarterly* 11 (fall 1958): 201–203.

———. "The Quality of Evil in Faulkner's 'Sanctuary.'" *Tennessee Studies in Literature* 4 (1959): 99–107.

Hudson, Tommy. "William Faulkner: Mystic and Traditionalist." *Perspective* 3 (autumn 1950): 227–235.

Humphrey, Robert. "Faulkner's Synthesis." In *Stream of Consciousness in the Modern Novel,* 17–21, 64–70, 104–111, *et passim.* Berkeley: University of California Press, 1954.

———. "Form and Function of Stream of Consciousness in William Faulkner's 'The Sound and the Fury.'" *University of Kansas City Review* 19 (autumn 1952): 34–40.

Hunt, John W. *William Faulkner: Art in Theological Tension.* Syracuse, N.Y.: Syracuse University Press, 1965.

Hunter, Edwin R. *William Faulkner: Narrative Practice and Prose Style.* Washington, D.C.: Windhover, 1973.

Inge, M. Thomas, ed. *William Faulkner: The Contemporary Reviews.* Cambridge: Cambridge University Press, 1995.

Irwin, John T. *Doubling and Incest/Repetition and Revenge: A Speculative Reading of Faulkner.* Expanded edition. Baltimore, Md.: Johns Hopkins University Press, 1996.

Izard, Barbara, and Hieronymous, Clara. *Requiem for a Nun: On Stage and Off.* Nashville and London: Aurora Pubs., 1970.

Jackson, James Turner. "Delta Cycle: A Study of William Faulkner." *Chimera* 5 (autumn 1946): 3–14.

Jacobs, Robert D. "Faulkner and the Tragedy of Isolation." *Hopkins Review* 6 (spring–summer 1953): 162–183. Reprinted in *Southern Renascence: The Literature of the Modern South,* edited by Louis D. Rubin Jr. and Robert D. Jacobs, 170–191. Baltimore; Md.: Johns Hopkins University Press, 1953.

———. "How Do *You* Read Faulkner?" *Provincial* (April 1957): 3–5.

Jehlen, Myra. *Class and Character in Faulkner's South.* New York: Columbia University Press, 1976.

Jenkins, Lee Clinton. *Faulkner and Black-White Relations: A Psychoanalytic Approach.* New York: Columbia University Press, 1981.

Johnson, C. W. M. "Faulkner's 'A Rose for Emily.'" *Explicator* 6 (May 1948): item 45.

Johnson, M. Suzanne Paul. *William Faulkner's* Pylon: *Annotations for the Novel.* Ann Arbor, Mich.: UMI, 1993.

Jones, Diane Brown. *A Reader's Guide to the Short Stories of William Faulkner.* New York: G. K. Hall, 1994.

Jones, Leonidas M. "Faulkner's 'The Hound.'" *Explicator* 15 (March 1957): item 37.

Junior, Junius. *Pseudo-Realists.* New York: Outsider Press, 1931.

Kang, Hee. *The Snopes Trilogy: Reading Faulkner's Masculine and Feminine.* Dissertation Abstracts International 53 (January 1993): 7.

Kartiganer, Donald M. "The Farm and the Journey: Ways of Mourning and Meaning in *As I Lay Dying.*" *Mississippi Quarterly* 43 (1990): 251–303.

———. *The Fragile Thread: The Meaning of Form in Faulkner's Novels.* Amherst: University of Massachusetts Press, 1979.

———, ed. *Faulkner and the Natural World.* Jackson: University of Mississippi Press, 1999.

Kartiganer, Donald M., and Ann J. Abadie, eds. *Faulkner and the Artist.* Jackson: University Press of Mississippi, 1996.

———. *Faulkner in Cultural Context.* Jackson: University Press of Mississippi, 1997.

———. *Faulkner and Gender.* Jackson: University Press of Mississippi, 1996.

———. *Faulkner and Ideology.* Jackson: University Press of Mississippi, 1995.

———. *Faulkner and Psychology.* Jackson: University Press of Mississippi, 1997.

Kawin, Bruce. *Faulkner and Film.* New York: Ungar, 1977.

Kazin, Alfred. "Faulkner: The Rhetoric and the Agony." *Virginia Quarterly Review* 18 (summer 1942); 389–402. Reprinted in *On Native Grounds,* 453–470. New York: Reynal & Hitchcock, 1942.

———. "Faulkner in His Fury." In *The Inmost Leaf*, 257–273. New York: Harcourt, Brace, 1955.

———. "Faulkner's Vision of Human Integrity." *Harvard Advocate* 135 (November 1951): 8–9, 28–33.

———. "In the Shadow of the South's Last Stand." *New York Herald Tribune* (Books) (February 20, 1938): 5.

———. "Mr. Faulkner's Friends, The Snopeses." *New York Times Book Review* (May 5, 1957): 1, 24.

———. "The Stillness of 'Light in August,'" *Partisan Review* 24 (fall 1957): 519–538. Reprinted in *Twelve Original Essays on Great American Novels*, edited by Charles Shapiro, 257–283, Detroit: Wayne State University Press, 1958; and in *William Faulkner: Three Decades of Criticism*, edited by Frederick J. Hoffman and Olga W. Vickery, 247–265, New York: Harcourt, Brace & World, 1963; and also in *Faulkner A Collection of Critical Essays*, edited by Robert Penn Warren, 147–162, Englewood Cliffs, N.J.: Prentice Hall, Inc., 1966.

———. "A Study in Conscience." *New York Herald Tribune* (Books) (January 22, 1939): 2.

Kerr, Elizabeth M. *William Faulkner's Gothic Domain*. Port Washington, N.Y.: Kennikat Press, 1979.

———. *William Faulkner's Yoknapatawpha: "A Kind of Keystone in the Universe."* New York: Fordham University Press, 1976.

———. *Yoknapatawpha: Faulkner's "Little Postage Stamp of Native Soil."* Rev. ed. Amherst: University of Massachusetts Press, 1963.

King, Roma, Jr. "The Janus Symbol in 'As I Lay Dying.'" *University of Kansas City Review* 21 (summer 1955): 287–290.

Kinney, Arthur F. *Critical Essays on William Faulkner: The Compson Family*. Boston: G. K. Hall, 1982.

———. *Critical Essays on William Faulkner: The Sutpen Family*. New York: G. K. Hall & Co., 1996.

———. *Faulkner's Narrative Poetics: Style as Vision*. Amherst: University of Massachusetts Press, 1978.

———. *Go Down, Moses: The Miscegenation of Time*. New York: Twayne, 1996.

Kirk, Robert W., and Marvin Klotz. *Faulkner's People*. Berkeley: University of California Press, 1963.

Knoll, Robert E. "'The Unvanquished' for a Start." *College English* 19 (May 1958): 338–343.

Kohler, Dayton. "William Faulkner and the Social Conscience." *College English* 11 (December 1949): 119–127. Also appeared in *English Journal* 38 (December 1949): 545–553.

Kreiswirth, Martin. *William Faulkner: The Making of a Novelist*. Athens: University of Georgia Press, 1983.

Kronenberger, Louis. "Faulkner's Dismal Swamp." *Nation* 146 (February 19, 1938): 212, 214.

Kubie, Lawrence S. "William Faulkner's 'Sanctuary': An Analysis," *Saturday Review of Literature* 11 (October 20, 1934): 218, 224–226. Reprinted in *Faulkner A Collection of Critical Essays*, edited by Robert Penn Warren, 137–146. Englewood Cliffs, N.J.: Prentice Hall, Inc., 1966.

Labor, Earle. "Faulkner's 'The Sound and the Fury.'" *Explicator* 17 (January 1959): item 29.

LaBudde, Kenneth. "Cultural Primitivism in William Faulkner's 'The Bear.'" *American Quarterly* 2 (winter 1950): 322–328.

LaLonde, Christopher A. *William Faulkner and the Rites of Passage*. Macon, Ga.: Mercer University Press, 1996.

Leary, Lewis. *William Faulkner of Yoknapatawpha County*. New York: Crowell, 1973.

Leaver, Florence. "Faulkner: The Word as Principle and Power." *South Atlantic Quarterly* 57 (autumn 1958): 464–476. Reprinted in *William Faulkner: Three Decades of Criticism*, edited by Frederick J. Hoffman and Olga W. Vickery, 199–209. New York: Harcourt, Brace & World, 1963.

Leavis, F. R. "Dostoevsky or Dickens?" *Scrutiny* 2 (June 1933): 91–93.

Lee, Edwy B. "A Note on the Ordonnance of 'The Sound and the Fury.'" *Faulkner Studies* 3 (summer–autumn 1954): 37–39.

Lee, Robert, ed. *William Faulkner: The Yoknapatawpha Fiction*. New York: St. Martin's, 1990.

Lemay, Harding. "Faulkner and his Snopes Family Reach the End of their Trilogy." *New York Herald Tribune* (Books) (November 15, 1959): 1, 14.

Levins, Lynn Gartrell. *Faulkner's Heroic Design: The Yoknapatawpha Novels*. Athens: University of Georgia Press, 1976.

Lewis, R. W. B. *The Picaresque Saint*. Philadelphia: J. B. Lippincott, 1958.

———. "The Hero in the New World: William Faulkner's 'The Bear.'" *Kenyon Review* 13 (autumn 1951): 641–660. Reprinted in *Interpretations of*

American Literature, edited by Charles Feidelson Jr. and Paul Brodtkorb Jr., 332–348. New York: Oxford, 1959.

Lewis, Wyndham. "The Moralist with a Corn-cob: A Study of William Faulkner." *Life and Letters* 10 (June 1934): 312–328. Reprinted in *Men Without Art,* 42–64. London: Cassell, 1934.

Lilly, Paul R., Jr. "Caddy and Addie: Speakers of Faulkner's Impeccable Language." *Journal of Narrative Technique* 3 (1973): 170–182.

Lind, Ilse Dusoir. "The Design and Meaning of 'Absalom, Absalom!'" *PMLA* 70 (December 1955): 887–912. Reprinted in *William Faulkner: Three Decades of Criticism,* edited by Frederick J. Hoffman and Olga W. Vickery, 278–304. New York: Harcourt, Brace & World, 1963.

———. "The Calvinistic Burden of 'Light in August.'" *New England Quarterly* 30 (September 1957): 307–329.

———. "The Teachable Faulkner." *College English* 16 (February 1955): 284–287, 302.

Linn, James W., and Houghton W. Taylor. "Counterpoint: 'Light in August.'" In *A Foreword to Fiction,* 144–157. New York: Appleton-Century, 1935.

Linn, Robert. "Robinson Jeffers and William Faulkner." *American Spectator* 2 (1933): 1. Reprinted in *The American Spectator Year Book,* edited by George Jean Nathan, Ernest Boyd, et al., 304–307. New York: Frederick A. Stokes, 1934.

Lisca, Peter. "Some New Light on Faulkner's 'Sanctuary.'" *Faulkner Studies* 2 (spring 1953): 5–9.

Litz, Walton. "William Faulkner's Moral Vision." *Southwest Review* 37 (summer 1952): 200–209.

Lockyer, Judith. *Ordered by Words: Language and Narration in the Novels of William Faulkner.* Carbondale: Southern Illinois University Press, 1991.

Longley, John Lewis, Jr. *The Tragic Mask: A Study of Faulkner's Heroes.* Chapel Hill: University of North Carolina Press, 1963.

———. "Galahad Gavin and a Garland of Snopeses." *Virginia Quarterly Review* 33 (autumn 1957): 623–628.

———. "Joe Christmas: the Hero in the Modern World." *Virginia Quarterly Review* 33 (spring 1957): 233–249. Reprinted in *William Faulkner: Three Decades of Criticism,* edited by Frederick J. Hoffman and Olga W. Vickery, 265–278. New York:

Harcourt, Brace & World, 1963. Also reprinted in *Faulkner: A Collection of Critical Essays,* edited by Robert Penn Warren, 163–174. Englewood Cliffs, N.J.: Prentice Hall, Inc., 1966.

Lowrey, Perrin. "Concepts of Time in 'The Sound and the Fury.'" *English Institute Essays 1952,* edited by Alan S. Downer, 57–82. New York: Columbia University Press, 1954.

Luce, Dianne C. *Annotations to Faulkner's* As I Lay Dying. New York: Garland, 1990.

Lydenberg, John. "Nature Myth in Faulkner's 'The Bear.'" *American Literature* 24 (March 1952): 62–72.

Lytle, Andrew. "Regeneration for the Man," *Sewanee Review* 57, no. 1 (winter 1949): 120–127. Reprinted in *Faulkner: A Collection of Critical Essays,* edited by Robert Penn Warren, 231–237. Englewood Cliffs, N.J.: Prentice Hall, Inc., 1966.

———. "'The Town': Helen's Last Stand." *Sewanee Review* 65 (summer 1957): 475–484.

Machlachlan, John M. "William Faulkner and the Southern Folk." *Southern Folklore Quarterly* 9 (June 1945): 153–167.

MacLeish, Archibald. "Faulkner and the Responsibility of the Artist." *Harvard Advocate* 135 (November 1951): 18, 43.

MacLure, Millar. "William Faulkner: Soothsayer of the South." *Queen's Quarterly* 63 (autumn 1956): 334–343.

Madge, Charles. "Time and Space in America." *London Mercury* 32 (May 1935): 83.

Malin, Irving. *William Faulkner: An Interpretation.* Stanford, Calif.: Stanford University Press, 1957.

Marcus, Steven. "Faulkner's Town: Mythology as History." *Partisan Review* 24 (summer 1957): 432–441.

Marvin, John R. "'Pylon': The Definition of Sacrifice." *Faulkner Studies* 1 (summer 1952): 20–23.

Massey, Linton. "Notes on the Unrevised Galleys of Faulkner's 'Sanctuary.'" *Studies in Bibliography* 8 (1956): 195–208.

Matthews, John T. "*As I Lay Dying* in the Machine Age." *Boundary* 2 (1992).

———. *The Play of Faulkner's Language.* Ithaca, N.Y.: Cornell University Press, 1982.

Maxwell, Allen. "'The Wild Palms.'" *Southwest Review* 24 (April 1939): 357–360.

Mayes, Martha. "Faulkner Juvenalia." In *New Campus Writing, No. 2,* 135–144. New York: Bantam, 1957.

McCamy, Edward. "Byron Bunch." *Shenandoah* 3 (spring 1952): 8–12.

McClennan, Joshua. "'Absalom, Absalom!' and the Meaning of History." *Papers of the Michigan Academy of Science, Arts, and Letters* 42 (1956), 357–369.

———. "William Faulkner and Christian Complacency." *Papers of the Michigan Academy of Science, Arts, and Letters* 41 (1956): 315–322.

McCole, Camille J. "The Nightmare Literature of William Faulkner." *Catholic World* 141 (August 1935): 576–583.

———. "William Faulkner: Cretins, Coffinworms, and Cruelty." In *Lucifer at Large,* 203–228. New York: Longmans, 1937.

McCorquodale, Marjorie K. "Alienation in Yoknapatawpha County." *Forum* 1 (January 1957): 4–8.

McDonald, Hal. "Faulkner's *Sanctuary.*" *Explicator* 55, no. 4 (summer 1997): 222–223.

McElderry, B. R., Jr. "The Narrative Structure of 'Light in August.'" *College English* 19 (February 1958): 200–207. Reprinted in *Mississippi Quarterly* 11 (fall 1958): 177–187.

McGrew, Julia. "Faulkner and the Icelanders." *Scandinavian Studies* 31 (February 1959): 1–14.

McHaney, Thomas L. *William Faulkner's* The Wild Palms: *A Study.* Jackson: University Press of Mississippi, 1975.

McIlwaine, Shields. "Naturalistic Modes: The Gothic, The Ribald, and the Tragic." In *The Southern Poor-White from Lubberland to Tobacco Road,* 217–240. Norman: University of Oklahoma Press, 1939.

McLaughlin, Richard. "Requiem for Temple Drake." *Theatre Arts* 35 (October 1951): 50, 77.

Meriwether, James B., ed. *A Faulkner Miscellany.* Jackson: University Press of Mississippi, 1974.

Meriwether, James B. "Snopes Revisited." *Saturday Review* 40 (April 27, 1957): 12–13.

———. "William Faulkner." *Shenandoah* 10 (winter 1959): 18–24.

Merwin, W. S. "William Faulkner." In *Nobel Prize Winners,* edited by L. J. Ludovici, 43–60. Westport, Conn.: Associated Booksellers, 1957.

Millgate, Michael. *The Achievement of William Faulkner.* Lincoln: University of Nebraska Press, 1978.

———. *Faulkner's Place.* Athens: University of Georgia Press, 1997.

———. *New Essays on "Light in August."* New York: Cambridge University Press, 1987.

———. *William Faulkner.* New York: Grove, 1961.

Miner, Ward L. *The World of William Faulkner.* Durham, N.C.: Duke University Press, 1952.

Moloney, Michael F. "The Enigma of Time: Proust, Virginia Woolf, and Faulkner." *Thought* 32 (spring 1957): 69–85.

Monteiro, George. "Bankruptcy in Time: A Reading of William Faulkner's 'Pylon,'" *Twentieth Century Literature* 4 (April–July 1958): 9–20.

———. "Initiation and the Moral Sense in Faulkner's 'Sanctuary.'" *Modern Language Notes* 73 (November 1958): 500–504.

Moreland, Richard C. *Faulkner and Modernism: Rereading and Rewriting.* Madison: University of Wisconsin Press, 1990.

Morris, Welsey, and Barbara Alverson Morris. *Reading Faulkner.* Madison: University of Wisconsin Press, 1990.

Morris, Wright. "The Function of Rage: William Faulkner." In *The Territory Ahead,* 171–184. New York: Harcourt, Brace, 1958.

———. "The Violent Land: Some Observations on the Faulkner Country." *Magazine of Art* 45 (March 1952): 99–103.

Mortimer, Gail L. *Faulkner's Rhetoric of Loss: A Study in Perception and Meaning.* Austin: University of Texas Press, 1983.

Moseley, Edwin M. "Christ as Social Scapegoat: Faulkner's *Light in August.*" In Edwin M. Moseley, *Pseudonyms of Christ in the Modern Novel: Motifs and Methods.* Pittsburgh: University of Pittsburgh Press, 1962.

Moses, W. R. "The Unity of 'The Wild Palms.'" *Modern Fiction Studies* 2 (autumn 1956): 125–131.

———. "Water, Water Everywhere: 'Old Man' and 'A Farewell to Arms.'" *Modern Fiction Studies* 5 (summer 1959): 172–174.

———. "Where History Crosses Myth: Another Reading of 'The Bear.'" *Accent* 13 (winter 1953): 21–33.

Mueller, W. R. "The Theme of Suffering: William Faulkner's 'The Sound and the Fury.'" In *The Prophetic Voice in Modern Fiction,* 110–135. New York: Association Press, 1959.

Mumbach, Mary Katherine. "Remaining Must Remain": Patterns of Christian Comedy in Faulkner's "The Mansion." Abstract in *Dissertation Abstracts International* (October 1981): 42–44.

Neville, Helen. "The Sound and the Fury." *Partisan Review* 5 (June 1938): 53–55.

Nicholson, Norman. "William Faulkner." In *Man and Literature*, 122–138. London: SCM Press, 1943.

———. "William Faulkner." In *The New Spirit,* edited by E. W. Martin, 32–41. London: Dobson, 1946.

Nilon, Charles H. *Faulkner and the Negro.* New York: Citadel, 1965.

Nordanberg, Thomas. *Cataclysm as Catalyst: The Theme of War in William Faulkner's Fiction.* Uppsala, Sweden: Almqvist, 1983.

Oakley, Helen. *The Recontextualization of William Faulkner in Latin American Fiction and Culture.* Lewiston, N.Y.: Edwin Mellen Press, 2002.

O'Connor, William Van. *The Tangled Fire of William Faulkner.* Minneapolis: University of Minnesota Press, 1954.

———. *William Faulkner.* (Pamphlets on American Writers, No. 3), Minneapolis: University of Minnesota Press, 1959.

———. "Faulkner's Legend of the Old South." *Western Humanities Review* 7 (autumn 1953): 293–301.

———. "Hawthorne and Faulkner: Some Common Ground." *Virginia Quarterly Review* 33 (winter 1957): 105–123.

———. "The Old Master, the Sole Proprietor." *Virginia Quarterly Review* 36 (winter 1960): 147–151.

———. "Protestantism in Yoknapatawpha County." *Hopkins Reviews* 5 (spring 1952): 26–42. Reprinted in *Southern Renascence: The Literature of the Modern South,* edited by Louis D. Rubin Jr. and Robert D. Jacobs, 153–169. Baltimore: Johns Hopkins University Press, 1953.

———. "Rhetoric in Southern Writing: Faulkner." *Georgia Review* 12 (spring 1958): 83–86.

———. "A Short View of Faulkner's 'Sanctuary.'" *Faulkner Studies* 1 (fall 1952): 33–39.

———. "'The Sound and the Fury' and the Impressionistic Novel." *Northern Review* 6 (June–July 1953): 17–22.

———. "The Wilderness Theme in Faulkner's 'The Bear.'" *Accent* 13 (winter 1953): 12–20. Reprinted in *William Faulkner: Three Decades of Criticism,* edited by Frederick J. Hoffman and Olga W. Vickery, 322–330. New York: Harcourt, Brace & World, 1963.

———. "William Faulkner's Apprenticeship." *Southwest Review* 38 (winter 1953): 1–14.

O'Donnell, George Marion. "Faulkner's Mythology." *Kenyon Review* 1 (summer 1939): 285–299. Reprinted in *William Faulkner: Three Decades of Criticism,* edited by Frederick J. Hoffman and Olga W. Vickery, 82–93. New York: Harcourt, Brace & World, 1963. Also reprinted in *Faulkner A Collection of Critical Essays,* edited by Robert Penn Warren, 23–33. Englewood Cliffs, N.J.: Prentice Hall, Inc., 1966.

O'Faolain, Sean. "William Faulkner: More Genius than Talent." In *The Vanishing Hero: Studies in Novelists of the Twenties,* 73–111. Boston: Little, Brown, 1956.

Page, Sally. *Faulkner's Women: Characterization and Meaning.* Deland, Fla.: Everett/Edward, 1972.

Parker, Robert Dale. *Faulkner and the Novelistic Imagination.* Urbana: University of Illinois Press, 1985.

Pearson, Norman Holmes. "Faulkner's Three 'Evening Suns.'" *Yale University Library Gazette* 29 (October 1954): 61–70.

———. "Lena Grove." *Shenandoah* 3 (spring 1952): 3–7.

Peavy, Charles. *Go Slow Now: Faulkner and the Race Question.* Eugene: University of Oregon Press, 1971.

Peek, Charles A., and Robert W. Hamblin. *A Companion to Faulkner Studies.* Westport, Conn.: Greenwood Press, 2004.

Penick, Edwin A., Jr. "The Testimony of William Faulkner." *Christian Scholar* 38 (June 1955): 121–133.

Perdeck, A. "William Faulkner." *Critisch Bulletin* (1934): 209–213.

Peters, Erskine. *William Faulkner: The Yoknapatawpha World and Black Being.* Darby, Penn.: Norwood, 1983.

Peyre, Henri. "American Literature through French Eyes." *Virginia Quarterly Review* 23 (summer 1947): 421–437.

Phillips, Gene D. *Fiction, Film, and Faulkner: The Art of Adaptation.* Knoxville: University of Tennessee Press, 1988.

Pilkington, James Penn. "Faulkner's 'Sanctuary.'" *Explicator* 4 (June 1946): item 61.

Podhoretz, Norman. "William Faulkner and the Problem of War: His Fable of Faith." *Commentary* 18, no. 3 (September 1954): 227–232. Reprinted in *Faulkner: A Collection of Critical Essays,* edited by Robert Penn Warren, 243–250. Englewood Cliffs, N.J.: Prentice Hall, Inc., 1966.

Pilkington, John. *The Heart of Yoknapatawpha.* Jackson: University of Mississippi, 1981.

Poirier, William R. "'Strange Gods' in Jefferson, Mississippi: Analysis of 'Absalom, Absalom!'" In *William Faulkner: Two Decades of Criticism,* edited by Frederick J. Hoffman and Olga W. Vickery, 217–243. East Lansing: Michigan State University Press, 1951.

Polk, Noel. *Children of the Dark House: Text and Context in Faulkner.* Jackson: University Press of Mississippi, 1996.

———.*An Editorial Handbook for William Faulkner's "The Sound and the Fury."* New York: Garland Publishers, 1985.

———. *Faulkner's "Requiem for a Nun": A Critical Study.* Bloomington: Indiana University Press, 1981.

———, ed. *"Intruder in the Dust": A Concordance to the Novel.* West Point, N.Y.: Faulkner Concordance Advisory Board, 1983.

———. *New Essays on "The Sound and the Fury."* New York: Cambridge University Press, 1993.

———. *"Requiem for a Nun": A Concordance to the Novel.* Ann Arbor, Mich.: UMI Research Press, 1979.

Polk, Noel, and Ann J. Abadie, eds. *Faulkner and War.* Jackson: University Press of Mississippi, 2006.

Polk, Noel, and John D. Hart, eds. *"Absalom, Absalom!": A Concordance to the Novel.* 2 vols. Ann Arbor, Mich.: UMI Research Press, 1989.

———. *"The Hamlet": A Concordance to the Novel.* 2 vols. Ann Arbor, Mich.: UMI Research Press, 1990.

———. *The Mansion: A Concordance to the Novel.* 2 vols. Ann Arbor, Mich.: UMI Research Press, 1988.

———. *"Pylon": A Concordance to the Novel.* Ann Arbor, Mich.: UMI Research Press, 1989.

———. *"The Reivers": A Concordance to the Novel.* Ann Arbor, Mich.: UMI Research Press, 1990.

———. *"The Unvanquished": A Concordance to the Novel.* Ann Arbor, Mich.: UMI Research Press, 1990.

Polk, Noel, and Kenneth L. Privratsky, eds. *"A Fable": A Concordance to the Novel.* 2 vols. Ann Arbor, Mich.: UMI Research Press, 1981.

———. *"The Sound and the Fury:" A Concordance to the Novel.* 2 vols. Ann Arbor, Mich.: UMI Research Press, 1980.

Polk, Noel, and Lawrence Z. Pizzi, eds. *"The Town": A Concordance to the Novel.* Ann Arbor, Mich.: UMI Research Press, 1985.

Poster, Herbert. "Faulkner's Folly." *American Mercury* 73 (December 1951): 106–112.

Powell, Sumner C. "William Faulkner Celebrates Easter, 1928." *Perspective* 2 (summer 1949): 195–218.

Powers, Lyall H. *Faulkner's Yoknapatawpha Comedy.* Ann Arbor: University of Michigan Press, 1980.

Prescott, Orville. "The Eminently Obscure: Mann, Faulkner." In *In My Opinion,* 75–91. Indianapolis: Bobbs-Merrill, 1952.

Pritchett, V. S. "Books in General." *New Statesman and Nation* 41 (June 2, 1951): 624, 626.

———. "The Hill-Billies." In *Books in General,* 242–247. New York: Harcourt, Brace, 1953.

———. "Time Frozen: A Fable." *Partisan Review* 21, no. 5 (September–October 1954): 557–561. Reprinted in *Faulkner: A Collection of Critical Essays,* edited by Robert Penn Warren, 238–242. Englewood Cliffs, N.J.: Prentice Hall, 1966.

Pusey, William Webb III. "William Faulkner's Works in Germany to 1940: Translations and Criticism." *Germanic Review* 30 (October 1955): 211–226.

Putzel, Max. *Genius of Place: William Faulkner's Triumphant Beginnings.* Baton Rouge: Louisiana State University Press, 1985.

Ragan, David Paul. *William Faulkner's Absalom, Absalom!: A Critical Study.* Ann Arbor, Mich.: UMI, 1987.

Randall, Julia. "Some Notes on 'As I Lay Dying.'" *Hopkins Review* 4 (summer 1951): 47–51.

Ransom, John Crowe. "William Faulkner: An Impression." *Harvard Advocate* 135 (November 1951): 17.

Rascoe, Burton. "Faulkner's New York Critics." *American Mercury* 50 (June 1940): 243–247.

Reaver, J. Russell. "This Vessel of Clay: A Thematic Comparison of Faulkner's 'As I Lay Dying' and

Latorre's 'The Old Woman of Peralillo.'" *Florida State University Studies* 14 (1954): 131–140.

Redman, Ben Ray. "Faulkner's Double Novel." *Saturday Review of Literature* 19 (January 21, 1939): 5.

———. "Flights of Fancy." *Saturday Review of Literature* 11 (March 30, 1935): 577, 581.

Reed, John Q. "Theme and Symbol in Faulkner's 'Old Man.'" *Educational Leader* 21 (January 1958): 25–31.

Reed, Joseph W., Jr. *Faulkner's Narrative*. New Haven, Conn.: Yale University Press, 1973.

Rice, Philip Blair. "Faulkner's Crucifixion." *Kenyon Review* 16 (autumn 1954): 661–670. Reprinted in *William Faulkner: Three Decades of Criticism*, edited by Frederick J. Hoffman and Olga W. Vickery, 373–381. New York: Harcourt, Brace & World, 1963.

Richardson, H. Edward. "The 'Hemingwaves' in Faulkner's 'Wild Palms.'" *Modern Fiction Studies* 4 (winter 1958–1959): 357–360.

Richardson, Kenneth E. *Force and Faith in the Novels of William Faulkner*. The Hague, Netherlands: Mouton, 1967.

Riedel, F. C. "Faulkner as Stylist." *South Atlantic Quarterly* 56 (autumn 1957): 462–479.

Robb, Mary Cooper. *William Faulkner: An Estimate of His Contribution to the American Novel*. Pittsburgh: University of Pittsburgh Press, 1957.

Roberts, Diane. *Faulkner and Southern Womanhood*. Athens: University of Georgia Press, 1994.

Robinson, Fred Miller. *The Comedy Of Language: Studies in Modern Comic Literature*. Amherst: University of Massachusetts Press, 1980, 51–88.

Robinson, Owen. *Creating Yoknapatawpha: Readers and Writers in Faulkner's Fiction*. New York: Routledge, 2006.

Rolle, Andrew F. *"William Faulkner: An Inter-disciplinary Examination."* Mississippi Quarterly 11 (fall 1958): 157–159.

Rollyson, Carl E. *Uses of the Past in the Novels of William Faulkner*. Ann Arbor, Mich.: UMI Research Press, 1984.

Ross, Stephen M. *Fiction's Inexhaustible Voice: Speech and Writing in Faulkner*. Athens: University of Georgia Press, 1983.

Ross, Stephen M., and Noel Polk. *Reading Faulkner: The Sound and the Fury*. Jackson: University Press of Mississippi, 1996.

Roth, Russell. "The Brennan Papers: Faulkner in Manuscript." *Perspective* 2 (summer 1949): 219–224.

———. "The Centaur and the Pear Tree." *Western Review* 16 (spring 1952): 199–205.

———. "Ideas and Queries." *Faulkner Studies* 1 (summer 1952): 23–26.

———. "William Faulkner: The Pattern of Pilgrimage." *Perspective* 2 (summer 1949): 246–254.

Rousselle, Melinda McLeod. *Annotations to William Faulkner's* Sanctuary. New York: Garland, 1989.

Rubin, Louis D. Jr. "Snopeslore: Or, Faulkner Clears the Deck." *Western Review* 22 (autumn 1957): 73–76.

Rueckert, William H. *Faulkner from Within: Destructive and Generative Being in the Novels of William Faulkner*. West Lafayette, Ind.: Parlor Press, 2004.

Rugoff, Milton. "Faulkner's Old Spell in a New Novel of Yoknapatawpha." *New York Herald Tribune* (Books) (May 5, 1957): 1.

Runyan, Harry. "Faulkner's Poetry." *Faulkner Studies* 3 (summer–autumn 1954): 23–29.

Ruppersburg, Hugh M. *Voice and Eye in Faulkner's Fiction*. Athens: University of Georgia Press, 1983.

Ruzicka, William T. *Faulkner's Fictive Architecture: The Meaning of Place in the Yoknapatawpha Novels*. Ann Arbor, Mich.: UMI Research Press, 1987.

Ryan, Marjorie. "The Shakespearian Symbolism in 'The Sound and the Fury.'" *Faulkner Studies* 2 (autumn 1953): 40–44.

Sandeen, Ernest. "William Faulkner: Tragedian of Yoknapatawpha." In *Fifty Years of the American Novel*, edited by Harold C. Gardiner, 165–182. New York: Scribners, 1952.

Sartre, Jean-Paul. *Literary and Philosophical Essays*. Translated by Annette Michelson. London: Rider & Co., 1955.

Sawyer, Kenneth B. "Hero in 'As I Lay Dying,'" *Faulkner Studies* 3 (summer–autumn 1954): 30–33.

Schappes, Morris U. "Faulkner as Poet." *Poetry: A Magazine of Verse* 43 (October 1933): 48–52.

Schwartz, Delmore. "The Fiction of William Faulkner." *Southern Review* 7 (summer 1941): 145–160.

Schwartz, Lawrence H. *Creating Faulkner's Reputation: The Politics of Modern Literary Criticism*. Knoxville: University of Tennessee Press, 1988.

Scott, Arthur L. "The Faulknerian Sentence." *Prairie Schooner* 27 (spring 1953): 91–98.

———. "The Myriad Perspectives of 'Absalom, Absalom!'" *American Quarterly* 6 (fall 1954): 210–220.

Scott, Evelyn. *On William Faulkner's "The Sound and the Fury."* New York: Cape & Smith, 1929.

Scott, Nathan A. Jr. "The Vision of William Faulkner." *Christian Century* 74 (September 18, 1957): 1,104–1,106.

Sensibar, Judith L. *The Origins of Faulkner's Art.* Austin: University of Texas Press, 1984.

Serafin, Joan M. *Faulkner's Uses of the Classics.* Ann Arbor, Mich.: UMI Research Press, 1983.

Sewall, Richard B. "'Absalom, Abasalom!'" In *The Vision of Tragedy,* 133–147. New Haven: Yale University Press, 1959.

Sherwood, John C. "The Traditional Element in Faulkner." *Faulkner Studies* 3 (summer–autumn 1954): 17–23.

Simon, John K. "What Are You Laughing At, Darl?: Madness and Humor in *As I Lay Dying.*" *College English* 25 (1963): 104–110.

Singal, Daniel J. *William Faulkner: The Making of a Modernist.* Chapel Hill: University of North Carolina Press, 1997.

Skei, Hans H. *William Faulkner: The Novelist as Short Story Writer.* Oslo: Universitetsforlaget, 1985.

Slatoff, Walter J. *Quest for Failure: A Study of William Faulkner.* Ithaca, N.Y.: Cornell University Press, 1960.

———. "The Edge of Order: The Pattern of Faulkner's Rhetoric." *Twentieth Century Literature* 3 (October 1957): 107–127. Reprinted in *William Faulkner: Three Decades of Criticism,* edited by Frederick J. Hoffman and Olga W. Vickery, 173–198. New York: Harcourt, Brace & World, 1963.

Smith, Hallett. "Summary of a Symposium on 'Light in August.'" *Mississippi Quarterly* 11 (fall 1958): 188–190.

Smith, Henry Nash. "William Faulkner and Reality." *Faulkner Studies* 2 (summer 1953): 17–19.

Smith, Thelma M., and Ward L. Miner. "Faulkner." In *Transatlantic Migration,* 122–145. Durham: Duke University Press, 1955.

Snead, James A. *Figures of Division: William Faulkner's Major Novels.* New York: Methuen, 1986.

Snell, George. "The Fury of William Faulkner." *Western Review* 11 (autumn 1946): 29–40. Reprinted in *The Shapers of American Fiction,* 87–104. New York: E. P. Dutton, 1947.

Spiller, R. E. "The Uses of Memory: Eliot, Faulkner." In *The Cycle of American Literature,* 291–300. New York: Macmillan, 1955.

Stallings, Lawrence. "Gentleman from Mississippi." *American Mercury* 34 (April 1935): 499–501.

Stavrou, C. N. "Ambiguity in Faulkner's Affirmation." *The Personalist* 40 (spring 1959): 169–177.

Stewart, George R., and Joseph M. Backus. "Each in Its Ordered Place: Structure and Narrative in 'Benjy's Section' of 'The Sound and the Fury.'" *American Literature* 29 (January 1958): 440–456.

Stewart, James T. "Miss Havisham and Miss Grierson." *Furman Studies* 6 (fall 1958): 21–23.

Stewart, Randall. *American Literature and Christian Doctrine,* 136–142. Baton Rouge: Louisiana State University Press, 1958.

———. "Hawthorne and Faulkner." *College English* 17 (February 1956): 258–262.

Stone, Geoffrey. "'Light in August.'" *Bookman* 75 (November 1932): 736–738.

Stonesifer, Richard J. "In Defense of Dewey Dell." *Educational Leader* 22 (July 1958): 27–33.

———. "Faulkner's 'Old Man' in the Classroom." *College English* 17 (February 1956): 254–257.

Stonum, Gary Lee. *Faulkner's Career: An Internal Literary History.* Ithaca, N.Y.: Cornell University Press, 1979.

Sullivan, Walter. "The Tragic Design of 'Absalom, Absalom!'" *South Atlantic Quarterly* 50 (October 1951): 552–566.

Sundquist, Eric. *Faulkner: The House Divided.* Baltimore, Md.: Johns Hopkins University Press, 1983.

Swallow, Alan. "A General Introduction to 'Faulkner Studies.'" *Faulkner Studies* 1 (spring 1952): 1–3.

Swiggart, Peter. *The Art of Faulkner's Novels.* Austin: University of Texas Press, 1962.

———. "Moral and Temporal Order in 'The Sound and the Fury.'" *Sewanee Review* 61 (spring 1953): 221–237.

———. "Time in Faulkner's Novels." *Modern Fiction Studies* 1 (May 1955): 25–29.

Swisher, Clarice, ed. *Readings on William Faulkner.* San Diego, Calif.: Greenhaven Press, 1997.

Taylor, W. F. "A Wider Range." In *The Story of American Letters*, 471–481. Chicago: Henry Regnery, 1956.

Taylor, Walter. *Faulkner's Search for a South*. Urbana: University of Illinois Press, 1983.

Thomas, Douglas M. "Memory-Narrative in 'Absalom, Absalom!'" *Faulkner Studies* 2 (summer 1953): 19–22.

Thompson, Alan R. "The Cult of Cruelty." *Bookman* 74 (January–February 1932): 477–487.

———. "'Sanctuary.'" *Bookman* 73 (April 1931): 188–189.

Thompson, Lawrence. *William Faulkner: An Introduction and Interpretation*. New York: Barnes & Noble, 1963.

———. "Mirror Analogues in 'The Sound and the Fury.'" In *English Institute Essays 1952*, edited by Alan S. Downer, 83–106. New York: Columbia University Press, 1954. Reprinted in *William Faulkner: Three Decades of Criticism*, edited Frederick J. Hoffman and Olga W. Vickery, 211–225. New York: Harcourt, Brace & World, 1963. Also reprinted in *Faulkner: A Collection of Critical Essays*, edited by Robert Penn Warren, 109–121. Englewood Cliffs, N.J.: Prentice Hall, Inc., 1966.

Thorp, Willard. "Four Times and Out?" *Scrutiny* 1 (September 1932): 172–173.

Tilley, Winthrop. "The Idiot Boy in Mississippi: Faulkner's 'The Sound and the Fury.'" *American Journal of Mental Deficiency* 59 (January 1955): 374–377.

Torchiana, Donald T. "Faulkner's 'Pylon' and the Structure of Modernity." *Modern Fiction Studies* 3 (winter 1957–58): 291–308.

———. "The Reporter in Faulkner's 'Pylon.'" *History of Ideas News Letter* 4 (spring 1958): 33–39.

Towner, Theresa M. *Faulkner on the Color Line: The Later Novels*. Jackson: University Press of Mississippi, 2000.

Towner, Theresa M., and James B. Carothers. *Reading Faulkner: Collected Stories*. Jackson: University Press of Mississippi, 2006.

Tritschler, Donald. "The Unity of Faulkner's Shaping Vision." *Modern Fiction Studies* 5 (winter 1959–60): 337–343.

Tredell, Nicholas. The Sound and the Fury *and* As I Lay Dying: *Essays, Articles, Reviews*. New York: Columbia University Press, 2000.

Troy, William. "The Poetry of Doom." *Nation* 143 (October 31, 1936): 524–525.

———. "And Tomorrow." *Nation* 140 (April 3, 1935): 393.

Urgo, Joseph R. *Faulkner's Apocrypha: "A Fable," Snopes, and the Spirit of Human Rebellion*. Jackson: University Press of Mississippi, 1989.

Urgo, Joseph R., and Ann J. Abadie, eds. *Faulkner and the Ecology of the South*. Jackson: University Press of Mississippi, 2005.

Utley, Francis Lee, Lynn Z. Bloom, and Arthur F. Kinney, eds. *Bear, Man, and God: Seven Approaches to William Faulkner's "The Bear."* New York: Random House, 1964.

Vanderwerken, David L. *Faulkner's Literary Children: Patterns of Development*. New York: Peter Lang, 1997.

Van Doren, Mark. "'Pylon.'" *New York Herald Tribune* (Books) (March 24, 1935), 3.

Vickery, John B. "William Faulkner and Sir Philip Sidney?" *Modern Language Notes* 70 (May 1955): 349–350.

Vickery, Olga W. *The Novels of William Faulkner: A Critical Interpretation*. 3rd ed. Baton Rouge: Louisiana State University Press, 1959.

———. "'As I Lay Lying.'" *Perspective* 3 (autumn 1950): 179–191.

———. "Faulkner and the Contours of Time." *Georgia Review* 12 (summer 1958): 192–201.

———. "Faulkner's First Novel." *Western Humanities Review* 11 (summer 1957): 251–256.

———. "Faulkner's Mosquitoes.'" *University of Kansas City Review* 24 (spring 1958): 219–224.

———. "Gavin Stevens: From Rhetoric to Dialectic." *Faulkner Studies* 2 (spring 1953): 1–4.

———. "The Making of a Myth: 'Sartoris.'" *Western Review* 22 (spring 1958): 209–219.

———. "'The Sound and the Fury': A Study in Perspective." *PMLA* 69 (December 1954): 1,017–1,037.

Visser, Irene. *Compassion in Faulkner's Fiction*. Lewiston, N.Y.: Edwin Mellen, 1996.

Volpe, Edmond L. *A Reader's Guide to William Faulkner: The Novels*. San Jose, Calif.: Authors Choice Press, 2001.

———. *A Reader's Guide to William Faulkner: The Short Stories*. New York: Syracuse University Press, 2004.

Wadlington, Warwick. As I Lay Dying: *Stories Out of Stories*. New York: Twayne, 1992.

———. *Reading Faulknerian Tragedy*. Ithaca, N.Y.: Cornell University Press, 1987.

Wagenknecht, Edward. "Erskine Caldwell and William Faulkner." In *Cavalcade of the American Novel*, 417–425. New York: Henry Holt, 1952.

Waggoner, Hyatt H. *William Faulkner: From Jefferson to the World*. Lexington: University of Kentucky Press, 1959.

———. "William Faulkner: The Definition of Man." *Books at Brown* 18 (March 1958): 116–122.

———. "William Faulkner's Passion Week of the Heart." In *The Tragic Vision and the Christian Faith*, edited by Nathan A. Scott Jr., 306–323. New York: Association Press, 1957.

Wagner, Linda W., ed. *William Faulkner: Four Decades of Criticism*. East Lansing: Michigan State University Press, 1973.

Wagner-Martin, Linda, ed. *New Essays on "Go Down, Moses."* New York: Cambridge University Press, 1996.

Warren, Robert Penn, ed. *Faulkner: A Collection of Critical Essays*. Englewood Cliffs, N.J.: Prentice Hall, 1966.

———. "Cowley's Faulkner." *New Republic* 115 (August 12, 1946): 176–180; continued (August 26, 1946): 234–237.

———. "Faulkner: The South, the Negro, and Time." *Southern Review* 1 (summer 1965): 501–529. Reprinted in *Faulkner: A Collection of Critical Essays*, edited by Robert Penn Warren, 251–271. Englewood Cliffs, N.J.: Prentice Hall, Inc., 1966.

———. "William Faulkner." In *Selected Essays*, 59–79. New York: Random House, 1958. Reprinted in *William Faulkner: Three Decades of Criticism*, edited by Frederick J. Hoffman and Olga W. Vickery, 109–124. New York: Harcourt, Brace & World, 1963.

Wasiolek, Edward. "'As I Lay Dying': Distortion in the Slow Eddy of Current Opinion," *Critique* 3 (spring–fall 1959): 15–23.

———. "Dostoevsky and 'Sanctuary.'" *Modern Language Notes* 74 (February 1959): 114–117.

Watkins, Floyd C. "The Gentle Reader and Mr. Faulkner's Morals." *Georgia Review* 13 (spring 1959): 68–75.

———. "The Structure of 'A Rose for Emily.'" *Modern Language Notes* 69 (November 1954): 508–510.

Watson, James G. *William Faulkner, Letters and Fictions*. Austin: University of Texas Press, 1987.

Watson, James G. *William Faulkner: Self-Preservation and Performance*. Austin: University of Texas Press, 2000.

Watson, Jay. *Forensic Fictions: The Lawyer Figure in Faulkner*. Athens: University of Georgia Press, 1993.

Weinstein, Philip. *Faulkner's Subject: A Cosmos No One Owns*. New York: Cambridge University Press, 1992.

———. *What Else But Love: The Ordeal of Race in Faulkner and Morrison*. New York: Columbia University Press, 1996.

Wells, Dean Faulkner. *The Ghosts of Rowan Oak: William Faulkner's Ghost Stories for Children*. Oxford, Miss.: Yoknapatawpha Press, 1980.

Wells, Dean Faulkner, and Lawrence Wells. "The Trains Belonged to Everybody: Faulkner as Ghost Writer." *Southern Review* 12 (autumn 1976): 864–871.

Welty, Eudora. *On William Faulkner*. Afterword by Noel Polk. Jackson: University Press of Mississippi, 2003.

West, Anthony. "A Dying Fall." *New Yorker* 35 (December 5, 1959): 236–243.

West, Ray B., Jr. "Hemingway and Faulkner." In *The Short Story in America, 1900–1950*, 85–106. Chicago: Henry Regnery, 1952.

———. "Atmosphere and Theme in Faulkner's 'A Rose for Emily.'" *Perspective* 2 (summer 1949): 239–245. Reprinted in *William Faulkner: Two Decades of Criticism*, edited by Frederick J. Hoffman and Olga W. Vickery, 259–267. East Lansing: Michigan State University Press, 1951.

———. "Faulkner's 'A Rose for Emily.'" *Explicator* 7 (October 1948): item 8.

———. "William Faulkner: Artist and Moralist." *Western Review* 16 (winter 1952): 162–167.

West, Ray B., Jr., and R. W. Stallman. "Theme through Atmosphere." In *The Art of Modern Fiction*, 270–275. New York: Rinehart, 1949.

Whan, Edgar W. "'Absalom, Absalom!' as Gothic Myth." *Perspective* 3 (autumn 1950), 192–201.

Wheeler, Otis B. "Faulkner's Wilderness." *American Literature* 31 (May 1959): 127–136.

Whicher, Stephen E. "The Compsons' Nancies—A Note on 'The Sound and the Fury' and 'That Evening Sun.'" *American Literature* 26 (May 1954): 253–255.

White, William. "One Man's Meat: Societies and Journals Devoted to a Single Author." *The American Book Collector* 8 (November 1957): 22–24.

Whittemore, Reed. "Notes on Mr. Faulkner." *Furioso* 2 (summer 1947): 18–25.

Wilder, Amos N. "Faulkner and Vestigial Moralities." In *Theology and Modern Literature*, 113–131. Cambridge: Harvard University Press, 1958.

William, Cecil B. "William Faulkner and the Nobel Prize Awards." *Faulkner Studies* 1 (summer 1952): 17–19.

Williams, David. *Faulkner's Women: The Myth and the Muse*. Montreal, Canada: McGill Queen's University Press, 1977.

Wilson, Paul A. "Faulkner and Camus: Requiem for a Nun." *Odyssey: A Journal of the Humanities* 3, no. 2 (1979): 3–9.

Wittenberg, Judith Bryant. *Faulkner: The Transfiguration of Biography*. Lincoln: University of Nebraska Press, 1979.

Woodward, C. Vann. *The Burden of Southern History*. Baton Rouge: Louisiana State University Press, 1960.

———. *Origins of the New South, 1877–1913*. Baton Rouge: Louisiana State University Press, 1951.

Wright, Austin M. *Recalcitrance, Faulkner, and the Professors: A Critical Fiction*. Iowa City: University of Iowa Press, 1990.

Wykes, Alan. "The Perceptive Few and the Lost Generation." In *A Concise Survey of American Literature*, 165–174. London: Arthur Baker, 1955.

Young, T. D., and Floyd C. Watkins. "Faulkner's Snopeses." *Mississippi Quarterly* 11 (fall 1958): 196–200.

Yonce, Margaret J. *Annotations to Faulkner's Soldiers' Pay*. New York: Garland, 1990.

Zender, Karl F. *The Crossing of the Ways: William Faulkner, the South, and the Modern World*. New Brunswick, N.J.: Rutgers University Press, 1989.

Zink, Karl E. "Faulkner's Garden: Woman and the Immemorial Earth." *Modern Fiction Studies* 2 (autumn 1956): 139–149.

———. "Flux and the Frozen Moment: The Imagery of Stasis in Faulkner's Prose." *PMLA* 71 (June 1956): 285–301.

———. "William Faulkner: Form as Experience." *South Atlantic Quarterly* 53 (July 1954): 384–403.

Zoellner, Robert H. "Faulkner's Prose Style in 'Absalom, Absalom!'" *American Literature* 30 (January 1959): 486–502.

6. Web Sites

The major Web site for Faulkner studies is William Faulkner on the Web. Available online. At URL: http://www.mcsr.olemiss.edu/~egjbp/faulkner/faulkner.html (From this web site, there are links to others, including the Center for Faulkner Studies at http://www.semo.edu/cfs.) Accessed September 27, 2007.

7. Societies, Centers, and Conferences

Center for Faulkner Studies, Southeast Missouri State University, One University Plaza, Cape Girardeau, MO 63701-4799. The center possesses the Louis Daniel Brodsky collection of Faulkner material and promotes educational and research projects relating to Faulkner's work and life. It also publishes twice annually the very useful pamphlet *Teaching Faulkner*, edited by Robert W. Hamblin, the Center's director, and Charles A. Peek. Web site: http://www.semo.edu/cfs/ and E-mail:cfs@semovm.semo.edu

Faulkner E-mail discussion group. To subscribe, send the message "subscribe faulkner" to md@listserv.olemiss.edu

Faulkner and Yoknapatawpha Conference, a weeklong conference sponsored by the English Department and the Center for the Study of Southern Culture at the University of Mississippi, Oxford, Mississippi. It is usually held during the last week of July. Web site: http://www.mcsr.olemiss.edu/~egibp/faulkner/fyconference.html

William Faulkner Foundation, Rennes University, Rennes, France, is the major European center for Faulkner studies and research. It is located at 6, avenue Gaston Berger, 3500 Rennes, France. Web site: http://www.uhb.fr/faulkner/WF/index.htm and E-mail: Foundation Faulkner@uhb.fr

The William Faulkner Society promotes Faulkner scholarship and the critical study of his works. Its annual meeting is held at the American Literature Association Convention; this society is affiliated with *The Faulkner Journal.* For membership contact Evelyn Jaffe Schreiber, 5508 Devon Road, Bethesda, MD 20814. Web site: http://www.acad.swarthmore.edu/faulkner/

The William Faulkner Society of Japan, contact Professor Yamashita, Faculty of Humanities, Soai University 4–4–1 Nankou-naka, Suminoe-ku, Osaka City, 559–0033 Japan; E-mail: yamasita@soai.ac.jp

DAY-BY-DAY CHRONOLOGY OF EVENTS IN *AS I LAY DYING*

As I Lay Dying takes place over a ten-day period. Though Faulkner's arrangement of the chapters does not follow a strict chronological order, a relative sequence of events can be discerned. The following is an outline of events with chapter (or episode) numbers inserted. Faulkner, however, does not number the episodes of the novel. The time period of Addie's only monologue, chapter 40, is indeterminable. It takes place either on (or shortly before) the day of her death or sometime in the indefinite past, but Faulkner situates this critical chapter five days after her death. Addie's spectral presence in the midst of her burial journey to Jefferson seems a blunt reminder of her continuing hold on her family and a compelling vindication of herself and thoughts ironically associated with the stench of her rotting corpse. The novel's chronology is also interrupted by chapter 39, "Cora," which narrates events that occurred sometime in the indefinite past, and by chapter 41, "Whitfield," which narrates events that occurred just before and the day after Addie's death.

Another issue that confuses the chronology is the day the Bundrens leave for Jefferson. That day cannot be determined with complete accuracy. According to Vernon Tull, the Bundrens started their journey late on the third day after Darl and Jewel left to haul lumber (92), namely, the fourth day in the novel's chronology. But Samson, in chapter 29, sees the Bundrens pass by on their way to Jefferson on the third day after the funeral (113), namely, the fifth day in the novel's chronology. The outline below follows Tull's reckoning. (Also

see Edmond L. Volpe, *A Reader's Guide to William Faulkner*, 379, where he touches upon this same question of the novel's chronology.)

Day One (chapters 1–19):

As Addie lies dying, her daughter Dewey Dell fans her. Cora Tull, Addie's neighbor, and Cora's daughters, Eula and Kate, are also in the room making small talk. Outside the window, Cash is building a coffin. (It was not uncommon to build a family member's coffin, a practice that can be seen in other works such as *Riders to the Sea* by the Irish playwright John Millington Synge, 1871–1909.) Addie's husband Anse is with Vernon Tull as her sons Darl and Jewel come into the yard. Although reluctant at first because Addie is near death, Anse agrees to let Darl and Jewel haul a load of lumber, for which they will receive three dollars. They know they can use the money when they travel to Jefferson to bury Addie. The two brothers expect to be back by sundown the next day.

Jewel does not admit that his mother is dying and becomes irritated with the Tulls for visiting her so frequently. Sometime after Darl and Jewel leave for the job and the Tulls go home, Dr. Peabody, whom Addie does not care to see, arrives. He is a heavy man and has to leave his buggy at the bottom of the hill leading to the Bundrens' house. With the assistance of Anse and his son Vardaman, Peabody is helped up the hill with a rope. Vardaman, who is with his mother when she dies, blames her death on Dr. Peabody and in retaliation chases his horses off.

Dewey Dell prepares dinner for the family and their guest. Cash, however, is still fashioning the coffin as evening and the rain come. Around midnight the distressed, confused, and soaking wet Vardaman appears at the Tulls'. Once Vernon and his wife realize that Addie must have died, they take Vardaman back home in the driving rain. Shortly before dawn, the rain stops as Cash is finishing the coffin. Anse, Peabody, Tull, and Cash carry the coffin into Addie's room and place it by the bed. Faulkner's description of their march into the house is poetic and poignant: They "raise the coffin to their shoulders and turn toward the house. It is light, yet they move slowly; empty, yet they carry it carefully; lifeless, yet they move with hushed precautionary words to one another, speaking of it as though, complete, it now slumbered lightly alive, waiting to come awake" (79–80).

Meanwhile, Darl and Jewel are caught in the rainstorm with a disabled wagon filled with soggy lumber. Although they had expected to return home before sundown the next day, they do not arrive until the third day after they left.

Day Two (chapter 20):

It is the day of Addie's funeral. With Dr. Peabody's horses hitched to his wagon, Vernon Tull arrives at the Bundrens' at 10 in the morning. Others are already there: Peabody; Quick, who found Peabody's buckboard; Armstid, who thinks Anse should bury Addie's body at New Hope because the old bridge is too risky to cross with the rising river; Uncle Billy; Houston; and Littlejohn. Jewel and Darl, however, have not returned from hauling the lumber. Cash is meticulously trimming plugs to fill in the auger holes that Vardaman bored into the coffin thinking that his mother needed air. Dressed in her wedding gown, Addie is laid head to foot "so the dress could spread out" (88), and a veil is placed over her face to hide the auger marks on it that Vardaman unintentionally caused. When the preacher Whitfield arrives, the service begins. After it is over, the Tulls leave for home and spot Vardaman sitting on the edge of a slough fishing alone. Tull suggests that he go home with them and fish the next morning in

the river where Tull will take him, but Vardaman stays by himself.

Day Three: (chapter 20, p. 92):

Specific events for this day cannot be adequately discerned. Addie, according to Tull, lay in the coffin for three days, during which time Darl and Jewel came home and left again with a new wagon wheel. This activity probably took place on the third day in the novel's chronology. The period of time that Addie lay in the coffin, therefore, includes the day of her funeral, the day after, and the day the Bundrens started out late on their journey.

Day Four (The journey begins on this day: chapters 21–29.)

As Darl and Jewel return home from hauling lumber, buzzards are circling high above the house. Cash cautions his father and brothers, in particular the impetuous Jewel, to take it easy with the coffin, but Jewel, nonetheless, rushes down the hill leaving Anse and the hobbling Cash behind. Darl himself can hardly keep up and at the last minute is no longer holding the coffin as Jewel single-handedly shoves it onto to the wagon bed. Against his father's objections, Jewel goes back to get his horse. Dewey Dell carries a basket and a package that she tells her father contains Mrs. Tull's cakes (see below, Day Nine), but in fact the package contains a change of clothes. Anse makes a remark to her similar to the one he made to Jewel when Jewel got his horse to ride on the burial trip to Jefferson: "'It aint right. . . . It's a flouting of the dead" (102).

They start off and pass Tull's lane, and to Anse's chagrin, Darl begins to laugh. In recognition of the Bundrens' passing by, Tull lifts his hand and watches Jewel catch up to the wagon. As they pass a sign pointing out that New Hope Church is three miles away, Cash comments that Addie's body will begin to smell, indicating that he would prefer burying her at New Hope. Darl, who is narrating this episode (chapter 27), seems sympathetic to Cash's preference. Cash is also concerned about the coffin not being properly balanced for such a long trip to Jefferson.

Once the Bundrens find that the bridge at Tull's is impassable, they travel on to the bridge at Samson's only to discover that that bridge too is gone. Samson, who is sitting on the porch of his store with Quick and MacCallum as the Bundrens pass by, has little choice but to offer the Bundrens lodging for the night, for it is getting dark and their home is eight miles away. Although they take dinner, the Bundrens decline to sleep in the house but stay with the wagon, which was driven into the barn at Samson's request because of the threat of rain.

Day Five (The second day of the journey: chapter 29, pp. 118–119, chapters 30–31, 33–38, 42, and chapter 43, pp. 184–186; chapter 32, although taking place within the novel's chronology, is Darl's flashback to the time Jewel bought his horse from Quick.)

Early in the morning, the Bundrens, without saying good-bye to their hosts, depart in the rain and head back toward New Hope and Tull's bridge. Samson detects the stench from Addie's corpse, and when he goes into the barn to check, he spots a buzzard that he watches as it finds its way out.

As the Bundrens pass the sign for New Hope, Cash once again stares at it and Vardaman asks his father why they are not going there. Anse offers no reply. They pass Tull's farm and go on to the end of the levee from where they can see the partly-submerged bridge. Tull, who by this time has stopped plowing his field, goes up to them and, thinking that the river has reached its crest, suggests that the Bundrens wait another day before attempting to cross it. Jewel snaps at Tull for this idea but instead would like the use of his mule, an idea that Tull peremptorily dismisses. Anse decides that he, Dewey Dell, and Vardaman will cross over the bridge to the other side and that Cash, Darl, and Jewel will ford the river. Tull, who is narrating this episode, chapter 33, crosses with Anse. With Tull's help from the other side, the three brothers find the spot to ford the river, but their attempt almost becomes a debacle. The mules separate from the wagon and drown. Darl jumps from the wagon and ends up on the riverbank. Cash is forced out of the wagon, fractures his leg, is rescued from drowning,

and loses the tools that he brought along on the journey. Meanwhile, Jewel, who is also fighting the current, miraculously saves the wagon and coffin from being washed away and with help from Tull and Darl recovers Cash's tools.

Jewel heads off to Armstid's farm for a team of mules. When he comes back, the Bundrens hitch the mules to the wagon and go to Armstid's where they are given supper and spend the night. Armstid proposes the use of his mules, but Anse declines the offer. Anse, however, is mulling over Armstid's earlier suggestion to buy a span of mules from Snopes. After supper, Jewel rides to Frenchman's Bend to find Dr. Peabody, but the doctor is out of town. Jewel returns around midnight with Uncle Billy, who sets Cash's leg.

Day Six (The third day of the journey: chapter 43, pp. 186–192)

Sometime in the early morning, Anse takes Jewel's horse and rides to Frenchman's Bend to bargain with Snopes over a span of mules. Meanwhile, the putrid odor from Addie's coffin is getting worse and attracting buzzards that the young Vardaman chases after in Armstid's yard. Upset by the condition of Addie's corpse and the delay in burying it, Lula demands that her husband do something. Armstid naively thinks that he can get the petulant Jewel to take one of the mules to see about his father, but his intentions backfire. Realizing what Armstid is really concerned about—the offensive smell of the corpse—Jewel moves the wagon by himself. Darl does not lend a hand.

Armstid, who is narrating chapter 43, describes Anse's demeanor upon his return: "He looked kind of funny: kind of more hangdog than common, and kind of proud too. Like he had done something he thought was cute but wasn't so sho now how other folks would take it" (189). Part of Anse's trade with Snopes involved Jewel's horse, something that so infuriates Jewel that he rides off in anger. Anse again declines Armstid's offer to use his mules except to move the wagon about a mile down the road where he and his family spend the night. Cash is in a pallet on top of the coffin. Anse also declines supper.

Day Seven (The fourth day of the journey: chapter 43, pp. 192–193, and chapter 44)

After breakfast, Eustace Grimm, who works for Snopes, arrives at Armstid's with a team of mules for the Bundrens. Without telling anyone (and to Armstid's surprise, for he assumed that Jewel was on his way to Texas), Jewel had left his horse in Snopes's barn where Eustace found it earlier in the morning when he went to feed. The Bundrens continue their journey to Jefferson as buzzards circle high above. With support under his knee and a rolled-up quilt under his head, Cash lies on the coffin feeling every bump the wagon goes over.

Day Eight (The fifth day of the journey: chapters 45–51)

The Bundrens arrive at Mottson and park their wagon in front of Grummet's hardware store. Dewey Dell, awkward and hesitant but determined to buy an abortifacient, goes to Moseley's drugstore where she is flatly denied any kind of medication that would produce an abortion and told by Moseley to use the ten dollars that she got from her boyfriend Lafe "and get married with it" (203). Dewey Dell leaves the store to go back to the wagon where townsfolk with handkerchiefs covering their noses have already gathered to hear the marshal argue with Anse to move on. Anse rejoins by saying that he is on a public street and has as much a right as anyone to stop and buy what he needs. Darl comes from Grummet's with ten cents worth of cement to mix into a cast for Cash's leg.

When Dewey Dell returns from Moseley's, the Bundrens leave Mottson and stop at a farmhouse where they borrow a bucket in which Darl mixes the cement for Cash's leg. As Darl and the others are finishing with Cash, they spot Jewel in the distance walking up to the wagon. He joins them and they move on to Gillespie's farm where they spend the night. The coffin is put under an apple tree, but when the wind shifts Jewel, Darl, and Gillespie's son, Mack, take it into the barn and put it on sawhorses. Vardaman, who is with his sister on the porch, watches them move the

coffin and later when she is asleep sneaks off to find out where the buzzards stay at night. While he is looking for them, he sees Darl set fire to Gillespie's barn, and when he tells his sister, she forbids him to say anything to anybody. Jewel rushes into the burning barn and momentarily stops at the coffin but is told by Darl to start saving the horses; he is followed by Mack and Gillespie. After the horses and the other animals are rescued, Jewel at great risk to his own life saves the coffin. His back is badly burned which Dewey Dell treats with butter and soot. Others carry the coffin to the apple tree, and later Vardaman finds Darl lying on the coffin, crying. Meanwhile, because of the cement, Cash's leg and foot have turned black.

Day Nine (The sixth day of the journey: chapters 52–58 and chapter 59, pp. 258–259)

About a mile from Jefferson, Dewey Dell asks her father to stop. He does so reluctantly, and she walks off with her package into the woods and disappears for a while. When she returns, she is wearing a change of clothes. (Her Sunday dress was in the package that she has been carrying on the trip and not Mrs. Tull's cakes as she had told her father; see above, Day Four.) As the Bundrens are coming into Jefferson, they pass three negroes and then 10 feet in front of them a white man, all walking into town. In horror, the negroes turn and look at the wagon as one utters a comment. Jewel angrily responds by cursing, but—because the wagon is still moving—it is the white man who gets the brunt of Jewel's rage. Prompted by his brother Cash, Darl holds back Jewel, who, nevertheless, swings at the man and struggles with Darl to free himself. Seeing that the white man has pulled a knife, Darl attempts to diffuse the situation. Anse steps down from the wagon, and Dewey Dell holds Jewel back as Darl bravely faces the man to explain that because his brother was burned in a fire the night before he is not himself. The altercation comes to an end when Jewel, who thought the white man spoke out, apologizes, and the Bundrens continue into Jefferson.

Anse knows that Gillespie will sue him for Darl's arson and believes that he (Anse) has no choice but to give Darl up to the authorities to be taken to the mental institution in Jackson, but only after Addie is buried and not before as Jewel would like it. Cash will see Dr. Peabody after the burial, too.

The Bundrens yet need to dig Addie's grave. Anse, however, brought no spade and objects to Darl's buying one at the local hardware store. He insists on borrowing a spade and stops at a house where music is playing from a graphophone. (In *Annotations to Faulkner's As I Lay Dying*, Dianne C. Luce points out that a graphophone "was a trade-mark for a phonograph" and that Calvin Brown has noted that "all the phonographs in the 1902 Sears catalogue are designated graphophones.") This house, as Cash identifies in his narrative, chapter 53, is where (the second) Mrs. Bundren lives. (It is not, however, until the next day, the day when Anse unexpectedly introduces this woman as "Mrs. Bundren" to his family right before leaving Jefferson for home, that Cash finds out her name.) After what seems to be an inordinate amount of time, especially by Jewel, Anse comes back to the wagon with two spades and the Bundrens proceed to the cemetery to dig a grave and bury Addie.

Immediately after the Bundrens leave the cemetery, Darl is approached by two men, who tell him that they are there to apprehend him. Darl steps back—and before the men can get hold of him, Dewey Dell jumps on him "like a wild cat" (237) and has to be restrained by one of the men as the other one, Anse, and Jewel force Darl to the ground. As Darl is struggling, he looks up at Cash and wonders aloud why he had not been told that he would be taken away. After Jewel, who is particularly infuriated with Darl, is pulled away from his brother, Darl sits on the ground and laughs as Cash explains that he will be better off in the state institution in Jackson. In this episode, 53, Cash believes that Dewey Dell is the one who told Gillespie that Darl set fire to the barn (237), though Cash does not suggest a motive. Knowing

that Darl most certainly would be sent to Jackson in order to avoid a lawsuit that Anse would never want to pay, Dewey Dell may have wanted to assure herself that Darl—the only Bundren who knows—would not wittingly or unwittingly reveal the secret of her pregnancy that she is seeking to terminate.

Darl is taken away by the two men and travels by train to Jackson. In the last chapter that he narrates, chapter 57, Darl speaks of himself in the third person. After he is escorted away, Cash goes to Dr. Peabody to have his leg taken care of and Dewey Dell goes to a drugstore in her quest for medication to end her pregnancy. She speaks with the clerk Skeet MacGowan, who pretends to be a medical doctor. Dewey Dell is given a small dose of a liquid that smells like turpentine and told to come back at 10 P.M. for the rest of the medicine and "the operation" (247), the same kind of "operation" she had before. In between the time Dewey Dell leaves the drugstore and returns, Anse discovers that she has $10 and, against her pleading, takes it from her as a loan to spend on himself.

When Dewey Dell returns to the drugstore at the appointed time, Skeet meets her at the door and notices a boy—her brother Vardaman—sitting on the curb and asks whether he wants anything; Vardaman looks up and offers no reply. On the way back to the hotel where the Bundrens are staying the night, Dewey Dell realizes that she has been had and that what happened to her in the cellar of the drugstore was not a remedy at all.

Day Ten (The seventh day, returning home, chapter 59, pp. 260–261)

In the morning, Anse goes out for a while. When he comes back, he tells his family to get ready to leave and to meet him at a particular corner on the square. As they are waiting, he is seen coming toward them, carrying a suitcase. He looks different because of his new teeth, and he also has a woman with him carrying a graphophone. To their astonishment, he introduces her to Cash, Jewel, Dewey Dell, and Vardaman as Mrs. Bundren.

Diagrammatic Outline of *As I Lay Dying*

1st day (chapters 1–19)	2nd day (chapter 20)	3rd day (chapter 20, p. 92)	4th day (chapters 21–29)	5th day (chapter 29, pp. 118–119, chapters 30–31, 33–38, 42, and chapter 43, pp. 184–186)	6th day (chapter 43, pp. 186–192)	7th day (chapter 43, pp. 192–193, and chapter 44)	8th day (chapters 45–51)	9th day (chapters 52–58) and chapter 59, pp. 258–259	10th day (chapter 59, pp. 260–261)
Addie lies dying as Cash is making her coffin. Darl and Jewel leave to haul lumber. Addie dies.	Addie's funeral.	Darl and Jewel come home for a new wagon wheel.	Darl and Jewel return home from hauling lumber. Later, the Bundrens leave for Jefferson to bury Addie. They stay the night at Samson's.						
			1st day of journey	**2nd day of journey**	**3rd day of journey**	**4th day of journey**	**5th day of journey**	**6th day of journey**	**7th day, returning home**
				The Bundrens leave Samson's farm to return to Tull's bridge. They ford the river. Their mules drown and Cash fractures his leg. They spend the night at Armstid's; Uncle Billy sets Cash's leg.	Anse goes to French-man's Bend to bargain with Snopes for a team of mules. The deal includes Jewel's horse. The Bundrens spend the night about a mile away from Armstid's.	Eustace Grimm arrives at Armstid's with a span of mules for the Bundrens. They continue their journey to Jefferson.	The Bundrens arrive at Mottson and stop in front of Grummet's hardware store. Dewey Dell goes to Moseley's drugstore where she unsuccessfully tries to purchase medication to cause an abortion. The townsfolk cover their noses near the Bundren wagon. The marshal orders Anse to move on. He leaves only after Darl returns from Grummet's with cement for Cash's leg. Jewel catches up to them on the way to Gillespie's farm. During the night Darl sets fire to Gillespie's barn. The animals are rescued and Jewel saves the coffin but his back is severely burned. Cash's leg and foot turn black because of the cement.	The Bundrens arrive in Jefferson and bury Addie, after which Darl is taken to a mental institution in Jackson. Cash's leg is reset by Dr. Peabody and Dewey Dell again fails in her attempt to get medication for an abortion. The Bundrens stay in a hotel for the night.	Before the Bundrens leave Jefferson for home, Anse gets new teeth and introduces a woman as Mrs. Bundren to Cash, Jewel, Dewey Dell, and Vardaman.

Faulkner's Appendix to *The Sound and the Fury*

In an interview at the University of Virginia, Faulkner explained that the appendix to *The Sound and the Fury* was written about 20 years after the novel was published in 1929 as another attempt at trying "to make that book . . . match the dream" (*Faulkner in the University*, 84). Entitled "1699–1945 The Compsons," the appendix first appeared in *The Portable Faulkner* (1946). When *The Sound and the Fury* was published together with *As I Lay Dying* by The Modern Library in 1946, the appendix appeared as a foreword entitled "Compson 1699–1945."

1699–1945 The Compsons

IKKEMOTUBBE. A dispossessed American king. Called *l'Homme* (and sometimes *de l'Homme*) by his fosterbrother, a Chevalier of France, who, had he not been born too late, could have been among the brightest in that glittering galaxy of knightly blackguards who were Napoleon's marshals, who thus translated the Chickasaw title meaning "The Man"; which translation Ikkemotubbe, himself a man of wit and imagination as well as a shrewd judge of character, including his own, carried one step further and anglicized it to "Doom." Who granted out of his vast lost domain a solid square mile of virgin north Mississippi dirt as truely angled as the four corners of a cardtable top (forested then because these were the old days before 1833 when the stars fell and Jefferson, Mississippi, was one long rambling one-storey mudchinked log building housing the Chickasaw Agent and his trading-post store) to the grandson of a Scottish refugee who had lost his own birthright by casting his lot with a king who himself had been dispossessed. This in partial return for the right to proceed in peace, by whatever means he and his people saw fit, afoot or ahorse provided they were Chickasaw horses, to the wild western land presently to be called Oklahoma: not knowing then about the oil.

JACKSON. A Great White Father with a sword. (An old duellist, a brawling lean fierce mangy durable imperishable old lion who set the well-being of the nation above the White House, and the health of his new political party above either, and above them all set, not his wife's honor, but the principle that honor must be defended whether it was or not because defended it was whether or not.) Who patented, sealed, and countersigned the grant with his own hand in his gold tepee in Wassi Town, not knowing about the oil either: so that one day the homeless descendants of the dispossessed would ride supine with drink and splendidly comatose above the dusty allotted harborage of their bones in specially built scarlet-painted hearses and fire-engines.

These were Compsons:
QUENTIN MacLACHAN. Son of a Glasgow printer, orphaned and raised by his mother's people in the Perth highlands. Fled to Carolina from Culloden Moor with a claymore and the tartan he wore by day and slept under by night, and little else. At eighty, having fought once against an English king and lost, he would not make that mistake

527

twice and so fled again one night in 1779, with his infant grandson and the tartan (the claymore had vanished, along with his son, the grandson's father, from one of Tarleton's regiments on a Georgia battlefield about a year ago) into Kentucky, where a neighbor named Boon or Boone had already established a settlement.

CHARLES STUART. Attained and proscribed by name and grade in his British regiment. Left for dead in a Georgia swamp by his own retreating army and then by the advancing American one, both of which were wrong. He still had the claymore even when on his homemade wooden leg he finally overtook his father and son four years later at Harrodsburg, Kentucky, just in time to bury the father and enter upon a long period of being a split personality while still trying to be the schoolteacher which he believed he wanted to be, until he gave up at last and became the gambler he actually was and which no Compson seemed to realize they all were, provided the gambit was desperate and the odds long enough. Succeeded at last in risking not only his neck but the security of his family and the very integrity of the name he would leave behind him, by joining the confederation headed by an acquaintance named Wilkinson (a man of considerable talent and influence and intellect and power) in a plot to secede the whole Mississippi Valley from the United States and join it to Spain. Fled in his turn when the bubble burst (as anyone except a Compson schoolteacher should have known it would), himself unique in being the only one of the plotters who had to flee the country: this not from the vengeance and retribution of the government which he had attempted to dismember, but from the furious revulsion of his late confederates now frantic for their own safety. He was not expelled from the United States; he talked himself countryless, his expulsion due not to the treason but to his having been so vocal and vociferant in the conduct of it, burning each bridge vocally behind him before he had even reached the place to build the next one: so that it was no provost marshal nor even a civic agency but his late co-plotters themselves who put afoot the movement to evict him from Kentucky and the United States and, if they had caught him,

probably from the world too. Fled by night, running true to family tradition, with his son and the old claymore and the tartan.

JASON LYCURGUS. Who, driven perhaps by the compulsion of the flamboyant name given him by the sardonic embittered woodenlegged indomitable father who perhaps still believed with his heart that what he wanted to be was a classicist schoolteacher, rode up the Natchez Trace one day in 1820 with a pair of fine pistols and one meagre saddlebag on a small light-waisted but stronghocked mare which could do the first two furlongs in definitely under the halfminute and the next two in not appreciably more, though that was all. But it was enough: who reached the Chickasaw Agency at Okatoba (which in 1860 was still called Old Jefferson) and went no further. Who within six months was the Agent's clerk and within twelve his partner, officially still the clerk though actually halfowner of what was now a considerable store stocked with the mare's winnings in races against the horses of Ikkemotubbe's young men which he, Compson, was always careful to limit to a quarter or at most three furlongs; and in the next year it was Ikkemotubbe who owned the little mare and Compson owned the solid square mile of land which some day would be almost in the center of the town of Jefferson, forested then and still forested twenty years later, though rather a park than a forest by that time, with is slave quarters and stables and kitchen gardens and the formal lawns and promenades and pavilions laid out by the same architect who built the columned porticoed house furnished by steamboat from France and New Orleans, and still the square intact mile in 1840 (with not only the little white village called Jefferson beginning to enclose it but an entire white county about to surround it, because in a few years now Ikkemotubbe's descendants and people would be gone, those remaining living not as warriors and hunters but as white men—as shiftless farmers or, here and there, the masters of what they too called plantations and the owners of shiftless slaves, a little dirtier than the white man, a little lazier, a little crueller—until at last even the wild blood itself would have vanished, to be seen only occasionally in the nose-shape of a Negro on a cottonwagon or a white sawmill hand or trapper or locomotive fireman); known as the Compson Domain then, since now it was fit to breed princes, statesmen and generals and bishops, to avenge the dispossessed Compsons from Culloden and Carolina and Kentucky; then known as the Governor's house because sure enough in time it did produce or at least spawn a governor—Quentin MacLachan again, after the Culloden grandfather—and still known as the Old Governor's even after it had spawned (1861) a general—(called so by predetermined accord and agreement by the whole town and county, as though they knew even then and beforehand that the old governor was the last Compson who would not fail at everything he touched save longevity or suicide)—the Brigadier Jason Lycurgus II who failed at Shiloh in '62 and failed again, though not so badly, at Resaca in '64, who put the first mortgage on the still intact square mile to a New England carpetbagger in '66, after the old town had been burned by the Federal General Smith and the new little town, in time to be populated mainly by the descendants not of Compsons but of Snopeses, had begun to encroach and then nibble at and into it as the failed brigadier spent the next forty years selling fragments of it off to keep up the mortgage on the remainder: until one day in 1900 he died quietly on an army cot in the hunting and fishing camp in the Tallahatchie River bottom where he passed most of the end of his days.

And even the old governor was forgotten now; what was left of the old square mile was now known merely as the Compson place—the weed-choked traces of the old ruined lawns and promenades, the house which had needed painting too long already, the scaling columns of the portico where Jason III (bred for a lawyer, and indeed he kept an office upstairs above the Square, where entombed in dusty filingcases some of the oldest names in the county—Holston and Sutpen, Grenier and Beauchamp and Coldfield—faded year by year among the bottomless labyrinths of chancery: and who knows what dream in the perennial heart of his father, now completing the third of his three avatars—the one as son of a brilliant and gallant statesman, the second as battleleader of brave

and gallant men, the third as a sort of privileged pseudo Daniel Boone-Robinson Crusoe, who had not returned to juvenility because actually he had never left it—that that lawyer's office might again be the anteroom to the governor's mansion and the old splendor) sat all day long with a decanter of whiskey and a litter of dogeared Horaces and Livys and Catulluses, composing (it was said) caustic and satiric eulogies on both his dead and his living fellowtownsmen, who sold the last of the property, except that fragment containing the house and the kitchengarden and the collapsing stables and one servant's cabin in which Dilsey's family lived, to a golfclub for the ready money with which his daughter Candace could have her fine wedding in April and his son Quentin could finish one year at Harvard and commit suicide in the following June of 1910; already known as the Old Compson place even while Compsons were still living in it on that spring dusk in 1928 when the old governor's doomed lost nameless seventeen-year-old great-greatgranddaughter robbed her last remaining sane male relative (her uncle Jason IV) of his secret hoard of money and climbed down a pear tree and ran off with a pitchman in a travelling streetshow, and still known as the Old Compson place long after all traces of Compsons were gone from it: after the widowed mother died and Jason IV, no longer needing to fear Dilsey now, committed his idiot brother, Benjamin, to the State Asylum in Jackson and sold the house to a countryman who operated it as a boarding house for juries and horse- and muletraders; and still known as the Old Compson place even after the boardinghouse (and presently the golfcourse too) had vanished and the old square mile was even intact again in row after row of small crowded jerrybuilt individually owned demiurban bungalows.

And these:

QUENTIN III. Who loved not his sister's body but some concept of Compson honor precariously and (he knew well) only temporarily supported by the minute fragile membrane of her maidenhead as a miniature replica of all the whole vast globy earth may be poised on the nose of a trained seal. Who loved not the idea of the incest which he would not commit, but some presbyterian concept of its eternal punishment: he, not God, could by that means cast himself and his sister both into hell, where he could guard her forever and keep her forevermore intact amid the eternal fires. But who loved death above all, who loved only death, loved and lived in a deliberate and almost perverted anticipation of death, as a lover loves and deliberately refrains from the waiting willing friendly tender incredible body of his beloved, until he can no longer bear not the refraining but the restraint, and so flings, hurls himself, relinquishing, drowning. Committed suicide in Cambridge Massachusetts, June 1910, two months after his sister's wedding, waiting first to complete the current academic year and so get the full value of his paid-in-advance tuition, not because he had his old Culloden and Carolina and Kentucky grandfathers in him but because the remaining piece of the old Compson mile which had been sold to pay for his sister's wedding and his year at Harvard had been the one thing, excepting that same sister and the sight of an open fire, which his youngest brother, born an idiot, had loved.

CANDACE (CADDY). Doomed and knew it; accepted the doom without either seeking or fleeing it. Loved her brother despite him, loved not only him but loved in him that bitter prophet and inflexible corruptless judge of what he considered the family's honor and its doom, as he thought he loved, but really hated, in her what he considered the frail doomed vessel of its pride and the foul instrument of its disgrace; not only this, she loved him not only in spite of but because of the fact that he himself was incapable of love, accepting the fact that he must value above all not her but the virginity of which she was custodian and on which she placed no value whatever: the frail physical stricture which to her was no more than a hangnail would have been. Knew the brother loved death best of all and was not jealous, would have handed him (and perhaps in the calculation and deliberation of her marriage did hand him) the hypothetical hemlock. Was two months pregnant with another man's child, which regardless of what its sex would be she had already named Quentin after the brother whom they both (she and the brother) knew was already the same as dead, when she married (1910) an extremely eligible young Indianian she and her mother had met while vacationing at French Lick the summer before. Divorced by him 1911. Married 1920 to a minor moving picture magnate, Hollywood, California. Divorced by mutual agreement, Mexico 1925. Vanished in Paris with the German occupation, 1940, still beautiful, and probably still wealthy too, since she did not look within fifteen years of her actual forty-eight, and was not heard of again. Except there was a woman in Jefferson, the county librarian, a mouse-sized and -colored woman who had never married, who had passed through the city schools in the same class with Candace Compson and then spent the rest of her life trying to keep *Forever Amber,* in its orderly overlapping avatars, and *Jurgen* and *Tom Jones* out of the hands of the highschool juniors and seniors who could reach them down, without even having to tiptoe, from the back shelves where she herself would have to stand on a box to hide them. One day in 1943, after a week of a distraction bordering on disintegration almost, during which those entering the library would find her always in the act of hurriedly closing her desk drawer and turning the key in it (so that the matrons, wives of the bankers and doctors and lawyers, some of whom had also been in that old highschool class, who came and went in the afternoons with the copies of the *Forever Ambers* and the volumes of Thorne Smith carefully wrapped from view in sheets of Memphis and Jackson newspapers, believed she was on the verge of illness or perhaps even loss of mind), she closed and locked the library in the middle of the afternoon and with her handbag clasped tightly under her arm and two feverish spots of determination in her ordinarily colorless cheeks, she entered the farmers' supply store where Jason IV had started as a clerk and where he now owned his own business as a buyer of and dealer in cotton, striding on through that gloomy cavern which only men ever entered—a cavern cluttered and walled and stalagmite-hung with plows and discs and loops of tracechain and singletrees and mulecollars and sidemeat and cheap shoes and horse linament and flour and molasses, gloomy because the goods it contained were not shown but hidden rather since those who supplied Mississippi farmers, or at least Negro Mississippi farmers, for a share of the crop did not wish, until that crop was made and its value approximately computable, to show them what they could learn to want, but only to supply them on specific demand with what they could not help but need—and strode on back to Jason's particular domain in the rear: a railed enclosure cluttered with shelves and pigeonholes bearing spiked dust-and-lint-gathering gin receipts and ledgers and cotton samples and rank with the blended smell of cheese and kerosene and harness oil and the tremendous iron stove against which chewed tobacco had been spat for almost a hundred years, and up to the long high sloping counter behind which Jason stood, and, not looking again at the overalled men who had quietly stopped talking and even chewing when she entered, with a kind of fainting desperation she opened the handbag and fumbled something out of it and laid it open on the counter and stood trembling and breathing rapidly while Jason looked down at it—a picture, a photograph in color clipped obviously from a slick magazine—a picture filled with luxury and money and sunlight— a Riviera backdrop of mountains and palms and cypresses and the sea, an open powerful expensive chromium-trimmed sports car, the woman's face hatless between a rich scarf and a seal coat, ageless and beautiful, cold serene and damned; beside her a handsome lean man of middleage in the ribbons and tabs of a German staff-general—and the mouse-sized mouse-colored spinster trembling and aghast at her own temerity, staring across it at the childless bachelor in whom ended that long line of men who had had something in them of decency and pride, even after they had begun to fail at the integrity and the pride had become mostly vanity and selfpity: from the expatriate who had to flee his native land with little else except his life, yet who still refused to accept defeat, through the man who gambled his life and his good name twice and lost twice and declined to accept that either, and the one who with only a clever small quarterhorse for tool avenged his dispossessed father and grandfather and gained a principality, and the brilliant and gallant governor, and the general who, though he failed at leading in battle brave and gallant men,

at least risked his own life too in the failing, to the cultured dipsomaniac who sold the last of his patrimony, not to buy drink but to give one of his descendants at least the best chance in life he could think of.

"It's Caddy!" the librarian whispered. "We must save her!"

"It's Cad, all right," Jason said. Then he began to laugh. He stood there laughing above the picture, above the cold beautiful face now creased and dogeared from its week's sojourn in the desk drawer and the handbag. And the librarian knew why he was laughing, who had not called him anything but Mr. Compson for thirty-two years now, ever since the day in 1911 when Candace, cast off by her husband, had brought her infant daughter home and left the child and departed by the next train, to return no more, and not only the Negro cook, Dilsey, but the librarian too, divined by simple instinct that Jason was somehow using the child's life and its illegitimacy to blackmail the mother not only into staying away from Jefferson for the rest of her life, but into appointing him sole unchallengeable trustee of the money she would send for the child's maintenance, and had refused to speak to him at all since that day in 1928 when the daughter climbed down the pear tree and ran away with the pitchman.

"Jason!" she cried. "We must save her! Jason! Jason!"—and still crying it even when he took up the picture between thumb and finger and threw it back across the counter toward her.

"That Candace?" he said. "Don't make me laugh. This bitch ain't thirty yet. The other one's fifty now."

And the library was still locked all the next day too when at three o'clock in the afternoon, footsore and spent yet still unflagging and still clasping the handbag tightly under her arm, she turned into a neat small yard in the Negro residence section of Memphis and mounted the steps of the neat small house and rang the bell and the door opened and a black woman of about her own age looked quietly out at her. "It's Frony, isn't it?" the librarian said. "Don't you remember me—Melissa Meek, from Jefferson—"

"Yes," the Negress said. "Come in. You want to see Mama." And she entered the room, the neat yet cluttered bedroom of an old Negro, rank with the smell of old people, old women, old Negroes, where the old woman herself sat in a rocker beside the hearth where even though it was June a fire smoldered—a big woman once, in faded clean calico and an immaculate turban wound round her head above the bleared and now apparently almost sightless eyes—and put the dogeared clipping into the black hands which, like those of the women of her race, were still as supple and delicately shaped as they had been when she was thirty or twenty or even seventeen.

"It's Caddy!" the librarian said. "It is! Dilsey! Dilsey!"

"What did he say?" the old Negress said. And the librarian knew whom she meant by "he"; nor did the librarian marvel, not only that the old Negress would know that she (the librarian) would know whom she meant by the "he," but that the old Negress would know at once that she had already shown the picture to Jason.

"Don't you know what he said?" she cried. "When he realized she was in danger, he said it was her, even if I hadn't even had a picture to show him. But as soon as he realized that somebody, anybody, even just me, wanted to save her, would try to save her, he said it wasn't. But it is! Look at it!"

"Look at my eyes," the old Negress said. "How can I see that picture?"

"Call Frony!" the librarian cried. "She will know her!" But already the old Negress was folding the clipping carefully back into its old creases, handing it back.

"My eyes ain't any good any more," she said. "I can't see it."

And that was all. At six o'clock she fought her way through the crowded bus terminal, the bag clutched under one arm and the return half of her roundtrip ticket in the other hand, and was swept out onto the roaring platform on the diurnal tide of a few middle-aged civilians, but mostly soldiers and sailors enroute either to leave or to death, and the homeless young women, their companions, who for two years now had lived from day to day in pullmans and hotels when they were lucky, and in daycoaches and busses and stations and lobbies and public restrooms when not, pausing only long

enough to drop their foals in charity wards or policestations and then move on again, and fought her way into the bus, smaller than any other there so that her feet touched the floor only occasionally, until a shape (a man in khaki; she couldn't see him at all because she was already crying) rose and picked her up bodily and set her into a seat next the window, where still crying quietly she could look out upon the fleeing city as it streaked past and then was behind, and presently now she would be home again, safe in Jefferson, where life lived too with all its incomprehensible passion and turmoil and grief and fury and despair, but there at six o'clock you could close the covers on it and even the weightless hand of a child could put it back among its unfeatured kindred on the quiet eternal shelves and turn the key upon it for the whole and dreamless night. *Yes* she thought, crying quietly, *that was it; she didn't want to see it know whether it was Caddy or not because she knows Caddy doesn't want to be saved hasn't anything any more worth being saved for nothing worth being lost that she can lose.*

JASON IV. The first sane Compson since before Culloden and (a childless bachelor) hence the last. Logical, rational, contained and even a philosopher in the old stoic tradition: thinking nothing whatever of God one way or the other, and simply considering the police and so fearing and respecting only the Negro woman who cooked the food he ate, his sworn enemy since his birth and his mortal one since that day in 1911 when she too divined by simple clairvoyance that he was somehow using his infant niece's illegitimacy to blackmail her mother. Who not only fended off and held his own with Compsons, but competed and held his own with the Snopeses, who took over the little town following the turn of the century as the Compsons and Sartorises and their ilk faded from it (no Snopes, but Jason Compson himself, who as soon as his mother died—the niece had already climbed down the pear tree and vanished, so Dilsey no longer had either of these clubs to hold over him—committed his idiot younger brother to the state and vacated the old house, first chopping up the vast once splendid rooms into what he called apartments and selling the whole thing to a countryman who opened a boardinghouse in it), though this was not difficult since to him all the rest of the town and the world and the human race too except himself were Compsons, inexplicable yet quite predictable in that they were in no sense whatever to be trusted. Who, all the money from the sale of the pasture having gone for his sister's wedding and his brother's course at Harvard, used his own niggard savings out of his meagre wages as a storeclerk to send himself to a Memphis school where he learned to class and grade cotton, and so established his own business, with which, following his dipsomaniac father's death, he assumed the entire burden of the rotting family in the rotting house, supporting his idiot brother because of their mother, sacrificing what pleasures might have been the right and just due and even the necessity of a thirty-year-old bachelor, so that his mother's life might continue as nearly as possible to what it had been; this not because he loved her but (a sane man always) simply because he was afraid of the Negro cook whom he could not even force to leave, even when he tried to stop paying her weekly wages; and who despite all this, still managed to save $2840.50 (three thousand, as he reported it on the night his niece stole it) in niggard and agonized dimes and quarters and halfdollars, which hoard he kept in no bank because to him a banker too was just one more Compson, but hid in a locked steel box beneath a sawn plank in the floor of his locked clothes closet in the bedroom whose bed he made each morning himself, since he kept the room's door locked all the time save for a half hour each Sunday morning when, himself present and watching, he permitted his mother and Dilsey to come in long enough to change the bedlinen and sweep the floor. Who, following a fumbling abortive attempt by his idiot brother on a passing female child, had himself appointed the idiot's guardian without letting their mother know and so was able to have the creature castrated before the mother even knew it was out of the house, and who following the mother's death in 1933 was able to free himself forever not only from the idiot brother and the house but from the Negro woman too, moving into a pair of offices up a flight of stairs above the supplystore containing his cotton ledgers and samples, which

he had converted into a bedroom-kitchen-bath, in and out of which on weekends there would be seen a big, plain, friendly, brazenhaired pleasantfaced woman no longer very young, in round picture hats and in its season an imitation fur coat, the two of them, the middleaged cottonbuyer and the woman whom the town called, simply, his friend from Memphis, seen at the local picture show on Saturday night and on Sunday morning mounting the apartment stairs with paper bags from the grocer's containing loaves and eggs and oranges and cans of soup, domestic, uxorious, connubial, until the late afternoon bus carried her back to Memphis. He was emancipated now. He was free. "In 1865," he would say, "Abe Lincoln freed the niggers from the Compsons. In 1933, Jason Compson freed the Compsons from the niggers."

BENJAMIN. Born Maury, after his mother's only brother: a handsome flashing swaggering workless bachelor who borrowed money from almost anyone, even Dilsey although she was a Negro, explaining to her as he withdrew his hand from his pocket that she was not only in his eyes the same as a member of his sister's family, she would be considered a born lady anywhere in any eyes. Who, when at last even his mother realized what he was and insisted weeping that his name must be changed, was rechristened Benjamin by his brother Quentin (Benjamin, our lastborn, sold into Egypt). Who loved three things: the pasture which was sold to pay for Candace's wedding and to send Quentin to Harvard, his sister Candace, firelight. Who lost none of them, because he could not remember his sister but only the loss of her, and firelight was the same bright shape as going to sleep, and the pasture was even better sold than before, because now he and Luster could not only follow timeless along the fence the motions which it did not even matter to him were human beings swinging golfsticks, Luster could lead them to clumps of grass or weeds where there would appear suddenly in Luster's hand, small white spherules which competed with and even conquered what he did not even know was gravity and all the immutable laws, when released from the hand toward plank floor of smokehouse wall or concrete sidewalk. Gelded 1913. Committed to the

State Asylum, Jackson, 1933. Lost nothing then either because, as with his sister, he remembered not the pasture but only its loss, and firelight was still the same bright shape of sleep.

QUENTIN. The last. Candace's daughter. Fatherless nine months before her birth, nameless at birth and already doomed to be unwed from the instant the dividing egg determined its sex. Who at seventeen, on the one thousand eight hundred ninety-fifth anniversary of the day before the resurrection of Our Lord, swung herself by a rainpipe from her window to the locked window of her uncle's locked and empty bedroom and broke a pane and entered the window, and with the uncle's firepoker ripped off the locked hasp and staple of the closet door and prized up the sawn plank and got the steel box (and they never did know how she had broken the lock on it, how a seventeen-year-old girl could have broken that lock with anything, let alone a poker) and rifled it (and it was not $2840.50 or three thousand dollars either, it was almost seven thousand. And this was Jason's rage, the red unbearable fury which on that night and at intervals recurring with little or no diminishment for the next five years, made him seriously believe it would at some unwarned instant destroy him, kill him as instantaneously dead as a bullet or a lightningbolt: that although he had been robbed not of a mere petty three but of almost seven, he couldn't even report it; he could not only never receive justification—he did not want sympathy—from other men unlucky enough to have one bitch for a sister and another for a niece, he couldn't even demand help in recovering it. Because he had lost four thousand dollars which did not belong to him he couldn't even recover the three thousand which did, since those first four thousand dollars were not only the legal property of his niece as a part of the money supplied for her support and maintenance by her mother over the last sixteen years, they did not exist at all, having been officially recorded as expended and consumed in the annual reports he submitted to the district Chancellor, as required of him as guardian and trustee by his bondsmen: so that he had been robbed not only of his thievings but his savings too, and by his own victim; he had

been robbed not only of the four thousand dollars which he had risked jail to acquire, but of the three thousand which he had hoarded at the price of sacrifice and denial, almost a nickel and a dime at a time, over a period of almost twenty years: and this not only by his own victim but by a child who did it at one blow, without premeditation or plan, not even knowing or even caring how much she would find when she broke the drawer open; and now he couldn't even go to the police for help: he who had considered the police always, never given them any trouble, had paid the taxes for years which supported them in parasitic and sadistic idleness; not only that, he didn't dare pursue the girl himself because he might catch her and she would talk, so that his only recourse was a vain dream which kept him tossing and sweating on nights two and three and even four years after the event, when he should have forgotten about it: of catching her without warning, springing on her out of the dark, before she had spent all the money, and murdering her before she had time to open her mouth) and climbed down the pear tree in the dusk and ran away with the pitchman who was already under sentence for bigamy. And so vanished; whatever occupation overtook her would have arrived in no chromium Mercedes; whatever snapshot would have contained no general of staff.

And that was all. These others were not Compsons. They were black:

TP. Who wore on Memphis' Beal Street the fine bright cheap intransigent clothes manufactured specifically for him by the owners of Chicago and New York sweatshops.

FRONY. Who married a pullman porter and went to Saint Louis to live and later moved back to Memphis to make a home for her mother since Dilsey refused to go further than that.

LUSTER. A man, aged 14. Who was not only capable of the complete care and security of an idiot twice his age and three times his size, but could keep him entertained.

DILSEY.

They endured.

FAULKNER'S INTRODUCTION TO SANCTUARY

In his introduction to the edition of Sanctuary *published by The Modern Library in 1932, Faulkner gave a misleading explanation of his intentions in writing the novel. He withdrew it from later editions.*

This book was written three years ago. To me it is a cheap idea, because it was deliberately conceived to make money. I had been writing books for about five years, which got published and not bought. But that was all right. I was young then and hard-bellied. I had never lived among nor known people who wrote novels and stories and I suppose I did not know that people got money for them. I was not very much annoyed when publishers refused the mss. now and then. Because I was hard-gutted then. I could do a lot of things that could earn what little money I needed, thanks to my father's unfailing kindness which supplied me with bread at need despite the outrage to his principles at having been of a bum progenitive.

Then I began to get a little soft. I could still paint houses and do carpenter work, but I got soft. I began to think about making money by writing. I began to be concerned when magazine editors turned down short stories, concerned enough to tell them that they would buy these stories later anyway, and hence why not now. Meanwhile, with one novel completed and consistently refused for two years, I had just written my guts into *The Sound and the Fury* though I was not aware until the book was published that I had done so, because I had done it for pleasure. I believed then that I would never be published again. I had stopped thinking of myself in publishing terms.

But when the third mss., *Sartoris*, was taken by a publisher and (he having refused *The Sound and the Fury*) it was taken by still another publisher, who warned me at the time that it would not sell, I began to think of myself again as a printed object. I began to think of books in terms of possible money. I decided I might just as well make some of it myself. I took a little time out, and speculated what a person in Mississippi would believe to be current trends, chose what I thought was the right answer and invented the most horrific tale I could imagine and wrote it in about three weeks and sent it to Smith, who had done *The Sound and the Fury* and who wrote me immediately, "Good God, I can't publish this. We'd both be in jail." So I told Faulkner, "You're damned. You'll have to work now and then for the rest of your life." That was in the summer of 1929. I got a job in the power plant, on the night shift, from 6 P.M. to 6 A.M., as a coal passer. I shoveled coal from the bunker into a wheelbarrow and wheeled it in and dumped it where the fireman could put it into the boiler. About 11 o'clock the people would be going to bed, and so it did not take so much steam. Then we could rest, the fireman and I. He would sit in a chair and doze. I had invented a table out of a wheelbarrow in the coal bunker, just beyond a wall from where a dynamo ran. It made a deep, constant humming noise. There was no more work to do until about 4 A.M., when we would have to clean the fires and get up steam again. On these nights, between 12 and 4, I wrote *As I Lay Dying* in six weeks, without changing a word. I sent it to Smith and wrote him that by it I would stand or fall.

I think I had forgotten about *Sanctuary*, just as you might forget about anything made for an immediate purpose, which did not come off. *As I Lay Dying* was published and I didn't remember the mss. of *Sanctuary* until Smith sent me the galleys. Then I saw that it was so terrible that there were but two things to do: tear it up or rewrite it.

I thought again, "It might sell; maybe 10,000 of them will buy it." So I tore the galleys down and rewrote the book. It had been already set up once, so I had to pay for the privilege of rewriting it, trying to make out of it something which would not shame *The Sound and the Fury* and *As I Lay Dying* too much and I made a fair job and I hope you will buy it and tell your friends and I hope they will buy it too.

Faulkner's Nobel Prize Acceptance Speech Stockholm, December 10, 1950

I feel that this award was not made to me as a man but to my work—a life's work in the agony and sweat of the human spirit, not for glory and least of all for profit, but to create out of the materials of the human spirit something which did not exist before. So this award is only mine in trust. It will not be difficult to find a dedication for the money part of it commensurate with the purpose and significance of its origin. But I would like to do the same with the acclaim too, by using this moment as a pinnacle from which I might be listened to by the young men and women already dedicated to the same anguish and travail, among whom is already that one who will some day stand here where I am standing.

Our tragedy today is a general and universal physical fear so long sustained by now that we can even bear it. There are no longer problems of the spirit. There is only the question: When will I be blown up? Because of this, the young man or woman writing today has forgotten the problems of the human heart in conflict with itself which alone can make good writing because only that is worth writing about, worth the agony and the sweat.

He must learn them again. He must teach himself that the basest of all things is to be afraid; and teaching himself that, forget it forever, leaving no room in his workshop for anything but the old verities and truths of the heart, the old universal truths lacking which any story is ephemeral and doomed—love and honor and pity and pride and compassion and sacrifice. Until he does so, he labors under a curse. He writes not of love but of lust, of defeats in which nobody loses anything of value, of victories without hope and, worst of all, without pity or compassion. His griefs grieve on no universal bones, leaving no scars. He writes not of the heart but of the glands.

Until he relearns these things, he will write as though he stood among and watched the end of man. I decline to accept the end of man. It is easy enough to say that man is immortal simply because he will endure; that when the last ding-dong of doom has clanged and faded from the last worthless rock hanging tideless in the last red and dying evening, that even then there will still be one more sound: that of his puny inexhaustible voice, still talking. I refuse to accept this. I believe that man will not merely endure: he will prevail. He is immortal, not because he alone among creatures has an inexhaustible voice but because he has a soul, a spirit capable of compassion and sacrifice and endurance. The poet's, the writer's, duty is to write about these things. It is his privilege to help man endure by lifting his heart, by reminding him of the courage and honor and hope and pride and compassion and pity and sacrifice which has been the glory of his past. The poet's voice need not merely be the record of man, it can be one of the props, the pillars to help him endure and prevail.

CHRONOLOGY OF WILLIAM FAULKNER'S LIFE

1897

William Cuthbert Falkner born (in New Albany, Mississippi, September 25)

Havelock Ellis publishes *Studies in the Psychology of Sex*

H. G. Wells publishes *The Invisible Man*

1902

The Falkner family moves to Oxford, Mississippi

John Steinbeck is born

Emile Zola dies

Beatrix Potter publishes *Peter Rabbit*

1905

Falkner enters the first grade on his eighth birthday

First movie theatre opens in Pittsburgh, Pennsylvania

Edith Wharton publishes *The House of Mirth*

The Bloomsbury Group is founded

1911

Falkner enters the eighth grade (September)

Marie Curie awarded Nobel Prize in chemistry

Roald Amundsen reaches South Pole

1913

Faulkner draws ten cartoons for a proposed Oxford High School yearbook

1914

Falkner begins long-lasting friendship with Phil Stone

Archduke Francis Ferdinand is assassinated in Sarajevo and World War I begins

James Joyce publishes *Dubliners*

Tennessee Williams is born

1915

Falkner drops out of school

Franz Kafka publishes *Der Verwandlung* (*The Metamorphosis*)

Edgar Lee Masters publishes *Spoon River Anthology*

Germany sinks *Lusitania*

D. W. Griffith's film *The Birth of a Nation* opens

1916

James Joyce publishes *A Portrait of the Artist as a Young Man*

1917

Falkner drawings appear in *Ole Miss* yearbook

United States declares war on Germany

T. S. Eliot publishes *Prufrock and Other Observations*

C. G. Jung publishes *Psychology of the Unconscious*

1918

Falkner is rejected by the U.S. Army; in June changes spelling of his name to *Faulkner* when enlisting in the Royal Air Force; attends School of Military Aeronautics in Toronto; is discharged when World War I ends (November 11); returns to Oxford, Mississippi

Irving Berlin's *Yip Yip Yaphank* opens on Broadway

James Joyce's *Ulysses* begins serialization in the *Little Review*

Willa Cather publishes *My Antonía*

World War I ends

1919

Faulkner's first national publication, the poem "L'Après-midi d'un Faune," appears in *The New Republic* (reprinted in *The Mississippian*)

Racehorse Man o' War loses only race

Sherwood Anderson publishes *Winesburg, Ohio*

1921

John Dos Passos publishes *Three Soldiers*

1922

James Joyce publishes *Ulysses*

1924

Faulkner publishes *The Marble Faun*

Ottoman Empire ends

André Breton publishes *Manifeste de surréalisme* (*Manifesto of Surrealism*)

1925

Faulkner travels in Europe

The Charleston becomes a popular dance

Hitler publishes volume one of *Mein Kampf*

Scopes "Monkey Trial" takes place

F. Scott Fitzgerald publishes *The Great Gatsby*

1926

Faulkner's first novel, *Soldiers' Pay*, is published

Magician Harry Houdini dies

1927

Faulkner publishes *Mosquitoes*

Sinclair Lewis publishes *Elmer Gantry*

Babe Ruth sets major league baseball's single-season record with 60 home runs

1929

Faulkner publishes *Sartoris*; marries Estelle Franklin; publishes *The Sound and the Fury*

Thomas Wolfe publishes *Look Homeward, Angel*

Ernest Hemingway publishes *A Farewell to Arms*

1930

Faulkner buys Rowan Oak; publishes *As I Lay Dying*

Noël Coward publishes *Private Lives*

Dashiell Hammett publishes *The Maltese Falcon*

D. H. Lawrence dies

Sinclair Lewis wins the Nobel Prize in literature

1931

Faulkner and Estelle's daughter Alabama is born; she dies nine days later. Faulkner publishes *Sanctuary* and *These 13* (a collection of short stories)

Robert Frost wins Pulitzer Prize for *Collected Poems*

Salvador Dali paints "Persistence of Memory"

1932

Faulkner writes for Metro-Goldwyn-Mayer (MGM); publishes *Salmagundi* (prose and poetry) and *Light in August*

Franklin Delano Roosevelt elected president of the United States

Adolf Hitler becomes German citizen

Amelia Earhart is first woman to make transatlantic solo flight

Aldous Huxley publishes *Brave New World*

1933

Faulkner publishes *A Green Bough* (collection of poems); daughter Jill is born

Faulkner receives screen credit for coscripting *Today We Live*, the film adaptation of his short story "Turn About"; does additional scriptwriting in Hollywood

Hitler comes to power in Germany; first concentration camps built

C. G. Jung publishes *Modern Man in Search of a Soul*

1934

Faulkner publishes *Doctor Martino and Other Stories*; works for Universal Studios

F. Scott Fitzgerald publishes *Tender is the Night*

Luigi Pirandello wins Nobel Prize in literature

1935

Faulkner publishes *Pylon*; works for Twentieth Century-Fox; begins affair with Meta Dougherty Carpenter

Alcoholic Anonymous starts in New York City

Persia is renamed Iran

1936

Faulkner publishes *Absalom, Absalom!*

Faulkner coauthors screenplay filmed as *The Road to Glory*

King Edward VIII abdicates

Margaret Mitchell publishes *Gone With the Wind*

Baseball Hall of Fame opens in Cooperstown, New York

Eugene O'Neill wins Nobel Prize in literature

1937

Faulkner returns to Oxford, Mississippi, from California

John Steinbeck publishes *Of Mice and Men*

Amelia Earhart is lost in the Pacific

1938

Faulkner publishes *The Unvanquished;* buys Greenfield Farm

Kristallnacht

Eddie Arcaro wins his first Kentucky Derby

Thornton Wilder wins Pulitzer Prize for *Our Town*

1939

Faulkner is elected to the National Institute of Arts and Letters; publishes *The Wild Palms*

James Joyce publishes *Finnegans Wake*

World War II begins

1940

Faulkner publishes *The Hamlet* (the first of the Snopes trilogy)

F. Scott Fitzgerald dies

1941

James Joyce dies

Joe DiMaggio sets major league record by hitting safely in 56 consecutive games

1942

Faulkner publishes *Go Down, Moses;* writes for Warner Brothers

Enrico Fermi splits atom

1944

Faulkner coauthors screenplay for *To Have and Have Not*

1945

Faulkner walks out on Warner Bros. contract and returns to Oxford

First atomic bomb is detonated in New Mexico

United States drops atomic bombs on Hiroshima and Nagasaki, Japan

1946

The Portable Faulkner is published

Faulkner receives screen credit for coauthoring script of *The Big Sleep*

Victor Emmanuel III abdicates as King of Italy

1948

MGM buys screen rights to *Intruder in the Dust,* two months before novel is published in September; Faulkner is elected to the American Academy of Arts and Sciences

Indian nationalist leader Mohandas Gandhi is assassinated

Babe Ruth dies

1949

Faulkner publishes *Knight's Gambit*

Arthur Miller receives Pulitzer Prize for *Death of a Salesman*

1950

Faulkner is awarded the American Academy's Howells Medal for Fiction; *Collected Stories of William Faulkner* is published; Faulkner wins the 1949 Nobel Prize in literature

George Bernard Shaw dies

Alger Hiss convicted of perjury

1951

In Hollywood, Faulkner writes scripts for Howard Hawks; publishes novella *Notes on a Horsethief;* wins National Book Award for Fiction (for *Collected Stories*); publishes *Requiem for a Nun*

J. D. Salinger publishes *The Catcher in the Rye*

James Jones publishes *From Here to Eternity*

Rachel Carson publishes *The Sea Around Us*

1954

Faulkner publishes *A Fable*

Ernest Hemingway wins Nobel Prize in literature

Charles A. Lindbergh wins Pulitzer Prize for *The Spirit of St. Louis*

1955

Faulkner receives the National Book Award for *A Fable* (novel also wins the Pulitzer Prize); on invitation of State Department participates in Nagano Seminar, Japan; publishes *Big Woods*

James Agee dies

Vladimir Nabokov publishes *Lolita*

Thomas Mann dies

Albert Einstein dies

1957

Faulkner begins Writer-in-Residence at the University of Virginia (1957–1958); travels to Athens on invitation of State Department; awarded the Silver Medal of Greek Academy; publishes *The Town* (the second novel of the Snopes trilogy)

Stage version of *Requiem for a Nun* plays in London

Jack Kerouac publishes *On the Road*

Dr. Seuss publishes *The Cat in the Hat*

Bernard Malamud publishes *The Assistant*

1958

Faulkner participates in Council on Humanities at Princeton University

John Kenneth Galbraith publishes *The Affluent Society*

1959

Requiem for a Nun opens on Broadway; Faulkner publishes *The Mansion* (the third of the Snopes trilogy)

De Gaulle becomes president of the Fifth Republic in France

Hawaii becomes fiftieth state

1960

Faulkner appointed to University of Virginia faculty

John F. Kennedy–Richard Nixon presidential debates are televised

Students conduct nonviolent sit-ins at all-white lunch counters in Greensboro, North Carolina

Harper Lee publishes *To Kill a Mockingbird*

1961

Faulkner travels to Venezuela on invitation of State Department

Ernest Hemingway dies

Soviet cosmonaut Uri Gagarin orbits Earth

Alan Shepard flies in first United States space flight

Civil rights Freedom Riders in Alabama are beaten

1962

Faulkner receives the Gold Medal for Fiction of the National Institute of Arts and Letters; publishes *The Reivers*; dies of heart attack

John Steinbeck wins Nobel Prize in literature

Alexander Solzhenitsyn publishes *One Day in the Life of Ivan Denisovich*

Adolf Eichmann is hanged

Hermann Hesse dies

e. e. cummings dies

Eleanor Roosevelt dies

Rachel Carson publishes *Silent Spring*

Black student James Meredith is escorted to the University of Mississippi by federal marshals

INDEX